# JAPAN

## FOR THE IMPOVERISHED

## A Travel Guide

## by Jim Rickman

**PUBLISHED BY**
**BORGNAN CORPORATION**

JAPAN FOR THE IMPOVERISHED

by Jim Rickman

with assistance from Toshishige Kusunoki

Illustrations by 'Nickle' (Yuko Katahara)

Copyright © 1995 by Borgnan Corporation

First Edition: August 1995

Published by Borgnan Corporation,
Dai-san Taihei Building, 1-25-3 Higashi Ikebukuro,
Toshima-ku, Tokyo 170, Japan.
Tel. 03-3983-7151

Distributed in Japan by Yohan (Western Publications Distribution Agency),
3-14-9 Okubo, Shinjuku-ku, Tokyo 169, Japan.
Tel. 03-3208-0181

ISBN 4-938749-01-7

Printed in Japan

# PREFACE

What is different about this book? That is what you will want to know when you pick it up in the bookshop.

Briefly, it puts more emphasis on accommodation and transportation, which are the ways in which money can be saved in Japan, and less emphasis on the details of sightseeing attractions, which are relatively easy to find out about locally. That is not to say, however, that we have no information about what to see in Japan. On the contrary, if you visit all of the spots mentioned in this book, it will probably take at least three months, but we have tried to distinguish the important places from those of marginal interest, which competitive books, though sometimes encyclopædic in their contents, do not always manage to achieve.

For each spot mentioned, we have told you how to get there - which bus to take (and both bus destinations and bus stop names are always given in Japanese, as well as in English, since they will be marked in Japanese when you need to use them), how long it takes and even the times of departures, if they are few. We have tried to put detailed maps wherever it seemed necessary and to think of everything from the readers' point of view.

There are suggestions for suitable discount tickets, although note now that, if you are eligible for a 'Japan Rail Pass', you should not neglect to purchase one before you come. It cannot be bought in Japan. There are also model itineraries according to length of stay in Japan, desired speed of travel and ticket availability.

But perhaps this book's strongest claim to be purchased is the accommodation section. We have listed 300 youth hostels and for every one there is a map to help you to find it. We have listed 60 Japanese-style inns and for every one there is a map. We have listed private hostels and hotels of reasonable price in Tokyo and Kyoto and for every one there is a map. We have listed about 200 'business hotels' and provided a map for each major city in which they are located, so at any level of moderately-priced accommodation, we do not think that there is a book in English which offers more.

Finally, we have tried very hard indeed to avoid mistakes. The author hates errors. Having travelled in various countries, his opinion is that if there is anything worse than a book which fails to give the information needed, it is one which gives it incorrectly and therefore he has been to considerable lengths to avoid being accused of the same fault. Of course, prices will rise and timetables will change, but inflation is slow in Japan and major revisions to train times are infrequent, although bus timetables do change periodically, so should be regarded as a general guide only. However, the author has tried very hard to avoid real mistakes and to emphasize what he always wants to know when arriving in a strange place. Where shall I stay? How do I get there? We hope that this book will truly be a help to you in your travels. You do not need to be absolutely impoverished in order to use it, but, if you are, this is certainly the book for you.

# CONTENTS

## PART 1 INTRODUCTION

## PART 2 SIGHTSEEING



## PART 3 ACCOMMODATION



## PART 4 ITINERARIES

# THANKS

A few words of thanks are in order – first and most importantly to the publisher for having the confidence to get this book into print when all around him advised that it would never sell. Also, thanks are due to him for writing parts of the introduction dealing with Japanese culture and history, about which his knowledge far exceeds that of the author.

Next to 'Nickle' for the charming little illustrations of impoverished travellers which appear in odd corners of the book from time to time as well as, more conspicuously, on the front and back covers. At the foot of this page, there is an illustration of Nickle illustrating (watched by the author?).

We are grateful to the Japan Youth Hostels Association for giving us considerable assistance by keeping our information up to date, and even giving us some encouragement also. In particular, our thanks go to Mr. S. Imai, Mr. O. Mizuno and Mr. A. Kobayashi. Mr. I. Sawa of Sawanoya Ryokan gave us valuable assistance with other parts of the accommodation section, while Mr. Noliyuky Nacano checked some of the manuscript and found undreamt of errors.

Thanks too to the ladies of the Educational Section of Borgnan Corporation who have tolerated the author's presence in their midst for nearly a year and even assisted kindly from time to time with the gathering of information and provided boundless quantities of those essential ingredients for writing a book – coffee and commiseration.

# PART 1 INTRODUCTION

## A FEW WORDS ABOUT THE BOOK

The author was in the Tourist Information Centre in Tokyo one day and overheard one visitor saying to another, "Get a copy of that pamphlet, 'Accommodation for Paupers', or whatever. That's what we need." The comment stuck in my mind and I went to the publisher next day and said, "I have decided to call our book 'Japan for the Impoverished'." "Yes, all right," he replied, rather to my surprise. "At least people will remember the title." So here it is, a book by an impoverished author, written for an impoverished publisher to be read by the impoverished traveller. Actually, you do not need to be completely poverty-stricken in order to read on. We hope that this work will be of use to anybody whose budget is limited, even if it is limited only to the extent that you want to stay in moderately-priced hotels rather than luxury accommodation and prefer to find your own way around rather than join a group tour.

The number of visitors to Japan increases year by year, and yet very many people are deterred by the idea that it is 'the most expensive country in the world' and 'you cannot find anywhere cheap to stay.' "There are no hotels under $100 per person per night." "It costs $300 just to go from Tokyo to Kyoto and back." "You have to pay $5 for a cup of coffee." These are variations on the same theme and they are simply not true. Of course, you *can* easily pay such prices if you wish, but there is no need to do so. As at the time of printing, all accommodation listed in this book costs a maximum of ¥10,000 ($100) for two people or ¥5,000 ($50) for one person per night (i.e. it satisfies at least one of these two criteria), including all taxes and service charges. The 300 youth hostels listed cost an average of ¥2,500 and are generally good places to stay. There are private hostels as cheap as ¥1,100. To be sure, you can pay $300 to go to Kyoto and back on the *shinkansen* (bullet train), but this book will also tell you how to cover those 1,000 kilometres by train for less than $50. You can buy a cup of coffee for $5 if you wish – or you can have a lunch including soup and coffee for the same price. It just depends how you approach the country. On the whole, the author believes that Japan is no more expensive than western Europe, for example. Follow some of the suggestions in this book and even the impoverished can see Japan reasonably economically. Of course, prices are not in the same category as those in other parts of south-east Asia, but having a look at Japan should not be out of the question for anybody who can afford to buy an air ticket here in the first place. Read on and discover how to travel around in the most economical manner available to correspond with your basic requirements.

"But the language. How can I manage?" Well, of course, in Japan people speak Japanese. However, this is a country with a high class education system and virtually everybody spends at least six years learning English at school, so it is almost always possible to find somebody who can speak a few words of the language, even though linguistic standards are generally not high. In particular, people can nearly always read something written in Roman script, as long as it is printed, not in cursive handwriting. More important, though, Japanese people are always willing to help and to go out of their way to do so. It is true that Japan is a little harder to travel than some other countries because of the fact that the visitor can never read anything, but this is more than compensated for by people's willingness to do everything possible to assist the visitor. Armed with this book (which includes names in Japanese whenever it seems useful) you will manage very well – and the more you succeed in getting away from the tracks of other western visitors, the more you will surprise yourself with your ability to manage and the more helpful you will find that people are, as in most countries.

This book is divided into four parts. First this, the introductory section, with general information about the country, its history, culture, address system, money, communications systems, business hours, entertainment and other types of useful (we hope) information.

Next is the part dealing with sightseeing, area by area and place by place. The third section deals in detail with accommodation and the fourth has suggested itineraries. It is hoped that this is a convenient arrangement of the contents, but one is never quite sure what is ideal and cross-referencing can be done to only a limited extent, otherwise the book would never get published before everything became out of date!

Now what are the author's credentials for writing a book like this, apart from being impoverished, the reader will want to know. The author came here as a detour on a journey from Australia to England in 1980. He was in Bangkok and was told by other travellers that, if he made a trip to Japan and stayed for, say, six months, he would be able to do some odd jobs teaching English (illegally!) and be able to earn enough to cover living expenses and probably the air fare as well. That seemed appealing and so I came. I was offered a one-year contract to work legally and thought, "Well, just another six months." And then another six months and months stretched into years and years into decades. I always say that I am leaving soon.

Probably unlike other writers of travel books, I did not travel Japan with the idea of writing a book in mind. Whether that is an advantage or a disadvantage, I am unsure, but it probably resulted in my seeing more of the out of the way spots and less of the major tourist attractions than would otherwise have been the case.

It may or may not be a claim to fame, but the author has travelled every Japan Railways line in the country, something which most Japanese find difficult to believe when told. I have not yet travelled all of the private lines, but am working on it! The reader will understand, therefore, that the author has something of a preference for trains. In my opinion, they are the economical and comfortable way to see Japan, particularly if used with a Japan Rail Pass. Maybe this is a biased opinion (although the author thinks it objective!), but no other method of travel can offer the short-term visitor such speed, comprehensive service and enjoyable scenery. Therefore, there is no doubt that this is a book for those who are willing to join the author on some enjoyable train jaunts. Come with me then and enjoy the railways of Japan.

## FOR THE TRULY IMPOVERISHED

How to live at the bottom end of the impoverishment scale? Well, the ways that expenses can be cut to the closest possible level to zero are by hitch-hiking and camping.

Hitch-hiking is easy in Japan, mainly because Japanese never do it. The hardest part is finding a suitable starting point when in larger cities. Japanese drivers tend to be very kind and you may find yourself offered refreshments along the way, and even a night's accommodation is not unheard of. Usually the driver's reason for such generosity goes beyond the western desire for a little company along the way. Nor is it simple kindness, although, of course, that is a part of the character of almost anybody who gives a fellow human a ride. Most of all, though, it is the Japanese desire to meet people from other lands and find out about them and their culture, so do not forget your duty to your host to satisfy his curiosity in return for your transportation. Although this is a cheap way to travel, and is very safe, in terms of the motives of your host, compared with the same method of transportation in other lands, the author does not completely recommend it. The disadvantages are these. You have to get to and from your points of origin and destination, which is often a time-consuming nuisance, and your travel will mostly be along the 'expressways' of Japan. Now these are, at best, rather boring, allowing you to see comparatively little of the country through which you are passing. At worst, they can be dangerous, for there are 10,000 people killed in road accidents in Japan every year, or anything but express, especially in the vicinity of large cities and at holiday times. So speed is not a predictable element of hitch-hiking, but it will enable you to travel cheaply and to stave off total impoverishment for a while.

For eating, you can try bread crusts. See the section on food, but this is serious. You can buy a huge bag of crusts for ¥50 and then purchase something cheap in a supermarket to go with your crusts. There is probably no cheaper way to survive in Japan, although it can become rather a monotonous diet.

As for camping, that is a little more difficult, and not always cheap. The Japanese idea of camping is a fairly luxurious one, offering novelty principally. Moreover, it is regarded as a summertime recreation and summer equals July and August. Also, it is for those with their own vehicles, who drive to camping areas which are often not easily accessible by public transport or on foot.

For the visitor, all of these aspects pose problems. The high standard of camping sites tends to mean that they are quite expensive. Generally, though, tents or other accommodation can be hired, so it is not essential to bring your own. If there is a choice, municipally-operated sites will usually be cheaper than privately-operated ones, but the lowest fee is usually about ¥1,000 per person, not including a tent, in addition to which hot water for showers and gas for cooking will be metered.

The locations mean that, in many cases, considerable energy, time, and even money, will be expended in reaching them. When they are useful, though, is when you have a vehicle at your disposal, but how many of the readers of this book will be in that position? On the whole, it is best to consider camping if you reach a place and happen to discover somewhere suitable to do so, but it is doubtful whether it is worthwhile carrying a tent round Japan for these odd occasions. It is difficult to camp on unclaimed ground, as in other countries, because there is none. Only in Hokkaido and on some of the very remote islands is that possible and in many cases you will still need transport to reach such locations. What is possible and cheap sometimes, though, is to camp innocently in official camping grounds when they are closed. Of course, there will be no luxuries like hot water and gas, but you probably did not want those anyway. One last word of warning on the topic of camping is that, in Japan, camping does not necessarily mean in tents. It may well mean in huts or other buildings of a temporary nature, with no accommodation for tents, and it may also mean in groups or families, without suitably priced facilities for individuals.

If you have a Japan Rail Pass, you will be able to find certain overnight trains with seats, on which you can sleep free, but not necessarily very comfortably. You will need to read the transportation section of this introduction to find out about other tickets, but with a *shu-yu-ken* (excursion ticket), you can also sleep on certain overnight trains and there are even a few which can be used with Blue Spring tickets.

For those with Japan Rail Passes, the following three overnight trains are specially recommended. First, the train called 'Midnight' which runs between Hakodate and Sapporo in Hokkaido. Ask to be accommodated in the 'carpet car' and you should get quite a reasonable night's sleep. This train is popular, so you need to book as far in advance as possible. Next is the train called *Naha* which runs between Shin Osaka and Nishi Kagoshima in the south of Kyushu. It has seats which recline very far back and are quite tolerable for sleeping. Thirdly, the *Akatsuki* train between Kyoto and Nagasaki has identical seating. All three of these trains have some accommodation reserved for ladies only.

Most usefully for Blue Spring, the 'Midnight' train mentioned above between Hakodate and Sapporo can be used on payment of just the reservation fee of ¥500. Then there is an overnight train called 'Moonlight' between Tokyo and Niigata and on to Murakami. This has reclining seats and is not too uncomfortable. You pay just the seat reservation fee of ¥500. Thirdly, there is a train between Tokyo and Ogaki, well on the way to Kyoto. This has upright seats and is terribly uncomfortable, but, if you have a Blue Spring ticket, you can continue all the way to Kyoto, Osaka, Hiroshima and even to Kyushu if you want to, all for ¥2,260 including a whole night of communal discomfort. Well, that is how it is when you are truly impoverished!

If you are really desperate for somewhere to sleep, small rural unmanned stations usually have an enclosed shelter of some sort which is not locked at night. Moreover, within the Tokyo area, there has recently been an accumulation of ramshackle temporary sleeping quarters around Shinobazu-no-ike, near Ueno station, occupied by the homeless. Should you feel like joining this community, at the present time, at least, the police seem to have given up trying to discourage such camping. A hostel is more comfortable, though, and safer for your possessions, if any.

## FOR THE ORDINARILY IMPOVERISHED

For those who are not absolutely destitute, but want to limit expenditure, best suggestions are to buy a Japan Rail Pass and to stay in youth hostels. Because you have bought the pass before coming to Japan, it will assure you of comfortable travelling and will not seem like an expense to be reckoned with whilst here.

As for the youth hostels, they are often very pleasant places to stay, especially if you can manage to get away from the large institutional ones where so many other visitors from overseas are to be found. As a general rule, the smaller and more remote the hostel, the more unique, interesting and friendly it is. Whatever the size or location, however, you will find there information in abundance and young Japanese who are interesting to talk to and learn about – and, after all, why did you come to Japan but to see the sights and meet the people? See the sights in the day and meet some of the people in the hostels in the evenings. Do not let age be a deterrent. Even if you happen not to be so young, you will be welcomed just the same at the hostels. In any case, young people rarely think about age. It has yet to creep up on them. And, as always, they will always want to widen their horizons by talking to guests from overseas. Sometimes the problem is to escape and get enough sleep.

If you are travelling alone (and, incidentally, the author believes that that is always the best way to meet people), then youth hostels are for you. However, for pairs and couples, you may find that some of the cheaper hotels are not much more expensive. If you would prefer privacy occasionally, check through the lists given and combine youth hostels with some cheap hotels. If you do this, the author's suggestion is to take hotels in the major sightseeing spots and hostels in the more remote locations. That way you will probably get the best of both worlds – some pleasant little hostels with real character combined with convenient, more centrally located, but still not too expensive, hotels in the larger cities.

One final suggestion for the partially impoverished who have sufficient time is to use Blue Spring tickets in addition to or instead of the Japan Rail Pass. See the section on transportation for more information on Blue Spring, but remember that, if you choose this option, you must plan to be in Japan during one of the Blue Spring seasons, that is December and January, March and early April or late July to early September. Blue Spring is an excellent way to see the country if only you are not in a hurry and come in the right season. Whilst Blue Spring itself is very economical, the problem is that the pace is more leisurely than with a Japan Rail Pass and then the necessary accommodation costs money.

## FOR THE ONLY MARGINALLY IMPOVERISHED

The author envisages that this group will comprise those who simply want to take a holiday in Japan without paying luxury prices and without being part of a group tour. Welcome to this book and congratulations on not being deterred by the title. Although you are not quite the type of reader for whom the information herein was compiled, you can surely benefit from it. Sightseeing activities are detailed and are just as suitable for you as for the less pecunious fraternity, especially if you do not mind doing some walking, which is always the best way to get the feel of a place in any case.

For travelling you should purchase a Japan Rail Pass covering about half of the total time which you wish to spend in the country and then base your tour plans on one of the itineraries given at the end of this book. Remember that it needs time to look at Tokyo and Kyoto in particular and that it is not good use of a rail pass to have your time ticking away while you are doing that, so try to visit one (probably Tokyo, since that is the arrival point for most people) before you start using your pass and arrive in the other with the last journey on the pass.

You will probably be most interested in the Japanese inns and business hotels for accommodation. The Japanese inns mostly offer Japanese style accommodation, with *futon* on a *tatami* floor, and give you much more of a sense of being in Japan. You should certainly try them. Most are very small and friendly establishments. Business hotels are, by contrast, usually western style, with beds, although the cheaper ones will offer only a communal bathroom in most cases. These hotels are quite adequate and only half of the price of what your travel agent is likely to be able to offer. It is advisable, though, always to reserve in advance for major cities.

## PRICES AND TIMES

Unfortunately, prices and times do change, so how reliable is the information in this book?

Prices first. Information is correct, to the best of our research abilities, as of January 1995. Inflation is slow in Japan, so it will be sufficient to add 5% per annum to the rates given in this book for use in 1996 and thereafter. At the time of writing, there is also a threat to increase the rate of 'consumption tax' from the current 3% to 7%. Rail fares have not increased for three years and so are likely to go up in the spring of 1995, while bus, taxi and subway operators in many cities applied for increases in 1994 and were refused on the grounds that, whilst the economy was not particularly healthy, an effort should be made to keep basic costs down. The transportation operators responded that the result of such a policy would be that the increases, when they came, would be large ones. They probably will come during 1995. In Tokyo, for example, the request was that the minimum subway fare should be raised from ¥140 to ¥170 and no doubt it will be soon. Please expect these inevitable increases and allow for them when budgeting.

As for times, you will note that this book has been far more specific about such matters than is usual. That is a calculated risk. As long as there are not too many timetable changes, it should assist the reader, but if there are major revisions, it will become a nuisance to him. JR introduces new timetables about every two years and did so last on 3rd December 1994. Therefore, with luck, the JR schedules in this book should remain reliable until the end of 1996. Even thereafter, there will probably be alterations of only a few minutes here and there, if recent precedent is followed, so, if you allow those few extra minutes, about 90% of the information given should still be correct until, say, the end of 1998. After that, maybe you should enquire whether there is not a later edition of this book available. Write to the publisher if in doubt.

Private railways tend to fit their times to suit JR connexions, so do not revise timetables independently very often. However, buses do change and should be regarded as the least reliable element in this book. In particular, many bus services have seasonal variations. Therefore, where bus times are given, they should be regarded as a general guide only and should always be checked. If you stay at youth hostels, you will find that there is always somebody in your dormitory who has a timetable. Ask him or her to check your next day's schedule for you.

Times are all given according to the 24 hour clock, as this seems the easiest way to avoid any confusion.

## GETTING TO JAPAN

Unfortunately, there are not so many really cheap air fares to Japan and the country is quite a long way from the usual points of origin of western travellers. Moreover, it is not on routes where a stopover can be taken easily.

From London, the cheapest flights to Japan cost about £500 return or £300 single at the time of writing (1995 prices). There are, of course, seasonal fluctuations and the prices mentioned are low season rates (winter). The cheapest airline is usually Aeroflot, via Moscow. Next cheapest, at about £550 return, are Bangladesh Biman, via Dhaka (change aircraft), Bangkok and Singapore, and Pakistan International via Karachi (change aircraft), Bangkok and Manila or via Islamabad (change aircraft) and Peking. The flight with Aeroflot takes about 15 hours, half of the time taken by the other two airlines mentioned. China Airlines sometimes has cheap flights via Taipei too and there are many other airlines offering different stops at about £600 return.

From Australia, cheapest prices are about $A1,200 return from any of the major cities. Flights are direct, or via Jakarta in the case of Garuda. There is also an offer from Australia or New Zealand of a stopover in Japan on flights to Europe with Japan Air Lines. This is not particularly expensive at around $A2,000 return and is perhaps the most attractive offer for a visit to Japan, since, if you are on your way to Europe, the stop costs nothing extra. Sadly, no similar stopover is available on a cheap ticket from Europe.

From North America, prices start at about $700 from the west coast of the United States. It is also possible to get stopovers on the way to Hong Kong, Seoul, Taipei and Bangkok, but not necessarily at the cheapest rates.

Note that an onward or return ticket is a requirement when entering Japan, although it is not usually inspected, as long as you do not appear excessively impoverished. Even though you will probably not be asked to show it, though, you will need such a ticket because cheap one-way air tickets are not available in Japan (only cheap returns). Incidentally, the airlines offering cheap tickets from Japan are mostly different from those offering cheap tickets to Japan. From Japan to Europe, the cheapest of the cheapies are Malaysian, Korean and again Aeroflot. To Australia only Malaysian, with Qantas in second place but far behind. To North America Malaysian again, followed by Korean. Cheapest return prices to Europe are ¥80,000, to Australia ¥100,000 and to North America ¥60,000, but nearly all such tickets are limited in validity to 35 or 60 days.

The cheapest place on a main route from which to reach Japan is Bangkok. Bangladesh Biman offers a return ticket via Singapore for 8,800 baht ($350 – stopover in Singapore $50 extra), a price which has not increased in 15 years.

As for shipping, there are ferries between Japan and Taiwan, China, Korea and, occasionally, Russia. The most interesting route is probably to take a ferry from Kagoshima, in the south of Kyushu, to Okinawa, thence to Taiwan, from where there is a ferry to Macao. From Macao, one can go through China or take a launch to Hong Kong, where cheap air tickets are available. However, this route, although interesting, is by no means cheap. Total cost from Kagoshima to Hong Kong will be $400 one way, in return for which expenditure you will see a lot of interesting parts of Japan which most visitors miss, plus the beauty of Taiwan and the tiny and unique colonies of Macao (if you go before 1999) and Hong Kong (if you go before 1997).

Customs regulations permit the visitor to bring three bottles of spirits and 400 cigarettes into Japan free of duty. These comparatively generous allowances are probably because virtually every Japanese businessman smokes and has to bring back bottles of whisky for his friends whenever he goes overseas. There is nothing much which can be brought into Japan and sold at a profit. Even imported alcohol is now available in discount stores in Japan (see Akihabara in Tokyo section of this book) for little more than one pays in an airport duty-free shop and Scotch whisky can often be purchased here more cheaply than in Scotland.

## VISAS

The immigration rules have changed several times recently and are quite likely to change again, so anybody thinking of coming to Japan should check that what is stated in the next few paragraphs is still correct.

Some nationalities need visas to visit Japan and some do not. Those who do not include citizens of the U.S.A., the U.K., Canada, New Zealand and most European countries. However, on arrival, assuming that the visa has been obtained by those who require it, all nationalities are usually treated the same and given a ninety-day stay as a 'temporary visitor'. This category seems to include almost anybody who is not earning money or studying here. It used to be possible to obtain one ninety-day extension, but now it seems to be more difficult to do so. For citizens of the U.S.A., it appears to be impossible. If one wants to stay longer under this status, one may have to leave the country and come back. There are relatively cheap air tickets, particularly to Seoul, which seem designed specifically for this purpose.

If you want to work in Japan, you will need either a working visa or a working holiday visa. The latter are issued only to young people who are nationals of countries with reciprocal arrangements with Japan. At present, this means Australia, New Zealand or Canada. The age limit is usually thirty. The period of stay granted is initially six months. One extension is relatively easy to obtain and a second extension is possible but more difficult. One is expected to combine part-time work with sightseeing, but there is little check on what proportion of each one does.

A working visa needs much more formality. It can be obtained before one comes to Japan, or one can apply for a 'Certificate of Eligibility to a Status of Residence' inside Japan once one has found an employer. However, in the latter case it is necessary to leave Japan to obtain the visa and then return using it. It does not have to be obtained in one's home country. Any place outside Japan will do. To obtain a working visa, one requires a university degree, where it seems an appropriate qualification for the work to be performed, and a contract for at least one year from an acceptable employer to perform an acceptable job. One also needs to produce one's *curriculum vitae* and one's academic qualifications (originals to be sighted and copies to be retained by the authorities). Certain other documents are required from your employer, including his business registration, his annual financial report, a letter giving his reason for wishing to employ you and letters offering certain guarantees regarding his new employee. It may take up to three months before the visa or Certificate of Eligibility is ready, although the applicant is usually told that it will not be as long as that. The working visa is generally granted for one year initially and is extendable annually thereafter. If one leaves Japan for any reason, one must first obtain (buy!) a re-entry permit if one wishes to retain one's current status. This applies to any type of status, in fact.

Those who are studying can obtain a cultural visa. This needs various documents from the institution where one is studying, including one to state that all fees due have been paid. The institution must be one recognized by the immigration authorities. Importantly, one also needs a guarantee letter from a private sponsor, preferably a Japanese. This letter is to say that the guarantor will take responsibility for any debts which one may incur, for repatriation if it becomes necessary and for ensuring that one's conduct remains within the limits of the law. (How is he supposed to do that, one wonders?) Cultural visas are usually granted initially for six months and are extendable until the authorities think that one has been studying for long enough. One year visas are also available. If one studies Japanese, one will usually be expected to demonstrate some proficiency in the language when applying for a visa extension. Those with cultural visas are permitted to do some part-time work to help to support themselves. This is not an automatic right. Permission must first be obtained from the authorities. It seems, incidentally, to be becoming more difficult to obtain a cultural visa. The authorities are examining the services offered by the schools more carefully now and scrutinizing the true purposes of the applicants. In particular, it seems that a request to change from temporary visitor status to cultural activities status is regarded with suspicion. Those with a cultural visa will also need to purchase a re-entry permit if they wish to leave the country and return with the same status.

There are other types of visa too, of course. If one is married to a Japanese, one will qualify for a spouse visa, these days available to males as well as females. Then there are visas for entertainers, missionaries and trainees. Most of those reading this book, however, will be interested in one of the types already dealt with.

In connexion with visas, it should be mentioned that there are plenty of people in Japan without the correct visa. The majority of these are from Asian countries. They arrive in Japan and are permitted short stays, following which they obtain employment, often involving manual labour for men or 'hostess' work for women, and then they stay until they feel that they have earned enough. When they leave the country, they are usually fined for overstaying, although they can also or alternatively be imprisoned, and are blacklisted from returning. There are also those with western backgrounds who work in the teaching or other industries without working visas and leave the country and return every three or six months.

Those who stay in Japan for more than three months, or have permission to stay for more than three months, must obtain a 'Certificate of Alien Registration' from the local government office in the area where they are residing and must carry this certificate at all times. Those who are staying for less than three months are required to carry their passports at all times. Police and certain other officials are entitled to ask to see such documents and, if one does not have either the certificate or the passport, one is likely to find a lot of one's time being wasted at the local police station.

Below is a list of various types of status of residence, activities permitted with each and periods of stay allowed, with the most common period granted listed first. Please note that this is not a comprehensive list. We have included only the categories most likely to be of interest to readers and have summarized the types of activities permitted. For complete information, a book succinctly entitled 'A Guide to Entry, Residence and Registration Procedures in Japan for Foreign Nationals', published by the Japan Immigration Association is available in Japanese and typical Japanese English (both languages in the same volume) for ¥1,500.

## STATUS OF RESIDENCE LIST

| Status of Residence | Activities Permitted | Period of Stay |
|---|---|---|
| Investor/Business Manager | Activities to commence or continue international trade | 1 year, 6 mths., 3 years |
| Legal/Accounting Services | Activities required by attorneys or certified public accountants recognized under the Foreign Lawyers' Law or the Accountant Law | 1 year, 6 mths., 3 years |
| Researcher | Research on basis of contract with public or private organization in Japan | 1 year, 6 months |
| Instructor | Language instruction or other education | 1 year, 6 mths. |
| Engineer | Engineering work on basis of contract with public or private organization in Japan | 1 year, 6 months |
| Specialist in Humanities/ International Services | Activities requiring knowledge of jurisprudence, economics, sociology, human science or foreign culture on basis of contract with public or private organization in Japan | 1 year, 6 months |
| Intra-Company Transferee | Work permitted for Engineer or Specialist in Humanities/ International Services, but as temporary transferee to an office legally established in Japan | 1 year, 6 months |
| Skilled Labor | Activities requiring industrial techniques or skills belonging to special fields on basis of contract with public or private organization in Japan | 1 year, 6 months |
| Cultural Activities | Academic or artistic activities providing no income, studying Japanese culture or arts | 6 months, 1 year |
| College Student | College or equivalent education | 6 mths., 1 year |
| Dependent | Daily activities for spouse or unmarried minor child of person legally residing in Japan under one of above categories | 1 year, 6 mths., 3 mths., 3 yrs. |
| Trainee | Learning technology, skills or knowledge at public or private organizations in Japan | 6 mths., 1 year, 3 months |
| Spouse or Child of Japanese National | Unrestricted | 1 year, 6 mths., 3 years |
| Temporary Visitor | Sightseeing, recreation, sports, visiting relatives, inspection tours, lectures, meetings, business contact, similar activities | 90 days, 15 days |

## GEOGRAPHY

Japan consists of four main islands and a string of over 3,000 minor ones. The four main islands are Honshu (meaning 'main island') in the centre, with Hokkaido to the north, Shikoku to the south and Kyushu to the south-west. From the south of Kyushu, a string of islands runs down almost to Taiwan. In all the chain which constitutes Japan stretches 3,000 kilometres from 45 degrees 31minutes north to 20 degrees 25 minutes north and covers a land area of 377,682 square kilometres. That makes it about 50% bigger than Great Britain or slightly smaller than the American state of California, for example.

Honshu has 61% of the total area and 80% of the population. The next island in terms of size is Hokkaido, which accounts for 22% of Japan's land area, but only 5% of its population. Kyushu represents 11% of the area and Shikoku 5%.

The total population is about 130,000,000, a number which is slowly increasing still, but only because lifespan continues to be extended. In fact, the current birthrate is only about 1.5 children per female, a figure which is so low that it has begun to cause some concern (although it seems to the author that having rather fewer people around might not be such a bad idea!).

Much of Japan is mountainous and many of these mountains are volcanoes, of which several are still active. From time to time a volcano erupts, causing considerable excitement and sometimes a few fatalities. At the time of writing, the most recent eruption was of Mt. Unzen, in the northern part of Kyushu. The lava flow down the eastern side of the mountain will be clearly evident to any visitor during the next few years.

Because of its location in an area of volcanic activity and shifting submarine plates, Japan is also subject to earthquakes. These can be quite sizeable and nobody enjoys them very much. However, Japanese buildings are constructed in the knowledge that they will be subjected to shaking, so serious damage and loss of life are much less than one might expect considering the magnitude of some of the earthquakes. In the three months prior to the writing of this paragraph, for example, there have been earthquakes measuring 8.1, 7.3 and 7.5 on the Richter Scale, all of which might well have caused serious loss of life in many parts of the world and the first of which, in particular, was of world-class size. In fact, however, a total of three people died in Japan in those three earthquakes and one of those perished of a heart attack brought on by the shock.

Then, however, followed the major earthquake in Kobe in January 1995. This earthquake registered only 7.2 according to Mr. Richter, but was shallow and sudden, putting great stress on buildings, so that even structures thought to be earthquake-proof succumbed and 5,400 lives were lost and a huge amount of damage was caused. There is always a fear of *tsunami* (tidal waves) following any earthquakes.

Should you have the misfortune to be in a major earthquake, you should turn off any appliances such as heaters which might cause fires and remember to use stairs, not lifts. If you are near the sea, it would be a good idea to move away as quickly as possible. If you then switch on a television or radio, you will discover what an excellent warning system has been developed. Within seconds of a major earthquake anywhere in the country, all normal broadcasting will have been suspended on all stations in favour of information and warnings likely to be of benefit to viewers and listeners. Both NHK (national) television channels will have information in English on their alternative language frequencies, although this will be only a recorded message at first. The Japanese service is really extremely precise, with information such as the following, "The Meteorological Agency advises that there is a strong fear of *tsunami*. The first *tsunami* is expected to reach Kushiro at precisely 23:00. The time is now 22:48. Residents of Kushiro have twelve minutes to evacuate to higher ground." However, whilst it is wise to know what to do if such a disaster should occur, do not become paranoid about it. Remember that, even in Kobe, 99.6% of the people survived, according to the author's calculations.

Because of the mountainous terrain, only about 20% of Japan is under cultivation and the part which is agricultural is devoted mainly to rice production by small-scale farmers (resulting in rice prices which are probably the highest in the world). Japan has few mineral resources, so depends upon importing raw materials and exporting finished products.

For sightseeing purposes, however, the geography of Japan is really very attractive, offering both mountain and coastal scenery in a compact area. Wherever you go, to famous natural beauty spots, or just travelling at random, it is still a most appealing landscape. Unfortunately, though, amidst all this beauty, the route most frequently travelled by visitors, the one between Tokyo and Kyoto, and that by *shinkansen*, which restricts the views and includes many tunnels, is one of the least interesting. So do try to get a little off the *shinkansen* routes and take a little time to admire the most attractive Japanese landscape, in which endeavour this book will assist you.

## CLIMATE

'Temperate' is a one-word description, but that hides the fact that Japan has a surprising range of climate. The highest temperature ever recorded is 40.8 ℃ in Yamagata (Tohoku, to the north of Tokyo) in 1933 and the lowest −41.0 ℃ in Kamikawa (Hokkaido) in 1902.

In Tokyo, summer is hot and humid, winter cool but not excessively cold. Snow falls on about ten days each winter. Places to the south of Tokyo tend to be rather warmer, of course, and those to the north somewhat cooler. The Japan Sea (northern) coastline is cooler than the Pacific (southern) coastline. In winter, however, Hokkaido is more than somewhat cooler than Tokyo, with even daytime maxima staying well below freezing in many places and night minima sometimes descending to the minus twenties and thirties centigrade. Actually, though, the factor which affects temperature most throughout Japan is altitude, rather than latitude.

As for visiting the country, any season is satisfactory, although if asked to choose the least appealing the author would opt for summer, because of the high level of humidity. If asked to choose the most attractive time, he would select autumn, when the leaves are in their russet beauty, slightly later in Japan than one might expect. November is quite a good time to come – and the trains are not too crowded then either. Spring is also pretty, as the cherry blossom dances through the land – and all the drunkards follow it! But actually the author is a winter eccentric and loves the northern areas of Hokkaido and Tohoku in that season, when the snow lies deep and unblemished and, much to their credit, the trains still manage to run on time, unlike in some western countries which invented this excellent means of transportation and should now be ashamed of their inabilities to deal with mildly unfavourable conditions. Remember, though, that Japan stretches quite far north, so that, in Hokkaido in particular, hours of daylight are short in winter (and long in summer).

Japan has a rainy season from mid-June until early July which tends to deter visitors at that time. However, the author rather likes rain (and, indeed, weather in general) and cannot see what all the fuss is about. Just bring an umbrella. It is, in his opinion, considerably better than the unrelieved humidity which follows during high summer.

In summary, Japan has plenty of seasonal variety, but do not be put off by it. Rather enjoy it and come at any time which suits you. The country will still be beautiful.

## TRANSPORTATION

It will be no surprise to discover that the author believes that trains are the best choice for long-distance travel. Despite recent pruning, the JR network covers the whole of Japan. It offers a fast and highly efficient service. Moreover, although it is not exactly cheap, there is not really anything cheaper. In fact, JR is not a single company, but a group of regional companies made from the old Japan National Railways (JNR). However, since the regional companies co-operate closely with each other, it is hardly apparent that JR is not a single organization. The JR service is supplemented by private lines, in the countryside as well as in the cities, so that if a place does not have a railway station, it must be very small indeed. Let us first, though, look at the other possibilities, which do exist.

### *By Car or Motor-Cycle*

Japan's roads are frequently congested, the 'expressways', for which huge tolls are exacted, as well as the ordinary highways, so driving is not only expensive but also not much fun. However, if that is what you decide to do, cars are available for hire at moderate rates. Since charges vary considerably, however, you should shop around before making a decision.

Hire of motor-cycles is less common, but there are many Japanese who travel Japan on their own machines ('bike' in Japanese, the word never being used to refer to non-motorized bicycles). This method of transport is economical and it allows you to see out of the way places which public transport does not reach or which are very expensive to get to by public transport. As anywhere else in the world, though, it is not a particularly safe method of travelling, especially as many of Japan's roads are so narrow and crowded. Moreover, it will be difficult to find anywhere where a motor-cycle is available for hire.

### *By Bus*

Long-distance buses have started operations in the last few years on a limited number of routes. Many of these run only at night. Prices are similar to, or just a little lower than, those for express trains. However, if you travel by night, you will save the cost of accommodation. The most popular route is between Tokyo and Kyoto or Osaka. In the daytime, you must change buses at Nagoya, but services are frequent. JR operates the buses between Tokyo and Nagoya, in competition with its own trains! Between Nagoya and Kyoto, again JR runs buses, but there are other operators too, while between Nagoya and Osaka there is a slightly less frequent service, again shared by JR and other operators. At night JR runs buses right through between Tokyo and Kyoto and between Tokyo and Osaka. On these night services, however, there is a seat reservation charge of ¥1,400 (waived for Japan Rail Pass users) and you cannot travel without a reservation.

### *By Air*

The air service offered is comprehensive and efficient. There are three major domestic airlines: Japan Air Lines (JAL), All Nippon Airways (ANA) and Japan Air System (JAS). Some smaller airlines offer supplementary services in more remote areas and to places which can accommodate only small aircraft. Note that in Tokyo nearly all domestic services use

Haneda Airport, not Narita International Airport. Haneda is much more conveniently located, within the Tokyo city limits, and is reached by a monorail from Hamamatsucho on the Yamanote Line or by a branch line of the Keihin Kyuko Private Railway which is joined to the Toei Asakusa subway line. Air travel is, of course, comparatively expensive. The airlines do not generally offer cheap tickets, but there are agents, usually operating from miniscule shops, or even, occasionally, just on the street, who will sell tickets at discount prices. These agents, it should be said, are more reliable than they appear!

For those who are short of time, there are sometimes cheap air 'tours' available, seasonally, to various destinations. Typically, for about the same price as the usual airfare, these include an hotel for two or three nights and a few meals, but not usually any actual tour.

***By Hitch-Hiking***

As mentioned previously, for those who are really short of money, hitch-hiking is very easy and pleasurable in Japan, because it is a rather un-Japanese thing to do. If you should try this method of transportation, you are likely to experience the overwhelming hospitality of the Japanese at its very best.

***By Ferry***

Then there are ferries. Perhaps surprisingly, Japan retains an extensive ferry service, not merely for short crossings between islands, but for long-distance travel too, in competition with land transport. The problem with ferries is that they are slow. However, prices compare favourably with land transportation in many cases and, of course, accommodation, albeit of a rather basic kind, on carpeted or *tatami*-mat floors in the lowest classes, is included. Since seas are rarely rough in Japan, it is a pleasant way to travel if you have enough time and if there is a service going to your destination. There are also regular international ferry services to Korea (from Fukuoka and Shimonoseki), to Taiwan (from Naha in Okinawa) and to China (from Nagasaki, Yokohama, Osaka and Kobe) as well as an occasional service from Yokohama or Niigata to Russia.

***By Train***

Which brings us back to trains. To plan your journey, the best thing to do is to purchase a railway timetable. Various versions are published in Japanese and JR gives away a rudimentary timetable in English. This version lists only express trains in most cases and only for main or tourist-oriented services. Also, it is sometimes out of date. If you need to go only to main centres and only by express trains, it will prove helpful, but often those who have this timetable do not appreciate that there are cheaper alternative services available. If you buy the Japanese version, you may not be able to read the names of the stations, but, by looking at the maps at the start of the book and comparing with a map in Japanese and Roman script, you will easily find your destination. The number of the page which you should consult is written on the railway line. Turn to that page and you will find all the trains available. The timetable is published by two different companies (JR and the Japan Travel Bureau - JTB) in three different sizes. The larger versions are easier to read. The timetable lists every rail service in Japan, all major long-distance and local bus routes, ferries, pleasure-boat trips, air services including international flights, funicular railways, monorails, ropeways and just about any other form of public transport you could imagine, except taxis. And it is very rare indeed to

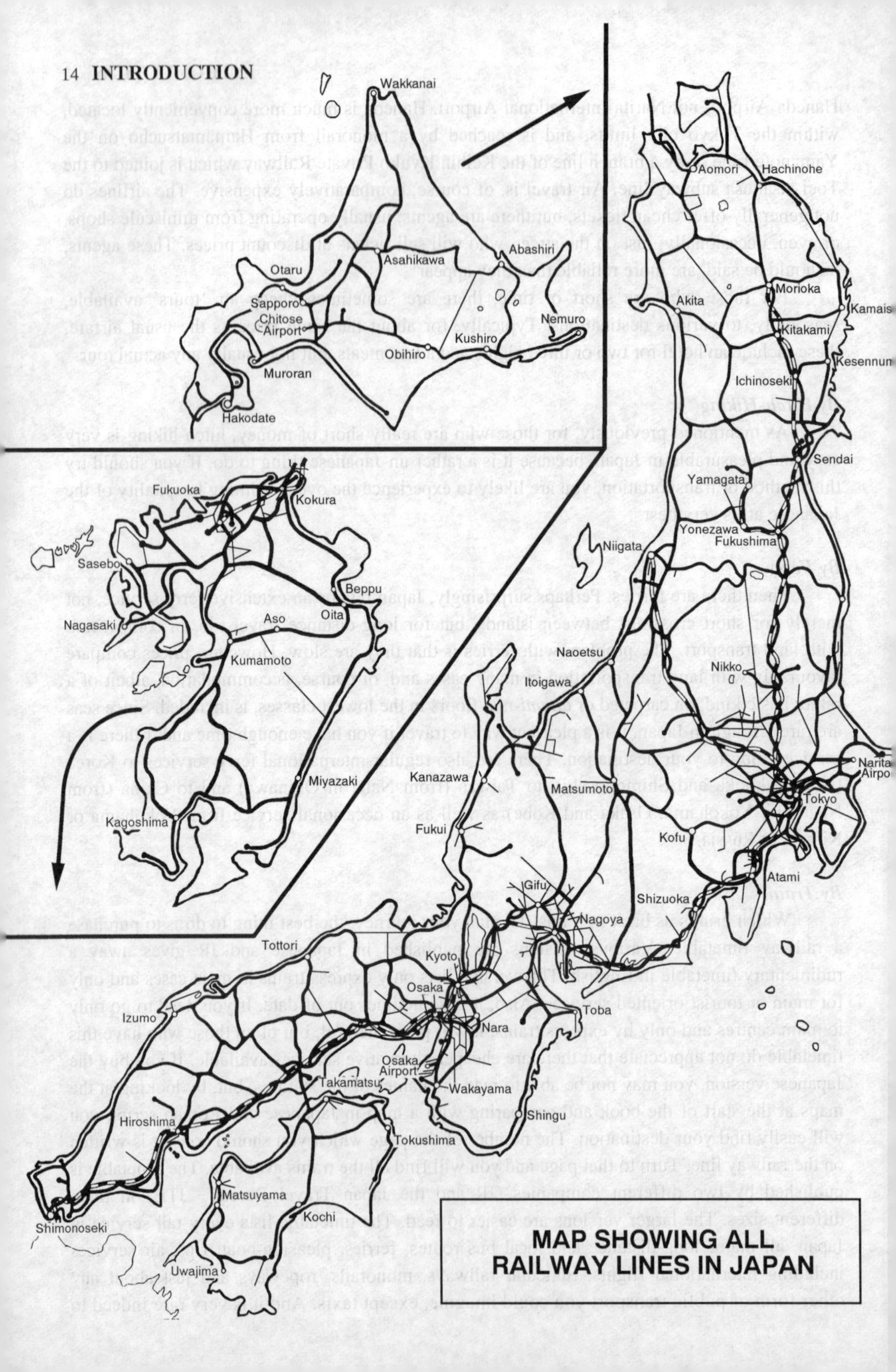


**MAP SHOWING ALL RAILWAY LINES IN JAPAN**

find a mistake in the thousand or so pages which make up this monthly publication. It is a remarkable book.

If all of this seems too complicated, in Tokyo JR operates an information service by telephone in English. The telephone number is 03-3423-0111 and the service is available from 10:00 until 18:00 on Monday to Friday. This is very convenient, of course, but you should not forget that, by using such a service, you get somebody else's opinion of what you should do, rather than what you yourself might have chosen had you known all the facts and possibilities. If your finances are limited, it might be better to investigate the choices by yourself - or read on in this book!

The system with JR trains is that first you buy a basic fare ticket to wherever you want to go. That ticket is enough to get you there, but if you want to use any express trains, you will need a supplementary ticket, of course at supplementary charge. If you want a reserved seat, there will be an additional charge for that. If you want to travel in the 'green car' (first class - 'green car' are the actual words used in Japanese; they are not a translation), that will cost still more. Most people buy their supplementary tickets before they start their journeys, but it is usually possible to get on the train and then pay the conductor.

Let us now look at the various trains available and the costs which will be involved in taking them. First, as a rough guide, you can reckon that travel in Japan using an ordinary ticket will cost about ¥15 per kilometre. It does not get appreciably cheaper with distance. The train which everybody associates with Japan, of course, is the *shinkansen* (bullet train). These magnificent monsters whizz along at up to 270 kilometres per hour and, in the thirty years for which they have been operating, there has never been a fatal accident involving a passenger on a train (over 200 suicides in front of trains, though, and a fair sprinkling of inattentive railway workers dispatched). They operate on a totally separate system from the rest of the trains, and there is a good reason for that, for they use a standard 4 feet 8½ inches track, while all the other JR services use a 3 feet 6 inches gauge. Even the west Japan (blue) trains and the north Japan (green) trains cannot use the same tracks, because the frequency of the electric current is different. This separation extends to there being barriers within the stations to prevent passengers without *shinkansen* tickets from entering the *shinkansen* section (although you can get in with just a platform ticket). If you want to travel by *shinkansen,* you will have to pay a very sizeable surcharge. As a rough guide, reckon that the supplement will add about two-thirds of the basic fare. The train is divided into reserved and unreserved sections, with the reserved section being the larger. If you want a reserved seat, it will add another ¥300, ¥500 or ¥700, depending on the season. On the platform the places to queue for unreserved seats will be marked.

The next fastest type of train is known as a *tokkyu* (limited express). It can usually be recognized by its high-level driver's cab. In general, *tokkyu* trains do not run where there are *shinkansen* routes. This type of train too attracts a sizeable surcharge, which may add something like 50% to the basic fare. However, if you change from the *shinkansen* to a *tokkyu* or *vice versa* on the same day, the *tokkyu* charge will be reduced by half. There are also night *tokkyu* trains which offer sleeping accommodation for another extra charge of ¥5,150 for the lowest class of accommodation, a class which is not necessarily available on all trains. These trains are quite comfortable and they travel at speeds of up to 130 kilometres per hour.

Next is the *kyuko* (express). These are fairly ordinary types of trains which stop at only a limited number of stations and usually offer some reserved seating. The number of such trains

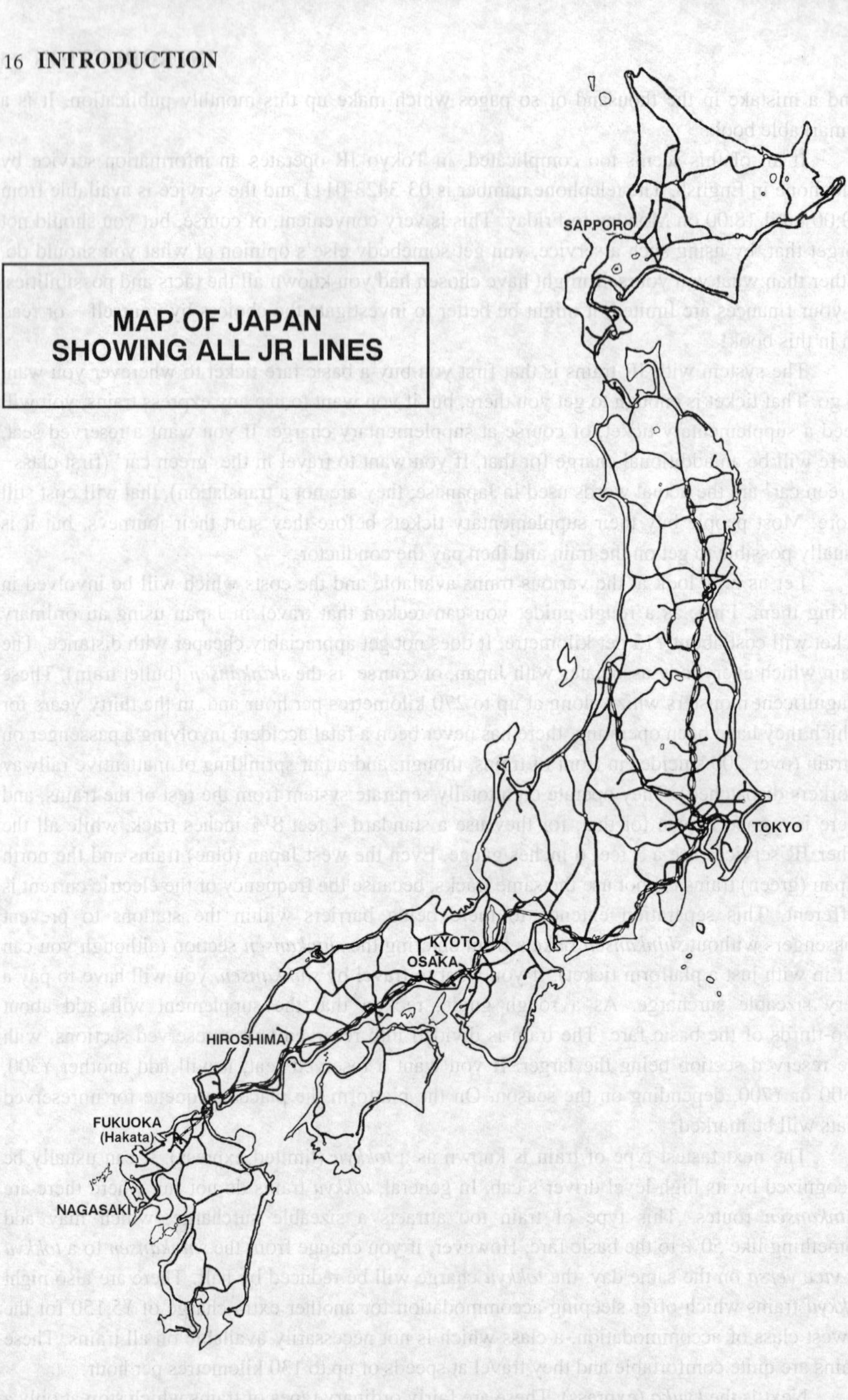
SAPPORO
TOKYO
KYOTO
OSAKA
HIROSHIMA
FUKUOKA
(Hakata)
NAGASAKI

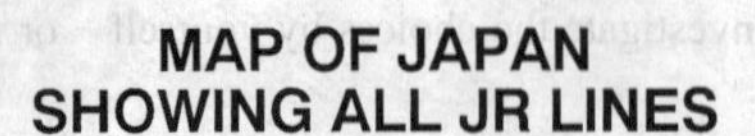
MAP OF JAPAN
SHOWING ALL JR LINES

has been reduced considerably in recent years, so that they now run mainly on lines where conditions do not permit the operation of trains fast enough to be deemed *tokkyu*. There are supplements for travelling on *kyuko* trains too. As a general guide, add a third to the basic fare for using a *kyuko*.

Next down the list are *kaisoku* (rapid) trains. These are trains which simply skip some stations and may or may not be a little more comfortable than ordinary trains. There is no supplement for using a *kaisoku*.

And, finally, there are *futsu* (ordinary) trains which stop at every station and for which there are, of course, no supplements.

It should be noted that the above categories apply to JR, not necessarily to private railways, which may use some different terms for their trains, commonly, for example, inserting a *junkyu* (semi-express) below the *kyuko*. Also, the express categories of private railways do not necessarily require supplementary charges. Usually, if a private railway train requires a supplement, it looks as though it does – and, indeed, this is generally true with JR too.

Well, now, how do we save money on long-distance trains? Yes, it is possible, for there are some special tickets available, mostly designed with the needs of sightseers, Japanese or from overseas, in mind. To use these tickets to the best advantage, and to avoid some financial catastrophe, it is very important to understand the rules for each, so the following sections will go into some detail on these points. It is also important with a pass of any type to plan your itinerary carefully in advance, otherwise you will find yourself wasting the pass on cheap short-distance work and discovering that it has expired when you really need it for expensive long-distance journeys. Here then are some of the special tickets most useful for visitors to Japan.

***Japan Rail Pass***

This pass is well known to almost every person who comes to Japan. It offers unlimited rail travel on JR for a period of one, two or three weeks. The Japan Rail Pass must be purchased abroad and is not available in Japan. Ordinary and 'Green' (first class) passes are available. The price is quoted in yen and then converted to the local currency, usually at a rate slightly favourable for the sales agent. The one week ordinary pass, for example, currently costs ¥27,800, the two weeks ordinary pass ¥44,200 and the three weeks ordinary pass ¥56,600. Since the cost of a one week pass is only a little more than the return fare from Tokyo to Osaka by *shinkansen*, the pass is really rather good value, expensive though it may seem when prices are converted into your local currency. It is important to note, though, in relation to this pass, that it can be used only by those with entry permits as temporary visitors. It cannot be used, for instance, by those with working visas. When you purchase the pass overseas, you will be issued with a voucher which is exchangeable at certain JR offices for the pass itself. The offices most commonly used for this purpose are at Tokyo station (Yaesu side) and at Narita Airport. There your passport will be checked to ensure that you are a temporary visitor. If you use one of the other JR offices which are authorized to make the exchange you *might* not get checked as strictly, but, there again, you might. Once you have exchanged your voucher for the actual pass, you can change your reservations as many times as you wish, but you cannot change the dates of validity on the pass, even, it seems, if you have not started using it. However, you can cancel the pass if you turn it in before the first day of validity. In this case, you will lose 10% of the value.

Basically, the Japan Rail Pass includes all express supplements and reservation charges. Note carefully, therefore, what it does not include. It does not include travel on the *Nozomi shinkansen* trains (running on the Tokaido and Sanyo *shinkansen* between Tokyo and Hakata) and it does not include sleeping accommodation on any train. Be very careful about this, because, if you want to use a sleeper, you must pay not only the sleeper charge, but also the express charge, which makes it very expensive - usually around ¥10,000. Similarly, if you erroneously travel on a *Nozomi* train, you will be liable not just for the difference in fares, but for the entire express supplement. The exact amount will depend upon the distance travelled, but it will certainly be several thousands of yen.

The pass itself is sufficient authority to travel. You can just go into any station, get onto any train and travel in unreserved accommodation. However, if you reserve, which costs nothing, you will be spared the necessity of being on the platform early enough to ensure a good seat. You will be issued with a ticket allocating you a specific seat. A and D seats are window seats or, in the *shinkansen*, A and E in most ordinary carriages. If you want to travel in non-smoking accommodation, you should say so. The booking office clerk will probably understand the words 'no smoking', but, in case not, the Japanese is *kin-en*. The Japanese for 'smoking' is *kitsu-en.* If you choose a 'Green' pass, it is worth noting that on some trains there is no non-smoking green car accommodation available.

At the end of your pass, you are permitted to complete any journey commenced within the validity of the ticket, as long as no change of train is involved. In other words, you may take an overnight train for your last journey and arrive at your destination on the day after the one on which your ticket expired.

### *Shu-yu-ken*

Now the Japan Rail Pass, although so well known, is not the only bargain available and, in any case, there may be those who are not eligible for such a pass. There are other special tickets, less well publicized overseas, which are available to Japanese sightseers too. One of these is the *shu-yu-ken*, which might reasonably be translated as an 'excursion ticket'. It is particularly suitable for those who wish to visit only one area of Japan. Suppose that you arrive in Tokyo and want to go only to the Kyoto, Nara and Osaka area. You can buy a ticket, for about the same price as the ordinary return fare, which will permit you to go there and come back and also to travel freely within a fixed area for a certain period of time. In this particular case, the free area would include all JR lines in and around Osaka, Kyoto, Nara and Kobe. The time allowed depends on the distance from the point of origin. In this case, it would be a week. Travel to and from the area is by ordinary train, or by *kyuko*, but if you want to take a faster train, you may do so by paying just the supplement. If the free area chosen is a large one, such as Hokkaido or Kyushu, then travel within the area by *tokkyu* is permitted, as long as unreserved accommodation is used. If it is a smaller area, only ordinary and *kyuko* trains are allowed, unless appropriate supplements are paid. Most JR buses within the area can also be used. These *shu-yu-ken* are available for almost any area of Japan from any major starting point, as long as the area being visited is far enough away from your point of origin for the journey to be considered an excursion. It is permissible to stop off on the way there or back or both, as long as you stay within the validity of the ticket. It is also permissible to start back at the very end of the period of validity and to arrive on the next day, as long as you do not take any unnecessary stops.

What you should be very careful about with a *shu-yu-ken* is travelling in reserved accommodation. If you do so, you will be liable for the entirety of any express supplement, in addition to the reservation charge itself.

***Blue Spring (Sei-shun ju-hachi kippu* -青春 *18* きっぷ*)***

For those who really want to economize, there is a JR ticket called the *sei-shun ju-hachi kippu*. The author refers to it as the Blue Spring ticket, because *sei-shun* literally translated means just that. In fact, though, the real meaning is 'youth' and *ju-hachi* means eighteen. (*Kippu* means ticket.) However, there is no age limit for this ticket; it is just a name. For ¥11,300, Blue Spring gives you five one-day tickets. You can go wherever you like in Japan from midnight until midnight. This is really excellent value for ¥2,260 per day and this is one of the author's favourite types of ticket. The catch is that you can use only ordinary and *kaisoku* trains. If you want to take any sort of express, you must pay the full fare, including the supplement, for that journey (not just the supplement, please note). However, unlike with the Japan Rail Pass, time is not ticking away on your ticket while you are stationary. You do not have to use your five tickets on consecutive days, nor do they all have to be used by the same person. They can be used by anybody at any time within the period of validity. Blue Spring tickets are available only around school holiday times, however, and can be used during the periods 1st March until 10th April, 20th July until 10th September and 10th December until 20th January. Sales of the tickets cease ten days before the end of each period and tickets cannot be carried over into the next Blue Spring season.

Throughout this book, reference has been made to how trips can be undertaken using Blue Spring tickets. They really are an excellent way of experiencing the real Japan and give a chance to see and appreciate the beauty of the Japanese countryside, because, on ordinary trains, one moves at a leisurely pace.

It is very important to note, though, that the term 'Blue Spring' is just the author's joke. Nobody in Japan is going to understand what is intended if you go to the ticket counter and ask for 'Blue Spring' tickets (although people may think it quite amusing when they do finally comprehend!). Officially, these are called *sei-shun ju-hachi kippu*, the *kanji* (Chinese characters) for which are given above, just in case the words do not seem to trip off the end of your tongue, and that is what must be requested at the booking office.

***Other Special Tickets***

There is quite a range of other special tickets, of which some brief mention may be made here. There is a ticket called a **'Full Moon'** ticket (this time it is the real name, not the author's joke). It allows travel for various periods for a husband and wife travelling together whose combined ages total at least 88 years. Travel is in 'green car' (first class) reserved seat accommodation by day and in the lowest class of sleeper at night. Any trains may be used, except the *Nozomi shinkansen*. The advantage of this ticket is the sleeping accommodation, of course, which is not available with a Japan Rail Pass. The ticket might suit a middle-aged-plus couple planning a fairly intensive itinerary and who would appreciate the benefits of first-class seats during the day. The tickets available are valid for 5 days for ¥79,000, for 7 days for ¥98,000 or for 12 days for ¥122,000 (prices are for two people). A 5% discount is given if one of the travellers is over 70 years of age.

There is another ticket called a '**Nice Midi Pass**'. This is for two or more ladies over the age of 30 travelling together. There are two types – ordinary and 'green car' – valid for unlimited travel in Japan for three days, except by *Nozomi shinkansen* and the airport express trains. The 'green car' pass includes the lowest class of sleeper, and, for this reason only, might just possibly interest two females with a very short stay in Japan. In any other case, a Japan Rail Pass would seem better value. The ordinary pass costs ¥56,000 for two and *pro rata* for more ladies. The 'green car' pass costs ¥76,000 for two and *pro rata* for more ladies.

Around Tokyo, there is a ticket called an '**Holiday Pass**' available on Saturdays, Sundays and holidays. This gives unlimited travel for the day on ordinary trains within the area shown below for the sum of ¥2,000. There is another ticket called a '**Super Holiday Pass**' which gives unlimited travel within the larger area shown on the opposite page for ¥4,000. The latter is not a bargain, of course, if it is during Blue Spring season when you can go anywhere in the country by ordinary train for ¥2,260. However, there is the distinction that, with the 'Holiday Pass' and 'Super Holiday Pass', one may use expresses, except the Tokaido *shinkansen* (the Tohoku and Joetsu *shinkansen* may be used), on payment of the appropriate supplement, whereas with Blue Spring one must not use expresses at all. Recently, other areas in Japan have started to develop their own 'Holiday Passes' too, so, if it happens to be a holiday and you need a ticket for local travel, you might enquire whether an 'Holiday Pass' is available for the area where you happen to be.

***Ordinary Tickets***

If you just want to go somewhere and come back, you will get a 10% reduction by buying a return ticket if the single journey is over 600 kilometres. The validity of the ticket will depend on the length of the journey. You get two days for the first 200 kilometres and one day for each 200 kilometres or part thereof after that. This applies to single tickets as well as to returns. Stopovers are permitted, except within the actual cities of departure and destination.

If you want to take the *shinkansen* on a popular route, such as Tokyo to Osaka, you can

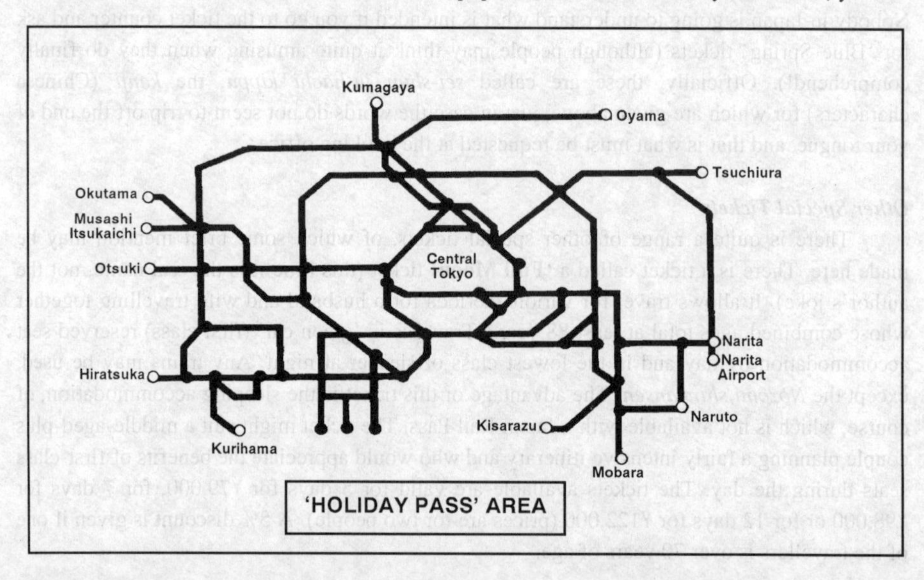

go to one of those miniscule travel agents mentioned above in connexion with cheap air tickets. They have cheap rail tickets too. If one buys tickets in bulk, one can get a discount, so these agents purchase fifty and retail them cheaply, sharing the savings with their customers. You can usually obtain a reserved *shinkansen* ticket rather more cheaply than you would be able to buy an unreserved one from the station. You then have to take the ticket to the booking office to make the reservation (no charge), otherwise you would still have to travel in the unreserved accommodation. All this is quite legal, in case you worry. You have until the date marked on the ticket to use it, usually quite a generous allowance, although the exact time will depend on when the agent bought his tickets. It should be noted that these bulk tickets, as well as some of the special tickets mentioned above, cannot be used for about ten days in each of the three peak travelling seasons, that is at New Year, in 'Golden Week' (at the end of April and beginning of May) and at *o-bon*, in the middle of August.

This is not an exhaustive list of cheap rail tickets available, but it covers most types likely to be of interest to our readers. If none of them suits your own requirements, try telephoning the JR information service, but the chances are that there is nothing quite designed for you. For most people, the most useful tickets are the Japan Rail Pass, the *shu-yu-ken* and Blue Spring.

## ACCOMMODATION

Accommodation is likely to be a major concern for all readers of this book, even the only marginally impoverished. If you want a first-class hotel, there will be no problems at all, but then if you wanted that, you probably would not have purchased this book.

In the Accommodation section of this book, you will find four types of accommodation listed. First are youth hostels, more than 300 of them, with an individual map for each. Youth hostels are very fine places to stay in Japan, especially the smaller, more remote and more unusually Japanese ones, for example temple hostels. There is a lengthy introduction to this section, so the information will not be repeated here, except to make two or three important

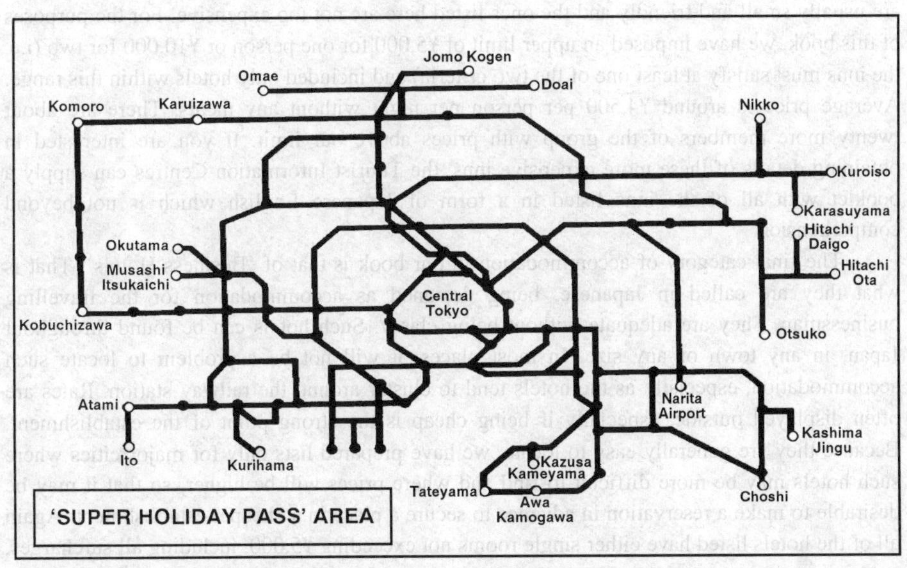

points. The first is that you must make reservations by telephone for these hostels, not just turn up hopefully. A Japanese hosteller will help you to do this, upon supplication. The second is that the maps are *not to scale*. It is vital to understand this in advance, rather than say all sorts of unrepeatable things about this book after the disaster. It is the Japanese way of drawing maps and it works quite well once you get used to it! And thirdly, please do read the introduction to youth hostel accommodation *before* trying to use the hostels. It really will help, since Japanese hostels have their own special character. Average price is around ¥2,500 and older people will find themselves just as welcome as younger, provided they take the precaution of becoming youth hostel members before arriving, or failing that, buy a Youth Hostelling International Card (¥2,800) as soon as they get here.

The second category of accommodation listed is private hostels. These are available only in Tokyo and Kyoto. They tend to have fewer rules, more character, more dirt and a lower tariff than the youth hostels. Those in Tokyo are often so crowded, however, that they are not very interested in new guests, as you may discover when trying to telephone them. The ones in Kyoto, though, will be more interested in having your custom. The main advantage of these places, really, is that they are comparatively cheap, so they will be of particular interest to those at the lower end of the scale of impoverishment. Individual maps are given for all, again many of them not to any very accurate scale, since they were mostly taken from hand-drawn sketches. Prices start at ¥1,100 and average about ¥2,000. This section also includes some cheaper hotels, mostly Japanese-style, in Tokyo and Kyoto, which did not fit into any of the other categories.

The third category is that of the 'Japanese Inn Group'. This is not a group in the sense of a chain under the same management. It is a loose association of Japanese-style hotels which would welcome guests from overseas. There is a brief introduction to the particular features of Japanese-style accommodation, which it would be wise to read before deciding that this is the style of accommodation which would suit you. However, most people enjoy these hotels, or *ryokan* as they are termed in Japanese, because they give a real feeling of being in Japan and are usually small and friendly and the ones listed here are not too expensive. For the purposes of this book, we have imposed an upper limit of ¥5,000 for one person or ¥10,000 for two (i.e. the inns must satisfy at least one of the two criteria) and included only hotels within this range. Average price is around ¥4,500 per person per night without any meals. There are about twenty more members of the group with prices above our limit. If you are interested in obtaining details of these more expensive inns, the Tourist Information Centres can supply a booklet with all of the inns listed in a form of Japanese English which is not beyond comprehension.

The final category of accommodation in our book is that of 'Business Hotels'. That is what they are called in Japanese, being designed as accommodation for the travelling businessman. They are adequate without being classy. Such hotels can be found throughout Japan, in any town of any size. In most places, it will not be a problem to locate such accommodation, especially as the hotels tend to cluster around the railway station. Rates are often displayed outside, especially if being cheap is the strong point of the establishment. Because they are generally easy to locate, we have prepared lists only for major cities where such hotels may be more difficult to find and where prices will be higher, so that it may be desirable to make a reservation in advance to secure a place in a cheaper establishment. Again all of the hotels listed have either single rooms not exceeding ¥5,000, including all surcharges, or, more usually, double or twin rooms not exceeding ¥10,000. In larger cities, such as Tokyo, it was, in fact, quite difficult to locate any hotels satisfying these criteria. Two warnings are necessary. The first is that many of the rooms at these prices in major cities do not have bathrooms attached. There is, of course, a communal Japanese-style bathroom available. More information about Japanese-style bathing is given in the introduction to the Youth Hostels, but be assured that it is a pleasurable experience once one becomes accustomed to it. The second warning is that hotel rates have been increasing disproportionately rapidly recently. If this trend continues, you may well find prices considerably higher than stated in this book. As usual, take 1995 as a base and add 5% per annum for subsequent years.

## HISTORY

### *Early Days*

It is believed that the Japanese archipelago became separated from the mainland of Asia about 20,000 years ago, at the end of the last Ice Age. Therefore, the inhabitants of Japan are of basically the same ethnic origin as the nearby Asian peoples, perhaps mixed to some extent with seafaring migrants from Polynesia.

Over a period of some 8,000 years a distinctive form of civilization evolved of which the surviving features are shell mounds (*kaizuka iseki*) and a form of pottery bearing patterns made with ropes. This is known as Jomon earthenware and, because of its distinctiveness, this period of Japanese history is usually referred to as the Jomon Era. The people of this time were hunters and fishers who also gathered wild fruits and vegetables.

The period covering the third century B.C. to the second century A.D. is known as the Yayoi Era. Yayoi is a place in the Tokyo area where pottery dating from this period was discovered. At this time, people started to live on farms and to cultivate crops, adopting from the Asian continent the system of paddy-farming to produce rice. Metal implements started to be used and the population began to gather into local communities, leading to the development of a system of village leaders and priests. Gradually provinces started to be formed with their own leaders.

***Kofun or Yamato Era*** (From end of 3rd century B.C. until 7th century A.D.)

Yamato is the name of a place near the present Nara. Yamato became central in the process of unification of the nation, which first occurred during this period, albeit on a rather loose and informal basis. The history books claim that the first Emperor of Japan was Jimmu, who was enthroned on 11th February in the year 660 B.C. 11th February is still a national holiday to commemorate the founding of the nation. In fact, however, there is little reason to suppose that there is any accuracy in the date chosen or the year given. Modern thought is that they simply happened to fit with a cycle of auspicious events according to the Chinese calendar.

It was during the Yamato Era that the Emperor of Japan really started to be recognized as a figurehead. He gradually gained in power as the unification proceeded and at this time the title of Emperor was first used. Various burial mounds (*kofun*) attest to the power and wealth which the Imperial family gradually gained. Accordingly, archaeologists sometimes refer to this period as the Kofun Era, while the word Yamato is still used to this day to describe something which is distinctively Japanese. For example, a picture in a uniquely Japanese style is referred to as *yamato-e*, a Japanese spirit as *yamato damashii* and a Japanese lady as *yamato nadeshiko*.

***Asuka Era*** (From mid-6th century until early 8th century)

In the year 538, Buddhism was introduced to Japan from China and Prince Shotoku (573 – 620) adopted it as the state religion, building the famous temple named Horyu-ji just outside Nara as a centre for the faith. Prince Shotoku was a particularly capable and enlightened leader who worked hard to establish a strong centralized nation with a single leader. He promulgated the 'Seventeen Articles' defining the concept of a nation. He also developed the 'Twelve Ranks' system whereby ordinary people could win promotion to higher positions. He sent students and priests to China to broaden their horizons and to improve diplomatic ties and he was the first person to use the phrase 'The Nation of the Rising Sun' to refer to Japan in diplomatic correspondence.

After the death of Prince Shotoku, Prince Nakono Oe carried out reforms in 645 leading to the further centralization of authority. In 701 all land and servants of the court and nobles were placed under the control of the central government, following the example of China, and a taxation system was introduced. For the first time original coinage was minted.

***Nara Era*** (710 – 784)

Until this time, the location of the national capital had changed every time there was a new Emperor. This was because the land of the old capital was thought to be polluted by the death of the former Emperor. However, this was a rather inconvenient system, as can be imagined, so, in 710, it was decided to establish a permanent capital in Nara. Thus Nara remained the capital of Japan until 784.

Under the guidance of another enlightened leader, the Emperor Shomu, the capital grew steadily and increased in prosperity. Buddhism was promoted and the temple of Todai-ji was constructed with its famous Big Buddha image. Also, all around the country were constructed temples named Kokubun-ji, the word meaning 'nationally-proliferated temples', sponsored by the government.

However, as the century progressed, the constitutional government system gradually began to collapse and the court nobles once again started to own land and servants privately. These people increased in wealth and power and started to create their own aristocratic culture.

***Heian Era*** (794 – 1185)

In order to restructure the system of government, as well as to sever the strong influential ties between Buddhism and government, the Emperor Kanmu decided to move the Imperial capital to Kyoto, which remained the seat of Emperors for more than a millennium, until the beginning of the Meiji Era in 1868. Like Nara, Kyoto was modelled on the system used in China.

It is at this stage in Japanese history that we find the word *shogun* first being used. In the early ninth century, the border of Japan was extended as far north as the tip of the present nation's main island of Honshu. To do this, it was necessary to push back the Ainu people who were already living in the northern areas of Honshu. Campaigns were waged and the generals in charge were given the title of *Sei-tai Shogun* ('Great Barbarian-Crushing Generalissimo').

At the successful conclusion of the campaign, the title would be relinquished and returned to the Emperor, who would usually grant some favour by way of thanks.

Now, however, the Emperors began to neglect politics and to spend much of their time at leisure or in pursuit of studies of the arts, literature or culture. Taking advantage of this change in interests, the noble family of Fujiwara began to gain influence by controlling the political scene. The peak of the power of the Fujiwaras came in the eleventh century. They married into the royal family and managed to monopolize almost all of the important government positions. As time went on, however, the Fujiwara family too became corrupted by luxury and this allowed the rise of the *samurai* (warrior) class to positions of political strength.

The first *samurai* to come to power were the Taira family, but their supremacy was short-lived, as they were defeated by the Minamoto clan first at the bloody battle of Yashima, near Takamatsu in Shikoku, in 1184, and then, finally, a year later, at the battle of Dan-no-ura, near Shimonoseki at the western tip of Honshu.

In terms of culture, this period saw Japan loosening her ties with China and developing her own distinctive culture. The system of dispatching regular scholarly and diplomatic missions to China ceased in 894.

***Kamakura Era*** (1192 – 1333)

Minamoto's victory spelt the end for aristocratic court government with the Emperor as the central figure. Instead, Japan was now to have a military administration. Minamoto Yoritomo persuaded the Emperor to appoint him as *shogun*, a title which he did not return at the end of any campaign, and he became the first administrative *shogun* in the country's history. To avoid the bad example of his predecessors in power, he decided to shift his base away from the affluent atmosphere of Kyoto and chose Kamakura, a short distance west of the present Tokyo, for his administrative headquarters (*bafuku*). For the next 700 years, Japan was to be ruled by the *samurai* class under a feudal system by which the *shogun* would divide the land among the local lords (*daimyo*), in return for which they would pledge absolute allegiance to him.

The control of the Minamoto family lasted for three generations, until Minamoto Sanemoto, the grandson of Yoritomo, was assassinated in Kamakura in 1219 as part of a family feud. As the result of the plotting of the Hojo family (the family of Yoritomo's wife), all of the possible Minamoto successors were eliminated and power moved into the hands of the Hojos, who controlled the Kamakura government for the next 140 years. To do this, they invited a member of the Fujiwara family to accept the nominal title of *shogun* and kept the reigns of actual power firmly within their own circle.

It was at this time that Japan faced its first ever serious threat of invasion. The Mongols, under Kublai Khan, the descendent of Genghis Khan, the founder of the Mongolian Empire, had already conquered most of central Asia, and had established an empire which stretched from China to eastern Europe, the most extensive that the world had ever seen. Kublai Khan sent a letter to Japan demanding that the country pay tribute to him or risk the threat of invasion. Japan refused and the Mongols sent a first expeditionary force to Hakata (Fukuoka) in Kyushu in 1274. With the assistance of a typhoon, Japan repelled the troops. However, the threat was not ended, for in 1281 a much larger force was dispatched, an huge army of over

100,000 soldiers. Fortunately, a typhoon occurred again at the vital moment and the Mongolian fleet was wrecked, with the assistance of a defensive wall which the Japanese had built. The typhoon which had been instrumental in the destruction of the Mongolian fleet was referred to as a 'Divine Wind' (*kamikaze*), a term which was resurrected at the end of the Second World War to describe those who were prepared to give their lives in support of their nation and in the hope of divine assistance. Following the *kamikaze* of 1281, both the troops involved and the priests who claimed that they had prayed for divine intervention awaited their reward from the Kamakura government, but Kamakura had nothing to offer and a feeling of discontent began to spread. The Emperor Godaigo in Kyoto was not slow to notice this change in the political situation and made an attempt to regain real power from these favourable circumstances. At his second attempt, he managed to set up an administration in 1334. For a brief period, imperial power was restored.

***Muromachi Era*** (1338 - 1573)

Unfortunately for him, the Emperor Godaigo respected and rewarded only nobles and priests. Thus the warriors came to bear a grudge against him and the warlord Ashikaga Takauji, who had assisted the Emperor to regain power, set up his own military government in Kyoto in defiance of Imperial authority. In 1338, he invited the Emperor to name him the first Muromachi *shogun* and, when that invitation was accepted, there followed a period of 54 years when two Imperial courts existed. However, by the time of the third Muromachi *shogun*, Ashikaga Yoshimitsu, the man who built Kinkaku-ji in Kyoto, the courts had been reunified and both nobles and the Imperial court had lost real power once more. The Imperial opportunity had been missed.

Yet, by the time of the eighth Muromachi *shogun*, Ashikaga Yoshimasa, the man who built Ginkaku-ji, the shogunate had also lost power and from this time poor administration coupled with excessive taxation was to result in civil chaos.

A problem regarding the succession to the shogunate led to a major war in 1467 and this was followed by a century of feuding when powerful lords tried to expel or kill their masters in order to grasp higher positions, in total defiance of the *bushido* code of chivalry, which was based on absolute loyalty to one's master. This period is often referred to as the 'Warring States' period.

Finally, in 1573, a relatively minor warlord, Oda Nobunaga, expelled the fifteenth Muromachi *shogun* and the Muromachi Era came to an end. Although the political administration had been unstable during the Muromachi Era, culture had flourished and the popularity of *Noh, Kyogen*, Zen Buddhism, Tea Ceremony and Flower Arrangement, for example, had increased very considerably, especially amongst the nobility.

***Azuchi Momoyama Era*** (1582 - 1600)

Firearms had been introduced to Japan in 1543 and Oda Nobunaga's great merit was that he was able to make effective use of such weapons to maintain his supremacy. He was on the verge of complete reunification of the nation when he was assassinated by one of his generals in 1582. Another general, Toyotomi Hideyoshi, took vengeance on the assassin and succeeded his former master, completing the reunification process. Toyotomi was the son of a farmer who rose through the ranks and was just beginning to prove himself an able leader when he suddenly died whilst supervising an invasion force heading for Korea. Initially he was succeeded by his son, but Tokugawa Ieyasu, a commissioner of the Toyotomi government, mounted a challenge, resulting in the battle of Sekigahara, a town some way east of Kyoto, in 1600. The victor was Tokugawa and the reunification of Japan became a fact under his administration. A Japanese saying is that, 'Nobunaga made the pie and Hideyoshi baked it, but Ieyasu was the man who ate it.'

***Edo Era*** (1603 - 1867)

Tokugawa Ieyasu, possibly the most famous man in Japanese history, was appointed *shogun* in 1603. He immediately moved the administrative government to Edo (Tokyo), leaving the Emperor and his court in Kyoto without power. The Tokugawa shogunate proved to be the longest warrior class government in Japanese history, lasting for some 260 years. This became known as the Edo Era. The stability of this period of history resulted from various decisions made by Tokugawa Ieyasu himself. He organized his government very efficiently and used able advisors in various fields, amongst them an Englishman, William Adams, who had been shipwrecked here, as naval advisor. He also became aware of the threat posed by Jesuit Christianity, introduced by St. Francis Xavier in 1549, which was becoming well established in Kyushu and seemed likely to threaten the established feudal system. He was later proven right, for in 1637 there was a rebellion in Nagasaki which had to be crushed by Ieyasu's grandson, Iemitsu. Strict division of governmental powers was introduced. The Tokugawa family took control of major cities, ports and mines, while 270 *daimyo* were each given their own territory, scattered throughout Japan so as to ensure political security. Society was clearly divided into four classes. The warriors (*shi*) were at the top. Next came the farmers (*no*), then the artisans (*ko*) and finally the merchants (*sho*). To ensure security, the *shogun* insisted that each *daimyo* pay a visit to Edo once every two years and that the *daimyo*'s wives and children remain in the city permanently. There they were virtually hostages to ensure the good behaviour of the *daimyo* themselves. Moreover, the arrangement put a severe economic burden on the *daimyo*, so that they could never consider rebellion and remained loyal to the Tokugawa government at all times. Believing that foreign influences, and Christianity in particular, would have a destabilizing effect on society, the third Tokugawa *shogun*, Iemitsu, decided to close the country completely, except for a single trade route with the Dutch and Chinese through the small island of Dejima in Nagasaki. This seclusion policy lasted for 220 years, starting in 1639.

Because of these policies established by his predecessors, the reign of the fifth *shogun*, Tsunayoshi, saw the peak of political stability and cultural advancement. A series of reforms carried out in 1716 - 1745, followed by others in 1787 - 1793 and 1841 - 1843 resulted in the regaining of much of the prosperity of past ages.

All of this pattern of government was disturbed when, in 1853, during the administration of the fourteenth Tokugawa *shogun*, Commodore Perry of the U.S. Navy came to Uraga, near the present U.S. Navy base at Yokosuka, not far west of Tokyo, bearing a letter from the president of the United States demanding that Japan open its ports to foreign trade. Since for centuries no foreign warships had been seen in Japan, great consternation was caused by the arrival of the four 'Black Ships'. The Japanese government promised to give a response the following year and Perry withdrew. He returned the next year with seven ships to assist him in giving a strong hint to the Japanese government. In 1858, the Chief Minister, Naosuke Ii, without consultation with the Emperor and without obtaining a consensus from the influential *daimyo*, signed a treaty of amity and commerce and opened a limited number of ports to foreign trade. Because of his dictatorial attitude, Ii was assassinated shortly afterwards. However, the centuries of isolation had been brought to an end. Society was in turmoil because of opposition to the change in policy and it became evident that the days of the Tokugawa shogunate were numbered.

*Meiji Era* (1868 – 1911)

A strong anti-government revolt centred in Satsuma (now Kagoshima in Kyushu) and Choshu (now Yamaguchi in extreme western Honshu) forced the fifteenth Tokugawa *shogun*, Yoshinobu, to step down from his position. The Emperor Meiji took control and proceeded, over the years of his reign, to carry out a series of enlightened reforms which established Japan as a modern nation and one to be reckoned with.

In 1868, the Emperor transferred the Imperial Palace from Kyoto to Tokyo (as he renamed the city of Edo) and established a strong government led by himself with the assistance of many able advisors. That this, the 'Meiji Restoration', was achieved without bloodshed is a great tribute to the wisdom of the leaders of both sides. The Emperor restored the lands of the provincial feudal lords and appointed them governors of their prefectures. He replaced Buddhism with Shintoism as the state religion, the latter regarding him as a living god, under whom four new classes of citizens were established, these being the Emperor's family and relatives (*kozoku*), the ex-*daimyo* (*kazoku*), the ex-warriors (*shizoku*) and the ordinary people (*heimin*). However, the Emperor's hold on power was still tenuous and there was always the threat of revolt until 1877 when Saigo Takamori, who had left the government as a result of disagreements over foreign policy, reluctantly led a major rebellion by ex-*samurai* in the south of Kyushu. He was defeated in Kumamoto, where he attempted to besiege government troops in the castle, and retreated to Kagoshima, where he killed himself in a cave after an unsuccessful rearguard action.

The Emperor was intent upon the advancement of the country. He developed heavy industries, including steel, mining and cotton. He established an army based upon the German model and a navy based upon the British one. Telephones were introduced in 1869 and the first railway was opened between Shinbashi in Tokyo and the port of Yokohama in 1872. In the same year, a compulsory education system was introduced, enabling all citizens to receive six years of basic primary education. A western-style constitution was introduced in 1889. To assist with these reforms, a group of foreign advisors was invited to Japan and scholars were sent abroad to study.

The confidence derived from the establishment of strong military forces, in combination with diplomatic recognition, led to an upsurge in nationalism and militarism, both of which were further stimulated by successes in the Sino-Japan War of 1894 and the Russo-Japan War of 1904. Having demonstrated its new-found strength, the military demanded an increased role in domestic politics, a dangerous precedent to establish.

The Emperor Meiji died in 1912, but an impressive legacy remained. More than any other Emperor in Japanese history, he had left his mark upon the nation and was to be remembered and revered by his people as none of his predecessors ever had been.

***Taisho Era*** (1912 – 1926)

Although the Emperor Taisho was weak both physically and mentally, he was supported by able ministers and his reign passed without any major difficulties arising. In 1914, the First World War started and Japan supported the Allies, which resulted in various economic benefits and a general international acceptance of the country. Following the war, in 1920 Japan joined the League of Nations.

The greatest set-back to the country during this period was a natural disaster, for in 1923 the Great Kanto Earthquake occurred, killing 100,000 people in and around Tokyo.

***Showa Era*** (1926 – 1989)

On Christmas Day 1926 the Emperor Showa came to power. The choice of the name Showa ('Brilliantly Peaceful') for his reign was to prove unfortunate, for it turned out to be neither brilliant nor peaceful.

The Great Depression started in the U.S.A. in 1929 and spread throughout the world, affecting Japan just as it did all other industrialized nations. Partly to divert attention from these problems, the military leaders developed the Far East Co-Prosperity Scheme, a thinly veiled attempt at imperialistic expansion. Within Japan a propaganda campaign was trying to convince the population that the nation was the chosen vanguard to lead Asia on the path to success. A feeling of extreme nationalism pervaded the atmosphere and the military gained in power. In 1931, Manchuria was invaded and a puppet régime installed. The League of Nations demanded Japan's withdrawal from the province, but instead, in 1933, Japan chose to leave the League of Nations. The military became audacious enough to engineer the assassination of the prime minister in 1932 and of other top ministers in 1936.

By 1937, Japan was at war with China and in 1939 the Second World War started. Japan's excursions into Asia brought about severe conflicts of interest with other nations and finally, in 1941, the nation committed the ultimate folly of attacking the U.S. navy at Pearl Harbor, thereby committing itself to a major war which it had little chance of winning. 1,860,000 military personnel were lost and there were 670,000 civilian casualties by the time that Japan surrendered unconditionally in 1945 following the atomic bombing of Hiroshima and Nagasaki. It was the first time in its history that the country had been occupied by a foreign force.

Following this defeat, Japan was rebuilt and restructured under the American occupation. The governmental, economic, social and educational systems were completely revised. In 1946, a new constitution was promulgated, declaring that the three basic principles of the country were national sovereignty, the granting of basic human rights and the renunciation of war. In 1947, an education system was adopted giving six years of primary education, three years of lower secondary education, a further three years of upper secondary education and four years of tertiary education. In 1951, at San Francisco, Japan concluded peace treaties with 48 nations, not, however, including the U.S.S.R., which held, as Russia now continues to hold, certain islands off the east coast of Hokkaido which had always been regarded as Japanese territory.

Japan's determined efforts to rebuild its economy have brought the nation a new wave of prosperity. The speed of this recovery has surprised the whole world and can be attributed principally to five factors: firstly to the hard-working ethics of the Japanese character;

secondly to the high levels of education and technical skills; thirdly to the concerted effort to rebuild, by pouring most of the nation's capital into industrial reconstruction and development; fourthly to the policy of total disarmament and the surrender of colonial territories, which released the country from a huge burden of expenditure; and fifthly to the unique management system offering, amongst other benefits, secure lifetime employment.

Economically, Japan has become one of the world's major powers. In 1954, the Japanese government felt in a position to start offering overseas aid and, by the close of the Showa Era, the country had become the world's second largest donor, providing about eight billion dollars annually to 25 countries.

Towards the end of 1988, the Emperor Showa became ill, with his condition deteriorating day by day. He died in the first week of 1989 and his son succeeded him, becoming Japan's 125th Emperor. The Showa Era had lasted for 62 years and two weeks, by far the longest reign in Japanese history.

***Heisei Era*** (1989 – )

The new Emperor chose to call his reign the Heisei Era, meaning the 'Era of Spreading Peace'. He brings to the throne a rather different background from that of past Emperors, for he undertook post-graduate education in England and is the first Emperor to be married to a commoner.

The economic miracles of Japan have continued into his reign, but the 'Bubble Economy' of the end of the Showa Era eventually burst and this resulted in a recession minor by world standards, but, nevertheless, a shock to Japan, which had become accustomed to an unrelieved diet of success.

Politically, too, changes have come recently. For 38 years until 1993, the government had been formed by members of the Liberal Democratic Party, the only matter in dispute being which faction of the party would hold control at any particular time. However, a series of political scandals disenchanted voters, starting with the Lockheed bribes involving the prime minister of the time, Mr. Tanaka, and continuing with the Recruit Cosmos scandal, involving the sales to politicians of shares certain to rise very rapidly in value, and the Sagawa Delivery Service payments made to various politicians in high positions. In 1993, the Liberal Democratic Party failed to win a majority in the general election and was replaced by a coalition of opposition parties. However, this has proven to be a fragile coalition unable to enact any controversial legislation due to the necessity of appeasing the views of various members with different backgrounds. Nevertheless, it has shattered the myth that the Liberal Democratic Party is invincible.

The recent recession and the steady rise in the value of the yen have certainly made economic conditions less favourable for Japan, but the nation's response has been to rationalize and economize where possible, and there was plenty of scope for such measures, so that products still remain of high quality and competitive in price and, for a while at least, the prosperity of the nation seems assured.

## CHRONOLOGICAL TABLE OF JAPANESE HISTORY

| *International Events* | *Year* | *Events in Japan* |
|---|---|---|
| Rome unifies Italy | 272 BC | |
| | 1st C. | Over 100 small kingdoms compose Japan |
| | 239 | Princess Himiko establishes kingdom of Yamatai and sends mission to China |
| Germanic migrations | 375 | |
| | 400 | Japan beginning to take form of unified nation |
| | 538 | Arrival of Buddhism |
| | 593 | Prince Shotoku becomes Regent |
| | 603 | Establishment of system of 12 ranks for court officials |
| | 604 | Constitution of 17 articles |
| | 607 | Foundation of Horyu-ji |
| | 645 | Establishment of system of centralized monarchy |
| Rise of Islamic Empire | 661 | |
| | 701 | Reform of administrative and penal codes |
| | 710 | Permanent capital established in Nara |
| | 743 | Big Buddha at Nara started |
| | 794 | Imperial capital moved to Kyoto |
| | 894 | Discontinuance of official missions to China |
| | 1053 | Byodo-in constructed at Uji by Fujiwaras |
| Crusades begin | 1096 | |
| | 1185 | Minamotos defeat Tairas at Battle of Dan-no-ura |
| | 1192 | Minamoto Yoritomo becomes first administrative *shogun* |
| | 1221 | Emperor Gotoba tries but fails to regain power |
| | 1274 | First Mongolian attack |
| | 1281 | Second Mongolian attack thwarted by *kamikaze* |
| | 1333 | End of Kamakura Era |
| | 1334 | Emperor Godaigo briefly regains power |
| | 1338 | Start of Muromachi shogunate |
| | 1392 | Unification of government |
| | 1467 | Most of Kyoto destroyed |
| | 1467 | Start of 'Warring States' period |
| Columbus discovers America | 1492 | |
| | 1543 | Introduction of firearms |
| | 1549 | Arrival of St. Francis Xavier and Christianity |
| | 1573 | End of Muromachi shogunate |
| | 1582 | Oda Nobunaga, on point of unifying country, assassinated |
| | 1590 | Toyotomi unifies Japan |
| | 1600 | Battle of Sekigahara. Start of Tokugawa shogunate |
| | 1603 | Tokugawa Ieyasu establishes headquarters in Edo (Tokyo) |
| | 1637 | Christian uprising in Kyushu |
| | 1641 | Isolation policy instituted |
| King Charles I beheaded | 1649 | |
| King James II deposed | 1688 | |

| U.S. War of Independence | 1776 | |
|---|---|---|
| French Revolution | 1789 | |
| | 1853 | Commodore Perry arrives with demand to open country |
| | 1858 | U.S. – Japan treaty of amity and commerce |
| | 1860 | Chief Minister Ii assassinated |
| | 1867 | *Shogun* agrees to step down |
| | 1868 | Meiji Restoration |
| | 1871 | Feudal fiefs become prefectures |
| | 1872 | Class system abolished except for aristocracy |
| | 1877 | Rebellion led by Saigo Takamori put down |
| | 1889 | New western-style constitution promulgated |
| | 1890 | First session of diet (parliament) opened |
| | 1894 | Sino – Japan War won by Japan |
| | 1902 | Anglo – Japanese treaty concluded |
| | 1904 | Russo – Japan War won by Japan |
| | 1912 | Death of Emperor Meiji. Start of Taisho Era |
| | 1914 | Japan involved in First World War as ally of Britain |
| Russian Revolution | 1917 | |
| | 1923 | Great Kanto Earthquake reduces Tokyo to ashes |
| | 1926 | Death of Emperor Taisho. Start of Showa Era |
| The Great Depression | 1929 | |
| | 1931 | The 'Manchuria Incident' |
| | 1932 | Attempted coup d'état |
| | 1933 | Japan leaves League of Nations |
| | 1936 | Attempted coup d'état |
| | 1937 | The 'China Incident' |
| Second World War starts | 1939 | |
| | 1940 | Japan enters pact with Germany and Italy |
| | 1941 | Pacific War starts |
| | 1945 | Japan surrenders unconditionally |
| | 1946 | Present constitution promulgated |
| | 1947 | Basic Education Law passed |
| | 1951 | Peace treaty signed |
| | 1972 | Reversion of Okinawa to Japan |
| | 1989 | Death of Emperor Showa. Start of Heisei Era |

## CULTURE

Superficially, Japan seems very western in many ways, especially in the major cities. However, there are certain elements of traditional Japanese culture which have been preserved even in the cities and which continue to flourish in the modern-day atmosphere. Here are just a few of the traditions which the visitor may come across, or, if he is sufficiently interested, may wish to search out.

*Sado (Tea Ceremony)*

Also called *cha-no-yu*, or, more colloquially, *o-cha*, which simply means tea, *sado* refers to the typically Japanese way of serving and drinking tea, in accordance with certain set rules of etiquette. Thus it is considered a discipline for mental composure, elegant manners and high etiquette rather than merely a hobby or pastime. The ceremony is thought to have originated in Buddhist monasteries in the south of China and was perfected by Sen Rikyu in Japan in the sixteenth century.

Powdered tea is whisked in hot water and then served to each guest in turn. It is customary to turn the cup round before sipping from it and to admire the cup and utensils used as objects of art, rather than to drink the tea in one gulp and ask for more! Japanese style sweets are usually served with the tea and are eaten before the tea is drunk.

Many girls take classes in tea ceremony if they have sufficient time, especially when of university or early working age.

***Ikebana (Flower Arrangement)***

*Ikebana* is the traditional Japanese art of arranging cut flowers. Originally it was closely associated with the tea ceremony, as the room used for the ceremony was carefully decorated with flowers. However, there are now many different techniques and conflicting principles concerning arrangement. This too is an art often studied by girls in their late teens and twenties.

***Japanese Gardens***

Gardening in Japan is essentially an æsthetic pursuit rather than a question of getting a good crop of beans. Even flowers are not generally found in traditional Japanese gardens. The object is rather to create a microcosm of the world around us, with, for example, a pond representing the sea and mounds representing mountains. Often a stone lantern, of the type found at temples, is included. The garden is designed to be looked at from the house and must be balanced without hinting at artificial symmetry. Of course, these days any Japanese who is rich enough to have a garden will delight in designing it to the proper specifications, for that will be a symbol of his affluence. It will also serve to soothe his troubled mind as he gazes at it on Sunday afternoons, forgetting the worries of his business and enjoying his temporary union with nature.

Older and larger formal Japanese gardens often take this symbolism of the real world in miniature a step further, having recognizable features of Japan in them. For example, Suizenji Garden in Kumamoto in Kyushu represents the major features of the old Tokaido, the road between Edo (Tokyo) and Kyoto, in its landscaping, with a miniature Mt. Fuji prominent, while Rikugi-en Garden in Tokyo represents 88 beauty spots of the nation.

***Bonsai***

*Bonsai* are miniature potted trees, dwarfed by special means of cultivation to restrain their growth. The owner then further develops twisted growth by the application of clips and similar devices ('torturing the trees', the author calls it!), his aim being to produce a form of semi-natural elegance and beauty suited to the limited size of a Japanese garden. In recent years *bonsai* have become well known and popular throughout the western world. They are now much sought after and attract high prices.

### *Kabuki*

*Kabuki* is a traditional form of stage drama which developed and flourished in the Edo Era. Although this genre of theatre was originally performed by females, it has long been the custom for all roles to be played by males. The action is accompanied by music played on traditional Japanese instruments and by songs. The actors speak their lines in artificial sing-song voices and actions are performed with exaggerated gestures. Costumes are gorgeous, make-up colourful and stage settings elaborate. It used to be a form of entertainment aimed at the ordinary people and it is still popular today, although not exactly the working man's daily form of relaxation. At performances it is customary for members of the audience to encourage the actors by shouting out their names in a manner which would be thought unacceptable in western theatre.

### *Noh*

*Noh* is another form of classical theatre, but, unlike *kabuki*, it involves little movement of the actors and has a simple stage setting. It was developed in the fourteenth and fifteenth centuries by two great actors, Kiyotsugu Kan-ami and his son Motokiyo Ze-ami, who wrote most of the plays currently performed. The style of performance has not changed significantly since the sixteenth century. Actors are all male and the principal actor is nearly always masked. The action is accompanied by music played on pipes and drums and by the chanting of a chorus. The audience tends to be composed entirely of connoisseurs of this form of theatre these days and has always been so to some extent, for this was never a popular form of drama, but rather one for the court aristocracy.

### *Bunraku*

This is a form of classical puppet theatre performed to the accompaniment of ballad music called *joruri*. The puppets are about two-thirds of life size, weighing up to 10 kilograms and with elaborate costumes. They are manipulated by three puppeteers each, of whom the two minor ones will wear black costumes and hoods in order to be unobtrusive. The puppeteers are always visible.

This type of entertainment probably developed from puppet shows given by strolling entertainers in the Heian Era. The accompanying music was developed in the sixteenth century and the plays performed today were mostly created in the eighteenth century. The puppets were refined at the same time. To be a puppeteer requires great skill and a lifetime of studying, working through the positions of second and first assistant to become eventually the main manipulator of the puppet.

### *Rakugo*

*Rakugo* is a form of one-man entertainment. The entertainer appears on stage seated on a *zabuton* (cushion), dressed in traditional Japanese costume, usually with only a fan as a prop, and recounts humorous stories, taking all the parts in a conversation. This type of entertainment remains quite popular among ordinary Japanese and can be found at certain theatres and on television. The actor, of course, requires great skill to be able to take the parts of various characters all at the same time and to convey the action without ever shifting from his seat.

*Geisha*

The job of a *geisha* is to entertain at formal parties and to keep the atmosphere happy and encourage conversation. Prospective *geisha* are trained in such skills as music, singing, dancing, tea ceremony, flower arrangement and etiquette. This period lasts for up to ten years, although they usually work at the same time. After they have graduated to the position of *geisha* their services are, of course, extremely expensive, so that our impoverished visitor will not want to consider frequenting any of the establishments where they work. He may, however, possibly see a *geisha* going to work in the entertainment districts of Gion in Kyoto or Ginza in Tokyo if he happens to be in one of those areas in the early evening.

## FOOD

One of the excellent features of Japan is its eating establishments. One can find all types of cuisine and at all prices. If one wants a lavish high-class meal, one can have it, but the great thing is that one does not have to spend a lot on food if one does not want to. In fact, considering the country's reputation for high prices, food is really rather reasonable.

One type of establishment which always does give a shock with its prices is the coffee shop. Such businesses are everywhere throughout Japan and a cup of coffee or similar usually costs at least ¥300, sometimes considerably more. What one is paying for is not the coffee, but the space to chat and stay as long as one wishes, and space is expensive in Japan, especially in the big cities. Go into a coffee shop in the morning, however, and you will usually find a bargain available known as 'morning service' (that is the Japanese name, not a translation). For only slightly more than you would pay for your cup of coffee you can have a light breakfast, typically a boiled egg with toast and maybe a small salad, and, of course, the cup of coffee.

When lunch-time comes, there are numerous small restaurants offering a special lunch menu. Since this is known, in Japanese, as *lunchi*, your linguistic powers will not be overstrained by ordering. Sometimes such exotic choices are offered as *Lunchi A* and *Lunchi B*. Restaurants almost always have their delicacies on display in the window in the form of very skilfully made wax models. However, since the lunch menu changes every day, it is not usually so displayed. Some restaurants put a real meal on display outside under a plastic cover. Others just write the day's dishes on a blackboard, or even just on a special lunch menu on the table. What you can expect, however, is soup, a main course with rice, perhaps a small salad and coffee or tea. If you find that you are being asked a question after ordering your *lunchi*, it is most likely to be whether you want tea or coffee and whether you want it hot or iced. The Japanese for coffee is 'coffee' (pronounced *kohi*) and the Japanese for tea is *ko-cha*, but 'tea' will be understood by everybody. The Japanese for hot is 'hot' (pronounced *hotto*) and the Japanese for iced is 'ice'. You will be beginning to think that this is not such a difficult language after all! *Lunchi* starts at the cheapest restaurants at ¥450 and can be had for about ¥600 in an ordinary class of establishment. Better class restaurants also offer a lunch menu at around ¥1,000 to ¥1,200. Whichever you choose, *lunchi* is a bargain by Japanese standards.

For the impoverished and very hungry, there is the famous Shakey's Pizza Parlor. Branches can be found throughout Japan and all offer an eat-all-you-can lunch of pizza, fried potatoes and spaghetti for ¥600. You can do this for a couple of days, after which you will not want anybody even to mention pizza for the next month! One catch is that eating a lot of pizza makes you very thirsty and, of course, drinks are not included and there is no water around.

Even so, it is a real bargain for a starving foreigner.

Dinner is a little more difficult, for there are fewer special offers at this time. If you want to eat a reasonable meal at a moderate price, however, try the top floors of department stores. There you will often find such a range of eating establishments that you will not know which to choose. If you are hungry, you will probably get best value from one of the 'set' menus, that is one which offers a combination of two or three smaller dishes with rice and maybe with coffee or similar to follow. A reasonable meal is likely to cost ¥1,000 to ¥1,500 in such a restaurant.

If you want to go out for a drink, there are many cheap drinking places in certain areas. The cheaper it looks, the better it will usually be (and the cheaper!). If you drink in such an establishment, the rule usually is that you must eat something as well, but you are likely to find it difficult to read the menu, which will be on pieces of paper stuck on the wall. If in doubt, try *yakitori*, grilled chicken on skewers. All such places will serve beer, which is 'beer' in Japanese. However, in Japan people do not generally go drinking by themselves, and you are likely to enjoy this experience more if you go with an experienced guide. Places to avoid are those with hostesses or with touts outside. They are likely to be very expensive indeed, so be careful.

If you need a quick and cheap snack at any time, a noodles shop is usually the solution. These can be found in many places, including, quite often, the platforms of railway stations. There is usually a variety of dishes and a choice of *soba* (thin noodles) or *udon* (thick noodles). A fairly standard choice is *tempura soba* or *tempura udon*. Cheaper is *kitsune soba* or *kitsune udon*. A bowl of noodles is likely to cost about ¥350.

Another relatively cheap way to eat, especially when travelling, is to indulge in *o-bento*, a type of lunch-box which can be purchased at small shops which usually display an illustrated menu outside or above the counter. It can also be bought at railway stations, either from kiosks or from vendors on the platforms. *O-bento* bought at stations is often known as *eki-ben* (station lunch-box). Unfortunately, this type of *o-bento* has become rather expensive in recent years, as has that sold actually on the train. It is usually better to purchase outside the station and get better value. Supermarkets and 'convenience stores' usually sell *o-bento* also.

There are plenty of pseudo-European bakeries around in Japan too. There is almost always one in or just outside a main railway station, for example. If one purchases a few items at such an establishment, the cost will not be outrageous. Since this is Japan, however, not Europe, there will be a few surprises. One to watch out for is that something which is heavy and looks as though it might contain a chocolatey substance may well have *anko* (sweet bean paste) in it. You might immediately fall in love with *anko* – and, there again, you might not!

If you have occasion to shop and cook for yourself, you may be surprised to find that, as long as you are willing to adapt your diet to the local conditions, you can eat quite cheaply. This adaptation principally means cutting out expensive meat, especially beef, but you can still eat chicken and pork. If you look around supermarkets at closing time, you can find a lot of bargains in the form of ¥100 off stickers on items that will not be at their best the next day. You can also find bargain plates outside greengrocers' shops, usually a little assortment of items which will not remain fresh for much longer, for ¥100 or so. However, these goods need eating quickly, of course, because shopkeepers know when things will last and when they will not. Bakeries sell the crusts of bread very cheaply, or even sometimes give them away, because nobody in Japan wants to lower himself to eat crusts. These are called *pan no mimi*. *Pan* is the French word *pain* and *mimi* means ears. A large bag of crusts typically costs about ¥50.

To assist in the restaurant or drinking establishment, here is a brief list of Japanese dishes which you may come across, or may wish to order, during the course of your stay.

***Sushi***

Best known of Japanese food, *sushi* consists of an oval-shaped ball of rice flavoured with vinegar with a slice of raw fish or similar on top. *Norimaki* is a type of *sushi* roll with cucumber or other filling inside a cylinder of rice with dried seaweed (*nori*) on the outside. *Sushi* can be eaten with the fingers or with chopsticks and the fish side is usually dipped lightly in soy sauce before one eats.

If you visit a *sushi* shop, you will usually have the choice of ordering a set menu or selecting different types of *sushi* by name. When ordered in the latter way, which is generally more expensive, *sushi* always come in pairs. Some *sushi* shops do not display prices and these should be treated with caution as owners sometimes gain a reputation for adjusting their prices to suit their own estimates of their customers' pockets.

You can also find interesting *sushi* shops with revolving conveyor belts. These are generally known as *hyaku yen zushi* ('¥100 *sushi*') from the days when one plate used to cost ¥100. At present a more common price is ¥120 or ¥130 per plate. Sometimes there are different colours of plates at varying prices, but such information is always displayed. If this appeals to you, go in, sit at the counter, help yourself to Japanese tea using the mug and tap provided and take from the conveyor belt whatever you fancy as it passes by. When you have finished, take your plates to the entrance where you will be charged accordingly. You may find that tax, currently 3% but likely to increase, will be added at this point.

***Sashimi***

*Sashimi* is perhaps the most traditional food of Japan, consisting simply of sliced raw fish which is eaten after being dipped in soy sauce mixed with *wasabi*, a type of Japanese horseradish.

***Tenpura***

*Tenpura* is food dipped in batter and deep fried in vegetable oil. Typical ingredients are shrimps, prawns, small fish, cuttlefish and various types of vegetables. The *tenpura* is dipped in a sauce immediately before it is eaten. This dish was brought to Japan by Portuguese missionaries in the sixteenth century, but the origin of the word *tenpura* itself is uncertain.

***Sukiyaki***

*Sukiyaki* is a type of beef stew. Tender beef is cut into thin slices and then boiled briefly in a pot with such vegetables as leeks and mushrooms together with *tofu* in a sauce made from soy sauce, sugar and a little Japanese alcohol. Before eating, those participating take from the large pot and put a small helping in a personal dish, then usually dip in raw egg before eating.

Since meat was not eaten in Japan until the end of the nineteenth century, *sukiyaki* is a relatively modern invention.

### *Shabu-Shabu*

*Shabu-shabu* is similar to *sukiyaki*, but the beef is only dipped briefly into boiling stock. It is then dipped into one of two sauces before being eaten. One of the sauces provided is vinegary and the other is a thicker sauce flavoured with sesame.

### *Nabe*

There are various types of *nabe* and, although there are many similarities between *sukiyaki* and *nabe*, the former is always thought of as rather a luxury meal and the latter as a poor man's dish. *Nabe* is cooked in a much deeper pot with a considerable amount of water and a variety of ingredients which may include fish and chicken as well as meat and vegetables. Sometimes noodles are put into the pot when most of the other ingredients have been finished and then, after being cooked in the broth, are eaten as the conclusion of the meal.

### *Soba and Udon*

*Soba* is a type of long, brownish noodles made from buckwheat flour. *Udon* is made from kneaded wheat flour. It is thicker than *soba* and white in colour. Noodles come with various other ingredients, so it is necessary to specify when ordering both which type of noodles and which flavourings are required.

### *Gyoza*

*Gyoza* is a Chinese dish of meat (usually pork) and vegetables in a pastry casing which is then fried. They are small two-bites crescent shaped morsels tasting quite strongly of garlic. When one orders a plate of *gyoza*, one usually gets about five of them. They should be dipped in the hot orange-coloured sauce provided before they are eaten.

### *Shumai*

*Shumai* are also of Chinese origin and are similar to *gyoza* in content, but without the strong garlic taste. They are cylindrical in shape and are steamed, not fried. An order is usually from three to five, depending on the size. They are dipped in soy sauce, with or without mustard added, before being eaten.

### *Ramen*

*Ramen* is a type of thin noodles of Chinese origin made from wheat flour, eggs and salt. It is served in pork or chicken broth seasoned with *miso* (soy bean paste) or salt.

### *Yaki Soba*

*Yaki soba* is fried noodles mixed with some vegetables and meat.

### *Yakitori*

Yakitori

Traditionally, *yakitori* is small pieces of chicken skewered on bamboo and grilled over charcoal. However, other ingredients can also be cooked in the same way. They are cooked either *shio* (with salt) or *tare* (with soy-based sauce) as requested.

### *Oden*

*Oden* is an assortment of ingredients boiled for a long time in a seasoned fish broth.

Typical fare includes eggs, potatoes, *tofu*, *konnyaku* (devil's tongue jelly), Japanese radish and *konbu* (a type of seaweed). Although *oden* is sometimes served in restaurants, it is also available from stalls in winter or even from convenience stores. At restaurants and stalls it is usually eaten accompanied by warm Japanese alcohol to take the edge off cold winter evenings, which it accomplishes very well. It is inexpensive and filling.

***Tonkatsu***

*Tonkatsu* is a breaded pork cutlet, usually served with grated cabbage. If it is served with rice, the dish is known as *katsu-don* (*don* always means 'with rice'), and this is a good stand-by if you want to order something not too expensive but cannot comprehend the menu!

***Miso-Shiru***

*Miso* is a brownish paste made from fermented, steamed, salted soy beans, together with rice, wheat and various other ingredients. Although it is used in many aspects of Japanese cooking, it is most famous in *miso-shiru* or *miso* soup, as it is often called in English. A bowl of this soup accompanies most Japanese meals.

***Natto***

*Natto* is a dish with a strong smell, which westerners generally find unpleasant, made from steamed fermented soy beans. It is often served with breakfast in the eastern and northern parts of Japan, but is not popular in the west or south. If you can stand the smell, it is supposed to be a very healthy dish.

***Okonomi-Yaki***

This is a type of pancake including egg, cabbage, meat, cuttlefish, ginger and whatever else the chef happens to put in. At *okonomi-yaki* restaurants, you order the ingredients from a menu and are left to cook them by yourself on a hotplate provided in the middle of the table. However, *okonomi-yaki* is also available from street stalls and then you get a standard menu. It is cheap and filling.

***Takoyaki***

*Takoyaki* is balls of batter containing octopus. This delicacy is usually served from street stalls in plastic containers with ten or twelve such balls covered with a sweet sauce and eaten by means of toothpicks provided. Cost ranges from ¥300 to ¥500.

***Yaki Nikku***

*Nikku* means meat, so this is cooked meat. The difference in *yaki nikku* restaurants is that you cook it yourself on a hotplate in the centre of the table, after first selecting the type of meat which you require from the menu offered. This type of restaurant originated in Korea, so the meat is dipped in a Korean-style sauce flavoured with garlic before being eaten.

***Onigiri***

*Onigiri* is a rice ball with something in the middle and dried seaweed around the outside. Most commonly it is found as part of a packed lunch or bought in convenience stores. There are various shapes, but the most popular is triangular. Those bought in stores have the seaweed in a separate plastic wrapping to avoid its becoming damp and it requires a genius to unravel the correct pieces of plastic to get the seaweed onto the *onigiri* without dropping the whole lot on the floor. Typical fillings are *umeboshi* (salted dried sour plums), *tarako* (salted cod roe), *shiojake* (salted salmon) and *katsuo-bushi* (dried bonito flakes). A usual price in a store is ¥120.

Onigiri

## DRINKS

Most people know Japanese alcohol as *sake*, but the term *o-sake* ('honourable alcohol') is used in Japan to describe any type of alcohol, i.e. as a generic rather than specific term. Japanese-style alcohol is usually referred to as *Nihon-shu*, meaning exactly that, 'Japanese alcohol'. *Nihon-shu*, of which there are many variations, is made from fermented rice and has an alcohol content of about 15%. It is most commonly served warm in porcelain flasks which are poured into porcelain cups. The custom in Japan is to fill everybody else's cup or glass and rely on others to fill yours and these cups are small enough to keep everybody alert.

Another Japanese drink is *shochu*, made from sweet potatoes, rice or other cereals and then distilled. It is clear and colourless and generally comes with alcohol content of 20% or 25%, although up to 35% or 40% is possible. It is sometimes drunk with hot water and lime or lemon juice, especially in winter. Alternatively, it may be served cold with soda water, flavoured syrup and ice. Then it is called *chuhai*, which is evidently an abbreviation of *shochu* highball. More commonly, drinking shops may call it according to its flavouring, lime sour, lemon sour, etc.

As far as non-alcoholic drinks are concerned, a Japanese meal is usually accompanied by Japanese green tea, called *o-cha*, for which there is no charge. Coffee ('*kohi*') or western tea (*ko-cha*) may be ordered and sometimes come as part of a set menu.

## FINDING AN ADDRESS

Newcomers to Japan are usually confused by the address system and claim that they can never find any place. Those who have been here for a while, however, usually decide that the system, while different, is quite manageable. The first thing to remember is that in Japanese the address is written in exactly the reverse order of that used in English. That is to say that the prefecture or city comes first and the addressee's name comes last. Although the Japanese are kind enough to use the English order when writing in Roman script, some confusion sometimes arises.

Let us suppose that you have an address which you want to find, for example 'Dai-san Taihei Building, 1-25-3 Higashi Ikebukuro, Toshima-ku, Tokyo 170.' The number 170 is just a postcode. Tokyo is divided into 23 *ku* or wards, of which Toshima is one. If you manage to reach the nearest railway station, in this case the Higashi Ikebukuro subway station, you will almost inevitably find a large map of the immediate area on the wall. Of course, it will be in Japanese, but it is the numbers which are most important and if in doubt you can always ask assistance. Higashi Ikebukuro, like most other towns, is divided into *chome*. The *chome* is the first number in the Romanized form of the address, 1 in this case. There are usually about six to eight *chome* in each town. Once you ascertain that you are in the correct *chome*, by using the map on the wall to direct you, things become easier. The second number in the address, 25 in this case, represents the block. In Japan, only main streets have names and addressing is done by block, not by street. This means that people living on opposite sides of the same road will have only the *chome* number in common. They will be in different blocks. Even if you do not know the relationship of one block number to another, with a little walking around, you will soon discover the pattern. Look on the telegraph poles and you will find signs with white lettering on a green or blue background showing the number of the *chome* and block. If you see 1-3, for example, you will know that you are still quite a long way from 1-25. When you see 1-24, you will expect it to be in the next block one way or another. Once you have located the correct block, you will find that the buildings are numbered in consecutive order around the block. Walk round until you come to the number which you want. Little signs with white lettering usually on a blue background are attached to most buildings showing the block and number. In addition, in this case you have the name of the building, which may well be displayed in Roman characters, since that method has become fashionable. If there is a fourth number in the address, it will indicate that it is an apartment. The first digit in an apartment number almost always represents the floor on which it is situated.

So, you see, addresses are not so difficult after all. You just have to get used to the system!

## USING THE TELEPHONE

The telephone system is remarkably efficient in Japan and there are public telephones available everywhere. Local calls cost ¥10 for three minutes until recently. The minimum charge is still ¥10, but now the time has been reduced drastically to one minute. Long distance calls can be surprisingly expensive, although a discount is given for calls made after 19:00.

There are various types of public telephone, but the most common ones now are those which are green or grey in colour. Most will accept either coins or cards, but some of the green ones take only one or the other. The coins which can be used are the ¥10 and the ¥100.

In recent years, the monopoly of a single domestic telephone company (Nippon Telegraph and Telephone Corporation – NTT) has been broken and competitors have been permitted. If you stay in Japan for a long time, this is something to bear in mind, but for the visitor the only relevance will be in relation to the purple or white public telephones which you will find at main railway stations. These are operated by the JR group of companies, using spare lines on the railways' own communications system. At the destination, the call is plugged into the NTT network and the railways pay NTT the cost of a local call. For long distance calls, these telephones are cheaper than the NTT telephones and are worth taking advantage of. Do not use them for local calls, however, as they are considerably more expensive if used in that way.

International calls can be made from grey telephones and from those green public telephones which have a gold panel on the front. They are usually housed in boxes which display the words 'International Telephone'. To make an international call first dial 001 or 0041 or 0061, followed by the country code and the number, usually minus the initial 0. The three different initial numbers represent three different companies. There used to be only 001 (Kokusai Denshin Denwa – KDD), but this market too was opened up and the two competitors offered so much lower rates that KDD was forced to reduce its prices to compete, which is worth remembering if you are in doubt as to which company to use. 0041 (International Telecom Japan – ITJ) and 0061 (International Digital Communications – IDC) still offer cheaper services, in most cases, than 001, but they do not have lines to all countries. It is cheaper to make international calls after 19:00 and cheaper still between 23:00 and 8:00. To make international calls from a public telephone, you need ¥100 coins or a telephone card. ¥10 coins cannot be used and in the case of the card the cost will be charged in ten-unit blocks, so cards with less than ten units remaining cannot be used.

Telephone cards are available in denominations of ¥500 and ¥1,000. The ¥500 card gives 50 ¥10 units, but the ¥1,000 card gives 105 ¥10 units, so offers a slight advantage. The cards are often attractively decorated and are collected by certain people. They are available from tobacconists, souvenir shops, machines in or near some telephone boxes, and a wide variety of stores. It is almost always possible to buy a telephone card at a railway station. The Japanese for telephone card is 'telephone card' (pronounced *terehon cardo*) and, although the word for telephone is *denwa*, telephone would be understood.

There are, of course, telephone directories in Japan, but it is an odd feature of the country that nobody seems to use them. Asked why, most people reply that they can never find what they want because of the difficulties associated with the Japanese writing system. Whenever anybody wants to find out a number, he telephones directory enquiries. This service used to be free, but it became so costly for the telephone company to operate that now there is a charge of ¥30 per number. There is a directory enquiries service in English too. The number is 03-3586-0110. The cost is as for an ordinary telephone call.

## ENTERTAINMENT

Entertainment tends to be terribly expensive in Japan. It costs about ¥2,000 for a cinema seat, for instance, and for live entertainment the cheapest seats are often as expensive as ¥5,000.

There is plenty of low-class television entertainment. In Tokyo there are six channels, but only Channels 1 and 3, operated by the non-commercial NHK, profess to offer any intellectual stimulation. When films are broadcast, often late at night at weekends, the original soundtrack may be broadcast on a second frequency. Most channels also offer a news programme with an English version, but it could hardly be said to be a professional-sounding presentation. In any case, much of the Japanese news seems to consist of politics and such reports are somewhat less than thrilling.

The only local radio in English is the Far East Network (FEN) operated by the American armed forces for those of their number who are stationed here. Its intellectual level is about what one might expect, considering its audience. If you have a short-wave radio, you can listen to Voice of America at certain hours. It is also possible to tune in to the BBC, Radio Australia and Radio Moscow, but reception is often a problem with these stations.

## BUSINESS HOURS

Business hours in Japan are mostly similar to those in western countries. Offices usually work from 9:00 until 17:30 or 18:00. Sunday is a holiday. For larger companies Saturday is also a holiday, but for smaller companies Saturday may be a half day, or two Saturdays in a month may be worked.

Shops tend to open late and stay open late. Fairly typical hours for a large store would be 10:00 until 19:00 or 20:00. Smaller shops will be open later, maybe until 22:00. In larger towns now, it is usually possible to find 'convenience stores' which are open 24 hours a day, 365 days a year, so nobody is likely to starve in Japan!

## MONEY AND BANKS

At the time of writing the Japanese currency, the yen (pronounced *'en'*) has a value of about ¥100 to the U.S. dollar. That means that it has approximately doubled in value against the dollar in the last decade and its strength seems likely to continue for a while yet.

Notes are issued in denominations of ¥10,000, ¥5,000 and ¥1,000. There are coins for ¥500, ¥100, ¥50, ¥10, ¥5 and ¥1.

When arriving in Japan, it is not a bad idea to change quite a lot of money at the airport. You are sure to need quite a lot, rates do not vary much among the banks, including those at the airport, and you will be able to make the change much more quickly there than at any other bank.

Most banking in Japan, for the ordinary citizen, is done by machine. Machines are quick, efficient and even polite, for they often boast little recorded messages. If you have to do business inside the bank, however, it will be quite different. The most simple transaction will take twenty minutes, because, while machines can be trusted, the actions of humans must be checked and rechecked to ensure that no mistakes have been made. If possible, therefore, try to avoid Japanese banks or do everything possible in a single visit. It should also be noted that the fees charged by banks for their services are sometimes quite a shock. It is best to ask first. There are several overseas banks in the area of Otemachi in Tokyo and, where it is permitted by government regulations, their charges are often somewhat lower.

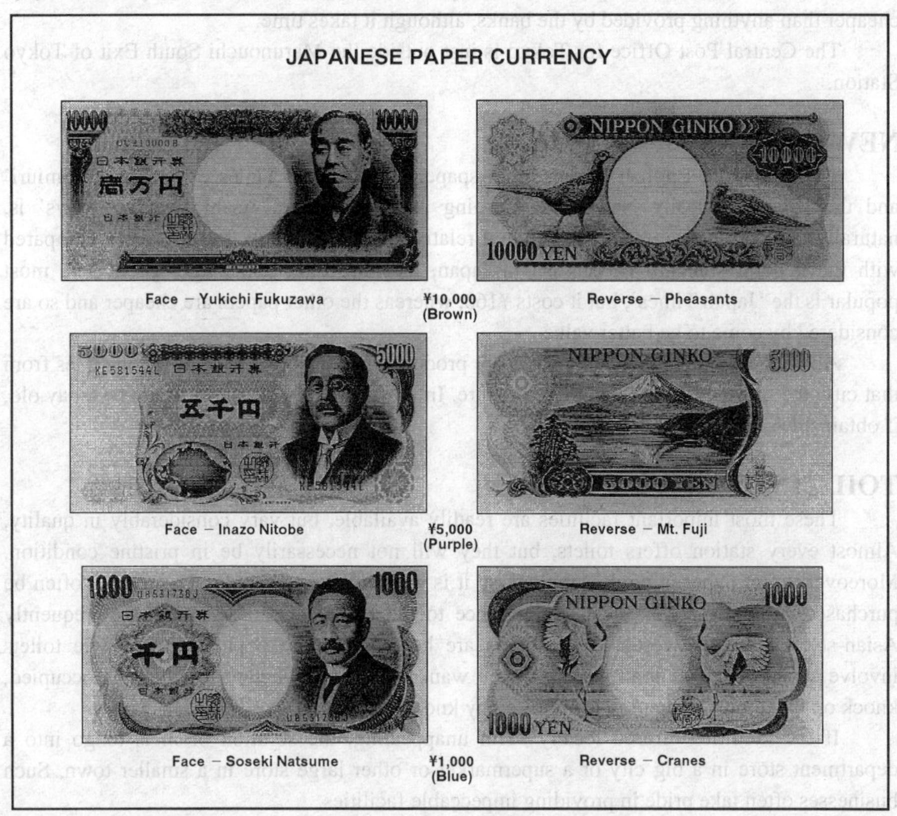


Face – Yukichi Fukuzawa | ¥10,000 (Brown) | Reverse – Pheasants

Face – Inazo Nitobe | ¥5,000 (Purple) | Reverse – Mt. Fuji

Face – Soseki Natsume | ¥1,000 (Blue) | Reverse – Cranes

## POSTAL SERVICES

Postal services are very reliable and safe, but not particularly quick. Postage rates within Japan are ¥80 for a letter and ¥50 for a postcard. These rates increased in 1994 after remaining unchanged for more than twelve years. It is common to use express mail to ensure rapid delivery, but this costs ¥270 extra. Express mail is delivered even on Sundays and holidays and reaches all reasonable destinations the next day if posted by a stated time, usually about 17:00. It can be posted in a postbox, if it is clearly marked, in red, as express mail.

International letters cost ¥130 to South America and Africa, ¥110 to Europe, North America, Australasia and the Middle East and ¥90 to most Asian countries. Rates are for 10 grams by airmail. Postcards cost ¥70. Air letter forms (aerogrammes) are available for ¥90 and can be sent for that price to anywhere in the world. Moreover, if you spoil an air letter form or a pre-paid postcard or anything else with pre-paid postage, you can take it back to the Post Office and obtain a refund, minus a small handling charge.

When international mail is posted in a postbox, and there are two slots, it should be put into the slot marked 'Other Mail', or something similar, not into the one for letters and postcards. The same applies to all express mail. Rates for international mail to Europe have actually decreased four times in the last decade, from ¥170 to ¥110. Is there any other country in the world where such a phenomenon has occurred?

The Post Office also operates a money transfer service internationally which is far cheaper than anything provided by the banks, although it takes time.

The Central Post Office for Tokyo is just outside the Marunouchi South Exit of Tokyo Station.

## NEWSPAPERS

There are four English language newspapers. The 'Japan Times', the 'Daily Yomiuri' and the 'Mainichi Daily News' are morning papers and the 'Asahi Evening News' is, naturally, an evening paper. All maintain a relatively high standard. In fact, when compared with the general standard of English in Japan, they are quite amazingly good. The most popular is the 'Japan Times', but it costs ¥160, whereas the other papers are cheaper and so are considered by some to be better value.

All of the English language papers are produced in Tokyo, so the further one goes from that city, the more difficult they are to procure. In more remote places, they may be a day old, if obtainable at all.

## TOILETS

These most important facilities are readily available, but vary considerably in quality. Almost every station offers toilets, but they will not necessarily be in pristine condition. Moreover, toilet paper is rarely supplied, so it is wise to carry a supply. Tissues can often be purchased from a machine near the entrance to the toilets. Japanese toilets are frequently Asian-style, although western-style toilets are becoming more popular. Asian-style toilets involve squatting rather than sitting. If you want to find out whether a cubicle is occupied, knock on the door. Occupation is indicated by knocking back.

If the facilities offered locally seem unappealing, the solution often is to go into a department store in a big city or a supermarket or other large store in a smaller town. Such businesses often take pride in providing impeccable facilities.

## SPORTS AND GAMES

When the author is asked what the national sport of Japan is, he usually replies, "*Pachinko*." If you do not know *pachinko*, you will after you have been in Japan for a short while. It is, in any case, described hereunder. In truth, the most popular spectator sport is probably baseball, while the most popular participation sport is either baseball or golf. The most popular indigenous spectator sport is sumo, which also will be described below.

### *Baseball*

It was the American occupation after the Second World War which really made baseball popular in Japan. There are two professional leagues, each consisting of six teams, named the 'Pacific League' and the 'Central League' (and which the Japanese, with their passion for abbreviation, manage to shorten to the 'Pa League' and the 'Se League'). The six teams in each league compete over a long series of matches to decide the champion and then the two champions compete to decide the grand champion. Each league thinks that it has a higher standard than the other, so, in reality, they are pretty equal. The standard of professional baseball in Japan is high, but obviously not yet quite as high as in North America, since players from that continent who are just past their best or who cannot quite get to the top often come to Japan to be paid very well for their services here.

Baseball is played at schools, with an annual high school tournament attracting a great deal of attention. It is also played on an amateur basis among companies (for which there is another annual tournament), but there are not as many village or town teams as one might expect, possibly because the sport needs space or because people feel too busy.

### *Golf*

Golf is the compulsory sport of the businessman. He often does not seem to enjoy it much, but he regards proficiency as an essential for his business career. Now golf needs a great deal of space and that is at a premium in Japan, so the average businessman-golfer learns to play at the practice ranges which you can see throughout the big cities, looking like giant aviaries. When the author first came to this country, I had never seen such an invention and wondered what these grassy areas enclosed by high nets could be – and, however hard I looked, I could never see any birds inside! Our businessman-golfers can be found here driving away (often on two levels) after work and on Saturdays and Sundays. Even this type of practice is not cheap, though. Therefore, the businessman is also to be found standing out in the street late at night, driver in hand, firing an imaginary ball straight and true all the way into the bright 'Seven-Eleven' window in the distance. Even on the platform of Shinjuku station, you will see him adjusting his grip on a non-existent club and flexing his knees, to ensure that they bend at exactly the angle prescribed by last night's television golf clinic.

Then, one day, after much hard practice, the fledgling golfer will graduate to a real course. Now, of course, he is not going to find such a facility in the centre of Tokyo, so, to make up a foursome (he always plays in a foursome), he has to get up at 3:00, leave at 3:30 and drive for three hours to the course where he and his business partners are due to tee off at 7:08 precisely.

And yet, amazing though it may seem, after several years of this, he may actually begin to enjoy the sport and to become quite good at it and to feel that all of this self-deprivation was actually worth while. Then he wants to join a club. Now the cost of membership of a golf club is phenomenal, running into many millions of yen, so this is attainable only by company directors, politicians, gangsters and similar pillars of the Japanese society. Just think of the pride which one can secretly feel when admitting with reluctance that one is actually a member of a golf club. Some companies take out a corporate membership to allow suitable members of their staff to use the facilities of a golf club. It is certainly a strange sport, as practised in Japan.

Professionally, of course, some Japanese have become very good in recent years and the standard is likely to become higher still. A golf tournament can be seen on television, either live or recorded, almost every weekend. If timings are suitable, overseas events are often broadcast live late at night, enabling the visitor from overseas to feel suitably homesick as he watches the swaying palm trees of Florida or the gales howling across St. Andrews.

***Sumo***

In Japan, sumo is the most popular of the sports native to the country. People from overseas tend to have a superficially poor impression of this sport – 'overweight people with little or no skill pushing each other around'. However, most of those who stay in Japan for a while come to realize that there is, in fact, a great deal of skill involved and they gradually gain in interest until the bi-monthly tournaments become events to look forward to with excitement.

The basic rules are simple. A ring is constructed about 4.55 metres (15 *shaku*) in diameter, the edge marked by a raised straw ridge. The two competitors, clad only in loincloths, grapple with each other and the loser is the first person to touch the ground with any part of his anatomy other than his feet or to touch the ground outside the ring. Around these simple rules, however, a great deal of ceremony has been built. The competitors in the professional tournaments parade wearing a type of elaborate and very expensive apron. Then, before his contest, each will warm up with a set of ritual exercises which include the throwing around of quantities of salt, believed to be a purifying element. A referee (*gyoji*), clad in elaborate formal dress, supervises the proceedings and tells the contestants when it is time to start, but he does not actually say "Go," as one might expect. He merely says, "It's time now," and the two competitors have to synchronize their own start. They are also free to start at any earlier time, by mutual agreement, and occasionally do so. Should the two fail to start together, the *gyoji* will order a restart, but the Sumo Association, the body which controls the professional sport, will fine them for their failure to co-ordinate.

Each sumo competitor belongs to a training school, almost always managed by a retired champion, and is given food and accommodation by the school. He is ranked by the Sumo Association according to his past performances and paid a salary when he enters the top two divisions of the sport. His salary will then increase every time he wins more than half of his contests in a tournament or wins a prize or beats a champion. In addition, in the top division, people or companies may offer a reward to the winner of a particular contest, in return for which the name of the donor is paraded round the ring before the contest starts. This reward is currently fixed at ¥60,000, of which half goes to the winner immediately, offered by the *gyoji* on his fan in an envelope at the end of the contest and received with reluctance by the victor, and half is put into a retirement fund for his later benefit.

The ranks of sumo competitors are divided into east and west, which has no particular significance, except to ensure that there are two holders of each rank. The top division is called *makunouchi* and consists of 40 competitors. The top rank is *yokozuna* and to this rank, exceptionally, only special promotions are made, so that there may be more or fewer *yokozuna* than the general guideline of two. A *yokozuna* can never lose his rank, so, if his performance is inadequate, he will be forced to retire. The second rank is called *ozeki* and this too is a specially appointed rank, so that there may be more or fewer than the standard number of two *ozeki*. An *ozeki* will lose his rank if he fails to win more than half of his contests in two consecutive tournaments. The third rank is called *sekiwake* and the fourth *komusubi*. Thereafter, the competitors in the top division are called *maegashira* and ranked from *maegashira* 1 to *maegashira* 15 or 16.

A professional tournament lasts for fifteen consecutive days, Sunday to Sunday, and those in the top two divisions, *makunouchi* and *juryo*, compete once every day. Those in lower divisions have seven contests during the tournament. Each competitor's first aim is to win more than half of his contests (*kachikoshi*). If he achieves that, he will be promoted. If he wins fewer than half (*makekoshi*), he will be demoted. The interest in a tournament lies in seeing each competitor's progress day by day.

There are several interesting features to this sport, of which perhaps the most unusual is that there are no weight classifications. Somebody weighing 90 kilograms has to compete on equal terms with somebody weighing 270 kilograms. Nor is the result a foregone conclusion, for the great champions are not usually the heavy men. They are those with muscle and technique. Perhaps this is one of the reasons why the sport has such a great following, for it is certainly amazing to see some of the small competitors throw down opponents two or three times their size. Another interesting point is that, in general, injury is not considered an acceptable excuse for non-participation. If you do not compete, you will be regarded as having lost. And perhaps one of the most valuable of the sport's unwritten rules is that no decision is ever to be disputed.

Professional sumo tournaments take place six times a year, in odd numbered months. Alternate tournaments are in Tokyo, with the others in Osaka, Nagoya and Fukuoka. Seats are extremely expensive and are always sold out in any case, although one can go along on the day and stand for a moderate fee. However, the best (and cheapest) seat is at home in front of the television with a bottle of beer! The last 2 or 2½ hours of each day's action, from about 15:30 until 18:00 is shown on NHK television every day during the tournaments and, of course, the cameras give an excellent view of the contests. Some of the more amusing moments of the broadcast occur when competitors are interviewed after particularly outstanding wins, for they are, by tradition, modest, emotionless and reticent and so generally have nothing at all to say when hauled in front of the camera. The commentators must dread the days when they are assigned to interview duty and find it a great relief when they encounter the occasional victor with something to say about his triumph. For example, the following recent interview was seen when a tiny man defeated a truly huge and highly-ranked opponent. "Congratulations." "Thank you very much." "Well, that was an excellent win, wasn't it? Had you thought out your tactics carefully? Did it go according to plan?" "Plan? Heck, no! What happened was I looked up and saw him bearing down on me and I thought, 'Oh, my god!' So I moved out of the way, like this, and he just kept going into the third row of the spectators!" One sometimes wonders just how many contests are won by such refined strategies, but each win is always matched with an accepted technique when announced.

Sumo competitors start young, often entering their training school in their early teens, and their career is usually finished by the time that they are about 30 years of age. The great champion Chiyonofuji managed to compete at the highest level recently until he was nearly 36 and, at a lower level, but still in the *Makunouchi* Division, Takamiyama retired a few years ago when just short of his fortieth birthday. The oldest man in the sport at the moment of writing is 35 and clearly past his peak. The names used by those in professional sumo, incidentally, are ring names, although those in lower divisions sometimes use their real names. As they improve, they are at liberty to change their names to those judged more suitable for senior ranks. At the time of writing there are almost exactly 1,000 professional sumo competitors.

Sumo is mainly a spectator sport, of course, not the sort of activity in which the average businessman surreptitiously engages at weekends. However, amateur sumo does exist, particularly at universities, where it is of quite a high standard and sometimes used as an alternative route into the professional world.

### *Judo*

More famous, but less popular in Japan as a spectator sport, is judo. Basically it is an art of self-defence which has been developed into a sport, the object being to use the opponent's momentum against him or her. It has now become an Olympic sport and seems to be just as popular in other countries as in Japan.

Here it is mostly practised at school and university level, after which only those with very special talent opt to continue.

### *Karate*

Surprisingly, karate did not come to the main part of Japan until 1922, although it existed in Okinawa much earlier, having been introduced from China. It is not really a popular discipline, although training is often available in schools and universities.

### *Aikido*

Another method of self-defence, *aikido* too is not popular with the average Japanese, although he may have been instructed in such techniques at school or university.

### *Kendo*

*Kendo* is a type of fencing using a stout bamboo pole. It is perhaps the most popular of the self-defence sports and is generally practised in schools. *Kendo* started as a method of training in swordsmanship, with a wooden sword used as the weapon. However, since the eighteenth century, a bamboo pole has been used and protective clothing has been worn. Points are scored by striking an opponent's head, wrist or body or by a successful thrust at his neck.

### *American Football*

American football has a minor following in Japan and is played at school and university levels.

### *Association Football*

Until recently, association football was a very minor sport in Japan. However, a professional league, the 'J-League', has now been formed and the result has been a great increase in popularity. The Japanese national team has become one of the best in Asia, vying with that of South Korea for local honours, and now Japan has ambitions of staging the World Cup in the near future.

One feature of the sport in Japan is that the Japanese are thought to have a desire for a definite result, so draws are not permitted in the J-League, every match being decided by the playing of extra time and then, if necessary, by penalty kicks. Despite the importation of a large number of star professional players from overseas, most matches in Japan are decided by goals scored as the result of defensive errors.

***Tennis***

Tennis has increased greatly in popularity since the present Emperor met his commoner wife on a tennis court. Unfortunately, no similar fairy tales have been heard recently, but the sport remains popular, especially among girls, for whom it is perhaps the most common form of outdoor recreation.

***Gateball***

This is a Japanese form of croquet and is very popular amongst the retired, who display quite amazing energy in rushing around the ground to hammer opponents' balls out of play. The game is played not on grass but on a gravel surface, but otherwise, except sometimes in the speed at which and animosity with which it is played, it seems to differ little from its croquet ancestor. Because of the similarity in names, the Japanese almost always equate cricket with croquet and, having no acquaintance with the former, assume that it is a sport like Japanese gateball, which upsets those, like the author, with Commonwealth backgrounds.

***Horse Racing***

Horse racing is popular in Japan as a betting sport. The Japanese like a little flutter now and then and, according to the latest figures, flutter to the tune of ¥3.8 trillion a year at present. Betting is mostly done in computerized shops operated by the Japan Racing Association around the country.

***Cycle Racing***

This is another betting sport. Meetings are held in various places around the country and those who attend are almost exclusively working-class men.

***Shogi***

This is a Japanese form of chess, played on a nine by nine board. It is a popular and skillful game, which evidently originated in China.

***Igo*** **(or *Go*)**

In Japan, the game is known as *igo,* although in other parts of the world it is often called *go*. It is played on a board nineteen by nineteen, with stones, black or white according to the player, being placed on the intersections of the lines, not in the squares. The object is to surround territory. If an opponent's piece also becomes surrounded, it is removed from the board. This game also originated in China, but it is very popular in Japan. You will see columns in the newspaper every day about it and businessmen sit in trains studying strategy on their way home.

***Mah-Jong***

This is another popular game which originated in China. It is played with 136 bamboo-backed ivory tiles (usually plastic, in fact, these days). Four players compete to be the first to obtain a winning hand of 13 tiles by discarding one by one those which are unwanted in their hand and replacing them with others drawn at random from the pool. The game is sufficiently popular for there to be shops which operate solely by providing facilities for playing the game, together with refreshments, if required. People often continue playing long into the night.

***Pachinko***

Last but not least, the Japanese national sport of *pachinko*. In fact, though, it is suggested that this game originated in Korea and, although it is not so popular there, many of those who operate *pachinko* parlours in Japan are said to be of Korean extraction.

*Pachinko* is a form of pinball and the name is said to derive from the whirring noise made by the machines in action. A *pachinko* parlour is a noisy, smoky shop filled with the sound of stirring military music and with hypnotized men (mostly) and women fascinated by the sight of metal balls whizzing around the machine and hopefully opening the right gates and hitting the correct levers to release thousands more such balls as prizes. Tobacco fumes are an essential element of the concentration necessary for this delicate process. Of course, there is also a man with a microphone to announce the advent of big winnings in stentorian tones '*pour encourager les autres*'.

Perhaps surprisingly, '*pachinko* professionals' exist, people who have the skill necessary to pick the right machines and make their living by this sport. The author is told that it is a hard life, however, necessitating long hours of intense concentration in an unfavourable atmosphere for only a moderate living and the probability of an early onset of arthritis in the fingers of the right hand. To combat the professionals, the *pachinko* parlour owners employ their own professionals who come along in the middle of the night and adjust the pins of those machines which have been making a loss during the day. A fair proportion of Japan's very limited number of hold-ups is carried out at *pachinko* parlours, so it is to be presumed that the owners are not losing too much money in the battle of the professionals.

When you enter a *pachinko* parlour, you insert money into a machine to purchase as many balls as desired. At the close of play, or when you have had enough, you take your remaining balls back to the management, where a machine counts them with such amazing rapidity that one tends to doubt the accuracy of the result (recounts are not permitted). Then one can select gifts to the value of the number of balls. One cannot, according to the law, have cash instead. This is something of a handicap for the professional, so a system has been devised whereby a voucher is issued for the number of balls. One then takes this voucher outside and round the back there is a tiny window (no connexion at all with the *pachinko* parlour, of course!) which will surreptitiously exchange the voucher for cash at somewhat less than the rate which you had to pay to purchase the balls in the first place. So the law is satisfied and the professional can stay in business. Pachinko parlours are generally open from 10:00 until 22:00.

## WORKING IN JAPAN

Japan has long been famous as the refuelling stop for travellers passing through Asia. Here it is possible to rest and recuperate for a time whilst earning some much needed cash by teaching English in the evenings. Indeed, that is how the author first came here.

Well, that is how it used to be, but things have changed somewhat over the last decade. First of all, it is not as easy to find an English-teaching position as it used to be, there being a great deal of competition these days, enabling schools to be more selective, although one feels that their standards for selection are sometimes rather dubious.

Secondly, the immigration officials are no longer as welcoming as they used to be and are more likely to want to ask questions of those who return quickly for a second or subsequent visit.

Thirdly, though, a large number of opportunities has opened up in addition to the old stand-by of teaching English. Non-Japanese are now employed in a whole range of professions to give advice in matters where Japanese may lack experience, or to make up for an insufficiency of skilled labour, or, in some cases, simply to perform duties which Japanese do not relish. The fact is that, if you want to work in Japan, you will probably find an opportunity to do so, even if you have to wait a while for that opportunity, while if you are really serious about working here and are prepared to commit yourself for a period of at least two or three years, there are some interesting opportunities available. It is not the purpose of this book to go into detail about such matters, but this company has already published a book on the topic, entitled *Japan – For Businessman and Job-Hunter*, which we recommend to anybody wishing to delve into the employment prospects.

If, however, all you want is a part-time English teaching position, the best place to look for one is the 'Japan Times' on Mondays. Start telephoning early, because there will be many applicants besides yourself.

If you require a longer-term position, bear in mind that the immigration authorities will almost certainly require of you a university degree, although if you are Australian, Canadian or a New Zealander and under thirty, you may be eligible for a working holiday visa. For further information, see the Visas section on page 7.

## JAPANESE LANGUAGE

One sometimes hears that Japanese is considered one of the world's most difficult languages. In fact, though, it is not particularly difficult to struggle along in speaking a few words or to understand when spoken to. What is so hard is to learn to read and write. So difficult is it that the Japanese themselves, when presented with the name of an unknown town, for example, cannot necessarily read it!

This is not intended to be the start of a course in practical Japanese, particularly as the writer himself cannot claim any great proficiency in the language, but a little explanation of the system may at least help the reader to understand the problems. First of all, there are three ways of writing things in Japanese. There are two phonetic alphabets and there is the Chinese character system. Any Japanese word can be written phonetically using the *hiragana* alphabet of 48 characters. In fact, this is how children do first learn to read and write. The first five characters in the alphabet represent vowel sounds. The remainder, with one exception, represent a combination of a consonant plus a vowel, for example *ka, ki, ku, ke, ko*. The only consonant which can exist independently is that single exception *n*. This system means, of course, that not only is the number of vowels used in Japanese limited to five, but also the number of consonants recognized as distinct is limited too. This is the cause of much mispronunciation of English and other languages, as we shall see in the next paragraph.

The second phonetic alphabet is called *katakana* and it is used to distinguish nasty foreign words which have crept into Japanese, of which there are very many. The *hiragana* characters tend to be rounded and the *katakana* characters angular. *Katakana* represents exactly the same sounds as *hiragana*. Because of the limited number of consonants, and because of the necessity of placing a vowel between any two consonants, *n* excepted, *katakana* leads to mutilation of the English language, from which most words are stolen, and of other languages too. It is well-known that Japanese cannot distinguish l and r. It is less well-known that they cannot distinguish b and v, or f and h, or s and th. They are also unable to distinguish the vowels a and u. Thus, when expressed in *katakana*, the words 'bus' and 'bath' are identical. Moreover, when loan-words are too long, the Japanese shorten them, without regard, of course, to the etymology. So 'television' is, in Japanese, *terebi* and 'mass communications' is *masukomi*. One detestable favourite of this writer is *remicon*, which is, believe it or not, 'ready-mixed concrete'. This butchering of one's language is sometimes hard to forgive, especially as it is often carried over when people are actually speaking English. It can also mean that even though an English word is being used, a native speaker of the language may not readily comprehend it. Moreover, if you say something in English, even though the person to whom you are speaking knows the word, he may not understand it because of your strange pronunciation (!), principally your failure to insert a few extra vowels. However, if you want to learn something Japanese, the *katakana* alphabet is a good place to start, because, as soon as you have mastered it, you will be able to read and understand what you have read. You will, for example, be able to read the names of the western dishes on a menu, because they are usually written in *katakana*, and that is a very useful ability! You will probably find yourself mouthing the words to try to imagine what they might have been before they underwent the *katakana* metamorphosis, but in most cases you will get there in the end.

The third way of writing is to use Chinese characters. This is regarded as being much more sophisticated than using *hiragana*, but it is also much more difficult. The characters themselves take a good deal of memorizing. About 2,000 are taught at school and about 3,000 are in common use. They are often used in combination with *hiragana*, with the Chinese characters, or *kanji* as they are usually called, expressing the root meaning and *hiragana* showing the verb endings, particles and prepositions. The real problem with *kanji*, though, is an historical one. Japanese already existed in spoken form when *kanji* were imported from China in order to write it down. Of course, the Japanese words were different from the Chinese words for the same things, but when the *kanji* arrived, they brought with them both the meaning and the Chinese sound. For example, the Japanese word for 'east' is *higashi*, but the character meaning east ( 東 ) can also be read, in compounds, *to*. If you show that character to a Chinese, even now, he will read *ton*, almost like the Japanese alternative pronunciation. Virtually all Japanese *kanji* have at least two possible readings, therefore, and sometimes more. For example, that *kanji* for 'east' can also be read *azuma*. Thus, when dealing with compounds, which most words are, Japanese are not necessarily sure how to read their own language, if the compound is not one with which they are familiar. You will often see *kanji* with small *hiragana* characters over the top to tell the reader how to pronounce them, especially in the case of place or personal names. Well, you may be thinking, if the Japanese cannot read their own language, what hope have I, a mere foreigner? But do not despair! This book will only suggest that you manage to recognize a very few of the most useful characters. *Kanji* are really quite fun – and a sort of detective game into the bargain!

There are just a few more things to mention. Now Japanese is, luckily, not a tonal language, like Chinese or Thai, for instance. In fact, it is somewhat like English in terms of speech. If you pronounce words in an absolutely flat way without any stress or accent, that may not be ideal, but you will generally be understood. The same would apply in English. If, however, you put stress or accent in the wrong place, you probably will not be understood, again as in English. English-speakers, particularly certain nationalities, sometimes feel an overwhelming temptation to stress the penultimate syllable. This is nearly always wrong in Japanese and is apt to lead to total incomprehension, when the same pronunciation, even if not quite correct, would probably be understood if rendered without any stress at all. This, then, is what the author would regard as the golden rule for reading Romanized Japanese:

**DO NOT STRESS THE PENULTIMATE SYLLABLE.**

Also note that, when Japanese is written in Roman script, a final u is nearly always weak, just as a final e is in English. Sometimes it is weak even in the middle of the word, particularly if it is at the end of one of the *kanji* which make up the word. Thus, when you are looking for the Tourist Information Center at Yurakucho, you will want to ask, not for 'Yura*ku*cho', as many people do, but for 'Yurakcho'. A final e in the Romanized form of Japanese, however, is pronounced.

People learning a few words of a foreign language often seem to study rather unnecessary formalities or politenesses, asking, for example, "What is the Japanese for 'Thank you'?" In fact, Japanese often use the English term 'Thank you' themselves (or, more phonetically, *san-kyu*), but would, in any case, understand an expression of gratitude without any Japanese words. When people ask what is most important in a foreign language, the author always advises, "Learn to ask 'How much?' and learn to count. They are the most important words in any language." Therefore this little section tries to give just a few practical words. Counting is a little difficult in Japanese. The words given are for ordinary numbers, for money or for time, but they cannot be used for counting objects. That is to say that they cannot be used for saying, "I want two of those." A different set of words is used for that purpose, and they are more difficult. If you want two, try holding up two fingers, or even saying 'two' in English. Note that there are two words for 'four' and two words for 'seven'.

Questions are made in Japanese by putting *-ka* at the end of the sentence, so when you hear *-ka*, panic, because an answer is required!

*Hai* means 'yes', but it is a deceiving word, because it is also quite likely to mean 'I understand', or even 'I beg your pardon', when asking for a repetition. It is not safe to assume that somebody means 'yes' just because he says *hai*. Much safer is *so desu* (it is so). That is usually a definite statement of agreement. Japanese people do not like to say 'no', so it is difficult to give a translation for this apparently simple word. *Iie* is used in the sense of 'not at all'. Thus, "You are very kind." "*Iie* (not at all)." *Chigai masu* is used to disagree politely. Thus, "Is this the train for Kyoto?" "*Chigai masu* (no, it is not)." *Kekko desu* (literally, 'it's all right' and also used to mean that, so again confusing) is for 'no, thank you', to decline an offer, but it needs to be said with a negative tone of voice, or some negative gesture. Thus, "Do you want to subscribe to a newspaper?" "*Kekko desu* (no, thank you)." And close the door firmly!

Three short lists follow. The first is of spoken Japanese which might be useful. The second gives Japanese readings and translations of *kanji* which might be encountered in everyday life. The third is a 'Bus Stop Vocabulary' list.

***(a) Useful Spoken Words and Phrases***

| ***English*** | ***Japanese*** |
|---|---|
| How much (is it)? | *Ikura (desu-ka)?* |
| At what time? | *Nan ji-ni?* |
| train | *densha* |
| bus | *basu* |
| taxi | *takushi* |
| hotel | *hoteru* |
| Excuse me. / I am sorry. / Thank you. | *Sumi masen.* |
| yes | *hai / so desu* |
| no | *iie / chigai masu / kekko desu* |
| I understand. | *Wakari mashita.* |
| I do not understand. | *Wakari masen.* |
| Where is . . . . . ? | *. . . . . . doko desu-ka?* |
| ticket | *kippu* |
| no smoking | *kin-en* |
| single (room) | *shinguru (rumu)* |
| double | *daburu* |
| twin | *tsuin* |
| bath | *o-furo* or *basu* |
| dining-room | *shoku-do* |
| (I made a) reservation. | *Yoyaku (shi-mashita).* |
| name (one's own) | *namae* |
| name (somebody else's) | *o-namae* |
| address | *jusho* |
| English (language) | *eigo* |
| Japanese (language) | *nihon-go* |
| Japan | *nihon* |
| this | *kore* |
| that | *sore* (further away) / *are* (nearer) |
| expensive | *takai* |
| cheap | *yasui* |
| map | *chizu* |
| police | *keisatsu* |
| please / yes, please | *o-negai shimasu* |
| breakfast | *cho-shoku* or *asa gohan* |
| dinner | *yu-shoku* |
| water | *o-mizu* |
| coffee | *kohi* |
| tea | *ko-cha* |
| Japanese (green) tea | *o-cha* |

***(b) Useful kanji***

| ***Kanji*** | ***Japanese*** | ***English*** |
|---|---|---|
| 一 | *ichi* | one |
| 二 | *ni* | two |
| 三 | *san* | three |
| 四 | *shi* or *yon* | four |
| 五 | *go* | five |
| 六 | *roku* | six |
| 七 | *shichi* or *nana* | seven |
| 八 | *hachi* | eight |
| 九 | *ku* or *kyu* | nine |
| 十 | *ju* | ten |
| 十一 | *ju-ichi* | eleven |
| 二十 | *ni-ju* | twenty |
| 百 | *hyaku* | one hundred |
| 二百 | *ni-hyaku* | two hundred |
| 千 | *sen* (or *i-sen*) | one thousand |
| 二千 | *ni-sen* | two thousand |
| 一万 | *ichi-man* | ten thousand |
| 一万一千 | *ichi-man i-sen* | eleven thousand |
| 十万 | *ju-man* | one hundred thousand |
| 百万 | *hyaku-man* | one million |
| 円 | *en* | yen |
| 年 | *nen* | year |
| 月 | *gatsu* | month |
| 日 | *nichi* | day or date |
| 時 | *ji* | hour or o'clock |
| 分 | *hun* or *pun* | minute(s) |
| 駅 | *eki* | station |
| 空港 | *kuko* | airport |
| 入口 | *iri-guchi* | entrance |
| 出口 | *de-guchi* | exit |
| 男 | *otoko* | men |
| 女 | *onna* | ladies |
| 指定席 | *shitei seki* | reserved seat |
| 自由席 | *jiyu seki* | unreserved seat |
| 新幹線 | *shinkansen* | *shinkansen* ('bullet train') |
| 北 | *kita* | north |
| 南 | *minami* | south |
| 東 | *higashi* | east |
| 西 | *nishi* | west |
| 上 | *ue* or *kami* | top (or upper) |
| 下 | *shita* or *shimo* | bottom (or lower) |
| 中 | *naka* or *chu* | middle |
| 行 | *yuki* | to (destination of train or bus) |

*(c) 'Bus Stop Vocabulary'*

These are words referring to geography, buildings or locations which may be encountered in names of bus stops or similar and where it may be helpful to know what landmarks to be watching for.

| *Japanese* | *Kanji* | *English* | *Japanese* | *Kanji* | *English* |
|---|---|---|---|---|---|
| *-yama* | 山 | mountain | *-shi* | 市 | city |
| *-san* | 山 | mountain | *-machi* | 町 | town |
| *-ko* | 港 | port | *-cho* | 町 | town |
| *minato* | 港 | port | *-mura* | 村 | village |
| *-ko* | 湖 | lake | *-chome* | 丁目 | division of town |
| *misaki* | 岬 | cape | *shi yaku-sho* | 市役所 | city hall |
| *-saki* | 崎 | promontory | *machi yaku-ba* | 町役場 | town hall |
| *hanto* | 半島 | peninsula | *byoin* | 病院 | hospital |
| *-oka* | 丘 or 岡 | hill | *sho-gakko* | 小学校 | primary school |
| *-tani* | 谷 | valley | *chu-gakko* | 中学校 | middle school |
| *-ya* | 谷 | valley | *koko* | 高校 | high school |
| *onsen* | 温泉 | spa | *daigaku* | 大学 | university |
| *-mae* | 前 | in front of | *-dera* | 寺 | temple |
| *iriguchi* | 入口 | entrance to | *-ji* | 寺 | temple |
| *koen* | 公園 | park | *jingu* | 神宮 | shrine |
| *-numa* | 沼 | lake | *-miya* | 宮 | shrine |
| *-ike* | 池 | pond / lake | *hakubutsu-kan* | 博物館 | museum |
| *kogen* | 高原 | heights | *dobutsu-en* | 動物園 | zoo |
| *-hashi (-bashi)* | 橋 | bridge | *shako* | 車庫 | bus depot |
| *keiyu* | 経由 | via | *mawari* | 回り | circular |

***The Katakana Alphabet*** (for imported words)

| | A | I | U | E | O |
|---|---|---|---|---|---|
| | ア a | イ i | ウ u | エ e | オ o |
| **K** | カ ka | キ ki | ク ku | ケ ke | コ ko |
| **S** | サ sa | シ shi | ス su | セ se | ソ so |
| **T** | タ ta | チ chi | ツ tsu | テ te | ト to |
| **N** | ナ na | ニ ni | ヌ nu | ネ ne | ノ no |
| **H** | ハ ha | ヒ hi | フ hu | ヘ he | ホ ho |
| **M** | マ ma | ミ mi | ム mu | メ me | モ mo |
| **Y** | ヤ ya | | ユ yu | | ヨ yo |
| **R** | ラ ra | リ ri | ル ru | レ re | ロ ro |
| **W** | ワ wa | ヰ wi* | | ヱ we* | ヲ wo |
| | ン n | * not in common use | | | |

## COMMON JAPANESE WORDS

Here are a few Japanese words which you may come across in the course of your stay. They are divided here by subject. To search for a word alphabetically, please use the index at the end of the book.

### ACCOMMODATION

***Ryokan*** – A *ryokan* is a traditional Japanese inn usually with the outward appearance of a large ordinary house. The interior is most commonly in typical Japanese style and the price generally includes dinner and breakfast. Most *ryokan* put emphasis on quality of service and food and are not cheap.

***Minshuku*** – A *minshuku* is a Japanese inn operated by private individuals in their own home. It is the nearest Japanese equivalent to bed and breakfast. Dinner and breakfast are usually included in rates stated, but can often be omitted, with a small reduction in price, upon request. *Minshuku* pride themselves on having a homely atmosphere and moderate prices.

### ABOUT THE HOUSE

***Tatami*** – The floors of typical Japanese rooms are covered with *tatami*, which are thick mats made of rice straw with a covering of rushes. They are rectangular and come in two standard sizes, of which the more common is now 180 cms. by 90 cms. An attractive cloth strip is used to decorate the edges. Neither shoes nor slippers are permitted on *tatami*. Only socks may be worn. Sizes of rooms in Japanese houses are usually quoted by the number of *tatami* mats. The most common sizes are 8 mats, 6 mats, 4½ mats and 3 mats.

***Futon*** – A *futon* is a thick quilt padded with cotton wool which is used for bedding. A more rigid *futon* is used under the sleeper with a softer, more flexible one as the cover. *Futon* are placed on the *tatami* floor at night and put away in the cupboard during the day when not in use.

***Zabuton*** – A *zabuton* is a small square cushion laid on the *tatami* floor and used for sitting on.

***Fusuma*** and ***Shoji*** – These are types of sliding doors used in Japanese houses. *Fusuma* are wooden-framed paper doors, while *shoji* are doors with wooden latticework covered with thin, translucent paper. Such doors are used to divide rooms and *fusuma* are also used for cupboard doors. Since they are easily damaged, one needs to be careful about putting excessive pressure on them or scraping them with rigid objects. Such doors are not usually lockable.

***Tokonoma*** – The *tokonoma* is an alcove found in the main room of a Japanese house. It is a place of honour and is used to display a picture scroll, a vase of flowers or some precious object. It is not to put one's luggage in or to sit in!

### CLOTHING

***Kimono*** – Most people know that the *kimono* is a traditional Japanese garment with long sleeves. The *kimono* folds over at the front so as to be double-breasted. It has no buttons and is held in place by means of a belt called an *obi*. Most people wear a *kimono* only on special occasions such as New Year's Day, for weddings and for other formal ceremonies. *Kimono* are elaborate and very expensive garments.

***Yukata*** – The *yukata* is an informal type of *kimono* and it is popular as home wear or for relaxation or casual wear, especially in summer. It is particularly favoured by those on holiday to wear while cooling off after a bath and a *yukata* is almost always provided by a *ryokan* to be used for this purpose and as sleeping wear.

## EVERYDAY LIFE

***Hanko*** – A *hanko* is a seal engraved with the user's name. It is used instead of a signature and is the legal method of identification in Japan. Most people have two *hanko*, a formal one for use in official and legal matters and a less formal one for everyday affairs. The former will be made of wood, but the latter may be rubber. At work there may be yet another type of *hanko* to be used for company business.

***Janken*** – This is a game played by children (and by adults too) especially when deciding who shall take some reward or perform some necessary duty or in deciding an order of priority. It is the Japanese equivalent of tossing a coin. The game is generally known in English as scissors, paper, stone. In time to a rhythmic chant, the equivalent of ready, steady, go, the participants thrust out their hands held in one of three attitudes, representing scissors, paper or stone. Scissors cut paper, paper wraps up stone and stone blunts scissors. If necessary the process is repeated many times with participants gradually being eliminated.

## SHOPS

***Noren*** – The *noren* is a short cloth found hanging at the entrance to shops, restaurants or even kitchens in private homes. The writing on the cloth shows the nature of the business in which the owner is engaged and owners regard it as a very serious matter to keep the *noren* as long as possible, for it shows how many years they have been in business.

***Chochin*** – A *chochin* is a Japanese lantern made of bamboo and either paper or cloth. It is hung at the entrance to shops, especially restaurants. Cheap drinking establishments are often distinguished by having a red lantern at the entrance.

***Hashi*** and ***Waribashi*** – *Hashi* is the Japanese word for chopsticks. *Waribashi* are disposable chopsticks which are very common in Japan (and particularly wasteful of timber which is generally imported and not regrown). They come in a single piece, split up the middle, but not completely separated. You complete the separation by pulling them apart. The end which you split yourself is for holding. The machined end does the transportation of the food.

## HISTORICAL

***Kofun*** and ***Haniwa*** – A *kofun* is a tomb constructed as a mound and built generally for an ancient political administrator. Such burials started around the time when Christ was living and the mounds are usually surrounded by moats and topped with *haniwa*. *Haniwa* are clay figures in the shape of men, women and animals, especially horses. They were apparently for ritual use and were buried with the dead as funerary objects. Since similar mounds are found in Korea and Mongolia, it seems reasonable to suppose that there is a connexion between the culture of those areas and of Japan.

***Kojiki*** and ***Nihon-shoki*** – These are the two most ancient chronicles of Japan. They were written in the eighth century. *Nihon-shoki* provided a complete chronology of national history as far back as the accession of the first Emperor, Jimmu, on 11th February in the year 660 B.C. Unfortunately, most of this chronology is probably fictitious.

***Shogun*** – *Shogun* literally means *generalissimo*. Originally, the temporary title of *sei-tai shogun* (barbarian-quelling great general) was given to the commander-in-chief of an expeditionary army sent to crush any forces rebelling against the emperor. However, from the twelfth century the title became an official one given to the administrative head of the *samurai* (warrior class) feudal government appointed by the emperor to govern the nation. Except for a brief period during the reign of the Emperor Godaigo, this system lasted until the Meiji Restoration in 1868.

***Daimyo*** – The *daimyo* were the feudal lords who held local power under the *shogun*.

***Samurai*** – *Samurai* originally and literally meant 'one who serves'. During the Heian Era, *samurai* served, guarded and fought for the nobles, that is to say for government officials. Later, however, they used their military strength to become very influential in the political arena also.

***Ronin*** – A *ronin* was originally a warrior who had no lord. He would wander around the country searching for mercenary work or for a permanent master. Nowadays the term is frequently used humorously to describe a student who has failed the entrance examinations for university and is preparing for his next opportunity to sit them, or, in times of recession, to refer to the unemployed.

***Ainu*** – The Ainu are the indigenous people of Japan, who once inhabited much of the country but were gradually pushed northwards by the military-minded Yamato race spreading from Kyushu. Nowadays only about 15,000 Ainu remain and it is doubtful whether many of those are full-blooded Ainu. The few are to be found in remote corners of Hokkaido, where they strive to keep alive their language and culture.

## RELIGION

***Shintoism*** – This is the religion which is unique to Japan. It is based upon the worship of nature, of ancestors and of ancient heroes. It became the state religion following the Meiji Restoration (from 1868) and remained so until the end of the Second World War. Most Japanese marriages are conducted according to Shinto rites and people visit shrines on festive occasions, but otherwise Shinto doctrines do not have a great effect upon the lives of the average Japanese citizen.

***Buddhism*** – Buddhism came to Japan via India and China in the sixth century. It teaches how to overcome the sufferings of this world through self-improvement. Most Japanese have Buddhist funerals and the religion has influenced many aspects of Japanese culture, from literature and architecture to morals and philosophy.

***Zen*** and ***Za-zen*** – Zen is a sect of Buddhism. It emphasizes that enlightenment should be obtained through silent meditation (*za-zen*) and places relatively less weight on Buddhist scriptures and rites. It has influenced greatly many aspects of Japanese culture, including tea ceremony, dry landscape gardening and flower arrangement. *Za-zen* is a form of meditation performed in a cross-legged sitting posture to attain the ideal state of supreme enlightenment.

***O-saisen Bako*** – This is a large wooden offertory box found at every shrine and temple. It is placed in front of the sanctuary and worshippers throw money into it when praying for good fortune.

***Omikuji*** – *Omikuji* are paper oracles telling one's fortune. They can be purchased for a small fee in shrines and temples. Those who buy usually tie the *omikuji* to the branch of a tree, particularly if it is an unfavourable fortune.

***Mikoshi*** – *Mikoshi* are portable shrines in which the spirit of a divinity or guardian is supposed to repose temporarily during the period of a festival. The *mikoshi* is carried gleefully around the streets by teams of willing bearers bouncing it up and down in a manner which involves considerable expenditure of energy and must be most uncomfortable for the divinity within.

***O-bon*** – This is the time when the spirits of deceased ancestors are supposed to return to the family home and be entertained there for a period of three days. The festival is observed usually in mid-August (but in mid-July by some who still reckon by the old Chinese calendar). People make a bon-fire (excuse the pun) to guide the spirits home and performances of *bon odori* (*bon* dancing) are given as a welcome. People also visit the graves of their ancestors at this time to comfort the spirits. Although *o-bon* is not a national holiday, most people feel obliged to return to their 'home towns' at this time. Companies usually suspend operations for a day or two and the whole country is on the move. It is a particularly bad time to be going anywhere. All transport (except ordinary trains) is packed, sometimes beyond belief and reserved seats are sold out as soon as they go on sale, a month in advance. Many young people who are less religiously minded have adopted the custom of searching for their ancestors in such places as Hawaii or Europe, so international flights are crowded too. On the other hand, it is a very good time to have a look round Tokyo or other business cities, as these are almost deserted.

***Shichi Go San*** – This is a festival held on 15th November when girls of seven, boys of five and three-year-olds of either sex are taken to a shrine by their parents in order to pray for long life and healthy and prosperous futures. The words '*shichi go san*' mean 'seven, five, three.' The children are dressed in beautiful and costly *kimono* and special types of red and white sweets are available, known as *chitose-ame* ('thousand year sweets'). See the coloured pages for a photograph of *Shichi Go San*.

## ADVICE AND INFORMATION

Here is a list of telephone numbers where English (or another language, as indicated) should be spoken and which can be used to obtain advice and information, or in case of emergency.

| *Service* | *Number* |
|---|---|
| Japan Helpline – emergencies, counselling, 24 hours, free | 0120-46-1997 |
| Tokyo English Lifeline – emergencies, counselling, 9-13, 19-23 | 03-3264-4347 |
| Police (Japanese) – free | 110 |
| Fire, ambulance (Japanese) – free | 119 |
| Hospital Information | 03-3212-2323 |
| Tourist Information Centre – assistance, 9-17, in Tokyo | 03-3502-1461 |
| Tourist Information Centre – assistance, 9-20, Narita Airport | 0476-34-6251 |
| Tourist Information Centre – assistance, 9-17, in Kyoto | 075-371-5649 |
| Tourist Information Centre – assistance, 9-17, East Japan, free | 0088-22-2800 |
| Tourist Information Centre – assistance, 9-17, West Japan, free | 0088-22-4800 |
| Teletourist Service – forthcoming events, Tokyo | 03-3503-2911 |
| Teletourist Service (French) – forthcoming events, Tokyo | 03-3503-2926 |
| Teletourist Service – forthcoming events, Kyoto | 075-361-2911 |
| JR East Infoline – railway services | 03-3423-0111 |
| Tokyo Subway Information | 03-3502-1461 |
| Postal Services Information – 9.30-16.30 | 03-5472-5851 |
| Japan Hotline – directory enquiries, general information | 03-3586-0110 |
| NTT Telephone Information, Tokyo | 03-3277-1010 |
| NTT Telephone Information, Narita | 0476-28-1010 |
| NTT Telephone Information, Yokohama | 045-322-1010 |
| NTT Telephone Information, Osaka | 06-313-1010 |
| NTT Telephone Information, Nagoya | 052-541-1010 |
| NTT Telephone Information, Hiroshima | 082-262-1010 |
| NTT Telephone Information, Sapporo | 011-219-1010 |
| NTT Telephone Information, Sendai | 022-232-1010 |
| NTT Telephone Information, Fukuoka | 092-632-1010 |
| Tokyo City Air Terminal – flight information | 03-3665-7111 |
| Foreign Residents' Advisory Centre – 9.30-12, 13-16 | 03-5320-7744 |
| Foreign Residents' Advisory Centre (French) | 03-5320-7755 |
| Foreign Residents' Advisory Centre (Chinese) | 03-5320-7766 |
| Foreign Residents' Advisory Centre (Korean) | 03-5320-7700 |
| Tokyo Regional Immigration Bureau – information, 9.30-12, 13-16 | 03-3213-8527 |
| Immigration Office – computerized information | 03-3213-8141 |
| Central Immigration Office | 03-3580-4111 |
| Tokyo Regional Immigration Bureau | 03-3213-8111 |
| Narita District Immigration Office | 0476-32-6812 |
| Osaka Regional Immigration Bureau | 06-941-0771 |
| Osaka Immigration Information (English, Chinese, Spanish, Portuguese) | 06-774-3409 |
| Tokyo City Air Terminal Immigration Office – re-entry permits | 03-3664-3046 |

| | |
|---|---|
| Tokyo Bar Association (English and Chinese) – legal advice | 03-3581-2302 |
| Ministry of Justice (English, German, Chinese) – legal advice | 03-3214-0424 |
| Labor for Foreign Laborers Rights (English, Chinese, Korean, Spanish, Port.) | 03-3357-5506 |
| Legal Assistance – 11-19 | 03-3591-1301 |
| HELP – for Asian women with problems | 03-3368-8855 |
| Kaigai Nikkei Koryu Centre (English, Spanish, Port.) – for workers, 16-17 | 03-5256-5301 |
| Yokohama International Tourist Association – information, 9-17 | 045-641-4759 |
| YOKE (multilingual) – for Yokohama residents, Mon., Wed., Fri., 10-16 | 045-671-7209 |
| Kobe International Community Centre (English and Chinese) | 078-322-0030 |
| Kobe Community House and Information Centre | 078-857-6540 |
| AIDS Hotline – Saturdays, 19-22 | 03-3359-2477 |
| AIDS Information – Saturdays, 13-18 | 03-5256-3002 |
| AIDS Information, Osaka area | 0720-48-2044 |
| Alcoholics Anonymous | 03-3971-1471 |

# FESTIVALS

| Date | Place | Name | Features |
|---|---|---|---|
| **January** | | | |
| 1st to 3rd | National | New Year | Time to visit temple or shrine. Holiday |
| Early January | Yokote, Akita | Kamakura | Igloo construction |
| 6th | Tokyo | Dezome-shiki | Firemen's acrobatics |
| 15th | National | Coming of Age | 20 year olds' day. Many kimonos to be seen. Holiday |
| **February** | | | |
| 3rd | National | Setsubun | Bean-throwing festival to encourage good luck |
| From 1st weekend | Sapporo | Snow Festival | Snow and ice sculptures |
| 11th | National | National Foundation Day | Holiday |
| **March** | | | |
| 3rd | National | Girls' Day | Dolls Festival |
| Early March | Nara | Todai-ji O-mizu Tori | Water-drawing ceremony |
| 13th | Nara | Kasuga Shrine Festival | |
| 21st | National | Vernal Equinox | Visiting graves of ancestors. Holiday |
| **April** | | | |
| 14th to 15th | Takayama | Spring Festival | Famous parade |
| 29th | National | Greenery Day | Holiday |
| **May** | | | |
| 2nd to 4th | Fukuoka | Hakata Dontaku Festival | |
| 3rd | National | Constitution Day | Holiday |
| 5th | National | Boys' Day | Holiday. Carp flags flown |
| 12th to 16th | Tokyo | Kanda Festival | |
| 15th | Kyoto | Aoi Festival | Parade of ox-carts |
| 3rd Sunday | Tokyo | Sanja Festival | Many portable shrines |

| Date | Place | Festival | Description |
|---|---|---|---|
| **June** | | | |
| 10th to 16th | Tokyo | Sanno Festival | |
| 15th | Morioka | Chagu Chagu Umako | Procession of horses |
| **July** | | | |
| 7th | Hiratsuka | Tanabata | Star Festival |
| 16th to 17th | Kyoto | Gion Festival | Major Procession |
| Mid-July | Hiroshima | Kangen-sai | Ancient music festival on Miyajima |
| 23rd to 24th | Soma, Fukushima | Soma Nomaoi | Horseriders in ancient costume |
| 25th | Osaka | Tenjin Festival | Parade on land and river, fireworks |
| **August** | | | |
| 3rd to 7th | Hirosaki | Nebuta | Illuminated floats |
| 5th to 7th | Akita | Kanto Festival | Lanterns on poles in balancing act |
| 6th to 8th | Sendai | Tanabata | Star Festival |
| 6th | Hiroshima | Peace Ceremony | Commemorating atomic bombing |
| 15 to 18th | Tokushima | Awa Odori | All-night comic dancing |
| Mid-August | National | O-bon | Welcoming back spirits of ancestors |
| 15th | Nara | Kasuga Mandoro | Stone lanterns lit at Kasuga Taisha |
| 16th | Kyoto | Daimonji | Bonfires on hills |
| **September** | | | |
| 14th to 16th | Kamakura | Yabusame | Horseback archery |
| 15th | National | Respect for Aged Day | Holiday |
| 23rd | National | Autumnal Equinox | Holiday |
| **October** | | | |
| 7th to 9th | Nagasaki | O-kunchi Festival | Festival with strong Chinese element |
| 8th to 10th | Akan-ko | Marimo Festival | Ainu Festival |
| 9th to 10th | Takayama | Autumn Festival | Famous parade |
| 10th | National | Sports Day | Holiday. |
| 17th | Nikko | Grand Autumn Festival | |
| 22nd | Kyoto | Jidai Matsuri | Procession in ancient costume |
| 31st to 3rd Nov. | Tokyo | Meiji Shrine Festival | |
| **November** | | | |
| 3rd | National | Culture Day | Holiday |
| 3rd | Hakone | Daimyo Gyoretsu | Procession in ancient costume |
| 15th | National | Shichi Go San | Kimono-clad children visit shrines |
| 23rd | National | Labour Thanksgiving Day | |
| Late November | Tokyo | Asakusa Cock Festival | Sale of good-luck bamboo rakes |
| **December** | | | |
| 23rd | National | Emperor's Birthday | Holiday. Palace grounds open |
| 31st | Oga | Namahage Festival | Masked 'ogres' visit local homes |

## WHICH PLACES SHOULD YOU VISIT?

The following lists, mainly subjective opinions, of course, are in order of precedence without consideration of geography.

### TEN CITIES OR TOWNS

1. Kyoto 2. Nara 3. Tokyo 4. Nikko 5. Kamakura 6. Hiroshima 7. Nagasaki 8. Takayama 9. Hakodate 10. Yokohama

### THREE FAMOUS CASTLES

1. Himeji (Kansai District) 2. Matsumoto (Chubu) 3. Matsuyama (Shikoku)

### THREE PRETTY GARDENS (Official List)

1. Kenroku-en, Kanazawa 2. Koraku-en, Okayama 3. Kairaku-en, Mito

### THREE PRETTY GARDENS (Author's Opinion)

1. Kenroku-en, Kanazawa 2. Ritsurin Koen, Takamatsu 3. Koraku-en, Tokyo

### THREE NATURAL BEAUTY SPOTS (Official List)

1. Matsushima 2. Miyajima (Hiroshima) 3. Amano Hashidate

### THREE NATURAL BEAUTY SPOTS (Author's Opinion)

1. Miyajima 2. Hakone 3. Daisetsu-zan National Park (Hokkaido)

### THREE ATTRACTIVE LAKES

1. Towada-ko (Tohoku) 2. Mashu-ko (Hokkaido) 3. Shoji-ko (Fuji Five Lakes)

### THREE IMPRESSIVE MOUNTAINS

1. Mt. Fuji 2. Mt. Aso (Kyushu) 3. Mt. Bandai (near Aizu Wakamatsu, Tohoku)

### TEN FAMOUS TEMPLES

1. San-ju-san Gen-do (Kyoto) 2. Kiyomizu-dera (Kyoto) 3. Todai-ji (Nara) 4. Horyu-ji (near Nara) 5. Zenko-ji (Nagano) 6. Enryaku-ji (Kyoto) 7. Senso-ji (Asakusa, Tokyo) 8. Kinkaku-ji (Kyoto) 9. Ginkaku-ji (Kyoto) 10. Ryoan-ji (Kyoto)

### THREE FAMOUS SHRINES

1. Ise Grand Shrines (Ise) 2. Toshogu (Nikko) 3. Izumo Taisha (Izumo)

### THREE BIG CAVES

1. Akiyoshi-do (Chugoku) 2. Ryuga-do (Shikoku) 3. Ryusen-do (Tohoku)

### THREE SCENIC COASTLINES

1. Sanriku (Tohoku) 2. Noto Peninsula (Chubu) 3. Kii Peninsula (Kansai)

### THREE FAMOUS SPAS *(Onsen)*

1. Beppu (Kyushu) 2. Kusatsu (Chubu) 3. Noboribetsu (Hokkaido)

**TEN SCENIC JR MAIN LINES**

1. Joetsu Line (Chubu) 2. Takayama Line (Chubu) 3. San-in Line (Chugoku) 4. Dosan Line (Shikoku) 5. Sekisho Line (Hokkaido) 6. Ou Line (Tohoku) 7. Shinetsu Line (Chubu) 8. Uetsu Line (Tohoku) 9. Chuo Line (Chubu) 10. Kagoshima Line (Kyushu)

**TEN SCENIC JR MINOR RAILWAY LINES**

1. Shinmei Line (Hokkaido) 2. Iiyama Line (Chubu) 3. Hohi Line (Kyushu) 4. Kisuki Line (Chugoku) 5. Tadami Line (Chubu / Tohoku) 6. Gono Line (Tohoku) 7. Hisatsu Line (Kyushu) 8. Koumi Line (Chubu) 9. Hanawa Line (Tohoku) 10. Kyudai Line (Kyushu)

**THREE INTERESTING PRIVATE RAILWAYS**

1. Oigawa Railway (Chubu) 2. Kurobe Gorge Railway (Chubu) 3. Hakone Tozan Railway (Tokyo Area)

**THREE ENJOYABLE BUS RIDES**

1. Matsuyama to Kochi (Shikoku) 2. Kitami to Akan-ko (Hokkaido) 3. Nikko to Chuzenji (Tokyo Area)

**THREE TALLEST BUILDINGS**

1. Landmark Tower, Yokohama — 296 metres 2. Metropolitan Government Offices, Shinjuku, Tokyo — 243 metres 3. Sunshine 60, Ikebukuro, Tokyo — 240 metres

## TWO SUGGESTIONS FOR THE TRAVELLER

To tell people how to do their travelling is, of course, presumptuous. Each does best travelling in his own way, at his own speed, looking at what he wants to see. Nevertheless, the author would like to offer just two general suggestions.

**① Bring half of what you consider essential**

People always travel with too many possessions. Therefore, decide on an absolute minimum — and then bring only half of that. The things to cut out are bulky items. Basically, you can bring as much underwear and as many pairs of socks as you wish, but do not bring spare pairs of trousers and several thick sweaters "in case it turns a bit chilly." Unnecessary encumbrances will turn out to be a real nuisance. Trousers and similar can be washed overnight and worn again the next morning. If you bring a sweater, you should make it a very light one, or else be prepared to wear it most of the time. Moreover, the more you bring, the more you are likely to forget or lose somewhere along the way. If you do find that you have brought too much, try to leave the excess somewhere while you travel round Japan. Remember that the happiest travellers are usually those who are carrying the least. The author recalls once meeting an Australian who had had all his possessions stolen in India. "I had only a change of shirt," he said. "I was never so relieved in all my life! I had a really good time from then on."

**② Get up and get moving early**

This is always the best way, whether you are travelling or sightseeing. Get on the road before the masses do. It always helps to arrive at your destination early and find somewhere to stay before it gets dark. It is especially important in Japan, because it gets light so early here.

# PART 2 SIGHTSEEING

## INTRODUCTORY

The following pages deal with sightseeing in Japan. Generally the author has made the supposition that you will follow his suggestion that travelling by train wherever possible is the best way to see Japan, so routes are designed to fit with one of the special types of rail tickets available. Most people will probably use a Japan Rail Pass, so this type of ticket is given priority, but attention is always given to those who will use a *shu-yu-ken* or Blue Spring tickets (really called *sei-shun ju-hachi kippu*, in case you need to ask for them at the ticket office). For more information on these tickets, see the section starting on page 13 in the text.

Headings give the names of main places to visit. Each is then followed by the same name in *kanji* (Chinese characters), which you can show to anybody who cannot understand where you want to go. It may also help you to locate the correct train at the railway station, or to find your intended destination on a map or in the railway timetable. The words in inverted commas which follow this are a literal translation of the place name and are really just for amusement and interest. Please do not take them too seriously, or complain that sometimes a word has been taken to be an adjective and sometimes a noun, or that the same Chinese character has been given different meanings in different places. This has sometimes been necessary to make some sense out of the names, and remember that this is just for fun. Beneath, in smaller italic type, is the apparently true derivation of the name, although some of these derivations certainly sound far-fetched to the author. The most dubious of them are so marked.

Also indicated is the railway line on which each place lies and the time needed to reach it from Tokyo or some more appropriate major centre. Note that where there is a direct service from the Tokyo area, this is the time given, but it may, in some cases, be possible to reach the place more quickly by taking the *shinkansen* and then changing to a local express.

Whenever it is necessary to take a bus, the destination of the bus and the stop at which you should alight are given in *kanji*. This is because buses are very rarely marked in Roman letters in Japan. Unfortunately, they do not often bear the convenience of route numbers either.

Many train and bus times have been given, as the author believes that these will be helpful. Very considerable effort has been made to ensure that they are correct at the time of publication, but, as stated earlier, times do change, so one needs to check the information given. In particular, bus times tend to change both seasonally and from year to year, so should always be treated with suspicion. Fares are sure to change, but that does not usually cause great inconvenience, as long as one is prepared. Regard 1995 as a base and add 5% per year.

It is not the author's intention to deprecate other books, but the fact is that, although each has its merits, you will find quite a lot of factual mistakes in them. Even in the 'recognized' guide books, you will find maps showing railway lines which were abandoned years ago, for example. This generally happens because the author has not noticed the changes which have taken place since the book was first written and, indeed, even in the year which has elapsed during the preparation of this book, it has been difficult to keep up with the changes taking place. However, this is a new book and we believe that the information contained herein is fresh and reliable. We have certainly gone to pains to try to make it so.

# TOKYO (東京)
# ('Eastern Capital')

## Access

For most visitors, the arrival point in Japan is Narita Airport, outside Tokyo. Note that Narita Airport is a long way from Tokyo. The journey of some 70 kilometres takes an hour by the fastest possible routes, which are the JR 'Narita Express' and the Keisei 'Skyliner'. From the airport to the city, there are, in fact, three choices: the 'limousine bus', a Japan Railways line or the Keisei Private Railway.

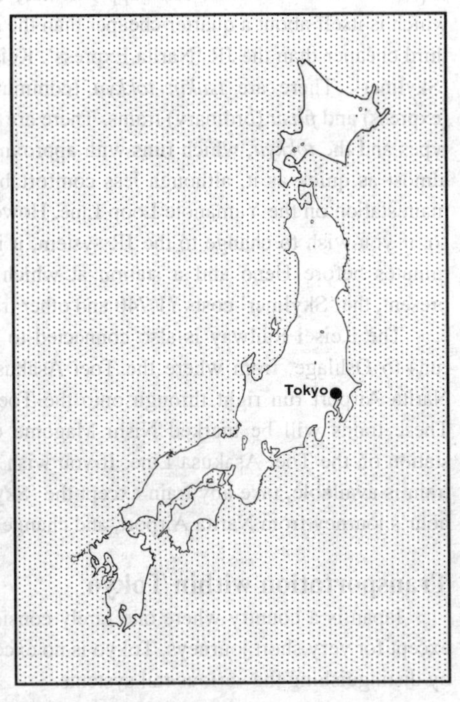


The bus is expensive and susceptible to the vagaries of traffic conditions. Most journeys go to the Tokyo City Air Terminal, which is itself not in a particularly convenient location, although it has now been connected to the subway system (Suitengu-mae station on the Hanzomon Line), which makes it much more accessible. Certain journeys go to a selection of the most expensive hotels, which is convenient if you wish to stay in one of those. There are also occasional trips to Tokyo Station, to Yokohama and to Haneda (mainly domestic) Airport. At present the bus costs approximately ¥3,000.

The Japan Railways line departs from the basement of each of the two terminal buildings and has two types of train, the 'Narita Express', which is a supplementary fare limited express (*tokkyu*) train, and a rapid (*kaisoku)* train. Departures for the limited express are every half-hour during the early morning, afternoon and early evening and every hour in the middle of the day and during the late evening. Departures are at 13 and 43 minutes past the hour (just 13 minutes past at hourly-service times). The *kaisoku* train runs every hour on the hour. There is a very great difference in price between the two, with the limited express costing more than twice as much as the *kaisoku* train. However, if your budget is not limited, the express is quick and comfortable and you have a reserved seat. If you want to economize, however, the *kaisoku* train is not so slow, taking about 90 minutes to Tokyo, and it will not be crowded on leaving Narita Airport, although it may become so later in the journey at some times of the day. The express runs to Tokyo station, where most trains are divided, one half of the train continuing to Yokohama, with occasional journeys extended to Ofuna, and the other half going round Tokyo's Yamanote loop line to the major centre of Shinjuku. A few runs continue on to Ikebukuro, further round the Yamanote Line. The *kaisoku* train follows the same route, but with stops on the way, to Tokyo. Then most journeys go on also to Yokohama, Ofuna, Kamakura and beyond. At the time of writing, the 'Narita Express' costs ¥2,890 to Tokyo and the *kaisoku* train costs ¥1,260.

The Keisei Private Railway is cheapest of all. It also departs from the basements of the terminal buildings, sharing the stations there with the Japan Railways line. The Keisei Railway also offers an express, named the 'Skyliner'. It runs every forty minutes until 22:00. It is not as expensive as the JR train. The supplementary charge amounts to about 85% of the basic fare, which is itself about a quarter cheaper than the JR fare. Overall the Keisei 'Skyliner' is about a third cheaper than the JR 'Narita Express'. Keisei offers a selection of trains in addition to the 'Skyliner'. There are *tsukin tokkyu* (commuter express), *tokkyu* (limited express), *kyuko* (express) and *futsu* (ordinary) trains. There are no supplementary charges for any of these four types and the *tokkyu*, which runs with approximately the same frequency as the 'Skyliner', is almost as quick as it, although less comfortable. The Keisei Railway runs to Ueno, another main station on the Yamanote Loop Line. However, the station is separate from the JR station, so, if you wish to change to the JR system, it is preferable to do so at Nippori, reached three minutes before Ueno and a station at which all trains, including the 'Skyliner', stop. At present, the 'Skyliner' costs ¥1,740 and other trains cost ¥940.

The Keisei Railway is also connected to the subway system. From Aoto, a branch line runs to Oshiage, from where the Toei Asakusa Line commences. Some Keisei trains from Narita Airport run right through onto the Toei Asakusa Line, without any change of train. These trains will be marked Nishi Magome on the destination board, that being the final station on the Toei Asakusa Line. If you wish to get onto the subway, but no Nishi Magome train is available, take any train except the 'Skyliner' (which does not stop) to Aoto, about an hour's journey from Narita Airport, and change to any train leaving from platform 1.

## Transportation within Tokyo

Japan is a country where one rarely considers any mode of transport other than railway, except for very short journeys. Tokyo is no exception. It is a maze of railway lines. Let us start by distinguishing the various rail systems.

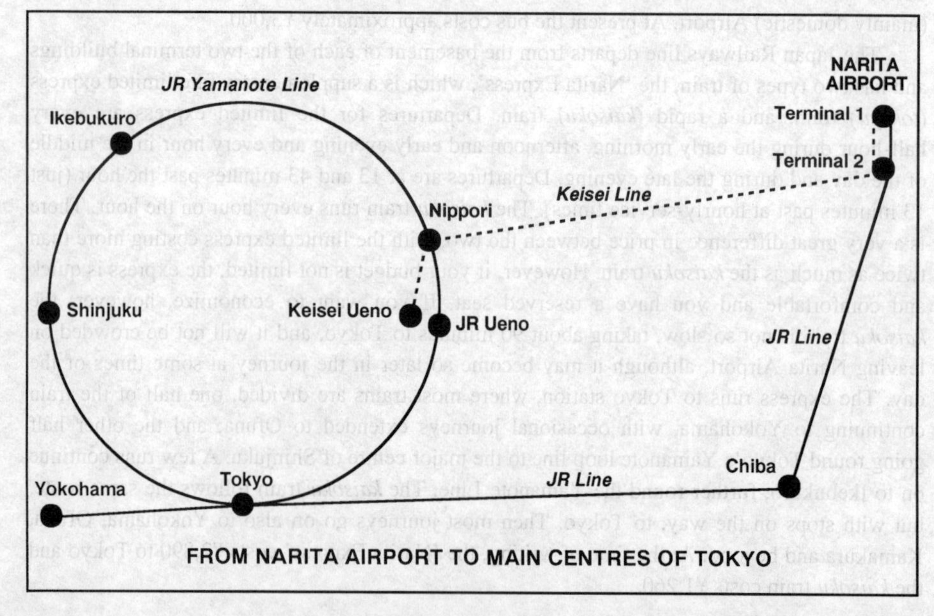

FROM NARITA AIRPORT TO MAIN CENTRES OF TOKYO

First of all, there are the lines operated by Japan Railways (JR). There is the circular Yamanote Line (green striped trains) running round Tokyo and passing through many of the main centres. This is bisected by another line which carries both Chuo Line (orange) trains and Sobu Line (yellow) trains. Paralleling the Yamanote Line for about half of its route is the Keihin Tohoku Line (blue trains). This is the central area. The Chuo, Sobu and Keihin Tohoku Lines all extend further, while from the main centres of Shinjuku, Tokyo and Ueno various other suburban and long-distance trains start. *Shinkansen* (bullet train) services start from Tokyo station and run west (blue trains) to Nagoya, Kyoto, Osaka, Kobe, Hiroshima and Hakata (Fukuoka). They run north (green trains) to Niigata, Fukushima, Yamagata, Sendai and Morioka.

Next there is the subway system. Now the subway is operated not by a single company, as one might expect, but by two separate companies, known as Toei and Eidan. Toei, the municipal authority, also operates buses in the central area of Tokyo and the single remaining tram route. The names of its subway lines are usually prefixed by the word 'Toei'. There are four such lines. Eidan operates eight subway lines. There is no free interchange between Toei and Eidan lines. However, if one buys a ticket for a journey which involves the use of both systems, a discount of ¥40 is given on the addition of the two fares. One must, however, purchase the correct type of ticket for this journey. The Eidan lines are generally a little cheaper than the Toei lines, if one has a choice.

Then there is the private railway network. There are several private companies operating in the Tokyo area. Many of the lines start at stations on the Yamanote loop line and run to destinations not served by JR, although some of them run in direct competition with JR. We have already met the Keisei Line from Narita Airport and there are, for example, two companies running to Yokohama in competition with the JR service. In general, the private railways are cheaper than JR.

With one of the railway systems, one can reach almost anywhere in the Tokyo area. Consult the subway map which we have provided on the first of the colour pages in the centre of this book and decide which route to follow, remembering that it will usually be more simple and cheaper to keep to one system as far as possible.

Buses are generally used in Tokyo only to supplement the rail system, that is to say to get from the nearest station to one's precise destination. Because of the clogged condition of Tokyo's roads, they are generally too slow for anything else. Considering the short distances for which most people use buses, they are surprisingly expensive, most now having a flat fare of ¥200 within the city area. There is no transfer system.

Taxis are also expensive. At the time of writing, they start at ¥600, including the first two kilometres or waiting time in lieu thereof. Even though they are so costly, they are well patronized and, indeed, if there are four or five people, it may be cheaper to take a taxi than a bus, as well as being more convenient. Tipping is not expected.

For the rail system, tickets are nearly always purchased from machines. These machines are very clever. They can give change and issue quite a variety of different tickets. Most of them will accept ¥1,000 notes as well as coins and some will now accept ¥5,000 and ¥10,000 notes also. Just put your money in and press the appropriate button for the value of ticket which you require. Out will come your ticket and your change. Somewhere around most subway stations, there is usually a notice in English showing fares, but if you cannot find it do not worry. Just buy a minimum price ticket and pay the difference at the other end. It is always acceptable to do this on any of the railway systems. If a conductor happens to come through your train, you can pay him instead. If you should be unlucky enough to have a problem with a ticket machine, you will find two buttons, usually at the top left. Press the bottom one to have your money refunded. Press the top one to report some malfunction. Many stations now have automatic gates into which you insert your ticket to enter and exit. If you do not have the correct ticket for exiting, you should put the ticket which you do have into the excess fare machine which will then tell you how much more you have to pay. Put in the extra money and you will be issued with a new ticket which will open the automatic gates for you to leave the station. At stations where there are no automatic gates, present your ticket at the window by the exit to be told how much excess fare is owing.

For buses, there are two different fare systems. If you enter at the front of the bus, as in central Tokyo, you pay the fare to the driver as you go in. There is a plastic box into which you drop the correct money and a notice below the box telling you how much to pay. If you do not have the correct money, there is a machine which will change coins or ¥1,000 notes. Put your coin or note into the slot and the change will come out below. In central Tokyo, you put in enough money for the full fare and the change is returned. However, where the flat fare system is not in operation, the machine will just give you small change for the coin or note which you inserted and you then have to put the fare into the fare box. If you entered at the front of the bus, you exit towards the rear. However, if you enter towards the rear of the bus, as in Tokyo suburbs or more rural locations, you will find a different system in operation. From a machine by the door you accept the proffered slip of paper. On the slip is a number. Keep this piece of paper carefully. On a display at the front of the bus a series of fares is shown. Your fare is the one under the number on your slip of paper. You can watch it increase frighteningly minute by minute! When you get off, drop into the box the appropriate fare and your numbered ticket. If you get on at the start of the route, sometimes the machine does not offer you a ticket. In that case your fare will be displayed beneath the number 0. If you lose your ticket, you are supposed to pay the highest fare on the board, so try not to!

How about saving money? Yes, there are ways – legal ways, that is. First of all, if you are going to be travelling the same route regularly you can buy a season ticket. These are available for one, three or six months and can be purchased for any rail or bus journey. They are sold at most railway stations and at bus company offices. For Toei buses in central Tokyo, the season ticket does not specify a route, but permits free travel on any Toei bus within the period of validity. If a month is too long, there are other possibilities. You can buy eleven tickets for the price of ten for any rail journey involving only a single company. These tickets are valid for two months, or three months in the case of JR. Slightly different rules apply depending on the company. Sometimes the tickets are issued in the form of a strip, but usually they are individual tickets nowadays. If they are in the form of a strip, you may have to present what remains of the whole strip when entering, after which you tear off the end ticket and surrender it when you exit at your destination. You cannot present a single torn-off ticket when entering in cases where the expiry date is marked only on the last ticket. However, if the expiry date is marked on all tickets then individual use will be allowed. With all systems, it is permitted for two or more people to use tickets on the same strip, including when travelling together. Tickets are valid for travel in either direction between the two points marked on them, including intermediate stops, but one cannot break one's journey. The ticket must be surrendered when one leaves the station. It should also be noted carefully that one cannot use such tickets for a longer journey than the one specified by paying the difference in fares. If one goes beyond the station marked on the ticket, one must pay the *full* fare for the additional journey (with the exception of the subway system – see after). These tickets are called *kai-su-ken* and they are usually bought from the ticket window, although some major stations now have machines which can issue them.

There are two special types of *kai-su-ken* offered by JR. One is called *Yamanote kai-su-ken*. These tickets allow one to enter and exit at any JR station on or within the Tokyo Yamanote line. At the time of writing they cost ¥1,600 for eleven tickets, making them economical for any but the shortest journeys. They are also convenient, of course, since one does not have to queue for a ticket every time one travels. The other type is called *Tokyo-to ku-nai kai-su-ken*. These tickets are valid for any JR journey within Greater Tokyo, that is within the 23 wards (*ku*) of Tokyo. The exact area is marked on the tickets. They currently cost ¥2,900 for eleven tickets.

The subway *kai-su-ken* system is a little different. One purchases eleven tickets at a certain value for the price of ten. Then, as one enters the station, the automatic gate marks on the ticket your starting point. If you go beyond the limits of the area for which your ticket is valid, in this case, unlike with other railway systems, you can just pay the excess. So these tickets are particularly useful, since, if you purchase minimum price tickets, they can be used for any subway journey, as long as you pay any excess charge on leaving the station at your destination. Toei and Eidan both have this system, although, of course, you cannot use Toei tickets on Eidan lines or *vice versa*. For subways, *kai-su-ken* can be purchased from a machine at most stations.

There are *kai-su-ken* for buses too. In this case they consist of books or strips of tickets marked with certain values. They can be used on any bus services operated by the issuing company. In central Tokyo, there are books of tickets currently priced at ¥1,000 and ¥3,000 which can be used on the services of any of the variety of companies which operate in the area. Most of the tickets are priced at the current bus fare. Alternatively, one can buy books of tickets, currently costing ¥1,000 or ¥4,000, for a particular company. In general, the higher the cost of the book of tickets, the greater the discount, but the least that you can expect is eleven tickets for the price of ten. As one moves from central Tokyo into the suburbs, where there is no flat fare, one finds that the various companies have different types of *kai-su-ken*, but usually they offer a book of mixed tickets or a strip of eleven tickets at a particular value for the price of ten, or both. Bus *kai-su-ken* do not have a time limit and they can be used in combination with coins or other *kai-su-ken.* They can be bought from the offices of the bus company, and usually from bus drivers also, although the choice carried by drivers is necessarily limited.

There are also four types of one-day ticket available in central Tokyo. The one which is likely to be most useful to readers is that sold by the Eidan company. It permits use of all that company's eight subway lines for the price of ¥650, at the time of writing. Since the minimum fare at present is ¥140, one has only to make five journeys in a day to benefit from this ticket. Called an *ichi-nichi jo-sha-ken* (one day ticket), it can be purchased from a machine at many stations now, for use on the same day. Otherwise, it can be bought at one of the company's offices. Tickets sold at the office do not have to be used on the date of sale. If there is no suitable machine at your station and no office, you are entitled to purchase a ticket to the nearest station with an office, getting your ticket stamped with a special rubber stamp as you enter the station, then retain the ticket on exiting at the other end and get a refund when you purchase your one-day ticket. The same rule applies to season tickets and *kai-su-ken* if they cannot be issued at your station, and in these cases you can also ask for a ticket home if necessary.

The Toei company also has an *ichi-nichi jo-sha-ken* (one-day ticket). For the same price of ¥650, this permits use of the four Toei subway lines, as well as the Toei buses (green and cream) which run in the central area and the single tram route, known as the Arakawa Line, which runs between Waseda and Minowa. It can be purchased from machines and at Toei offices.

JR also offers a one-day ticket for use on its services within the area of Greater Tokyo, the 23 wards (*ku*) mentioned previously. This ticket is called a *to-ku-nai free kippu* and it costs ¥720 and is available at any station within the area.

The last ticket offers a combination of all the above three tickets. It is called a *Tokyo Free Kippu*. Although this sounds appealing, the ticket costs ¥1,480 for a day and the fact is that you can reach most places with just one of the tickets. However, if this ticket is your choice, it is available from any JR station in the area and from subway offices.

One more way of saving money and time is to purchase a pre-paid card to use instead of cash for the purchase of tickets. Such cards are offered by JR, the Eidan subway company and some of the private railway companies. The JR card is called an 'Orange Card' (this is the name in Japanese, not a translation) and it is available in denominations of ¥1,000, ¥5,000 and ¥10,000. Perhaps you will not be surprised to hear that it is not usually orange! The ¥1,000 card offers no discount, but with the ¥5,000 card you can purchase tickets to the value of ¥5,300 and with the ¥10,000 card, you get ¥10,700 of purchasing power. It used to be the case that only one machine at a station would accept cards – and in front of that machine there always seemed to be a little old lady searching her handbag for the last ¥10 necessary to make up her fare. Now, however, more machines have been installed which accept cards, including some which accept only cards. Since relatively few people use the card system, one can usually purchase one's ticket rapidly, in addition to having the opportunity to save a little money. Where there are excess fare machines near the exits to stations, you can also use your card to pay any excess owing.

The Eidan subway company offers cards called 'Metrocards' in denominations of ¥1,000, ¥2,000 and ¥3,000. There is, however, no discount, only convenience. The private railways vary, but a typical offering is ¥1,000, ¥3,000 and ¥5,000 cards, with the last providing ¥5,300 of tickets. The pre-paid cards offered by the various companies are usually quite colourful and there are now collectors of such cards. If one goes somewhere in Japan, an Orange Card showing local scenery makes a good souvenir for Japanese friends. It can be used anywhere on the JR system.

## Accommodation

Tokyo has a variety of hostel-style accommodation available. Cheapest are some of the private hostels listed on pages 464 to 466. There are more such hostels, but many prefer to take only long-term guests, so we have omitted them from our list. The fact is that some of such accommodation has been spoilt by an excess of demand. Often nobody bothers to answer the telephone or the person who answers has no idea whether accommodation is available or not, nor when the owner will be back. Several hostels said that they had plenty of permanent guests and were not interested in inclusion in this book. Even some of the better known names, such as Kimi Ryokan (Ikebukuro), were not interested in supplying a map or current information. Therefore, we have included only hostels which appeared relatively reliable and interested in having short-term guests. Even so, you may still encounter some of the problems which we have just described.

Much more reliable, if somewhat institutional, are three Youth Hostels in the area. That at Iidabashi, Tokyo Kokusai (International) Hostel, is central and easily reached by JR or subway. Note that JR Chuo Line (orange) trains do not usually stop at Iidabashi. Sobu Line (yellow) trains stop. The transfer from Chuo to Sobu Line can be made at Ochanomizu to the east or Yotsuya to the west. The hostel is in a tall building right next to the station platform. Just look for the only building around with eighteen floors.

Yoyogi Hostel was built as part of the facilities for the 1964 Olympic Games. It has just been refurbished and improved, but it is still cheaper than Tokyo Kokusai and it offers self-catering facilities, which is rare in Japan. To reach the Yoyogi Hostel, one needs to go to Shinjuku, a major station on the JR Yamanote Loop Line, also on the JR Chuo, Sobu and Saikyo Lines and the Marunouchi and Toei Shinjuku Subway Lines, and then take the Odakyu Private Railway two stations to Sangu-bashi. Only local trains stop.

The third hostel is quite a way out of the city at Takao on the western side. It is reached by taking the Keio Private Railway, also from Shinjuku, to Takaosan-guchi, the terminus for that particular branch of the railway. Note that the Keio Main Line runs to Hachioji and those trains do not go to Takaosan-guchi. However, there are regular direct trains from Shinjuku. Although the distance is 45 km and the journey takes an hour, fortunately the Keio Railway is not too expensive by Japanese standards. Those using Japan Rail Passes can go as far as Takao by JR Chuo Line, from where it is only one station to Takaosan-guchi by Keio Line, but if one is not using a pass or similar ticket, this will be a much more expensive route. The hostel is in semi-rural surroundings at the foot of Mt. Takao, a popular spot for hiking expeditions on holidays.

As stated above, the problem with central Tokyo accommodation is that it tends to be very popular, especially in summer. Those arriving late in the day may well not be able to find a place anywhere, so be sure to book ahead. However, the Takao Hostel is large and usually has spare beds. If even it is full, try Kanagawa Youth Hostel in Yokohama. If travelling by JR, from Nippori, Ueno, Tokyo or many other stations on the Yamanote Loop Line, take a Keihin Tohoku Line (blue) train, to Sakuragicho, one station beyond Yokohama, a 40 minute journey from Tokyo. If you are not using a rail pass, however, it may be cheaper to use the Tokyu Private Railway Toyoko Line from Shibuya, on the JR Yamanote Line, for which line Sakuragicho is the terminus.

At the next level of pricing, there are seven members of the Japanese Inn Group in the Tokyo area, mostly in quiet and traditional spots. These are certainly very pleasant places to stay, if one can afford around ¥4,500 per person. See pages 473 to 475. There are also some similar inns which are not members of the group and these are included in the private hostel listing on pages 464 to 466.

There are a few reasonably priced Business Hotels too. See the list on pages 489 to 490 and expect to pay a little more than for one of the Japanese Inns. Most of these hotels are western style and are on the fringes of the main centres of the city.

Then there are capsule hotels, which can be found around main railway stations, although not always very conspicuously. Since the Japanese for capsule hotel is, of course, 'capsule hotel', you can try asking at the station or at a police box. Likely price is ¥4,000 for one person. However, sometimes such hotels do not have any accommodation for females.

If all else fails, Tokyo has plenty of Love Hotels, catering to a lively trade. Some main centres are between Nippori and Uguisudani (on the route from Narita Airport), between Shinjuku and Shin Okubo and between Ikebukuro and Otsuka, all being stations on the JR Yamanote Loop Line. Although prices for a couple are likely to be somewhat lower than at the Japanese Inns or Business Hotels, remember that, unless an hourly surcharge is paid, occupation will not usually be permitted until 22:00 or 23:00 and that you can stay in a particular room for one night only, since that room will be needed again during the day-time.

## Sightseeing in Tokyo

As can be seen from the heading to this section, the name Tokyo means Eastern Capital. Until the Meiji Restoration of 1868, the capital of Japan was Kyoto, but, when he took back the reigns of power, the Emperor Meiji decided to symbolize the change with a shift to the city of Edo, as it had been known until then. Since Kyoto was considerably to the west, the new capital was renamed 'Eastern Capital' — Tokyo.

These days the population of the city is around 12,000,000, but the conurbation of which Tokyo is the centre sprawls far beyond the city's official limits, linking it in one unending sea of unattractive concrete and plaster dwellings tied together with telegraph wires, to the cities of Kawasaki, Yokohama, Chiba and many others, so that only administrative officials know which is which.

Tokyo is by no means the most interesting city in Japan, but its sheer size gives it a vitality and variety that no other city in the country can match. Although those who live in Tokyo tend to think that there is not much to see, in fact there is enough to keep the visitor busy for several days and his problem will probably be to select from the list the few attractions for which he has sufficient time and money. Here are some of the more important areas for sightseeing within the city limits.

### ASAKUSA (浅草 — 'Slight Grass')

**Derivation of Name:** *This is a sandy area beside the Sumida River where little grass grew.*

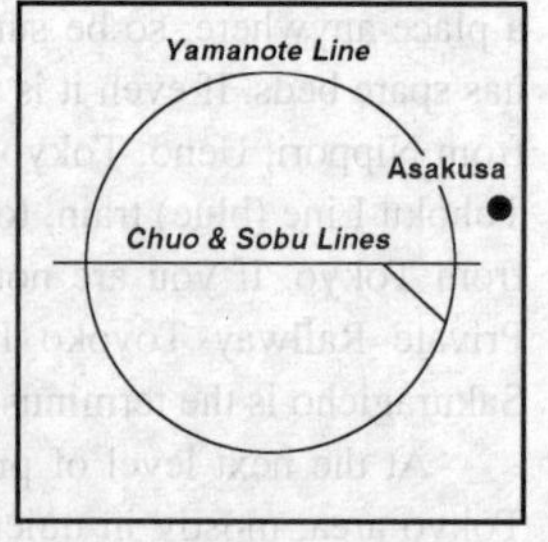


#### *Senso-ji (Asakusa Kannon Temple)*

Although this temple claims to be the oldest in Tokyo, the present buildings are post-war. A huge red lantern hangs beneath the ornate gateway named **Kaminari-mon** (Thunder Gate), which is guarded by the gods of wind and thunder, looking suitably fierce. Passing through the gate, one then walks along a narrow lane (**Nakamise Dori**) lined with souvenir shops selling all types of goods from rice crackers and toys to swords and *kimonos*. Usually this lane is crowded with visitors. At the end is another gate, with Buddha's sandals hanging on the far side, and then an incense burner, the smoke from which is supposed to do wonders for various ailments, so you will see people rubbing it onto any afflicted parts of their bodies. Beyond this is the main hall and, to one side, a five-storey pagoda. **Senso-ji** is the official name of this temple, although it is also known as 'Asakusa Kannon Temple' because 'Asakusa' is another way to read the Chinese characters

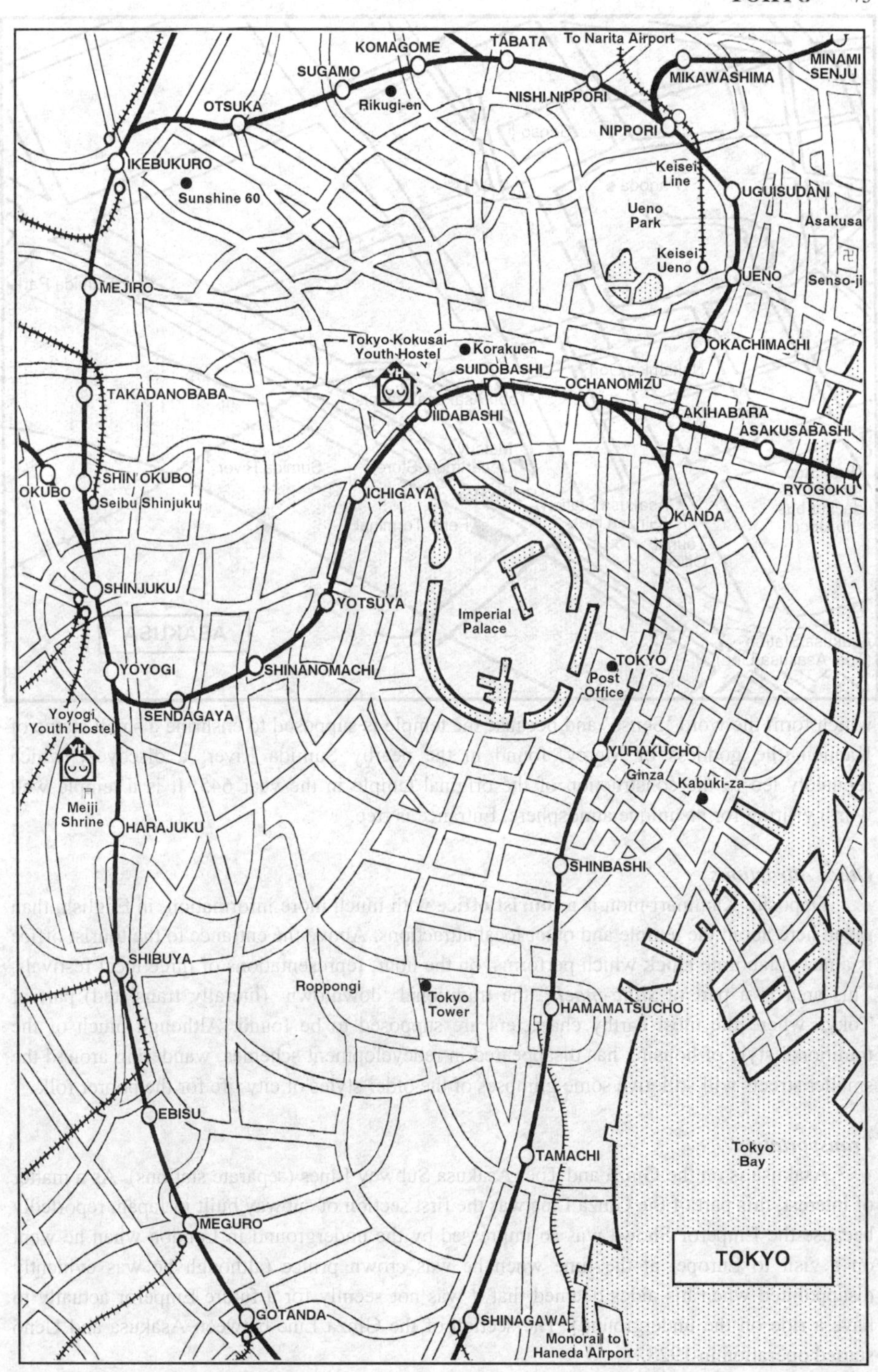
TABATA
To Narita Airport
KOMAGOME
SUGAMO
MINAMI SENJU
MIKAWASHIMA
Rikugi-en
NISHI NIPPORI
OTSUKA
NIPPORI
IKEBUKURO
Sunshine 60
Keisei Line
UGUISUDANI
Ueno Park
Asakusa
Keisei Ueno
MEJIRO
UENO
Senso-ji
Tokyo-Kokusai Youth Hostel
Korakuen
OKACHIMACHI
YH
SUIDOBASHI
OCHANOMIZU
TAKADANOBABA
IIDABASHI
AKIHABARA
ASAKUSABASHI
SHIN OKUBO
OKUBO
Seibu Shinjuku
ICHIGAYA
RYOGOKU
KANDA
SHINJUKU
YOTSUYA
Imperial Palace
YOYOGI
SHINANOMACHI
TOKYO
Post Office
SENDAGAYA
Yoyogi Youth Hostel
YURAKUCHO
Ginza
Kabuki-za
Meiji Shrine
HARAJUKU
SHINBASHI
SHIBUYA
Roppongi
Tokyo Tower
HAMAMATSUCHO
EBISU
TAMACHI
Tokyo Bay
MEGURO
TOKYO
GOTANDA
SHINAGAWA
Monorail to Haneda Airport

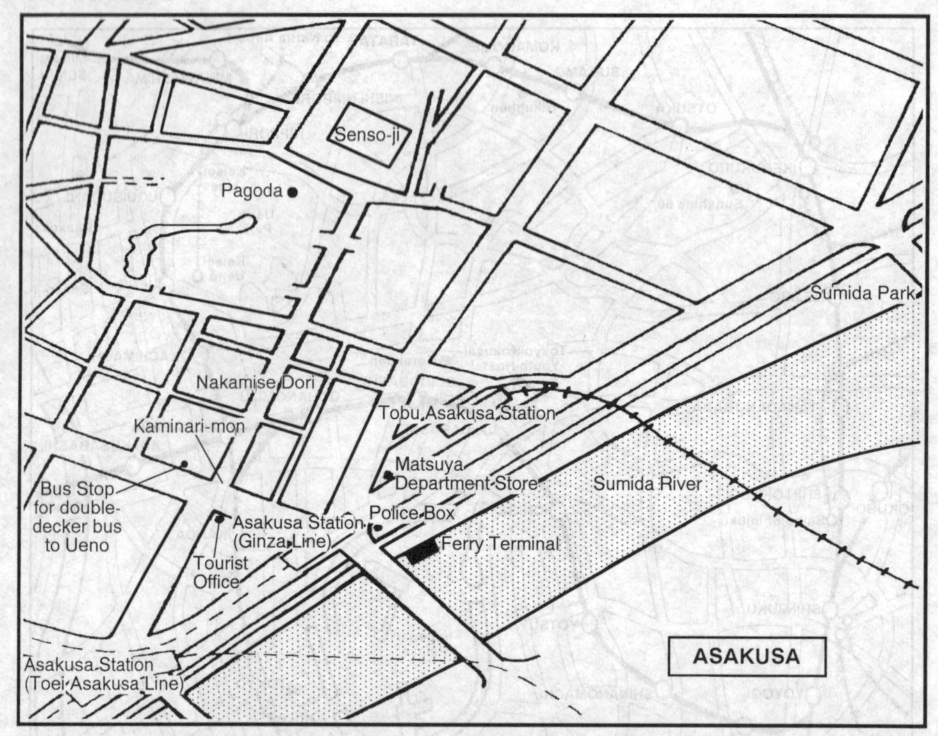


which form the word 'Senso' and because the temple is supposed to enshrine a small statue of Kannon, the goddess of Mercy, found in the nearby Sumida River, a discovery which reputedly led to the construction of the original temple in the year 645. It is a temple well worth visiting for its unique atmosphere. Entrance is free.

### *Other Attractions*

Opposite Kaminari-mon is a **tourist office** with much more information, in English, than given here about the temple and other local attractions. Above the entrance to the tourist office is a new, elaborate **clock** which performs, on the hour, representations of three local festivals. This area is a part of ***shita-machi***, the traditional 'downtown' (literally translated) part of Tokyo where the most earthy characters are supposed to be found. Although much of the traditional style of housing has disappeared in redevelopment schemes, wandering around the smaller streets will still give some glimpses of the older styles of city life for the poorer folk.

### *Transportation*

Asakusa is on the Ginza and Toei Asakusa Subway Lines (separate stations). As a matter of interest, this part of the Ginza Line was the first section of subway built in Japan, reportedly because the Emperor Showa was so impressed by the underground in London when he went on a visit to Europe, at the time when he was crown prince (although he was evidently disappointed when his aides deemed that it was not seemly for a future Emperor actually to have a ride on the underground). The section of the Ginza Line between Asakusa and Ueno started operation in 1928.

There is a sightseeing ferry service along the Sumida River, just beside the subway stations, to Hama Rikyu and Hinode, the latter being a 7 minute walk from Hamamatsucho on the JR Yamanote Line. This service costs ¥560 for a 40 minute journey.

The Tobu Private Railway to Nikko begins in Asakusa too, in the Matsuya Department Store building (upstairs!) next to the river.

Finally, there is a double-decker bus service, one of only two in Tokyo, to and from Ueno. This is a tourist service really, for those who have never travelled upstairs before, and people are willing to queue for some time for the experience, so it is not particularly recommended unless you like queues and children. It is also relatively expensive, at ¥200 for a 15 minute journey. However, it is less crowded from Asakusa than from Ueno, especially early in the day, so, if you do want to take the bus, this is the better direction in which to do so. It starts from a point very near Kaminari-mon (see map).

## UENO (上野 – 'Top Field')

**Derivation of Name:** *Town was on a small plateau slightly higher than surrounding fields.*

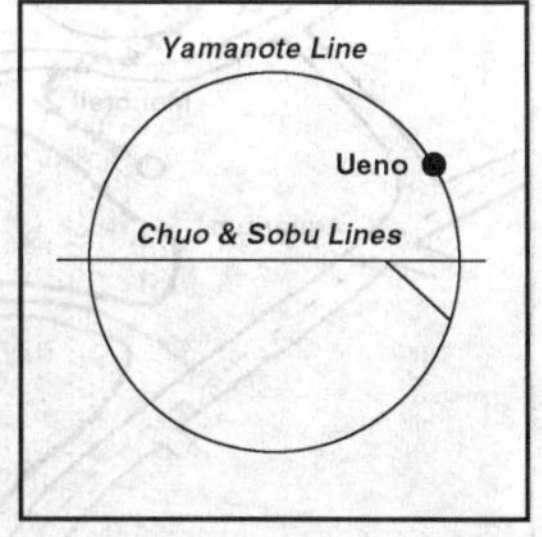


### *Ueno Park*

As a park, Ueno is not so special, although it is a pleasant oasis in the midst of all the traffic of the city. However, within the confines of the 210 acre park is a selection of museums, a zoo, two temples and an important shrine.

As one emerges from the Koen Guchi (Park Exit, upstairs) of JR Ueno station, immediately ahead across the road is the **Tokyo Culture Hall**, often used for classical concerts in the evenings, although these are relatively expensive, with tickets often starting at as much as ¥5,000. Steer to the right of this building and you will see the **National Museum of Western Art**, with Rodin sculptures outside. Although it has a good collection of western art, and particularly of the works of Rodin, the gallery can be very crowded indeed (and expensive) when special exhibitions are held and even ordinarily it is best to be there when the gates open at 9:30, if one does wish to visit. ¥400 (considerably more during special exhibitions). Open from 9:30 until 17:00.

Continuing past the art gallery and turning right at its corner, one will come to the **National Science Museum**, an imposing building with a steam engine on one side and a whale on the other. ¥400. Open from 9:00 until 16:30.

Just beyond the whale is a main road. Turn left for a few metres and the **National Museum** will be reached, on the other side of the road. This is perhaps the most interesting museum in the country concerning Japan. It is certainly the most extensive. ¥400. Open from 9:00 until 16:30.

Returning across the road into the park, if one turns right, one reaches the **Concert Hall of the Old Tokyo School of Music**, an attractive western-style building which has been moved to this site and restored. Its organ is unique in Japan. ¥200. Open from 9:30 until 16:30 on Sundays, Tuesdays and Thursdays and on other days, except Mondays, if the hall is not in use.

Pass this building and turn left, incidentally noticing on the right, across the road, the entrance to the old underground Keisei Private Railway terminus. This station is still in use, one stop from the current terminus at the other end of the park, and is known now by the

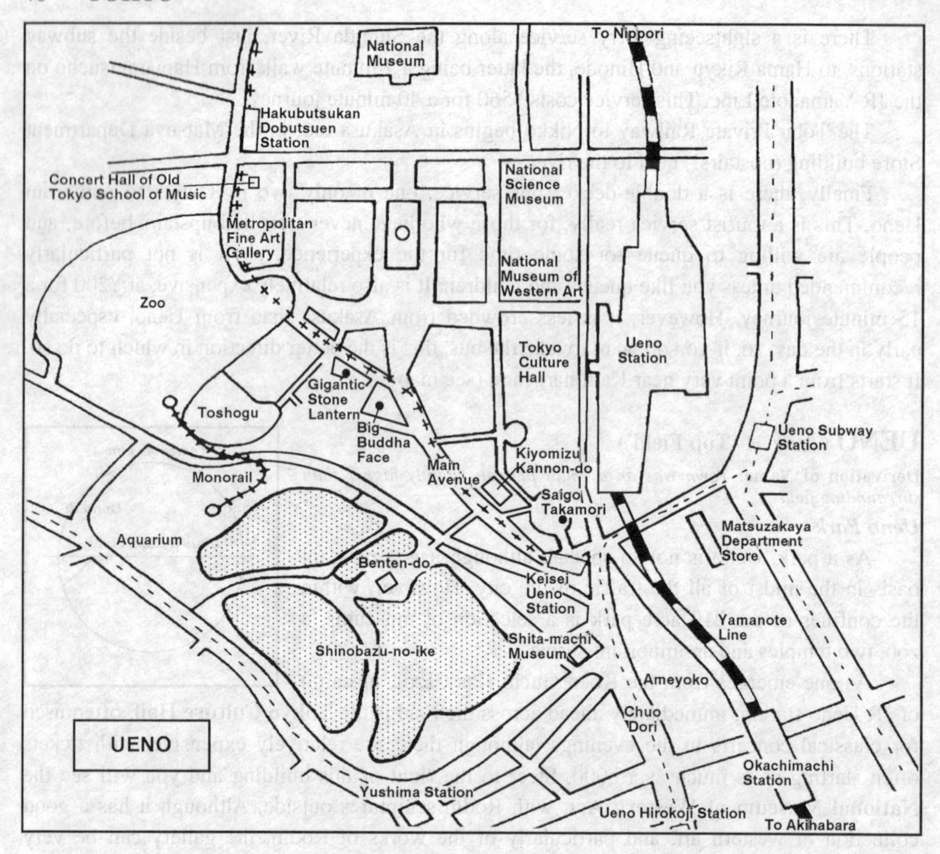


simple name of Hakubutsukan Dobutsuen ('museum and zoo')! Unfortunately, the interior is dilapidated now and only a few trains stop because the station can accommodate only four carriages. The last train is at 18:00.

Having turned left after the Concert Hall, one is walking past the **Metropolitan Fine Art Gallery**, where Japanese art is exhibited. The entrance is on the other side. On the right is another unused entrance to the Keisei station and now one is walking next to the **zoo**. The entrance can be reached by following round to left and then right. Although this is a zoo with limited space and older-type accommodation, it has quite a range of exhibits. However, it is crowded, of course, and the best time to go, if visiting a zoo should happen to appeal, is at 9:30 on a rainy or snowy weekday outside the school holidays! There is a monorail within the zoo, to reach an extension across the road. ¥500 (¥100 extra for monorail). Open from 9:30 until 16:30.

Passing beyond the entrance to the zoo, one will find, on the right after a left bend, the paved avenue leading to **Toshogu**. Here the great leader of the nation in the early seventeenth century, Tokugawa Ieyasu, is enshrined, although the principal, and magnificently ornate, shrine dedicated to him will be found in Nikko. The avenue is lined with stone lanterns and the shrine, despite its importance and beauty, is not visited as much as one might expect, especially considering its accessibility and the fact that Nikko is just crawling with tourists.

Here one can experience a few moments of tranquility, for a modest charge of ¥200, and also look at a small museum of Tokugawa relics – armour, a note in his own hand, et cetera. Recommended.

If one returns along the lantern-lined avenue and then bears right, one will see first a truly **gigantic stone lantern** and then a mound with the remains (just the face) of a **Big Buddha statue** which was destroyed in the earthquake of 1923. The Buddha is not very conspicuous and is easy to miss. Look for the mound.

Now you will reach the **main avenue** of the park, lined with cherry trees and the scene of much revelry at cherry blossom time, usually the first week in April. At this time the whole avenue is occupied by raucous 'flower-viewing parties'. Early in the morning, a representative of each group will be delegated to spread a plastic sheet on the ground and reserve a place all day for the coming evening's celebration. At night, one party touches another. Vast quantities of alcohol are imbibed and the noise of music (taped) and singing can be heard from a considerable distance, although one wonders how much appreciation of the besieged blossoms actually takes place. If you are lucky, however, it will not be early April and the avenue will be more peaceful. Bear right and you will see a temple, **Kiyomizu Kannon-do**, above on the left. Steps lead up to it and, although it is not special, it offers a view over the surrounding area.

Beyond the temple and slightly to the right is an open area with a **statue of Saigo Takamori**, an Imperial general who saved Edo (the old name for Tokyo) from destruction by averting a major battle in 1868. His dog is also featured. From this elevated area, a good view over the other and busier side of Ueno can be obtained, with the railway station dominating the foreground.

We have not finished yet, though. If you return to Kiyomizu Kannon-do, the temple just visited, and go back down the stone steps, across the main avenue and down another set of steps, you will come to a road and, on the other side of that, **Shinobazu-no-ike**, a pond famous for its lotus flowers, at their best in August, although they began to take over the whole pond and have been reduced in extent in recent years. The pond also has a number of species of duck, some of them migratory species from Siberia.

Pressing ahead, one crosses a bridge to an island on which is a temple named **Benten-do**, which is a pleasant spot to sit down for a rest. Continuing on, across another small bridge, one reaches a fork where boats are available for hire on the distant part of the pond. Let us fork left at this junction along a cherry tree lined path which curves between the two parts of the pond, also very attractive at the beginning of April. Keep left and walk three-quarters of the way round the pond and you will come to the small **Shita-machi Museum**, a museum devoted to the traditional life of the poorer people living in this part of the 'downtown' area of Tokyo.

If you now leave the pond and the park, a walk of only 100 metres will bring you to Chuo Dori, the main road running through Ueno (with McDonald's on the corner). Turn left to return to JR Ueno station, or to the Keisei Private Railway, which is underground here, or to Ueno station on the Ginza or Hibiya Subway Lines. Turn right to reach Ueno Hirokoji on the Ginza Line.

***Ameyoko***

If, however, you still have energy, cross Chuo Dori and follow any one of the small streets leading to the railway line (straight ahead). Between Ueno and Okachimachi stations, under and adjacent to the railway, is Ameyoko, an area of bargain stores selling just about everything. If you turn right on reaching the railway viaduct, a walk of only five minutes will bring you to Okachimachi station, next to which you will find more cheap stores. If you keep going, you will come to Akihabara, the electrical appliance centre, in another 20 minutes.

***Transportation***

JR Ueno station is the main line terminus for the Takasaki, Tohoku and Joban Lines. It is also served by the Tohoku and Joetsu *shinkansen* trains, which mostly terminate at Tokyo. For suburban services, the Yamanote and Keihin Tohoku lines pass through. The Keisei Private Railway terminates at Keisei Ueno. The Hibiya and Ginza Subway Lines pass through Ueno, so there should be no difficulty in reaching this area of Tokyo.

The double-decker bus service to Asakusa leaves from a stop on Chuo Dori towards Ueno Hirokoji subway station.

## AKIHABARA (秋葉原 – 'Autumn Leaves Field')

**Derivation of Name:** *Probably ancient elegant name for garden with abundant harvest in autumn.*

***Electrical Appliance Stores***

Akihabara's claim to fame lies in its concentration of electrical appliance stores. No directions are needed. They advertise themselves and start, in any case, right outside the JR Akihabara station.

Yamanote Line
Akihabara
Chuo & Sobu Lines

If purchasing, note that there are 'duty-free' goods (for visitors) and discounted goods, but you cannot usually have both. Very often the discounted goods are cheaper than the duty-free ones. Also remember that goods sold for the domestic market are 100 volts, 50 or 60 hertz (usually adjustable between the two frequencies), not a

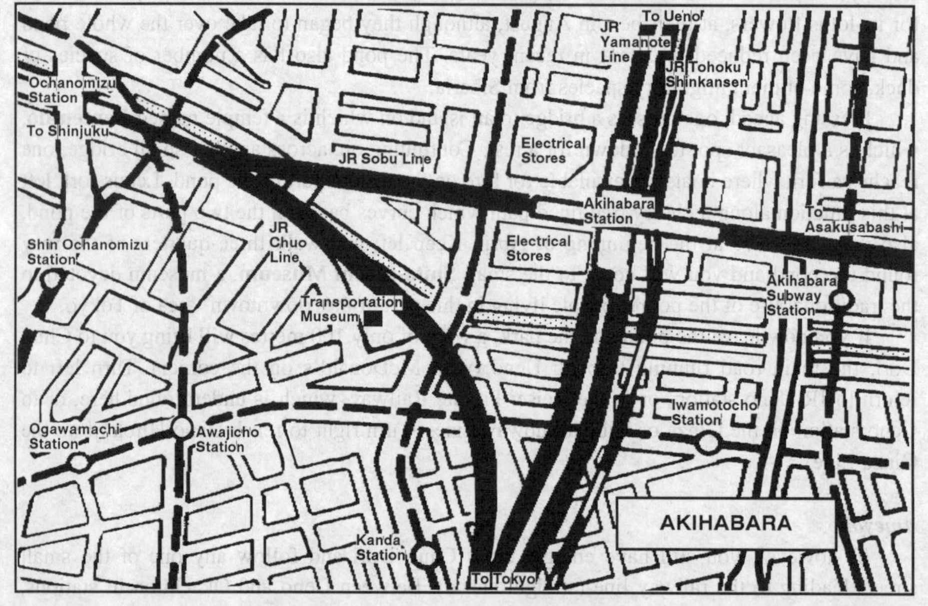

popular type of current in other parts of the world. Before you buy, make sure that you are purchasing something which can be used when you get home. Also, Akihabara is one of the few places in Japan where gentle bargaining is acceptable. Visit two or three stores and find the lowest price for what you want. Then ask for a better price. Usually it is forthcoming.

***Transportation Museum***

A 5 minute walk from Akihabara will bring you to the Transportation Museum, which has quite an interesting collection, for those who are interested in various means of transport. The first subway train in Tokyo is there, as is the first *shinkansen*, for example. To reach this museum, take the main exit from JR Akihabara station (by the Akihabara Department Store) and walk beside the elevated Sobu Line (yellow trains) to the first main road. Turn left, cross the river and the museum is on the right immediately after the railway viaduct conveying Chuo Line (orange) trains.

***Other Attractions***

Right in front of the main exit from JR Akihabara station, along a short passage, is the Akihabara Department Store where very reasonably priced alcohol can be purchased, if one has exhausted one's duty-free supply. There is also a selection of cheap food stalls. Try *okonomi-yaki* at ¥280 for a moderately-priced hot lunch or afternoon snack (standing up only, though).

***Transportation***

Akihabara is on the JR Yamanote, Keihin Tohoku and Sobu Lines. It is also on the Hibiya Subway Line, but the exit from the subway is not as conveniently located in relation to the electrical stores. The Transportation Museum is also within walking distance of Awajicho (Marunouchi Line), Ogawamachi (Toei Shinjuku Line), Kanda (Ginza Line) and Shin Ochanomizu (Chiyoda Line) subway stations, but it is more difficult to give directions from any of these.

## TOKYO (東京 – 'Eastern Capital')

**Derivation of Name:** *Literal. Name given by Emperor Meiji and originally pronounced 'Toke'.*

***Railway Station***

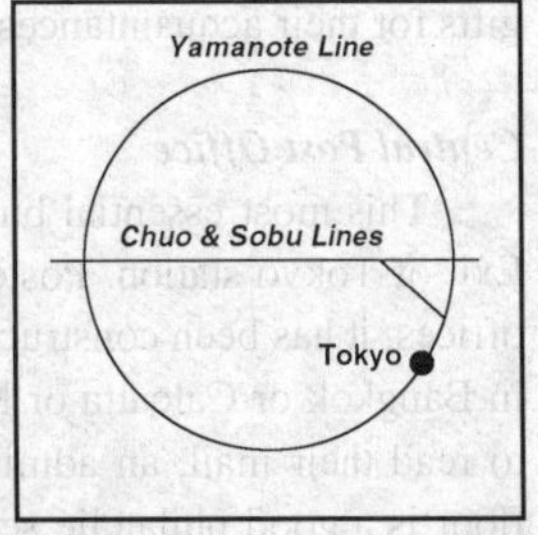


Tokyo station is in the business district of the city, the railway line forming a type of boundary, with the more imposing business area on the Marunouchi side. The station itself is an object of interest, for it is a copy of Amsterdam Railway Station. It was built in 1914. There is an hotel in the station with the windows of some of the rooms overlooking a busy concourse, presumably to keep guests entertained at all times. The hotel also offers expensive, but rather luxurious, restaurant, coffee shop and bar. In the station building (outside the ticket barrier) are other moderately-priced restaurants and drinking places. There is also an art gallery, inside the station, where those with time to spare between trains can spend a few pleasant minutes. On the Yaesu side of the station an underground shopping complex is to be found. Above ground, near the Yaesu Central Exit, is the **Travel Centre** at which Japan Rail Pass vouchers can be exchanged and

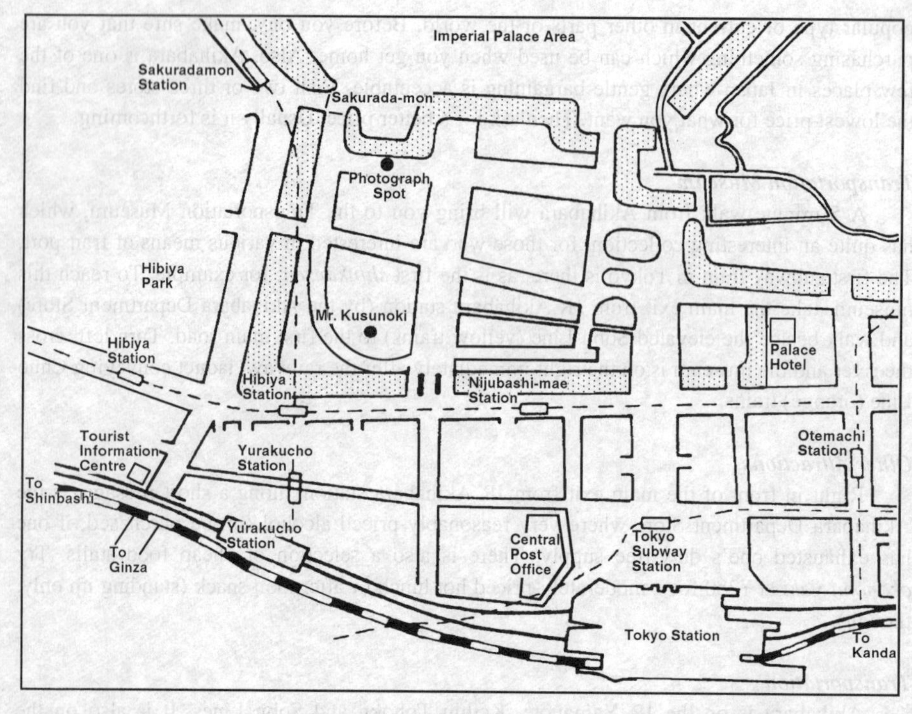


**TOKYO**

long-distance tickets purchased and where somebody will speak English. Outside the Yaesu North Exit, on the left, is a building called the **Kokusai Kanko-kan** (National Sightseeing Centre), where almost every prefecture in Japan maintains an office with tourist information, mostly in Japanese, but some in English. Amusingly and conveniently, these offices also sell regional produce, so that Japanese holidaymakers do not have to carry back all the required gifts for their acquaintances. They can just call in here and purchase them on their return!

### *Central Post Office*

This most essential building for travellers is located right outside the Marunouchi South Exit of Tokyo station. Poste Restante is in the basement. In the true tradition of all main post offices, it has been constructed with steps leading up to the main entrance, so that travellers, as in Bangkok or Calcutta or Melbourne or many other places around the world, can sit on them to read their mail, an admirable thought on the part of post office architects. On the ground floor is a good philatelic section and there is also a shop selling older postal items at inflated prices, for those who like such souvenirs.

### *Transportation*

It is hardly a problem to reach Tokyo station, as can be imagined. Nearly all *shinkansen* trains terminate here and so do the JR Tokaido Line, Chuo Line and Keiyo Line. The Yamanote Line, Keihin Tohoku Line and Yokosuka Line and Sobu *kaisoku* (rapid) trains all pass through, as does the Marunouchi Subway Line.

*Imperial Palace*

The Imperial Palace is a huge area of some 250 acres right in the centre of the city. If the Emperor ever feels like selling it off, he will certainly get a good price for it! The palace, however, is a modern building constructed after the old one was destroyed during the war. Moreover, because it is on a higher level, surrounded by a moat and impressive stone walls, the palace can only be glimpsed from outside. In fact, when high office buildings were constructed in the nearby Marunouchi business district, there was much dispute over whether the Emperor's privacy was going to be invaded because it would be possible to see into the palace area. However, it appears that most of the Marunouchi businessmen do not spend their time sitting at their desks with trained binoculars eagerly trying to ascertain what the Emperor might be having for lunch today (especially as he does not actually live there at present, the premises being occupied by his mother, the Dowager Empress, i.e. the previous Emperor's widow). No subway lines have been allowed to pass under the palace grounds, though.

The approved thing to do is to cross the wide space in front of the palace entrance, officially designated the Imperial Palace Outer Garden, and have one's photograph taken in front of **Niju-bashi**, the 'double bridge'. One may have to wait one's turn for this honour, for the picture is a requisite for all Japanese visitors. It is, however, quite a pretty scene. The palace grounds are open to the public only on the Emperor's birthday (23rd December) and New Year's Day, when the Emperor and his family usually come out onto the balcony to acknowledge the greetings of well-wishers. If you are able to visit at one of these times, you will, of course, find that several other people are visiting too!

Across the road in front of the palace, in the Imperial Palace Outer Garden, you will discover a statue of Kusunoki Masashige, regarded as one of the most loyal of the Emperor's warriors. He died a while ago, in 1336 to be precise, perishing in a battle fought in Kobe in that year to try to maintain the imperial power.

***Transportation***

The Imperial Palace Outer Garden can be reached by a 10 minute walk from Tokyo station. Use the Marunouchi Central Exit and walk down the wide road straight ahead on the other side of the greenery and taxi turning area in front of the station. This road is so wide, incidentally, because the central part is to be driven along only by the Emperor and his entourage, which makes it seem something of a waste of space. At the end, turn left and you will see the palace gate and the official photographic spot beyond.

Closer is Nijubashi-mae station on the Chiyoda Subway Line. From here it is a 5 minute walk. Also near, on the other side of Niju-bashi, is Sakuradamon on the Yurakucho Subway Line. From here, walk through Sakurada-mon, which is the name of a gate ('Cherry Blossom Field Gate') and turn right, then left, to reach the photograph area.

If you need somewhere to relax after your exertions, **Hibiya Park** is next to the Imperial Palace grounds. It is a pleasantly laid-out western-style park with fountains and greenery, as well as a concert area, a garden shop and even a couple of restaurants. If you visit this park, your nearest stations will now be JR Yurakucho or subway Hibiya, Yurakucho, Uchisaiwaicho or Kasumigaseki, all of which are at corners of the park. If you walk back to JR Yurakucho, you will pass the **Tourist Information Centre** on the way. If you continue from there under the railway bridge, instead of turning left to reach the station, you will reach the Ginza shopping and expensive nightclubs area.

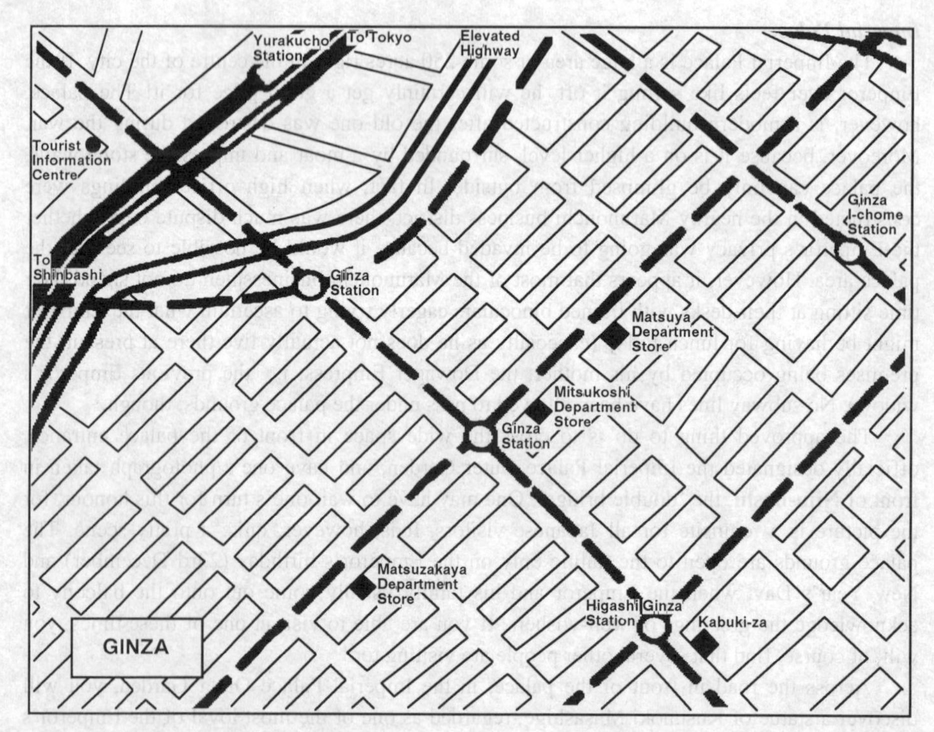


## GINZA (銀座 – 'Silver Seat')

**Derivation of Name:** *During Meiji Era, mint for production of silver coins was located here.*

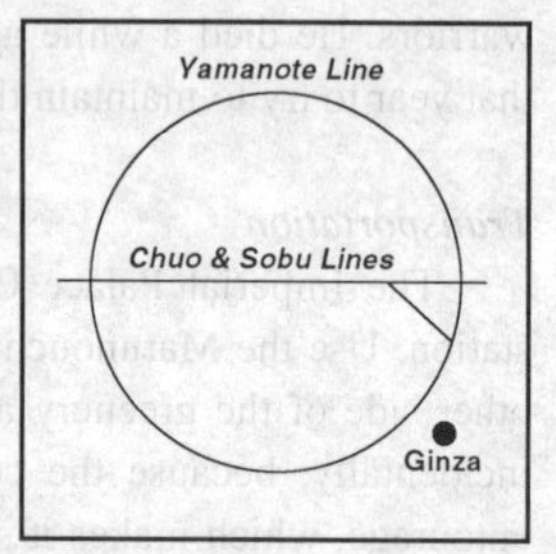


### *Shopping*

Ginza is one of the areas of Tokyo which visitors seem to know of in advance of their arrival. It is a district of department stores and fashionable shops, where you can buy almost anything at double the price which you will pay anywhere else. The streets are wide and tree-lined, although the willows which were originally planted here were all killed off by the traffic fumes and have had to be replaced by more resilient species.

At night this is also an expensive nightclub area, where companies from the nearby business district used to entertain their distinguished guests. Even *geisha* establishments could still be found here. However, most of these businesses have fallen upon harder times recently, as expense accounts are no longer as unlimited as they used to be.

As can be seen above, the name Ginza ('Silver Seat') is derived from the fact that this place used to have a mint for silver coins. The opulence associated with silver is certainly still visible today.

### *Kabuki-za*

*Za*, meaning seat, has come, by extension, to mean also a theatre, which has a large number of seats, of course. *Kabuki-za* is a theatre specialising in *kabuki* plays, a traditional

Japanese form of entertainment. Since the action is very formalized and the dialogue recited in sing-song voices, the casual observer is unlikely to understand much, nor to be able to sit through the long performance patiently, to combat which the theatre offers overseas visitors tickets for a single act and an earphone hire service to give an idea of the action. Earphones with an English commentary cost ¥600 for the duration of the performance, plus a deposit of ¥1,000. The single act charge varies according to the play being performed, but is usually about ¥1,000. An entire performance costs ¥2,500 for a seat in the balcony.

***Transportation***

Ginza station is on the Ginza, Marunouchi and Hibiya Subway Lines. The nearest JR station is Yurakucho on the Yamanote Line, from where walk for about 7 minutes away from the station outside the Yamanote Line (i.e. in a south-easterly direction).

Kabuki-za is immediately outside Higashi Ginza station on the Hibiya and Toei Asakusa Subway Lines.

## SHIBUYA (渋谷 – 'Astringent Valley')

**Derivation of Name:** *'Shibu' used to have the meaning of 'rust' and this was a valley where things easily went rusty (doubtful).*

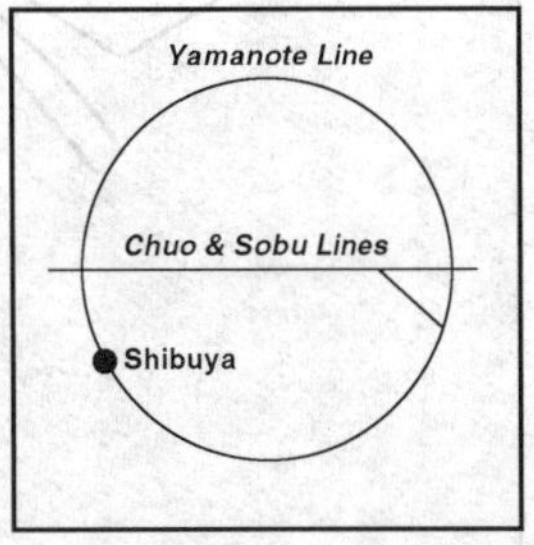


***Hachiko***

Shibuya is one of the fashionable centres popular with young people. The area around the station never ceases to be a depiction of what the word 'crowded' really means in Japan. Hachiko Square is the most famous meeting place in Tokyo. Hachiko was a dog who used to meet his master at the station every evening (not Shibuya, but in a distant part of the country), until one day his master died and failed to return. Undeterred, Hachiko used to visit the station every evening for the rest of his own life, patiently awaiting his master's return. It is a story which everybody knows and which has even been made into a film. A statue of the dog stands outside Shibuya station and, if you want a meeting place for your date, where else would you choose? It is a very apt symbol too, as the dog's patience is rivalled by that of those waiting interminably for their overdue partners. In practice, the area is so crowded with would-be daters that it is hard to locate anybody at all.

***NHK Broadcasting Centre***

If you walk north (towards Harajuku), paralleling the JR Yamanote Line, and then bear left, you will pass many of the department stores and fashionable retailers located in this area and then, after about 12 minutes, reach a major junction. On your right can be seen the top of the **Yoyogi Sports Centre**, built for the 1964 Olympic Games, while ahead and slightly to the left is the **NHK Broadcasting Centre**. It is possible to visit this centre, open from 10:00 until 18:00 (17:00 in winter). Admission is free. If you continue walking, to the right of NHK, you will reach **Yoyogi Park**, which is mentioned in the following Harajuku section. The park can be entered by a bridge over the main road, from which bridge, if you are lucky, you may be able to see **Mt. Fuji** on a clear day. Turn right, once in the park, to reach Harajuku station by the shortest route, but almost any path will bring you there eventually.

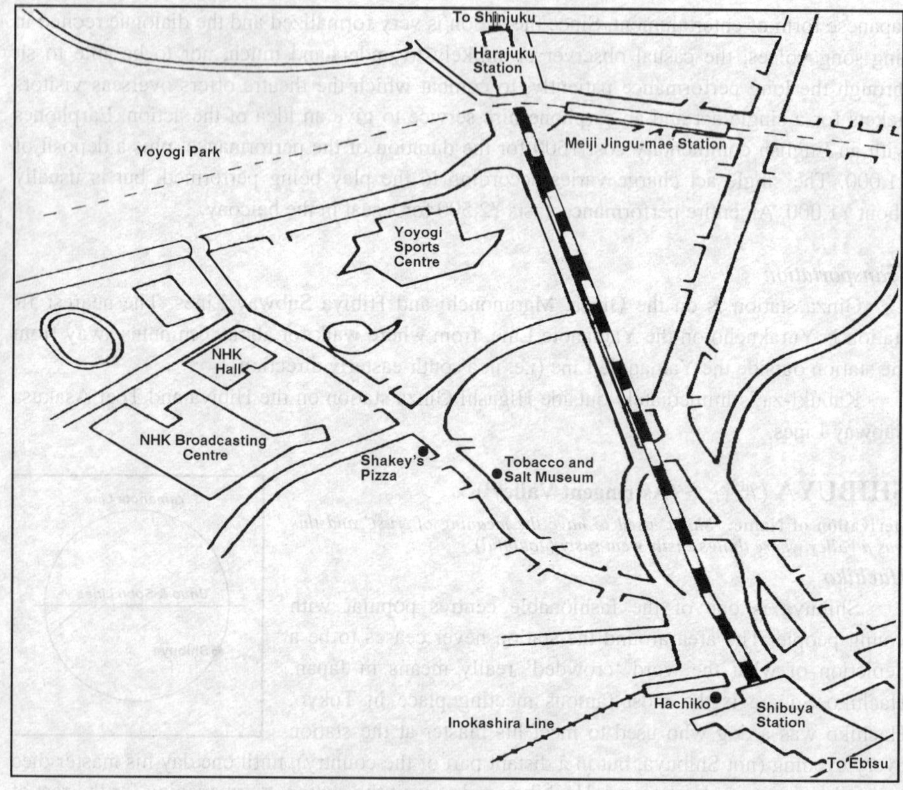


SHIBUYA

*Transportation*

As well as being on the JR Yamanote Line, Shibuya is served by the Ginza and Hanzomon Subway Lines. It is also the terminus for the Tokyu Private Railway Toyoko and Shin Tamagawa Lines, although, in fact, all of the trains on the Shin Tamagawa Line continue onto the Hanzomon Subway Line and *vice versa*. The Inokashira Line operated by the Keio Private Railway terminates at Shibuya also.

## HARAJUKU (原宿 – 'Field Lodging Place')

**Derivation of Name:** *This was a lodging place, in the fields, for travellers on one of the main highways.*

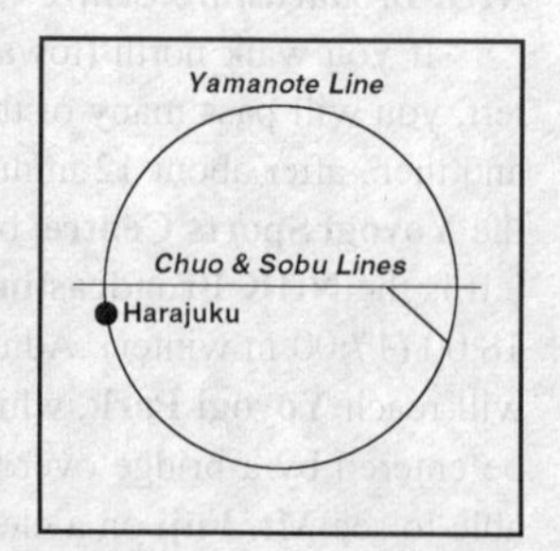


*Shops*

Harajuku is even more fashionable than Shibuya and the area is crowded with boutiques, coffee shops and restaurants. If one takes the smaller exit (downstairs) from JR Harajuku station, crosses the road and continues ahead along a narrow street called **Takeshita Dori**, one will get a taste of the character of the area. The major road, however, is **Omote Sando**, reached by taking the main exit (upstairs) and turning left.

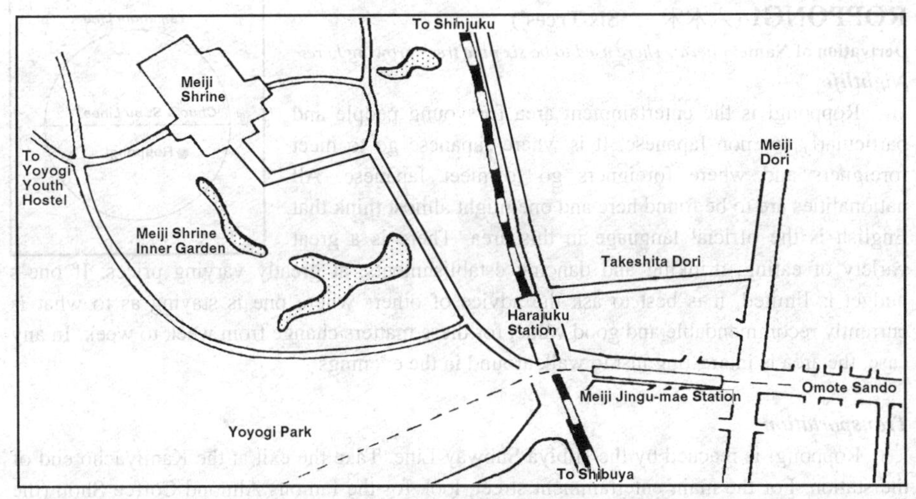

HARAJUKU

### *Meiji Shrine*

Take the upstairs exit from JR Harajuku and turn sharp right and you will be on the long wooded approach road to the Meiji Shrine. This Shinto shrine is dedicated to the Emperor Meiji, the man who overturned the *shogunate* in the Meiji Restoration of 1868 and laid the foundations for the modern Japan. He is generally regarded as one of the greatest of all Japanese Emperors. The shrine was completed in 1920, following the death of the Emperor Meiji in 1912, and is worth visiting at any time, but, on the first three days of the New Year, it is crowded beyond belief. The shrine itself is free, but to visit the Treasure Museum costs ¥200 and to visit the Meiji Gardens costs ¥300.

### *Yoyogi Park*

Adjoining the Meiji Shrine is Yoyogi Park. To reach it, one takes the upstairs exit from Harajuku station and turns right less sharply than for the Meiji Shrine. This was the site of the Tokyo Olympic Village in 1964. During the week, it is a pleasant place for a stroll, but it is at its most exciting on Sundays when frequented by groups of young people dancing, singing and just watching. Performers include the *takenoko-zoku* ('Bamboo Shoot Group') dancers and bunches of imitation Elvis Presleys. On holidays, the main road is closed to traffic and these free performances can be witnessed at the entrance to the park, both along the road outside and within the park confines. It is some of the most amusing free entertainment in Tokyo, although the area is crowded, of course. Some of the performers are really very good indeed.

### *Transportation*

JR Harajuku station, on the Yamanote Line, is immediately adjacent to the Meiji Shrine and Yoyogi Park. Meiji Jingu-mae on the Chiyoda Subway Line is also close. The main shopping area lies between Meiji Jingu-mae station and Omote Sando station, the latter being on the Ginza and Hanzomon Subway Lines, in addition to the Chiyoda Line. The Meiji Shrine is walking distance from Yoyogi Youth Hostel, which stands on land borrowed from the shrine gardens.

## ROPPONGI (六本木 – 'Six Trees')

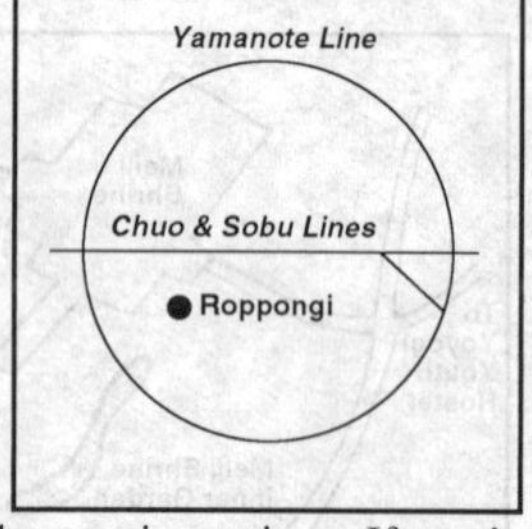


**Derivation of Name:** *Literal. There used to be six pine trees growing here.*

### *Nightlife*

Roppongi is the entertainment area for young people and particularly for non-Japanese. It is where Japanese go to meet foreigners and where foreigners go to meet Japanese. All nationalities are to be found here and one might almost think that English is the official language in this area. There is a great variety of eating, drinking and dancing establishments, at greatly varying prices. If one's budget is limited, it is best to ask the advice of others where one is staying as to what is currently recommendable and good value, for these matters change from week to week. In any case, the area is interesting just to walk around in the evenings.

### *Transportation*

Roppongi is reached by the Hibiya Subway Line. Take the exit at the Kamiyacho end of the station. For the main entertainment street, look for the famous Almond Coffee Shop (the traditional meeting place here, so you will see many people waiting, both inside and out) and turn right into the major street just after it.

## SHINJUKU (新宿 – 'New Lodging Place')

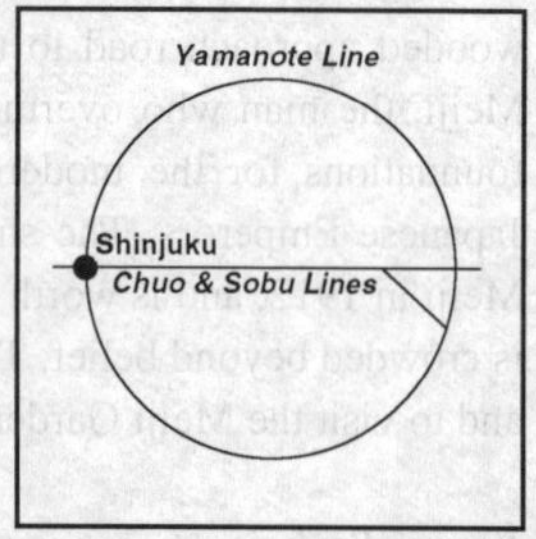


**Derivation of Name:** *This place was at an intersection of major highways, a location where many new inns quickly became established to cater for travellers.*

### *Shopping*

Shinjuku is a major centre on the Yamanote Line offering a variety of department stores and smaller shops. It also has the best bookstore in Japan for books published abroad. This is **Kinokuniya Bookstore**, not very far from the east exit of JR Shinjuku station and closer still to Shinjuku San-chome on the Marunouchi Subway Line. On the west side of the station are to be found some of the top hotels in the city, as well as the skyscrapers which are the new offices of the Tokyo Metropolitan Government. 'Wherever did they get the money to build those?' one wonders, until the realization comes suddenly. 'From me!'

Clustered around the station on both sides are cheap **camera stores**, selling also items such as tape, watches, video equipment, computers and games.

### *Tall Buildings*

Shinjuku has a whole cluster of tall buildings, although not the tallest in Japan, in fact, which is Landmark Tower in Yokohama. These buildings offer good possibilities for viewing the city and several have free observation platforms, as well as restaurants and coffee shops where prices are not too inflated, by Tokyo standards.

Take the west exit from Shinjuku station, at the lowest level. There you will find ornamental fountains surrounded by a road circumnavigated by taxis. There is also a police box, which is the traditional meeting point on this side of the station. Take the road which runs directly away from the station and which is underground at this point, and so rather noisy,

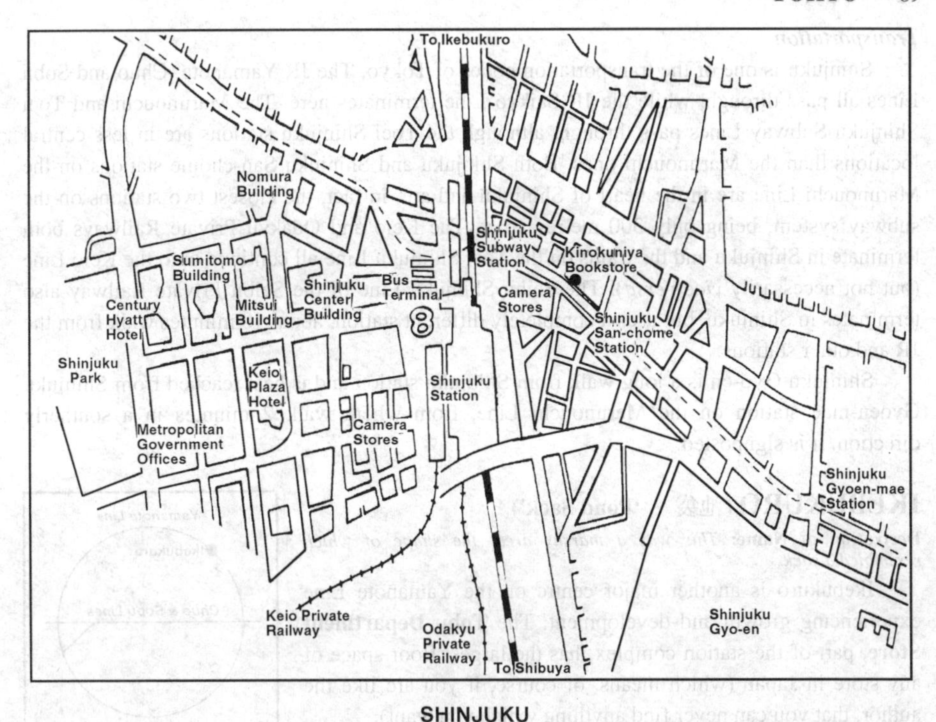

SHINJUKU

unfortunately. When you emerge from the tunnel section, you will just have passed **Shinjuku Center Building**, a 54 storey structure on the right with a free observation platform on the 53rd floor. If you continue, you will come to **Sumitomo Building**, also on the right. This 52 storey building has perhaps the best free observation deck, on the 51st floor. The floors immediately below have medium-priced restaurants with good views. Behind and to the right is **Mitsui Building** with 55 floors. There is no free observation area here, but the top two floors have restaurants. Behind and to the right again is **Nomura Building**, 50 storeys, with a free observation platform on the top floor.

*Shinjuku Park*

If you continue along the road which started underground at the west exit of Shinjuku station, beyond Sumitomo Building you will come to Shinjuku Park, which is a pleasant oasis, rather than a special place to visit. It is about 15 minutes from the station.

*Shinjuku Gyo-en*

Shinjuku Gyo-en is also a park, an imperial garden open to the public for a small charge. This extensive area is much more worthy of a visit. It is difficult to imagine that one is in the midst of a busy city when walking or sitting in this park which incorporates both Japanese and western elements. Because it is so large, Shinjuku Gyo-en requires at least a period of one to two hours for a reasonable examination. ¥160. Open from 9:00 until 16:30.

*Transportation*

Shinjuku is one of the transportation nodes of Tokyo. The JR Yamanote, Chuo and Sobu Lines all pass through, while the JR Saikyo Line terminates here. The Marunouchi and Toei Shinjuku Subway Lines pass through, although the Toei Shinjuku stations are in less central locations than the Marunouchi ones. Both Shinjuku and Shinjuku San-chome stations on the Marunouchi Line are in the heart of Shinjuku and are, in fact, the closest two stations on the subway system, being only 300 metres apart. The Keio and Odakyu Private Railways both terminate in Shinjuku and the trains on the Toei Shinjuku Line all continue onto the Keio Line (but not necessarily *vice versa*). The Seibu Shinjuku Line of the Seibu Private Railway also terminates in Shinjuku, but uses a completely different station, about 10 minutes walk from the JR and other stations.

Shinjuku Gyo-en is a long walk from Shinjuku station and is best reached from Shinjuku Gyoen-mae station on the Marunouchi Line, from where walk 2 minutes in a southerly direction. It is signposted.

## IKEBUKURO (池袋 – 'Pond Sack')

**Derivation of Name:** *This was a marshy area, the shape of which resembled a sack.*

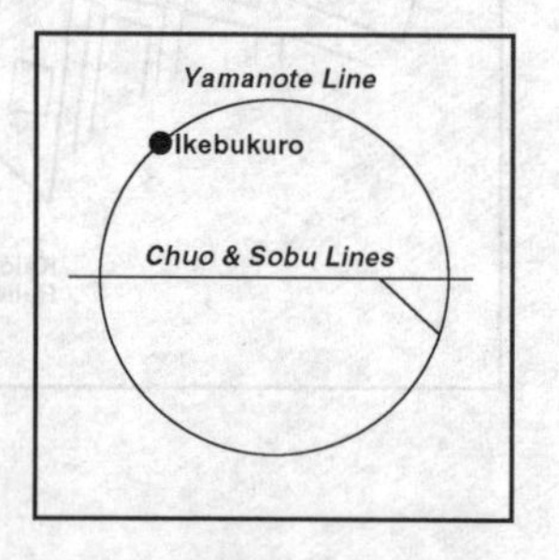


Ikebukuro is another major centre on the Yamanote Line experiencing growth and development. The **Tobu Department Store**, part of the station complex, has the largest floor space of any store in Japan (which means, of course, if you are like the author, that you can never find anything which you want).

*Sunshine City*

Ikebukuro's main claim to fame is the Sunshine City complex, which used to include the tallest building in Japan, although it has recently been outgrown by Landmark Tower in Yokohama. The Ikebukuro building is known as **Sunshine 60**, as it has sixty floors. There is a lift which takes one to the top (240 metres) in 35 seconds, but this is not a free observation point, unlike the observation platforms in Shinjuku. It fact, it costs a fairly hefty ¥620. Within the same complex are a shopping centre, a department store, the 'World Import Mart', which has displays of goods being imported into Japan, of varying interest according to the particular theme on display, a **planetarium** and an **aquarium**, the last two quite expensive. The planetarium costs ¥800 and the aquarium is a very costly ¥1,440. There is a combination ticket, somewhat discounted, for aquarium and observation platform. This costs ¥1,850. The two are not near each other, but on opposite sides of the complex, the aquarium being located on the tenth floor of the Mitsukoshi Department Store Building. There are also restaurants to suit all pockets, the cheapest ones being located in the basement.

To reach Sunshine City, take the east exit from JR Ikebukuro station, cross the main road (Meiji Dori) and proceed ahead for about 100 metres before branching left. Since your objective is the tallest building in the area, you will not get too lost. Sunshine City can also be reached from Higashi Ikebukuro station on the Yurakucho Subway Line. Take exit 2 and turn right at the first small street. The route is signposted. From Ikebukuro, it is a walk of about 10 minutes, from Higashi Ikebukuro about 5 minutes.

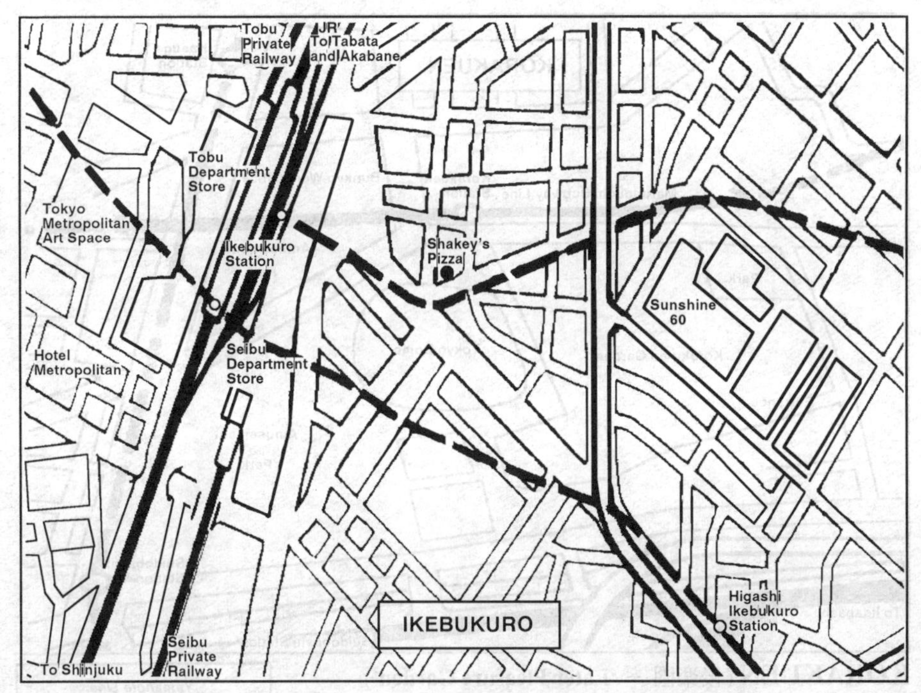


*Transportation*

Ikebukuro is on the JR Yamanote and Saikyo Lines. A few middle-distance Tohoku and Takasaki Line trains terminate here also, although most terminate at Ueno. Ikebukuro is served by the Marunouchi and Yurakucho Subway Lines, being the terminus for the Marunouchi Line and for the express trains which operate on the Yurakucho Line. Note that the three subway stations (Marunouchi Line, Yurakucho Line and Yurakucho Line express) are all separate. The Seibu and Tobu Private Railways both have lines for which Ikebukuro is the terminus – the Tobu Tojo Line and the Seibu Ikebukuro Line.

## KOMAGOME (駒込 – 'Putting Ponies')

**Derivation of Name:** *Literal. This was originally an area in which ponies were confined.*

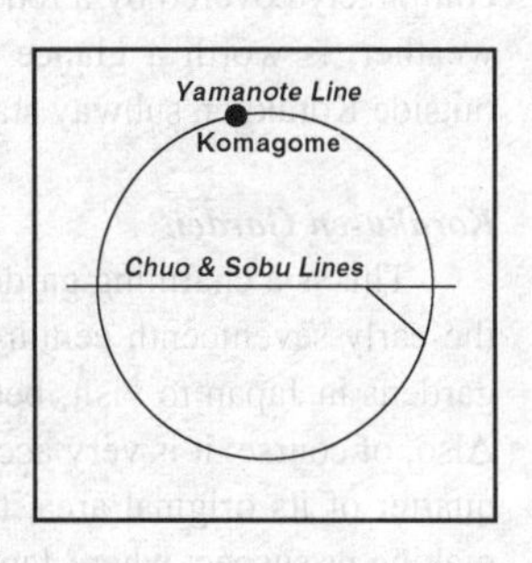


*Rikugi-en Garden*

This garden, originally private, is supposed to have representations of the 88 most scenic spots in Japan, so it will be a very economical way of viewing the country, if that can satisfy your curiosity! Hopefully, however, you may still feel that some of them will be worth seeing in actuality on a somewhat grander scale. The garden is 5 minutes walk from Komagome station.

*Transportation*

Komagome is on the JR Yamanote Line, and is an attractive station in spring when the flowers along the railway cutting are in bloom. It is also on the Nanboku Subway Line.

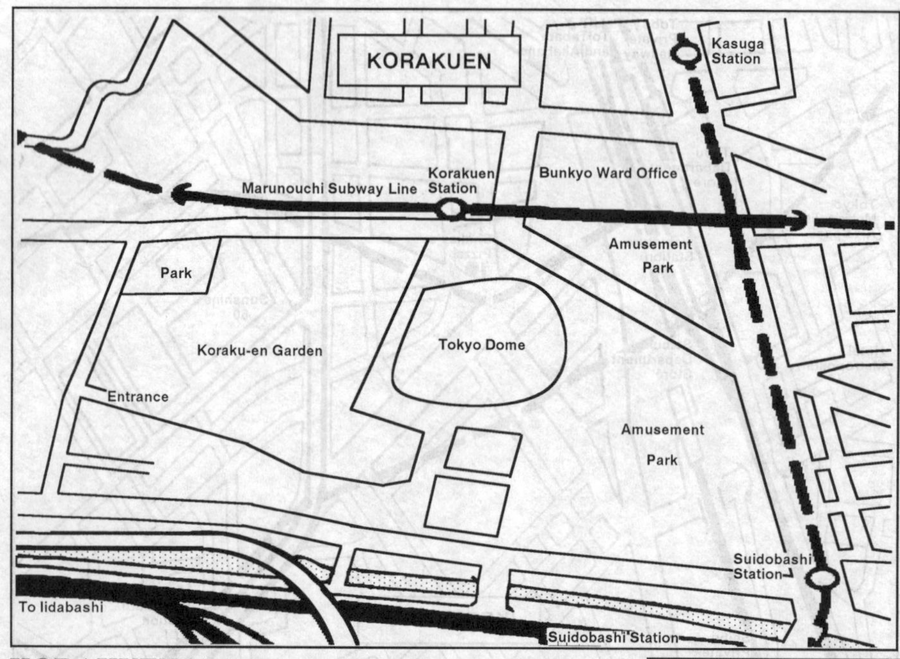


# KORAKUEN (後楽園 – 'Later Pleasure Garden')

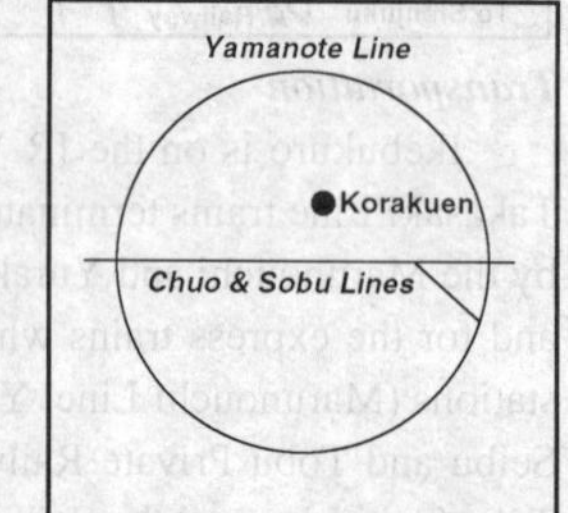


**Derivation of Name:** *Believed to be from Chinese poem which stated, 'People should concern themselves with the problems of the world first and pleasure should wait until later.'*

### *Sports and Amusement Facilities*

Amongst Japanese, Korakuen is best known for its baseball stadium, **Tokyo Dome** (also known, semi-officially, as 'The Big Egg') and its amusement park, neither of which is likely to appeal particularly to the visitor, although the stadium, completely covered by a retractable metal roof, so that it can continue to function in inclement weather, is worth a glance as one passes by. Both stadium and amusement park are right outside Korakuen subway station.

### *Koraku-en Garden*

This is a charming garden, usually not too crowded, again by Tokyo standards, laid out in the early seventeenth century. In the opinion of the author, it is one of the most worthwhile gardens in Japan to visit, better than some of the more famous ones, although less extensive. Also, of course, it is very accessible compared with others in distant places. It is, in fact, only a quarter of its original area, the baseball stadium and other facilities having stolen most of it, making us suspect where Japanese priorities may lie. Details of the garden are given in English on various notices and on the entrance ticket, so will not be repeated here. Entrance costs ¥200. Recommended.

The garden is adjacent to the baseball stadium. If you stand at Korakuen station facing the stadium, the garden is to the right. The problem is that the entrance is on the other side, so you must turn right and walk immediately beside the Marunouchi Line viaduct and then turn left at the first road and continue along one more side of the garden. The entrance is reached at the farthest corner of the garden from your starting point. It should be made clear that this garden is quite different from the Koraku-en in Okayama which is amongst the official Three Famous Gardens of Japan. Okayama is 700 kilometres west of Tokyo and the only connexion is that the names of the two gardens are the same.

***Transportation***

Korakuen station is on the Marunouchi Subway Line, which is above ground at this point. The station used to have an attractive arched roof, but it was removed a few years ago. On arrival from Hongo San-chome, you can see very clearly the amusement park in the foreground and the baseball stadium behind. Also close are JR Suidobashi on the Sobu Line and both Suidobashi and Kasuga on the Toei Mita Subway Line.

## SHIBA (芝 – 'Turf')

**Derivation of Name:** *Uncertain, but probably literal. This was a well turfed area.*

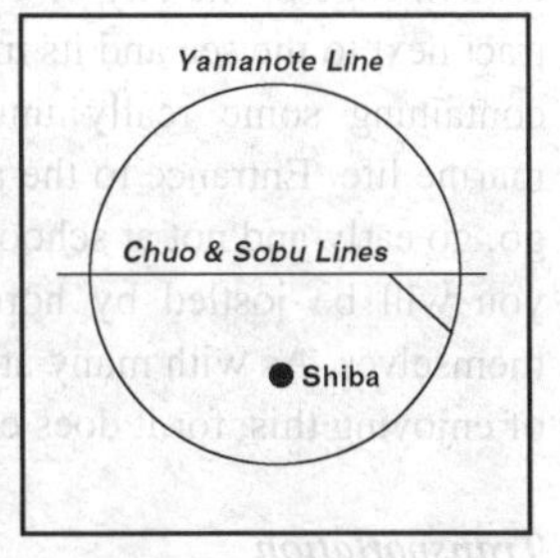


***Tokyo Tower***

Tokyo Tower is the tallest structure, as opposed to building, in Japan. It appears to be a modern copy of the Eiffel Tower, 333 metres high, which is slightly taller than its French counterpart, and it is used for transmitting television broadcasts. There are two observation decks, one at 150 metres and a second at 250 metres. It costs ¥800 to go up by lift to the first deck and a further ¥600 to proceed from there to the higher platform.

If you walk from Onarimon or Shiba Koen station, you will pass through Shiba Park and may like to look at **Zojo-ji**, an impressive temple, on the way. This was originally the family temple of the famous Tokugawa family. The main gate dates from 1605.

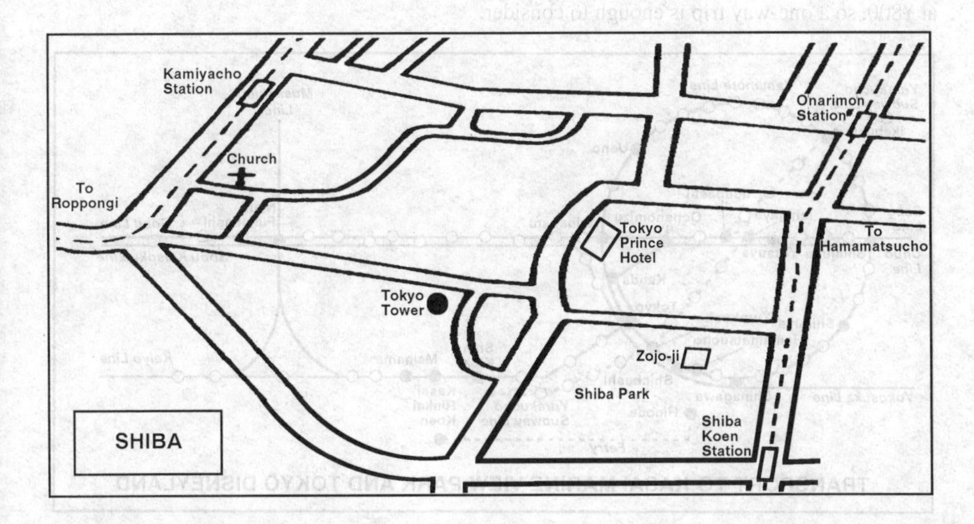

***Transportation***

The nearest stations to Tokyo Tower are Kamiyacho on the Hibiya Subway Line and Onarimon or Shiba Koen on the Toei Mita Subway Line. From Kamiyacho, take exit no. 1 and walk towards Roppongi for about 5 minutes and then branch left. From Onarimon or Shiba Koen, walk through Shiba Park for about 7 minutes. The tower, being the tallest structure in the country, is not too difficult to locate. The nearest JR station is Hamamatsucho on the Yamanote Line, but it is not very convenient. Walk directly away from the station inside the Yamanote Line until Shiba Park is reached. Total walking time is about 15 minutes.

## KASAI (葛西 – 'West Arrowroot')

**Derivation of Name:** *Uncertain, but possibly arrowroot grew in this area.*

***Kasai Marine View Park***

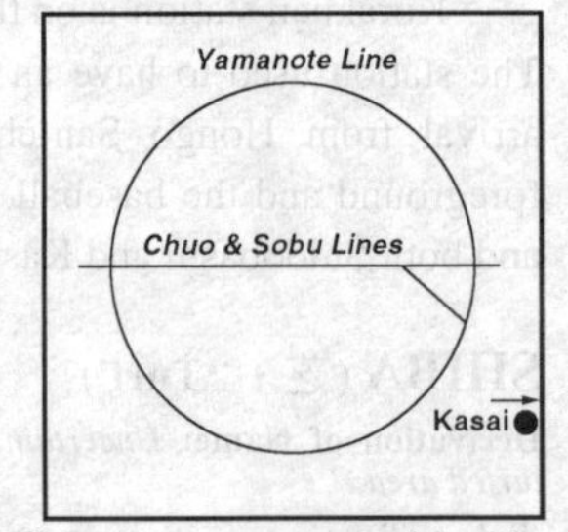


Kasai Rinkai Koen (Kasai Marine View Park) is on the very eastern edge of the city of Tokyo on reclaimed land. It is a large tract next to the sea and its main point of interest is an **aquarium** containing some really unusual (even horrifying) species of marine life. Entrance to the aquarium costs ¥600. If you want to go, go early and not at school holiday time. Even so, there may well be long queues and inside you will be jostled by hordes of schoolchildren being given an official chance to enjoy themselves. As with many attractions in Japan, the worse the weather, the more chance there is of enjoying this, for it does contain a magnificent collection of sea dwellers.

***Transportation***

Kasai Rinkai Koen station is on the JR Keiyo Line and the park is immediately outside. The Keiyo Line starts underground in a remote part of Tokyo station.

There is also a ferry service to and from Hinode, 7 minutes walk from Hamamatsucho station on the JR Yamanote Line. This is quite an interesting journey of 45 minutes, winding along the channels among the artificial islands in Tokyo Bay. However, it is rather expensive at ¥800, so a one-way trip is enough to consider.

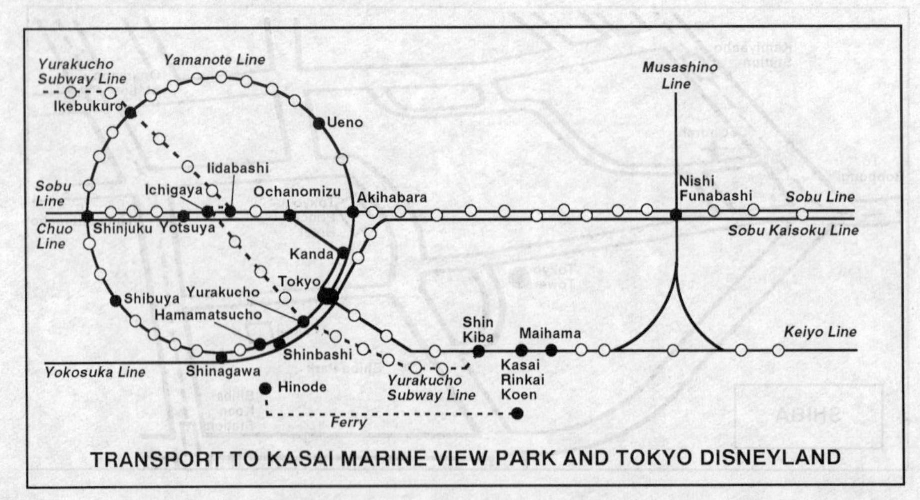

TRANSPORT TO KASAI MARINE VIEW PARK AND TOKYO DISNEYLAND

# SIGHTSEEING ALMOST IN TOKYO

The following locations are not actually within the boundaries of the city of Tokyo, but are so close that most visitors would think of them as part of the city.

## TOKYO DISNEYLAND (東京ディズニーランド)

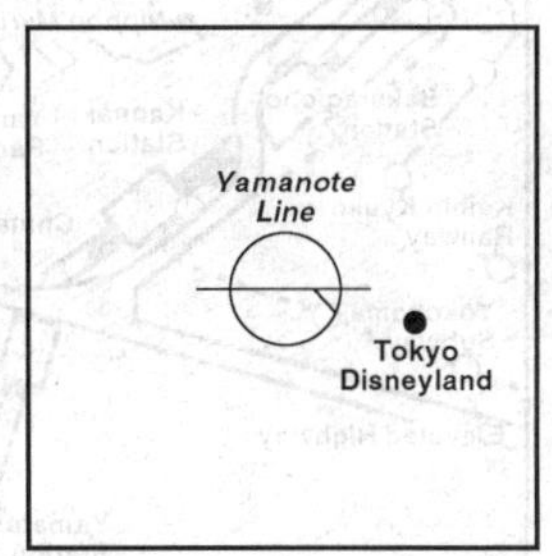


'But I thought that Disneyland was in America' is one of the most frequently heard comments among visitors, some of whom are not aware of the huge success of the Tokyo version of Disneyland, in contrast with the European attempt at the same. Indeed, its very success is its problem, for it is generally very crowded and, of course, at school holiday times unbelievably so. This Disneyland has all of the attractions which you might expect and at certain times of the year it stays open late and there is an 'electrical parade' or a fireworks display. Most people buy a one day 'passport', allowing unlimited use of most attractions (within the bounds of the limitations imposed by queuing). This costs ¥4,800. There are other types of tickets available too. Bear in mind that it is not uncommon to have to wait for thirty minutes for any of the more popular attractions. As usual, the best time to go is on a wet weekday in the middle of winter. One needs a whole day for an adequate visit and should be sure to arrive early.

***Transportation***

Tokyo Disneyland is just outside Maihama station on the JR Keiyo Line, Maihama being the first station outside the Tokyo metropolitan area. The journey takes 15 minutes from Tokyo station (and another 15 minutes to find the Keiyo Line at Tokyo, for it is not conveniently located). It is suggested that the name of Maihama (literally 'Dancing Beach') came phonetically from the first syllable of Miami in combination with the Japanese for beach and that it was hoped that this would become a popular tourist spot. That hope was fulfilled.

## YOKOHAMA (横浜 – 'Horizontal Beach')

**Derivation of Name:** *Located near a long sandbar.*

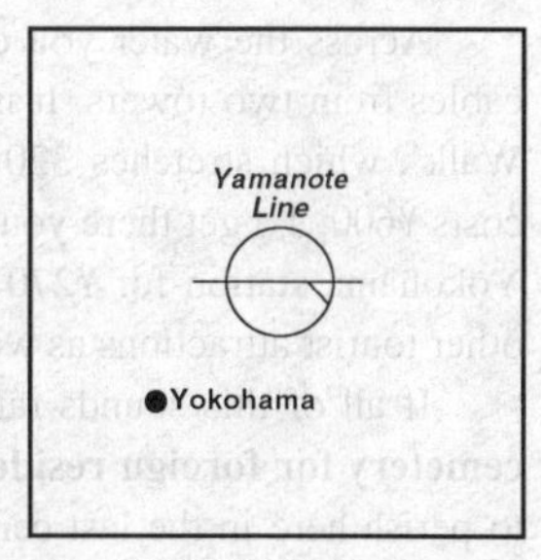


Actually, Yokohama is a completely separate city from Tokyo, of course, the capital of Kanagawa prefecture. However, since Tokyo merges into Kawasaki and Kawasaki into Yokohama, one might pass from one to another these days without ever suspecting that they were separate entities. In fact, if considered separately, Yokohama is the second most populous city in Japan. It is a modern city, having been little more than a marshy port 150 years ago, but has some interesting recent history to offer, for it was one of the places opened to foreign trade in 1858, following the strong hints given by Commodore Perry in 1853. Here the influence of non-Japanese has been strong.

Yokohama station is in the centre of the city, but the areas which are more interesting historically are a little distant from here.

Perhaps the most famous feature of Yokohama is that it has the best known **Chinatown** in Japan, although there is quite an interesting one in Nagasaki too. Chinatown is a 7 minute

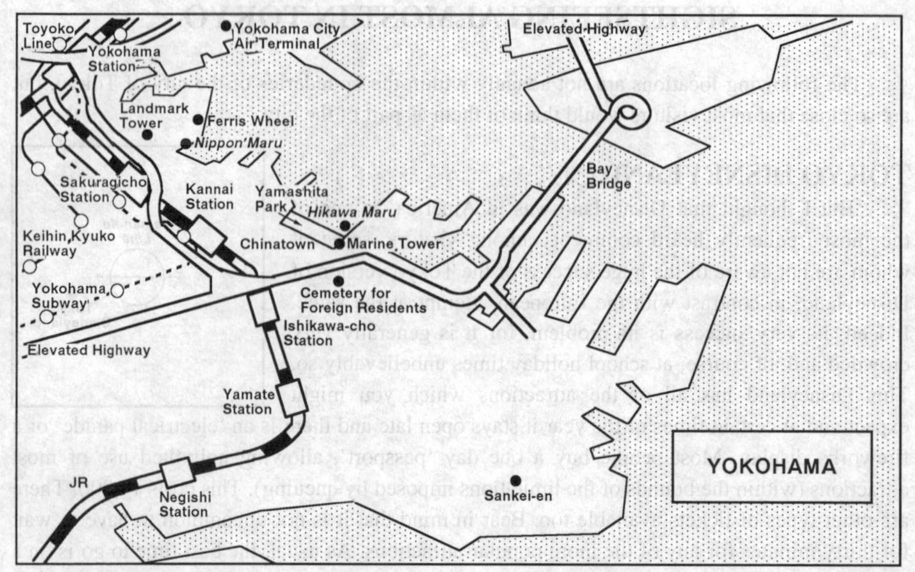


walk from Kannai or Ishikawa-cho, consecutive stations on the JR Negishi Line, which is an extension of the Keihin Tohoku Line (no change of train necessary). Kannai is two stations beyond Yokohama. Follow the railway towards Ishikawa-cho until you see a Chinese gateway on the left. Then turn left. Another Chinese gateway proclaims the entrance to a whole street of Chinese restaurants (some cheap, but some not, so take care) and a variety of stores selling Chinese and other imported products. At the end of this interesting street is **Yamashita Park** and the terminal for various types of passenger ships offering bay cruises or, like the ***Hikawa Maru***, just anchored (¥800 to go on board and look at a floating museum or ¥300 to visit only the deck area, where there is a beer garden in summer). There is also a **silk museum** (¥300) and the **Marine Tower** viewpoint, 106 metres high (¥700). A discounted ticket is available for the combination of the *Hikawa Maru* and Marine Tower (¥1,300).

Across the water you can see the new **Bay Bridge**, 860 metres long and suspended by cables from two towers. It is the biggest bridge of its type in the world. To cross on the 'Sky Walk', which stretches 320 metres between the two towers and is 50 metres above the sea, costs ¥600. To get there you can take a 'Blue Line' bus from bus stop no. 14 at the east exit of Yokohama station for ¥270 each way, or ¥600 for an all day ticket for the bus, which visits other tourist attractions as well.

If all of this sounds rather expensive, a walk of about 10 minutes will bring you to the **cemetery for foreign residents**, containing the graves of those who were unfortunate enough to perish here in the last century and this. Residents from more than forty countries of origin are interred here. First walk to the southern end of Yamashita Park. Just beyond the park is a small concrete-enclosed river, which you need to follow until the second bridge, where turn left and walk up the hill, through a park, to the cemetery on the hill top, commanding a fine view of the city, not that those interred there are able to enjoy it fully, one imagines. The residents here include Mr. Morel, a pioneer of the Japanese railway system. From the cemetery, it is 20 minutes walk back to Ishikawa-cho station through the fashionable shopping area of **Moto-machi**.

Further out still is **Sankei-en**, an attractive and large park well worth a visit. However, it is necessary to take a bus to reach here. The nearest station is Negishi on the JR Negishi Line, five stations beyond Yokohama, from where it is a 10 minute ride. Entry costs ¥300. There are also buses from Sakuragicho and from the east exit of Yokohama station.

If we return now towards the city of Yokohama, we shall come back to Sakuragicho, one station south of Yokohama on the Negishi Line. Here there are some more interesting sites and sights. The Yokohama Exposition was centred here when it was held in 1989. At that time the ***Nippon Maru*** was rebuilt and this sailing vessel now lies at anchor about 5 minutes walk from the station next to the **Yokohama Maritime Museum**. Entry to both costs ¥600. Open from 10:00 until 17:00 (16:30 in winter).

Opposite the *Nippon Maru* is **Landmark Tower**, the tallest building in Japan, with a height of 296 metres and a total of 70 storeys. There is an observation deck on the 69th floor, but it costs ¥1,000 for the privilege of visiting. The lift takes 40 seconds to whisk you up and is able to display a certificate from Mr. Guinness to say that it is the fastest lift in the world. It should be at that price.

Beyond Landmark Tower is the **Yokohama Art Gallery**. ¥500. Open from 10:00 until 18:00. If you walk out further along the peninsula here you will come to the an amusement park which has another Guinness certificate displayed. This is for the largest **Ferris Wheel** in the world. It is 100 metres in diameter, with the top 105 metres above the ground, offering another good view. This one will cost you ¥600. One revolution of the big wheel, which is what you get for your money, takes 15 minutes. Beyond the amusement park is the terminal for ferries to Tokyo and, if you continue walking, you will come to the Marine Park area.

***Transportation***

Yokohama can be reached from Tokyo by three different railway companies. Whichever company is used, the journey time will be about 40 minutes. For those with Japan Rail Passes, JR offers rapid service by its Tokaido and Yokosuka Lines and local service by its Keihin Tohoku Line (blue trains), which is called the Negishi Line south-west of Yokohama. The Tokaido Line leaves from platforms 7 to 9 at Tokyo station and stops also at Shinbashi and Shinagawa within the Tokyo area. The Yokosuka Line departs from underground platforms 1 to 4 (not to be confused with above ground platforms 1 to 4 or Keiyo Line underground platforms 1 to 4!) at Tokyo and stops at Shinbashi underground platforms and at Shinagawa platform 14. Thereafter the two lines take different routes, but there is not much difference in travelling time. The Keihin Tohoku Line parallels the Yamanote Line for about half of its circle, but, in the middle of the day, approximately from 10:30 until 15:30, Keihin Tohoku trains stop only at Tabata, Ueno, Akihabara, Tokyo, Tamachi and Shinagawa. After Shinagawa all trains stop at every station on the way to Yokohama. At Tokyo, the Keihin Tohoku Line departs for Yokohama from platform 6. At Ueno, it leaves from platform 4. Most Narita Express trains, from Narita Airport, have a section which goes to Yokohama. However, Shin Yokohama station, on the *shinkansen* route, is not near the centre of Yokohama. From Tokyo to Yokohama costs ¥440. To Sakuragicho costs ¥530. From Shinagawa to Yokohama or Sakuragicho costs ¥370.

The Toyoko Line of the Tokyu Private Railway runs to Yokohama and on to Sakuragicho. It is cheaper than JR, but leaves from Shibuya. The Hibiya Subway Line ends at Naka Meguro on the Toyoko Line, where changing is just a matter of crossing the platform.

Some trains from the Hibiya Line continue onto the Toyoko Line, but they never go as far as Yokohama. The Toyoko Line offers both *kyuko* (express) and ordinary trains. There is no supplement for using the *kyuko*, which can be identified by having the destination marked in red instead of black. It is usually faster to wait for a *kyuko*, but the ordinary train tends to be less crowded. From Shibuya to Yokohama costs ¥230. To Sakuragicho costs ¥260.

The third service is offered by the Keihin Kyuko Private Railway, which operates from Shinagawa. Some services run through from the Toei Asakusa Subway Line. There are various types of train – in ascending order of speed *futsu* (ordinary), *kyuko* (express), *tokkyu* (limited express) and *kaisoku tokkyu* (rapid limited express). There are no supplementary charges for any type of train, except for some rush hour guaranteed seat services termed 'KQ Wing' (¥200 supplement). All trains stop at Yokohama. The Keihin Kyuko Railway costs ¥270 from Shinagawa to Yokohama, the *kaisoku* train making only one stop (Kawasaki) *en route* and being quite comfortable.

It is worth bearing in mind that JR offers a special ticket for those who want to make a day trip to the Yokohama area from the Tokyo area. It is called a *Yokohama Free Kippu* and it includes return travel from the station of origin to Yokohama and unlimited travel between Yokohama and Shin Sugita, seven stations beyond Yokohama. Cost varies according to the station of origin, but, for example, from Tokyo it costs ¥880, from Shinagawa ¥560 and from Shinjuku ¥1,040. This ticket is good value, especially from Shinagawa, to reach which station from anywhere else on the Yamanote Line you can use *Yamanote kai-su-ken* (see page 71).

There are also ferry services between Tokyo and Yokohama, but not many. They leave from Hinode in Tokyo, 7 minutes walk from Hamamatsucho on the JR Yamanote Line, at 13:50 and 17:10, not very convenient timings. There are two stops in Yokohama, but the more useful one is the second, called MM21, which is about 15 minutes walk from Sakuragicho station. Departures from MM21 for Tokyo are at 12:00 and 15:20. The journey takes 1 hour 45 minutes and costs ¥2,600 one way.

There is another ferry service between Yokohama station (east exit) and Yamashita Park, which takes 15 minutes and costs ¥500. The ferry calls at MM21 on the way and it costs ¥300 from there to either end of the route.

Within Yokohama, a one-day ticket is offered for use on city buses for ¥600 (*'bus ichi-nichi jo-sha-ken'* – バス一日乗車券) or for use on city buses and subway for ¥830 (*'bus chika-tetsu ichi-nichi jo-sha-ken'* – バス地下鉄一日乗車券).

# ONE DAY EXPEDITIONS FROM TOKYO

The following are journeys which can conveniently be made in a single day using Tokyo as a base, although some are worthy of a longer visit if time permits.

## KAMAKURA (鎌倉 – 'Scythe Warehouse')

**Derivation of Name:** *Original meaning was 'cave shaped like a scythe', but Chinese characters became changed (doubtful).*

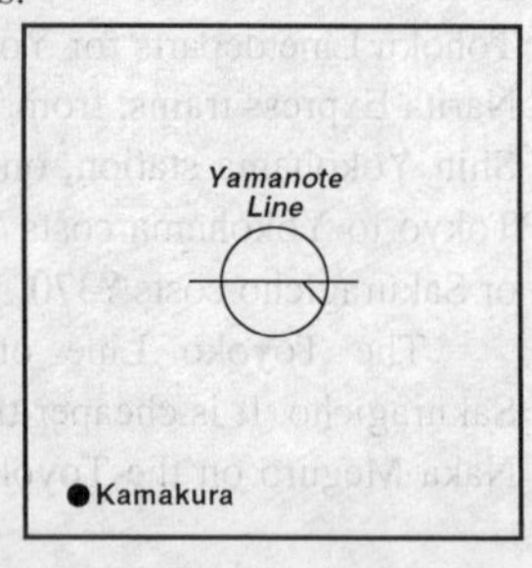


Kamakura, only about an hour from the centre of Tokyo by train, is one of the essential places in Japan to visit. If one had a single day stopover in Tokyo, this would be the place to go. The city is overflowing with history and really in a single day one can just pick out a few of the most important sights and scratch the surface. Kamakura was the administrative capital of Japan from 1192 until 1333 and so contains a wealth of temples. Since the city declined in importance after its golden age, some of these have survived the centuries relatively undamaged.

In 1184, Minamoto Yoritomo expanded his position as chief of the armed forces and took on administrative functions also. He established his seat of government in Kamakura. By 1192, he had been recognized as the first administrative *shogun* of Japan, while the emperor in Kyoto had become merely a ceremonial figurehead. In 1219, Yoritomo's grandson and successor, Minamoto Sanetomo, was assassinated in Kamakura and the Hojo family took over the reigns of power. The Kamakura Era lasted until the imperial army besieged the city in 1333 and Hojo Takatoki was forced to commit suicide, along with 870 supporters, at a temple in the city.

This section will try to suggest an itinerary which will include some of the most important sights in Kamakura along a roughly semi-circular route, building up gradually towards the most famous. If the reader does not like this itinerary, he has only to wander off in almost any direction to find less frequented temples. Remember, though, to go on a weekday. Kamakura will be crowded enough even then, but at the weekend it will be far worse. Anyway, here are the author's suggestions.

First take the JR Yokosuka Line to Kita Kamakura. At the previous station, Ofuna, incidentally, notice the huge modern white statue of **Kannon**, the Goddess of Mercy, up on the hill on the right. Although this is worth a look if you have time, there is a great deal to see in Kamakura, so a glance from the train may be all that can be afforded. It is difficult to get a good photograph from the station, though, because of the electric wires, a common complaint in Japan. At Kita Kamakura, alight and walk forward on the left side of the railway. Very soon you will come to **Engaku-ji**, up a flight of steps on the left, a temple dating from 1282, although most of the buildings are much later. The gate, however, is a most impressive and sturdy antique structure. To an extent, this gate symbolizes the differences between the architecture here in Kamakura and that which you will see later when you visit Kyoto, for Kyoto is an expression of elegance, the finest example of the refined and aristocratic taste of its age. Kamakura, by contrast, is a *samurai* city where the architectural style is simple and practical. It is an interesting contrast. The string of temple buildings runs back towards the hills, to a pond with tortoises and a building where the tea ceremony can be performed for the sum of ¥500. As at most of the temples here in Kamakura, the admission ticket gives information in English and there are notices in the same language explaining the features of various buildings. Admission to the complex costs ¥200.

Leave Engaku-ji by the same route and continue along beside the railway. The next temple which you will reach is **Meigetsu-in**, sometimes known as the hydrangea temple, a short distance down a road on the left. This is an optional visit, because other than at hydrangea time (May and June), the temple is not so special, and at that time it is crowded, of course. However, it is set in pleasant gardens and has, at the end, some old tombs in caves in the hillside. ¥200.

Continue towards Kamakura, keeping the railway on your right, although it soon drops out of sight now. After about 10 minutes, you will come to **Kencho-ji**, one of the most famous of Kamakura's temples. The temple was founded in 1253, but again the present buildings are not that old. The main temple hall was built in 1646. There is also a large temple bell on display. Here, you can keep walking back towards the hills for a long way, coming upon other interesting sites as you go. Finally you reach a long flight of steps with another pleasant little temple at the top. From here a hiking trail begins. Of course, if you happen to enter here rather than by the main entrance, it is unlikely that anybody is going to think of demanding an admission fee. Otherwise, from the front entrance, admission to the temple complex costs ¥300.

Leaving Kencho-ji and continuing in the same direction as before, you walk downhill through a tunnel which is not a tunnel, for the top is open to the elements and its purpose really is protection from falling rocks, and after 10 minutes you will come to a flight of steps on your left leading up to **Hachiman-gu**, Kamakura's most famous shrine. It was founded in 1063 and moved to its present site in 1191. As was appropriate at the time, it was dedicated to the Emperor Ojin, the guardian of warriors. The present building dates from 1828. At the top of the steps is the shrine and a treasure house with some historical relics (¥100). A long steep flight of steps leads down to a wide open area below. One can feel the history here, for at the foot of the steps on the right is the place where the *shogun* Sanetomo was assassinated by his nephew, who was the chief priest at the shrine. The nephew is supposed to have hidden behind the huge ginkgo tree which is still there and waited for the *shogun* to return from his visit to the shrine. The assassinated *shogun* was a great loss to Japan for he had considerable literary talent and his poetry is still read today. He was only 28 years old. Down below is also a stage, reconstructed after being destroyed in the 1923 earthquake, where Shinto dances are performed on ceremonial occasions. Proceeding towards the official entrance, for actually, of course, we started from the rear, we come to an interesting bridge. Everybody used to try to walk across it without taking a run-up. It could be done, but it is not really what one would call the most practical of bridges. Perhaps that is why it crosses a pond which does not really need to be crossed in any case. Recently, however, the bridge has been sealed off, so that one can no longer attempt the challenge of crossing. Entrance to Hachiman-gu is free, except for the treasure house.

From here, a wide avenue with trees and a path down the centre leads into town. Notice **McDonald's** on the way. This particular branch evidently claimed the world record for the most hamburgers sold on one day. The day was New Year's Day, so you will know that that is a good day not to come here! Soon you will reach Kamakura station. Go underneath the railway line and, on the other side, you will find the station for the **Enoden** Private Railway. This is a charming little line, particularly in its early stages, twisting and turning among back gardens, sometimes touching the foliage on both sides. The third station is Hase, our destination. The distance is not so great (1.7 km), so it would be possible to walk, but the railway is fun.

After alighting at Hase, cross the railway line and proceed inland to come to Kamakura's most famous attraction, the **Big Buddha** (*Daibutsu*) which appears on the cover of this book. This is not the biggest Buddha in the country, one in Nara being larger, but it is the most beautiful of the large statues. It is reputed to have been made in 1292, cast in bronze and apparently gilded originally, although all of the gilding has now disappeared. Big Buddha used to be housed in a temple, but the temple has gone too, supposedly washed away in 1495 by a tidal wave which left the 120 tons of Buddha unmoved. However, the Buddha is so far inland that it is difficult to believe this story. Perhaps, therefore, the coastline was in a different place at that time. Whatever the reason for the disappearance of the temple, its absence is a boon for

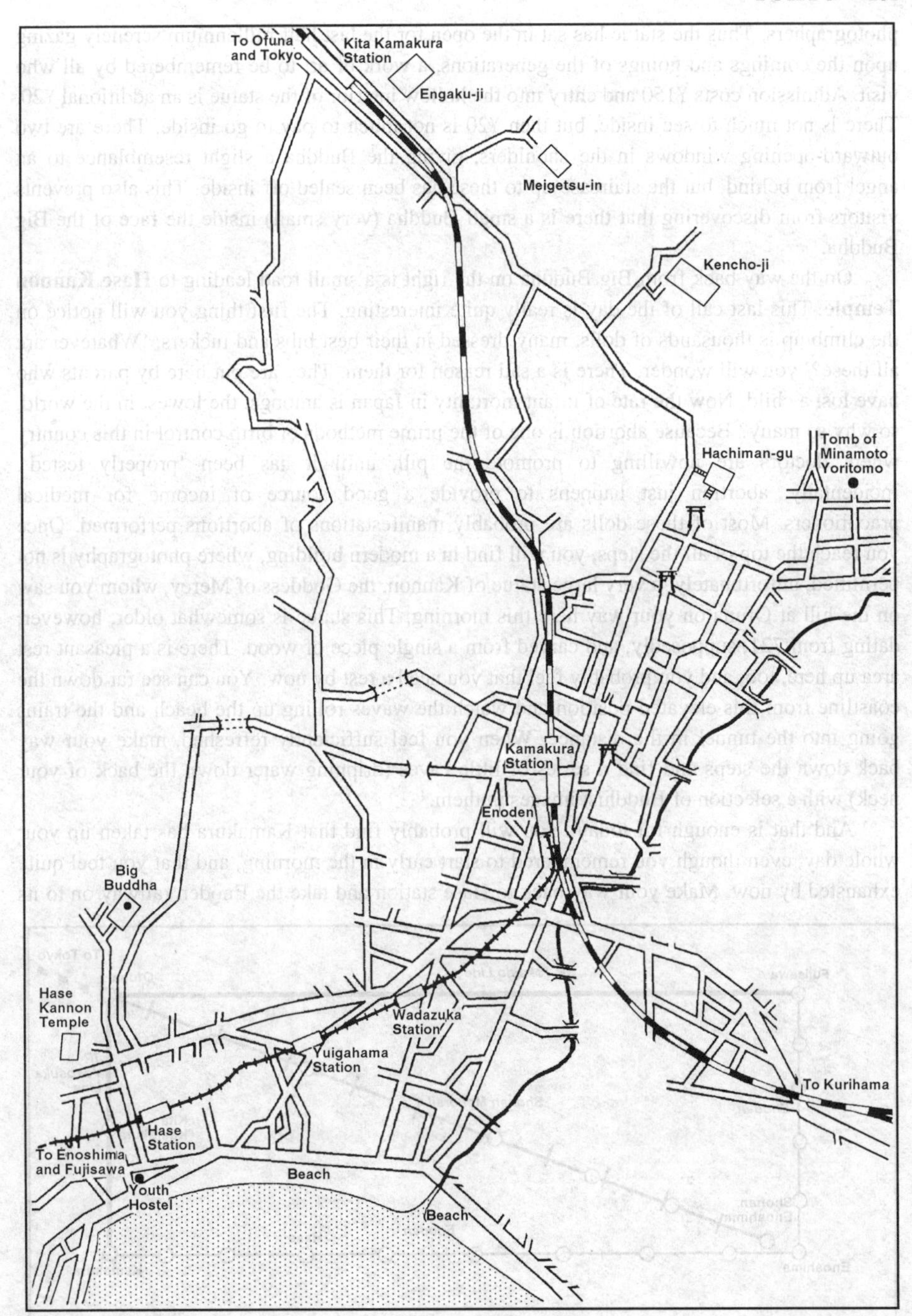
To Ofuna
and Tokyo
Kita Kamakura
Station
Engaku-ji
Meigetsu-in
Kencho-ji
Hachiman-gu
Tomb of
Minamoto
Yoritomo
Kamakura
Station
Enoden
Big
Buddha
Hase
Kannon
Temple
Wadazuka
Station
Yuigahama
Station
Hase
Station
To Enoshima
and Fujisawa
Youth
Hostel
Beach
Beach
To Kurihama

KAMAKURA

photographers. Thus the statue has sat in the open for the last half millennium serenely gazing upon the comings and goings of the generations, a work of art to be remembered by all who visit. Admission costs ¥150 and entry into the hollow interior of the statue is an additional ¥20. There is not much to see inside, but then ¥20 is not much to pay to go inside. There are two outward-opening windows in the shoulders, giving the Buddha a slight resemblance to an angel from behind, but the staircase up to these has been sealed off inside. This also prevents visitors from discovering that there is a small Buddha (very small) inside the face of the Big Buddha.

On the way back from Big Buddha on the right is a small road leading to **Hase Kannon Temple**. This last call of the day is really quite interesting. The first thing you will notice on the climb up is thousands of dolls, many dressed in their best bibs and tuckers. 'Whatever are all these?' you will wonder. There is a sad reason for them. They are put here by parents who have lost a child. Now the rate of infant mortality in Japan is amongst the lowest in the world, so why so many? Because abortion is one of the prime methods of birth control in this country where doctors are unwilling to promote the pill, until it has been 'properly tested'. Incidentally, abortion just happens to provide a good source of income for medical practitioners. Most of these dolls are probably manifestations of abortions performed. Once you reach the top of all the steps, you will find in a modern building, where photography is not permitted, unfortunately, a very large statue of Kannon, the Goddess of Mercy, whom you saw on the hill at Ofuna on your way here this morning. This statue is somewhat older, however, dating from 721, supposedly, and carved from a single piece of wood. There is a pleasant rest area up here, too, and you probably feel that you need a rest by now. You can see far down the coastline from this elevated position and watch the waves rolling up the beach and the trains going into the tunnel in the distance. When you feel sufficiently refreshed, make your way back down the steps and find a series of little caves (dripping water down the back of your neck) with a selection of Buddhist images in them.

And that is enough for today. You will probably find that Kamakura has taken up your whole day, even though you remembered to start early in the morning, and that you feel quite exhausted by now. Make your way back to Hase station and take the Enoden railway on to its

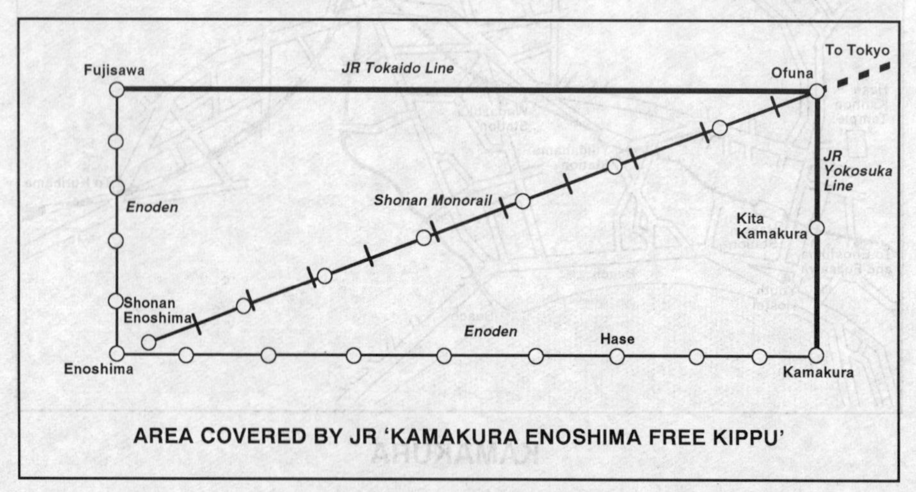

AREA COVERED BY JR 'KAMAKURA ENOSHIMA FREE KIPPU'

terminus at Fujisawa or just to Enoshima, where you can transfer to the Odakyu Private Railway or to the monorail which runs back to Ofuna. At Enoshima, Enoden finally runs out of room and makes its triumphal way right down the middle of the main street, but more about transportation in the following section.

*Transportation*

To follow the route above, take the JR Yokosuka Line from the underground platforms at Tokyo or Shinbashi stations or from platform 14 at Shinagawa, all stations on the Yamanote Line.

To return from Fujisawa, where Enoden ends, there is a choice of the JR Tokaido Line, running back to Yokohama, Shinagawa, Shinbashi and Tokyo, or the Odakyu Private Railway, running to Shinjuku, on the JR Yamanote Line, with connexions at Yoyogi Uehara onto the Chiyoda Subway Line.

If you prefer to take Enoden only as far as Enoshima, a beach resort, from that town there is a choice of the Odakyu Private Railway or a monorail service to Ofuna, from where one can rejoin the JR Tokaido or Yokosuka Line for the journey back to the Tokyo area.

JR offers a special two-day ticket for the Kamakura area, called a *Kamakura Enoshima Free Kippu*. It provides return travel from the station of origin and unlimited travel within the area bounded by Ofuna, Kamakura, Enoshima and Fujisawa, including free travel on Enoden and the monorail. For the two days, it costs ¥1,900 from any station on or within the JR Yamanote Line. It is available from other stations too, at varying rates.

The Odakyu Private Railway has similar tickets. ¥1,350 buys a two-day ticket giving a return journey from Shinjuku to Fujisawa, plus unlimited travel between Fujisawa and Enoshima with the Odakyu Railway and unlimited travel on Enoden. If you do not need the return journey from Shinjuku, just the unlimited travel area can be purchased for ¥540. The ticket is also available from any other Odakyu station for ¥540 plus the return fare from that station to Fujisawa. A second type of ticket includes Enoden buses and Keihin Kyuko buses (both) within the city of Kamakura, as well as all described above, and costs ¥1,980 from Shinjuku or ¥1,170 from Fujisawa. These tickets are all called 'Enoshima Kamakura Free

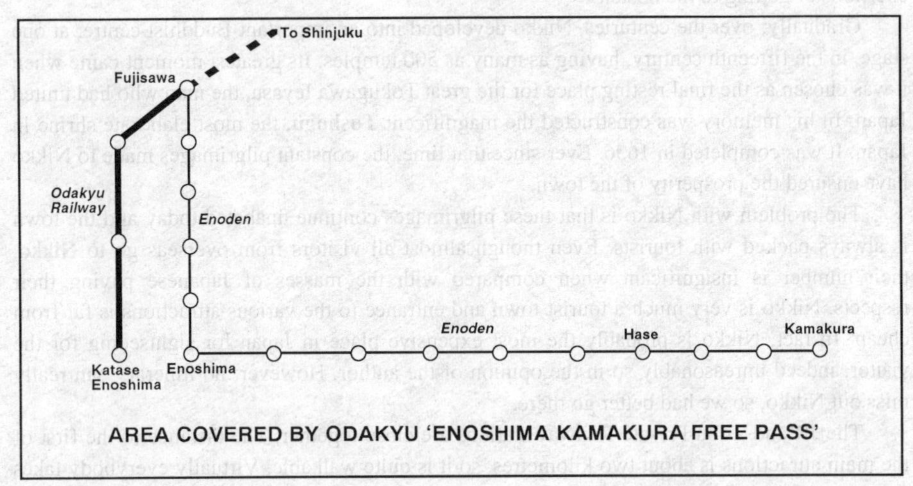


AREA COVERED BY ODAKYU 'ENOSHIMA KAMAKURA FREE PASS'

Pass' (江の島鎌倉フリーパス) and are available at Odakyu stations. 'Free Pass A' includes the buses, while 'Free Pass B' is for trains only.

Enoden also offers special tickets. ¥530 buys an all-day ticket for the railway (*'ichi-nichi jo-sha-ken'* ——日乗車券), while, for ¥780, there is an all-day ticket for the railway plus bus between Kamakura and Ofuna. Tickets are available at Enoden stations.

Keihin Kyuko and Enoden both offer one-day passes for their own buses (no trains and only their own buses, not each other's) within the city of Kamakura. These tickets are called 'Bus Free Kippu' (バスフリーきっぷ) and cost ¥700. They are available at each bus company's offices, for example at Kamakura station.

## NIKKO (日光 – 'Light of the Sun')

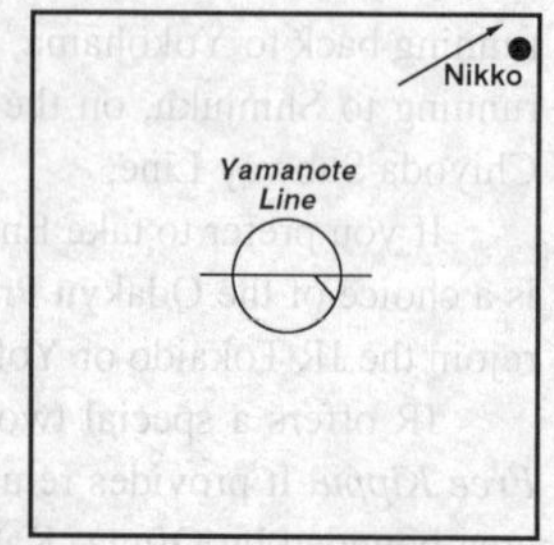


**Derivation of Name:** *Originally named for Futara-san, the famous shrine here. 'Futara' can also be read as 'Nikko'. Later the Chinese characters used for the name became changed.*

Most people regard a visit to Nikko as an essential of any stay in Tokyo. It is another historic town, but quite different in character from Kamakura. Usually it is visited as a one day trip from Tokyo, but, in fact, it is a long day and really the town merits a more extended visit because of the attractive countryside nearby. However, for most of us, time is limited and it is certainly possible to see the historical attractions of Nikko in a single day, and to have a glimpse of the surrounding countryside as well.

If you do decide to stay, there are three youth hostels in and around Nikko, so there is usually no problem in finding accommodation. As usual, though, one must reserve in advance, even if only a day or two beforehand.

Nikko had its origin in the year 782, when a Buddhist priest succeeded in climbing Mt. Nantai, which overlooks the town, and established a temple on the mountain. Incidentally, if you stay at any temple hostels during your time in Japan, you will find that Buddhist priests have the same policy today, so that you feel that you have earned your stay just by the exertions of getting to the hostel.

Gradually, over the centuries, Nikko developed into an important Buddhist centre, at one stage, in the fifteenth century, having as many as 500 temples. Its greatest moment came when it was chosen as the final resting place for the great Tokugawa Ieyasu, the man who had united Japan. In his memory was constructed the magnificent **Toshogu**, the most elaborate shrine in Japan. It was completed in 1636. Ever since that time, the constant pilgrimages made to Nikko have ensured the prosperity of the town.

The problem with Nikko is that these pilgrimages continue unabated today and the town is always packed with tourists. Even though almost all visitors from overseas go to Nikko, their number is insignificant when compared with the masses of Japanese paying their respects. Nikko is very much a tourist town and entrance to the various attractions is far from cheap. In fact, Nikko is probably the most expensive place in Japan for sightseeing for the visitor, indeed unreasonably so in the opinion of the author. However, no itinerary can really miss out Nikko, so we had better go there.

The JR and Tobu Private Railway stations are close together. The distance to the first of the main attractions is about two kilometres, so it is quite walkable. Virtually everybody takes

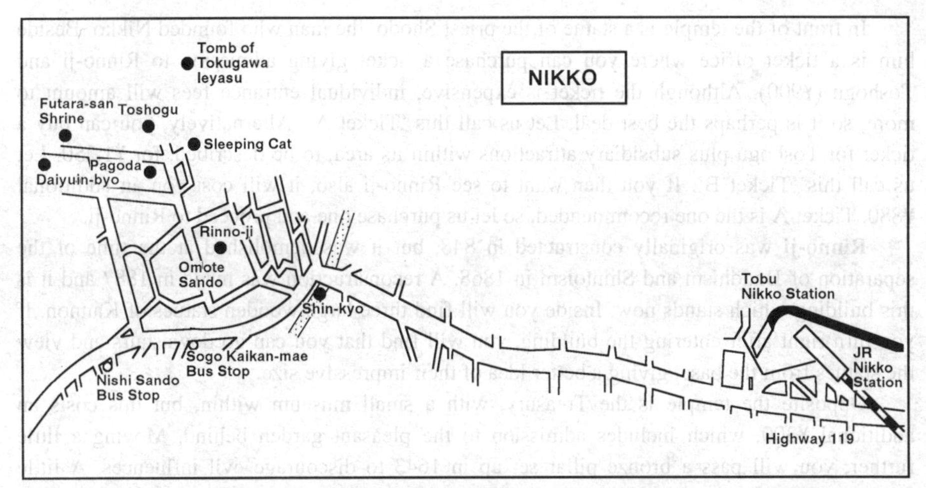


a bus, however, on which it is a 7 minute ride, at the excessive cost of ¥300, to Sogo Kaikan-mae (総合会館前). You will not miss this stop, because most of the passengers will get off there. Better, though, to get off at Shin-kyo (神橋), where there is something else to see. This is reached after 5 minutes at a slightly more reasonable cost of ¥190. The stop is immediately before a bridge where the road turns sharp left, if you have any chance to look out of the front of the bus. Almost all buses from the stations will be travelling this route.

However, if you are game to walk, turn right as you leave either station and follow the main road through the town. It is gently uphill all the way. Because Nikko is inland and at some altitude, you will find it cool here and in the winter there is likely to be some snow around. Walk right through the town and at the very end you will come to **Shin-kyo**, a bridge. Now, despite its attractive, and even practical, appearance, this is not a bridge for crossing the river which it spans, as you might perhaps suppose. Actually its main purpose these days seems to be to earn ¥300 per visitor for the bridge-keeper who will rush out and shout at you if you venture to set foot upon it without paying him first. Just in case you should be tempted to use the bridge for crossing the river, it is blocked at the end, to make it seem an even more futile exercise in construction. However, this bright orange wooden bridge makes a good photograph from the bridge which really is used, and crossing the latter is free, fortunately. The photograph which you will take here is the image of Nikko which frequently appears on tourist literature, so it is an almost obligatory snapshot!

Of course, the bridge has a history, which ought to be mentioned. The original was constructed in 1636, as the access route to the shrine of Toshogu. However, even then it was not used, except by an Imperial Messenger during the shrine festival. Then, in 1902, the bridge was destroyed by a great serpent, if one believes the story, although, incidentally, there was a fierce storm and flood at the same time. It was rebuilt in 1907 and that is the bridge there now. One wonders whether the bridge-keeper rushes out to collect his ¥300 from the Imperial Messenger too.

Having crossed the road bridge, both you and the main road turn sharp left to avoid running into the cliff and soon afterwards, while the main road continues beside the river, you should branch right and then Rinno-ji will become visible, the largest temple in Nikko and the one with the longest history.

In front of the temple is a statue of the priest Shodo, the man who founded Nikko. Beside him is a ticket office where you can purchase a ticket giving admission to Rinno-ji and Toshogu (¥900). Although the ticket is expensive, individual entrance fees will amount to more, so it is perhaps the best deal. Let us call this 'Ticket A'. Alternatively, you can buy a ticket for Toshogu plus subsidiary attractions within its area, to be described, for ¥1,250. Let us call this 'Ticket B'. If you then want to see Rinno-ji also, it will cost you an additional ¥880. Ticket A is the one recommended, so let us purchase one and proceed to Rinno-ji.

**Rinno-ji** was originally constructed in 848, but it was demolished at the time of the separation of Buddhism and Shintoism in 1868. A reconstruction was made in 1887 and it is this building which stands now. Inside you will find three large wooden statues of Kannon. If you turn right after entering the building, you will find that you can go downstairs and view the statues from the base, giving a better idea of their impressive size.

Opposite the temple is the Treasury, with a small museum within, but this costs an additional ¥300, which includes admission to the pleasant garden behind. Moving a little further, you will pass a bronze pillar set up in 1643 to discourage evil influences. A little further still, and down some steps, you will reach Omote Sando, the main avenue leading to the principal attraction, Toshogu itself. Turn right and there is the entrance to the shrine. If you came all the way by bus, this is the avenue by which you will approach on foot after crossing the road from the bus stop. There is another ticket box here where you can purchase either Ticket A or Ticket B.

The shrine complex is entered through a decorated gate known as Nio-mon. Turning left, one passes several storerooms and stables. Do not just pass them by, for here on the left are the original **three wise monkeys** busily engaged in seeing, speaking and hearing no evil. They are quite small, on the second of several monkey panel decorations, and there is always a crowd gathered around them. Opposite you can see some more interesting carving, this time a pair of elephants, carved by a man who had reputedly never seen any elephants – and it looks like it too! Reports of these enormous strange beasts had been brought back from distant lands, and some elephants had actually been shipped to Japan, but it seems as though this carver had not had the pleasure of meeting any. In this area the sacred horse is stabled. It will accept eagerly any gratuitous contributions (which can be purchased for ¥50) and is kept in case God needs to use a horse, but it seems that He does not often need to do so these days, both JR and Tobu being available. The sacred horse, for its part, appears quite satisfied by this state of affairs and munches away happily until such time as it is required for celestial duties.

Continuing, one will pass, after turning right, the holy water fountain, as at all religious edifices in Japan. Incidentally, although Japanese visitors purify themselves by washing out their mouths here, there is no obligation to follow suit. On the other hand, if one is feeling thirsty, the water comes straight from a mountain spring.

On the left here is **Yakushi-do**, also known sometimes as Honji-do. It is a Buddhist temple, which exemplifies the combination of Buddhism and Shintoism which formerly existed. Though the temple looks old, in fact most of the original construction was burnt down in 1961 and the present building dates from 1968. This temple can be entered with Ticket B, but not with Ticket A. On the ceiling is a drawing of a dragon. If you stand below it, in the centre of the floor, and clap your hands, you can hear the dragon roar. To help you in this endeavour, the spot is marked and you will be at the end of a long queue of people waiting their turn to be processed in the minimum possible time. "Right, stand there. Clap. Donation?

Next!" You do not have to succumb to the pressure to make a 'voluntary' donation, although all Japanese will do so. It *is* voluntary and you have, after all, paid for your ticket to come in in the first place.

Now you will come to **Yomei-mon,** the most elaborately decorated gate in Japan. It really is a remarkable structure which has to be seen to be appreciated. In former times only high-ranking warriors could pass this gate, and, even then, only if unarmed. However, the others would still have had something worth looking at whilst they waited for their superiors. Notice that the rear of one of the columns is carved upside-down, not a mistake, but done to frustrate evil spirits.

In contrast with Yomei-mon is **Kara-mon,** also known as the Chinese Gate. Instead of being decorated in bright colours, it is mostly white. Another contrast is that it is always closed, except during shrine festivals, when it is used by the Shinto priests.

After climbing the steps and passing through Yomei-mon, you will be in the Inner Courtyard. On your left is the building where the portable shrines (*mikoshi*) are kept. They are carried in two processions each year, on 18th May and 17th October, and each of the three requires 50 people to carry it.

Across the courtyard, you will reach the entrance to the oratory (*haiden*) and sanctuary (*honden*). This is the shoes-off point. Put them in one of the pigeon-holes provided and proceed along a short corridor. Beyond this point, visitors enter in shifts to a brief ceremony of great import of which you will understand nothing. Participate if you wish, or just observe, but fringe participation gives a somewhat better view of the interior, which is beautifully decorated.

Emerging again from the building and replacing shoes, you will pass one more point of interest. This is the entrance to the **tomb of Tokugawa Ieyasu**. This area requires another separate ticket, as if to prove just what a touristy place Nikko is. Unfortunately, it is not included on Ticket A, although it is part of Ticket B. If you are entitled to enter, or buy another ticket to do so, you will first observe a famous carving of a **sleeping cat** over the doorway to the entrance. This carving is rather small and something of a disappointment, considering its fame, after all that has gone before. It is said to ensure that no mice are ever to be found in the buildings of the shrine. The ticket office is strategically placed so that it is just far enough away from the carving to ensure that you cannot really see it without paying. Now you climb a large number of steps – 207 to be precise – to reach the tomb itself. When you get there, you will find that it is a very plain tomb, quite a contrast with the magnificence down below. This is also a rather peaceful spot, because, of the thousands of tourists who visit Toshogu, relatively few seem to muster the energy to climb up here.

If you now return to the entrance to Toshogu, turn right and a short walk will bring you to **Futara-san Shrine**, the shrine which originally gave Nikko its name. Mercifully, admission is free. The shrine was constructed in 1617 and this is the oldest building in Nikko. It is dedicated to the gods of the nearby mountains and so is a shrine for worshipping nature, whereas Toshogu, of course, is for the worship of a national hero. Actually, this building is only part of the Futara-san Shrine complex. A second building will be found near Lake Chuzenji, if you go that far, while the third is near the summit of Mt. Nantai.

Almost opposite the Futara-san Shrine is another construction which you should not miss. This is the **Daiyuin-byo**, the mausoleum of Tokugawa Iemitsu, the third Tokugawa *shogun*, who died in 1651. He is the man who built Toshogu, regardless of the enormous expense (one reason for this being that it helped to keep the *daimyo*, the local lords, poor, and so assisted him in retaining his strong authority over them). He requested that his own mausoleum should be inferior to that of Ieyasu, his grandfather, and so it is, but only a little. One of the principal distinctions is that this is only a mausoleum, not a shrine, for Iemitsu was never elevated to divine status. However, the design is not so different from that of Toshogu and a great advantage in viewing it is that many visitors do not even bother to come here, as this mausoleum is of much less fame, despite its beauty.

There are plenty of other sights in and around Nikko, for those who have time. There are, for example, museums, botanical gardens, waterfalls and several other temples and monuments. Maps and information (including those in English) are available at the railway stations for those who have sufficient time or at the youth hostels, for those who are staying there. However, if you have only a single day and you still want to see some of the countryside, you had better press on. Be warned, though, that from now on the journey is going to become even more expensive. Return to the main road and locate a bus stop for buses heading away from the town of Nikko (i.e. on the far side of the road). The nearest stop to Daiyuin-byo is called Nishi Sando ( 西参道 ). Some buses terminate here, but those which continue will mostly be marked Chuzenji Onsen ( 中禅寺温泉 ) or Yumoto Onsen ( 湯本温泉 ). Either of these will do. They run irregularly, but once or twice an hour. The 40 minute journey (if there is no traffic jam) to Chuzenji is spectacular, as well as being spectacularly expensive. It costs ¥1,100 from Nikko station or slightly less from here. Do not forget to take a numbered ticket when boarding, to determine your fare at the end of the journey, or else you will have to pay the maximum fare.

To reach Chuzenji, the bus must climb what is known as **Iroha-zaka**. The road constructed up to Chuzenji in 1954 had 48 hairpin bends, corresponding with the number of letters in the classical Japanese alphabet, *i*, *ro*, and *ha* being the first three letters in that alphabet. However, that road is not the one which you will be travelling now, as it became overcrowded and is now used only for down traffic, so you will see it later. The up road was built in 1961. The steepest gradient is one in seven. The bus has to struggle sometimes, if crowded.

Just before Chuzenji is reached, the bus makes a stop at **Akechi Daira** ( 明智平 ). If the weather is good, it is worth getting off here. A ropeway runs up to a lookout on the hilltop (only 300 metres) for a cost of ¥310 one way. From here one can obtain a good view of Lake Chuzenji and Kegon Falls, the exit from the lake, in the distance. If you wish, and if time permits, instead of taking the ropeway back down to Akechi Daira, you can walk along a trail to the lake, or to the top of another ropeway which descends to near Kegon Falls. It will take 90 minutes to the ropeway or about two hours to the lake. The ropeway, from a place called Chanoki Daira ('Tea Tree Plateau') costs ¥440 one way for a journey of one kilometre.

**Chuzenji** is a small spa town, the main attraction of which is **Kegon Falls**, where the water spills out of the lake into the valley 96 metres below. Although the falls are quite spectacular, especially during the summer months, they can only be glimpsed from the top and so a lift has been built to take observers to the foot to appreciate the true power of the water flow (¥520). During the winter, comparatively little water flows and the falls are usually frozen. However, they are still attractive to view from the base and there are not so many visitors around during the cool weather. Incidentally, the shape of this waterfall was changed a few years ago when an earthquake dislodged some of the rocks at the top.

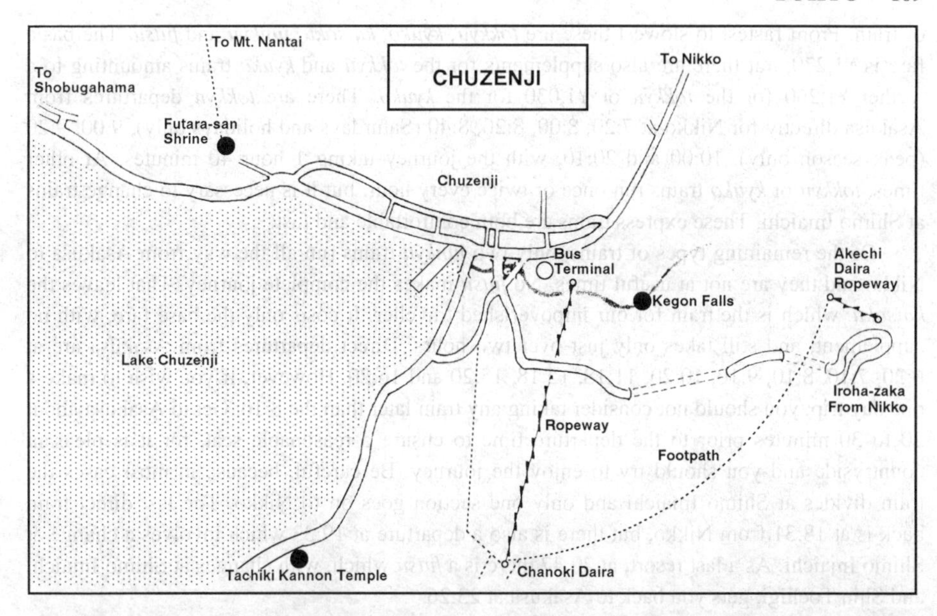


If you now walk back and through the town, you can visit the second part of **Futara-san Shrine**, although it is set back from the lake on the right and somewhat of a climb. It was this shrine which originally bore the name of Chuzen-ji, but it became so important that the name was applied to the town too, and then even to the lake. Now, since the separation of Buddhism and Shintoism in 1868, the shrine has borne a different name, but still it is frequently referred to as Chuzen-ji and, of course, both town and lake now have that name officially. A track continues from here right to the top of Mt. Nantai, where the third part of the shrine is located, supposedly on the site where the priest Shodo originally established his temple twelve centuries ago. However, this walk will take about three hours each way, for **Mt. Nantai** is 2,484 metres in height, and can be attempted only in good weather.

Alternatively, there are boat rides on Lake Chuzenji in the summer months. A circuit of the lake takes 55 minutes and costs ¥900. A ferry to Shobugahama takes 20 minutes and costs ¥450. From there, one could walk back to Chuzenji town in about one hour and would pass the path to Futara-san Shrine on the way.

Further round the lake is **Tachiki Kannon Temple**, actually now known properly as Chuzen-ji, but more commonly called by the former name. It was originally part of the Futara-san Shrine, until the separation of Buddhism and Shintoism, and contains a 5½ metre tall statue of Kannon which is said to have been carved, at least in part, by the priest Shodo himself from a living tree. This temple is not actually the original one, which was destroyed in the floods of 1902, but a reconstruction. The Kannon statue, however, is the original. The current site of the temple is a good spot for viewing the lake. Admission costs another ¥300.

***Transportation and Tickets***

Although both JR and the Tobu Private Railway run trains to Nikko, the more convenient service is with Tobu. It is also considerably cheaper. Departures are from the Matsuya Department Store in the Asakusa area of Tokyo (see map on page 76) and there are five types of train. From fastest to slowest these are *tokkyu*, *kyuko*, *kaisoku*, *junkyu* and *futsu*. The basic fare is ¥1,270, but there are also supplements for the *tokkyu* and *kyuko* trains amounting to a further ¥1,260 for the *tokkyu* or ¥1,030 for the *kyuko*. There are *tokkyu* departures from Asakusa directly for Nikko at 7:20, 8:00, 8:20, 8:40 (Saturdays and holidays only), 9:00, 9:20 (peak season only), 10:00 and 20:10, with the journey taking 1 hour 40 minutes. At other times, *tokkyu* or *kyuko* trains run once or twice every hour, but it is necessary to change trains at Shimo Imaichi. These express trains are both comfortable and fast.

Of the remaining types of trains, only two *junkyu* trains run all the way from Asakusa to Nikko and they are not at useful times. No *futsu* makes the complete journey. That leaves the *kaisoku*, which is the train for our impoverished traveller. It costs only the base fare, with no supplement, and still takes only just over two hours. Direct departures from Asakusa are at 6:20, 7:10, 8:10, 9:10, 10:20, 11:18, 12:18, 15:20 and 16:20. However, if you wish to make a one day trip, you should not consider taking any train later than the 8:10. Get to Asakusa about 20 to 30 minutes prior to the departure time to ensure a reasonable seat, for it is pleasant countryside and you should try to enjoy the journey. Be careful, because in most cases the train divides at Shimo Imaichi and only one section goes on to Nikko. The last direct train back is at 18:31 from Nikko, but there is also a departure at 19:33 which involves a change at Shimo Imaichi. As a last resort, at 20:47 there is a *futsu* which, with changes at Shimo Imaichi and Shin Tochigi, gets you back to Asakusa at 23:26.

If you prefer to travel by JR, perhaps because you have time left on a Japan Rail Pass, the fastest way is to take the *shinkansen* to Utsunomiya, where you change to the JR Nikko Line. The journey from Tokyo to Utsunomiya takes between 52 minutes and one hour by the Tohoku *shinkansen* . Be careful, as there are a few trains which do not stop at Utsunomiya. Trains from Utsunomiya to Nikko run about every hour and take approximately 45 minutes. If you arrange a good connexion, therefore, you will reach Nikko from Tokyo in about two hours. However, if you have to buy a ticket for this journey, it will cost ¥4,830 with unreserved seating or ¥500 more for a reserved seat as far as Utsunomiya.

Alternatively, you can travel by ordinary train. This will cost ¥2,470 each way and take approximately three hours, with a change at Utsunomiya. In the Tokyo area, trains to Utsunomiya depart frequently from Ueno and about once an hour from Ikebukuro. Of course, if you use a Blue Spring ticket (see page 19), the return journey can be done for ¥2,260 with JR, as long as it is a day trip.

In summer and autumn, there is one JR *tokkyu* (limited express) train from Yokohama, Shinjuku and Ikebukuro directly to Nikko on Saturdays and Sundays only. At the time of writing, this train leaves Yokohama (platform 10) at 9:26, Shinjuku (platform 3) at 10:08 and Ikebukuro at 10:13 on Saturdays, reaching Nikko at 12:17. On Sundays, it leaves Yokohama (platform 10) at 6:57, Shinjuku (platform 4) at 7:35 and Ikebukuro at 7:41, reaching Nikko at 9:56. It departs from Nikko at 17:14 on both Saturdays and Sundays, reaching Ikebukuro at 19:47 and Shinjuku at 19:53. It does not go on to Yokohama. However, these timings change from year to year and should be checked. This train would cost ¥4,120 each way for an unreserved seat. In October and early November, JR has started to use a special 'Super View' train for this run now, to give a good view of the autumn leaves.

In the Nikko area, one can purchase at the Tobu station a bus ticket from the station to Chuzenji, or some other destinations, which permits one to stop at will *en route*. The price is the ordinary bus fare (¥1,100 each way to Chuzenji), but by stopping on the way one would usually pay more, so it does offer a small saving provided that one is not planning to walk any part of the route. It is also convenient, of course.

As mentioned above, there are two types of somewhat discounted entrance ticket for Nikko's main attractions. One ticket offers admission to Toshogu and Rinno-ji for ¥900. The other provides entry into the three areas of Toshogu – the Roaring Dragon, the shrine itself and the tomb – for ¥1,250. The former ticket is recommended. Of course, one can also buy tickets for individual attractions if one prefers, but for most visitors that will be less cost-effective.

## MT. FUJI (富士山 – 'Affluent Warrior Mountain')

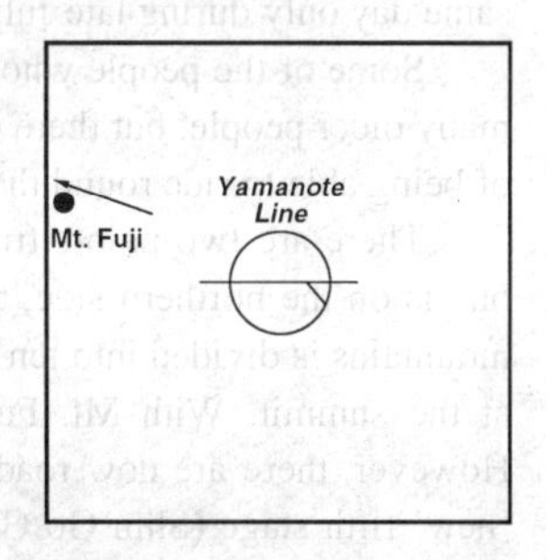


**Derivation of Name:** *Corruption of Ainu word 'pushi', meaning 'fire spirit' (doubtful).*

Mt. Fuji is 3,776 metres high and can be seen from a distance of 150 kilometres on a fine day, which is to say from Tokyo and considerably beyond. This dormant volcano, which last erupted in 1707, and covered Tokyo with more than 10 centimetres of ash, is considered one of the world's most perfectly shaped mountains. Every visitor wants to see it and many want to climb it.

If the first desire will satisfy you, in reasonable weather you will be able to get quite a good view from the JR Tokaido Line as you travel between Tokyo and Kyoto, for example, or even just between Tokyo and Shizuoka. The *shinkansen* lies a little closer to the mountain than the ordinary line, but, of course, progress is much more sedate on the ordinary train, so you get more time to appreciate the beauty. If you want to get closer, you may wish to visit the area known as the Fuji Go-ko ('Fuji Five Lakes') to the north of the mountain. However, be warned that, although you are nearer, you will not necessarily get a better view, as the mountain tends to be 'shy', as a local resident explained it to the author.

If you actually want to climb the mountain, though, you should visit Japan in July or August, for those two months alone comprise the official climbing season. Before July there will probably still be snow on the peak, but climbing is generally possible into September, in fact, before the weather deteriorates too much. The climb is usually attempted from a point about half-way up, where the road ends, and can take up to about eight hours up and five hours down, although the superbly fit may manage to do it in considerably less. The weather is very changeable, so one needs to be prepared for rain and cold, particularly if climbing after dark. Although it is possible to buy most necessities on the mountain, at inflated prices, of course, to take a good supply of water would be wise.

The 'proper' way to do the climb is to start in the afternoon and spend the night in one of the huts near the top. It will be nice and cozy there, with very many other climbers sharing the sardine can with you, and not even cheap, at perhaps ¥4,000 for each sardine. Moreover you will be awakened fairly early in the morning (say 3:00 or 3:30!) as everybody else gets up to climb the last section of the mountain to see the sunrise from the top. At this unfriendly hour, indeed, there will be a traffic jam with the zig-zag track to the top clogged with dawn-seekers, so that, if you are not careful, you will be too late anyway. And even if you do get there on time, it is quite probable that weather conditions will prevent you from seeing the actual sunrise.

Of course, you do not have to follow the official procedure. If you start climbing in the evening, you should be able to reach the summit without the need for overnight accommodation, although it is not so safe to be climbing at night. Alternatively, if you start early in the morning, you should be able to get up and down in a single strenuous day, although foregoing the thrill of sunrise at the summit. You will also be going in the opposite direction to the masses by adopting such a plan. On the way down, speed is increased if one slides on the volcanic ash, but one needs some protection from cinder burns. Note, however, that the bus schedule permits one sufficient time to climb the mountain and return by bus the same day only during late July and August.

Some of the people whom you will see climbing will surprise you. Not only will there be many older people, but there will also be those with bicycles on their backs, for the excitement of being able to ride round the crater at the top.

There are two points from which to attempt the ascent of the mountain. The traditional one is on the northern side, the new one on the southern. By Japanese custom, the ascent of mountains is divided into ten stages and the stages are numbered from one near the base to ten at the summit. With Mt. Fuji, the walk used to begin at Kawaguchi-ko or Fuji Yoshida. However, there are now roads to the fifth stage (Go Gome – 五合目) on the north and the 'new' fifth stage (Shin Go Gome – 新五合目) on the south. The road to the northern route runs from Kawaguchi-ko, that to the southern route from Gotenba, Mishima or Fujinomiya.

Obviously, if you intend to climb Mt. Fuji, your visit there will not be a day trip. However, if you decide just to visit the five lakes, that can be done in a day. If you have more time, though, there is plenty to see and there are three youth hostels in the area and another at Gotenba, for those who require accommodation.

**The five lakes**, from east to west, which is how they would be approached from Tokyo, are Yamanaka-ko, Kawaguchi-ko, Sai-ko, Shoji-ko and Motosu-ko. The last three are at 902 metres above sea level, but Yamanaka-ko is at 982 metres and Kawaguchi-ko at 833 metres. They vary in depth from the 21 metres of Kawaguchi-ko to the 138 metres of Motosu-ko. They also vary considerably in size and character. Yamanaka-ko is the biggest and most developed, with guest houses all along its shore and recreational facilities surrounding and on the lake. It is still beautiful, but hardly peaceful. Kawaguchi-ko is also developed, but this time many of the attractions are not directly connected with the lake. Amongst the Japanese, this town is best known for its amusement park, called 'Fuji-kyu Highlands'. This is also the transportation hub for the area. The Fuji Kyuko Private Railway ends at Kawaguchi-ko station and it is the terminus for many of the bus routes, including that to Go Gome, for climbing Mt. Fuji.

The remaining three lakes are more peaceful. There is a youth hostel on the shore of Sai-ko. Buses to Motosu-ko and Fujinomiya do not call, but there is a regular service from Kawaguchi-ko station which does come here. Shoji-ko is often cited as the most beautiful of the five lakes and it is also the smallest. Buses to Motosu-ko stop there.

In the area there are also many caves. These are lava tube caves, formed by the cooling of molten lava with air trapped inside. The most visited are Narusawa Hyoketsu (鳴沢氷穴), the **'Ice Cave'**, and Fugaku Fuketsu (富岳風穴), the **'Wind Cave'**, not far apart along the main road in the vicinity of Sai-ko. Buses to Motosu-ko and Fujinomiya will stop at the caves and one can walk between the two in about 25 minutes. Of 263 known lava tube caves over 30 metres in length in the world, 81 are in Japan and, of those, 75 are in the vicinity of Mt. Fuji.

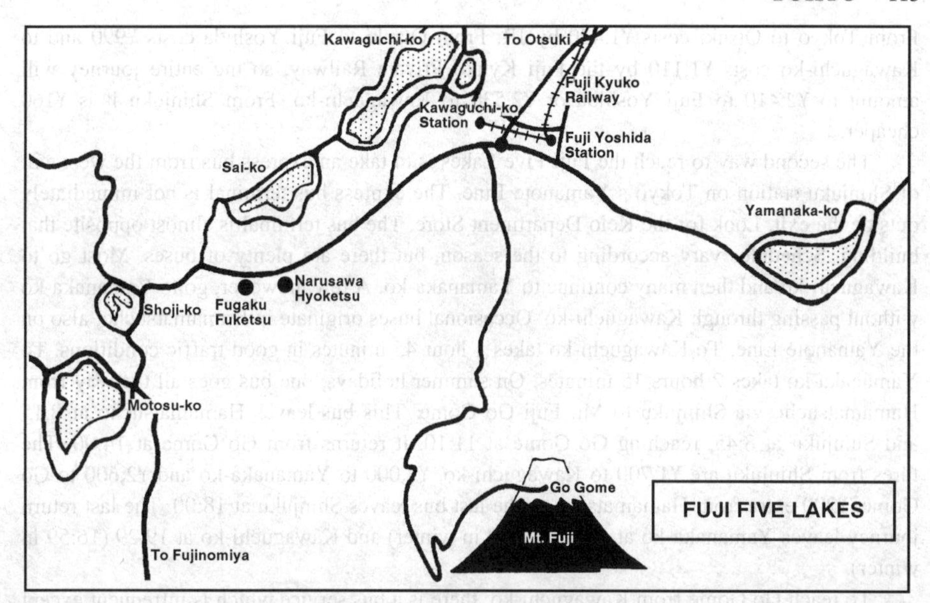


The most impressive cave of this type, however, is on Cheju Island in South Korea, for those who are going there later.

There are several **waterfalls**, the most popular being Shira Ito no Taki, 'White Thread Falls', which can be reached from Kawaguchi-ko station in 33 minutes by bus, at a cost of ¥570 each way.

There is a **lookout** near Kawaguchi-ko station from which a good view of Mt. Fuji can be obtained, weather permitting. A ropeway runs up, at a cost of ¥340 for a 3 minute ride.

There are also boat cruises on Kawaguchi-ko. A 30 minute ride can be had for the exorbitant price of ¥900.

Another possibility is hiking. A hiking course runs through the entire area, visiting all of the five lakes. The complete journey would require about three days.

***Transportation and Tickets***

There are two simple ways to reach the Fuji Five Lakes. The first is to take the JR Chuo Line to Otsuki and change to the Fuji Kyuko Private Railway, which runs to Fuji Yoshida and on to Kawaguchi-ko. Most express trains on the Chuo Line run from Shinjuku, but, for many of the ordinary services, it is necessary to take a suburban Chuo Line train (orange) from Tokyo or Shinjuku as far as Tachikawa or Takao and then change to a medium-distance train. However, a few of these suburban services are extended all the way to Otsuki. There are also three trains every day which run through from the JR Chuo Line onto the Fuji Kyuko Private Railway without any change of train. The first starts from Takao at 7:48 and reaches Kawaguchi-ko at 9:30. The other two run all the way from Tokyo, starting at 18:05 and 19:10 and arriving at 21:00 and 21:59. Return trains leave Kawaguchi-ko at 5:53 and 6:23 for Tokyo, arriving at 8:46 and 9:18, and at 10:50 for Tachikawa, a little further into Tokyo than Takao, arriving at 12:40. On holidays there are some additional direct trains, including, at peak periods, one which follows an unusual route originating in Omiya, to the north of the Tokyo.

From Tokyo to Otsuki costs ¥1,420 by JR. From Otsuki to Fuji Yoshida costs ¥990 and to Kawaguchi-ko costs ¥1,110 by the Fuji Kyuko Private Railway, so the entire journey will amount to ¥2,410 to Fuji Yoshida or ¥2,530 to Kawaguchi-ko. From Shinjuku it is ¥160 cheaper.

The second way to reach the Fuji Five Lakes is to take an express bus from the west exit of Shinjuku station on Tokyo's Yamanote Line. The express bus terminal is not immediately outside the exit. Look for the Keio Department Store. The bus terminal is almost opposite that building. Schedules vary according to the season, but there are plenty of buses. Most go to Kawaguchi-ko and then many continue to Yamanaka-ko. A few, however, go to Yamanaka-ko without passing through Kawaguchi-ko. Occasional buses originate in Hamamatsucho, also on the Yamanote Line. To Kawaguchi-ko takes 1 hour 45 minutes in good traffic conditions. To Yamanaka-ko takes 2 hours 15 minutes. On summer holidays, one bus goes all the way from Hamamatsucho via Shinjuku to Mt. Fuji Go Gome. This bus leaves Hamamatsucho at 8:15 and Shinjuku at 8:45, reaching Go Gome at 11:10. It returns from Go Gome at 14:00. The fares from Shinjuku are ¥1,700 to Kawaguchi-ko, ¥2,000 to Yamanaka-ko and ¥2,600 to Go Gome. ¥200 extra from Hamamatsucho. The last bus leaves Shinjuku at 18:00. The last return journey leaves Yamanaka-ko at 19:00 (16:30 in winter) and Kawaguchi-ko at 19:29 (16:59 in winter).

To reach Go Gome from Kawaguchi-ko, there is a bus service which is infrequent except in mid-summer. Three buses per day (four at weekends) operate from April until October. In November, there are two buses at weekends only. However, in late July and August there are as many as twelve journeys per day. In this season, the first bus leaves Kawaguchi-ko at 8:20 (7:20 on holidays) and the last departs at 21:05. The first return journey, from Go Gome, is at 9:25 (8:30 on holidays) and the last is at 20:35. The journey is supposed to take 55 minutes up and 50 minutes down, but is very much dependent upon traffic conditions. The fare is very high at ¥1,610 each way.

To reach Shin Go Gome, on the south side of Mt. Fuji, there is a bus service from Gotenba. Usually there are two buses per day, but in July and August the service is augmented to a maximum of eleven journeys. Note, however, that buses go to two slightly different destinations, although both are at approximately the same altitude. In mid-summer, the first bus from Gotenba is at 7:10 and the last at 16:45. The first return trip is at 9:20 and the last at 19:05. The journey takes 45 or 70 minutes, depending on the destination of the bus, and costs ¥1,020 or ¥1,420. In July and August only there are also three buses per day (more on holidays) from Shin Fuji, a *shinkansen* station, via Fujinomiya to Shin Go Gome. These buses use yet another slightly different destination on the mountain. Journey time is just over two hours and cost ¥2,270. Finally, there is a mid-summer only service of four buses per day from another *shinkansen* station, Mishima, to Shin Go Gome. The fare is ¥2,260 and again the journey takes just over two hours.

For travel around the Five Lakes area, the Fuji Kyuko Bus Company offers a selection of three-day tickets, one of which may be worth purchasing if you are intending to stay for that long. Note, however, that none of these tickets includes the buses to Go Gome or to Gotenba. The widest area is covered by the *Fuji Isshyu Free Pass*, which allows unlimited travel between Yamanaka-ko and Fujinomiya or Mishima. It costs ¥3,800. This ticket probably represents the best value available.

The easiest way to reach Gotenba from the Tokyo area is to take one of the four daily *tokkyu* trains named *Asagiri* which operate from Shinjuku along the Odakyu Private Railway as far as Matsuda, where they switch to the JR Gotenba Line. These trains run to Gotenba and then on to Numazu. However, the fare to Gotenba is quite high at ¥2,420. If you take this express train only to Matsuda and then change to an ordinary train, the cost will be reduced to ¥1,620, but a wait at Matsuda will be involved. Cheaper still is to take a *kyuko* train on the Odakyu Line to Shin Matsuda and change to JR Matsuda (3 minutes walk) for the ordinary train to Gotenba. This costs ¥1,120. Taking JR all the way, starting from Tokyo by the JR Tokaido Line and changing at Kozu to the Gotenba Line, costs ¥1,850. There are also express buses, but most go only to a stop on the expressway, not to the town itself. However, the expressway stop is within walking distance of the youth hostel. Buses are operated both by JR (from Tokyo station) and by Odakyu (from Shinjuku station west exit) and the fare by either operator is ¥1,500. By *Asagiri*, the journey takes about 1 hour 40 minutes. The express bus takes a similar time. Other methods would take about an hour longer if good connexions were planned, but note that trains run only about hourly on the Gotenba Line.

Mishima and Shin Fuji are both on the Tokaido *shinkansen* route, but notice that usually only *Kodama* trains stop, although there are just a few *Hikari* trains which stop at Mishima. The journey to Mishima takes 60 to 70 minutes from Tokyo. To Shin Fuji it takes about 80 minutes. Mishima is also a stop on the conventional JR Tokaido Line, but Shin Fuji is not.

## HAKONE (箱根 – 'Box Root')

**Derivation of Name:** *Shape of surrounding mountains resembled a box (very doubtful).*

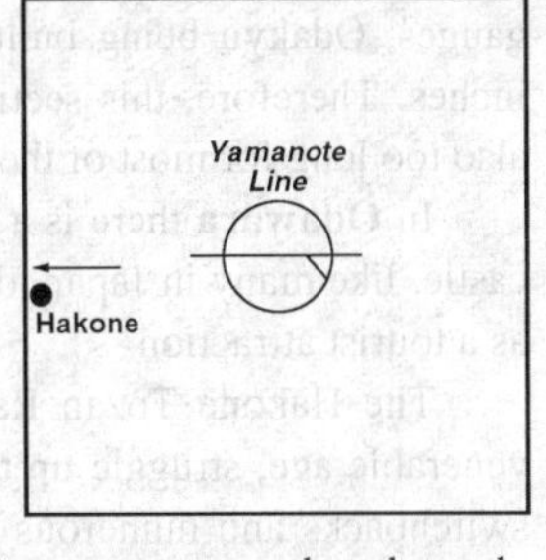


Hakone is a hot springs area located about two hours west of Tokyo by train. Because it is in the hills, it is cool even in summer and it also commands some beautiful views of Mt. Fuji if the weather is clear, which is by no means always.

Japanese love spas and this is one of the closest spa resort areas to Tokyo, so it is very popular and crowded at most times of the year. Accommodation will always be a problem here, and more so now that the only youth hostel in the area closed recently. The closest hostel now is in Gotenba, to the north.

It is not too difficult to have a look at Hakone in a single day, but one of the temptations to stay is that the Odakyu Private Railway Company offers two special tickets, one valid for two days and one for three, which include a variety of transport in the area – trains, buses, boats, a funicular railway and a ropeway. They also give discounts on the admission fees to almost all attractions in Hakone. Just show your pass conspicuously when paying and a magical reduction will usually be made. These tickets are good value, so the following itinerary is designed to fit with the use of one of them. Even for a day visit, they are economical, but since they are available for two or three days, why not take advantage of the extra time available?

The 'Hakone Free Pass' is a three-day ticket which includes the return journey from the point of origin (most people choose Shinjuku) to Odawara by Odakyu Private Railway and then unlimited use of the Hakone Tozan Private Railway, the Hakone Tozan Funicular Railway, the Hakone Ropeway, Hakone Tozan buses in an area bounded by Gotenba, Numazu, Atami and Odawara, the Odakyu express bus between Togendai and Gotenba and a sightseeing boat on Lake Ashi. It costs ¥5,400 from Shinjuku or ¥4,050 from Odawara.

The 'Hakone Weekday Pass' is a two-day ticket, available to start on any Monday to Thursday, offering the same as the above, except that the bus area is limited to that bounded by Sengoku, Hakone-machi and Odawara. It costs ¥4,600 from Shinjuku or ¥3,340 from Odawara. This ticket is not available during popular holiday periods.

If, by any chance, you choose not to use one of the above tickets, you can still find discount coupons for main attractions available on the platform of the Hakone Tozan Private Railway at Odawara station.

It is also possible to tour this area and then move on to Mt. Fuji via Gotenba. There are buses from Gotenba to the Fuji Five Lakes area or to Shin Go Gome from which point the mountain can be climbed.

For those with limited time, a circuit of the Hakone area can be performed in a single day, provided that one leaves Tokyo early in the morning. From Shinjuku, take the Odakyu Private Railway, which offers a remarkably cheap service, by Japanese standards. There are four types of train — in ascending order of speed *futsu*, *junkyu*, *kyuko* and *tokkyu*. Only the *tokkyu* has a supplementary charge. *Futsu* and *junkyu* trains are rather slow, because there is so much traffic on the Odakyu Railway, so, in practice, the choice lies between a *kyuko* and a *tokkyu*. Although Odawara is the end of the Odakyu Line, some trains, both *tokkyu* and *kyuko*, continue onto the Hakone Tozan Private Railway as far as Hakone Yumoto, one of the main spa resort towns. This is an interesting extension, because the two railways use different gauges, Odakyu being built to 3 feet 6 inches and Hakone Tozan to a standard 4 feet 8½ inches. Therefore, this section of the line has had to be dual-gauged. The Odakyu trains are also too long for most of the carriages to be adjacent to the platforms at the small stations.

In **Odawara** there is a castle and the city was the scene of a battle in 1590. However, the castle, like many in Japan, dates mainly from the antiquity of 1960, having been reconstructed as a tourist attraction.

The Hakone Tozan Railway is much more exciting. Its little trains, many of them of venerable age, struggle up to Gora, a distance of 15 kilometres, at a cost of ¥570, with three switchbacks and numerous tunnels *en route*, for this is a steep climb after Hakone Yumoto, with a maximum gradient of 8%, which seems impossibly steep when you are on the train. The main towns on the way are Hakone Yumoto and Miyanoshita, the latter offering the attraction of the colonial-style **Fujiya Hotel**, where you may not be able to afford to stay, but could have morning tea, if you felt so inclined. Actually, at the time of writing, the Fujiya Hotel is offering, to visitors from overseas only, a twin room for US$133, except on Saturday nights, which is not so expensive as to be beyond the range of all readers. Even for those for whom it is rather costly, it might be an enjoyable extravagance, for this is exactly the type of hotel which tends to appeal to western taste, whereas Japanese would usually prefer modern super-comfort.

Just before the end of the railway is a station called **Chokoku-no-mori**, where there is an outdoor exhibition of sculptures. Unfortunately, the admission charge is ¥1,500.

From Gora, a funicular railway runs up to So-unzan. The ride of 1.2 kilometres takes 10 minutes and costs ¥400. Next is a ropeway which goes to Owakudani and on via Ubako to Togendai. The distance is 4 kilometres, which takes 26 minutes at a cost of ¥1,300 if you go all the way. However, you will probably want to get off at **Owakudani** ('Big Gushing Valley') on the way. This is one of the few places in Hakone where volcanic activity is conspicuous. On the approach, you will see a valley which looks like a sulphur factory,

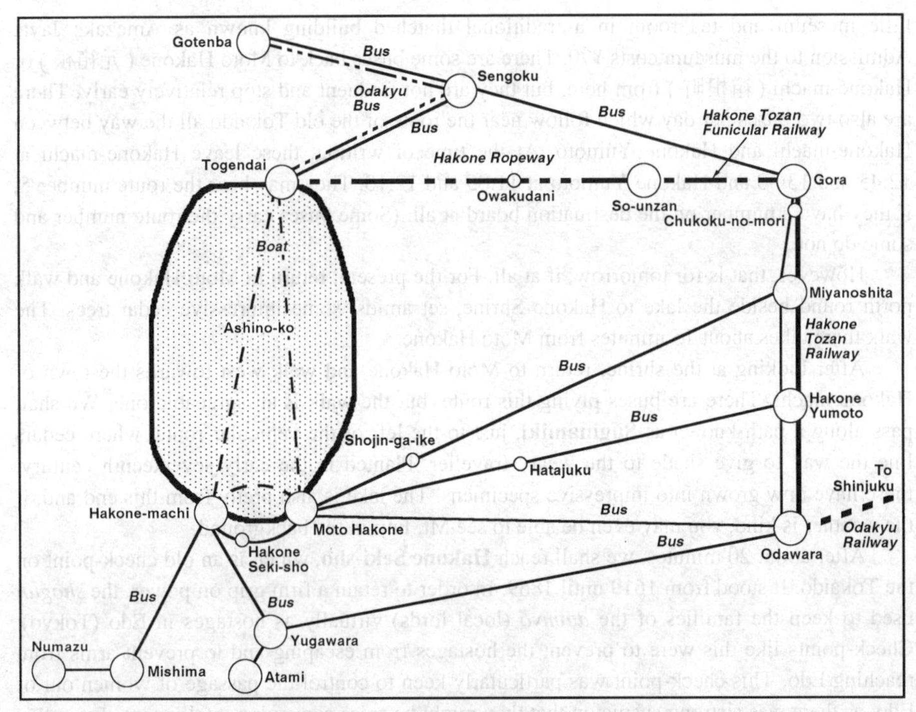


**DIAGRAM OF MAIN SERVICES AVAILABLE WITH 'HAKONE FREE PASS'**

although most of the holes drilled are to release gases and avoid an explosion. As you wander around you will find steam spurting from the rocks, bubbling hot mud and, of course, natural hot water which is piped away to various hotels, some quite distant from this spot. If you are lucky, you will have a view of Mt. Fuji from here. There is a museum near the ropeway station. Admission costs ¥400.

Continuing to Togendai, without alighting at Ubako, which has no special attractions, you will reach the shores of **Ashino-ko** (Lake Ashi). There is a small town here, with bus services available, but it is more interesting to continue by boat. The boat leaves every 30 to 40 minutes for Hakone-machi and Moto Hakone. You will be surprised by its appearance, but, after all, Hakone is a tourist area. The journey takes 30 minutes to Hakone-machi and 40 minutes to Moto Hakone and costs ¥950 to either town. To get our money's worth, let us go to Moto Hakone, the second stop.

After disembarking from the boat, cross the Hakone Tozan bus station and take the road straight ahead. Walk a short distance up the hill and you will find, on your left, the entrance to a piece of the **old Tokaido** trunk road, which connected Tokyo with Kyoto. Cross the overhead bridge and you will come to a section on a steep hill. It has been paved with stones and so has survived the intervening century since it was last in regular use. You can walk along the old Tokaido all the way to Hakone Yumoto, a distance of 9 kilometres, which will take about three hours. If you are staying overnight, why not do this tomorrow? If that seems too far, walk half way, to Hatajuku, from where there are plenty of buses to Hakone Yumoto (箱根湯本). If even that seems too far, if you just walk for about 30 minutes, you will reach a little museum and tea room in a traditional thatched building known as Amezake Jaya. Admission to the museum costs ¥70. There are some buses back to Moto Hakone (元箱根) or Hakone-machi (箱根町) from here, but they are not frequent and stop relatively early. There are also two buses per day which follow near the route of the old Tokaido all the way between Hakone-machi and Hakone Yumoto. At the time of writing, these leave Hakone-machi at 12:45 and 13:50 and Hakone Yumoto at 11:05 and 12:10. They may bear the route number 5, if they have a number on the destination board at all. (Some buses carry the route number and some do not.)

However, that is for tomorrow, if at all. For the present, return to Moto Hakone and walk north round beside the lake to Hakone Shrine, set amidst some impressive cedar trees. The walk there takes about 15 minutes from Moto Hakone.

After looking at the shrine, return to Moto Hakone and walk west towards the town of Hakone-machi. There are buses plying this route, but the walk is an agreeable one. We shall pass along a path known as **Suginamiki**, just to the left of the vehicular route, where cedars line the way to give shade to the weary traveller. Planted in the early seventeenth century, these have now grown into impressive specimens. The lake is also pretty from this end and, if the weather is kind, you may even be able to see Mt. Fuji in the background.

After about 20 minutes, we shall reach **Hakone Seki-sho**, which is an old check-point on the Tokaido. It stood from 1619 until 1869. In order to retain a firm grip on power, the *shogun* used to keep the families of the *daimyo* (local lords) virtually as hostages in Edo (Tokyo). Check-points like this were to prevent the hostages from escaping and to prevent arms from reaching Edo. This check-point was particularly keen to control the passage of women out of Edo, as there was a strong suspicion that they might be spies conveying intelligence. From this direction we shall come first to a small museum on the right of the road just after the end of the avenue of cedars. In English, it is curiously signposted as the 'Museum of Material', but if you are expecting to find cloth inside, you will be disappointed. Your ¥200 admission fee (¥150 if you have an 'Hakone Free Pass' or 'Hakone Weekday Pass') includes entry to Hakone Seki-sho, which you will find if you continue walking a short distance towards Hakone-machi. The check-point which is there now is a modern re-creation, complete with all the officials.

For our next stop, we need to take a bus. You can take it from the bus stop on the main road near Hakone Seki-sho, or you can continue your walk for 5 minutes more to Hakone-machi, where you will find the bus station outside the boat terminal. You need a bus going to Odawara (小田原) via Miyanoshita (宮ノ下). Be careful, as there are other routes to Odawara too. Remember that, if you are using an 'Hakone Free Pass', you can use only Hakone Tozan buses (blue and white), not Izu Hakone buses. The Hakone Tozan buses run approximately every 20 minutes and may well bear the route number 1. Your destination is **Shojin-ga-ike** (精進ヶ池), a small lake which will appear after about 7 minutes on the left side. The bus follows the road which you have just walked from Moto Hakone and then continues up the hill.

Get off at the lake and just beyond it there is a path to the left leading to some stone **Buddha images** about seven centuries old. On the other side of the road is a carving of **Jizo**, who is the Japanese St. Christopher, amongst other functions, patron saint of travellers. You are now on one of the most difficult sections of the old Tokaido. Until the time of the Meiji Restoration (1868), ordinary citizens could not own horses and so travelled only on foot. Jizo is here to guard them on their difficult and dangerous journey, although one cannot help thinking, as the traffic whizzes past, that he is needed more today than he ever was then.

If this is just a one day trip, you need to take another bus on the same route to Odawara or Hakone Yumoto, from either of which trains return to Shinjuku. To Hakone Yumoto (箱根湯本) takes 35 minutes and costs ¥700. To Odawara (小田原) takes 55 minutes and costs ¥950.

However, if you decide to spend the night at the youth hostel in Gotenba, you should take the bus back to Hakone-machi or Moto Hakone (any Hakone Tozan bus) and then take the boat back to Togendai. Next take the bus for Gotenba (御殿場) to Ni-no Oka (二の岡), which takes 45 minutes and costs ¥860. Be careful! The last bus is at 16:25, to catch which you must be on the boat which leaves Hakone-machi at 15:20 or 15:30 (according to the season) and Moto Hakone at 15:30 or 15:40. If you should have the misfortune to miss that bus, there is an Odakyu bus at 17:30 going to Shinjuku (新宿) in Tokyo and that will stop at Tomei Gotenba (東名御殿場), at the entrance to the expressway, a stop which is just a little further from the hostel. You are allowed to use this bus with an 'Hakone Free Pass'. There are also two more buses to Gotenba from Sengoku (仙石), to reach which there is a frequent bus service from Togendai, destination Odawara (小田原), sometimes bearing the route number 2. The last bus from Sengoku to Gotenba is at 18:10.

If you find yourself short of time, though, a faster route to Gotenba from Lake Shojin is to take the bus for Odawara as far as Miyanoshita and then change to a bus for Togendai (桃源台), route number 2, and alight at Sengoku (仙石). From Lake Shojin to Miyanoshita takes only 20 minutes and from there to Sengoku takes 15 minutes. From Sengoku to Gotenba is a journey of 30 minutes. Remember that, if you are using the 'Hakone Weekday Pass', the limit of your area is Sengoku, from where it costs ¥630 to Gotenba.

To locate the Gotenba Youth Hostel, consult the map in our Youth Hostels section, but be warned that some of the roads shown are not very major, while the path indicated by a dashed line is quite small and really needs the use of a torch after dark. From Ni-no Oka bus stop, go back a few metres to the corner with traffic signals and turn left. There are signs to the hostel from here, but, if you want to take the short cut, turn right at the first road and follow signs for the Y.M.C.A., crossing one major road on the way. After reaching the gate of the Y.M.C.A., follow the road left (lake on your left), then right and you will come to a T junction with a rustic shrine ahead. Walk up to the shrine and pass to the left of it along a very small path. The first building that you come to is the youth hostel. From the door there is a beautiful view of the sunset behind Mt. Fuji, if you arrive at the right time.

There is also a youth hostel in Ito. An Hakone Tozan bus runs from Moto Hakone, via Hakone-machi, to Atami, from where it is five stations (¥310) by JR to Ito. This bus route is included on the 'Hakone Free Pass', but not on the 'Hakone Weekday Pass'. The last bus leaves Moto Hakone at 16:50 and Hakone-machi at 16:55. The first half of this bus ride too is most impressive, with slightly more magnificent views to be had from the left of the bus.

Other attractions in the Hakone area include many hiking courses and even a cycling course, as well as several more museums and gardens and, of course, many of the hot spring resorts that the Japanese love. There are also ropeways or funicular railways to two viewpoints at Komagatake and Ju-koku Toge, but they are not included on the 'Hakone Free Pass', nor is the bus route to the latter, so visiting these places would be quite expensive. Anyway, this schedule is sufficient to give a taste of the area and will most certainly be more than enough for one day, even if you are willing to leave the Tokyo area very early in the day and return very late. In any case, you should leave as early as possible, because Hakone is a popular place and it gets crowded as the day wears on.

***Transportation and Tickets***

As mentioned above, it is best to purchase one of the tickets offered by the Odakyu Private Railway which give discounted travel from Shinjuku and back and unlimited travel for two or three days within the Hakone area. Even if you go for only a day trip, you will find one of these two tickets advantageous.

If you prefer not to travel with Odakyu, the tickets are still available from Odawara and they are also available from any other Odakyu station by adding the return fare from that station to Odawara to the Odawara price (no discount, except from Shinjuku). If you take a *tokkyu* train on the Odakyu Line, you must pay the supplement in addition.

A *kyuko* from Shinjuku to Odawara takes about 90 minutes and costs ¥750 for a journey of 82 kilometres. Departures are frequent. The *tokkyu* does the journey in 75 minutes, or 90 minutes to Hakone Yumoto. The supplement is ¥800 to either destination. Even with the supplement, the service is good value, for the Odakyu *tokkyu* trains are quite comfortable. If you wish to sit in a 'special' seat, equivalent to first class and available on some trains only, there is a further supplement of ¥650.

If you prefer JR, ordinary trains run to Odawara in 90 minutes from Tokyo station. Departures are frequent. There are also *kaisoku* (rapid) trains named *Acty*, which do the journey in 75 minutes (no supplement). Then there are *tokkyu* trains, named *Odoriko* ('Dancing Girl') which take about one hour and the *shinkansen* which takes about 40 minutes, these last two only really for the consideration of Japan Rail Pass holders. Note that generally only *Kodama* trains stop on the *shinkansen*. The problem with JR is that it is expensive compared with Odakyu. The ordinary train costs ¥1,420, while the *shinkansen* costs ¥3,070 for an unreserved seat and ¥500 more for a reservation and the Dancing Girl costs ¥2,350 unreserved.

One more possibility is an express bus which runs from the west exit of Shinjuku station (bus stop no. 35) to Togendai. Departures are hourly at 10 minutes past the hour. The journey takes about 2 hours 15 minutes, traffic permitting, and costs ¥1,850. Late afternoon and evening departures travel via Gotenba station, as do early morning return journeys. All services stop at the entrance to the expressway at Gotenba, walking distance from the youth hostel. Returns are hourly from Togendai at half past each hour. One additional express bus each day runs, from April until November only, from Shinjuku to Moto Hakone via Hakone Yumoto. It leaves Shinjuku at 10:30, reaching Hakone Yumoto at 12:12 and Moto Hakone at 12:41. It leaves Moto Hakone at 15:00 and Hakone Yumoto at 15:40, reaching Shinjuku at 17:20. The one-way fare is ¥1,300 to Hakone Yumoto and ¥1,830 to Moto Hakone. All of these express buses are operated by Odakyu. The 'Hakone Free Pass' can be used on these services between Gotenba and Togendai (between Sengoku and Togendai for the 'Hakone Weekday Pass'). Also, if you have an 'Hakone Free Pass', you may travel between Shinjuku and Gotenba (from where any further travel is included on your pass) for the reduced fare of ¥830.

There is also a rival special ticket. This is called an 'Hakone Wide Free'. It includes a completely different set of transport from the 'Hakone Passes'. With this ticket, within the Hakone area you can use Izu Hakone buses (but not Hakone Tozan buses), the ropeway and funicular railway which run up to Komagatake (one from each side of the mountain), the funicular railway to Ju-koku Toge and a rival boat service on Lake Ashi. This boat goes from Kojiri, a walk of about 5 minutes from Togendai, to Hakone-machi and Moto Hakone via Hakone-en (Hakone Park), which is the starting point for the ropeway to Komagatake. Whilst these are useful services, offering some attractive extra scenery, this ticket does not include the Hakone Tozan Railway, the Hakone Tozan Funicular Railway or the Hakone Ropeway, without which a visit to the area seems somewhat incomplete, while to buy both types of pass is rather too expensive. However, if this pass appeals to you more, it costs ¥3,100 and is valid for four days. It does not include transport to or from the Tokyo area, but Odakyu offers the return journey for ¥1,500, of course. The 'Hakone Wide Free' is available from Izu Hakone bus offices or from the Japan Travel Bureau (JTB) and probably from most other major travel agents too.

Finally, there is a pass for Izu Hakone buses only within this area. This is called an 'Hakone Bus Free' and it costs ¥1,800 for four days.

## TOKYO BAY (東京湾)

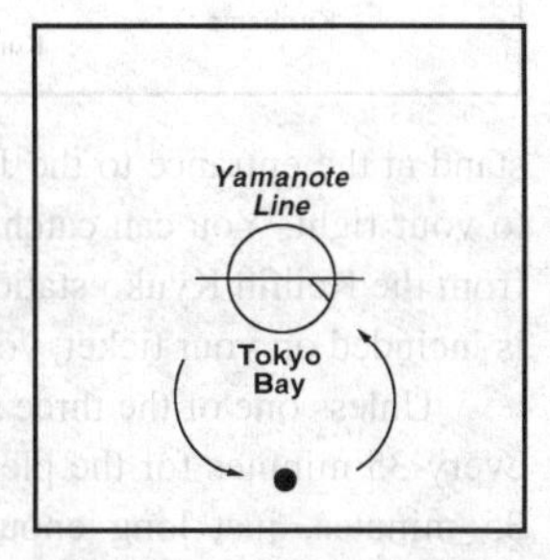


This is rather a pleasant one-day jaunt, for which JR provides a special ticket which can be purchased at any station on or within the Yamanote Line or on the route to be described. This is a tour around Tokyo Bay and, perhaps surprisingly, it will need a whole day and will cover a considerable distance. As usual, you need to start fairly early.

First buy your ticket. You want a *Tokyo Wan Free Kippu*, which costs ¥3,020. You can start at any point on the route and proceed in either direction, but let us assume that Tokyo is the point of origin and that we have decided to go in an anti-clockwise direction.

From Tokyo, take the Yokosuka Line from underground platforms 1 to 4 or the Tokaido Line from above ground platforms 7 to 9. If you want to go more slowly, you can take a Keihin Tohoku Line (blue) train from platform 6. You are free to stop wherever you wish along the route. We shall proceed, by way of Yokohama, to Ofuna. It is on all of the lines mentioned and is the terminus for the Keihin Tohoku Line. Here, on the hill on the right, is the modern **statue of Kannon**, the Goddess of Mercy. If you did not have time to look at it properly when visiting Kamakura, this is your chance. It is 10 minutes walk from the station and admission costs ¥100. The interior is hollow and houses a small temple. It is worth a short visit.

Return to Ofuna station and take the Yokosuka Line onwards. Soon you will come to **Kamakura**. You do not have time to explore this historic city now, for that needs a day in itself, but, if you have no other plan to visit, which would be a mistake, you could just go to the most famous of its attractions, the Big Buddha at Hase (see directions on page 100). However, if your duty to see Kamakura has been discharged, then you may proceed with a clear conscience to **Yokosuka**, the site of a large American naval base, and on to Kurihama, the end of the line. In some cases it is necessary to change trains at Zushi and in other cases not all of the train goes as far as Kurihama, so be alert.

If you wish, you can take a look around the town of **Kurihama** before catching a Keihin Kyuko bus to the ferry terminal, called Kurihama-ko (久里浜港 – 'Kurihama Port'). If you

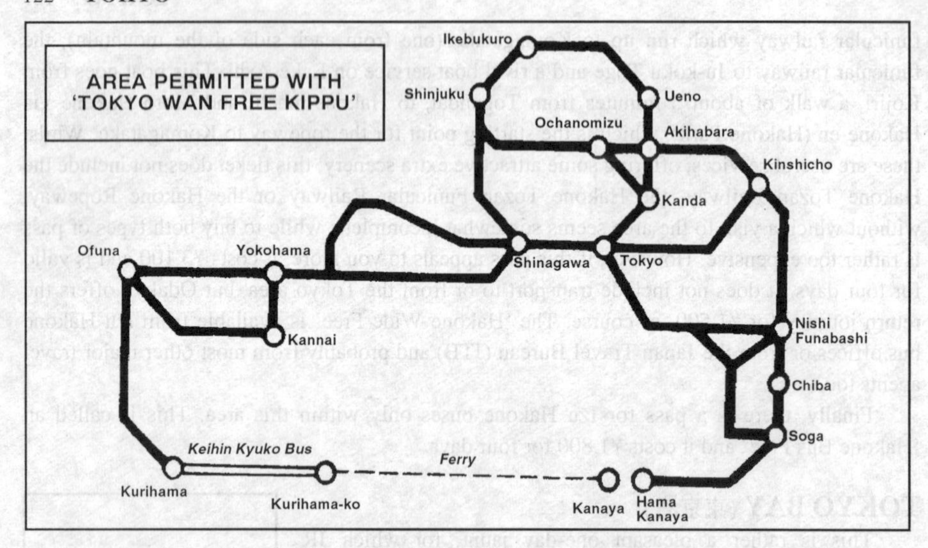


stand at the entrance to the JR station, you will see the Keihin Kyuko Private Railway station to your right. You can catch the bus from either of the two stations, but there are more buses from the Keihin Kyuko station. Actually it is within walking distance, but since the bus service is included on your ticket, you might as well use it.

Unless one of the three ships plying this route is away for its annual refit, the ferries leave every 35 minutes for the pleasant crossing from Kurihama to Kanaya. The journey also takes 35 minutes, just long enough to have lunch outside on the upper deck. You could buy something for lunch in Kurihama, although food is available on the ferry too.

From the small port of **Kanaya** to the station of Hama Kanaya is a few minutes walk. There is also a ropeway here – **Nokogiriyama Ropeway**. Look up and to your right. If you wish to ascend, there is a good view across the bay, if it is not too misty. The single fare is ¥500 and the return ¥900. However, show your *Tokyo Wan Free Kippu* and you will get a 10% discount. It is possible to ride up and walk down.

Trains run irregularly, but on average about every 45 minutes, from Hama Kanaya. They go as far as Chiba, from where there is a choice of routes. You can return to Tokyo by the Sobu Line by changing at Chiba, but it is recommended that you change instead at Soga, two stations before Chiba, and take the much more picturesque Keiyo Line which was completed in March 1990 and which runs along the waterfront. The journey from Hama Kanaya to Soga will take approximately 75 minutes. From Soga to Tokyo takes 45 minutes to one hour.

The Keiyo Line has *kaisoku* (rapid) trains as well as those which stop at every station. You can take either type. If it is still daylight, you may wish to stop at Maihama and gaze at all the cloud-capped towers and gorgeous palaces which comprise **Tokyo Disneyland**. The next station is **Kasai Rinkai Koen**, with its seafront park and aquarium. A little while later, the line goes underground, where it remains until reaching its remote corner of Tokyo station.

So we end where we began. Remember though that you can still use your ticket to go anywhere else you wish on or within the Yamanote Line in Tokyo, or, indeed, anywhere at all on today's route. By showing your *Tokyo Wan Free Kippu*, you can also have a discount on a sightseeing cruise in Yokohama. Departures are from Yamashita Park.

# TOHOKU (東北)
## ('North-East')

The Japanese refer to the part of Honshu, the main island of Japan, which lies north of the Tokyo area as Tohoku – the north-east, or, to be absolutely accurate to the Japanese, the east-north. This area is comparatively little frequented by visitors from overseas, perhaps with the exception of Matsushima. However, it is a very attractive area, in fact, with some impressive mountain and coastal scenery, as well as the deepest lake in Japan (Tazawa-ko) and the lake which claims to be the most beautiful (Towada-ko). It also has friendly, hospitable people and is one of the author's favourite areas, perhaps because it is not over-touristed.

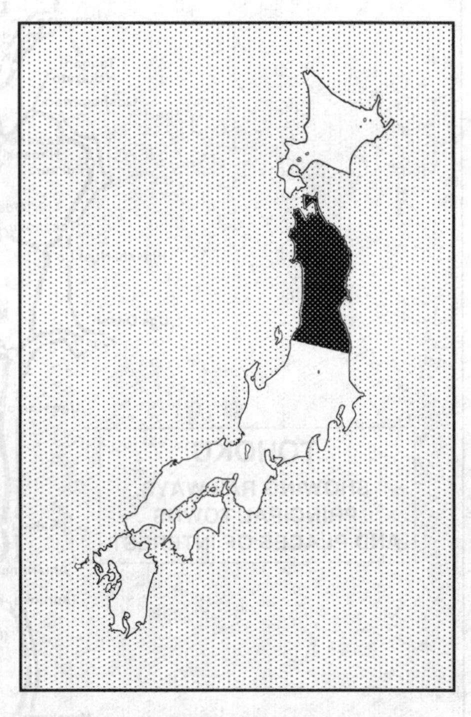

As you travel through Tohoku, you will constantly be reminded about the travels of Matsuo Basho, a poet who made a famous journey to this region in 1689. He wrote a book of *haiku* poetry entitled *Basho's Narrow Road to a Distant Land*. Before the days of JR's efficiency, this journey was quite an undertaking, as the title of Basho's work suggests. He travelled for 156 days, covering over 2,400 kilometres, entirely on foot. Every place along the way is proud to claim that Basho wrote a poem about it. One almost expects to see little notices stating 'Basho's bin 'ere.' And when Basho did not write a poem there, we can even find in tourist literature claims such as that Basho was too overcome by the beauty of the place to write any poem about it!

We shall proceed around Tohoku in an anti-clockwise direction. If you plan to visit Hokkaido, break off when you reach Aomori, travel around Hokkaido and then resume this section on your return.

This book concentrates on the principal attractions, the 'must-sees' and the 'should-sees-if-time-permits'. Of course, there are other points of interest too, but it is our wish to distinguish those which are of lesser interest and to keep our book to a reasonable size and price. If you have spare time in any place, there is usually a tourist information office in or near the main railway station. In addition, youth hostels are excellent sources of information and, if you plan in advance to stay for a while in a particular area, consult the Tourist Information Centre in Tokyo, Narita Airport or Kyoto before leaving. In any case, you should ask one of these offices for a map, for they can provide beautiful colour maps of Japan, and of particular areas, far better than anything to which our budget can run!

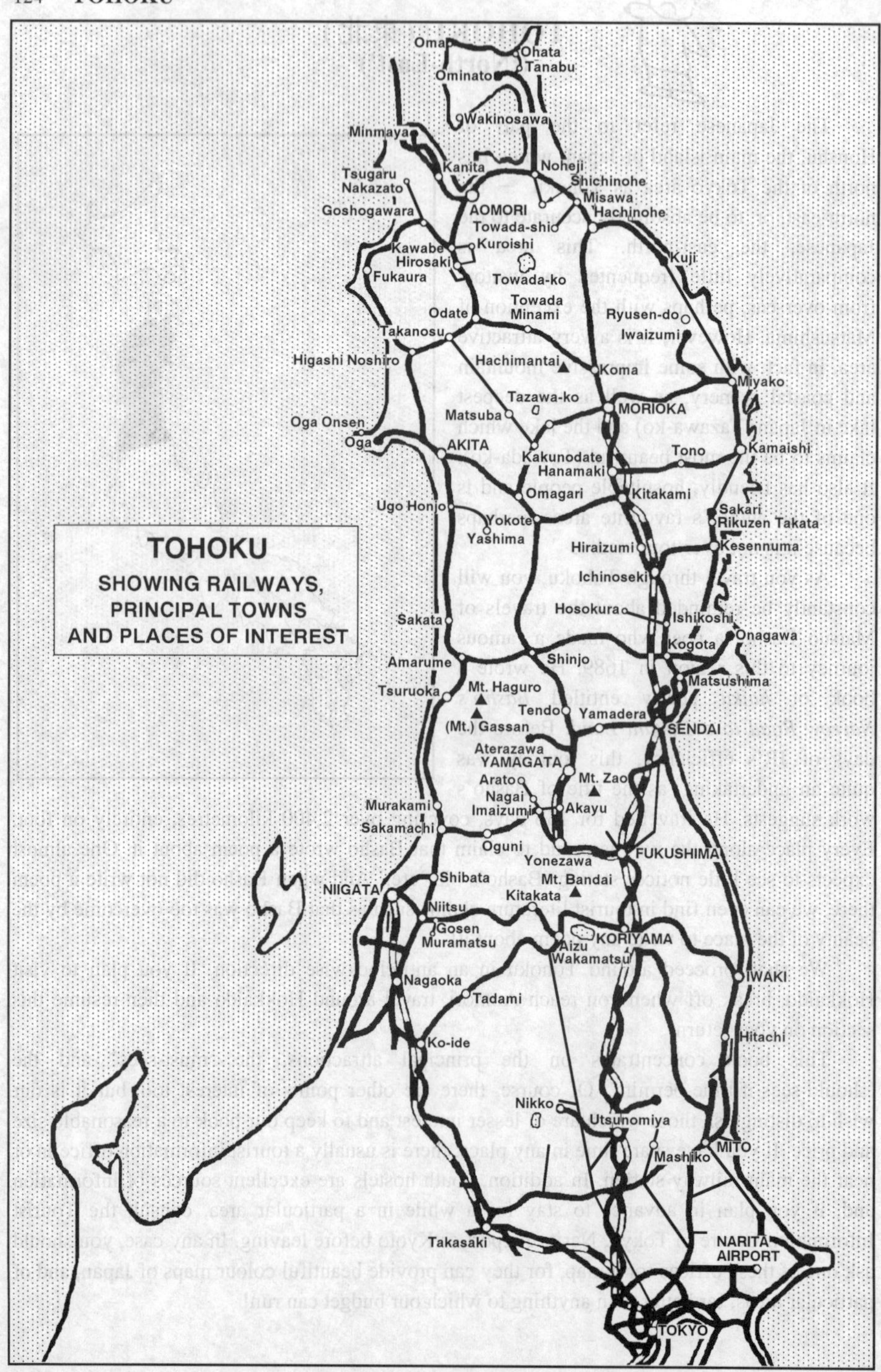
TOHOKU
SHOWING RAILWAYS,
PRINCIPAL TOWNS
AND PLACES OF INTEREST
Oma
Ohata
Tanabu
Ominato
Wakinosawa
Minmaya
Kanita
Noheji
Tsugaru
Nakazato
Shichinohe
AOMORI
Misawa
Goshogawara
Hachinohe
Towada-shi
Kawabe
Kuroishi
Hirosaki
Kuji
Fukaura
Towada-ko
Towada
Minami
Odate
Ryusen-do
Iwaizumi
Takanosu
Higashi Noshiro
Hachimantai
Koma
Miyako
Tazawa-ko
MORIOKA
Matsuba
Oga Onsen
Oga
AKITA
Kakunodate
Tono
Kamaishi
Hanamaki
Kitakami
Omagari
Ugo Honjo
Sakari
Rikuzen Takata
Yokote
Yashima
Hiraizumi
Kesennuma
Ichinoseki
Hosokura
Ishikoshi
Sakata
Onagawa
Kogota
Shinjo
Amarume
Matsushima
Tsuruoka
Mt. Haguro
Tendo
Yamadera
(Mt.) Gassan
SENDAI
Aterazawa
YAMAGATA
Arato
Mt. Zao
Nagai
Murakami
Imaizumi
Akayu
Sakamachi
Oguni
FUKUSHIMA
Yonezawa
Shibata
NIIGATA
Mt. Bandai
Kitakata
Niitsu
Gosen
KORIYAMA
Muramatsu
Aizu
Wakamatsu
IWAKI
Nagaoka
Tadami
Ko-ide
Hitachi
Nikko
Utsunomiya
MITO
Mashiko
NARITA
AIRPORT
Takasaki
TOKYO

***Transportation and Tickets***

Distances are quite substantial in this area, so it is a good place to be using a 'Japan Rail Pass', especially if you are going on to Hokkaido. If you came without one, however, and it is not Blue Spring season, there are still plenty of possibilities.

JR issues a *Tohoku Wide Shu-yu-ken* (excursion ticket) which allows you to explore the area of Honshu north of Niigata, Koriyama and Iwaki freely for 10 days for the sum of ¥22,650 from any point in the Tokyo area. Similar tickets are available from other points of origin throughout Japan. As long as unreserved seating only is occupied, *tokkyu* trains can be used without any supplement within the designated Tohoku area (see map below), as can the Yamagata *shinkansen* between Fukushima and Yamagata. JR buses can also be used, except long-distance overnight services. To reach the Tohoku area, however, if you wish to use *tokkyu* trains or the *shinkansen*, you must pay the appropriate supplement, as the *shu-yu-ken* provides only conveyance by ordinary train or by the unreserved sections of *kyuko* trains between the point of origin and the start of the free area. However, there are no regular *kyuko* services on the access routes to the Tohoku area (only seasonal services).

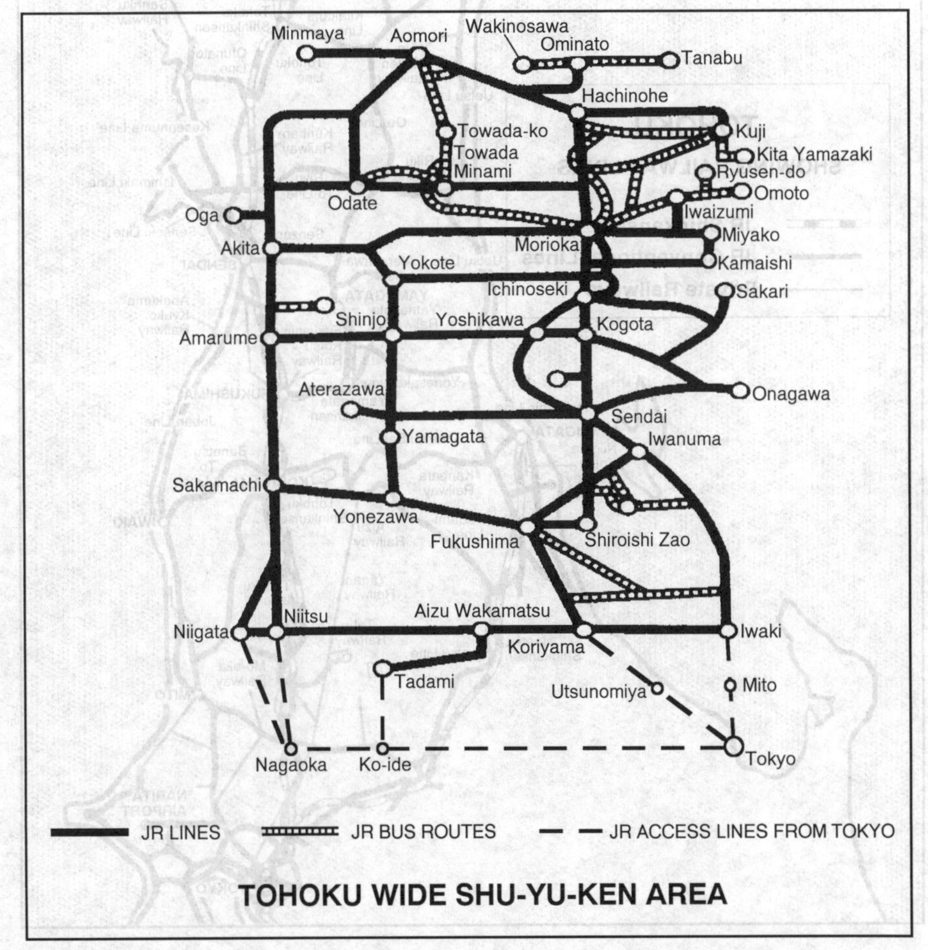

TOHOKU WIDE SHU-YU-KEN AREA

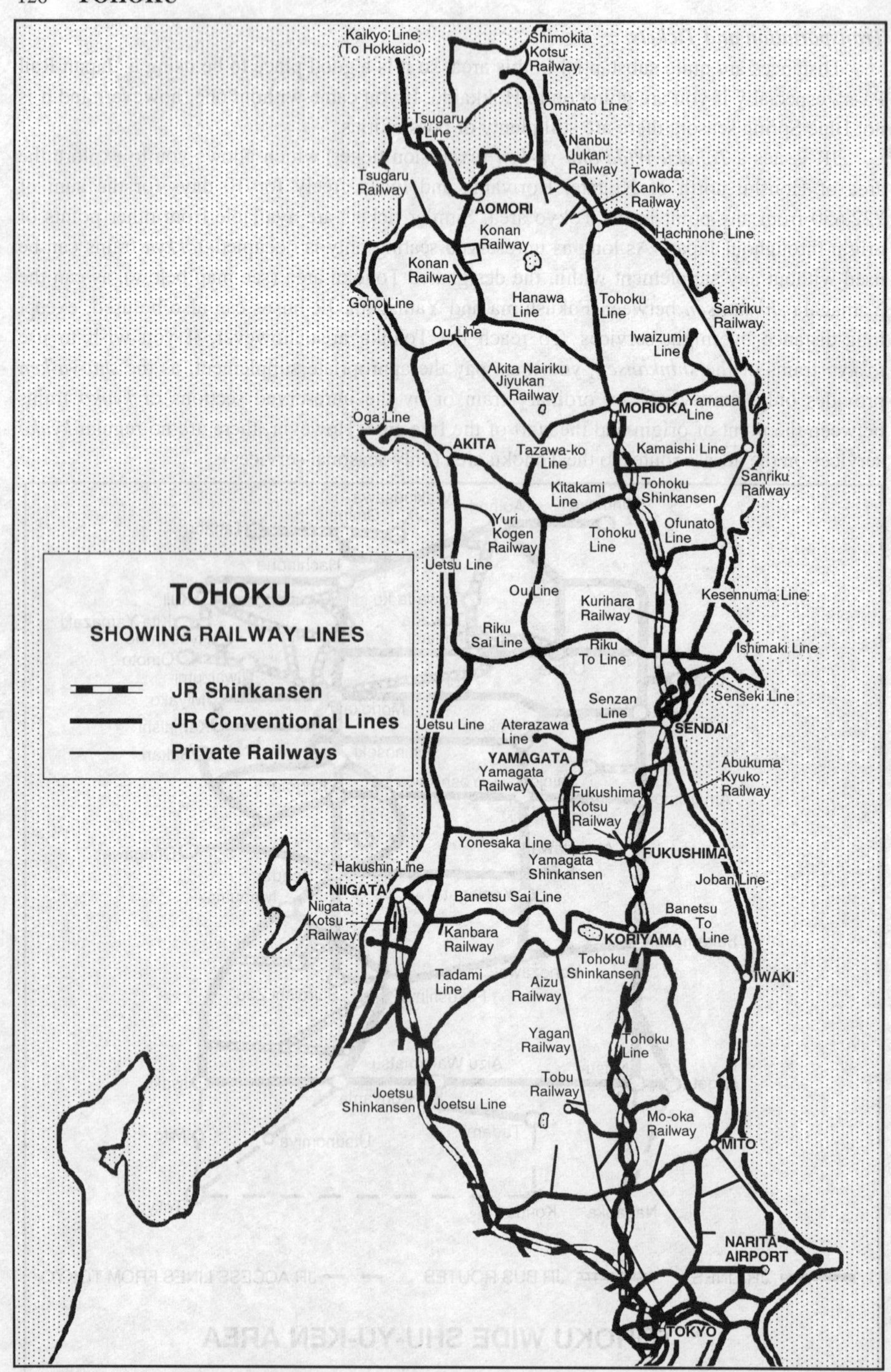
TOHOKU
SHOWING RAILWAY LINES
JR Shinkansen
JR Conventional Lines
Private Railways
Kaikyo Line (To Hokkaido)
Shimokita Kotsu Railway
Ominato Line
Tsugaru Line
Nanbu Jukan Railway
Tsugaru Railway
Towada Kanko Railway
AOMORI
Konan Railway
Hachinohe Line
Konan Railway
Gono Line
Hanawa Line
Tohoku Line
Sanriku Railway
Ou Line
Iwaizumi Line
Akita Nairiku Jiyukan Railway
MORIOKA
Yamada Line
Oga Line
AKITA
Tazawa-ko Line
Kamaishi Line
Kitakami Line
Tohoku Shinkansen
Sanriku Railway
Yuri Kogen Railway
Tohoku Line
Ofunato Line
Uetsu Line
Ou Line
Kesennuma Line
Kurihara Railway
Riku Sai Line
Riku To Line
Ishimaki Line
Senseki Line
Senzan Line
Uetsu Line
Aterazawa Line
SENDAI
YAMAGATA
Yamagata Railway
Abukuma Kyuko Railway
Fukushima Kotsu Railway
Yonesaka Line
FUKUSHIMA
Hakushin Line
Yamagata Shinkansen
Joban Line
NIIGATA
Banetsu Sai Line
Niigata Kotsu Railway
Banetsu To Line
Kanbara Railway
KORIYAMA
Tohoku Shinkansen
IWAKI
Tadami Line
Aizu Railway
Yagan Railway
Tohoku Line
Tobu Railway
Joetsu Shinkansen
Joetsu Line
Mo-oka Railway
MITO
NARITA AIRPORT
TOKYO

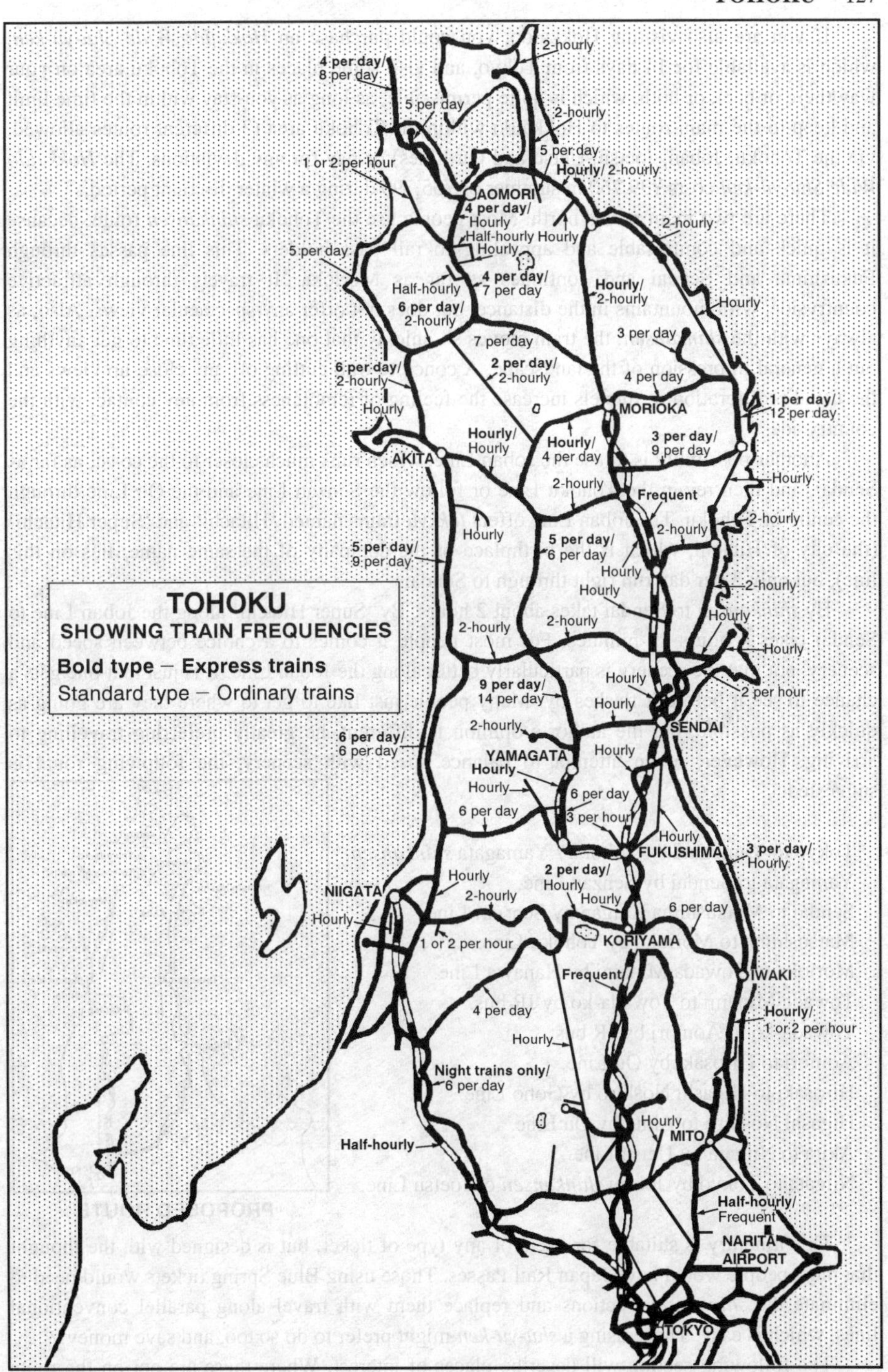
TOHOKU
SHOWING TRAIN FREQUENCIES
Bold type – Express trains
Standard type – Ordinary trains
AOMORI
MORIOKA
AKITA
SENDAI
YAMAGATA
FUKUSHIMA
NIIGATA
KORIYAMA
IWAKI
MITO
NARITA AIRPORT
TOKYO
4 per day/ 8 per day
2-hourly
5 per day
1 or 2 per hour
5 per day
Hourly/ 2-hourly
4 per day/ Hourly
Half-hourly
Hourly
4 per day/ 7 per day
6 per day/ 2-hourly
7 per day
2 per day/ 2-hourly
Hourly/ 2-hourly
3 per day
4 per day
1 per day/ 12 per day
3 per day/ 9 per day
Hourly/ Hourly
Hourly/ 4 per day
Frequent
5 per day/ 9 per day
5 per day/ 6 per day
9 per day/ 14 per day
6 per day/ 6 per day
6 per day
3 per hour
3 per day/ Hourly
2 per day/ Hourly
2 per hour
1 or 2 per hour
Hourly/ 1 or 2 per hour
Night trains only/ 6 per day
Half-hourly
Half-hourly/ Frequent

If you are also visiting Hokkaido, you could purchase an *Hokkaido Wide Shu-yu-ken*, which is available for 14 days from Tokyo, and visit some places in the Tohoku area on your way there or back or both, which is quite permissible, as long as you stay within the time limit and keep to the main routes to Hokkaido within the Tohoku area (3 different routes allowed, via the Tohoku, Joban, Joetsu, Uetsu and Ou Lines) or pay for any deviations. The *Hokkaido Wide Shu-yu-ken* costs ¥39,760 in summer or ¥35,790 during a winter discount period.

There are two main routes north. Most people use the Tohoku *shinkansen* route, because it is quick and comfortable and appealing to rail pass holders. This line passes through Fukushima and Sendai and continues as far as Morioka. It travels through attractive countryside, with mountains in the distance, but does not offer any spectacular views. Also, as always with the *shinkansen*, the train moves so quickly that one has little time to get anything but a general impression of the landscape. A concrete wall cutting off any close-up views and the usual proliferation of tunnels increase the feeling of remoteness from any contact with the countryside.

Another possibility is to use the Joban Line, which runs much closer to the coast, as far as Sendai, and then rejoin the Tohoku Line or follow the Senzan Line and the Ou Line through the centre of Tohoku. The Joban Line offers *tokkyu* trains named 'Hitachi' and 'Super Hitachi' (the city of Hitachi, which is the birthplace of the company of the same name, lies on this line), but only 3 per day run right through to Sendai.

By *shinkansen* to Sendai takes about 2 hours. By 'Super Hitachi' along the Joban Line to Sendai takes 4 hours 15 minutes. For most people it comes to a choice between speed and scenery, not that the scenery is particularly better along the Joban Line. It is just that one gets a chance to see it before it flashes by. Many people just like to get to where they are going as quickly as possible, but the author's opinion is different, he greatly preferring travelling to arriving. However, in an attempt to balance speed with scenery, the following route is suggested:

Tokyo to Yamagata by Tohoku / Yamagata *shinkansen*.
Yamagata to Sendai by Senzan Line.
Sendai to Matsushima Kaigan by Senseki Line.
Matsushima to Morioka by Tohoku Line.
Morioka to Towada Minami by Hanawa Line.
Towada Minami to Towada-ko by JR bus.
Towada-ko to Aomori by JR bus.
Aomori to Hirosaki by Ou Line.
Hirosaki to Higashi Noshiro by Gono Line.
Higashi Noshiro to Akita by Ou Line.
Akita to Niigata by Uetsu Line.
Niigata to Tokyo by Joetsu *shinkansen* or Joetsu Line.

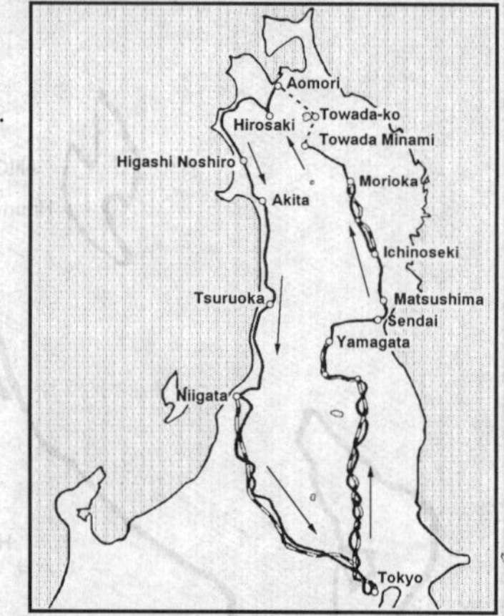


**PROPOSED ROUTE**

This itinerary is suitable for users of any type of ticket, but is designed with the thought that most people would have Japan Rail Passes. Those using Blue Spring tickets would need to eliminate the *shinkansen* sections and replace them with travel along parallel conventional lines, which is easy. Those using a *shu-yu-ken* might prefer to do so too, and save money.

The following section will describe places of interest. Where these are not on the route above, it is not too difficult to make the required detours.

It should be mentioned that there are also long-distance express bus services to the Tohoku area from Tokyo. These services run only at night, to such cities as Morioka, Akita and Aomori. Cost is approximately ¥10,000 one way to any of these places. The author's own opinion is that these services cannot really be recommended for the visitor. They deprive him of any chance to see the scenery and give him a not-so-comfortable night. However, there are those who are pleased to save the cost of a night's accommodation and who did not really want to look at the scenery anyway. The bus services are operated by a variety of companies and start from different locations in Tokyo. The Tourist Information Centre can provide information, as can anybody who has an up-to-date railway timetable.

## MITO (水戸 — 'Water Door') Joban Line, 65 mins. from Tokyo

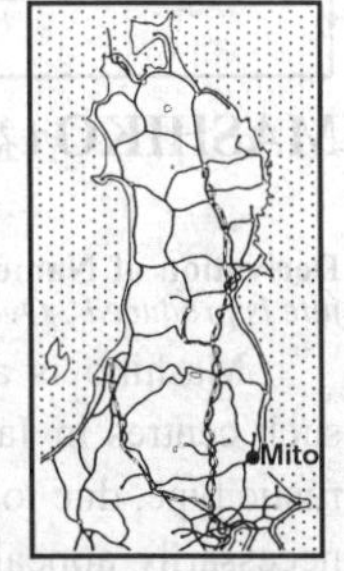


**Derivation of Name:** *There used to be a gate here to control the flow of water in the Nakagawa River.*

The main attraction of Mito is a garden called **Kairaku-en**, famous for its plum blossom in March. Although this is one of the three famous gardens of Japan, other than in March it does not have so much to offer — and in March it has more people than plum trees. Although it seems impolite to Mito to say so, the author believes that this garden can be left out of your itinerary without too much loss, especially if you are planning to visit Kanazawa or Takamatsu (or Okayama, the official list would say).

If you do wish to visit Kairaku-en, 'Hitachi' and 'Super Hitachi' *tokkyu* trains start from Ueno station in Tokyo, run every half hour and take between 65 and 90 minutes to reach Mito. Ordinary trains also start from Ueno. They are frequent and take about 2 hours to get to Mito. During plum blossom season, most down trains stop at a special temporary station called Kairaku-en. The station is right beside the garden. At other times, you will see the garden on the left as you approach Mito. Alight at Mito station and walk back keeping near the railway. The distance is quite walkable, about 20 minutes, but there are buses available too.

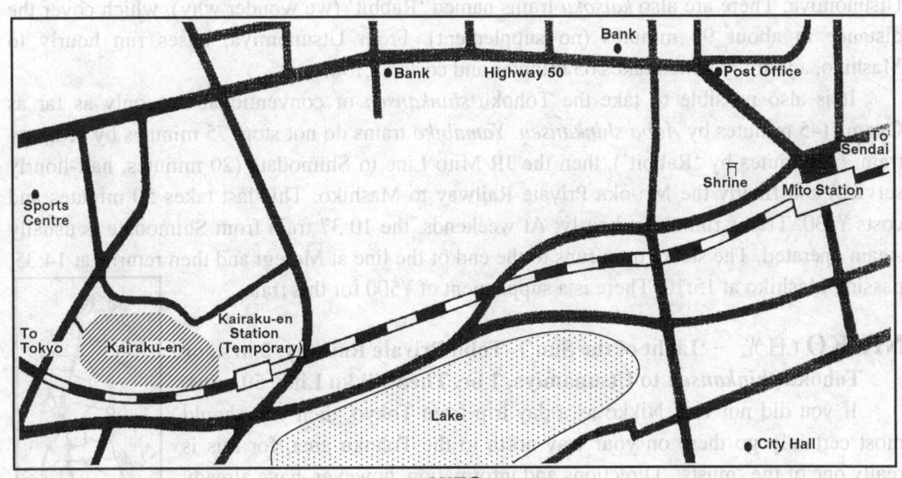

MITO

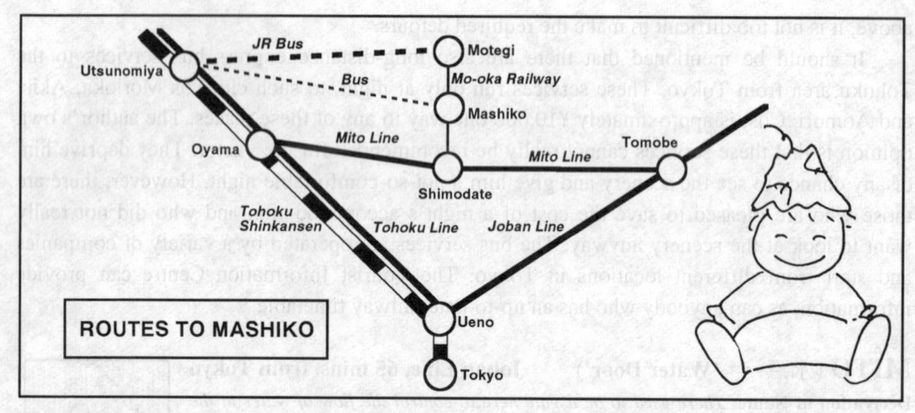


## MASHIKO (益子 — 'Profitable Children') Tohoku *shinkansen* to Utsunomiya, 1 hour from Tokyo. Then bus, 65 mins.

**Derivation of Name:** *The town used to be called 'Masoko', meaning 'the place where jute is produced'. Over time, the pronunciation became distorted to 'Mashiko'.*

Mashiko is a pottery centre, the nearest one to Tokyo of very many such centres in Japan. The pottery produced here, although famous, is of a rustic type, due to the relatively poor quality of the soil in the area and is not necessarily appealing to western taste, it should be mentioned. One might think of Mashiko, therefore, as the poor man's pottery centre. It is a small town which used to be served by a JR railway line. However, JR gave up the line in 1988 and it is now operated semi-privately with local municipality support.

The easiest way to reach Mashiko is to take a Tohoku *shinkansen* train from Tokyo to Utsunomiya, which takes about an hour, and then change to a bus. All *Aoba* trains stop at Utsunomiya, but some *Yamabiko* trains do not, so be careful. Ordinary trains run frequently along the conventional Tohoku Line, starting in Ueno and taking about 1 hour 45 minutes to Utsunomiya. There are also *kaisoku* trains named 'Rabbit' (we wonder why), which cover the distance in about 90 minutes (no supplement). From Utsunomiya, buses run hourly to Mashiko, a journey which takes 65 minutes and costs ¥1,150.

It is also possible to take the Tohoku *shinkansen* or conventional line only as far as Oyama (45 minutes by *Aoba shinkansen*. *Yamabiko* trains do not stop. 75 minutes by ordinary train. 65 minutes by 'Rabbit'), then the JR Mito Line to Shimodate (20 minutes, half-hourly service) and finally the Mo-oka Private Railway to Mashiko. This last takes 50 minutes and costs ¥730. Trains run about hourly. At weekends, the 10:37 train from Shimodate is usually steam operated. The steam train runs to the end of the line at Motegi and then returns at 14:35, passing Mashiko at 15:10. There is a supplement of ¥500 for this train.

## NIKKO (日光 — 'Light of the Sun') Tobu Private Railway, 2 hrs., or Tohoku *shinkansen* to Utsunomiya, 1 hr. Then Nikko Line, 50 mins.

If you did not visit Nikko as a day trip from Tokyo, then you should most certainly go there on your way north to the Tohoku area, for this is really one of the 'musts'. Directions and information, however, have already been given on page 104.

## AIZU WAKAMATSU (会津若松 – 'Meeting Port Young Pine')

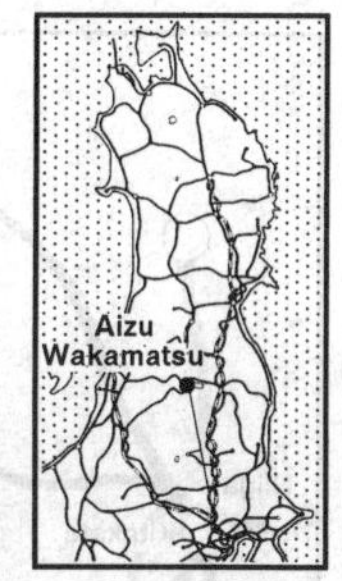


**Tohoku *shinkansen* to Koriyama, 90 mins. from Tokyo.**
**Then Banetsu Sai Line, 1 hr.**

**Derivation of Name:** *'Aizu', which is the name of the area, means 'the meeting place of rivers'. 'Wakamatsu', the name of the city, is literal. Young pines were regarded as sacred trees and portended good fortune.*

Aizu Wakamatsu is a city surrounded by attractive countryside. It lies on the Banetsu Sai Line (Banetsu West Line) one hour by the fastest trains west of the Tohoku Line. Change trains at Koriyama. It is worth making the trip just for the train ride. The journey begins through drab semi-urban landscape as far as Bandai Atami, where many of the passengers alight, for this is a spa resort and that is very appealing to the Japanese. The town is also famous for a type of lacquerware known as *Aizu-nuri*. As soon as those passengers have left for their day at the baths, the rural scenery begins and the railway starts to climb. If you are travelling on an ordinary train, you will find a switch-back station next, Naka Yamajuku, but, now that this line is electrified, the expresses by-pass the station and rush on up the hill. After a while, Mt. Bandai will appear on the right and you will see **Lake Inawashiro** on the left, a popular summer resort area, with boating, water-skiing and similar sports facilities available. In the winter, there is skiing nearby.

Aizu Wakamatsu was largely destroyed when it became a centre of resistance to the Meiji Restoration in 1868. There is a castle, but it is one of the new ferro-concrete type, a reconstruction of that which disappeared a century ago. There is a similar reconstruction of *samurai* houses and there are other historical sites connected with the opposition to the Meiji Restoration. However, it is the natural scenery which one tends to remember from a visit here, rather than the history, for Aizu Wakamatsu seems overshadowed by Mt. Bandai.

In 1888, **Mt. Bandai** suddenly and unexpectedly exploded. It had lain dormant for a millennium and there had been no hint of the build-up of gases within which led to this catastrophe. The top was blown right off the mountain and about 500 people were killed. This was not an eruption, but an explosion, so one can still see the scars and the changed shape of the mountain. The pieces of mountain were scattered over a large area, changing the landscape there too. A youth hostel is located in the centre of this interesting area, beside **Goshiki-numa** (Lake Goshiki), the name meaning 'the lake of five colours'. This is Ura Bandai Hostel, which professes to speak English and which is in an attractive location. It is an ideal base from which to explore. There is a hiking course starting here and in summer there are boat rides available, although they are, as usual, expensive – ¥1,000 for a 40 minute circuit of Lake Hibara, for example.

To reach the youth hostel, alight from the train at Inawashiro and catch a bus bound for Bandai Kogen (磐梯高原). It takes about 30 minutes to Goshiki-numa Iriguchi (五色沼入口), the nearest bus stop to the hostel. Occasional buses run through from Aizu Wakamatsu, but the journey is expensive at ¥1,470 for a 75 minute ride. There is also a summer-only bus service from the west exit of Fukushima station to Bandai Kogen via Goshiki-numa Iriguchi. This costs ¥2,610 and takes three hours, including a 30 minute sightseeing stop at **Jodo Daira** on the way. The journey is a pretty one and there are volcanic attractions at Jodo Daira, including Mt. Azuma Kofuji, a volcano which can be climbed in the time allowed, and Mt. Issaikyo, with steam gushing out. Buses leave Fukushima at 8:00 (holidays only), 10:40 and 13:10. They leave Goshiki-numa Iriguchi for Fukushima at 9:10, 13:17 (holidays only) and 14:47.

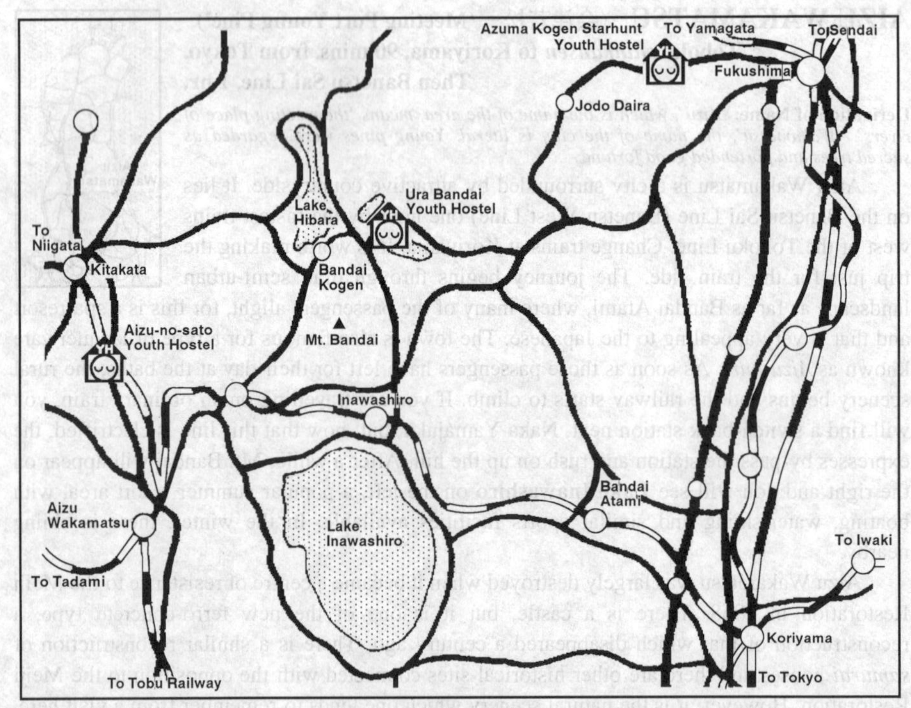


**AIZU AREA**

These buses also pass Azuma Kogen Starhunt Youth Hostel on the way, about 30 minutes before reaching Fukushima.

There is another route to Aizu Wakamatsu from Tokyo and this is via the Tobu Private Railway and its affiliates. This is useful for anybody visiting Nikko *en route*. From Tobu Asakusa station in Tokyo, there are connecting services all the way to Aizu Wakamatsu, although it is always necessary to change trains at least once, as the section from Aizu Tajima to Aizu Wakamatsu is not electrified. This last section used to be a JR line, but JR abandoned it and the line was taken over by a semi-private company. A new section of track was built in the middle, by yet another company, as a link, and then a service could be run all the way from the Tokyo area, in collaboration with Tobu. This is an interesting and pretty alternative to the JR route and you will pass over track owned by four different companies, including JR for the last 3 kilometres. Unfortunately, that means that you must pay fares to four different companies (although you can purchase a through ticket, of course), but it is still cheaper than using the JR route. A convenient train to catch is the 9:10 from Asakusa to Aizu Tajima, which it reaches at 12:45. The connexion leaves Aizu Tajima at 12:49 and arrives in Aizu Wakamatsu at 14:10. Cost is ¥4,170. If you prefer the luxury of an express, there is a *kyuko* from Asakusa at 10:10 which reaches Aizu Tajima at 13:24. All seats are reserved, so you must purchase a reservation ticket before departure. The connexion departs at 13:27 and reaches Aizu Wakamatsu at 14:29. Cost is ¥5,760. There are plenty of other trains too, but these are early and convenient and involve only one change. From Nikko, travel to Shimo Imaichi (30 minutes) and then change to a train for Aizu Tajima.

## KITAKATA (喜多方 – 'Very Happy Direction') Tohoku *shinkansen* to Koriyama, 90 mins. from Tokyo. Then Banetsu Sai Line, 90 mins.

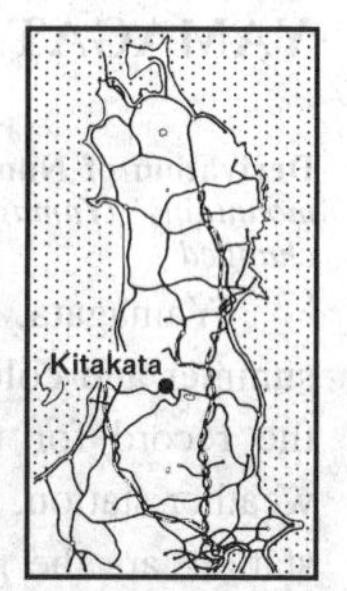


**Derivation of Name:** *Original meaning was 'in the northern direction' (Kitakata was north of the main centre at Aizu Wakamatsu). Later the first Chinese character of the name became changed.*

Kitakata is famous as a typically traditional Japanese country town, although one wonders whether a place can be both famous and typical. It offers a number of traditionally-styled buildings and warehouses and is the centre of a *geta* manufacturing industry. *Geta* are traditional Japanese open-top wooden footwear, not as uncomfortable as they look, but apparently used nowadays mainly by the owners of expensive *sushi* restaurants and by *sumo* competitors. Therefore, one would not expect the demand for these products to be great, but there are piles of pieces of *geta* around the town, in various stages of processing. The piles of the finished product, incidentally, are supposedly constructed so that a *geta* can be removed from any place without the collapse of the whole edifice. The visitor is advised not to put this to the test, however, just in case! Kitakata is quite small enough to be toured on foot, but there are horse-drawn carriages, mostly of odd design, available for hire at high prices too (about ¥1,500 for a one-hour tour).

More recently, Kitakata has also become famous for its variety of Chinese noodles (*ramen*) shops, so, if you are thinking of having lunch here, you will know what to put on the day's menu.

Although Kitakata is only 90 minutes from Koriyama, in fact there are few trains which go right through. No expresses do so. If you have to change trains at Aizu Wakamatsu, beware that there may be a long wait before you can travel the last 15 kilometres to Kitakata.

Beyond Kitakata, the railway extends to Niigata. The line continues to pass through attractive scenery and offers an enjoyable ride. From Kitakata to Niigata takes 2½ hours. Ordinary and *kaisoku* trains only, no expresses. There is a youth hostel at Shiokawa, between Aizu Wakamatsu and Kitakata, named Aizu-no-sato Hostel. English is spoken.

## FUKUSHIMA (福島 – 'Lucky Island') Tohoku *shinkansen*, 1 hr. 40 mins. from Tokyo

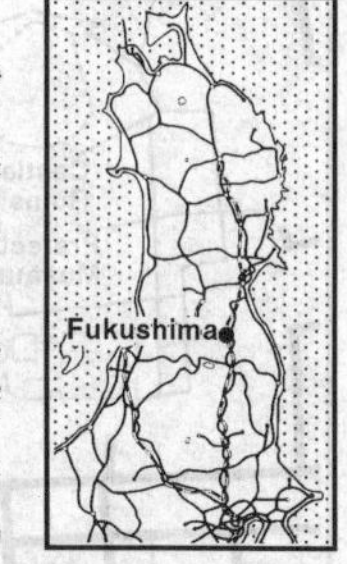


**Derivation of Name:** *The city was built on raised ground in the centre of a basin, regarded as a form of island. 'Fuku' (lucky) is often used to indicate a centre of development.*

Despite its name, Fukushima is by no means an island, being far inland, the capital of Fukushima prefecture. Although not special as a city, it lies within easy reach of some scenic routes and interesting volcanic terrain. If you took the bus here from Ura Bandai Youth Hostel, you will already have sampled these attractions. If not, it is possible to make a round trip to **Jodo Daira** (see under Aizu Wakamatsu) from Fukushima. In summer only, there is a bus which leaves from the west exit of Fukushima station at 13:00. It reaches Jodo Daira at 14:10 and stays there for one hour, departing again at 15:10 and returning to Fukushima station at 16:50. The return journey is by a different route. The fare is ¥1,310 one way or ¥2,610 for the complete tour. This bus travels via Azuma Kogen Starhunt Youth Hostel on the outward journey only.

# YAMAGATA (山形 – 'Mountain Shape')

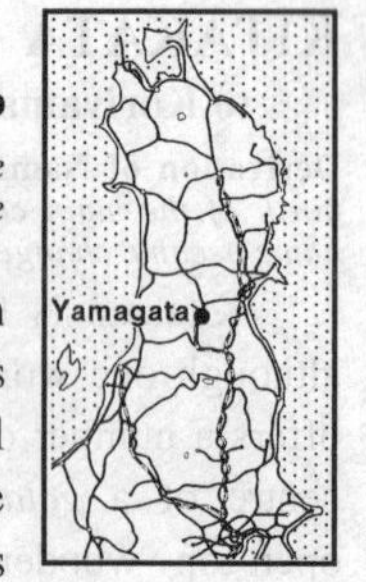


**Yamagata *shinkansen*, 2 hrs. 45 mins. from Tokyo**

**Derivation of Name:** *Originally the Chinese characters meant 'in the direction of the mountains' (Yamagata lies at the foot of Mt. Zao), but the second character became changed.*

Yamagata, the capital of the prefecture of the same name, is hot in summer and cold in winter, due to its location in a basin. In fact, it claims the record for the highest temperature recorded in Japan at an official weather station, 40.8 ℃ in 1933. Just beside the railway, to the north of the station, are the ruins of a castle in what is now a park. The main gate has been reconstructed, but not yet the buildings. Yamagata is a pleasant enough city, but it has been included in our itinerary not so much for the city itself as for the journey here from Fukushima.

When the author first made this journey, he had no knowledge of the terrain and no particular expectations. It was a beautiful trip. The old locomotive-hauled train climbed slowly up and up into the mountains, stopping at a variety of switch-back stations where the snow lay deep. Tohoku folk always seem friendly and natural. On this crowded train, the lady opposite gave me *umeboshi* (preserved sour plums) to keep me going on this enjoyable journey! However, I probably enjoyed it so much because I was not expecting anything spectacular. The reader will be going with this description in mind and will now be disappointed. That is how these things always happen. Moreover, circumstances have changed now.

In 1989, it was decided to build a spur from the Tohoku *shinkansen* to Yamagata. In the past, all *shinkansen* lines had been freshly constructed, as they use standard gauge, instead of the 3 feet 6 inches to which the rest of the JR system is built. In this case, however, a money-saving compromise was adopted which, in retrospect, seems to have given the traveller the worst of all worlds. The existing narrow gauge track was converted to standard gauge and

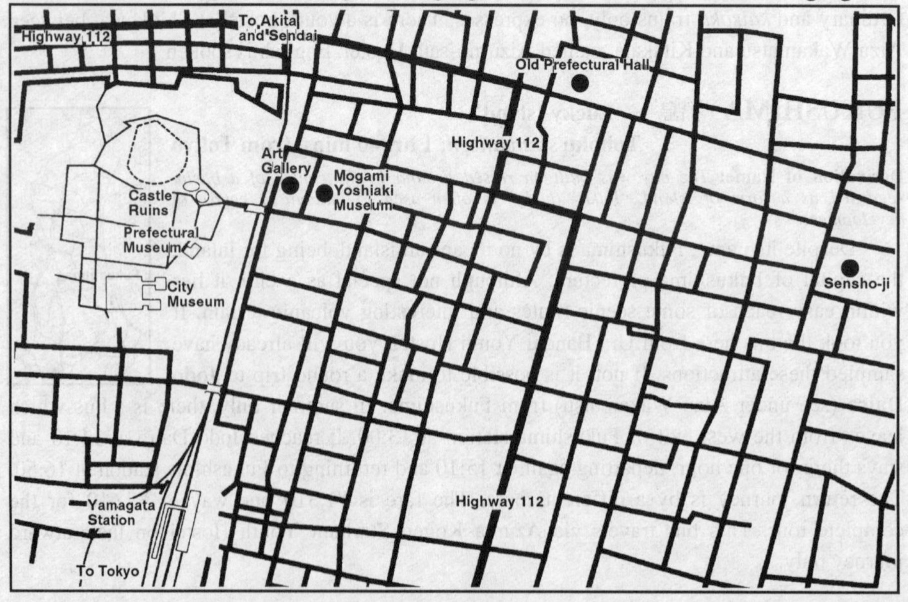


YAMAGATA

Yamagata *shinkansen* trains usually run from Tokyo to Fukushima as the front section of certain Tohoku *shinkansen* departures. For a start this looks odd, as the Yamagata section is silver, while the Sendai or Morioka section is green and cream and the two are of a different design. Also, there is no corridor between the two sections. Moreover, the Yamagata section has to be narrower than the rest of the train because of the clearance limits imposed by tunnels on the converted track. Worst of all for the passengers is the fact that, whilst the train runs at 245 kilometres per hour up to Fukushima, it has to be limited to 130 kilometres per hour between Fukushima and Yamagata, a speed only a fraction greater than that which was attainable by the narrow gauge expresses in any case. The only real advantage to the new service, which commenced on 1st July 1992, is that passengers no longer have to change trains. As for the ordinary trains, they too had to be converted to standard gauge, of course. As a result, the old locomotive-hauled service has disappeared and shiny new electric multiple units now work the route. This is the only place on the JR network where there are standard gauge ordinary trains and the only place where ordinary trains share tracks with *shinkansen* rolling stock. Another disadvantage of this arrangement is that through services to other lines can no longer be made. For example, there used to be a service between Yamagata and Niigata, but now it is necessary to change *en route* from a standard gauge train to a narrow gauge one.

Even the charming switch-back stations have gone, ironed out in the reconstruction work. They were, in any case, unnecessary for electric trains which could cope with steeper gradients. So this line no longer has the character which endeared it to the writer a few years ago. However, it is still a pretty ride, even if you may no longer be offered *umeboshi* along the way! It is also the only place where *shinkansen* trains run on a single-track line, for two brief sections of the route. Notice also a short part of the line between Yamagata station and Zao station which is dual gauged for the purpose of serving freight customers at Zao.

When you take your train from Tokyo station, remember to go to the front part of the train, the shiny silver section. If you mistakenly get into the rear green and cream section, you will not be able to get through to your seat once the train has started, a mistake which has been made by many passengers before you. Recommended and fastest services leave Tokyo at 6:32 and 7:28. The former goes only to Yamagata (i.e. there is no Tohoku *shinkansen* portion) and arrives at 9:07. The latter makes only one stop, at Fukushima, and arrives in Yamagata at 9:55. With either of these two trains, you will then have the whole day to explore your destination. However, if early rising does not suit you, there are, in fact, trains every hour throughout the day. Most leave Tokyo at 28 minutes past the hour.

A *Tohoku Wide Shu-yu-ken* entitles you to use the Yamagata *shinkansen* route between Fukushima and Yamagata without incurring a supplementary charge. However, you will have to pay a supplement if you travel on the *shinkansen* between Tokyo and Fukushima, and it is a substantial supplement too − ¥3,500 from Tokyo to Fukushima for an unreserved seat. If you wish to avoid this supplement, it is necessary to take ordinary trains between Tokyo and Fukushima, which will require about 4½ hours.

If you are using a Blue Spring ticket, of course, you must take ordinary trains all the way. Bear in mind that there are only 6 through or connecting services per day on the section of line between Fukushima and Yamagata, so the journey needs to be planned carefully. Ordinary trains leave Fukushima at 7:00 and 8:30 and it is necessary to change at Yonezawa. The next train is not until 13:15 and this is the one to catch if coming from Tokyo. You need to leave

Ueno on the 7:36 ordinary train and to change trains at Utsunomiya (9:21 / 9:22) and Kuroiso (10:12 / 10:27). You reach Fukushima at 12:20, so have time to get lunch there. Be back at the train to Yamagata well before its departure at 13:15 though, as it will be a short and crowded train. It reaches Yamagata at 15:02.

There is a pleasant youth hostel in Yamagata, but it is not in the central part of the city. If you take an ordinary train back to Zao, one station towards Fukushima, or, of course, if you are coming from Fukushima on an ordinary train, get off at Zao, you can walk to the hostel, although it is a little over 2 kilometres. Go out of the station exit and walk ahead the short distance to the main road. Turn right at the traffic signals and keep walking along the main road, keeping the railway on your right, until it starts to become rural. As you see the railway start to bend away to the right, there is a small car park on your left and the youth hostel is down the road immediately following it. This hostel has a natural hot spring bath in it. It is also possible to take a bus from Yamagata station (see the entry in the Youth Hostels section on page 414).

## MT. ZAO (蔵王山 – 'Warehouse King Mountain')

**45 mins. by bus from Yamagata**

**Derivation of Name:** *'Zao' is the name of an incarnation of Buddha. In 680, a Buddhist priest set up here a temple for the worship of Zao.*

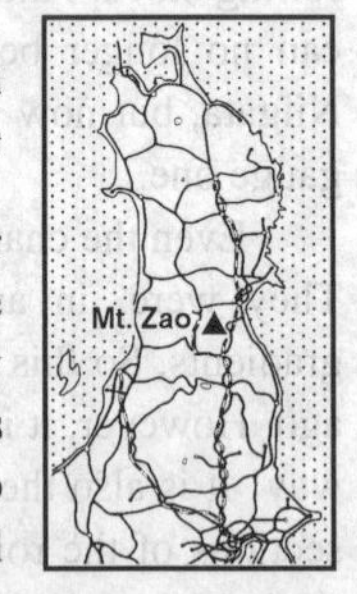


The Zao area is famous for its skiing facilities in winter and for mountain hiking in summer. Its most unusual feature is its ice-covered pine trees, which appear in the depths of winter. This phenomenon is caused by water-laden winds becoming cooled and having to discharge surplus moisture. The super-cooled water, at temperatures below freezing, clings to the trees and soon becomes completely frozen, forming weird and beautiful 'ice trees' (*juhyo*), looking like white monsters.

Also famous is **Okama**, a lake in the crater of a volcano set in desolate surroundings where almost no vegetation can survive. This can be reached on foot during the summer months.

To reach the Zao area, take a bus from Yamagata station to Zao Onsen (蔵王温泉), a journey which takes 45 minutes and costs ¥760. From here several ropeways and ski lifts operate (even in summer). If you walk for 15 minutes to the Zao Ropeway, a 7 minute ride will bring you to **Juhyo Kogen**, the base of the 'ice trees' area. A further 8 minute ride will take you to the top of this area. Cost is ¥650 to Juhyo Kogen or ¥1,300 to the top. A return journey is available for ¥2,200. When you reach the top station, you will see Mt. Sanpokojin on your left and Mt. Jizo on your right. Mt. Jizo is 1,736 metres, slightly the higher of the two. If you climb to the summit of either of these two, you will be rewarded by a fine view on a clear day. If you wish to visit Okama, it is a walk of about 45 minutes from the top of the ropeway.

## TENDO (天童 – 'Heavenly Children')

**Ou Line, 12 mins. from Yamagata**

**Derivation of Name:** *There was a legend that two children descended from heaven here.*

Tendo is the town where 90% of *shogi* (Japanese chess) pieces are made. Proud of its tradition, the town has made use of the pentagonal shape of the pieces for various purposes, including the design of its spa bath. The town is also known for its cherry blossom and for a large-scale *shogi* game played with people as pieces which takes place in the same season. You can watch craftsmen at work carving the *shogi* pieces. However, if you visit the museum, you will find that you have paid ¥500 to discover that Tendo appears to have no history!

It takes only 12 minutes from Yamagata to Tendo by *tokkyu*. All trains stop. By ordinary train the journey takes 20 minutes.

## YAMADERA (山寺 – 'Mountain Temple')

**Senzan Line, 20 mins. from Yamagata or 1 hr. from Sendai**

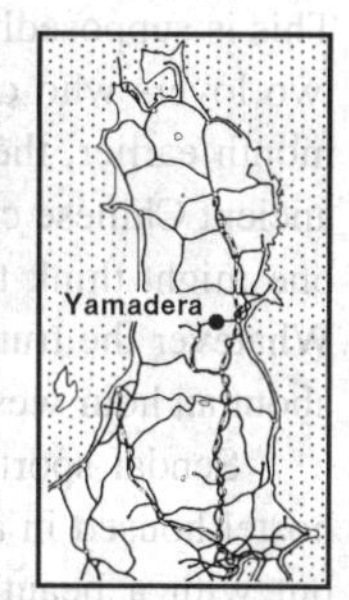


**Derivation of Name:** *Literal.*

In this case, the name is an exact description of what this small town has to offer. Indeed, the name has come about because of the attraction and, since the community seems to cater exclusively to tourism, it probably would not even exist but for the constant flow of visitors to the temple complex high above. Yamadera is well worth a visit and our route comes this way partly for the purpose of making a stop here, so try not to miss it.

It is obvious where to go. Just follow the others across the river and up the mountain. Remember the way that temples always seem to be on mountains. You are not likely to forget it after this visit, but actually the climb, although strenuous in parts, is quite manageable. The real name of this temple complex is Risshaku-ji ('Temple Standing on a Rock'), also an apt title, but it has become commonly known simply as Yamadera, the mountain temple. It was founded in 890, although there was a catastrophic fire in 1521, so none of the buildings dates from earlier than that, and it is a branch of Enryaku-ji in Kyoto, another temple which should not be omitted from your list of visits. The temple buildings here start at the very base of the mountain and straggle all the way up, with the best at the top, of course. This has the advantage that you will encounter fewer and fewer people as you go up, there being many who fall by the wayside (not too literally, fortunately). You have to climb more than 1,100 stone steps. Just think of the work which must have gone into making the steps, not to mention transporting all the materials for the temples up here and then constructing the buildings.

The complex has a beautiful rustic atmosphere, away from any big town and surrounded by cedar trees. When you finally reach the summit, you will be rewarded with a view of the landscape stretching down the valley and into the distance. Basho has been here, as you might suppose, and wrote his poem about the tranquility of the place. It is one of the most famous of Basho's works, so his statue also stands here. You should allow about three hours for your visit to Yamadera.

From Yamagata, take a train bound for Sendai along the Senzan Line. There are both *kaisoku* (rapid) and ordinary trains. All stop at Yamadera, except the 9:20 from Yamagata and the 18:01 from Sendai. It is a ride of about 20 minutes by ordinary train, or 15 minutes by *kaisoku*.

## SENDAI (仙台 – 'Wizard's Table')

**Tohoku *shinkansen*, 2 hrs. from Tokyo**

**Derivation of Name:** *Long ago, a Buddhist priest set up here a temple with a thousand images of Buddha. The words for '1,000 Buddhas' can be read as 'Sen Tai'. Over the years, pronunciation and then Chinese characters became changed (doubtful).*

Sendai is the major city of the Tohoku area. Its railway station always seems to be crowded beyond the capacity of the trains which serve it. The city was destroyed during the war, so not a great deal of history remains.

However, there are the ruins of a castle named **Aoba-jo** ('Green Leaf Castle'). This was destroyed in 1872, not in the last war. The **tomb of Date Masamune,** the man who built the castle, is nearby. However, this was destroyed during the war and has since been rebuilt. To reach this area, take a bus from bus stop no. 9 outside Sendai station.

Sendai is well known for its celebration of the **Tanabata Festival** on 6th to 8th August. This is supposedly the time when two stars meet in the sky and is associated with a legend of two lovers who could meet but once a year. Since the festival is celebrated in other places a month earlier, the discrepancy being due to whether one follows the modern calendar or the ancient Chinese calendar, one wonders about the accuracy of the timing of this event. After all, one might think that, on a particular date, either two stars do appear to meet or they do not. Whatever the truth of the matter, it is a good excuse to have two big celebrations (Hiratsuka, about an hour west of Tokyo, being most famous for the July celebration).

Sendai sports three youth hostels, of which the most interesting is Dochu-an, a unique hostel housed in a traditional, but rebuilt, farmhouse, including surprisingly modern facilities, but with a beautiful wooden interior. The hostel is on the edge of the city, in semi-rural surroundings, and the 'parent' grows his own rice which he uses for the hostel meals. The hostel is one of the most expensive in Japan, but it is also the most popular, so you need to book well ahead to stay here. It is a few minutes walk from Tomisawa, the southern terminus of the Sendai subway, but it can also be reached from JR Nagamachi station, one stop from Sendai towards Tokyo. Exit from the station and turn left. When the main highway crosses over the railway, branch right and refer to the map in the Youth Hostels section on page 412.

From Tokyo, it takes about 2 hours to reach Sendai by the Tohoku *shinkansen*. In fact, the fastest trains run non-stop between the two cities and cover the 325 kilometres in 1¾ hours. These trains leave Tokyo at 8:00 and 14:52, but there is a frequent service at all times. By the route suggested in this book, however, it will take about an hour from the previous stop at Yamadera.

There are also ferry services to and from Sendai. The most useful service is to Tomakomai in Hokkaido, but ferries also run to Nagoya. To Tomakomai takes about 15 hours (overnight) and costs ¥7,500. To Nagoya takes 22 hours and costs ¥6,200, both fares for the lowest class.

## MATSUSHIMA (松島 — 'Pine Islands')

**Tohoku and Senseki Lines, 25 mins. from Sendai**

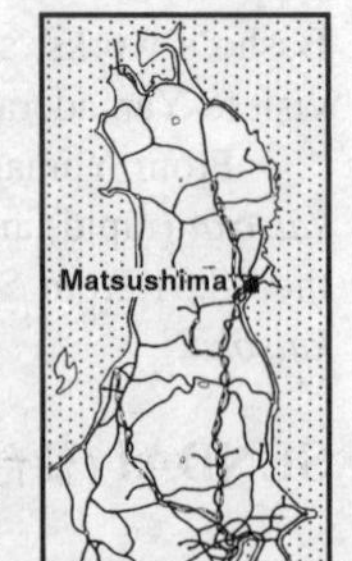


**Derivation of Name:** *Literal.*

Matsushima is exactly what its name implies — a cluster of pine-covered islands in an attractive bay. As it has, for the last 275 years, been reckoned as one of the three great natural beauty spots in Japan, ever since a gentleman named Hayashi so appointed it in a book called *Japan's Scenic Beauty*, it requires inclusion in our itinerary, as it did in Basho's, another of his famous poems being written about this spot. Its fame means that transportation and accommodation are no problem, but that it will always be crowded with visitors. There are two ways to view Matsushima — from the land or from the water. Probably it is a question of finances. From the land is cheap and quite adequate. From the water is expensive but better.

There are two railway lines serving Matsushima. The Tohoku Line and the Senseki Line cross each other and cross back, then run parallel. The Tohoku Line is the quicker of the two, but Matsushima station is a few minutes walk from the interesting parts of the bay. If you use this line, it will take about 25 minutes to Matsushima. Preferable, however, is the Senseki Line. First you have to find it at Sendai. It is not adjacent to the other platforms, but at right angles to them, along an underground passage. From the *shinkansen*, in particular, it is quite a long walk. There are two types of train: ordinary and *kaisoku*. The *kaisoku* trains depart every hour on the hour. Ordinary trains to Matsushima Kaigan usually depart at 17 minutes past each hour. The *kaisoku* takes 26 minutes, the ordinary trains about 40 minutes.

When you alight at Matsushima Kaigan, immediately in front of the station is an information office where you can find free leaflets in English. You can see the bay just ahead. The nearest attraction is an **aquarium**, the oldest in Japan, having been established in 1927. However, at ¥1,400 it is expensive and you will probably decide not to visit. If you go to the right, you will soon see the island of **Oshima**, reached by crossing a red bridge. Formerly a retreat for meditation, it has caves which were used for that purpose and Buddhist images carved into the rocks. This small island gives quite a good view of the bay.

A somewhat better view, though, is obtained from **Sokan-zan**, a little further round the bay, and a better one still from **Ogidani**, the hill behind you. There is also **Saigyo Modoshi-no Matsu Park** behind Matsushima Kaigan station offering a good view. All of these involve some walking, especially the last.

If you now return to the station area and go round the bay in the opposite direction (i.e. to the left as you face the bay), you will come to a **museum**, the **Kanrantei ('Wave-viewing') Tearoom** and then a **boat quay**. Admission to the museum costs ¥200. The boats run both as ferries and on pleasure trips, about both of which more soon.

Just beyond the boat quay are two more red bridges leading to the small island of **Godaido-jima**, which is just big enough for a Buddhist hall called **Godai-do**. This hall is opened only once every 33 years. Do not stand around waiting for it, because the next occasion will be in 2006.

Proceeding further, you will reach the long (252 metres) red bridge to **Fukuura-jima**.

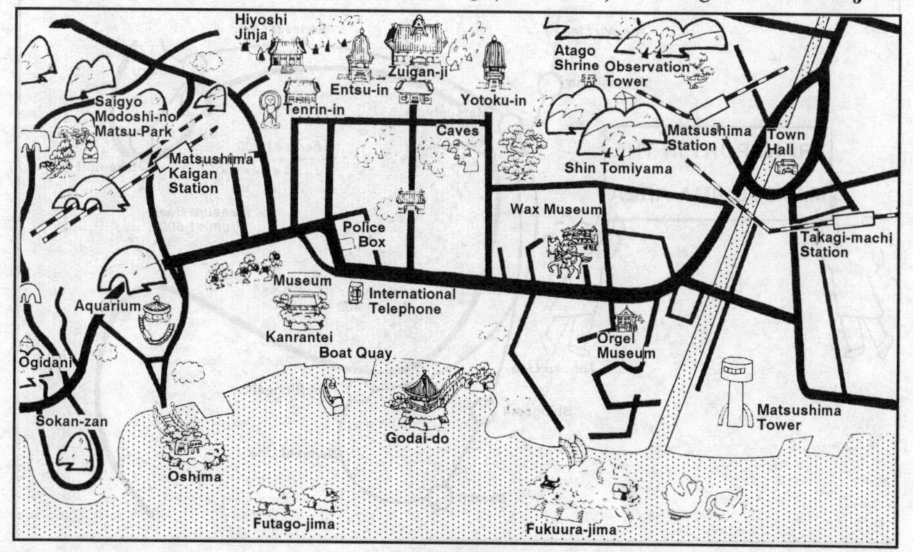


MATSUSHIMA

This is a natural botanical garden where a colony of swans lives. A good view can be obtained from the bridge, to cross which there is a ¥150 toll (no charge to come back).

If you now return to the main street and walk a short way back towards Matsushima Kaigan station, you will come to the entrance to a temple known as **Zuigan-ji**, the most famous Zen temple in Tohoku. Admission costs ¥500. The temple's history goes back to 828, but the original buildings were destroyed and the present ones date from 1609. There are several other places of interest nearby.

As you face Zuigan-ji, to the left is **Entsu-in,** the mausoleum of the grandson of Date Masamune, the latter being the man who built Aoba-jo in Sendai, and who was also responsible for rebuilding Zuigan-ji. This building is supposed to contain the oldest oil painting in Japan, brought here from Rome. There is also a rose garden. Admission costs ¥300. Next is **Tenrin-in**, the mausoleum of one of Date Masamune's daughters, and behind that is **Hiyoshi Jinja**, a shrine which, like Godai-do, is opened once every 33 years. To the right of Zuigan-ji is **Yotoku-in**, the mausoleum of one of the wives of Date Masamune.

Beyond Yotoku-in is a hill called **Shin Tomiyama**, another place offering a good view of the bay, this time over the rooftops. There is a short tower to improve the line of vision. Another viewpoint is Matsushima Tower, which can be seen near Takagi-machi station, one stop beyond Matsushima Kaigan. ¥400 to go up the tower, though. There is another hill beyond and behind Takagi-machi station, called **Tomiyama**, which again offers a view.

From here you can return to Sendai either by Senseki Line from Takagi-machi or by Tohoku Line from Matsushima. The latter is faster and offers a more frequent service. If you are staying at Matsushima Youth Hostel, you should take the Senseki Line onwards to Nobiru. The Matsushima Youth Hostel is completely new, opened in July 1994. Of course, it is also one of the more expensive hostels. Nearby, though, is **Otakamori**, another viewpoint, this one offering a completely different perspective on this bay of islands. If you are continuing north, and not staying in this area, you can take the Tohoku Line from Matsushima station.

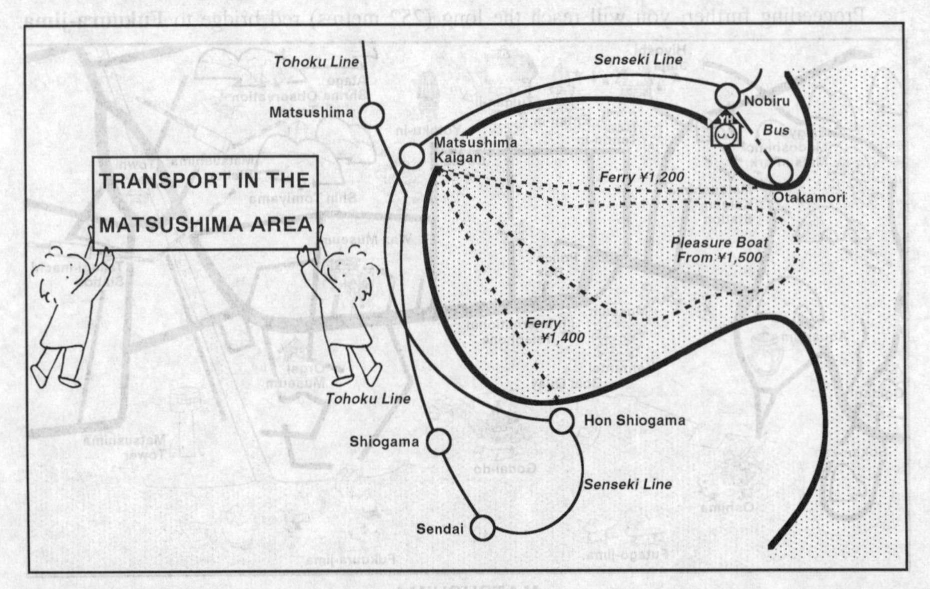

Now, what about the **boat trip**? From the boat quay at Matsushima Kaigan one can take a pleasure trip. Various routes are offered, but none of them is cheap. They start at about ¥1,500 for a one-hour trip. Alternatively, you can take a ferry ride. One way to do this is to alight from the Senseki Line train at Hon Shiogama (or at Shiogama station if you take the Tohoku Line) on the way here. All trains stop. Hon Shiogama is 16 minutes from Sendai by *kaisoku* or 26 minutes by ordinary train. From there you can take a ferry to Matsushima Kaigan. The cost is ¥1,400 for a one hour journey and boats depart every 30 minutes from 8:00. Of course, one can do this for the return journey instead if one prefers. The last boat back is at 16:00. Fewer boats operate in winter, however. Another possibility is to take the boat from Matsushima Kaigan to Otakamori, from where you can obtain a fine view of the bay, and then take a bus to Matsushima Youth Hostel or to Nobiru station (野蒜駅) on the Senseki Line. The ferry ride takes one hour and costs ¥1,200, but there are only two departures, and these in summer only. Boats leave Matsushima Kaigan at 9:00 and 12:00 and return from Otakamori at 10:05 and 13:05. There are not many buses from Otakamori either. Suitable departures from Otakamori Nobori-guchi are at 13:18 and 16:18 on weekdays and at 10:53, 13:53, 15:53 and 16:53 on holidays. It would be possible to walk to the Youth Hostel instead — about 45 minutes walk.

## HIRAIZUMI (平泉 – 'Plateau Spring')

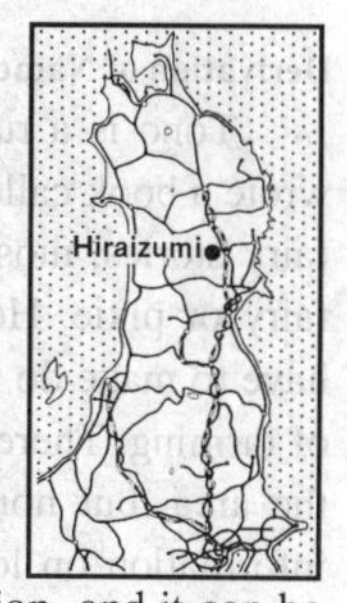


**Tohoku Line, 2 hrs. from Sendai**

**Derivation of Name:** *This was a flat place, subject to flooding, and with a spring which never dried up.*

On reaching Hiraizumi, you will find it difficult to believe that this tiny town was once the most important place in the Tohoku area. True, it was a while ago, in the eleventh and twelfth centuries, when it was the cultural and administrative capital of the district. The Fujiwara family, which controlled this part of Japan, built beautiful temples here, of which there is but a hint today. There is a youth hostel though, only a few minutes walk from the station, and it can be recommended, for Motsuji Hostel is within the grounds of the temple named **Motsu-ji**. To reach here, simply leave Hiraizumi station and walk straight ahead until the road bends sharp left. Motsu-ji used to be the largest and most important temple in Tohoku, but everything has been destroyed over the years. Foundations only remain, together with a garden dominated by a large pond and some relatively new, but still very attractive, temple buildings. There is an admission charge, but, if you stay in the hostel, you have to gain admittance somehow, so will not usually be asked to pay to view the temple (especially if you arrive after it officially closes at 17:00). The author got up rather earlier than was necessary to catch an early morning train and wandered around the grounds before 6:00. At that time, with the early morning light on the temple buildings and a thin mist hanging over the pond, it was a beautiful and peaceful sight and, of course, at that hour there was nobody else around to destroy the tranquility.

Nearby is **Chuson-ji**, a temple dating from 1105. Although most of the old buildings have disappeared over the years, a structure named **Konjiki-do** ('Golden Hall') has survived. It is surrounded by a new outer building and can be viewed through glass panels. Three of the Fujiwara rulers are buried within. In 1950, researchers checked to make sure that they were still there, an event which can be watched on film in the small museum nearby.

Another nearby attraction is **Geibi-kei**. It is a gorge up to 100 metres deep through which one can take a boat ride. The return journey takes 90 minutes and costs ¥1,300. Boats leave hourly throughout the year.

To reach Hiraizumi from Sendai, or, indeed, from Tokyo, take the Tohoku *shinkansen* to Ichinoseki. From Sendai the journey takes 30 to 45 minutes and from Tokyo 2½ to 2¾ hours. There are a few trains which do not stop, so take care. At Ichinoseki, change to the conventional Tohoku Line for two stations, 9 minutes, to Hiraizumi. If you are travelling from Matsushima, however, it is easier to take the ordinary train north from Matsushima than to return to Sendai to take the *shinkansen*. The two stations between Sendai and Ichinoseki on the *shinkansen* route do not lie on the conventional Tohoku Line, so it is not convenient to change at those. From Matsushima to Hiraizumi by Tohoku Line takes about 1 hour 45 minutes. It is necessary to change at Ichinoseki.

Chuson-ji (中尊寺) is only 5 minutes from Hiraizumi by bus (¥130). Geibi-kei, however, lies on the Ofunato Line, which starts in Ichinoseki. The service is approximately 2-hourly. There are both *kaisoku* and ordinary trains, but all stop at Geibi-kei. By ordinary train it takes about 35 minutes and by *kaisoku* 25 minutes.

## TONO (遠野 – 'Distant Field')

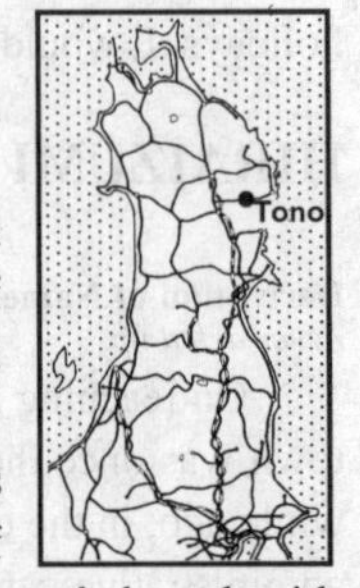


**Kamaishi Line, 70 mins. from Hanamaki**

**Derivation of Name:** *From Ainu 'tonupu', meaning 'marshy field'.*

Tono is a rustic farming town made famous because Kunio Yanagida wrote a book called *Tono Monogatari* ('Tales of Tono'). Since it is a book of fairy stories, most Japanese visit here hoping to catch a glimpse of the odd fairy or pixie. However, they have become scarce these days, so you may have to make do with some old thatched farmhouses and traditional methods of farming. There is a tourist information office near the station with maps of the area, but none of the attractions is near the station. There is also a youth hostel with information on local sights. That too is not near the station. See the directions in the Youth Hostels section on page 411. Tono Youth Hostel was among the top ten hostels in the most recent poll.

To reach Tono is, in any case, a deviation from our main route, but, if you wish to see the coastal scenery of Sanriku (see next entry), Tono is a reasonable place to spend the previous night, on the way there, although from here you cannot reach Jodogahama in time to take the boat service which runs to Otanabe in August only.

The Kamaishi Line runs from Hanamaki to Kamaishi, on the coast, formerly a steel-producing and fishing town, but one which is now surviving on fishing alone. It is a place which has seen better days, especially now that the steel industry is in such decline. There we join the Yamada Line which runs back to Morioka via Miyako. There are three *kyuko* trains between Hanamaki and Kamaishi, one of which is extended to Miyako. These trains take 60 minutes between Hanamaki and Tono. Ordinary trains, which run 9 times per day, take 70 minutes. The Tohoku *shinkansen* stops at Shin Hanamaki, which is also on the Kamaishi Line. The station is separate from the *shinkansen* station, but adjacent to it.

There is a youth hostel at Hanamaki too – Hanamaki Naranosato Hostel – but it is a long walk from Shin Hanamaki station. The hostel is a very pleasant little one in a farmhouse. When the author stayed here, I was told that I was the first non-Japanese guest to come alone. Maybe nobody else could face the long walk! This used to be the smallest hostel in Japan, but, although still small, it has expanded its capacity somewhat, no doubt due to increased demand.

## SANRIKU（三陸 − 'Three Lands'）

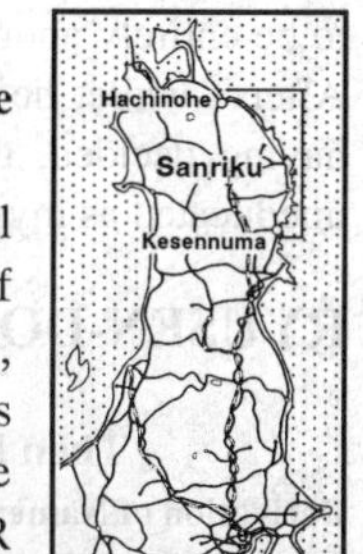


**Various Branch Lines off Tohoku Line**

**Derivation of Name:** *Includes parts of three prefectures.*

From Kesennuma north to Hachinohe extends an area of rugged coastal scenery known as Sanriku − the 'three lands' − because it includes parts of three prefectures − Miyagi, Iwate and Aomori. Most of the coast, however, is in Iwate. The problem with this area is that, although it is beautiful, it is not easily accessible by public transport. True, a railway runs the whole length of the coast, but, rather inconveniently, this railway is operated by JR as far north as Sakari, then by the Sanriku Private Railway to Kamaishi, by JR to Miyako, by the Sanriku Private Railway to Kuji and by JR north to Hachinohe. There are trains which run right through from Sakari to Kuji, including one through trip by a 'retro' diesel rail car originally used in the Yokohama Exposition in 1989 and designed to look a century old (but not really so, of course). However, even if one has a ticket for the JR portions, the private railway is expensive − ¥920 for the 37 kilometres from Sakari to Kamaishi and ¥1,600 for the 71 kilometres between Miyako and Kuji. Moreover, these are newly constructed lines and much of their lengths is in tunnels, so that one gets only glimpses of what is probably beautiful scenery. The JR section between Kamaishi and Miyako is older and above ground, but it does not run along the coast for very far, mostly taking an inland route. There are **boat services** from various points along the coast, of which the most accessible is probably Jodogahama (浄土ヶ浜) a 13 minute bus ride from Miyako station (¥150). However, the most scenic boat ride, from Jodogahama to Otanabe, runs only in August (at 9:00, 3 hours, ¥2,900). Otherwise, it is a short circular cruise (40 minutes, ¥1,000) or a voyage to Taro, 40 minutes north, ¥1,200 (summer only), from where by Sanriku Private Railway either back to Miyako (20 minutes, ¥390) or on to Kuji (75 minutes, ¥1,360). Although this scenery is spectacular in parts, it should be borne in mind that it will take at least a whole day to make the necessary detour to look at it.

Miyako can be reached either from Hanamaki via Kamaishi, where it is usually necessary to change trains, or directly from Morioka. From Morioka, however, there are only four trains per day, the first at 10:43, reaching Miyako at 12:41. This train is usually crowded, so, since it is not pleasant to stand for two hours, be sure to get there early. From Morioka one can also take a *kyuko* which starts at 8:36 and travels via Hanamaki (9:06) and Tono (10:05) along the Kamaishi Line to Kamaishi, which it reaches at 10:52. A connexion leaves Kamaishi at 11:00 and arrives in Miyako at 12:20.

If you decide to travel up the whole length of the coast, paying for the two private railway sections, there is a youth hostel at Rikuzen Takata. This large hostel with 96 beds is in quite an isolated location only a few metres from a relatively unfrequented beach. At night one can hear the sound of the waves breaking on the shore. When the author was here, there were only three hostellers staying. The 'parent' kindly said that he would collect me from the station, as it was already dark and quite a long walk, but I foolishly said that I would find my own way. Do not make the same mistake! This hostel is quite difficult to locate after dark. If you are offered a ride, you should accept it.

I recall too that, on the train journey here, the man opposite started a conversation with me. He was a very rural character and I had difficulty in understanding anything which he was saying because of his strong Tohoku accent. To make matters worse, his conversation proved to be entirely about fish, in which area my Japanese vocabulary turned out to be sadly lacking. After a while, he stopped talking and never spoke another word for the rest of the journey, having decided, no doubt, that he could not find anything in common with somebody as uneducated as myself who did not know about fish.

## RYUSEN-DO (竜泉洞 – 'Dragon's Spring Cave')

**Yamada Line, 1 hr. 40 mins. from Morioka to Mo-ichi.**
**Then Iwaizumi Line to Iwaizumi, 53 mins. Then bus, 18 mins.**

**Derivation of Name:** *Uncertain.*

Caves sometimes have such wonderful names. This one is of the limestone variety and is the third biggest in Japan. It is, however, rather difficult to reach, especially since JR withdrew the mid-day train to Iwaizumi. If you live in Iwaizumi and have the misfortune to miss the 7:58 train one morning, you will have to stand around waiting until 17:20 for the next. This situation rather limits visits to the cave, but there are also JR bus services and, if timetables do not change too much, a one-day circular trip can be made from Morioka, in summer only, incorporating a lot of pretty scenery, a look at the Sanriku coast and a visit to Ryusen-do. Get somebody to check this schedule carefully before following it. It does not involve any risky connexions, but there are several infrequent services and a change in one of those might leave the visitor stranded somewhere along the route. At the moment, however, in summer, it can be done like this:-

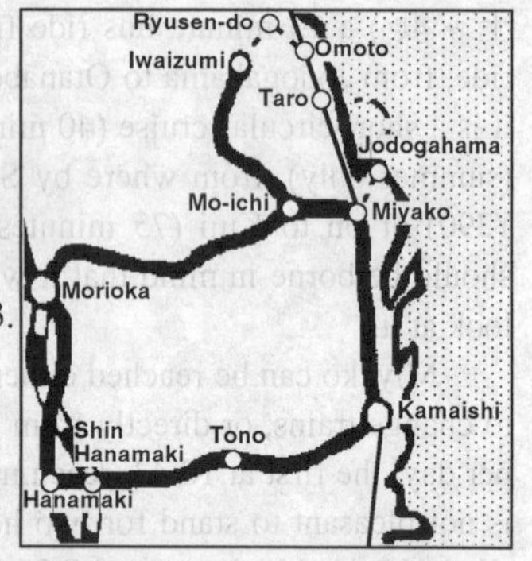


Morioka 8:36 *kyuko* to Kamaishi 10:52 (via Tono 10:05).
Kamaishi 11:00 ordinary train to Miyako 12:20.
Miyako 12:50 bus to Jodogahama (浄土ヶ浜) 13:03.
Jodogahama 13:10 or 13:40 boat to Taro 13:50 or 14:20.
Taro 14:43 train to Omoto 15:04.
Omoto station 15:09 JR bus to Ryusen-do (竜泉洞) 15:43.
Ryusen-do 16:35 or 17:03 JR bus to Iwaizumi station (岩泉駅) 16:47 or 17:15.
Iwaizumi 17:20 ordinary train to Mo-ichi 18:12.
Mo-ichi 18:31 ordinary train to Morioka 20:28.

Those with Blue Spring tickets cannot use the morning *kyuko* from Morioka and have the choice of taking an earlier ordinary train which runs along the same route, leaving Morioka at 6:23 and reaching Kamaishi at 9:16, or taking the 10:43 *kaisoku* from Morioka direct to Miyako along the Yamada Line, arriving at 12:41. Blue Springers also have to pay for the JR bus, which is quite expensive – about ¥500 from Omoto to Ryusen-do and ¥170 from the cave to Iwaizumi station. It is important to note, too, that the return to Morioka is not until 20:28, while youth hostels generally require check-in by 20:00. However, if you stayed at the hostel the previous night and have paid already, a return later than 20:00 will be all right. In other words, this schedule is suitable for a day trip from Morioka, but if you are arriving newly at the youth hostel there, you will need to ask for a special dispensation to check in late. Kami Morioka station, reached at 20:23, is actually much nearer to the hostel than Morioka station is.

Notice also that there is a 10 minute walk involved between Taro port and Taro station. However, sufficient time is allowed for this in the schedule.

For those who do not want the expense of the boat ride but would still like a glimpse of the coastline and a visit to Ryusen-do, there is another possibility, as hereunder, again a one-day trip from Morioka.

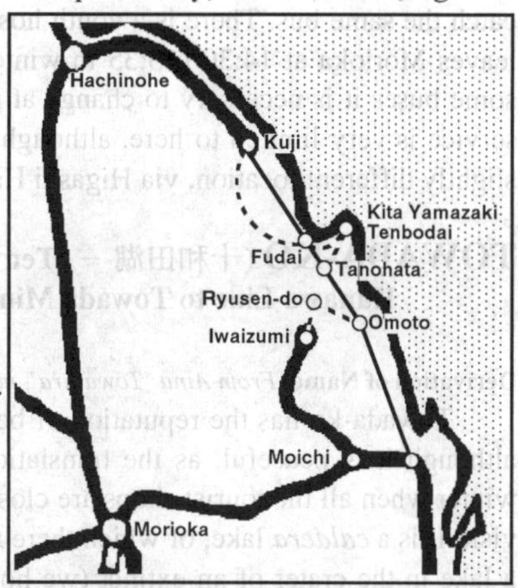


Morioka 8:25 *tokkyu* to Hachinohe 9:36.
Hachinohe 9:49 ordinary train to Kuji 11:55.
Kuji 12:00 JR bus to Fudai station (普代駅) 12:52.
Fudai station 13:00 JR bus to Kita Yamazaki
Tenbodai (Lookout) (北山崎展望台) 13:25.
Kita Yamazaki Tenbodai 13:36 bus to Tanohata
station (田野畑駅) 14:02 (**Not holidays**).
Tanohata 14:53 train to Omoto 15:04.
Omoto 15:09 JR bus to Ryusen-do (竜泉洞) 15:43.
Ryusen-do 16:35 or 17:03 JR bus to Iwaizumi
station (岩泉駅) 16:47 or 17:15.
Iwaizumi 17:20 ordinary train to Mo-ichi 18:12.
Mo-ichi 18:31 ordinary train to Morioka 20:28.

This tour is not particularly suitable for those using Blue Spring tickets. Although the *tokkyu* from Morioka can be replaced by an ordinary train leaving at 7:10 and reaching Hachinohe at 9:24, from Kuji all the buses would have to be paid for, as well as the train from Tanohata to Omoto. This would amount to approximately ¥2,500. Those using a Japan Rail Pass or a *shu-yu-ken* would have to pay only for the bus from the lookout to Tanohata (¥320) and the train from there to Omoto (¥330).

Kita Yamazaki Tenbodai is a lookout post specially designed to offer a good view of the coastline. It is a pity that you will have only 11 minutes there, but it cannot be helped. You will also get views of the coast on the journey south from Hachinohe by bus and train.

## MORIOKA (盛岡 – 'Quantity Hill')

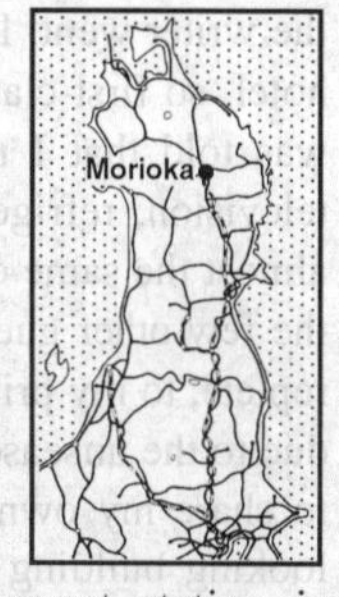


**Tohoku *shinkansen*, 3 hrs. from Tokyo**

**Derivation of Name:** *The local lord named this place 'forest hill' ('Morioka' — same pronunciation). Later the first Chinese character was changed because there seemed to be such a lot of forest!*

Morioka is at present the end of the Tohoku *shinkansen*, although the line is being extended to Aomori. The city's main attraction is the ruins of **Kozukata Castle**, now a park beside the river. The castle can be reached on foot from Morioka station in about 20 minutes. The area is pleasant, but not really worthy of a special visit. There is a youth hostel in Morioka. Directions are given in our Youth Hostels section, but actually the nearest station is Kuriyagawa, one stop north of Morioka, from where the hostel is within walking distance.

If you are coming from Hiraizumi, the *shinkansen* journey from Ichinoseki takes only 43 minutes. By ordinary train from Hiraizumi to Morioka takes 90 minutes.

## HACHIMANTAI (八幡平 – 'God of War Plateau')

**Hanawa Line to Obuke, 40 mins. from Morioka. Then bus, 65 mins.**

**Derivation of Name:** *An early general built here a temple to Hachiman, the God of War.*

The attractive mountainous area of Hachimantai lies north-west of Morioka. In the winter, this is a ski resort area. It is also well known for its hot springs.

Buses run direct from Morioka, but it is cheaper to take a train first to Obuke and then catch the same bus. There is a youth hostel in Hachimantai. Note that the last bus for this area leaves Morioka at 14:30 (13:35 in winter) and Obuke at 15:30 (14:32 in winter) and that on some buses it is necessary to change at Higashi Hachimantai (東八幡平). In winter, the bus service is very limited to here, although plenty of buses run to the ski resorts, which are in a slightly different location, via Higashi Hachimantai (20 minutes by bus from the youth hostel).

## TOWADA-KO (十和田湖 — 'Ten Peaceful Fields Lake')

**Hanawa Line to Towada Minami, 2 hrs. 30 mins. from Morioka. Then bus, 1 hr.**

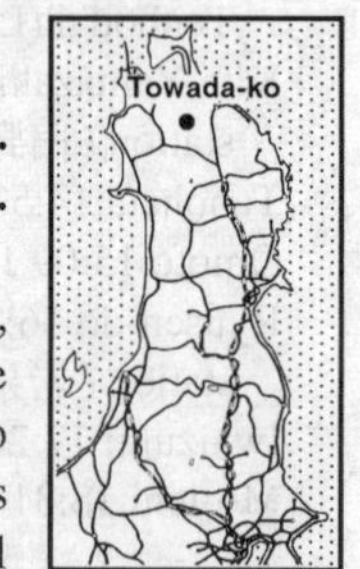


**Derivation of Name:** *From Ainu 'Towatara', meaning 'the lake surrounded by a cliff'.*

Towada-ko has the reputation of being the most beautiful lake in Japan, although it is peaceful, as the translation of its name suggests, only in the winter when all the tourist shops are closed and the masses think it too cold to visit. It is a *caldera* lake, of which there are many examples in Japan — that is a lake in the crater of an extinct (we hope!) volcano. It is indeed a beautiful lake if you can observe it without intrusion. The author was fortunate enough to visit in spring, a week before the tourist season started, when all the shopkeepers were just starting to take down the winter shutters and get out their paint-brushes. The snow still lay quite thick in places, especially on the narrow, twisting and dangerous road which runs from Towada Minami station and which must climb over the rim of the old volcano before descending to the lake. In the early morning, the mist hung low over the lake so that the mountain appeared to hover in mid-air above the clouds. Almost nobody was around at that time of the year. A week later, when the summer bus services started, no doubt it would have been transformed.

The town of Towada-ko (sometimes called Yasumiya) is very small, living only on the tourist business. There is a youth hostel here, called Hakubutsu-kan ('Museum') Hostel. When the writer went, I was told to report to the 'new building', which turned out to be a first-class hotel, so first-class that I felt embarrassed to go inside! However, when I asked hesitantly, I was told that I really was in the right place and I was given a normal hotel room, with television, refrigerator, etc., all to myself, as I was the only hosteller that day. Then I ate almost the same excellent dinner, served by friendly *kimono*-clad waitresses, as that for which the few other guests had surely paid three or four times as much as I had and retired, happily replete, to my private room and, later, to the huge communal bath, in which I was again alone, due to the unseasonable time of my visit. It was all very enjoyable. However, before you rush to share my own pleasant experience, I should warn that there is an old and rather shabby looking building which is generally used as the youth hostel and no doubt that has a very different atmosphere. I presume that it is not economical to heat it for the few guests who appear in winter.

There is a second youth hostel, called Towada Hostel, on the southern side of the lake, reached soon after the bus from Towada Minami turns right on arriving at the edge of the lake. This hostel is open in summer only. A third hostel is Kuromori-so in the spa town of Oyu Onsen, 17 minutes from Towada Minami on the way to Towada-ko. There is a natural spa bath in the hostel. Plenty of JR buses run this far all the year round, from Rikuchu Hanawa station, a little closer to Morioka, as well as from Towada Minami. Near this town is an interesting pre-historic **stone circle**, no doubt of religious significance. There is a fourth hostel, named Oirase Hostel, at Yakeyama, on the road from Towada-ko to Aomori or to Towada-shi, so this area is well served for low-cost accommodation.

Near the town of Towada-ko beside the lake is a small shrine and, just before you reach it, a sculpture entitled 'Maidens of the Lake'. The author thought that these two ladies must feel pretty chilly, with the snow accumulated round their feet and no clothes to keep them warm, but they seem to endure it well, no doubt looking forward to summer and the return of crowds of admirers.

There are several **lookout points** around the lake. There is one (Hakka Tenbodai – 発荷展望台) on the bus route from Towada Minami. The nearest one to Towada-ko town can be reached by walking along the road to Aomori or Towada-shi, or by taking a bus a short distance up the hill. There is another on the far side of the lake, Takinosawa Tenbodai (滝ノ沢展望台), to reach which you should take a bus bound for Hirosaki (弘前) for 25 minutes. There are three buses per day, in summer only. The first is at 8:20. Only this bus makes a good connexion for the return to Towada-ko (十和田湖) town, for it reaches the lookout at 8:55 and there is a bus back at 9:35. It is possible to continue round the lake and make a complete circuit by bus only for short periods at the beginning of August and in mid-October. In those brief periods, buses run from Takinosawa lookout to Nenokuchi (子ノ口) at 10:20 and 13:20. You can then return to Towada-ko town by another bus (most are JR buses) or by boat.

Several **boat routes** operate, but the most popular is between Towada-ko town and Nenokuchi. The ride takes an hour and during the summer boats leave half-hourly. The cost is ¥1,300. A one-hour circular trip on the lake is the same price.

A very popular walk is along the **Oirase valley**. The Oirase is the only stream which flows out of Towada-ko. It flows along a narrow green valley for 14 kilometres to the town of Yakeyama. To attempt this walk, first take a bus to Nenokuchi, a journey of 25 minutes. Most buses are JR buses bound for Aomori (青森). However, if you do not feel like so much

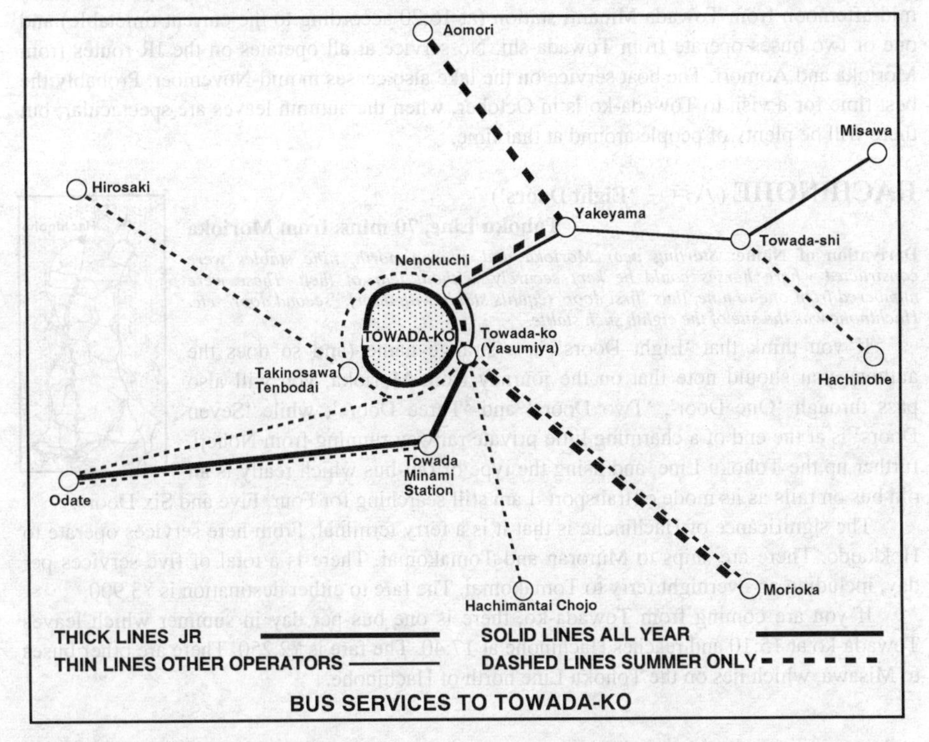

BUS SERVICES TO TOWADA-KO

walking, just look out of the bus window when you leave Nenokuchi, for the road to Aomori and Towada-shi also passes along this valley and you can get a good view of it without the need for physical exertion. Remember that there is a youth hostel in Yakeyama.

To reach Towada-ko from Morioka, take a train along the Hanawa Line to Towada Minami, which is a stub-end station where the train has to be turned round. Trains run about every two hours and the journey, which is a pretty one, takes approximately 2½ hours. A convenient departure from Morioka is at 11:01. This train is a *kaisoku* so it is a little quicker, reaching Towada Minami at 12:51. A JR bus leaves for Towada-ko (十和田湖) at 13:00 (summer only), the bus ride taking an hour.

If you prefer, there is also a direct bus service from Morioka to Towada-ko in summer. Three of the nine daily buses are operated by JR, these three departing at 11:00, 13:00 and 15:00. The journey takes 2 hours 15 minutes.

In summer, a direct bus service operates from the Hachimantai area. There are two buses per day from Hachimantai Chojo (八幡平頂上), so, if you are staying at the youth hostel, you first have to take a bus to there. There is a convenient connexion which leaves the Kanko Hotel at 11:04, reaching Hachimantai Chojo at 11:26. The bus to Towada-ko departs at 11:30, arriving at 13:59. To catch the later service, take the 13:19 from the Kanko Hotel to Hachimantai Chojo (13:40) and then the 14:25 bus from there to Towada-ko, where you will arrive at 16:54. These are not JR buses, so the journey will be expensive. From Hachimantai Chojo to Towada-ko costs ¥2,120, in addition to which you must buy a seat reservation ticket for ¥210. The entire journey from the Kanko Hotel to Towada-ko will cost about ¥2,700.

There are also buses to Towada-ko from Aomori (JR), Hachinohe, Misawa, Hirosaki and Odate. In winter, however, services are very limited. One JR bus per day operates in the mid-afternoon from Towada Minami station (at 16:20 according to the current timetable) and one or two buses operate from Towada-shi. No service at all operates on the JR routes from Morioka and Aomori. The boat service on the lake also ceases in mid-November. Probably the best time for a visit to Towada-ko is in October, when the autumn leaves are spectacular, but there will be plenty of people around at that time.

## HACHINOHE (八戸 – 'Eight Doors')

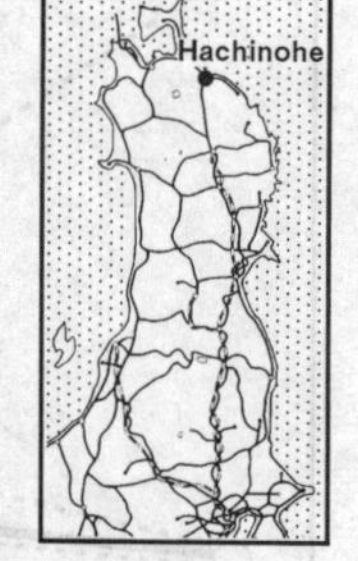


**Tohoku Line, 70 mins. from Morioka**

**Derivation of Name:** *Starting near Morioka and moving north, nine stables were constructed where horses could be kept securely, without fear of theft. These were numbered from one to nine, thus 'first door' (equals stable with door), 'second door', etc. Hachinohe was the site of the eighth such stable.*

If you think that 'Eight Doors' is a strange name (and so does the author), you should note that on the journey from Morioka, you will also pass through 'One Door', 'Two Doors' and 'Three Doors', while 'Seven Doors' is at the end of a charming little private railway running from Noheji, further up the Tohoku Line, and using the type of rail-bus which really is an old bus on rails as its mode of transport. I am still searching for Four, Five and Six Doors.

The significance of Hachinohe is that it is a ferry terminal. From here services operate to Hokkaido. There are ships to Muroran and Tomakomai. There is a total of five services per day, including an overnight ferry to Tomakomai. The fare to either destination is ¥3,900.

If you are coming from Towada-ko, there is one bus per day in summer which leaves Towada-ko at 15:10 and reaches Hachinohe at 17:40. The fare is ¥2,250. There are other buses to Misawa, which lies on the Tohoku Line north of Hachinohe.

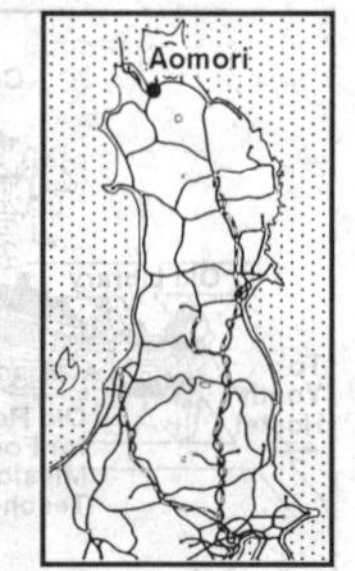


## AOMORI (青森 − 'Blue Forest') Tohoku and Ou Lines,

**2 hrs. 15 mins. from Morioka or 9 hrs. 15 mins. from Ueno (Tokyo)**

**Derivation of Name:** *Literal. There was green forest around, green and blue being almost synonymous in Japanese.*

Aomori is the northernmost large city on Honshu, Japan's main island. It used to be the departure point for JR ferries to Hokkaido until the Seikan Tunnel was opened on 22nd March 1988. One such ferry, the ***Hakkoda Maru***, is preserved as a relic of those days at the ferry terminal at the seaward end of Aomori station. In the sadly typical English of the tourist literature distributed by the Aomori City Council, "Display of history as a ferryboat linked Hakodate and Aomori is nice. Enjoy seeing water front atthe restaurant in this momrial ship."

The city is famous for its **Nebuta Festival** in early August, when huge floats parade through the streets. In case you arrive in the other 98% of the year, some of the floats are on permanent display at a place called Nebuta-no-sato (ねぶたの里). Unfortunately, it is 30 to 40 minutes by bus from Aomori station. However, JR runs 6 buses there per day and additional services are operated by Aomori city buses.

To reach Aomori from Towada-ko, take the JR bus which runs approximately hourly. The first bus is at 7:35 and the last at 16:30. The journey takes 3 hours. In winter, however, there is no service on this route, so one must take a bus to Towada-shi (¥1,650 − **not** JR) or Misawa (¥2,000). However, even on this bus route, there will be only one or two buses per day in winter. From Towada-shi, the Towada Kanko Private Railway runs to Misawa (¥560) and from Misawa the JR Tohoku Line runs north to Aomori.

There is no youth hostel in Aomori, unfortunately. The nearest are at Hirosaki or Mukaiyama, one station south of Misawa. The latter, Kawayo Green Hostel, can be recommended. It is only about 10 minutes walk from Mukaiyama station. It is located on a farm and it has a *rotenburo*, that is an outdoor spa bath. Some English is spoken. From Aomori to Mukaiyama takes 90 minutes by ordinary train. Expresses do not stop, although they stop at Misawa, so it is sometimes possible to save time by taking a *tokkyu* to Misawa and changing to an ordinary train there.

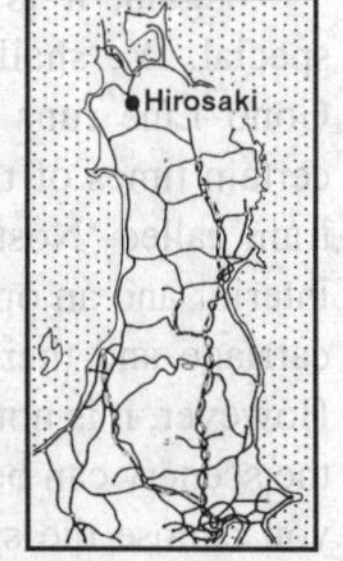


## HIROSAKI (弘前 − 'Clever Front')

**Ou Line, 2 hrs. 15 mins. from Akita or 12 hrs. from Ueno (Tokyo)**

**Derivation of Name:** *Originally a different Chinese character was used for 'hiro', meaning wide. Hirosaki was in front of a wide plain. The character was later changed to one with a better meaning.*

Hirosaki is a rather charming city with several old and unusual buildings, some of them displaying surprising western influence.

The primary attraction is the **castle**, which dates from 1610 and is a real one, not a modern reconstruction. It is in a park which is particularly attractive at cherry blossom time, rather later here than in the Tokyo area, occurring in late April. Since this timing coincides with the 'Golden Week' holiday, the park attracts huge crowds. There is also the old **Aomori Bank building**, a quite imposing **catholic church**, a five-storey pagoda in the grounds of **Saisho-in**, a **clock tower** on top of a watchmaker's shop, two **residences for foreign missionaries**, the **old library** and a **former army research centre.** It is an interesting city.

There is a youth hostel too, and, although its architecture is somewhat less impressive

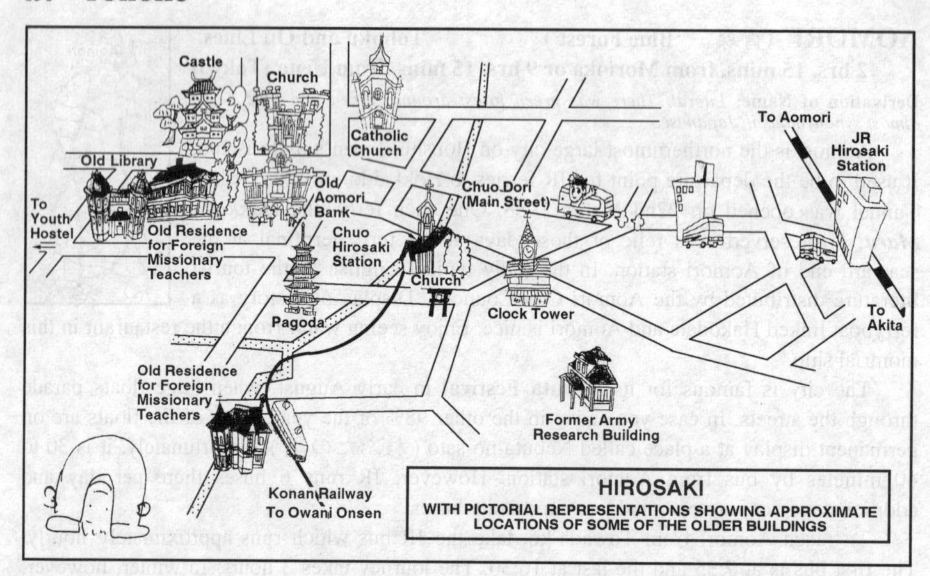


than that of the buildings already mentioned, it is very close to the castle, the old bank and several other historic buildings. It is a 20 minute bus ride from the JR station (there is a separate private railway station too, named Chuo Hirosaki), so a little inconvenient to reach and also not particularly easy to locate, being round a corner in a small dead-end street.

From Aomori it takes only about 35 minutes to Hirosaki by *tokkyu*. By ordinary train, it is a journey of some 45 minutes.

## AKITA (秋田 – 'Autumn Field')

### Ou and Uetsu Lines, 3 hrs. from Yamagata or 9 hrs. from Ueno (Tokyo)

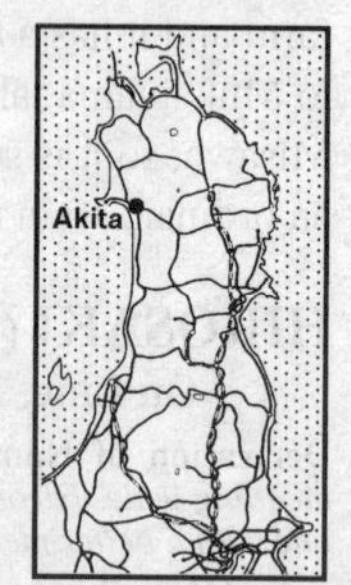


**Derivation of Name:** *Originally 'Akuta', meaning 'bad fields'. Because of the long winters, this area was not suitable for growing rice. Later the name was changed to make it sound more attractive.*

Again, it is not so much Akita itself as the journey there which is special. We shall take the Gono Line, rather than the Ou Main Line. The Gono Line runs around the coast and offers some very pretty views. At certain times of the year, there are morning and afternoon runs by a special train called 'Nostalgic View Train'. One carriage has an attractive wooden interior and an open observation deck at one end to enhance the views. This is a reserved seat carriage and there is a seat reservation charge of ¥500 (waived for Japan Rail Pass users). However, it is not a fast train – quite the opposite, in fact, as it goes deliberately slowly so that the scenery can be enjoyed – so it can be used even by Blue Springers. It is recommended that you choose the special carriage when it is available, as the journey will be more enjoyable. When the special train is not operating, a diesel multiple unit operates to the same timetable. The multiple units always terminate at Higashi Noshiro, where the Gono Line ends, but the special train sometimes continues to Akita. If deciding where to sit, remember that the train will be turned twice, once at Kawabe, near Hirosaki, and again at Higashi Noshiro, if the train continues to Akita. For the main part of the journey, from Kawabe to Higashi Noshiro, you want to be on the sea side.

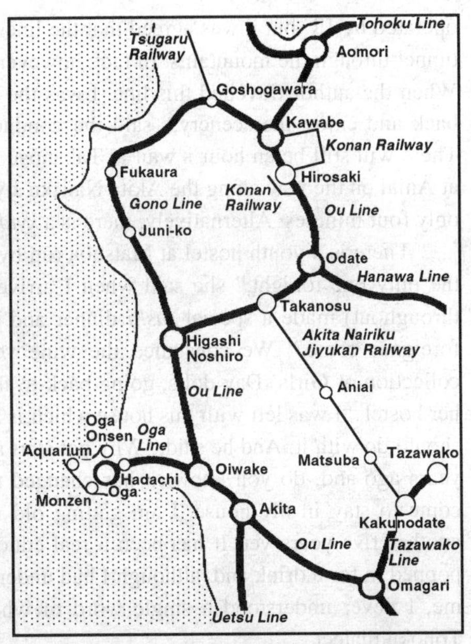


FROM AOMORI TO TAZAWA-KO

There are two options, then, from Hirosaki — a morning train or an afternoon train. If you spend a night in Hirosaki, the morning train will be suitable. If not, you may like to take the afternoon train as far as Fukaura and spend the night there. The morning train leaves Hirosaki at 9:19, proceeds round the coast in a leisurely fashion and reaches Higashi Noshiro at 13:58. The afternoon train leaves Hirosaki at 15:17 and reaches Higashi Noshiro at 19:31, on some days continuing to Akita where it arrives at 20:16. (Trains in the opposite direction leave Higashi Noshiro at 10:20 and 15:50 and arrive in Hirosaki at 14:48 and 21:33. The 10:20 sometimes originates in Akita at 8:53.)

About 50 minutes after starting from Hirosaki and before reaching the coast, you will come to a place named Goshogawara, from where extends the Tsugaru Private Railway. The terrain through which this railway passes is not particularly exciting, but the company is known for continuing to run, in winter, its 'stove trains', heated by wood or coal fires, round which the passengers tend to congregate, for it is cool in this area in winter.

Some 2½ hours from Hirosaki is the fishing town of Fukaura. If you have taken the afternoon train, it will be 17:30 when you reach here and you may have decided that this is a suitable place to spend the night, for there is a youth hostel here, a pleasant temple hostel (so you know that you will have to climb to get to it!). The hostel itself is in a modern building, however, not a traditional temple building. When the author stayed here, I was the only hosteller, so the priest spent the evening teaching me card tricks!

A little further down the line are the **Juni-ko** ('Twelve Lakes'). These lakes were formed by a major landslide. You will find plenty of information on them in Fukaura Youth Hostel, but you do not really need much information for walking around and enjoying the attractive scenery. Take the 7:53 train from Fukaura to Juni-ko station, a 30 minute ride. There is a bus to the lakes at 9:35 in the summer only (sorry about the bad connexion). It takes 10 minutes and costs ¥240, so you could probably walk there if you preferred in the hour which you will spend waiting for the bus. The return bus leaves from the lakes at 12:20, so you will have 2½ hours to look around. You will reach Juni-ko station again at 12:30, just in time to take the 12:45 'Nostalgic View Train', if it is running, for the remainder of the journey round to Higashi Noshiro. If it is not running, a diesel multiple unit will appear running to the same timetable. From Higashi Noshiro, at 14:11, there is a *tokkyu* to Akita and on to Morioka via Tazawako. Blue Springers will have to wait nearly two hours, though, for an onward connexion to Akita. There is, however, an ordinary train at 14:30 to Takanosu, half an hour in the opposite direction, from where the **Akita Nairiku Jiyukan Private Railway** runs through the mountains on a beautiful journey.

This railway is as long as its name suggests that it should be — and so quite expensive. It will cost ¥1,590 for the 94 kilometre trip to Kakunodate. Both ends of this line used to be operated by JR, but it was agreed that the lines should become private and be linked by a long tunnel through the mountains. In fact, however, not many passengers travel the central section. When the author travelled this line, I was the only passenger for this part of the journey. "Sit back and enjoy the scenery," said the conductor, "since you are the only one." And I did. There will still be an hour's wait at Takanosu for the 16:00 train and it is necessary to change at Aniai on the way along the Akita Nairiku Jiyukan Private Railway, but the delay this time is only four minutes. Alternatively, there is a *kyuko* from Takanosu at 15:27 for ¥300 extra.

There is a youth hostel at Matsuba run by a very pleasant lady in her seventies. "You are the only one tonight," she said when I arrived, "so the old lady (as she referred to herself throughout) made a special *sushi* dinner and bought a bottle of wine in honour of having a foreigner come." We consumed the wine very cheerfully between us and I admired her collection of Girls' Day dolls, going back to the last century. Then she told me the history of her hostel. "I was left with this house which is far too big for me, so I asked my nephew what I should do with it. And he said, 'Why not start a youth hostel?' So I did. That was about fifteen years ago and, do you know, it has changed my whole life. People from all over the world come to stay in my house. I am getting old now, but I think that I can continue for about another five years yet. It has been a real education for me." Later, incidentally, a neighbour popped in for a drink and, although I had understood fairly well what 'the old lady' had said to me, I never understood a single word of what she said to the neighbour, so strong is the Tohoku dialect.

However, if you choose to go to Akita in preference to Matsuba, the city has a park named Senshu Park near the station with the ruins of **Kubota Castle**, but maybe you are getting tired of castle ruins by now. What the city is most famous for is its **Kanto Festival** in early August when men balance on their heads, shoulders and various other parts of their anatomy bamboo poles with huge numbers of lighted lanterns attached to the rigging.

Unfortunately, Akita does not even have a youth hostel now. Apart from Matsuba, the nearest are on the Oga Peninsula, down the coast at Kisakata or at Tazawa-ko.

## OGA (男鹿 – 'Man Deer') Oga Line, 1 hr. from Akita

**Derivation of Name:** *Original meaning was 'summit', because this was the top of a sand peninsula, but the Chinese characters used became changed.*

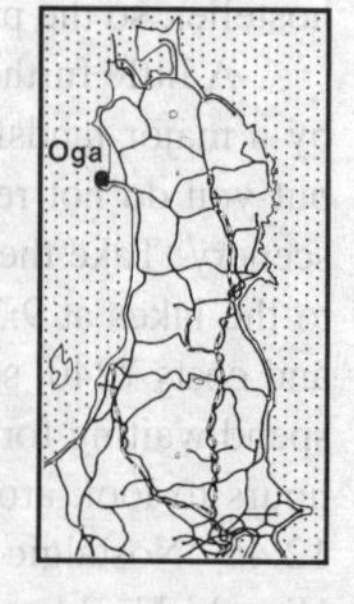


The Oga Peninsula lies just north of Akita, an hour by ordinary train. It is known for beaches, spas, coastal scenery and, very appropriately considering its name, for a form of local ogre. These Oga ogres are named ***namahage***. Because of the shortage of genuine *namahage* these days, men sometimes dress up in black *namahage* costumes and masks. At New Year they visit homes to try to frighten the children (and others?) into being good for the whole year, although it does not seem to be completely effective.

Oga also has a youth hostel. Although this hostel seems on the map to be near the city of Akita, actually it takes quite a while to get there. From Akita, take a train to Hadachi, the penultimate station on the Oga Line. From there it is necessary to take a bus to the spa resort of Oga Onsen (男鹿温泉), a journey of 50 minutes at a cost of ¥640. Buses connect well with trains. For example, trains leave Akita at 14:40, 15:45 and 16:43, reaching Hadachi at 15:35, 16:36 and 17:37. Buses leave Hadachi at 15:47, 16:42 and 17:52 and arrive at Oga Onsen at

16:35, 17:30 and 18:44. Nearly all buses turn round at Oga Grand Hotel (男鹿グランドホテル), your destination, to go back to the main road, so you are not likely to miss the stop. A few, however, continue on and the next bus stop (Youth Hostel-mae), as you reach the sea, is right outside the hostel. The hostel itself is not special, but it has a pleasant view looking out over the sea. There are also three buses a day directly from Akita. The last leaves Akita station at 16:30 and reaches Oga Onsen at 18:20. The fare is ¥1,000.

The area near the hostel could not really be called beach, but the popularity of the hostel with the sea bathing fraternity makes the author believe that there must be beaches somewhere nearby. There is also an aquarium on the tip of the peninsula, to where it is 15 minutes by bus (¥310). From there, to admire the coastal scenery, one can take a boat to Monzen (summer only) and then a bus back to Oga, the final station on the Oga Line, having circumnavigated the peninsula. There are few good connexions, but try using this suggestion which does not involve any very long delays. Take the 7:55 bus from Oga Onsen going to Kamo (加茂) as far as Oga Suizoku-kan (男鹿水族館 – Oga Aquarium), where you arrive at 8:10. The boat leaves for Monzen at 9:00 (summer only). It is a 50 minute journey which costs ¥1,650. The bus leaves Monzen at 9:52, which is a tight connexion. If you miss it, unfortunately you must wait until 11:27 for the next. The journey to Oga (男鹿) costs ¥520 and takes 32 minutes. There are trains to Akita at 11:12 and 12:13, arriving at 12:11 and 13:12.

## TAZAWA-KO (田沢湖 – 'Field Marsh Lake') **Tazawako Line, 35 mins. from Morioka or 70 mins. from Akita. Then bus, 15 mins.**

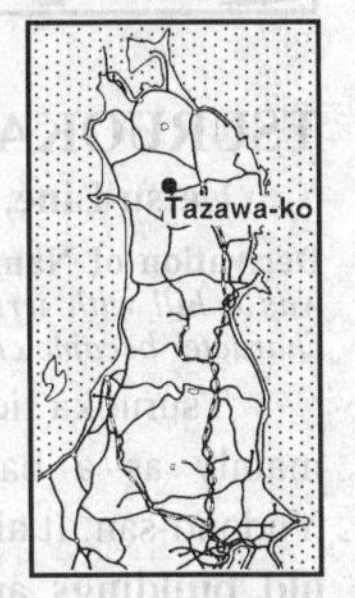


**Derivation of Name:** *There was a marsh here which was later developed into rice paddies.*

Tazawa-ko is the deepest lake in Japan – 423.4 metres, to be precise, not that the author has actually checked it (fortunately). Like Towada-ko, it is a *caldera* lake, that is a lake in the cone of an extinct volcano, and, like Towada-ko, it is a touristy place, so it is not a bad idea to go out of season, for it certainly has natural beauty. If you choose to go in the summer tourist season, however, Tazawa-ko offers swimming, hiking and the inevitable boat rides on the lake (40 minutes, ¥1,150).

To reach the lake, one takes a train along the Tazawako Line to Tazawako station. *Tokkyu* trains run hourly, but there are very few ordinary trains to Tazawako from the Morioka end of the line, so take care if you are approaching from that direction. Ordinary trains leave Morioka for Tazawako at 5:32, 13:53 and 17:54 only, taking one hour over the journey. To reach Tazawako from Morioka, trains have to pass through a very long tunnel under the mountains, so most ordinary trains terminate at the previous station. From the opposite (Omagari) end of the line, there is a two-hourly service of ordinary trains. From Tazawako station, one takes a bus for the 15 minute journey (¥340) to Tazawa-ko (田沢湖). The buses run approximately hourly but the last bus is at 17:35. The youth hostel is on this bus route just as one reaches the lake.

Another nearby hostel is Matsuba, mentioned in the Akita section. To reach there, change trains at Kakunodate, west of Tazawako. *Tokkyu* trains stop. This change will also give you the chance to look at an interesting street of *samurai* houses in Kakunodate.

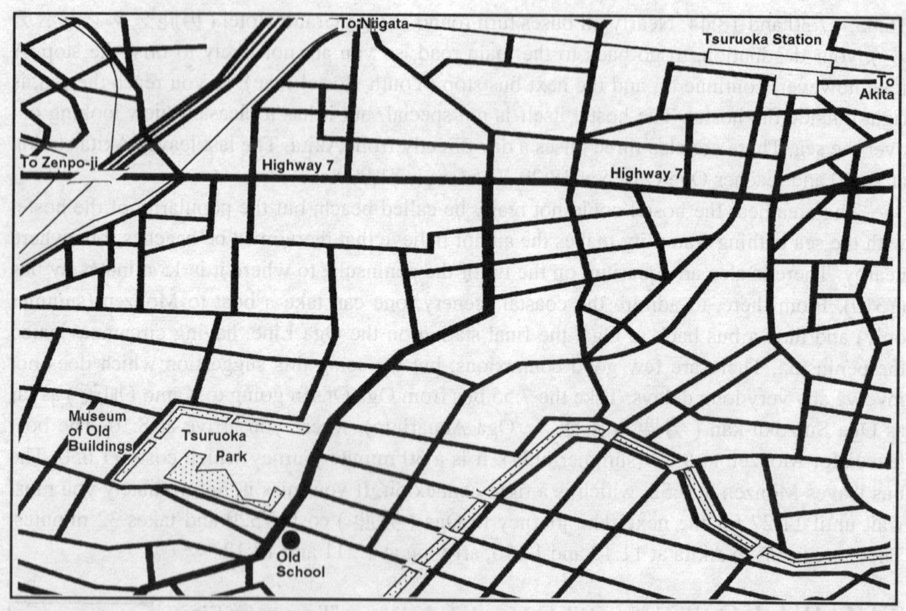


TSURUOKA

## TSURUOKA (鶴岡 — 'Crane Hill')

**Uetsu Line, 1 hr. 45 mins. from Niigata or 7 hrs. from Ueno (Tokyo)**

**Derivation of Name:** *'Tsuru', written in a different way, also meant 'irrigation'. This was a hill with irrigation channels for the cultivation of rice. Over time, the Chinese character became changed.*

Tsuruoka lies on the Japan Sea side of the Tohoku region and is useful mainly as a base for the nearby mountains, Haguro-san, Gassan and Yudono-san. It also has the ruins of a **castle**, now a park, a small **museum of old buildings** and the temple known as **Zenpo-ji**. The castle ruins and museum of buildings can be reached on foot in about 20 minutes, but it is necessary to take a bus for 20 minutes to Zenpo-ji ( 善宝寺 ). The temple is in the midst of cedar trees and has an old five-storey pagoda. Zenpo-ji dates from about 1450.

There is a youth hostel, but it is not in the city. You need to take an ordinary train three stations south to Sanze, a journey of 20 minutes, from where it is a walk of one kilometre (see page 414). Trains run rather less frequently than hourly.

## MT. HAGURO (羽黒山 — 'Black Feather Mountain')

**55 mins. by bus from Tsuruoka**

**Derivation of Name:** *Originally 'Hakura', meaning 'edge place'. The shrine here was built on the edge of the mountain. Over a period of time, the name became changed to 'Haguro'.*

On Haguro-san (Mt. Haguro) is the principal shrine of the *shugendo* sect of mountain ascetic Buddhism. Although Buddhist, this is generally called a shrine, since it was originally constructed as a Shinto shrine in the seventh century. Gradually, it became a place of pilgrimage for Buddhists, especially at the time when Buddhism and Shintoism were more closely related than nowadays. At present it belongs solely to a sect of Buddhism, but is still referred to as a shrine, to add confusion to the issue of religion in the minds of visitors. The shrines on Gassan and Yudono-san (see following sections) are similar. Haguro-san is only 414 metres high and so the summit is accessible throughout the year, although there are quite heavy falls of snow in the winter. There is a flight of 2,446 stone steps leading to the summit from near Haguro Centre (羽黒センター) bus stop in the town of Haguro. You should walk either up or down the mountain as, on the way, there is a very beautiful and old pagoda. Even without that, the walk would be well worth while as it is through a glade of 500 year old cedar trees and beside a small river with a scenic waterfall. Of course, the proper way is to walk up. Look for a gateway which indicates the start of the route. Go down a few steps to the river, relishing those few, because they are the only steps down on the whole journey, and follow the path. The walk will take about 45 minutes to an hour. At the summit is a large thatched shrine. You may meet pilgrims in white climbing up or down, but the author's experience was that there was almost nobody else around to disturb the natural beauty.

An easier alternative, of course, is to take the bus up and walk down. You will see exactly the same, but with less expenditure of energy. Buses run approximately hourly in the winter and half-hourly in the summer and cost ¥610 from Tsuruoka to Haguro Centre and ¥920 to the summit. It takes 40 minutes to Haguro Centre and 55 minutes to the top of the mountain. A few journeys start from Zenpo-ji in Tsuruoka.

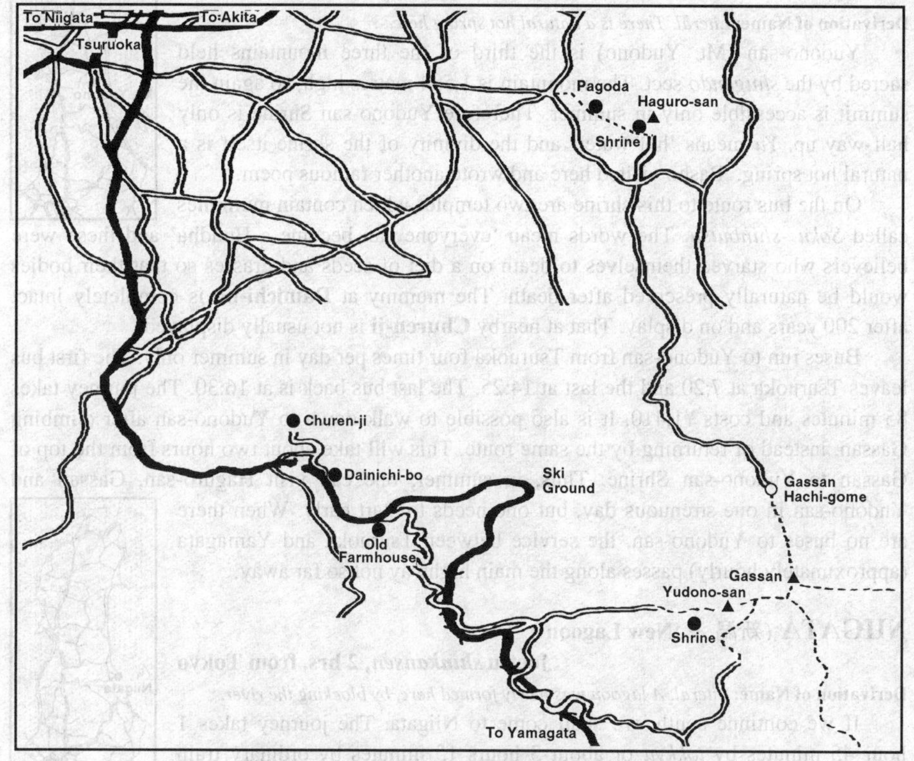


HAGURO-SAN, GASSAN AND YUDONO-SAN

## GASSAN (月山 – 'Moon Mountain') 90 mins. by bus from Tsuruoka

**Derivation of Name:** *Originally called 'Tsukiyama', meaning 'overhanging mountain'. Over time, the first Chinese character was changed to that meaning moon (same pronunciation). Finally, the name became changed to 'Gassan', which is an alternative reading for the same two Chinese characters.*

At 1,979 metres, Gassan is much higher than Haguro-san. Because of the heavy snows, the summit can be reached only in summer. There is a shrine at the top and white-robed pilgrims may be seen making their way there. You can go as far as the eighth stage by bus. Remember that Japanese mountains are always divided into ten stages. From the eighth stage the walk to the top of the mountain will take about three hours and is scenic, with a good view from the summit in favourable weather.

The bus ride to the eighth stage (月山八合目 – 'Gassan Hachi-gome') will take about 90 minutes from Tsuruoka and costs ¥1,580. Buses run only from July until September. However, if you wish to climb the mountain the only suitable departures from Tsuruoka are at 6:00 (mid-July to mid-August only) and 7:00. There are other buses which start from the top of Haguro-san at 10:20 (mid-July to mid-August only) and 11:30 and reach Gassan at 11:10 and 12:20 (¥1,170). The last bus back to Tsuruoka from Gassan is at 16:30.

## MT. YUDONO (湯殿山 – 'Hot Water Place Mountain') 85 mins. by bus from Tsuruoka

**Derivation of Name:** *Literal. There is a natural hot spring here.*

Yudono-san (Mt. Yudono) is the third of the three mountains held sacred by the *shugendo* sect. The mountain is 1,504 metres high, so again the summit is accessible only in summer. Therefore Yudono-san Shrine is only half-way up. *Yu* means 'hot water' and the divinity of the shrine itself is a natural hot spring. Basho visited here and wrote another famous poem.

On the bus route to this shrine are two temples which contain mummies called *Soku -shinbutsu*. The words mean 'everyone can become a Buddha' and these were believers who starved themselves to death on a diet of seeds and grasses so that their bodies would be naturally preserved after death. The mummy at **Dainichi-bo** is completely intact after 200 years and on display. That at nearby **Churen-ji** is not usually displayed.

Buses run to Yudono-san from Tsuruoka four times per day in summer only. The first bus leaves Tsuruoka at 7:20 and the last at 14:25. The last bus back is at 16:30. The journey takes 85 minutes and costs ¥1,410. It is also possible to walk down to Yudono-san after climbing Gassan, instead of returning by the same route. This will take about two hours from the top of Gassan to Yudono-san Shrine. Thus, in summer, one can visit Haguro-san, Gassan and Yudono-san in one strenuous day, but one needs to start early. When there are no buses to Yudono-san, the service between Tsuruoka and Yamagata (approximately hourly) passes along the main highway not so far away.

## NIIGATA (新潟 – 'New Lagoon') Joetsu *shinkansen*, 2 hrs. from Tokyo

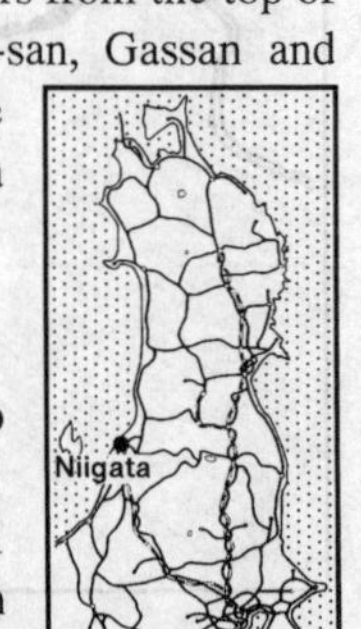


**Derivation of Name:** *Literal. A lagoon was newly formed here, by blocking the river.*

If we continue south, we shall come to Niigata. The journey takes 1 hour 45 minutes by *tokkyu* or about 3 hours 15 minutes by ordinary train from Tsuruoka. By ordinary train, it is usually necessary to change at Murakami. The service by ordinary train is very limited. Ordinary train departures from Tsuruoka for Niigata are at 7:37, 13:09, 15:04, 16:21, 17:54 and 20:41. The last connects at Murakami with a *kaisoku* train called 'Moonlight' which runs overnight via Niigata all the way to Ikebukuro and Shinjuku in Tokyo, arriving at Shinjuku at 5:10. This is a three-carriage all-reserved train, so, if you wish to travel on it, you must reserve well in advance. (From Murakami to Niigata, however, you can use it without a reservation.) There are a few seats kept only for ladies (non-smoking). When reserving, specify 'Ladies Seat' if you are of the correct sex and wish to have one of those. Because this train is a *kaisoku*, it can be used by Blue Spring ticket holders, on payment of the ¥500 reservation fee, but you need Blue Spring tickets for both the day on which it starts and the day on which it arrives, since it travels overnight. It is reasonably comfortable, with reclining seats, so you will probably be able to snatch a few minutes sleep along the way.

Niigata is a large city, but one which does not seem to have such a lot to offer to the visitor. Most people come here only because it is a place for changing trains, especially now that it is the terminus for the Joetsu *shinkansen*, or to go to Sado Island, for which see the next entry.

## SADO ISLAND (佐渡ケ島 – 'Helpful Crossing Island')

**2 hrs. 20 mins. from Niigata by ferry**

**Derivation of Name:** *Original meaning was 'narrow gate', because the sea crossing from the mainland was a short one. The Chinese characters used became changed, however.*

Sado-ga-shima (Sado Island) is a relatively large and pleasant rural island blessed with no less than six youth hostels, all of them small. It is the fifth largest island in Japan, 'the beegest of the littluns', as the author's maths teacher would have put it (referring to highest common factors).

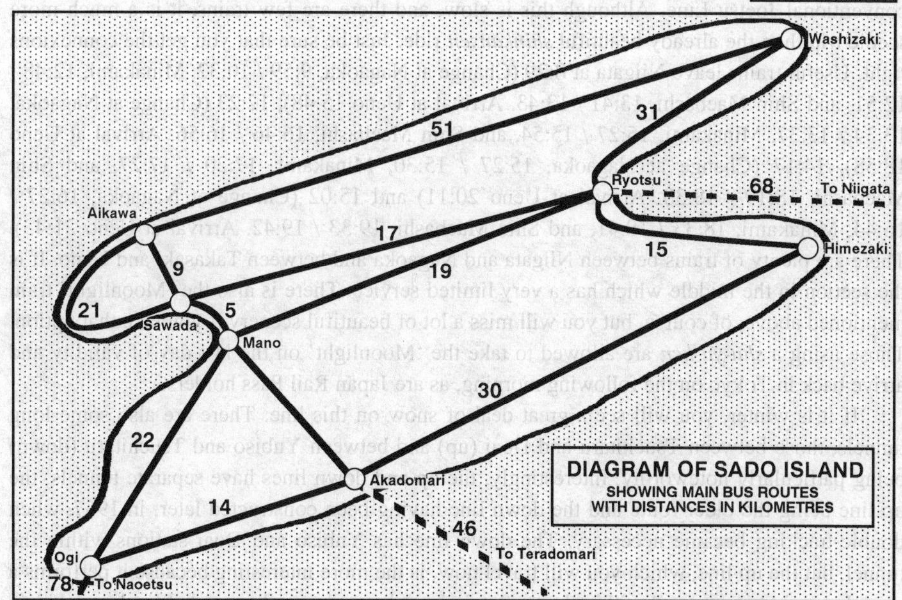

During the Edo Era, Sado was famous for two reasons. Firstly, it was a popular place to send prisoners and, secondly, it had the most important gold mines in Japan. These two claims to fame were connected, of course, the prisoners being forced to work in the mines. There is no risk of being condemned to such activities these days, whatever crimes you may have perpetrated whilst in Japan, as most of the mines are closed now, so you may visit in safety.

To reach Sado, there are ferries and a jet-foil which depart from within walking distance of Niigata station. The ferry runs six times per day to Ryotsu on Sado Island. It takes 2 hours 20 minutes and costs ¥1,780. The jet-foil runs hourly in summer, but less frequently in winter. It takes one hour and costs ¥5,460 in summer, or ¥5,130 in winter.

Ferries and jet-foil also run from Naoetsu, further down the coast, to Ogi on Sado. The jet-foil goes only twice per day, in summer only. Again it takes one hour and prices are the same as from Niigata. The ferry operates four times per day. It takes 2 hours 30 minutes and costs ¥1,960. There is also a ferry from Teradomari, a station on the Echigo Line south of Niigata, to Akadomari on Sado which takes 2 hours, runs two or three times per day and costs only ¥1,220.

The return from Niigata to Tokyo takes only 2 hours by Joetsu *shinkansen*. It is probably the most scenic of the *shinkansen* journeys, passing through the rugged mountains which form the backbone of central Japan. The trouble really is that it literally does pass through them. 91% of the total length of this line is either elevated or in tunnels. Through the mountains, there is a series of long tunnels and snow sheds, so that one gets only glimpses of the magnificent scenery.

Those using a *Tohoku Wide Shu-yu-ken* have now reached the limit of their territory and must pay the supplement if they wish to return to Tokyo by *shinkansen*. This supplement will amount to ¥4,220 for an unreserved seat or ¥500 more for a reserved seat. The alternative, and the only possibility for Blue Spring ticket users, is to take an ordinary train along the conventional Joetsu Line. Although this is slow, and there are few trains, it is a much more scenic trip than the already beautiful *shinkansen* ride. Just be sure that you get the connexions right. Useful trains leave Niigata at 8:29 (Change at Nagaoka, 9:59 / 10:32, Minakami, 12:48 / 12:51, and Shin Maebashi, 13:41 / 13:43. Arrival at Ueno 15:48), 12:23 (Change at Nagaoka, 13:34 / 13:37, Minakami, 15:27 / 15:54, and Shin Maebashi, 16:46 / 16:56. Arrival at Ueno 18:58), 14:17 (Change at Nagaoka, 15:27 / 15:30, Minakami, 17:20 / 17:27, and Shin Maebashi, 18:19 / 18:30. Arrival at Ueno 20:11) and 15:02 (Change at Nagaoka, 16:27 / 16:44, Minakami, 18:33 / 18:41, and Shin Maebashi, 19:33 / 19:42. Arrival at Ueno 21:43). There are plenty of trains between Niigata and Nagaoka and between Takasaki and Ueno. It is the section in the middle which has a very limited service. There is also the 'Moonlight' train mentioned above, of course, but you will miss a lot of beautiful scenery if you take that option. Those using a *shu-yu-ken* are allowed to take the 'Moonlight' on the last day of validity and arrive back in Tokyo on the following morning, as are Japan Rail Pass holders.

If it is winter, you will see a great deal of snow on this line. There are also some long tunnels, those between Tsuchitaru and Doai (up) and between Yubiso and Tsuchitaru (down) being particularly noteworthy. Interestingly, the up and down lines have separate tunnels, the up line being the older route and the down line having been constructed later, in 1967, when double-tracking became necessary. The down line has Yubiso and Doai stations within the tunnel, but the up line, which you will travel now, is the more interesting because it performs a complete spiral in a tunnel within the mountain in order to descend towards Minakami. If you sit on the right of the train, you will be able to see your line far below for a moment just before you enter the last tunnel and descend. When the down line was constructed, methods permitted the building of a much longer tunnel and rendered such masterpieces of engineering as the up line spiral unnecessary.

If you are using a Japan Rail Pass, you may decide that it is not necessary to return to Tokyo and that it would be preferable to continue along the Japan Sea coast, perhaps to Kanazawa. If you do this, you will miss some particularly attractive scenery, but the line to Kanazawa runs beside the sea for part of its length and is also pretty.

**Hirosaki Castle at Cherry Blossom Time**

▲ Daisetsu-zan Shirakaba-so Youth Hostel

Foreign Influence in Hakodate Architecture ▼

# HOKKAIDO (北海道)
## ('North Sea Route')

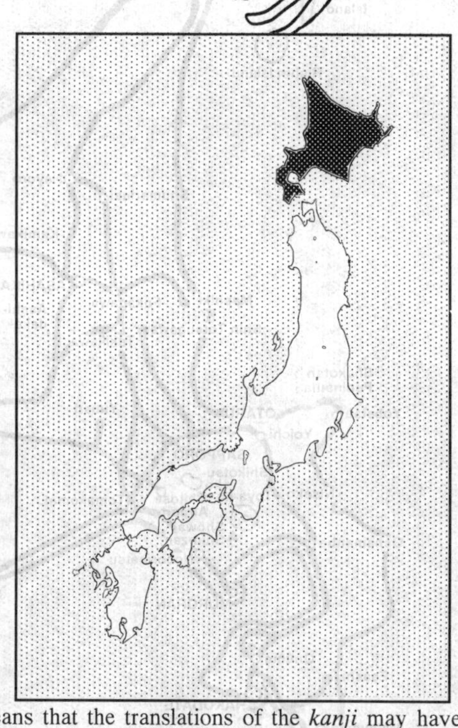

Hokkaido, the northernmost of Japan's four main islands, is quite different in character from the rest of Japan. It offers wide open spaces with a relatively sparse population. Farming is the main industry, both dairy and cereal. Sometimes one sees people stop to take photographs of cows, so unfamiliar are they with such beasts. Much of Japan's milk supply comes from here, some of it being transported in powdered form and then reconstituted. Grain silos too dot the wide open landscape of certain parts of the island.

Hokkaido is the most recent of the main islands to be developed. Until the last century, indigenous people known as the Ainu were the principal inhabitants and the plight of these people, dispossessed by later settlers and regarded as second-class citizens, is now, somewhat belatedly, giving some concern.

Many of the place names originated in the Ainu language and have been transformed into *kanji* phonetically. This means that the translations of the *kanji* may have little relevance to the original Ainu meaning. Moreover, in many cases *kanji* giving a phonetic approximation to the Ainu sounds could not easily be found, so the Chinese characters used are unfamiliar to most Japanese and sometimes cannot even be read by people who do not know the area.

The weather is special here too, with the winters being distinctly on the cool side and plenty of snow evident. At Kamikawa, near Asahikawa, roughly in the middle of the island, Japan's lowest temperature ever, −41 ℃, was recorded. In February, drift ice (*ryuhyo*) comes south, a present from Russia, and can be seen on the northern and eastern shores of Hokkaido.

Hokkaido is also famous for its wildlife. As you travel through the island, you are likely to see foxes from the train. When the author travelled the railway lines of Hokkaido, it was winter. The foxes were curled up in the snow and would glance up accusingly at the passing train, which had disturbed their slumber, then let the matter go and return to sleep. There are also herds of deer, which, although shy, may be glimpsed from time to time. In the less populated areas, there are Hokkaido bears, which you would probably prefer not to meet, although they can be seen in captivity, usually rather restricting captivity, in certain places. Then there are birds of various types, particularly in winter, when certain species migrate here from Siberia. The most famous of these are the cranes which can be observed in sanctuaries near Kushiro or around the Shiretoko peninsula.

Most people enjoy a visit to Hokkaido. If you have sufficient time, you should certainly put it on your itinerary. Since the Seikan Tunnel was opened for traffic in March 1988, linking the island with Honshu by rail, it has become much more accessible. Even just a couple of days will give you a taste of what Hokkaido has to offer, but if you have more time you will be able to visit some of the less frequented places which make it special.

***Transportation and Tickets***

The obvious way to go to Hokkaido is by train. It used to be necessary to take a JR ferry from Aomori to Hakodate, a four-hour journey which could be rough, although it could also offer the opportunity for a short night's free accommodation. Now, however, you can pass through the world's longest under-sea tunnel (53.85 kilometres, about a kilometre longer than the Channel Tunnel) in a mere 45 minutes and in comfort. It was originally intended that the *shinkansen* should run through this tunnel and on to Sapporo, but the idea was abandoned even before the tunnel was completed, so only conventional trains operate. The tunnel, incidentally, took 24 years to build and is by no means horizontal, dipping down to 240 metres below sea level. The line is electrified as far as Hakodate, but north of there trains are diesel powered. As a result, it is usually necessary to change trains at Hakodate. However, sleeper trains named *Hokutosei* run through from Ueno (Tokyo) to Sapporo. There are also sleepers from Osaka to Sapporo and there is a night *kyuko* between Aomori and Sapporo, a modern equivalent of the ferry, on which everybody tries to stretch out and get forty winks. These trains, of course, all have to change engines at or near Hakodate, which is, in any case, a stub-end station.

As part of the development of Hokkaido, it was thought essential to provide a comprehensive railway network. Thus the island, despite its lack of population, had one of the most extensive rail systems in the country. And then, suddenly, in the early 1980s, policy changed. Railways must make a profit. All uneconomical lines must be amputated. And so the rail network of Hokkaido is gradually disappearing. Now only a few branch lines remain to supplement the main routes. Even those few are endangered. It is still possible to reach the main areas of Hokkaido by train, but now it is often necessary to take a bus to get to the less frequented places. Those buses are expensive and not usually operated by JR, so we shall try to avoid them as much as possible.

If you have a Japan Rail Pass, you will be able to work your way up through the Tohoku region until you reach Aomori and then continue to Hokkaido. If you choose to travel straight through Tohoku, however, you can leave Tokyo in the morning by *shinkansen* and be in Hokkaido by early afternoon. Note, though, that you cannot use the sleeper trains which run to Hokkaido unless you pay a very high supplement, for you will be required to pay the express charge as well as the berth charge, amounting to a minimum of ¥8,240.

If you are not using a rail pass, there is an *Hokkaido Wide Shu-yu-ken* available. From Tokyo it is valid for 14 days and costs ¥39,760, or ¥35,790 during certain winter discount periods. These periods are from 1st October until 31st January and from 1st April until 31st May. Note carefully, however, that the periods specified are discount **sales** periods. Now you can purchase JR tickets up to a month in advance. That means, for example, that you can purchase a ticket on 31st January for use for 14 days starting on 28th February, or on 31st May for use from 30th June until 13th July. The starting date must be stipulated when purchasing the ticket, however. As long as you have not started using a ticket and it has not yet expired, you can obtain a refund, if necessary, less a small handling charge of ¥210. Sadly, the *Hokkaido Wide Shu-yu-ken* is no longer the bargain which it used to be, for, when the author used this ticket, there was a 20% winter discount and the ticket was valid for 20 days. Thus I paid approximately ¥30,000 for 20 days, which is only ¥1,500 per day, whereas now one must pay ¥35,000 for 14 days, or ¥2,500 per day. Since a 14-day Japan Rail Pass is almost the same price and offers much more, that seems a better option, but some visitors may not be eligible for the pass or may have omitted to purchase one prior to arrival.

The *Hokkaido Wide Shu-yu-ken* offers the use of any trains within Hokkaido, including *tokkyu*, provided one sits in an unreserved seat. If one sits in a reserved seat, one must pay not only the reservation charge, but the very substantial express charge as well. The ticket is available from almost any place in Japan, of course, not just from Tokyo. Going to and returning from Hokkaido, one must use ordinary or *kyuko* trains. If one uses *tokkyu* or *shinkansen*, one must pay the appropriate supplements. Remember, incidentally, that if one uses both *shinkansen* and *tokkyu* on the same day for a through journey, the supplement for the cheaper one, usually the *tokkyu*, is halved. There used to be two night *kyuko* trains between Ueno (Tokyo) and Aomori by different routes, but these run now only occasionally, at holiday

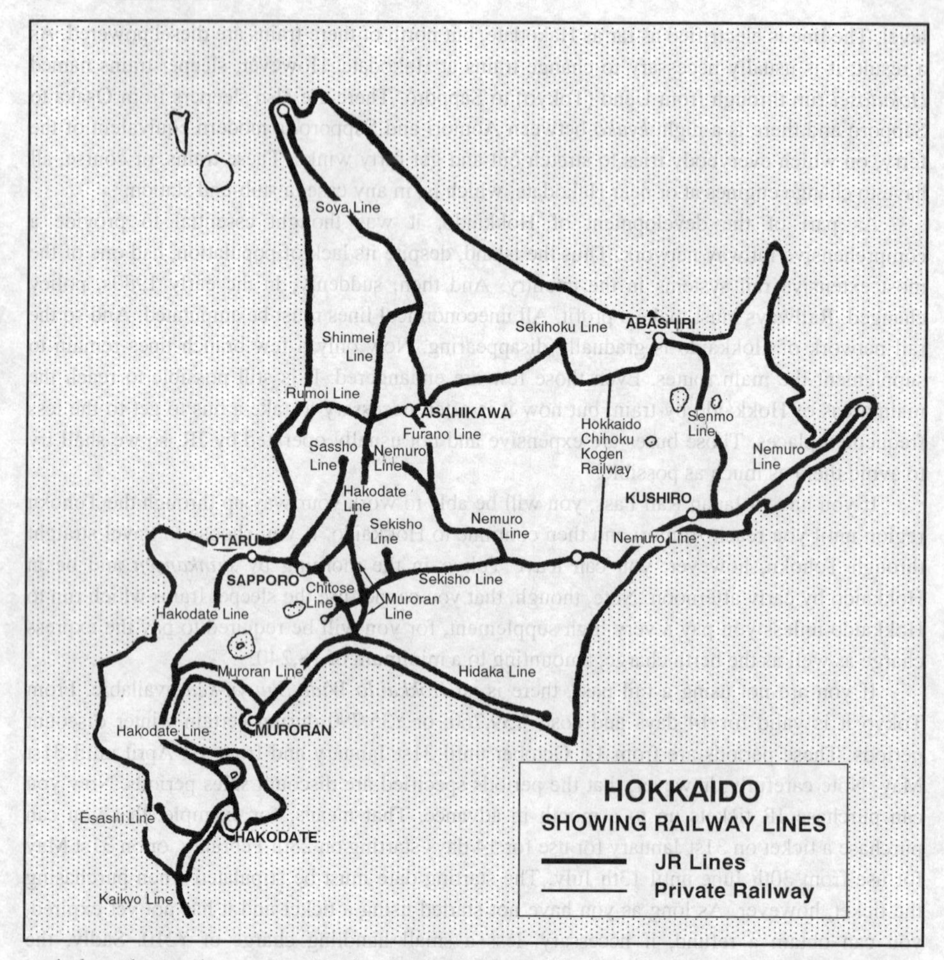


periods and sometimes at weekends. If one of them is running, you may use it, but, by doing so, you will be using up the first day of your pass and be well into the second by the time you reach Aomori. However, one of these trains might be useful for the return journey, when you are allowed to start on the last day of your pass and return to your point of origin the following day. When operating, the *kyuko Hakkoda* leaves Ueno at 22:17 and reaches Aomori via the Tohoku Line at 9:09 the next morning, just in time for the 9:20 *kaisoku* named *Kaikyo* to Hakodate, where it arrives at 11:59. When running, the *kyuko Tsugaru* departs from Ueno at 22:34 and travels via the Tohoku, Senzan and Ou Lines, arriving at Aomori at 11:28. The *Kaikyo kaisoku* connexion to Hokkaido departs at 12:05 and reaches Hakodate at 14:49. The return *Hakkoda* leaves Aomori at 19:52, arriving in Ueno at 6:58. The *Tsugaru* leaves Aomori at 16:47 and reaches Ueno at 5:52.

Three main routes are permitted from Tokyo to Aomori with an *Hokkaido Wide Shu-yu-ken*. The following lines may be used:- Tohoku, Joban, Joetsu, Uetsu and Ou (see Tohoku map on page 126). There is a special arrangement for those who would like to visit

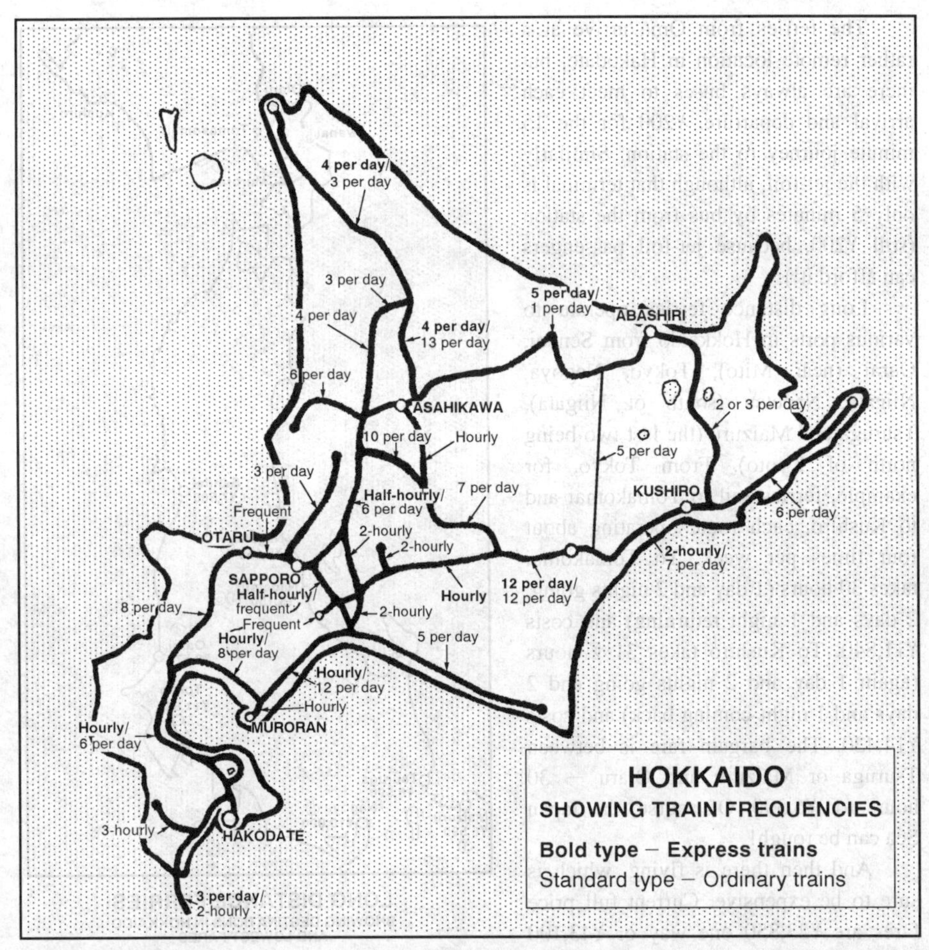


Towada-ko (Lake Towada) *en route*. This may be done, using JR buses, either on the way to Hokkaido or on the way back, on payment of an extra ¥2,880. The requirement for the detour must be specified when purchasing the ticket. It cannot be added later.

There are other ways to go to Hokkaido, of course. Ferries operate from a variety of locations to a range of ports in Hokkaido. The following relatively short distance services operate, in a clockwise direction round the coast of Aomori prefecture:

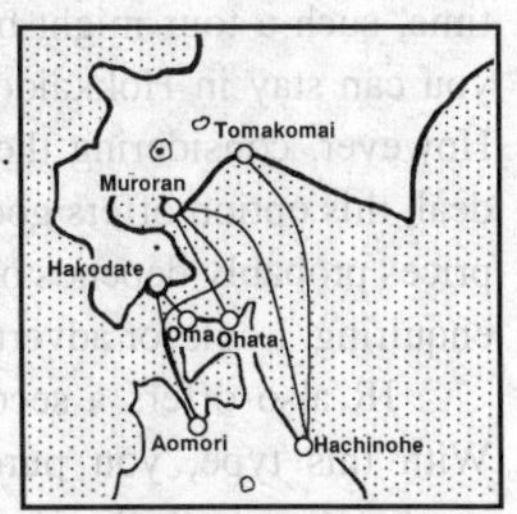


Aomori to Hakodate – 10 per day, 3 hrs. 40 mins., ¥1,400.
Aomori to Hakodate, jet-foil – 1 or 2 per day, 1 hr. 40 mins., ¥6,300.
Aomori to Muroran – 2 per day, 7 hrs., ¥3,400.
Oma to Hakodate – 2 or 3 per day, 1 hr. 40 mins., ¥1,000.
Ohata to Muroran – 1 per day, 4 hrs. 20 mins., ¥1,400.
Hachinohe to Muroran – 2 per day, 8 hrs., ¥3,900.
Hachinohe to Tomakomai – 3 per day, 9 hrs., ¥3,900.

The ferries from Oma arrive at a rather remote location in Hakodate, but there are always buses to meet each arrival and departure. ¥200 for the 15 minute journey to the station. Similarly with the jet-foil, although that terminal is only 5 minutes by bus from the station (still ¥200, because jet-foil passengers can afford it!).

Long distance ferries operate to various ports in Hokkaido from Sendai, Oarai (near Mito), Tokyo, Nagoya, Niigata, Naoetsu (south of Niigata), Tsuruga and Maizuru (the last two being north of Kyoto). From Tokyo, for example, ferries sail to Tomakomai and to Kushiro, each route operating about four times per week. To Tomakomai takes 30 hours (1 day and 2 nights going, 2 days and 1 night returning) and costs ¥11,840. To Kushiro takes 31½ hours (again 1 day and 2 nights going and 2 days and 1 night coming back) and costs ¥14,420. The bargain fare is between Tsuruga or Maizuru and Otaru – 30 hours for ¥6,590. Of course, the Japan Sea can be rough!

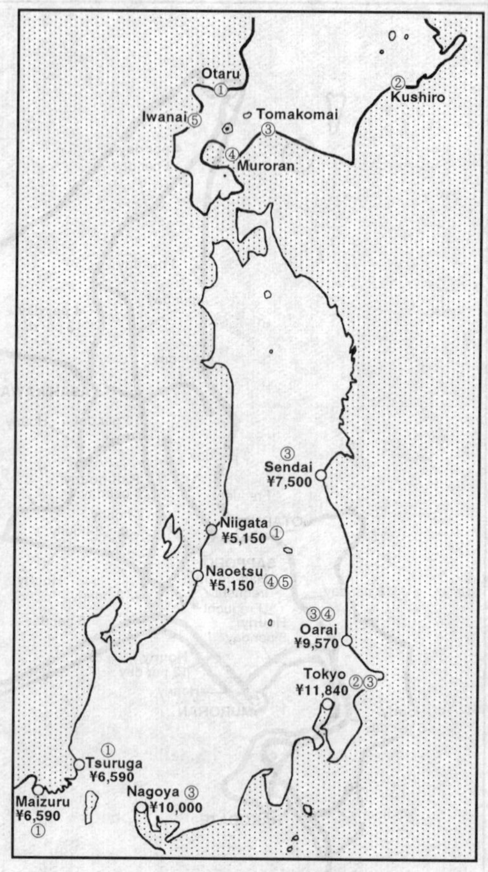


**LONG DISTANCE FERRIES**
**SHOWING DESTINATIONS IN HOKKAIDO AND LOWEST FARES**

And then there is flying, which is sure to be expensive. Current full price fares are ¥23,850 one way or ¥43,100 return between Tokyo and Sapporo (Chitose Airport). You can find discount tickets, but they are not going to be really cheap.

At the time of writing, though, there is a variety of relatively modestly priced group tours available to Hokkaido. Generally these include a return airfare, plus two or three nights accommodation in good hotels and a few meals. Despite the title of 'tour', usually not much sightseeing is included. The cost is similar to the ordinary airfare. For somebody with limited time, such a tour might be attractive. Its restriction, of course, is that, with most such tours, you can stay in Hokkaido for only the prescribed length of time, usually three or four days. However, considering the price and the fact that comfortable accommodation is part of the deal, this option offers good value. Whether such tours will continue to be available at bargain prices probably depends on the state of the economy, as well as the time of year, but it is worth enquiring. Look for advertisements in the newspapers and outside travel agents.

JR also offers a second type of *shu-yu-ken* called an *Hokkaido New Wide Shu-yu-ken*. With this type, you purchase a return ticket to Hokkaido by train, ferry or aircraft, in combination with the *shu-yu-ken*, which allows you to roam freely in Hokkaido for 5 or 10 consecutive days. It costs ¥13,320 for a 5-day *shu-yu-ken* and ¥21,360 for a 10-day one. In addition, you get a discount of 20% from the cost of a rail ticket and the cost of a short-distance ferry ticket, if used, and a discount of 10% from other modes of transport. The return ticket to Hokkaido must be purchased at the same time as the *shu-yu-ken*. This ticket has the advantage that you can plan a rail route through Tohoku which does not keep to the main access lines for Hokkaido, but otherwise it offers little that cannot be achieved with the *Hokkaido Wide Shu-yu-ken* and it is almost certain to be a more expensive option.

There is one more type of ticket available, which might well be of interest to those with limited time available for Hokkaido. It is called an *Hokkaido Free Kippu*. This ticket does not include travel to or from Hokkaido, but it offers unlimited travel for 7 days on trains and most buses operated by JR Hokkaido, including the Kaikyo Line (the Seikan Tunnel) as far south as Naka Oguni, one station north of Kanita at the northern tip of Honshu. Two types of ticket are available – *futsu-sha* (ordinary carriages) and *green-sha* ('green' first class carriages). With both types of ticket, you can use reserved carriages of *tokkyu* and *kyuko* trains (after making suitable reservations, of course). With the *green-sha* ticket you can also use B type sleepers on trains operating within Hokkaido, but not on trains originating in or bound for Honshu. The ticket costs ¥22,500 for *futsu-sha* and ¥33,400 for *green-sha*. If two people are travelling together, they can buy a slightly discounted *Hokkaido Pair Kippu* for ¥41,100 *futsu-sha* or ¥60,600 *green-sha*. The *Hokkaido Free Kippu* and *Hokkaido Pair Kippu* are not available during certain holiday periods.

This book suggests and follows a circular route clockwise around Hokkaido, as outlined below:

Aomori to Hakodate by Kaikyo Line.
Hakodate to Asahikawa via Oshamanbe, Otaru and Sapporo by Hakodate Line.
Asahikawa to Wakkanai by Soya Line.
Wakkanai to Soya Misaki and return by bus.
Wakkanai to Nayoro by Soya Line.
Nayoro to Fukagawa by Shinmei Line.
Fukagawa to Asahikawa by Hakodate Line.
Asahikawa to Asahi-dake by free bus.
Asahi-dake to So-unkyo on foot.
So-unkyo to Kamikawa by bus.
Kamikawa to Abashiri by Sekihoku Line.
Abashiri to Shari by Senmo Line.
Shari to Iwaobetsu or Rausu (Shiretoko) and return by bus.
Shari to Mashu by Senmo Line.
Mashu to Mashu-ko and return by bus.
Mashu to Kushiro by Senmo Line.
Kushiro to Nemuro by Nemuro Line.
Nemuro to Nosappu Misaki and return by bus.
Nemuro to Obihiro via Kushiro by Nemuro Line.
Obihiro to Hiro-o by bus.
Hiro-o to Samani via Erimo Misaki by JR bus.

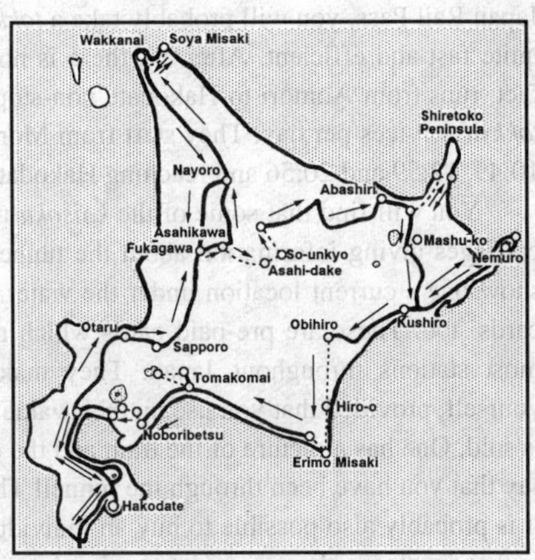


**PROPOSED ROUTE**

Samani to Tomakomai by Hidaka Line.
Tomakomai to Chitose by Chitose Line.
Chitose to Shikotsu-ko by youth hostel minibus (or public bus).
Shikotsu-ko to Tomakomai by youth hostel minibus (or public bus).
Tomakomai to Noboribetsu by Muroran Line.
Noboribetsu to Noboribetsu Onsen by bus.
Noboribetsu Onsen to Showa Shinzan by bus.
Showa Shin-zan to Toya via Toya-ko Onsen by bus.
Toya to Hakodate by Hakodate Line.
Hakodate to Aomori by Kaikyo Line.

## HAKODATE (函館 – 'Box Mansion')

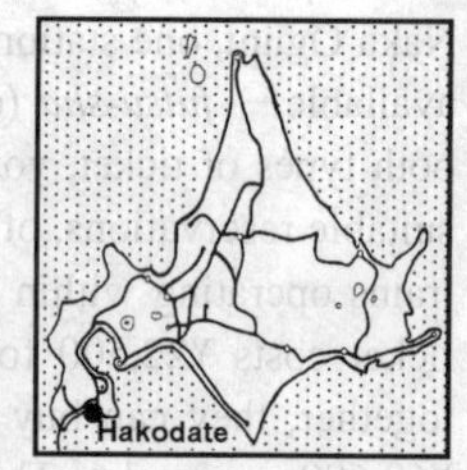


**Kaikyo Line, 12 hrs. from Tokyo**

**Derivation of Name:** *In 1454, the first settlers here built a square box-like mansion for their accommodation.*

To reach Hakodate, you will pass through the **Seikan Tunnel**, the world's longest under-sea tunnel. "That must be exciting," said somebody to the author. Well, for about the first two or three minutes. After that it becomes rather boring. The tunnel starts fairly well inland and slopes down at a gradient of 1.2%, with the engine braking steadily against the incline. There is a short almost flat section at the bottom, which is 240 metres below sea level and 100 metres below the sea bed at that point, and then a steady climb to the other side. If you have a Japan Rail Pass, you will probably take a *tokkyu*. Otherwise, you will use the *kaisoku*, which is quite fast and efficient. After all, there is not much to stop for under the sea. The *tokkyu*, in fact, runs from Aomori to Hakodate non-stop in about 2 hours. However, there are only three *tokkyu* services per day. They start from Morioka at 8:25, 10:44 and 18:40, leaving Aomori at 10:49, 12:59 and 20:56 and reaching Hakodate at 12:46, 14:53 and 22:59.

You will find that some of the *kaisoku* trains have an indicator board at the ends of some carriages giving information about the tunnel. After each kilometre, another light goes on to show one's current location under the water. The conductor may come round selling 'orange cards' too. These are pre-paid cards which may be used to buy JR tickets from machines at most stations throughout Japan. They make good souvenirs for Japanese friends, or for yourself, provided that you use up their value before departure. On this train, a set of two cards is sold. One has a picture of the train and the other a little certificate (in Japanese, of course) to say that you have been through the tunnel! The cards are ¥1,000 cards, so the set costs ¥2,000. It is probably also possible to buy an individual card. Another interesting feature of the tunnel is that in places there are pictures in electric lights which run along beside the train at the correct speed. (There is something similar in the tunnel to Narita Airport near Tokyo and in the tunnel to Chitose Airport near Sapporo.)

What will surprise you most of all, though, is that there are two stations in the tunnel. "Now that is strange," you may think. "I know that Japan is overcrowded, but surely not many people live down here." The stations are used by maintenance workers, but it is also possible to get off here and have a tour of the tunnel facilities. This costs ¥820 and must be booked in advance. Those on the tour go to a special carriage (all smoking seats) where their seats are reserved (no additional charge) and the doors of that carriage only are opened at the tunnel

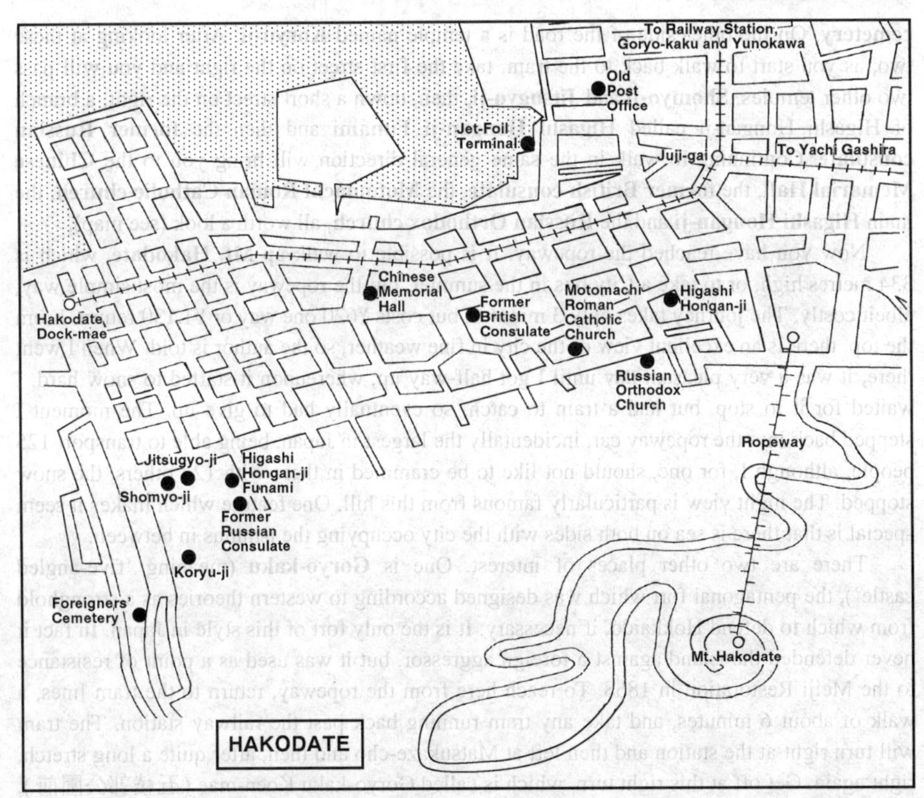


station. Tours are available on the *kaisoku* trains which leave Aomori at 9:20, 10:56, 12:05 and 14:07. Tourists then continue on to Hakodate on the next train.

When you come out of the tunnel, you will be in rural Hokkaido. The train runs around the Tsugaru Strait to Hakodate and, as that city is approached, there are some pleasant views across the water. To see these best, naturally one should be on the sea side of the train, that is to say on the right.

Hakodate is an interesting city. Because it is a port and in the south of Hokkaido, it has long been one of the main access routes to the island. At the end of the last century, when Hokkaido was being expanded, Europeans were invited to Hakodate to assist in this development. The result is a variety of western architecture, including brick constructions, rarely found in other parts of Japan. There is a lot to look at in Hakodate, mainly buildings, and good seafoods are available here as well. About half a day is the minimum to allow here.

As at Aomori, the railway station is right next to the sea and you can see at the end of the platform the place where the JR ferries used to dock, so that passengers could walk from the ship straight into the station and onto their trains. There is one of the old ferries berthed here too, the ***Mashu Maru***, which can be visited.

Exit from the station and along the main road in front of the bus terminal you will find trams running. Take a tram no. 5 going towards your right to Hakodate Dock-mae (函館どっく前 or ドック前). Go all the way to the terminus, which should take 11 minutes. Then take the street to your left and walk uphill for about 10 minutes. On your right is the **foreigners'**

**cemetery**. On the other side of the road is a temple named **Koryu-ji**. After looking at these two, as you start to walk back to the tram, take the first street on the right and you will pass two other temples, **Shomyo-ji** and **Jitsugyo-ji**, then, down a short street on the right, a branch of Higashi Hongan-ji called **Higashi Hongan-ji Funami** and then the **former Russian consulate**. Continuing to walk in the same general direction will bring you to the **Chinese Memorial Hall**, the **former British consulate**, the **Motomachi Roman Catholic church**, the main **Higashi Hongan-ji** and the **Russian Orthodox church**, all worth a look (see map).

Now you have reached the ropeway. It is possible to walk up **Mt. Hakodate**, which is 334 metres high, or to take a City bus in the summer, but the ropeway is the most simple way, albeit costly. The journey takes only 3 minutes, but costs ¥620 one way or ¥1,130 return. From the top, there is an excellent view of the city in fine weather, so the author is told. When I went there, it was a very pleasant day until I got half-way up, whereupon it started to snow hard. I waited for it to stop, but had a train to catch, so eventually had to give up. The moment I stepped back into the ropeway car, incidentally the largest in Japan, being able to transport 125 people, although I, for one, should not like to be crammed in there with 124 others, the snow stopped. The night view is particularly famous from this hill. One feature which makes it seem special is that there is sea on both sides with the city occupying the isthmus in between.

There are two other places of interest. One is **Goryo-kaku** (meaning 'five-angled castle'), the pentagonal fort which was designed according to western theories as a stronghold from which to defend Hokkaido, if necessary. It is the only fort of this style in Japan. In fact it never defended the island against a foreign aggressor, but it was used as a point of resistance to the Meiji Restoration in 1868. To reach here from the ropeway, return to the tram lines, a walk of about 6 minutes, and take any tram running back past the railway station. The tram will turn right at the station and then left at Matsukaze-cho and then, after quite a long stretch, right again. Get off at this right turn, which is called Goryo-kaku Koen-mae (五稜郭公園前). The journey is scheduled to take 23 minutes (or 18 minutes from the railway station). From there it is a walk of about 10 minutes to the fort, first in the direction in which the tram was travelling before it turned, then along a street to your right which is signposted in English. If in doubt, head towards a tower which is visible from some distance and is near the fort. Entry to the fort area is free, as only ramparts remain, no original buildings.

The last major attraction is the **Trappistine Convent**, the first nunnery in Japan and the only Trappistine convent in the country. There is a Trappist monastery too, the first monastery

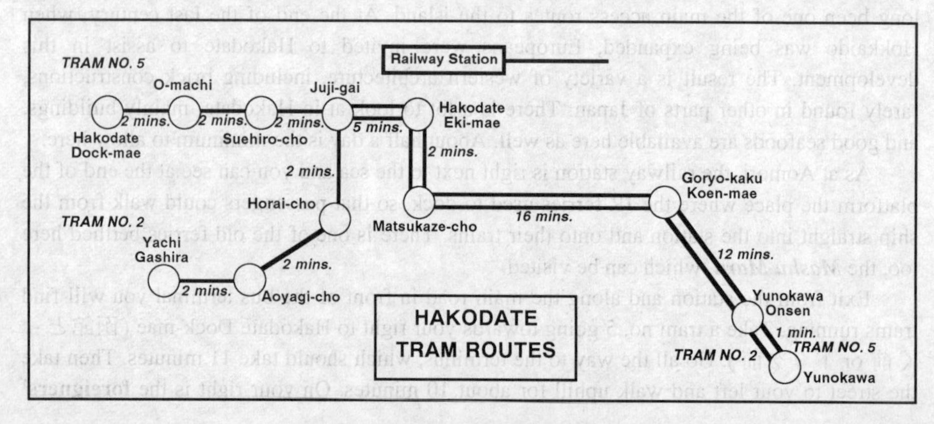

in Japan, but it is about 25 kilometres away. The brick buildings themselves with their green roofs are attractive and the convent is also famous for its butter and confectionery products, which can be purchased. To get here you can take a City bus no. 19 or 39, destination Hakodate Airport (函館空港 – 'Hakodate Kuko'), to Yunokawa Danchi Kita Guchi (湯の川団地北口) and walk for 15 minutes, or an Hakodate bus no. 59 to Trappistine Iriguchi (トラピスチヌ入口) and walk for 8 minutes, or an Hakodate bus no. 10-2 to Trappistine-mae (トラピスチヌ前), which stop is right outside the convent. From Goryo-kaku, City buses nos. 19 and 39 run along the same street as the tram, so can be taken from a stop on that street. Each service operates hourly. The journey takes 19 minutes from there, or 35 to 40 minutes from Hakodate station. **Yunokawa**, incidentally, through which you will pass and which is the terminus for the tram, is the oldest spa in Hokkaido.

Hakodate City Transport offers a one-day ticket (一日乗車券 – '*ichi-nichi jo-sha-ken*') for unlimited use of trams and City buses for the sum of ¥1,000. Fares are by distance here, starting at ¥190 and going up to ¥230, so if you are planning to take more than five trams or buses during the day this ticket will be worth while. A two-day ticket (二日乗車券 – '*futsu-ka jo-sha-ken*') costs ¥1,700. Tickets can be purchased at the bus terminal right outside the railway station, in advance or on the day of use. Bus and tram drivers usually have them too. Note that the ticket allows the use of City buses only. Those are the cream and orange ones. Hakodate buses, which are silver and red, are not included. Services stop completely, both buses and trams, at about 21:00. The one-day and two-day tickets also give a 10% discount on the ropeway fare and on admission prices to certain other attractions. If in doubt, just show the ticket when paying and hope! Incidentally, Hakodate used to have more tram routes, but they too have disappeared recently. Now only routes nos. 2 and 5 remain.

There is a youth guest house in Hakodate. Note that this is different from a youth hostel, although youth hostel membership is still required. The principal difference is that it is more expensive. As usual, see our Youth Hostels section. If you decide to stay in the youth guest house, take a tram no. 2 from Yunokawa or from Hakodate station. The tram will be going to Yachi Gashira (谷地頭) and your stop is Horai-cho (宝来町), the first stop after the tram turns left after leaving the railway station – not the stop on the corner where it turns left, but the next one. It takes 38 minutes from Yunokawa or 7 minutes from Hakodate station. Then walk for 3 minutes. It is also quite possible to walk all the way from the station.

If this youth guest house is too expensive for you, there is a pleasant enough youth hostel, at more usual prices, a short way up the railway at Onuma, for which see the following section.

There is also a night *kaisoku* train from Hakodate to Sapporo. This train has one carriage of all-reserved non-smoking reclining seats and two all-reserved 'carpet cars', that is to say carpeted carriages without seats where weary travellers can stretch out and get some sleep during the night, a very good idea. A blanket and pillow is provided for every passenger and shoes must be left at the door (slippers provided), so it is quite clean within. Usually this train runs non-stop between Hakodate and Sapporo, but in certain seasons it makes a few stops on the way. In either case, it leaves Hakodate at 23:30 and reaches Sapporo at 6:30 (and the same times in the opposite direction). Since it is a *kaisoku*, it can be used with any type of ticket, even a Blue Spring ticket, on payment of the ¥500 reservation fee (waived for holders of Japan Rail Passes). Moreover, as long as it is not making any stops on the way, it may be used with only a Blue Spring ticket for the date of departure (ticket for date of arrival not required).

## ONUMA (大沼 – 'Big Marsh')

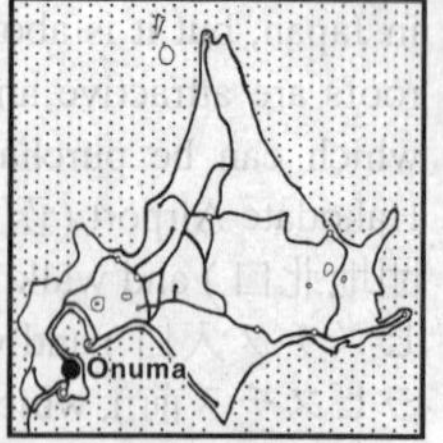


**Hakodate Line, 20 mins. from Hakodate**

**Derivation of Name:** *Literal.*

Onuma is really much more attractive than the translation of its name suggests. It is a collection of lakes, of which the largest is Onuma and the next biggest Konuma ('Little Marsh'). The scene is dominated by Komagatake, a volcano with the top blown off, which often forms a pretty reflection in the lakes. The lakes can be toured at any time of the year on foot or by rented bicycle.

There is an agreeable youth hostel here, only 20 minutes from Hakodate by *tokkyu*, so a suitable base also for those who still want to see more of that city, but would prefer not to pay the rather higher charges of Hakodate Youth Guest House. The hostel here is called Exander Onuma and some English is spoken. 'Exander' is evidently an approximation to an Ainu word for the area, "which sounded a bit like 'Alexander' without the 'Al', so that is how we spelt it." To reach the hostel, take a train to either Onuma or Onuma Koen. It is between the two and easy walking distance from either. Some *tokkyu* trains stop at Onuma Koen, including one which leaves Hakodate at 17:24 and reaches Onuma Koen at 17:44. If you are using a Blue Spring ticket there is an ordinary train from Hakodate at 16:35, reaching Onuma at 17:17 and a *kaisoku* at 17:00 which reaches Onuma at 17:30 and Onuma Koen at 17:38.

Exander Onuma Hostel has plenty of information on walks around the Onuma area and in the evening a slide show of the scenery in various seasons is often given and is certainly worth seeing. The hostel will also keep its doors open late so that you can go to Mt. Hakodate and see the lights of the city in the evening, and will give you a ticket for a 10% discount on the ropeway too. The last train back is at 22:32, reaching Onuma at 23:10 and Onuma Koen at 23:16.

## MATSUMAE (松前 – 'Pine Front') Kaikyo Line to Kikonai, 2 hrs. from Aomori or 1 hr. from Hakodate. Then bus 95 mins.

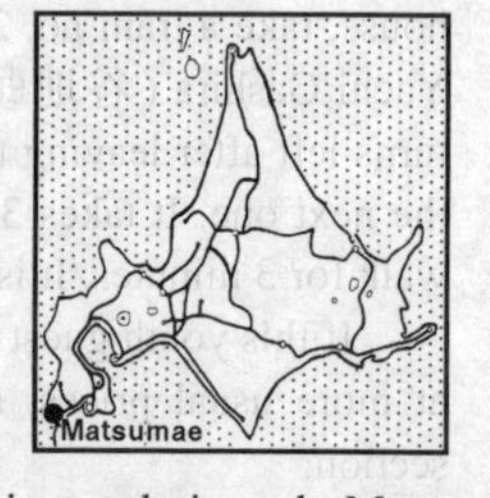


**Derivation of Name:** *From name of local feudal lord, Matsumae Yoshihiro, in 1593, when name of town changed.*

Matsumae is only a small town these days, but it used to be the capital of Hokkaido and is one of the few places here with a long history, having been settled as many as 500 years ago. There is a castle, the only one in Hokkaido, but it is a modern concrete reproduction. The town is also famous for its cherry blossom, which arrives only in early May.

Located on the south-western tip of Hokkaido, Matsumae used to have both a railway and a youth hostel until recently, but both have now disappeared. The youth hostel closed in 1994, but the railway was abandoned when the Seikan Tunnel was opened in 1988, although the new line uses the old route for parts of its length. From the train you can see sections of the abandoned line weaving around the new straightened route in certain places. Now, however, it is necessary to take a bus from Kikonai, usually the first stop inside Hokkaido for the train coming from Honshu. The bus takes 95 minutes and runs eleven times per day. It costs ¥1,240. You could visit by alighting from the train here on the way to Hakodate, or you could make a day trip from Hakodate. On the way, the bus passes Shiriuchi station and you could save money by taking the train to this point instead of Kikonai. The problem is that only two trains in each direction stop here every day. Those trains are the 7:29 and 16:08 departures from Aomori and the 7:53 and 17:20 departures from Hakodate.

If you are making a day trip from Hakodate, the economical way would be to take the 7:53 from Hakodate (connexion from Onuma at 7:11), which reaches Shiriuchi at 8:48. A bus leaves from the bus company's office at 8:57 (not the station, and the town is a little distance away, although the bus passes along the main road near the station on its way to Shiriuchi, if you can find a bus stop) and reaches Matsumae (松前) at 10:17. The return is from Matsumae at 15:50, arriving at Shiriuchi at 17:10. The train leaves at 17:55 and arrives in Hakodate at 18:49. The connexion to Onuma is not until 19:52, reaching Onuma at 20:43. Taking the bus from Shiriuchi instead of Kikonai will save about ¥200 in each direction.

## OTARU (小樽 – 'Little Barrel')

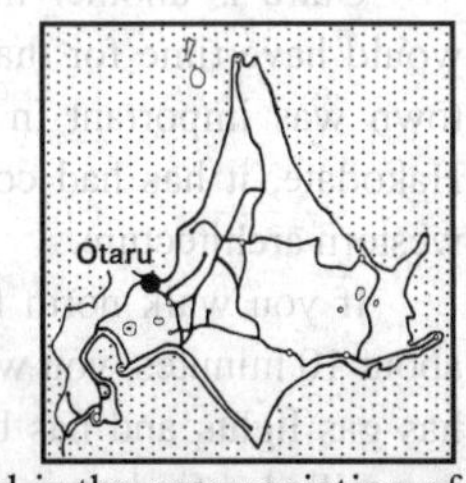


**Hakodate Line, 35 mins. from Sapporo**

**Derivation of Name:** *Originally 'Otarunai', name of river in Ainu language.*

As we go north from Onuma, the railway line divides, with one part going to the sea side of Lake Onuma and one part going to the inland side. The lines reunite at Mori, then follow the coastline north to Oshamanbe, where there is another division. Oshamanbe, incidentally, is a name that even most Japanese cannot read, so unusual is the pronunciation of its *kanji*. The Hakodate Main Line takes the northern route and some express trains used to run this way to Sapporo. Now, however, despite the naming of the lines, all express trains follow the southern route, the Muroran Main Line, and the Hakodate Main Line has really become a branch line with only an infrequent service of ordinary trains. However, since we have to both go and come back along this route, it makes sense to go one way and return the other. Let us take the Hakodate Line this time, therefore. We can start on the 7:44 *tokkyu* from Hakodate which reaches Oshamanbe at 8:54. This train does not stop at Onuma Koen, so from Exander Onuma Hostel take the 7:12 from Onuma, 7:15 from Onuma Koen, to Mori (7:44), and wait for the *tokkyu* to arrive at 8:16. From Oshamanbe, there is an ordinary train at 9:02. It reaches Otaru at 12:08. On the way, you will pass **Niseko** (10:33), which is a very popular ski resort in the winter and has a youth hostel, if you wish to stay. You will also pass **Yoichi** (11:41), from where buses run to the **Shakotan Peninsula** and Shakotan Youth Hostel at Yobetsu (余別). The bus takes 1 hour 40 minutes and costs ¥1,100. There is a bus at 12:21. It is a no. 21 bus, but not all no. 21s go as far as Yobetsu.

For those who think that this means getting up too early, there is a slightly later *tokkyu* train at 9:15 from Hakodate. For most of the year, this train stops at Onuma Koen at 9:35, but in March

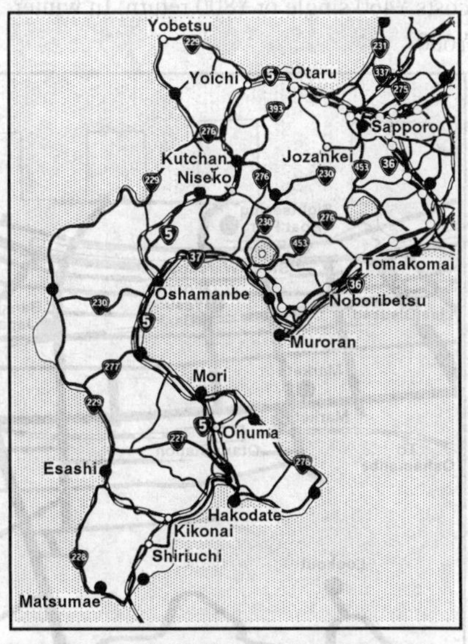


**FROM MATSUMAE TO SAPPORO**
SHOWING RAILWAYS AND MAIN ROADS
(Shields show Highway Numbers)

and April it does not stop and there is no suitable connexion, unless one takes the 8:18 from Onuma Koen, 8:23 from Onuma, to Hakodate to catch the *tokkyu* there. The *tokkyu* reaches Oshamanbe at 10:32 and an ordinary train leaves at 10:35, reaching Niseko at 12:07, Yoichi at 14:05 and Otaru at 14:34. On the way, the train has a rest at Kutchan for 40 minutes, if you want a look round that town. There is a no. 21 bus from Yoichi to Yobetsu at 14:51.

Blue Spring ticket users will just have to get up early. Best is to take the 6:48 train from Onuma round by the coast all the way to Oshamanbe, which will be reached at 9:17. You then have to wait until the 10:35 ordinary train, as above. If you prefer, you can take the 7:12 from Onuma, 7:15 from Onuma Koen, by the inland route to Mori (7:44) and change to the ordinary train which was the 6:48 from Onuma and which reaches Mori at the same time.

Otaru is another interesting port worthy of a visit of a couple of hours, at least. You would have time for that if you followed the schedule suggested above. Like Hakodate, this town was important in the development of Hokkaido at the end of last century and, like Hakodate, it has had considerable western influence and has several attractive examples of western architecture.

If you walk north from the station (the exit and bus terminal are on the north side) for about 10 minutes, you will come to a canal along which are built **stone warehouses**. This area has gas lights and has been preserved in its turn-of-the-century condition. Around the town you will also find several Meiji period bank buildings and churches.

Ferries run between Otaru and the towns of Tsuruga and Maizuru, north of Kyoto, and are mentioned in the 'Transportation and Tickets' section of this chapter. They are comparatively cheap. Ferries also run to Niigata. There is a youth hostel in Otaru. To reach it, take a bus no. 9 from bus stop no. 3 in front of the station to Tenguyama (天狗山), which is the terminus. It is a 20 minute ride (¥180). Here you will also find a ski area and a ropeway running up **Mt. Tengu** to a fine viewpoint over the city. The ropeway takes 4 minutes and costs ¥460 single or ¥800 return. In winter, a single journey is offered for ¥360 and a return for ¥600.

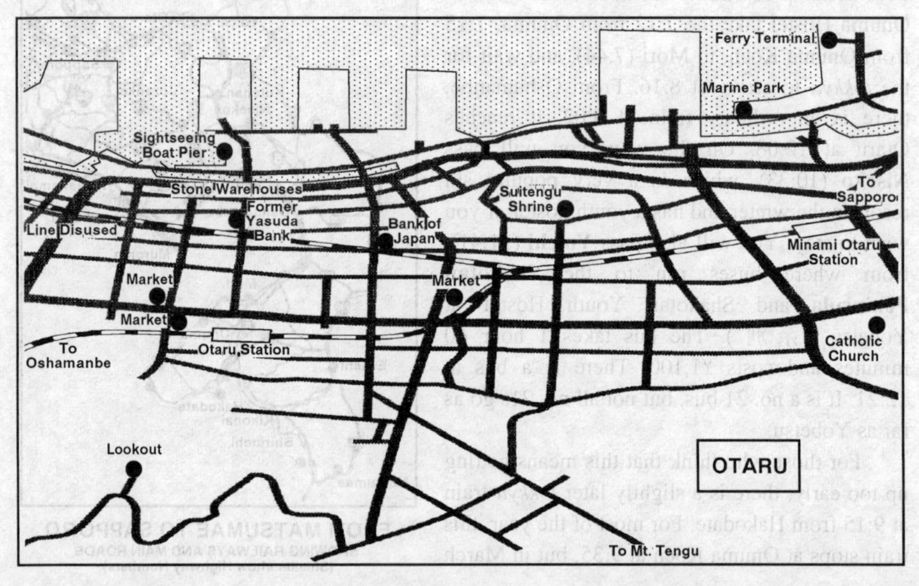

If you intend to take a bus from Otaru to Shakotan Youth Hostel at Yobetsu (余別), you need bus no. 21 starting from bus stop no. 5 at the station. Remember that not all no. 21 buses go that far, so check the destination also. The fare from Otaru to Yobetsu is ¥1,400.

The Hokkaido Chuo Bus Company offers a one-day ticket (一日乗車券 – '*ichi-nichi jo-sha-ken*') for use within the city area only, for ¥650. There is a special circular bus route operated by buses painted a pretty blue and pink and marked 'Marine-go' (マリン号) which travels to many of the points of interest in the town. This too can be used with the one-day ticket. All buses within the city area cost ¥180, whether pretty or not.

If you prefer not to stay in Otaru, it takes only about 35 minutes to Sapporo by *kaisoku* train or 50 minutes by ordinary train. Departures are frequent. There are also JR (and other) buses which run between Otaru and Sapporo in 50 or 55 minutes (express buses) or 90 minutes (ordinary buses).

## SAPPORO (札幌 – 'Strip of Canvas')

**3 hrs. 30 mins. from Hakodate, 16 hrs. from Ueno (Tokyo)**

**Derivation of Name:** *Ainu word meaning 'large, dry river'.*

Sapporo is Japan's biggest city north of Tokyo. It has a population of about 1.5 million and, unlike most Japanese cities, it is relatively new and carefully planned, having been established in 1869 on the Toyohira River. In Sapporo, streets tend to run at right angles to each other, with O-dori ('Big Avenue') as the main reference point. **O-dori** is a boulevard with a grassy area in the centre and the Television Tower at the eastern end. It runs east and west and divides north Sapporo from south Sapporo. Its eastern extremity also marks the boundary between west Sapporo and east Sapporo.

The symbol of Sapporo is an 1881 **clock tower** of Russian design, the only Russian-style building left in the city now as a reminder of the influence of pioneers from that country in the early days of Sapporo's establishment. It is two blocks north of O-dori.

There is a **botanical garden** in the city with two museums, the University Museum, which is a natural history museum, and the Ainu Museum, based on a collection of 20,000 artifacts made Dr. Batchelor, who was an English minister working here.

**Hokkaido University** is well known because of its high standards. In the campus is a bust of Dr. William Clark, an American who taught here for just a single year in 1876-77. His Christian principles and high expectations made such an impression that he has been remembered ever since, especially for his parting words, "Boys, be ambitious", which are engraved on his bust.

Sapporo is famous for its **Snow Festival** in early February, when huge sculptures made of snow are constructed all the way along O-dori. These structures are truly amazing – for example one-third scale reproductions of famous buildings which take an army of men a week to prepare. In fact, the army (actually styled 'ground self-defence force') is an organization which is rather good at this sort of operation and has the necessary man-power to produce some of the most imposing exhibits year after year. Teams now come from all over the world to try their hands at this novel, but rather transient, art form and the festival can no longer be contained in a single area, so has spread to various other venues throughout the city, with specialities which include sculptures in ice, a totally different medium, as well as in snow. If you are in Japan in winter, this is a visit which should be placed high upon your itinerary. In the author's opinion, though, the time to come is the week before the festival starts, when you can see all the excitement of the construction of the sculptures without having to fight the crowds, battle your way onto the overcrowded trains and search vainly for somewhere to stay.

Another attraction is the **Sapporo Brewery**, on the edge of the city. Tours of the works naturally include sampling of the products.

**Susukino** is the entertainment district. It lies about 10 minutes walk south of O-dori. It is also one end of Hokkaido's only remaining tram route, which runs round three-quarters of a loop, the other end of which you will pass between O-dori and Susukino.

Only 30 kilometres south-west of the city of Sapporo is the famous spa resort of **Jozankei**. *Kei* means gorge and the resort was developed in 1871 by a priest named Jozan. As one might suppose, it lies in a wooded gorge with very attractive surrounds. However, as you might also suppose, because of its proximity to Sapporo and its ease of access, coupled with the Japanese love of spa resorts, it is rather touristy. The spring water is exceptionally hot (so be careful, if you visit!) and contains a variety of minerals, thought to do wonders for rheumatism and a range of other ailments. There are buses to Jozankei (定山渓) at least every half hour from Sapporo station at a cost of ¥750. The journey takes 65 minutes. Nakayama Toge Youth Hostel lies a further half hour west on the same road.

Sapporo has a subway system consisting of three lines. The trains run on rubber tyres instead of steel wheels. Two types of one-day ticket (一日乗車券－*'ichi-nichi jo-sha-ken'*) are available. One costs ¥950 and is for use on subway, buses and the remaining tram route. The other costs ¥750 and is available for use on the subway system only.

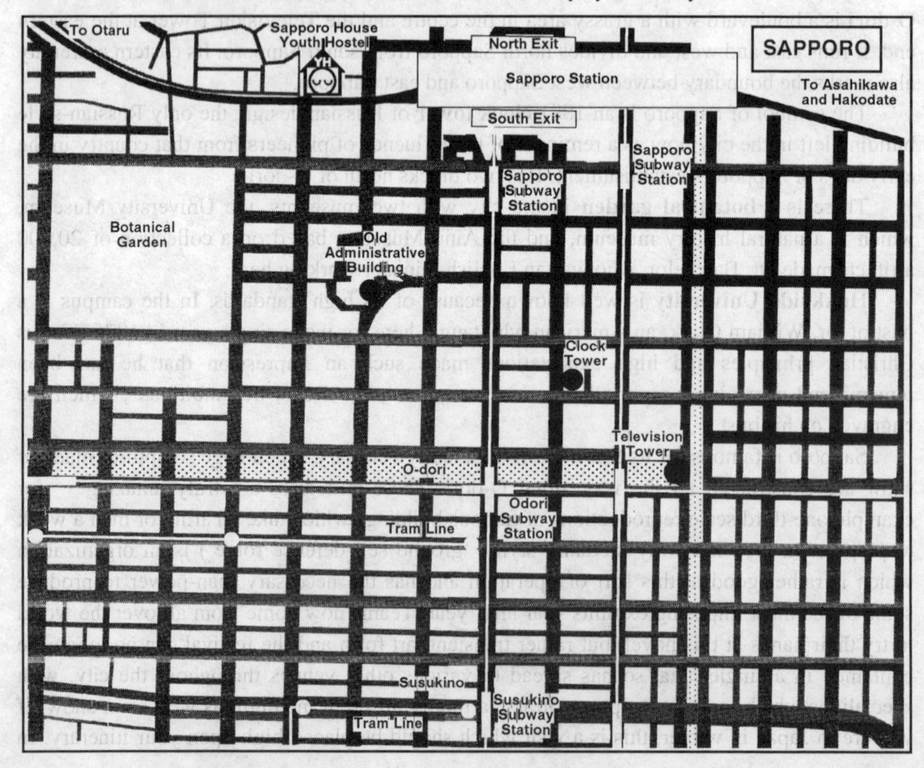

There are three youth hostels in Sapporo, although Miyagaoka Hostel, where English is spoken, is open only in summer. Most people stay at Sapporo House, because it is just at the end of the railway station, with the trains passing almost overhead, a most convenient location. However, as a result, it is usually crowded and the author found it noisy (from internal sounds, not external) and found some of the inmates somewhat obnoxious.

A more pleasant hostel, again in the author's biased opinion, is Sapporo Lions. Its merit and demerit is that it is rather less accessible. First one needs to take the subway to Odori, only one stop from Sapporo station by Nanboku or Toho Line. Then one changes to the Tozai Line westbound for a further three stations to Maruyama Koen, from where one takes a no. 14 bus to Morinomiya Schanze (森の宮シャンツェ), one of the ski jumps used for the 1972 Winter Olympics. From Morinomiya Schanze bus stop, where the bus turns round, to the hostel is a walk of about 7 minutes, steadily uphill. The hostel is a smart building on a sharp bend, not usually very full, and pleasant and clean inside. Having located its whereabouts, you may decide that you can walk to the station in the morning and save the bus fare. The walk takes 30 to 40 minutes downhill, not a great deal longer than waiting for and catching the bus. You can walk through Maruyama Park on the way. Miyagaoka Hostel lies on the same route, but much nearer to the station, if it is open when you are in Sapporo.

## ASAHIKAWA (旭川 – 'Morning Sun River')

**Hakodate Line, 80 mins. from Sapporo**

**Derivation of Name:** *Literal.*

Asahikawa is one of the major cities of Hokkaido, connected to Sapporo by express trains which run every thirty minutes during most of the day. It is not in itself a particularly exciting city, but it is centrally positioned on the island, so you may find yourself staying there at some stage.

There is a youth hostel, to reach which it is necessary to take a bus. Go out of the station and cross the main road ahead and one more small road. On the corner of the next main street, you will find Malsa Department Store. Turn left here and there are three bus stops, for three different companies. You want the last one, with a blue top, located outside a small terminal for longer distance buses. This is the stop used by the Dohoku Bus Company, and you need bus no. 550, going to Shi Yaku-sho (市役所) via Inosawa (伊の沢). Buses generally leave from this stop at 3 and 33 minutes past each hour, but this is not their starting point. They come along this main street, so you must be alert. You must also note the surroundings, so that you can remember to get off here when you come back. The main part of the city is in this area too, if you want to explore.

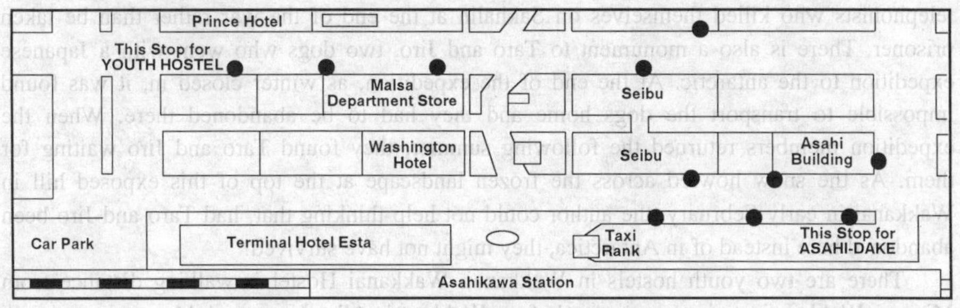

**BUS STOPS IN ASAHIKAWA**

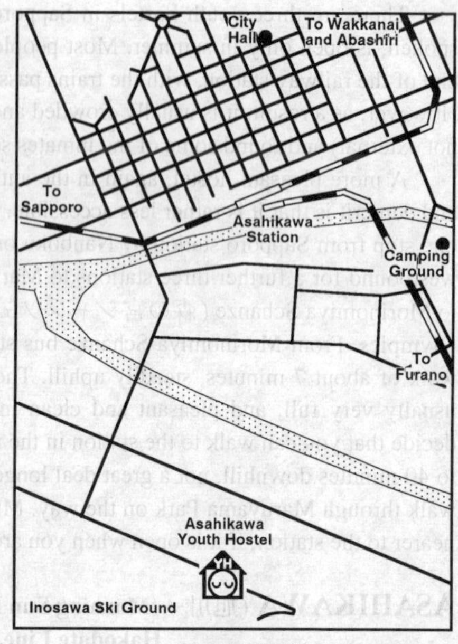


Get off the bus at Yuriana Yochien (ユリアナ幼稚園), a pre-school. The youth hostel is a large one right beside a ski area. If you look out of the window during the winter, you will wonder how many times errant skiers have come through it and into the lounge of the hostel. When the author stayed here, there was only one other hosteller, however. The 'parent' kindly said that he would teach me to ski if I wished, except at the weekend, when the slope is crowded, but I had a schedule to keep to, so I never learnt. Ski equipment is available for hire at the hostel and hostellers get a discount for the skiing facilities.

Although there are plenty of express trains between Sapporo and Asahikawa, Blue Springers will discover that there are not many ordinary trains. Convenient departures from Sapporo are at 9:09, 12:40, 14:40 and 16:10. By express the journey takes only 80 minutes, but by ordinary train it takes 2½ hours.

## WAKKANAI (稚内 — 'Infant Inside')

**Soya Line, 6 hrs. from Sapporo**

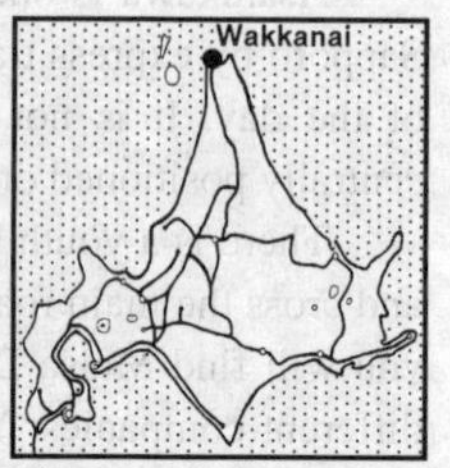


**Derivation of Name:** *From Ainu language, meaning 'cold water river'.*

Wakkanai is on the northern tip of Hokkaido. Its main claim to fame is that it is Japan's most northerly city, which seems a good reason for making a visit. It is an agreeable small city, sheltering between the sea and a hill on which is a park and, in winter, a ski area. Wakkanai is a port and ferries sail from here to the islands of Rebun and Rishiri. Before the war, they used to go to Sakhalin too, when the southern part of that island was a Japanese possession. It is a distance of only about 50 kilometres. At the end of the port you can see the dome-covered protective area from which those ships used to depart.

There is a ropeway up to the **park**, for which the youth hostel sometimes has discount coupons. Once up there you will find a variety of monuments, including one to the telephonists who killed themselves on Sakhalin at the end of the war rather than be taken prisoner. There is also a monument to Taro and Jiro, two dogs who went with a Japanese expedition to the antarctic. At the end of the expedition, as winter closed in, it was found impossible to transport the dogs home and they had to be abandoned there. When the expedition members returned the following summer, they found Taro and Jiro waiting for them. As the snow howled across the frozen landscape at the top of this exposed hill in Wakkanai in early February, the author could not help thinking that, had Taro and Jiro been abandoned here instead of in Antarctica, they might not have survived!

There are two youth hostels in Wakkanai. Wakkanai Hostel is walking distance from Minami Wakkanai station, one stop before Wakkanai. All trains stop. More conveniently located, though, and a very pleasant and popular hostel, is Wakkanai Moshiripa, only a short distance from Wakkanai station and in the main part of the town.

Four *kyuko* trains run to Wakkanai every day, three of them from Sapporo via Asahikawa and one just from Asahikawa. One of these is an overnight train leaving Sapporo at 22:00 and reaching Wakkanai at 6:00. This train carries sleepers, although, of course, it is expensive to use them. There is a morning express from Asahikawa at 8:49, for which a *tokkyu* connexion leaves Sapporo at 7:05, and there is a mid-day express which leaves Sapporo at 11:32. The last express leaves Sapporo at 16:32. Journey time from Sapporo is about 6 hours. If you are using Blue Spring tickets, however, there are only two possibilities. A *kaisoku* train leaves Asahikawa at 11:02 and arrives in Nayoro at 12:31, from where a connexion leaves at 12:41, reaching Wakkanai at 16:39. Alternatively, there is a train from Asahikawa at 11:43, reaching Nayoro at 13:14, and a train from Nayoro to Wakkanai at 13:29. However, this train stops for 1½ hours on the way at Otoi Neppu, so does not reach Wakkanai until 18:34.

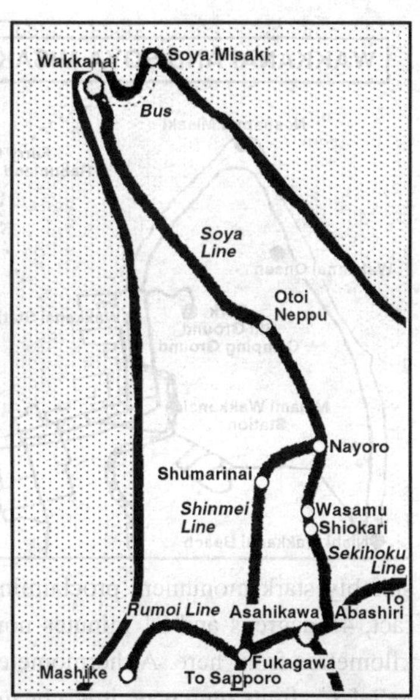

NORTH TO WAKKANAI

As one approaches Wakkanai by train, there is a pretty view over the sea. The train usually stops here for a moment for passengers to take photographs — very kind! The conductor may make an announcement when the time comes.

## SOYA MISAKI (宗谷岬 – 'Cape Principal Valley')

**52 mins. by bus from Wakkanai**

**Derivation of Name:** *Originally name of nearby island, from Ainu language, meaning 'rocky shore'*

Having got to Wakkanai, one feels an obligation to visit Soya Misaki (Cape Soya), which is the most northerly point on the mainland of Japan. To get there, take a bus from the bus terminal near Wakkanai railway station. The bus passes Minami Wakkanai station, too, on the way. There are only four buses per day. Their destination is O-misaki (大岬), a few minutes beyond Soya Misaki (宗谷岬). The journey to Soya Misaki takes 52 minutes and costs ¥1,230 each way. However, if you buy a return ticket ('*ofuku*') at the bus terminal before boarding the bus, you will get a 10% discount. If you are arriving in Wakkanai on the 12:45 *kyuko* train, note that there is a bus to Soya Misaki at 13:00 and that the next is not until 16:00. If you take the 13:00, you will probably be back in Wakkanai at 15:15. The only other useful bus departure is at 8:10.

Soya Misaki seems like not just the end of Japan, but the end of the world. At least, it did when the author went there in February, and that notwithstanding the fact that he has lived in the Orkney Isles for a while. It is a bleak windswept point with nothing but a couple of monuments and a group of souvenir shops and cafés huddled together to keep warm. (Soya Misaki, I mean, not Orkney!) Maybe it is more appealing in summer. On the shore is the

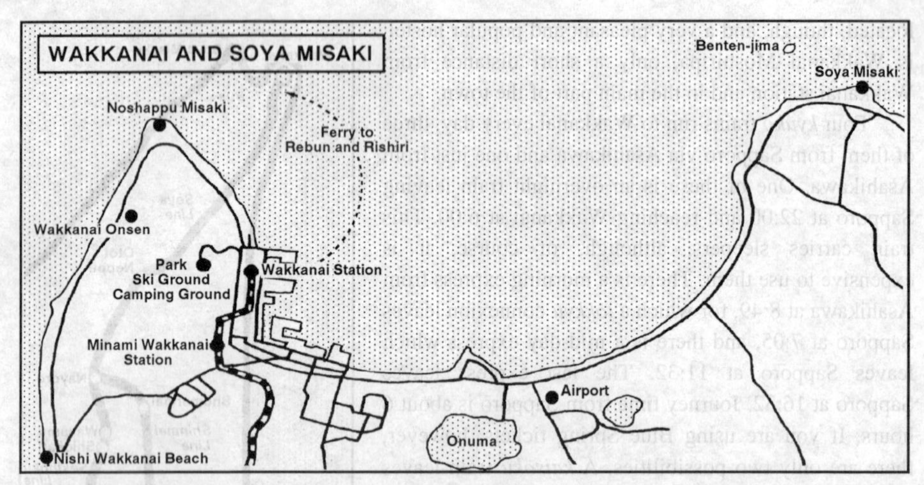


suitably stark monument proclaiming the fact that this is as far north as you can go. It is, in fact, 45 degrees and 31 minutes north. In reasonable weather Sakhalin can be seen, only 43 kilometres from here. A thermometer shows that, however cold you may feel, it is really only −2.4 ℃ . In its own way, it is a beautiful spot.

To add to the atmosphere, on the hill behind is another monument, this to those who perished on the Korean Air flight shot down near Sakhalin by the U.S.S.R. in 1983. This is the nearest land outside Russia to the place where the disaster occurred. It is also the area from which many of the bodies were recovered.

Since the attractions of Soya Misaki are limited in number, you will probably be able to take the same bus going back to Wakkanai. That would give about half an hour here, which is usually enough, especially with the limited bus service available. Useful departures from here to Wakkanai are at 9:35, 14:20, 17:27 and 18:50.

## REBUN (礼文 − 'Thankful Writing') and RISHIRI (利尻 − 'Profitable Buttocks')

**2 hrs. by ferry from Wakkanai**

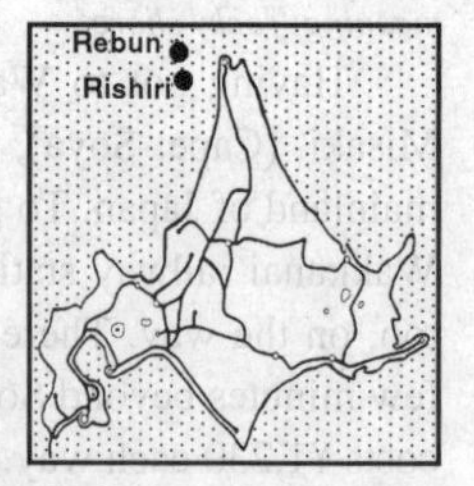


**Derivation of Names:** *Rebun — From Ainu language, meaning 'far away island'. Rishiri — From Ainu language, meaning 'high island'.*

Rebun and Rishiri are two islands lying to the west of Wakkanai. They are quite different in character, Rebun being a long, thin, relatively flat island and Rishiri being a circular volcanic island. However, both have some pretty scenery and walking courses are available, as well as limited bus services. Ferries take varying times to reach the islands, but 2 hours is about the average. If Wakkanai is not remote enough for you, try one of these two islands. They are quite popular with Japanese holidaymakers in summer and accommodation is available. Probably only Blue Spring ticket users will be really attracted by the proposition of going here, however, because others will not want to have time ticking away on their rail tickets. That, of course, is one of the great merits of Blue Spring.

In summer, ferries leave Wakkanai four times a day for Oshidomari on Rishiri and four times for Kabuka on Rebun. In winter, there are two departures for Rishiri and three for Rebun. In addition, there are two ferries each way between Kabuka and Oshidomari and one between Kabuka and Rishiri's western port of Kutsugata. This last service does not operate in winter. Between Wakkanai and Oshidomari costs ¥1,850. Between Wakkanai and Kabuka costs ¥2,060. Between Oshidomari or Kutsugata and Kabuka costs ¥720.

There is one youth hostel on Rishiri, walking distance from the port of Oshidomari. There are three hostels on Rebun, for which see our Youth Hostels section. Rebun Hostel is within walking distance of the port. Momoiwa-so Hostel will collect hostellers on request and return their luggage to the port, but asks them to walk back to Kabuka themselves because there are sights to be seen on the way. For Rebun-to Funadomari Hostel, it is necessary to take a bus to the north of the island.

## SHUMARINAI (朱鞠内 – 'Scarlet Ball Inside')

**Shinmei Line, 1 hr. from Nayoro**

**Derivation of Name:** *Presumably from Ainu language, but meaning uncertain.*

It is, of course, quite possible just to return directly to Asahikawa or Sapporo by *kyuko* after one's expedition to Wakkanai, but the author is always averse to repeating a journey when an alternative is available. There is a branch line, which may well not survive much longer, from Nayoro to the town of Fukagawa, on the main line between Sapporo and Asahikawa (see map on page 179). This is pleasant scenery, especially the sunset over the hills which you will see along the way if you follow the plan suggested. You have to follow the plan proposed here, or not attempt this deviation at all, because there is only one through train per day in each direction and the one going the other way leaves Fukagawa at 5:10, which is rather too early for convenience.

Take the 12:56 *kyuko* from Wakkanai as far as Nayoro, which it reaches at 15:42. The ordinary train for Shumarinai and Fukagawa leaves Nayoro at 16:00. It reaches Shumarinai at 17:03 and stops there for 9 minutes for a breather before continuing to Fukagawa, where it arrives at 18:58. There is a *tokkyu* to Asahikawa at 19:02, arriving at 19:20, or, if you are going the other way, a *tokkyu* to Sapporo at 19:19, arriving at 20:20.

For Blue Springers it is a little more difficult. From Wakkanai, take the 10:48 ordinary train to Nayoro, arriving at 14:13, and wait there for the 16:00 to Shumarinai and Fukagawa. But then you are stuck, because there are no connexions on ordinary trains from there unless you wait for two hours. You would just have to take the *tokkyu* to Asahikawa and pay ¥1,280 for that section (or hope that nobody noticed!). Or you could take a bus from the bus terminal at 19:39, reaching Asahikawa at 20:25, for ¥610.

When the author travelled this Nayoro to Fukagawa route, there were only two passengers on the train. The conductor asked each of us our destinations and, since we were both going to the terminus at Fukagawa, he then sought our consent to his not bothering to announce every stop on the way. Instead, he told us stories of the winter a few years ago when the lowest temperatures ever had been recorded here and the trains had struggled on, with the heating turned up to its maximum setting, but with passengers and crew still freezing. He also talked about all the beautiful lines in Hokkaido which have now been abandoned. The author suspects that this will be the next to join that long list, so why not go and see it while you can?

If you think that this whole diversion is not worth while, though, there are *kyuko* trains from Wakkanai to Asahikawa and Sapporo at 7:52, 12:56 and 22:05 and to Asahikawa only at 16:06. 4 hours to Asahikawa; 6 hours to Sapporo (8 hours on the night train). The ordinary trains leave Wakkanai at 6:42, 10:48, 13:54 and 16:51. The last two are very slow, stopping for long periods on the way, but the 6:42 will get you to Asahikawa at 11:23 (change at Nayoro, 9:58 / 10:00) and the 10:48 will enable you to reach Asahikawa at 15:52 (change at Nayoro, 14:13 / 14:27).

There is also a youth hostel on the way back to Asahikawa from Wakkanai. This is Shiokari Onsen Hostel, just beside Shiokari station, which is one station south of Wassamu ('Peacefully Cold'), where all trains stop, except the 8:49 *kyuko* from Asahikawa and the 16:06 *kyuko* from Wakkanai. However, only ordinary trains stop at Shiokari and it is 8 kilometres from Wassamu. From Asahikawa, it takes one hour to Shiokari by ordinary train. There are nine trains per day. The youth hostel has a spa bath.

## ASAHI-DAKE (旭岳 – 'Morning Sun Peak')

**95 mins. by bus from Asahikawa**

**Derivation of Name:** *Literal, meaning that if one climbs the mountain here, one can enjoy the morning sun.*

This is a very pleasant mountain hot spring resort. Try it! It has a youth hostel with a spa bath inside and the bus service to there is free. What more could you ask? This is a place worth visiting in any season. In winter you can sit in the spa bath while the snow falls outside and in summer there are some beautiful mountain hiking courses. In June and July, wildflowers cover the plateau above the resort, one of the most beautiful sights in Japan.

First you must find the free bus. It leaves from the main road outside Asahikawa station. If you face the road, with the station at your back, you will see three bus stops on your side of the road. You want the one on the right. There are two buses per day throughout the year, at 9:00 and 15:00. In summer, there is a third, at 13:00. Be there in good time, especially for the afternoon bus, because there may be gaggles of middle-aged ladies who will claw your eyes out to be on that bus first! As long as you are going to one of the two resort areas served by the bus, you do not have to pay for the journey. Only short distance passengers pay. The bus goes to the other resort, **Tennin-kyo,** first, then turns round and retraces its path for a while before turning right to go up to Asahi-dake (旭岳) – quite steeply up, in fact. In winter, even if there is not much snow down below, there will be plenty up here. Many passengers will alight at Tennin-kyo and you may just have time to get off the bus and have a glimpse of the impressive gorge there. There is a public toilet and, with luck, somebody will need to use it, which will give you the desired opportunity, but ask the driver's permission, lest you get left behind.

The youth hostel is called Daisetsu-zan Shirakaba-so. It is also a *minshuku* (small private hotel). **Daisetsu-zan** ('Big Snowy Mountains') is the name of this area, which is the largest national park in Japan. You should get off the bus at Camp-jo (キャンプ場), which means camping ground. It is the stop after everybody else has got off at the posh hotel! Even if you miss it, the bus terminates just up the road at the ropeway. It has no choice, as the road just ends there. It takes 7 minutes to walk from the ropeway back to the hostel.

If you go back to Asahikawa (旭川) on the bus at a later stage, you will need a ticket, which will be given to you by the youth hostel (or any other hotel where you may choose to stay) when you leave. Do not forget it, or you will have to pay for the journey back (¥1,250).

In summer, however, there is an alternative to going back by bus and that is to walk over the mountains to So-unkyo. You can walk all the way or you can take the ropeway up, walk

across a relatively flat area at the top, heading east towards Kurodake, and either walk or take the chair-lift and ropeway down into So-unkyo. This is quite a long walk, even though not particularly demanding, so allow sufficient time. Six hours might be suitable for those walking the entire route at a leisurely pace. You can also perform a circuit and return to Asahi-dake, if you prefer. Nobody lives up here, so do not set out late in the day and get stranded, although there is a hut near the top of Kurodake. Nor, of course, should you attempt the walk in winter. When the author was here in February, the thermometer outside the bottom station of the ropeway proclaimed that the temperature at 9:00 was −12 ℃. Skiing is available in this area even until mid-May. The Asahi-dake Ropeway is in two stages. The first takes 7 minutes and costs ¥650. The second takes 5 minutes and costs another ¥650. At So-unkyo, there is a ropeway for the lower section, taking 7 minutes and costing ¥800, and a chair-lift for the top section taking 15 minutes and costing ¥360.

## SO-UNKYO (層雲峡 – 'Layers of Clouds Gorge') Sekihoku Line to Kamikawa, 45 mins. from Asahikawa. Then bus 30 mins.

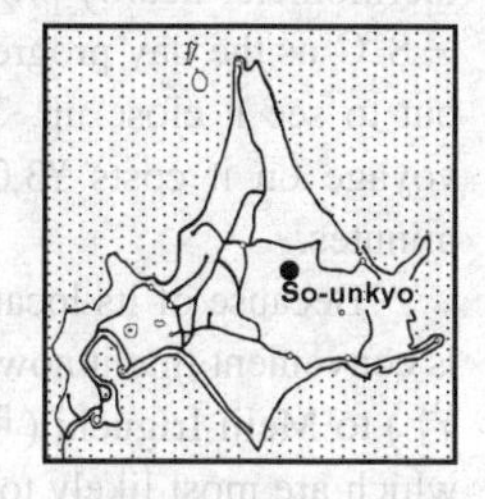


**Derivation of Name:** *From 'so-unpetsu', meaning, in Ainu language, 'river with many waterfalls'.*

So-unkyo is a small town which offers some gorgeous scenery, if the pun may be excused. It is situated in a gorge, through which the road in both directions runs. This road is now kept open for all of the year, so the town may be approached from either direction, although rather expensively from the east.

Following our route, however, we have a choice of approaching on foot over the mountains from Asahi-dake, a long but not difficult walk if the ropeways are used and the weather is favourable, or by train to Kamikawa and then by bus. Kamikawa, incidentally, holds the record for the lowest temperature ever recorded at an official weather station in Japan, −41.0 ℃ on 25th January 1902. From Sapporo, *tokkyu* trains run to Kamikawa, *en route* for Abashiri four times per day and once during the night, taking 2 hours 20 minutes. From Asahikawa, there are 9 ordinary trains and 1 *kaisoku*, taking 50 to 80 minutes. From Kamikawa, buses run about hourly, most of them originating in Asahikawa, if you prefer to go by bus all the way. The fare is ¥750 from Kamikawa, or ¥1,800 from Asahikawa. The journey takes 30 minutes from Kamikawa, or 1 hour 50 minutes from Asahikawa.

A little further down the road from So-unkyo are two waterfalls, frozen in winter but pretty in any season, while, from the town itself, a ropeway and chairlift run up to the mountains, as mentioned in the Asahi-dake section above. Skiing is possible here too until well into May. Keep to the trails, though, as there is some dangerous countryside around. In February, there is a festival with structures made out of ice and snow. Sprinklers are used to water the trees and the water immediately turns to ice, creating a magical environment.

There are two youth hostels in So-unkyo. The larger one had a notice on the door when the author visited, stating, in English (not in Japanese), that hostellers without reservations would not be accommodated. In any case, the hostel was closed. The other hostel is a small hotel with a spa bath, since this is also a spa resort. At festival time, it may not be able to accept hostellers and at other times it may prefer to accommodate them as hotel guests, rather than as hostellers.

## ABASHIRI (網走 – 'Net Running')

**Sekihoku Line, 5 hrs. 30 mins. from Sapporo**

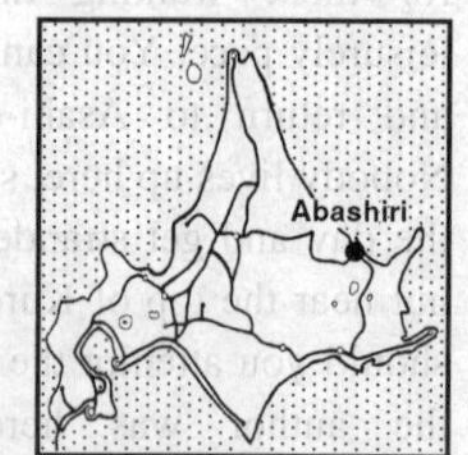


**Derivation of Name:** *From Ainu language, meaning 'land which we discovered'.*

Abashiri is a sizeable fishing town. In winter it has a snow festival like that held in Sapporo, although on a much smaller scale. It is also one of the first places from which the **drift ice** (*ryuhyo*) can be seen in February. This ice forms in the sea further north around Russia and floats down to the coast of Hokkaido, much of it ending piled up around the northern shore of the Shiretoko Peninsula. There is a hill from which the ice can be spotted as it first appears and which has on it a Drift Ice Museum (*Ryuhyo-kan* – 流氷館), in case it is not the right season when you visit. There are buses, but only four per day, in summer only. In winter, Abashiri can be quite cool. When the author visited, the harbour was frozen and the thermometer nearby proclaimed that the temperature was −13 ℃, although it did warm up to −8 ℃ as the day progressed. When the drift ice arrives, an ice-breaker, the *Aurora*, runs trips out to see it close up. This vessel operates from mid-January until the end of March and a voyage on it costs ¥3,000 for an expedition lasting 60 minutes, with departures every 90 minutes.

Because of its location, Abashiri is a place through which most people have to pass, so it is convenient that it now has a youth hostel. To get there, take a bus marked Futatsu Iwa (二ッ岩) to Meiji Iriguchi (明治入口), a journey of 8 minutes. There are not many buses. Those which are most likely to be useful leave from the bus terminal, about 5 minutes walk from the station, at 13:55, 15:20 and 17:05. Only the 15:20 travels via the station. There are also hostels a little further down the coast at **Kitahama** (Gensei Kaen Hostel), **Hama Koshimizu** (Okhotsk Koshimizu Hostel) and **Shari** (Shari Hostel). Gensei Kaen is particularly pleasant, with a beautiful view of the sunrise from the windows of the females' dormitories. Males just have to get up and go outside for their photograph! In spring, the area from here to Shari is famous for its wildflowers, so will be crowded. The railway line runs right along the beach, and gives a good view of both sea and flowers. There is even a special stop, used only in the wildflower season, for getting the ideal photograph.

Abashiri is the end of the Sekihoku Line and the limit for express trains. South from here to Kushiro only ordinary trains operate. From Sapporo to Abashiri, there are four expresses by day and one more at night. Journey time is 5½ hours. The night train has both seats and sleepers and takes 7 hours.

If coming from So-unkyo, you have the choice of returning to Kamikawa (上川) and taking the train from there, which is the cheaper option, or continuing through the gorge via Onneyu Onsen (spa), which features a bear farm, as far east as Rubeshibe (留辺蘂). This route costs ¥2,000 for a journey of 80 minutes. By *tokkyu* from Kamikawa to Abashiri takes 3 hours. From Rubeshibe takes 1 hour. The useful trains from Kamikawa are at 9:22 and 12:01.

Using a Blue Spring ticket, one has no choice. There is just one train from Kamikawa, a *kaisoku* at 15:51, which reaches Kitami at 18:07. A connexion from there at 18:10 arrives in Abashiri at 19:12. The same train continues south to the three hostels along the coast, reaching Kitahama at 19:36, Hama Koshimizu at 19:45 and Shari at 20:02.

Going east, there are buses from So-unkyo to Rubeshibe at 9:47 and 11:47 giving reasonable connexions with the *tokkyu* trains at 11:17 and 13:56. The destination of the buses is actually Kitami (北見), if you prefer to continue that far (¥2,450). For Blue Springers, there is no connexion from the 9:47 bus, but the 11:47 makes an ideal connexion with the 13:14 ordinary train from Rubeshibe to Abashiri, arriving at 14:51. This is actually quicker than waiting for the express. The 15:47 bus from So-unkyo connects with the 17:23 ordinary train to Abashiri, Kitahama, Hama Koshimizu and Shari, which is the train mentioned in the previous paragraph.

## SHIRETOKO (知床—'Knowledgeable Floor')

**Bus, 2 hrs. from Shari or 3 hrs. 30 mins. from Kushiro**

**Derivation of Name:** *From Ainu language, meaning 'end of the land'.*

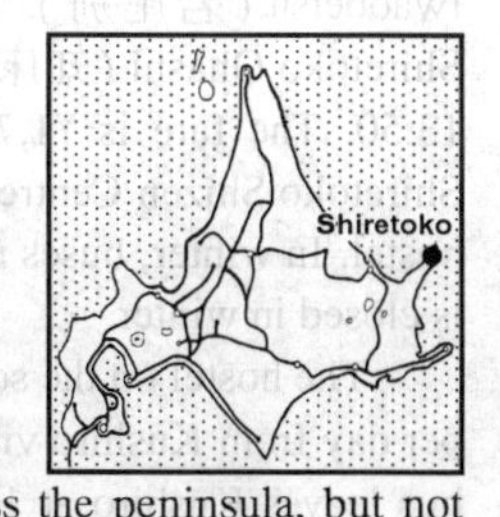


The great advantage of the Shiretoko Peninsula is that it is difficult to reach, so it remains a relatively unpopulated and not over-touristed area. It is a national park and the further you go, the better it gets. There are roads along both north and south sides of the peninsula, but neither goes right to the end. There is one road across the peninsula, but not near the tip.

The attractions are the mountains which run through the centre of the peninsula, of which one, Io-san ('Mt. Sulphur'), is an active sulphur-producing volcano, the Shiretoko Go-ko (five

EASTERN HOKKAIDO

lakes) and the coastal scenery, as well as natural hot spring pools where you can just stop and hop in. Nobody maintains these natural pools, so there is no charge for bathing in such places. In winter, Shiretoko is one of the best places for viewing the drift ice (*ryuhyo*) which finds its path obstructed and piles up along the coast of the peninsula. It is also a good location for viewing wildlife, including the species of bear which is native to Hokkaido, so be careful! The odd tourist occasionally makes a tasty lunch for a hungry bear.

Buses run in summer on all of the roads mentioned above, although not frequently. In winter, however, services finish at Utoro on the north and Rausu on the south. Boats for viewing the coastal scenery leave from Utoro in summer. A 90 minute tour operates five times per day and costs ¥2,400. A tour lasting 3¾ hours departs at 12:10 only and costs ¥6,000.

There are two youth hostels on the Shiretoko Peninsula. The one on the northern side is at Iwaobetsu. To get there, take a bus from Shari station, on the Senmo Line, for 70 minutes to Iwaobetsu (岩尾別). The destination of the bus will be Shiretoko Go-ko (知床五湖) or Shiretoko Ohashi (知床大橋). There are only four buses per day and the last leaves Shari at 13:50. The fare is ¥1,700. There is another bus at 14:50 on which you can go as far as Shiretoko Shizen Centre (知床自然センター), from where it is a walk of 4 kilometres to the hostel. In winter, buses run only to Shiretoko Shizen Centre, and, in any case, the youth hostel is closed in winter.

The hostel on the southern side of the peninsula is at Rausu (羅臼). There are three buses per day from Kushiro via Naka Shibetsu and a further three from Naka Shibetsu only. The last bus leaves Kushiro at 15:45 and Naka Shibetsu at 17:40. The journey takes 3½ hours from Kushiro and costs ¥4,500. If you are approaching from the north, there are two buses per day, in summer only, from Shari and two more from Utoro. The last bus leaves Shari at 14:50 and Utoro at 15:45. The journey from Shari takes 1¾ hours and costs ¥2,340.

## MASHU-KO (摩周湖 – 'Rubbing Around Lake')

**Senmo Line, 1 hr. 30 mins. from Kushiro**

**Derivation of Name:** *From Ainu language, possibly meaning 'lake filled with ducks' (doubtful).*

Mashu-ko (Lake Mashu) claims to have the clearest water in the world, transparent to a depth of over 30 metres, a depth which is slowly diminishing, however, with the influences of modern civilization. The lake is another *caldera*, that is a lake in the cone of an extinct volcano. This cone has steeply sloping sides, so that it is impossible to approach the lake. It can be viewed only from the rim of the cone. From that vantage point, however, it is an impressive and beautiful sight, when visible, although the lake is often covered with mist.

The station called Mashu is about 15 kilometres from the main lookout over the lake, so it is necessary to take a bus. Incidentally, this station used to be called Teshikaga, the name of the nearby town, but few people could pronounce correctly the combination of *kanji*, so, a few years ago, the station name was changed to Mashu, which was more familiar to visitors.

There are only ordinary trains on the Senmo Line. From Abashiri, there are four trains per day, at 6:44, 10:00, 15:40 and 18:02. The journey takes about 2 hours. From Kushiro, there are eight trains per day and the journey takes about 90 minutes. Buses run from the station to the lookout over the lake (Mashu Dai-ichi Tenbodai – 摩周第一展望台) in summer only (¥690), but there are more buses from Teshikaga bus terminal, to locate which see the map for

Mashu-ko Youth Hostel on page 402. In winter, buses run from the bus terminal only.

An alternative and much more interesting route to Mashu-ko, but unfortunately a rather costly one, is by bus from Bihoro. This route serves a double function as a sightseeing service and a means of transportation for local people. There is a taped commentary (in Japanese, of course) and the bus stops at several attractions along the route. First along the way is **Bihoro Toge** (Bihoro Pass), from which a magnificent view extends in all directions. When the author was there, it was fascinating to be able to look down on those who were hang-gliding. The next stop is at **Kussharo-ko** (Lake Kussharo), a lake which is always warm, even in the depths of winter, because of the volcanic activity around and the fact that it is fed with hot water from the nearby springs. It is consequently popular with wildlife and has a colony of happy swans. Nearby is another **Io-san** ('Sulphur Mountain'), where the bus makes a further exciting halt. Steam hisses from the crevices in the mountain side and a smell of sulphur, almost overpowering at times, fills the atmosphere. Yellow fungus-like growths deform the mountainside to give evidence of the principal element available here. As usual in such places, ladies are selling sulphur-vapour steamed eggs, which, they assure prospective customers, are good for every known ailment, and probably some unknown ailments too! The bus journeys on to Kawayu Onsen, where it may stop for lunch, if that time of the day has been reached. From here, it is a short ride to the **Mashu-ko lookout**, where there is another pause, and then down into the spa town of Teshikaga (弟子屈). If you have enough time and money, the route continues on to **Akan-ko** (阿寒湖), for which see the next entry. This bus runs at least once a day throughout the year. In summer it operates three times a day, with the first service returning to Bihoro (美幌) by a more direct route after a lengthy stop at Akan-ko. The fares from Bihoro are ¥3,420 to Mashu-ko, ¥3,830 to Teshikaga and ¥5,490 to Akan-ko. To return to Bihoro by the direct route costs another ¥2,040.

There is a youth guest house at Kussharo, near the lake, and a youth hostel at Mashu-ko, for details of which see the Youth Hostels section. There is also a youth hostel in Bihoro.

## AKAN-KO (阿寒湖 – 'Cold Sycophant Lake')

**Nemuro Line to Kushiro, 5 hrs. from Sapporo. Then bus 2 hrs.**

**Derivation of Name:** *Corruption and abbreviation of 'rakanpetsu', meaning, in Ainu language, 'river where dace spawn'.*

Akan-ko is another attractive lake, famous for scenery, for its Ainu population and for *marimo*. If you arrive by bus from Mashu-ko, you will see much of the scenery on the way. The **Ainu** here can be found mainly in a special village at one end of the town (see youth hostel map on page 403). Their conditions seem somewhat better than in some other places in Hokkaido, although they are still regarded mainly as tourist attractions. In their small village they are engaged principally in handicrafts. If one wishes to see something of the traditions and appearance of the Ainu, this is probably the best place to do so.

***Marimo*** is a type of weed which flourishes in the lake. Its unique quality is that every few minutes it rises to the surface to breathe. It looks like little green balls of sponge and, although this is not the only place where *marimo* is found, the weed is rare and this is the largest known variety. There is a small museum opposite the bus terminal which has *marimo* in a glass tank. Whilst the author stood and stared at it intently for fifteen minutes, no piece budged even a millimetre. When I decided that it was only a myth and gave up, it probably bobbed up and down behind my back for all it was worth. I suspect that it is like a party game where no piece of *marimo* should ever be caught moving when anybody is watching!

Unlike Mashu-ko, for example, Akan-ko freezes in winter and it was feared that a particularly severe winter recently may have damaged the *marimo* by causing it to be crushed by the weight of ice. In winter, the lake is used for snowmobile races and fishing (through holes drilled in the ice). Fish caught in winter are supposed to be particularly succulent.

There are various ways of reaching Akan-ko (阿寒湖) by bus. The most scenic is from Teshikaga (Mashu-ko), a journey of 1 hour which costs ¥1,990. Also attractive is the ride from Kushiro, which takes approximately 2 hours and costs ¥2,490. Then there are buses directly from Bihoro which operate twice per day, in summer only, at 7:20 and 16:00. The journey takes 70 minutes and costs ¥2,040.

There is a youth hostel at Akan-ko (Akan Angel Hostel). It includes a spa bath and English is spoken. Directions are in the Youth Hostels section.

## KUSHIRO (釧路 – 'Bracelet Road')

**Nemuro Line, 5 hrs. from Sapporo**

**Derivation of Name:** *Corruption of Ainu 'kusuri', meaning 'the road we are travelling'.*

Kushiro's main point of interest is that it is a ferry terminal with services to and from Tokyo. There is also a reserve for cranes (the feathered type) at **Tsuru Koen** (鶴公園 – 'Crane Park') about an hour along the bus route towards Akan-ko (¥850). Numbers of birds are greatly augmented during the winter when cranes migrate here because of the mild and friendly conditions. Cranes' standards must differ from those of humans, so wrap up warm if you want to go and take pictures of these birds. It is a popular place for such activities, particularly during the cooler time of year.

Kushiro is blessed with two youth hostels. The nearer to the station is Hoshino Makiba, where some English is allegedly spoken. It is a pleasant hostel and easier to locate than Kushiro Hostel, which involves a bus ride or a lengthy and complicated walk. However, English is spoken at the latter hostel also and it is the cheaper of the two.

Kushiro is a 5 hour journey from Sapporo by *tokkyu*. There are six trains per day and another at night, via the Sekisho Line. By ordinary train, the route is different. One leaves Sapporo at 6:59 and travels to Takikawa, arriving at 8:42. The connexion leaves at 9:35, reaching Kushiro at 16:59, with a 16 minute pause in Shintoku and a 22 minute rest in Obihiro, in case you want to go shopping. If you are coming from the north, however, there are four through trains from Abashiri and a total of eight trains from Mashu. Journey time is 3½ hours from Abashiri or about 90 minutes from Mashu. Most of these services are operated by single carriage trains which are sometimes crowded.

## NEMURO (根室 – 'Root Room')

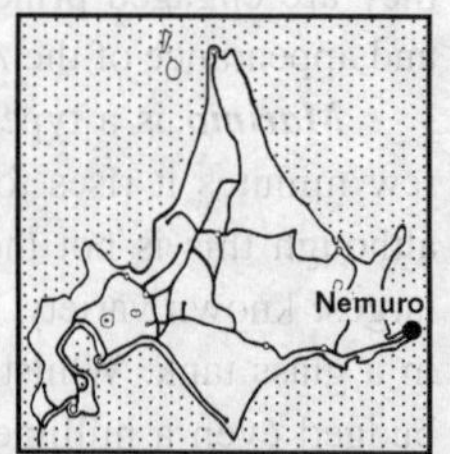


**Nemuro Line, 7 hrs. 30 mins. from Sapporo**

**Derivation of Name:** *From Ainu language. Meaning uncertain.*

If you continue east from Kushiro, you will reach the end of the railway at Nemuro, a city with a population of 40,000. No express trains run beyond Kushiro, but most of them make connexions with the ordinary trains there. From Kushiro, it is a run of approximately 2 hours 15 minutes to Nemuro. There are six trains per day. If you have a similar experience to the author, you may find your train having to make an emergency stop because of deer on the line.

From Nemuro station, there is a bus service to **Nosappu Misaki** (Cape Nosappu) where there is an observation tower. Nosappu Misaki (納沙布岬) is the easternmost point of the Japanese mainland (146 degrees and 49 minutes east, to be precise). Beyond lie the islands which Japan claims but which have been occupied by the U.S.S.R., and now by Russia, since 1945. The continuing dispute over these islands, historically a part of Japan, has been the reason why a peace treaty was never signed between Japan and the Soviet Union. If you climb the observation tower and look through the binoculars provided, you may be able to see the Russians watching you watching them. However, if you do not want such expense, you can see the disputed islands even from ground level. It is another pleasantly desolate spot. When the author took the bus here, he recalls remarking to the bus driver that maybe the islands would soon revert to Japan, for it seemed at that time that a solution might be near. "I hope not!" he replied, to my surprise. "Pardon?" "Well, if those islands come back to Japan, nobody is going to come on my bus any more." Which goes to show that there are different ways of looking at these matters. There are ten buses per day and the fare is ¥960 each way. The journey takes 40 minutes.

There is a youth hostel in Nemuro. When the author stayed, I was alone there. The nearest station is Higashi Nemuro, the easternmost railway station in Japan, one stop before Nemuro. From there the hostel is within walking distance. However, if you are coming on the 17:50 arrival from Kushiro (15:33 departure from Kushiro, connecting rather poorly with the 9:53 *tokkyu* from Sapporo), the 'parent' will be willing to collect you from the station. If you are coming back on the bus from Nosappu Misaki, there is no need to return all the way to Nemuro station. When the bus meets the main road and turns right, you want to get off and walk in the opposite direction (i.e. as though the bus had turned left). After a few minutes you will reach Higashi Nemuro station, from where follow the map on page 402.

## ERIMO MISAKI (襟裳岬 – 'Cape Collar Dress')

**Hidaka Line, 3 hrs. from Tomakomai. Then bus 1 hr.**

**Derivation of Name:** *Corruption of Ainu 'enrumu', meaning 'cape'.*

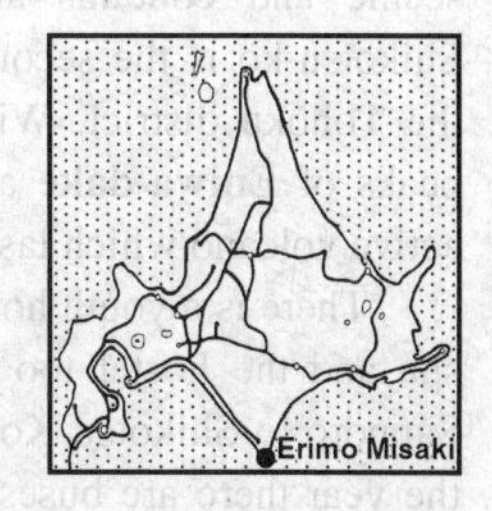


Erimo Misaki (Cape Erimo) is the southern tip of the central part of Hokkaido, another windswept and agreeable spot. It is frequented by a large colony of seals who may be seen basking in the sun if there happens to be any. If not, the youth hostel has a video of them made by NHK, the national broadcasting service.

Erimo Misaki may be reached from east or west, so it seems logical to arrive from one direction and depart in the other. Since our previous entry was for Nemuro, let us arrive from the east. Take a train to Obihiro, changing at Kushiro. From Obihiro station buses run to Hiro-o, a journey of 2 hours costing ¥1,700. Buses run approximately hourly. Along the way, you will see the abandoned railway line, with many of the stations looking as though they are just waiting for the next train. In Hiro-o, the former railway station is being used as the bus terminal, again, it appears, merely as a temporary measure until the rail service resumes. One fears that it will be a long wait, however. From Hiro-o, a JR bus continues, so those with a Japan Rail Pass or a *shu-yu-ken* will not need to pay for this section (otherwise ¥1,450). The

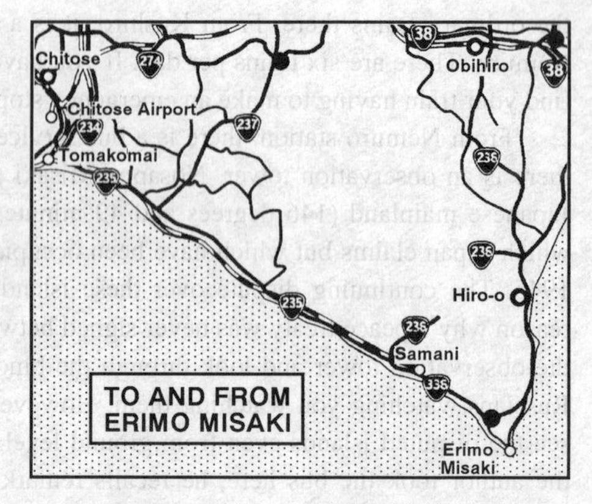


ride takes an hour to Erimo Misaki, although the destination of the buses is Samani (様似). It is a pretty journey, right beside the sea for much of the route, so sit on the left. In fact, the road runs so close to the water that one feels in danger of being swept away by the waves breaking over the low wall in even slightly rough conditions. It is an enjoyable trip.

There is a friendly and pleasant youth hostel here, one of those which sometimes has the custom of waving hostellers off with flags, even very early in the morning in the author's case. For the hostel, alight from the bus at Misaki Sho-gakko (岬小学校 – Misaki Primary School), just before the small town begins. For the cape itself, go a little further, to the stop called Erimo Misaki (えりも岬), right on the point.

From Higashi Nemuro, one may start at 8:21, reaching Kushiro at 10:36. A *tokkyu* leaves at 11:04 and arrives in Obihiro at 13:02. The bus to Hiro-o is at 13:30, arriving at 15:29. Finally, the JR bus leaves at 16:25 and gets to Erimo Misaki at 17:25. For those using Blue Spring tickets, however, the journey cannot be done in a day. Instead one must stay in Kushiro and start from there on the 7:22 train, reaching Obihiro at 10:03. The bus departs at 10:30 and arrives in Hiro-o at 12:29. The JR bus leaves at 13:10 and reaches Erimo Misaki at 14:10.

## SHIKOTSU-KO (支笏湖 – 'Supporting Mace Lake')

**80 mins. by bus from Sapporo**

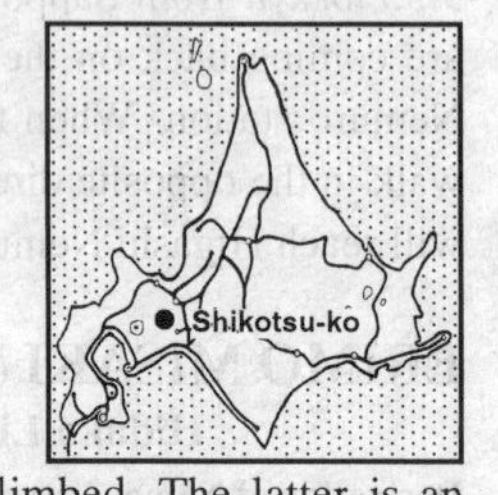


**Derivation of Name:** *From Ainu language. Meaning unknown.*

We now return to the area south of Sapporo which is particularly scenic and contains also some interesting volcanic countryside. Shikotsu-ko is the second deepest lake in Japan, after Tazawa-ko in the Tohoku district. With a depth of 360 metres, it lies beside the peaks of **Eniwa-dake** and **Tarumae-dake**, both of which can be climbed. The latter is an active volcano which last erupted in 1979.

There is a youth hostel in Shikotsu Kohan, the main town beside the lake. The town has a spa and the hostel too contains a spa bath. In summer, there are six buses per day from Sapporo to Shikotsu Kohan (支笏湖畔), 80 minutes, at a cost of ¥1,150, while throughout the year there are buses from Chitose Airport, which serves Sapporo and has also a railway station, and from Tomakomai, the number of buses varying according to the season. From Chitose Airport (Shin Chitose Kuko station) takes 52 minutes and costs ¥770 while from Tomakomai takes 40 minutes and costs ¥580. In addition, if you are staying at the youth hostel, by prior arrangement the 'parent' will collect hostellers from Chitose station at 19:00 and return them to Tomakomai station, in the morning, leaving at 8:30, which will save a considerable sum of money. Note that Chitose is a different station from Chitose Airport (see map) and that if you want to be collected you must telephone before lunch on the day of collection at the latest.

If you are coming from Erimo Misaki, according to our route, take a JR bus to Samani

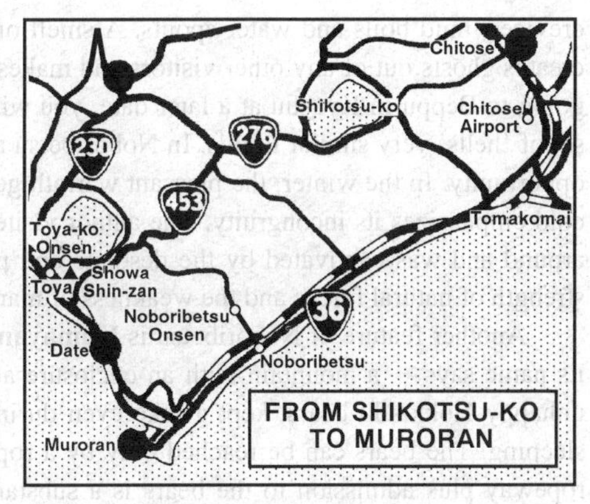


(様似), a journey of one hour, and then a train to Tomakomai, which takes a little in excess of three hours more. Only ordinary trains operate. From Tomakomai to Chitose is five stations, which takes 20 minutes by express or 25 minutes by ordinary train. If you want to reach Chitose Airport, however, you must change once more, at Minami Chitose, four stations north of Tomakomai. From Tomakomai and Minami Chitose trains are frequent.

For an early morning departure, leave Erimo Misaki Shigai at 6:41 (note that this bus starts from Shigai, a few minutes walk from the youth hostel, and does not pass the hostel itself) and reach Samani at 7:36. The train starts at 8:28 and reaches Tomakomai at 11:39. Although the bus times are subject to change, at the time of writing the next service is at 13:45, reaching Shikotsu Kohan at 14:25.

To connect with the youth hostel bus to Shikotsu-ko Hostel, there is a bus starting from Erimo Misaki Shigai (not from the youth hostel) at 13:01 (not Saturdays). It reaches Samani at 13:56. The train departs at 14:22, arriving in Tomakomai at 17:50. There is a *tokkyu* from there at 17:55, stopping at Minami Chitose at 18:11. There you must change again to the 18:16 ordinary train which terminates at Chitose at 18:21. Alternatively, you can wait at Tomakomai for the 18:23 ordinary train, which reaches Chitose at 18:47.

Tomakomai, along this route, is another ferry port and services run from here to Aomori, Ohata, Hachinohe, Sendai, Oarai, Tokyo and Nagoya.

## NOBORIBETSU (登別 – 'Climbing Separately')

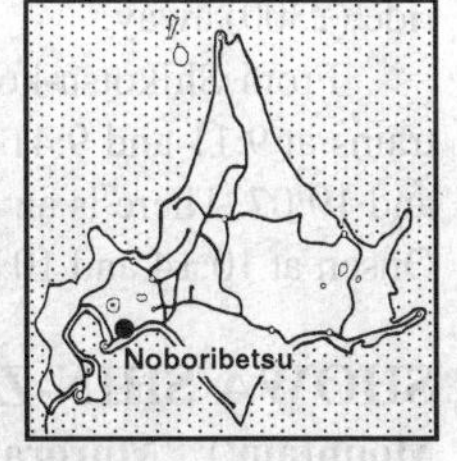


**Muroran Line, 70 mins. from Sapporo**

**Derivation of Name:** *Corruption of Ainu 'nupuru-petsu', meaning 'river of dark colour'.*

Noboribetsu is one of those spa towns which the Japanese love to visit. However, it is also not a bad one for the visitor from overseas to go to, to sample this aspect of Japanese culture. One of its features is that the enormous **spa bath** of one of the principal hotels is open to non-residents, at least until the evening rush-hour starts. Noboribetsu is not the only town which offers this feature, but it is not so common, so worth taking advantage of during a visit, if only because of the impressive architecture of the bath hall. The hotel is the Dai-ichi Takimoto Hotel, at the top end of the town, which is built on a hill. Take bathing materials with you. Make sure that you have got the appropriate entrance for your sex and then take off shoes and put them in a locker, taking the key with you, before entering and paying. Undress in the ante room, leaving your clothes and towel in another locker there. Then proceed to the inner sanctum and have at least a quick scrub before plunging into any one of the many pools. Be careful! Test the temperature before boiling yourself alive.

Beyond the hotel is an interesting area which you should be certain to visit. This is **Jigokudani** ('Hell Valley'). You will soon find why it is called that. Steam issues from crevices, mud boils and water spouts. A smell of sulphur hangs over all and a volcanic mist creates ghosts out of any other visitors and makes drops of vapour cling to the hair. If you are going to Beppu in Kyushu at a later date, you will find that you are charged ¥2,000 to visit a set of 'hells' very similar to this. In Noboribetsu all is free, however, so make the most of this opportunity. In the winter, the pleasant warmth generated here in the midst of the surrounding cold emphasizes its incongruity. The author visited early one morning when nobody else was around and was captivated by the desolate and potentially dangerous scenery displaying the strength of natural forces and the weakness of man.

Another feature of Noboribetsu is **Kumayama** ('Bear Mountain'), which is exactly what its name says – a mountain with an enclosure at the top containing a substantial number of unhappy Hokkaido bears, kept awake even during the winter when they should properly be sleeping. The bears can be reached only by a ropeway, unfortunately, and the charge for the ropeway plus admission to the bears is a substantial ¥2,300 return. A 10% discount can be obtained with a voucher available at the youth hostel. Also in this bearland are some Ainu houses and, if you are lucky, some Ainu to go along with them. In winter, however, the Ainu seem to be allowed to hibernate, even though the bears cannot. There is also a museum relating to bears and to the geography of the region and a look-out tower from which a fine view of the surrounding area can be obtained in reasonable weather.

There is a youth hostel in Noboribetsu, although the very pleasant one at which the author stayed is now closed, unfortunately. However, Akashiya-so Hostel is a small Japanese-style hotel and offers a spa bath in the hostel, if you prefer not to go to the big hotel bath hall, or arrive too late.

To reach Noboribetsu, take a train to Noboribetsu station. This takes about 70 minutes from Sapporo by *tokkyu* or 2½ hours by ordinary train, of which there are few. By ordinary train, a change is necessary at Tomakomai. However, Noboribetsu town, where the station is located, is not the same as Noboribetsu Onsen (登別温泉), the spa, which is a 13 minute bus ride (¥300) away.

From Shikotsu-ko, take the youth hostel or public bus to Tomakomai. There are *tokkyu* trains at 9:11 and 9:41 (and fairly regularly throughout the day), reaching Noboribetsu at 9:32 and 10:07. There is an ordinary train at 9:58, arriving at 10:41. There are buses to Noboribetsu Onsen at 10:14 and 10:46 and throughout the day.

## SHOWA SHIN-ZAN (昭和新山 – 'Brilliantly Peaceful New Mountain')

**Muroran Line, 1 hr. 45 mins. from Sapporo to Toya. Then bus 15 mins. to Toya Onsen and bus 15 mins. to Showa Shin-zan**

**Derivation of Name:** *See below.*

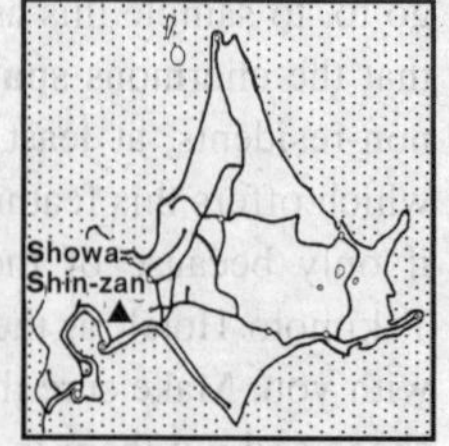


Showa Shin-zan is a remarkable sight. The reign of the previous Emperor (1926-1989), was known as the Showa Era – 'the Age of Brilliant Peace', although unfortunately it did not quite live up to its title. Thus this is the 'new mountain of the Showa Era'. One day at the end of 1943, there were earthquakes and Showa Shin-zan started to sprout from the ground, much to the irritation, no doubt, of the farmer on whose land it sprouted. From then on, it just 'growed and growed', until today it has reached a height of 402 metres, which is perhaps 200 metres higher than the land around it. It is still steaming and growing slowly.

The real culprit behind – or, rather, beside – this new mountain is **Usu-san**, which stands nearby, at 737 metres towering over its infant prodigy. There is a ropeway which runs almost to the top of Usu-san. The 6 minute journey costs ¥1,450 return and offers a good view on the way. At the base of the ropeway is a museum containing information and displays on the eruptions of Usu-san in 1977 and 1978.

From Noboribetsu, the scenic way to reach Showa Shin-zan is by bus over the mountains. In summer there are five such buses per day and even in winter one service operates. The destination of the buses is Toya-ko Onsen (洞爺湖温泉) and you should alight at Tozan Guchi (登山口). The journey takes 90 minutes and costs ¥1,400. Especially in winter, the journey is a memorable one. Tozan Guchi is about 3 kilometres from Showa Shin-zan. The distance is walkable, although uphill, but in summer there are buses every hour. Any bus going along this road will do, for it leads only to Showa Shin-zan (昭和新山), which will be the destination marked on the bus. In winter, though, there are no buses. The author walked, and came across a most memorable accident involving no less than four tour buses and two cars, all except one of which found that they could not stop on the slippery downhill slope (and the driver of the one in front no doubt regretted subsequently that he could!). However, such entertainment cannot be promised to all pedestrians. This accident also resulted in my being given a ride back from the mountain in a police car (no handcuffs!), but again this cannot be guaranteed.

There is a youth hostel right by the turn-off to Showa Shin-zan. It has a spa bath.

## MURORAN (室蘭 – 'Room Orchid')

**Muroran Line, 1 hr. 45 mins. from Sapporo**

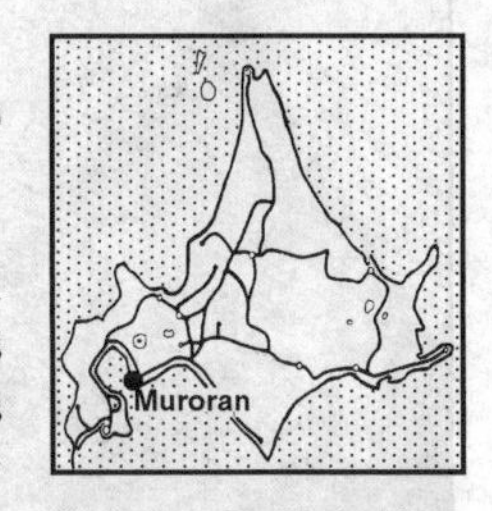


**Derivation of Name:** *From Ainu 'mo ruerani', meaning 'gentle descent'. Muroran is on a slight slope down to the sea.*

As a city, Muroran is not so exciting, but it is a ferry terminal with services to Hachinohe in Tohoku and Oarai near Mito. Express trains run from Sapporo five times per day. They actually operate as expresses as far as Higashi Muroran and then continue as ordinary trains for the last four stops to Muroran. At other times, one may take an express for Hakodate as far as Higashi Muroran and change to an ordinary train there. Ordinary trains mostly originate in Tomakomai, where it is necessary to change if coming from Sapporo using only ordinary services.

From Showa Shin-zan Youth Hostel, first take a bus into Toya-ko Onsen (洞爺湖温泉), an 8 minute journey. Then change to a bus for Toya station (洞爺駅), which takes 15 minutes at a cost of ¥290. Toya-ko is a pretty lake and the best view of it is obtained from the bus as it climbs out of Toya-ko Onsen on its way to Toya station. To go to Muroran, take an express train bound for Sapporo or an ordinary train for Higashi Muroran as far as Higashi Muroran and change to a train for Muroran. A very few ordinary trains go through to Muroran without the need for a change.

However, if you have finished in Hokkaido now and are returning to Honshu, you need to take a train in the opposite direction. Expresses will be going to Hakodate, but with ordinary trains it will be necessary to change in Oshamanbe and connexions there are poor. For those using rail passes or a *shu-yu-ken*, a suggested schedule is to catch the 9:20 bus from Showa Shin-zan Youth Hostel to Toya-ko Onsen and the 9:45 bus from there to Toya station. There is a *tokkyu* from Toya at 10:06 reaching Hakodate at 11:36. The *kaisoku* to Aomori leaves

Hakodate at 11:50, arriving at 14:23, but this is a good opportunity to have a tour of one of the underwater stations, if you missed that chance when travelling in the opposite direction. The train stops at Tappi Kaitei ('Underwater Flying Dragon') at 13:20 and you will be picked up by the next *kaisoku* at 14:10, arriving in Aomori at 15:15. The stop is worthwhile just for the name of the station! If you do not take it, however, there is a *tokkyu* leaving Aomori at 14:26 and reaching Hirosaki, where there is a youth hostel, at 14:55. If you do stop underwater, to search for the flying dragon, there is an ordinary train from Aomori to Hirosaki at 15:56, arriving at 16:46.

Those with Blue Spring tickets should take the same buses, then the 10:39 ordinary train from Toya to Oshamanbe, arriving at 11:39. There will be a long wait there until the 13:17 train for Hakodate which reaches Onuma at 15:37 and Hakodate at 16:21. For those who want to get further, there is a bus at 7:05 for Muroran ( 室蘭 ), that is going away from Toya-ko Onsen, not towards it. Alight at Date Monbetsu station ( 伊達紋別駅 ) after about 30 minutes and take the 7:49 train to Oshamanbe, arriving at 8:58. Your connexion leaves at 10:34 and reaches Hakodate at 13:22. From there you can take the 13:58 *kaisoku* arriving in Aomori at 16:36 and then the 17:18 ordinary train to Hirosaki, arriving at 18:00, for the youth hostel there.

**'When Icicles Hang by the Wall' So-unkyo, Hokkaido**

# CHUBU (中部)
## ('Central Part')

The area lying between Tokyo and Kyoto is known as Chubu, the 'central part', and since it is indeed the central part of Japan, that is a reasonable name. Almost every visitor to Japan wants to go to Tokyo and to Kyoto, and therefore travels between the two. Most people do the journey by *shinkansen*, which takes only three hours, along the coast for much of the journey. Although there are glimpses of attractive scenery – the sea, Mt. Fuji and some mountains as Kyoto is approached – the general impression is that one long conurbation stretches most of the way between the two cities. However, if one travels by an inland route, or crosses to the Japan Sea, the impression gained is quite different. There is beautiful mountain scenery in the Japan Alps and the unpredictable Japan Sea has a character quite different from that of the relatively placid Pacific Ocean. The journey to Kyoto can still be done in a day, if necessary, although it is a very long day by ordinary train, so better to use two days or longer, and one will see so much more.

***Transportation and Tickets***

This book proposes a round trip going through the Japan Alps and along the Japan Sea side, before cutting back inland, with return along the Pacific Ocean. If you have insufficient time for this, the *shinkansen* is, of course, fast and efficient, but if you can spare an extra day or two, the route proposed will allow you to see much more of rural Japan – and also satisfies the author's preference for going and returning by different routes.

Here is the route proposed by this book:

Tokyo to Takasaki by Takasaki Line.
Takasaki to Naoetsu via Nagano by Shinetsu Line.
Naoetsu to Kanazawa by Hokuriku Line.
Kanazawa to Toyama by Hokuriku Line.
Toyama to Gifu (or Nagoya) via Takayama by Takayama Line.
Gifu or Nagoya to Kyoto by Tokaido *shinkansen* or Tokaido Line.
Kyoto to Nara by Nara Line.
Nara to Kameyama by Kansai Line.
Kameyama to Taki by Kii Line.
Taki to Toba and return by Sangu Line.

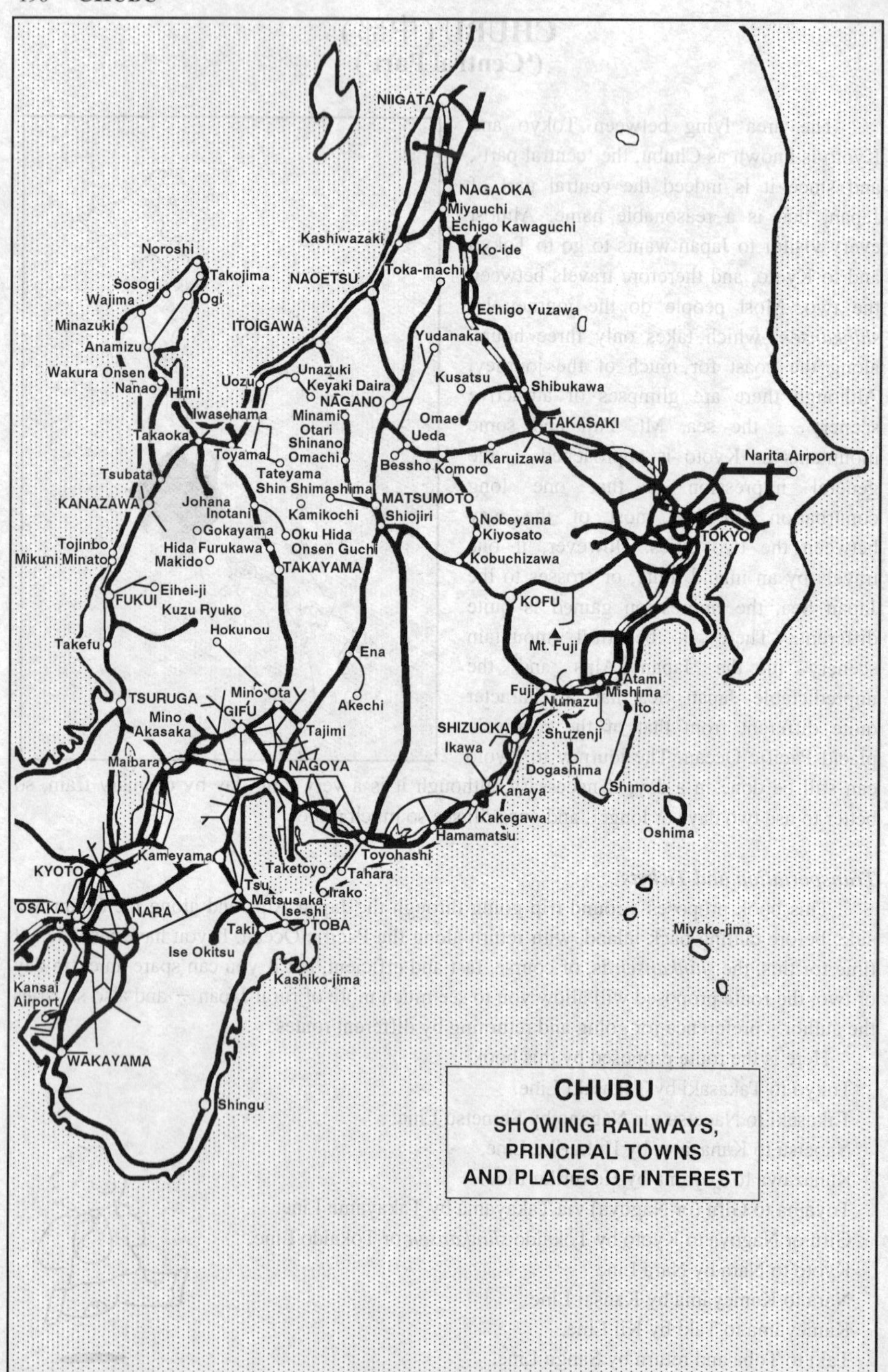
NIIGATA
NAGAOKA
Miyauchi
Echigo Kawaguchi
Kashiwazaki
Ko-ide
Noroshi
Takojima
Sosogi
Ogi
Wajima
NAOETSU
Toka-machi
Echigo Yuzawa
Minazuki
ITOIGAWA
Anamizu
Yudanaka
Wakura Onsen
Nanao
Himi
Uozu
Unazuki
Keyaki Daira
NAGANO
Kusatsu
Shibukawa
Iwasehama
Minami Otari
Omae
TAKASAKI
Takaoka
Toyama
Shinano Omachi
Ueda
Bessho
Komoro
Karuizawa
Narita Airport
Tsubata
Tateyama
Shin Shimashima
MATSUMOTO
KANAZAWA
Johana
Inotani
Kamikochi
Shiojiri
Nobeyama
Kiyosato
TOKYO
Gokayama
Oku Hida
Tojinbo
Mikuni Minato
Hida Furukawa
Makido
Onsen Guchi
TAKAYAMA
Kobuchizawa
Eihei-ji
FUKUI
Kuzu Ryuko
KOFU
Hokunou
Takefu
Mt. Fuji
Ena
Fuji
Atami
Mino Ota
Akechi
Numazu
Mishima
Ito
TSURUGA
GIFU
Mino Akasaka
Tajimi
SHIZUOKA
Shuzenji
Ikawa
Maibara
NAGOYA
Dogashima
Shimoda
Kanaya
Kakegawa
Oshima
Hamamatsu
Kameyama
Toyohashi
KYOTO
Taketoyo
Tahara
Tsu
Irako
OSAKA
NARA
Matsusaka
Ise-shi
TOBA
Taki
Miyake-jima
Ise Okitsu
Kashiko-jima
Kansai Airport
WAKAYAMA
Shingu
CHUBU
SHOWING RAILWAYS, PRINCIPAL TOWNS AND PLACES OF INTEREST

Taki to Tsu by Kii Line.
Tsu to Kawarada by Ise Private Railway.
Kawarada to Nagoya by Kansai Line.
Nagoya to Kakegawa by Tokaido *shinkansen* or Tokaido Line.
Kakegawa to Kanaya by Tokaido Line.
Kanaya to Ikawa by Oigawa Private Railway.
Ikawa to Shizuoka by bus.
Shizuoka to Tokyo by Tokaido *shinkansen* or Tokaido Line.

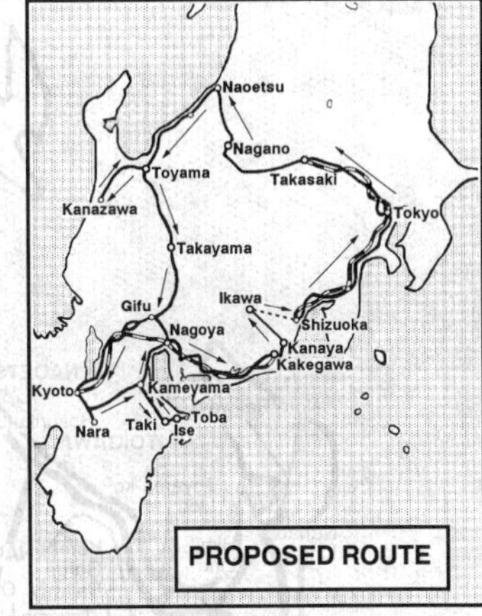


There are several possible deviations suggested, but they are easily added to the above itinerary.

Although most visitors will probably be using rail passes, distances in the Chubu region are not so great and this is quite a suitable area to be using Blue Spring tickets, in particular, if it happens to be Blue Spring season. Those with rail passes could consider exploring this area either before starting or after finishing their passes. Bear in mind, especially, that Kyoto and Nara need time to see and it is a waste of a rail pass to be sitting in Kyoto with your pass time ticking away. Much better to use Blue Spring tickets to travel in a leisurely manner to Kyoto, through an area with plenty of ordinary trains, take time to look at that city and then start using the rail pass.

There is a *shu-yu-ken* (excursion ticket) which allows most of the route proposed in this section. It is called an *Hokuriku Wide Shu-yu-ken*. Hokuriku is the name given to the area facing the Japan Sea within which this ticket allows unlimited travel. The ticket costs ¥14,730 from Tokyo and is valid for 7 days. Note carefully, though, that if you buy it from Chiba, on the eastern edge of the Tokyo suburban sprawl, it costs the same but is valid for 10 days. It may be difficult to persuade a station in Tokyo to sell you a ticket from Chiba, but you need to go only as far as Ichikawa on the JR Sobu Line or Maihama on the JR Keiyo Line in order to be able to purchase, since these stations are outside the Tokyo metropolitan area and within the prefecture of Chiba, so Chiba conditions apply and you get your extra three days for the cost of only two short suburban train journeys. There is a map on page 201 showing the area of free travel and the permitted access routes. You are allowed to stop anywhere on the access routes as well as within the free travel area. Express trains (unreserved sections) can be used within the free travel area. On the access routes, however, you can use only *kyuko* trains without supplement. For other expresses the applicable supplements will be charged.

## KUSATSU (草津 – 'Grassy Port') Agatsuma Line, 2 hrs. 30 mins. from Ueno (Tokyo) to Naganohara Kusatsu Guchi. Then bus 30 mins.

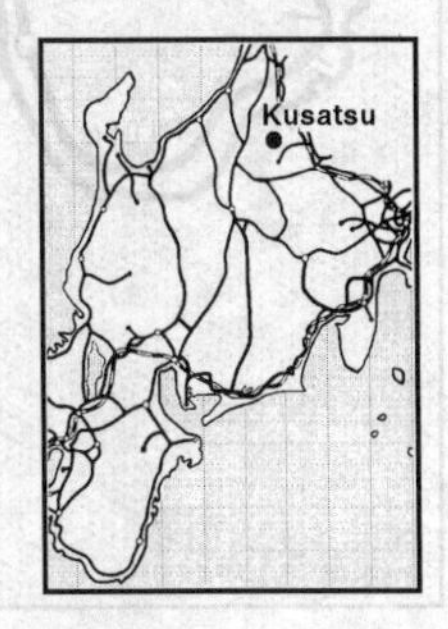


**Derivation of Name:** *Originally called 'Kusa Mizu', meaning 'smelly water'. In time, such an unappealing name became changed to one more inviting.*

Kusatsu is a spa town all the year round and a ski resort in winter. It is a very typical Japanese resort town, within easy reach of Tokyo and set in pretty mountain scenery, so popular at all times. There are many places like this and Kusatsu is not recommended more than another, but it is the sort of town that needs a mention at least and it has

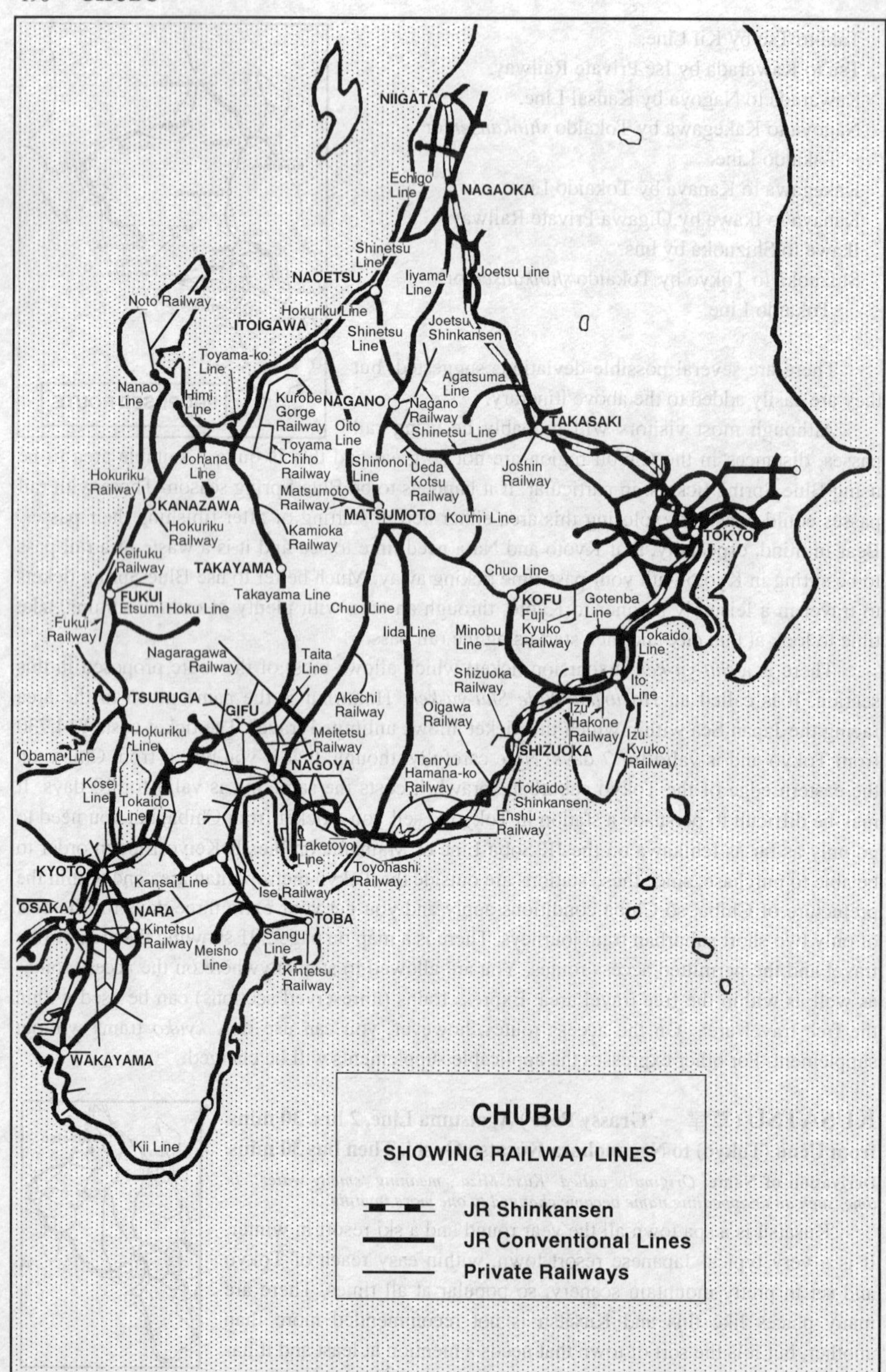
NIIGATA
Echigo Line
NAGAOKA
Shinetsu Line
Iiyama Line
Joetsu Line
NAOETSU
Noto Railway
Hokuriku Line
ITOIGAWA
Shinetsu Line
Joetsu Shinkansen
Toyama-ko Line
Nanao Line
Himi Line
Kurobe Gorge Railway
NAGANO
Nagano Railway
Agatsuma Line
TAKASAKI
Oito Line
Shinetsu Line
Toyama Chiho Railway
Johana Line
Shinonoi Line
Ueda Kotsu Railway
Joshin Railway
Hokuriku Railway
Matsumoto Railway
KANAZAWA
MATSUMOTO
Koumi Line
Hokuriku Railway
Kamioka Railway
TOKYO
Keifuku Railway
TAKAYAMA
Chuo Line
FUKUI
Takayama Line
KOFU
Gotenba Line
Etsumi Hoku Line
Chuo Line
Fuji Kyuko Railway
Fukui Railway
Iida Line
Minobu Line
Tokaido Line
Nagaragawa Railway
Taita Line
Shizuoka Railway
Ito Line
TSURUGA
Akechi Railway
Oigawa Railway
Izu Hakone Railway
GIFU
Hokuriku Line
Meitetsu Railway
SHIZUOKA
Izu Kyuko Railway
Obama Line
NAGOYA
Kosei Line
Tokaido Line
Tenryu Hamana-ko Railway
Tokaido Shinkansen
Enshu Railway
Taketoyo Line
Toyohashi Railway
KYOTO
Kansai Line
Ise Railway
OSAKA
NARA
TOBA
Kintetsu Railway
Sangu Line
Meisho Line
Kintetsu Railway
WAKAYAMA
Kii Line
CHUBU
SHOWING RAILWAY LINES
JR Shinkansen
JR Conventional Lines
Private Railways

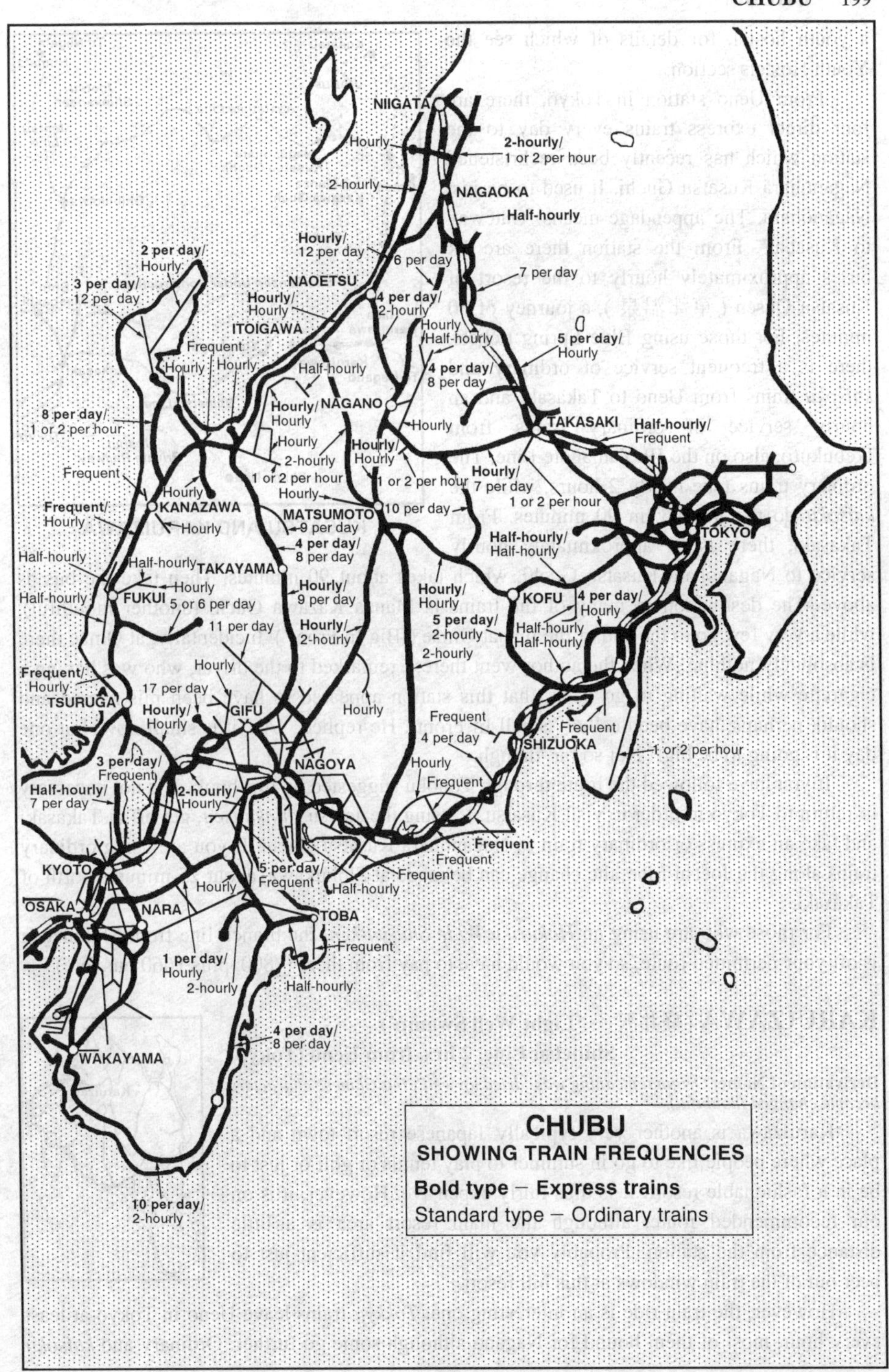
NIIGATA
Hourly
2-hourly/
1 or 2 per hour
2-hourly
NAGAOKA
Half-hourly
Hourly/
12 per day
6 per day
7 per day
2 per day/
Hourly
3 per day/
12 per day
NAOETSU
4 per day/
2-hourly
Hourly/
Hourly
ITOIGAWA
Hourly
Half-hourly
5 per day/
Hourly
Frequent
Hourly
Hourly
Half-hourly
4 per day/
8 per day
Hourly/
Hourly
NAGANO
8 per day/
1 or 2 per hour
Hourly
TAKASAKI
Half-hourly/
Frequent
Hourly
2-hourly
Hourly/
Hourly
Frequent
1 or 2 per hour
1 or 2 per hour
Hourly/
7 per day
Hourly
1 or 2 per hour
KANAZAWA
Hourly
Frequent/
Hourly
Hourly
MATSUMOTO
10 per day
9 per day
TOKYO
4 per day/
8 per day
Half-hourly/
Half-hourly
Half-hourly
Half-hourly
TAKAYAMA
Hourly
FUKUI
Half-hourly
5 or 6 per day
Hourly/
9 per day
Hourly/
Hourly
KOFU
4 per day/
Hourly
11 per day
Hourly/
2-hourly
5 per day/
2-hourly
Half-hourly
Half-hourly
2-hourly
Frequent/
Hourly
Hourly
TSURUGA
17 per day
Hourly/
Hourly
GIFU
Hourly
Frequent
4 per day
Frequent
SHIZUOKA
1 or 2 per hour
3 per day/
Frequent
NAGOYA
Hourly
Half-hourly/
7 per day
2-hourly/
Hourly
Frequent
Frequent
Frequent
KYOTO
5 per day/
Frequent
Frequent
Hourly
Half-hourly
OSAKA
NARA
TOBA
Frequent
1 per day/
Hourly
2-hourly
Half-hourly
4 per day/
8 per day
WAKAYAMA
10 per day/
2-hourly
CHUBU
SHOWING TRAIN FREQUENCIES
Bold type – Express trains
Standard type – Ordinary trains

a youth hostel, for details of which see the Youth Hostels section.

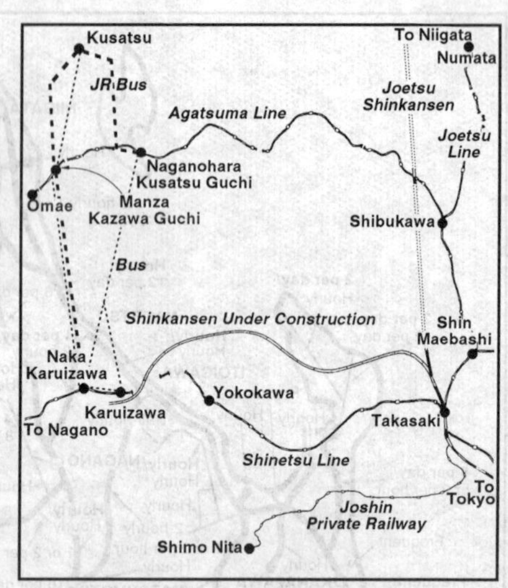


KUSATSU AND KARUIZAWA

From Ueno station in Tokyo, there are four direct express trains every day to the station which has recently been rechristened Naganohara Kusatsu Guchi. It used to be just Naganohara. The appendage means 'Gateway to Kusatsu'. From the station there are JR buses approximately hourly to the resort of Kusatsu Onsen (草津温泉), a journey of 30 minutes. For those using Blue Spring tickets, there is a frequent service of ordinary and *kaisoku* trains from Ueno to Takasaki and an hourly service of ordinary trains from Ikebukuro, also on the JR Yamanote Line. The ordinary trains take nearly 2 hours, while the *kaisoku* do the journey in 90 minutes. From Takasaki, there is an approximately hourly service to Naganohara Kusatsu Guchi, which takes about 90 minutes. Then take the bus as above. The destination of many of the trains is Manza Kazawa Guchi (another mouthful), while a very few go to the end of the line at Omae ('Big In Front'). Incidentally, at Omae there is absolutely nothing. When the author went there, I remarked to the driver, who was having a cigarette while waiting to go back, that this station appeared to have been mis-named and should, perhaps, have been called 'Small In Front'. He replied, "Ah, it is small now, but one day it is going to be big." Not so far, though.

If you have followed the route through Tohoku suggested by this book, it is not necessary to return to Tokyo in order to visit Kusatsu. If using the Joetsu *shinkansen*, get off at Takasaki and take an express or ordinary train to Naganohara Kusatsu Guchi. If you are using ordinary trains along the Joetsu Line, the change can be made at Shibukawa, about 25 minutes north of Takasaki.

For those who are using an *Hokuriku Wide Shu-yu-ken*, the branch line from Shibukawa is off your permitted route, so you would have to pay from there (¥800, plus ¥660 bus fare).

## KARUIZAWA (軽井沢 – 'Light Well Swamp')

**Shinetsu Line, 2 hrs. from Ueno (Tokyo)**

**Derivation of Name:** *Original meaning was 'dried up well', but Chinese characters became changed (doubtful).*

Karuizawa is another very typically Japanese resort town and a place where people like to go in summer to play tennis or golf or just to be in a fashionable resort. It is thus fairly expensive. However, it is on our recommended route, although the main resort area is a little distance from the station. Probably you will find it sufficient just to peer out of the train windows at this hill resort.

However, the train ride is an interesting one. *Tokkyu* trains leave Ueno in Tokyo at least every hour, most of them bound for Nagano although some go further. Ordinary and *kaisoku* trains run frequently from Ueno and Ikebukuro to Takasaki, from where only a very few ordinary trains go through to Karuizawa. Those which do mostly continue to Nagano.

The landscape from Tokyo to Takasaki is generally unstimulating, as the train passes through a string of dormitory towns. On leaving Takasaki, however, the scenery slowly improves as the train starts to climb gradually. On reaching Yokokawa, about 30 minutes beyond Takasaki, all trains stop. They have to do this because the train is now to tackle the steepest grade anywhere on the JR network (6.67%). Many years ago this section used to be operated with a cog system, but nowadays an extra engine is attached at the rear and the train struggles up the steep incline with only that support. In the opposite direction, the extra engine is still attached, this time to the front of the train to give extra braking capability (otherwise, of course, there would be an awful lot of spare engines in Karuizawa!). The distance between Yokokawa and Karuizawa is 11 kilometres and it takes the train 17 minutes to cover this section of track through a series of 17 tunnels, emerging from which one gets glimpses of very attractive countryside. Go quickly though if you want to experience this enjoyable journey. In 1998, the Winter Olympics are to be held in Nagano and JR hopes to complete a new *shinkansen* line to the city in time for that big event. When the *shinkansen* route is opened, JR intends to abandon the section of ordinary track between Yokokawa and Karuizawa, leaving the ends of two lines dangling either side of the series of tunnels through which you are now passing and forcing all through passengers to pay the price and travel this section by *shinkansen*. Whether this will really happen is not yet certain, for naturally there is opposition

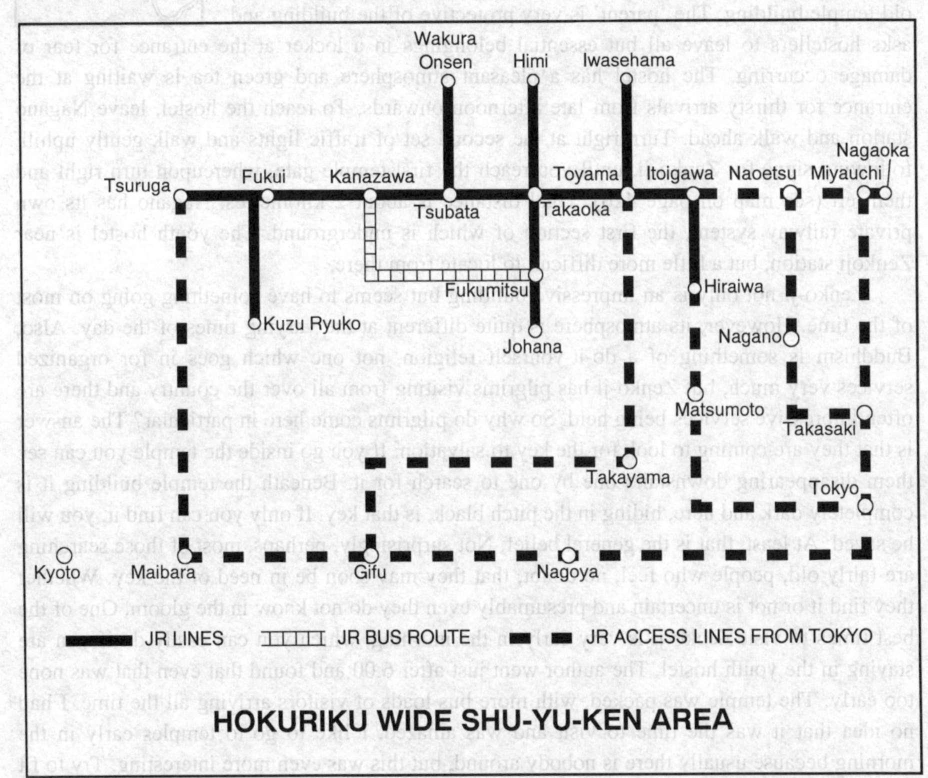

HOKURIKU WIDE SHU-YU-KEN AREA

to the abandonment, but, of course, this system of adding extra locomotives to all trains constitutes an expense of which JR would be happy to relieve itself.

Again, if coming from the tour of Tohoku suggested by this book, it is not necessary to return to Tokyo in order to commence this route. Take the Joetsu *shinkansen* or Joetsu conventional line from Niigata as far as Takasaki and then an express or ordinary train along the Shinetsu Line to Karuizawa or on to Nagano.

If you are coming from Kusatsu and using a rail pass, in summer there is one JR bus from Kusatsu Onsen at 8:45 every day to Naka Karuizawa ( 中軽井沢 ), one station beyond Karuizawa and within the same town. It arrives at 11:24. There are other buses to Karuizawa (軽井沢 ) run by different companies too, but they are expensive at ¥2,160. Of course, if you take this option you will miss the interesting section of railway described above.

## NAGANO (長野－'Long Field')

**Shinetsu Line, 3 hrs. from Ueno (Tokyo)**

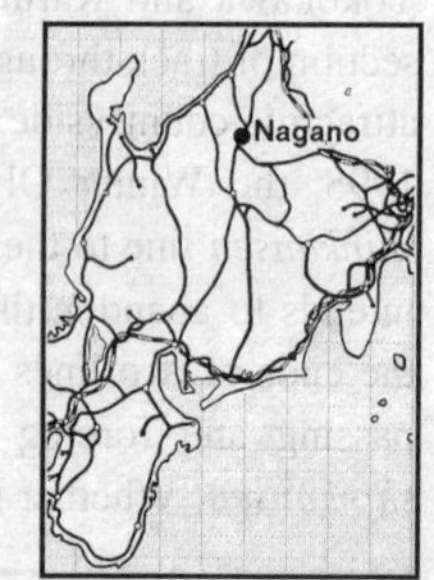


**Derivation of Name:** *Literal.*

Nagano is the major city in the Japan Alps area. It lies in a valley itself, but is surrounded by mountains in all directions. One of the most interesting features of the city is its great temple, **Zenko-ji**. There is a youth hostel and not only is this hostel in the most interesting part of the city adjacent to the temple, but it is actually housed in a 200 year old temple building. The 'parent' is very protective of the building and asks hostellers to leave all but essential belongings in a locker at the entrance for fear of damage occurring. The hostel has a pleasant atmosphere and green tea is waiting at the entrance for thirsty arrivals from late afternoon onwards. To reach the hostel, leave Nagano station and walk ahead. Turn right at the second set of traffic lights and walk gently uphill, following signs for Zenko-ji, until you reach the first temple gate, whereupon turn right and then left (see map on page 426). Total distance is about 2 kilometres. Nagano has its own private railway system, the first section of which is underground. The youth hostel is near Zenkoji station, but a little more difficult to locate from there.

Zenko-ji not only is an impressive building but seems to have something going on most of the time. However, its atmosphere is quite different at the varying times of the day. Also, Buddhism is something of a do-it-yourself religion, not one which goes in for organized services very much, but Zenko-ji has pilgrims visiting from all over the country and there are often impressive services being held. So why do pilgrims come here in particular? The answer is that they are coming to look for the key to salvation. If you go inside the temple you can see them disappearing downstairs one by one to search for it. Beneath the temple building it is completely dark and here, hiding in the pitch black, is that key. If only you can find it, you will be saved. At least, that is the general belief. Not surprisingly, perhaps, most of those searching are fairly old, people who feel, no doubt, that they may soon be in need of the key. Whether they find it or not is uncertain and presumably even they do not know in the gloom. One of the best times to visit Zenko-ji is very early in the morning, which you can easily do if you are staying in the youth hostel. The author went just after 6:00 and found that even that was none too early. The temple was packed, with more bus loads of visitors arriving all the time. I had no idea that it was the time to visit and was amazed. I like to go to temples early in the morning because usually there is nobody around, but this was even more interesting. Try to fit

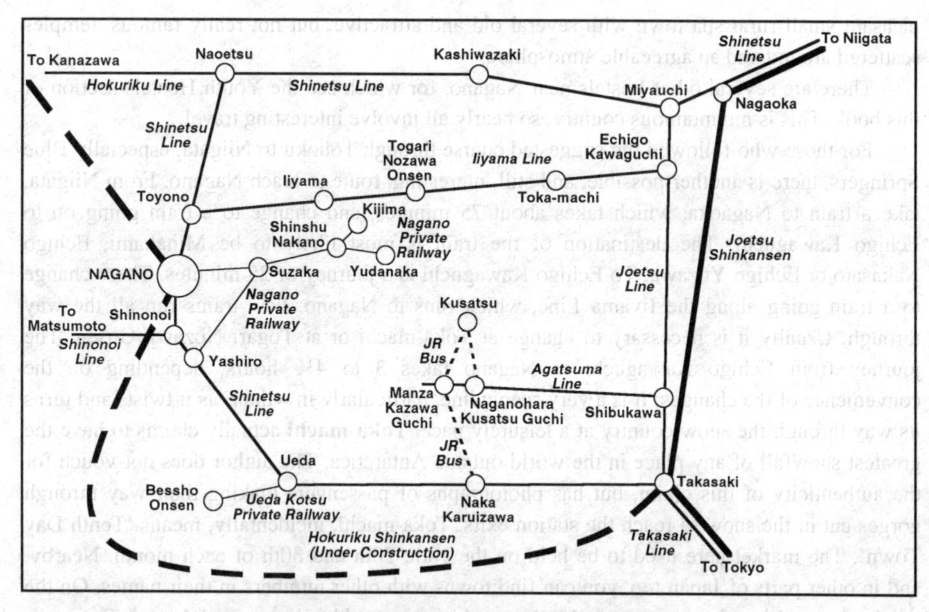


**RAILWAY LINES AROUND NAGANO**

it into your itinerary, if possible.

Only five minutes walk to the east of the hostel is a hill overlooking the city and from here there is a good view, particularly in the evening when the lights of the whole city are spread out beneath one.

The Nagano Private Railway offers a two-day ticket giving unlimited travel on its lines for ¥2,710, although there is still a ¥100 supplement for using a *tokkyu*. However, since the ticket is quite expensive and the routes rather limited, most visitors will probably not consider this a worthwhile investment.

To reach Nagano, take an express train from Ueno station in Tokyo for the 3 hour journey. Trains run at least hourly. From 1998, there should be a *shinkansen* service and the expresses will be discontinued. Blue Spring ticket users or those with a *shu-yu-ken* should take one of the frequent *kaisoku* or ordinary trains from Ueno or Ikebukuro to Takasaki and then change to an ordinary train to Nagano, a journey of 2 hours to Takasaki and a further 2½ hours from there to Nagano. As mentioned previously, those coming from Niigata need not return to Tokyo, but can change trains at Takasaki. There are few ordinary trains from Takasaki to Nagano. Current departures from Takasaki are at 7:13, 11:18, 14:06, 16:15, 18:40 and 20:48 (change at Karuizawa). You need to catch a train from Ueno about 2¼ hours earlier in order to be sure of making a connexion.

The journey as far as Karuizawa has already been described above. From there, you will continue through pretty countryside. Look for Mt. Asama, an active volcano, on your right after passing Karuizawa. As you journey along, you will also see the construction of the new *shinkansen* line to Nagano and eventually to Kanazawa. For those who like quieter places, there is also a youth hostel in **Bessho** (Ueda Mahoroba Hostel). Alight at Ueda and take the Ueda Kotsu Private Railway to its terminus at Bessho Onsen (30 minutes, ¥570). Bessho is a pleasant small rural spa town with several old and attractive, but not really famous, temples scattered around and an agreeable atmosphere.

There are several other hostels near Nagano, for which see the Youth Hostels section of this book. This is mountainous country, so nearly all involve interesting travel.

For those who followed the suggested course through Tohoku to Niigata, especially Blue Springers, there is another possible, and still interesting, route to reach Nagano. From Niigata, take a train to Nagaoka, which takes about 75 minutes, and change to a train going on to Echigo Kawaguchi. The destination of the train is most likely to be Minakami, Echigo Nakasato or Echigo Yuzawa. To Echigo Kawaguchi is a journey of 25 minutes. There change to a train going along the Iiyama Line, which runs to Nagano. Few trains run all the way through. Usually it is necessary to change at Toka-machi or at Togari Nozawa Onsen. The journey from Echigo Kawaguchi to Nagano takes 3 to 4½ hours, depending on the convenience of the changes. It is a very scenic line, particularly in winter, as it twists and turns its way through the snow country at a leisurely pace. **Toka-machi** actually claims to have the greatest snowfall of any place in the world outside Antarctica. The author does not vouch for the authenticity of this claim, but has photographs of passengers making their way through gorges cut in the snow to reach the station exits. Toka-machi, incidentally, means 'Tenth Day Town'. The market here used to be held on the 10th, 20th and 30th of each month. Nearby, and in other parts of Japan too, you can find towns with other numbers in their names. On the nearby Joetsu Line, for example, is Muika-machi, a town with a large youth hostel. The name means 'Sixth Day Town' and, of course, the market used to be on the 6th, 16th and 26th of each month.

There are not many connecting services on the Iiyama Line and times tend to change, so please check before making the journey. At the time of writing, however, convenient departures from Echigo Kawaguchi are at 10:10 (change at Toka-machi and Togari Nozawa Onsen; connexions are at 8:43 from Nagaoka and 7:07 from Niigata; arrival in Nagano is at 13:44), 12:45 (change at Togari Nozawa Onsen; connexions at 12:17 from Nagaoka, 10:35 from Niigata; arrival in Nagano 15:31), 14:05 (change at Toka-machi and Togari Nozawa Onsen; connexions at 13:37 from Nagaoka and 12:23 from Niigata; arrival in Nagano 18:47) and 15:55 (change at Toka-machi; connexions at 15:30 from Nagaoka, 14:17 from Niigata; arrival in Nagano at 19:53). If you have a Japan Rail Pass, you will be able to take the *shinkansen* between Niigata and Nagaoka and shorten the connexion time somewhat.

## NAOETSU (直江津 – 'Straight Bay Port')

**Shinetsu Line, 4 hrs. from Ueno (Tokyo)**

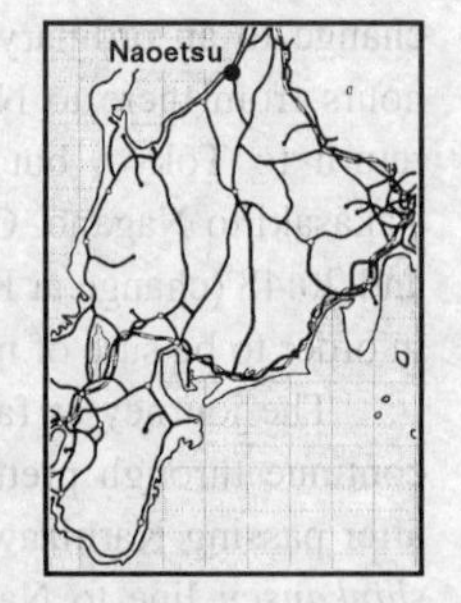


**Derivation of Name:** *There appeared to be an unending straight seashore here stretching away from the port.*

Naoetsu is a small port town, not special but it is where you will meet the sea if following the suggested route through Nagano via the Shinetsu Line. It is also the port from which one of the regular ferry services to Sado Island departs (see page 157). If you visited the island from Niigata, you may choose to return to Naoetsu and start your tour of Chubu from here.

The train journey from Nagano continues to be scenic and in winter quite substantial amounts of snow will be lying along the line. You pass through several ski resorts and, of course, this is the area where the 1998 Winter Olympics are to be held. By express, it takes 72 minutes from Nagano to Naoetsu. There are four trains per day, the first at 9:53 and the last at 15:49, and one train in the middle of the night. The night train and the 11:20 *tokkyu* both go right through to Kanazawa and, since Kanazawa is our next major stop, the 11:20 might be a good train to catch. The night train, incidentally, now continues even beyond Kanazawa, all the way to Fukui.

For those using a *shu-yu-ken* or Blue Spring tickets, there are eleven ordinary trains per day between Nagano and Naoetsu. Morning departures are at 6:34, 7:54 and 9:57. The journey takes about 95 minutes and you will even get a switch-back station, for no very obvious reason, at Nihongi. There is also a train at 7:00 which starts from Nagano as an ordinary train, but is magically transformed into a *kyuko* on the way. Those using a *shu-yu-ken* are permitted to travel on this train without supplement as long as they sit in unreserved seats.

## TOYAMA (富山 – 'Prosperous Mountain')

**Hokuriku Line, 5 hrs. 25 mins. from Ueno (Tokyo)**

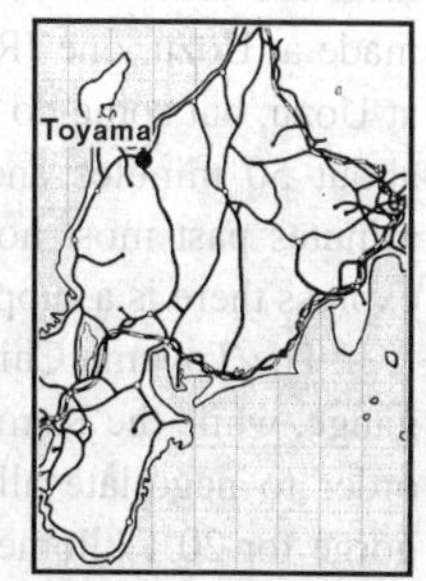


**Derivation of Name:** *Said to be from name of temple called Fusen-ji. The Chinese characters for 'Fusen' can also be read as 'Toyama'.*

Toyama is not really a special city to visit, but there is a youth hostel, although not in the city itself (see Youth Hostels section). There is also a private railway system, operated by the Toyama Chiho Railway Company, which leads to Kurobe Gorge, amongst other places (see next entry). The station is separate from, but next to, the JR station. The Toyama Chiho Railway offers a special two-day ticket giving unlimited travel on all of its lines. This costs ¥4,000, and, although that seems expensive, if you are thinking of both travelling the Kurobe Gorge Railway and making a journey to Tateyama (see 'Alpine Route' section, under), it would be worth buying this ticket and making those two expeditions on consecutive days.

From Naoetsu to Toyama takes 75 minutes by express or 2 hours 15 minutes by ordinary train. Both types of service operate approximately hourly. Those using an *Hokuriku Wide Shu-yu-ken* will be entitled to use express trains without supplement when they reach Itoigawa, about 40 minutes from Naoetsu by ordinary train.

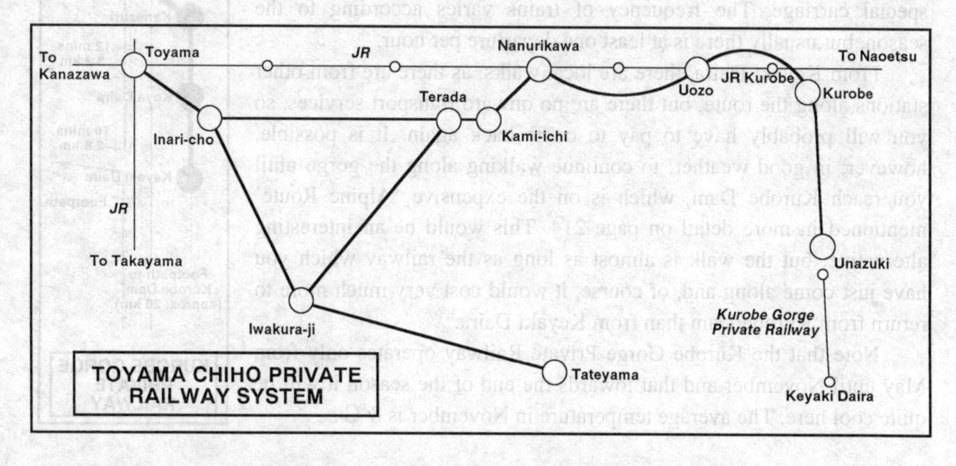

## KUROBE GORGE (黒部峡谷 – 'Black Part Gorge Valley')

### Kurobe Gorge Railway, 90 mins. from Toyama

**Derivation of Name:** *Literal. The gorge is steep with many trees, so that very little sunlight can enter.*

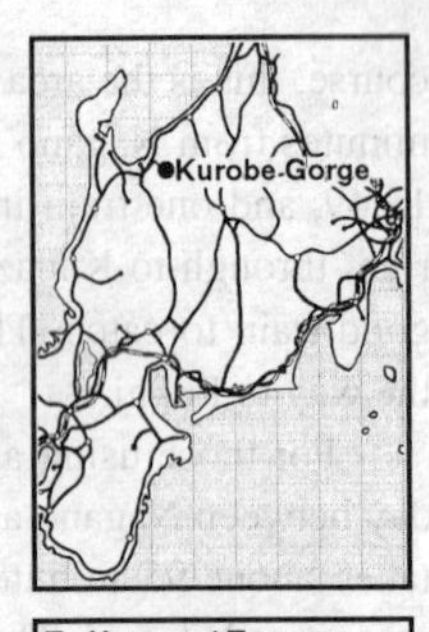


Here is a truly memorable rail journey – by narrow gauge railway along the Kurobe Gorge. The start of the railway is at Unazuki, another spa resort. Unazuki is reached by the Toyama Chiho Private Railway, which starts, not surprisingly, in Toyama. However, if you are following the suggested route, it is not necessary to go all the way to Toyama, as the line runs parallel to the JR track for some distance to the east of Toyama (see diagram on previous page). The easternmost town at which a transfer can be made is Kurobe, but the two stations there are some distance apart. If you prefer an easy change, it can be made at Uozu, one JR station further west. Most JR *tokkyu* trains stop at Uozu, but some do not stop at Kurobe. From Uozu to Unazuki takes about 50 minutes and costs ¥830. There is an ordinary train at 30 minutes past most hours and an express at 54 minutes past. For the express there is a supplement of ¥150.

The Toyama Chiho Private Railway operates on a 3 feet 6 inches gauge, while the Kurobe Gorge Private Railway uses 2 feet 6 inches in order to negotiate all the tight corners. The railway runs along the gorge for 20.1 kilometres, although about half of the total length is in tunnels. The trains do not rush, managing to cover the scenic route in about 90 minutes. In the course of the journey, you will pass through a total of 41 tunnels and cross 28 bridges. The carriages used are designed to give as good a view as possible, so have either open sides or plenty of glass. The fare is ¥1,410 from Unazuki to the terminus at Keyaki Daira. This, however, is the fare in an ordinary carriage, that is in an open-sided carriage. If you want glass, there will be a supplement of ¥360, ¥510 or ¥610, depending upon the luxury of the carriage. Most trains offer a choice of ordinary carriages and one of the types of special carriage. The frequency of trains varies according to the season, but usually there is at least one departure per hour.

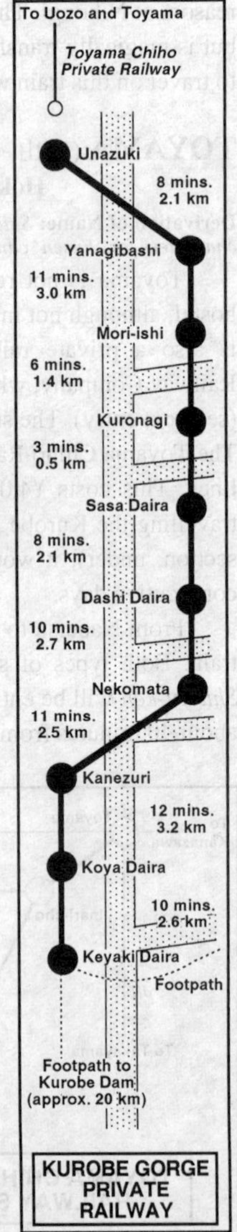


From Keyaki Daira, there are local walks, as there are from other stations along the route, but there are no onward transport services, so you will probably have to pay to come back again. It is possible, however, in good weather, to continue walking along the gorge until you reach Kurobe Dam, which is on the expensive 'Alpine Route' mentioned in more detail on page 214. This would be an interesting alternative, but the walk is almost as long as the railway which you have just come along and, of course, it would cost very much more to return from Kurobe Dam than from Keyaki Daira.

Note that the Kurobe Gorge Private Railway operates only from May until November and that towards the end of the season it will be quite cool here. The average temperature in November is 8 ℃.

## TAKAOKA (高岡 − 'High Hill')

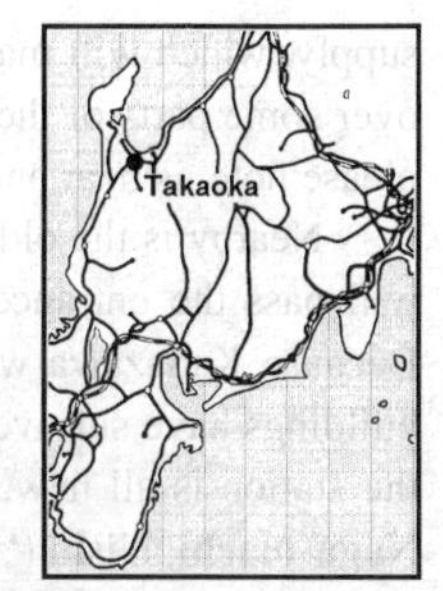


**Hokuriku Line, 5 hrs. 40 mins. from Ueno (Tokyo)**

**Derivation of Name:** *Formerly called Sekino, but in 1609 a famous daimyo of the Maeda family built a castle and wrote a poem referring to the place as the 'high hill'. The name stuck.*

Takaoka is a medium-sized city between Toyama and Kanazawa. It retains a tram line − only one − but its most important feature is an impressive temple named **Zuiryu-ji**, about 10 minutes walk from the South Exit of Takaoka station. Conveniently, this temple is also a rather pleasant youth hostel, so see the map in the Youth Hostels section on page 424 for directions to both. If you are using the hostel, note that the entrance is at the back, near the railway line. Although this hostel makes no claim to be familiar with English, actually the wife of the priest operating it speaks English well and their daughter has been to England to study and so is even better. In fact, it is the only hostel in Japan where the author has really been spoken to in English. At the time of writing, however, this hostel is closed temporarily while certain temple buildings are being reconstructed. Let us hope that it will be open again by the time that this is read.

Takaoka also boasts the third largest **Buddha statue** in Japan, on the other side of the station, but it is not really special, particularly as you are almost certain to visit one of the two larger ones, at Nara or Kamakura.

## KANAZAWA (金沢 − 'Gold Swamp')

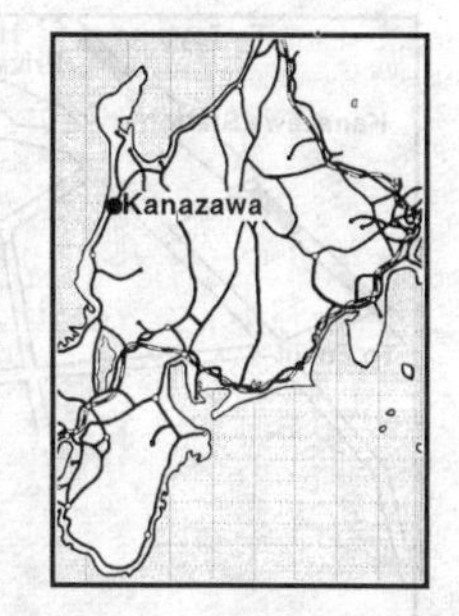


**Hokuriku Line, 6 hrs. from Ueno (Tokyo)**

**Derivation of Name:** *There was a swamp here where gold found in the area was washed.*

Kanazawa had always been regarded as rather a backwater for overseas visitors, although popular with Japanese. Recently, however, it has received more publicity and now everybody seems to want to go to Kanazawa. Whilst it was under-rated previously, it is now in danger of being over-rated. What it offers is a famous garden which is certainly worth seeing, the ruins of a castle, some old houses and, in places, the remains of a traditional life-style. It is also a good place for rice, if that interests you. However, do not come expecting too much. The garden is the main attraction.

The garden is called **Kenroku-en** ( 兼六園 ). It is some distance from the station, although it is possible to walk in about 30 minutes. Alternatively, there is a bus from near the station. Kenroku-en is one of the official Big Three gardens in Japan, the Japanese always liking to have three of everything. Even in the opinion of the author, either this garden or Ritsurin Koen in Takamatsu on the island of Shikoku (not included in the official Big Three) is the best garden in Japan, so try to put this on your itinerary if possible. It is usually buzzing with activity, rather too much so, in fact, so good times to go are early in the morning or late in the afternoon, rather than at the more popular times of day. In summer it is open from 7:00 until 18:00, in winter from 8:00 until 16:30. One of the best features of this garden is that it is big, so the huge numbers of visitors are not too much of a problem, especially as most of them tend to stay near the main entrance, because the tour bus will be leaving in precisely six minutes and don't be late, please! Another interesting feature is the original piped water supply, which will make you think, for the garden is on a hill. There is also quite a good view over some parts of the city. Admission costs ¥300. The official place to take your photograph, please note, is near and including the stone lantern not far from the main entrance.

Nearby is the old **castle**, but there is not much left. Most has been destroyed by fire. You will pass the entrance to the castle ruins if you walk between the station and Kenroku-en. Because Kanazawa was not really important enough to bomb during the war, a lot of older buildings have survived and can reward casual walking around the city, although the area near the station is all new. The areas with the most interesting traditional buildings are known as **Naga-machi**, **Nishi** ('west') and **Higashi** ('east'), the last two being *geisha* districts.

There are several other lesser attractions, in the form of museums, gardens, shrines and temples. There is an information office just outside the station. If you have time, **Oyama Jinja** (shrine) is interesting, the gate combining Chinese architecture with stained glass, but designed by a Dutchman. Also interesting is the temple **Myoryu-ji**, which is full of secret passages, since it was the family temple of the ruling Maeda clan. However, it is expensive (¥700) and busy.

There are two youth hostels in Kanazawa. The JYH Hostel is in **Utatsuyama Koen**, a park area full of shrines and temples to the east of Kenroku-en. It is a pleasant location and it is possible to walk from the station or from Kenroku-en, although both are walks of about 30 minutes. The privately operated hostel is more central, near the Naga-machi area, again about 30 minutes walk from the station, but only about 15 minutes west of Kenroku-en.

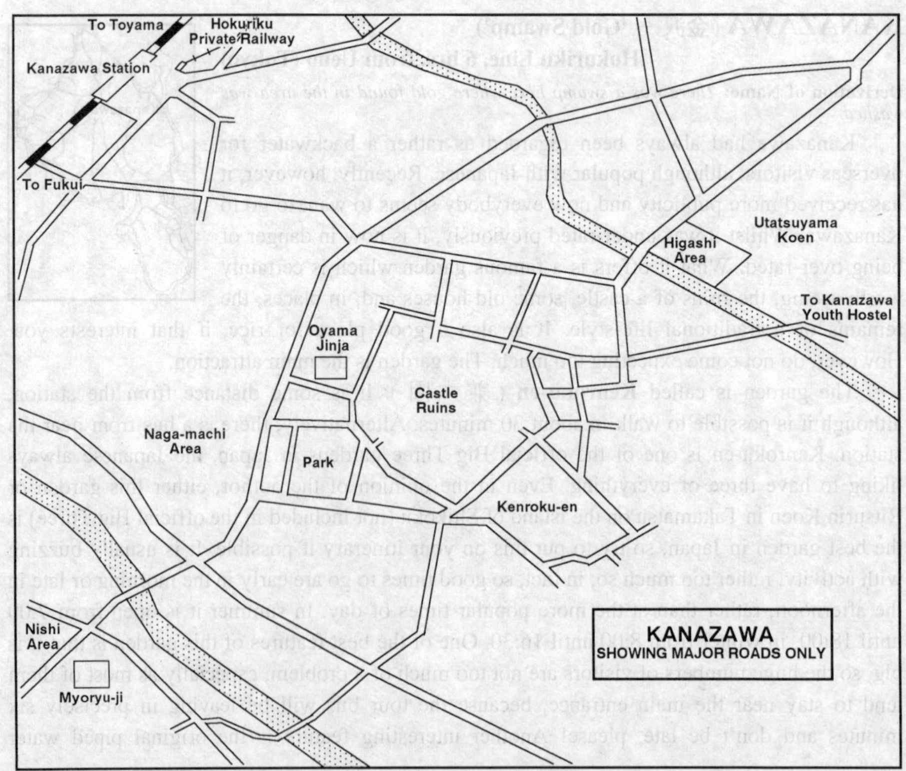

From Ueno in Tokyo, there is one *tokkyu* train every day at 8:30 direct to Kanazawa. The journey takes 6 hours. There are also two overnight trains, a *tokkyu* carrying sleepers only and a *kyuko* with seats only. At other times, one takes the Joetsu *shinkansen* to Nagaoka and changes to a *tokkyu* there. Certain trains are arranged as connexions. Using this route, the journey can be done within 5 hours. Along the Japan Sea coast, there are plenty of both express and ordinary trains. From Naoetsu to Kanazawa, for example, takes 2 hours by *tokkyu* or about 3½ hours by ordinary train. Usually it is necessary to change at Toyama when travelling by ordinary train.

If you are coming from travel in the Tohoku area and want to save time, you can simply travel from Niigata straight through to Kanazawa, which takes 3½ hours by *tokkyu* or about 7 hours by ordinary train if you plan good connexions. There is one *tokkyu* which leaves Aomori at 6:11 and travels along the Japan Sea via Niigata and Kanazawa all the way to Osaka. This train connects with the overnight *tokkyu* from Sapporo to Aomori. It reaches Kanazawa at 15:46 and Osaka at 18:38. There are also overnight sleeper trains on this route, including the very expensive 'Twilight Express' which runs in certain seasons between Sapporo and Osaka.

## NOTO PENINSULA (能登半島 – 'Very Good Climbing Half Island') Noto Private Railway, 2 hrs. from Kanazawa

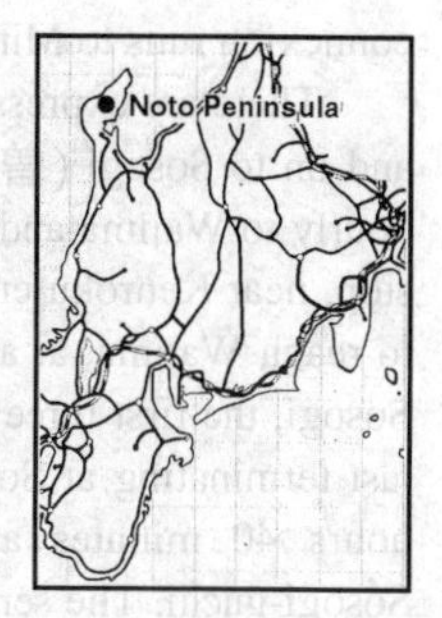


**Derivation of Name:** *Originally, Noto meant 'very good gateway (to the sea)', but Chinese characters became changed.*

The Noto Peninsula is an area of attractive coastal scenery which is not over-touristed, although its merits are quite well known among Japanese. The outer side of the peninsula (on the left as one leaves Kanazawa) is the more rugged and spectacular. The inner coast (on the right) is also pretty, but more peaceful. There are four youth hostels dotted around the peninsula, so it is not too difficult to find accommodation here. Also, every village seems to have *minshuku* (small private hotels). Railway lines run to Wajima, roughly in the top centre of the peninsula, and Takojima ('Octopus Island') on the easternmost tip. Unfortunately, however, JR has abandoned these lines to a private company, the Noto Private Railway, so they are not included in any of the rail tickets which visitors are likely to be using.

The rather odd arrangement is that JR has retained the spine of the line as far as the spa resort of Wakura Onsen. However, although JR expresses, *tokkyu* and *kyuko*, run through to that station, and sometimes beyond, all of the ordinary trains terminate at Nanao, the previous station, from where the Noto Railway trains start. Of course, if you have a valid JR ticket, you will be charged only for travel beyond Wakura Onsen. From Wakura Onsen, the line runs up to Anamizu, where it divides to Wajima and Takojima. Fares from Wakura Onsen are ¥910 to Wajima and ¥1,520 to Takojima. The express surcharge is ¥310 to Wajima and ¥520 to Takojima. There used to be an overnight express train all the way to Wajima from Ueno (Tokyo) on certain days, but the timetables on these lines have changed considerably since JR gave up the routes. *Tokkyu* trains now run as far as Wakura Onsen from Osaka, Nagoya and Nagaoka, all passing through Kanazawa *en route*. The only through services to the ends of the lines are *kyuko* trains which leave Kanazawa at 8:02 and 16:11 for Wajima, arriving at 10:19 and 18:25. The 16:11 train divides on the way, with part going to Suzu, 4 kilometres short of Takojima. By ordinary train, journey times are 90 minutes from Kanazawa to Nanao, 80 minutes from Nanao to Wajima and approximately 2½ hours from Nanao to Takojima. Trains run about hourly as far as Nanao and somewhat less frequently beyond. In most cases there are good connexions at Nanao, but onward trains do not necessarily serve both the Wajima Line and the Takojima Line.

The railway line is pretty and it crosses from one side of the peninsula to the other, so that first you get glimpses of the sea on the left, then the water reappears on the right. If you continue up to Wajima, you pass through wooded areas with few people and some steep climbs for the train. The author was fortunate enough to travel this route just a few days before it was given away by JR, although I had no idea that a change was about to take place. At the time, it was diesel operated, but, concurrently with the hand-over, electrification was introduced on the section as far as Wakura Onsen which remained JR territory.

However, if you want a change from trains, there are express buses from Kanazawa to major places on the peninsula. Unfortunately, though, these do not run close enough to the coast to give really good views in most cases.

If you decide to stay in Noto Minazuki Hostel, there are buses approximately hourly from Anamizu to Monzen (門前), a 35 minute journey which costs ¥640. From there an infrequent connexion runs to Minazuki (皆月), which takes 30 minutes and costs ¥520.

There are express buses from Kanazawa to Wajima (輪島), where there is another hostel, and on to Sosogi (曽々木), where there is a third. In the middle of the day, departures are hourly to Wajima and from 12:20 until 17:30 these services originate at Kenroku-en Shita bus stop, near Kenroku-en garden, passing Kanazawa station 15 minutes later. They take 2 hours to reach Wajima, at a cost of ¥2,100. The 12:20, 14:20, 15:20 and 17:30 departures go on to Sosogi, the first three stopping right outside the youth hostel, which is beside the sea, and the last terminating at Sosogi-guchi (曽々木口), a few minutes walk away. Journey time is 2 hours 40 minutes and cost ¥2,400. There are also local buses between Wajima and Sosogi-guchi. The service runs approximately 2-hourly, takes 35 minutes and costs ¥700. The destination of most such buses will be Ushitsu (宇出津). In the morning, there is a convenient bus at 7:28 from right outside Sosogi Kajiyama Youth Hostel direct to Kanazawa station (金沢駅), where it arrives at 10:06. It continues to Kenroku-en Shita (兼六園下), reaching there at 10:15.

**Wajima** is famed for its hand-made lacquerware, a skillful (and expensive) process, of which you will find many examples throughout the town. The journey on to Sosogi is quite attractive, with views of the coast interspersed with views of rice fields. At Sosogi, you will find a village of traditional Japanese houses, most of them now serving as *minshuku*, and two particularly impressive **old farmhouses**. These are a short walk along the road which leads to Ushitsu, the older one being about 300 years old. If you go inside, you will find information available in English.

Continuing along the coast beyond Sosogi, at Takaya you will reach the start of a **walking course** beside the sea. The author walked this path and enjoyed it. The route, which leads from Takaya to Noroshi ('Wolf Smoke') is 11 kilometres long. In practice, this will occupy a whole day by the time that one has got to the start and returned or gone on from the end. Unfortunately, public transport is not convenient for allowing a walk from west to east, but it can be done from east to west. If you stay at Tsukumo Wan Youth Hostel, on the Takojima branch of the Noto Private Railway, take the 9:44 train from Tsukumo Wan Ogi to Takojima, which it reaches at 10:17 (¥470). There you will have to wait until 11:52, when a JR bus will pass outside the tiny station going to Kinoura (木ノ浦), which take as far as Noroshi (狼煙 – 35 minutes, ¥600). On your right you will see steps leading up to Rokugo Misaki (Cape Rokugo) and here, after you have taken a few minutes to admire the lighthouse and the view from the cape, the walk begins. There is only one bus continuing west from Takaya, so be careful. It leaves Takaya at 16:35 for Sosogi-guchi (曽々木口). The journey takes 40 minutes and costs ¥700. The bus actually starts at Kinoura at 16:30 and runs along the road near the walking course, so as long as you have passed Kinoura by 16:30, you are safe. The last stop before the terminus is Sosogi (曽々木), right outside Sosogi Kajiyama Youth Hostel. However, if you want to return to Tsukumo Wan, perhaps because of not wishing to carry luggage, there is a bus to Ushitsu (宇出津) at 18:13, a 50 minute journey for ¥750. From there, it is a 20 minute train journey back to Tsukumo Wan Ogi.

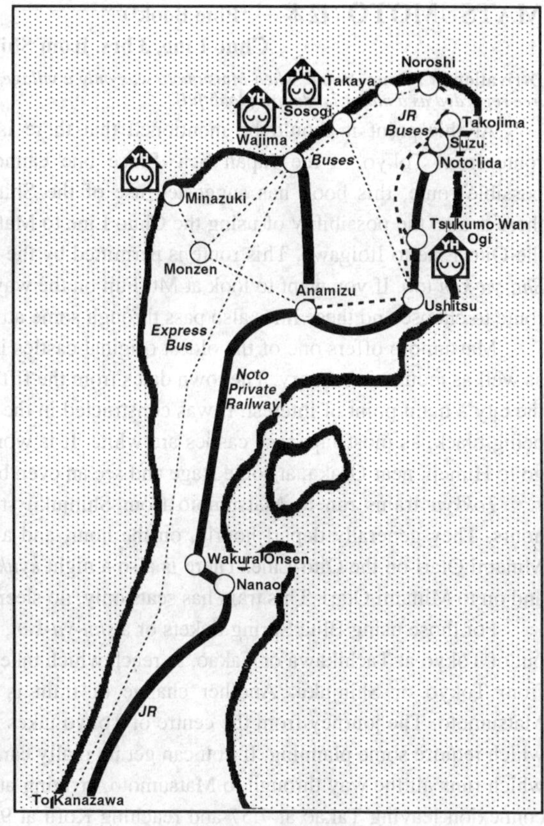


**NOTO PENINSULA**
**SHOWING RAILWAYS AND RELEVANT BUS SERVICES**

Those using rail passes and wishing to save a little money, but not time, could note that there are some JR bus services in this area. The bus from Takojima to Noroshi, for example, is operated by JR, and so is free to those with Japan Rail Passes. There are also JR services from Anamizu to Ushitsu and from Ushitsu to Noto Iida, some of which buses, but only some, pass Tsukumo Wan Ogi station. For the route suggested above, a bus can be substituted in the morning, but the timing is not very convenient. From Tsukumo Wan Ogi station, take the JR bus at 7:26 destination Suzu (珠洲) to Noto Iida (能登飯田), where it arrives at 8:08. From there at 11:40 will depart the bus which you were to catch as it passed Takojima station. Alternatively, you can stay on your bus until the terminus at Suzu (8:12) and catch your connexion there at 11:43. Note, however, that for users of the *Hokuriku Wide Shu-yu-ken*, these JR buses are not within your area.

On the sheltered side of the Noto Peninsula, there is Tsukumo Wan Youth Hostel, as mentioned above, and from nearby there are **boat trips** around Tsukumo Wan (Tsukumo Bay). These trips run about every half hour in the summer and five times per day in winter, take 30 minutes and cost ¥750.

# MATSUMOTO (松本 – 'Pine Book')

**Chuo Line, 3 hrs. from Shinjuku (Tokyo)**

**Derivation of Name:** *At time when Matsumoto was only a village, there was a pine tree regarded as a major landmark (doubtful).*

At this point it should be mentioned that there is an alternative route from Tokyo to the Japan Sea. Since one cannot travel every possible route, this book has suggested use of the Shinetsu Line, but there is also the possibility of using the Chuo Line to Matsumoto, thence the Oito Line to Itoigawa. This route is permitted by the *Hokuriku Wide Shu-yu-ken* too. If you want to look at Mt. Fuji on the way, this is a good route to choose and these lines also pass through some attractive countryside.

Matsumoto offers one of the oldest original castles in Japan and some nearby spa resorts, as well as mountain scenery. The town dates from the fifth century, but it is the **castle** which is the city's main point of interest. It was constructed in the sixteenth century and it is unusual in being black, as most Japanese castles are white. It is worth a visit, although most people will go to Himeji, near Osaka, at some stage and see an even better castle there.

*Tokkyu* trains run to Matsumoto from Shinjuku station in the Tokyo area and take 3 hours. They generally depart hourly, on the hour, and a few continue beyond Matsumoto to Minami Otari on the Oito Line. There is also a night *kyuko* at 23:50 which goes to Matsumoto and on to Minami Otari. This train has seats only, no sleepers.

For those using Blue Spring tickets or a *shu-yu-ken*, most ordinary trains start a little way out of Tokyo at Tachikawa or Takao, to reach which take a suburban Chuo Line train (orange) from Tokyo or Shinjuku. Another change of train is usually required along the way to Matsumoto. The journey from the centre of Tokyo takes about 5 hours with good connexions, which require some planning. If you can get up really early, there is a train at 6:44 from Takao which runs all the way through to Matsumoto, arriving at 10:20. Alternatively, there is a good connexion leaving Takao at 7:57 and reaching Kofu at 9:39. The onward departure is at 9:47 arriving in Matsumoto at 11:32. From Shinjuku, you should allow 45 minutes to reach Tachikawa and an hour to get to Takao. Moreover, Chuo Line trains tend to be crowded, so you need to be on board your train some while before departure if you wish to sit down.

There used to be a *kaisoku* train at night, generally fairly empty, from Shinjuku to Matsumoto. However, this train now runs on an occasional basis only and has become extremely popular. Since it leaves Shinjuku at 0:02, only the new day's Blue Spring ticket is

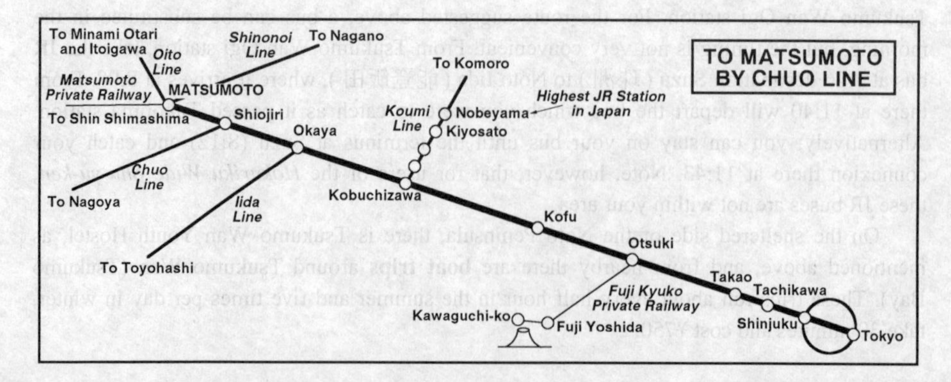

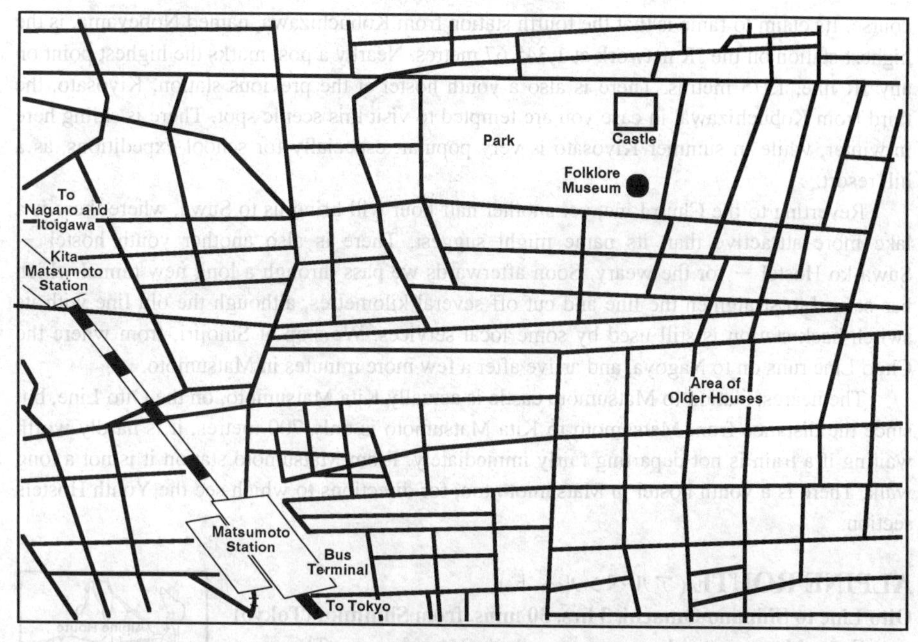


MATSUMOTO

required in order to use it. However, when the author last went on this train (and thought 'never again'), there were people standing for almost the whole five hours and the entire floor space was filled with inert but uncomfortable bodies, mostly belonging to mountain climbers and hikers who got off in the hour preceding arrival in Matsumoto at 4:45. I was very lucky indeed to get the last seat in my carriage. If you wish to use this train, check when it is operating (usually only Friday or Saturday night at holiday times) and be at Shinjuku station at least 90 minutes prior to departure. Bring a newspaper to sit on while queueing. Those using an *Hokuriku Wide Shu-yu-ken* can use the 23:50 *kyuko*. If you get on at Tachikawa, the first stop, which is reached after midnight, you will gain an extra day on your ticket. This train is not usually so crowded that you would be unable to get a seat at Tachikawa.

After the Chuo Line reaches Takao, the edge of the Tokyo suburbs, it starts to climb and, between the tunnels, the views commence. After about 30 minutes by express from Takao, Otsuki ('Big Moon') is reached. From here, the Fuji Kyuko Private Railway extends to the foot of Mt. Fuji at Fuji Yoshida and Kawaguchi-ko. If you are making this detour now, see the directions already given on page 111. Continuing along the Chuo Line, we pass through a fruit-growing and wine-making area. From the train you will see the grapes, peaches, pears and apples growing. In spring, special trains run along this line for viewing the variety of blossom. It is a very pretty line in April especially. A further half hour by *tokkyu* brings us to Kofu, the major city of the area, where those on ordinary trains may be obliged to change.

After Kofu, the slow but steady climb continues and 30 minutes more by express will take us to Kobuchizawa, another town where those on ordinary trains might have to change. A branch line, named the Koumi Line, runs from here to Komoro, on the Shinetsu Line. This is another pretty line, although you will not have time to take all the pretty lines in Japan, of course. Its claim to fame is that the fourth station from Kobuchizawa, named Nobeyama, is the highest station on the JR network at 1,345.67 metres. Nearby a post marks the highest point on any JR line, 1375 metres. There is also a youth hostel at the previous station, Kiyosato, the third from Kobuchizawa, in case you are tempted to visit this scenic spot. There is skiing here in winter, while in summer Kiyosato is very popular, especially for school expeditions, as a hill resort.

Reverting to the Chuo Line, yet another half hour will bring us to Suwa, where there is a lake more attractive than its name might suggest. There is also another youth hostel – Suwa-ko Hostel – for the weary. Soon afterwards we pass through a long new tunnel which has served to straighten the line and cut off several kilometres, although the old line with its switch-back station is still used by some local services. We stop at Shiojiri, from where the Chuo Line runs on to Nagoya, and arrive after a few more minutes in Matsumoto.

The nearest station to Matsumoto castle is actually Kita Matsumoto, on the Oito Line, but since the distance from Matsumoto to Kita Matsumoto is only 700 metres, it is hardly worth waiting if a train is not departing fairly immediately. From Matsumoto station it is not a long walk. There is a youth hostel in Matsumoto too, for directions to which see the Youth Hostels section.

## ALPINE ROUTE (アルペンルート)

**Oito Line to Shinano Omachi, 3 hrs. 30 mins. from Shinjuku (Tokyo)**

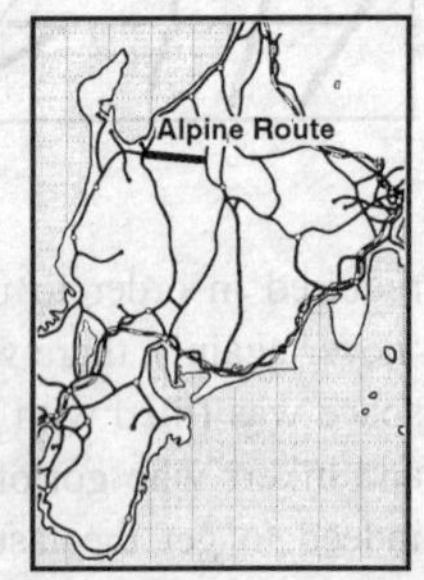


From Matsumoto, there are several choices of route. The most obvious is along the Oito Line to Minami Otari and on to Itoigawa. This is the route prescribed by the *Hokuriku Wide Shu-yu-ken* and it is the easiest and cheapest, whilst still being very scenic, particularly in winter, when the snow will lay thick here and the mountains on your left form beautiful reflections in the lakes. Expresses run occasionally as far as Minami Otari, about 75 minutes from Matsumoto, which is the border between JR East and JR West. The expresses cannot go any further because the line is not electrified beyond this point. By ordinary train from Matsumoto to Minami Otari takes about 2 hours, with trains running approximately every 90 minutes. From Minami Otari to Itoigawa there are ordinary trains only, the journey taking 50 minutes and again trains operating about every 90 minutes. For economy combined with beautiful scenery, this is the recommended route. On the way, there is a youth hostel, Kizaki-ko Hostel, near Shinano Kizaki station. This is a station at which only ordinary trains stop. It is about 75 minutes from Matsumoto, two stations beyond Shinano Omachi, which is the starting point for the 'Alpine Route' described in some detail below. From Itoigawa, those using an *Hokuriku Wide Shu-yu-ken* will be able to avail themselves of express trains without paying any supplement.

The second possibility is to cut across by the Shinonoi Line from Matsumoto to Nagano and then follow the Shinetsu Line route recommended in the previous pages. There are express and ordinary trains running on the Shinonoi Line, each approximately hourly. This is yet another attractive line, despite its having been ironed out, with the addition of several tunnels, in recent years. For ordinary trains, there remains one switch-back station. In particular, watch for the view prior to descending to Shinonoi and Nagano. From the elevated level of the railway line, one can indeed 'see the vision splendid of the sunlit plains extended'. For the best view, you should sit on the right. Those using the *Hokuriku Wide Shu-yu-ken* are not permitted to traverse the Shinonoi Line. Moreover, if the fact that you have had a stop at Matsumoto is noticeable from your ticket (i.e. if it has been stamped at Matsumoto), you cannot then have one at Nagano, since the two stations are on different permissible routes.

The third possibility is the one with which this section will deal principally, and that is travel via the 'Alpine Route'. That is the Japanese name, not a translation. The 'Alpine Route' is a relatively newly opened way through the heart of the mountains using an exciting combination of modes of transportation – bus, train, trolley-bus, ropeway and cablecar. This most appealing journey has one major draw-back and that is the price. From JR line at one end to rejoining JR at the other end will cost over ¥10,000. The route operates from late April until early November. For those with ¥10,000 to spare, here is how it is travelled. From Matsumoto, take the Oito Line to Shinano Omachi, which takes 1 hour by ordinary train or 35 minutes by *tokkyu*. From the station there are hourly buses to Ogisawa (扇沢), a 40 minute journey which costs ¥1,300 for 18 kilometres. If you think that that is expensive, just wait! Next is a trolley-bus through a tunnel in the mountain. It is the only trolley-bus route in Japan, but does that justify a price of ¥1,240 for a journey of 6.1 kilometres completed in 16 minutes? The trolley-bus will bring you to Kurobe Dam, an impressive structure, across which you must now walk, the only short part of the route (600 metres) where there is no transportation. From Kurobe-ko (Lake Kurobe), on the other side of the dam, the Kurobe Cablecar will whisk you part-way up the hill to Kurobe Daira, from where there is a good view of the dam below, 800 metres for ¥820 in 5 minutes. Tateyama Ropeway will then take you further up to Daikanho, 1.7 kilometres in 7 minutes for a mere ¥1,240. And now the biggest shock of all, the Tateyama Tunnel Bus, only 3.6 kilometres in 10 minutes, for which you will have to pay ¥2,060 to reach Murodo. There are some walks which can be made from Murodo, if you have time, including one to the **Jigokudani** ('Valley of Hell') area of volcanic activity and one to the top of Mt. Tateyama. The latter, however, is a long and strenuous walk which will take 4 to 5 hours for a return journey. The next ride on our journey is probably the best value, a 23 kilometre trip along twisting narrow roads to Bijo Daira ('Beautiful Lady Plateau'). It takes 50 minutes and

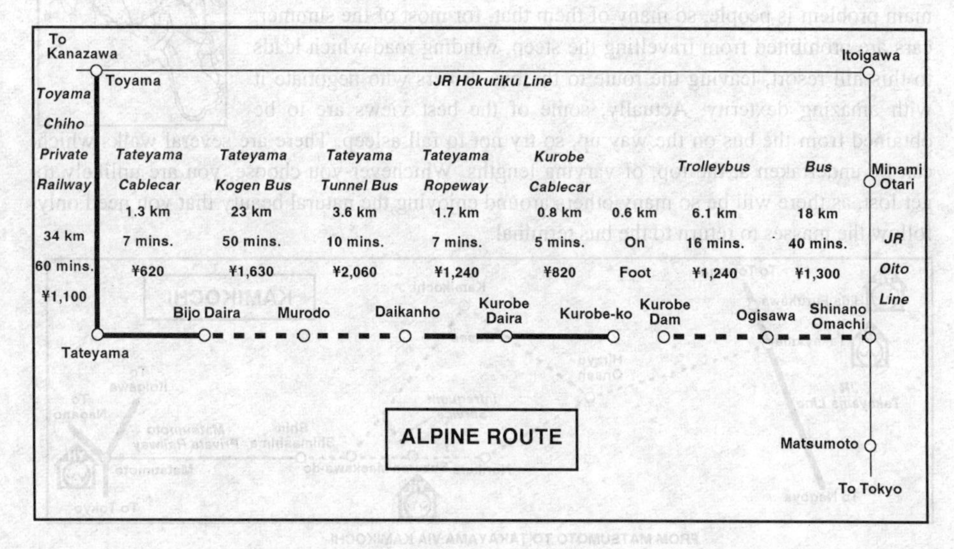

costs ¥1,630. Not only are there fine views of the countryside as one descends, but, if one goes early in the season, the road will be cut through several metres of snow in places. Sit near the front of the bus for the best views. On the way you will pass a bus stop called **Shomyo Taki** (称名滝). If you walk 900 metres from this stop, you will find a waterfall which claims to be Japan's highest. However, although it bounces 350 metres down the cliff face, the fall is in four steps, so it all depends how you measure a waterfall really. From Beautiful Lady Plateau (search, if you wish, and perhaps you will find her!), the final descent is by the Tateyama Cablecar to the town of Tateyama, 1.3 kilometres in 7 minutes at a cost of ¥620. Now you are on the level, more or less, and can complete your journey to the coast at Toyama by the Toyama Chiho Private Railway, which will seem quite cheap after the rest of this route. From Tateyama to Toyama, trains run at least every hour, usually on or just after the hour. The journey of 34 kilometres takes an hour and costs ¥1,100.

JR issues certain tickets which include travel through the 'Alpine Route', but, although they offer some discount, they are not really very suitable for visitors from overseas, since what they provide is simply a round trip from Tokyo, Nagoya or Osaka to Toyama, one way by the 'Alpine Route' and one way by JR express trains.

Because the journey through the 'Alpine Route' is so expensive, an alternative is to start from Toyama and go only as far as Murodo before returning to Toyama. This is the cheapest and best part of the route and the cost will be only half of that for going all the way through.

There is one more possibility, for travel between Matsumoto and Takayama, and that will be the topic of the next section.

## KAMIKOCHI (上高地 – 'Upper Highlands')

**Matsumoto Private Railway to Shin Shimashima,**
**30 mins. from Matsumoto. Then bus 75 mins.**

**Derivation of Name:** *Originally Kami Kawauchi, meaning 'top end of the river'.*

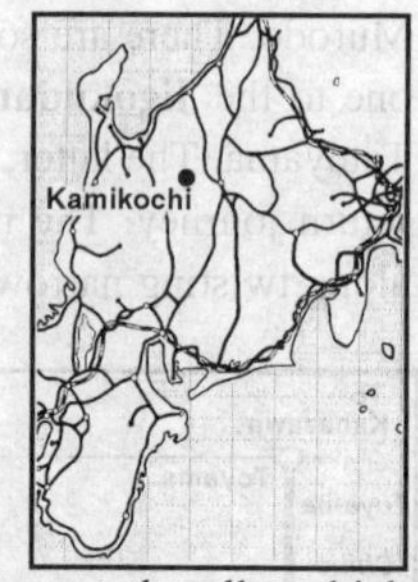


Kamikochi is supposed to be one of the great sights of Japan. The main problem is people, so many of them that, for most of the summer, cars are prohibited from travelling the steep, winding road which leads to this hill resort, leaving the route to the bus drivers who negotiate it with amazing dexterity. Actually, some of the best views are to be obtained from the bus on the way up, so try not to fall asleep. There are several walks which can be undertaken at the top, of varying lengths. Whichever you choose, you are unlikely to get lost, as there will be so many others around enjoying the natural beauty that you need only follow the masses to return to the bus terminal.

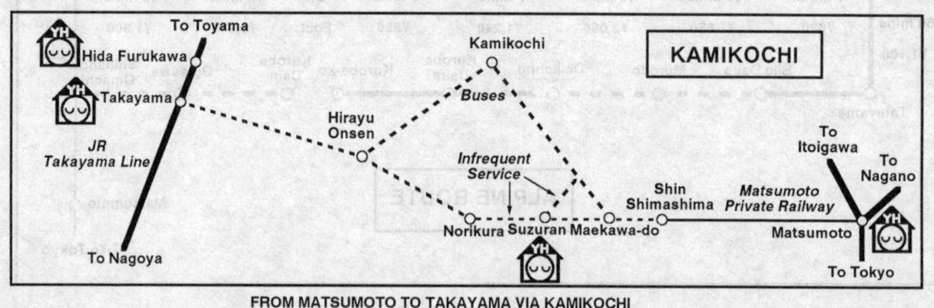


FROM MATSUMOTO TO TAKAYAMA VIA KAMIKOCHI
(Note that most bus services run in summer only)

From Matsumoto, take the Matsumoto Private Railway to Shin Shimashima, a journey of 30 minutes costing ¥670. Trains run about hourly. From Shin Shimashima, take a bus to Kamikochi (上高地), which takes 75 minutes and costs ¥2,050 single or ¥3,500 return. Buses connect with trains in most cases, but in winter there is no service.

When you have finished admiring the sights of Kamikochi, you have the choice of returning to Matsumoto and continuing to the Japan Sea from there or going by bus from Kamikochi on to Takayama, a route which is outlined in the following section on Takayama.

## TAKAYAMA (高山 – 'High Mountain') Takayama Line, 2 hrs. 20 mins. from Nagoya or 90 mins. from Toyama

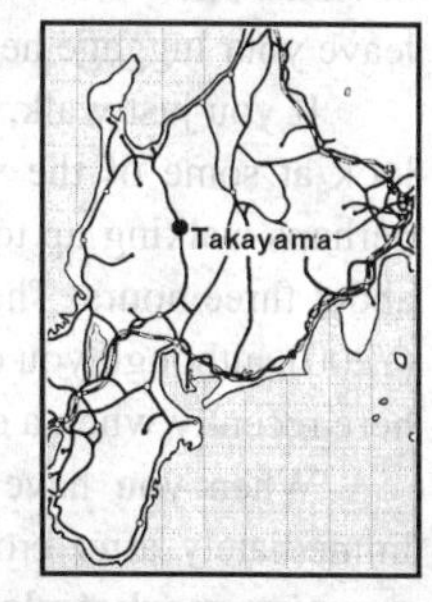


**Derivation of Name:** *Literal.*

Takayama has become a popular place to visit. It is a traditional Japanese town with a long history set in a valley amidst the hills. In the centre of the town beside the little river are several streets of old wooden houses, nearly all now functioning as souvenir shops or small museums. This area, together with the area of temples and shrines to the east of the town, make Takayama seem like a miniature Kyoto. The great advantage of Takayama is that everything is within walking distance.

There is a youth hostel and, appropriately enough, it is operated by one of the temples, Tensho-ji. It is a pleasant enough hostel, but always busy. It has information about the town in English and bicycles for hire at only a fraction of the price which you will pay elsewhere in the town. One oddity is that the author cannot recall ever staying in an hostel where the bathroom was so far from the dormitories.

On arrival at Takayama station, or Takayama Bus Terminal, which is next to the station, you will find, immediately outside, the Hida Tourist Information Service office. This should be your first port of call, for there are maps and information leaflets available in English. Having picked up what you require, if you are staying at the youth hostel, you can see some of the sights on your way there. With the station behind you, turn left and walk to the first major corner. On this corner, incidentally, is an hotel named the Orion Plaza Business Hotel which was advertising accommodation at ¥3,500 per person when the author was in Takayama, a reasonable alternative to the youth hostel. Turn right here and after another 2 or 3 minutes you will reach **Kokubun-ji** on your left, with a three storeyed pagoda outside. This is the most ancient temple in Takayama, dating from 746, but the oldest building presently in existence is the main hall, built in the sixteenth century. The ginkgo tree near the pagoda, however, is said to be 1,200 years old.

Continuing along the same street, another 5 minutes will bring you to the river, named the Miyagawa. Immediately after it on the left is the **morning market** of local produce, while on the right is the area of traditional wooden buildings known as **San-machi Suji**, with nearly all of the traditional little shops selling traditional little souvenirs, including pottery, lacquerware and local alcohol. The alcohol shops are indicated by rather quaint balls of cedar twigs hung outside. There is also an amazing number of private little museums and art galleries. Look in the tourist literature available at the station and you are almost certain to find something which will stimulate your interest – wild birds, dolls, toys, medicine boxes, archaeology, folk arts and crafts, lacquerware, architecture, art, local history, dances and more. You can just walk up one street and down the next to gain a taste of this area.

Once more continuing along our original street, you will cross another small river, the Enakogawa, and then, as the main road turns right, reach the start of the **Higashiyama Walking Course** (see map below). This is a very pleasant semi-rural walk among the temples and greenery which surround the town, one which the author enjoyed, meeting hardly anybody else on the way. The course is marked frequently with signposts in Japanese. It matters not that you cannot read them, for all that they say is 'This Way'. Even though there are plenty of these signs, it is advisable to take a map, for there are some places where the route is not entirely obvious. After a few temples, you will come to Tensho-ji, where the youth hostel is. You can leave your luggage here, if staying, before continuing with the course.

If you just walk, you can probably complete the course in an hour, but if you take time to look at some of the very attractive temples on the way, and have a rest or two, as well as perhaps walking up to look at the ruins of the castle in **Shiroyama Park**, you can stretch it to about three hours. The only charge on the route is for admission to the main hall of **Shoren-ji** (¥200), although you can look at the rest of the temple without any fee. The temple was moved here recently when a dam was constructed which flooded its original site.

When you have finished the course, walk back towards the station and the turn left immediately after crossing the river. Soon you will come to **Takayama Jinya** and another **morning market-place** outside. Takayama Jinya is the restored seat of local government, the only one of its type remaining in Japan. The site was used for that purpose from 1615 until 1969, but, although the form of the administration centre has not changed much, several reconstructions have taken place. There is also a large granary, for taxes were collected in the form of rice and had to be stored somewhere. Information is given in English on the admission ticket and throughout the displays. Look for the quaint little rabbit's head decorations around the walls! Entry costs ¥360.

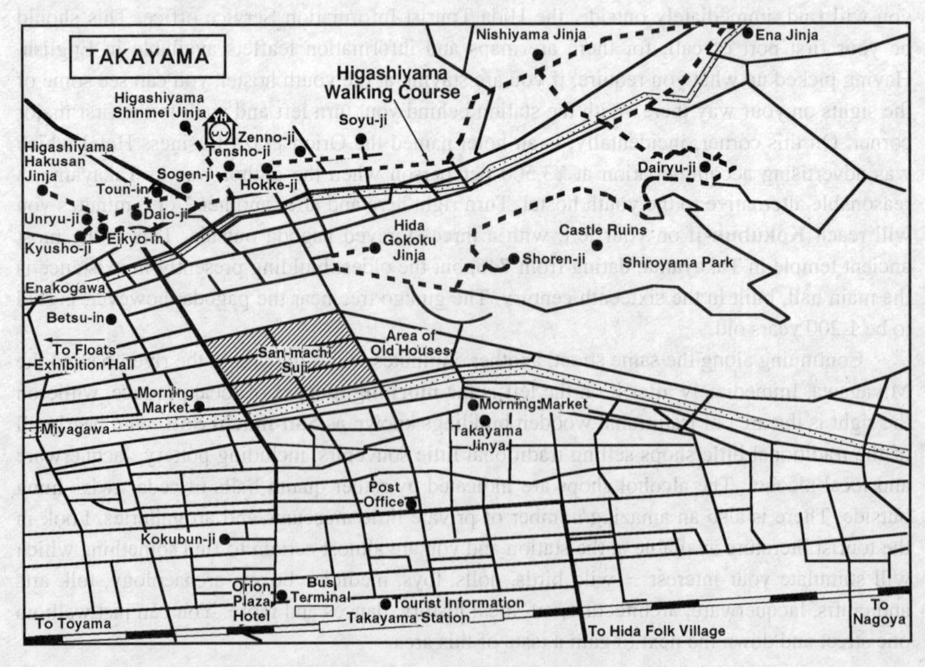

On the other side of the station is **Hida Folk Village**, a collection of old houses brought from various parts of the surrounding area. Some are simply displayed, while others are used as workshops or souvenir shops. This is quite a good collection, but, since admission costs ¥700, the village merits having some time devoted to it if you decide to go there. It is about 20 minutes walk from the station.

Takayama is famous for its **spring and autumn festivals**, when huge floats are paraded through the streets, many with elaborate puppets on them. These puppets need eight puppeteers to control each one, and, of course, working them is a truly skillful operation. Since most visitors do not manage to be present at the times of the festival, there is an exhibition hall where four floats are on display at any one time. The hall is a few minutes walk to the north of the main part of the town and admission costs ¥600. Most of the floats are about 200 years old.

The area around Takayama is known as Hida and has several other places which can be visited. Takayama itself is often referred to as Hida Takayama and nearby is **Hida Furukawa**, where there is a street of old warehouses, as well as other old buildings, and another youth hostel. There are also several spa resorts in the area. However, Takayama is the main attraction. About 24 hours is the minimum period to allow here in order to see most of its interesting features.

To reach Takayama from Kanazawa, return north-eastwards as far as Toyama, 45 minutes by *tokkyu* or about 75 minutes by ordinary train, and then take the Takayama Line, which is well known for its scenic beauty, although in the opinion of the author it is no better than many other lines. Probably the difference is that this one has fast comfortable express trains from which the view can be admired. The journey from Toyama to Takayama takes about 90 minutes by *tokkyu* and 2 hours 15 minutes by ordinary train. There are four *tokkyu* trains per day, all going to Nagoya, and six ordinary trains. At the time of writing, *tokkyu* departures from Toyama are at 8:20, 12:43, 14:49 and 16:52. Ordinary trains leave at 6:06, 7:34, 10:23, 13:39, 15:46 and 19:14. Those using an *Hokuriku Wide Shu-yu-ken* will be leaving their free area and starting their return journey as soon as they begin to travel along the Takayama Line.

To approach Takayama from Kamikochi, take a bus for Hirayu Onsen (平湯温泉) or Norikura (乗鞍) as far as Hirayu Onsen, a journey of 65 minutes at a cost of ¥1,500. Departures are approximately hourly in summer. There change to a bus for Takayama (高山), 55 minutes at a cost of ¥1,430. Departures are again hourly, at 10 minutes past the hour.

## GOKAYAMA (五箇山 – 'Five Pieces Mountain')

**Johana Line, 50 mins. from Takaoka. Then bus 45 mins.**

**Derivation of Name:** *There are five valleys and mountains in this area.*

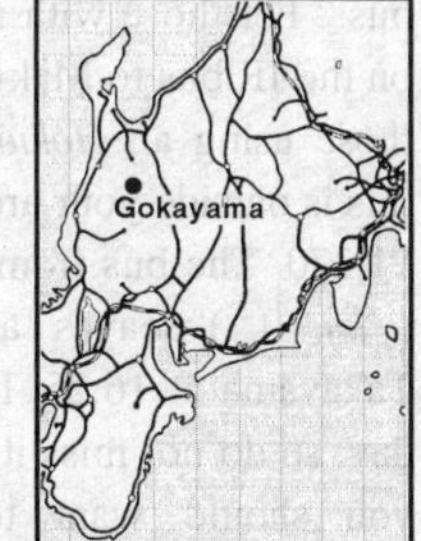


Here is an alternative route from Kanazawa or Takaoka to Takayama for those who would like to see some old traditional country buildings and even stay in one. **Ecchu Gokayama Youth Hostel** is very popular because it is housed in a traditional old thatched farmhouse of a design unique to this area of Japan. As usual with places slightly off the beaten track, the problem is the expense of the buses which must be taken. However, if you follow the plan given here, the expense will at least be minimized. Note, though, that some of these services run in summer only and that even the hostel is closed in the middle of winter.

Make your way to Takaoka, 15 minutes from Kanazawa by express or 25 minutes by ordinary train. From there, take the 11:40 train along the Johana Line, arriving in Johana, the final station, at 12:27. From the bus stop right outside the station exit, take the bus which will appear at 12:46, destination Gokayama (五箇山), and go as far as Suganuma (菅沼). This 45 minute journey costs ¥970. It is a scenic ride, somewhat more so if you sit on the right of the bus. You will travel through mountain scenery, passing through several long tunnels on the way. It would be a good idea to ask the driver about your stop when you feel that you are approaching, because there is not much to identify it. It is merely a place to pull the bus off the busy highway for a few seconds. A road runs off diagonally and downwards on the right, but you are unlikely to notice it until you have gone past. Having got off at the right place, however, that is the road which you want to take. You will immediately see a little cluster of thatched farmhouses in the valley below you. To the youth hostel it is a walk of 20 minutes. Directions are given in the Youth Hostels section. You may well find that you are not the only visitor from overseas staying there that night, despite the apparent remoteness of the hostel.

There is one further bus which can be used. Take the 16:26 train from Takaoka which reaches Johana at 17:13. The bus leaves from outside at 17:14, so there is no time to waste. There are also occasional buses from Kanazawa, destination Nagoya (名古屋), which travel via Suganuma, but, of course, they cost more.

When you want to continue your journey, probably next day, return to the same bus stop and take the same bus at 13:25 to Hatogaya (鳩ケ谷), where you will arrive at 13:53, incidentally passing some more settlements of thatched houses along the way and especially in Hatogaya itself. These places are likely to be swarming with visitors. When the author passed here, other passengers on the bus had come all the way from Tokyo to look at the houses. A JR bus will be waiting beside the public toilet opposite Hatogaya bus stop. Get on and it will depart at 14:00 in summer only for Mino Shiratori station (美濃白鳥駅). You should get off at Makido (牧戸), where it arrives at 14:57. You will not miss Makido, because there is a bus station there in which the bus pulls up. Note, however, that your connecting bus to Takayama leaves not from this bus station but from a stop on the road along which the bus was running before turning right and then left into the bus station. If in doubt, keep muttering, "Takayama bus, Takayama bus." For those with rail passes, the journey on the JR bus to Makido will be free, but for those using an *Hokuriku Wide Shu-yu-ken*, this is outside your area again, so it will cost ¥1,270. The bus from Makido to Takayama (高山) leaves at 15:10 and reaches Takayama at 16:25. It is the last bus of the day, so do not miss it. The fare is ¥1,840. If you should want to stop and look at Hatogaya, there is an earlier bus, destination Nagoya, at 11:10 from Suganuma in summer only.

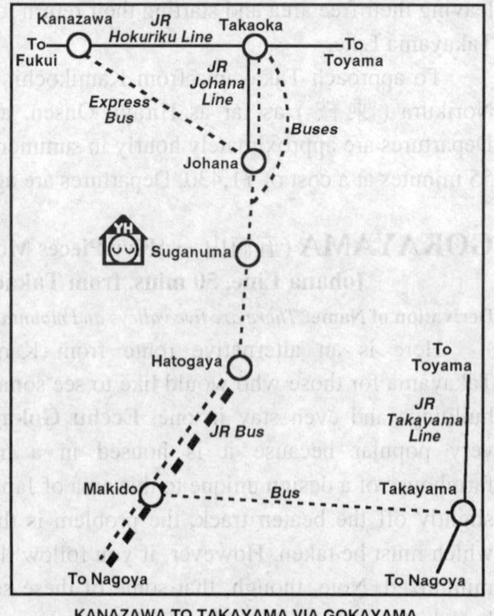


KANAZAWA TO TAKAYAMA VIA GOKAYAMA
(Connexions available only in summer)

## FUKUI (福井－ 'Lucky Well')

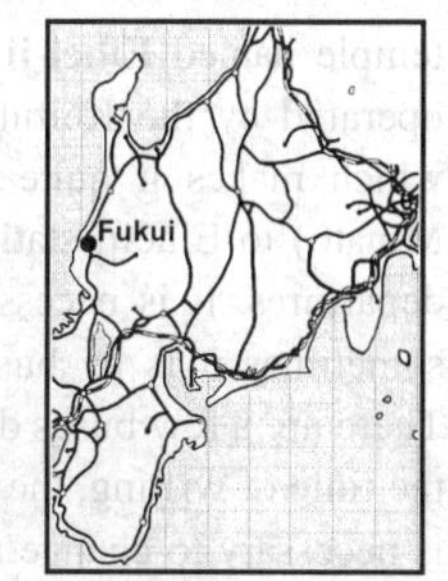


**Hokuriku Line, 8 hrs. from Ueno or Tokyo**

**Derivation of Name:** *Originally called Kitano-sho, meaning 'north residence'. However, the mention of north is considered to be a bad omen, so the name was changed to 'lucky residence', pronounced 'Fukui'. In time, the second Chinese character became changed.*

Those using an *Hokuriku Wide Shu-yu-ken*, in particular, will probably want to explore the limits of their territory, so may well make an expedition to Fukui, 50 minutes beyond Kanazawa by *tokkyu*, or 90 minutes by ordinary train. This pleasant city and its neighbour, Sabae, are the capitals of the spectacle frames industry in Japan. In Fukui, a tram line still runs down the middle of the main street, the trams turning themselves into trains a little further on and continuing as the Fukui Private Railway to the city of Takefu.

The main attractions of Fukui lie a little distance away from the city centre. There is another private railway called the Keifuku Private Railway running to Mikuni Minato, a journey of 45 minutes which costs ¥880. From there it is a walk of about 2 kilometres, or a short bus ride, to **Tojinbo** (東尋坊), a series of rocks jutting into the sea. This coastal scenery would be rather attractive but for the number of visitors there at any time. It can best be seen from the sea, so boats leave frequently for a 30 minute jaunt at a cost of ¥800. Tojinbo Youth Hostel is not far away, near Mikuni station, Mikuni being one stop before Mikuni Minato (Mikuni Port). Some buses from Tojinbo to Awara Onsen (芦原温泉) go past the hostel, but not all so be careful. You need a bus travelling via Mikuni station (三国駅). After the station, it will turn left and you should alight at Youth Hostel Iriguchi (ユースホステル入口), shortly afterwards. See the map in the Youth Hostels section. A slightly cheaper route to Tojinbo is to alight from the JR train at Awara Onsen, reached 11 minutes before Fukui by *tokkyu*, and to take a bus from there. Buses run to Tojinbo at least twice an hour at a cost of ¥700 for the 40 minute journey.

The rather more interesting second attraction of Fukui is an imposing and famous old

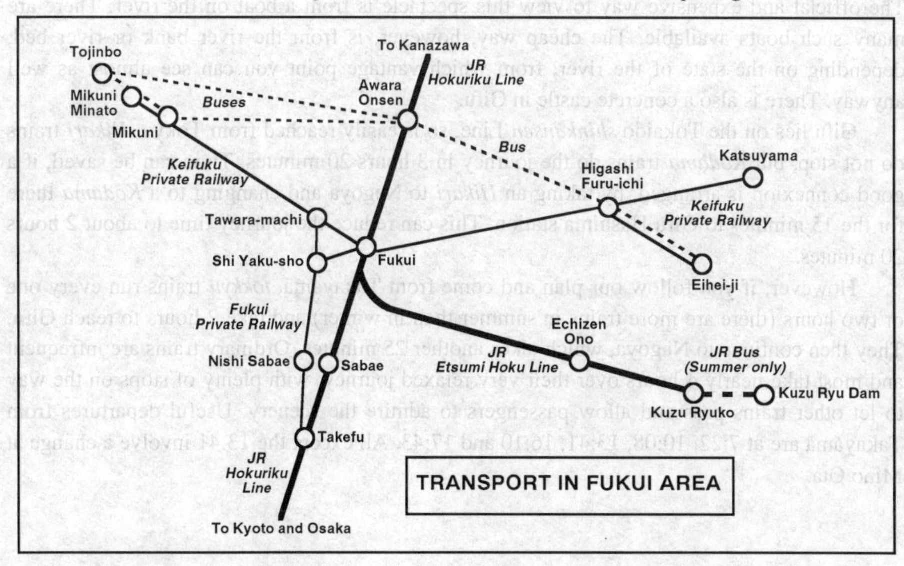

temple named **Eihei-ji**, which is certainly worth seeing. This lies at the end of another line operated by the Keifuku Railway Company. To reach it you have to return to Fukui first, which makes it quite an expensive journey. The fare just from Fukui (not from Mikuni Minato) to Eiheiji station is ¥710 and that journey takes 35 to 40 minutes, with half-hourly departures. It is necessary to change on the way. Sometimes the connexion is by train and sometimes it is by bus. The rumour is that this private line's existence is endangered too. There are a few buses direct from Tojinbo to Eihei-ji (永平寺), 80 minutes, for ¥1,350, but, at the time of writing, the only departures are at 10:10, 11:10, 12:27 and 13:27. At other times, it is necessary to change at Awara Onsen (芦原温泉), which makes it more expensive, as well as less interesting, than the train.

There is another youth hostel at Eihei-ji, named Eihei-ji Monzen Yamaguchi-so. It is only a short walk from station and temple. There is also a hostel in the city of Fukui, Fukui-ken Fujin Seinen Kaikan. It is conveniently located in the heart of the city, only a short walk from the station, and a pleasant place to stay, with small rooms and even a *yukata* provided.

There is a JR branch line running from Fukui to **Kuzu Ryuko**. In winter, the snow will lie deep along this line and it is an attractive journey. For a brief period in mid-summer, there are JR buses running up to Kuzu Ryu Dam (九頭竜ダム, 10 minutes, ¥360), a picnic spot.

## GIFU (岐阜 – 'Junction Town')

**Tokaido *shinkansen*, 3 hrs. 20 mins. from Tokyo**

**Derivation of Name:** *Named after a mountain of good omen in China, but exact reason for name unknown.*

Gifu is not a particularly exciting city, but it is known for the **cormorant fishing** (*ukai*) which takes place on the river in summer. Fish are attracted by blazing torches in the fishing boats and then caught by trained cormorants on pieces of string. The birds have rings round their necks so that they cannot deprive the fishermen of their suppers! The official and expensive way to view this spectacle is from a boat on the river. There are many such boats available. The cheap way, however, is from the river bank or river bed, depending on the state of the river, from which vantage point you can see almost as well anyway. There is also a concrete castle in Gifu.

Gifu lies on the Tokaido *shinkansen* Line, so is easily reached from Tokyo. *Hikari* trains do not stop, but *Kodama* trains do the journey in 3 hours 20 minutes. Time can be saved, if a good connexion is arranged, by taking an *Hikari* to Nagoya and changing to a *Kodama* there for the 15 minutes to Gifu Hashima station. This can reduce the journey time to about 2 hours 20 minutes.

However, if you follow our plan and come from Takayama, *tokkyu* trains run every one or two hours (there are more trains in summer than in winter) and take 2 hours to reach Gifu. They then continue to Nagoya, which takes another 25 minutes. Ordinary trains are infrequent and most take nearly 4 hours over their very relaxed journey, with plenty of stops on the way to let other trains pass and allow passengers to admire the scenery. Useful departures from Takayama are at 7:22, 10:08, 13:41, 16:10 and 17:43. All except the 13:41 involve a change at Mino Ota.

## KYOTO (京都 – 'Capital City')

**Tokaido *shinkansen*, 2 hrs. 45 mins. from Tokyo**

**Derivation of Name:** *Literal.*

It is natural that everybody will want to visit Kyoto, the most interesting city in Japan, and, for that reason, a separate section is devoted to the Kansai area, which includes Kyoto. Here we shall merely mention how to include the city in a tour of the Chubu region.

Having reached Gifu, those with Japan Rail Passes can continue to Kyoto by *shinkansen*. Note, however, that Gifu station, where conventional services stop, is not the same as Gifu Hashima station, where the *shinkansen* stops. To get there it is necessary to go next door to Shin Gifu station and take a Meitetsu Private Railway train to Shin Hashima, a journey of 25 to 30 minutes costing ¥390. If you are arriving in Gifu by *tokkyu*, it is more simple to stay on board until Nagoya is reached and then take the *shinkansen* from there. From Nagoya to Kyoto is a journey of 45 minutes to 1 hour.

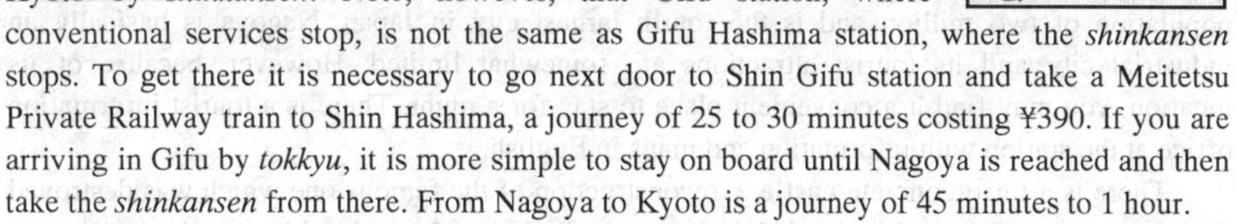

Those using Blue Spring tickets need to continue from Gifu to Maibara, where it is necessary to change trains to go on to Kyoto. There are plenty of trains from Gifu to Ogaki, but it would be better to wait for one going through to Maibara. These run approximately hourly. From Maibara to Kyoto there are again plenty of trains. Both *kaisoku* and *shin kaisoku* ('new' rapid) trains operate. You can take whichever is available first, but the *shin kaisoku* trains are often more comfortable. As far as Kyoto, the *kaisoku* trains stop at every station, while the *shin kaisoku* skip some. Trains do not terminate at Kyoto. Likely destinations are Kakogawa, Himeji and Aboshi. From Gifu to Maibara takes 50 minutes, while from Maibara to Kyoto takes about an hour.

For those using an *Hokuriku Wide Shu-yu-ken*, Gifu certainly lies on your route back to Tokyo, but you are not allowed to visit Kyoto. Therefore you are supposed to pay from Gifu. However, Maibara also lies on a permitted return route to Tokyo, so once you reach Kyoto, it is quite likely that nobody will know for sure which route you took and that you will be charged only from Maibara (¥1,090), therefore. If you decide not to visit Takayama, from Fukui you can go directly to Kyoto. There are frequent *tokkyu* trains which you can use from Fukui to Tsuruga, where the *Hokuriku Wide Shu-yu-ken* area ends. If you continue to Kyoto, beside Lake Biwa, the largest lake in Japan, the cost will be ¥2,720, including the express supplement. The fastest trains cover the journey from Fukui to Kyoto non-stop in 90 minutes. Others trains stop two or three times and take a few minutes longer. If you prefer, you can get off the *tokkyu* at Tsuruga and take an ordinary train to Nagahama, then a *kaisoku* or *shin kaisoku* via Maibara to Kyoto. By this route, you would be charged only from Maibara (¥1,090). From Fukui to Tsuruga, including a journey through a long, long tunnel drilled through the hills some years ago to shorten the route, takes 35 minutes by *tokkyu*. From Tsuruga to Nagahama takes about 45 minutes and from Nagahama to Kyoto takes about 75 minutes. Allow some time for connexions also.

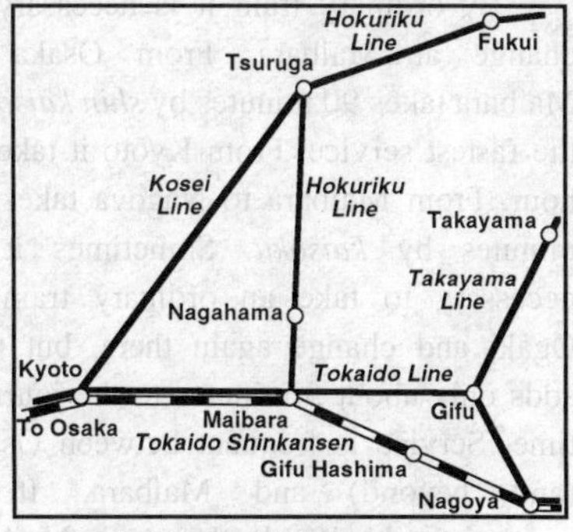


ROUTES TO KYOTO

## NAGOYA (名古屋 – 'Old Name House')

**Tokaido *shinkansen*, 2 hrs. from Tokyo**

**Derivation of Name:** *Original meaning was 'place where waves become calm'. Then Chinese characters used became changed.*

Having completed your sightseeing in the Kansai area (Kyoto, Nara, Osaka, Kobe and surroundings), you will want to return to Tokyo by a different route. Let us use the direct route beside the Pacific Ocean this time, making one or two stops along the way.

Nagoya is the major city between Kyoto and Tokyo. It has a population of two million and is the fourth largest city in Japan. Nagoya is basically an industrial city and its tourist attractions are somewhat limited. However, because of its location, you may find it a convenient place to stay for a night. There is a tourist information office at the station with information and maps in English.

There is a ferro-concrete **castle**, a reconstruction of the famous one which was destroyed during the war. The most renowned features are the two **golden dolphins** on the roof, often regarded as the symbols of the city. Then there is the **television tower**, which is 180 metres high and has an observation deck half way up, while the **Tokugawa Art Gallery** has an illustrated version of the famous 'Tales of Genji'.

There are two youth hostels. Aichi-ken Seinen Kaikan is the more conveniently located, within walking distance of the station, but it is sometimes full. Nagoya Hostel is on the Higashiyama Line of the subway. The line runs through Nagoya station. To Higashiyama Koen station, where the hostel is located, takes 16 minutes and the hostel is a further 8 minutes walk uphill from there. See the Youth Hostels section for directions. This hostel is in quite a pleasant location next to the zoo and botanical gardens. When the author stayed here at cherry blossom time, the surroundings, and particularly the path up to the hostel looked very pretty.

To reach Nagoya from Osaka or Kyoto is easy. For those with rail passes, *shinkansen* trains are frequent and all stop at Nagoya. From Shin Osaka, the journey takes exactly 1 hour by *Hikari* or 75 minutes by *Kodama*. From Kyoto, journey times are 45 minutes by *Hikari* or 1 hour by *Kodama*. Remember that, with a rail pass, you are not allowed to use *Nozomi* services, according to the current regulations.

By ordinary train it is necessary to change at Maibara. From Osaka to Maibara takes 90 minutes by *shin kaisoku*, the fastest service. From Kyoto it takes 1 hour. From Maibara to Nagoya takes 66 minutes by *kaisoku*. Sometimes it is necessary to take an ordinary train to Ogaki and change again there, but that adds only about 5 minutes to the journey time. Service is frequent between Osaka (and beyond) and Maibara. It is approximately hourly between Maibara and Nagoya.

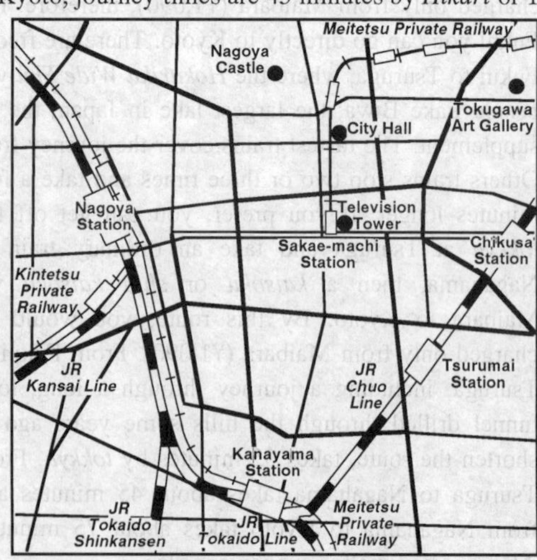

NAGOYA CITY CENTRE

There is also a line from Nara to Nagoya, although this route would be expensive for those using an *Hokuriku Wide Shu-yu-ken*, because they would not rejoin their permitted route until Nagoya, instead of at Maibara. From Nara, ordinary trains run to Kameyama ('Tortoise Mountain'), sometimes with a change at Kamo. They take approximately 1 hour 45 minutes and run about hourly. From Kameyama to Nagoya takes about 75 minutes with trains running hourly again and usually making reasonable connexions with trains from Nara. There is a single *kyuko* which runs right through from Nara to Nagoya. It leaves Nara at 16:34 and reaches Nagoya at 18:48. (In the opposite direction, it leaves Nagoya at 8:50 and reaches Nara at 11:02.)

Nagoya has a one-day ticket for use on buses and subways. This costs ¥820. On the tenth of the month only, a one-day ticket is available for the subway for ¥500. The object is to encourage people not to use their cars on that day.

## ISE (伊勢 – 'This vigour') Sangu Line, 1 hr. 35 mins. from Nagoya

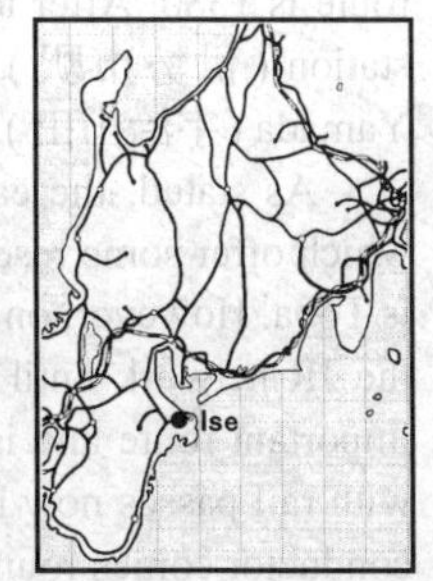


**Derivation of Name:** *Originally 'Iso', meaning 'seashore'. Became corrupted to Ise.*

Nagoya is the nearest major city to the interesting area of Ise, although this region can also be reached conveniently from Osaka or Kyoto, about which more in a few paragraphs.

At Ise can be found the two most important shrines of the Shinto religion – the so-called **Grand Shrines of Ise**. Until the end of the Second World War, Shintoism had been the national religion. The Emperor was divine and all the priests at the Ise shrines were top government officials. After the war, the Emperor was demoted to a mere mortal and state and religious functions were separated. However, that has not changed the fact that these are the most important shrines in the Shinto faith. Moreover, they remain the family shrines of the Imperial Household, so all major events which concern the Imperial Family are reported here and the members of the family still visit periodically. Since all Japanese are supposedly descended from the royal family, these are, in a sense, their shrines too and they are regarded, especially by older people, with especial reverence.

The two shrines are known as the **Inner Shrine** (*Naiku*) and the **Outer Shrine** (*Geku*), but this is not a reference to their geographical positions, for they are actually 6 kilometres apart and it is the Outer Shrine which is in the centre of Ise town and the Inner Shrine which is outside the town. Rather it is a reference to their relative degrees of holiness, for the latter enshrines Amaterasu Omikami, the sun goddess, whose grandson was the first Emperor of Japan (very appropriately called Jim). The sun goddess gave him a sacred mirror, one of the three symbols of imperial authority, and this mirror is kept in the Inner Shrine, wrapped in silk and placed in a beautiful cypress-wood box. It has been kept here since the year 5 B.C. and is never shown to the general public. This mirror is the most venerated object in the Shinto religion. Of course, the events related in this paragraph are not all proven historically, but they are the basis of the Shinto faith.

The buildings of the two shrines are all made traditionally and ceremonies are all carried out exactly as they have been for centuries. Here you will find pure Shinto architecture. The thatched buildings are all made of wood, mostly cypress, with no paint used and no nails. Moreover, it has been the tradition to demolish them every twenty years and construct new buildings. There are two sites, side by side, for this purpose. While one site is in use, the other is waiting for rebuilding. Traditionally, the pillars of the roof of the old sanctuaries are then used to make the *torii* (arched gateways) for the new shrines.

Visitors are allowed only as far as the outer gate of the shrine. Sometimes Shintoists can go as far as the inner gate when accompanied by a priest. Beyond that, however, is sacred ground, for the use only of high-ranking priests, Emperors, members of the Imperial Family and the like. Even photographs are not allowed.

The Outer Shrine (*Geku*) is only a short walk from Ise-shi station (JR and Kintetsu), although there are plenty of buses if you feel lazy. The ride to Geku-mae (外宮前) takes 2 minutes and costs ¥150. From the Outer Shrine to the Inner Shrine (*Naiku*), though, you will need to take the bus. There are two routes, both circular. Buses leave from Geku-mae for Naiku-mae (内宮前) frequently and take 15 to 20 minutes over the journey. The fare by either route is ¥380. After looking at the Inner Shrine, you will want to take the bus back to Ise-shi station (伊勢市駅), which again costs ¥380 and takes 18 minutes. The bus travels via Uji Yamada (宇治山田), a major station on the Kintetsu Private Railway.

As stated, the easiest way to travel to Ise is from Nagoya. JR now runs *kaisoku* trains which offer some reserved seats and reach Ise-shi in 90 minutes. The destination of such trains is Toba. However, on the way, they travel via the Ise Private Railway, which used to be part of the JR network until given to private enterprise, a strange decision really, for the line is an important route and is still used by many JR *tokkyu* and *kaisoku* trains. However, even those with rail passes now have to pay for this section of the journey. The cost is ¥440. Usually the conductor comes round at this stage to search for those who need to pay. *Kaisoku* trains depart from Nagoya hourly, on the hour. If you wish to avoid the ¥440 charge, you have to take an ordinary train to Kameyama and change to a train for Ise-shi and Toba there, which is time-consuming, particularly as connexions are usually not good.

There is also the possibility of taking the Kintetsu Private Railway from Nagoya to Ise. The Kintetsu line runs right beside the JR route for much of the way and operates in direct competition with it. *Kyuko* trains (no supplement) cover the journey to Ise-shi in about 1 hour 45 minutes at a cost of ¥1,260. There are also *tokkyu* trains with supplements of ¥1,020 or ¥1,330. The fastest trains cover the distance in 78 minutes, but stop not at Ise-shi, but at Uji Yamada, the next station, from where there are buses to both the Inner Shrine and the Outer Shrine. Departures are frequent for all types of train.

Kintetsu also offers direct *tokkyu* services to Ise from Kyoto (hourly, 2 hours) and from Osaka (from Kami Hon-machi station, frequent service, 1 hour 45 minutes). Then there are *kaisoku kyuko* services hourly from Kami Hon-machi (no supplement, 2 hours), but from Kyoto it is necessary to change trains *en route* at Yamato Yagi if you do not take the *tokkyu*. From Kami Hon-machi, the basic fare is ¥1,550 (supplements as from Nagoya) and from Kyoto ¥1,740 (supplements ¥1,270 or ¥1,580).

Since the author likes to avoid travelling the same route twice as far as possible, a suggestion is that from Kyoto you go to Nara and view the sights there and then travel via the JR Kansai Line to Kameyama (details in the Nagoya section above), from where trains run about hourly to Ise-shi, the journey taking approximately 90 minutes. Although that route is an indirect and awkward one from Nagoya, from Nara it is reasonably direct. If you then return to Nagoya later, only a small part of the journey will be duplicated. Even for those using an *Hokuriku Wide Shu-yu-ken*, the cost of this diversion would not be so much more from Nara than from Nagoya, assuming that you would want to pay a visit to Nara in any case.

There are special tickets offered too. From Tokyo there is a ticket called an *Ise Shima Free Kippu*. The rules for this are almost the same as those which apply to a *shu-yu-ken*. The ticket offers a return journey by JR ordinary or *kyuko* trains, in unreserved seats, to Ise-shi. If you want to use faster trains, then you pay just the applicable supplements. From Ise-shi onwards around the peninsula, you can use all JR trains, Kintetsu trains, Mie Kotsu buses and Kintetsu ferries, which covers almost all transport available except purely sightseeing buses and boats. If a Kintetsu *tokkyu* train is used, the supplement must be paid. The ticket also gives discounts on various admission fees. It is valid for eight days and costs ¥16,040 from Tokyo or ¥15,000 from Yokohama.

For those who have already reached this part of the world, similar tickets are offered from Kyoto (¥6,600), Osaka (¥6,340) and Nagoya (¥5,860). In these cases, travel is by Kintetsu only, both for the return journey and within the 'free' area and the tickets are valid for four days only.

Kintetsu also offers a more limited ticket, called an 'Ise Toba Joy Free' (or maybe it is an 'Ise Toba Joy-free'! The Japanese does not make it clear which is intended). This is similar to the ticket just mentioned, but it includes only the area from Ise-shi to Toba, not beyond, Kintetsu only, and only bus routes which start at one of the stations included in the area. No ferries are included. Prices are ¥4,490 from Kyoto, ¥4,170 from Osaka and ¥3,670 from Nagoya. The ticket is valid for two days.

There is a youth hostel at Matsusaka, on the way to Ise − Atago-san Hostel − for details of which see the Youth Hostels section.

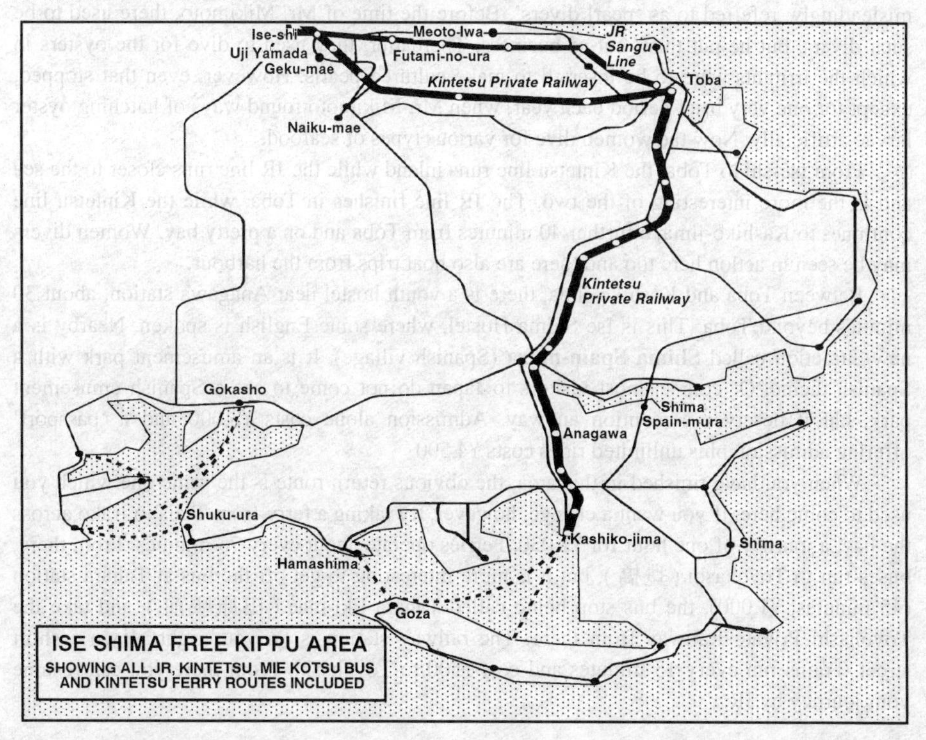

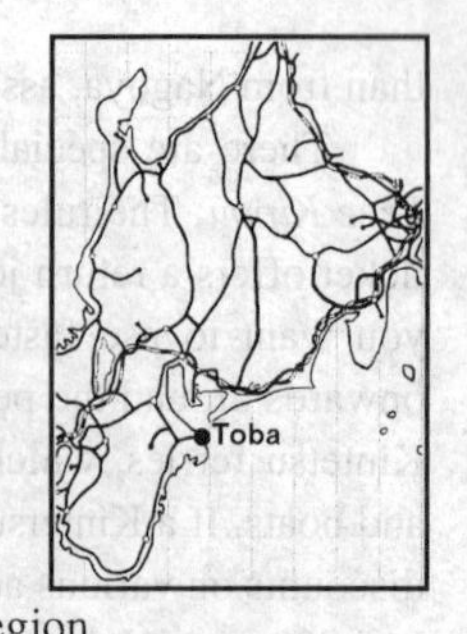


## TOBA (鳥羽 – 'Bird Feather')

**Sangu Line, 1 hr. 45 mins. from Nagoya**

**Derivation of Name:** *According to legend, the sun goddess, Amaterasu Omikami, came down to this place in a ship made of eagles' feathers.*

Proceeding south from the town of Ise, you will come, after another 15 minutes by *kaisoku*, to Toba. There is one place on the way which is worth a stop – and, indeed, the *kaisoku* makes one. This is **Meoto Iwa**, near the station of Futami-no-ura. This station is served only by JR, not by Kintetsu. Indeed, the JR Sangu Line is rather attractive as it makes its way beside the sea towards Toba through this region.

Meoto Iwa, the 'married rocks', are regarded as sacred by Shintoists and represent a husband and wife. The nuptial knot is tied fairly literally with a huge straw rope, replaced three times every year. In a temple nearby, there is another youth hostel, named Taiko-ji Hostel.

Toba itself is world-famous as the home of **cultured pearls** and of the Mikimoto company. Mr. Mikimoto was born here in 1858. He believed that it should be possible, by introducing an irritant inside the shell of an oyster, to produce a pearl of quality equal to that of the natural article. After several failures, he finally succeeded in this endeavour in 1893. The Mikimoto Pearl Island lies on the site of that first success and shows the processes used in the production of cultured pearls. It is a fascinating place to spend a couple of hours. The island is connected to the mainland by a bridge, about 200 metres long.

Toba is also known for its **women divers**, sometimes erroneously, or perhaps deliberately misleadingly, referred to as 'pearl divers'. Before the time of Mr. Mikimoto, there used to be such divers, but he put them out of business. Thereafter, they used to dive for the oysters in which the irritants were to be inserted to make cultured pearls. However, even that stopped, except for one very brief period each year, when Mr. Mikimoto found ways of hatching oyster larvae artificially. Now the women dive for various types of seafood.

From Ise-shi to Toba, the Kintetsu line runs inland while the JR line runs closer to the sea and is the more interesting of the two. The JR line finishes in Toba, while the Kintetsu line continues to Kashiko-jima, a further 40 minutes from Toba and on a pretty bay. Women divers may be seen in action here too and there are also boat trips from the harbour.

Between Toba and Kashiko-jima, there is a youth hostel near Anagawa station, about 30 minutes beyond Toba. This is Ise Shima Hostel, where some English is spoken. Nearby is a new attraction called **Shima Spain-mura** (Spanish village). It is an amusement park with a Spanish theme. Of course, most visitors to Japan do not come to see a Spanish amusement park, but it deserves a mention anyway. Admission alone costs ¥3,000 and a 'passport' offering admission plus unlimited rides costs ¥4,500.

When you have finished in this area, the obvious return route is the same one which you used to come here. If you want a change, however, try taking a ferry from Toba to Irako across the bay, a journey of one hour for ¥1,030. Ferries operate about every 75 minutes. From there, buses run to Toyohashi (豊橋), but it is more interesting to get off the bus at Tahara station (45 minutes, ¥1,000), the bus stop being called Tahara Eki-mae (田原駅前), and take the Toyohashi Private Railway from there. The railway station is on your right, down a short street. Trains run every 15 minutes and cost ¥500 to Toyohashi. From there you can resume your journey by JR.

## OIGAWA (大井川 – 'Big Well River')

**Tokaido Line to Kanaya, 30 mins. from Shizuoka**

**Derivation of Name:** *Originally 'Ohokigawa', meaning 'river with a big bank'.*

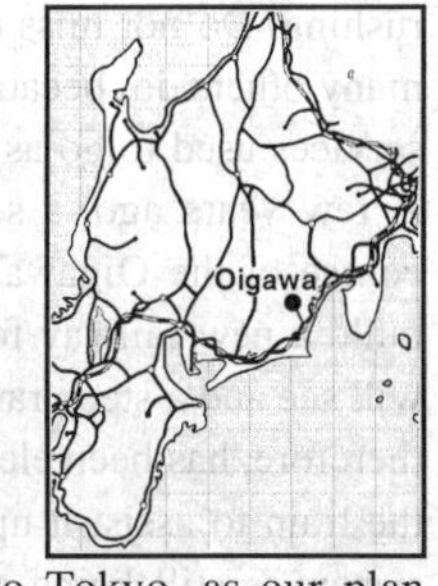


Here is another of the beautiful private railways of Japan, a really enjoyable day's entertainment, if you can afford it! Oigawa is the name of a river, and the railway follows the course of the river valley for its whole length, a total of 65 kilometres.

The **Oigawa Private Railway** starts from Kanaya, on the Tokaido Line between Hamamatsu and Shizuoka. If you are travelling west, the best *shinkansen* station to use is Shizuoka, but if you are returning to Tokyo, as our plan suggests, the nearest *shinkansen* station is Kakegawa, at which only *Kodama* trains stop. The journey takes 70 minutes from Nagoya or 35 minutes from Toyohashi. From Kakegawa to Kanaya by ordinary train takes 14 minutes. By ordinary train it takes about 2½ hours from Nagoya to Kanaya and it is usually necessary to change at Toyohashi (or sometimes at Hamamatsu). As far as Toyohashi, there are actually three types of train – *shin kaisoku*, *kaisoku* and ordinary (*futsu*). None requires a supplement, so all can be used with Blue Spring tickets. The *shin kaisoku* and *kaisoku* are quite comfortable. There are plenty of trains in this area. From Toyohashi to Kanaya there are only ordinary trains, but still plenty of them, and the journey takes about 85 minutes, sometimes involving a change at Hamamatsu.

The Oigawa Railway runs a few of its services using steam locomotives, the exact number and timing depending on the season and the day of the week. However, the service which operates most frequently leaves Kanaya at 11:45 and goes as far as Senzu, where it arrives at 13:03. It returns from Senzu at 14:50, reaching Kanaya at 16:08. In addition to the steam service, there are departures from Kanaya to Senzu approximately hourly by ordinary train or *kyuko*. The journey takes 1 hour by *kyuko* or 70 minutes by ordinary train. The *kyuko* trains are old *tokkyu* rolling stock from the Odakyu Private Railway in Tokyo and are quite comfortable. The journey to Senzu costs ¥1,620. There is a supplement of ¥150 for the *kyuko* and a supplement of ¥500 for the steam train ('S.L.' in Japanese).

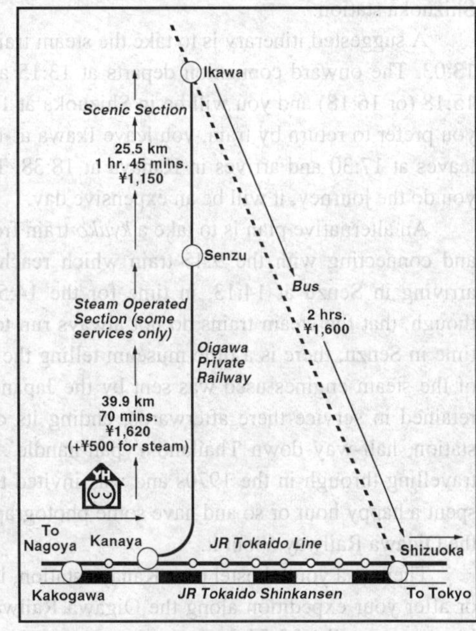

EXPEDITION ALONG OIGAWA PRIVATE RAILWAY

Senzu, however, is not the end of the line. The most scenic part is yet to come. As far as Senzu, the line is electrified, but from here a small diesel locomotive (made in Germany) will pull specially built miniature carriages through a series of tunnels, over bridges across gorges and up into the mountains for another 25 kilometres, a journey which takes a further 1 hour 45 minutes, without any pretence of rushing. Do not miss this by taking the steam train to Senzu and then going straight back, as many others do, because this part of the line is what you should have come to see. Some steam services used to go as far as Oku Izumi, another 7 kilometres, but they all stop at Senzu now. A few years ago, a series of dams was constructed along the river, with the result that the course of the Oigawa Railway would be submerged. The constructors of the dam agreed to build a new railway for that section, including a couple of rather splendid bridges which you will see and a steep ramp, too steep for a conventional locomotive to tackle. That short section, therefore, has been electrified and an electric locomotive operating on a cog system is added to the train to assist it up the ramp, all very exciting! It is the only place in Japan where a cog system is still being operated. As you proceed upon your leisurely journey, admiring some magnificent views, the conductor will give a commentary (in Japanese, of course, but just look in the direction in which everybody else is looking!), pointing out some of the sights. This commentary includes such instructions as, "Look up in the trees on your left now and you will see the monkeys sitting on the branches." During the course of the ride, you will cross one particularly impressive bridge more than 100 metres high. As you look out of the little carriage, you cannot see the track or bridge, so there is nothing between you and the tops of the trees far below. There is also nothing much at Ikawa, the end of the line. However, if you walk a short distance downhill you will come to a large dam with a generating station beside it. The journey from Senzu to Ikawa costs ¥1,150 and now, of course, you have little alternative but to go back again. If you want to economize a little, though, there is a bus back to Shizuoka. Note carefully that that is exactly what there is – a single bus, or two buses in mid-summer. The bus leaves from outside Ikawa station at 15:18 for most of the year, or at 14:13 and 16:18 in mid-summer. It costs ¥1,600 for the journey of 2 hours 20 minutes to Shizuoka station.

A suggested itinerary is to take the steam train from Kanaya at 11:45, arriving at Senzu at 13:03. The onward connexion departs at 13:15 and reaches Ikawa at 14:59. Take the bus at 15:18 (or 16:18) and you will be in Shizuoka at 17:39 (or 18:36). Total cost will be ¥4,870. If you prefer to return by train, you leave Ikawa at 15:40, reaching Senzu at 17:26. A connexion leaves at 17:30 and arrives in Kanaya at 18:38. Total cost will be ¥6,040, so whichever way you do the journey, it will be an expensive day.

An alternative plan is to take a *kyuko* train from Kanaya at 8:35, arriving in Senzu at 9:36 and connecting with the 9:45 train which reaches Ikawa at 11:29. The return is at 12:30, arriving in Senzu at 14:13, in time for the 14:50 steam train back to Kanaya. Remember, though, that the steam trains do not always run to this schedule. If you happen to have spare time in Senzu, there is a little museum telling the history of the line and its rolling stock. One of the steam engines used was sent by the Japanese to work in Thailand during the war and retained in service there afterwards, ending its career working in the sidings at Chumphon station, half-way down Thailand's 'pan-handle'. There, by chance, the author saw it while travelling through in the 1970s and was invited to come and ride round on it as it worked. I spent a happy hour or so and have some photographs of the engine at work, but I have not told the Oigawa Railway about it.

There is a youth hostel near Kanaya station, in a suitable location for staying either before or after your expedition along the Oigawa Railway. This is Sayo-no Nakayama Hostel. It is, however, a walk of 3.5 kilometres from the station.

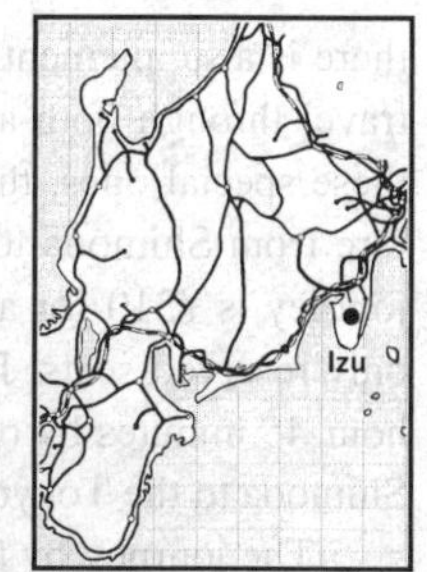


## IZU (伊豆 – 'This Bean') Ito Line, 1 hr. 45 mins. from Tokyo

**Derivation of Name:** *Originally 'Yuzu', meaning 'a place where hot water comes out'.*

The Izu Peninsula extends south of the Tokaido Main Line between the stations of Numazu and Atami. It is an area much loved by residents of Tokyo because it contains some very attractive countryside, as well as several spa resorts, and is within easy reach of the big city. It is especially popular for annual company outings. (The author has been obliged to go there twice for such fraternization.) These same reasons make it somewhat less attractive to visitors from overseas. There are always so many people around, especially in summer, and the scenery, although certainly pretty, can be matched by that in some less frequented areas. Thus it is really a place for the locals rather than for overseas visitors, but if you have time you can take a look.

The best way to see the peninsula is probably to perform a loop round it. From Mishima, the Izu Hakone Private Railway runs down to Shuzenji. Trains take 35 minutes and cost ¥470. From Shuzenji, take a bus to the western coast of Izu. The destination of the bus will be Matsuzaki (松崎), but it might be a good idea to get off at Dogashima (堂ヶ島), reached after 1 hour 35 minutes at a cost of ¥1,920. Buses run about twice an hour. **Dogashima** has what is probably the best coastal scenery in Izu. Boat trips from here take you, in calm weather, through natural arches and into caves accessible only from the sea. The voyage takes 20 minutes and costs ¥850. Even if that is beyond your budget, the eroded landscape is pretty from the shore. You will already have seen some pleasant coastal scenery on your way down the coast from Toi on the bus. An alternative to the route so far is to get off the train at Numazu and take an expensive high-speed ferry down the coast. Ferries run about every 2 hours and cost ¥2,270 to Toi (55 minutes), ¥3,090 to Dogashima (80 minutes) and ¥3,290 to Matsuzaki (90 minutes).

From Dogashima there are two bus routes to Shimoda (下田). It is suggested that you take the coastal one. Departures are approximately once an hour until 15:45. The journey takes 1 hour 45 minutes and costs ¥1,700.

You have now reached the south-east of the peninsula. Here you might like to visit the temple known as **Ryosen-ji**, which has some interesting sculptures. It is walking distance from the station. Shimoda also has the best beach in Izu. It is known as **Yumigahama** (弓ヶ浜), but is a 30 minute bus ride (¥560) from the town centre.

There are several youth hostels around Izu, but the nearest to Shimoda is Gensu Hostel which deserves a mention because on the bus route recommended from Dogashima you will actually pass this hostel. Alight from the bus at Minami Izu-machi Yaku-ba (南伊豆町役場), about 1 hour 20 minutes from Dogashima. There is a spa bath in the hostel which is also not too far from Yumigahama.

From Shimoda, the Izu Kyuko Private Railway runs north to the JR terminus at Ito. However, trains from Shimoda do not necessarily terminate at Ito. Most continue to Atami, where the Tokaido Line is rejoined, and the *tokkyu* trains go on all the way to Tokyo, Shinjuku or Ikebukuro. These *tokkyu* departures are called *Odoriko* ('Dancing Girl') or *Super View Odoriko* and operate about hourly in the summer and somewhat less regularly in other seasons. There are also trains called 'Resort 21' and 'Royal Box' running between Shimoda and Atami. These offer special carriages, including, on the 'Royal Box' trains, a 'Salon Car' for which there is a supplement of ¥750 within the Izu Kyuko area or ¥740 within the short JR area. For travel through both areas, the charge is ¥1,000, to be paid on the train. For seats other than these special ones, there is no supplement and the carriages are still of a special design. The fare from Shimoda to Ito is ¥1,440. The *tokkyu* supplement for the Izu Kyuko section of the journey is ¥310 for an unreserved seat, or ¥410 for a reserved seat. Some *tokkyu* trains have only reserved seats. Journey time from Shimoda to Atami is 85 minutes by *tokkyu* or about 1 hour 45 minutes by ordinary train. Ordinary trains run approximately every 45 minutes. From Shimoda to the Tokyo area by *tokkyu* takes 2 hours 45 minutes.

The journey by train along the eastern coast of Izu is a pretty one, although quite a lot of the trip is in tunnels. For the best views, sit on the right of the train from Shimoda. If it is a 'Resort 21' or 'Royal Box' train, try to get a seat at the front on the right.

To the east of the Izu Peninsula are the **Izu Seven Islands** (actually more than seven, but that is what they are called). The most popular one is called Oshima ('Big Island'), which is reasonable, since it is, in fact, the largest. It can be reached from Tokyo by ferry in 8 hours at a cost of ¥3,310. The same ferry, which leaves Tokyo at 22:00 every night, continues to some of the other islands. There are also ferries to Oshima from Atami, Ito and Inatori, near Shimoda. From Atami the ferry takes 2 hours and costs ¥2,380. From Ito it takes 90 minutes and costs ¥2,070. From Inatori it takes 70 minutes and costs ¥2,010. High-speed ferries operate very expensively from Atami and Inatori. From Atami takes 1 hour and costs ¥5,350. From Inatori (summer only) takes 40 minutes and costs ¥4,610. There is a youth hostel – Mihara Sanso – on Oshima, near the port of Motomachi, where most ferries arrive.

Further down the chain of islands is Miyake-jima, which also has a youth hostel and to where there is another direct ferry service from Tokyo. Ferries leave Tokyo at 22:30 every night and reach Miyake-jima at 5:30 at a cost of ¥4,980. Other islands do not have youth hostels, but accommodation is available on all. In summer, the main islands offer camping facilities too.

To reach the Izu Peninsula from Tokyo, one has the choice of the Dancing Girl *tokkyu* trains or the *shinkansen* to Atami, which takes 50 minutes by *Kodama*, and then local transportation. By ordinary train, there is a frequent service to Atami, which takes 2 hours, and there are also occasional *kaisoku* trains, named *Acty*, which travel the distance in 90 minutes.

Coming from the west, as our route supposes, by *Kodama shinkansen* it takes only 30 minutes from Shizuoka to Mishima or 40 minutes to Atami. Trains run two or three times per hour. Sit on the left and, if the weather is kind, you will have a good view of Mt. Fuji. By ordinary train, it takes an hour to Mishima and 80 minutes to Atami. Again trains run two or three times per hour.

There are some special tickets available for Izu. The ticket offered by JR is called an *Izu Free Q Kippu*. It includes return travel from the Tokyo area in unreserved seats of the Dancing Girl or *shinkansen* and unlimited travel by JR, the Izu Kyuko Private Railway and the Izu Hakone Private Railway in the area south of and bordered by the Tokaido Line between Atami and Numazu. It also includes travel on Tokai buses, Izu Hakone buses and Izu Shimoda buses within the same area. The cost is ¥12,860 from Tokyo or ¥11,820 from Yokohama and the ticket is valid for four days. With this ticket, no stop is permitted outside the unlimited travel area.

The Odakyu Private Railway offers two tickets called a *Nishi Izu Free Pass* (West Izu Free Pass) and a *Naka Izu Free Pass* (Central Izu Free Pass). These both include one-way travel from Shinjuku (or another Odakyu station) to Numazu by *Asagiri tokkyu* train, via the Odakyu Railway and the JR Gotenba Line. The journey takes two hours. The West Izu area is bounded by Numazu, Mishima, Shuzenji and Kumomi, just south of Matsuzaki. Travel is permitted by JR between Numazu and Mishima only, by Izu Hakone Railway between Mishima and Shuzenji, by Izu Hakone bus and Hakone Tozan bus between Numazu station and Numazu Port only, by Tokai bus within the unlimited travel area and by the ferries operating between Numazu and Heda and between Numazu and Toi. If a Tokai express bus is used, a ¥200 supplement is payable. The Central Izu area is bounded by Numazu, Mishima, Shuzenji and surrounds including the Cycle Sports Centre, and Mito. Travel is permitted by JR between Numazu and Mishima only, by Izu Hakone Railway between Mishima and Shuzenji and by Tokai bus and Izu Hakone bus within the unlimited travel area. If a Tokai express bus is used, the ¥200 supplement must be paid. Remember that neither ticket includes the return journey to Tokyo and that neither permits anything approximating to the circuit of Izu suggested earlier in this section. The *Nishi Izu Free Pass* costs ¥8,230 from Shinjuku and the *Naka Izu Free Pass* costs ¥5,030 from Shinjuku. Both passes are valid for three days.

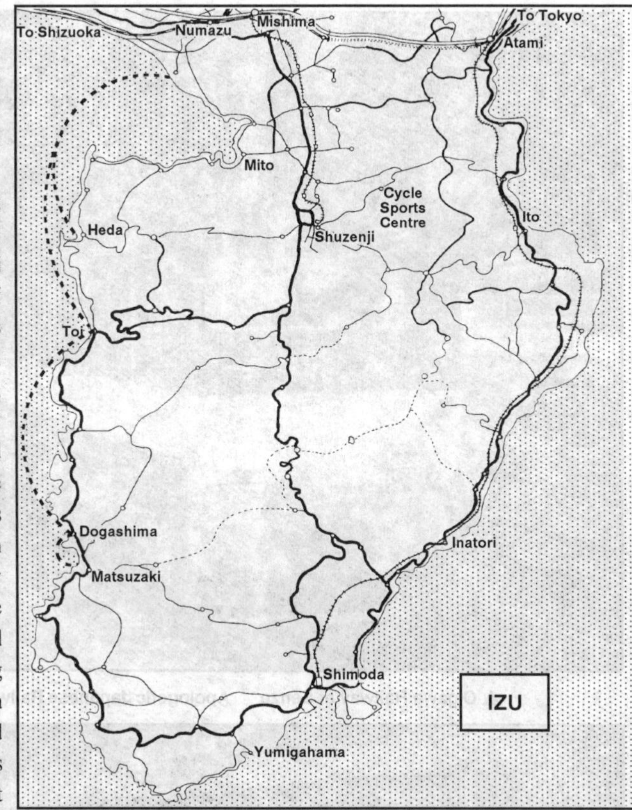


If you decide not to make a stop in Izu, but choose to return directly to Tokyo, those with Japan Rail Passes can take either *Hikari* or *Kodama shinkansen* trains from Shizuoka to Tokyo. *Hikari* trains take 64 minutes, while *Kodama* trains take about 90 minutes. By ordinary train, you will usually have to change at either Numazu or Atami. If you are starting in Kanaya, you may have to change in Shizuoka too. From Kanaya to Shizuoka takes 20 minutes. From Shizuoka to Tokyo with a change *en route* takes about 3½ hours. If you are using an *Hokuriku Wide Shu-yu-ken*, you are entitled to travel in the unreserved section of *kyuko* trains along the designated access routes, and there is a *kyuko* service on this section. Trains leave Shizuoka for Tokyo at 10:29 and 16:54, arriving at 12:57 and 19:30.

▲ Oigawa Railway at Senzu Apologetic Japanese Railway Station ▼

# KANSAI (関西)
## ('West of the Border')

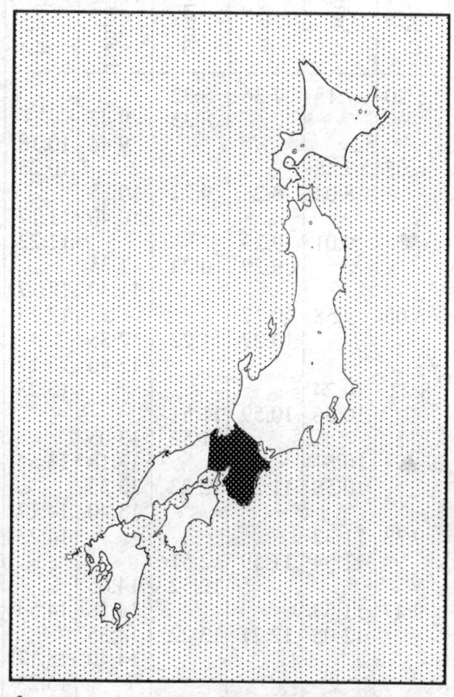

The area around Kyoto, Nara, Osaka and Kobe is generally known as Kansai. In feudal times, checkpoints were set up along the Tokaido, the road which ran between Edo (Tokyo) and Kyoto, and the credentials of all travellers were examined at these points. The principal checkpoint was the one in Hakone which you will have seen if you visited there. In those times, places to the east of that checkpoint were known as Kanto ('East of the Border') and places to the west were Kansai ('West of the Border'). The names have survived, although the definition of Kansai, in particular, is now more limited than it was in feudal times.

The four cities mentioned above are quite different in character. Kyoto and Nara are old historical cities. Osaka is the business city and Kobe is the port. The most interesting, of course, are Kyoto and Nara. If one had to choose a single place in Japan to visit, Kyoto would surely be that place.

Because of its popularity amongst visitors from overseas, as well as amongst Japanese, Kyoto offers a number of private hostels which are listed on pages 467 to 469, together with some lower-priced *ryokan* (Japanese-style hotels). The hostels are generally cheaper than the official youth hostels and popular among overseas visitors. Japanese rarely use such hostels. Probably they do not know of their existence, but, in any case, they would tend to be deterred by their less official atmosphere and worried about the fact that they seem rather cheap.

The cities of Kyoto, Osaka and Kobe spread out and meet one another in the same way as Tokyo, Kawasaki, Yokohama, Chiba and other surrounding cities, making it difficult to know when one passes from one to another. The Kansai area is the territory of private railways, so rail transportation is efficient and cheap, especially along the main corridor running from Kyoto, through Osaka, on to Kobe and beyond to Himeji. More about transport below.

***Transportation and Tickets***

Those with Japan Rail Passes will probably travel directly from Tokyo to Kyoto by *shinkansen*, despite the suggestions made in the preceding 'Chubu' section. Maybe a few people will follow the Chubu plan – and then there will be those who want to get to the Kansai area cheaply and fairly quickly without using a rail pass. Maybe these people have only a short time in Japan, or maybe they are those who have sensibly decided to take their time looking at Kyoto and Nara before commencing the use of their passes.

It is quite possible to travel along the Tokaido Line from Tokyo to Kyoto, and beyond, by

# FROM TOKYO TO KYOTO AND BEYOND BY ORDINARY TRAIN

| Tokyo | Atami | Numazu | Shizuoka | Hamamatsu | Toyohashi | Ogaki | Maibara | Kyoto | Osaka | Himeji | Total Time to Kyoto |
|---|---|---|---|---|---|---|---|---|---|---|---|
| 5:20 | 7:15 | 7:36 | 8:32 | | | | | | | | |
| | | | 8:33 | 9:42 | | | | | | | |
| | | | | 9:44 | 10:18* | | | | | | |
| 6:07 | 7:58 | | | | 10:23 | 11:54 | 12:29 | | | | |
| | 8:04 | 8:26 | 9:22 | 10:35 | | | 12:32 | 13:40 | 14:21 | 15:53* | 8hr 20m |
| | | | | 10:40 | 11:17* | | 12:51 | 13:44 | 14:14 | 15:16 | 8hr 24m |
| ♥ | 9:01 | 9:23 | | | 11:23 | 12:54 | 13:28 | | | | |
| | | 9:29 | 10:22 | 11:35 | | | 13:32 | 14:40 | 15:21 | 16:53* | 8hr 33m |
| | | | | 11:40 | 12:17* | | 13:51 | 14:44 | 15:14 | 16:16 | 8hr 37m |
| 8:03 | 9:58 | 10:17 | | | 12:23 | 13:54 | 14:28 | | | | |
| | | 10:27 | 11:22 | 12:35 | | | 14:32 | 15:40 | 16:21 | 17:53* | 8hr 40m |
| | | | | 12:40 | 13:17* | | 14:51 | 15:44 | 16:14 | 17:16 | 8hr 44m |
| 8:22 | 10:24 | | | | 13:23 | 14:54 | 15:28 | | | | |
| | 10:36 | 10:59 | 11:51 | | | | 15:32 | 16:40 | 17:19 | 18:53* | 8hr 37m |
| | | | 11:52 | 13:05 | | | 15:51 | 16:44 | 17:14 | 18:15 | 8hr 41m |
| ♠ | 10:51 | | | 13:18 | 13:54 | 15:22 | 15:56 | | | | |
| | 10:58 | 11:27 | 12:22 | 13:35 | | | 16:02 | 17:10 | 17:49 | 19:23* | 8hr 48m |
| | | | | 13:40 | 14:17* | | 16:21 | 17:14 | 17:44 | 18:46 | 8hr 52m |
| 9:33 | 11:32 | | | | 14:23 | 15:54 | 16:28 | | | | |
| | 11:34 | 11:59 | 12:51 | | | | 16:32 | 17:40 | 18:19 | 19:54 | 8hr 30m |
| | | | 12:52 | 14:05 | | | 16:51 | 17:44 | 18:14 | 19:16 | 8hr 34m |
| 9:47 | 11:57 | | | 14:18 | 14:54 | 16:22 | 17:01 | | | | |
| | 12:05 | 12:27 | 13:22 | 14:35 | | | 17:02 | 18:10 | 18:49 | 20:26* | 8hr 37m |
| | | | | 14:40 | 15:17* | | 17:21 | 18:14 | 18:44 | 19:46 | 8hr 41m |
| | | | | | 15:23 | 16:54 | 17:28 | | | | |
| 10:43 | 12:37 | 12:56 | | | | | 17:32 | 18:40 | 19:19 | 20:53* | 8hr 53m |
| | | 12:59 | 13:52 | 15:05 | | | 17:51 | 18:44 | 19:14 | 20:15 | 8hr 57m |
| 11:03 | 12:53 | 13:14 | | 15:18 | 15:54 | 17:22 | 17:56 | | | | |
| | | 13:28 | 14:22 | 15:35 | | | 18:02 | 19:10 | 19:49 | 21:23* | 8hr 27m |
| | | | | 15:40 | 16:17* | | 18:21 | 19:14 | 19:44 | 20:45 | 8hr 31m |
| 11:47 | 13:34 | 13:55 | | | 16:20 | 17:59 | 18:33 | | | | |
| | | 13:59 | 14:52 | 16:04 | | | 18:51 | 19:44 | 20:14 | 21:15* | 8hr 41m |
| 11:53 | 13:53 | | | 16:18 | 16:54 | 18:28 | 19:04 | | | | |
| | 13:55 | 14:17 | | | | | 19:21 | 20:14 | 20:44 | 21:48 | 8hr 27m |
| | | 14:27 | 15:22 | 16:35 | | | | | | | |
| | | | | 16:40 | 17:18 | | | | | | |
| 13:40 | 15:12 | | | | 17:23 | 18:56 | 19:31 | | | | |
| | 15:14 | 15:33 | 16:30 | 17:40 | | | 19:37 | 20:45 | 21:24 | 22:54* | 8hr 52m |
| | | | | 17:42 | 18:16* | | 19:56 | 20:49 | 21:19 | 22:25* | 8hr 56m |
| 14:45 | 16:33 | 16:54 | 17:48 | | 18:41 | 20:00 | 20:34 | | | | |
| | | | 18:00 ¶ | 19:01 | | | 20:36 | 21:29 | 21:59 | 23:00* | 7hr 49m |
| | | | | 19:04 | 19:38 | | | | | | |
| 15:03 | 16:51* | | | | 19:41 | 21:00 | 21:34 | | | | |
| | 16:55 | 17:15 | 18:10 | 19:25 | 19:56 | | 21:56 | 22:29 | 22:59 | 24:00* | 7hr 44m |
| | | | | | 20:05 ♦ | 21:59 | 22:38 | | | | |
| | | | | | | | 22:58 | 0:46 | | | 9hr 03m |
| 23:40 ♣ | 1:24 | 1:47 | 2:40 | 4:15 | 4:52 | 6:56 | | | | | |
| | | | | | | 7:03 | 7:50 | 9:01 | 9:36* | | 9hr 21m |
| | | | | | | | 8:19 | 9:14 | 9:44 | 10:46 | 9hr 34m |

Notes: *Train does not terminate at this station. ♥ Starts at Shinagawa at 7:15. ♠ Starts at Shinagawa at 9:27. ¶ 17:50 on holidays. ♦ Change also at Okazaki at 20:39*/ 20:50. ♣ Starts at Shinagawa at holiday times. For details see text.

# FROM KYOTO AND BEYOND TO TOKYO BY ORDINARY TRAIN

| Himeji | Osaka | Kyoto | Maibara | Ogaki | Toyohashi | Hamamatsu | Shizuoka | Numazu | Atami | Tokyo | Total Time from Kyoto |
|---|---|---|---|---|---|---|---|---|---|---|---|
| | | 5:29 | 6:38 | | | | | | | | |
| | | | 6:43 | 7:20 | 9:31 | 10:04 | | | | | |
| | | | | | | 10:20 | 11:31 | 12:22 | | | |
| | 6:23 | 7:02 | 8:15 | | | | | 12:23 | 12:42* | | |
| | | | 8:20 | 8:53 | 10:24 | 10:58 | | | 13:00 | 14:33 | 9hr 04m |
| 6:00 | 7:32 | 8:09 | 9:19 | | | 11:00 | 12:11 | 13:06* | | | |
| | | | 9:21 | 9:53 | 11:24 | 11:58 | | 13:07 | 13:33 | 15:26 | 8hr 24m |
| 6:18 | 7:51 | 8:27 | 9:39 | | | 12:00 | 13:11 | 14:07 | 14:28 | | |
| 6:40 | 7:52 | 8:23 | 9:24* | | | | | | 14:37 | 16:31 | 8hr 22m |
| | | | 9:44 | 10:24 | | | | | | | |
| 7:15 | 8:27 | 8:56* | | 10:41 | 12:00 | | | | | | |
| 6:54 | 8:31 | 9:08 | 10:17 | | 12:04 | 12:40 | 13:51 | 14:49 | 15:05 | | |
| | | | 10:20 | 10:53 | 12:24 | 12:58 | | | 15:07 | 16:37 | 8hr 10m |
| 7:24 | 9:04 | 9:40 | 10:47 | | | 13:00 | 14:11 | 15:13 | 15:31 | | |
| 7:45 | 9:00 | 9:30 | 10:24* | | | | | | 15:39 | 17:30 | 8hr 22m |
| | | | 10:48 | 11:20 | | | | | | | |
| | | | | 11:41 | 13:00 | | | | | | |
| 8:57 | 10:00 | 10:30 | 11:22* | | 13:04 | 13:40 | 14:50 | | | | |
| | | | 11:25 | 11:59 | | | 14:51 | 15:50 | 16:08 | | |
| | | | | 12:11 | 13:30 | | | | 16:14 | 18:10 | 8hr 30m |
| | | | | | 13:44 | 14:18 | | | | | |
| | | 10:35 | 11:43* | | | 14:20 | 15:30 | | | | |
| | | | 11:50 | 12:22 | 13:52 | | 15:31 | 16:28 | 16:45 | | |
| 9:57 | 11:00 | 11:30 | 12:22* | | 14:04 | 14:40 | 15:49 | | 16:47 | 18:38 | 8hr 08m |
| | | 11:35 | 12:43* | | | | 16:01 | 16:54* | | | |
| | | | 12:50 | 13:22 | 14:52 | | | 17:05 | 17:25* | | |
| 10:57 | 12:00 | 12:30 | 13:22* | | 15:04 | 15:40 | 16:50* | | 17:30 | 18:59 ¶ | 8hr 40m |
| | | 12:35 | 13:43* | | | | 17:21 | 18:15 | 18:35 | 20:29 | 8hr 54m |
| | | | 13:50 | 14:22 | 15:52 | | | | | | |
| 11:57 | 13:00 | 13:30 | 14:22* | | 16:04 | 16:48 | 18:04 | 18:57 | | | |
| | | 13:35 | 14:43* | | | | | 18:58 | 19:28 | 21:25♥ | 8hr 50m (8hr 28m) |
| | | | 14:50 | 15:22 | 16:54 | | | | | | |
| 12:57 | 14:00 | 14:30 | 15:22* | | 17:06 | 17:39 | | | | | |
| | | 14:35 | 15:43* | | | 17:40 | 18:54 | 19:59 | 20:26 | | |
| | | | 15:50 | 16:22 | | | | | 20:38 | 22:28 | 8hr 53m |
| | | | | 16:41 | 18:02 | | | | | | |
| 14:27 | 15:30 | 16:00 | 16:54 | | 18:18 | 18:53 | | | | | |
| | | 16:05 | 17:13* | | | 18:55 | 20:03 | | | | |
| | | | 17:14 | 17:52* | | | 20:07 | 21:04 | 21:27 | | |
| | | | | 18:14 | 19:35 | | | | 21:39 | 23:17 ¶ | 9hr 00m |
| | | | | | 19:37 | 20:10 | | | | | |
| 19:28 | 20:30 | 21:00 | 21:54 | | | 20:17 | 21:22 | 22:10 | | | |
| | | | 22:05 | 22:37 | | | | 22:15 | 22:34 | 0:10 ¶ | 8hr 25m |
| | | | | 22:40 | 0:36 | 1:03 | 2:00 | 2:56 | 3:14 | 4:42 | 7hr 42m |

Notes: * Train does not terminate at this station.
¶ Terminates at Shinagawa.
♥ Change at Odawara at 19:49 / 19:51 to arrive in Tokyo at 21:03.

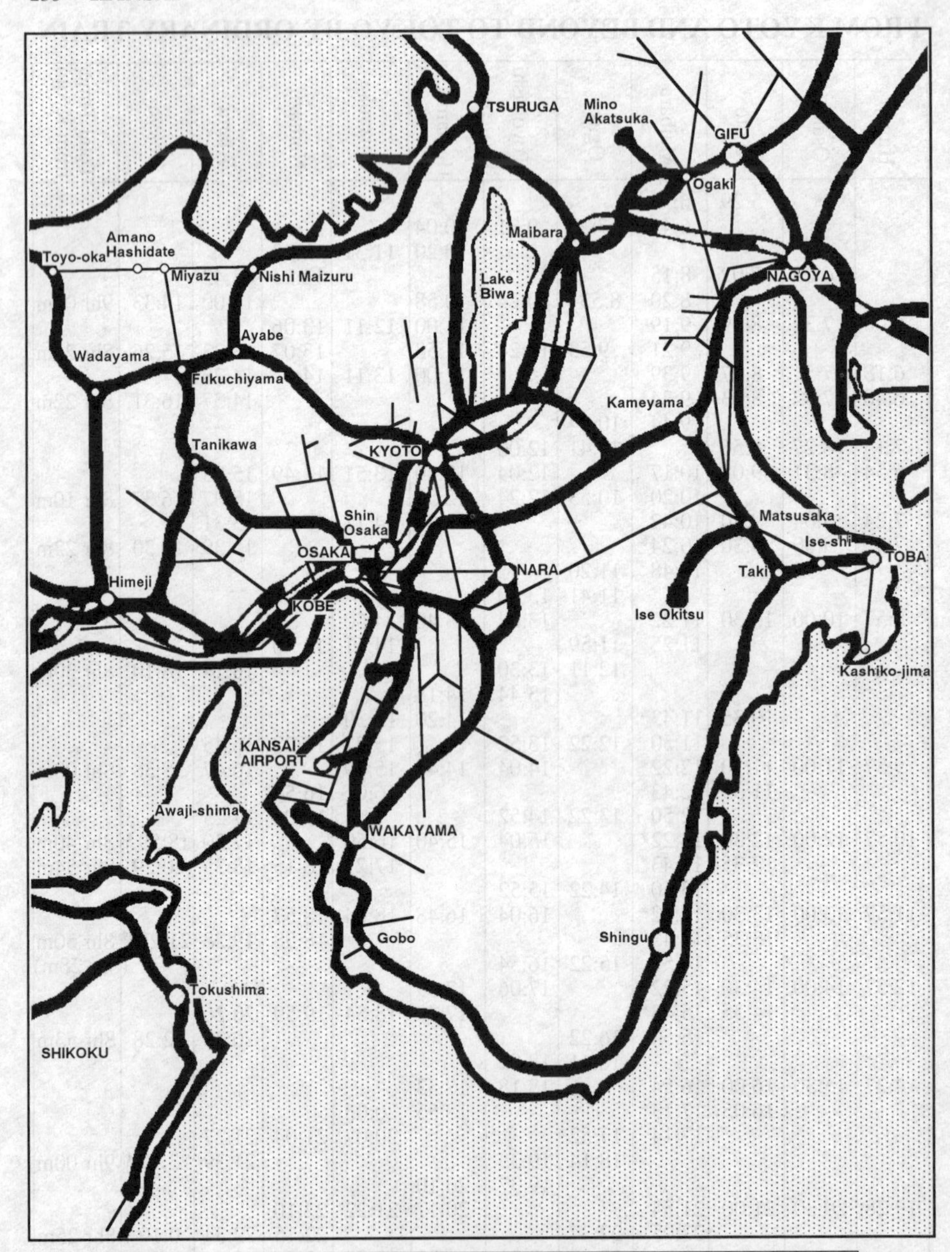


**KANSAI**

**SHOWING RAILWAYS, PRINCIPAL TOWNS AND PLACES OF INTEREST**

ordinary trains in a single day. If it is Blue Spring season, this can be done at a cost of ¥2,260, which is really very good value. If it is not Blue Spring season, it will cost ¥7,830, but you will have four days in which to complete the journey, so can stop along the way if you wish. The Tourist Information Centres even distribute sheets showing ordinary train connexions for this route. The author is uncertain whether these show all suitable trains or not, but offers his own schedule on pages 236 and 237. A change of line indicates a change of train. By day, one must change trains several times *en route*, but by night there is a train, rather famous and popular amongst young people especially, which runs from Tokyo all the way to Ogaki, where a single change will take you to Kyoto, Osaka and beyond. This night train is particularly crowded and uncomfortable, especially at school holiday times, which correspond with Blue Spring seasons. The seats are absolutely upright and far from conducive to a good night's sleep. Queues start to form on the platform hours before the train's departure. If you want a seat at all, be there at least an hour before the train is due to leave. If you want a good seat, which means a window seat, so that you have something against which to rest your head, it would be better to arrive two hours in advance. On the whole, the author suggests the use of day trains. Although the scenery is not spectacular, you will get a glimpse of Mt. Fuji, if the weather is kind, and see a little of the coast. If you do decide to travel by night, note that at holiday times two trains operate, so popular is this choice, and that, to avoid congestion of the platforms at Tokyo, the trains start during these periods at Shinagawa station, also on the Yamanote Line. If you are using Blue Spring tickets, also note that the night train starts from Tokyo at 23:40, while your Blue Spring ticket will start at midnight. Therefore, buy an ordinary ticket from Tokyo, or your station of origin, to Yokohama, the first stop after midnight. Do not, however, decide to board the train at Yokohama, for you will not be likely to get a seat there, or certainly not a comfortable seat. When two trains are operating, the schedule is arranged so that the second departure overtakes the first along the way, at Hamamatsu, encouraging those who want to go no further to take the first train and those who are travelling beyond to take the second, thus spreading the load more evenly. At such times, you need buy an ordinary ticket only as far as Kawasaki, which is reached by both trains after midnight.

If you are buying an ordinary return ticket for the journey to Kansai, remember that there is a 10% reduction on return tickets where the single journey is over 600 kilometres. Now the distance from Tokyo to Kyoto is 514 kilometres, so the return ticket costs ¥15,660 and you have eight days in which to complete the return journey. If you buy a return ticket as far as Himeji, however, which you will almost certainly want to visit, the distance is 645 kilometres and the cost is ¥16,870 with the return journey to be completed in ten days, which represents better value. As usual, though, better still is a *shu-yu-ken* (excursion ticket).

There are two special tickets available for this area. The first, and the one which is recommended, is the *Kei-han-shin Mini Shu-yu-ken*. The reason for the name is that *kei* is an alternative reading for the *kyo* of Kyoto. *Han* is an alternative reading for the *saka* of Osaka and *shin* is an alternative reading for the *ko* of Kobe. The ticket includes a return journey from Tokyo, or a variety of other starting points, to the Kansai area by ordinary or *kyuko* train and unlimited travel within the area shown on the map on page 242. This area includes Kyoto, Nara, Osaka and Kobe and continues as far west as Nishi Akashi, 32 kilometres short of Himeji. Because the ticket is a 'mini' *shu-yu-ken*, express trains other than *kyuko* cannot be used even within the unlimited travel area. If you wish to use the *shinkansen* to reach the Kansai area or return from it, you pay just the supplement. The cost of a *Kei-han-shin Mini*

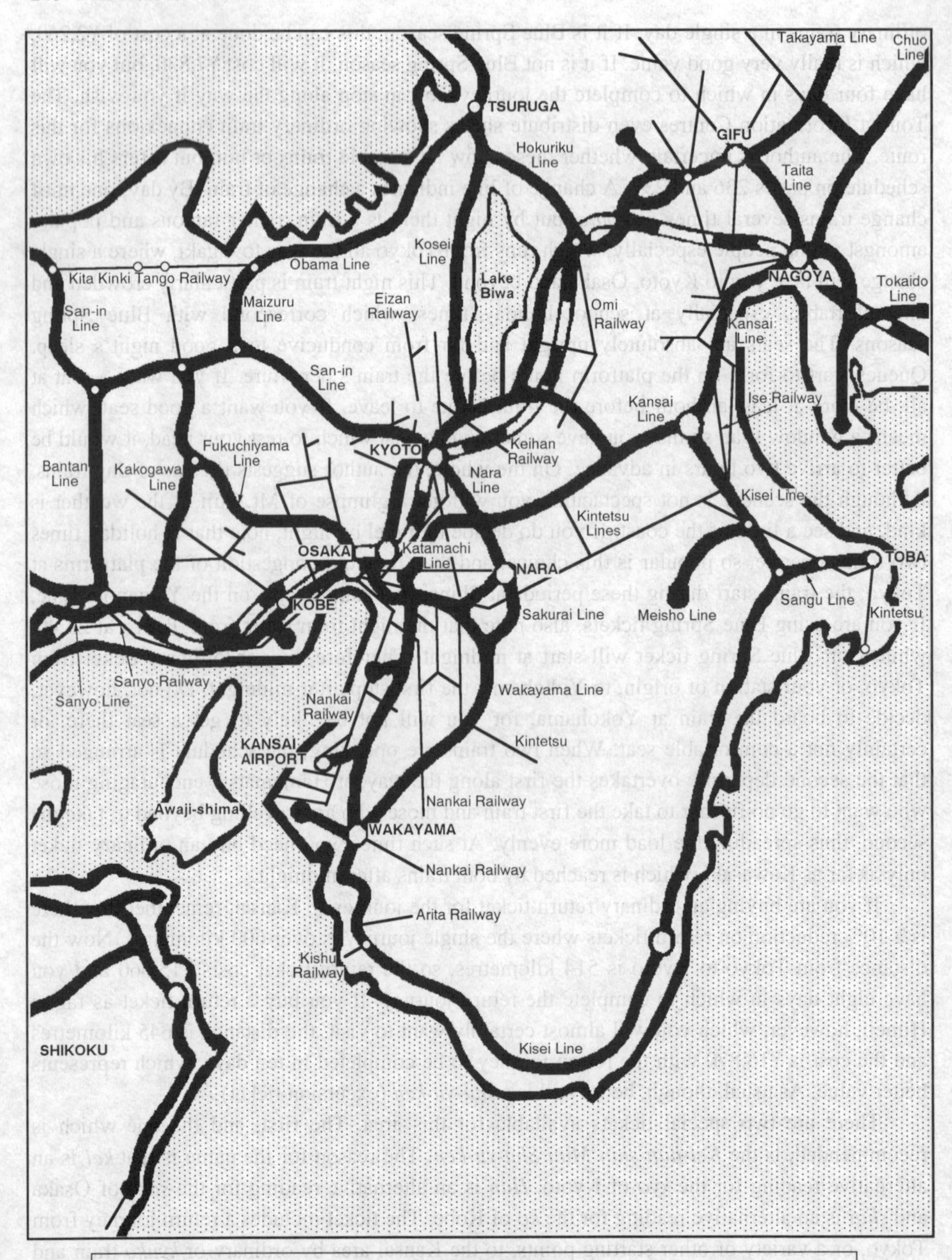


## KANSAI
### SHOWING RAILWAY LINES

JR Shinkansen
JR Conventional Lines
Private Railways

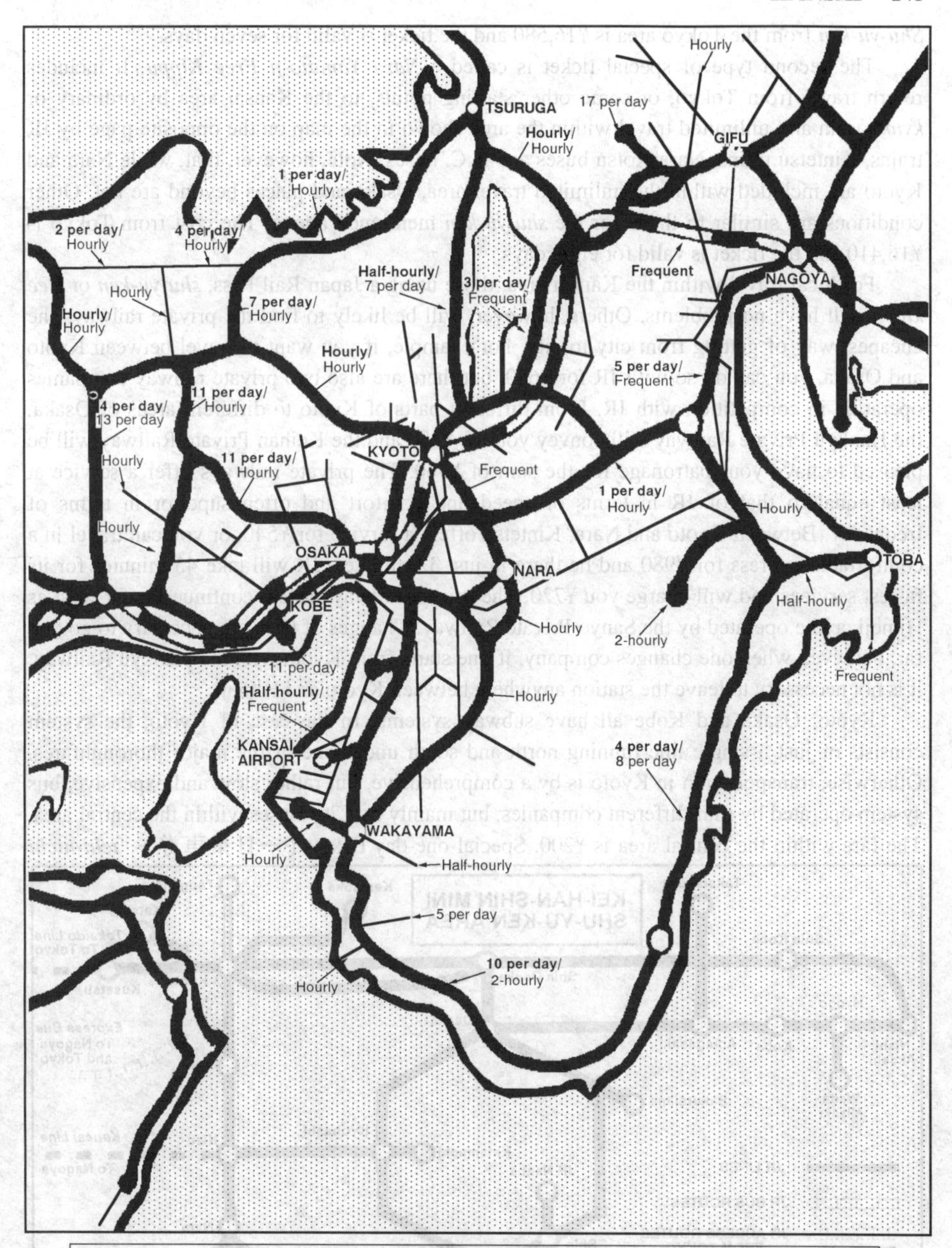


## KANSAI

**SHOWING TRAIN FREQUENCIES**

**Bold type – Express trains**

Standard type – Ordinary trains

(Where not indicated, services are frequent)

*Shu-yu-ken* from the Tokyo area is ¥16,580 and the ticket is valid for seven days.

The second type of special ticket is called a *Nara Yamato-ji Free Kippu*. It includes return travel from Tokyo, or some other starting points, to the Kansai area by ordinary or *kyuko* train and unlimited travel within the area shown in the map on the opposite page by JR trains, Kintetsu trains, Nara Kotsu buses and N.C. buses. Note, however, that, while Nara and Kyoto are included within the unlimited travel area, Osaka and places beyond are not. Other conditions are similar to those for the *shu-yu-ken* mentioned above. The cost from Tokyo is ¥16,410 and the ticket is valid for eight days.

For local travel within the Kansai area, those using a Japan Rail Pass, *shu-yu-ken* or *free kippu* will have no problems. Others, however, will be likely to find the private railways the cheapest way of getting from city to city. For example, if you want to travel between Kyoto and Osaka, you can do so with JR for ¥680, but there are also two private railway companies operating in competition with JR. From different parts of Kyoto to different areas of Osaka, the Hankyu Private Railway will convey you for ¥350 and the Keihan Private Railway will be pleased to have your patronage for the sum of ¥360. The private railways offer a service at least equal to that of JR in terms of speed and comfort and often superior in terms of frequency. Between Kyoto and Nara, Kintetsu offers a service for ¥540, or you can travel in a comfortable express for ¥980 and be there in just 32 minutes. JR will take 45 minutes for its fastest services and will charge you ¥720. The private railway system continues as far west as Himeji, a line operated by the Sanyo Private Railway. Changes of train are necessary to go that far, but, even when one changes company, if one starts from Kyoto with the Hankyu Railway, it is not necessary to leave the station anywhere between Kyoto and Himeji.

Kyoto, Osaka and Kobe all have subway systems. In the case of Kyoto, the system consists of just a single line running north and south under one of the major thoroughfares. Otherwise, transportation in Kyoto is by a comprehensive, but rather slow and expensive, bus system operated by four different companies, but mainly by City Buses within the central area. The fare within the central area is ¥200. Special one-day tickets (一日乗車券 – *'ichi-nichi*

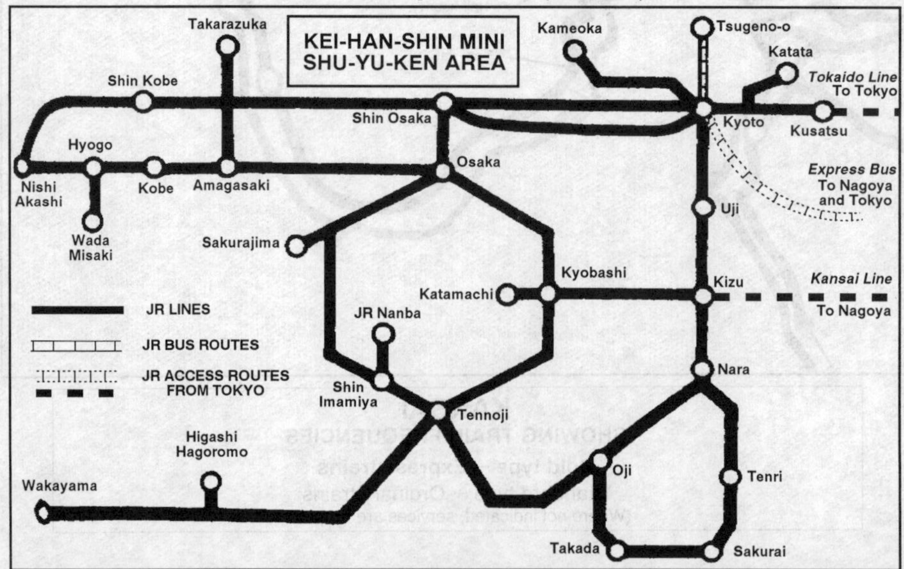

*jo-sha-ken'*) and two-day tickets (二日乗車券－ *'futsu-ka jo-sha-ken'*) are offered for use on City Buses, Kyoto Buses within the city area and the subway. However, they are rather expensive at ¥1,200 for one day and ¥2,000 for two days. Kyoto also offers a bus plus subway single-journey ticket, for those who need to change from one to the other. It gives a discount on the combination of the two fares. At subway stations, it can be purchased from a machine (but remember to take the ticket from the automatic gate when you leave the station). On the bus, it can be purchased by telling the driver what you want (*'bus plus chika-tetsu kippu'*), although, of course, you can buy such a ticket only when getting off at a subway station. You will be given a voucher which you then insert into the ticket machine in the subway station. The voucher is for the minimum subway fare, so, if you want to go further, you add coins for the extra amount. Then press the appropriate fare button and out pops your ticket.

In Osaka, the subway system is quite comprehensive. A map is shown on the last of the colour pages. The system is supplemented by buses and, as in Kyoto, in some cases a bus plus subway ticket is available. A one-day ticket (一日乗車券－ *'ichi-nichi jo-sha-ken'*) is available for Osaka buses, subway and 'new tram' (an elevated train running on rubber tyres without rails) for ¥850. On the 20th of each month (or the next day if the 20th is a holiday), the ticket is available for ¥600, in an effort to discourage the use of cars for one day.

The Keifuku Private Railway in Kyoto offers a one-day ticket (*'Arashiyama-sen ichi-nichi kanko jo-sha-ken'*－嵐山線一日観光乗車券) for ¥550.

In Kobe, there is just a single subway route. Although there are three 'lines', in fact most trains just run through from one end of the system to the other.

It should be mentioned that, since the opening of the new Kansai Airport in September 1994, Osaka has become an increasingly possible entry point into Japan. It is the nation's only 24 hour airport. If you arrive here, transportation is not difficult. The airport is on an artificial island in the bay and new railway lines have been constructed to it. Services are operated by both JR and the Nankai Private Railway. JR runs a *tokkyu* named *Haruka* to Kyoto via Osaka. It takes 45 minutes to Shin Osaka and 75 minutes to Kyoto. JR also runs ordinary trains to Osaka in 65 minutes. The Nankai Private Railway operates *tokkyu* and *kyuko* trains to Nanba, in the south of Osaka, 30 to 35 minutes by *tokkyu* or 45 minutes by *kyuko*. There are buses to Nara, a journey which takes 95 minutes. More detailed information is given in the section on the Kansai Airport on page 263.

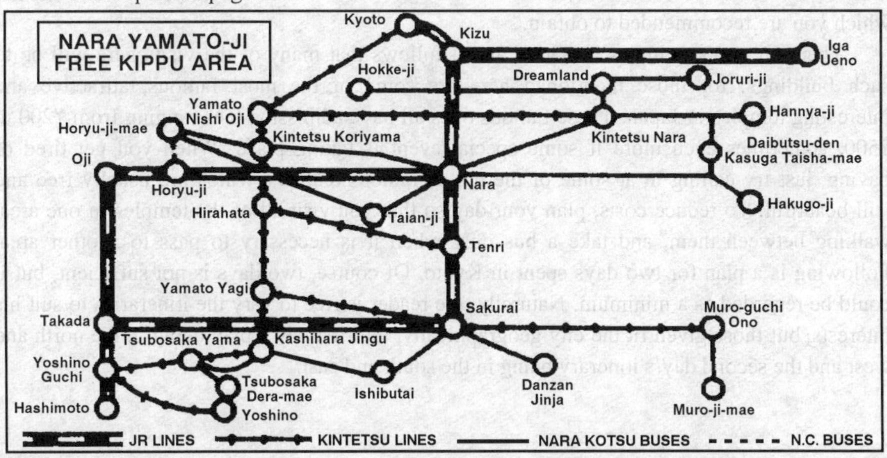

# KYOTO (京都 – 'Capital City')

**Tokaido *shinkansen*, 2 hrs. 45 mins. from Tokyo**

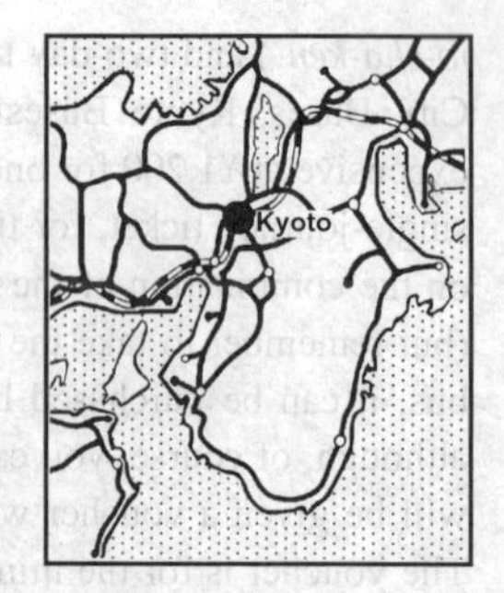


**Derivation of Name:** *Literal.*

Kyoto, 'Capital City', was just that from 794 until the Meiji Restoration in 1868. It is the single most important and interesting place in Japan to visit and, whatever else you have to leave off your itinerary, you should not omit Kyoto. Although it is the seventh largest city in Japan, with a population of almost 1.5 million, Kyoto often has the atmosphere of a town rather than a city. If it were not for the incessant and noisy traffic, it would be a tranquil place to visit. There is so much to see that one feels that one could spend weeks here. For more than a thousand years, Kyoto has been the cultural and Buddhist centre of Japan and such traditions can hardly fail to create a special atmosphere. In addition, Kyoto was the only major city to be spared serious damage during the war, mainly because it was not an important industrial centre, so the centuries-old temples and other buildings have survived here when they have been destroyed in other places. This is not to say that today's Kyoto is just as it was a century ago. When you step out of the railway station (which has the longest platform in Japan, incidentally), you will see a bustling modern city and think that what you have read about the sustaining of tradition here is all a joke. However, Kyoto has a Jekyll and Hyde personality. The bustling centre hides the tradition which exists geographically, as well as figuratively, all around, for the old temples ring the city and seem to define its limits. Even in the centre, though, a stroll away from the main streets will bring you to little alleys hiding unsuspected beautiful little temples and traditional wooden homes crowded together. Kyoto is indeed a fascinating city and one which the visitor soon comes to love and to want to explore more. It is a place to which one keeps coming back, if possible, making it a halt on any trip. However, of course, most visitors do not have infinite time, so this book will try to pick out just a few of the many attractions which should not be missed.

Your first stop in Kyoto should be the **Tourist Information Centre**, which is very near the station. Cross the bus terminal and walk a few metres along the street straight ahead. The Tourist Information Centre is on your left and can provide colour maps and plenty of other useful pieces of paper, including a leaflet of suggested walks in the city, which is a sheet which you are recommended to obtain.

There are 1,600 temples in Kyoto and it follows that many of the visits here will be to such buildings, for those mentioned here are some of the most famous, attractive and interesting temples in Japan. These famous ones all have admission fees ranging from ¥200 to ¥500, sometimes even more if some special event is taking place. When you get tired of paying, just try calling in at some of the not-so-famous temples, which are usually free and still beautiful. To reduce costs, plan your day so that you visit all of the temples in one area, walking between them, and take a bus only when it is necessary to pass to another area. Following is a plan for two days spent in Kyoto. Of course, two days is not sufficient, but it could be regarded as a minimum. Naturally, the reader is free to vary the itineraries to suit his interests, but those given fit the city geographically, the first day's plan being in the north and west and the second day's itinerary being in the south and east.

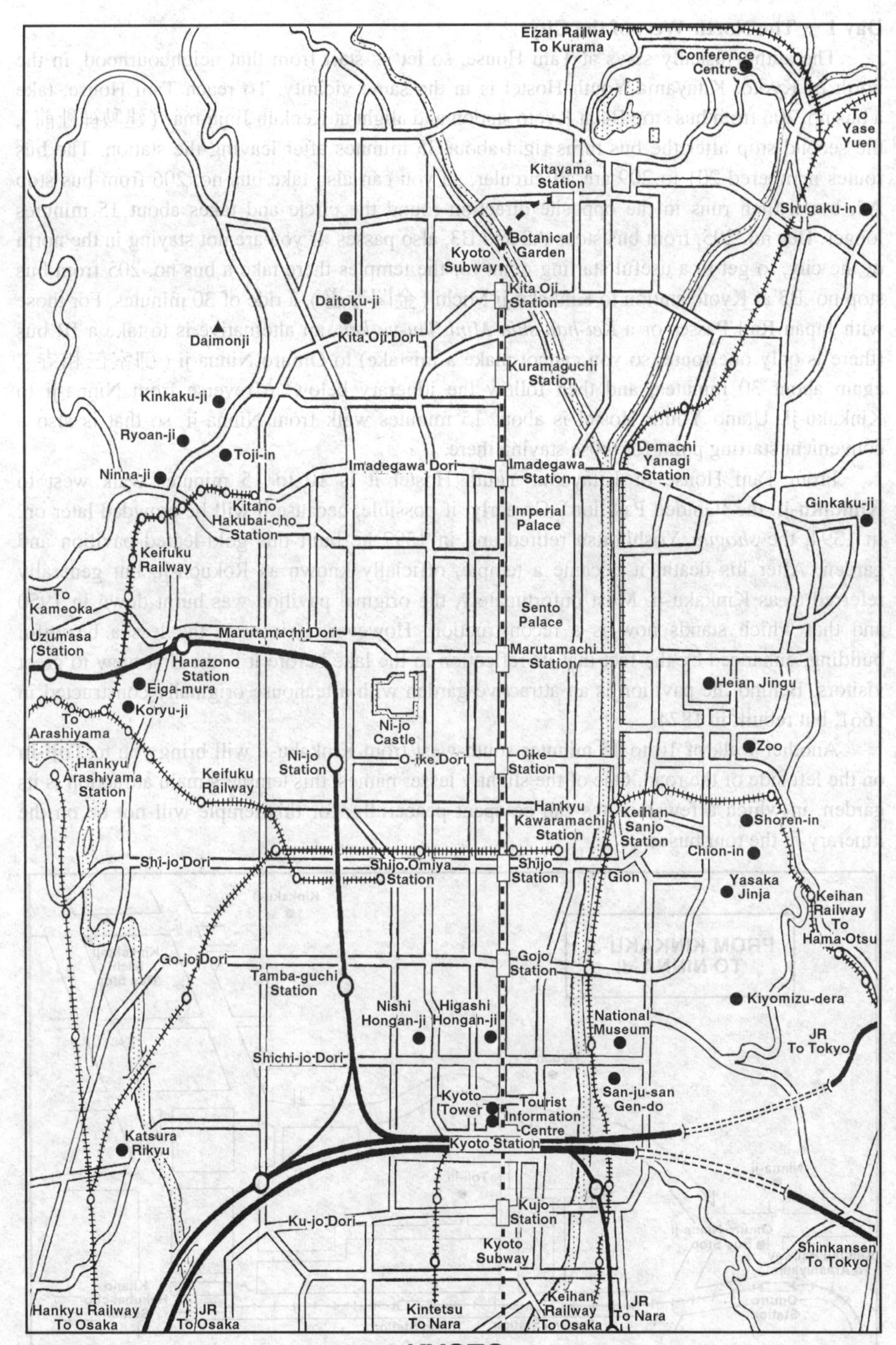

Eizan Railway
To Kurama
Conference Centre
To Yase Yuen
Kitayama Station
Shugaku-in
Botanical Garden
Kyoto Subway
Kita Oji Station
Daitoku-ji
Kita Oji Dori
Daimonji
Kuramaguchi Station
Kinkaku-ji
Ryoan-ji
Toji-in
Demachi Yanagi Station
Imadegawa Dori
Imadegawa Station
Ninna-ji
Kitano Hakubai-cho Station
Imperial Palace
Ginkaku-ji
Keifuku Railway
To Kameoka
Sento Palace
Uzumasa Station
Marutamachi Dori
Hanazono Station
Marutamachi Station
Eiga-mura
Koryu-ji
Heian Jingu
To Arashiyama
Ni-jo Castle
Zoo
Hankyu Arashiyama Station
Ni-jo Station
O-ike Dori
Oike Station
Keifuku Railway
Hankyu Kawaramachi Station
Keihan Sanjo Station
Shoren-in
Chion-in
Shi-jo Dori
Shijo Omiya Station
Shijo Station
Gion
Yasaka Jinja
Keihan Railway To Hama-Otsu
Go-jo Dori
Gojo Station
Tamba-guchi Station
Kiyomizu-dera
Nishi Hongan-ji
Higashi Hongan-ji
National Museum
JR To Tokyo
Shichi-jo Dori
San-ju-san Gen-do
Kyoto Tower
Tourist Information Centre
Katsura Rikyu
Kyoto Station
Kujo Station
Ku-jo Dori
Kyoto Subway
Shinkansen To Tokyo
Hankyu Railway To Osaka
JR To Osaka
Kintetsu To Nara
Keihan Railway To Osaka
JR To Nara


KYOTO

**Day 1 – The North-West of the City**

The author usually stays at Tani House, so let us start from that neighbourhood, in the north of Kyoto. Kitayama Youth Hostel is in the same vicinity. To reach Tani House, take a bus no. 206 from bus stop B4 at Kyoto station and alight at Kenkun Jinja-mae (建勲神社前), the second stop after the bus turns right about 35 minutes after leaving the station. The bus routes numbered 201 to 209 are all circular, so you can also take bus no. 206 from bus stop A2, but it then runs in the opposite direction round the circle and takes about 15 minutes longer. Bus no. 205, from bus stops A3 and B3, also passes. If you are not staying in the north of the city, to get to a useful starting point for the temples there take a bus no. 205 from bus stop no. B3 at Kyoto station to Kinkaku-ji Michi (金閣寺道), a ride of 30 minutes. For those with Japan Rail Passes or a *Kei-han-shin Mini Shu-yu-ken*, an alternative is to take a JR bus (there is only one route, so you cannot make a mistake) to Omuro Ninna-ji (御室仁和寺), again about 30 minutes, and then follow the itinerary below in reverse from Ninna-ji to Kinkaku-ji. Utano Youth Hostel is about 15 minutes walk from Ninna-ji, so that is also a convenient starting point for those staying there.

From Tani House or Kitayama Youth Hostel it is 10 to 15 minutes walk west to **Kinkaku-ji**, the 'Golden Pavilion'. Go early, if possible, because it will be crowded later on. In 1394, the *shogun* Yoshimitsu retired and in 1397 he built this gold-leafed pavilion and garden. After his death, it became a temple, officially known as Rokuon-ji, but generally referred to as Kinkaku-ji. Most unfortunately, the original pavilion was burnt down in 1950 and that which stands now is a reconstruction. However, it is none the less a beautiful building, enhanced by the fact that its reflection in the lake before it is the first view to greet visitors. Behind the pavilion is an attractive garden with a teahouse originally constructed in 1661, but rebuilt in 1874.

Another walk of 10 to 15 minutes south-west from Kinkaku-ji will bring you to **Toji-in** on the left side of the road. One of the slightly lesser names, this temple's main attraction is its garden, in which a few minutes can be spent peacefully, for this temple will not be on the itinerary of the tour buses.

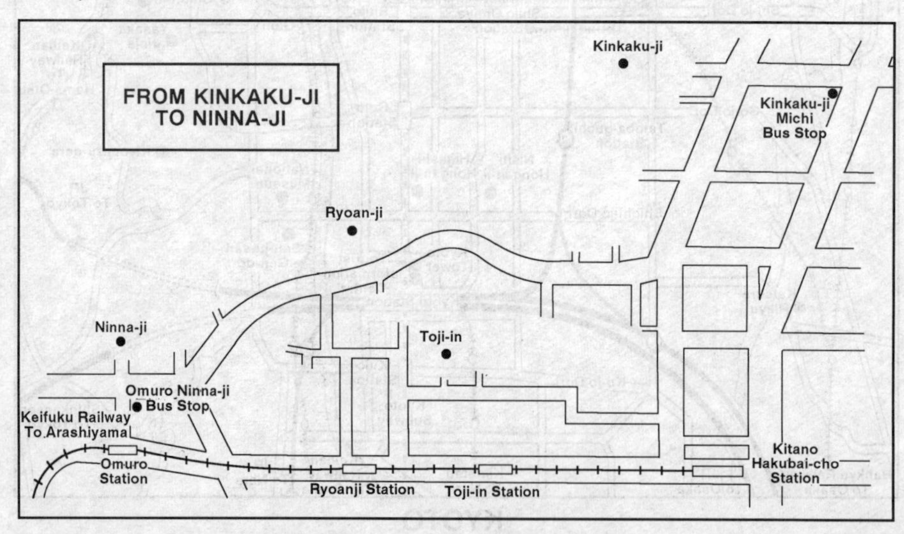

Return to the main road and in 5 minutes you will reach **Ryoan-ji**, which offers the most famous rock garden in Japan. The temple, from the verandah of which you will view the garden, was constructed in 1448. However, it was destroyed by fire and the present building dates from the eighteenth century. The garden, though, is just sand and rocks, so suffered no damage and is believed to be unchanged from the time when it was constructed in about 1450. It is not as big as you might expect, about 30 metres by 15 metres, but it contains no foliage at all, which was the fashion at the time of its design. It is customary to sit on the steps provided and meditate about such matters as the meaning of the garden, the meaning of life itself and perhaps the price which you have had to pay to view this revelation. If the atmosphere is peaceful, some of the admirers may seem to drop into something a little deeper than meditation. Usually, however, the peace is being shattered by the next tour bus load of arrivals. Again it is best to go early, if possible. Do not just leave by the front entrance after viewing the temple and rock garden. Outside there is a pretty garden of the more traditional kind which you can wander through on your way out.

Next is **Ninna-ji**, another temple not quite at the top of the tour bus list and extensive enough to seem uncrowded. The main features are the huge gate, which you can hardly miss, as it is on the main street, the gods which guard the gate and some of the interior decoration.

Strike south now and in a very short time you will come to Omuro station on the charming little Keifuku Private Railway. Take a train in a westerly direction to Keifuku Arashiyama. You will have to change trains on the way when you meet the main Keifuku Line at Katabira-no Tsuji. The total journey is 4 kilometres, which will cost ¥190. If you have visited the above temples in reverse order, from Kinkaku-ji walk south along the main road (Nishi Oji Dori) for about 15 minutes until you reach, on your right, Kitano Hakubai-cho station, which is the terminus of the Keifuku Railway, and take the train to Arashiyama from there, a journey of 6 kilometres at a cost of ¥210.

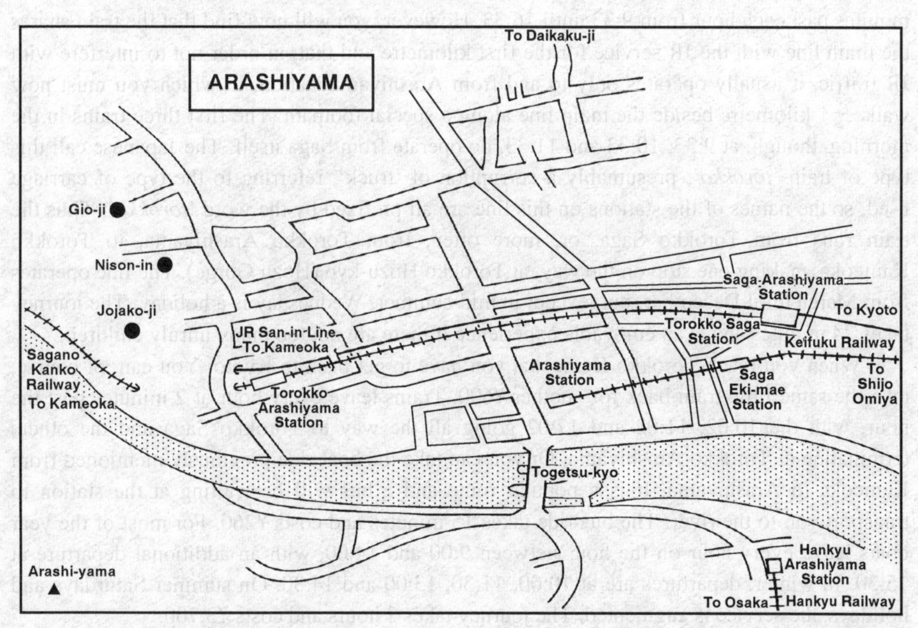

**Arashiyama** is a famous area of Kyoto. The Emperors used to come here on their days off as long ago as the end of the eighth century. It is a particularly beautiful place at cherry blossom time and in autumn, when the steep riverside is ablaze with red and orange maple leaves. Of course, at such times it is even more crowded than usual. Just wander around and you will start to get the feel of the area. There are several attractive temples on the hill a little beyond where the railway ends. Try visiting Jojako-ji, Nison-in and Gio-ji (see map), or walk further up on to the hill. Togetsu-kyo, the traditional bridge which spans the river, is frequently featured in tourist literature. There are expensive boat rides along the river, but only from Kameoka to Arashiyama, not in the other direction. However, we shall be going to Kameoka soon, so you can take the boat for the return journey if you wish, and have sufficient money.

When you have finished admiring Arashiyama, make your way to JR Saga Arashiyama station, which lies on the San-in Line. Over a period of years, JR and its predecessor, JNR, have been trying to make improvements to this route. It is still an awkward line, as it has electrified sections interspersed with non-electrified areas, so that, by ordinary train, it is necessary to keep changing. Expresses use diesel units and run right through electrified and non-electrified sections. The San-in Line passes through some hilly countryside and so it was originally built with many twists and turns. A few years ago, however, parts of the line were straightened out by the construction of long tunnels. Following this, comments were heard that, although the new line was fast, the scenic beauty of the old one had been lost and it was decided to run a train solely for tourist purposes on the old line, a venture which has proven quite unexpectedly successful. This tourist railway is called the Sagano Kanko Railway (Sagano Sightseeing Railway). A diesel engine pulls four small carriages slowly along the old scenic track, at a cost of ¥600 for the 7 kilometre journey. There is a special station to the left of the main JR Saga Arashiyama station and there you must go to reserve your seat (included in the charge). You cannot just get on the train without a reservation. Trains leave at 33 minutes past each hour from 9:33 until 16:33. However, you will now find that the train shares the main line with the JR service for the first kilometre and that, in order not to interfere with JR traffic, it usually operates only to and from Arashiyama station, to which you must now walk – 1 kilometre beside the main line along a special footpath. The first three trains in the morning, though, at 9:33, 10:33 and 11:33, do operate from Saga itself. The Japanese call this type of train '*torokko*', presumably a corruption of 'truck', referring to the type of carriage used, so the names of the stations on this line are all prefixed by the word '*torokko*'. Thus the train runs from Torokko Saga, or, more often, from Torokko Arashiyama, to Torokko Kameoka, making one stop on the way, at Torokko Hozu-kyo (Hozu Gorge). The line operates from March until December, but, except in mid-summer, Wednesday is a holiday. The journey takes 24 minutes and is an enjoyable experience if there are not too many unruly children.

When you reach Torokko Kameoka, you have to get back to Kyoto. You can, of course, take the same little train back for another ¥600. Trains leave every hour at 2 minutes past the hour, with the 10:02, 11:02 and 17:02 going all the way to Torokko Saga and the others terminating at Torokko Arashiyama. Or you can take the boat ride previously mentioned from Kameoka to Arashiyama. It is a popular route and a bus will be waiting at the station to transport you to the river. The bus ride takes 15 minutes and costs ¥260. For most of the year boats leave every hour on the hour between 9:00 and 14:00, with an additional departure at 15:30. In winter, departures are at 10:00, 11:30, 13:00 and 14:30. On summer Saturdays and holidays, the service is augmented. The journey takes 2 hours and costs ¥3,700.

Or, of course, one can take the JR service back to Kyoto, which is the cheap way to return. There is not much in the vicinity of Torokko Kameoka station, but it has been constructed in that place because, a little further on, the course of the old line crossed the new one and so it would create problems to continue any further. If you look along the new line, you can see Umahori station about 600 metres down the track. This is also a new station. The old one is over to the left, in the heart of the village. It is a pity, really, that the disused station could not have become the terminus for the tourist railway, but it is on the wrong side of the main line. If you walk to Umahori station, you can catch a train back to Kyoto. If you prefer, you can have a look at the rural community on the side of the hill on your left before returning. Trains run about every 20 minutes, taking 8 minutes back to Saga Arashiyama or about 30 minutes to Kyoto. For those with a *Kei-han-shin Mini Shu-yu-ken*, this is within your area, which extends to Kameoka, the station beyond Umahori.

If you find yourself unable to get a seat on the Sagano Kanko Railway from Torokko Saga or Arashiyama, take a JR train to Umahori and travel back on the tourist train. You can nearly always get a seat in that direction because many people choose a one-way journey starting in Saga. And that will be enough sightseeing for one day, you will find. Tomorrow, let us start near Kyoto station.

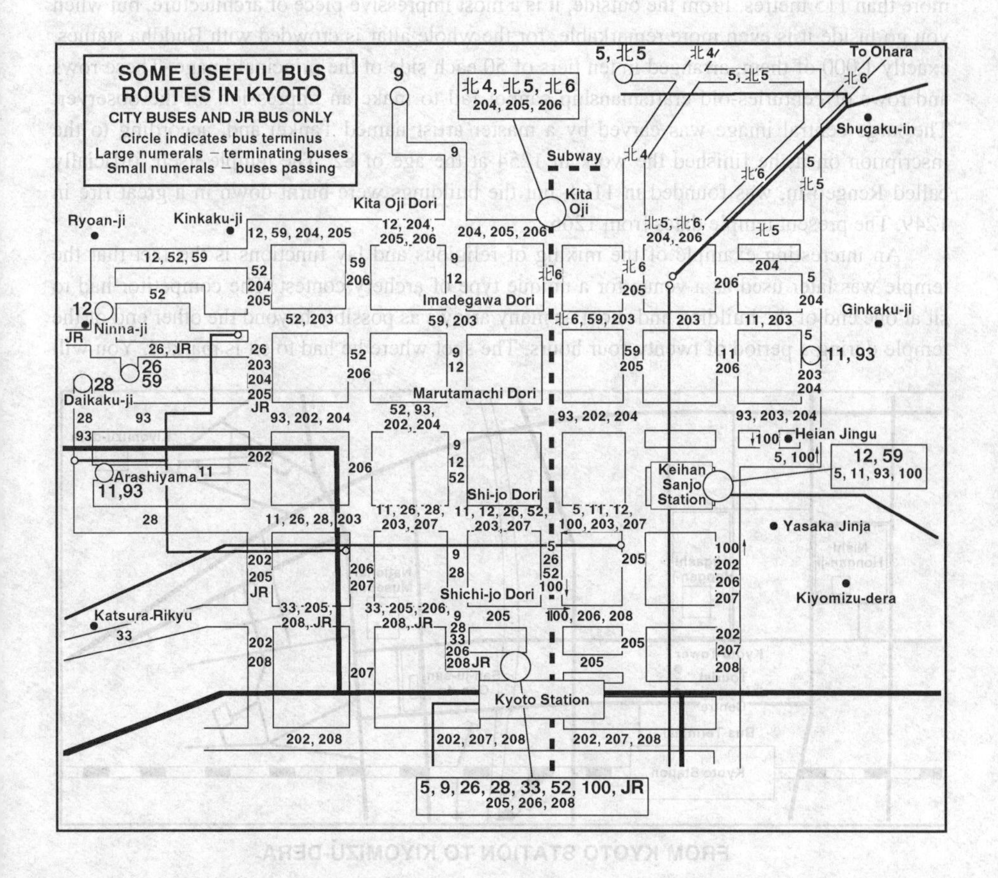

**Day 2 – The South-East of the City**

Standing in the bus terminal area, we have the station at our back and the Central Post Office on our left. Let us advance to the main road ahead (Shiokoji Dori) and turn left and then right at the first major junction. From here a walk of 5 minutes, a total of 10 minutes from the station, will bring us to **Nishi Hongan-ji** ('West Hongan Temple') on the left, sometimes claimed to be the best example of Buddhist architecture in Japan. It was constructed in 1591, but burnt down later, so that the present buildings date from the seventeenth and eighteenth centuries. Some of the buildings can be seen only on guided tours at fixed times.

Proceeding due east from here for five minutes will bring you to **Higashi Hongan-ji** ('East Hongan Temple'), which temple was separated from Nishi Hongan-ji in 1602. It is now the headquarters of the largest Buddhist sect in the country. However, the present buildings, which are quite impressive, date only from 1895.

Following the main street and still proceeding east, we shall come to **San-ju-san Gen-do**, on our right, its lengthy name meaning '33 Alcoves Hall'. 33 is an auspicious number in Buddhism, so this temple has been constructed with 33 spaces between the pillars along its altar. This makes the front of the building very wide, so wide that, before you go inside, you might think that the front is the side and vice versa. It is, in fact, the widest temple in Japan – more than 115 metres. From the outside, it is a most impressive piece of architecture, but when you go inside it is even more remarkable, for the whole altar is crowded with Buddha statues, exactly 1,000 of them, arranged in ten tiers of 50 each side of the principal image. These rows and rows of centuries-old craftsmanship cannot fail to make an impression on the observer. The large central image was carved by a master artist named Tankei and, according to the inscription on it, he finished the work in 1254 at the age of 82. The temple itself, officially called Rengeo-in, was founded in 1164, but the buildings were burnt down in a great fire in 1249. The present temple dates from 1266.

An interesting example of the mixing of religious and lay functions is the fact that the temple was later used as a venue for a unique type of archery contest. The competitor had to sit at one end of the building and shoot as many arrows as possible beyond the other end of the temple during a period of twenty-four hours. The spot where he had to sit is marked. You will

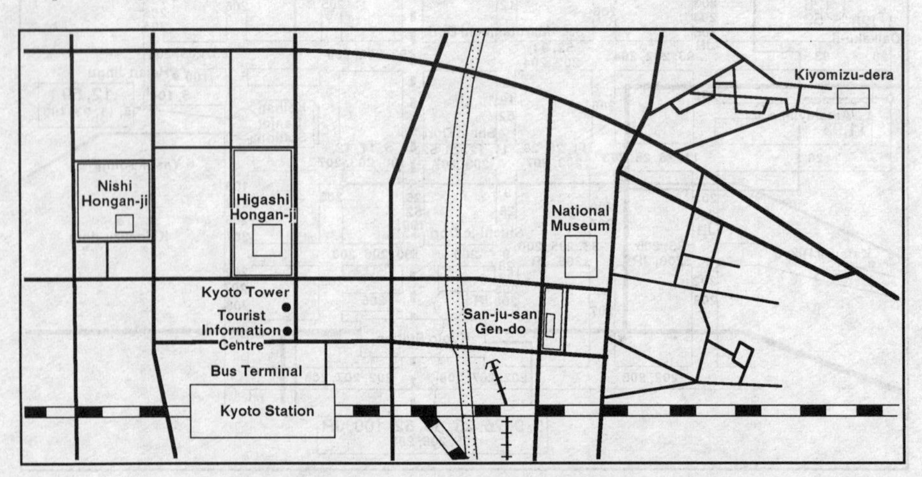


**FROM KYOTO STATION TO KIYOMIZU-DERA**

# MAP OF TOKYO SUBWAY SYSTEM

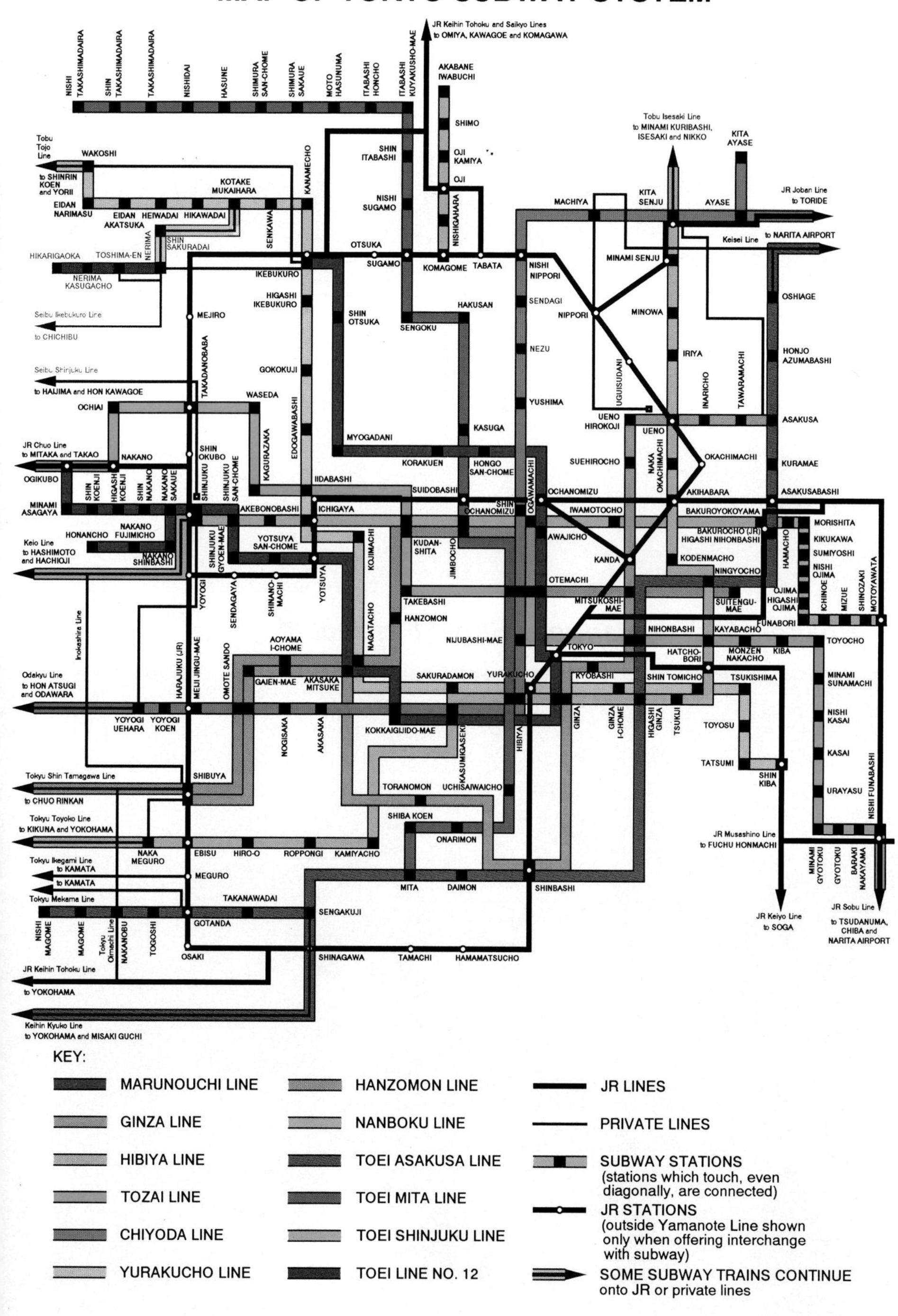

Hokkaido ▲ Sapporo Snow Festival ▼

Around Kyoto ▲Ginkaku-ji In Kurama▼

*Hiroshima* ▲ *Itsukushima Jinja* *'A-Bomb Dome'* ▼

Shichi Go San Festival

Shikoku ▲ Ritsurin Koen Matsuyama Castle ▼

Kyushu ▲ 'Aso Boy' at Miyaji Directions to Toilets at Dazaifu ▼

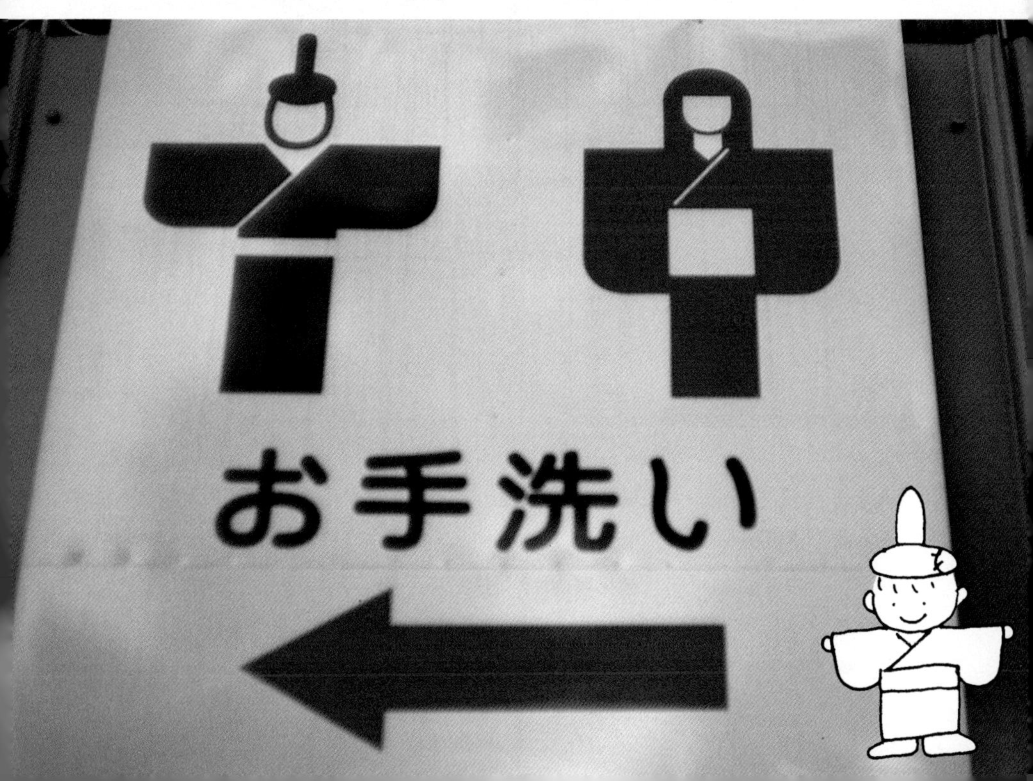

# MAP OF OSAKA SUBWAY SYSTEM

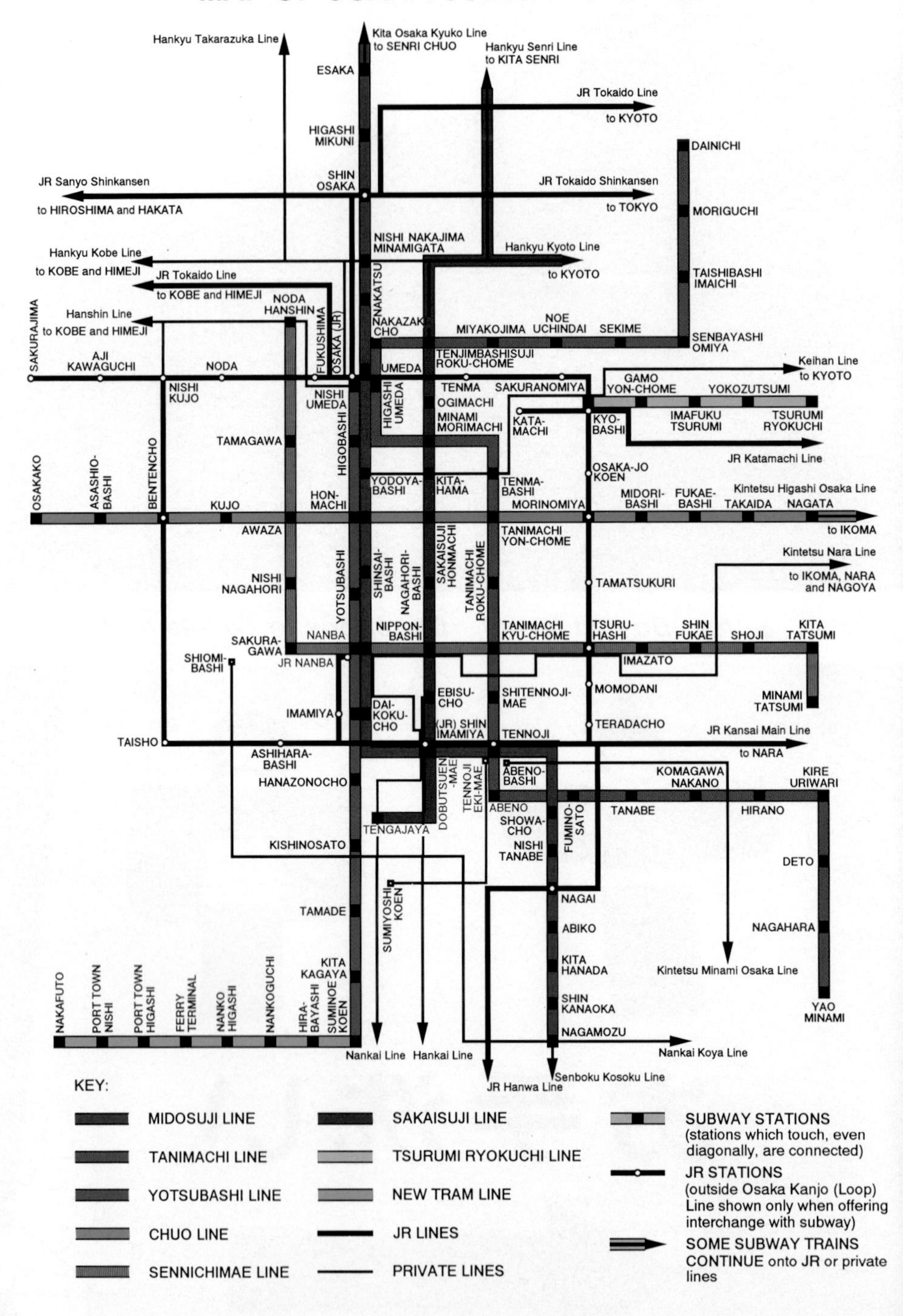

observe how the eaves of the building restrict the angle of elevation which can be used, so that considerable strength is required to get the arrows to travel the required distance. You will also observe the holes in the eaves from mis-judged trajectories. The record for this competition was set in 1686 by a man named Wasa who managed to get 8,153 arrows beyond the mark out of 13,053 launched. Just consider that that means shooting an arrow once every eight seconds for the whole twenty-four hours! Actually, Mr. Wasa's batting average was not as good as that of some previous champions, but his total output was prodigious.

Continuing beyond the location of the archery contest, you will pass behind the altar back down the width of the hall. Here there are statues of the 28 followers of Kannon, also carved in the thirteenth century. Many are considered masterpieces. They were evidently brightly painted originally, but there is little trace of colour now. When you have finished inside, take a few minutes to walk round this building outside also and be impressed by its massive elegance. This is a temple not to be left off your itinerary. Many visitors say that this above all others is the image which they retain in their minds from Kyoto, just contemplating the work which went into the carving of those rows upon rows of Buddhas centuries ago.

Our next stop is one of Kyoto's most famous temples, **Kiyomizu-dera**. It takes about 20 to 25 minutes to walk, first east, then north, then east again. Although the route is signposted once one gets near, it is best to be carrying the map which the Tourist Information Centre can provide, in beautiful colour and detail! Kiyomizu-dera ('Pure Water Temple') is approached along a narrow road of stalls selling souvenirs of every description. This walk, in itself, is interesting. You may arrive by a more southern route, but, even if so, you will be returning along the souvenir lane.

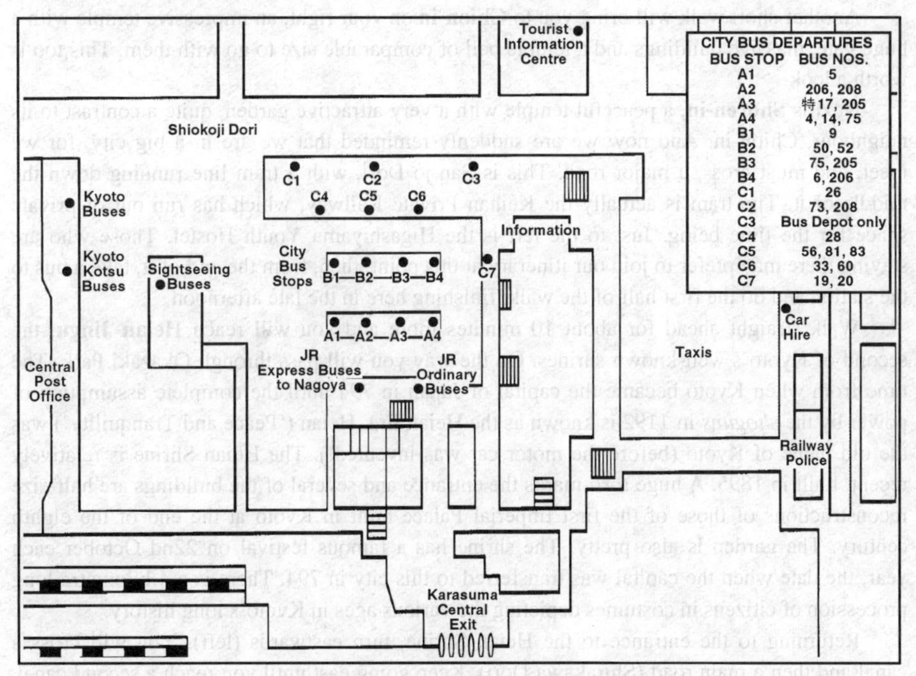

KYOTO STATION BUS TERMINAL

Kiyomizu-dera is most unusual in that it is constructed on the edge of a cliff and appears to have grown beyond its original expectations, expanding right over the edge of the cliff. Parts of the structure are supported, therefore, by an amazing wooden scaffolding. According to the stories told, this temple was founded in 778 and expanded and given its current name in 805. The present buildings, however, are reconstructions dating from 1633, although they appear to follow closely the designs of the eighth and ninth century originals.

Beneath the temple are three springs. They are said to bring long life, beauty and wisdom, but you can drink from only one and must choose which. You will see people queueing to make their choice.

Leave Kiyomizu-dera along the main route ('Kiyomizu-zaka') lined with its souvenir shops and then turn right, down some steps, into San-nen-zaka ('Three Year Hill'). In this area, you will find a large number of pottery shops selling 'Kiyomizu-yaki', the local type of ceramic ware. You will also find traditional Japanese tea shops, where you can stop if feeling the need to sit down. In fact, this is one of the most interesting areas of Kyoto for just wandering around. Indeed, you may find yourself doing just that, for it is quite easy to get lost in these back alleys, even with a map. As the small road bends left, you want to turn right again, down some more steps, into Ni-nen-zaka ('Two Year Hill'). At the end of this road, there is a choice. We need to go left. If you turn right, you will get to **Ryozen Kannon**, a pleasant but modern statue. Have a look if you wish and then return. Now turn right again to go past Kodai-ji, which lies on the right of the small road. Now right and left and we have reached **Yasaka Jinja**. There are not many famous Shinto shrines in Buddhist Kyoto, but this is one of the three well-known ones, so is worth looking at. Next to it is **Maruyama Park**.

Another short walk will bring you to **Chion-in** on your right, an impressive temple with a huge gate, massive buildings and a temple bell of comparable size to go with them. This too is worth a look.

Next is **Shoren-in**, a peaceful temple with a very attractive garden, quite a contrast to its neighbour, Chion-in. And now we are suddenly reminded that we are in a big city, for we meet, and must cross, a major road. This is San-jo Dori, with a tram line running down the middle of it. The tram is actually the Keihan Private Railway, which has run out of private space for the time being. Just to the left is the Higashiyama Youth Hostel. Those who are staying there may prefer to join our itinerary at this point, then, from the end of it, take a bus to the station and do the first half of the walk, finishing here in the late afternoon.

Walk straight ahead for about 10 minutes more and you will reach **Heian Jingu**, the second of Kyoto's well-known shrines. On the way you will pass through Okazaki Park. The time from when Kyoto became the capital of Japan in 794 until the complete assumption of power by the *shoguns* in 1192 is known as the Heian Era. Heian ('Peace and Tranquility') was the old name of Kyoto (before the motor car was invented!). The Heian Shrine is relatively recent, built in 1895. A huge *torii* marks the entrance and several of the buildings are half-size reconstructions of those of the first Imperial Palace built in Kyoto at the end of the eighth century. The garden is also pretty. The shrine has a famous festival on 22nd October each year, the date when the capital was transferred to this city in 794. There is a 4 kilometre long procession of citizens in costumes depicting the various ages in Kyoto's long history.

Returning to the entrance to the Heian Shrine, turn eastwards (left). You will cross a canal and then a main road (Shirakawa Dori). Keep going east until you reach a second canal. Now turn left and head north along the path which runs on the near side of the canal, nicknamed the **'Philosophers' Path'**. This is a pleasant walk of about 20 to 30 minutes. On the way you will pass Reikan-ji and Honen-in a short distance on the other side of the canal, but these are not special temples. When the canal makes an abrupt turn to the left, you want to go right and in 5 minutes more you will come to **Ginkaku-ji**, the 'Silver Pavilion', another of Kyoto's big names.

Actually there is not much silver to be seen here, but the name forms a contrast with that of Kinkaku-ji, which we saw yesterday. This is another old villa become a temple, again offering an attractive garden. Ginkaku-ji will be on the itinerary of every tour bus, so is sure to be crowded.

When you have finished here, you will probably have had enough for today. You will have walked about 8 kilometres and will probably be ready to take a bus home. Return along the road which led up to Ginkaku-ji and, after about 10 minutes, you will come back to Shirakawa Dori. If you want to go to the station, you can take bus no. 5. If you want to go to the north of the city, use bus no. 204.

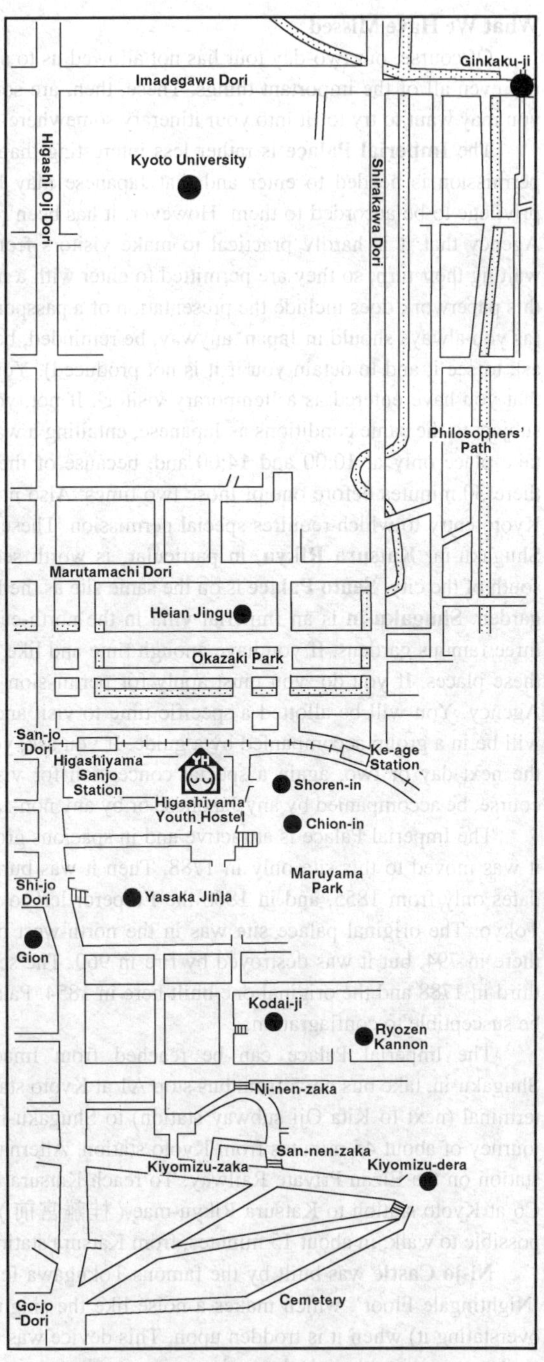

FROM KIYOMIZU-DERA TO GINKAKU-JI

**What We Have Missed**

Of course, our two-day tour has not allowed us to see everything that Kyoto has to offer, nor even all of the important things. These, then, are some of the important omissions which you may want to try to fit into your itinerary somewhere.

The **Imperial Palace** is rather less interesting than you might expect. Note that special permission is needed to enter and that Japanese may have to wait several months for this privilege to be accorded to them. However, it has been recognized by the Imperial Household Agency that it is hardly practical to make visitors from overseas stand around for months waiting their turn, so they are permitted to enter with a minimum of paperwork. Nevertheless, this paperwork does include the presentation of a passport, so be sure to take it along with you (as you always should in Japan, anyway, be reminded, because any police officer is entitled to ask to see it and to detain you if it is not produced). Your passport will be checked to ensure that you have entered as a 'temporary visitor'. If not, you will not be allowed in and will be subject to the same conditions as Japanese, entailing a waiting period of several months. Tours take place only at 10:00 and 14:00 and, because of the paperwork involved, you should be there 30 minutes before one of those two times. Also note that there are three other places in Kyoto entry to which requires special permission. These are Katsura Rikyu, Sento Palace and Shugaku-in. **Katsura Rikyu**, in particular, is worth seeing. It is an Imperial garden in the south of the city. **Sento Palace** is on the same site as the Imperial Palace and also has a famous garden. **Shugaku-in** is an Imperial villa in the north-east of the city which has no less than three famous gardens. If you have enough time and like gardens, you might want to see all of these places. If you do, you must apply for permission now, here at the Imperial Household Agency. You will be allotted a specific time to visit and can go only at that time, when you will be in a group accompanied by a guide. If you ask, you can usually be given a time within the next day or two, again a special concession for visitors from overseas. You cannot, of course, be accompanied by any Japanese or by any non-Japanese working in Japan.

The Imperial Palace is attractive and in spacious grounds, but not really very historic, for it was moved to this site only in 1788. Then it was burnt down, so that the present building dates only from 1855, and in 1868 the Emperor left to make his home in the new capital of Tokyo. The original palace site was in the north-west of the city. The first palace was built there in 794, but it was destroyed by fire in 960. The second palace burnt down in 1177, the third in 1788 and the original one built here in 1854. Palaces, it seems, as in England, seem to be susceptible to conflagration.

The Imperial Palace can be reached from Imadegawa subway station. To get to Shugaku-in, take bus no. 5 from bus stop A1 at Kyoto station or bus no. 北5 from Kita Oji bus terminal (next to Kita Oji subway station) to Shugaku-in Rikyu Michi (修学院離宮道), a journey of about 45 minutes from Kyoto station. Alternatively, you can walk from Shugakuin station on the Eizan Private Railway. To reach Katsura Rikyu, take bus no. 33 from bus stop C6 at Kyoto station to Katsura Rikyu-mae (桂離宮前). It takes about 20 minutes. It is also possible to walk, in about 15 minutes, from Katsura station on the Hankyu Private Railway.

**Ni-jo Castle** was built by the famous Tokugawa Ieyasu in 1603. It is best known for its 'Nightingale Floor', which makes a noise like the singing of a bird (perhaps 'nightingale' is overstating it) when it is trodden upon. This device was used in the corridors, reputedly to try to detect spies, although the author suspects that an ingenious builder might just have been trying to find a good excuse for an unfortunate squeak. The castle, which is not very defensive in nature, in fact, was expanded in 1626 and then used as a prefectural office, following the Meiji Restoration, from 1871 until 1884, suffering considerable damage as a result. You may choose to visit just castle or castle and garden. The garden is quite attractive.

On the way to Arashiyama, and not so far from Utano Youth Hostel, is **Eiga-mura** ('Movie Village'), where you can visit the film studios to see the sets and watch films actually being made. The Japanese film-making industry originated in Kyoto at the beginning of this century and now specializes in *samurai* films and Edo period sets. The nearest station is Uzumasa on the Keifuku Private Railway. On the JR San-in Line, Eiga-mura lies between Hanazono and Uzumasa stations. Or you can take a City Bus no. 11 or Kyoto Bus no. 61, 62, 63, 71, 72 or 73 to Uzumasa Koryu-ji (太秦広隆寺). The last three buses start from Kyoto station (bus stop near the Central Post Office) and the first four originate at Keihan Sanjo station. All also operate from Arashiyama. Youth hostels and hotels in Kyoto can often provide you with a discount coupon for entry to Eiga-mura.

If you are going to visit Eiga-mura, you should go to **Koryu-ji** as well, since it is almost next door. The temple itself was founded in 603 and some of the present buildings were built in the twelfth and thirteenth centuries. There are many very old Buddhist carvings on display, some dating from the temple's foundation.

**Fushimi Inari Taisha**, the third of Kyoto's limited number of well known Shinto shrines, is famous for all the *torii* which line the path up the hill. The *torii* are donated by supplicants and may be seen at many shrines, but you will probably never see as many at one time as here. The shrine is very close to Inari station, two stops from Kyoto on the JR Nara Line. Since it is on the way to Nara, it can be seen quite conveniently when you are also on your way there.

**Kyoto Tower** is quite near the railway station. You will not easily miss it, since it is 131 metres tall. There is a lookout at a point 100 metres up, but, as it costs ¥730 to go up, you may well decide that Kyoto can be seen well enough from ground level.

The famous entertainment district is **Gion**, on the eastern side of Kyoto, not far from Yasaka Jinja. *Geisha* can still be found here and, although one would not want to frequent the establishments where they work, unless one happens to have an unlimited company expense account, they can occasionally be seen tripping to work in the evening, *kimono*-clad. In Gion is held one of Kyoto's major festivals too, with truly huge floats pulled through the streets by gangs of willing labourers. This festival is held on 17th July, if you happen to be around at that time.

Another famous festival is **Daimonji**, so called because fires are used to make the *kanji* reading *dai* (大), and meaning 'big', on five different hillsides visible from the city. This occurs on 16th August as part of the festivities associated with *o-bon*, when the spirits of deceased ancestors have to be welcomed back into the family home and entertained for a period of three days.

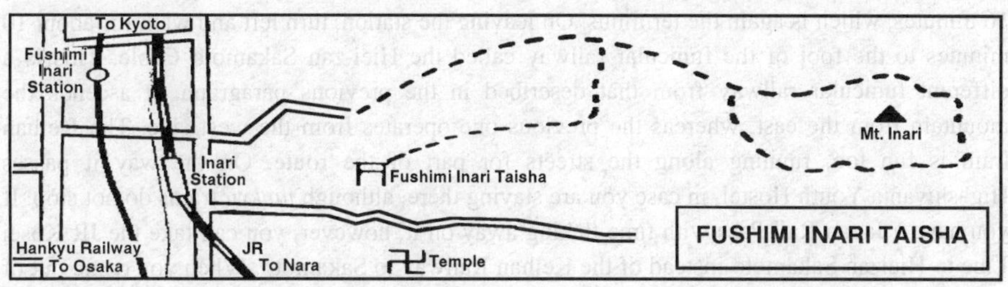

**A Day Trip**

If you have a spare day, an expedition thoroughly to be recommended is a visit to **Hiei-zan** and its magnificent mountain temple complex. There are several ways to reach the mountain. The cheapest is by bus. There are regular departures in summer from either Kyoto station or Keihan Sanjo, operated by Kyoto Bus and Keihan Bus. In winter there are few buses, but, according to the current timetable, there is a useful departure from Kyoto station at 10:20 and from Keihan Sanjo at 10:41 (the same bus). A special ticket is available for ¥800 for the purpose of visiting Hiei-zan. It is called an *'Hiei-zan-nai ichi-nichi free jo-sha-ken'* ( 比叡山内一日フリー乗車券 ) and you should purchase one at the bus company office before boarding the bus. Otherwise, the bus costs ¥730 each way to Enryaku-ji ( 延暦寺 ), its final destination being Hiei-zan Cho ( 比叡山頂 ), a few minutes further on. The journey to Enryaku-ji takes about an hour. The last return journey leaves from Enryaku-ji at 17:56 in summer and 15:57 in winter, as at the time of writing. More interesting, however, is to take the Eizan Private Railway to Yase Yuen (15 minutes, ¥220) and then go up the mountain by funicular railway and ropeway. The line to Yase Yuen is a branch line. Sometimes trains run directly from the start of the railway at Demachi Yanagi and sometimes it is necessary to change trains at Takara-ga-ike, the fifth stop, where a train will be waiting to go the other two stations to Yase Yuen. When you leave the station, turn left and a short walk will bring you to the funicular railway. This carries you part of the way up the mountain and then the ropeway can be taken to complete the journey. The cost of the funicular railway is ¥520, while the ropeway costs ¥300. Note, however, that the summit of the ropeway is not near the temples. To reach Enryaku-ji requires a walk of 30 minutes, although it is a pleasant walk downhill through wooded mountain terrain. On the way, you will pass the second part of the temple (turn off to the left over the bridge across the toll road), so if you want an enjoyable, if slightly expensive, round trip, this is a good way to do it. You can also walk from the top of the funicular railway, without taking the ropeway to the summit. This walk is almost the same distance as that from the upper station of the ropeway. When the author went up the mountain by this route early one November morning, a thick autumn mist shrouded the landscape, limiting visibility to about ten metres. I was the only passenger on the funicular train and the driver carefully described for me every detail of the beautiful landscape which I might have enjoyed in more favourable conditions. Thus I enjoyed it vicariously anyway. The forest walk was also beautiful without any other specimens of humanity visible and in the solitude and stillness which only thick mist can bring.

The third route is that which the author would recommend if you can travel only one. First take the Keihan Private Railway from Keishin Sanjo (which is almost the same place as Keihan Sanjo) to the terminus of that train at Hama Otsu, 27 minutes, where you change to another train, running in the opposite direction to the one on which you arrived, to Sakamoto, 16 minutes, which is again the terminus. On leaving the station, turn left and walk for about 10 minutes to the foot of the funicular railway called the Hiei-zan Sakamoto Cable. This is a different funicular railway from that described in the previous paragraph. It ascends the mountain from the east, whereas the previous one operates from the west side. The Keihan train is fun too, running along the streets for part of the route. On the way it passes Higashiyama Youth Hostel, in case you are staying there, although *junkyu* trains do not stop. If you have a Japan Rail Pass with time ticking away on it, however, you can take the JR Kosei Line to Hieizan Sakamoto instead of the Keihan Railway to Sakamoto. When you come out of

Hieizan Sakamoto station, you want to go left compared with the direction in which your train was travelling on the elevated tracks. The map for Saikyo-ji Youth Hostel may help you to get your bearings. The walk to the funicular railway is much longer from here — about 20 minutes. On the way, you will pass Sakamoto station. The Keihan Private Railway is more interesting than the JR route and cheaper, as well as being more convenient. The funicular railway takes 11 minutes and costs ¥820. A return ticket is available for ¥1,550.

The temples on Hiei-zan had their origin 1,150 years ago and developed into a force of monks so large and powerful that it was able to challenge even the power of the *shogun*. This led to the burning of all the temples in 1571, so the buildings existing now are from later than that date. The principal temple is **Enryaku-ji** and it is in three main parts. From the top of the Hiei-zan Sakamoto Cable, it is only a short walk to the first, and principal, site of Enryaku-ji. You will encounter a ticket box on the way and the ticket which you will be sold there entitles you to enter all three sites, if you can find them and get to them. You should be given a map as well to assist with your exploration. When the author went, I was not given one and had to ask. I was told that the supply of maps in English had been exhausted and replied that if I had one in Japanese it might give me a sporting chance of finding the other two locations of the temple

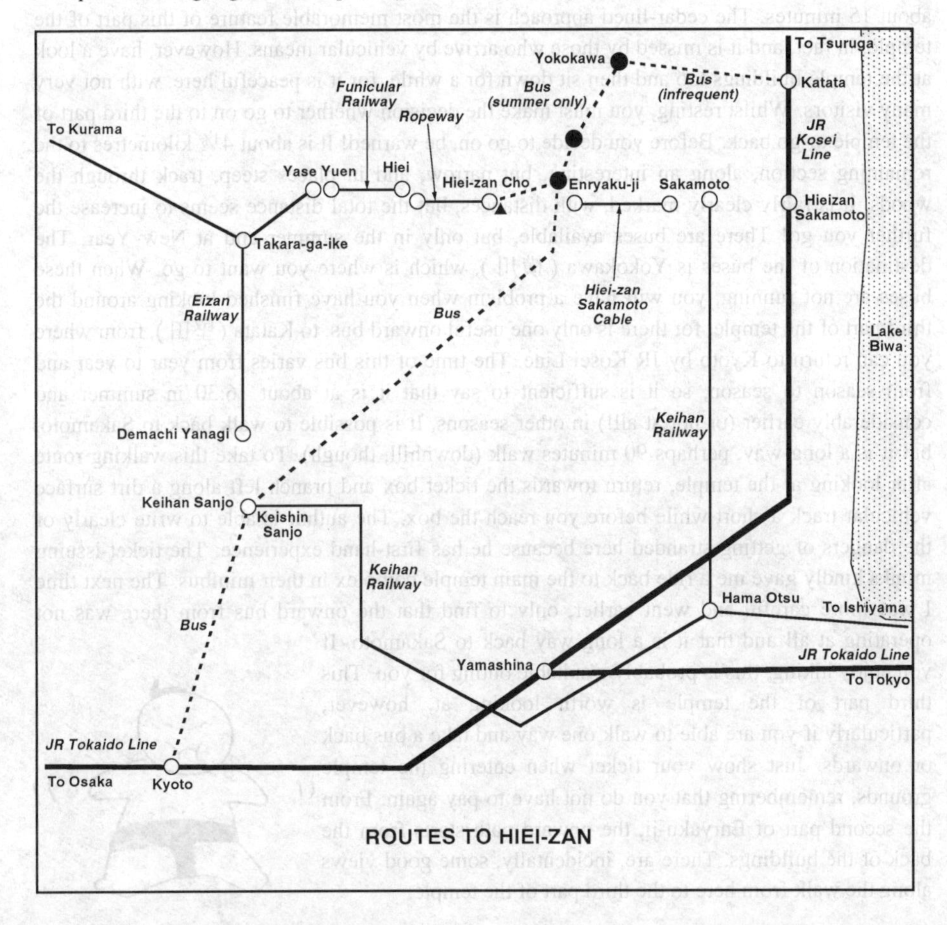

ROUTES TO HIEI-ZAN

buildings. Without a map, it is quite a difficult task, as you will soon perceive. First let us look around this area though. It is a beautiful setting and, however many temples you may have seen in Kyoto over the last few days, you are sure to be impressed by the natural surroundings of this one and to think what a splendid choice of site was made more than a millennium ago. When the author last visited, although the weather was fine down below in Kyoto, it was snowing up here. Temple buildings seem to look their best with a covering of snow, but, even if it is summer, come up and experience the tranquility and coolness of this forest location. There are several buildings to see in addition to the main temple hall. When you have visited all, return to the ticket box and fork right, instead of left, which would lead you back to the funicular railway. You will now see, on your left, a picturesque, but modern, shrine, which is worth a look. Shrines are usually free moreover! At this point, most people consider the visit finished and go home. Do not do so, however, but continue along the path which leads away from the temple buildings. You will see the toll road down below on the right and then come to a bridge across it. Cross and walk down the steps through an avenue of magnificent cedar trees to the second part of Enryaku-ji. Not many visitors walk this far, although some come along the toll road in their cars. The distance, however, is not much over a kilometre, a walk of about 15 minutes. The cedar-lined approach is the most memorable feature of this part of the temple, in fact, and it is missed by those who arrive by vehicular means. However, have a look at the temple buildings too and then sit down for a while, for it is peaceful here, with not very many visitors. Whilst resting, you must make the decision whether to go on to the third part of the temple or go back. Before you decide to go on, be warned! It is about 4½ kilometres to the remaining section, along an interesting, but narrow, and in places steep, track through the woods. It is fairly clearly marked, with distances, but the total distance seems to increase the further you go! There are buses available, but only in the summer and at New Year. The destination of the buses is Yokokawa (横川), which is where you want to go. When these buses are not running, you will have a problem when you have finished looking around the third part of the temple, for there is only one useful onward bus, to Katata (堅田), from where you can return to Kyoto by JR Kosei Line. The time of this bus varies from year to year and from season to season, so it is sufficient to say that it is at about 16:30 in summer and considerably earlier (or not at all!) in other seasons. It is possible to walk back to Sakamoto, but it is a long way, perhaps 90 minutes walk (downhill, though). To take this walking route after looking at the temple, return towards the ticket box and branch left along a dirt surface vehicular track a short while before you reach the box. The author is able to write clearly of the dangers of getting stranded here because he has first-hand experience. The ticket-issuing monks kindly gave me a ride back to the main temple complex in their minibus. The next time I was more careful and went earlier, only to find that the onward bus from there was not operating at all and that it is a long way back to Sakamoto. If you enjoy hiking, this is probably a suitable outing for you. This third part of the temple is worth looking at, however, particularly if you are able to walk one way and take a bus back or onwards. Just show your ticket when entering the temple grounds, remembering that you do not have to pay again. From the second part of Enryaku-ji, the onward path starts from the back of the buildings. There are, incidentally, some good views along the walk from here to the third part of the temple.

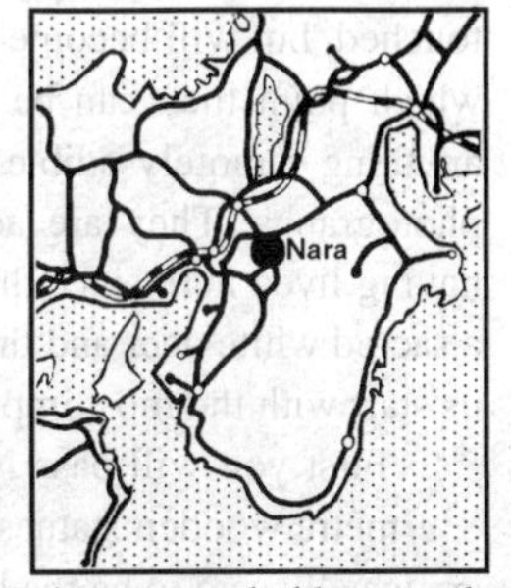


## NARA (奈良 – 'Especially Good') JR Nara Line or Kintetsu Private Railway, 32 to 45 mins. from Kyoto

**Derivation of Name:** *Original meaning of 'nara' (with different Chinese characters) was 'make flat'. Long ago, the people cleared the grass here and made the area flat.*

Whilst visiting Kyoto, you certainly should not neglect Nara. Nara was the capital of Japan before Kyoto, from 710 until 784. Prior to that time it was customary for the capital to move every time the Emperor changed, a system which was found to be somewhat inconvenient, so Nara became the first permanent capital. It is a city of 350,000 people, very much smaller than Kyoto. It is surrounded by a park and in that park most of the buildings of interest are to be found, which makes the sightseeing here much more pleasant than in certain other cities. Although there are bus services, it is possible to walk almost anywhere in Nara.

Many people choose to make a day visit, but there are places to stay, including two youth hostels. If you are including Nara as part of the extended Chubu tour suggested earlier in this book, then you probably should stay in Nara, and then take Kintetsu to Ise and Toba. There are also two ways to reach Nara from Kyoto – by JR or by Kintetsu. Although Kintetsu is faster and cheaper, the JR Nara Line has the advantage of passing two additional sightseeing spots. The first is **Fushimi Inari Taisha**, which has already been mentioned in the section on Kyoto. The second is in the town of **Uji**, only 17 minutes from Kyoto by *kaisoku. Kaisoku* trains run hourly, at 45 minutes past each hour. In between, there is a frequent service by ordinary trains taking about 30 minutes. There is also a frequent service by the Keihan Private Railway, which journey takes 45 minutes but costs only ¥280. Your objective is **Byodo-in**, not so far from either station. From Keihan Uji, cross the river. Byodo-in is a temple dating from 1053 and is famous for its long hall, the shape of which is supposed to symbolize a mythical bird akin to a phœnix. At this point, remove a ¥10 coin from your pocket, assuming that you are not too impoverished to own even one of those, and you will see that this is the selfsame building which appears on the coin. It is a stylish piece of architecture, considered to be one of the best examples of its period, but its main interest comes from the fact that it is the '¥10 temple'. Having spent a few minutes looking at it, you can return to the station and continue to Nara.

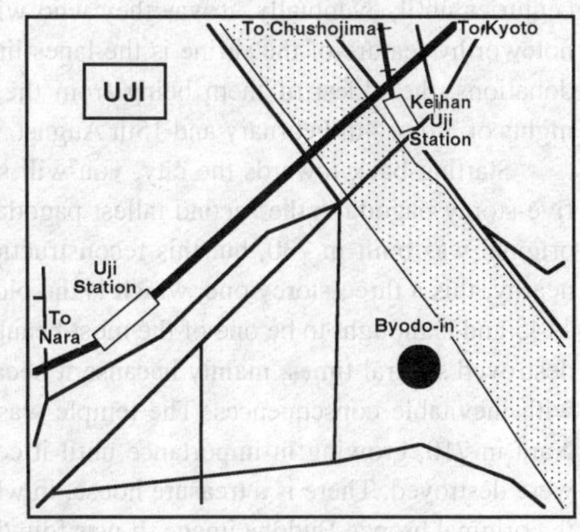


If you arrive in Nara by Kintetsu, you can easily walk to the park. If you come by JR, it will take about 20 minutes to reach the edge of the park, but it is still quite walkable. The youth hostels are both in the northern part of the city, also walking distance from the park, but not on the way there. The first thing you will notice upon reaching **Nara Park** is that it has deer, about 1,200 of them, in fact. They are semi-tame and actually roam in the park only during the day, returning to their bed quarters at night when summoned by horn by the deer-keeper. They do not like much to be touched, but will become your great friends whenever you decide to have something to eat, at which point they can be really quite insistent about the merits of sharing. Never put down anything remotely edible unless you have similar opinions. However, the deer are good for photographs. They are actually the divine messengers of Kasuga Taisha (Kasuga Shrine), having lived here since the principal deity of the shrine moved in in 768. He arrived riding on a sacred white deer and these are its descendants. We shall look at that shrine later, but now let us start with the most important temple in the city, Todai-ji.

First you will pass **Nandai-mon**, the 'Great South Gate', which is 21 metres high. The 8½ metre wooden statues on each side of the gate are the largest wooden statues in Japan and are usually said to be the best examples of Kamakura period sculpture. The gate was originally built in the eighth century, but it was knocked down by a typhoon and rebuilt in 1199.

**Todai-ji** is one of the great temples of Japan. It was founded in 733, and soon became the major centre for Buddhism in the country. Between 745 and 749 was cast the huge Buddha image which is now within the main hall. However, both hall and Buddha have endured some hard times. The form of the hall at which you are now looking dates from a major reconstruction which took place in 1709. However, the hall itself was rebuilt in 1903. As for the **Big Buddha**, the largest one in Japan, only the pedestal and part of the legs are original. In 855, the head fell off in an earthquake and many other mishaps followed over the centuries. Most of the image dates from 1692. You will notice that it does not have the serenity of the Big Buddha at Kamakura. Therefore, although this Buddha is larger and older, it is generally thought to be inferior to the Kamakura Buddha. It is also difficult to take photographs of it since it is inside the hall. This image weighs 450 tons and is nearly 22 metres tall, including the pedestal. The hall in which it is housed claims to be the largest wooden structure in the world. It is nearly 50 metres tall and 55 metres by 50 metres. Even so, it is only two-thirds of the size of the hall which originally stood here.

Let us move on now to **Kasuga Taisha** (Kasuga Shrine), an attractive building in the usual orange and white Shinto colours. This shrine looks its best in the late afternoon as the rays of the setting sun bring out the bright colour of its paintwork. That, at least, is how the author remembers it, backed by woodland and with few visitors around. The shrine was founded in 768 and was the family shrine of the Fujiwaras, who were closely related to the Imperial family and gradually became increasingly influential in the eighth to eleventh centuries until, eventually, it was they who wielded the real power in the country. The most noteworthy feature of the shrine is the lanes lined with lanterns leading to it. The lanterns are donations, the oldest of them being from the eleventh century. They are lit on the festival nights of 3rd or 4th February and 15th August.

Starting back towards the city, you will see the pagoda of **Kofuku-ji** on your left. This five-storey pagoda is the second tallest pagoda in Japan, measuring 50 metres in height. The original was built in 730, but this reconstruction dates from 1426. There is a second pagoda nearby, this a three-storey one, which is the oldest surviving part of the temple. It was built in 1145 and is thought to be one of the most beautiful pagodas in the country. Kofuku-ji has been destroyed several times, mainly because it became too powerful and was involved in feuding, with inevitable consequences. The temple was founded elsewhere in 669 and was moved to Nara in 710, growing in importance until it could boast 175 different buildings. All of them were destroyed. There is a treasure house, in which is exhibited, amongst other items, a part of the original bronze Buddha image. It was found in 1937 during repair work.

There is one more important place to see, but it is not in the city, so let us hurry back to the JR station in order to take a train for the 12 kilometre journey taking 12 minutes by JR Kansai Line to Horyu-ji (¥210). The train will be going to Osaka or JR Nanba. Alternatively, there is a bus to Horyu-ji ( 法隆寺 ), from either the Kintetsu station or the JR station, but it costs ¥680 and takes 54 minutes. The bus goes right to the temple, though, whereas from the station there is some walking to be done. Despite its being out of the city, **Horyu-ji** is a temple not to be missed because it claims to contain the oldest wooden buildings in the world. It was founded in 607, but burnt down in 670. It was then rebuilt, although the exact date is uncertain, and that rebuilt temple was destroyed by fire in 925. However, the main hall and pagoda were spared by this fire and these are the buildings which you can see now, so they date from about 700. The main hall was dismantled during the war for fear that it would suffer damage. The pieces were all numbered and then it was reassembled later. Unfortunately, in 1949, there was a fire which damaged the famous paintings of the Paradise of Buddha on the walls of this hall. Inside the hall, the three main bronze images bear inscriptions stating that they were made in 623. The pagoda is of antiquity similar to that of the main hall.

Well, having spent several days looking round Kyoto and Nara, you will probably have had enough of temples for a while, so let us see something different tomorrow.

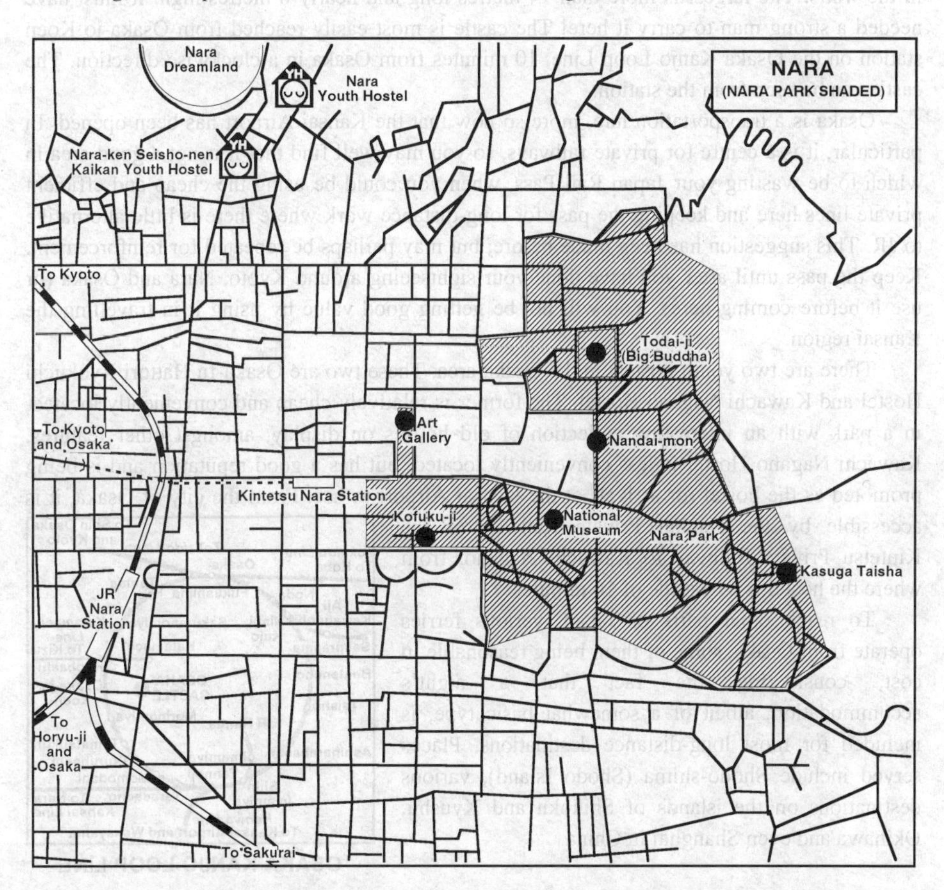

# OSAKA (大阪 – 'Big Slope')

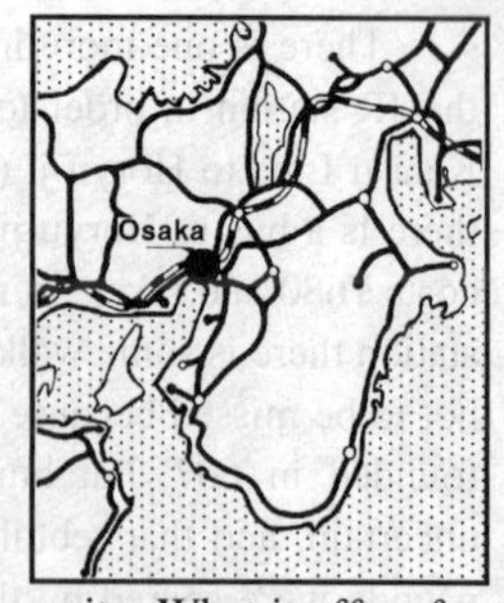


**Tokaido *shinkansen*, 3 hrs. from Tokyo**

**Derivation of Name:** *At end of fifteenth century, a temple called Ishiyama Hongan-ji was established on a hill ('big slope') which became centre of city. It was later turned into a fortress and then a castle.*

Osaka is Japan's third largest city, Yokohama being the second. However, if you consider Yokohama to be merely an extension of Tokyo, that makes Osaka second in size only to the Tokyo sprawl. Osaka sprawls too, merging with Kobe to the west and several other smaller cities on other sides. Osaka itself has a population of 2.5 million. However, Osaka is an industrial and business city. What it offers for sightseeing is rather limited.

**Osaka Castle** is now the city's main tourist attraction, but only the foundations are original. The rest is ferro-concrete, as so often in Japan. The original castle was constructed in 1575 by Toyotomi Hideyoshi, a famous leader in the process of the unification of Japan, and was thought to be impregnable. In 1615, it proved not to be so. The original castle was huge and what is there now is but a tiny part of the original. Noteworthy are some of the stones used in the walls. The largest is more than 14 metres long and nearly 6 metres high. It must have needed a strong man to carry it here! The castle is most easily reached from Osaka-jo Koen station on the Osaka Kanjo Loop Line, 10 minutes from Osaka in a clockwise direction. The castle can be seen from the station.

Osaka is a transportation hub, more so now that the Kansai Airport has been opened. In particular, it is a centre for private railways, so you may well find that it is not a good area in which to be wasting your Japan Rail Pass, when you could be using the cheap and efficient private lines here and keeping the pass for long-distance work where there is little alternative to JR. This suggestion has been made before, but may perhaps be repeated for reinforcement. Keep the pass until after you have done your sightseeing around Kyoto, Nara and Osaka (or use it before coming here). You will not be getting good value by using it in travelling the Kansai region.

There are two youth hostels in the Osaka area. These two are Osaka-fu Hattori Ryokuchi Hostel and Kawachi Nagano Hostel. The former is relatively cheap and conveniently located, in a park with an interesting collection of old houses on display, amongst other features. Kawachi Nagano Hostel is less conveniently located, but has a good reputation and is being promoted as the hostel for arrivals at the Kansai Airport to use. From the city of Osaka, it is accessible by the Nankai Private Railway or the Kintetsu Private Railway to Kawachi Nagano, from where the hostel is a bus ride of 16 minutes.

To reach other parts of Japan, various ferries operate from Osaka, some of them being reasonable in cost, considering the fact that a night's accommodation, albeit of a somewhat basic type, is included for most long-distance destinations. Places served include Shodo-shima (Shodo Island), various destinations on the islands of Shikoku and Kyushu, Okinawa and even Shanghai in China.

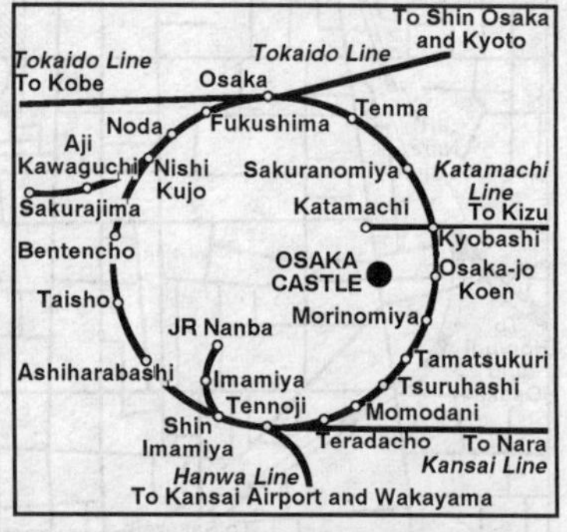


OSAKA KANJO LOOP LINE

## KANSAI AIRPORT (関西空港)

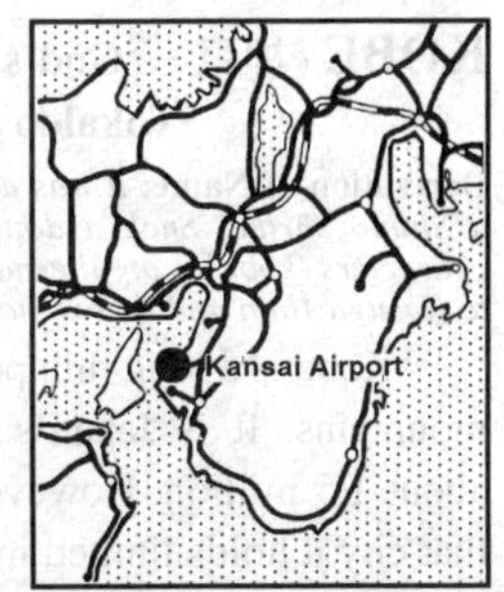


**JR Kansai Kuko Line or Nankai Railway, 45 mins. from Osaka**

Kansai Airport was opened in September 1994 and is Japan's first 24-hour international airport. It is built on an artificial island in the bay south of the city of Osaka and connected to the mainland by an impressive bridge 3 kilometres long used by both rail and road traffic. At present, the airport is served by only a limited number of international flights, but it is anticipated that it will gradually become more popular because of its 24-hour availability.

If this is your arrival point in Japan, you will find a railway station shared by JR and the Nankai Private Railway. JR offers express services (all reserved seats) to Osaka and Kyoto. Trains run half-hourly, at 18 and 48 minutes past the hour and make three stops, at Tennoji, in the south of Osaka, at Shin Osaka, in the north of Osaka and the interchange point with the *shinkansen*, and at Kyoto. Some trains terminate at Shin Osaka. To Tennoji takes 30 minutes. To Shin Osaka takes 45 minutes and to Kyoto takes 75 minutes. However, unless you have a Japan Rail Pass, this will be an expensive train to use. The basic fare is ¥1,010 to Tennoji, ¥1,300 to Shin Osaka and ¥1,800 to Kyoto, but, in addition, there is an express supplement of ¥1,220 to Tennoji and ¥1,630 for destinations beyond. It is much cheaper to take an ordinary train and save the supplement. Some of these ordinary services run to Osaka, from where there is a *kaisoku* (rapid) service to Kyoto (no supplement), while some terminate at Tennoji, from where the Osaka Kanjo Loop Line (see diagrams below and on previous page) runs to Osaka. Since this is a circular route, it does not matter much which way round you go.

The Nankai Private Railway offers an express service to Nanba, in the south of Osaka. Trains run frequently, the fastest taking 30 to 35 minutes. *Tokkyu* trains cost ¥800 plus a seat reservation charge of ¥450. The *kyuko* service costs just the basic fare of ¥800 and takes 45 minutes.

To reach Kawachi Nagano and the youth hostel there from the airport, take a bus to Komyo Ike (光明池), which takes 40 minutes and costs ¥1,000. Then change to a bus for Kawachi Nagano (河内長野) and alight at Amano-san (天野山) after 30 minutes (¥450). From there, it is 15 minutes walk (see map in Youth Hostels section on page 437), but the hostel is willing to collect hostellers from the bus stop upon request. It would also be possible to take the Nankai Private Railway all the way to Kawachi Nagano station, changing either at Nanba or at a station called Kishinosato Tamaide, reached just a few minutes before the Nanba terminus, but where, unfortunately, the trains from the airport do not stop. The cost from the airport to Kawachi Nagano is ¥970, plus any express supplement.

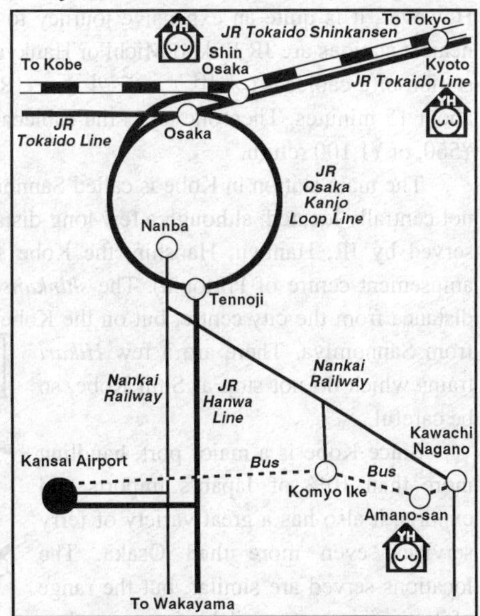


**TRANSPORT FROM KANSAI AIRPORT**
(Note that JR *Haruka* Express does not pass through Osaka station)

## KOBE (神戸 – 'God's Door')

**Tokaido *shinkansen*, 3 hrs. 15 mins. from Tokyo**

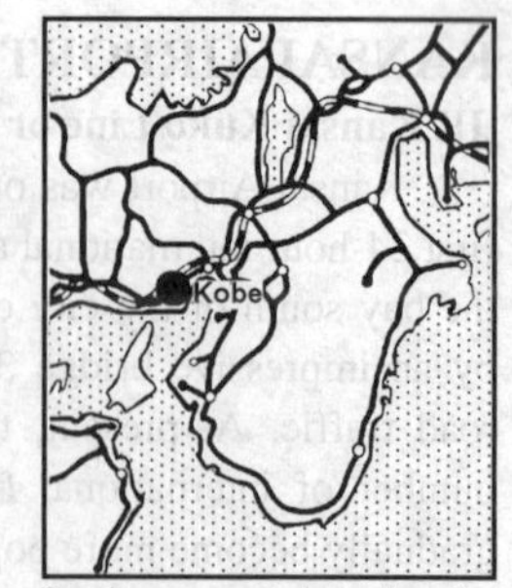


**Derivation of Name:** *It was a practice of wealthy people to donate a house to a Shinto shrine. Such a donation was called a 'kanbe', of which Chinese characters 'kobe' is an alternative reading. The Imperial Court gave a 'kanbe' to Kasuga Jinja and that is thought to be the origin of the name of the city.*

Kobe is a long thin port city, squeezed between the sea and the mountains. It is Japan's sixth largest city, with a population of about 1.5 million. However, although it is prettier than Osaka, like that city it holds limited interest for visitors from overseas.

In January 1995, an earthquake of magnitude 7.2 on the Richter Scale occurred under the sea off nearby Awaji-shima, causing major damage and serious loss of life in the city of Kobe. Over 5,000 people were killed and 50,000 dwellings, as well as many offices, were destroyed, either by the earthquake itself or by the resulting fires. In fact, though, the earthquake was of a magnitude not uncommon in Japan, but on this occasion it was in a shallow location and so the effects were unusually severe. In case this makes you feel insecure, it should be mentioned that this is an area not generally prone to earthquakes and that, now that such a disaster has already occurred, another is unlikely here for some time, so this is, actually, one of the safest areas of Japan to be visiting or in which to reside.

There is a street here known as **Kaigan Dori**, but sometimes referred to as 'The Bund', where many foreign residents formerly lived and where some of those old buildings still remain. It is still the main street for offices of foreign companies. There is also the **tomb of Kusunoki Masashige**, whose statue you saw outside the Imperial Palace in Tokyo. This is to be found at Minatogawa Jinja, also known as Nanko Jinja. He died here in Kobe, as the Commander of the Imperial Army, in a battle fought in 1336.

The view from **Mt. Rokko**, behind the city, is famous, particularly the twilight view. However, it is quite an expensive journey to reach the top of this 900 metre mountain. The nearest stations are JR Rokko Michi or Hankyu Rokko. From there, one takes a bus to the base station of a cablecar (六甲ケーブル下 – 'Rokko Cable Shita') which costs ¥200 and takes about 15 minutes. Then one takes the cablecar up the mountain, a 10 minute journey costing ¥560, or ¥1,100 return.

The main station in Kobe is called Sannomiya. There is a JR station called Kobe, but it is not centrally located, although a few long-distance *tokkyu* trains terminate there. Sannomiya is served by JR, Hankyu, Hanshin, the Kobe subway and Kobe Shin Kotsu (running to the amusement centre of Portopia). The *shinkansen* station is called Shin Kobe and it is a little distance from the city centre, but on the Kobe subway only one station (1.3 kilometres) away from Sannomiya. There are a few *Hikari* trains which do not stop at Shin Kobe, so be careful.

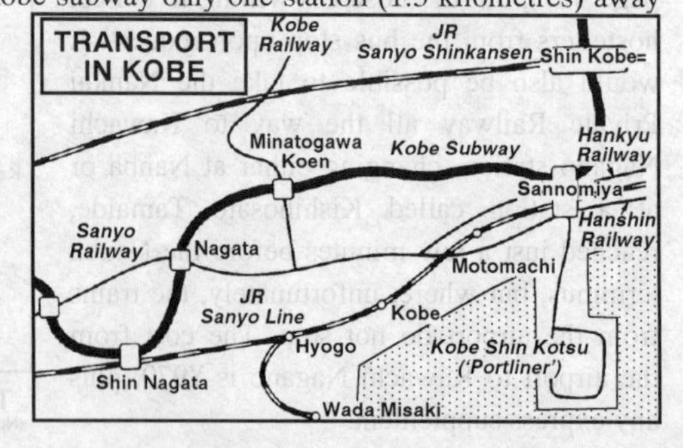


Since Kobe is a major port, handling more than 10% of Japan's imports and exports, it also has a great variety of ferry services, even more than Osaka. The locations served are similar, but the range of destination ports available is even wider.

## HIMEJI (姫路 – 'Princess Road')

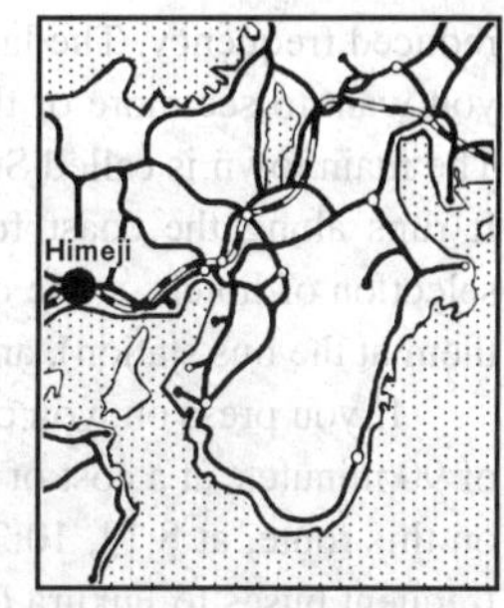


**Sanyo *shinkansen*, 3 hrs. 30 mins. from Tokyo**

**Derivation of Name:** *'Hime' can also mean small, so originally this was probably a 'small road'.*

Himeji is the site of the most magnificent castle in Japan. Once you have seen this one, you do not need to bother about any of the others. It is named Hakuro-jo ('White Egret Castle'), because, like most Japanese castles, it is white and its form is thought to resemble that of a bird of prey. It is most certainly a beautiful castle, standing majestically on top of a small hill clearly visible from the *shinkansen* platform and from near the north exit of the station, so directions are unnecessary. Entry costs ¥500. Information is given in English both on the admission ticket and on notices around the various buildings, so will not be repeated here, except to say that this is an original castle, not a concrete reproduction. Parts date from the sixteenth century, but the castle was gradually added to over the years, so some parts are more recent. If you have time to look at only one castle in Japan, this should be it. Do not miss it.

Himeji is easy to reach, for it is on the *shinkansen* route. Some *Hikari* trains stop and some do not, so exercise caution. All *Kodama* trains stop, of course. For those using a *Kei-han-shin Shu-yu-ken*, Himeji is just outside your area, which finishes at Nishi Akashi. You will probably find it most simple to stay on the *shin kaisoku* train and continue to Himeji, where you will be charged ¥560 in excess fare for the 32 extra kilometres. The journey takes 21 minutes from Nishi Akashi or 91 minutes from Kyoto. Himeji is also served by the Sanyo Private Railway, but the cost is about the same as by JR.

## AWAJI-SHIMA (淡路島 – 'Pale Road Island')

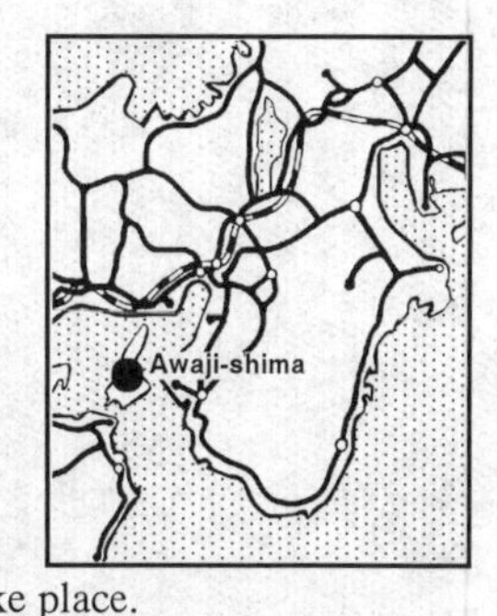


**Ferry, 20 mins. from Akashi**

**Derivation of Name:** *In Shikoku, there was a province named 'Awa'. Awaji was originally 'the road leading to Awa', but the Chinese characters have become changed.*

Awaji-shima is the sixth biggest island in Japan. It was the site of the earthquake in January 1995 which caused so much death and destruction in Kobe. Awaji-shima suffered too, of course, but, because the island is sparsely populated, the death toll was relatively low compared with that in Kobe. There was, however, a great deal of damage to property and much rebuilding has had to take place.

Awaji-shima can be reached by a short ferry ride of 20 minutes from Akashi, which lies between Kobe and Himeji, closer to the former. Those using a *Kei-han-shin Shu-yu-ken* will remember that Nishi Akashi is the western limit of your area. Akashi is one station east of that, so within the area. For those with rail passes, Nishi Akashi is a *shinkansen* stop. From there, take any train on the conventional tracks below for one stop back towards Osaka in order to reach Akashi.

The ferry is about 10 minutes walk from the station. Walk towards the sea (of course) and you will find it. The boat is a surprisingly small one, so small that when the author went across one stormy evening he wondered whether he was going to make it or not. The cost is ¥310 and the service at least half-hourly, except in the middle of the night, when it still runs, but with reduced frequency. The landing point on Awaji-shima is Iwaya which is a very small town. If you want to see more of the island, you will need to take a bus from the bus terminal nearby. The main town is called Sumoto ( 洲本 ) and a bus to there takes 65 minutes and costs ¥1,150. It runs along the coast for much of the route. Sumoto is not so huge either, but it has a selection of hotels, some of which are not too expensive (there is an information board listing them at the bus station), and a youth hostel 4 kilometres away.

If you press on, you can reach Shikoku by taking another bus to Naruto ( 鳴門 ), a journey of 90 minutes, at a cost of ¥1,450. At the time of writing there are only four departures per day on this route, at 8:14, 10:30, 14:44 and 16:44. At other times, it is possible to take one of the frequent buses to Fukura ( 福良 ) and change there to a bus for Naruto. There are also express buses from Iwaya direct to Fukura. They cover the journey in between 95 minutes and 2 hours and cost ¥1,600. From Naruto, there are trains, for which refer to the Shikoku section. On the way to Naruto, you will cross a rather magnificent bridge, with a spiralling approach, which connects the islands of Awaji-shima and Shikoku. Beneath this bridge are the Naruto whirlpools formed by the fast flowing waters at the change of tides. If you are lucky, you will

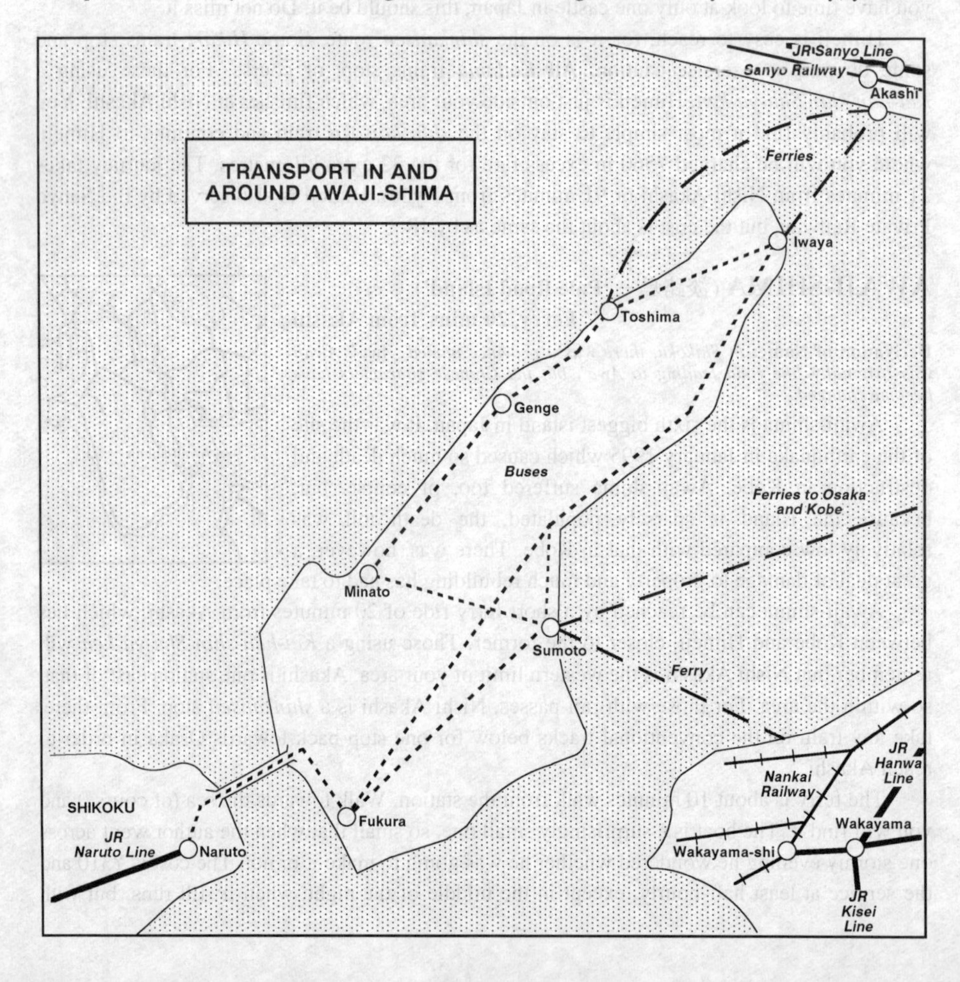

be able to see them from the bus. There is more information on this phenomenon under the Naruto heading in the section on Shikoku.

It is also possible to perform a partial circuit of Awaji-shima by taking a bus from Sumoto to Minato (湊), 45 minutes, ¥700, and another from there to Toshima (富島), 65 minutes, ¥1,200. However, this last bus runs through to Toshima only in mid-summer. At other times it is necessary to change at Genge (郡家), which will increase the fare to ¥840 plus ¥560, a total of ¥1,400 from Minato to Toshima. From Toshima, there is an hourly ferry service back to Akashi at a cost of ¥600. It takes 25 minutes. However, what you will see on Awaji-shima is pleasant but not spectacular rural and coastal scenery at considerable cost. It is worthwhile considering going through Awaji-shima to reach Shikoku, for it is a relatively quick and less frequented route, but to perform a tour of the island for itself may not be the best use of limited time and money.

There is a ticket called an 'Awaji-shima Free' (淡路島フリー) which gives unlimited travel by bus within the island for two days. It costs ¥3,120. Note, however, that it must be purchased from a travel agent in advance and cannot be bought on the island.

## KII PENINSULA (紀伊半島 – 'Description Half Island')

**Kise Line, 2 hrs. from Nagoya or from Osaka**

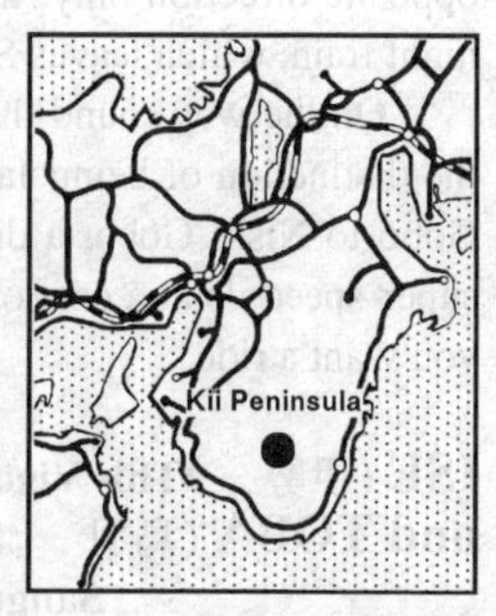


**Derivation of Name:** *Original meaning was 'tree country', but Chinese characters have been changed.*

The Kii Peninsula ('Kii Hanto') extends southwards between Nagoya and Kyoto. Except for visits to the area of Ise and Toba, at the eastern extremity of the peninsula, most people just cut across the top where the main railway lines run. However, if you have time, this is actually a pleasant area of relatively unpopulated countryside. The JR Kise Line runs all the way round by the coast, so, if you are not in too much of a hurry, why not travel round this pretty line instead of rushing along on the *shinkansen* and seeing so little of rural Japan? There are *tokkyu* trains, but they cannot run all the way round because the Osaka end of the line is electrified, while the Nagoya end is not. Trains from Nagoya generally go as far as Kii Katsuura, while those from Shin Osaka (sometimes Kyoto also) run to Shingu, so that there is a slight overlap in the middle. Shingu is the border between JR Tokai and JR West. It is also the limit of electrification from the Osaka direction. It is, of course, preferable to sit on the sea side, that is on the left from Nagoya or on the right from Osaka. Here are some suitable connexions:-

① Nagoya 8:15. Shingu 11:20 / 11:39. Shin Osaka 15:50.
② Nagoya 8:15. Shingu 11:20 / 12:41. Shin Osaka 16:51. Kyoto 17:16.
③ Nagoya 10:50. Shingu 14:03 / 14:40. Shin Osaka 18:53.
④ Tennoji (in southern Osaka) 9:20. Kii Katsuura 12:45 / 13:05. Nagoya 16:29.

There is an hourly service at the Osaka end of the line, but only a limited service at the Nagoya end. Trains to and from Nagoya travel by way of the Ise Private Railway, for which section one must pay ¥440, plus a *tokkyu* supplement of ¥250. If you prefer to stop on the way, there is a convenient youth hostel in Shingu (Shingu Hayatama Hostel), located very close to Hayatama Jingu, which is one of the most important shrines in the area.

Those using Blue Spring tickets will be obliged to stop somewhere *en route*, as it is impossible to get round in a single day and arrive at Nagoya or Osaka at a reasonable hour.

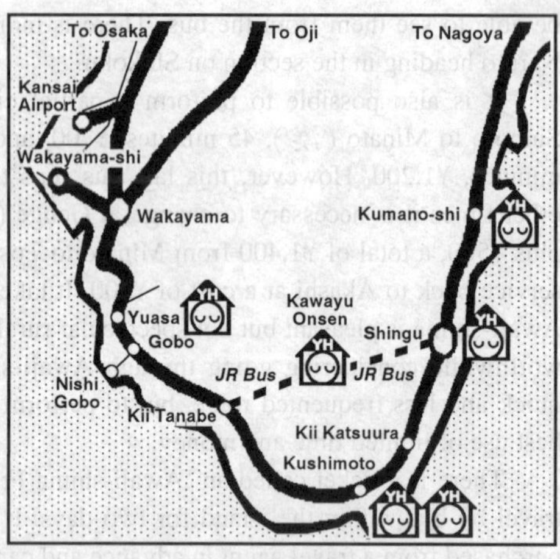


KII HANTO

Also, several changes of train are necessary. It is possible, however, leaving Tokyo at 6:47, to reach Shingu by ordinary train almost exactly twelve hours later. (Tokyo 6:47. Hiratsuka 7:49 / 7:56. Atami 8:40 / 8:41. Hamamatsu 11:15 / 11:18. Nagoya 12:49 / 13:10. Taki 14:19 (via Ise Private Railway, ¥440) / 15:19. Shingu 18:50.) Next day you can continue at 6:54, 8:07 (change at Kii Tanabe), 9:23 (change at Kii Tanabe) or 11:05 to Wakayama, a journey of 5 hours, and thence to Tennoji (Osaka), another hour, and on to Kyoto if you wish, another hour, taking the Osaka Kanjo Loop Line between Tennoji and Osaka. In the opposite direction only, there is an ordinary night train, which leaves Shin Osaka at 22:45 and reaches Shingu at 5:01.

On the way round the Kii Peninsula, you will pass the Kishu Private Railway which has the distinction of being Japan's shortest, if you are interested in such a curiosity. It runs from Gobo to Nishi Gobo, a distance of 2.7 kilometres, which it covers in 8 minutes (not exactly super-speedy!) at a cost of ¥160. Trains run about once an hour, if you want a ride.

## ISE (伊勢 – 'This Vigour') and TOBA (鳥羽 – 'Bird Feather')

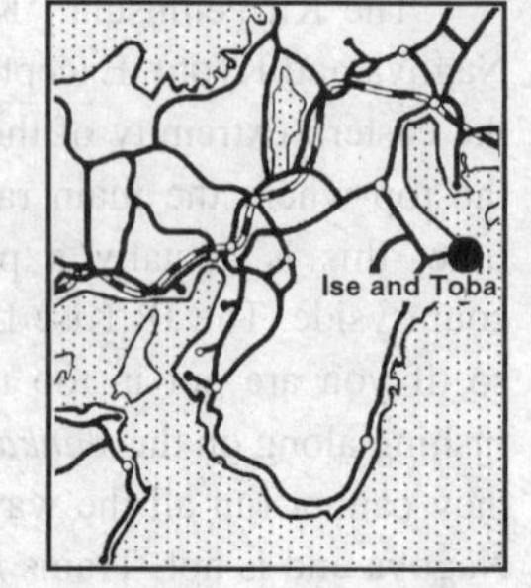


**Sangu Line, 90 mins. to Ise-shi from Nagoya**

These two towns were included in the section on Chubu, since they are most easily visited from Nagoya. See pages 225 to 228.

## AMANO HASHIDATE (天橋立 – 'Heavenly Standing Bridge')

**Kita Kinki Tango Private Railway, 2 hrs. 15 mins. from Kyoto**

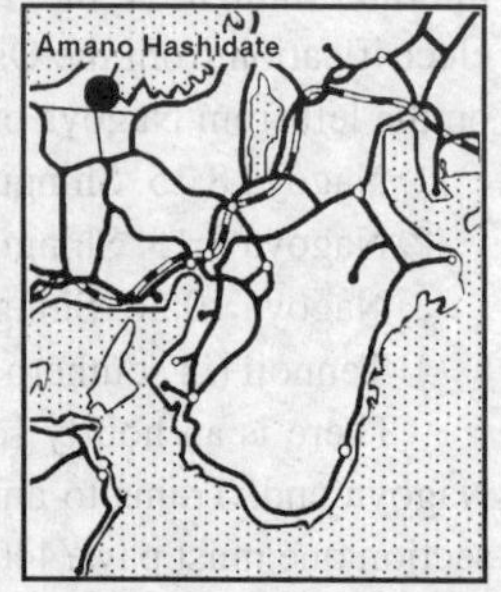


**Derivation of Name:** *According to legend, there was a ladder to heaven in this place, but it fell down, forming the famous sandbar now visible.*

Amano Hashidate lies rather more than two hours north of Kyoto on a railway which used to belong to JR, but was given away as unprofitable. That is a little surprising really because Amano Hashidate is one of Japan's top three natural scenic attractions, according to the official list, and people flock here in the summer especially, at which time extra trains are operated. The scenic beauty consists of a lengthy sandbar with pine trees growing on it. It is quite pretty, but even Japanese probably rank it as number three out of the three and others might be inclined to rank it somewhat lower than that.

Amano Hashidate can be visited as a day trip from Kyoto or Osaka, but it will be rather an expensive one now that the line is no longer JR. Alternatively, it can be fitted quite conveniently into the tour of the Chugoku region outlined in the next section. That would not be significantly cheaper but it would save time and avoid retracing trainsteps. However, if you decide to go from Kyoto, there are *tokkyu* trains at 9:30 and 10:25 and there are *kyuko* departures at 11:25 and 14:25. These trains use JR track as far as Nishi Maizuru and then switch to the private railway. The cost of the private railway section to Amano Hashidate is ¥610 and the supplement for the *tokkyu* is ¥720 for a reserved seat or ¥620 for an unreserved seat. For the *kyuko*, it is ¥310 for a reserved seat or ¥210 for an unreserved one. There is an alternative route along a line which runs between Fukuchiyama and Miyazu, if you want variety for the return. Miyazu is one station east of Amano Hashidate. This line also is operated by the Kita Kinki Tango Private Railway (no connexion with dancing. Tango is the name of this region). Express trains do not use this line, except in mid-summer and also except for one *tokkyu* train which leaves Amano Hashidate at 7:03 every morning and reaches Kyoto at 9:05. However, there are ordinary and *kaisoku* trains operating approximately an hourly service. Usually it is necessary to change at Miyazu.

If you travel all the way from Kyoto by ordinary train, take the San-in Line and change trains at Sonobe, where the electrification ends. The journey will take an hour. Next take a train to Fukuchiyama, about 80 minutes, and change to a private railway train to Miyazu, about 45 minutes. Then finally one more station west to Amano Hashidate. The fare from Fukuchiyama to Amano Hashidate is ¥730. Alternatively, from Sonobe take the train only to the small station of Ayabe, one hour, and change to a train in the opposite direction to Nishi Maizuru, 30 minutes, from where you can take the private railway to Amano Hashidate, 45 minutes. Whichever way you go, it is an awkward journey and there may come a stage when you begin to wonder whether it was worth it.

Once in Amano Hashidate, you still have some more travelling to do to reach the scenic viewpoints. First, you must get to Ichinomiya (一の宮), by walking (4 kilometres), by bus (10 kilometres, 20 minutes, ¥510) or by ferry (12 minutes, ¥510). If you take the bus, it will probably be going to Kyoga Misaki (経ヶ岬) or Hinode (日出) and you want to get off at Cable Shita (ケーブル下) which is, not surprisingly, the bottom of a cablecar and chairlift running up to a place named Kasamatsu ('Umbrella Pine') above, from where the view is to be beheld. The bus actually starts in Miyazu, if you find it more convenient to take it from there. It costs ¥630 from Miyazu. The cablecar or chairlift ride costs ¥310.

There are two youth hostels in Amano Hashidate (see page 435). The maps given there will also help you to find your way from the station to the cablecar. The hostels are both quite near the base station for the cablecar and chairlift.

▲ Sagano Kanko Railway, Kyoto

This tram was running in Hiroshima on the day when the first atomic bomb was dropped ▼

# CHUGOKU（中国）
## ('Middle Country')

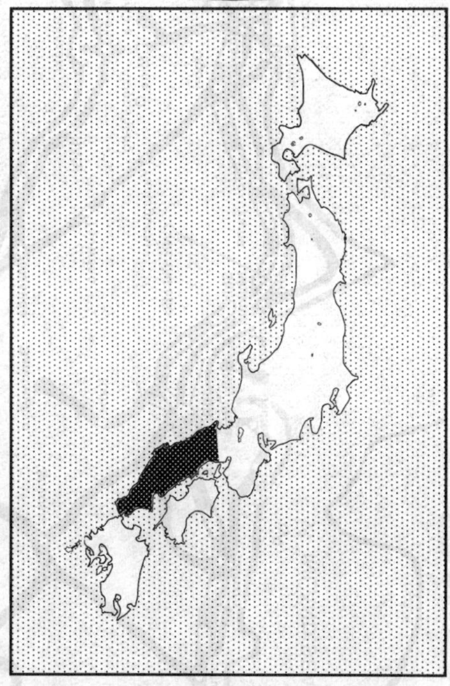

The part of Japan lying west of the Kansai area is known as Chugoku. Incidentally, the same word is used to mean China, so be sure that you have the right Chugoku before travelling there!

It is an area which people tend to travel through without really looking at, except that Hiroshima features on many itineraries. The Sanyo *shinkansen* line runs through the southern part of Chugoku and so a quick glance from a rapidly moving train window is all that can be managed by many visitors. This book too will make the assumption that you are passing through Chugoku in order to reach another area of Japan, probably Kyushu or Shikoku, and will suggest a few stops which can be made on the way. As usual, we shall describe a circle, this time in a clockwise direction, the outward journey beside the Seto Nai-kai (Inland Sea) and the return along the northern coast beside the Japan Sea. If you wish to visit Shikoku, break off after Okayama and continue with our Chugoku route on your return. Alternatively, you can take a ferry from Hiroshima to Matsuyama, travel round Shikoku and then take a ferry to Kyushu. If you intend to visit Kyushu but not Shikoku, continue from Shimonoseki around Kyushu, completing the Chugoku expedition when you come back.

***Transportation and Tickets***

If you do not have a rail pass, this is a good area to be using Blue Spring tickets or passing through with a *shu-yu-ken* for Kyushu. If you really want to explore Chugoku, however, there is one ticket which is very well suited to the Chugoku tour described here and which would also allow you to look at such places as Nagoya, Kyoto, Nara, Osaka, Kobe and Himeji *en route*. It is called a *Tsuwano Hagi Free Kippu* and the rules for it are almost the same as those governing the use of a *shu-yu-ken*. Ordinary or *kyuko* trains may be used to reach the area, or you can use faster trains and pay just the supplements. Within the area (i.e. between Asa and Masuda), you can use the unreserved seats of the *tokkyu* named *Oki* which runs between Shimonoseki and Yonago. One of the very good features of this ticket is that, within the area of unrestricted travel, you can use Bocho buses in addition to JR buses and trains. A second and excellent feature is that the ticket is valid for 16 days from Tokyo, the longest duration of any of the special tickets currently on offer. The area of this ticket and the permitted access routes are shown in the map on page 273. It costs ¥22,160 for 16 days from Tokyo.

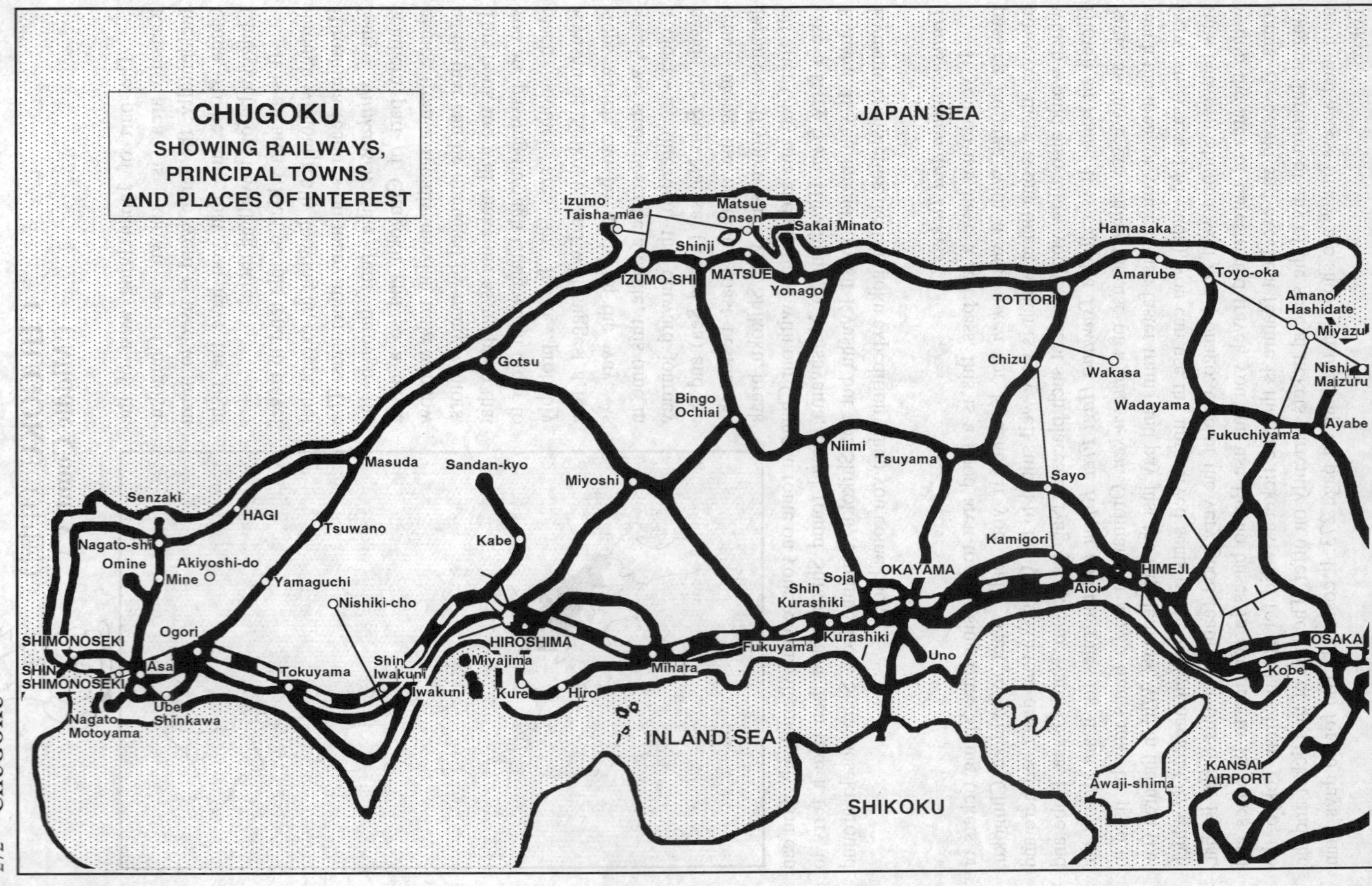
CHUGOKU
SHOWING RAILWAYS,
PRINCIPAL TOWNS
AND PLACES OF INTEREST
JAPAN SEA
Izumo Taisha-mae
Matsue Onsen
Sakai Minato
Hamasaka
Shinji
IZUMO-SHI
MATSUE
Yonago
Amarube
Toyo-oka
TOTTORI
Amano Hashidate
Miyazu
Gotsu
Chizu
Wakasa
Nishi Maizuru
Bingo Ochiai
Wadayama
Ayabe
Fukuchiyama
Niimi
Masuda
Sandan-kyo
Tsuyama
Miyoshi
Sayo
Senzaki
HAGI
Tsuwano
Kabe
Kamigori
Nagato-shi
Omine
Akiyoshi-do
Mine
Yamaguchi
Soja
OKAYAMA
HIMEJI
Nishiki-cho
Aioi
Shin Kurashiki
Ogori
SHIMONOSEKI
HIROSHIMA
Kurashiki
OSAKA
Fukuyama
Uno
SHIN SHIMONOSEKI
Asa
Tokuyama
Shin Iwakuni
Miyajima
Mihara
Kobe
Iwakuni
Kure
Hiro
Ube
Nagato Motoyama
Shinkawa
INLAND SEA
KANSAI AIRPORT
Awaji-shima
SHIKOKU

There is also a *shu-yu-ken* (excursion ticket) available. This is called a *Yamaguchi Akiyoshi-do Mini Shu-yu-ken*. The area covered, which is somewhat larger than that permitted by the *Tsuwano Hagi Free Kippu*, is shown in the map below. Since this is a 'mini' *shu-yu-ken*, the use of *tokkyu* trains, even within the area of unlimited travel, is not permitted unless major supplements are paid. Moreover, rather unusually, the ticket is not available from the Tokyo area. However, it is available from the Kansai region, costing ¥16,070 from Kyoto, ¥15,040 from Osaka or ¥14,010 from Kobe. The ticket is valid for 7 days. The nearest point of origin to Tokyo available for this *shu-yu-ken* is Shizuoka, from where it costs ¥19,470 and is valid for 10 days. Overall, especially as the time limit is much shorter, it does not seem to represent the same good value as the *Tsuwano Hagi Free Kippu*.

If you intend, or have only enough time, to go as far as Hiroshima and Iwakuni, there is an *Hiroshima Miyajima Mini Shu-yu-ken*. This ticket will also permit the side trip to Sandan-kyo. Again the use of *tokkyu* trains is not permitted unless substantial supplements are paid. The cost is ¥20,090 from Tokyo and the ticket is valid for 10 days. The area covered is shown in the map at the foot of page 280.

If you are using a *Shikoku Wide Shu-yu-ken*, you will be able to travel only the small section of our tour as far as Okayama. If you are using a *Kyushu Wide Shu-yu-ken*, you will be able to go all the way to Shimonoseki, but only by the southern route. The return along the Japan Sea coast will, unfortunately, not be permitted.

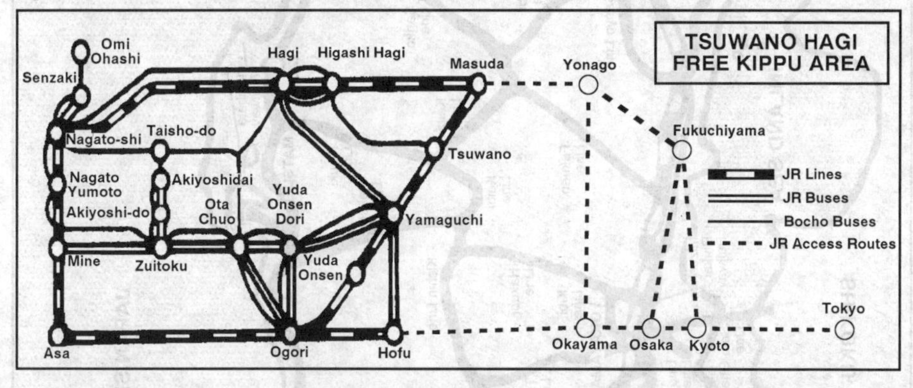


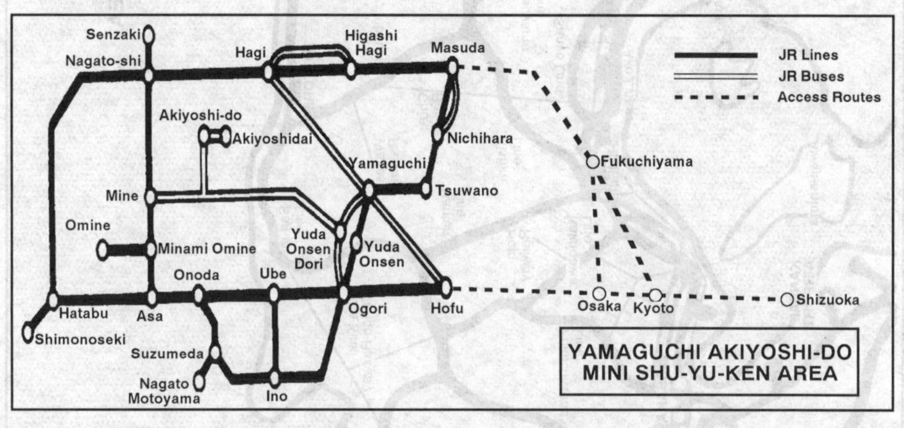

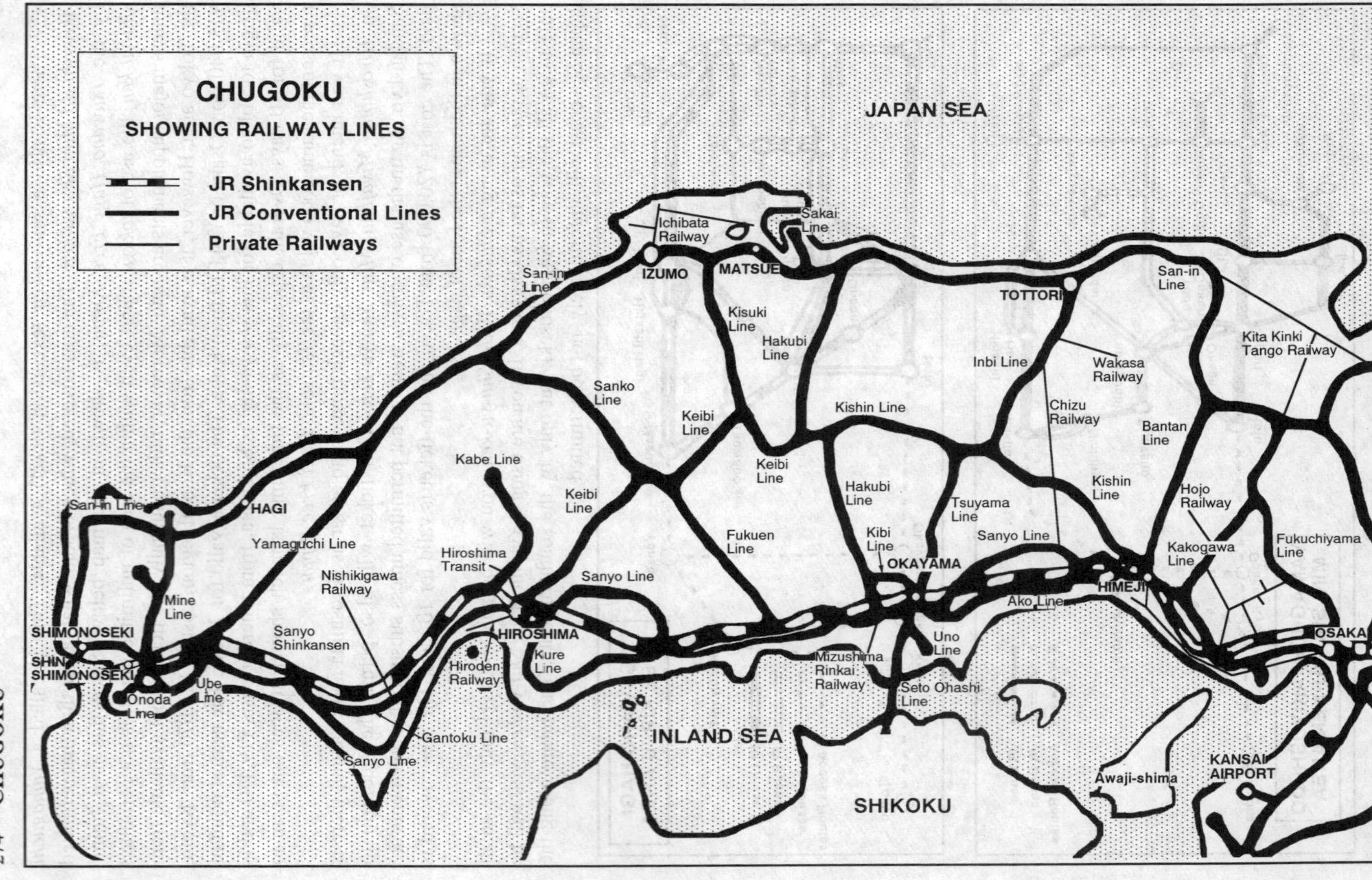
CHUGOKU
SHOWING RAILWAY LINES
JR Shinkansen
JR Conventional Lines
Private Railways
JAPAN SEA
Ichibata Railway
Sakai Line
San-in Line
IZUMO
MATSUE
TOTTORI
San-in Line
Kisuki Line
Hakubi Line
Kita Kinki Tango Railway
Inbi Line
Wakasa Railway
Sanko Line
Keibi Line
Kishin Line
Chizu Railway
Bantan Line
Kabe Line
Keibi Line
Keibi Line
Hakubi Line
Tsuyama Line
Kishin Line
Hojo Railway
San-in Line
HAGI
Yamaguchi Line
Hiroshima Transit
Fukuen Line
Kibi Line
Sanyo Line
Kakogawa Line
Fukuchiyama Line
Nishikigawa Railway
Sanyo Line
OKAYAMA
HIMEJI
Mine Line
Ako Line
SHIMONOSEKI
Sanyo Shinkansen
HIROSHIMA
Uno Line
OSAKA
SHIN SHIMONOSEKI
Kure Line
Mizushima Rinkai Railway
Hiroden Railway
Ube Line
Onoda Line
Seto Ohashi Line
Gantoku Line
INLAND SEA
Sanyo Line
KANSAI AIRPORT
Awaji-shima
SHIKOKU

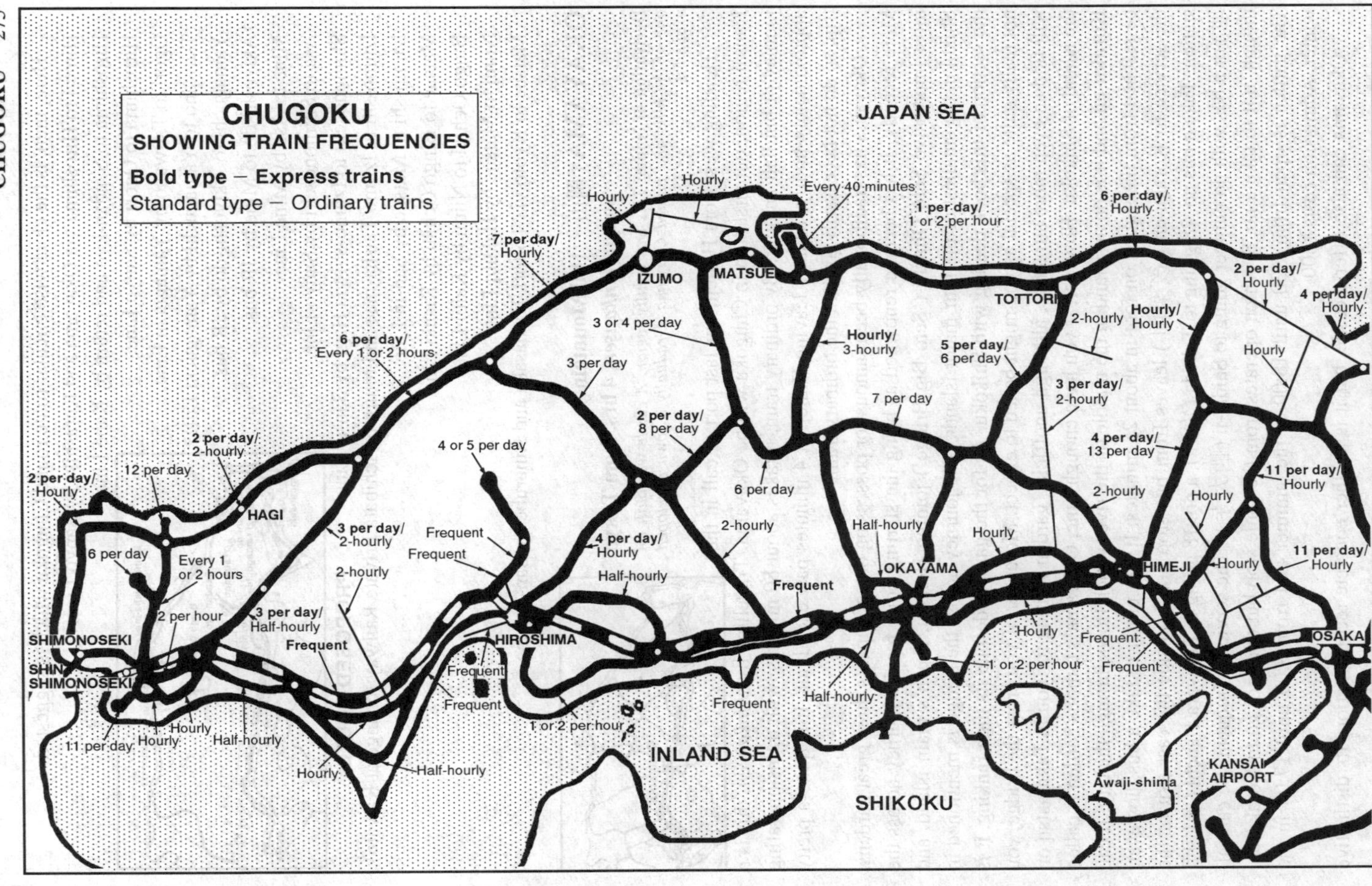
CHUGOKU
SHOWING TRAIN FREQUENCIES
Bold type – Express trains
Standard type – Ordinary trains
JAPAN SEA
Hourly
Hourly
Every 40 minutes
1 per day/
1 or 2 per hour
6 per day/
Hourly
7 per day/
Hourly
IZUMO
MATSUE
TOTTORI
2 per day/
Hourly
4 per day/
Hourly
3 or 4 per day
Hourly/
3-hourly
5 per day/
6 per day
2-hourly
Hourly/
Hourly
Hourly
6 per day/
Every 1 or 2 hours
3 per day
7 per day
3 per day/
2-hourly
2 per day/
8 per day
4 per day/
13 per day
2 per day/
2-hourly
4 or 5 per day
11 per day/
Hourly
2 per day/
Hourly
12 per day
6 per day
2-hourly
HAGI
Hourly
3 per day/
2-hourly
Frequent
Frequent
4 per day/
Hourly
2-hourly
Half-hourly
Hourly
6 per day
Every 1
or 2 hours
2-hourly
Hourly
HIMEJI
Hourly
11 per day/
Hourly
Half-hourly
OKAYAMA
Frequent
2 per hour
3 per day/
Half-hourly
SHIMONOSEKI
Frequent
HIROSHIMA
Hourly
Frequent
OSAKA
SHIN
SHIMONOSEKI
Frequent
1 or 2 per hour
Frequent
Frequent
Frequent
Half-hourly
Hourly
1 or 2 per hour
1 per day
Hourly
Half-hourly
INLAND SEA
Hourly
Half-hourly
KANSAI
AIRPORT
Awaji-shima
SHIKOKU

Here, then, is the clockwise circular route round Chugoku which is suggested:-
Himeji to Hiroshima via Okayama and Kurashiki by Sanyo Line.
Hiroshima to Sandan-kyo and return by Kabe Line.
Hiroshima to Ogori by Sanyo Line.
Ogori to Tsuwano by Yamaguchi Line.
Tsuwano to Yamaguchi by Yamaguchi Line.
Yamaguchi to Akiyoshi-do by JR bus.
Akiyoshi-do to Mine by JR bus.
Mine to Asa by Mine Line.
Asa to Shimonoseki by Sanyo Line.
Shimonoseki to Izumo-shi via Hagi by San-in Line.
Izumo-shi to Izumo Taisha-mae and return by Ichibata Private Railway (change at Kawato).
Izumo-shi to Matsue by San-in Line.
Matsue to Bingo Ochiai by Kisuki Line.
Bingo Ochiai to Niimi by Keibi Line.
Niimi to Matsue by Hakubi Line.
Matsue to Kyoto via Tottori, Hamasaka and Amarube by San-in Line.

**PROPOSED ROUTE**

## OKAYAMA (岡山 - 'Hill Mountain')

**Sanyo *shinkansen*, 4 hrs. from Tokyo**

**Derivation of Name:** *This was a hilly region. A castle was built on one of the hills and named Okayama. Gradually a town developed around it.*

Heading west from Himeji, our last port of call in the Kansai region, our first stop in Chugoku will be Okayama. Travelling by *shinkansen*, this is a journey of but half an hour. By ordinary train, it takes about 80 minutes, with trains operating approximately hourly, usually leaving Himeji at 4 minutes past each hour. It is quite a pretty trip, so do not necessarily disdain the ordinary train.

Okayama has traditionally been famous for possessing one of Japan's three great gardens. More recently, it has become renowned as being the starting point for the journey across the most impressive **Seto Ohashi** ('Seto Big Bridge') joining Honshu, Japan's main island, and Shikoku, the smallest of the four major islands. The journey across the bridge is mentioned in the section of this book dealing with Shikoku. As for the garden, despite its high ranking, it is not really quite as special as you might be led to expect. Moreover, if you cross the bridge, you will find an even more attractive, although unofficial, garden waiting for you in Takamatsu on the island of Shikoku. However, if you have enough time, Okayama's famous garden is called **Koraku-en** and it is on an island in the middle of the river which flows through the city. It can be reached from the station on foot in about 25 minutes. If you prefer to take a bus, however, the service to Koraku-en (後楽園) leaves from bus stop no. 2 outside the east exit of the station. Take a bus no. 28 going to Takeda (竹田), a no. 18 going to Fujiwara Danchi (藤原団地) or a bus with no number going to Saidai-ji (西大寺). The service is frequent. Be careful, though, **not** to take a no. 8, which operates from the same stop but does not go to Koraku-en. The garden is open from 7:30 until 18:00 in the summer and from 8:00 until 17:00 in the winter. Admission costs ¥300.

Okayama can also offer a castle, but it is another concrete reconstruction. Its distinctive

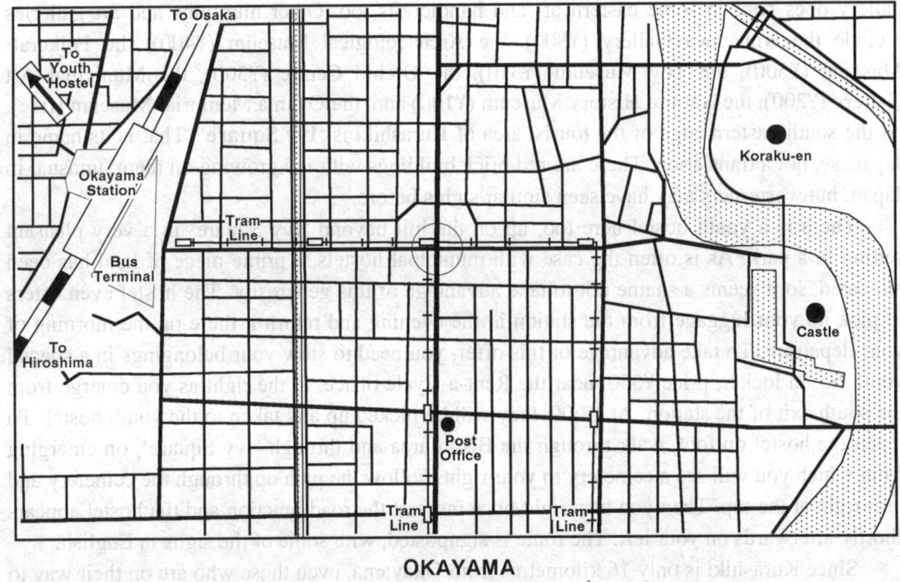

OKAYAMA

feature is that, like the castle in Matsumoto, it is black instead of the customary white.

The city has a youth hostel too, walking distance from the station. As usual, see the Youth Hostels section of this book.

## KURASHIKI (倉敷 – 'Laying Out Warehouses')

**Sanyo *shinkansen*, 4 hrs. 30 mins. from Tokyo**

**Derivation of Name:** *The city contained many warehouses for the storage of rice produced in the area.*

It should be noted that the Sanyo *shinkansen* stop is actually at Shin Kurashiki ('New Kurashiki'), which is two stations west of Kurashiki on the JR Sanyo Main Line. Since only *Kodama* trains, the slower type of *shinkansen* service, stop at Shin Kurashiki, the best way to reach the city, if travelling by *shinkansen*, is to alight at Okayama, where all trains stop, and take the ordinary train for three stations along the conventional Sanyo Line to Kurashiki, a journey of just 14 minutes. The service is frequent.

As stated above, Kurashiki is so named because of all the warehouses formerly used for keeping the rice produced in the area. Many of these, built of stone, can still be seen around the town in what is called the **Bikan** ('Beautiful Sights') **Area**. Some have been converted into small museums and galleries. There is also a tree-lined canal with stone banks passing the warehouses, so that the rice could be shipped away. All is very pretty and the town is certainly worth a visit for these unique features.

The most famous of the museums and galleries is the Ohara Art Gallery. Mr. Ohara was a prosperous textile producer who was attracted by western art and this is his collection. Probably you did not come to Japan to admire western art though, and the admission charge is a high ¥800, so you may decide not to put this on your list of daily expenses, even though the gallery does contain some eastern art and handicrafts too. Other museums and art galleries include the Ninagawa Gallery (¥800), the Archaeological Museum (¥400), the Folkcraft Museum (¥500), the Toy Museum (¥310), the Orchid Centre (¥300), the Municipal Art Gallery (¥200), the Natural History Museum (¥100) and the Oyama Memorial Museum (free). At the south-eastern edge of the tourist area of Kurashiki is **'Ivy Square'**. That is its name in Japanese, not a translation. There are red brick buildings with ivy growing on them, unusual in Japan, but westerners may have seen similar sights before.

There is a youth hostel here too, up on the hill beyond 'Ivy Square' in a very pleasant setting in a park. As is often the case with municipal hostels, a prime piece of land has been allocated, so it seems a shame not to take advantage of this generosity. The hostel even offers to pick up your luggage from the station in the evening and return it there on the morning of your departure. To take advantage of this offer, you need to stow your belongings in a special youth hostel locker, price ¥350, near the Rent-a-Cycle office, to the right as you emerge from the south exit of the station. At 17:00, they will be picked up and taken to the youth hostel. To reach the hostel on foot, walk through the Bikan area and through 'Ivy Square', on emerging from which you will see a cemetery to your right. Follow the path up through the cemetery and turn right at the top. Then you turn right once more at the road junction and the hostel appears shortly afterwards on your left. The route is signposted, with some of the signs in English.

Since Kurashiki is only 16 kilometres from Okayama, even those who are on their way to Shikoku should consider making the detour here. It costs only ¥310 each way on the train, a price which is certainly worth paying to see a little of traditional Japan. If you are then travelling to Shikoku, take the train south from Okayama. When you have looked at the island of Shikoku, you can return to Okayama and continue west or you may prefer to take a ferry from Matsuyama to Hiroshima, which is our next stop in Chugoku, or one of the variety of ferry services from Shikoku to Kyushu.

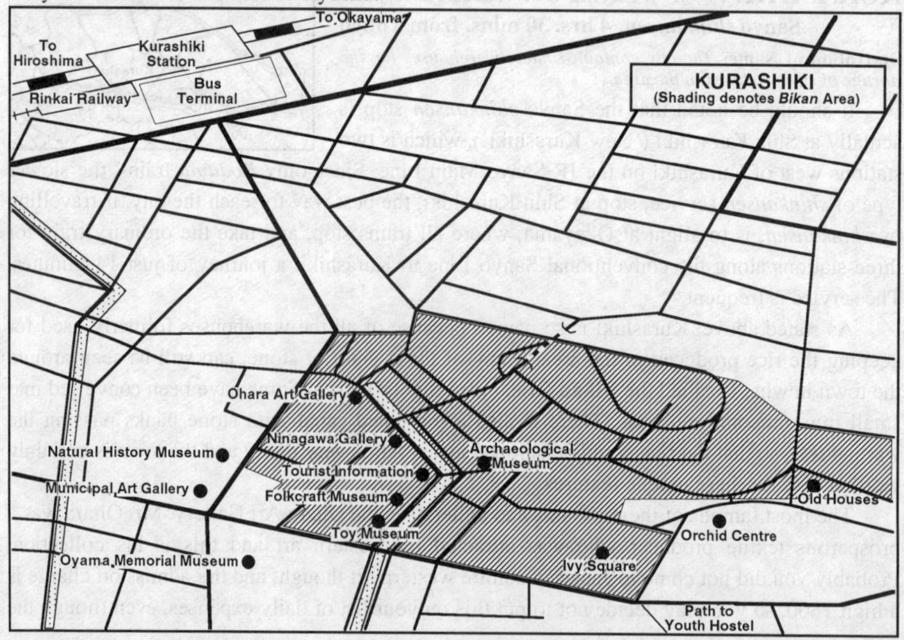

# HIROSHIMA (広島 – 'Wide Island')

**Sanyo *shinkansen*, 5 hrs. from Tokyo**

**Derivation of Name:** *There were two great warriors named Hiromoto and Fukushima who came from this area. The word Hiroshima is reputed to be an amalgam of their names.*

By *shinkansen*, Hiroshima is only 45 minutes from Okayama. By ordinary train, however, it takes nearly 3 hours and it is sometimes necessary to change trains on the way. Trains run about every 30 minutes. *En route*, at the port of Mihara, the line divides. The Sanyo Main Line cuts inland, while the Kure Line runs round the coast and is, of course, the more scenic route. However, if you choose it you will add an hour to your travelling time, it taking two hours from Mihara to Hiroshima by the Kure Line, compared with one hour by the Sanyo Line. You will probably have to add some time for changing trains too. Departures on the Kure Line are once or twice an hour, often involving another change on the way at Hiro.

Hiroshima, of course, achieved notoriety as the victim of the first atomic bomb. For that reason it is on everybody's itinerary and it caters well for those speaking English, both for tourist information and for accommodation. This is a good point to issue a warning, therefore, that the city has really only two attractions to offer – the remains and reminders of that terrible bombing and the nearby island of Miyajima. Otherwise, it is a rather ordinary city, and, of course, a new one, for little remained after 6th August 1945. By all means make a pilgrimage here, but do not make the mistake of thinking that it will take several days to see the sights. A day or a little less is quite sufficient to allow.

**'Peace Park'** lies below where that first atomic bomb exploded in 1945. It was a residential area at the time, but it was decided to convert it into a park to serve as a memorial to the event. An attempt was made to erect a map showing the homes and names of all those who perished in what is now the park. However, this effort reveals pitifully that insufficient people survived for their collective memories even to assign names to half of those who were

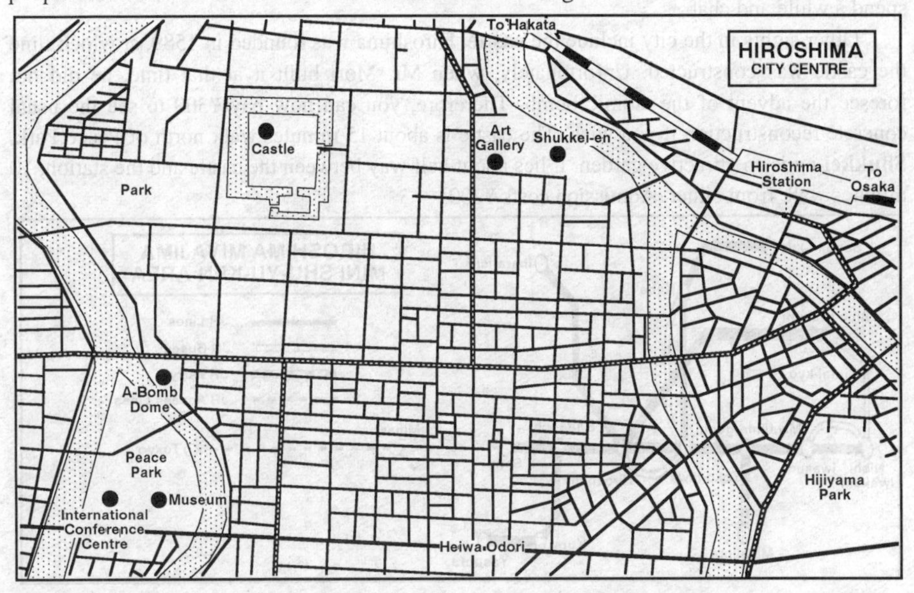

consumed by the devastation. The symbol of Hiroshima famous throughout the world, the **'A-Bomb Dome'**, lies in one corner of the park. This building was originally the Industrial Promotion Hall and was of a very atypical architectural style, being of western influence. Probably it is a great tribute to its strong construction that it still exists at all, for it was almost exactly beneath the spot where the B-29 bomber dropped its historic load. The atomic bomb exploded about 580 metres above the Industrial Promotion Hall and the temperature is thought to have reached 300,000 ℃, hot enough to melt concrete (and people, of course). However, the shell of this building still remains, and has been allowed to remain as a permanent reminder of what happened and in the hope that it will never happen again. The metal skeleton of this building was twisted by the force of the blast and in recent years it has been propped up to maintain it in a state of ruin, if that be not too much of a contradiction.

Around Peace Park are various monuments which need not be listed here. You can wander round and look at them, but the place which you have to visit, of course, is the **museum**. Admission costs a token ¥50. It should be said that a visit to this museum is a duty rather than a pleasure. It is, in fact, an harrowing experience and you are likely to leave pondering just what the destiny of humanity may be and wondering whether we are more or less civilized than a millennium or so ago. Hiroshima, it must be acknowledged, has done an excellent job of turning its fearful experience to good use by terming itself the 'City of Peace' and trying to publicize its devastation in such a way as to warn the world of what may happen if another such bomb is dropped. Moreover, of course, the bomb which was dropped here is but a small toy compared with what is available fifty years on.

To reach Peace Park, take a tram from the station. Trams marked 2, 6 or 宮 ('*Miya*') will take you in 15 minutes to Genbaku Dome-mae ('Atomic Bomb Dome'). Alternatively, you can walk in about 30 minutes. When you have finished looking at the museum and park, the **International Conference Centre**, near the museum, houses a place called the International Lounge, just up some steps from the entrance, where visitors from overseas are welcome to spend a while and chat.

Other sights in the city include the **castle**. Hiroshima was founded in 1589, at which time the castle was constructed. Unfortunately, when Mr. Mori built it at that time, he did not foresee the advent of the atomic bomb. Therefore, you can now pay ¥300 to see the usual concrete reconstruction if you wish. The castle is about 15 minutes walk north of Peace Park. **Shukkei-en** is an attractive garden. It lies about half way between the castle and the station, 10 minutes walk from either. Admission costs ¥200.

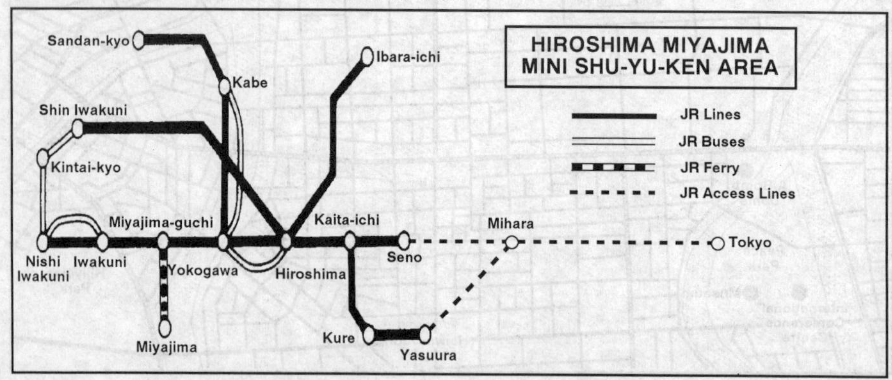

Hiroshima has a fairly comprehensive tram network, a diagram of which is shown below. A one-day ticket is available, details of which are given on the next page. Some of the trams have been brought here from cities around the world, but most of those are used only on special occasions and are not in regular service. The author was interested to travel on one tram (on route 9, which is short and independent of the other routes) which bore a small notice at one end stating, in Japanese, of course, 'This tram was in service on the day when the atomic bomb was dropped on the city of Hiroshima. At 8:15 on 6th August 1945, it had just left the depot to start its day's work. It was about 7 kilometres from the spot where the bomb detonated. It was blown from the track and all windows were smashed, but it did not otherwise suffer serious damage and was later restored to regular service.' Sturdy vehicles are trams! However, I could not help wondering just how much radioactivity I was absorbing during my brief ride on the vehicle.

The second main attraction of the Hiroshima area lies not within the city itself, but eight stations west on the JR Sanyo Line or at the very end of the Hiroshima tram system. This is **Miyajima**, a small and attractive island lying just a short ferry ride off the coast. Along with Matsushima, near Sendai in the Tohoku district, and Amano Hashidate, two hours north of Kyoto, this is one of the three official natural beauty spots of Japan. Its reputation is well deserved. The only negative feature is, as usual in Japan, that there may be a large number of other people there at the same time as you.

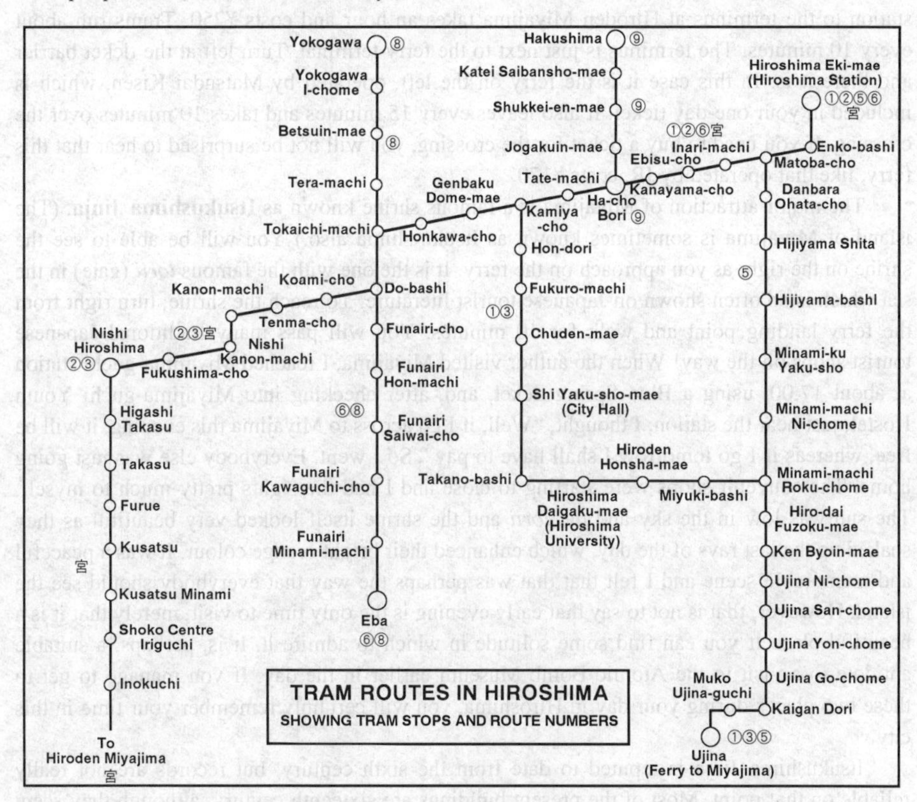

If you have a Japan Rail Pass or if you are using a *shu-yu-ken*, you will naturally travel to the JR station of Miyajima-guchi, 30 minutes from Hiroshima. From the exit, you can see the ferry terminal straight ahead, about 3 minutes walk if the traffic lights are kind to you. There are two ferry companies operating services, with boats leaving every few minutes. The ferry on the right is operated by JR and you can use it free with a Japan Rail Pass, an *Hiroshima Miyajima Mini Shu-yu-ken* or a Blue Spring ticket. Otherwise, it costs ¥170 each way. The crossing takes 10 minutes and ferries leave every 15 minutes during the main part of the day.

If you do not have a Japan Rail Pass or other suitable JR ticket, what you should do is purchase a one-day tram ticket ('*ichi-nichi jo-sha-ken*') before you begin your day's sightseeing. These are available at an office outside Hiroshima station (and at Hiroden Miyajima station, at the other end of the tram line, for those starting there). Two types are available. The first type gives the freedom of the tram system for a day and costs ¥600. The second type includes the ferry to and from Miyajima and costs ¥840. If you purchase this ticket, you can look around Hiroshima first and then use it to come to Miyajima later in the day – or *vice versa*, of course. It will be an economical way of taking care of your transportation expenses for the day. If you are using the tram system for your visit to Miyajima, take a tram marked 宮 ('*Miya*'). These trams start from Hiroshima station, run past Peace Park, then go to Nishi Hiroshima station and continue from there as a private railway system running parallel to and beside the JR Sanyo Line. The entire journey from Hiroshima station to the terminus at Hiroden Miyajima takes an hour and costs ¥250. Trams run about every 10 minutes. The terminus is just next to the ferry terminal. Turn left at the ticket barrier and there it is. In this case it is the ferry on the left, operated by Matsudai Kisen, which is included in your one-day ticket. It also leaves every 15 minutes and takes 10 minutes over the crossing. If you need to buy a ticket for the crossing, you will not be surprised to hear that this ferry, like that operated by JR, costs ¥170.

The major attraction of Miyajima is a famous shrine known as **Itsukushima Jinja**. (The island of Miyajima is sometimes known as Itsuku-shima also.) You will be able to see the shrine on the right as you approach on the ferry. It is the one with the famous *torii* (gate) in the sea which is so often shown on Japanese tourist literature. To reach the shrine, turn right from the ferry landing point and walk for 10 minutes. You will pass many traditional Japanese tourist shops on the way! When the author visited Miyajima, I reached Miyajima-guchi station at about 17:00, using a Blue Spring ticket, and, after checking into Miyajima-guchi Youth Hostel, just near the station, I thought, "Well, if I go across to Miyajima this evening, it will be free, whereas if I go tomorrow I shall have to pay." So I went. Everybody else was just going home. The souvenir shops were starting to close and I had the sights pretty much to myself. The sun was low in the sky and the *torii* and the shrine itself looked very beautiful as they soaked up the last rays of the day, which enhanced their bright orange colour. It was a peaceful and memorable scene and I felt that that was perhaps the way that everybody should see the island. However, that is not to say that early evening is the only time to visit, merely that it is a beautiful place if you can find some solitude in which to admire it. It is, perhaps, a suitable antidote to a visit to the Atomic Bomb Museum earlier in the day. If you manage to get to these two places during your day in Hiroshima, you will certainly remember your time in this city.

Itsukushima Jinja is reputed to date from the sixth century, but records are not really reliable on that point. Most of the present buildings are sixteenth century, although they seem to be accurate reconstructions of earlier buildings dating from the twelfth century. The pagoda nearby was constructed in 1533, while the famous *torii* in the sea was rebuilt in 1875. The shrine is most unusual in that most of it is on piles over the sea and the passages are similarly like gangways just above the water. The central part of the shrine is a *Noh* stage, the oldest in Japan, although it has been rebuilt at least once. From the point of view of the audience, it is not really in an ideal location, unless one happens to be amphibious. Admission to Itsukushima Jinja costs ¥200.

There are other places to visit on the island too, if you have time. Various trails lead up the hills and maps are available at the ferry terminal. The forest is in a comparatively natural state and comes with monkeys, deer and other wildlife. There is a ropeway to near the top of Mt. Misen (530 metres). It costs ¥900 one way or ¥1,500 return. There are also beaches, if it is a suitable season for bathing. The beaches are reached by proceeding from the ferry landing point in the direction opposite to that which leads to Itsukushima Jinja, that is to say by turning left when leaving the pier.

There is also a ferry service from Hiroshima to Miyajima, but it is an expensive way of reaching the island, costing ¥1,440 one way. The journey is by an high-speed vessel and takes only 25 minutes. Boats run about hourly, with an augmented service on Saturdays and holidays (which is, incidentally, exactly contrary to information being distributed at the time of writing by the Tourist Information Centres in Tokyo and Kyoto). Boats leave from Ujina Pier in Hiroshima, at the end of the no. 1, 3 and 5 tram routes.

There are no fewer than five youth hostels in the Hiroshima area, for details of which see the Youth Hostels section. Most visitors from overseas stay in the hostel which is called

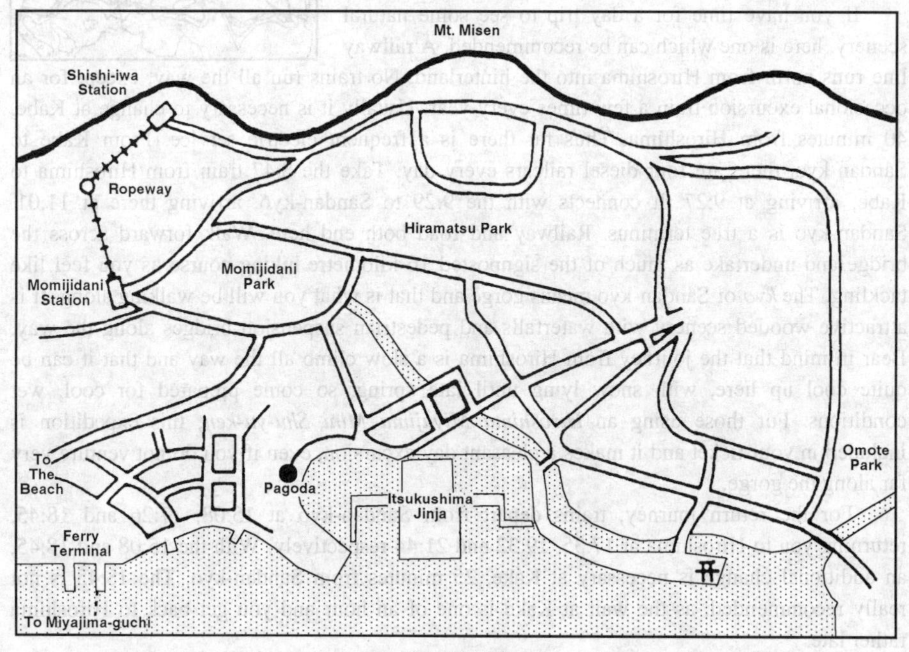


MIYAJIMA

simply Hiroshima and which is by far the largest of the five. To reach it one needs to take a bus from bus stop no. 22 at Hiroshima station. All buses except the green bus go to Ushita Shin-machi I-chome bus stop, from where it is an 8 minute walk, well signposted, to the hostel. However, a pleasant alternative which can be recommended is the small and friendly hostel at Miyajima-guchi. This hostel was opened a few years ago by the man who was for several years the 'parent' at Hiroshima Hostel and who decided to try a similar venture on his own behalf. He understands the needs of hostellers well, therefore, and his hostel offers several advantages. First, it is only 2 minutes walk from JR Miyajima-guchi station or Hiroden Miyajima, the terminus of the tram line, so it is very easy to locate. Then it permits check-in until midnight, which is exceptional and very useful. Finally, it will accept hostellers without prior reservations, space permitting. Be careful about this last advantage, however, for there are only 30 beds and it is, not surprisingly, a popular hostel. Make a reservation if at all possible, for at popular times the hostel is often full. Its one disadvantage is that it is situated right on a major highway with heavy traffic, so it is certainly preferable not to be allocated a front room. It should be added that Miyajima-guchi is a very convenient place to stay, just as convenient as Hiroshima itself, for it is right by one of the two major attractions of the area and the use of the one-day tram and ferry ticket will enable you to see everything you need to see in the Hiroshima area without any additional transportation expenses.

## SANDAN-KYO (三段峡 - 'Three Steps Gorge')

### Kabe Line, 2 hrs. 15 mins. from Hiroshima

**Derivation of Name:** *Literal. The cliffs of the gorge are cut away in three steps.*

If you have time for a day trip to see some natural scenery, here is one which can be recommended. A railway line runs north from Hiroshima into the hinterland. No trains run all the way, except for an occasional excursion train a few times every year. Usually it is necessary to change at Kabe, 40 minutes from Hiroshima. Thus far there is a frequent electric service. From Kabe to Sandan-kyo, there are four diesel railcars every day. Take the 8:47 train from Hiroshima to Kabe, arriving at 9:27. It connects with the 9:29 to Sandan-kyo, arriving there at 11:01. Sandan-kyo is a true terminus. Railway and road both end here. Walk forward across the bridge and undertake as much of the signposted 16 kilometre hiking course as you feel like tackling. The *kyo* of Sandan-kyo means gorge and that is what you will be walking along. It is attractive wooded scenery with waterfalls and pedestrian suspension bridges along the way. Bear in mind that the journey from Hiroshima is a slow climb all the way and that it can be quite cool up here, with snow lying until late spring, so come prepared for cool, wet conditions. For those using an *Hiroshima Miyajima Mini Shu-yu-ken*, this expedition is included in your ticket and it makes a pleasant day excursion, even if you do not venture very far along the gorge.

For the return journey, trains depart from Sandan-kyo at 15:08, 17:26 and 18:45, returning you to Hiroshima at 17:35, 19:32 and 21:44 respectively. With the 15:08 and 18:45, an additional change is necessary at Kake, 25 minutes from Sandan-kyo. The 18:45 is not really recommended, as the wait at Kake is one of an hour and you get back to Hiroshima rather late.

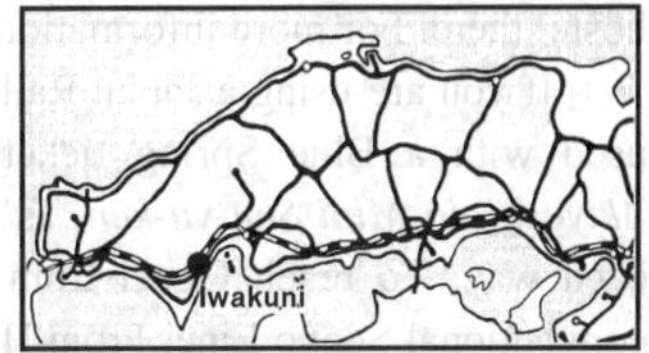


## IWAKUNI (岩国 – 'Rock Country')

**Sanyo *shinkansen*, 5 hrs. 30 mins. from Tokyo**

**Derivation of Name:** *Literal. There are many rocky mountains in this area.*

Iwakuni is famous for a bridge known as **Kintai-kyo**. It is worth a visit as it is really more Japanese than Japan itself is – so Japanese, in fact that crossing it is quite hard work. One has to climb and descend the arches five times, so that it can be traversed only on foot. The bridge lies about half way between Iwakuni station, used by conventional JR services, and Shin Iwakuni, used by the *shinkansen*. From Iwakuni station, there is a frequent bus service. Of these buses, those going to Shin Iwakuni station are operated by JR and so are free for holders of a Japan Rail Pass or an *Hiroshima Miyajima Mini Shu-yu-ken*, for the latter of whom this is the limit of your territory. If you arrive by *shinkansen*, there is the same JR bus service going to Iwakuni station and passing Kintai-kyo on the way. However, the nearest station is actually Kawanishi, two stops west of Iwakuni on the Gantoku Line. Trains run to there from Iwakuni approximately hourly. From Kawanishi station, it is about 15 minutes walk to Kintai-kyo.

Kintai-kyo is a toll bridge, with a little toll booth at each end, where your ¥100 will be collected. However, the toll collectors work office hours, outside which time you are invited to drop your coin into a box. Not so many people accept this kind invitation. This is not the original bridge, built in 1673, for that was swept away by a flood. However, it is an imposing reconstruction. Having crossed the bridge, you will find on the other side some gardens dotted with statues, monuments and a museum and, high up on your right, a castle (but, again, not an original one), reached by a ropeway. If you go through the gardens and turn left, you will come to the youth hostel, which, although not special in itself, is set in a pleasant wooded location, having been given a prime position, like so many municipal hostels.

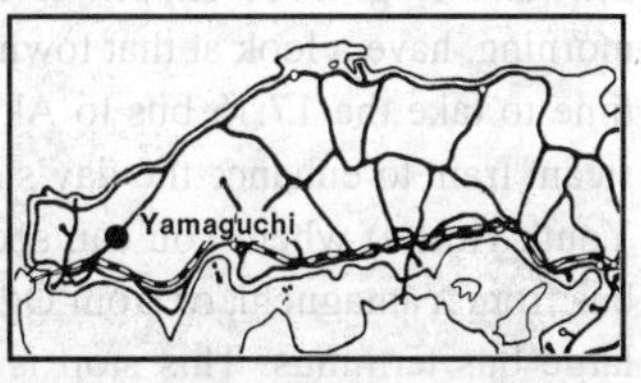


## YAMAGUCHI (山口 – 'Mountain Mouth')

**Sanyo *shinkansen* to Ogori, 5 hrs. 30 mins. from Tokyo.**
**Then Yamaguchi Line, 25 mins.**

**Derivation of Name:** *This is the entry route to a mountainous area.*

The JR Yamaguchi Line is famous because it is one of only two JR lines to have retained occasional steam services. (The other line is the Hohi Line between Kumamoto and Oita in Kyushu.) Trains run at weekends and during holiday periods, but not throughout the year, so check first if you wish to experience this service. At the time of writing, the train, when it is operating, leaves Ogori at 10:30 and goes as far as Tsuwano, where it arrives at 12:30. It departs from Tsuwano for the return journey at 15:21, reaching Ogori at 16:57. (It is downhill going back!) However, this timetable also varies a little, although the train usually leaves Ogori in the mid-morning and returns from Tsuwano in the mid-afternoon. It uses not only a type C57 steam engine, but also refurbished old carriages. The first part of the journey, as far as Yamaguchi, is through rather ordinary semi-suburban countryside, but then the train climbs up into the mountains through some long tunnels and the landscape, when visible, becomes steep and forested. When the author last passed this way, the snow started to fall heavily as we gained height, enhancing the natural beauty of the area. When you reach Tsuwano, there are some sights to see there, so you can either view them and return with the steam train or stay overnight, for there is a youth hostel there. For more information on Tsuwano, see a little further on in this section.

If you are using a Japan Rail Pass, the steam train is included in your pass. It can also be used with a Blue Spring ticket or with a *Tsuwano Hagi Free Kippu* or a *Yamaguchi Akiyoshi-do Mini Shu-yu-ken*, as long as you pay the seat reservation charge, which is ¥500 each way. To reach Ogori from Hiroshima or Iwakuni, take the Sanyo *shinkansen* or the conventional Sanyo Line. From Hiroshima, the journey takes 40 minutes by *Hikari shinkansen* train (not all trains stop), an hour by *Kodama shinkansen* train or nearly three hours by ordinary train. From Shin Iwakuni, travelling time is 35 minutes by *Kodama shinkansen* train. *Hikari* trains do not stop at Shin Iwakuni. From Iwakuni it takes two hours to Ogori by ordinary train.

## AKIYOSHI (秋吉 - 'Autumn Fortune')

**Bus from Ogori, 40 mins.**

**Derivation of Name:** *'Akiyoshi' used to have the meaning of 'privately owned land' and probably that is the derivation here. The Chinese character used for the name of the cave (only) was changed by the Emperor Showa when, as crown prince, he paid a visit here in 1926, but there was no change in pronunciation.*

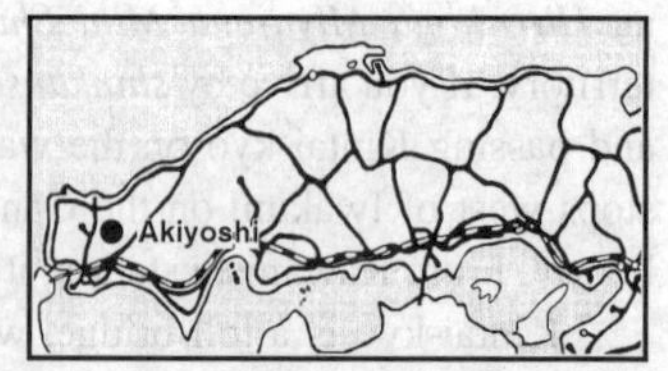


Akiyoshi is famous for having the largest cave in Japan. It is an impressive cavern and well worth a visit, but perhaps its greatest surprise is the admission fee which is ¥1,050. To be sure, it must cost money to light the cave and quite extensive walkways have been constructed and guards stationed at strategic points. Nevertheless, there are very many visitors each day and those ¥1,050s must soon add up.

The cave can be reached by bus from Ogori or from Yamaguchi. The buses from Yamaguchi are operated by JR, as are some of the buses from Ogori. There is also a service from Hagi in the north, operated by the Bocho Bus Company, which is available with a *Tsuwano Hagi Free Kippu*. If the steam train is running, you can go to Tsuwano in the morning, have a look at that town and return with the afternoon steam service to Yamaguchi in time to take the 17:15 bus to Akiyoshi. That is a recommended route, especially if there is a steam train to enhance the day's adventures. There is a youth hostel at Akiyoshi (Akiyoshidai Youth Hostel) where you can spend the night before looking at the cave in the morning. The bus from Yamaguchi, or from Ogori, will turn right after about 40 to 45 minutes and arrive at a large bus terminus. This stop is called Akiyoshi-do ( 秋芳洞 ) and it is where you should alight. Buses from Ogori terminate here, but most of the ones from Yamaguchi turn round and continue to the town of Akiyoshi and on to Mine (美祢 ). You do not want to go to the town of Akiyoshi as both the cave and the youth hostel are near Akiyoshi-do bus terminal. *Do* means cave and Akiyoshi-do is the name of the cave which you have come to see. If you take the 17:15 bus from Yamaguchi, you will arrive at Akiyoshi-do at 18:11. It is then 20 minutes walk to the youth hostel (see map in Youth Hostels section). If, however, you are coming from Ogori, the buses leave from outside the *shinkansen* entrance of the station. JR buses operate at 9:50, 11:50, 14:05 and 16:20. In between, there are departures operated by the Bocho Bus Company, making up a half-hourly service in the morning which tapers off in the afternoon. The 16:20 is the last bus of the day. Journey time from Ogori is 45 minutes.

**Akiyoshi-do** has three entrances. Most people use the one nearest to the bus terminal and that is recommended as it is rather impressive due to the fact that there is a substantial river pouring out of the cavern into which you want to find a route. However, do not despair, for the gods and cave authorities, with the help of all those ¥1,050s, have found a way and a wooden staircase and platform have been constructed above the rushing, foaming waters, making a spectacularly unnatural entrance to this natural phenomenon. The author found that he took an excellent photograph looking out of the cave over the river from this point, whereas his pictures taken inside appeared like sketches of the interior of a coal mine without the aid of artificial illumination. No doubt it just emphasizes how weak the efforts of man are when compared with natural light. Yes, I did remember to turn the flash on, but the cave is big. The cave is the biggest in the country, actually, in terms of length, rather than volume, but it has some very high caverns too. As usual, there are stalagmites (up) and stalactites (down), many given fanciful titles, and an interesting variety of huge open spaces and narrow passages. You can proceed for about one kilometre, at which point the cave forks into a left and a right chamber. You can go a little way down either. If you choose the left chamber, you will reach the Kurotani ('Black Valley') Exit, about 10 minutes walk from the youth hostel. It is suggested that you go this way first and then retrace your steps to take the exit in the right chamber. This exit is by lift. You do not have to pay to be taken to the surface, but if you wish to return to the cave later, there will be a charge of ¥103 (i.e. ¥100 plus tax) for the second lift ride. Some people do return, after viewing the landscape from the nearby lookout, which is a small metal construction near a building offering refreshments. It is a short walk uphill from the cave exit. Rides in a very slow horse-drawn cart are also available, if the antique and despondent-looking horse feels up to it. This cave exit is only some five minutes from the youth hostel. There are also JR buses back to Akiyoshi-do ( 秋芳洞 ), although only about once every hour.

To avoid retracing our steps, let us take a JR bus on to **Mine** ( 美祢 ) when we have finished here, instead of returning to Yamaguchi or Ogori. Not all buses which go this way are JR buses, but many are. Convenient morning departures from Akiyoshi-do are at 8:18, 11:10

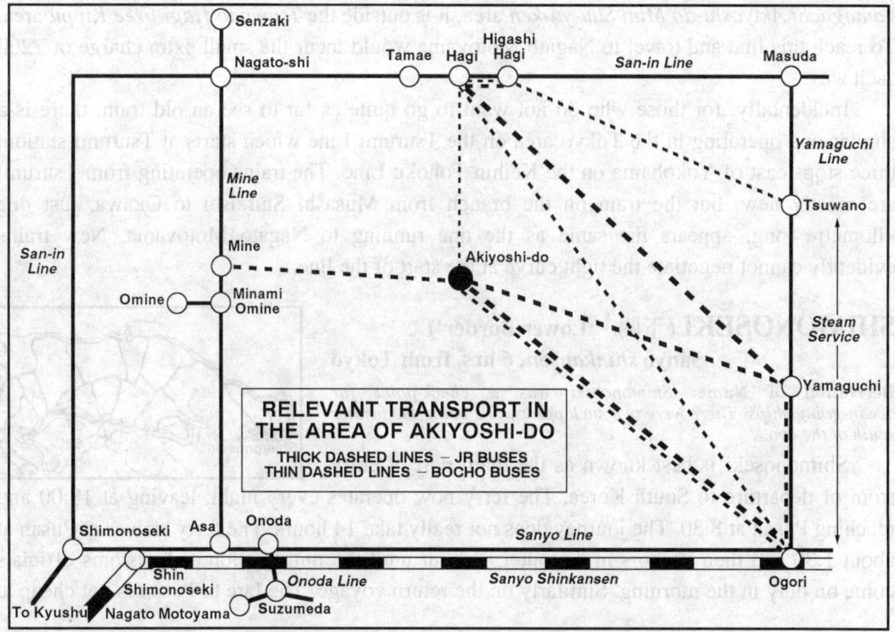

and 12:41. The journey takes 25 minutes. (There are other buses too, but they do not connect with trains.) From Mine, the railway runs south to Asa. Connecting departures from Mine are at 8:58, 12:01 and 13:43. The journey to Asa takes approximately 30 minutes. On the way, one station south of Mine, you will pass a station called Minami Omine, from where a short branch line runs 2.8 kilometres to Omine. This line has survived because of mining activities, but, since these have now stopped, its future is uncertain. However, it is a old line and, at both **Omine** and **Minami Omine**, you can see unusual distance markings on the sides of the platforms in the miles and chains system used by the British engineers who built the line.

From Asa, it is a matter of another 35 minutes to Shimonoseki, the port at the western tip of Honshu. For those eccentrics who, like the author, like odd trains, one of JR's oldest in regular service operates on a branch near here. The Onoda Line loops round from Onoda station, one stop east of Asa, and trains travel as far as Ube Shinkawa, on the Ube Line. About half way round the Onoda Line, a branch (also part of the Onoda Line) runs just two stations from Suzumeda to Nagato Motoyama, a long name for a very small station. This is where the old train runs. It is an electric railcar, just a single brown carriage, and it operates only at rush hours, not that there is so much rush around here. When the author travelled on this service, I found that plates inside the vehicle seemed to indicate that it was built in the 1950s and confirmed this with the driver. "Oh, no," he said. "I should think that it must be much older than that. That was probably when it was last refurbished." It looks as though it dates from the 1920s and it is probably kept in service because it can negotiate some part of the line which modern trains cannot. The total journey is 2.3 kilometres, which takes 5 minutes. During the day, the train rests from its exertions at Suzumeda, but at night it returns to Ube Shinkawa to sleep. The first train of the evening rush hour, for those who want to ride this unusual service, leaves Suzumeda at 16:29 and is back there at 16:45, after a 6 minute break in Nagato Motoyama, where there is not a great deal to see. Although this route is included in the *Yamaguchi Akiyoshi-do Mini Shu-yu-ken* area, it is outside the *Tsuwano Hagi Free Kippu* area. To reach this line and travel to Nagato Motoyama would incur the small extra charge of ¥200 each way.

Incidentally, for those who do not want to go quite as far to see an old train, there is a similar one operating in the Tokyo area on the Tsurumi Line which starts at Tsurumi station, three stops east of Yokohama on the Keihin Tohoku Line. The trains operating from Tsurumi are mostly new, but the train on the branch from Musashi Shiraishi to Okawa, just one kilometre long, appears the same as the one running to Nagato Motoyama. New trains evidently cannot negotiate the tight curve at the start of the line.

## SHIMONOSEKI (下関 - 'Lower Border')

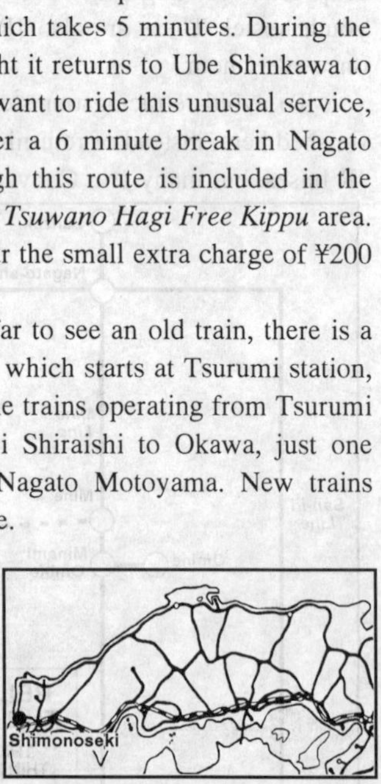

**Sanyo *shinkansen*, 6 hrs. from Tokyo**

**Derivation of Name:** *Shimonoseki was a check-point for ocean-going ships. There were two such points, this being the further south of the two.*

Shimonoseki is best known as the main port of entry from or departure to South Korea. The ferry now operates every night, leaving at 18:00 and reaching Pusan at 8:30. The journey does not really take 14 hours. The ferry arrives at Pusan at about 1:30 and then anchors in the outer harbour until the immigration and customs officials come on duty in the morning. Similarly on the return voyage. The fare to Pusan is not cheap at

¥8,500, in addition to which you will be asked for a ¥600 port terminal fee. If you are coming from Korea to Japan, it is somewhat cheaper in that direction. If you are leaving Japan now to go to Korea, there are a couple of points to note. Firstly, if you purchase two bottles of Johnnie Walker Black Label whisky, you may be lucky enough to find somebody at the Pusan Ferry Terminal willing to purchase them for 20,000 won each, although this trade seems to have been declining recently. Secondly, there is also a ferry service to Pusan from Hakata Port in Fukuoka in Kyushu, where there is no ¥600 port terminal fee. The ferry from Hakata operates on only three nights per week, however (Mondays, Wednesdays and Fridays).

If you are coming from Korea to Japan, you should be sure that there is no reason for the Japanese immigration officials to take objection to you, for those at Shimonoseki have something of a reputation for finding objections even where you thought that none could exist. The ferry to and from Pusan is the cheapest route in and out of Japan, and so is used by those with the least money and by those whose time in Japan has expired but who want to stay longer and Japan no longer seems pleased to entertain such guests. Traditionally this route has been used by those working illegally in either country. Nowadays, however, unless one is working near Shimonoseki, it is cheaper to fly to Korea and back. However, the officials have not forgotten their duty to discourage unwelcome arrivals, so, if you have anything at all in your passport which may not please immigration officials, this is probably not the best way to enter Japan.

Shimonoseki has a municipal youth hostel in the usual magnificent surroundings. This one is on the hill overlooking the Kanmon Strait which divides Honshu from Kyushu. The hostel itself is not so special, but the view is splendid. If you sit in the dining room, or go outside and further up the hill, you can watch the ships passing, as they do frequently all day and night. The name of the hill on the side of which the hostel is perched is **Hinoyama** ('Fire Mountain'). Hostel directions say to take a bus for Hinoyama (火の山) from stop no. 1 at the railway station as far as the ropeway. Since there are not so many of these buses (only one per hour with the last at 18:00), you can take others from the same bus stop to Mimosuso-gawa (みもすそ川). Even if you cannot pronounce it, it is the stop immediately after you pass under the huge and lofty Kanmon Bridge, which can hardly be missed. However, the distance is walkable, so why not walk? If you do so, you will pass on the way the most interesting shrine in Shimonoseki. It is called **Akama Jinja** ('Red Gate Shrine'), so you will not be surprised to see that it has a red gate. If you walk along Highway 9, you will see the shrine on your left about half way to the hostel.

The ropeway to the top of Fire Mountain starts from very near the youth hostel and costs ¥200. You can ride up and then walk down. The view from the top is similar to that from the hostel, but even better. If you feel like a brief visit to Kyushu, there is a pedestrian tunnel under the Kanmon Strait just beside the bridge. The strait is just over a kilometre in width here, so the walk takes only 10 minutes. The tunnel is free for pedestrians (¥20 for bicycles). The other end of the tunnel is in Moji, but it is a long walk from there to the town and buses, although they exist, are few. However, if you are going to visit Kyushu seriously, and the island is certainly worthy of having a few days devoted to its scenery, you should break off from this section of the book now, travel around Kyushu and then resume here on your return.

For those using a *Tsuwano Hagi Free Kippu*, your area finishes at Asa. If you want to have a look at Shimonoseki, as you probably do, you will be charged ¥560 for the journey here.

## HAGI (萩 - 'Bush Clover')

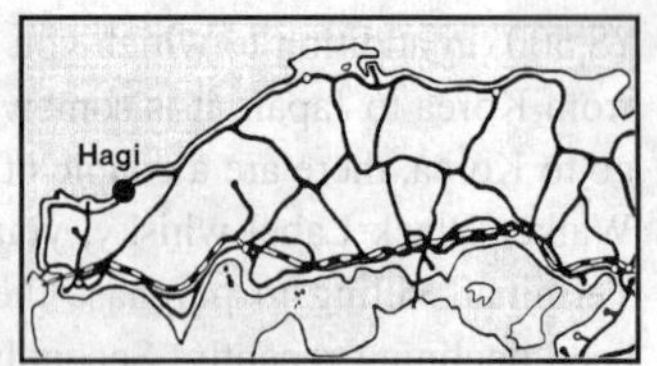


**San-in Line, 1 hr. 45 mins. from Shimonoseki**

**Derivation of Name:** *The plant known as bush clover grew abundantly here.*

Shimonoseki is the farthest west point in Honshu, so we now begin our return journey along the northern coast of Chugoku. This will be a complete contrast with the first half of our journey, for whereas the south of the region is developed and populated, the north is rural and only sparsely inhabited. For much of the way, the railway runs near the sea, so that the scenery on both sides is attractive. However, the sparse population results in a sparse railway service. For rail pass users, there is one *tokkyu* along this line every day and there is also one *kyuko*. The *tokkyu* originates in Kokura in Kyushu at 9:15 and passes through Shimonoseki at 9:29. It reaches Higashi Hagi at 11:17 and continues thereafter as far as Yonago, where it terminates at 15:30. The *kyuko* can also be used by those with a *Yamaguchi Akiyoshi-do Mini Shu-yu-ken*, provided they sit in unreserved seating. It also departs from Kokura, leaving at 12:11 and passing Shimonoseki at 12:33. It reaches Tamae at 14:27 and Higashi Hagi at 14:34, continuing to Tottori, where it arrives at 21:28. If you are using a Blue Spring ticket, it is nearly always necessary to change trains at Nagato-shi. Suitable connexions are as follows:

① Shimonoseki 6:42. Nagato-shi 8:47 / 9:04. Tamae 9:36. Higashi Hagi 9:46.
② Shimonoseki 7:26. Nagato-shi 9:32 / 10:27. Tamae 10:57. Higashi Hagi 11:07.
③ Shimonoseki 10:37. Nagato-shi 12:31 / 12:44. Tamae 13:14. Higashi Hagi 13:24.
④ Shimonoseki 12:45. Nagato-shi 14:41 / 15:07. Tamae 15:39. Higashi Hagi 15:50.
⑤ Shimonoseki 14:34. Kogushi 15:18 / 15:21. Nagato-shi 16:36 / 16:50. Tamae 17:29. Higashi Hagi 17:39.
⑥ Shimonoseki 15:29. Nagato-shi 17:43 / 17:52. Tamae 18:24. Higashi Hagi 18:32.
⑦ Shimonoseki 16:43. Tamae 19:26. Higashi Hagi 19:35 (no change necessary).

Those using a *Tsuwano Hagi Free Kippu* are not permitted to travel this route, although you can go to Hagi. Therefore, you must make this single compromise regarding our plan. There are three choices for you to reach Hagi from Shimonoseki, in addition to which you could just skip Shimonoseki and take a bus from Akiyoshi-do to Hagi (萩), a matter of 70 minutes. Buses run four times per day throughout the year and more often on holidays and in summer. As for the three possibilities from Shimonoseki, the most comfortable way to travel would be to take the 7:44 ordinary train from Shimonoseki to Asa, where it arrives at 8:18, and then catch the 8:50 *tokkyu* named *Oki* to Masuda. It reaches Masuda at 10:59 and at 11:07 there is a *kyuko* arriving at Higashi Hagi at 12:09 and Tamae at 12:16. The second possibility is to take a train as far as Ogori and then catch the *Hagi* express bus to the town of its name. The bus runs approximately hourly and takes between 70 and 90 minutes, Bocho buses being faster than the JR buses with which the route is shared. There is a reservation charge of ¥200 on these buses, which you must pay before boarding. The third possible route is back up the Mine Line from Asa all the way to Nagato-shi. Morning connexions are as follows:-

① Shimonoseki 6:54. Asa 7:30 / 7:36. Nagato-shi 8:41 / 9:04. Tamae 9:36. Higashi Hagi 9:46.
② Shimonoseki 7:44. Asa 8:18 / 8:32. Nagato-shi 9:37 / 10:27. Tamae 10:57. Higashi Hagi 11:07.
③ Shimonoseki 10:45. Asa 11:20 / 11:26. Nagato-shi 12:26 / 12:44. Tamae 13:14. Higashi Hagi 13:24.

Hagi is a town built on a bay, round which the railway curves. There are three stations, Tamae, Hagi and Higashi Hagi. The nearest of these to the main points of interest is Tamae, from where it is about 15 minutes walk to the castle ruins. Alternatively, one can continue to one of the other two stations and then walk back through the town, where there some old houses to see. From Higashi Hagi station, the walk back to the castle ruins takes about 35 minutes, not including any stops.

Hagi is famed as a traditional old Japanese town and many people, both Japanese and visitors from overseas, come long distances to look either at this town or at Tsuwano, nearby. It should be said that many of the overseas visitors, in particular, are rather disappointed, especially when they consider the amount of travelling necessary to reach this rather out of the way place. Hagi is pleasant enough, but it is not really worth a long trip if you just want to see a traditional Japanese town. Takayama, for example, is much more accessible and has more to offer. Indeed it is rather odd that so many overseas visitors do come here expecting so much. There must, one supposes, be a guide book which specially recommends the town, but this writer is not aware of which book it is. Much better to enjoy the coastal scenery from the train and just make Hagi an overnight stop with time for a brief look around.

What Hagi used to have was a castle. It was built in 1604 by the Mori family, which was particularly powerful in this area. Now Hagi just has the **ruins of the castle**, for it was pulled down at the time of the Meiji Restoration, when castles represented potential centres of opposition. The ruins are located within what is now Shizuki Park. There is an admission charge of ¥200, which also covers entry to a nearby ***samurai* house**. Another little park beside the sea has a collection of sculptures. Usually few people are around, even though there is no charge for admission to this park.

Other attractions include **Toko-ji**, the temple of the Mori family (admission ¥100) and **Shoin Jinja** together with **Shokason Juku**. These have an interesting history. Yoshida Shoin ran a private school where he educated several people who played major roles in the Meiji Restoration. Best known of these was Ito Hirobumi, a statesman whose portrait graced the ¥1,000 note until designs were changed a few years ago. Mr. Yoshida was executed for his trouble and Shoin Jinja (a shrine) now stands in memory of him. This group of attractions is quite a long walk from the castle area.

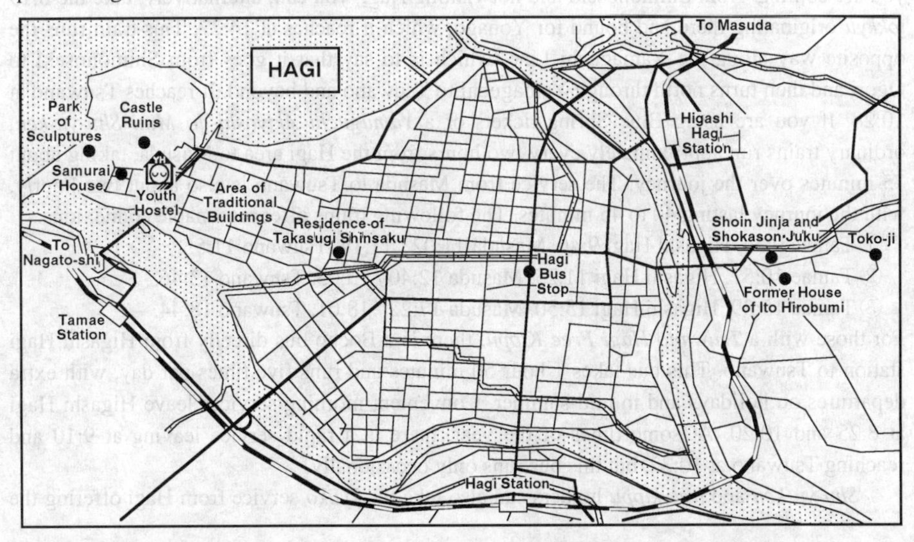

A third area for exploration lies near the castle on the way to Hagi town. Here there are several old and traditional buildings. The former **residence of Takasugi Shinsaku** is a good example of such a building. It can be viewed for ¥100. There are other similar houses and warehouses nearby. Probably about half a day is an appropriate time to allow to have a look at Hagi.

There is a youth hostel located conveniently near the castle ruins. It has plenty of information about the area and is accustomed to English-speaking guests. By the way, be careful to pronounce the name of this town correctly – Hagi, not Hage, the latter meaning bald!

## TSUWANO (津和野 – 'Port Peaceful Field')

**Yamaguchi Line, 65 mins. from Ogori**

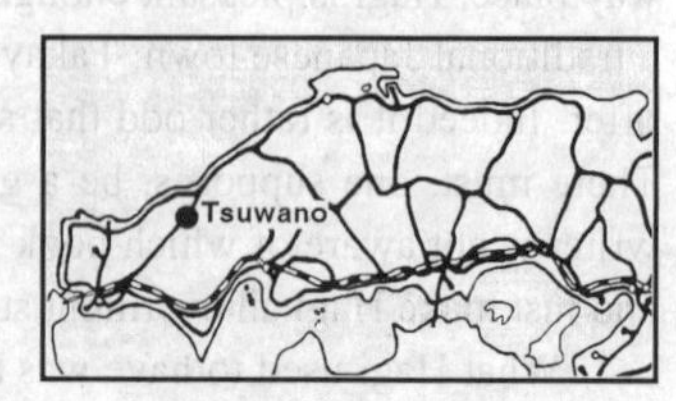


**Derivation of Name:** *A plant known as 'tsuwabuki' was growing in the fields here, so the town was called 'Tsuwabukino'. In time, this was corrupted to Tsuwano.*

The town of Tsuwano has already been mentioned under the heading of Yamaguchi, above. It has two claims to fame. The first is the **steam train service** which operates from Ogori. As stated previously, this service runs only on certain days. During the summer holidays, it often goes every day. At other times it operates on Sundays and holidays only and in the winter it usually does not run at all. However, if its operation days happen to fit with your schedule, it is a pleasant and enjoyable trip and you will have sufficient time in Tsuwano to look at the town before returning on the steam service to Yamaguchi and continuing by JR bus to Akiyoshi Cave, as suggested above in the Yamaguchi and Akiyoshi sections. However, it is also possible, and quicker, to reach Tsuwano from the Japan Sea end of the Yamaguchi Line and this is possibly the better option if the steam service is not running at the time of your visit.

If you are coming from Hagi (or from Kyushu or Shimonoseki), and have a rail pass, take the 11:17 *tokkyu* from Higashi Hagi (9:15 from Kokura, 9:29 from Shimonoseki) to Masuda, where it arrives at 12:16, and change to the 12:45 *tokkyu* which reaches Tsuwano at 13:16. If you are coming from Shimonoseki and not visiting Hagi, you can, alternatively, take the 8:19 *tokkyu* originating there and bound for Yonago, which it reaches at 14:27. This train runs the opposite way along the Yamaguchi Line, which is to say that it goes from Shimonoseki to Ogori and then turns north through Yamaguchi to Tsuwano and beyond. It reaches Tsuwano at 10:28. If you are using Blue Spring tickets or a *Yamaguchi Akiyoshi-do Mini Shu-yu-ken*, ordinary trains run approximately every two hours from the Hagi area to Masuda, taking about 75 minutes over the journey. The service from Masuda to Tsuwano is also about two hourly, with the journey lasting 40 to 45 minutes. The following trains offer reasonable connexions:

① Tamae 9:36. Higashi Hagi 9:46. Masuda 11:02 / 11:14. Tsuwano 11:55.

② Tamae 10:57. Higashi Hagi 11:25. Masuda 12:40 / 13:03. Tsuwano 13:46.

③ Tamae 15:39. Higashi Hagi 15:50. Masuda 17:22 / 18:01. Tsuwano 18:44.

For those with a *Tsuwano Hagi Free Kippu*, there is a Bocho bus directly from Higashi Hagi station to Tsuwano. This bus takes 1 hour 50 minutes and runs five times per day, with extra departures on holidays and in mid-summer. Convenient morning services leave Higashi Hagi at 8:25 and 10:20. At some times of the year, there is a rapid service leaving at 9:10 and reaching Tsuwano at 10:32, but this bus runs only occasionally.

*Shu-yu-ken* and *free kippu* holders can also take the *kyuko* service from Hagi offering the following connexion: Tamae 14:27. Higashi Hagi 14:34. Masuda 15:37 / 16:27. Tsuwano 17:08. Note that the *kyuko* does not stop at Hagi.

The other attraction for which Tsuwano is famous is fish – **carp** in particular. You will find these ornamental fish in ornamental ponds everywhere in Japan and the prices which they fetch are quite amazing, especially considering that they will never find their way onto the dinner table. Their sizes are surprising too, but then it is to be supposed that they live contented and placid lives, with plenty of nourishment and nothing much else to do but grow. Even so, the carp in Tsuwano are quite prodigious in size and are to be found absolutely everywhere in the town. The author has a friend who always tends to assess fish in terms of luncheon, which can occasionally be embarrassing, so, if you do not want any accusing looks from these huge specimens, remember that the fish in Tsuwano are to be admired, not eaten.

Tsuwano is also known for **Inari Jinja**, a shrine with a particularly large *torii* outside. If you use the steam service to travel to and from Tsuwano, you will have nearly three hours in the town, which is just about the right time for looking round. If you come by other means, you should try to allow about the same – or perhaps a little less will suffice.

Tsuwano has a youth hostel, for details of which see the Youth Hostels section of this book. Although the directions recommend taking a bus to the hostel, it is also possible to walk.

## IZUMO (出雲 –'Departing Cloud') San-in Line, 13 hrs. 30 mins. from Tokyo, or 3 hrs. from Okayama

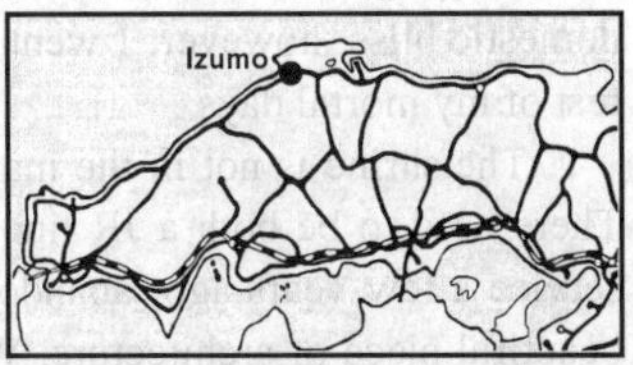


**Derivation of Name:** *Because of atmospheric conditions, clouds tend to form here.*

If you are coming from the east, *tokkyu* trains run to Izumo about every two hours from Okayama, a major stop on the Sanyo *shinkansen* route. The journey takes three hours. There are also two overnight sleepers from Tokyo. Coming from the west, however, as we are doing, the service is more limited. If you are travelling from Tsuwano and using a rail pass, there are *tokkyu* trains at 10:28, 12:55 and 15:56, reaching Izumo-shi ('Izumo City') station at 13:20, 15:40 and 18:51 respectively. All then continue to Yonago, which is reached about an hour later. If you are using Blue Spring or a *free kippu* or *shu-yu-ken*, it is best to start early and make use of some trains which are slightly faster than those later in the day. Here are the recommended services:

① Tsuwano 6:55. Masuda 7:34 / 7:49. Izumo-shi 10:35. Train continues to Yonago (12:06).

② Tsuwano 7:57. Masuda 8:37 / 9:24. Izumo-shi 12:15.

Other possibilities are:

③ Tsuwano 11:31. Masuda 12:11 / 12:25. Izumo-shi 16:03.

④ Tsuwano 13:18. Masuda 14:01 / 14:41. Hamada 15:37 / 16:40. Izumo-shi 19:06.

Those using a *Yamaguchi Akiyoshi-do Mini Shu-yu-ken* or a *Tsuwano Hagi Free Kippu* have one additional good connexion, using the *kyuko* service along the San-in Line:

Tsuwano 14:24. Masuda 15:04 / 15:45. Izumo-shi 18:12. Train continues to Tottori (21:28).

If you are coming from Hagi using a rail pass, you should take the 11:17 *tokkyu* from Higashi Hagi, reaching Izumo-shi at 14:31. (Train continues to Yonago, 15:30) or the *kyuko* from Tamae at 14:27 or Higashi Hagi at 14:34, reaching Izumo-shi at 18:12. (Train continues to Tottori, 21:28). By ordinary train, there are services about every two hours, but connexions are generally poor, except with the early morning services, which are recommended, therefore:

① Tamae 5:49. Higashi Hagi 6:19. Masuda 7:35 / 7:49. Izumo-shi 10:35. (Train continues to Yonago, 12:06.)

② Tamae 7:35. Higashi Hagi 7:47. Masuda 9:04 / 9:24. Izumo-shi 12:15.

*Shu-yu-ken* and *free kippu* holders can also use the *kyuko* service above, of course.

If you are coming directly from Shimonoseki, you have a choice of three express trains: the 8:19 *tokkyu* via the Yamaguchi Line, reaching Izumo-shi at 13:20, the 9:29 *tokkyu* running beside the Japan Sea all the way and reaching Izumo-shi at 14:31 and the 12:33 *kyuko* running beside the Japan Sea and reaching Izumo-shi at 18:12. If you want to do the journey by ordinary train, it will take most of the day and you will have to change several times. Useful departures from Shimonoseki are at 5:45, 6:42 and 10:37. The last has the best connexions. You must change at Nagato-shi (12:31 / 12:44), Masuda (14:40 / 14:41) and Hamada (15:37 / 16:40) and you will reach Izumo-shi at 19:06.

Well, after all that trouble, what does Izumo have to offer that we should be making a special stop here? What it has is **Izumo Taisha**, a rather special shrine second in importance only to the shrines at Ise. This is where the Shinto gods traditionally spend their holidays, all coming here for an annual reunion during the month of October. The author was also told that it is customary to visit this shrine with one's girl (or boy) friend and then the couple will be destined to get married and live happily ever after. Not altogether relishing that scenario of domestic bliss, however, I went alone and am now condemned to a solitary existence for the rest of my mortal days.

The shrine is not in the main part of the city of Izumo, but a train or bus journey away. There used to be both a JR line and a private line, but JR conceded defeat and withdrew its service a few years ago, abandoning the line. That was a pity, because Taisha station was a beautiful piece of architecture. When the author used the JR service there (it might have been JNR at the time), he found an ornate wooden booking office and photographs around the wall of special excursion trains at New Year and of the Emperor arriving at the station to visit the shrine. Maybe the station still stands, but there have been no trains for several years now, sadly. Instead, therefore, you can take a bus or travel by the Ichibata Private Railway. Let us do the latter, since the Ichibata Private Railway service also has character, due to the antiquity of some of the trains. This railway uses a different station from JR. On arrival at JR Izumo-shi, go to the exit and turn right. A short walk will bring you to the Ichibata Private Railway station, which lies right beside the JR line. To reach Izumo Taisha-mae station, it is necessary to change trains at Kawato *en route*. At Izumo Taisha-mae station, again turn right and 5 minutes walk will bring you (with your girl/boyfriend?) to the shrine.

Izumo Taisha is a massive piece of traditional architecture, set in wooded and peaceful surroundings. When the author arrived here, it was dusk and everybody had gone home, leaving the world to darkness and to me. It was one of those moments to savour. However, the grounds of the shrine are spacious and are unlikely to seem terribly crowded at any time, so it is not necessary to arrive at dusk to enjoy a visit. In fact, most of the buildings here are nineteenth century, although the style of architecture used is centuries old. Like most shrines in Japan, Izumo Taisha is free.

Ebisuya Youth Hostel is just near Izumo Taisha-mae station. Ebisu, incidentally, is one of the seven principal Shinto gods. He is the one who enjoys eating and drinking, which are popular pastimes in Japan. There is another youth hostel beside the Ichibata Private Railway if you return to Kawato and then take the train towards Matsue Onsen. At the last stop before the

Matsue Onsen terminus, at a small station called Furue, is Matsue Lakeside Youth Hostel. It is indeed, as its name suggests, beside Lake Shinji. Of course, if you already have a JR ticket, you may feel that you do not want to pay ¥750 to go from Izumo Taisha-mae station to Furue, but, in fact, it would cost as much and take considerably more time to return to Izumo-shi, go to Matsue by JR and then get back to Matsue Lakeside Hostel. The Ichibata Private Railway, incidentally, has a one-day ticket ('*free jo-sha-ken*' - フリー乗車券) available for ¥1,500.

From Izumo-shi to Osaka there is a night train, leaving at 21:42, which runs as far as Kurayoshi as a *kaisoku*. It reaches Kurayoshi at exactly midnight and, just like something from the story of Cinderella, it is magically transformed into a *kyuko* with reserved seats available. It reaches Osaka at 7:09. Even though this may sound like a good way to save a night's accommodation, you will miss a lot of attractive scenery if you take this option and be quite uncomfortable too, as the author can testify. Both sitting carriages (reserved and unreserved) are smoking carriages. The train also carries sleepers, but those are expensive, of course. In the opposite direction, this train leaves Osaka at 22:55 and reaches Izumo-shi at 7:28.

## MATSUE (松江 - 'Pine Bay') San-in Line,

### 13 hrs. from Tokyo, or 2 hrs. 40 mins. from Okayama

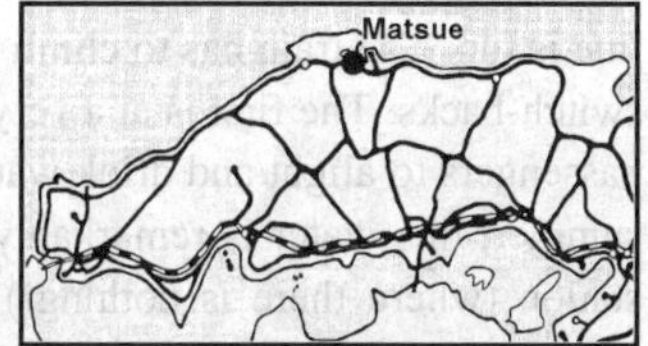


**Derivation of Name:** *The location of the city was thought to resemble that of a beauty spot called Zungefu in China. Matsue is the Japanese pronunciation of those same Chinese characters.*

Matsue is most famous for having been the place where an English writer named **Lafcadio Hearn** lived at the end of the last century. He wrote about contemporary Japan and is famous among the Japanese as much as among readers of English literature. Matsue is very proud of him and in this city you can visit his former home and a museum of his writings and other items connected with his life.

There is also a **castle** and note that this is an original castle, not a modern concrete reproduction. It dates from 1611 and sits on a hill not far from Mr. Hearn's home. Admission costs ¥400. These attractions are all considerably nearer to Matsue Onsen station of the Ichibata Private Railway than JR Matsue station, from where they are 20 to 30 minutes walk.

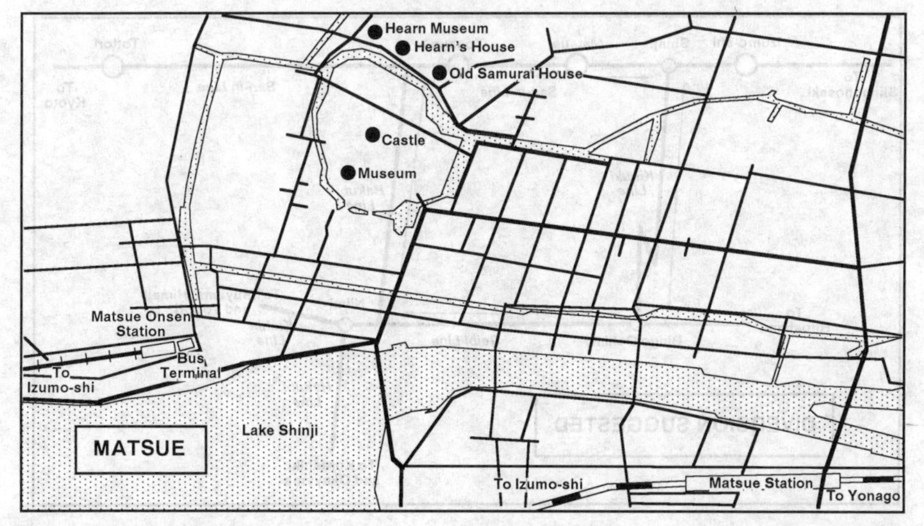

The city of Matsue lies in a pleasant location straddling the river at the mouth of Lake Shinji. The Ichibata Private Railway skirts this lake to the north, while the JR San-in Line skirts it to the south. Either railway can be used to travel from Izumo-shi to Matsue, but most people will probably already hold some sort of JR ticket. JR *tokkyu* trains run between the two cities somewhat irregularly, but, on average, about every hour. They take only 30 minutes over the journey. Ordinary trains operate approximately hourly and take 40 minutes.

The Ichibata Private Railway Company offers a one-day ticket (‘*ichi-nichi free jo-sha-ken*’ — 一日フリー乗車券) for the buses which it operates within the limits of Matsue city. This costs ¥800.

If you should feel like an interesting diversion from the main route, and have sufficient time for one, a small line runs inland from a place called Shinji (like the lake), between Izumo-shi and Matsue, to Bingo Ochiai, a place which has no connexion with the game played by housewives on Wednesday nights. Bingo is the old name for the area south-west of Matsue. This is the Kisuki Line and the ideal train to take (the only one, really, as there are not many on this route) leaves Matsue at 11:24 and departs from Shinji at 11:45. The last section of this line is fun. The train has to climb steeply up to Bingo Ochiai, which it does with the aid of two switch-backs. The first is at a very small station where the train stops for two minutes to allow passengers to alight and drink water from the sacred spring at the end of the platform. Even in summer, this water is remarkably cold. The train will finish its steep climb at Bingo Ochiai station (where there is nothing!) at 14:11 and, very conveniently, another train will depart three minutes later for Niimi. Alternatively, you can stay at Dogo Sanso Youth Hostel which is accessible by bus from Bingo Ochiai. If you take the onward train, you will reach Niimi at 15:42. From here you can choose to go back northwards to rejoin the San-in Line near Yonago (*tokkyu* at 16:26, reaching Yonago at 17:37 and continuing to Matsue at 18:06 and Izumo-shi at 18:39; ordinary train at 16:04, reaching Yonago at 18:01) or to go south to Kurashiki and Okayama (*tokkyu* at 16:03, reaching Okayama at 17:01; ordinary train at 16:27, reaching Okayama at 17:55). It should be mentioned, though, that this detour would not be permitted with a *Yamaguchi Akiyoshi-do Mini Shu-yu-ken* or a *Tsuwano Hagi Free Kippu*.

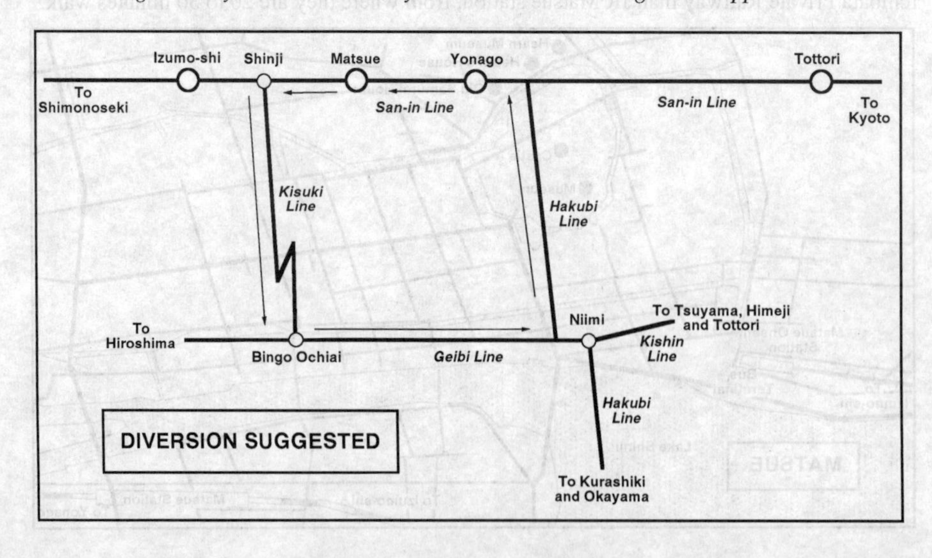

## TOTTORI (鳥取 – 'Bird Catching') San-in Line, 10 hrs. 30 mins. from Tokyo, or 4 hrs. from Kyoto

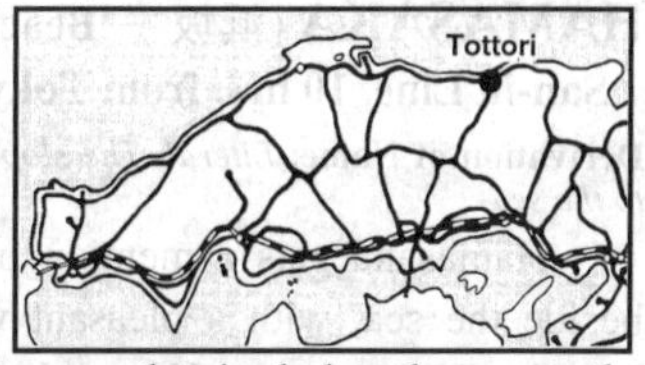


**Derivation of Name:** *The servants who used to catch birds for the Emperor lived in this region.*

Tottori is best known for its sand dunes which stretch along the coast for some 15 kilometres. They reach back from the sea for about 2 kilometres and are quite impressive, gently rippled and apparently stretching into infinity, although probably worth a stop only if you have plenty of time. After all, most people have seen sand dunes before and, if time is limited, it is best to concentrate on those sights which are distinctively Japanese. To get there, take a bus from Tottori station. In the summer, such buses run at least four times an hour. Some go only to Sunaoka (砂丘 – 'Sand Hills') or to Sunaoka Centre (砂丘センター)and some continue to Iwai Onsen (岩井温泉), in which case you should alight at Sunaoka Higashi Guchi (砂丘東口). The fare is ¥300 by any of these services and the journey takes 20 minutes.

When travelling from Matsue to Tottori, it is usually necessary to change trains at Yonago. From Matsue to Yonago takes 25 minutes by *tokkyu* or 35 minutes by ordinary train. From Yonago to Tottori takes 70 minutes by *tokkyu* or about 2 hours by ordinary train. However, there is only one useful *tokkyu* service, leaving Yonago at 7:00 and reaching Tottori at 8:09. It continues to Kyoto, arriving at 11:51. There is a *tokkyu* connexion from Matsue at 6:29, originating in Izumo-shi at 6:03. There is just one useful ordinary train which runs right through from Matsue to Tottori. It leaves Matsue at 6:36 and reaches Tottori at 9:36. Otherwise, it is always necessary to change in Yonago when travelling by ordinary train from Izumo-shi or Matsue to Tottori. However, there are plenty of trains.

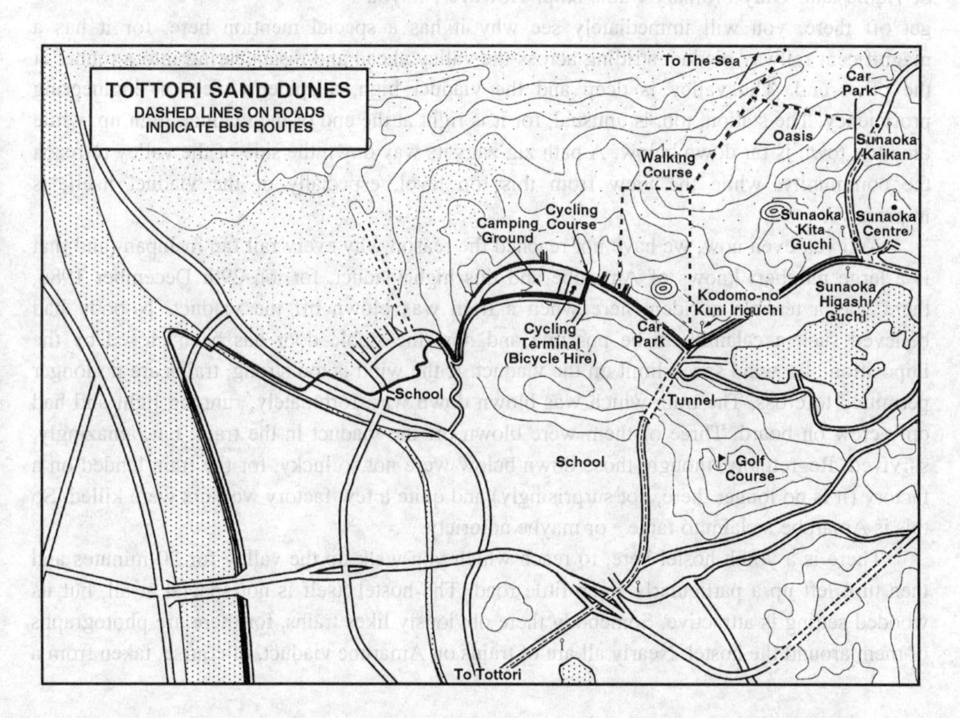

## HAMASAKA (浜坂 – 'Beach Slope')

### San-in Line, 10 hrs. from Tokyo, or 4 hrs. from Osaka

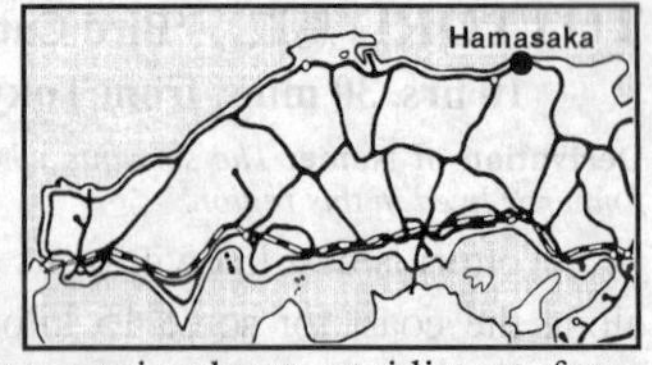


**Derivation of Name:** *Literal. The slopes here continued right down to the sea.*

Hamasaka gets a mention in this book because it is beside the sea, with a pleasant view, and has two youth hostels. The two are Hamasaka and Moroyose-so. The former is about equidistant from Hamasaka and Moroyose stations, Moroyose being one stop west of Hamasaka. Moroyose-so is near Moroyose station, as one might expect. However, it should be noted that *tokkyu* trains, which run about every two hours, do not stop at Moroyose.

Hamasaka, like other towns along this coast, is known for its seafood and Hamasaka Youth Hostel offers a special crab *sukiyaki* evening meal in winter. It also invites you to sit in the dining room and watch the lights of the fishing boats in the evening. Since you may need a stop somewhere along this stretch of coast, this is not a bad place to take it.

Hamasaka is only 30 minutes from Tottori by *tokkyu*, or 50 minutes by ordinary train. The latter are not frequent. There is a train every one to two hours, so plan in advance.

## AMARUBE (餘部 – 'Redundant Part')

### San-in Line, 15 mins. from Hamasaka

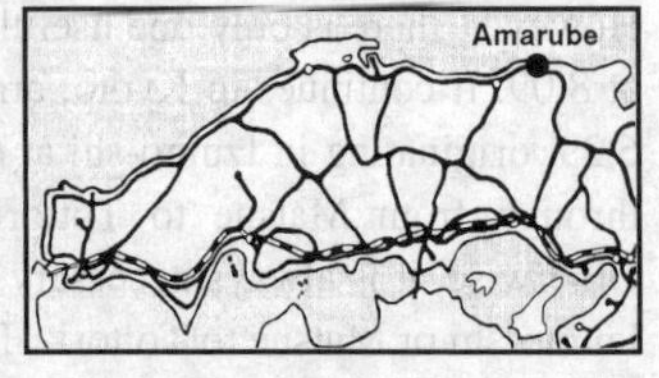


**Derivation of Name:** *During administrative reorganization long ago, any village with fewer than fifty households was known as 'amarube'.*

Amarube is a very small place, just two stations east of Hamasaka. Only ordinary trains stop. However, if you get off there, you will immediately see why it has a special mention here, for it has a magnificent railway viaduct striding across the valley ahead and disappearing into a tunnel at the other end. The valley is deep and the viaduct high, a spider's web of engineering proficiency. The station, too, is unusual, for it is right at the end of the viaduct, high up, while the little town is far down below. A path zig-zags its way down the side of the valley to reach the community, while the view from this top level, especially of the viaduct itself, is impressive.

And yet, even now, we have not reached the reason why every rail fan in Japan (and that is a large number) knows of Amarube and this high viaduct, for, on 29th December 1986, there was a terrible accident here when a train was blown off the viaduct. Nobody had believed such a calamity to be possible and now the stable door has been closed by the imposition of a wind speed limit on the viaduct. If the wind is too strong, trains are no longer permitted to cross. The train which was blown down was, fortunately, running light and had only crew on board. Three of them were blown off the viaduct in the train, but, amazingly, survived. Regrettably, though, those down below were not so lucky, for the train landed on a factory (it is no longer there, not surprisingly) and quite a few factory workers were killed. So this is Amarube's claim to fame – or maybe notoriety.

There is a youth hostel here, to reach which you walk up the valley for 20 minutes and then turn left up a particularly steep little road. The hostel itself is not special at all, but its wooded setting is attractive. Somebody there obviously likes trains, for there are photographs of them around the hostel. Nearly all are of trains on Amarube viaduct, of course, taken from a fine vantage point even higher up, and presumably with a camera several classes better than the author's.

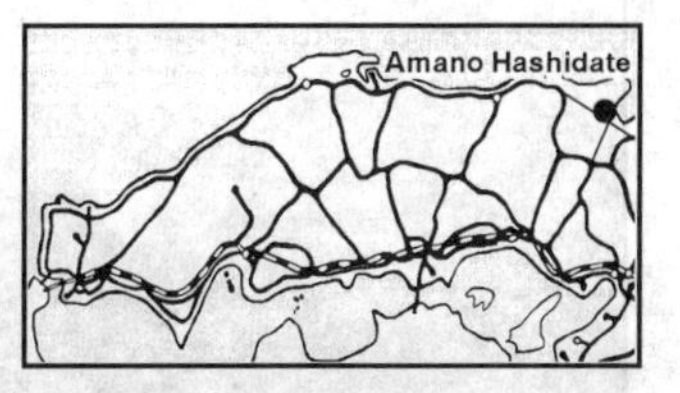


## AMANO HASHIDATE (天橋立 - 'Heavenly Standing Bridge') Kita Kinki Tango Private Railway, 2 hrs. 15 mins. from Kyoto

Amano Hashidate, one of the official three great natural scenic beauty spots of Japan, has already been described in the Kansai section of this book, which see for further information. It should be mentioned here, though, that it can easily be reached, as part of the Chugoku tour, from the station at Toyo-oka which is the western terminus of the Kita Kinki Tango Private Railway. Ordinary trains run from Toyo-oka every one to two hours, taking about 80 minutes, while at 9:56 there is a *kyuko* taking 66 minutes and at 15:49 a *tokkyu* taking 59 minutes. The basic fare from Toyo-oka to Amano Hashidate is ¥1,140 for the 55 kilometre journey and the supplements are ¥310 for the *kyuko* and ¥930 for the *tokkyu*, or ¥100 more if you want a reserved seat.

After seeing Amano Hashidate, of course, you can continue to Kyoto or Osaka via Fukuchiyama or Nishi Maizuru, as described in the Kansai section, without the necessity of coming back to Toyo-oka.

Alternatively, you can proceed from Amarube, Hamasaka or Tottori straight down the San-in Line to Kyoto, or down the Fukuchiyama Line, which branches off the San-in Line, to Osaka. The route to Kyoto, which readers are most likely to follow, is an attractive one through forested countryside and is well worth travelling. There are three *tokkyu* trains per day (and others from Kinosaki, two stations on the Tottori side of Toyo-oka) to Kyoto. To Osaka, there is one *tokkyu* from Kurayoshi, west of Tottori, and one from Hamasaka. There are also two other *tokkyu* trains which run to Osaka via the Bantan Line, that is to say via Himeji. Again there are several other *tokkyu* trains to Osaka from Kinosaki. Then there is the previously mentioned night *kyuko* to Osaka which starts from Izumo-shi as an ordinary train at 21:42 and reaches Osaka at 7:09. From Hamasaka to Kyoto takes 3½ hours by *tokkyu*. To Osaka takes about 3¾ hours. *Tokkyu* trains do not stop at Amarube. They stop at Hamasaka to the west and Kasumi to the east.

If you are travelling by ordinary train, because of the partial electrification of this line you must change trains three times, at Kinosaki (or Toyo-oka), Fukuchiyama and Sonobe. With reasonable connexions, it will take about 6 hours from Hamasaka to Kyoto (or Osaka). However, there are not so many trains between Toyo-oka and Fukuchiyama, so you must be careful of connexions on this section, where trains operate at intervals of about 90 minutes.

▲ The Summit of Ishizuchi-san Kotoden ▼

# SHIKOKU (四国)
## ('Four Countries')

Shikoku is the smallest of the four main islands of Japan, lying under the belly of Honshu. It is also the island most often missed by travellers with limited time - or even those who do have the time, but just have the impression that Shikoku is not interesting enough. That is a pity, because Shikoku is a very pretty island, which rewards with pleasant scenery and a gentle pace of life those who give it some of their time. It is understandable that people leave it out though, because there is nothing in Shikoku that absolutely must not be missed, just a lot of things that are well worth seeing if you have enough time.

If you have a rail pass and are heading west, why not go through Shikoku, instead of taking the *shinkansen* straight to Hiroshima? Even if you have only one day to spare, you can make a sweep through the island in that single day, finishing at Matsuyama, from where you can take a ferry for the crossing to Hiroshima next morning. Of course, if you can spare two or more days rather than one, you will enjoy Shikoku even more, but at least make the effort to pass through.

The name Shikoku means four countries and the island is so called because it has always been divided into four prefectures (or the equivalent of prefectures, which is actually a modern term). The current names of these four are Kagawa, Tokushima, Kochi and Ehime. We shall go round the island in that order, that is to say in a clockwise direction. Because it has to be accepted, with regret, that most people do have limited time for Shikoku, we shall suggest a minimum course, which could be accomplished in about two days, and a number of interesting deviations which can be made.

Somewhere on your travels around the island, you are sure to see pilgrims dressed in white. These people are making their way round Shikoku too, visiting 88 temples on the way. Most of these temples are not so special, although one or two are worth seeing and will be mentioned later. The temples are traditionally visited in a particular order, so you will see the number of each one on the official route written by its name - and it is usually considerably easier to read its number than its name! 88 is a number of good omen in Japan and 88 is thought to be a special age to attain, so it is probably not at random that this total number of temples was selected. Actually, they are all temples connected with a priest named Kobo Daishi. By tradition the pilgrims make their way around the island on foot, which should take a minimum of about a month. Since nobody in Japan can take a month's holiday, most of the

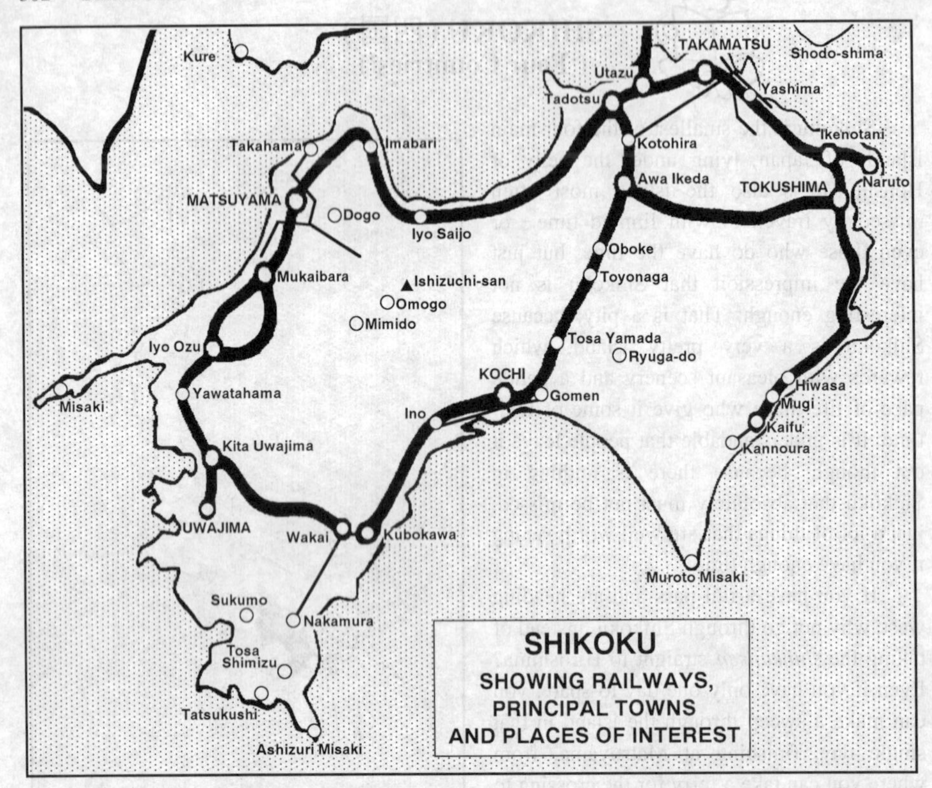


pilgrims are retired people, who possibly feel too that it is time to improve their spiritual status. Nowadays, however, it seems to be acceptable to make one's way around by any convenient means of transport. Because of the elevated location of most temples, a fair amount of exertion is going to be necessary anyway to visit the 88 locations. Some people now go around by bicycle, in which case the tour can be accomplished in about two weeks with some energetic pedalling. In other cases, one sees the pilgrims on buses or trains, although one always feels that one should ask whether the gods are aware of this conduct or not. Actually, the author has thought that this tour would be rather an interesting challenge, if only I could find time. If you fancy the idea, all you need is the uniform – a white coat, a stick, and a straw hat – and a map, easily obtainable, marking the 88 sites for your pilgrimage.

Because there are always these pilgrims making their way round Shikoku in search of salvation, most of the temples are obliged to provide accommodation. Pilgrims usually donate whatever they can afford for their bed and food. However, since accommodation is being offered in any case, several of these temples also act as youth hostels, in which case their fee is fixed, of course. Therefore, if you can spare time to visit Shikoku, this is a good opportunity to stay in one or two of the less conventional hostels.

***Transportation and Tickets***

If you are using a rail pass, you will find that Shikoku has a good network of express trains which are modern, efficient and comfortable. If you are using Blue Spring tickets, though, you will find that you need time, because the local services do not rush, and you need to plan because many of the local services are not frequent. As long as you do plan, however, you should not encounter problems, for all of the lines are reasonably served.

If you are looking for a suitable *shu-yu-ken*, there is an ideal one for you to use to visit Shikoku. It is called, reasonably enough, a *Shikoku Wide Shu-yu-ken*. It is valid for 10 days and it costs ¥27,400 from Tokyo. With this excellent, if slightly expensive, ticket, you can visit Nara, Osaka, Kobe, Himeji and Okayama (with a short excursion to Kurashiki, ¥310 each way) on the way to Shikoku, then spend about five days on the island, travelling by express train, which is permitted, as long as unreserved seating is used, before setting out on the return journey to Tokyo. This *shu-yu-ken* allows return by ferry to Kobe or Osaka (no extra charge), with a stop at the island of Shodo-shima (see later in this section) on the way. Then you can return to Tokyo via Kyoto, stopping to look at the sights there as well. It is a ticket which lets you see a very good selection of the famous and of the less frequented but still very attractive spots in Japan. To be sure, a Japan Rail Pass is better, but if you do not have one available, this is one of the best of the *shu-yu-ken* offers. The author used this ticket to visit Shikoku and Shodo-shima and had a particularly enjoyable time.

As in the case of Hokkaido, there is also a *Shikoku New Wide Shu-yu-ken*. This must be purchased in combination with a return ticket to Shikoku by train, aeroplane or ferry. For journeys by train and short distance ferry you will be given a 20% discount and for travel by other means of transport a 10% discount. The *shu-yu-ken* will be valid for 5 days within Shikoku at a cost of ¥12,570. It is not likely that this ticket will represent better value than the ordinary *Shikoku Wide Shu-yu-ken*, but you may find some reason to prefer it.

There are also many ferry services to Shikoku, too many to list, although a few will be mentioned in connexion with various cities in this section. Most useful of the longer distance ferries are those from Tokyo. Ferries leave Tokyo for Kochi on odd dates at 18:20, reaching Kochi at 15:40 on even dates. They leave Kochi at 18:10 on even dates and arrive in Tokyo at 14:40 on odd dates. There is also a service to Tokushima (final destination Kita Kyushu). It leaves Tokyo at 18:20 on even dates and reaches Tokushima at 12:30 on odd dates. It leaves Tokushima at 11:00 on odd dates and arrives in Tokyo at 5:00 on even dates. The fare between Tokyo and Kochi is ¥13,910 in the lowest class, but between Tokyo and Tokushima it is considerably cheaper at ¥8,200.

There are two other potentially useful overnight ferries to Shikoku. One leaves Higashi Kobe ('East Kobe') at 22:40 every night and reaches Imabari, in the centre of the north coast of Shikoku at 6:00 every morning. It then continues to Matsuyama, arriving at 8:10. It costs ¥3,600 to Imabari and ¥4,430 to Matsuyama. It returns by day, but another ship makes a night run at similar price from Imabari only to Higashi Kobe, leaving at 22:20. The other useful service is between Kobe and Matsuyama direct, leaving Kobe at 20:00 and 22:00 every night and arriving in Matsuyama at 4:10 and 6:05, before continuing to Oita in Kyushu. The return voyages leave Matsuyama at 20:35 and 22:40. The fare between Kobe and Matsuyama is ¥4,170. Of course, there are many other ferry voyages to and from a variety of ports in Shikoku. The above are just some of the less expensive overnight routes. You will usually be able to sleep quite well on the mats provided on these ferry services.

Here now is the suggested route, in clockwise direction, round the island of Shikoku:-

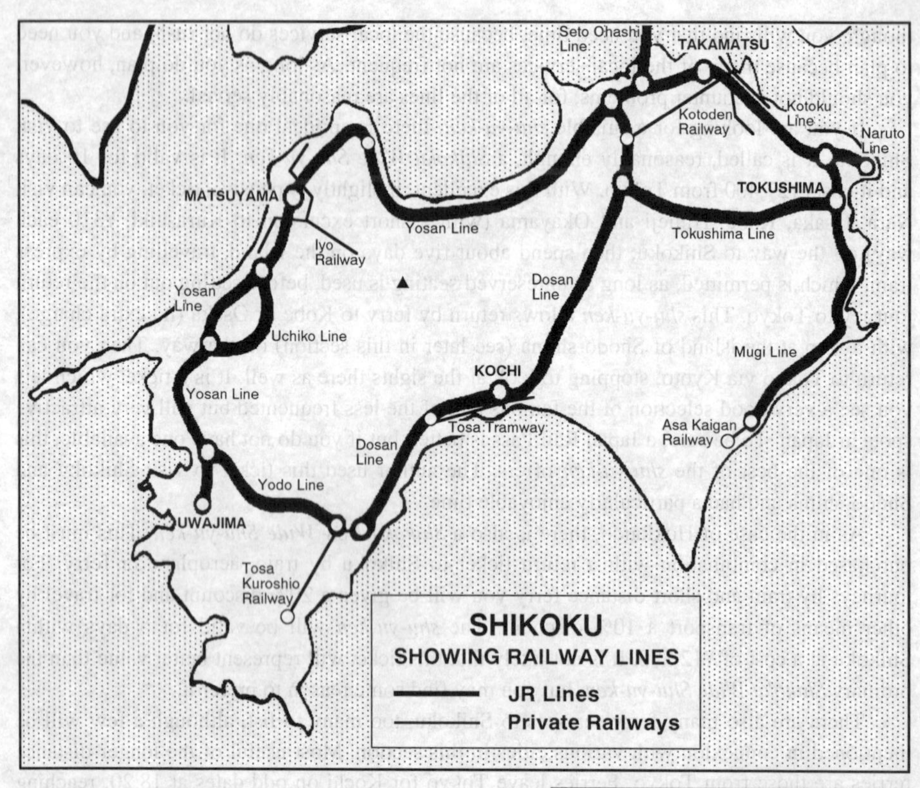


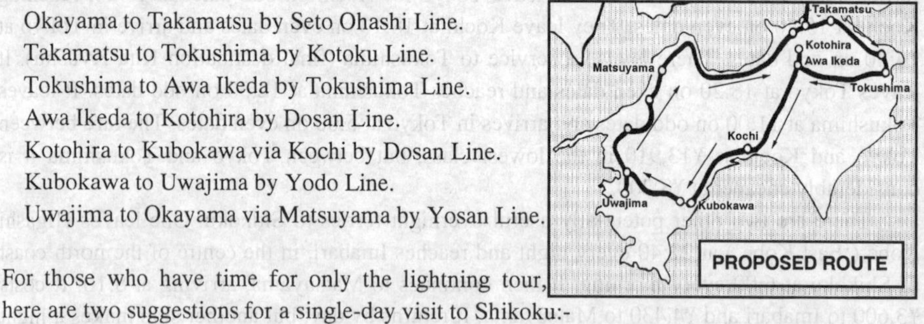


Okayama to Takamatsu by Seto Ohashi Line.
Takamatsu to Tokushima by Kotoku Line.
Tokushima to Awa Ikeda by Tokushima Line.
Awa Ikeda to Kotohira by Dosan Line.
Kotohira to Kubokawa via Kochi by Dosan Line.
Kubokawa to Uwajima by Yodo Line.
Uwajima to Okayama via Matsuyama by Yosan Line.

For those who have time for only the lightning tour, here are two suggestions for a single-day visit to Shikoku:-

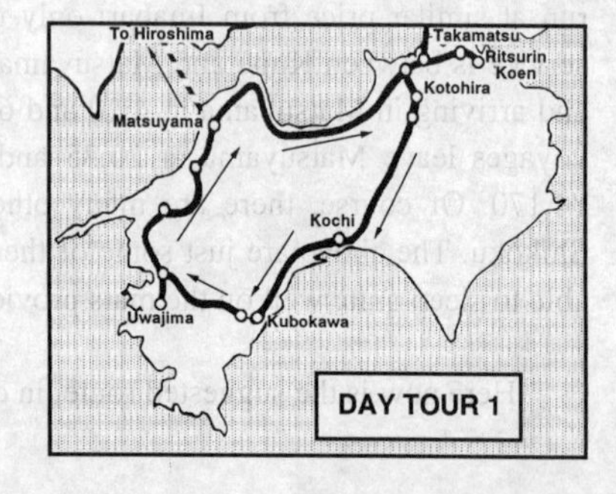


**DAY TOUR 1**

Okayama 6:14 *kaisoku* to Takamatsu 7:10.
Takamatsu 7:25 ordinary train to Ritsurin Koen Kita Guchi 7:31.
Visit to Ritsurin Koen.
Ritsurin Koen Kita Guchi 8:37 ordinary train to Takamatsu 8:43.
Takamatsu 8:51 *tokkyu* to Kotohira 9:26.
Visit to Kompira-san (shrine).

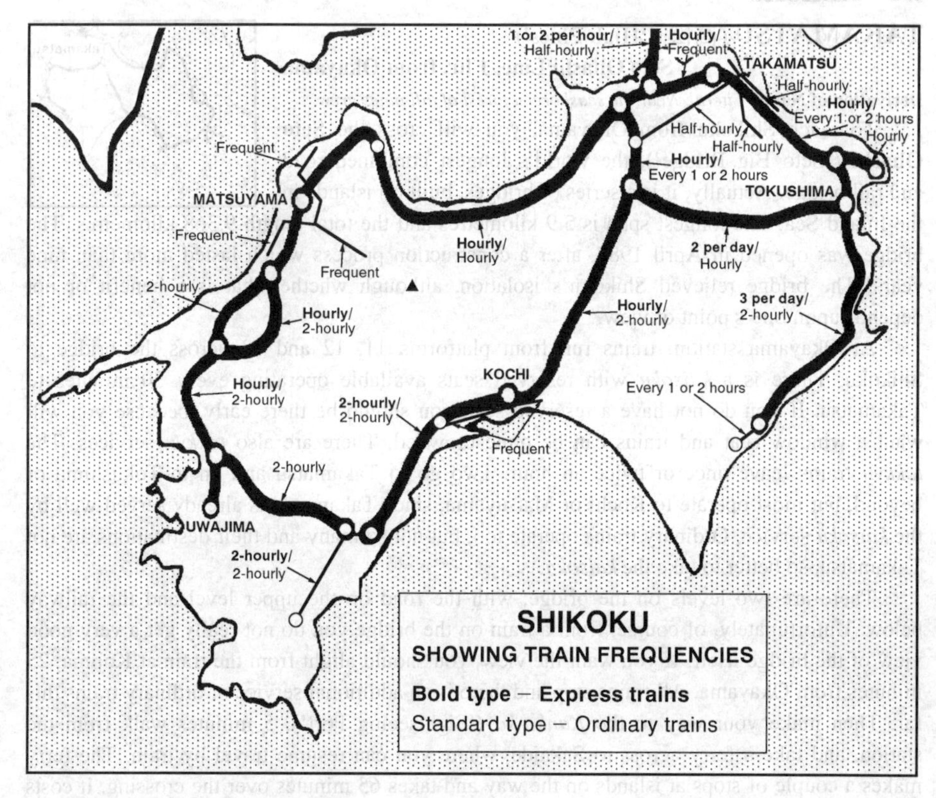


Kotohira 11:52 *tokkyu* to Kubokawa 14:32.
Kubokawa 14:41 ordinary train to Uwajima 16:40.
Uwajima 17:09 *tokkyu* to Matsuyama 18:37.
Tram to Dogo Onsen for Matsuyama Youth Hostel.
(Next day 7:25, 8:55 or 10:05 ferry to Hiroshima 10:25, 11:55 or 13:05.)
**or** Matsuyama 18:42 *tokkyu* to Okayama 21:35.

**DAY TOUR 2**

Okayama 6:14 *kaisoku* to Takamatsu 7:10.
Takamatsu 7:25 ordinary train to Ritsurin Koen Kita Guchi 7:31.
Visit to Ritsurin Koen.
Ritsurin Koen Kita Guchi 8:37 ordinary train
to Takamatsu 8:43.
Takamatsu 8:51 *tokkyu* to Kotohira 9:26.
Visit to Kompira-san (shrine).
Kotohira 11:52 *tokkyu* to Kochi 13:24.
Kochi 14:00 JR *kyuko* bus to Dogo Onsen 17:19
(for Matsuyama Youth Hostel).
**or** Kochi 14:00 JR *tokkyu* bus to Matsuyama 17:04.
Matsuyama 17:24 *tokkyu* to Okayama 20:01.

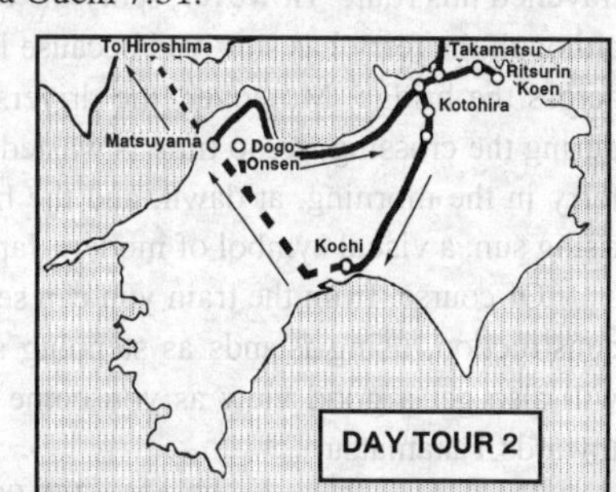

# TAKAMATSU (高松 – 'High Pines')

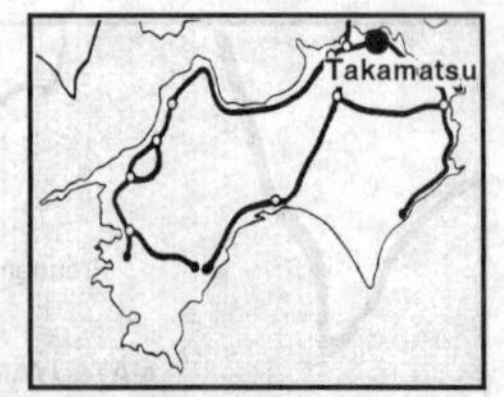


**Seto Ohashi Line, 1 hr. from Okayama**

**Derivation of Name:** *Literal. Near the seashore, a forest of tall pines grew.*

To reach Shikoku from Okayama, you will cross the **Seto Ohashi** ('Seto Big Bridge'), the world's longest combined road and rail bridge. Actually, it is a series of bridges, built on islands in the Inland Sea. The longest span is 5.9 kilometres and the total length 9.368 kilometres. The bridge was opened in April 1988, after a construction process which lasted more than nine years. The bridge relieved Shikoku's isolation, although whether that is a benefit or not depends upon one's point of view.

At Okayama station, trains run from platforms 11, 12 and 13 across the bridge to Shikoku. There is a *kaisoku* with reserved seats available operating every 30 minutes to Takamatsu. If you do not have a reserved seat, you should be there early, because you will want a window seat and trains can be quite crowded. There are also *tokkyu* services. The *tokkyu* trains leave once or twice an hour. Two go to Takamatsu and on to Tokushima or beyond, but most operate to Kochi or Matsuyama, since Takamatsu is already served well by the *kaisoku* service. Ordinary trains operate too, but not so many and their destinations are not Takamatsu, so better to take the *kaisoku*.

There are two levels on the bridge, with the road on the upper level and the railway below. Unfortunately, of course, from a train on the bridge you do not really get a very good view of the bridge itself. If you want the view, you should alight from the train at Kojima, 25 minutes from Okayama. All trains stop and there is an additional service of ordinary trains this far. Then make your way to the *Kanko-ko* ('Sightseeing Port'), 5 minutes walk from the station, and take a ferry across to Sakaide, where you can resume travel by train. The ferry makes a couple of stops at islands on the way and takes 65 minutes over the crossing. It costs ¥870. This service runs three times per day throughout the year, at 7:30, 11:00 and 15:05. In summer, there may be additional sailings.

An alternative is to take a bus from Kojima station to Shimotsui, 25 minutes at a cost of ¥300, and then a ferry to Marugame, which takes 65 minutes, calling at one island on the way, and costs ¥770. The ferry sails nine times per day and buses are mostly timed to connect. To catch suitable morning ferries, take the bus at 7:10, 8:55 or 10:50 from Kojima station. This means taking a train from Okayama at 6:14, 8:22 or 10:09. From Marugame, ordinary trains run to Takamatsu frequently. The service between Kojima and Shimotsui, now covered by bus, used to be operated by a small 2 feet 6 inches gauge train, which is how the author travelled this route. However, sadly the opening of the bridge signalled the end for this service, although the ferry has survived because it is cheaper for trucks to cross by this route than to go across the bridge. Moreover, the drivers can be having their breakfast and a statutory break during the crossing, so no time is wasted by the slower service. The author crossed on the first ferry in the morning, at dawn, and the bridge looked most impressive silhouetted against the rising sun, a visual symbol of modern Japan.

Of course, from the train you can see something of the bridge, especially as its method of construction, using islands as stepping stones, means that it is not completely straight. You will also get a good view as you come off the bridge and the train turns to the left to head towards Takamatsu.

Takamatsu is a city of about 350,000 people and is most famous for a garden known as

Ritsurin Koen. It is also known for the production of lacquerware and toilet paper, there being, however, no connexion between the two. It is the capital of Kagawa Prefecture.

**Ritsurin Koen** is not one of the official three famous gardens of Japan. However, in the opinion of many people, including the author, it is better than two of the official Big Three. Perhaps only Kenroku-en in Kanazawa surpasses this garden in its beauty. Naturally, you will find plenty of people here, as usual in Japan, so it is better to visit early, if possible. The garden is constructed around thirteen small hills and six ponds and is one of those gardens which is supposed to represent a miniature Japan. It was built in the sixteenth century, enlarged in the seventeenth, opened to the public in 1875 and reconstructed in 1897. Admission costs ¥310 and the garden is always open at least from 7:00 until 17:00. In the summer it is open from 5:30 until 19:00.

To reach Ritsurin Koen, take a JR train from platform 0 or 1 (occasionally 2 also) at Takamatsu to Ritsurin Koen Kita Guchi (Ritsurin Park North Entrance), which is the second stop, a journey of only 6 minutes. Trains run once or twice an hour, but note that only ordinary trains stop. The *tokkyu* stops at Ritsurin, the next station, but it is 10 minutes walk from the garden, whereas the ordinary train stops right outside. Walk down from the narrow platform and you will see notices directing you the short distance to the entrance. Before leaving the station, check the times of onward trains, which are on a notice on the platform. You will require 60 to 90 minutes to look round the garden. Also note that the 12:05 departure from Takamatsu does not stop at Ritsurin Koen Kita Guchi.

There are the remains of a castle in Takamatsu too, if you have spare time there. What is left of the castle has been converted into a park with an admission fee of ¥100. It is called **Tamamo Koen** and is just outside Takamatsu station.

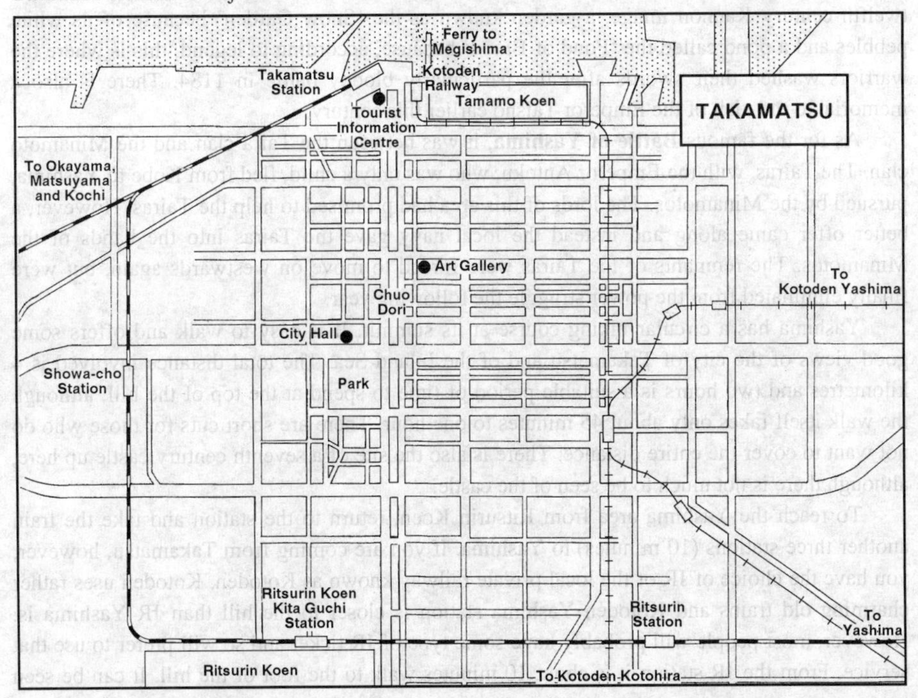

Only 4 kilometres from Takamatsu is an island called **Megishima**, but also known as **Onigashima** ('Demons' Island'). It is a popular place to visit because it is associated with a Japanese children's story about a boy called Momotaro ('Peach Boy'). He was supposedly discovered in a peach by an old couple who then reared him. When he grew up, he set off, accompanied by a dog, a monkey and a pheasant, to eliminate a group of demons who were terrorizing the population from their island home. Megishima is generally thought to have been this island and to have been inhabited by a group of pirates who made life difficult for the locals. There is a cave on the island where pirates probably once lived. There are ferries to Megishima every two hours, costing ¥320 and taking 20 minutes over the crossing. Bus tours to the cave operate every day in the summer and on holidays in other seasons, costing ¥600 and lasting 50 minutes.

## YASHIMA (屋島 - 'Roof Island')

**Kotoku Line, 15 mins. from Takamatsu**

**Derivation of Name:** *From shape of hill. See under.*

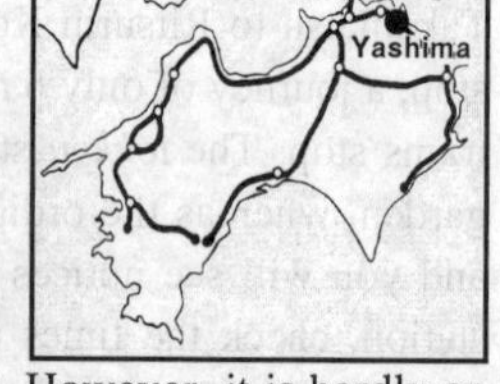


Yashima is only a short ride from Takamatsu. It is a large flat-topped hill 300 metres in height and its name probably comes from its shape, rather similar to that of the roof of a typical Japanese dwelling of former times, before ready-mixed concrete was invented. However, it is hardly an island, being separated from the mainland by only the narrowest of channels.

Yashima is famous both for having on it a temple with a long history and for the major battle which was fought here in 1184. The **temple** was supposedly founded by a Chinese religious teacher in 754. It is one of the 88 temples visited by the Shikoku pilgrims. There is a twelfth century Kannon image, a garden known as the 'Snow Garden' because of its white pebbles and a pond called the 'Pond of Blood' because, according to legend, this is where the warriors washed their swords after the particularly bloody battle in 1184. There is also a memorial to the visit of the Emperor Taisho earlier this century.

As for the famous **Battle of Yashima**, it was between the Taira clan and the Minamoto clan. The Tairas, with the Emperor Antoku, who was only a child, fled from Kobe to Yashima, pursued by the Minamotos. The lords of this area had promised to help the Tairas. However, a better offer came along and instead the local navy gave the Tairas into the hands of the Minamotos. The remnants of the Tairas were forced to move on westwards again, but were finally eliminated from the power struggle the following year.

Yashima has a circular hiking course at its summit. It is easy to walk and offers some good views of the city of Takamatsu and of the Inland Sea. The total distance involved is 4 kilometres and two hours is a suitable period of time to spend at the top of the hill, although the walk itself takes only about 45 minutes to one hour. There are short cuts for those who do not want to cover the entire distance. There is also the site of a seventh century castle up here, although there is not much to be seen of the castle.

To reach the Yashima area from Ritsurin Koen, return to the station and take the train another three stations (10 minutes) to Yashima. If you are coming from Takamatsu, however, you have the choice of JR or the local private railway known as Kotoden. Kotoden uses rather charming old trains and Kotoden Yashima station is closer to the hill than JR Yashima is. However, most people will probably have some type of JR ticket and so will prefer to use that service. From the JR station it is about 10 minutes walk to the foot of the hill. It can be seen clearly from either station. JR *tokkyu* trains all stop at Yashima. To reach the summit of the hill there is a funicular railway, as well as a bus service. Most people use the funicular railway. It operates every 20 minutes and costs ¥600, or ¥1,160 return, taking 5 minutes over the journey. The bus leaves from the lower funicular railway station at 9:52, 10:52, 12:52, 14:17 and 15:32. It costs ¥430 to the top of the hill (Yashima Sanjo - 屋島山上) and takes 10 minutes to get there. Return journeys are at 10:15, 11:15, 13:15, 14:45 and 15:50. The bus actually originates and terminates at Takamatsu Ferry Terminal, just near the JR station there, if you prefer to take it all the way. From Takamatsu it costs ¥700 and takes 38 minutes.

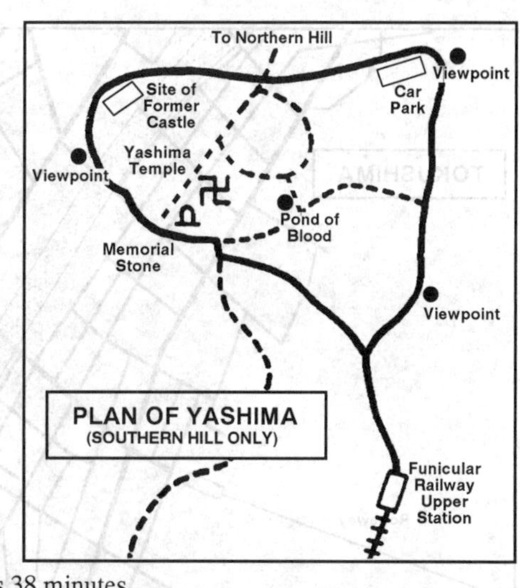


There is a youth hostel in Yashima, the nearest to Takamatsu. Named Takamatsu Yashima Sanso Hostel, it is just near the entrance to the lower station of the funicular railway. It is not special.

## NARUTO (鳴門 - 'Ringing Gate')

**Naruto Line, 90 mins. from Takamatsu**

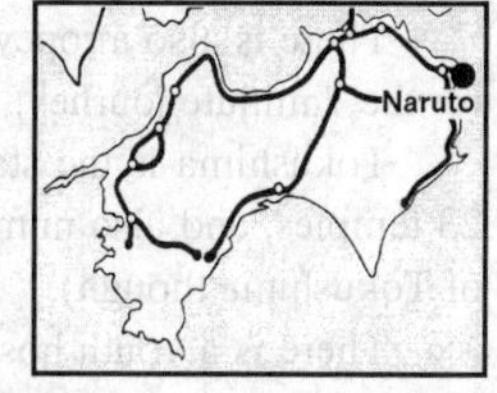


**Derivation of Name:** *Probably from the noise of the whirlpools and the fact that there is only a narrow space between the two islands here, forming a type of 'gate' through which the sea must pass.*

Naruto is a little north of Tokushima and is known for its **whirlpools** formed by the changing tide rushing through the narrow channel between Shikoku and Awaji-shima. If you come from Awaji-shima to Shikoku at the right time, these whirlpools can be observed quite well from the bridge which links the two islands. However, a better but more costly way is to take a sightseeing boat. This costs ¥1,500 for a 30 minute voyage and, in addition, you have to take a bus from Naruto station to Naruto Kanko-ko (鳴門観光港), the port from which it leaves, as it is rather too far to walk. You can also watch the whirlpools from the land by taking a bus to Naruto Koen (鳴門公園 - ¥300), where there is a good observation point. Buses run about hourly.

Trains to Naruto operate from Tokushima, with the journey taking 45 minutes. If you are coming from Takamatsu or Yashima, change trains at Ikenotani, an hour from Takamatsu by the *tokkyu* service, which runs approximately hourly, or about two hours by ordinary train. Trains to Naruto operate hourly. Sometimes connexions are good and sometimes they are not.

## TOKUSHIMA (徳島 - 'Virtuous Islands')

**Kotoku Line, 75 mins. from Takamatsu**

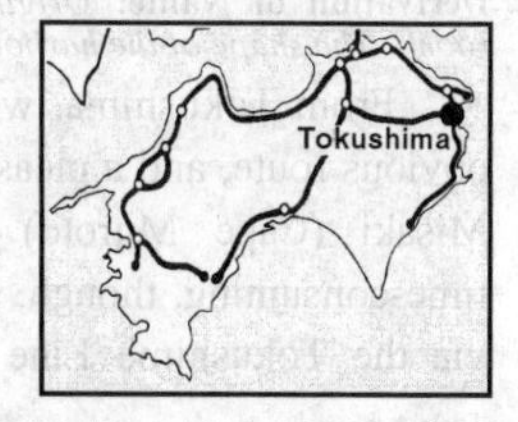


**Derivation of Name:** *There is a group of sand islands here and such islands are often described in poetic language as 'tokushima'.*

Tokushima is best known for its ***Awa Odori*** all-night festival of dancing in the middle of August, but, if it does not happen to be

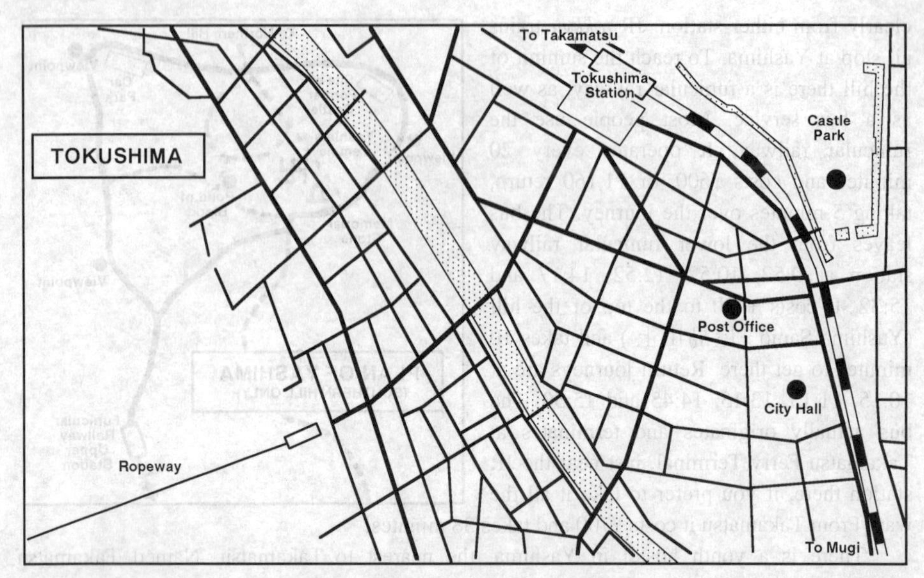


August when you are there, that will not excite you. There are the **ruins of a castle** and a pleasant garden in the grounds thereof. Admission to the two costs ¥50, although one must pay an additional ¥300 if one wishes to enter the castle museum.

There is also a ropeway up a hill overlooking the city. It costs ¥500 single or ¥800 return for the 7 minute journey.

Tokushima is the start of the pilgrimage around the 88 temples of Shikoku and the first 23 temples, and also number 66 on the route, are in the prefecture (not necessarily in the city of Tokushima though).

There is a youth hostel in Tokushima, but it is some way out of the main part of the city. There is also a hostel further south at Hiwasa, if you are continuing in that direction.

*Tokkyu* trains run approximately hourly to Tokushima from Takamatsu, taking 75 minutes over the journey, and there are also two trains per day from Okayama. These two leave Okayama at 11:49 and 16:48, arriving in Tokushima at 14:04 and 19:06. The latter continues further south to Mugi, which it reaches at 20:21, passing Hiwasa at 20:08.

As mentioned earlier, there is also a direct ferry service to Tokushima from Tokyo, operating every other day.

## MUROTO MISAKI (室戸岬 – 'Cape Room Door')

**Mugi Line to Kaifu, 1 hr. 45 mins. from Tokushima.**
**Then Asa Kaigan Railway to Kannoura, 11 mins. Then bus, 1 hr.**

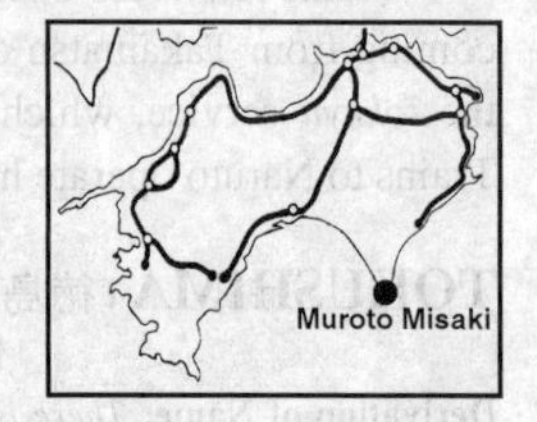


**Derivation of Name:** *Originally 'Muronoto', meaning 'a harbour like a room'. The shape of the harbour here was thought to resemble that of a room.*

From Tokushima, we have some choices to make. The most obvious route, and a pleasant one, is to keep going south to Muroto Misaki (Cape Muroto) at the tip of eastern Shikoku. This route is expensive and time-consuming, though, so most readers will probably opt for the alternative of heading west via the Tokushima Line to Awa Ikeda and Kochi, as described in the following entries.

However, for those who have time and money, here is the route south.

The Mugi Line continues south from Tokushima, through the town of Mugi to Kaifu, where the JR line, but not necessarily the train, ends. At this point, the Asa Kaigan Private Railway takes over and continues for two more stations (¥260) to Kannoura. There are bureaucratic reasons for this, of course, for most of the line was constructed during the days of railway expansion for the purpose of serving the community. When policy changed and it was decided that railways must pay their way, JNR, as it was at that time, was left with an incomplete line now suddenly stopped at nowhere in particular. Eventually it was decided to press on slowly, with support from the local authority. JR operates services to the point which the line had reached before the change of policy came, while a subsidized private company has laid track through the previously completed tunnels and added two more stations. Whether the line will ever get any further than the current rather unlikely mid-air terminus is doubtful. Indeed, there seems no particular reason why it should.

At present, most trains terminate at Mugi, although some run through to Kaifu and a few continue all the way to Kannoura. When trains terminate at Mugi or Kaifu, there is often a connexion to Kannoura. There is one *tokkyu* which starts from Takamatsu at 8:14 and runs all the way through to Kannoura, arriving at 11:31, although beyond Mugi the train is classified as an ordinary train. There are further *tokkyu* services to Mugi leaving Takamatsu at 14:01 and 17:49, the latter originating in Okayama at 16:48. These trains pass Tokushima at 15:17 and 19:13, arriving in Mugi at 16:24 and 20:21. Otherwise, there are ordinary trains from Tokushima to Kannoura, with or without a change, about every two hours. The journey is a pleasant one, with glimpses of the coast all along the way and with the train gradually becoming less and less populated.

From Kannoura, it is necessary to take a bus to get to Muroto Misaki. There are nine buses per day. Two afternoon trains connect particularly well with the bus services. If you take the 12:23 ordinary train from Tokushima, you will be in Kannoura at 15:22, having changed at Mugi. The bus leaves the station for Muroto Misaki (室戸岬) at 15:25, arriving at 16:15, at a cost of ¥1,500. The bus then continues to Kochi (高知), if you do not wish to stay at Muroto Misaki. It reaches Kochi at 18:43, at a cost of ¥3,940 from Kannoura.

The second service is by the *tokkyu* which leaves Takamatsu at 14:01 and Tokushima at 15:17, reaching Mugi at 16:24. A connecting ordinary train leaves Mugi at 16:25 and reaches Kannoura at 17:02. The bus departs at 17:19 and reaches Muroto Misaki at 18:12. It continues as far as a town named Aki (安芸).

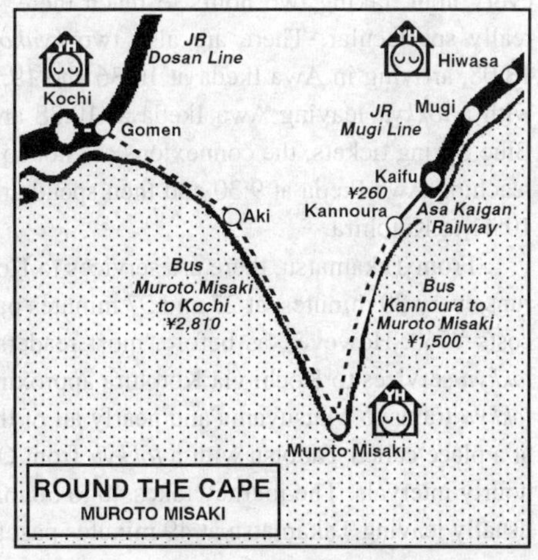


The bus runs along the coast almost all the way to Muroto Misaki, so it is a pleasant, if expensive, ride. At the cape, rocks straggle out into the sea and one of the hotels has a pond of little turtles. The cliff behind you is high and it has on it one of Japan's oldest lighthouses. Up there too is Hotsu Misaki-ji, number 24 in the circuit of 88 temples. It is also an agreeable youth hostel, although, as usual with temples, a hard climb to reach. The route up is a path only, not a road, although there is also a road, but involving a considerably longer walk. On the way up, you will go past a short path which leads to the lighthouse, from where there is a good view out to sea.

It is recommended that the earlier of the two buses mentioned above be taken, because you need a little time to look around Muroto Misaki in daylight and it would be a difficult walk up to the hostel, if you decide to stay there, in the dark.

In the morning, you will need to take a bus on to Kochi (高知). Bus times change periodically, of course, but, at the time of writing, there are buses at 5:32, 6:40, 7:30, 8:09 and 9:37. The journey takes 2 hours 30 minutes and costs ¥2,810. Some buses go to the station, but some terminate at Harimaya-bashi, two tram stops away in the city centre. Strangely, though, if you plan to travel in the opposite direction, note that all services start from Harimaya-bashi, and that none originates from the station.

The journey on to Kochi is still mostly beside the sea and again quite pleasant, although it deteriorates as the city is approached. Along the way you will be able to distinguish the signs of an abandoned railway route and then, when you reach Aki, where the bus company uses the old railway station as its terminal, you will notice the construction of a new rail route to the town, which seems indicative of some odd changes of policy over the years. However, despite the two rail routes, there are still no trains to Aki at present. When the new line is opened, it will be a private railway, but probably cheaper than the bus.

## KOTOHIRA (琴平 – 'Harp Plateau')

**Dosan Line, 40 mins. from Takamatsu**

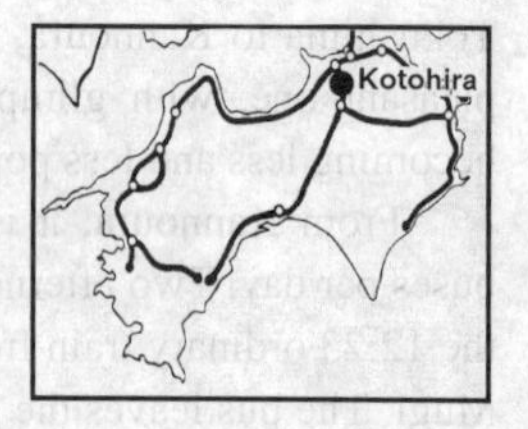


**Derivation of Name:** *Kompira is one of the twelve guardians of Buddha and Kotohira is a corruption of 'Kompira'.*

If time and money do not permit the journey round Muroto Misaki, which would be an understandable decision, the obvious alternative is to take the Tokushima Line from Tokushima west to Awa Ikeda and then turn north for a short while to our next port of call which will be Kotohira. Or you might even decide not to come any further down the east coast than Yashima. Let us look at both routes to Kotohira then. From Tokushima ordinary trains run to Awa Ikeda about every hour, taking two hours to reach there. The journey is pleasantly scenic without being really spectacular. There are also two *kyuko* services. They leave Tokushima at 9:18 and 18:08, arriving in Awa Ikeda at 10:36 and 19:28. The morning *kyuko* would connect perfectly with a *tokkyu* leaving Awa Ikeda at 10:38 and reaching Kotohira at 11:03. If you are using Blue Spring tickets, the connexions are not so good. Best is to take the 7:29 from Tokushima, reaching Awa Ikeda at 9:30 and then spend an hour looking at Awa Ikeda before catching the 10:41 to Kotohira.

From Takamatsu, there are services to Kotohira both with JR and with Kotoden. Kotoden runs every 30 minutes, at 27 and 57 minutes past each hour, takes an hour over the journey and costs ¥560. However, as before, most readers will already be committed to JR. JR operates *tokkyu* services to Kochi via Kotohira approximately every two hours, but in between there are *tokkyu* trains to Matsuyama and nearly all of those are arranged so that they make a connexion at a place called Tadotsu with a *tokkyu* from Okayama to Kochi, thus giving a service at about hourly intervals. The journey takes 40 to 50 minutes by *tokkyu*. The ordinary trains run hourly, usually leaving Takamatsu at 49 minutes past the hour and reaching Kotohira 65 to 70 minutes later. In addition, there are ordinary trains to Kannon-ji which make connexions at Tadotsu with other ordinary trains to Kotohira.

Kotohira is one place in Shikoku which should certainly not be left off your sightseeing list. It is famous for its shrine named **Kompira-san**. To reach it will involve some exertion, for there are 785 stone steps up to the main hall. From the JR station, walk ahead past Kotoden Kotohira station to the main street, with the post office on the corner. Turn left and walk for five minutes until you reach the entrance to the steps on your right at the end of a short street of expensive, but very traditional, *ryokan* (hotels). These are worth spending a moment looking at, for such buildings are not so often seen in a group like this.

Now the steps start, lined with souvenir shops for a while, until the exertion of lugging their wares up here becomes too much for the cajoling owners and the ascent takes on a more religious air. There are plenty of places to see on the way up, to break the strain of all the climbing. With a few minutes spent looking at the various buildings, it will probably take at least half an hour to reach the top. Outside the main hall is a platform from which a good view of the surrounding area can be obtained and, if you still have energy, you can keep climbing to some further shrine buildings of lesser importance, some of them quite a distance away. They are not so interesting, however, and probably not worth the effort, unless you want to get away from the masses. The author came up here at 6:30 in the morning, when it was not too crowded, but, even at that time, I was far from alone. Drizzle was falling, which restricted the view, but gave a fresh scent to the woods which lay below. Since this is one of Japan's famous shrines, try not to miss it.

There is a youth hostel here – Kotohira Seinen-no-ie Hostel. It is not so far from the start of the climb to Kompira-san. The location is fine, but it is housed in a concrete municipal building which is old, uninspiring and shabby. Nevertheless, even though the JYH gives it only one star on its scale of grading, it has a Happy Jim mark in this book. The author arrived here relatively late in the evening, tired and having had a hard job locating the hostel in the dark with the usual scaleless map. Finally finding my way, I opened the door and was greeted with, "Ah, there you are. Would you like a cup of tea?" Surely, it is the 'parents' who make each hostel good or bad, not the buildings. So, unless the management has changed, despite all of its shortcomings, this ranks, in the author's assessment, as a good hostel. Maybe no tea will be available when you arrive, though, and you will feel differently.

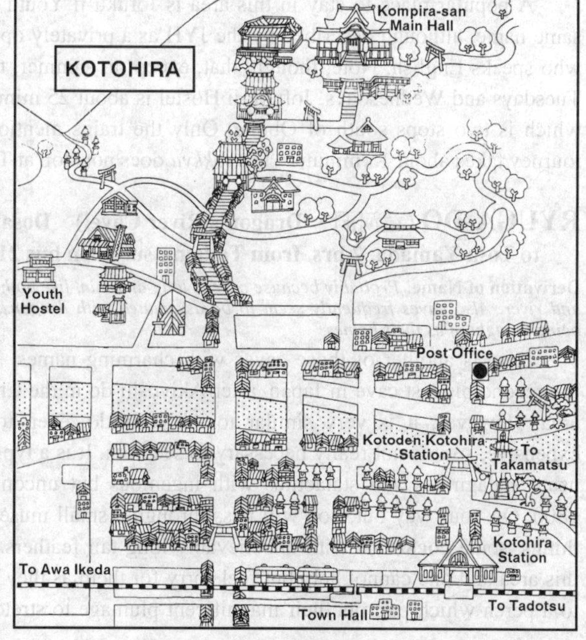

## OBOKE (大歩危 - 'Big Walking Danger')

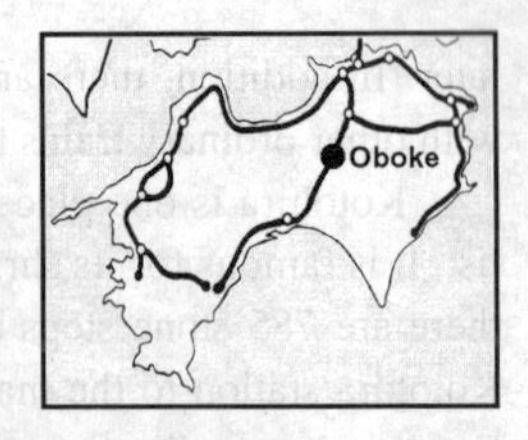


**Dosan Line, 85 mins. from Takamatsu**

**Derivation of Name:** *Originally 'Ohohoki', meaning 'big cliff'. Such a term is especially used in reference to places where there is a strong element of erosion, as here.*

As we now go south from Kotohira towards Kochi, we shall pass through some very attractive countryside, so try to ensure that you have a window seat on the train. The most inspiring section is when you travel through **Oboke Gorge**, starting about 15 minutes south of Awa Ikeda station. This is very scenic just from the railway carriage window, but, if you want more, there are boat rides available on the river down below, weather and water conditions permitting. The trip starts from near Oboke station and lasts a mere 30 minutes for the return journey. The fare is ¥1,000.

From Kotohira, there are *tokkyu* trains going south towards Kochi about every hour, but only a few stop at Oboke. Those which do so at useful times leave Kotohira at 8:05 and 12:34, arriving at Oboke at 8:48 and 13:19. Ordinary trains always stop, of course, but it is necessary to change trains at Awa Ikeda and connexions are generally poor. The following reasonable connexions are available:-

① Kotohira 7:03. Awa Ikeda 7:50 / 8:32. Oboke 9:04.
② Kotohira 9:39. Awa Ikeda 10:32 / 11:22. Oboke 11:55.
③ Kotohira 11:28. Awa Ikeda 12:40 / 13:24. Oboke 14:02.
④ Kotohira 13:18. Awa Ikeda 14:20 / 14:36. Oboke 15:08.

When you have finished at Oboke, you need to remember that onward trains are few too. Here is the current timetable from mid-morning until late afternoon. Trains leave Oboke going south at 11:55, 13:19 (*tokkyu*), 14:02, 15:08 and 18:34. All trains go to Kochi, which takes nearly two hours (55 minutes by *tokkyu*).

A popular place to stay in this area is Jofuku-ji Youth Hostel, part of the temple of the same name, although described by the JYH as a privately operated hostel. It is run by a priest who speaks English. Note, though, that, except in summer, this hostel is closed on Mondays, Tuesdays and Wednesdays. Jofuku-ji Hostel is about 25 minutes walk from Toyonaga station, which is two stops south of Oboke. Only the trains mentioned above are available and the journey takes about 15 minutes. The *tokkyu* does not stop at Toyonaga.

## RYUGA-DO (竜河洞 - 'Dragon's River Cave') Dosan Line to Tosa Yamada, 2 hrs. from Takamatsu. Then bus 21 mins.

**Derivation of Name:** *Probably because cave is long and thin, like both dragon and river. Also caves frequently seem to be associated with dragons, maybe being thought of as their homes.*

Here is another of those caves with charming names. This is the second biggest cave in Japan, after Akiyoshi-do in the Chugoku area. However, it is very similar to Akiyoshi-do, even to the extent of being almost as expensive, so it is not really necessary to see both. It is a typical large limestone cave with the usual stalagmites and stalactites with ingenious but unconvincing names. Admission costs ¥800. On your way out, you will pass through a small museum which houses, amongst other things, some **cockerels** with unbelievably long tail feathers. Such birds are specially bred in this area and one cannot help but feel sorry for them as they sit all day in a glass case chained to a perch which permits their magnificent plumage to stretch down and be displayed two or three metres below their bodies. Some fortunate specimens are deceased and stuffed, but others are still awaiting that day of release.

Buses run to Ryuga-do (竜河洞) from Tosa Yamada station, reached about 15 minutes before Kochi by *tokkyu* or about 30 minutes by ordinary train. These buses are JR buses, so are free to holders of rail passes or *shu-yu-ken* (otherwise ¥430 each way). There are five buses per day, at approximately two hourly intervals. Since they turn round and go straight back, you will have two hours to look at the cave before the next bus comes. If you are coming from the north, bus services are timed to connect well with *tokkyu* arrivals. The 9:26 *tokkyu* from Kotohira arrives at Tosa Yamada at 10:52 and a bus departs at 10:58. The 11:52 *tokkyu* from Kotohira arrives at 13:12 and a bus departs at 13:17. The 12:34 *tokkyu* from Kotohira stops at Oboke at 13:19 and reaches Tosa Yamada at 14:00. A bus leaves at 14:09. If you are using ordinary trains, you have two services to choose from. The 8:32 from Awa Ikeda passes Oboke at 9:04 and Toyonaga at 9:24, reaching Tosa Yamada at 10:17, for the 10:58 bus. Alternatively, the 11:22 from Awa Ikeda passes Oboke at 11:55 and Toyonaga at 12:09, reaching Tosa Yamada at 13:08, for the 13:17 bus. This is perhaps the most convenient bus service, because it entails a stay of only one hour at the cave, which is sufficient. The bus ride takes 21 minutes and return services from the cave to Tosa Yamada (土佐山田) are at 11:22, 13:43, 14:39 and 17:10. There are plenty of trains between Tosa Yamada and Kochi, which means that this expedition can easily be managed from a base in Kochi. There is also a bus service between Ryuga-do and Kochi (Harimaya-bashi). There are seven buses per day, but they are not JR buses, so you must pay. The fare is ¥1,010 each way and the journey takes about an hour.

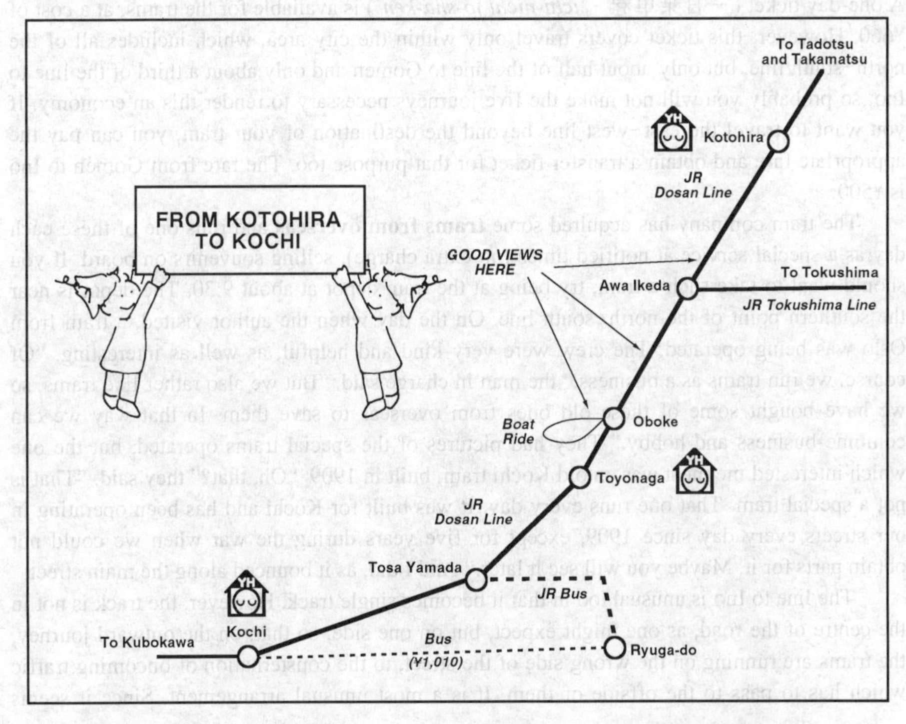

## KOCHI (高知 - 'High Knowledge')

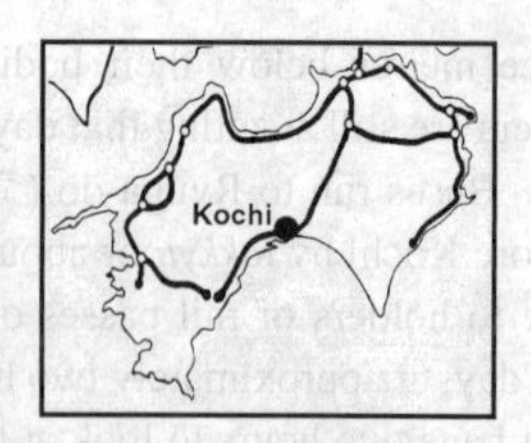


**Dosan Line, 2 hrs. 30 mins. from Okayama or 2 hrs. 10 mins. from Takamatsu**

**Derivation of Name:** *Originally 'Kawauchi', meaning 'inside the rivers'. Over time, changed to 'Kochi'.*

Kochi is the major city of the southern part of Shikoku, the capital of the prefecture of the same name. It is quite a pleasant city, with trams running in the streets, and its major attraction is its **castle**, which dates from 1748. It is on a hill to the west of the station, about 15 minutes walk away. Admission costs ¥350.

The centre of the city is **Harimaya-bashi** (はりまや橋), two stops by tram south of the station, or about 10 minutes walk. You will find a nice shiny traditional red bridge there and a place to sit down beside the river - or maybe it is a canal. The main bus terminal is here too, if you need to go anywhere by bus.

The tram system consists of only two lines, one running north and south with the railway station as its northern limit, and the other running east and west and much longer. This east-west line stretches from Gomen (後免) in the east, five stations away on the JR Dosan Line, to Ino (伊野) in the west, seven stations away on the same line. To travel the entire length of this line takes about 90 minutes, although, in fact, trams do not usually run the entire distance. The flat fare within the city area is ¥180 and if you wish to transfer from the east-west line to the north-south line, or vice versa, at Harimaya-bashi, where the two cross, you may do so, by asking for a transfer ticket (*norikai ken*) upon paying your fare as you exit from the first tram. A one-day ticket (一日乗車券 - '*ichi-nichi jo-sha-ken*') is available for the trams, at a cost of ¥660. However, this ticket covers travel only within the city area, which includes all of the north-south line, but only about half of the line to Gomen and only about a third of the line to Ino, so probably you will not make the five journeys necessary to render this an economy. If you want to travel the east-west line beyond the destination of your tram, you can pay the appropriate fare and obtain a transfer ticket for that purpose too. The fare from Gomen to Ino is ¥500.

The tram company has acquired some **trams from overseas** and runs one of these each day as a special service at notified times (no extra charge), selling souvenirs on board. If you should want to take such a tram, try being at the tram depot at about 9:30. The depot is near the southern point of the north-south line. On the day when the author visited, a tram from Oslo was being operated. The crew were very kind and helpful, as well as interesting. "Of course, we run trams as a business," the man in charge said. "But we also rather like trams, so we have bought some of these old ones from overseas to save them. In that way we can combine business and hobby." They had pictures of the special trams operated, but the one which interested me most was an old Kochi tram, built in 1909. "Oh, that?" they said. "That is not a special tram. That one runs every day. It was built for Kochi and has been operating in our streets every day since 1909, except for five years during the war when we could not obtain parts for it. Maybe you will see it later." And I did, as it bounced along the main street.

The line to Ino is unusual too in that it becomes single track. However, the track is not in the centre of the road, as one might expect, but on one side, so that, on the outward journey, the trams are running on the wrong side of the street, to the consternation of oncoming traffic which has to pass to the offside of them. It is a most unusual arrangement. Since it seems

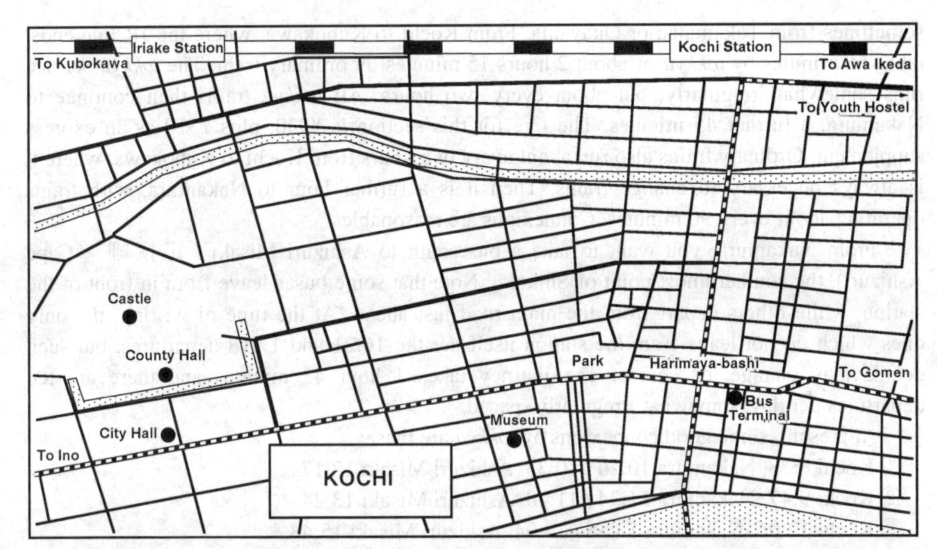


rather dangerous, it is fortunate that it does not last for long, for soon afterwards the track moves off the main road and runs beside it on a separate reservation. Most of the Kochi trams have notices inside giving details of their personal histories. Several of them came from Tokyo in the 1960s when that city gave up its tram system.

From Kotohira, it takes about 90 minutes to Kochi by *tokkyu*. From Oboke, it takes nearly two hours by ordinary train or one hour by *tokkyu*. From Toyonaga, it takes about 1 hour 45 minutes by ordinary train and from Tosa Yamada it takes 30 minutes by ordinary train.

There is a youth hostel in Kochi, a short walk from the station. English is spoken.

## ASHIZURI MISAKI (足摺岬 – 'Cape Scraping Legs')

**Tosa Kuroshio Railway to Nakamura, 4 hrs. 30 mins. from Okayama or 4 hrs. from Takamatsu. Then bus 1 hr. 45 mins.**

**Derivation of Name:** *Originally 'Ashisuri', meaning 'easy for legs to slip'. The cliffs here are dangerous.*

From Kochi we have decisions to make again. There are three main choices. The simple one is to take a JR express bus to Matsuyama. It is a scenic journey and the easy way back towards Japan's main island of Honshu, with the possibility of an interesting diversion to Ishizuchi-san, Shikoku's highest mountain, on the way. This is the recommended route for those in a hurry.

The second possibility is to travel round the western side of Shikoku by railway, via Uwajima. This is also quite a pretty trip and it can be done comfortably in a day if you are satisfied by looking at the scenery from inside a train.

The third possibility is to travel round the coast by train and bus. This will offer the most interesting scenery, but it needs time and is really quite an expensive undertaking. Let us deal with this possibility first.

The national railways line used to run west from Kochi all the way to Nakamura. However, it was regarded as unprofitable and was given away a few years ago to private enterprise. Nevertheless, *tokkyu* trains still run through to Nakamura from Kochi and sometimes from Takamatsu or Okayama. From Kochi to Kubokawa, where the JR line ends, takes 65 minutes by *tokkyu* or about 2 hours 15 minutes by ordinary train. The *tokkyu* service runs somewhat irregularly, but about every two hours. All *tokkyu* trains then continue to Nakamura, a further 45 minutes. The fare for this section is ¥930, plus ¥310 as an express supplement. Ordinary trains also run about every two hours from Kochi to Kubokawa, where it is always necessary to change trains. Then it is a further hour to Nakamura, with trains operating about every 90 minutes. Connexions are reasonable.

From Nakamura, you want to take a bus south to Ashizuri Misaki ( 足摺岬 - Cape Ashizuri), the southernmost point of Shikoku. Note that some buses leave from in front of the station, while others depart from the main road just ahead. At the time of writing, the only ones which do not leave from the station itself are the 16:21 and 17:18 departures, but such details may change, of course. The journey takes 1 hour 45 minutes and there are ten departures per day, somewhat irregularly spaced.

At present, some good connexions by *tokkyu* are these:

① Kochi 8:38. Nakamura 10:26 / 10:33. Ashizuri Misaki 12:17.
② Kochi 9:47. Nakamura 11:34 / 11:40. Ashizuri Misaki 13:24.
③ Kochi 12:06. Nakamura 13:58 / 14:04. Ashizuri Misaki 15:48.
④ Kochi 13:29 (originating in Okayama 10:49). Nakamura 15:13 / 15:18. Ashizuri Misaki 17:02.

If you are using ordinary trains, the best connexions are these:

① Kochi 6:45. Kubokawa 9:17 / 10:16. Nakamura 11:11 / 11:40. Ashizuri Misaki 13:24.
② Kochi 9:50. Kubokawa 11:46 / 12:29. Nakamura 13:33 / 14:04. Ashizuri Misaki 15:48.
③ Kochi 11:35. Kubokawa 13:47 / 13:49. Nakamura 15:01 / 15:18. Ashizuri Misaki 17:02.

The road first runs beside the **Shimanto River**, claimed to be the most pure in Japan. Then it cuts inland before returning to the coast and reaching Tosa Shimizu after about an hour. From here there are three different routes south to Ashizuri Misaki, all quite scenic. The journey will have been an expensive one, costing ¥1,980.

Ashizuri Misaki is an attractive area of rather wild coastal scenery. There is a short lookout tower on top of the cliffs, from where a good view of the Pacific Ocean may be obtained. When the author visited, there was a typhoon approaching and the sea was magnificently powerful. The wind swept one's hair back (what little remained to be swept back, that is) and the raindrops stung one's face. It was a beautiful contrast to much of Japan's rather tame scenery. As when one looks into an active volcano, it was a reminder of the strength of nature and the impunity of man.

There are two youth hostels here. Interestingly, one is operated by a shrine and one by a temple. The shrine hostel is Ashizuri Hostel in Shirao Shrine. The temple hostel is Kongofuku-ji Hostel. Kongofuku-ji has an history of more than a millennium (the temple, that is, not the youth hostel) and is number 38 on the pilgrimage round Shikoku. If you do not manage to get as far as Ashizuri Misaki, there is also a youth hostel in Kubokawa. This hostel is named Iwamoto-ji Hostel and it is also a temple hostel. Iwamoto-ji is number 37 on the pilgrimage. All of these hostels are easy to locate. For details, see the Youth Hostels section.

There is also a bus service to Ashizuri Misaki direct from Kochi. Buses leave the city (Sakai-machi - 堺町 ) at 7:02 and 14:00, arriving at Ashizuri Misaki at 11:51 and 18:32. The fare is a costly ¥4,190.

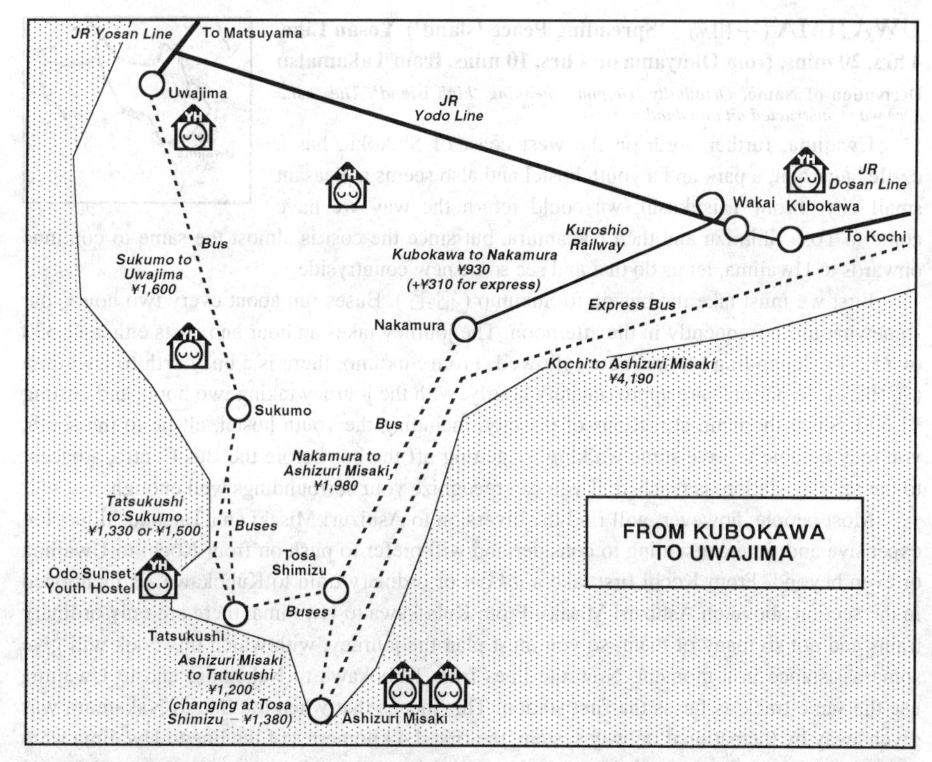


## TATSUKUSHI (竜串 - 'Dragon's Skewers')

**1 hr. by bus from Ashizuri Misaki**

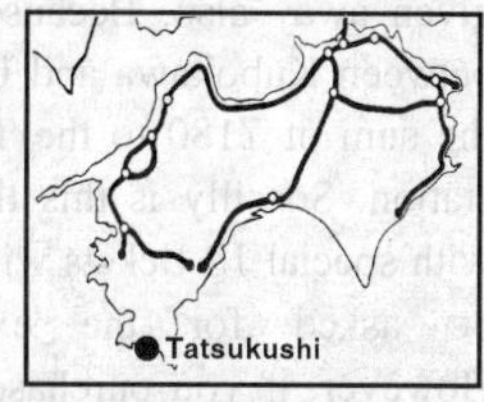


**Derivation of Name:** *The rock stacks formed here by erosion resemble giant red skewers of food ready for barbecuing.*

From Ashizuri Misaki, there is no choice but to turn north, so we proceed back to Tosa Shimizu and then move west to Dragon's Skewers, the name probably referring to the many tall thin columns remaining after weathering and sea erosion. Parts of this route are so narrow that it seems impossible that a bus service can be run along them. Indeed, difficulties do occur when two vehicles meet. The sea is on your left all the way, and rather picturesque, but it is at its best around Tatsukushi. Here you can go out in a glass-bottomed boat to watch the fish or you can descend a tower to the bottom of the sea and watch from there. The Emperor Showa, who was an enthusiast of marine biology, came here to do the latter. When the author visited, however, because of the impending typhoon the boats were not operating, while the tower was half price due to the limited visibility.

There are buses from Ashizuri Misaki to Tatsukushi (竜串) and on to Sukumo (宿毛), but not many. If there is no convenient departure, take a bus to Tosa Shimizu (土佐清水) and then a Sukumo or Tatsukushi bus from there. The fare from Ashizuri Misaki to Tatsukushi is ¥1,200. If you have to change buses at Tosa Shimizu, it will cost ¥820 plus ¥560, a total of ¥1,380.

## UWAJIMA (宇和島 - 'Spreading Peace Island') Yosan Line, 4 hrs. 20 mins. from Okayama or 4 hrs. 10 mins. from Takamatsu

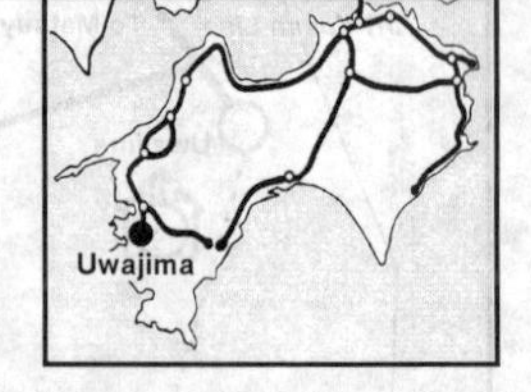


**Derivation of Name:** *Originally 'Uejima', meaning 'high island'. The castle here was constructed on an island.*

Uwajima, further north on the west coast of Shikoku, has a castle, a garden, a park and a youth hostel and also seems a pleasant small city. From Tatsukushi, we could return the way we have come to Tosa Shimizu and then Nakamura, but since the cost is almost the same to continue onwards to Uwajima, let us do that and see some new countryside.

First we must take the bus on to Sukumo (宿毛). Buses run about every two hours, but somewhat more frequently in the afternoon. The journey takes an hour and costs either ¥1,330 or ¥1,500, depending on the route followed. From Sukumo, there is a bus north to Uwajima (宇和島). Departures are approximately hourly, with the journey taking two hours and costing ¥1,600. Since the main attractions of the city, including the youth hostel, all lie to the south, you may be able to save some walking by getting off the bus before the Bus Centre, adjacent to the railway station, is reached, if you can recognize your surroundings well enough.

Most people, however, will find the diversion to Ashizuri Misaki and Tatsukushi just too expensive and time consuming to consider and will prefer to push on from Kochi to Uwajima or even beyond. From Kochi first take a *tokkyu* or ordinary train to Kubokawa, as mentioned in the section above on Ashizuri Misaki. From Kubokawa to Uwajima, there are only ordinary trains and not so many of them, so you must plan the journey, with which this book will give some assistance in a moment. Now the lines from Kubokawa to Nakamura and to Uwajima use the same track as far as the first station. This means that when the line to Nakamura was given away by the national railway system, the first 4.4 kilometres of the line to Uwajima were given away also. Because of this ridiculous situation, every time you travel on a JR train between Kubokawa and Uwajima, or any other destination on the Yodo Line, you must pay the sum of ¥180 to the Tosa Kuroshio Private Railway for use of its right of way for one station. So silly is this that travellers with special JR tickets will not usually be asked for the extra charge. However, if you purchase a ticket for this specific journey, it will include ¥180 to be paid to the Tosa Kuroshio Private Railway.

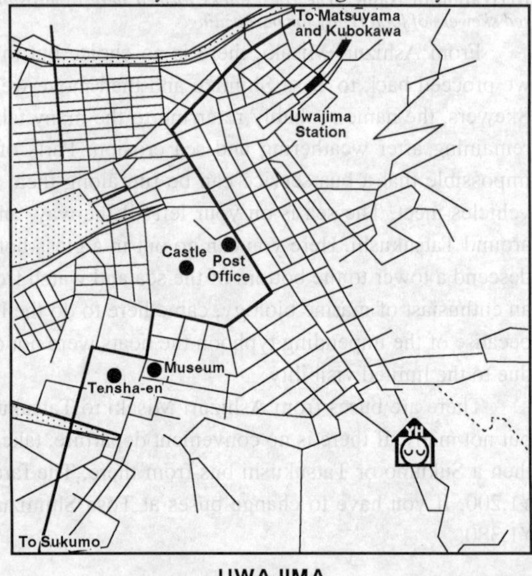

UWAJIMA

Just after you pass the first station (Wakai) on the Yodo Line, the two lines diverge, with the private railway entering a long spiraling tunnel which performs a full circle within the hills before descending to the plain below. Look out of the window on the left of your Yodo Line train and you will be able to see the Tosa Kuroshio Private Railway track emerging from this tunnel far below. The Yodo Line is quite scenic too, following the course of the **Shimanto River** for the early part of its route. This unusual name means '40,010 River', although the author does not know why it should be called by such a strange title. The journey from Kubokawa to Uwajima usually takes two hours, although some trains stop for a while *en route*, which increases the travelling time.

Assuming departure from Kochi in the morning, you should take the 6:45 ordinary train or the 8:38 *tokkyu*, reaching Kubokawa at 9:17 or 9:42. The train to Uwajima leaves Kubokawa at 10:01 and arrives at 11:58. A good afternoon connexion by *tokkyu* leaves Kochi at 13:29 (originating in Okayama at 10:49) and reaches Kubokawa at 14:32. The train to Uwajima leaves at 14:41, arriving at 16:40. To catch the same connexion using an ordinary train between Kochi and Kubokawa, departure from Kochi is at 11:35, with arrival at Kubokawa at 13:47.

The castle in Uwajima dates from 1665 and lies near the main road running to the south. A little further along the same road is the garden named Tensha-en. The youth hostel is near Atago Koen, the park from where a good view of the surrounding countryside and of the sea can be obtained. The route to the hostel gives the opportunity for some exercise!

## ISHIZUCHI-SAN (石鎚山 – 'Mt. Stone Hammer')

**3 hrs. by bus from Matsuyama**

**Derivation of Name:** *The shape of this rocky mountain was thought to resemble that of a hammer.*

Ishizuchi-san (Mt. Ishizuchi) is the highest mountain in Kyushu, standing 1,982 metres. It can be approached from either east or west, although neither is an easy journey and to climb to the top of the mountain and return requires a full day. Since we are now in the west of Shikoku on our tour of the island, let us ascend from that side and descend on the other.

There is a JR express bus service which runs between Kochi (高知) and Matsuyama (松山) and there are also some ordinary JR buses which operate in sections over the same route. From either end of the route, you should take a bus to Mimido (御三戸), 78 minutes from Matsuyama or 2 hours from Kochi. Buses leave from either end of the route hourly, on the hour. The bus ride is free for holders of a Japan Rail Pass or *Shikoku Wide Shu-yu-ken*, but the latter must pay a seat reservation charge of ¥400. From Mimido, you want to take a bus to Ishizuchi Tsuchi-goya (石鎚土小屋). There are only two buses per day and if you are intending to climb Ishizuchi-san, you must take the morning bus. It leaves Mimido at 9:37, reaching its destination at 11:08 at a cost of ¥1,500. Note that this bus runs every day to Ishizuchi Tsuchi-goya only in summer. In spring and autumn, it runs on holidays only and in winter it does not operate to Ishizuchi Tsuchi-goya at all, terminating at Omogo (面河). In order to make the connexion at Mimido, you must leave Kochi at 7:00 or Matsuyama at 8:00. For those who wish to avoid the ¥400 reservation charge, there is also an ordinary JR bus leaving Matsuyama station at 7:50 and reaching Mimido at 9:24 (¥1,480 if you do not possess a suitable JR ticket).

At Omogo, after a brief pause, the bus enters the toll road and starts the climb up to the base of Ishizuchi-san. This is quite a spectacular ride and you should, if possible, sit on the left of the bus. From the bus terminal your serious walking will begin. When the author came up here, he did not intend to climb the mountain, but instead wanted to take a different path leading across the base to another bus route. However, an unfortunate error in path selection led to my being the only person at the top of Ishizuchi-san with a briefcase and no water or food supply. Be warned, therefore, that although you can manage without food, you should certainly take water with you. I was very thirsty indeed after six hours on the mountain.

The climb starts off as a fairly gentle one and gradually gets harder. When one gets to the really stiff part, there is a chain up which one climbs (difficult with a briefcase!) and then one reaches a lookout and small shrine at the top. There is also a tiny shop selling cup noodles at inflated prices. Well, it must be quite a struggle to get them up here and where does the water come from? Just as you are relaxing from your exertions and admiring the magnificent view, you realize that this is not the top! A razor-back ridge stretches up to another summit from where those who have achieved it are waving happily. Although this little extra walk is not so strenuous, it is the most frightening part of the whole expedition, for on your left is a sheer drop of perhaps 300 metres. You can see the tops of the trees below if you are brave enough to venture to the extreme brink, where nothing but fear and common sense saves you from the extra fifty centimetres which will send you plummeting to be a mere blemish on the foliage beneath. When you reach the real top, however, you rejoice that you made the expedition, for you can see for ever and in all directions. Far away the industrial sprawl of Imabari is visible, with the Inland Sea stretching beyond and the outline of the coast of Honshu visible beyond that. The mountains stretching range after range in the opposite direction make the whole journey seem worthwhile and stay in the memory for ever.

Going down is easier. When you reach the base of the mountain proper, you can fork left, instead of taking the right path which you used on the way up, and you will come, after 45 minutes or so from the fork, to the top station of the ropeway which runs down the east side of Ishizuchi-san. The ropeway costs ¥900 (¥1,700 return) and takes 8 minutes to cover the journey. There is another magnificent view during the descent. From the bottom, you will find a bus service to transport you to Iyo Saijo station (伊予西条駅) at a cost of ¥950 (55 minutes). Buses run approximately two-hourly, with the last at 17:17. From Iyo Saijo, it will take an hour to Matsuyama by *tokkyu*, or two hours by ordinary train.

There is a youth hostel at Omogo (Kanmon Hostel), part of a small Japanese-style hotel. When the author stayed there, I was the only hosteller and I enjoyed my sojourn in the tiny village, apart from the fact that the shops were shut when I arrived and I could find nothing to eat! If you choose to stay here too, you will have time to look at **Omogo-kei** (Omogo Gorge) in the morning before taking the bus up to Ishizuchi-san. The bus leaves Omogo at 10:30. Omogo-kei is quite famous and is certainly worth a look. A circuit of the trail round the gorge will take about 90 minutes. There is also a camping ground (summer only) near a pretty waterfall. To reach these attractions, just walk along the small road leading on from the bus terminus. The camping ground is off to the left, through a short tunnel. The last bus (there are only four per day) from Mimido to Omogo (面河) is at 17:17. To reach Mimido in time, you should leave Matsuyama at 16:00 (tight connexion at Mimido) or Kochi at 15:00. There is also an ordinary bus from Matsuyama at 15:35 which reaches Mimido at 17:09, offering a safer connexion than the one above.

If you choose to travel in the opposite direction, the first bus from Iyo Saijo to Ishizuchi Ropeway (石鎚ロープウェイ) is at 7:41, to catch which you must leave Matsuyama on the 6:14 *tokkyu*. The next bus is at 10:20. Connexions from Matsuyama are by the 9:19 *tokkyu* or the 8:18 ordinary train. The last bus down the other side is at 16:30 from Ishizuchi Tsuchi-goya. It reaches Mimido (御三戸) at 17:50 and connexions are at 17:52 to Matsuyama

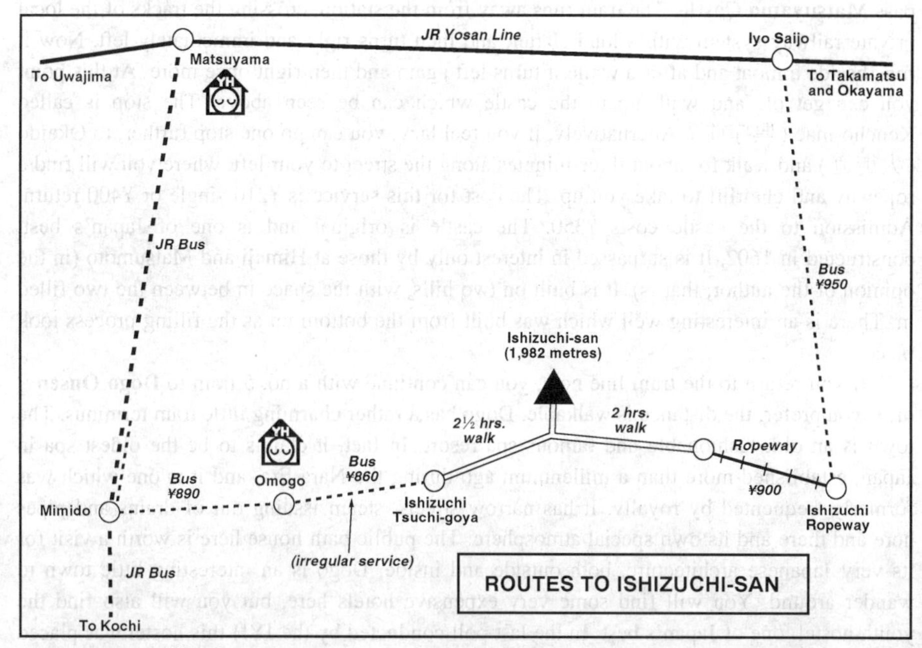


(松山), arriving at 19:12 (ordinary bus at 18:10, arriving at 19:44, not holidays) and at 18:18 to Kochi (高知), arriving at 20:20. Again the bus from Ishizuchi Tsuchi-goya runs every day only in summer. It runs on holidays in spring and autumn and not at all in winter. It is possible to walk down from Ishizuchi-san to Omogo, but it is a walk of about 10 kilometres, so you need to start early in the day if you are thinking of doing that.

## MATSUYAMA (松山 - 'Pine Mountain') Yosan Line, 2 hrs. 50 mins. from Okayama or 2 hrs. 40 mins. from Takamatsu

**Derivation of Name:** *Literal. Originally there were hills covered with pine trees.*

Matsuyama is perhaps the most interesting city in Shikoku. It offers a castle, a tram system, one of the oldest spas in Japan and an old temple, as well as one of the best and most popular youth hostels in the country.

From Uwajima it takes 90 minutes to Matsuyama by *tokkyu* or three hours by ordinary train. There are actually two routes. The older one goes round by the sea and is slightly longer and considerably slower. The new line goes through the mountains with long tunnels on the way and is used by all express services. Both routes are scenic.

From Kochi, you should take the JR express bus service to Matsuyama mentioned in the previous section on Ishizuchi-san. Those using a *Shikoku Wide Shu-yu-ken* will have to pay a ¥400 seat reservation fee for this service. Departures from Kochi are hourly and the journey takes 3 hours 30 minutes. This trip also is through scenic mountain countryside well worth travelling.

From Matsuyama station there are trams running. If you take a tram no. 5 going to Dogo Onsen (道後温泉), you will see most of the points of interest in the city. On the way you will pass **Matsuyama Castle**. The tram runs away from the station, crossing the tracks of the local private railway system with a loud clatter, and then turns right and immediately left. Now it runs beside a moat and after a while it turns left again and then right once more. At this point you can get off and walk up to the castle which can be seen above. The stop is called Kencho-mae (県庁前). Alternatively, if you feel lazy, you can go one stop further, to Okaido (大街道) and walk for about three minutes along the street to your left, where you will find a ropeway and chairlift to take you up. The cost for this service is ¥210 single or ¥400 return. Admission to the castle costs ¥350. The castle is original and is one of Japan's best, constructed in 1602. It is surpassed in interest only by those at Himeji and Matsumoto (in the opinion of the author, that is). It is built on two hills, with the space in between the two filled in. There is an interesting well which was built from the bottom up as the filling process took place.

If you return to the tram line now, you can continue with a no. 5 tram to **Dogo Onsen** – or, if you prefer, the distance is walkable. Dogo has a rather charming little tram terminus. The town is an old, fashionable and famous spa resort. In fact, it claims to be the oldest spa in Japan, established more than a millennium ago during the Nara Era, and it is one which was formerly frequented by royalty. It has narrow streets, steam issuing out of drains and pipes here and there and its own special atmosphere. The public bath house here is worth a visit for its very Japanese architecture, both outside and inside. Dogo is an interesting little town to wander around. You will find some very expensive hotels here, but you will also find the youth hostel, one of Japan's best. In the last poll conducted by the JYH this hostel was placed second and it always seems to be in the top three. It has small, clean rooms with free tea and coffee available in the lounge downstairs and even an English-language newspaper to peruse. If you have the Japan Youth Hostels handbook, you will immediately recognize the 'parent' from the sketch in the hostel's advertisement in the handbook. This is a hostel which can be

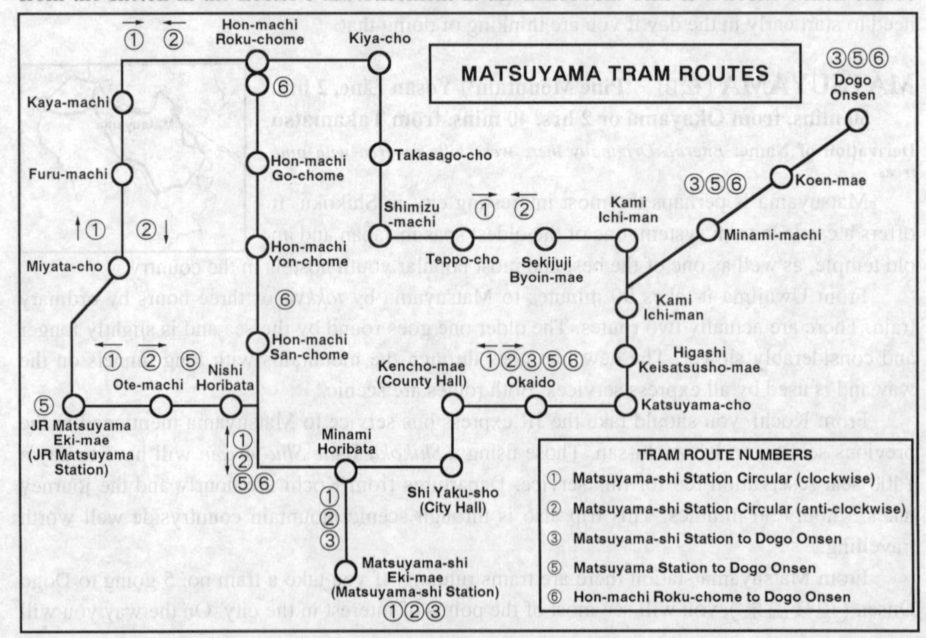

recommended without reservation.

Only a few minutes walk from the youth hostel is **Ishite** ('Stone Hand') **Temple**, number 51 on the circuit of Shikoku. This temple was founded in 728, but the oldest of the present buildings date from the fourteenth century. It is an attractive medium-sized temple straggling up the lower parts of a small hill, worth a visit if you have a few minutes to spare. Interesting are the records of past *sumo* tournaments at the entrance.

A one-day ticket is available for use on the Matsuyama trams (市電一日乗車券 - *'shi-den ichi-nichi jo-sha-ken'*). This ticket costs ¥450. Trams have a fixed fare of ¥170, so if you are planning to take three rides or more during the day, this ticket will be advantageous. It can be purchased from an office at the tram stop outside Matsuyama station, and at various other places. There is also a one-day ticket for Iyo Railway buses within the city of Matsuyama (バス一日乗車券 - *'bus ichi-nichi jo-sha-ken'*). This costs ¥560.

When you leave Matsuyama, the obvious route is to return eastwards along the north coast of Shikoku and cross once more over the Seto Ohashi (bridge) to Okayama. The journey to Okayama takes about 2 hours 50 minutes by *tokkyu*, and there are ten such services every day, as well as a similar number of connecting services. However, there are some other possibilities which should be considered. The most obvious of these, and the most appealing, is to take a ferry from Matsuyama to Hiroshima, a very pretty journey of about three hours across the Inland Sea. This route should be especially attractive to those using Blue Spring tickets who will not feel that they are wasting time and money on their passes by taking a ferry. Those using a *Shikoku Wide Shu-yu-ken*, who would also like a look at Hiroshima, Miyajima and Iwakuni will be interested too. (Another ferry can be used for the return from Yanai Minato, seven stations west of Iwakuni on the JR Sanyo Line, to Mitsuhama port in Matsuyama. This ferry operates about every 90 minutes and costs ¥2,310. The crossing takes 2

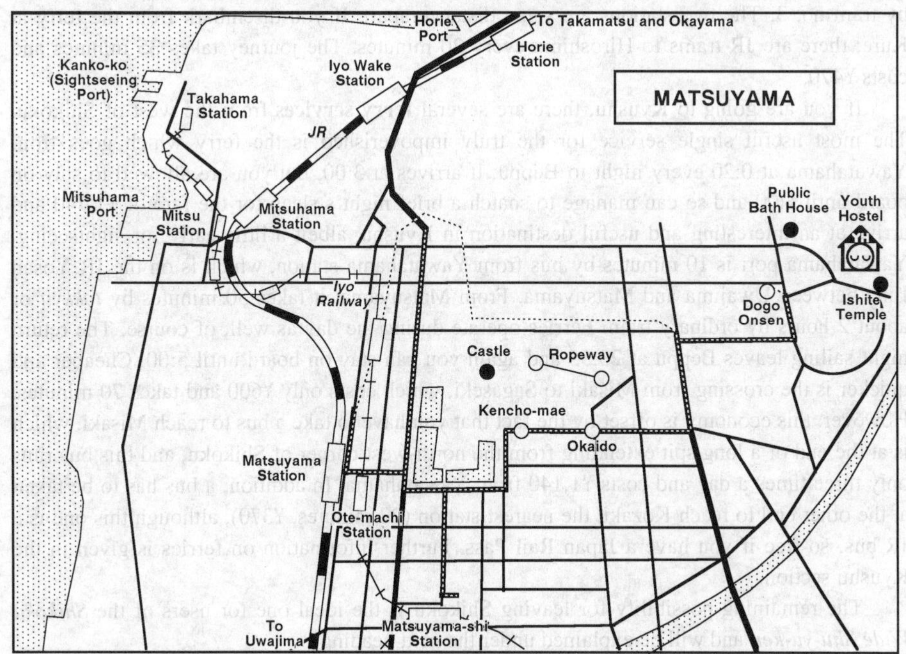

hours 25 minutes.)

From Matsuyama to Hiroshima there are two suitable services available, but note that there are three different ports in Matsuyama which are used for ferry services. The first service starts from Mitsuhama port, travels to Matsuyama Kanko-ko (Matsuyama Sightseeing Port) and then crosses first to Kure before continuing to Hiroshima. It costs ¥1,710 from either port in Matsuyama to Kure and ¥2,130 to Hiroshima. The ferry operates approximately every 90 minutes during the day. The second service operates from Horie port to Kure. It sails about hourly, except between 22:30 and 4:00, and takes 1 hour 50 minutes to reach Kure. The fare is ¥1,420. To reach Mitsuhama, take the Iyo Private Railway to Mitsu (14 minutes from Matsuyama-shi station, ¥290, train destination Takahama) and then walk for about 10 minutes towards the sea (i.e. from the station exit walk as nearly straight away from the station as you can within the constraints of having to cross some water). There is also a JR Mitsuhama station, one stop from Matsuyama by ordinary train, but it is further from the port. To reach Matsuyama Kanko-ko, take the Iyo Private Railway to its terminus at Takahama (21 minutes from Matsuyama-shi, ¥410) and walk forwards and towards the sea for about 5 minutes. To get to the Iyo Private Railway from Dogo, take a tram no. 3 to Matsuyama-shi station (松山市駅). Alternatively, take a tram no. 5 for Matsuyama station (松山駅) and alight where it crosses the private train lines with a great clatter. This stop is called Ote-machi (大手町). You will see Ote-machi station right next to the crossing. You want a train going to your right, that is from the platform on the far side of the line from Dogo. To reach Horie, take a JR ordinary train going towards Imabari for three stations (12 minutes) to Horie and then walk a short distance towards the sea. When taking a tram from Dogo, be careful to ensure that it is going to the correct railway station. Matsuyama station (松山駅) is the JR station and is served by tram no. 5. Matsuyama-shi station (松山市駅) is the Iyo Private Railway station and is served by tram no. 3. The two stations are some distance apart. If you disembark from the ferry at Kure, there are JR trains to Hiroshima every 20 minutes. The journey takes 35 minutes and costs ¥470.

If you are going to Kyushu, there are several **ferry services** from the west of Shikoku. The most useful single service for the truly impoverished is the ferry which goes from Yawatahama at 0:20 every night to Beppu. It arrives at 3:00, but you are allowed to stay on board until 5:00 and so can manage to snatch a brief night's sleep for the fare of ¥1,740 and arrive at an interesting and useful destination in Kyushu, albeit a little early for sightseeing. Yawatahama port is 10 minutes by bus from Yawatahama station, which is on the JR Yosan Line between Uwajima and Matsuyama. From Matsuyama, it takes 50 minutes by *tokkyu* or about 2 hours by ordinary train. Ferries operate during the day as well, of course. The return night sailing leaves Beppu at 23:55 and again you can stay on board until 5:00. Cheaper and quicker is the crossing from Misaki to Sagaseki, which costs only ¥600 and takes 70 minutes. However, this economy is offset by the fact that you have to take a bus to reach Misaki, which is at the end of a long spit extending from the north-west corner of Shikoku, and this bus runs only three times a day and costs ¥1,140 from Yawatahama. In addition, a bus has to be taken at the other end to reach Kozaki, the nearest station (22 minutes, ¥370), although this one is a JR bus, so free if you have a Japan Rail Pass. Further information on ferries is given in the Kyushu section.

The remaining possibility for leaving Shikoku is the ideal one for users of the *Shikoku Wide Shu-yu-ken* and will be explained under the next heading.

## SHODO-SHIMA (小豆島 - 'Little Bean Island') 75 mins. from Takamatsu or 4 hrs. 30 mins. from Osaka by ferry

**Derivation of Name:** *One of the island's main products used to be azuki beans – small red beans. These beans are still grown here, although they are no longer the main product.*

Shodo-shima is an island, not as small as it looks on the map, off the north-eastern shore of Shikoku. It is famous for the growing of olives in its Mediterranean-type climate and is popular as a holiday location, with the Japanese often seeing it as a day trip. Ferries, both conventional and high-speed, operate from many places – Takamatsu, Uno, Okayama, Hinase, Himeji, Kobe and Osaka – so you can go there from Takamatsu, for example, and return to Uno, the nearest point on Honshu, as you depart from Shikoku. The fare from Takamatsu to Tonosho or Ikeda on Shodo-shima is ¥430 and that from Tonosho to Uno or Shin Okayama is ¥820.

However, what will interest users of the *Shikoku Wide Shu-yu-ken* is that you are allowed to return from Shikoku (or arrive there) by utilizing the services of Kansai Kisen, a ferry operator, between Takamatsu and Kobe or Osaka, with a stop in Shodo-shima if you wish. When you purchase a *shu-yu-ken*, you are usually given two tickets. The 'A' ticket is for your journey to the chosen area. The 'B' portion is for free travel within that area and for your return. However, when you buy the *Shikoku Wide Shu-yu-ken* you are given a third voucher and this is to be surrendered in return for the ferry ticket. "There must be a catch," you think. Well, yes, there is a small one. You see, the only Kansai Kisen ferry from Takamatsu to Shodo-shima is at 6:20. That means that you really have to spend the previous night in Takamatsu, where there is no youth hostel. If you want to stay in a hostel, the only possibility is to stay in Kaigan-ji Hostel (see Youth Hostels section) and get up early in the morning to walk 4 kilometres to Tadotsu, from where the first train starts in the morning at 5:37, reaching Takamatsu at 6:06. It probably easier, though, to pay ¥430 for another company's ferry to Shodo-shima and pick up the Kansai Kisen service from there later.

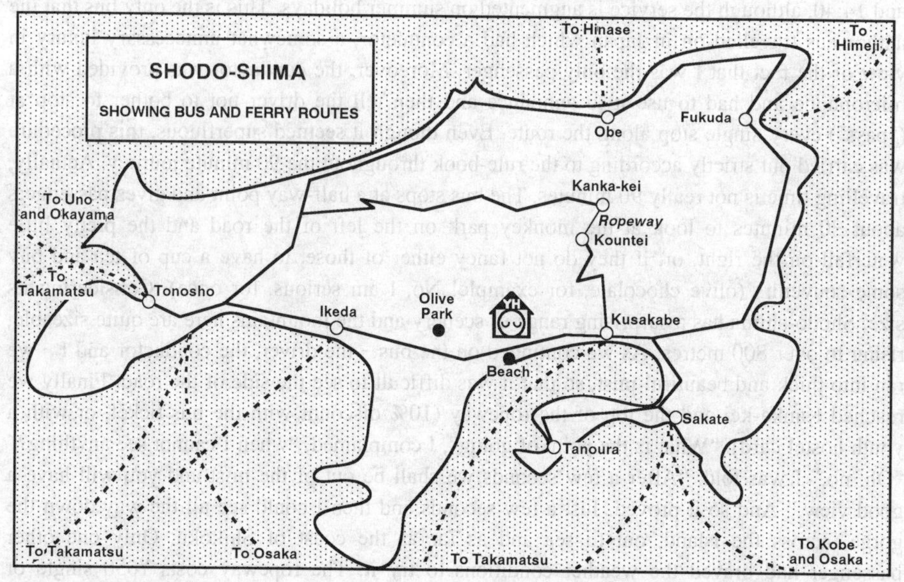

As mentioned above, Shodo-shima looks small on the map, but when you get there you will find it bigger than you had expected. For a start, if you take the Kansai Kisen ferry, you will be surprised at the size of the ship used. It has come from Beppu in Kyushu overnight, so serves quite a long-distance route. Even so, you might not have expected a vessel of 6,000 tons to be going into the tiny port of Sakate which is not even the main port of Shodo-shima. When the author went across on this service, I was the only passenger out on the deck to admire the beautiful misty view of Shikoku and nearby islands. Everybody else was inside sleeping, eating breakfast or playing cards (admittedly it was raining lightly). I enjoyed the 75 minute voyage greatly. Then, when we reached Sakate ('Sloping Hand'), everybody else rushed off the ship onto one of the flock of tour buses waiting there. I was the only person wishing to look round the island by myself. This is not hard to do, however, for it is well served by buses. Ask at the office at the small bus terminal near the port and you will be sold a one-day or two-day ticket allowing unlimited travel on the buses for whichever period you choose. The one-day ticket (フリー一日券 - *'free ichi-nichi ken'*) costs ¥1,700 and the two-day ticket (フリー二日券- *'free futsuka ken'*) ¥2,200. Any other way of getting around will be expensive. With the ticket you will be given a map of the island showing the bus routes and a list of places offering discounts to the holders of such tickets, which includes just about everywhere on the island.

You can start by taking the bus to Tonosho (土庄), to give you an idea of the character of Shodo-shima. Normally just this leisurely 45 minute journey would cost ¥760. On the way you will pass groves of olives, an olive farm and park open for inspection and the youth hostel, called, not surprisingly, Shodo-shima Olive Hostel. Nearby is a pleasant beach, if the season is suitable for bathing. Tonosho is the main town and principal port of the island, but it is still relatively small.

An interesting bus ride from here is the one up to the top of the ropeway at **Kanka-kei** (寒霞渓 - Kanka Gorge). There are only four buses which run every day, at 8:40, 10:45, 12:40 and 14:40, although the service is augmented on summer holidays. This is the only bus that the author has travelled on in Japan which had a conductor, a somewhat unnecessary luxury in view of the fact that I was the only passenger. Moreover, the conductor was provided with a microphone and had to use it to announce and then tell the driver not to bother to stop at ("pass") every single stop along the route. Even though it seemed superfluous, this procedure was carried out strictly according to the rule-book throughout the 90 minute journey. Actually, travelling time is not really 90 minutes. The bus stops at a half-way point and gives passengers about 30 minutes to look at the monkey park on the left of the road and the pretty little waterfall on the right, or, if they do not fancy either of those, to have a cup of tea and buy some souvenirs (olive chocolate, for example! No, I am serious, for once). Considering its size, Shodo-shima has a surprising range of scenery and the mountains here are quite sizeable, rising to over 800 metres. As we continued on the bus - the driver, the conductor and I - we ran into thick and beautiful mist, so that it was difficult to see the side of the road. Finally we reached Kanka-kei and the top of the ropeway (10% discount with the bus ticket, or with a youth hostel card). "What is the point of going", I complained, "when I cannot see anything?" "Oh, no," I was told. "After a few seconds we shall be out of the mist and you will have a good view." And so it proved. Just a few seconds and then I could see all the way down the gorge, across the island, out to sea and as far as the coast of Shikoku. Only one other passenger had braved the weather conditions to try it. The ropeway costs ¥650 single or

¥1,150 return and takes 5 minutes. From the bottom station at Kountei (紅雲亭), where there is nothing much, a bus service will take you back to Kusakabe (草壁), not very far from the youth hostel. There are also bus services from Tonosho to Fukuda (福田) via the north side of the island and from there back to Kusakabe, so you can explore the island well with your one- or two-day ticket. Most people enjoy a visit to Shodo-shima and find plenty to do to occupy a day or two, so put it on your schedule if you have time.

If you are continuing to Kobe or Osaka with Kansai Kisen, you have two services to choose from. One is the ferry on which you arrived and which leaves at 7:35 from Sakate (坂手), reaching Kobe at 10:35 and Osaka at 12:00. This service arrives at the south port of Osaka, from where you can catch the 'New Tram' connecting with the Osaka subway system. The second ferry is even bigger than the morning ship and towers above Sakate port. Manœuvering the vessel into the quay is quite a skillful business. This ship leaves at 14:45 and reaches Kobe at 17:45 and Osaka at 19:00. It arrives at Benten Futo, much nearer to the centre of the city. From there you can walk to Benten-cho station, on the Osaka Kanjo Loop Line, in about 15 minutes.

However, if you are heading west, you can travel back to Tonosho (土庄) and take one of the frequent ferries to Uno, from where JR trains run to Okayama, and continue with your travels. Let us continue too.

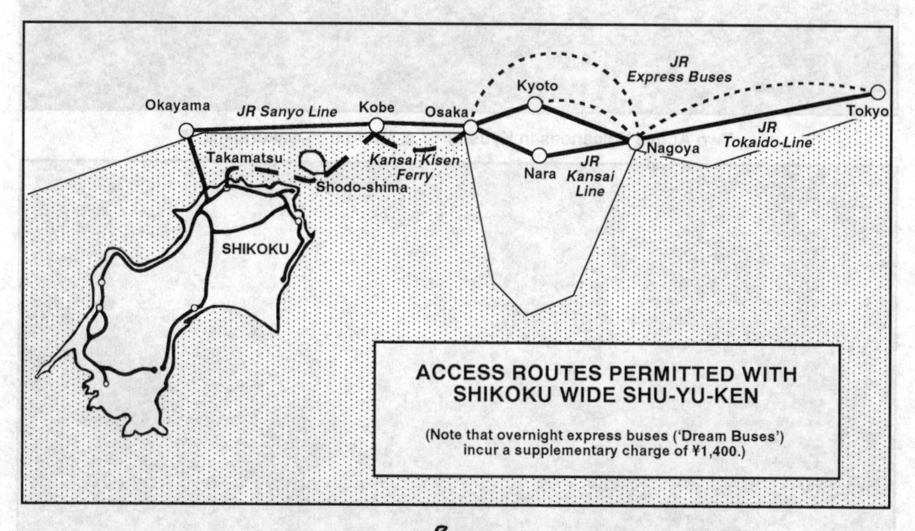


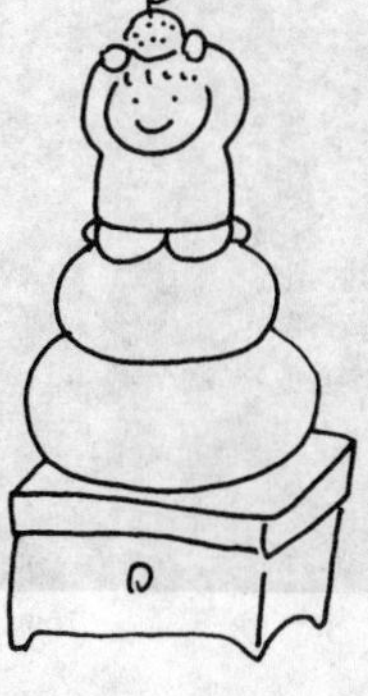

Two Active Volcanoes in Kyushu ▲ Mt. Aso Sakurajima ▼

# KYUSHU (九州)
## ('Nine States')

Although the name means 'Nine States' and Kyushu used to be divided into nine administrative areas, in fact there are now only seven prefectures in the island. Kyushu is the third biggest of Japan's four main islands and the farthest south. Therefore, of course, it is generally also the warmest. There is plenty to see on this island - an interesting variety of sea, mountains and historical sites. Most visitors try to put it on their itineraries if time can possibly allow and, because the *shinkansen* runs to Fukuoka (Hakata station) in the north of Kyushu in only six hours from Tokyo, it is not a difficult place to reach.

If time is limited, the two places in Kyushu which should not be missed are Nagasaki and Mt. Aso. If you visit the latter, then you will probably be able to return via Beppu and see the attractions there as well. In fact, though, the more you get off the beaten track in this island, the more you are likely to find it a beautiful place.

***Transportation and Tickets***

Kyushu has a good network of express trains. The Sanyo *shinkansen* extends as far as Hakata (Fukuoka) along the north coast and from there there are efficient and frequent express services to Nagasaki to the west and south to Kagoshima down the west coast of the island. There are also express trains running down the east coast of Kyushu. These start in Hakata and pass through Kokura. All trains run to Beppu and Oita, offering another efficient service that far. Some are extended to Miyazaki and four of the trains run all the way to Kagoshima, but the further they go, the slower they get, as the condition of the track deteriorates and time has to be spent waiting for crossings, there being only a single track beyond Oita.

For those using ordinary trains, there is a good service of both *kaisoku* and ordinary trains running between Moji-ko at the north-eastern tip of Kyushu or Shimonoseki on the western tip of Honshu and Kumamoto, half-way down the west coast of Kyushu. Elsewhere there is an adequate service on most lines, but you should plan your trip to avoid being stranded for long periods at unlikely spots.

For those interested in seeing Kyushu as a principal destination, there is, of course, a *shu-yu-ken* (excursion ticket) designed for your purposes. This is the *Kyushu Wide Shu-yu-ken*. It is available for 14 days from Tokyo and costs ¥35,500. As usual, you must travel to and from Kyushu by ordinary train or by *kyuko*, or pay the supplements for faster trains, but within the island you may use unreserved seats on any trains except the *shinkansen*. On the return

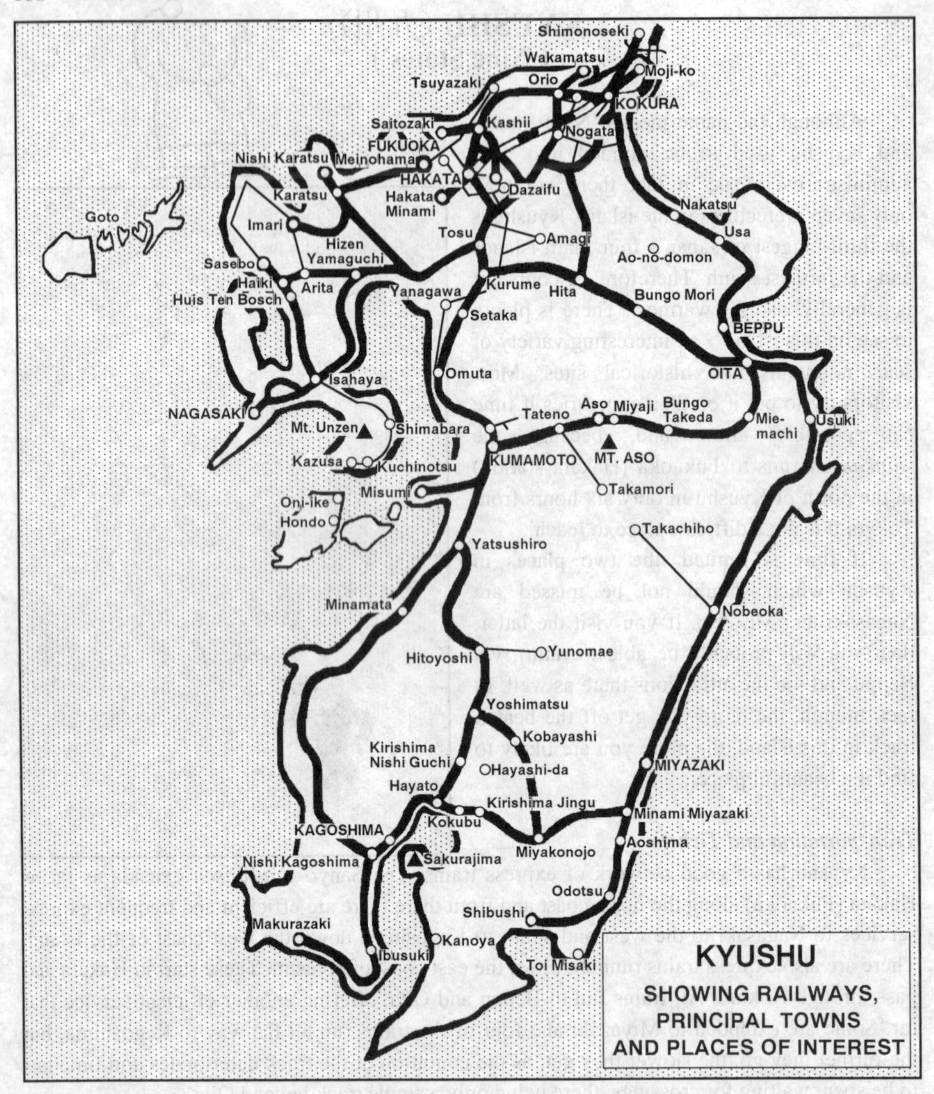


journey to Tokyo, or your point of origin, as long as you leave Kyushu within the validity of the ticket, you may complete your return journey by a direct route without unreasonable delay even though your ticket has expired by the time that you arrive. As long as you remain within the validity, you may make stop-overs on the outward and return journeys, so you can, for example, visit Kyoto, Nara, Osaka, Kobe, Okayama, Kurashiki and Hiroshima *en route*. However, in the case of this *shu-yu-ken*, the only route permitted is along the Tokaido and Sanyo Main Lines, with some very minor deviations where other lines run almost parallel, or by JR express bus operating between Tokyo and Osaka via Nagoya (where it is usually necessary to change buses).

There is also a *Kyushu Kita Wide Shu-yu-ken*. *Kita* means north and so it will be no surprise that this ticket covers only the northern half of Kyushu. The exact area is shown in the map at the bottom left of this page. This ticket will suit those who have time to see only Nagasaki, Mt. Aso and Beppu, but it seems something of a pity to use an excursion ticket to come all the way to Kyushu, 1,000 kilometres from Tokyo, and then see only half of the island. However, if this ticket suits you, it costs ¥30,060 from Tokyo and is valid for 14 days, with all other conditions the same as for the *Kyushu Wide Shu-yu-ken*.

There is a ticket for only the south of Kyushu too. This is called a *Kagoshima Miyazaki Mini Shu-yu-ken*. The difference with this ticket is that it is a 'mini' *shu-yu-ken*, so only *kyuko* trains can be used within the unlimited travel area, not *tokkyu*. That is not too serious an handicap, but what should be noted is that the ticket does not cover travel to Nagasaki or Mt. Aso. Since it is a 'mini' *shu-yu-ken*, however, it is cheaper than the ticket for the north of the island, costing ¥28,020 for departures from Tokyo. It is valid, though, for only 10 days. Would it not be better to buy a one week Japan Rail Pass at the same price and have the freedom to travel anywhere in Japan on almost any train? However, there may be some who are not eligible for the Japan Rail Pass, so the area covered by this ticket too is shown below right.

And there is yet another *shu-yu-ken*. As with the other islands, there is a *Kyushu New Wide Shu-yu-ken* too. As before, the rules are that it must be purchased in conjunction with a return ticket by rail, ferry or air and that a discount of 20% will be given for rail and short-distance ferry travel and a discount of 10% for all other travel. It is a long way to Kyushu, so this travel is sure to be expensive. The *shu-yu-ken* is valid for 5 days and costs ¥14,100. It gives free travel within Kyushu in unreserved seats on any trains except the *shinkansen*.

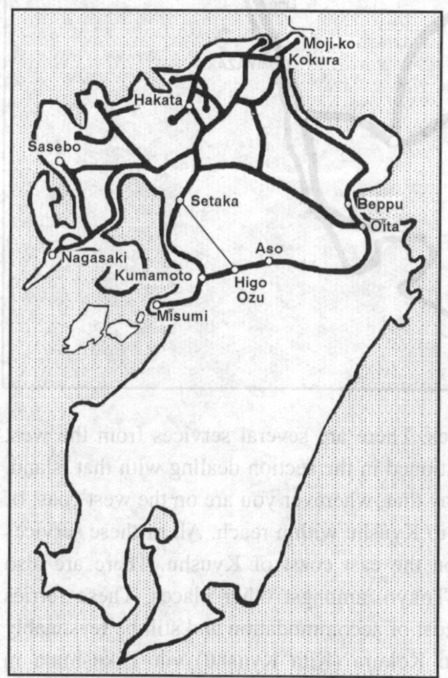

KYUSHU KITA WIDE SHU-YU-KEN AREA
THIN LINES INDICATE JR BUSES

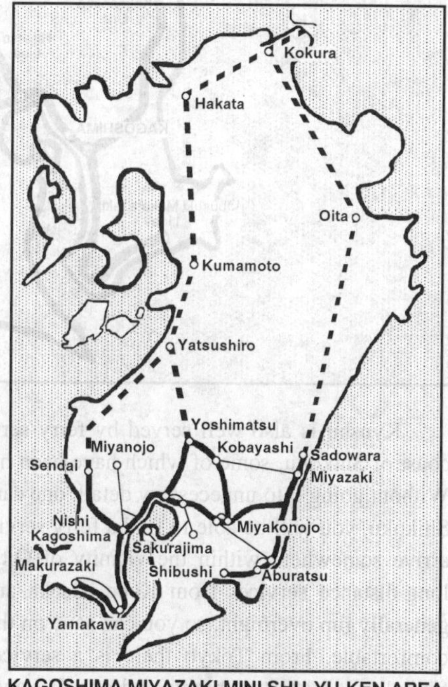

KAGOSHIMA MIYAZAKI MINI SHU-YU-KEN AREA
THIN LINES INDICATE JR BUSES
DASHED LINES INDICATE ACCESS ROUTES

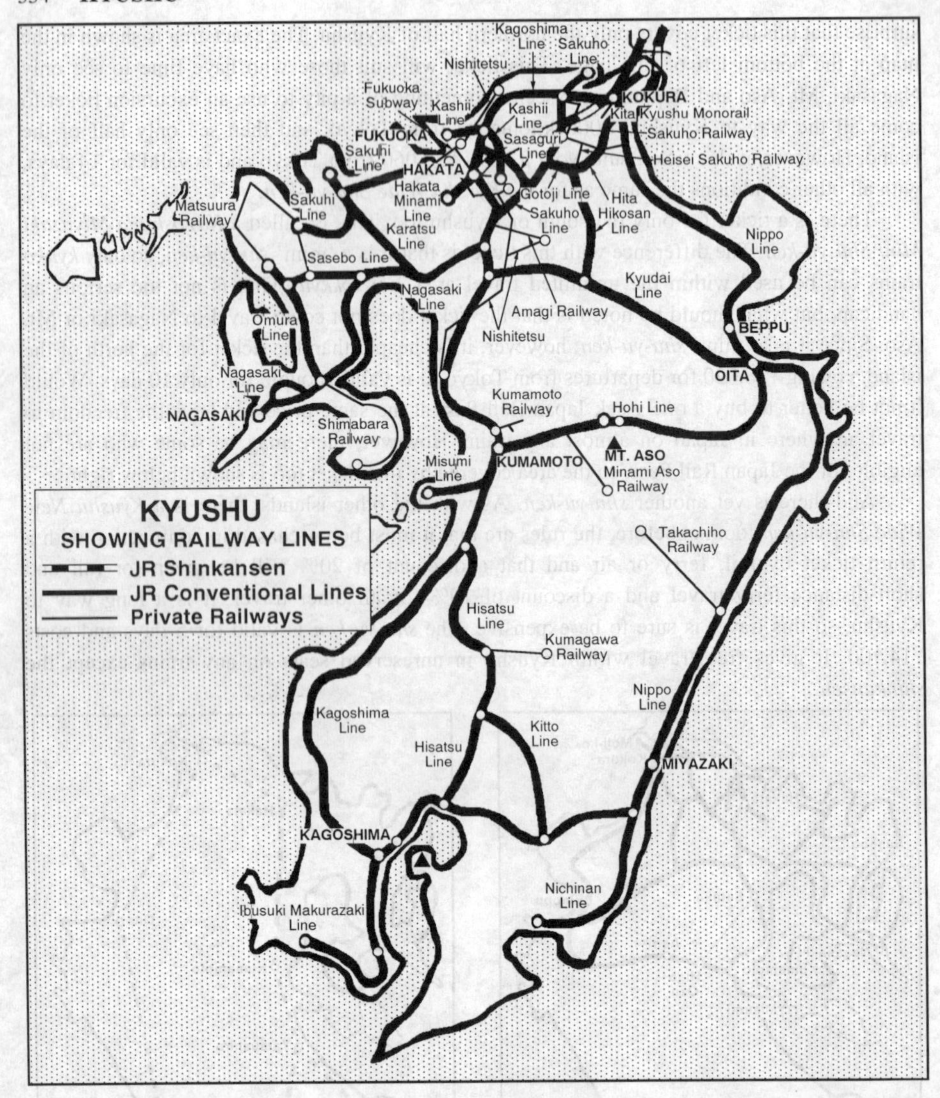


Kyushu is also well served by ferry services. There are several services from the west coast of Shikoku, some of which have been mentioned in the section dealing with that island. Without going into unnecessary detail, one can say that, wherever you are on the west coast of Shikoku, you will be able to find a ferry service to Kyushu within reach. All of these services arrive somewhere within the vicinity of Oita on the east coast of Kyushu. There are also long-distance services from Kobe, Osaka and Tokyo, amongst other places. These ferries generally run overnight, so you can save on the cost of accommodation and still be reasonably comfortable. From Tokyo there is a service to Kokura (Kita Kyushu) via Tokushima in Shikoku. It takes two nights and one day and costs ¥12,000. It leaves from both Tokyo and Kokura on even dates. If the weather is good, this ferry usually goes round the south of

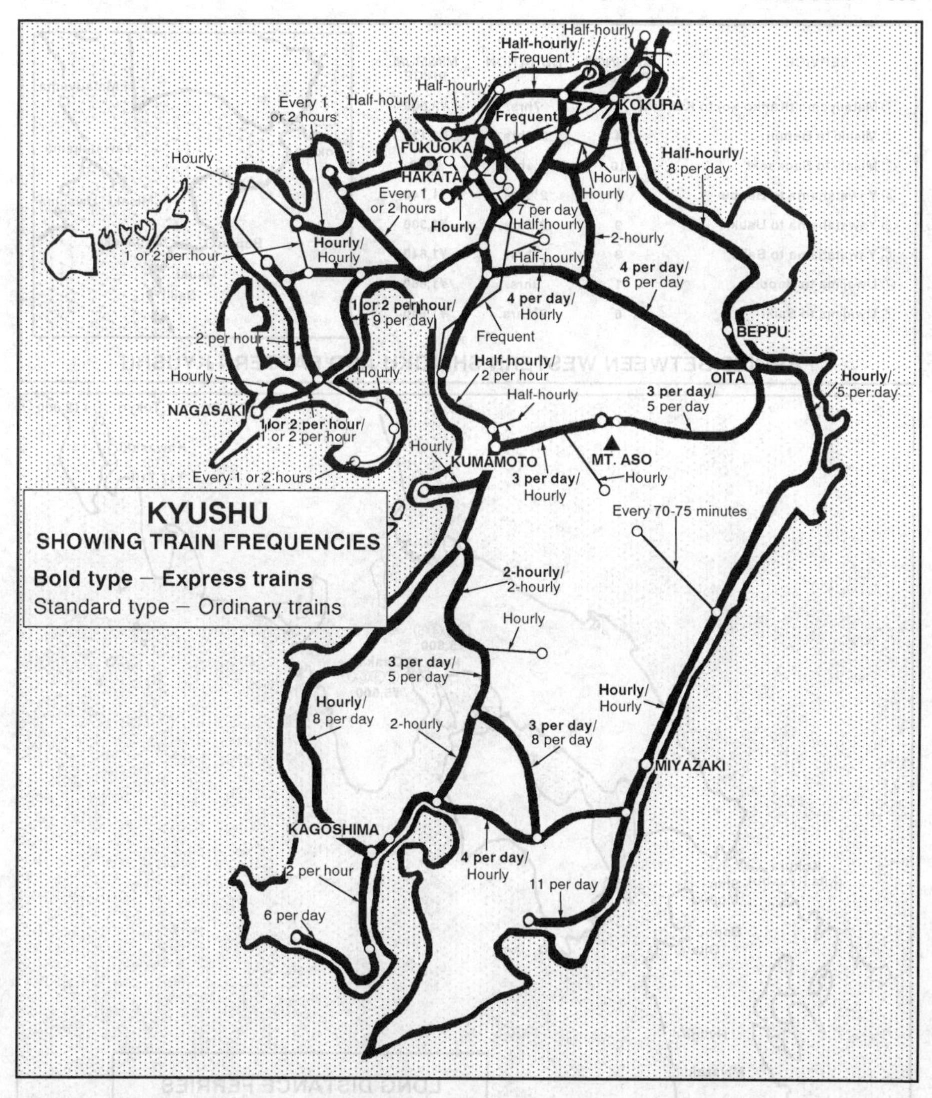


Shikoku and so does not pass through the very scenic Inland Sea. When the author took it, however, the weather was somewhat threatening, so it went by the sheltered scenic route. There is another service from Kawasaki (near Tokyo) to either Miyazaki or Hyuga (slightly north of Miyazaki). This service runs every night to one of the two destinations, leaving at 18:50 and arriving at about 16:00 the next afternoon, with similar times for the return. However, it is rather expensive at ¥17,710 and only one night on board is involved.

From Osaka and Kobe, there are several routes, all operating by night. Ferries go to Shin Moji, at the north-eastern tip of Kyushu, to Beppu, to Oita, to Hyuga, to Miyazaki and to Shibushi, some way south of Miyazaki. The cheapest fares are ¥5,600 (to Shin Moji). The journey takes about 12 hours. Further details of ferry services are given overleaf.

| SERVICE | SAILINGS PER DAY | DURATION | MINIMUM PRICE |
|---|---|---|---|
| ① Matsuyama (Kanko-ko) to Kokura | 1 | 7hrs. | ¥3,500 |
| ② Misaki to Beppu | 4 | 2¼hrs. | ¥1,120 |
| ③ Misaki to Sagaseki | 10 | 1¼hrs. | ¥600 |
| ④ Yawatahama to Beppu | 5 | 2½hrs. | ¥1,740 |
| ⑤ Yawatahama to Usuki | 9 | 2¼hrs. | ¥1,300 |
| ⑥ Yawatahama to Saiki | 3 | 3hrs. | ¥1,640 |
| ⑦ Uwajima to Beppu | 1 | 3hrs. | ¥1,860 |
| ⑧ Uwajima to Saiki | 6 | 2½hrs. | ¥1,640 |

Matsuyama
Kokura
Yawatahama
Misaki
Uwajima
Beppu
Sagaseki
Usuki
Saiki

FERRIES BETWEEN WESTERN SHIKOKU AND EASTERN KYUSHU

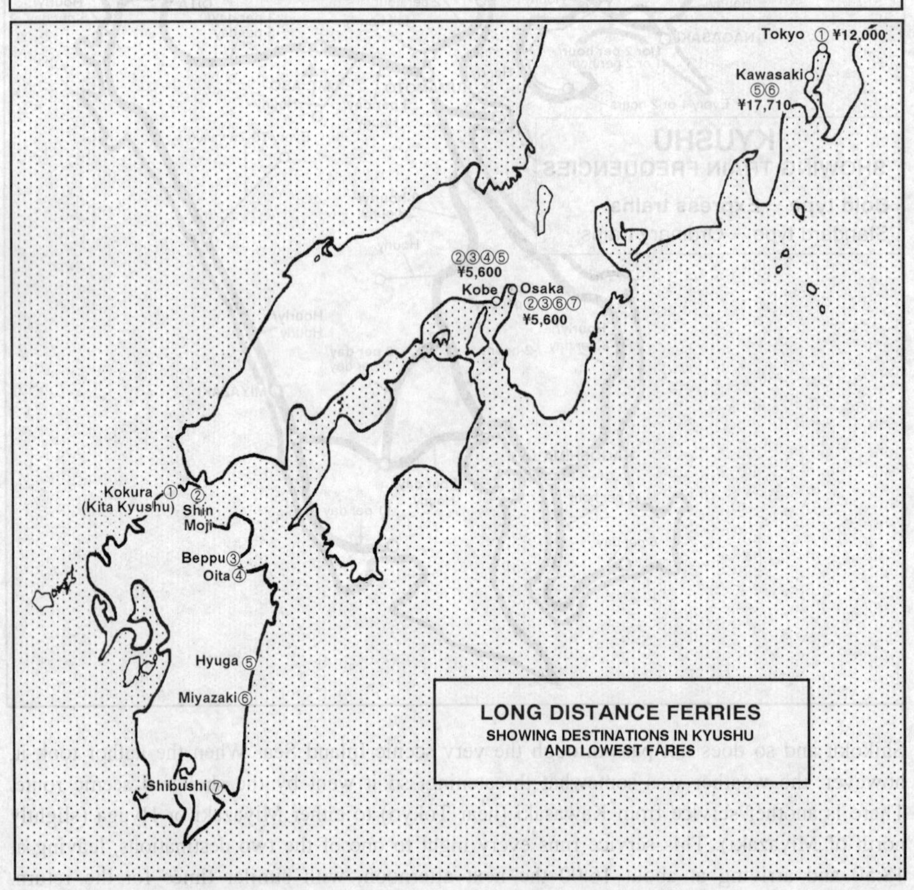

LONG DISTANCE FERRIES
SHOWING DESTINATIONS IN KYUSHU AND LOWEST FARES

There are overnight buses too. From Tokyo (Shinjuku) to Fukuoka takes 14½ hours and costs ¥15,000 single or ¥27,000 return. From Kyoto, Nara, Osaka or Kobe to various points in Kyushu takes 10 to 12 hours and costs ¥10,000 to ¥12,000. Taking one of these buses seems to the author a good way of spending an uncomfortable night and missing most of the scenery, but each person has his own preference.

Kyushu is also well served by overnight trains and some of these are worth mentioning. The overnight trains from Tokyo carry sleeping accommodation only, but there are two trains from the Kansai area which have seats as well as sleepers. A train called *Akatsuki* leaves Kyoto (platform 6) at 20:32 every evening and reaches Nagasaki at 8:47 the next morning. This is a *tokkyu* with one carriage of reserved seating. Thus it is suitable for use with a Japan Rail Pass, but not with a *shu-yu-ken* unless a large supplement is paid. If you have a Japan Rail Pass, you will find this train not too uncomfortable. The seats are all individual, with three seats across the carriage. They recline a long way towards the horizontal position. A blanket and slippers are provided (but no pillow) and the lights are almost completely extinguished at night. The carriage is non-smoking and one end is for ladies only, so if you are of the correct sex you can request one of the ladies' seats when reserving. The conductor will awaken you if you are alighting before the terminus. If you have to travel by night, this is not a bad train to choose. The return journey leaves Nagasaki at 19:50 and reaches Kyoto at 7:59.

A second train called *Naha*, also a *tokkyu*, leaves Shin Osaka at 20:26 every night and travels to Nishi Kagoshima, arriving at 10:31. This train has exactly the same features as the one just described. The return journey leaves Nishi Kagoshima at 19:05 and terminates in Shin Osaka at 9:26.

Within Kyushu itself, there are two more overnight trains with seats, although they do not offer the same level of comfort as those just mentioned. The *Dream Tsubasa* is a *tokkyu* which leaves Hakata at 23:59 every night and reaches Nishi Kagoshima at 6:05. It has reserved and unreserved seating, so is suitable for those with a *Kyushu Wide Shu-yu-ken* as well as those with a Japan Rail Pass, and it also has one carriage (reserved, non-smoking) for ladies only. You may request one of these seats when booking (if you are a lady, of course). The return journey leaves Nishi Kagoshima at 23:30 and reaches Hakata at 5:25, but you may stay on board until 6:00. The second train is again a *tokkyu* and is called *Dream Nichirin.* It runs down the east coast of Kyushu as far as Minami Miyazaki, leaving Hakata at 22:50 and reaching Miyazaki at 6:44 and Minami Miyazaki at 6:48. This train too has reserved and unreserved seating and one ladies' carriage (reserved, smoking). The return journey leaves Minami Miyazaki at 23:25 and Miyazaki at 23:30 and reaches Hakata at 6:57.

Because there are so many sights to see in Kyushu, the route proposed this time is not circular, but instead crosses the island and returns, as well as making loops and detours. There are several parts which involve the use of private railways or buses, thus adding to expense. Of course, these can be cut, but at the cost of some interesting sightseeing. Here then is the route suggested:-

Moji-ko to Hakata (Fukuoka) by Kagoshima Line.
Nishitetsu Fukuoka to Dazaifu and return by Nishitetsu Private Railway.
Hakata (Fukuoka) to Tosu by Kagoshima Line.
Tosu to Nagasaki by Nagasaki Line.
Nagasaki to Isahaya by Nagasaki Line.
Isahaya to Kuchinotsu by Shimabara Private Railway.
Kuchinotsu to Oni-ike by ferry.
Oni-ike to Hondo by bus.
Hondo to Misumi by bus.
Misumi to Kumamoto by Misumi Line.

PROPOSED ROUTE

Kumamoto to Aso by Hohi Line.
Aso to Aso-san and return by bus.
Aso to Mie-machi by Hohi Line.
Mie-machi to Usuki by JR bus.
Usuki to Nakatsu via Beppu by Nippo Line.
Nakatsu to Bungo Mori via Ao-no-domon by bus.
Bungo Mori to Kurume by Kyudai Line.
Kurume to Setaka by Kagoshima Line.
Setaka to Yanagawa by youth hostel minibus or by public bus.
Yanagawa to Omuta by Nishitetsu Private Railway.
Omuta to Yatsushiro by Kagoshima Line.
Yatsushiro to Kobayashi by Hisatsu and Kitto Lines.
Kobayashi to Ebino Kogen by bus.
Ebino Kogen to Hayashi-da by bus.
Hayashi-da to Kirishima Jingu by bus.
Kirishima Jingu to Nishi Kagoshima by Nippo Line.
Nishi Kagoshima to Ibusuki and return by Ibusuki Makurazaki Line.
Nishi Kagoshima to Minami Miyazaki by Nippo Line.
Minami Miyazaki to Shibushi and return by Nichinan Line.
Minami Miyazaki to Nobeoka by Nippo Line.
Nobeoka to Takachiho by Takachiho Private Railway.
Takachiho to Takamori by bus.
Takamori to Tateno by Minami Aso Private Railway.
Tateno to Kumamoto by Hohi Line.
Kumamoto to Shimonoseki by Kagoshima Line.

If you are really short of time and can spare only one day to rush round Kyushu, it is possible just to have a look from a train at virtually the whole island by circumnavigating it in either a clockwise or an anti-clockwise direction using express trains and one of the following plans:-

① Clockwise – Hakata 7:00 *tokkyu* to Miyazaki 13:00.
Miyazaki 13:30 *kyuko* to Kumamoto 18:18, via Kitto and Hisatsu Lines.
Kumamoto 18:45 *tokkyu* to Hakata 20:01.

② Clockwise – Kokura 6:40 *tokkyu* to Miyazaki 11:37.
Miyazaki 11:41 *tokkyu* to Nishi Kagoshima 13:49.
Nishi Kagoshima 14:10 *tokkyu* to Hakata 18:01.
Hakata 18:23 *tokkyu* to Kokura 19:18 (continues to Minami Nobeoka 23:14).

③ Anti-clockwise – Moji-ko 6:55 *tokkyu* to Nishi Kagoshima 12:07.
Nishi Kagoshima 12:50 *tokkyu* to Minami Miyazaki 14:49.
Minami Miyazaki 14:59 *tokkyu* to Kokura 19:59 (continues to Hakata 20:57).

④ Anti-clockwise – Hakata 7:00 *tokkyu* to Kumamoto 8:19.
Kumamoto 8:23 *kyuko* to Minami Miyazaki 13:18, via Hisatsu and Kitto Lines.
Minami Miyazaki 13:23 sleeper *tokkyu* to Oita 16:49.
Oita 16:56 *tokkyu* to Hakata 19:19.

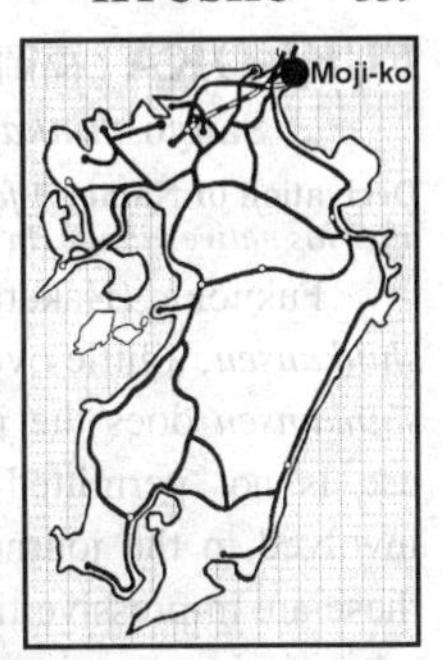


## MOJI-KO (門司港 - 'Gate Official Port')

**Kagoshima Line, 80 mins. from Hakata**

**Derivation of Name:** *A government official was stationed here to inspect all ships passing through the narrow Kanmon Strait which served as the gateway to the Inland Sea.*

Arriving from Honshu by train, the first place which we shall come to is Moji. Note that this is not the same as Moji-ko (Moji Port) which is two stations away on what is now a branch line. However, before the construction of the tunnel linking Honshu and Kyushu, it used to be the main line and Moji-ko used to be the place where the ferries from Honshu, even from as far away as Tokyo, would berth for passengers to transfer to trains to take them to their destinations in Kyushu. As a result, it has a beautifully ornate old **station** with a capacity far beyond present requirements and that is the reason that it is included in our list of places of interest. If you feel that a station is not worth a special visit, then you can skip Moji-ko, but if you have a few minutes to spare, well that is all that it needs. There is a frequent service from Moji to Moji-ko and the journey takes eight minutes. There is still a ferry service from Moji-ko to Shimonoseki in Honshu. It departs from near the station and the small boat takes only five minutes over the crossing. The service operates every 20 minutes and costs ¥260. The pier used in Shimonoseki, however, is not near the town centre, being about half-way between the station and the youth hostel. As mentioned in the section on Shimonoseki, it is also possible to walk in 10 minutes between Honshu and Kyushu, which is an exciting way to enter the island. A pedestrian tunnel runs under the Kanmon Strait. The Honshu entrance is at the foot of the hill on which the youth hostel is situated, almost underneath the most impressive bridge spanning the water. The Kyushu end of the tunnel, however, is a long walk from the centre of Moji-ko. Buses destination Mekari (和布刈) run about once an hour. Alight at Kanmon Tunnel Jindo Guchi (関門トンネル人道口).

A tram system used to operate from Moji-ko along the north of Kyushu as far as Orio. A few years ago, however, the section from Moji-ko to Kokura was discontinued and then, more recently, suddenly and unexpectedly, the service between Kokura and Kurosaki was withdrawn, leaving only a short section of 5 kilometres between Kurosaki and Orio, which is not really a tramway, since that part does not run in the street. The author was fortunate enough to travel between Orio and Kokura just a few weeks before the service was withdrawn, without any knowledge that the line was to be abandoned. It seems a pity, for it was well patronized and convenient, but the days of tramways seem to be numbered, even in Japan.

If you arrive in Kyushu by *shinkansen*, you will cross from Honshu by a separate railway tunnel and your first stop will be Kokura. Kokura is a port and industrial centre, but not actually a city in its own right. It is part of the city of Kita Kyushu which covers all of the north-eastern corner of the island and is an amalgam of various mainly industrial areas. Kokura is one station west of Moji on the conventional JR Kagoshima Line and so three stations (15 minutes) away from Moji-ko.

There is a youth hostel at Yahata, five stations west of Kokura on the Kagoshima Line. *Tokkyu* trains do not stop here, but all others do. The hostel is another of those municipal edifices built in magnificent locations. It is uphill all the way from the station to the hostel (25 minutes walk), but when you get there you can see all of the city of Kita Kyushu spread out below you. The view at night, as well as in the day, makes this a hostel worth staying in. Some English is spoken.

# FUKUOKA (福岡 – 'Lucky Hill')

### Sanyo *shinkansen* and Kagoshima Line, 6 hrs. from Tokyo

**Derivation of Name:** *A famous warrior built a castle here on a hill and named it after his native village. In time, the name came to be applied to the whole town.*

Fukuoka (Hakata station) is the western limit of the Sanyo *shinkansen*, a little over six hours from Tokyo by *Hikari*. The *Nozomi shinkansen* does the journey in five hours and four minutes, but its use is not permitted with a Japan Rail Pass. Since the distance involved in the journey from Tokyo to Hakata is 1,175 kilometres, these are impressive times – and, of course, *shinkansen* trains, like all others in Japan, are usually absolutely punctual.

Fukuoka is the name of the city, the largest in Kyushu, and Hakata is the name of the port. The JR station, some distance from the port, is, nevertheless, called Hakata. Fukuoka has a subway system, recently extended to the airport, which is a mere two stops from Hakata station. There are two lines, but the western extremity of the system is connected to the JR Chikuhi Line and some trains run through onto that line. The eastern edge of the subway system connects with a private line operated by Nishitetsu, but trains do not run through in this case. Nishitetsu also operates a line running south, more or less in direct competition with JR.

The centre of Fukuoka is really around **Tenjin**, three stations from Hakata on the subway. This is also the terminus for Nishitetsu (Fukuoka station). There is a shopping arcade running for a considerable distance underground, while, above ground, you can find some of Fukuoka's more impressive buildings, both new and old, and, in the evenings, a number of **noodles stalls** where a meal can be had at moderate cost and in an interesting atmosphere.

To the north of Fukuoka, land has been reclaimed and a sand spit stabilized by the planting of trees to make a recreational area which is now linked with the island of Shikanoshima. There is also a youth hostel here (Shikanoshima-so Hostel) and a government guest house (Kokumin Shuku-sha). A railway line runs round the spit to Saitozaki station.

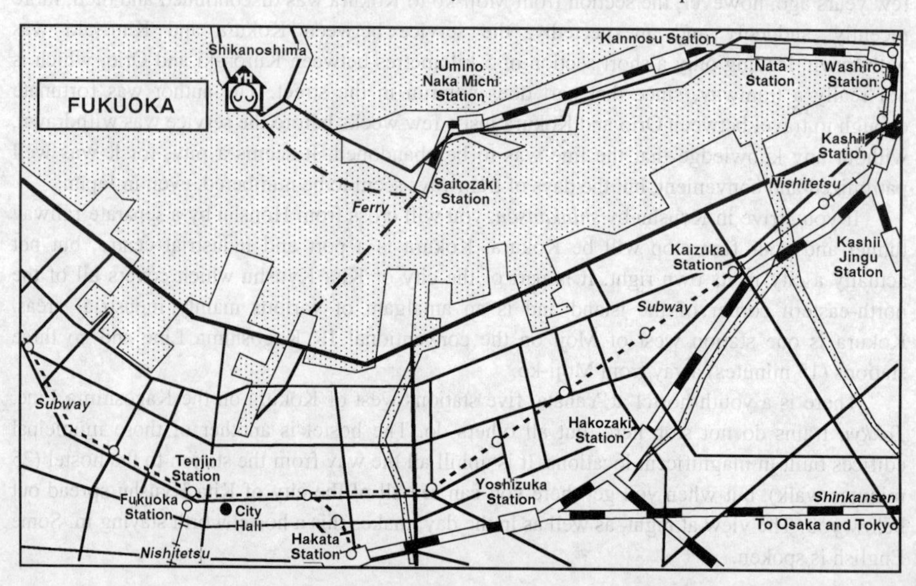

Occasional trains leave from Hakata, but usually it is necessary to take any train going east along the Kagoshima Main Line (towards Kokura) for three stations to Kashii and then change to a train going to Saitozaki. From Kashii to Saitozaki takes 20 to 25 minutes. Trains are frequent. If you want to go further, there are buses to Shikanoshima. There is also a ferry from Hakata port to Shikanoshima, calling at Saitozaki on the way. It takes 45 minutes and costs ¥560. From Saitozaki to Shikanoshima costs ¥190. The ferry runs approximately hourly, with the last sailing leaving Hakata at 20:00.

Also in the vicinity of Fukuoka, although a little distant from the city, is a famous shrine: **Dazaifu**. The easiest way to get there is with Nishitetsu, from Fukuoka station, near Tenjin subway station. First you take any train to Nishitetsu Futsuka-ichi, where all services stop. It takes 14 minutes by *tokkyu* (no supplement), on which trains it is the first stop, and about 30 minutes by the slowest trains. There you change to a small branch line which runs just two stations to Dazaifu, taking 5 minutes. The total fare from Fukuoka to Dazaifu is ¥360. There is a JR Futsuka-ichi station too, but it is about 10 minutes slightly convoluted walk from the Nishitetsu station. A map is displayed at the JR station showing the route to Nishitetsu. Study it carefully before setting out if you choose to use JR for the first part of the journey.

The shrine area is very near Dazaifu station and it is easy to see where to go. If in doubt, just follow everybody else! There is a pleasant garden, a rustic bridge and, of course, the shrine building itself dating from the sixteenth century.

There is also a youth hostel nearby, Dazaifu Hostel. It is a small one which was full when the author wanted to stay there, so no first-hand information is offered concerning it. However, it claims that English is spoken.

Nishitetsu issues a one-day ticket for the buses which it operates within the area of Fukuoka city. This costs ¥600 and is called an '*ichi-nichi free jo-sha-ken*' (一日フリー乗車券).

## NAGASAKI (長崎 - 'Long Peninsula')

**Nagasaki Line, 2 hrs. 15 mins. from Hakata**

**Derivation of Name:** *Literal. This is an elevated area on a long peninsula.*

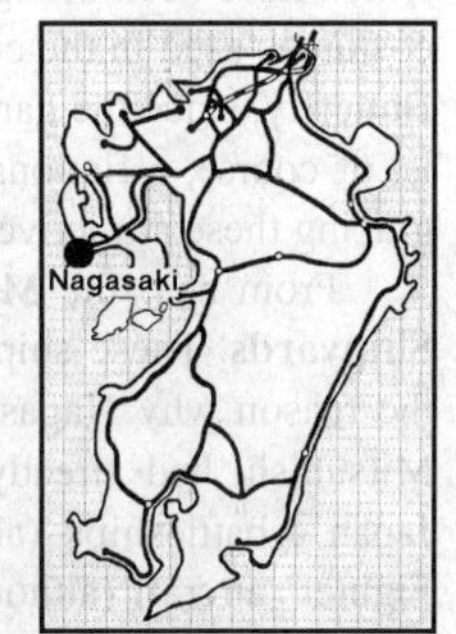


Nagasaki is one of the places not to be missed in Kyushu. However, the reason for visiting it is not so much the atomic bombing for which it has become famous as the interesting history which it had centuries prior to the events of the twentieth century. While all the rest of Japan was in a period of splendid isolation for over 200 years prior to the arrival of Commodore Perry in 1853, Nagasaki was the only port open to limited foreign trade. Even though attempts were made to restrict the scope of foreign influence by confining the traders to the single island of Dejima, Nagasaki has still had a cosmopolitan background that no other place in Japan has experienced over such a long period. It needs about a day to see most of what the city has to offer.

To reach Nagasaki from Hakata, take one of the *tokkyu* trains which run at least every hour, and usually every 30 minutes, taking about 2 hours 15 minutes to travel to Nagasaki. If you are using Blue Spring tickets, you should take a *kaisoku*, probably bound for Omuta or Arao, to Tosu, a journey of about 30 minutes, then change to an ordinary train. However, the route to be used and the changing points vary, so here are the current connexions available from early morning until late afternoon, by two different routes.

① Hakata 5:11. Tosu 5:50 / 6:14. Nagasaki 9:20.
② Hakata 6:33. Tosu 7:17 / 7:23. Haiki 9:04. (Caution: train divides *en route* and only part goes to Haiki) / 9:36. Nagasaki 11:08.
③ Hakata 8:20. Tosu 8:46 / 8:57. Hizen Yamaguchi 9:39 / 9:53. Haiki 10:47 / 11:00. Nagasaki 13:05.
④ Hakata 9:00. Tosu 9:26 / 9:58. Hizen Yamaguchi 10:39 / 11:12. Haiki 12:02 / 12:36. Nagasaki 13:58.
⑤ Hakata 11:00. Hizen Yamaguchi 12:08 (only part of train) / 12:20. Nagasaki 14:44.
⑥ Hakata 13:00. Hizen Yamaguchi 14:09 (only part of train) / 14:43. Nagasaki 16:52.
⑦ Hakata 15:00. Tosu 15:28 / 15:30. Nagasaki 18:46.
⑧ Hakata 16:36. Tosu 17:02 / 17:05. Nagasaki 20:09.

Some of the above connexions involve travelling via Haiki, on the west coast of Kyushu, just south of **Sasebo**, where there is an American naval base. After changing at Haiki, your first stop will be at a station called **Huis Ten Bosch**, a rather un-Japanese sounding name. In fact, it is an imitation of a Dutch town, complete with Dutch name and various thematic attractions. It is not the sort of place which most visitors from overseas come here to see, but deserves a mention in any case.

Well, now, having reached Nagasaki, let us start our explorations of the city in the west. **Glover Garden** will give a good idea of some of the more recent history. Mr. Glover was an enterprising Scotsman who came here in the nineteenth century and contributed greatly to the modernization of Japan. He brought the first steam engine to the country, for example, and used it in his mine. He built a shipyard and an ironworks, both of which he later sold to Mitsubishi Heavy Industries. He also started a brewery and made beer under the brand name of Kirin. This too he sold to Mitsubishi and now it is one of the most popular of Japanese beers (and still made by a Mitsubishi group company). And he lived here on this hill in this rather British house with a beautiful garden and a magnificent view. There are other similar houses which have been brought here also and there is an exhibition of *mikoshi* (portable shrines) and costumes used in the city's festivals, with films of the same. There is even a statue of Madame Butterfly, since the garden overlooking the harbour suits the operatic scene. Madame Butterfly is, of course, a fictional character, but no doubt Puccini would be flattered to find her statue gracing these attractive gardens.

From near the Mitsubishi Pavilion, you can look across the harbour at the **Mitsubishi Shipyards**. These shipyards were originally established by the Tokugawa *shogunate* and are the reason why Nagasaki was chosen as the target for the world's second atomic bombing. Mitsubishi had already been responsible for producing the *Musashi*, the second-greatest of Japan's battleships (although it was not produced here) and the highly successful 'Zero Fighter' aircraft (although again not here). On the day of the bombing, there was thick cloud and the crew of the aircraft, which had limited range, were on the point of giving up their mission when suddenly an opening appeared in the cloud cover and they saw the Mitsubishi Shipyards beneath. They dropped the bomb and turned back immediately. In fact, the bomb exploded not over the Mitsubishi Shipyards, but over the Mitsubishi Ironworks, 4 kilometres away. Every worker there was killed.

Entrance to the Glover Garden costs ¥600, but is worthwhile as there is enough to see here to keep you busy for about two hours, if you have enough time. At the least, it will take an hour. Nearby is House No. 16, which is similar, but will cost another ¥400, a sum which hardly seems worth while, unless you are particularly interested in Victoriana. Probably it is

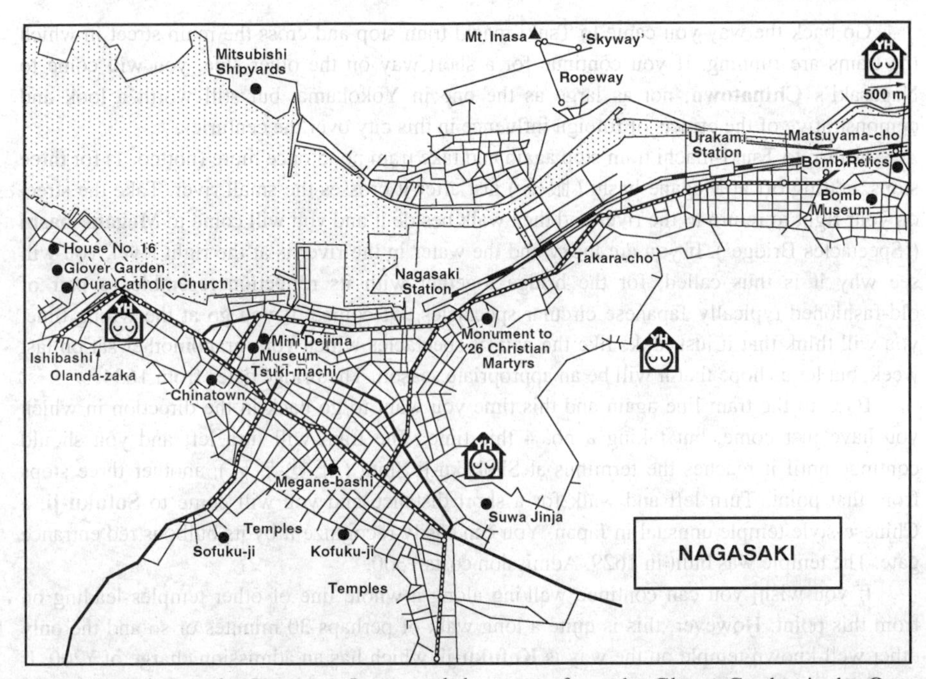


more interesting to the Japanese. Just round the corner from the Glover Garden is the **Oura Catholic Church**, built in 1865. Since it is historic and in memory of the 26 Christian martyrs crucified here in 1597 when Toyotomi Hideyoshi was trying to eradicate the potentially dangerous Christian political influence, there is an admission charge of ¥250.

If you are staying in Olanda-zaka Youth Hostel, these three attractions are on your doorstep. If not, then you can reach them by taking a tram no. 5. When the tram turns sharp left beside a canal, get off at Oura Tenshu-do Shita (大浦天主堂下) and cross the canal. You will soon come to Glover Garden on your left. Even if you miss the stop, the tram goes only one stop further.

When you have finished looking at the attractions mentioned, walk to the tram terminus at Ishibashi (石橋) and cross the street beside which the trams run. If you go up the hill ahead, you will come to several other older buildings of some slight interest. The narrow road curves to the left (youth hostel on your left) and descends **Olanda-zaka** ('Holland Slope'). Keep walking and you will return to the main road along which tram no. 5 is running. If you are not enticed by this walk of about 15 minutes, you can just take the tram from Ishibashi terminus.

Our next visit is near Tsuki-machi (築町) tram stop. That is the fourth stop from the tram terminus, but if you walked along Olanda-zaka, turn right at the main road and it is only 1½ tram stops away, so you might as well keep walking! From Tsuki-machi tram stop, however, walk back a few metres and turn right. About 5 minutes walk will bring you to **'Mini Dejima'**. This is approximately the site of the island to which the Dutch and Chinese traders were confined during Japan's period of isolation. The island has gone, because all was filled in long ago to create a harbour suitable for modern ships. Here now you can find a small scale reproduction of the foreigners' quarters of that period. There is also a museum here. Both the model of Dejima and the museum are free.

Go back the way you came to Tsuki-machi tram stop and cross the main street in which the trams are running. If you continue for a short way on the other side, you will come to Nagasaki's **Chinatown**, not as large as the one in Yokohama, but still worth a look and demonstrative of the effects of foreign influence in this city over the centuries.

Return to Tsuki-machi tram stop again and take tram no. 5 once more (not no. 1) for three stops, getting off at Megane-bashi (眼橋) just after it crosses the small river. Take the street on your right to return to the river and then walk beside it and you will come to **Megane-bashi** ('Spectacles Bridge'). If you are lucky and the water in the river is at the right level, you will see why it is thus called, for the bridge together with its reflection resembles a pair of old-fashioned typically Japanese circular spectacles. Of course, if you go at the wrong time, you will think that it just looks like the pair of spectacles which your grandmother sat on last week, but let us hope that it will be an appropriate season. The bridge dates from 1634.

Back to the tram line again and this time you want to go back in the direction in which you have just come, but taking a no. 4 this time. The tram will turn left and you should continue until it reaches the terminus at Shokaku-ji Shita (正覚寺下), another three stops from that point. Turn left and walk for a short distance and you will come to **Sofuku-ji**, a Chinese-style temple unusual in Japan. You can easily recognize it by its bulbous red entrance gate. The temple was built in 1629. Admission costs ¥300.

If you wish, you can continue walking along a whole line of other temples leading on from this point. However, this is quite a long walk of perhaps 30 minutes or so and the only other well-known temple on the way is **Kofuku-ji**, which has an admission charge of ¥200. If you follow this walking course, you will eventually come to another street with trams, from where you can take tram no. 3 and rejoin the route suggested in the next paragraph. Tram no. 3 joins the route followed by tram no. 1 just outside Nagasaki railway station.

If you do not bother with the other temples, return from Sofuku-ji to the nearby tram terminus and take a no. 1 this time. It will turn left at the end of the street, then right after passing Tsuki-machi, then right again past the railway station and, after a while, it will move from the street onto a separate track at the side of the road. You want to get off at the second stop after this happens. It is called Matsuyama-machi (松山町). As soon as you find the JR line on your left immediately next to the tram track, you will know that your stop is next. Turn right, cross the main road and walk ahead. You will soon come across a park with remains of the **atomic bombing**. The point above which the bomb exploded is marked and pieces from the Mitsubishi Ironworks, Urakami Catholic Cathedral and various other places are here on display. There is a **museum** a little further up the hill and, to your left a short distance, the **'Peace Park'**, which is a collection of statues and monuments, a good place to sit down, but not essential sightseeing. The museum is very similar to that which you will probably have seen in Hiroshima and you may not want to put yourself through the same ordeal twice. There is a notice to the effect that the purpose of these exhibits is to show the results of the bombing in the hope that mankind will never use such a weapon again. When the author visited the museum, there were parties of high school students laughing and joking over the relics, so that I had the impression that there was every chance that mankind might choose to indulge in similar experiments in the future. Admission to the museum, here as in Hiroshima, costs a token ¥50. You will notice, incidentally, that many more buildings survived the atomic blast in Nagasaki than in Hiroshima. That is because Nagasaki is hilly while Hiroshima is flat and the shadows of the hills protected buildings and, to some extent, people on the far sides of them.

Some seven or eight minutes walk from here is the new **Urakami Catholic Cathedral**. Although quite an imposing replacement for the one destroyed on 9th August 1945, it is the sort of building which is quite familiar to westerners, so again not an essential sight to see.

From this area, you can take a tram no. 1 or no. 3 to return to the railway station or beyond. Near the station is a **monument to the 26 Christian martyrs** who died here in 1597. Admission costs ¥250.

Alternatively, if you get off the tram at Takara-machi ( 宝町 ), six stops from Matsuyama-machi and two stops before the railway station, you can walk to your right across the railway and over the river, forking right to the base station of the ropeway which will take you up **Mt. Inasa** for a good view of the city. It is especially pretty at night. The ropeway costs ¥550 single or ¥1,000 return.

Nagasaki offers a one-day ticket for the trams for ¥500 (市電一日乗車券 - '*shi-den ichi-nichi jo-sha-ken*'), which can be purchased from the information office at the railway station, amongst other places. If you want to use such a ticket, it is a good idea to buy it as you arrive in the city, because sales points are limited and most are not open early in the morning. The ticket can be post-dated. If you follow the route suggested above, which will take most of a whole day, you can do all of the travelling conveniently by tram. However, if you do not mind walking, you only really need tramsport (actually it was a typing error, but I decided to leave it!) to and from the atomic bomb site, so you might take only three tram rides in the day. A single tram ride costs ¥100, remarkably cheap by Japanese standards, and you are allowed to change trams between routes nos. 1 and 5 without additional charge at Tsuki-machi only. Ask for a transfer ticket ('*norikai ken*') as you exit. There is also a one-day ticket for city buses (バス一日乗車券 - '*bus ichi-nichi jo-sha-ken*'), also ¥500.

There are four youth hostels in Nagasaki, all quite conveniently located. English is spoken at three of the four.

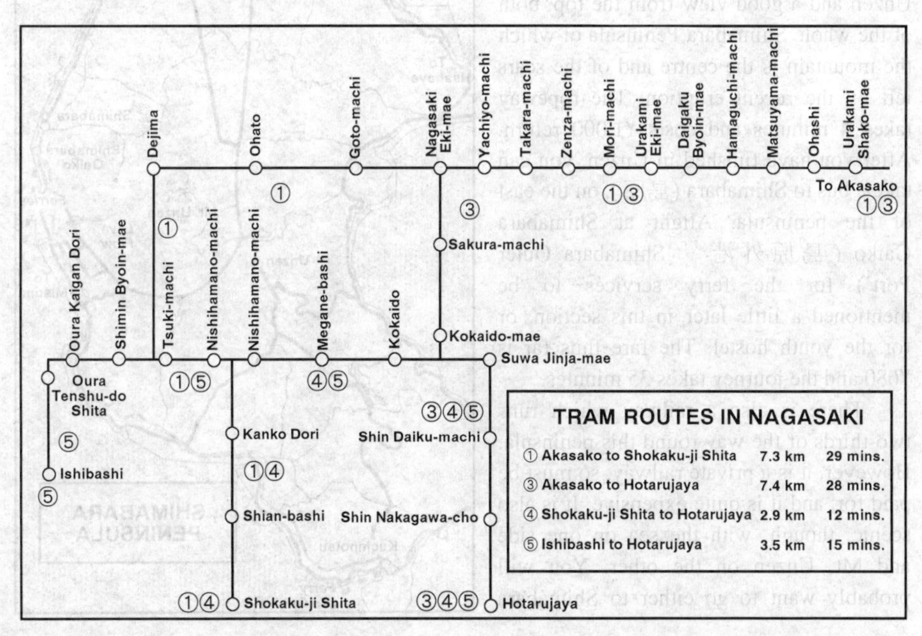

## MT. UNZEN (雲仙山 - 'Cloudy Wizard Mountain')

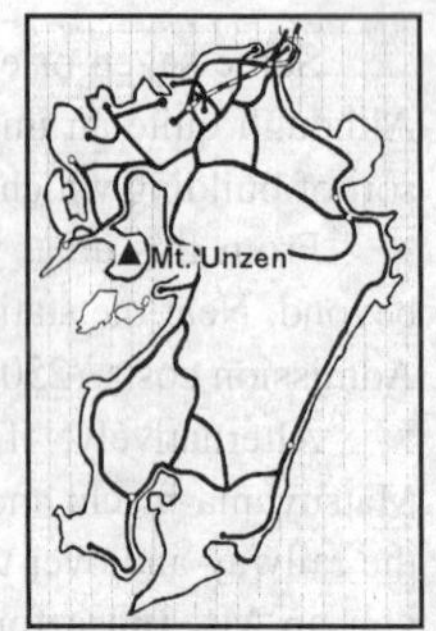


**Nagasaki Line to Isahaya, 2 hrs. from Hakata. Then bus 55 mins.**

**Derivation of Name:** *This place was originally called Onsen (spa). In time, the word was corrupted to Unzen.*

Mt. Unzen has long been a famous hill resort and spa, especially as it is conveniently near the port of Nagasaki and so used to appeal particularly to Europeans stationed in Hong Kong or Shanghai and to Americans in the Philippines. Recently, however, it has had fame of a different sort with the sudden and unexpected **eruption of Mt. Unzen**, which had lain dormant for two centuries. At the time of writing, the mountain is still smoking gently, but another eruption seems unlikely as most of its energy has now been dissipated, according to the experts. By way of caution, maybe it is worth adding that some of the experts were amongst those killed by venturing too near the mountain during a lull in proceedings in the course of the recent eruption. The lava flowed down the eastern side of the mountain and can be seen lying there.

To reach this area, first take a train to Isahaya. By *tokkyu*, this is the first stop from Nagasaki and the journey takes a mere 20 minutes. By ordinary train, it takes between 30 minutes and an hour, depending on which of two routes is used. There is also a *kaisoku* service taking 25 to 30 minutes. All trains from Nagasaki go to Isahaya and all stop there. The service is frequent. If you want to go to the town of Unzen (雲仙), near the top of the mountain, now take a bus going to Unzen Koen (雲仙公園). Buses run approximately hourly, take 55 minutes and cost ¥1,200. Most of the buses start at Nagasaki station, if you prefer to go by bus all the way. From there they take 90 minutes and cost ¥1,750. From Unzen Koen, there is a ropeway to the top of Mt. Unzen and a good view from the top, both of the whole Shimabara Peninsula of which the mountain is the centre and of the scars left by the recent eruption. The ropeway takes 4 minutes and costs ¥1,000 return. After you have finished in Unzen, you can take a bus to Shimabara (島原), on the east of the peninsula. Alight at Shimabara Gaiko (島原外港 - 'Shimabara Outer Port') for the ferry services to be mentioned a little later in this section, or for the youth hostel. The fare thus far is ¥680 and the journey takes 35 minutes.

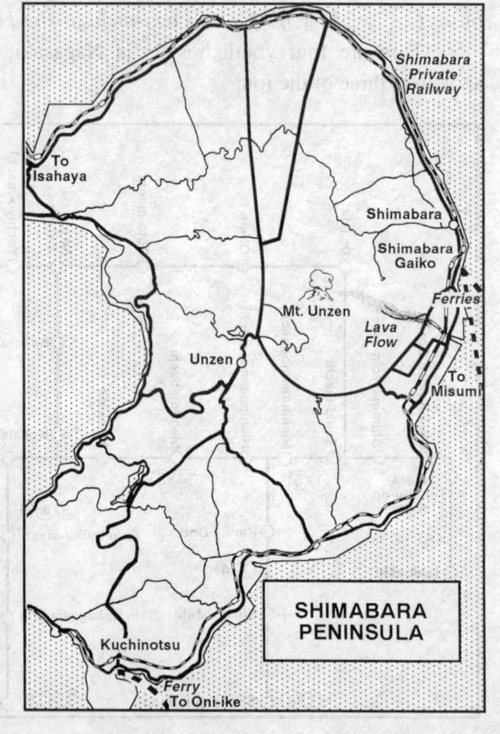


There is also a railway which runs two-thirds of the way round this peninsula. However, it is a private railway, so must be paid for, and it is quite expensive. It is also scenic, though, with the sea on one side and Mt. Unzen on the other. You will probably want to go either to Shimabara

Gaiko or to Kuchinotsu, from which two ports there are useful ferries. We already know about the eruption of Mt. Unzen and one does not want to exaggerate the dangers of this part of Kyushu, but there was recently an accident on this, the Shimabara Private Railway, when two trains met on a single track. The driver of one of the trains admitted that he had forgotten to check the signal before starting off. From Isahaya to Shimabara Gaiko takes 80 minutes and costs ¥1,170. To Kuchinotsu takes 2½ hours and costs ¥1,610. From Shimabara Gaiko, ferries operate to Kumamoto port approximately hourly at a cost of ¥580. The voyage takes an hour. Alternatively, there are ferries to Misumi, also costing ¥580 and taking one hour. This service sails six times per day. From Misumi to Kumamoto, there are ordinary trains about hourly. The journey takes an average of 50 minutes.

From Kuchinotsu, ferries run to Oni-ike on one of the islands of Amakusa, for which see the next entry. Ferries sail every 45 minutes and take 30 minutes to reach Oni-ike. The fare is only ¥320.

There is a youth hostel at Shimabara, right next to the port, for those who wish to stay in this area. In the town there is a reconstruction of **Shimabara Castle**, which was destroyed in the seventeenth century during the Christian revolt originating in Amakusa.

## AMAKUSA (天草 - 'Heavenly Grass') Misumi Line to Misumi, 50 mins. from Kumamoto. Then bus, 90 mins.

**Derivation of Name:** *A sweet type of grass grew here which was often used as a medicine.*

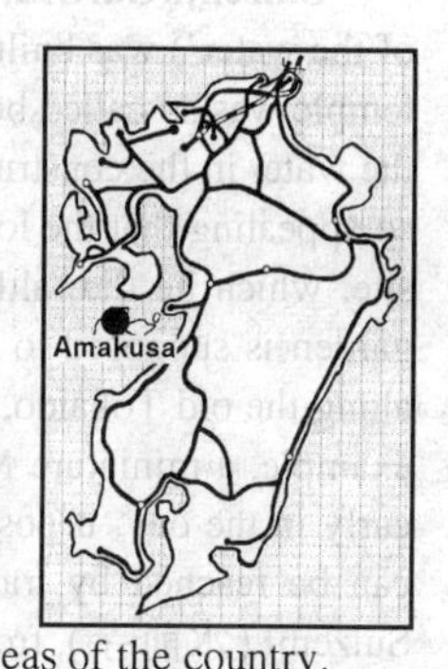


South of the Shimabara Peninsula, which has Mt. Unzen in its centre, lie the two main islands which comprise Amakusa. These islands were the focal point of a **Christian Revolt** in 1637 led by a 15 year old boy named Amakusa Shiro. The revolt resulted in a massacre of all the Christians in the area and on the Shimabara Peninsula and Christianity has never been quite as popular in Japan since that time. Even so, Kyushu still has a higher proportion of Christians than other areas of the country.

These days, Amakusa constitutes an agreeable rural backwater, pleasant to visit for just that reason and because of its interesting Christian history. If you arrive by ferry from the Shimabara Peninsula, you will need to take a bus from Oni-ike, where the service arrives, to the main town of Hondo (本渡). Buses are reasonably frequent and take 30 minutes to Hondo at a cost of ¥470. In Hondo, you will find, on a hill overlooking the town, memorials to those who died in the 1637 uprising and the graves of some of them.

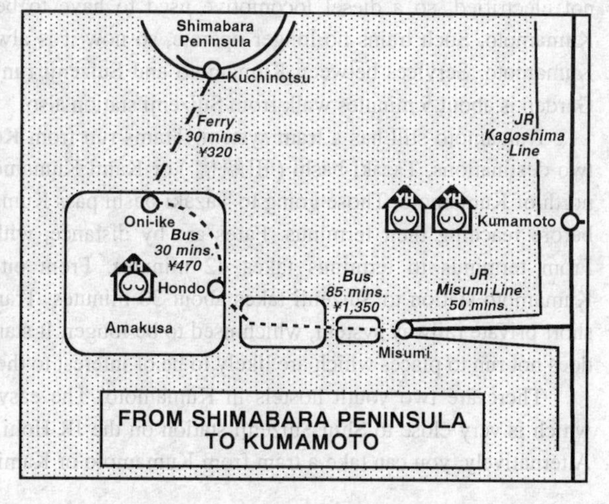


There is a youth hostel here, about 10 minutes walk from the Bus Centre. It is quite adequate without being really special.

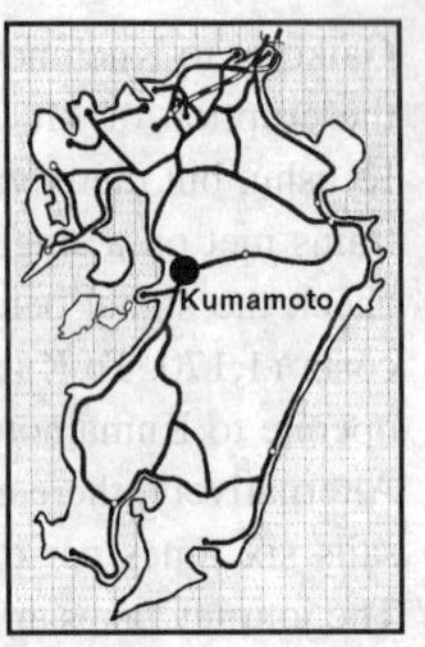


## KUMAMOTO (熊本 –'Bear Book')

**Kagoshima Line, 80 mins. from Hakata**

**Derivation of Name:** *The word 'Kumamoto', with the same pronunciation but different Chinese characters, meant a place lying on a crooked road. The characters used became changed with the passage of time.*

Lying half way down the west coast of Kyushu, Kumamoto is the capital of the prefecture of the same name and the third largest city in Kyushu, having a population of rather more than half a million. It is known for its castle and for Suizenji Garden.

**Kumamoto Castle** used to be reckoned as one of the strongest in Japan. It was built in 1607. However, in 1877 it was destroyed in a siege of government troops by a rebel force of former *samurai* led by Saigo Takamori who had resigned from the government over disagreements regarding foreign policy. The government troops withstood the siege and were victorious in the end, but, of the castle itself, only a small part survived. What is there now is another of those concrete reconstructions. This one dates from 1960.

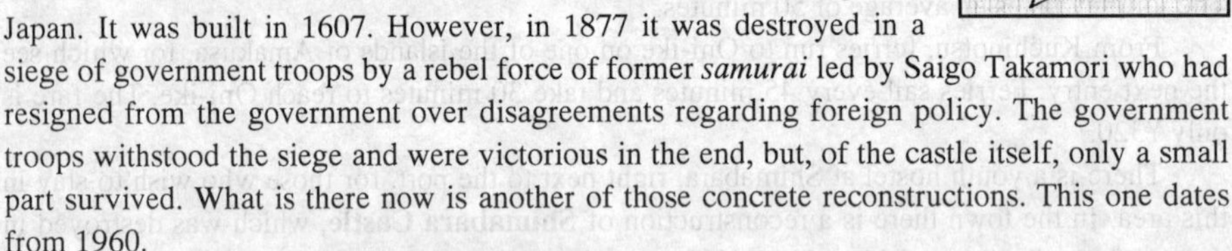

**Suizenji Garden**, however, really is quite old. A temple called Suizen-ji ('temple in front of the water') was built in 1632 by the lord who controlled the city, Hosokawa Tadatoshi. The temple was so called because it was built beside a spring of particular purity. The temple used the water in the construction of an attractive garden within its precincts and the garden became so appealing that the lord decided to move the temple and construct a house for himself on the site, which he did, although the name of the temple has been retained for the garden. This garden is supposed to be a miniature representation of the 53 'stations' (i.e. lodging places) along the old Tokaido, the road which ran between Edo (Tokyo) and Kyoto. You can see, for example, a miniature Mt. Fuji on one side. Admission costs ¥200 and it is a good idea to go early in the day, if possible, because there will be plenty of people here later on. The garden can be reached by tram easily enough. Take a tram marked Kengun-machi (建軍町) to Suizenji (水前寺), from where it is 5 minutes walk. There is also a station called Suizenji on the JR Hohi Line, four stops (8 minutes) from Kumamoto. *Tokkyu* trains used to run to Suizenji directly from Hakata, but that was an inconvenient practice because the Hohi Line is not electrified, so a diesel locomotive used to have to be attached to the electric train at Kumamoto. Such trains no longer operate, so now it is always necessary to change trains at Kumamoto. Services between Kumamoto and Suizenji run at least every half hour. Suizenji Garden is about 5 minutes walk from Suizenji station also.

Kumamoto still has a tram system. Trams run from Kengun-machi (建軍町) to one of two destinations, Tazaki-bashi (田崎橋) or Kami Kumamoto station (上熊本駅), one stop north of Kumamoto. Those going to Tazaki-bashi pass Kumamoto station (熊本駅) two stops before reaching their terminus. Fares are by distance, with the maximum fare being ¥190. From terminus to terminus takes 42 minutes. From either Kumamoto station or Kami Kumamoto station to Suizenji takes about 30 minutes. Trams run frequently. There is also a short private railway system, which used to be longer. It starts at Kami Kumamoto station, but does not run to places which are likely to be of interest to the short-term visitor.

There are two youth hostels in Kumamoto. The easy one to reach is Suizenji Hostel, which is very close to Shin Suizenji station on the JR Hohi Line, 6 minutes from Kumamoto. Alternatively, you can take a tram from Kumamoto or Kami Kumamoto station, in which case it is a ride of about 25 minutes. When the author stayed at this hostel, there was a 'meeting' in the evening at which each hosteller was invited to introduce himself to the others and to give one travel tip to everybody. The 'parent' next asked whether anybody would like to come on a free guided walking tour of some of the sights in the morning. Having obtained some participants, he then announced, "Right, the tour begins at 6:30. (general pandemonium!) Now, don't get so excited! We go first to Suizenji Garden, which is not far away. At that time in the morning, there is nobody to sell tickets, so we don't have to pay, but we can still get into the garden. Then we go to Kumamoto Castle. If we go in the exit there, we can avoid buying a ticket and nobody seems to notice early in the morning." And so the free tour continued. Suizenji definitely seemed to be a hostel with character! Of course, these things change over the years, but, at the least, it is conveniently located and has a pleasant atmosphere.

The other hostel is Kumamoto Shi-ritsu Hostel, another municipal hostel with a pleasant location next to a small park. The problem with this hostel is that it is a little difficult to reach. The youth hostel handbook suggests taking a tram and then a bus from Kumamoto station. If you do this, note that the end of bus route is circular, so you catch the bus from the same bus stop opposite the hostel when you want to go back. Also note that the route terminus is just before the hostel is reached, so your bus may well sit there for a while until the time scheduled for return. You do not have to get off or pay again. Just sit patiently until it is time to continue round the circle. However, this tram plus bus route is expensive and time consuming, as well as rather difficult, so the author's suggestion is to walk from Kami Kumamoto station. Notice, though, that some express trains do not stop at Kami Kumamoto, which is one station before Kumamoto. From Kami Kumamoto walk (or take a tram) until you see a large bridge overhead carrying a major highway, then turn right and follow the map in the Youth Hostels section on page 455. This hostel is not special, but it is cheap and quiet and, moreover, although this is not indicated in the youth hostel handbook, when the author stayed here, I was given a discount for being from overseas. I commented that it was cheap and the 'parent' responded, "Yes, isn't it? Shall we put the price up?" However, I assured him that that was not necessary, so hopefully this hostel remains good value.

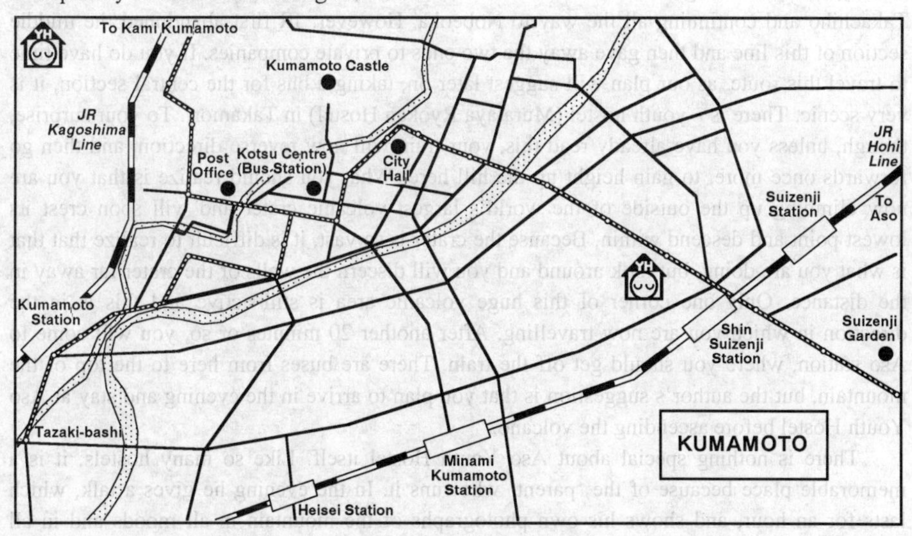

To reach Kumamoto from Hakata, there are *tokkyu* trains every 30 minutes, generally at 18 and 48 minutes past the hour. The journey takes about 80 minutes. Ordinary trains run approximately once an hour and take three hours. You can sometimes save time by catching a *kaisoku* as far as Omuta or Arao, which is the limit of the area served by such trains, and then transferring to an ordinary train.

If you are coming from Nagasaki, you do not need to return all the way to Hakata, but can change trains at Tosu. If you are coming from Amakusa, as our plan suggests, you will need to take a bus from Hondo to Misumi. This journey takes 85 minutes and costs ¥1,350. Buses operate about every 90 minutes. From Misumi trains run approximately hourly to Kumamoto taking 50 minutes over the journey. There are also buses which run from Hondo directly to Kumamoto. These operate every half hour. They take 2½ hours and cost ¥2,150.

## MT. ASO (阿蘇山 - 'Flattering Resuscitation Mountain')

**Hohi Line, 1 hr. from Kumamoto**

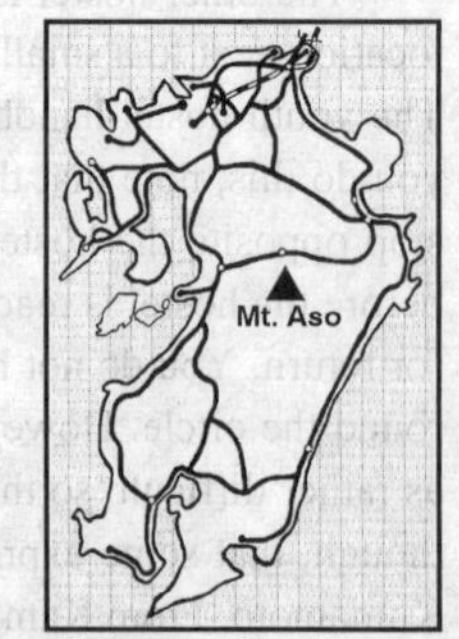


**Derivation of Name:** *From old word 'azu', meaning crumbling cliff.*

Mt. Aso is one of the great natural sights of Kyushu and one not to be missed. It is an active volcano located in one corner of what is claimed to be the largest volcanic crater in the world.

The journey to Mt. Aso starts at Kumamoto, as we take a train along the JR Hohi Line. Ordinary trains run as far as we want to go about every 90 minutes. If you are using a Japan Rail Pass or a *shu-yu-ken*, you can also take one of the three daily *tokkyu* services. These depart from Kumamoto at 8:31, 13:02 and 16:50. The journey takes about an hour to Aso by *tokkyu* or about 90 minutes by ordinary train. If you have a Japan Rail Pass and are using the *tokkyu* service, try asking for seat no. 13A or 13B in car 1 (non-smoking), or, failing that, seat no. 12A or 12B. It seems a fairly ordinary journey, although through pleasant countryside, until you reach Tateno. From here, a line runs ahead to Takamori. It used to be a JR line, and it used to go further than Takamori, joining up with the line which now finishes at Takachiho and continuing all the way to Nobeoka. However, JR first abandoned the middle section of this line and then gave away the two ends to private companies. If you do have time to travel this route, as our plan will suggest later on, taking a bus for the central section, it is very scenic. There is a youth hostel (Murataya Ryokan Hostel) in Takamori. To your surprise, though, unless you have already read this, your train will now reverse direction, and then go forwards once more, to gain height up the hill here. What you should realize is that you are now climbing up the outside of the world's largest volcanic crater and will soon crest its lowest point and descend within. Because the crater is so vast, it is difficult to realize that that is what you are doing, but look around and you will discern the walls of the crater far away in the distance. Only one corner of this huge volcanic area is still active and this is in the direction in which you are now travelling. After another 20 minutes or so, you will come to Aso station, where you should get off the train. There are buses from here to the top of the mountain, but the author's suggestion is that you plan to arrive in the evening and stay at Aso Youth Hostel before ascending the volcano.

There is nothing special about Aso Youth Hostel itself. Like so many hostels, it is a memorable place because of the 'parent' who runs it. In the evening he gives a talk, which lasts for an hour, and shows his own photographs of the mountain in all moods and in all

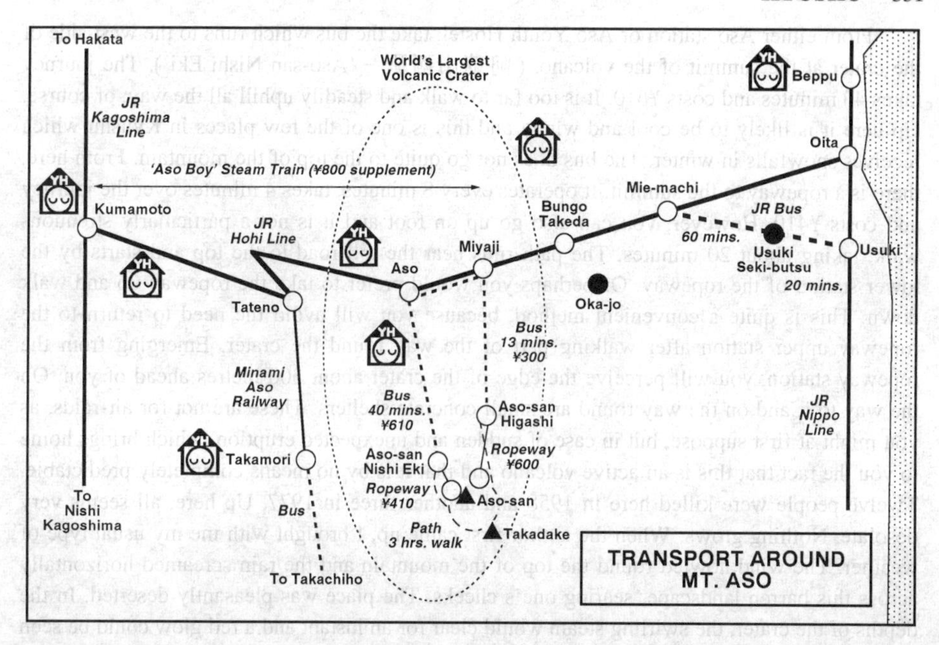


seasons. Now in his late sixties, he has run this hostel for thirty years and knows all there is to know about the volcano in the shadow of which half of his life has been spent. He is not only knowledgeable but also amusing. "Now there is a map in the youth hostel handbook and I have written clearly 'Walk for 16 minutes.' It is 1.3 kilometres. I have measured it carefully. But still once or twice every year I get a telephone call saying, 'This is Aso Central Hospital. We have one of your lost hostellers here.'" As he shows his photographs, he knows where and when every one was taken. "Now this is taken on the third Sunday in October. Come here on the fourth Sunday and all of these flowers will be gone." Even if you cannot understand Japanese, you should enjoy the 50 photographs which he shows, including those of the volcano erupting, and usually there is somebody kind and with sufficient English ability to convey the gist of what is being said, when necessary. The 'parent' has also had ten of his best pictures made into a set of postcards which are on sale at the hostel. He always begins his talk by saying, "I am too old for this job really. It should be done by a young person. Maybe I shall retire soon." Of course, he is quite wrong, so let us hope that he is still there giving his talk, which is famous amongst Japanese hostellers, when you visit.

Now, although you should stay at Aso Hostel and hear this talk, you should also remember that the Hohi Line is famous for being one of the two JR lines to retain a steam service, albeit irregular. The other line is the Yamaguchi Line in Chugoku (western Honshu). The train which runs along the Hohi Line is called 'Aso Boy' and it operates during holiday periods and at weekends in spring, summer and autumn, but not in winter. You will need to check whether it is operating at the time of your visit. When it runs, it leaves Kumamoto at 10:30 and reaches Aso at 12:50. It terminates at Miyaji, two stations further on, at 12:59. The return journey leaves Miyaji at 15:23, passes Aso at 15:34 and reaches Kumamoto at 17:18. 'Aso Boy' is a *kaisoku*, so can be used with any type of ticket. However, all seats are reserved and there is a seat reservation fee of ¥800.

From either Aso station or Aso Youth Hostel, take the bus which runs to the west side of the crater at the summit of the volcano. (阿蘇山西駅 - 'Aso-san Nishi Eki'). The journey takes 40 minutes and costs ¥610. It is too far to walk and steadily uphill all the way, of course. Up here it is likely to be cool and windy and this is one of the few places in Kyushu which receives snowfalls in winter. The bus does not go quite to the top of the mountain. From here, there is a ropeway to the summit. It operates every 8 minutes, takes 4 minutes over the journey and costs ¥410. However, you can also go up on foot and it is not a particularly strenuous walk, taking about 20 minutes. The path runs near the toll road to the top and starts by the lower station of the ropeway. Or perhaps you would prefer to take the ropeway up and walk down. This is quite a convenient method, because you will avoid the need to return to the ropeway upper station after walking part of the way round the crater. Emerging from the ropeway station, you will perceive the edge of the crater about 300 metres ahead of you. On the way to it and on the way round are small concrete shelters. These are not for air-raids, as you might at first suppose, but in case of sudden and unexpected eruption, which brings home to you the fact that this is an active volcano and that it is by no means completely predictable. Twelve people were killed here in 1958 and another three in 1977. Up here, all seems very desolate. Nothing grows. When the author first came up, I brought with me my usual type of weather. The wind howled round the top of the mountain and the rain screamed horizontally across this barren landscape, searing one's cheeks. The place was pleasantly deserted. In the depths of the crater, the swirling steam would clear for an instant and a red glow could be seen just for a second before all disappeared in the mists once more, a real-life witch's cauldron. When I came back in summer, however, the path was crowded with souvenir sellers and sightseers were everywhere. I cherish the first visit, displaying once more the power of nature. There are, in fact, five craters on the summit of the mountain, some more impressive than others. If you walk to your right, you will see the various orifices, all far below. Do not venture too near the edge, because it is a long and steep way down and there is not much to break one's descent. One suspects that it would be rather warm at the bottom too. It is possible to keep going and walk right round in an anti-clockwise direction to the east side of the volcano if you wish. It used to be possible to walk or take a bus in a clockwise direction, which is much easier and shorter, but this route has been closed for some years now. The anti-clockwise route will take about three hours and is not particularly well marked, but common sense says that one just keeps near (but not too near!) to the crater. On the way, you can ascend to the top of Takadake ('High Peak'), which is, reasonably enough, the highest peak in the area (1,522 metres), with only a slight detour, adding perhaps 20 minutes to the walking time. From here, if the weather is fine, as from various other places, you can appreciate the amazing size of this volcanic crater, for far, far away in the distance is the other side. If you feel like walking all the way round, it is reported to be a journey of 128 kilometres in total, so it will take you a while! After admiring the view from here, descend by the same route and then continue to the eastern side of the active crater. It should be said that, although this is not mountain climbing or anything akin to it, it is not just a stroll to be undertaken on the spur of the moment. Particularly after rain, when the author walked round, it is slippery and the volcanic soil tends to give way on the steeper sections. Eventually you will come to another ropeway on the east side. There is not much point in taking it for the descent, especially as there is a good path running beneath it, but if you attempt this walk in the opposite direction you might like to ascend by the ropeway, which costs ¥600 and takes 9 minutes. The service operates every 25 minutes. From the foot of the ropeway (阿蘇山東 – 'Aso-san Higashi'), buses operate to Miyaji station (宮地駅 – ¥300, 13 minutes) and then usually continue to Aso station (阿蘇駅 – ¥420, 26 minutes). There are only three buses per day, however. At the time of writing, they leave Miyaji station for Aso-san Higashi at 9:25, 13:10 (which connects perfectly with the arrival of 'Aso Boy') and 15:45. They return from Aso-san Higashi at 9:40, 13:25 and 16:05. These times are particularly subject to change, so please check them. There are lists of all relevant bus and train times in Aso Youth Hostel.

## BEPPU (別府 – 'Another Municipality') Nippo Line, 2 hrs. 30 mins. from Hakata or 1 hr. 30 mins. from Kokura

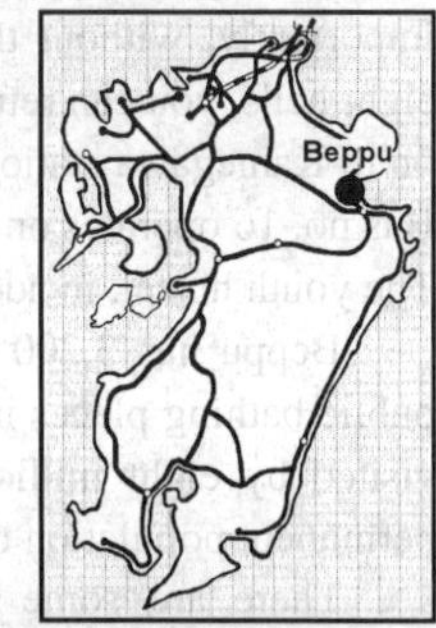


**Derivation of Name:** *Literal. This was a sub-capital of the prefecture.*

Beppu is the largest spa town in Kyushu and it is especially famous for its **hells**, not just one hell, as you might have supposed that there was, but a multitude of them. 'Hell' (*jigoku*) is the name generally given in Japanese to a place where interesting volcanic activity is evident.

To reach Beppu's hells, you need to take a bus no. 2, 7, 15, 16, 17, 20 or 26 to Kannawa (鉄輪), a journey of about 25 minutes from Beppu station or about 15 minutes by bus no. 16 from Kamegawa station, two stops north of Beppu. Although it is very expensive at ¥2,000, if you are going to look at the hells, it is best to buy a ticket which gives admission to eight different locations, which is to say nearly all of them. You can buy this ticket at any one of the eight and it is not difficult to find where to go, at least for the first six, for they are all in the same street and there are plenty of other visitors making their way round. The places, although interesting, are really rather touristy. Each offers its own variation on the theme. You will find, for example, a milky white pool, a green pool, boiling mud, a little zoo of animals which enjoy warm moist conditions, sculptures which can make use of steam, e.g. a dragon with steam issuing from its mouth, eggs boiled in

the natural hot water, fish which like hot water and plants which relish tropical conditions. To find the last two hells, return to the main street, turn left and walk for about 15 minutes. Alternatively, take a bus no. 16 going to Beppu (別府) via Kamegawa station (亀川駅) as far as Chino-ike (血の池). Here you will find, on the right of the road, a blood-red pool and, on the left, a geyser which spouts about every 25 minutes and a lot of people waiting for it to do so. Above the geyser a stone slab has been placed, so it does not spout very far into the air, in fact. Although all of this is interesting, maybe it is worth remarking that in Noboribetsu in Hokkaido, you can see similar volcanic activity without the touristy development and, more importantly, without the ¥2,000 admission charge. When you have finished looking at the eight hells, you can return by taking bus no. 16 in either direction to Beppu (別府) or continue on to Kamegawa station (亀川駅), either by bus no. 16 or on foot (about 25 minutes on foot). Bus no. 16 operates on a circular route and returns to Beppu after calling at Kamegawa station. The youth hostel, incidentally, lies on the route of most buses running from Beppu to Kannawa.

Beppu has 3,200 hot springs and the output of hot water is prodigious. There are 140 public bathing places in the city, apart from all the hotels with their own facilities. The city is visited by eight million people every year, which is not bad for somewhere which has a permanent population of only about 150,000.

There are some other attractions in the city which should be mentioned. On **Mt. Takasaki** is a temple named Manju-ji and 2,000 semi-tame monkeys in a park. Admission to the monkeys costs ¥500. They are happy to accept any refreshments offered.

In the rather pretty bay is anchored the former British ocean-going liner, the **S.S. Oriana**, a vessel of 42,000 tons, admission to which costs ¥2,050, for which price one might expect to be taken for a cruise, but actually the ship is used as a floating museum and restaurant. A voucher obtainable at the youth hostel, or at hotels, will give a discount for admission to the ship.

Then there are **sand baths**. Subterranean volcanic activity heats the sand in certain places and you can be buried and steamed if you wish, an experience which is better than it sounds! When the author last visited Beppu, however, the open-air sand baths were not in operation. There are similar attractions in Ibusuki, in the south of Kyushu, so see under that heading for more details regarding procedure.

There is a ropeway to the top of **Mt. Tsurumi** (1,375 metres) from where a good view of the city can be obtained. However, the ropeway costs ¥700 each way. To reach Mt. Tsurumi, (鶴見山) take a bus no. 32, 33, 36 or 37.

Beppu is easy to reach from the north of Kyushu. *Tokkyu* trains run every half hour from Hakata and Kokura. The journey takes 2½ hours from Hakata or 1½ hours from Kokura. Ordinary trains, however, mostly terminate before reaching Beppu. Only the following departures are available from Kokura to Beppu and Oita:- 5:44, 6:45, 8:20, 11:25, 15:25, 16:25, 16:50 and 18:25. The journey takes about 2 hours 45 minutes by ordinary train. For the return to Kokura, ordinary trains originate in Oita and pass through Beppu at 5:51, 7:15, 10:34, 12:33, 14:33, 16:07, 16:54, 18:06, 18:55 and 20:50 (change at Yanagigaura on the 20:50 only).

However, our plan envisages travelling from Mt. Aso to Beppu. There are three *tokkyu* trains on this route. They leave Aso at 9:28, 13:58 and 17:47 and take 1 hour 50 minutes to reach Beppu. For those using Blue Spring tickets, ordinary trains leave Aso at 6:58 (change at Bungo Takeda), 11:44 (change at Miyaji and Bungo Takeda), 16:02 (change at Miyaji and Bungo Takeda), 18:27 (change at Miyaji) and 20:01 (change at Bungo Takeda). The trains all terminate at Oita, to where it is a journey of about three hours. Trains run frequently between Oita and Beppu, taking 14 minutes.

This too is a very pretty journey and, if you are taking the *tokkyu*, you can again try asking for seat 13A or 13B in car 1. The train continues east across the floor of the volcanic crater to Miyaji, from where it has to begin the ascent over the rim of the volcano. This time it cannot manage without the assistance of a long tunnel cut through the rim and even this tunnel is on a considerable gradient. Just before the tunnel is entered, there is a good view across the huge crater from the left of the train. We are now in the highest area of Kyushu, passing through attractive sparsely populated countryside. This was a difficult line to build and it is a difficult line to keep open, especially as there are few passengers on this central section. Twice in recent years parts of the line have been closed for long periods as a result of weather damage and there is always a fear that they may never be re-opened, but so far the line has survived. Enjoy it while you can.

Near Bungo Takeda are the **ruins of Oka-jo** (Oka Castle). Although you have probably seen plenty of castle ruins by now, these are a little special, for the castle inspired a famous Japanese song, 'Moon over Oka-jo', by Taki Rentaro and the ruins now have a dilapidated beauty, reaching high up the hillside. There will probably be nobody else there. It takes about 30 minutes to walk from the station through the town to these ruins. There are also bus services, but you will still have to walk the harder part of the journey, from the entrance up to the ruins themselves, so it hardly seems worth taking a bus. If you make this stop, there is about an hourly service of trains from Bungo Takeda to Oita.

One more possible diversion on this journey is to see the interesting **stone Buddha carvings** (*seki-butsu*) near the town of Usuki. These Buddhas date from the tenth to twelfth centuries and are in good condition. There are about sixty complete or partial statues in a park and the admission fee is ¥520. To see them, alight from the train at Mie-machi and take a JR bus going to Usuki (臼杵) as far as Usuki Seki-butsu (臼杵石仏). Then, later, continue to Usuki station (臼杵駅), from where there are *tokkyu* trains every hour to Beppu and ordinary trains about every hour to Oita, some of them continuing to Beppu. For holders of a Japan Rail Pass or *shu-yu-ken*, this bus will be free. For Blue Spring users, however, it will cost ¥900, plus another ¥300 when you continue later to Usuki station. There are seven buses per day between Mie-machi and Usuki Seki-butsu. One example of a suitable itinerary is to leave Aso on the 9:28 *tokkyu*, reaching Mie-machi at 10:31. A bus leaves at 11:02 and arrives at Usuki Seki-butsu at 12:01. The next bus to Usuki station is at 13:39, arriving at 13:57. You can take a *tokkyu* at 13:59, reaching Beppu at 14:44.

Oita is the capital of the prefecture of the same name. It is a port and business city, not of great interest to visitors. However, the bay between Oita and Beppu is very pretty.

There is a youth hostel in Beppu, a long uphill walk from the station, so it is best to take a bus (see Youth Hostels section). The hostel is usually crowded and the author found the management not very friendly. Its principal merit is that it has a spa bath, so you can take the waters conveniently. Many visitors from overseas stay here, so you will not be lonely! If you prefer to be more centrally located, however, there are moderately priced hotels in the vicinity of Beppu station.

The Kamenoi Bus Company offers various special tickets, of which the cheapest is the '*mini free ken*' (ミニフリー券) giving free travel within a limited area for one day for ¥900. Other tickets give wider areas and longer periods.

## USA (宇佐 - 'Helpful Soul') Nippo Line, 55 mins. from Kokura

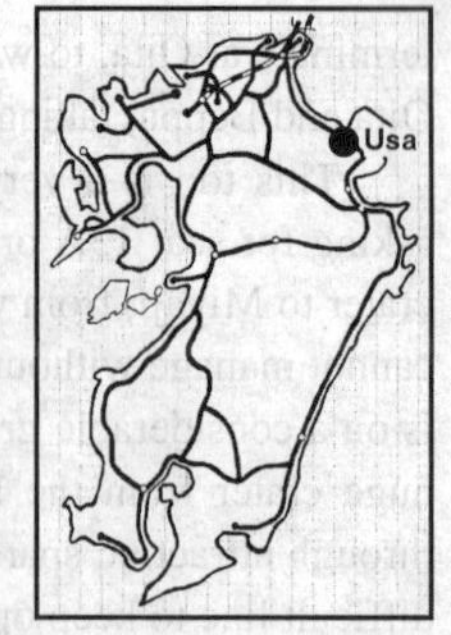


**Derivation of Name:** *Originally 'Isa', which was an old word for sandy land. Over time, corrupted to 'Usa'.*

Usa lies about 40 minutes north of Beppu by *tokkyu*. Departures are twice an hour. By ordinary train, only those services to Kokura mentioned above pass through Usa, the journey there taking an hour. This is a diversion from our main route, but, if you have time, you can visit Usa and Ao-no-domon (see next entry) in a day and then either return to Beppu or continue onwards to rejoin our main route at Hita or Bungo Mori.

The attraction of Usa is its important shrine, named **Usa Hachiman-gu**. It was founded in 725, although the present buildings are later, and is the head shrine of the Hachiman sect of shrines. It is rather a long walk from the station, so you may decide to take a bus, at least one way. The bus destination will be Usa Hachimangu (宇佐八幡宮) and the journey will take 9 minutes and cost ¥230. This is a pretty shrine, worth visiting if you have time. This and Dazaifu (for which see under Fukuoka) are the two most important shrines in Kyushu.

## AO-NO-DOMON (青ノ洞門 - 'Blue Cave Gate')

**Nippo Line to Nakatsu, 40 mins. from Kokura. Then bus, 30 mins.**

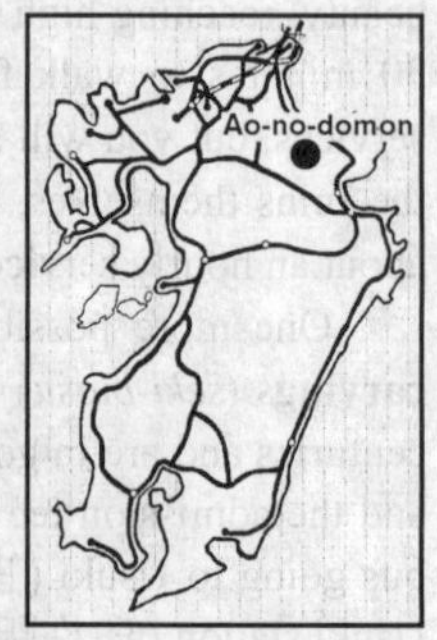


**Derivation of Name:** *Literal. This is the mouth of a tunnel in an area surrounded with greenery, green and blue being equated in Japanese.*

The author came to this place by accident, without knowledge of what was here, and was quite fascinated by the place. I was refused by a youth hostel in Nakatsu because I was a foreigner (incidentally the only time that this has happened and that hostel is now closed) and had to look for an alternative place to stay. Yamaguniya was the nearest alternative, so I came here. Yamaguniya proved to be a very pleasant hostel, a *ryokan* next to the river run by a kindly lady, so you could do much worse than spend the night in this out of the way spot, and just a short walk down the road was Ao-no-domon. **Ao-no-domon** is a tunnel, through which you will pass on the bus, but that part is not the original tunnel. The original lies immediately beside the vehicular section and is used now only by pedestrians. It was constructed by a Buddhist priest, using only a hammer and chisel, as a form of penance which, he hoped, would benefit the community by allowing road access to this little town. The job took thirty years. Inside the original tunnel is a little altar and memorial to the priest.

Here too **Yaba-kei** (Yaba Gorge) begins. You can climb the cliffs beside Ao-no-domon and get a good view, but it gets better later, although never really spectacular. However, if you come to see the tunnel, you should continue and see the gorge as well, even though the buses are expensive. The bus service originates in Nakatsu, taking 30 minutes to reach Ao-no-domon (青ノ洞門) at a cost of ¥580. It then continues to Kakisaka (柿坂), a further 17 minutes, passing through the gorge. On the way, just off the main route, lies a temple named **Rakan-ji** which has 3,770 stone Buddhist images on display. If you alight from the bus at Hon Yaba-kei (本耶馬渓), only three minutes from Ao-no-domon, so you can walk if you prefer, there are four buses per day to Rakan-ji (羅漢寺). Since this also is a short ride (only four minutes), you can walk this section too one or both ways before continuing to Kakisaka. Some buses

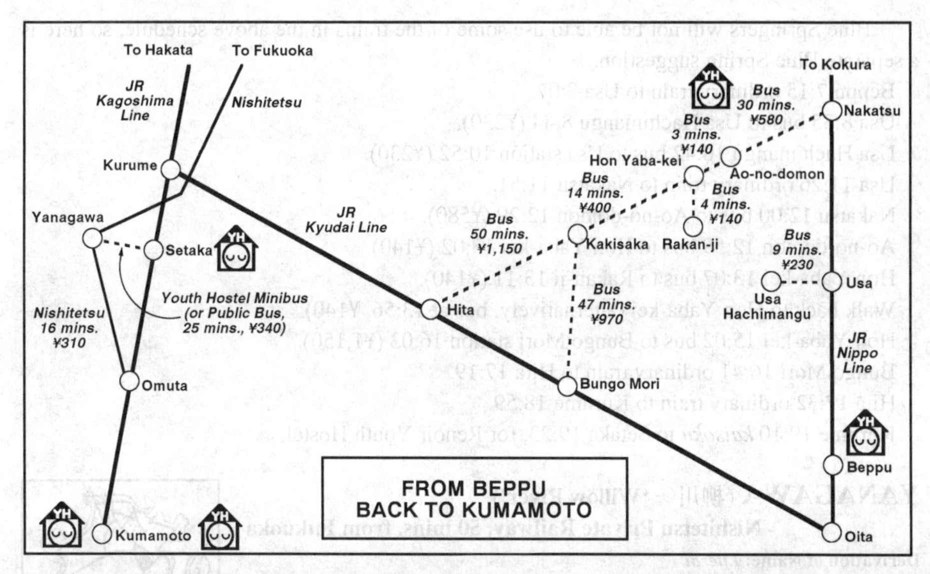


terminate at Kakisaka, while some continue to Hita station ( 日田駅 ) on the Kyudai Line. Others turn left and proceed through **Fuka Yaba-kei** ( 深耶馬渓 – 'Deep Yaba Gorge') to Bungo Mori station ( 豊後森駅 ), also on the Kyudai Line. This is the prettier route and is recommended. At Bungo Mori, we can rejoin the route suggested if this diversion to Usa and Ao-no-domon is not undertaken and proceed westwards. Here is a schedule based on current bus times which would allow this deviation to be made efficiently in a day. However, it would be wise to check the times, as some of the bus services are infrequent.

Beppu 8:44 *tokkyu* to Usa 9:21.

Usa 9:50 bus to Usa Hachimangu 9:59 (¥230).

Usa Hachimangu 10:42 bus to Usa station 10:52 (¥230).

Usa 11:21 *tokkyu* to Nakatsu 11:38.

Nakatsu 11:40 or 12:00 bus to Ao-no-domon 12:09 or 12:29 (¥580).

Ao-no-domon 12:59 bus to Hon Yaba-kei 13:02 (¥140).

Hon Yaba-kei 13:07 bus to Rakan-ji 13:11 (¥140).

Walk back to Hon Yaba-kei (alternatively, bus at 13:56, ¥140).

Hon Yaba-kei 15:02 bus to Bungo Mori station 16:03 (¥1,150).

Bungo Mori 17:26 *tokkyu* to Kurume 18:36. (Caution: this train is seasonal and has only reserved seats. When it is not operating, the following ordinary trains are available – Bungo Mori 16:41 to Hita 17:19. Hita 17:32 to Kurume 18:59.)

Kurume 18:55 ordinary train or 19:10 *kaisoku* to Setaka 19:13 or 19:23, for Renoir Youth Hostel.

The *tokkyu* train listed above from Bungo Mori to Kurume (the train continues to Hakata) is a special train named *Yufuin-no-mori*, of which further details are given in the following section on Yanagawa. This train has all reserved seats, so it must be booked in advance by Japan Rail Pass users and it cannot be used by those with a *shu-yu-ken* unless both the express supplement and the seat reservation charge are paid. Moreover it runs only at certain times of the year. If in doubt, take the ordinary train.

Blue Springers will not be able to use some of the trains in the above schedule, so here is a separate Blue Spring suggestion.

Beppu 7:15 ordinary train to Usa 8:07.
Usa 8:35 bus to Usa Hachimangu 8:44 (¥230).
Usa Hachimangu 10:42 bus to Usa station 10:52 (¥230).
Usa 11:26 ordinary train to Nakatsu 11:51.
Nakatsu 12:00 bus to Ao-no-domon 12:29 (¥580).
Ao-no-domon 12:59 bus to Hon Yaba-kei 13:02 (¥140).
Hon Yaba-kei 13:07 bus to Rakan-ji 13:11 (¥140).
Walk back to Hon Yaba-kei (alternatively, bus at 13:56, ¥140).
Hon Yaba-kei 15:02 bus to Bungo Mori station 16:03 (¥1,150).
Bungo Mori 16:41 ordinary train to Hita 17:19.
Hita 17:32 ordinary train to Kurume 18:59.
Kurume 19:10 *kaisoku* to Setaka 19:23, for Renoir Youth Hostel.

## YANAGAWA (柳川 – 'Willow River')

**Nishitetsu Private Railway, 50 mins. from Fukuoka**

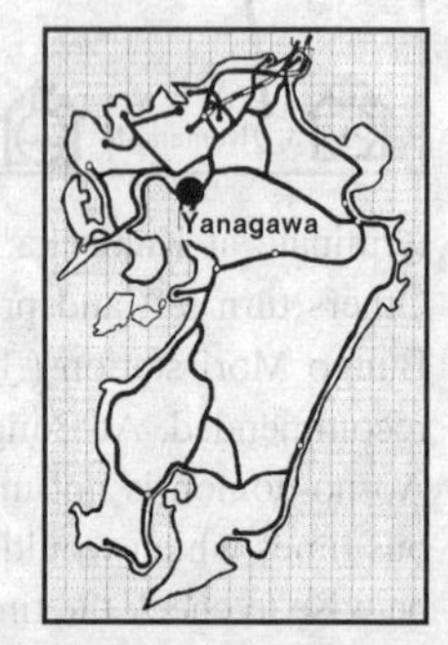


**Derivation of Name:** *Literal.*

Although the route is a slightly convoluted one, we shall now return to the west of Kyushu. We have done things this way in order to travel two pretty railway lines, first the Hohi Line from Kumamoto to Oita and now the Kyudai Line from Oita to Kurume. You can follow the plan above visiting Usa and Ao-no-domon and then looping round to meet the Kyudai Line at Bungo Mori, or, if you have insufficient time, money or interest for that, you can take the rather special *Yufuin-no-mori tokkyu* directly from Beppu. This is a converted diesel railcar with high level seats and, if you are in the front carriage, which you should ask to be, a view out of the front of the train. Food and drink are available on the train. There are two trains per day, one in the morning and one in the afternoon, but they do not run throughout the year, so you must check whether they are available or not. Moreover, they have only reserved seats, so must be booked in advance. Those using a *shu-yu-ken* will not want to take this service, because it will be necessary to pay both express supplement and seat reservation fee. However, Japan Rail Pass holders will probably enjoy the *Yufuin-no-mori* train. Departures from Beppu are at 10:19 and 15:53, according to current timetables. The trains go to Hakata, but we shall get off at Kurume at 12:58 or 18:36.

If you cannot take one of these trains, for one reason or another, then there are two other *tokkyu* services, which always run. These leave Beppu at 8:06 and 13:02, reaching Kurume at 10:42 and 15:39. If you are travelling by ordinary train, departures are from Oita and there are useful services at 7:25 (change at Yufuin and wait 53 minutes there), 12:43 and 13:52 (change at Hita). These trains take some relaxation along the way and complete the journey in four to five hours.

**Yanagawa** is a traditional Japanese town, with pretty river and canals running through it, slightly off the beaten track and worth a visit for that reason. It is served not by JR but by Nishitetsu and is near Renoir Youth Hostel at Setaka. It is suggested, therefore, that you stay at Renoir the night before going to Yanagawa. Renoir Hostel is itself interesting. It is in an old town house with considerable character. Climbing up to the dormitories is an experience. The 'parent' has a great love of Renoir's paintings; hence the hostel's name. You will find Renoirs around the rooms (not originals, the author suspects). After dinner, there is a 'meeting' at which the 'parent' will explain the arrangements which he has made for those who wish to visit Yanagawa. He has obtained discounts for everything you could possibly want to do, from taking a boat ride to having lunch, on production of your youth hostel card. He will also take you to Yanagawa free in the youth hostel minibus in the morning.

From Kurume to Setaka takes only 12 to 20 minutes, depending on the train. *Tokkyu* trains stop at Kurume at 17 and 47 minutes past each hour, but only the ones at 17 minutes past stop at Setaka (at 31 minutes past). There are plenty of ordinary and *kaisoku* trains. When you have finished in Yanagawa, take Nishitetsu south to Omuta (¥310, 16 minutes by the fastest trains) and continue south by JR from there. Even if Yanagawa does not appeal to you, Renoir Youth Hostel is still a pleasant place to stay.

## KIRISHIMA (霧島 – 'Misty Island')

**Kitto Line to Kobayashi, 3 hrs. from Kumamoto. Then bus, 70 mins.**

**Derivation of Name:** *This is an elevated area having the appearance of an island emerging from the clouds wreathed in mist.*

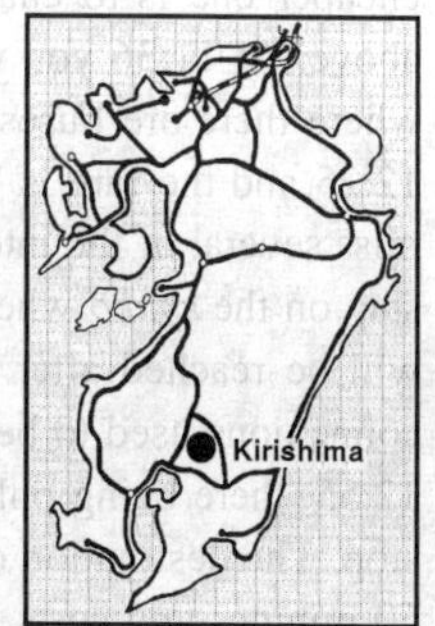


Let us move now to the southern part of Kyushu. There are two routes. One is the Kagoshima Line, which follows the west coast of the island and gives pretty glimpses of the sea. This line passes through Minamata, a city which has become notorious due to 'Minamata Disease', caused by an industrial company discharging its toxic waste into the river and sea whence it found its way into fish which were then eaten by the local inhabitants. Cases involving the resulting disorders of the nervous system are still wending their way slowly and painfully through the legal system. The *tokkyu* trains from Hakata to Kagoshima take this line.

The other route cuts inland from Yatsushiro, a short distance south of Kumamoto and is even more scenic. It is this route, the Hisatsu Line, which is recommended now. There are no *tokkyu* trains on this line, but there are three *kyuko* services every day in each direction between Kumamoto and Miyazaki. They leave Kumamoto at 8:26, 12:40 and 17:09, but, if we want to get to Kirishima, our destination, we had better take the morning service.

Immediately the train leaves the main line at Yatsushiro and starts to go inland, it joins a river called the Kumagawa, beside which it runs for a long time. It is a pretty river and the journey offers a variety of pleasant rural landscapes. There are **boat rides** along this river – shooting the rapids and similar fun – if you want to get off and spend your money. The trips start from the town of Hitoyoshi, the principal centre along this part of the line. The usual boat course starts from a point 20 minutes walk from Hitoyoshi station and lasts for 90 minutes. The cost is ¥2,500 or ¥2,600, depending on the time of year. In summer there are longer, and more expensive, courses available too. In winter the only departure is at 10:00, but in summer boats leave hourly or even more frequently. The boat ride finishes at Watari, two stations back towards Kumamoto.

At Hitoyoshi, the line divides and a branch runs east to Yunomae. This line is now privately operated, but it is another of those lines which used to belong to JR before being given away as being unprofitable.

We now proceed to the most enjoyable part of the line, as the train runs through more desolate country slowly gaining height, to do which it resorts to strategies such as full circles and switch-back stations. As there are few other services here, the express stops at all three stations on this section to Yoshimatsu, the next town of any size. At Yoshimatsu the line divides again. Our train will reverse direction and proceed eastwards to Miyakonojo and Miyazaki. If you are not so interested in the Kirishima National Park, you can stay on board and go to Miyakonojo, where you will arrive at 11:57. At 12:27, there will be a *tokkyu* to Nishi Kagoshima, reaching there at 13:45. Thereby you will reach Kagoshima by a scenic and comfortable route. If you want to get there more quickly, however, change to an ordinary train at Yoshimatsu. You will reach Yoshimatsu at 10:50 and the ordinary train to Hayato leaves at 11:09, arriving there at 12:01. There is an ordinary train from Hayato to Nishi Kagoshima at 12:03, arriving at 12:40.

However, if you want to see **Kirishima National Park**, there are still two choices. The cheaper one is to change at Yoshimatsu to the ordinary train for Hayato as just mentioned above. At 11:36 you will come to Kirishima Nishi Guchi ('Kirishima West Entrance'), from where there are buses to Hayashi-da ( 林田 ), the main town in the park. The next bus is at 12:25 and the fare is ¥480 for a 40 minute journey. However, if you use this route, you will miss several of the interesting volcanic features of the park. Therefore, it is suggested that you stay on the *kyuko* when it changes direction at Yoshimatsu and continue to Kobayashi, which will be reached after another half hour, at 11:22. When the author travelled this route, bus connexions used to be better than they are now, as, unfortunately, you will have to wait until 12:55, there being only four buses a day to Ebino Kogen ( えびの高原 ), which is our next stop. The destination of this bus is Hayashi-da ( 林田 ) and the journey to Ebino Kogen takes 50 minutes and costs ¥950. It is an interesting bus ride, climbing steadily up and up onto the volcanic plateau which is Kirishima.

You will probably know when you have reached **Ebino Kogen** by seeing the steam around. This is one of the areas of Japan known for its volcanic activity. Steam hisses out from the rocks here and there. There are hot pools and, if you walk just a short distance, you will find three small lakes coloured by the minerals through which their water has passed. Even though these three are close together, they are all quite different colours and of vivid hues. At least one can be seen from the bus, but better to get off and explore this area in more depth. You will be able to see the rugged peak of Mt. Karakuni in the background. You will arrive at Ebino Kogen at 13:45 and there are buses on to Hayashi-da at 15:05 and 16:05, a 20 minute journey at a cost of ¥310.

**Hayashi-da** is a small spa, with quite a good view from the little park in its centre. If you have spare time here, you can take the waters, for there is a public spa bath just near the bus station, with a steady stream of people sauntering in and out clutching towels and other necessaries. There is a youth hostel not far away from here at Kirishima Jingu (Kirishima Jingu-mae Hostel). According to the current timetable, the next – and last – bus to there is at 17:25. The destination of the bus is Kagoshima ( 鹿児島 ) and the journey to Kirishima Jingu ( 霧島神宮 ) takes 23 minutes and costs ¥360. If you prefer to go to Kagoshima, the cheap way is to take a bus to Kirishima Nishi Guchi station ( 霧島西口駅 ) and then travel by train, changing at Hayato. There is a bus from Hayashi-da to Kirishima Nishi Guchi at 15:30. However, if cost is no object, both of the buses originating in Ebino Kogen at 15:05 and 16:05 continue to Kagoshima, arriving at Nishi Kagoshima station ( 西鹿児島駅 ) at 16:40 and

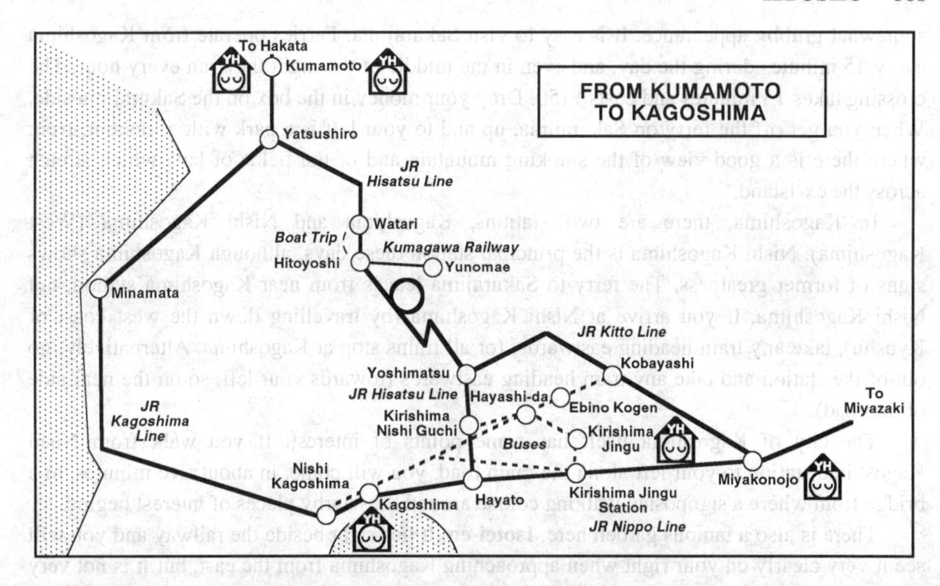


18:27. The fare is ¥1,200 from Hayashi-da or ¥1,500 from Ebino Kogen.

If you stay in Kirishima Jingu-mae Hostel, which has a spa bath, you will also have the chance to look at the nearby **Kirishima Jingu** (Kirishima Shrine), which is stately and imposing and built in a beautiful rustic setting surrounded by tall cedars. Forming an impressive backdrop is the mountain known as **Takachiho-no-mine**. This is an active volcano, with vapour rising from it. The top was blown off some millennia ago, so now it has an irregular, but nonetheless powerful, look. If you want to climb Takachiho-no-mine, you may do so tomorrow. The best starting point is at Takachiho Kawara, to where you may take a bus from Kirishima Jingu at 10:13 (or from Kirishima Jingu station at 10:00). The destination of the bus is Hayashi-da (林田) and the journey to Takachiho Kawara (高千穂河原) takes 24 minutes from Kirishima Jingu (37 minutes from Kirishima Jingu station) and costs ¥300 (or ¥400 from the station). There is only one bus per day, so do not miss it! Note also that the bus does not run in the months of December to February. The climb takes about two hours each way, so you should be back in good time to catch the return bus at 15:21. This bus reaches Kirishima Jingu (霧島神宮) at 15:40 and Kirishima Jingu station (霧島神宮駅) at 15:53. There is a *kaisoku* train to Nishi Kagoshima at 16:05 arriving at 16:58 or a *tokkyu* at 16:24 arriving at 17:14.

## KAGOSHIMA (鹿児島-'Baby Deer Island') Kagoshima Line, 4 hrs. from Hakata, or Nippo Line, 7 hrs. from Kokura

**Derivation of Name:** *Many fawns used to live here.*

Kagoshima is dominated by the active volcano of **Sakurajima**. 'Sakurajima' means 'cherry blossom island' and this used to be an island until the eruption of 1914, but then the enormous flow of lava was sufficient to connect the island to the mainland on the side farther from Kagoshima. Not only is Sakurajima still active, but it is still emitting a constant stream of fine ash which often gives Kagoshima a somewhat grubby appearance. It is easy to visit Sakurajima. Ferries operate from Kagoshima every 15 minutes during the day, and even in the middle of the night they run every hour. The crossing takes 13 minutes and costs ¥150. Drop your money in the box on the Sakurajima side. When you get off the ferry on Sakurajima, up and to your left is a park with a lookout, from where there is a good view of the smoking mountain and of the fields of lava which stretch across the ex-island.

In Kagoshima, there are two stations, Kagoshima and Nishi Kagoshima (West Kagoshima). Nishi Kagoshima is the principal station these days, although Kagoshima shows signs of former greatness. The ferry to Sakurajima leaves from near Kagoshima station, not Nishi Kagoshima. If you arrive at Nishi Kagoshima (by travelling down the west coast of Kyushu), take any train heading eastwards, for all trains stop at Kagoshima. Alternatively, go out of the station and take any tram heading eastwards (towards your left, so on the near side of the road).

The city of Kagoshima itself has some points of interest. If you walk from Nishi Kagoshima station to your left along the main road, you will come, in about five minutes, to a bridge from where a signposted walking course around the nearby places of interest begins.

There is also a famous garden here, **Isotei-en**. It lies right beside the railway and you will see it very clearly on your right when approaching Kagoshima from the east, but it is not very near a station. Kagoshima City Bus Company operates a special sightseeing bus every half hour which will take you there, as well as to other places of interest in the city. This bus is called the Kagoshima City View bus and it can be taken from outside Nishi Kagoshima station (also from Kagoshima station). The fare is ¥160 per ride. The garden dates from the seventeenth century and is next to the sea with a good view of Sakurajima across the water.

Other places to which you can be taken by the Kagoshima City View bus include **Shiroyama**, where the ruins of a castle are to be found and there is another good view of Sakurajima. The castle was built in 1602, but destroyed in 1877 after Saigo Takamori, who has been mentioned before, you will recall, retreated here following his unsuccessful siege of Kumamoto castle. The Satsuma rebels were no more successful here and Mr. Saigo was forced to commit suicide in a nearby cave which is another of the stops on the bus route.

Kagoshima still has two tram routes left. One runs from Kagoshima station west to just short of Taniyama station on the JR Ibusuki Makurazaki Line. This is route no. 1. Route no. 2 starts from Kagoshima station and runs via Nishi Kagoshima station to Korimoto, where it meets route 1 again and terminates. A one-day ticket (一日乗車券 - '*ichi-nichi jo-sha-ken*') is offered for Kagoshima city buses and trams for ¥500.

If you want a different view of Sakurajima, there are JR buses, free to holders of a Japan Rail Pass or *shu-yu-ken*, which run to the peninsula from Kokubu station. Kokubu is on the Nippo Line about 45 minutes by ordinary train or 30 minutes by *tokkyu* east of Kagoshima. It is one stop east of Hayato and one stop west of Kirishima Jingu. Direct buses leave Kokubu for Sakurajima port (桜島港) at 12:03 and 17:23 and leave Sakurajima port for Kokubu (国分) at 9:37 (final destination Kagoshima Airport (鹿児島空港 - 'Kagoshima Kuko')) and 11:11. At other times, it is necessary to change buses at Sakurajima Guchi (桜島口), but connexions are usually good. Total journey time is 80 minutes and there are good views of the volcano.

There is a youth hostel on Sakurajima. The hostel is a rather ordinary one, but it feels quite exciting to be sleeping on the side of an active volcano!

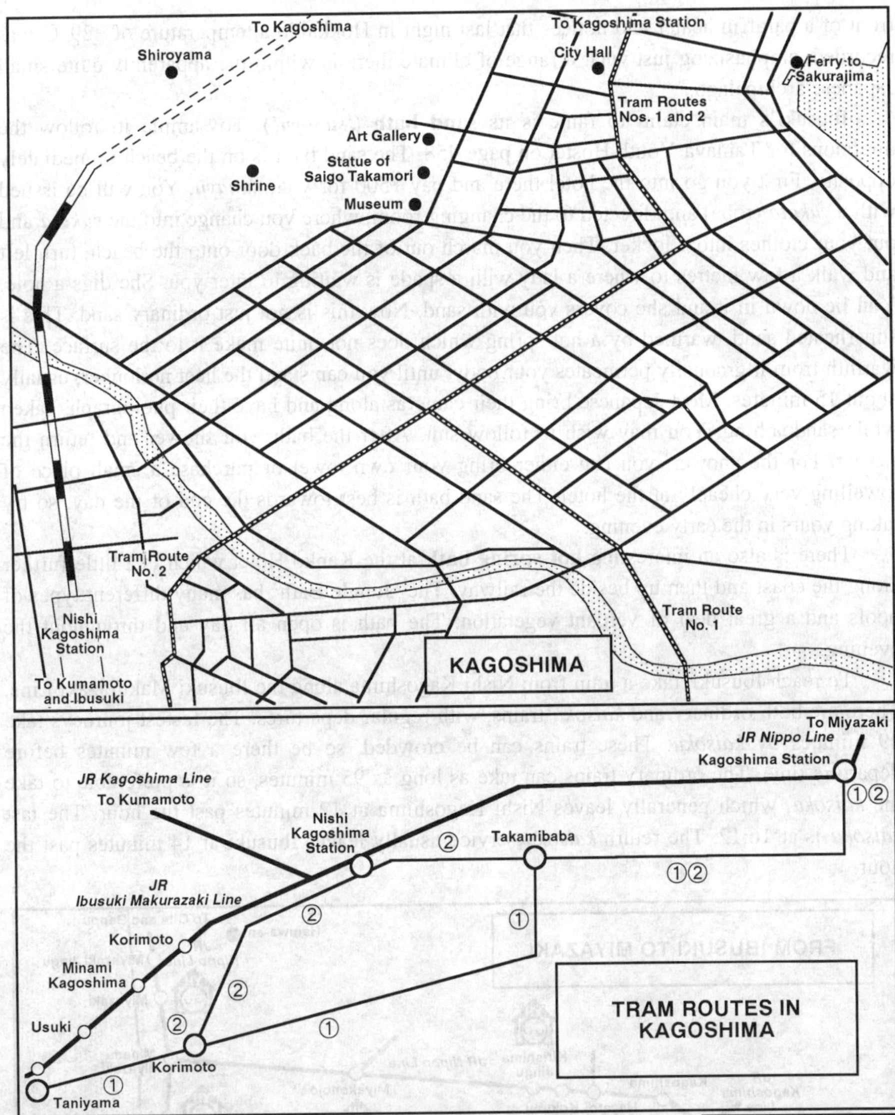


## IBUSUKI (指宿 – 'Pointing Out Lodging Place')

### Ibusuki Makurazaki Line, 1 hr. from Nishi Kagoshima

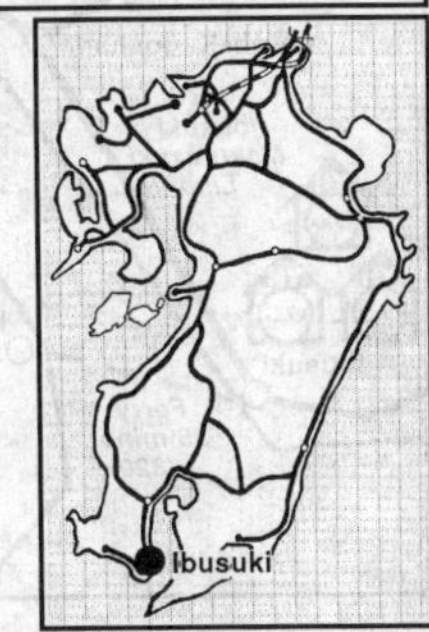


**Derivation of Name:** *Originally 'Yabusuki', meaning 'lodging place with abundant hot water', Ibusuki being a spa resort.*

Ibusuki is another spa town, but a rather likeable one. Since it is one of the southernmost towns on the main islands of Japan, it is comparatively warm. When the author was last there, in November, there was no need of more than a shirt (well, trousers too, to be decent), whereas now, in Tokyo in December, he is none too warm in front of a paraffin heater and notices that last night in Hokkaido a temperature of -29 ℃ was recorded, emphasizing just what a range of climate there is within the apparently quite small Japanese archipelago.

Ibusuki's main claim to fame is its **sand bath** ('*sunayu*'). To sample it, follow the directions for Tamaya Youth Hostel on page 458. The sand bath is on the beach immediately opposite. First you go into the hotel there and pay ¥500 for your *sunayu*. You will be issued with a *yukata* (robe) and directed to the changing room, where you change into the *yukata* and put your clothes into a locker. Then you march out of the back door onto the beach, turn left and walk a few metres to where a lady with a spade is waiting to inter you. She digs a hole. You lie down in it and she covers you with sand. Now this is not just ordinary sand. This is superheated sand, warmed by a hot spring which does not quite make it to the surface. The warmth from it gradually permeates your body, until you can stand the heat no longer, usually about 15 minutes. Most Japanese bring their cameras along and have their photographs taken while sandbathing. You may wish to follow suit. After the bath, you shower and return the *yukata*. For the shower, you can either bring your own towel or purchase a small piece of towelling very cheaply at the hotel. The sand bath is best towards the end of the day, so try taking yours in the early evening.

There is also an interesting **hot spring bath** at the Kanko Hotel which is a little further along the coast and then up beside the railway. The 'Jungle Bath' has many different types of pools and a great deal of verdant vegetation. The bath is open all day and throughout the evening.

To reach Ibusuki, take a train from Nishi Kagoshima along the Ibusuki Makurazaki Line. There are both ordinary and *kaisoku* trains, with regular departures. The fastest journeys take 49 minutes by *kaisoku*. These trains can be crowded, so be there a few minutes before departure time. The ordinary trains can take as long as 95 minutes, so it is preferable to take the *kaisoku*, which generally leaves Nishi Kagoshima at 12 minutes past the hour. The last *kaisoku* is at 16:12. The return *kaisoku* service usually leaves Ibusuki at 14 minutes past the hour.

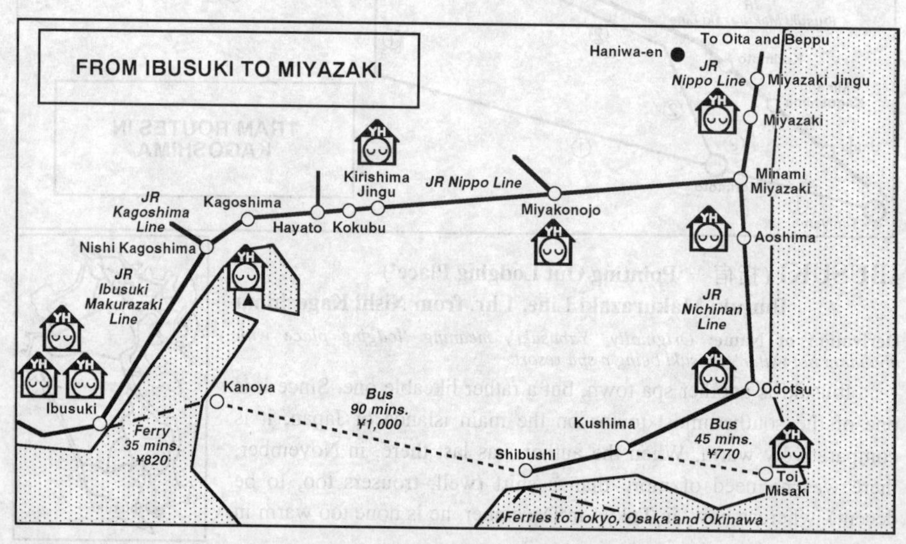

Ibusuki is not the end of the line. Services continue to Makurazaki, as you might have guessed from the name of the line. They used to go further, but amputation was performed some while ago now. Only six trains per day go as far as Makurazaki, but if you do go further than Ibusuki you will see an attractive volcano named **Kaimon-dake**.

There are three youth hostels in Ibusuki, although the author has never yet succeeded in getting Ibusuki Hostel to answer the telephone. Yunosato is a pleasant hostel. The author was the only hosteller when I stayed there and the 'parent', after explaining the night before that he might not manage to do so, very kindly got up at 6:00 to see me off. The hostel is new, clean and friendly and can be recommended.

## NICHINAN (日南 - 'South Sun')

**Nichinan Line, 2 hrs. from Miyazaki**

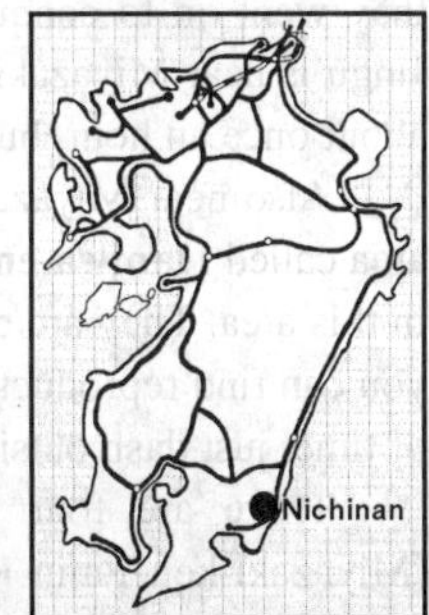


**Derivation of Name:** *The 'nichi' of this name uses the same Chinese character as the 'hyu' of Hyuga nearby, while 'nan' means south. This was the southern part of Hyuga Province.*

Nichinan is the name of an area, not a town. It is the south-eastern part of Kyushu. The simple way to move there from Ibusuki in the south-west is to return to Kagoshima and then take a train to Miyazaki (or Minami Miyazaki - South Miyazaki), from where the Nichinan Line starts. Here is the ideal schedule for the journey. Take the 8:04 ordinary train from Ibusuki to Nishi Kagoshima, where it arrives at 9:34. At exactly the same time another train will pull into the station bound for Miyazaki. Although it will not leave until 9:55, go and find your seat now and then look for your breakfast, if necessary. This train is a *kaisoku* and it will reach Minami Miyazaki at 12:12. Do not waste any time, for a Nichinan Line train will be just arriving at another platform to your right. It leaves at 12:14 (but do not panic, because it is a connexion). This train too is a *kaisoku*. It will reach Odotsu at 13:25, Kushima at 14:10 and Shibushi, at the end of the line, a port from which ferries run to Tokyo (on Sunday nights only), Osaka and Okinawa, at 14:31. If you have a suitable ticket and would prefer a higher degree of comfort for part of the journey, leave Ibusuki on the 7:49 ordinary train, which reaches Nishi Kagoshima at 9:07, and then take the 9:15 *tokkyu* to Miyazaki. It will reach there at 11:23. The *kaisoku* along the Nichinan Line leaves Miyazaki at 12:10.

However, for the adventurous, here is a more exciting (and more expensive!) route which avoids returning along the same line, for, as you should realize by now, the author always likes to avoid going back the same way. Stroll down to the harbour at Ibusuki and at 9:40 you will find a ferry leaving for Kanoya. It sails from the pier which extends quite a long way into the sea at the end of a parking area. The voyage lasts 35 minutes and costs ¥820. From Kanoya port, a short walk will bring you to a road along which buses run. You want a bus going to Shibushi (志布志). They run about every half hour and the fare is ¥1,000. The journey takes approximately 90 minutes so you will arrive in good time to take the 13:27 train to Miyazaki, alighting somewhere along the railway line if you prefer to stay on the Nichinan coast.

The **Nichinan coast** is semi-tropical, with waving palm trees beside sandy beaches, not the sort of place which appeals to the author too much, actually, because I cannot swim! From the train you get glimpses, but you really need to get off if you want to experience this area properly. Near Miyazaki, **Aoshima** is famous for its 'Devil's Washing Board' piece of upturned rock with the strata running diagonally instead of horizontally. Aoshima ('Blue

Island') is, in fact, what its name suggests, a small island covered with trees. It is now connected with the mainland by a causeway on top of the Devil's Washing Board so that it is accessible at all times, not just at low tide. There is a pleasant shrine on the island. Nearby is Aoshima Youth Hostel. Further down the coast, it is less touristy and **Toi Misaki**, in particular, is quite a wild area, where horses roam freely.

The city of Miyazaki has a shrine named **Miyazaki Jingu** where the author's namesake, Jimmu, the first Emperor of Japan, is enshrined. He lived a while ago (660 B.C.) and not much is known about him. Indeed, it is not even certain whether he really existed. However, the people of whom he was reputedly the leader, the Yamato, certainly lived in this area before they went on to conquer almost the whole of present-day Japan. Not surprisingly, Miyazaki Jingu is near Miyazaki Jingu station, which is one stop north of Miyazaki. Ordinary trains run about once an hour, but *tokkyu* and *kaisoku* trains do not stop there.

Also near Miyazaki Jingu station is a park called Heiwa Koen and within the park is an area called **Haniwa-en**. Here there is a collection of clay figures from old burial mounds found in this area. They are quite interesting and appealing, but, if you do not have time to visit here, you can find reproductions in other locations around the city and nearby. If you are really short of time, just dash outside Miyazaki station and there are some there!

There are four youth hostels in this area. There is one in the city of Miyazaki (Miyazaki-ken Fujin Kaikan Hostel), another just six stations away on the Nichinan Line at Aoshima (Aoshima Hostel), a third near Odotsu station on the same line (Nichinan Kaigan Hostel) and the last at Toi Misaki (Cape Toi) with the wild horses (Toi Misaki Hostel). Each location mentioned is a little more remote than the one preceding it.

## TAKACHIHO (高千穂 - 'High Thousand Ears of Grain')

**Nippo Line to Nobeoka, 3 hrs. 45 mins. from Kokura.**

**Then Takachiho Line, 90 mins.**

**Derivation of Name:** *The shape of the mountain nearby was supposed to resemble a pile of a thousand ears of rice stacked up (doubtful).*

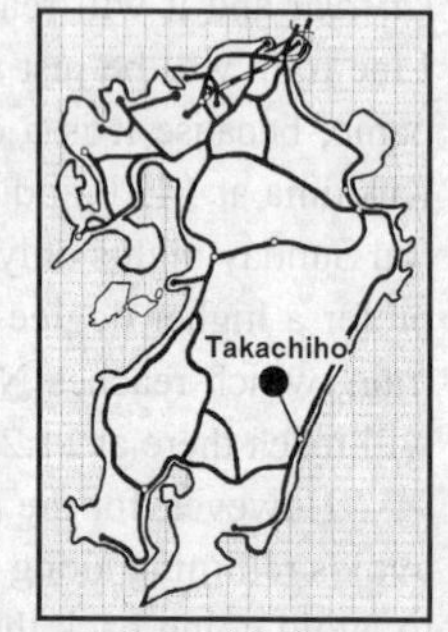


Takachiho is famous for its **gorge** which is a short distance from the town of the same name. This is a very pretty area, but the problem is that it is a little difficult and expensive to reach. From Miyazaki, proceed northwards until you reach Nobeoka. This takes 65 minutes by *tokkyu*, about 80 minutes by *kaisoku* or 1 hour 45 minutes by ordinary train. *Tokkyu* departures are generally at 20 minutes past each hour from Minami Miyazaki and 24 minutes past from Miyazaki. *Kaisoku* or ordinary trains also run approximately hourly. On the way north from Miyazaki look out of the right of the train and you will see the test track for the new **magnetically levitated train system** capable of extremely high speeds which is currently under development by the JR Group here. The track is 10 kilometres long. If you are lucky, you may see one of the experimental trains, but the author has had that privilege only once. On this test track speeds in excess of 400 kilometres per hour have been achieved.

The line from Nobeoka north-west to Takachiho is the lower end of what used to be a JR line from Tateno to Nobeoka. This line has been mentioned previously in the section on Mt. Aso. JR first abandoned the central section, then gave away the two ends to private enterprise. So now the Takachiho Private Railway operates the line, and charges the high price of ¥1,300 for travel along its 50 kilometres. Trains run about every 70 minutes and the journey takes approximately 90 minutes. It is a pretty line, although, as it gets near Takachiho, there are some long tunnels. As you emerge from the last of these, just before Amano Iwato station, three minutes before reaching Takachiho, there is a particularly famous and impressive high bridge. Takachiho station is a few minutes walk from the town. When you have climbed up to the road from the station, turn right and head downhill. Going in the opposite direction it took rather longer than the author had expected and I was fortunate that the station staff saw me coming and held the train for me. It is a walk of about 10 minutes down or 15 minutes up.

There are two youth hostels in Takachiho – Takachiho Hostel and Yamatoya Hostel. Yamatoya Hostel is near **Takachiho Shrine**, which is also worth visiting. Takachiho Hostel is very near Amano Iwato station.

Having paid to get this far from JR territory, rather than return by the same route, which you should know by this time that the author dislikes, when you have finished in Takachiho you can take a bus on to Takamori (高森), from where the Minami Aso Private Railway will return you to the JR Hohi Line at Tateno. Buses run to Takamori about every two hours and cost ¥1,280 for the 85 minute ride. It is another pretty, twisting, rural route. When the author travelled through here, I was the only passenger for most of the journey and thoroughly enjoyed the trip through the hills in the early morning mist. There is a youth hostel in Takamori too, if you need somewhere to stay in this small town. Murataya Ryokan is a Japanese-style hotel which also accepts hostellers.

From Takamori, the journey to Tateno takes 30 minutes in a diesel railcar. Trains run about every hour. Again there are pretty views and the train travels slowly at the appropriate moments, so that you can enjoy them. The driver gives a commentary as you go along (in Japanese, though, of course, but just look the same way as everybody else). From Tateno, JR will take you back to Kumamoto in about 45 minutes, or on to Oita and Beppu in just over 2 hours by *tokkyu* or about 4 hours by ordinary train, if you prefer.

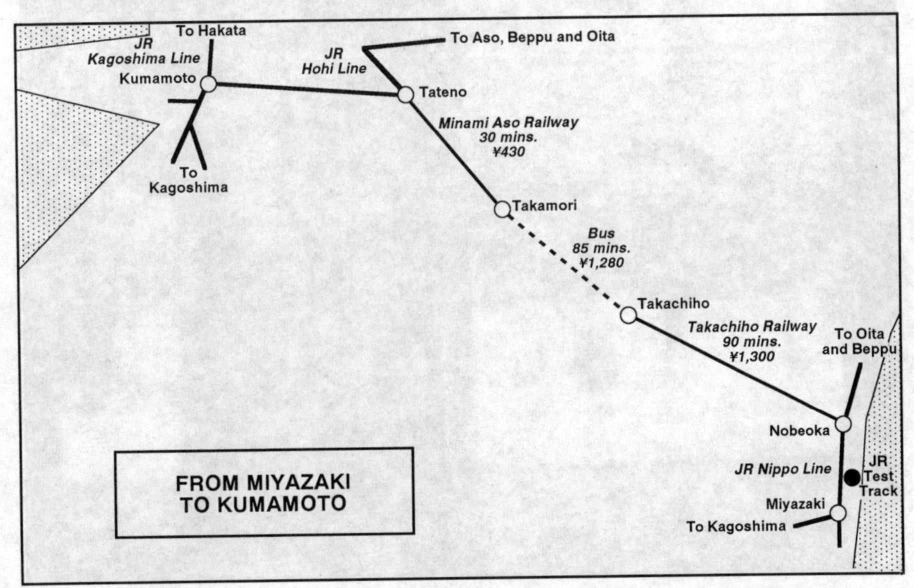

Well, that is our tour of Kyushu completed. Where will you go next? If you want to continue south to Okinawa, you need to go back to Kagoshima. From Kumamoto, you can take the coastal route by the Kagoshima Line this time, if you travelled inland before, as suggested. *Tokkyu* trains run hourly, mostly at 37 minutes past the hour, and take 2 ½ hours to reach Nishi Kagoshima. Or, if you travelled round the coast before, why not go inland via the scenic Hisatsu Line for this journey?

Or perhaps you are returning to Honshu to finish off our Chugoku plan. This is not a bad stage at which to be finishing a Japan Rail Pass either. Remember that there is a night *tokkyu* with relatively comfortable seats which runs from Nishi Kagoshima via Kumamoto and Hakata to Shin Osaka. Then you can spend a couple of days or more looking at Kyoto and the surrounding area without having to worry about your pass ticking away. You are allowed to take this train on the last night of your pass, even though the pass has expired by the time that you arrive in the morning. Timings are 19:05 from Nishi Kagoshima, 22:33 from Kumamoto and 00:11 from Hakata. Arrival in Shin Osaka is at 9:26. Even if you want to get on at Hakata, if this is the last night of your pass, remember to book from an earlier station, as it is after midnight when the train reaches Hakata, so the pass is not valid for travel from there. There is also a train from Nagasaki via Tosu and Hakata to Kyoto. Timings are 19:50 from Nagasaki, 22:03 from Tosu and 22:28 from Hakata. Arrival in Kyoto is at 7:59.

**Dazaifu Shrine, Kyushu**

# SOUTH TO OKINAWA (沖縄)
## 'Open Sea Rope'

From the south of Kyushu, a group of islands stretches further southwards. These are the Nansei Islands, the word meaning, reasonably enough, the 'south-west' islands. They are regarded as part of Kyushu until one reaches Okinawa, which is a separate prefecture. The further one goes, the more different the character of these islands seems from that of the rest of Japan. That is reasonable enough, too, for they have had much more foreign influence. Naha, the capital of Okinawa, is as close to Taiwan as it is to the southern tip of Kyushu and at one time Okinawa was claimed by both China and Japan.

***Transportation and Tickets***

If you are leaving Japan, this is an interesting way to go. There are ferries to Naha and from there one can take the twice weekly ship to Taiwan. From Kaohsiung another ferry operates to Macau, whence to Hong Kong by launch, or into or through China. Cheap air tickets are available in Hong Kong, of course.

However, if this is just a visit, then it is going to be an expensive one, unfortunately, although transportation is readily available. Ferries run to Okinawa from Tokyo, Osaka, Kobe, Hakata, Shibushi and Kagoshima. From Tokyo, ferries sail directly to Naha on Saturdays at 15:00, arriving at 14:00 on Mondays, and at 18:20 on Wednesdays they sail to Naha with two stops *en route*, arriving at 6:00 on Saturdays. The single fare by either route is ¥19,670. Sometimes a small discount is available for youth hostel members. Return voyages leave Naha at 12:00 on Wednesdays and 19:00 on Saturdays, arriving in Tokyo at 9:30 on Fridays and 7:30 on Tuesdays. From Osaka and Kobe, departures are about four times per week. The fare is ¥15,450.

Most popular, however, are the routes from Kagoshima. Some ferries go directly to Naha, leaving Kagoshima at 17:00 and arriving next day at 14:00, while others make some calls on the way, leaving Kagoshima at 18:00 and arriving in Naha at 18:40 the next day. Sailings on the latter route are daily and on the former about every three days. The fare is ¥11,840. The nearest islands to Kyushu are served by a different ferry service, which is daily, but these islands are not so popular with visitors.

One can also fly to Okinawa, but the single fare is ¥34,900 (¥63,000 return) from Tokyo or ¥21,050 (¥38,060 return) from Kagoshima, which is not within the budget of most of us.

There are bus services on the islands, but no railways south of Kyushu. Therefore, interesting tickets are unavailable for this part of Japan and the buses are quite expensive, a factor which tends to limit explorations.

## TANEGASHIMA (種子島 – 'Seedy Island')

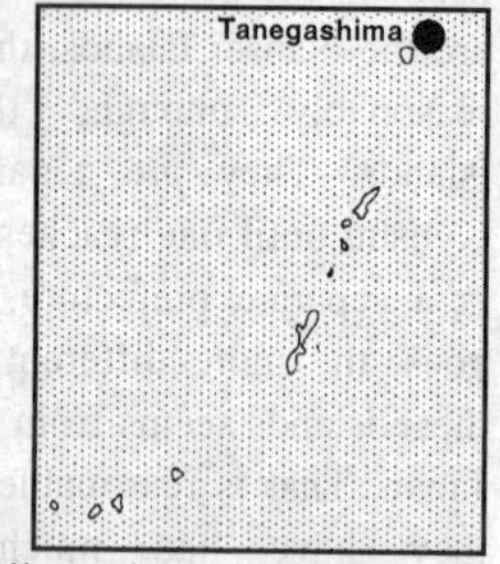


**4 hrs. from Kagoshima by ferry**

**Derivation Of Name:** *There was a legend that the first gods came to this place and planted rice seeds here.*

The nearest of the Nansei islands to Kyushu is called Tanegashima. The island has become famous recently because it is the site from which Japan's **space rockets** are launched. It can be reached by ferry from Kagoshima for the sum of ¥2,500. Ferries leave at 8:30 every day and sometimes there is also an afternoon service at 14:00. The journey takes four hours. There is also a jet-foil service which operates between two and four times per day, depending on the season. It takes two hours and costs ¥5,500. Sometimes one of the jet-foil services calls at Ibusuki on the way. You can also fly to Tanegashima for ¥6,400 (¥11,520 return). There are five flights per day from Kagoshima and the journey time is 40 minutes. There is a bus service from one end of the island to the other, taking 85 minutes and costing ¥1,450 if you travel all the way. The bus company also offers a three-day ticket (フリー三日乗車券 – '*free mika jo-sha-ken*') for ¥3,500.

## OKINOERABU (沖永良部 – 'Open Sea Long Good Part')

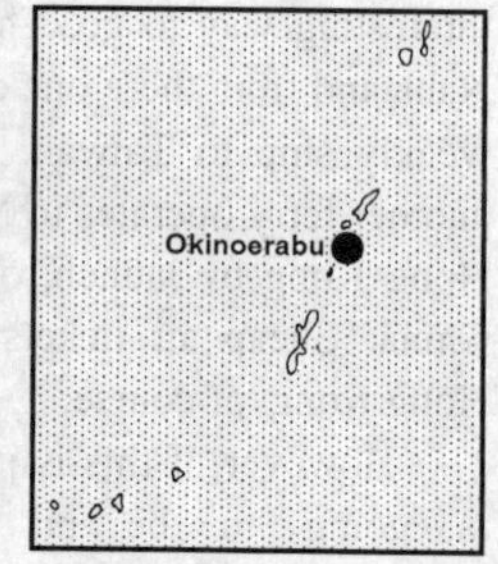


**18 hrs. from Kagoshima by ferry**

**Derivation Of Name:** *Unknown.*

Much further down the chain of islands lies Okinoerabu, a pleasant island to visit and one which has a youth hostel. The town where the ferry calls, which is not very big, is Wadomari (和泊). There is accommodation there, but, if you want to go to Okinoerabu Youth Hostel, walk into the town (to your left from the harbour) and catch a bus for Cheena (知名) as far as Furusato, a journey of 4½ kilometres taking about 15 minutes. The bus makes some detours on the way. Buses run about every 90 minutes. The youth hostel is inconspicuous, perched on the cliff top above a secluded beach. The 'parents' also run a café which is round the back and cannot be seen from the road. The hostel has seen better days, but the 'parents' are kind and pleasant and when the author was here there were hostellers who said that they came back every year because they liked the place so much. There are some pleasant spots to visit further down the island and these can be reached by bicycle or by bus and then on foot. The youth hostel will provide details. Okinoerabu is not a touristy island, so may appeal to those who want to visit somewhere quiet with a beach and a gentle pace of life.

Okinoerabu can be reached in 18 hours on the ferry to Okinawa which leaves Kagoshima at 18:00 every evening. There is another ferry which generally operates on Mondays and Wednesdays only, leaving Kagoshima at 17:20 and reaching Cheena (not Wadomari) at 14:20 on Tuesdays and Thursdays. Check the days of operation, however, as they may vary seasonally. The fare by either ferry is ¥9,890 from Kagoshima. Stopping off on the way to Okinawa does not add much to the total fare to there.

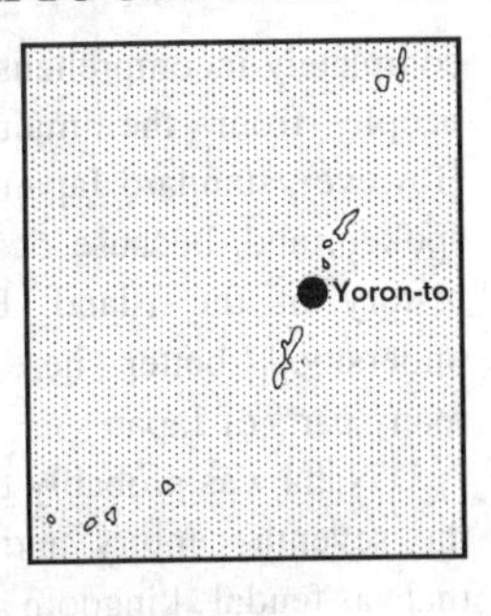


## YORON-TO (与論島 – 'Giving Discussion Island')

**20 hrs. from Kagoshima by ferry**

**Derivation Of Name:** *Unknown.*

Yoron-to is a much smaller island than Okinoerabu. It is the most southerly place in Kagoshima prefecture and is next stop for the ferry on the way down the string of islands to Okinawa. From Okinoerabu, it takes two hours. From Kagoshima, it is a voyage of 20 hours at a cost of ¥10,710. Yoron-to is more touristy than Okinoerabu, but still a relatively quiet little island with golden beaches and not much to disturb the tranquility.

There is a youth hostel here too – Yoron-to Takakura-so Hostel. It is quite a long walk from the port, or, at least, it seemed so in the heat of mid-summer. When the author visited, there were three hostellers staying and after dinner the jovial 'parent' produced a very large bottle of alcohol and insisted that everybody have a good drink first and then tell us all about himself. The reward was another drink. This procedure continued until the bottle was empty. I know not what was in the bottle, but I had a terrible headache the next day. The 'parent', however, seemed unaffected.

From the youth hostel, it is only about ten minutes walk to the beach, which is extensive and almost deserted, although there were signs of resort construction, so it may not always remain so. There is a bus on the island (only one!) and it circumnavigates almost the entire territory, either clockwise or anti-clockwise, about once an hour. The author was assured that the direction of travel does not depend entirely on the whim of the driver, but that there is a timetable. The fare is ¥500. Unfortunately, though, the bus does not go to the port. If one feels sufficiently energetic, one can, in fact, walk right round the island in a leisurely day or an athletic half day. Many people will like this island, compact and convenient and with beautiful beaches.

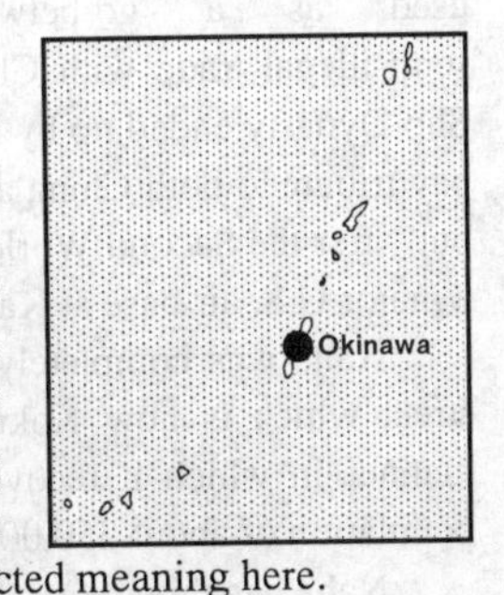


## OKINAWA (沖縄 – 'Open Sea Rope')

**2 days from Tokyo or 1 day from Kagoshima by ferry**

**Derivation Of Name:** *Originally 'Okinaba', meaning 'open sea fish place', but became corrupted to Okinawa.*

Okinawa can mean three different things. Most extensively, it is the name of a prefecture which includes all of the Japanese territory south of Yoron-to. Secondly, it can mean the group of islands extending as far south as Kume Island, but not including Miyako, Ishigaki or Iriomote. Thirdly, it is the name of the main island of the group just mentioned. We shall use it in the most restricted meaning here.

Okinawa is possibly most famous as the site of the final major struggle of the Second World War in April to June 1945. Most of the island was devastated by the Battle of Okinawa which took place in its southern part, although some communities in the north survived relatively unscathed. When Japan lost this battle, it had lost the war and, as a result, there are many memorials to those who killed themselves here knowing that the end had come. However, the present-day Okinawa has few obvious signs of the conflict which took place half a century ago.

Although the people of Okinawa are Japanese, there is a language spoken here which is completely incomprehensible to the people from the main islands. However, standard Japanese is also spoken, and, because of the recent history of the island, English is understood better here than in many parts of Japan.

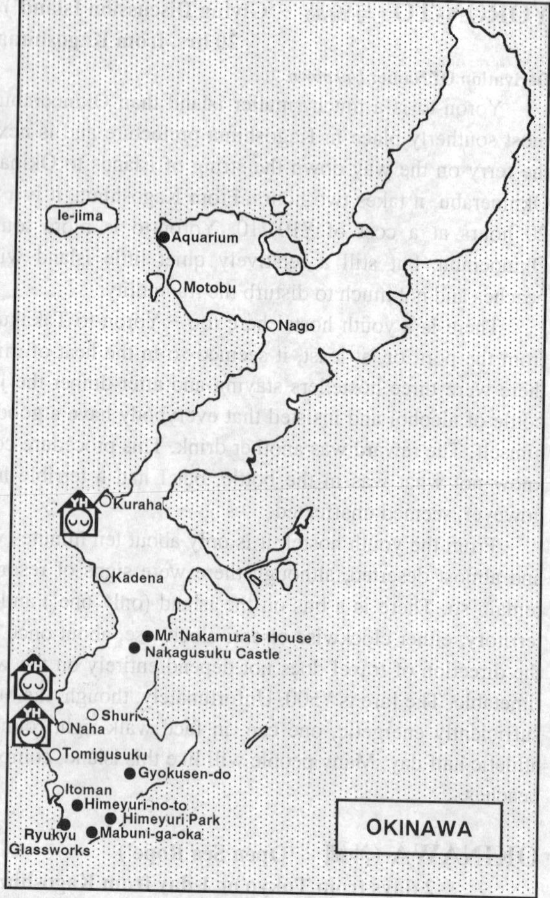


Naha was probably founded in the seventh century and it seems that a feudal kingdom was first established here in the twelfth century. In the fourteenth century Okinawa started to pay tribute to the Ming Dynasty in China. At the beginning of the fifteenth century, King Sho-hashi unified the kingdom, established his headquarters in Shuri and set up the Sho Dynasty whose rule lasted until the nineteenth century. The peak of prosperity was reached under King Sho-shin in the sixteenth century. In 1609 Okinawa was conquered by the Satsuma forces from Kyushu, but not annexed. Instead the kingdom was used as a go-between in semi-illegal trade with China. The Sho Dynasty ended up by having to pay tribute to both China and the Satsumas. In 1879, Okinawa became officially part of Japan, but, after the Second World War, it was occupied by the United States until 1972. There is still a major U.S. air base at Kadena on the island.

Naha was completely destroyed during the war, but was rebuilt as a shanty town. The street which is now Kokusai Dori was nicknamed 'The Miraculous Mile' because of the manner in which it recovered rapidly from its destruction in the war. The city now has a population of about 350,000.

Naha has three ports. The stopping ferry from Kagoshima arrives at the port conveniently located in the centre of the city, but the direct service from Kagoshima and the ferries from Tokyo, Osaka, Kobe and Taiwan, arrive at the 'New Port', quite a long way from where most people want to go. If you arrive there, you need to take bus no. 101 to get to the city. Buses run about every 20 minutes.

The ferry from Kagoshima to Naha departs from the 'New Port' in Kagoshima too. It is not close to either Kagoshima or Nishi Kagoshima station, but a bus can be taken from the latter. The fare from Kagoshima to Naha is ¥11,840 and the journey takes 21 hours by the direct ferry or about 25 hours by the stopping ferry.

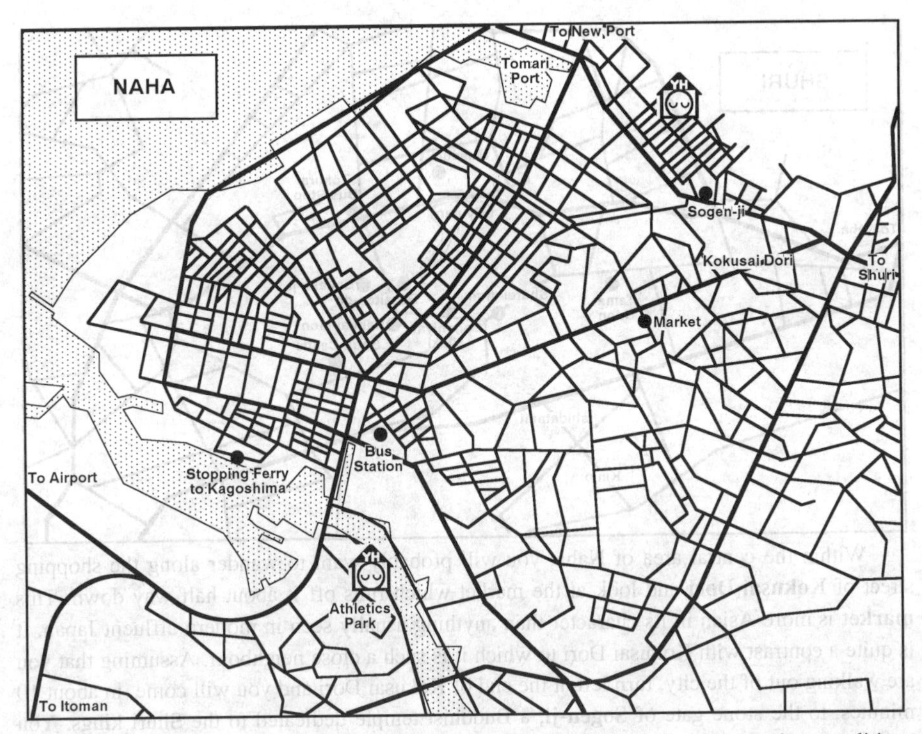


Okinawa offers only expensive bus services, so it is best to plan one's expeditions carefully to minimize travelling expenses. The stopping ferry calls in at Motobu, further north than Naha, on certain days, arriving at 16:50. The ferry fare from Kagoshima to Motobu is ¥10,970. **Motobu** was the site of the Okinawa Marine Exposition in 1975 and some attractions remain. Entrance to the park is free, but the **aquarium**, which is the main point of interest, costs ¥620. There is also a garden of tropical flowers, which again costs ¥620. To reach the park take bus no. 70 or 93 from Nago or from Motobu port. However, you will not have time to visit there today. To go south, take a bus no. 66, 70 or 93 to Nago and then a bus no. 20 or 120 south to Kuraha, where Maeda Misaki Youth Hostel is located, enabling you to see a little more of Okinawa at reduced cost. This bus continues all the way to Naha, in fact, but it would be getting rather late by the time you reached there. If the bus from Motobu is a no. 93, there should be no need to change at Nago, but there are very few such buses and those few operate only at weekends and in mid-summer. You should catch your bus from Motobu on the far side of the road, i.e. going to your right. Journey time to Nago is 40 minutes and cost ¥600. If you have time to look around, **Nago** has the ruins of a castle and what are claimed as the earliest blossoming cherry trees in Japan. The blossom appears at the end of January. From Nago to Kuraha takes 60 minutes and costs ¥900. Buses operate every 15 minutes. On the way, you will pass some of Okinawa's most popular and famous beaches.

The other two youth hostels in Okinawa are in the city of Naha. There used to be a third, where the author stayed, but it is now closed. Okinawa Kokusai Hostel is currently being rebuilt and will be re-opened as a completely new building in mid-1995, so will be waiting for you by the time that you read this.

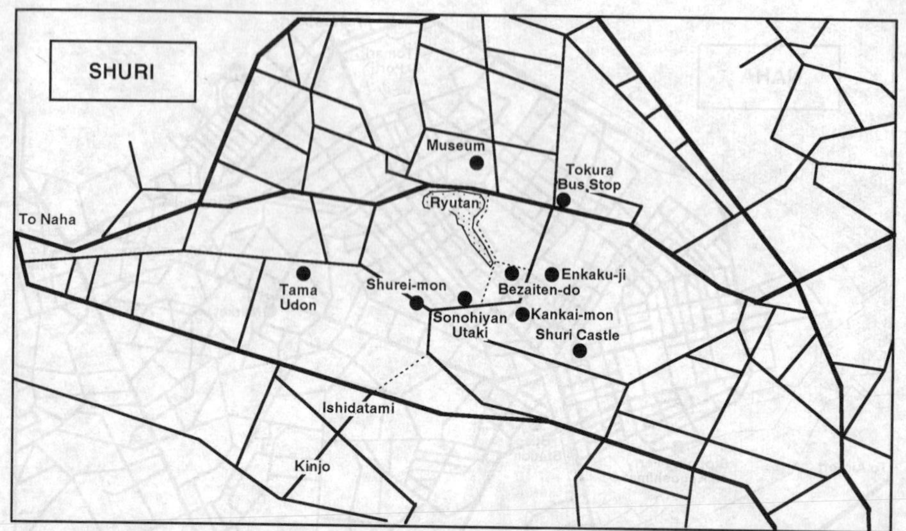


Within the central area of Naha, you will probably want to wander along the shopping street of **Kokusai Dori** and look at the market which runs off it about half way down. This **market** is more Asian in its character than anything usually seen in modern affluent Japan. It is quite a contrast with Kokusai Dori to which it is such a close neighbour. Assuming that you are walking out of the city, turn left at the end of Kokusai Dori and you will come, in about 10 minutes, to the stone gate of **Sogen-ji**, a Buddhist temple dedicated to the Shuri kings. You will also pass this on your left if taking bus no. 101 from the New Port. The temple was completely destroyed during the war, along with the tombs of kings buried there. Only a part of this gate survived. The remainder of the gate is a reconstruction.

A place which you will not want to miss is **Shuri**, reached by turning right at the end of Kokusai Dori or by taking a bus no. 1, 12, 13, 14 or 17 to Tokura (当蔵), as a fairly central starting point. **Shuri Castle** used to be the residence of the Sho Dynasty. It was a palace as much as a castle. However, everything was destroyed in the war. The main building of the palace has been reconstructed and this is impressive, displaying a typical Okinawan style of architecture, quite different from that of the rest of Japan and obviously influenced by Chinese styles as much as by Japanese. The reconstruction was completed in 1992. Unfortunately, it costs ¥800 to see it. Two of the gates have also been rebuilt, **Shurei-mon** and **Kankai-mon**, and there are other sites to visit, including the gate of **Enkaku-ji**, which was the temple of the Sho family, and a temple named **Bezaiten-do**. There is a stone gate named **Sonohiyan Utaki** where the kings used to pray before setting out on any journey or expedition and there is a stone path named **Ishidatami** built in 1522 to provide access to the castle. It leads through an area named **Kinjo** which has many old and traditional Okinawan houses. There is also a **museum** to visit (admission ¥200).

**Tama Udon** is nearby, not a type of noodles, as you might at first suppose, but the royal mausoleum on which work started in 1501. There were three crypts, with the royal body being stored in the middle one until it had decomposed. Then the bones were cleaned and put into the third chamber. Tama Udon was, of course, damaged during the war, but enough remains to be worth going to see.

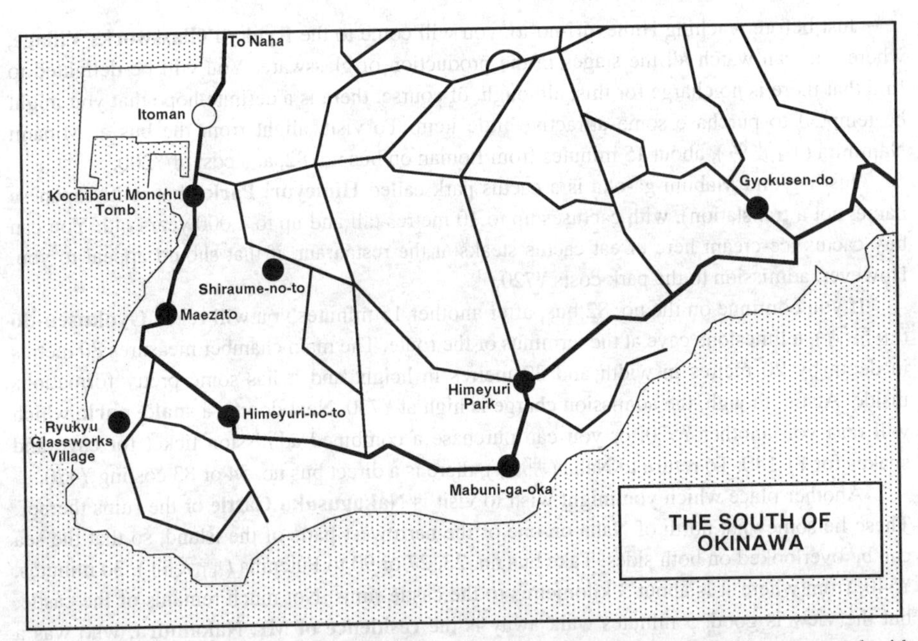


If you visit the southern part of the island, you will find many memorials connected with the war. The Japanese troops were gradually pushed to the south, where they made their last stand. General Buckner, the commander of the U.S. Tenth Army, was killed in action at **Maezato** and has a monument there. Nearby is **Shiraume-no-to,** a monument to 74 female students and 11 teachers who killed themselves in a cave here. The Japanese commander, Lt.-Gen. Ushijima, and Chief of Staff Cho killed themselves in a cave at their headquarters at **Mabuni-ga-oka** (Mabuni Hill), where their monuments, and many others, are to be found. The Okinawa Peace Prayer and Memorial Hall stands nearby now. Admission is ¥350. Not so far away is **Himeyuri-no-to** ('Princess Lily Tower') poignantly marking the place where 143 girl students and 15 teachers killed themselves.

Perhaps the most interesting reminder of the battle, though, is the **Headquarters of the Japanese Navy** at Tomigusuku (also called Tomishiro), south of Naha. This is an underground construction where you can see the commander's office, and various other rooms, as they were at that time, for an admission fee of ¥410. When the Americans finally discovered this underground shelter, they found the bodies of Vice-Admiral Ota, commander of the Japanese Navy in Okinawa, and 4,000 of his men, who preferred death to capture.

To reach Tomigusuku, take a bus no. 33 or 101 from Naha to Tomishiro Joshi Koen-mae (豊見城城跡公園前). The journey takes 25 minutes and costs ¥220. To reach any of the other monuments mentioned above, first take a bus no. 32, 33, 34, 35, 89 or 100 from Naha to Itoman (糸満). The fare is ¥470 and the journey takes 60 minutes. Then take a bus no. 82. To Himeyuri-no-to (姫百合の塔) costs ¥250 and takes 20 minutes. To Mabuni-ga-oka (摩文仁ヶ丘) costs ¥350 and takes 30 minutes. Buses run about every hour.

Since you are in the area, there are some other attractions which you can see at the same time. In Itoman is **Kochibaru Monchu Tomb**, a huge tomb not far from the centre of the city. It is designed like a house and accommodates 2,500 deceased members of the same family.

Just before reaching Himeyuri-no-to, you will come to the **Ryukyu Glassworks Village**, where you can watch all the stages in the production of glassware. You will be delighted to find that there is no charge for this, although, of course, there is a definite hope that you might be tempted to purchase some attractive little item. To visit, alight from the bus at Minami Namihira (南波平), about 15 minutes from Itoman on bus no. 82, at a cost of ¥200.

Just beyond Mabuni-ga-oka is a cactus park called **Himeyuri Park** (that is its Japanese name, not a translation), with cactuses up to 10 metres tall and up to 1,000 years old. You can buy cactus ice-cream here or eat cactus steaks at the restaurant, if that should appeal to you. However, admission to the park costs ¥720.

If you continue on the no. 82 bus, after another 15 minutes you will reach **Gyokusen-do** (玉泉洞), a limestone cave at the terminus of the route. The main chamber measures 80 metres in depth by 20 metres in width and 20 metres in height and it has some pretty formations inside. Again, though, the admission charge is high at ¥730. Next door is a **snake park**, which will cost you another ¥520, or you can purchase a combined admission ticket for cave and snakes for ¥1,140. To return to Naha (那覇), there is a direct bus no. 54 or 83 costing ¥470.

Another place which you might wish to visit is **Nakagusuku Castle** or the ruins thereof. These lie somewhat north of Naha on one of the narrowest parts of the island, so that the sea can be overlooked on both sides. Take bus no. 23, 27 or 90 to Futenma (普天間), 30 minutes, ¥540, from where it is about 3 kilometres to the castle ruins. Not much remains of the castle, but the view is good. 5 minutes walk away is the **residence of Mr. Nakamura**, who was a wealthy farmer here in the eighteenth century. It is one of the best examples of an Okinawan house and can be viewed for the sum of ¥300.

Other nearby islands can be reached fairly expensively by ferry, or even more expensively by air. The nearest island of size is **Ie-jima**. A ferry runs from Motobu at least four times a day and more frequently in busy seasons. It takes 30 minutes to make the crossing, at a cost of ¥570. **Kerama** is a group of islands where camp sites are available and tents and other necessities available for hire. To Kerama there is always at least one ferry per day, allowing about four hours on the islands if you want to make a day trip. It leaves from Tomari port in Naha, the middle one of the three ports, and takes 70 minutes to reach Kerama. The fare is ¥1,340. **Kume** is an island which somehow managed to escape the damage inflicted by the war on most other places in this area. There is always at least one ferry per day. The journey takes 4½ hours (or 2 hours by high-speed ferry) from Tomari port and costs ¥2,600 (or ¥2,960 by high-speed ferry).

## MIYAKO (宮古 – 'Old Shrine')

**10 hrs. 30 mins. from Naha by ferry**

**Derivation of Name:** *Originally 'Miyaku', which, in the local dialect, means 'eight islands'.*

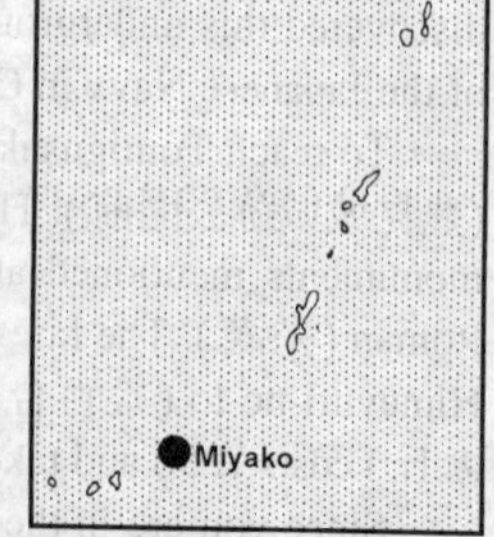


Miyako is the name given to a group of eight islands one night on a ferry south of Naha. The main island is also called Miyako and the principal town, to which the ferry runs, is Hirara. Miyako escaped damage in the war, so has an old and traditional lifestyle to offer and some old and traditional buildings. It suffered from harsh government in the past and the inhabitants were obliged to pay taxes to both the Chinese and the Japanese. There is a stone near the harbour called *Nintozei-seki*, 1.4 metres high. Anybody

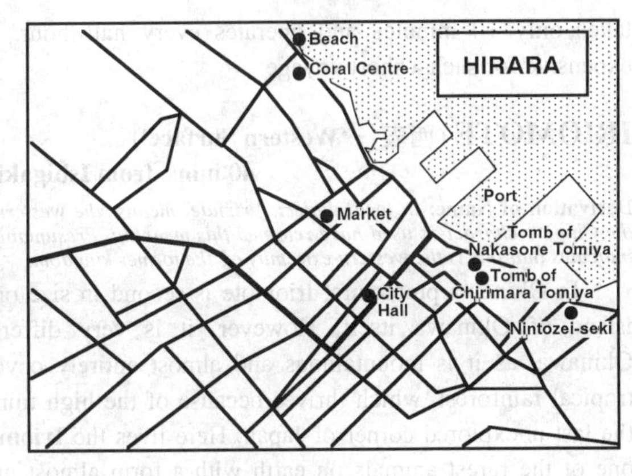


taller than this was liable for taxation. Miyako offers beaches, a botanical garden and its own distinctive culture. The main industry is the production of sugar cane.

There is now a youth hostel in Miyako, and it is also possible to camp or stay in *minshuku* or *ryokan*, of which there are plenty.

The ferry leaves Naha (New Port) at 20:00 about every other day and reaches Hirara at 6:00 or 6:30 the following morning. It returns by night also. The cost is ¥3,810. All of the ferry services continue to Ishigaki and some go on to Taiwan. There are bus services on Miyako Island but not on the smaller islands.

## ISHIGAKI (石垣 - 'Stone Fence') 12 hrs. from Naha by ferry

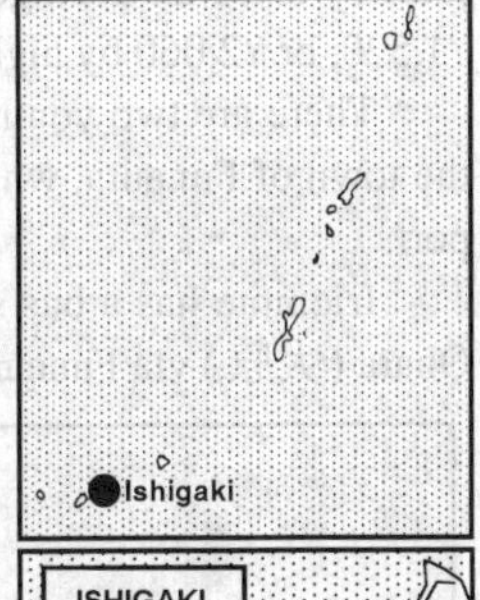


**Derivation of Name:** *Originally 'Ishinagira', which, in local dialect, means 'a place with many stones'.*

Ishigaki is further south still, the largest island in the group known as the Yaeyama Islands. The name of the main town is also Ishigaki. Ishigaki is again famous for its beaches, as well as for its cultured black pearls. There is a youth hostel named Trek Ishigaki-jima Hostel. It is not in the town of Ishigaki, but in Hoshino (星野), on the east coast, reached by bus in 30 minutes.

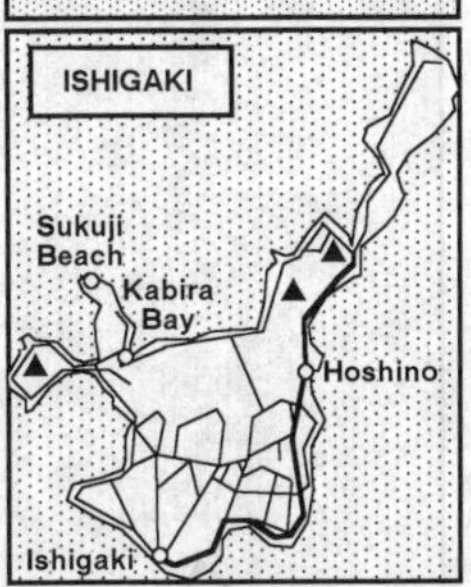


Ferries run to Ishigaki from Naha (New Port) about every two days, leaving at 20:00 (occasionally 18:30). The length of time taken depends on whether or not they stop in Miyako on the way. Most do, and remain there for two or three hours, which gives the opportunity to look at least at the town of Hirara. Such ferries take between 13½ and 15 hours in total between Naha and Ishigaki. Those which run directly, however, cover the journey in 12 to 14 hours. The fare is ¥5,250. On Ishigaki, there are several bus routes.

## TAKETOMI (竹富 - 'Prosperous Bamboo') 10 mins. from Ishigaki by ferry

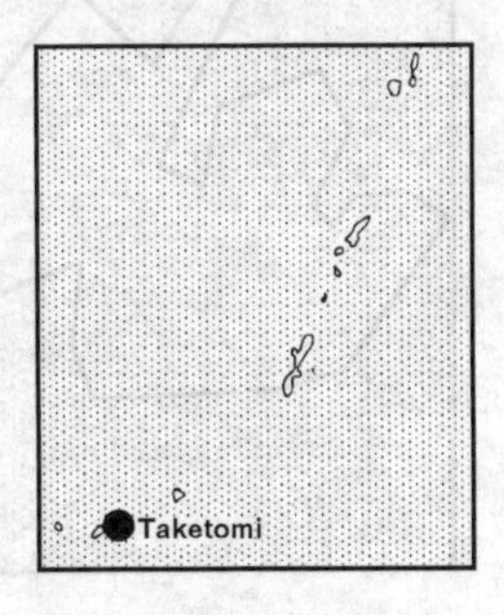


**Derivation of Name:** *Uncertain.*

The small island of Taketomi is famous for its **star-shaped sand**. It is quiet and traditional and with an area of only 6.3 square kilometres. Since it is surrounded by beaches, it is popular with one-day visitors. There are no buses. Buffalo carts are available for short distance travel and bicycles can be hired for longer distances.

There is a youth hostel on Taketomi. Tanaka Ryokan Hostel is part of a Japanese-style hotel. The ferry from Ishigaki to Taketomi takes only 10 minutes and operates every half hour. However, it costs ¥570, which is expensive for such a short voyage.

## IRIOMOTE (西表 – 'Western Surface')

**40 mins. from Ishigaki by ferry**

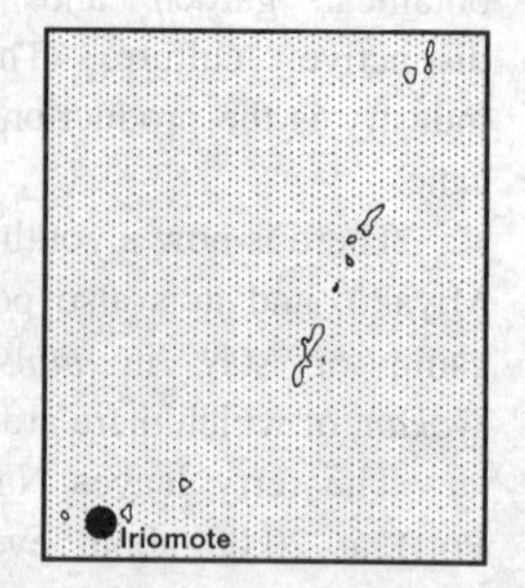


**Derivation of Name:** *In local dialect, 'irimute' means 'the western face' and the Chinese characters used have retained this meaning. Presumably the name indicates that this is the western extremity of the former kingdom.*

In Okinawa prefecture, Iriomote is second in size only to the island of Okinawa itself. However, it is very different from Okinawa, as it is mountainous and almost entirely covered with tropical rainforest, which thrives because of the high rainfall. It is the last unexplored corner of Japan. Here lives the **Iriomote lynx**, one of the rarest animals on earth with a form almost unchanged over the last five million years. One can take a ride on a boat up the Urauchi or Nakama Rivers to see forest and waterfalls or one can sit on the beach or dive in the coral.

The main town is called Funaura and it is here that the ferry arrives from Ishigaki. The journey takes an average of 40 minutes and ferries run eight times a day. The cost is a high ¥1,520, or ¥2,060 by high-speed ferry.

There are two youth hostels here at the limit of the JYH network. Irumote-so Hostel is in the town of Funaura, while Iriomote-jima Midori-so Hostel is about 30 minutes walk from the port.

Iriomote has a bus service on the road which runs about half way round the island, from Ohara (大原) via Funaura (船浦) to Shirahama (白浜).

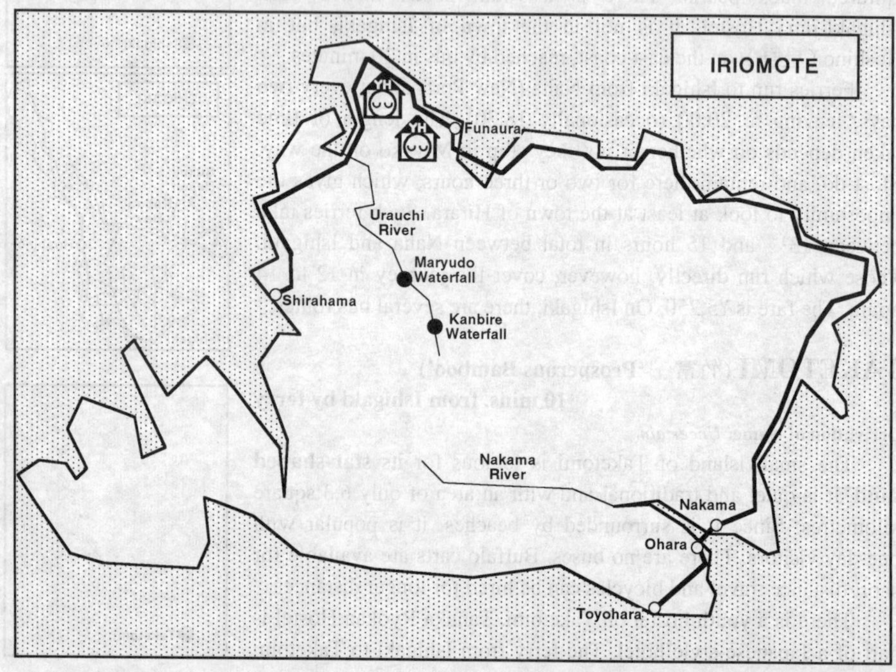

If you want to go even further in the Japanese archipelago, this group of islands has the most westerly point in Japan and the most southerly point in Okinawa (but not the most southerly point in Japan, which is on the island of Okinotori, much further east). The most southerly point in Okinawa is on the island of **Hateruma**. A ferry operates from Ishigaki on Tuesdays, Thursdays and Saturdays at 9:00. The voyage lasts 2 hours and costs ¥2,040 single or ¥3,880 return. The boat comes back at 14:00, giving three hours on the island if you do not want to stay there. Hateruma is only just north of the Tropic of Cancer. The most westerly point in Japan, at 122 degrees and 56 minutes east, is on the island of **Yonaguni**. The ferry runs from Ishigaki on Wednesdays and Saturdays at 10:00 and returns from Yonaguni on Mondays and Thursdays at 10:00. The voyage lasts 3 hours and costs ¥3,400 single or ¥6,450 return. The western tip of Yonaguni is only 127 kilometres from Taiwan.

If you want to travel on from here to **Taiwan**, there is a ferry from Naha. This ferry used to sail once a week, but at the time of writing it seems to be operating twice a week. If this proves to be a permanent change, it will go to Kaohsiung at 20:00 on Mondays, arriving at 9:00 on Wednesdays and to Keelung (pronounced *Chiloong*) at 20:00 on Fridays, arriving at 7:00 on Sundays. On the way, it calls at Miyako (8:00 on Tuesdays and Saturdays) and Ishigaki (15:00 on Tuesdays and 18:00 on Saturdays). Return sailings are at 16:00 on Wednesdays from Kaohsiung, arriving in Ishigaki at 16:00 on Thursdays, Miyako at 22:30 on Thursdays and Naha at 9:00 on Fridays, and at 16:00 on Sundays from Keelung direct to Naha (no stop in Ishigaki or Miyako), arriving at 14:00 on Mondays. Fares from Naha are ¥15,600 to Keelung and ¥18,000 to Kaohsiung. In the opposite direction, however, starting in Taiwan, they are about 25% cheaper. The ferry is operated by the Arimura Shipping Line and you must reserve, pay and present your passport at least two or three days prior to the sailing. Remember that you need a visa for Taiwan and you are not going to be able to obtain one in Ishigaki, for example, so plan well in advance if you are intending to take this route. Most of the passengers are Taiwanese who seem to be looking for bargains in Japan. When the author took this ferry, I found it crowded, noisy and very smoky inside. It was difficult to sleep during the night.

The alternative, of course, is to start back towards the main islands of Japan, which is also an expensive journey, but maybe you will think that it has been worth it, for this end of the Japanese archipelago certainly has a character and beauty all its own.

# PART 3 ACCOMMODATION

We have selected four different types of accommodation for this book, thinking thereby to be able to satisfy most categories of our impoverished readers. Youth hostels number over 300 throughout Japan and cost an average of about ¥2,500 per person. They have a great deal of character, especially the smaller and more remote ones, and are particularly suitable for the individual traveller. Please read the introduction to the Youth Hostels section before using them, since the special points of the Japanese system need to be noted. Rules are not excessive and most of the hostels are friendly and welcoming. We have listed almost every hostel in Japan and provided individual maps, not to scale, please note, for each.

Private hostels exist only in Tokyo and Kyoto, but in those two cities they are cheaper than youth hostels and with fewer rules (which is not always a merit, of course). Many also have cheap private rooms. In Tokyo, the market is glutted, but in Kyoto there is a good balance of supply and demand. Average price is ¥2,000 per night. Some private Japanese-style hotels are also included in this section. Rates are about ¥4,000 per person in Kyoto and ¥4,500 in Tokyo. We have listed 30 private hostels and hotels, with individual maps.

The Japanese Inn Group is a loose association of Japanese-style hotels which would welcome overseas guests. Usually a sprinkling of English is spoken, sometimes more. These hotels are throughout Japan and we have listed all which meet certain price limitations.

Business hotels are moderately priced but acceptable accommodation aimed at the businessman. They exist throughout Japan, but we have listed only major towns or cities, where they may be more difficult to locate and where also the price range tends to be higher, so that there is more need to know where to find the cheaper ones.

A few words also about the types of accommodation which we have not listed – and why. Camping grounds do exist in Japan and, indeed, are quite numerous. However, they tend to be difficult to reach, of a rather high standard (which means comparatively expensive) and seasonal. For a little more information on this topic, see the introduction on page 3.

Government Guest Houses (*Kokumin Shuku-sha*) exist at over 250 locations throughout Japan. They are comparatively economical and offer rather more privacy than youth hostels. However, it is customary to both book and pay in advance, with the payment to be made through a bank or post office, not an easy process. Usually you cannot just turn up and stay at a Government Guest House and many of them claim that they are not even authorized to handle money. On the other hand, there are some which will accept unexpected guests, so it may be worth trying if you are desperate. Also, while accommodation is economical, meals are relatively costly. Some of these guest houses will accept visitors without their taking meals, while others insist that meals must be included. Current rates are ¥3,605 per person per night for accommodation, ¥824 for breakfast and ¥2,060 for dinner, a total of ¥6,489 if you are obliged to subscribe to the whole package. The head office of the association is at 2-8-1 Toranomon, Minato-ku, Tokyo 105, in a building called Toranomon Denki Building. The telephone number is 03-3502-0480.

*Minshuku* are bed, breakfast and evening meal establishments, Japanese-style, in private homes. Although they are an interesting experience, usually the meals are included in the rates and the reduction for not taking them is not substantial. The price per night with two meals is around ¥8,000. In country areas, this will probably be the only type of accommodation.

Finally, of course, there are plenty of high-class hotels, which your travel agent can recommend to you. Service is usually very good, although rooms may be smaller than in other countries. Prices start at about ¥10,000 without meals and can go as high as you like.

# YOUTH HOSTELS
# [ユースホステル]

## PLEASE READ THIS SECTION BEFORE USING THE HOSTELS.

Japan claims to have more Youth Hostels than any other country outside Europe and, unlike the writers of some other travel books, the author of this one has found the hostels to be usually very good. However, the Japanese hostels have their own national flavour and the user needs to be aware of their differences in order to use the system smoothly.

**Reservations:** In Japan, one does not just turn up at a hostel and expect to be accommodated. Although, if a bed is available, one will not usually be turned away in such circumstances, one will often be told that it is necessary to book in advance and to please do so next time. Conventionally, reservations are made by telephone after one is fairly sure of one's plans. They can be made even on the day of arrival if space is still available, but it is best to reserve a few days in advance, if possible, or, at least, by the day before, so that one knows where one is going. Usually it is not a problem to find a suitable hostel with accommodation available, but at school and university holiday times, particularly in July and August, hostels can become crowded, so it is necessary to plan further ahead at those times.

Of course, telephoning is not so easy for somebody who does not speak Japanese. Not many hostels can manage sufficient English to cope with telephone reservations in that language, although a few major ones can do so. Note that hostels which claim English ability are so distinguished in the listing which follows by the 'We Speak English' mark (E). Where there is a language problem, the solution is to buy a telephone card and ask a Japanese fellow hosteller who speaks some English to make a few reservations for you. Since English is a compulsory university subject and many hostellers are of about university age, it is usually not too difficult to find somebody willing to assist. He or she will need the following information: your surname, the date(s) for which accommodation is required, the number and sexes of your party and whether or not you require dinner on your arrival day. Other possible questions are your nationality, where you are coming from that day and at what time you expect to arrive. Write these details down for the person who is assisting you. No advance payment is expected when you reserve by telephone and the system seems to work very well indeed. It is important to remember, therefore, that, having made the reservation, you have an obligation to turn up. If you cannot, it is essential that you let the hostel know that you wish to cancel your reservation, otherwise you may be depriving another hosteller of a bed and also reducing the revenue of the hostel. 'No shows' are rare at Japanese hostels, but when they occur, they are disproportionately frequent among non-Japanese. Please do not get a bad reputation for us all by abusing this very efficient and simple system.

There are other ways to reserve too, of which the most important for the overseas visitor is the International Booking Network (IBN). This computerized service allows reservations to be made at certain Japanese hostels from overseas. A small fee is payable and it is possible that certain discounts may not be available when bookings are made from overseas, but it certainly gives peace of mind to know that one's first few nights of accommodation are assured. This is particularly important in the busy centres of Tokyo, Osaka and Kyoto, which is where most visitors want to spend their first nights anyway. However, it is suggested that to arrange accommodation for the first few nights by this means may be sufficient. If you plan too far ahead before you have even seen Japan, you may find that your flexibility has been eroded and your costs increased. Also, you will be staying only at the major hostels and missing the charm of the small more remote and unconventional ones. It is not usually difficult to get reservations outside the major cities if one telephones a few days in advance. At present, there are 31 Japanese hostels participating in the IBN system. A list appears on page 397 and the hostels are marked in our listing with an IBN symbol (IBN). It is also possible to reserve accommodation in IBN hostels overseas from four centres in Japan.

Other ways to make reservations in Japan are by using the Youth Hostels Head Office or certain booking agencies or by sending a fax message, but since the Japanese themselves always use the telephone system, and it is simple and easy, with a little assistance, that seems the best method for visitors to the country too.

**Getting to the Hostel:** For each hostel mentioned in the subsequent pages, we have provided a map and directions from the nearest or most convenient station. The maps are based on those in the Japanese Youth Hostels Handbook and we are grateful to the Japan Youth Hostels Association for kind permission to use and modify such maps. Please note, most importantly, that **these maps make no pretence to any consistent scale**. Parts which are considered important are drawn to a large scale and parts which are considered unimportant are drawn to a small scale, all on the same map. It is vital to understand this, otherwise disaster will befall. The idea of inconsistent scale is alien to the western mind, but, in fact, it seems to work once one has got used to it. At first, however, it is easy to think, 'Oh, look, I have covered half of the distance in just two minutes. I shall be there in a moment or two.' When the tired hosteller finally arrives thirty minutes later, his comments about Japanese maps do not bear repetition! So use the maps as they are intended – to show the principal features along the way which will guide you, not to show relative distance. Distance or time required is mentioned in the information to the left of each map.

Since nearly everybody in Japan travels by train, our information shows which station you should use to reach the hostel and the line on which the station is situated if it is not in a major city or town. Unless stated otherwise, stations are all on lines operated by JR. Where they are not, we have indicated also the JR station or stations at which a transfer to the private company's line may most conveniently be made. The only exception to this is in a few major cities where private railway companies have major networks and transfers can be made at many places. If the hostel is within walking distance of the station, then just follow the map, remembering the warning about scale. If it is necessary to take a bus or tram, this is stated in the information section. 'Take bus for . . .' means that this is the destination which should be on the front of the bus. We have given it in both Roman and Japanese characters, so that you can identify your bus when it comes along, as well as asking passers-by if necessary. Unfortunately, except in some major cities, Japanese buses do not usually bear numbers, which would make them much easier to identify, and, even where they do, people do not seem to take much notice of the numbers. We have specially noted those buses which are operated by JR, as 'Japan Rail Pass' holders can use such services free of charge.

Once you are on the right bus, you then have to identify where to get off. First, do not forget to take a ticket from the machine as you board, if one is offered, as this will determine the fare to be paid when you alight. Buses usually have announcements for each stop, but it is unlikely that you will be able to identify your destination by this means. We have given it in Japanese characters again, as well as in Roman script, except when the words are basically English ones, as in the case of 'Youth Hostel-mae', for example, so that you can ask fellow passengers or the driver. People are usually very helpful in this way. Also we have mentioned the approximate duration of the journey, although this is not reliable, as it will depend upon traffic conditions. In addition, the map may provide assistance in showing identifiable features near the stop. There is a glossary of words which commonly appear in bus stop names on page 56 and this may help too in enabling you to identify a building or other feature at which you should get off. Although taking a bus is something of a traumatic experience, with constant anxiety about alighting at the correct place, the author has never yet missed his stop in these circumstances.

Regarding the names of bus stops, quite often the suffix '-mae' appears at the end of names of stops, for example 'Youth Hostel-mae'. This just means 'in front of' and seems to be an optional addition in many cases. Thus, even though this book has '-mae' at the end of the bus stop name, it might not appear on the stop itself. Similarly, and more commonly, we may have omitted '-mae', when it actually appears on the stop.

Buses are rather difficult in Japan, and also expensive. Therefore, when the option of using a bus or walking is given in the hostel directions, the author suggests that walking is preferable, unless you have a great deal of luggage, which would be a mistake in any case! You can get much less lost walking the wrong way than getting on the wrong bus. Moreover, you see a lot more of the place which you are visiting if you walk around it. In fact, even when walking is not suggested but the bus ride is ten minutes or less, the author often walks if the route seems reasonably clear.

**Arrival:** The triangular Youth Hostel mark usually, but not always, confirms that you have reached the right building. When you enter, the first things to look for are slippers, nearly always plastic pea-green ones. Never ignore this very strong hint that you should take off your shoes here and put on the slippers, even if they do not fit and there is a lengthy overhang! A few hostels with frequent non-Japanese visitors even provide specially marked 'foreigners' slippers'. If there are no slippers, but there is a congregation of shoes in the well before the front step, take off yours and add them to the heap. Then continue in socks. If there are no slippers and there is no pile of shoes and the floor looks dirty and institutional, only then may it be safe to continue wearing your shoes, but exercise great caution over this matter, as it would be a good way to offend your hosts before you have even checked in.

When you reach the front desk, you will be asked to write your particulars on a slip of paper. Often there is one type for males, one for females and one for non-Japanese, not, presumably, because they are regarded as a different sex, but because theirs is in English. Even if no such form is available, it is fairly obvious what to write – name, address, membership number, dates of arrival and intended departure and, at the end, previous and next hostels. You will also be asked at this point whether you want to take breakfast or not, for more about which see the section on food.

The hostel will stamp your Youth Hostel booklet. If you intend to leave very early in the morning, you can usually ask for it to be returned to you immediately. When your booklet is full, you will be given a card for additional stamps. Each hostel produces its own cards and some hostels take a great deal of trouble over it, so that these cards are almost worth collecting just for themselves.

**Prices:** The prices shown are correct for 1995 and are all-inclusive per person charges, we hope and believe. However, there is in Japan a consumption tax, currently 3%, which may sometimes be added to the bill (although we believe that we have included it in the rates given). Moreover, there are persistent rumours that this tax may soon be raised to 7%, which would add approximately ¥100 to the prices shown. Also, you may be using this book after 1995, in which case it would be prudent to add about 5% per year to allow for increases. At the time of writing, the most expensive hostel costs ¥3,200, plus a ¥150 spa fee. This spa fee is one of the few extra charges levied and it applies only at hostels which have natural hot water baths. There are also a few hostels which have them but do not charge extra. Sheets are not usually charged for, so most hostellers do not bother to bring their own sheet sleeping bag as they commonly do in Europe. The use of cooking facilities, however, will often be charged for (see following section) and it is very unusual to see Japanese hostellers cooking for themselves.

Some hostels offer a discount to hostellers from overseas. This generous gesture is in recognition of the fact that the recent appreciation of the yen has made it difficult for visitors to make ends meet here, even using only economical hostels for their accommodation. Where a discount is available to non-Japanese hostellers, the reduction offered is shown in brackets after the normal rate.

The average price for a night in a Youth Hostel is about ¥2,500. Rates given are for adult members. Non-members will be charged extra, usually ¥600 per night extra for the first six nights, after which they will have paid for a Youth Hostelling International Card, valid internationally in the same way as a membership card until the end of the current year. Alternatively, the full Youth Hostelling International Card can be purchased for ¥2,800 from the national or regional Youth Hostel offices, on production of a passport and the supply of one photograph. This is a preferable alternative, as some hostels may refuse to accommodate hostellers without a card. Youth Hostel Membership can be given in Japan only to those who have lived in the country legally for more than one year. Membership costs ¥2,500 per year and requires the production of an Alien Registration Card or passport showing legal residence in Japan. Those who cannot satisfy such conditions should, of course, apply for membership in their countries of residence before visiting Japan.

**Food:** Unlike hostels in most western countries, Japanese hostels do not usually offer self-catering facilities, so do not expect to be able to do your own cooking. When hostels do offer such facilities, they often charge for them. The amount varies between ¥50 and ¥200 per person.

Instead, meals are provided. Prices are shown in the information for each hostel, the maxima being ¥1,000 for dinner and ¥600 for breakfast. These rates have increased considerably recently. Youth Hostel meals used to be variable in quality, the best being very good, and always reasonable value. Now, however, they are a little expensive, but usually quite filling. Also, if you eat the hostel meal, it will provide a good opportunity to meet your fellow hostellers. If you want to save money, though, visit a nearby bakery or supermarket and buy some food which does not need cooking. When the hostel appears to be out in the country, you will need to think about this before getting there, but it is nearly always possible to buy something locally.

Also bear in mind that most hostels do not approve of food in the dormitories and that if you eat too conspicuously in common rooms, you may cause some embarrassment to Japanese who do not like to observe others eating or be observed while eating themselves, except when everybody present is engaged in the activity.

Some hostels also offer a special menu of local delicacies at dinner. Whilst this is a good way to try some interesting Japanese food, the price of such a meal is usually about ¥1,500. Of course, if you do want to try this special menu, it is essential to inform the hostel when making your reservation. Hostels offering local delicacies are so annotated in the listing which follows.

Breakfast is frequently Japanese-style and a Japanese breakfast does not always appeal to western taste. A typical menu might be rice with raw egg and seaweed, fish, *miso* soup and perhaps *natto* (fermented soya beans with a particularly strong smell), served with green tea. The author suggests that making an early start to the day's sightseeing or travels might be a better investment of time.

Note that if you want to eat the hostel dinner on the day of your arrival, it is always necessary to inform the hostel of that fact when making your reservation. It is also necessary to arrive by 18:30 at the latest. A decision about the next day's breakfast can usually be made upon arrival, although sometimes hostels ask at the time when the reservation is made.

**Dormitories:** Basically, there are two types of dormitory. One type consists of two-tiered bunk beds, very similar to those in western hostels. The hosteller is provided on arrival with sheets or a sheet sleeping bag and there are blankets neatly folded on the end of the bed and a pillow. Before using the blankets, note the manner in which they are folded, which is slightly unconventional in that two consecutive folds are made in the same direction, for you will be expected to fold them again the same way before leaving. Your sheets you will be expected to put in a place notified to you upon arrival. Usually it is near the entrance, so, if you are not told, leave them near the front desk.

The other type of dormitory is a *tatami* mat room, that is a conventional Japanese room. The first thing to remember is that one does not wear slippers on *tatami*. Take your slippers off as you enter the room and leave them on the wooden floor outside the sliding doors. Although no bedding is visible, it will be there, hiding in the capacious cupboards. When it is evening, you can take from there a *futon* to sleep on and another to put over you. The more rigid type of *futon* is the one to sleep on. Cover it with the sheet with which you will have been issued upon arrival. The softer type of *futon* is the covering one. If there are not too many hostellers, you may be able to use two under-*futon* if you wish. The sheet is again to be put in a specified place when you leave.

The convention is that you do not sleep with your head to the north, because that is the way in which the dead are laid out. However, if you can work out which direction is north at each hostel, you have a remarkable ability.

A few hostels have special family and guest rooms, at slightly higher rates. We have not identified such hostels. After all, what is the point of coming to Japan and then being segregated from the Japanese? The Japanese Youth Hostel Handbook (in Japanese) shows these hostels clearly, but there are not many of them.

**Bathing:** Bathing is one of the delights of Japanese hostels. Usually there will be only communal baths. Sometimes there is one for males and one for females and sometimes the same bath is used by both sexes at different times, in which case there will be a notice on the door defining the times for each. If there are very few hostellers present, it may just be a case of turning over a sign on the door to indicate which sex is using the bathroom at the present time.

The procedure for the bath is this. Go into the outer room and take off everything. Put your clothes into one of the baskets provided. Now, taking only essentials, such as soap, shampoo and a flannel, proceed to the main bathroom. Take one of the plastic stools and a plastic bowl and go to one of the pairs of taps sticking out of the wall. Often there are showers too for washing hair whilst seated. Have at least a perfunctory wash, ensuring that all soap is completely rinsed from your body. At this stage you may enter the bath. Be careful! It may be surprisingly hot. If it is really unbearable, it is permissible to run some cold water in to cool things down a little, but be cautious about this, because others are using the same bath and Japanese like to have their water pretty warm. You may soak there for as long as you can stand it. Then you can get out and have a more thorough wash or wash your hair or shave or any other business before having another dip — or, indeed, as many dips as you can tolerate. It is also quite permissible to sit around chatting if you wish. When you are thoroughly boiled or steamed, retreat to the ante-room and dry yourself on the towel which you should have remembered to take with you and leave there. Then return to your room. Remember never to allow any soap to get into the bath! Bathing will usually be available only in the evening and there will be a deadline for finishing, typically about 20:30.

Toilet facilities will usually be Japanese-style also, which means crouching, not sitting. Pointing towards the hooded end, ensure that you are properly positioned above the trough with no overhang. Then proceed. In Japan, it is usually all right to put toilet paper down the toilet, in moderate quantities, of course. When you have finished, flush by depressing the lever or button which is usually to be found behind the hood.

**Hours:** Japanese hostels expect hostellers to arrive earlier than in many other countries. Please note this fact because it is important. **You must check in by 20:00.** A few hostels in major cities allow a later check-in time, but if you are likely to arrive later than 20:00, you should always inform the hostel and ask permission. If you want to eat dinner, you must arrive by 18:30 at the latest. Having checked in, you can usually go out again, however, and stay out beyond 20:00. Most hostels close their doors at 21:00 to 22:00. A few have later times. Bear in mind, though, that you will not be able to have a bath if you come back late.

Opening times vary, often according to who runs the hostel and its location. If staff have to be employed, the hostel is likely to be closed during the day. Where it is an hotel, private home or temple, however, the operators are likely to be there during the day in any case, so the hostel may not insist on a closed period, particularly in inclement weather. Also, where public transport is limited the hostel will usually expect guests to turn up on the obvious bus or train and be ready for them.

Check-out time is usually 10:00, but varies. By check-out time, you should have departed or paid for the next night. Note that sometimes hostels do not allow you to pay several nights in advance, presumably because their accounting systems cannot cope with such intricacies. Sapporo House is one such. This means that, at such hostels, you cannot easily make a long day trip leaving early in the morning and coming back late in the evening.

**Hostel Classifications:** There are three types of classification given in our lists. Firstly, information is given as to who operates each hostel. The Japanese Youth Hostel Handbook further classifies according to who owns each hostel and whether it was purpose-built or not, but we felt that most hostellers did not need such detail. However, it is useful to know who is running the hostel and how big it is, because that gives some idea of its atmosphere. The JYH hostels tend to be large and somewhat institutional, but efficiently operated. They are mostly in major cities or well-known tourist spots. Because of that, they are often the ones most frequented by non-Japanese. However, they do not usually have the strong sense of character which some of the privately-operated hostels have.

Local Organization Hostels are similar in atmosphere, but may be housed in older and decaying buildings in some cases. Many are operated by local authorities, in which case it is sometimes possible to stay without a Youth Hostel card without penalty. Such youth hostels are indicated in our list by the 'Public Youth Hostel' mark ( ). It is permissible to stay at these hostels at the members' rate on production of an overseas passport. Other hostels are run by non-government community organizations. Some local authority buildings have been allocated locations with magnificent views which alone make a visit worth while. The value of the plots of land on which they are built, often surrounded by parkland, must be enormous. Local Organization Hostels are often cheaper than others, being partially subsidized, or, at least, not operated for profit.

Privately Operated Hostels, by contrast, are run as businesses. They vary considerably, but, in order to improve their businesses, they tend to be quickly responsive to hostellers' needs and are generally friendly places in which to stay, but prices tend to be a little higher than those of public hostels. Size varies too, and, of course, the smaller, the more friendly.

Hotel Hostels are usually parts of small Japanese-style inns, that is *ryokan* or *minshuku*. Sometimes the word *ryokan* (inn) or the suffix *-so* (house) appears in the hostel's name. These hotels are supplementing their income by taking hostellers in addition to hotel guests. The hostellers pay much less, of course, and share rooms. At off-peak seasons, especially, these can be very pleasant places to stay, as one may get a room to oneself perhaps, or shared with just one other hosteller, and otherwise be just like an hotel guest at a much reduced price. At busy times, on the other hand, one may feel like a sardine. These hostels tend to be in small towns and to have an individual atmosphere. The author recommends them.

Temple and Shrine Hostels are not overly religious in atmosphere and are sometimes housed in beautiful old wooden buildings, although sometimes they are just in modern annexes. Pilgrims often seek lodging in temple buildings and so, since accommodation is already available, some temples have chosen to extend their services to hostellers. They are usually in calm and peaceful surroundings, often with beautiful Japanese gardens outside, and have their own tranquil character. No religious activity or persuasion is expected of those who stay there, so do not be afraid to put such places on your list. At one such hostel, for example (Fukaura), the author was the only guest, so the priest who ran the hostel spent the evening teaching me card tricks! People who stay in Temple Hostels almost always enjoy the experience. The only point to remember is that temples are traditionally built on hills. That makes it nice and easy to walk to the station in the morning, but it is hard work the night before.

Private Homes are just that and are usually small hostels, where the owners have two or three spare rooms. Again they have their own character and are interesting because the owners are living there and are available to make contact with. This is more like being in lodgings than in a hostel. Again such hostels are recommended, but they are sometimes a little difficult to locate.

Additionally, the Youth Hostels have devised a star classification, with awards ranging from 1 ★ to 4 ★ . The classification has been based upon a combination of factors:- the building, the interior condition of the hostel, the amenities, services offered and the friendliness of the hostel. The classification awarded is shown for each hostel in our listing. If no star mark is shown, that does not necessarily imply a poor hostel. It means that no assessment has been made yet.

There is one more classification given and that is a 'Jim Mark', based on the author's personal impression of the hostel. There is a Happy Jim ( ) for hostels which he enjoyed, a Medium Jim ( ) for hostels which were quite satisfactory without having any special claim to fame and a Crying Jim ( ) for the occasional hostel which he did not enjoy very much. It should be said that this is not a very scientific classification and that it is completely subjective, one hosteller's opinion often being totally different from another's. However, it does offer a form of second opinion on the Youth Hostels' own classification system. The author has found many different reasons for giving favourable (or unfavourable) assessments of hostels. Most often the reason has been the attitude of those running the hostel. Sometimes it has been the behaviour of other hostellers. Sometimes it has been the surroundings or the view or the hostel building itself. Sometimes it has been the facilities offered. Many of these factors change from day to day and, in any case, one person may have a good experience and the next a bad one. One hosteller may think that the kindness of those running the hostel overcomes the inadequacies of the building while the next may be of the opinion that the cockroaches hiding under the bed cannot be made up for by any type of friendliness. It is all a matter of opinion, but, anyway, the author's opinion is there for what it is worth. Where no 'Jim Mark' appears, of course, that means that the author has not visited that particular hostel.

**Terminology:** There is not much terminology to learn in connexion with Japanese Youth Hostels – just a couple of words. Youth Hostels are known as 'Youth Hostels', just as in English, but, because of the lack of a 'th' sound in Japanese, and because of the Japanese delight in abbreviating foreign words, 'Youth Hostel' is often abbreviated to 'Youth' and then mispronounced as 'Yous', so, when you hear it, you will know what a 'Yous' is. In case you cannot easily be understood and need to show the words 'Youth Hostel' written in Japanese to somebody, when asking for directions, for example, they appear in the Japanese *katakana* alphabet under the heading at the start of this section of the book.

The second technical term to learn is that the person who runs each hostel, whom we would usually call the manager, is, in Japan, called the 'Parent'. (i.e. the English word 'Parent' is used. It is not a translation.) That is rather a friendly idea, for the word is not otherwise in common usage in Japan.

**Duties:** Most hostels do not assign any specific duties to hostellers. However, you will be expected to leave your sleeping quarters as you found them, with blankets neatly and properly folded or, if the dormitory was *tatami*, with the bedding folded and put away in the cupboard as found. Sheets should be put in the receptacle which will probably be near the entrance.

If you take dinner or breakfast, you may be expected to help with the washing-up afterwards. Otherwise, there is generally no duty requirement.

**Laundry Facilities:** Most of the larger hostels have coin-operated washing machines and driers. Smaller hostels, however, rarely offer such facilities, so plan to do your washing while in cities or large towns. There are commercial coin-operated laundries as well, of course, but the machines in the Youth Hostels are usually cheaper.

**Alcohol:** Most hostels now permit alcohol in moderation. Many sell beer, either as an optional extra with dinner or from vending machines in the hostel. However, the price tends to be high. Of course, the hostels prefer that you buy their beer, but there is usually no specific rule saying that you cannot go outside and purchase your own. In any case, if you buy the same brand as that offered in the hostel, who is to know where it came from?

**Meeting:** There may be a 'meeting' held in the evening, although this idea has been going out of fashion somewhat recently. The idea of the meeting may have been to draw together normally shy males and females to make some contact with each other. However, times change and perhaps it is being found that the sexes need no encouragement whatever to make contact with each other these days.

Some hostels still keep the tradition, though, and sometimes it is a very useful one, for the Parent may use the time to tell hostellers about the area, about what there is to see, about how they can get around and about what discounts are available to hostellers. One notable case is the meeting at Aso Hostel in Kyushu, where the Parent who has run the hostel for thirty years holds his guests spellbound for an hour as he shows them his own photographs of Mt. Aso in all of its moods in all seasons. Another example is Renoir Hostel, also in Kyushu, which has organized discounts on just about everything, even including lunch, in the interesting nearby town of Yanagawa and where the Parent introduces the options available during the meeting time. Exander Onuma Hostel, in Hokkaido, sometimes gives a slide show of the surrounding area in the various seasons. So, even though you do not speak Japanese, and even though the meeting, if one is held, is not usually compulsory, it is not necessarily to be shunned. Indeed, unless you have something particularly urgent to which to attend, it is probably worth going along and at least seeing what is on offer.

# POPULARITY POLL

From time to time the JYH organizes an informal poll amongst hostellers staying in certain hostels on certain nights to assess the relative popularity of hostels throughout the country. Here, for interest, are the results of the last such poll conducted.

| | Name | Location | Page |
|---|---|---|---|
| 1. | Dochu-an | Sendai, Tohoku | 412 |
| 2. | Matsuyama | Shikoku | 450 |
| 3. | Bibaushi Liberty | Hokkaido | 404 |
| 4. | Kawayo Green | Tohoku | 409 |
| 5. | Tono | Tohoku | 411 |
| 6. | Shiretoko Iwaobetsu | Hokkaido | 401 |
| 7. | Mashu-ko | Hokkaido | 402 |
| 8. | Wakkanai Moshiripa | Hokkaido | 400 |
| 9. | Furano White | Hokkaido | 405 |
| 10. | Azumino Pastoral | Chubu | 429 |
| 11. | Momoiwa-so | Hokkaido | 399 |
| 12. | Kiyosato Ihatov | Hokkaido | 402 |
| 13. | Saroma Kohan | Hokkaido | 400 |
| 14. | Urakami-ga-oka | Nagasaki, Kyushu | 454 |
| 15. | Ueda Mahoroba | Chubu | 427 |
| 15. | Utano | Kyoto, Kansai | 437 |
| 17. | Komoro | Chubu | 427 |
| 17. | Naka Shibetsu | Hokkaido | 401 |
| 19. | Okhotsk Koshimizu | Hokkaido | 400 |
| 20. | Shodo-shima Olive | Shikoku | 448 |
| 21. | M.G. | Chugoku | 444 |
| 22. | Rishiri Green Hill | Hokkaido | 399 |
| 23. | Abashiri Ryuhyo-no-oka | Hokkaido | 401 |
| 24. | Kurashiki | Chugoku | 443 |
| 25. | Shimantogawa | Shikoku | Unlisted |
| 25. | Jofuku-ji | Shikoku | 451 |
| 27. | Sahoro | Hokkaido | 405 |
| 27. | Ise Shima | Kansai | 434 |
| 27. | Higashiyama | Kyoto, Kansai | 436 |
| 30. | Kiso Ryojo-an | Chubu | 429 |

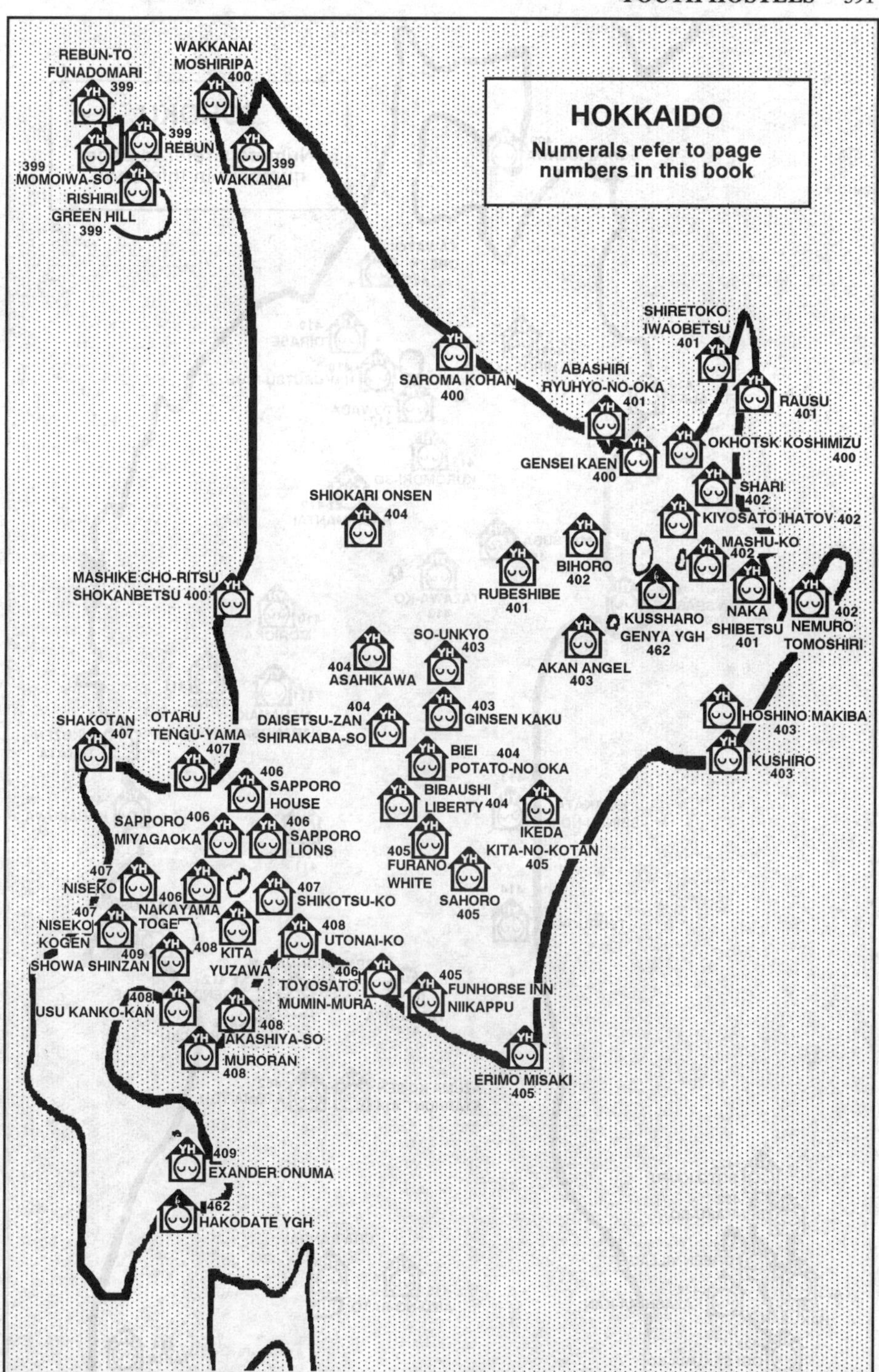
HOKKAIDO
Numerals refer to page numbers in this book
REBUN-TO FUNADOMARI 399
WAKKANAI MOSHIRIPA 400
399 REBUN
399 WAKKANAI
399 MOMOIWA-SO
RISHIRI GREEN HILL 399
SHIRETOKO IWAOBETSU 401
SAROMA KOHAN 400
ABASHIRI RYUHYO-NO-OKA 401
RAUSU 401
OKHOTSK KOSHIMIZU 400
GENSEI KAEN 400
SHARI 402
SHIOKARI ONSEN 404
KIYOSATO IHATOV 402
MASHU-KO 402
BIHORO 402
RUBESHIBE 401
MASHIKE CHO-RITSU SHOKANBETSU 400
KUSSHARO GENYA YGH 462
NAKA SHIBETSU 401
NEMURO TOMOSHIRI 402
SO-UNKYO 403
404 ASAHIKAWA
AKAN ANGEL 403
403 GINSEN KAKU
HOSHINO MAKIBA 403
SHAKOTAN 407
OTARU TENGU-YAMA 407
404 DAISETSU-ZAN SHIRAKABA-SO
BIEI 404 POTATO-NO OKA
KUSHIRO 403
406 SAPPORO HOUSE
BIBAUSHI LIBERTY 404
IKEDA KITA-NO-KOTAN 405
SAPPORO 406 MIYAGAOKA
406 SAPPORO LIONS
405 FURANO WHITE
407 NISEKO
407 SHIKOTSU-KO
SAHORO 405
406 NAKAYAMA TOGE
407 NISEKO KOGEN
408 UTONAI-KO
409 SHOWA SHINZAN
408 KITA YUZAWA
406 TOYOSATO MUMIN-MURA
405 FUNHORSE INN NIIKAPPU
408 USU KANKO-KAN
408 AKASHIYA-SO
MURORAN 408
ERIMO MISAKI 405
409 EXANDER ONUMA
462 HAKODATE YGH

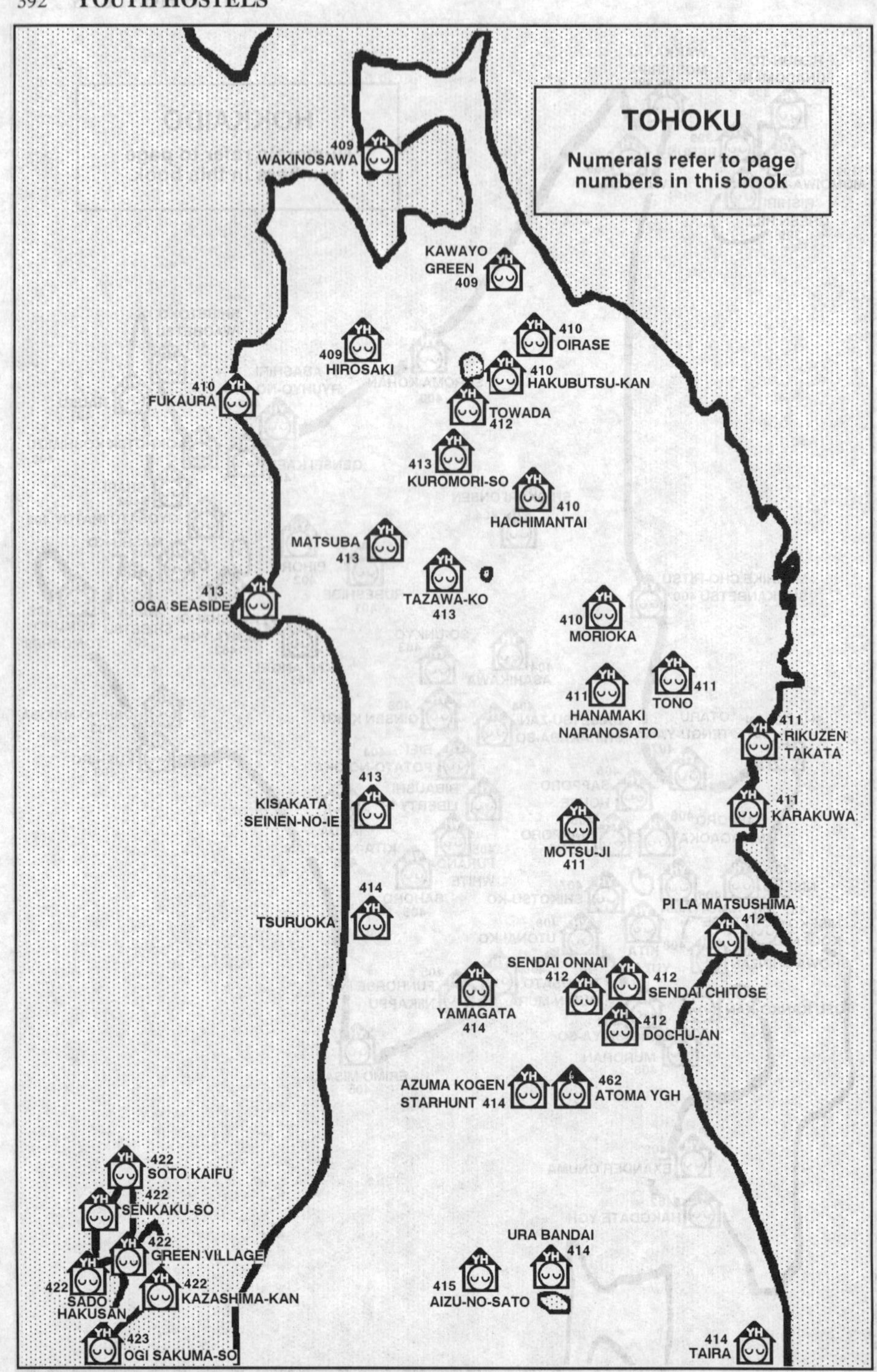
TOHOKU
Numerals refer to page numbers in this book
409 WAKINOSAWA
KAWAYO GREEN 409
410 OIRASE
409 HIROSAKI
410 HAKUBUTSU-KAN
410 FUKAURA
TOWADA 412
413 KUROMORI-SO
410 HACHIMANTAI
MATSUBA 413
TAZAWA-KO 413
413 OGA SEASIDE
410 MORIOKA
411 HANAMAKI NARANOSATO
TONO 411
411 RIKUZEN TAKATA
413 KISAKATA SEINEN-NO-IE
411 KARAKUWA
MOTSU-JI 411
414 TSURUOKA
PI LA MATSUSHIMA 412
SENDAI ONNAI 412
412 SENDAI CHITOSE
YAMAGATA 414
412 DOCHU-AN
AZUMA KOGEN STARHUNT 414
462 ATOMA YGH
422 SOTO KAIFU
422 SENKAKU-SO
422 GREEN VILLAGE
422 SADO HAKUSAN
422 KAZASHIMA-KAN
423 OGI SAKUMA-SO
URA BANDAI 414
415 AIZU-NO-SATO
414 TAIRA

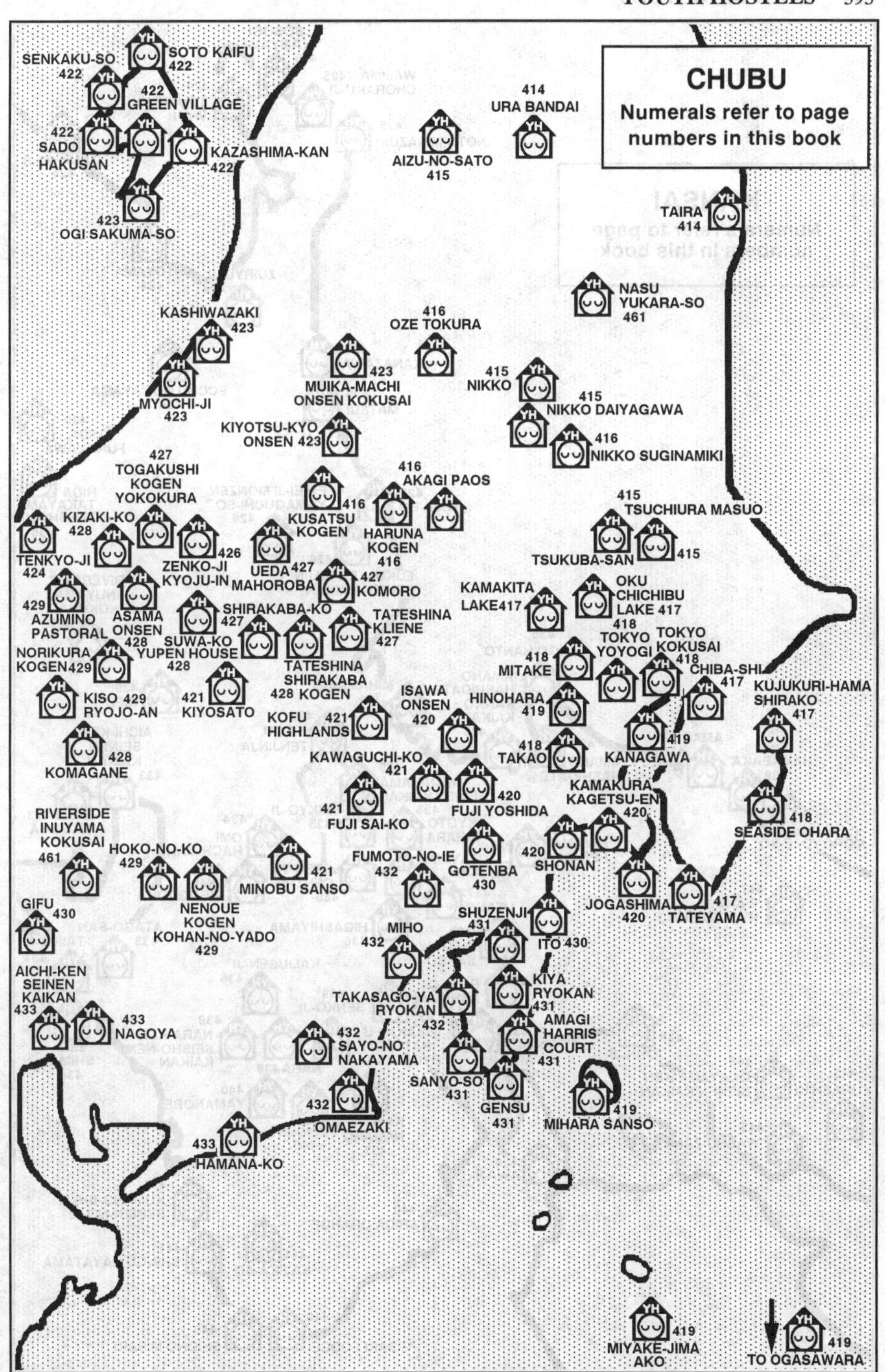
CHUBU
Numerals refer to page numbers in this book
SENKAKU-SO 422
SOTO KAIFU 422
422 GREEN VILLAGE
422 SADO HAKUSAN
KAZASHIMA-KAN 422
423 OGI SAKUMA-SO
414 URA BANDAI
AIZU-NO-SATO 415
TAIRA 414
NASU YUKARA-SO 461
KASHIWAZAKI 423
MYOCHI-JI 423
416 OZE TOKURA
423 MUIKA-MACHI ONSEN KOKUSAI
415 NIKKO
415 NIKKO DAIYAGAWA
416 NIKKO SUGINAMIKI
KIYOTSU-KYO ONSEN 423
427 TOGAKUSHI KOGEN YOKOKURA
416 AKAGI PAOS
416 KUSATSU KOGEN
HARUNA KOGEN 416
415 TSUCHIURA MASUO
TSUKUBA-SAN 415
KIZAKI-KO 428
TENKYO-JI 424
ZENKO-JI KYOJU-IN 426
UEDA MAHOROBA 427
427 KOMORO
429 AZUMINO PASTORAL
ASAMA ONSEN 428
SHIRAKABA-KO 427
TATESHINA KLIENE 427
KAMAKITA LAKE 417
OKU CHICHIBU LAKE 417
418 TOKYO YOYOGI
TOKYO KOKUSAI 418
NORIKURA KOGEN 429
SUWA-KO YUPEN HOUSE 428
TATESHINA SHIRAKABA 428 KOGEN
418 MITAKE
CHIBA-SHI 417
KUJUKURI-HAMA SHIRAKO 417
KISO 429 RYOJO-AN
421 KIYOSATO
ISAWA ONSEN 420
HINOHARA 419
KOFU 421 HIGHLANDS
418 TAKAO
419 KANAGAWA
428 KOMAGANE
KAWAGUCHI-KO 421
421 FUJI SAI-KO
420 FUJI YOSHIDA
KAMAKURA KAGETSU-EN 420
418 SEASIDE OHARA
RIVERSIDE INUYAMA KOKUSAI 461
HOKO-NO-KO 429
421 MINOBU SANSO
FUMOTO-NO-IE 432
GOTENBA 430
420 SHONAN
NENOUE KOGEN KOHAN-NO-YADO 429
JOGASHIMA 420
417 TATEYAMA
GIFU 430
SHUZENJI 431
MIHO 432
ITO 430
AICHI-KEN SEINEN KAIKAN 433
KIYA RYOKAN 431
TAKASAGO-YA RYOKAN 432
AMAGI HARRIS COURT 431
433 NAGOYA
432 SAYO-NO NAKAYAMA
SANYO-SO 431
GENSU 431
419 MIHARA SANSO
432 OMAEZAKI
433 HAMANA-KO
419 MIYAKE-JIMA AKO
419 TO OGASAWARA

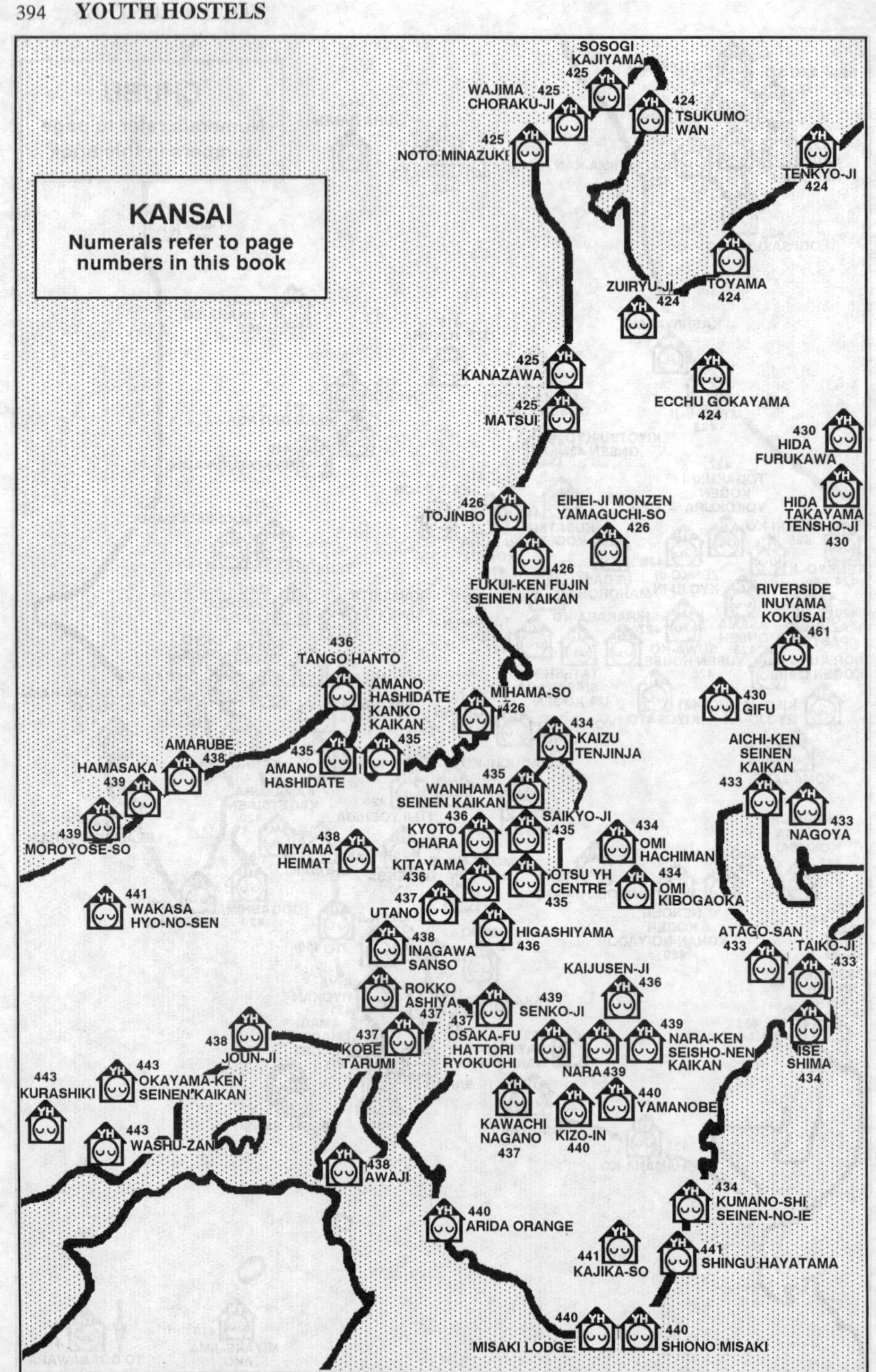
KANSAI
Numerals refer to page numbers in this book
SOSOGI KAJIYAMA 425
WAJIMA CHORAKU-JI 425
424 TSUKUMO WAN
425 NOTO MINAZUKI
TENKYO-JI 424
ZUIRYU-JI 424
TOYAMA 424
425 KANAZAWA
ECCHU GOKAYAMA 424
425 MATSUI
430 HIDA FURUKAWA
HIDA TAKAYAMA TENSHO-JI 430
426 TOJINBO
EIHEI-JI MONZEN YAMAGUCHI-SO 426
426 FUKUI-KEN FUJIN SEINEN KAIKAN
RIVERSIDE INUYAMA KOKUSAI 461
436 TANGO HANTO
AMANO HASHIDATE KANKO KAIKAN
MIHAMA-SO 426
430 GIFU
434 KAIZU TENJINJA
AMARUBE 438
HAMASAKA 439
435 AMANO HASHIDATE
435
AICHI-KEN SEINEN KAIKAN 433
435 WANIHAMA SEINEN KAIKAN
433 NAGOYA
439 MOROYOSE-SO
436 KYOTO OHARA
SAIKYO-JI 435
434 OMI HACHIMAN
438 MIYAMA HEIMAT
KITAYAMA 436
OTSU YH CENTRE 435
434 OMI KIBOGAOKA
441 WAKASA HYO-NO-SEN
437 UTANO
HIGASHIYAMA 436
ATAGO-SAN 433
TAIKO-JI 433
438 INAGAWA SANSO
KAIJUSEN-JI 436
ROKKO ASHIYA 437
439 SENKO-JI
438 JOUN-JI
437 KOBE TARUMI
437 OSAKA-FU HATTORI RYOKUCHI
439 NARA-KEN SEISHO-NEN KAIKAN
ISE SHIMA 434
NARA 439
443 KURASHIKI
443 OKAYAMA-KEN SEINEN KAIKAN
440 YAMANOBE
KAWACHI NAGANO 437
KIZO-IN 440
443 WASHU-ZAN
438 AWAJI
434 KUMANO-SHI SEINEN-NO-IE
440 ARIDA ORANGE
441 KAJIKA-SO
441 SHINGU HAYATAMA
440 MISAKI LODGE
440 SHIONO MISAKI

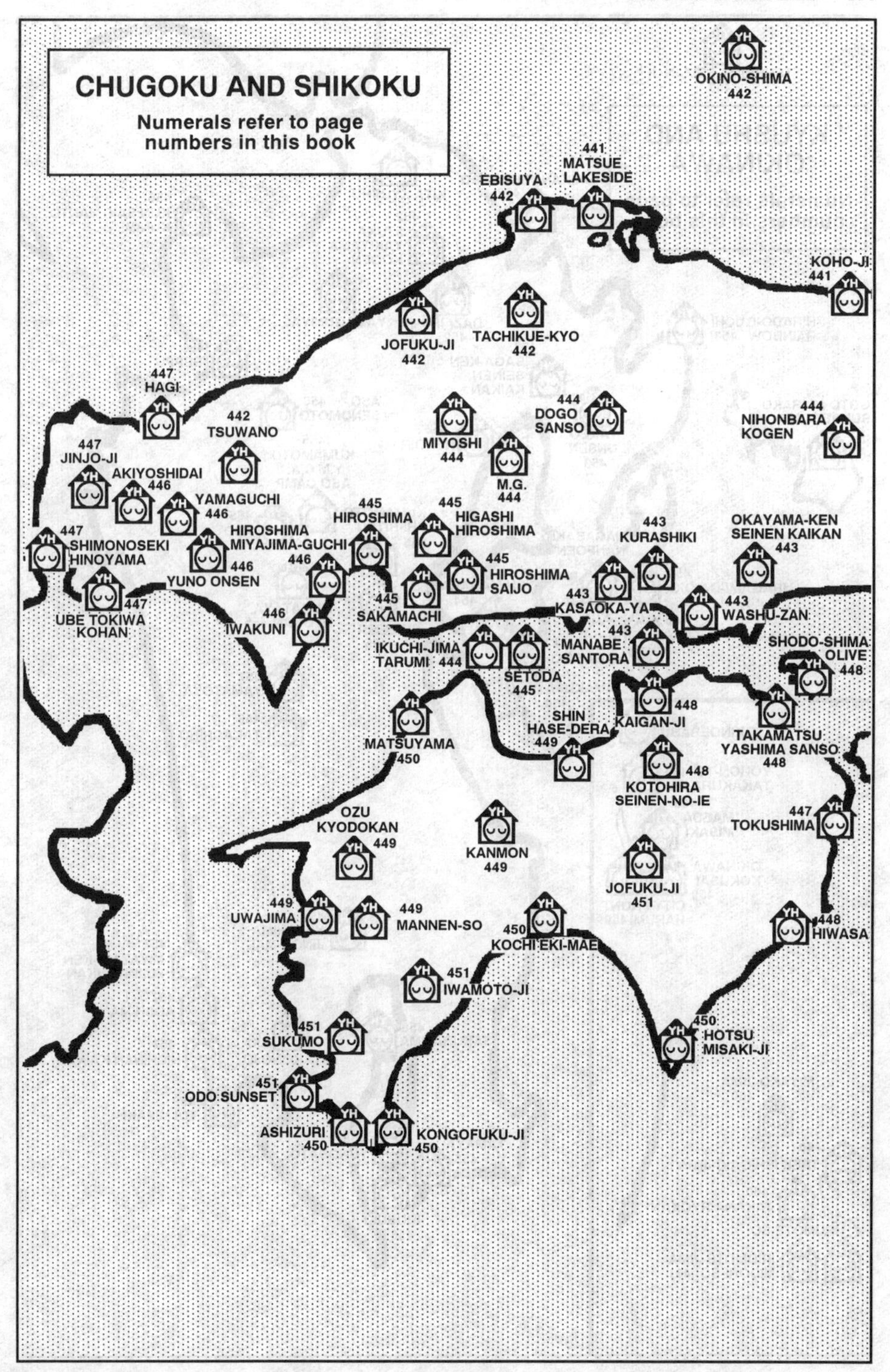
CHUGOKU AND SHIKOKU
Numerals refer to page numbers in this book
OKINO-SHIMA 442
441 MATSUE LAKESIDE
EBISUYA 442
KOHO-JI 441
JOFUKU-JI 442
TACHIKUE-KYO 442
447 HAGI
442 TSUWANO
444 DOGO SANSO
MIYOSHI 444
444 NIHONBARA KOGEN
M.G. 444
447 JINJO-JI
AKIYOSHIDAI 446
YAMAGUCHI 446
445 HIROSHIMA
445 HIGASHI HIROSHIMA
443 KURASHIKI
OKAYAMA-KEN SEINEN KAIKAN 443
447 SHIMONOSEKI HINOYAMA
HIROSHIMA MIYAJIMA-GUCHI 446
446
YUNO ONSEN
445 HIROSHIMA SAIJO
UBE TOKIWA KOHAN 447
446 IWAKUNI
445 SAKAMACHI
443 KASAOKA-YA
443 WASHU-ZAN
IKUCHI-JIMA TARUMI 444
SETODA 445
443 MANABE SANTORA
SHODO-SHIMA OLIVE 448
448 KAIGAN-JI
MATSUYAMA 450
SHIN HASE-DERA 449
TAKAMATSU YASHIMA SANSO 448
448 KOTOHIRA SEINEN-NO-IE
OZU KYODOKAN 449
KANMON 449
447 TOKUSHIMA
JOFUKU-JI 451
449 UWAJIMA
449 MANNEN-SO
450 KOCHI EKI-MAE
448 HIWASA
451 IWAMOTO-JI
451 SUKUMO
450 HOTSU MISAKI-JI
451 ODO SUNSET
ASHIZURI 450
KONGOFUKU-JI 450

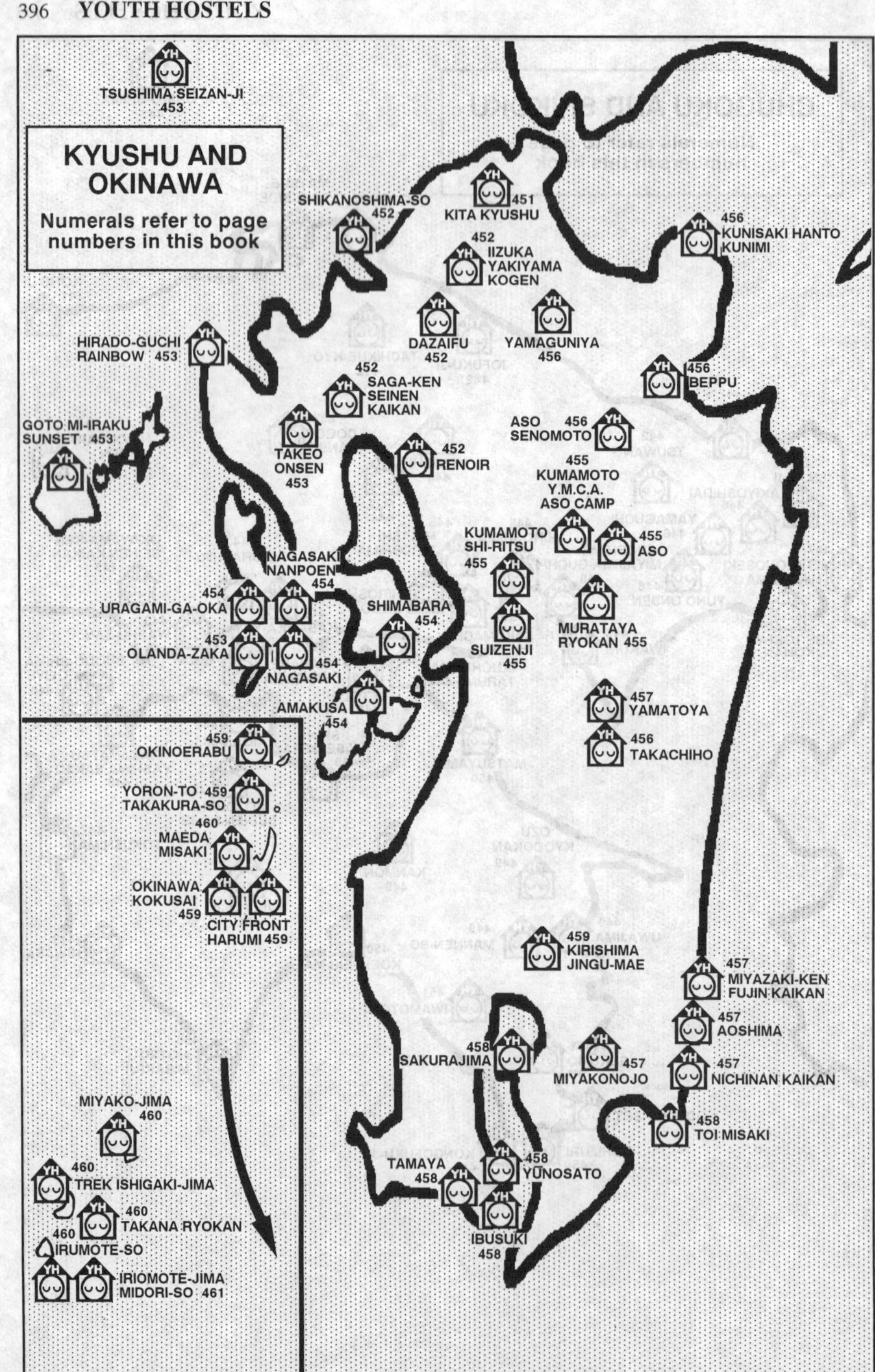
KYUSHU AND OKINAWA
Numerals refer to page numbers in this book
TSUSHIMA SEIZAN-JI 453
SHIKANOSHIMA-SO 452
KITA KYUSHU 451
452 IIZUKA YAKIYAMA KOGEN
456 KUNISAKI HANTO KUNIMI
HIRADO-GUCHI RAINBOW 453
DAZAIFU 452
YAMAGUNIYA 456
452 SAGA-KEN SEINEN KAIKAN
456 BEPPU
GOTO MI-IRAKU SUNSET 453
TAKEO ONSEN 453
452 RENOIR
ASO 456 SENOMOTO
455 KUMAMOTO Y.M.C.A. ASO CAMP
KUMAMOTO SHI-RITSU 455
455 ASO
NAGASAKI NANPOEN 454
454 URAGAMI-GA-OKA
SHIMABARA 454
453 OLANDA-ZAKA
454 NAGASAKI
SUIZENJI 455
MURATAYA RYOKAN 455
AMAKUSA 454
457 YAMATOYA
456 TAKACHIHO
459 OKINOERABU
YORON-TO 459 TAKAKURA-SO
460 MAEDA MISAKI
OKINAWA KOKUSAI 459
CITY FRONT HARUMI 459
459 KIRISHIMA JINGU-MAE
457 MIYAZAKI-KEN FUJIN KAIKAN
457 AOSHIMA
458 SAKURAJIMA
457 MIYAKONOJO
457 NICHINAN KAIKAN
458 TOI MISAKI
MIYAKO-JIMA 460
460 TREK ISHIGAKI-JIMA
TAMAYA 458
458 YUNOSATO
460 TAKANA RYOKAN
460 IRUMOTE-SO
IBUSUKI 458
IRIOMOTE-JIMA MIDORI-SO 461

# JAPANESE HOSTELS PARTICIPATING IN INTERNATIONAL BOOKING NETWORK (IBN)

**Numerals refer to page numbers in this book**

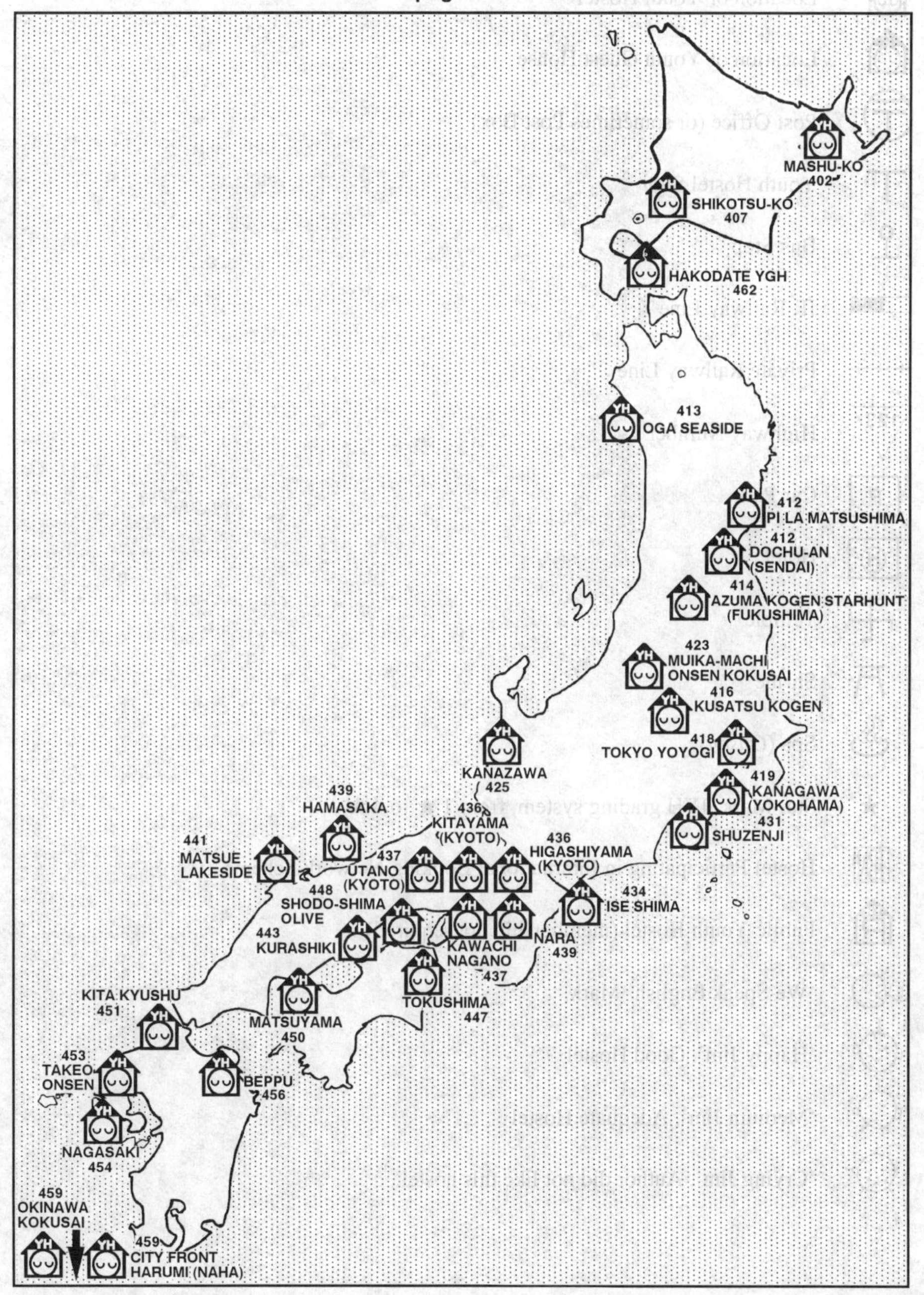

# SYMBOLS USED IN MAPS AND INFORMATION SECTIONS

Location of Youth Hostel

Location of Youth Guest House

Post Office (or sometimes Post Box)

Youth Hostel Sign

Bus Stop

JR Railway Line

Private Railway Line

Highway Number

Car Park

Hotel

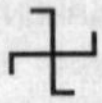

Temple

Shrine

Spa (*Onsen*)

★ Star Mark. JYH grading system, from 1★ to 4★

Hostel Participating in International Booking Network Scheme

Public Youth Hostel (membership not required)

'We Speak English' Mark

'Happy Jim'. Good Hostel

'Medium Jim'. Adequate Hostel

'Crying Jim'. Author did not like this hostel.

## RISHIRI GREEN HILL (利尻グリーンヒル)

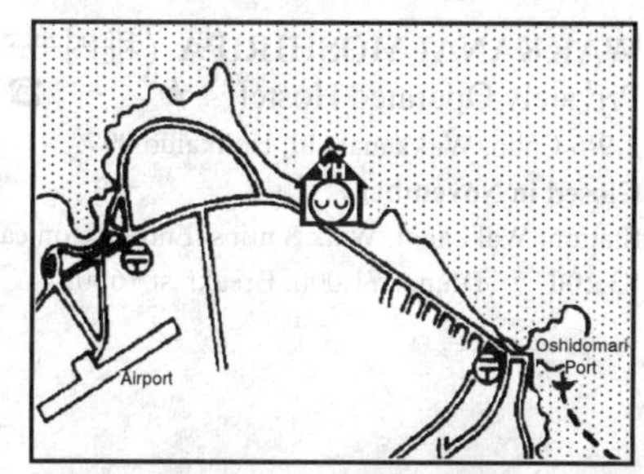


Privately Operated Hostel 3★ ☎ 01638-2-2507. Fax: 2383
35-3 Fujino, Oshidomari, Rishiri Fuji-cho, Rishiri-gun, Hokkaido 097-01. 46 beds
Station: Wakkanai. Walk to ferry, 5 mins. Ferry to Oshidomari, 2 hrs. Walk 25 mins. or take bus to Youth Hostel-mae, 5 mins. Hostel is adjacent to bus stop.
**¥2,600.** Dinner ¥1,000. Breakfast ¥600.

## REBUN (礼文)

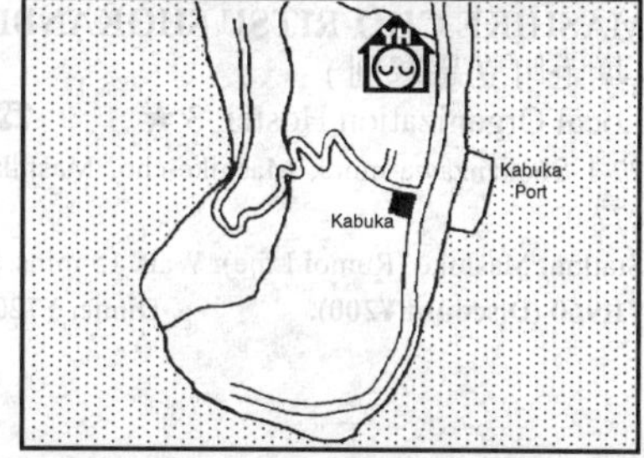


Privately Operated Hostel 3★ ☎ 01638-6-1608
Kabuka, Rebun-cho, Rebun-gun, Hokkaido 097-12. 80 beds
Station: Wakkanai. Walk to ferry, 5 mins. Ferry to Kabuka, 2 hrs. 10 mins. Walk 13 mins. (1.2 km).
**¥2,700.** Dinner ¥1,000. Breakfast ¥600.

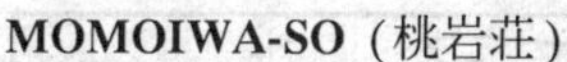

## MOMOIWA-SO (桃岩荘)

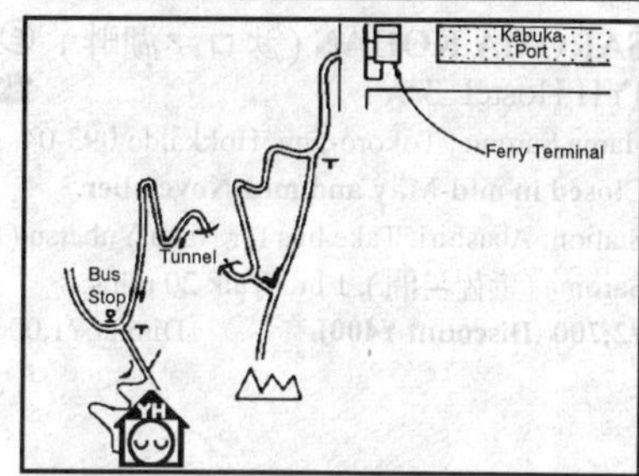


Hotel 3★ ☎ 01638-6-1421, 1390
Moto-chi, Kabuka, Rebun-cho, Rebun-gun, Hokkaido 097-12.
**Open from June until September.** 74 beds
Station: Wakkanai. Walk to ferry, 5 mins. Ferry to Kabuka, 2 hrs. 10 mins. Take bus for Moto-chi (元地) to Momoiwa-so Iriguchi (桃岩荘入口), 15 mins. Walk 7 mins. Or telephone hostel to be collected from ferry terminal. Or walk, 50 mins.
**¥2,700.** Dinner ¥1,000. Breakfast ¥600.

## REBUN-TO FUNADOMARI (礼文島船泊)

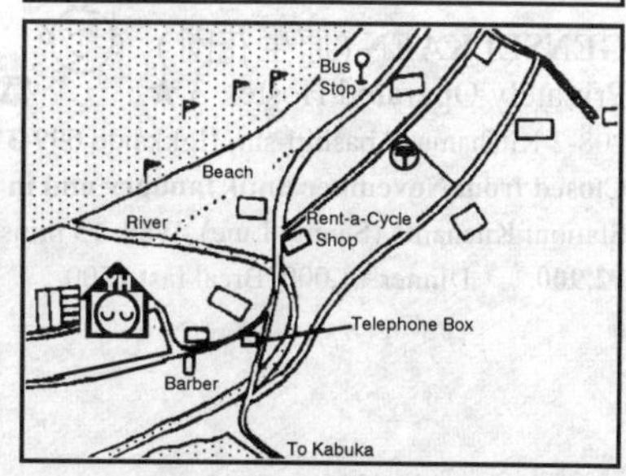


Privately Operated Hostel 2★ ☎ 01638-7-2717. Fax: 2183
Osonae, Funadomari, Rebun-cho, Rebun-gun, Hokkaido 097-11.
**Open from mid-May until mid-October.** 56 beds
Station: Wakkanai. Walk to ferry, 5 mins. Ferry to Kabuka, 2 hrs. 10 mins. Take bus for Sukoton Misaki (スコトン岬) or Funadomari (船泊) to Funadomari Hon-cho (船泊本町), 47 mins. Walk 2 mins.
**¥2,700.** Dinner ¥1,000. Breakfast ¥500. Local Delicacies ¥1,500.

## WAKKANAI (稚内)

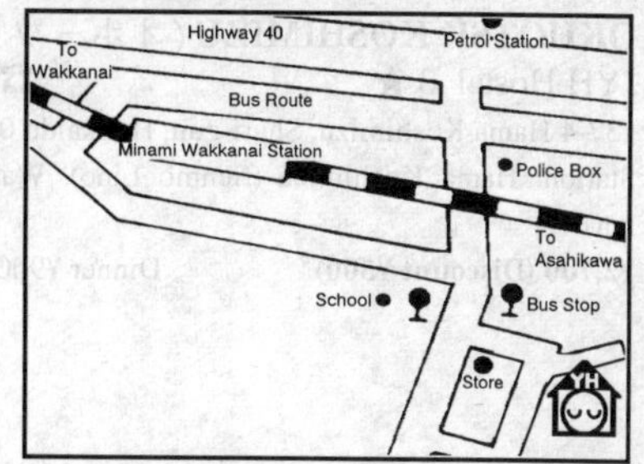


Privately Operated Hostel 3★ ☎ 0162-23-7162, 7179
3-9-1 Komadori, Wakkanai-shi, Hokkaido 097. 74 beds
Station: ① Minami Wakkanai. Walk 12 mins.
② Wakkanai. Take bus for Midori Roku-chome (緑6丁目) to Minami Sho-gakko (南小学校), 12 mins. Walk 2 mins.
**From ¥2,100.** Dinner ¥1,000. Breakfast ¥600.

## WAKKANAI MOSHIRIPA (稚内モシリパ)

Privately Operated Hostel 4★ ☎ 0162-24-0180

2-9-5 Chuo, Wakkanai-shi, Hokkaido 097.

**Closed in November.** 34 beds

Station: Wakkanai. Walk 8 mins. Entrance on east side.

**¥3,200** Dinner ¥1,000. Breakfast ¥600.

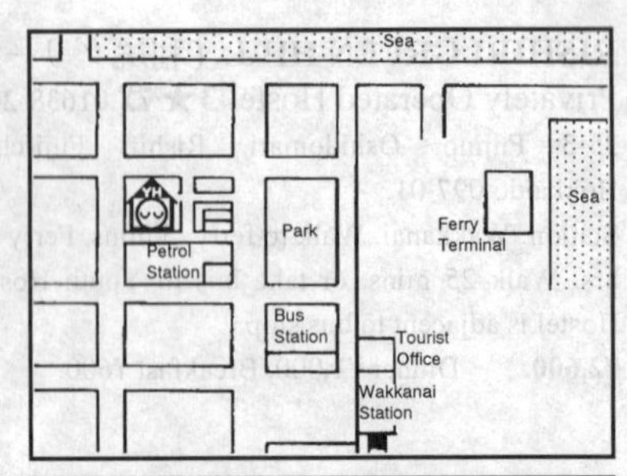


## MASHIKE CHO-RITSU SHOKANBETSU (増毛町立暑寒別)

Local Organization Hostel 3★ ☎ 0164-53-2396

77-1 Shokanzawa-mura, Mashike-cho, Mashike-gun, Hokkaido 077-02. 50 beds

Station: Mashike (Rumoi Line). Walk 15 mins. (1 km).

**¥1,960 (Discount ¥200).** Dinner ¥720. Breakfast ¥410.

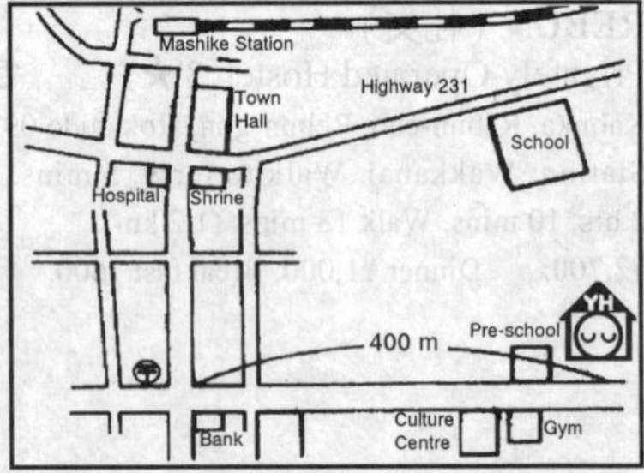


## SAROMA KOHAN (サロマ湖畔)

JYH Hostel 3★ ☎ 01587-6-2515

Hama Saroma, Tokoro-gun, Hokkaido 093-04.

**Closed in mid-May and mid-November.** 80 beds

Station: Abashiri. Take bus for Naka Yubetsu (中湧別) to Hama Saroma (浜佐呂間), 1 hr. Walk 20 mins.

**¥2,700 (Discount ¥400).** Dinner ¥1,000. Breakfast ¥600.

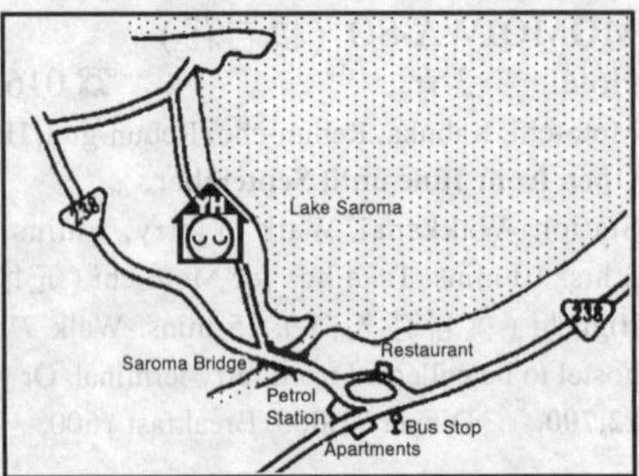


## GENSEI KAEN (原生花園)

Privately Operated Hostel 3★ ☎ 0152-46-2630

208-2 Kitahama, Abashiri-shi, Hokkaido 099-31. 44 beds

**Closed from November until January and in mid-April.**

Station: Kitahama (Senmo Line). Walk 15 mins. (800 m).

**¥2,900.** Dinner ¥1,000. Breakfast ¥500.

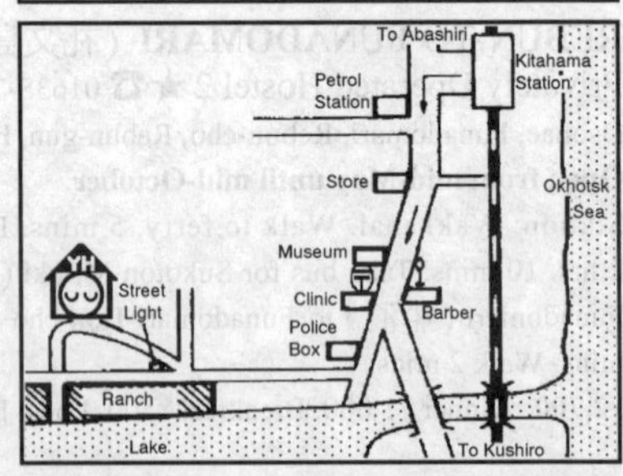


## OKHOTSK KOSHIMIZU (オホーツク小清水)

JYH Hostel 3★ ☎ 0152-64-2011

137-4 Hama Koshimizu, Shari-gun, Hokkaido 099-34. 75 beds

Station: Hama Koshimizu (Senmo Line). Walk 25 mins. (1.8 km).

**¥2,700 (Discount ¥500).** Dinner ¥900. Breakfast ¥500.

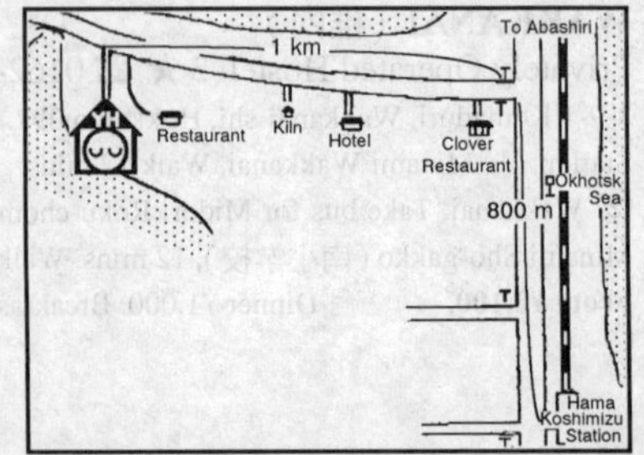

## ABASHIRI RYUHYO-NO-OKA (網走流氷の丘)

Privately Operated Hostel 4★ ☎ 0152-43-8558
22-6 Meiji, Abashiri-shi, Hokkaido 093. 28 beds
Station: Abashiri. Take bus for Futatsu Iwa (二ツ岩) to Meiji Iriguchi (明治入口), 8 mins. Walk 10 mins.
**¥3,200.** Dinner ¥1,000. Breakfast ¥600. Local Delicacies ¥1,500.

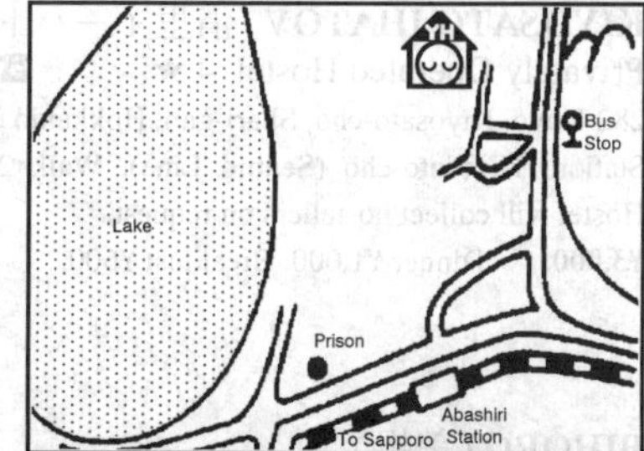


## RUBESHIBE (るべしべ)

JYH Hostel 3★ ☎ 0157-42-2268
24-12 Asahi Chuo-cho, Rubeshibe, Tokoro-gun, Hokkaido 091.
**Closed from November until January.** 80 beds
Station: Rubeshibe (Sekihoku Main Line). Walk 12 mins. (1 km).
**¥2,500 (Discount ¥200).** Dinner ¥850. Breakfast ¥500.

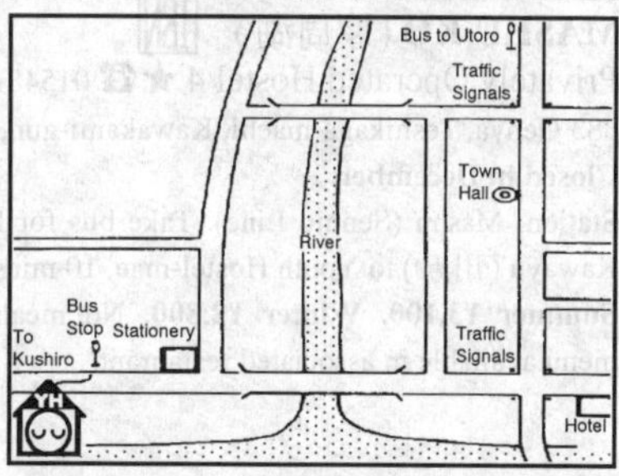


## RAUSU (ラウス)

Privately Operated Hostel 1★ ☎ 01538-7-2145
4 Hon-cho, Rausu, Menashi-gun, Hokkaido 086-18. 88 beds
Station: Kushiro. Take bus for Rausu (羅臼) to Rausu Hon-cho (羅臼本町), 3hrs. 40mins. Walk back 1 min.
**¥2,500.** Dinner ¥1,000. Breakfast ¥500.

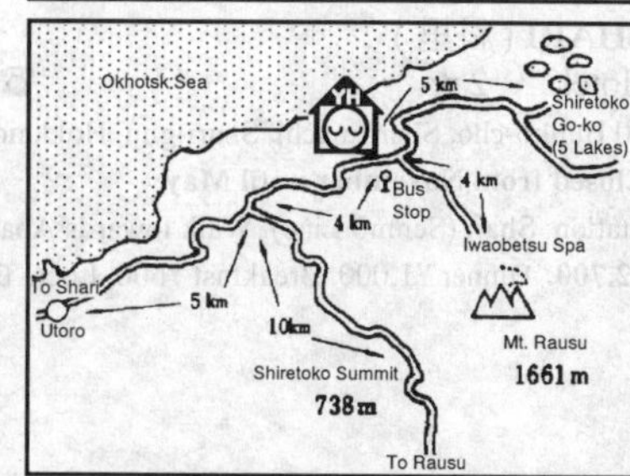


## SHIRETOKO IWAOBETSU (知床岩尾別)

Privately Operated Hostel 3★ ☎ 01522-4-2311
Iwaobetsu, Shari-machi, Shari-gun, Hokkaido 099-43.
**Open from June until October.** 91 beds
Station: Shari (Senmo Line). Take bus for Shiretoko Go-ko (知床五湖) to Iwaobetsu (岩尾別), 1 hr. 10 mins. Walk 1 min.
**¥2,900.** Dinner ¥1,000. Breakfast ¥600.

Okhotsk:Sea
5 km
Shiretoko Go-ko (5 Lakes)
Bus Stop
4 km
4 km
Iwaobetsu Spa
To Shari
5 km
Utoro
10km
Mt. Rausu
1661 m
Shiretoko Summit
738 m
To Rausu

## NAKA SHIBETSU (なかしべつ)

JYH Hostel 4★ ☎ 01537-2-7727. Fax: 7790
2-3 Kita 19-sen Naka Shibetsu, Naka Shibetsu-cho, Shibetsu-gun, Hokkaido 086-11. 24 beds
**Closed from November until January, except at New Year.**
Station: Kushiro. Take bus to Naka Shibetsu (中標津), 1 hr. 50 mins. Change to bus for Shibetsu (標津) or Rausu (羅臼) to Nishi Ju-kyu Sen (西 19 線). Walk 10 mins. Sometimes change of bus is not necessary. Hostel will collect hostellers from Bus Terminal on request.
**¥3,200.** Dinner ¥1,000. Breakfast ¥400.

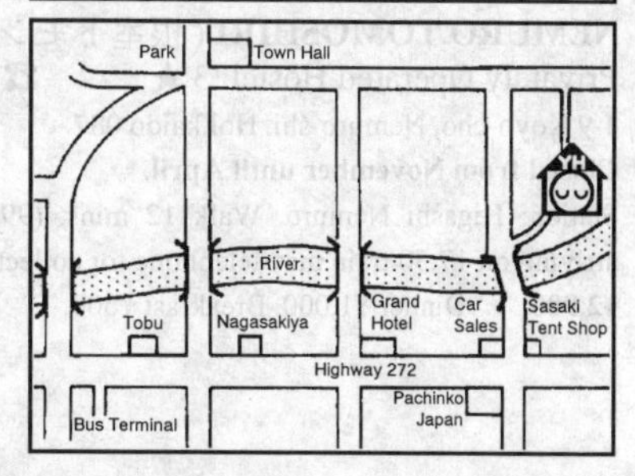

## KIYOSATO IHATOV (清里イーハトーヴ)

Privately Operated Hostel 4★ ☎ 01522-5-3995

282 Koyo, Kiyosato-cho, Shari-gun, Hokkaido 099-44. 24 beds

Station: Kiyosato-cho (Senmo Line). Walk 25 mins. (2 km). Hostel will collect hostellers on request.

**¥3,000.** Dinner ¥1,000. Breakfast ¥600.

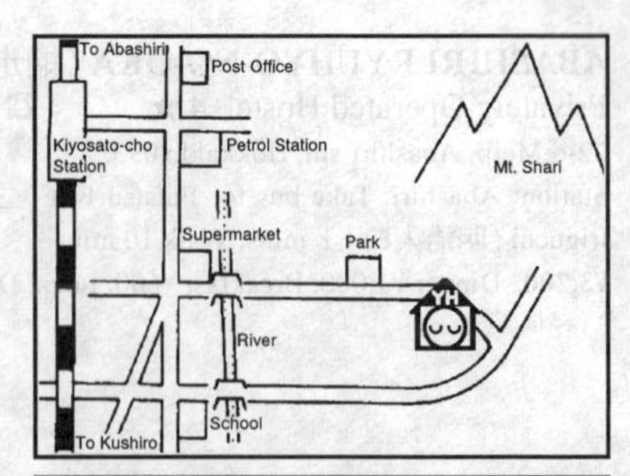


## BIHORO (美幌)

JYH Hostel 3★ ☎ 01527-3-2560

31 Moto-machi, Bihoro-cho, Hokkaido 092.

**Closed from late October until early November.** 80 beds

Station: Bihoro (Sekihoku Main Line). Take Kitami Bus for Tsubetsu (津別) or Ryoyo-sho (療養所) to Minami San-chome (南三丁目), 8 mins. Walk 10 mins. (800 m). Alternatively, walk from station along 'Koen Dori', 30 mins. (2 km).

**Winter ¥2,700. Summer ¥2,500 (Discount ¥200).**

Dinner ¥1,000. Breakfast ¥600.

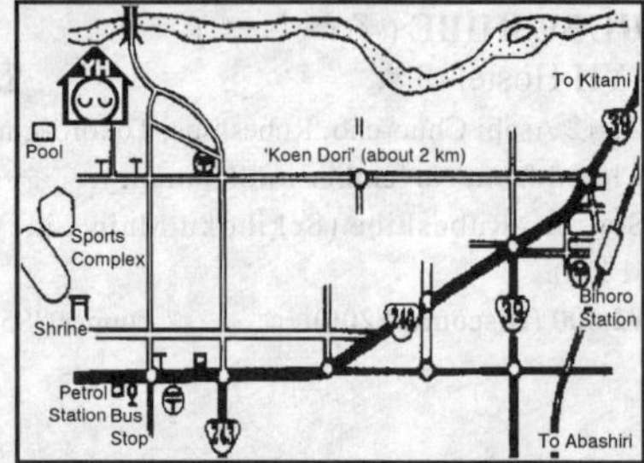


## MASHU-KO (摩周湖) IBN

Privately Operated Hostel 4★ ☎ 01548-2-3098. Fax: 4875

883 Genya, Teshikaga-machi, Kawakami-gun, Hokkaido 088-32.

**Closed in December.** 104 beds

Station: Mashu (Senmo Line). Take bus for Bihoro (美幌) or Kawayu (川湯) to Youth Hostel-mae, 10 mins. Walk 2 mins.

**Summer ¥3,100. Winter ¥2,800.** No meals, but economical menu available in associated restaurant.

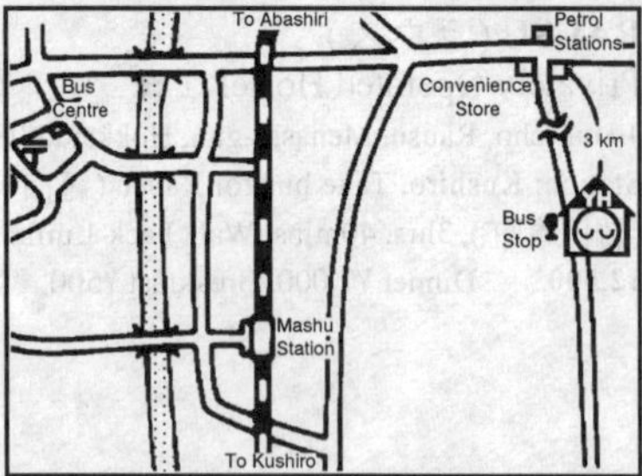


## SHARI (斜里)

Hotel 2★ ☎ 01522-3-2220

30 Bunko-cho, Shari-machi, Shari-gun, Hokkaido 099-41.

**Closed from November until May.** 55 beds

Station: Shari (Senmo Line). Walk towards Abashiri, 5 mins.

**¥2,700.** Dinner ¥1,000. Breakfast ¥600. Local Delicacies ¥1,500.

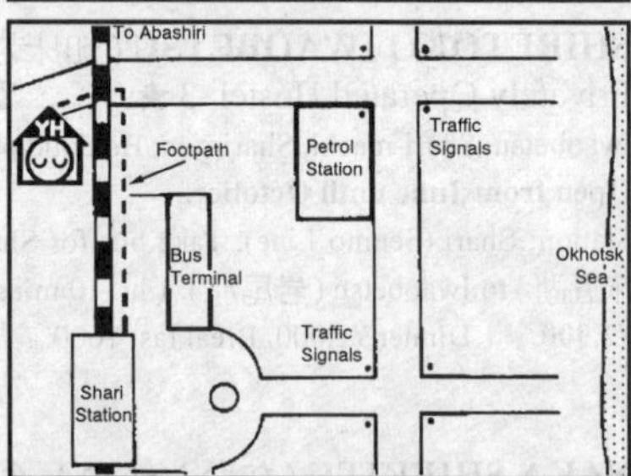


## NEMURO TOMOSHIRI (根室トモシリ)

Privately Operated Hostel 3★ ☎ 01532-2-2825

4-9 Koyo-cho, Nemuro-shi, Hokkaido 087. 24 beds

**Closed from November until April.**

Station: Higashi Nemuro. Walk 12 mins. (990 m). Hostellers arriving on 17:50 train may telephone for collection.

**¥2,900.** Dinner ¥1,000. Breakfast ¥600.

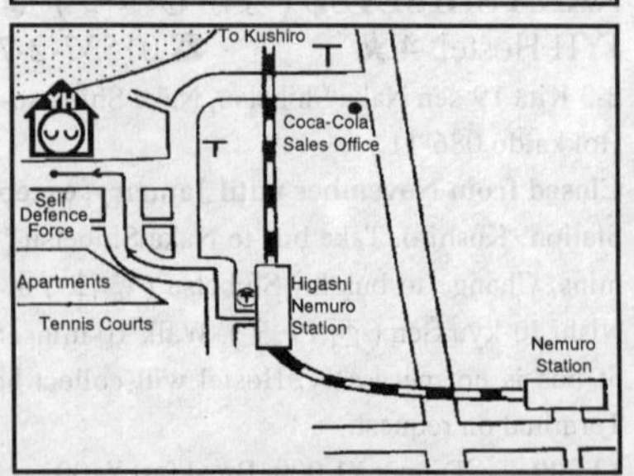

**HOSHINO MAKIBA** (星のまきば)
Privately Operated Hostel 3★☎ 0154-23-0852. Fax: 24-5141
7-23 Kawakita-cho, Kushiro-shi, Hokkaido 085. 44 beds
Station: Kushiro. Walk 15 mins. (1.5 km).
**¥2,400.** Dinner ¥1,000. Breakfast ¥450.

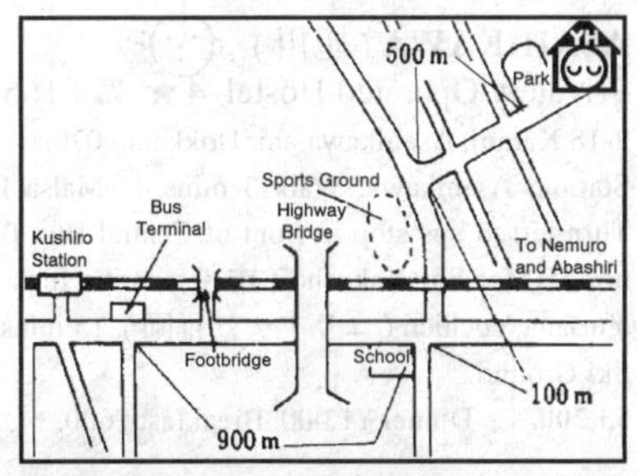


**KUSHIRO** (釧路)
JYH Hostel 3★ ☎ 0154-41-1676
3-7-23 Tsurugadai, Kushiro-shi, Hokkaido 085.
**Closed in mid-January and mid-May.** 50 beds
Station: Kushiro. Take Kushiro City Bus no. 27 or 30 to Youth Hostel-mae, 15 mins. Walk 2 mins. Or take bus no. 2, 8, 12 or 15 to Kogyo Koko (工業高校), 12 mins. Walk 7 mins. Or walk from station, 40 mins. (2.5 km).
**Winter ¥2,100. Summer ¥1,900.** Dinner ¥600. Breakfast ¥400.

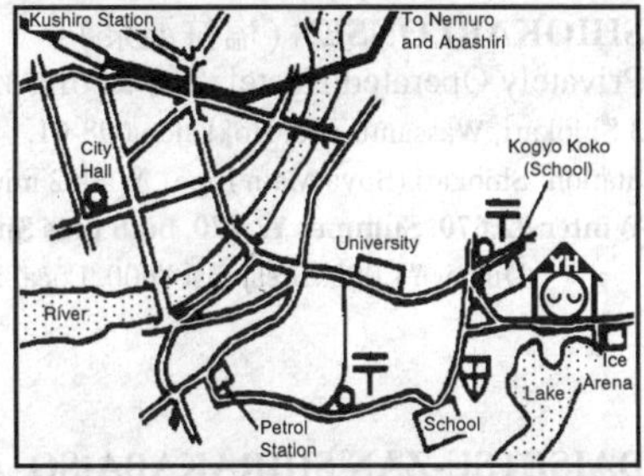


**AKAN ANGEL** (阿寒エンジェル)
Privately Operated Hostel 2★ ☎ 0154-67-2309, 2954
5-1 Shurikomabetsu, Akan-cho, Hokkaido 085-04. 90 beds
Station: Kushiro. Take bus for Akan-ko (阿寒湖) to Akan Kohan (阿寒湖畔) Bus Terminal, 1 hr. 50 mins. Walk 12 mins.
**¥2,700, plus Spa Fee ¥150.** Dinner ¥1,000. Breakfast ¥600.

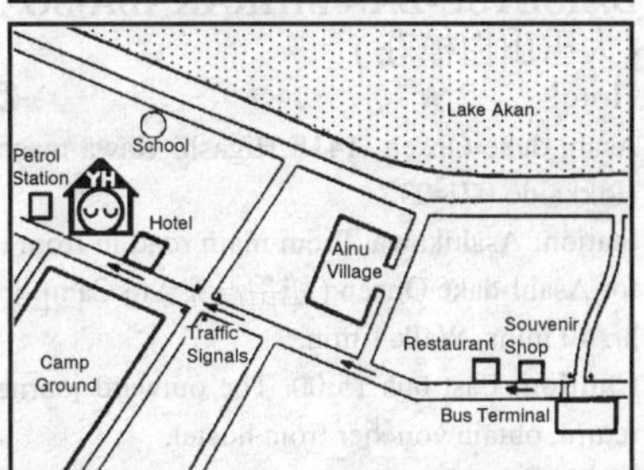


**SO-UNKYO** (層雲峡)
JYH Hostel 3★ ☎ 01658-5-3418. Fax: 3186
So-unkyo, Kamikawa-cho, Hokkaido 078-17. 90 beds
Station: Kamikawa (Sekihoku Main Line). Take bus for So-unkyo (層雲峡) or Kitami (北見) to So-unkyo Bus Centre, 35 mins. Walk 7 mins.
**Caution:** When the author visited this hostel, there was a notice on the door stating that hostellers would not be accepted without a prior reservation (presumably even if space were available).
**¥2,900.** Dinner ¥1,000. Breakfast ¥600.

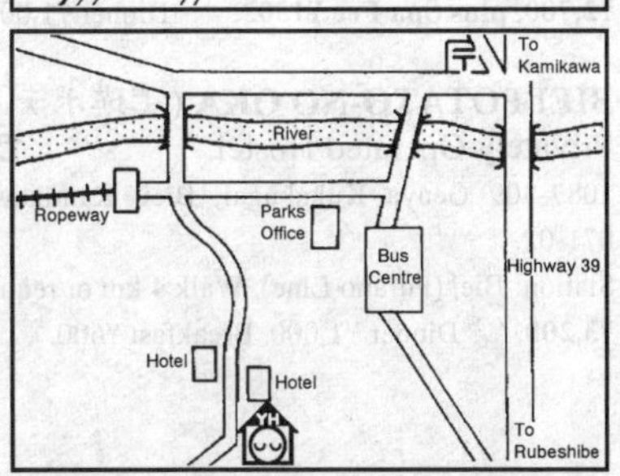


**GINSEN KAKU** (銀泉閣)
Hotel 3★ ☎ 01658-5-3003, 3501
So-unkyo, Kamikawa-cho, Hokkaido 078-17. 30 beds
Station: Kamikawa (Sekihoku Main Line). Take bus for So-unkyo (層雲峡) or Kitami (北見) to So-unkyo Bus Centre, 35 mins. Walk 5 mins.
**¥2,900, plus Spa Fee ¥150.** Dinner ¥1,000. Breakfast ¥600.

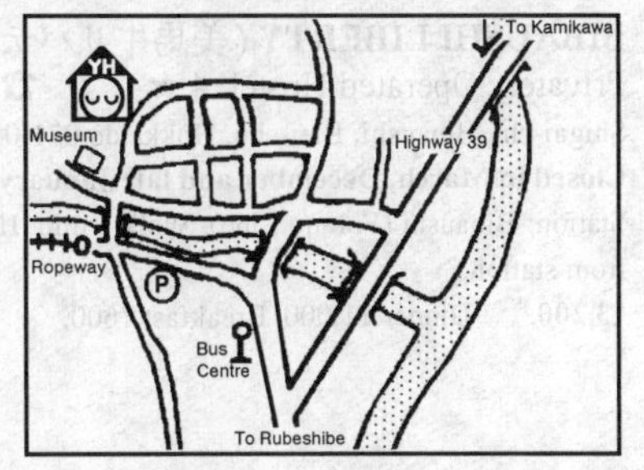

## ASAHIKAWA (旭川)

Privately Operated Hostel 4★ ☎ 0166-61-2751, 8886

7-18 Kamui, Asahikawa-shi, Hokkaido 070. 158 beds

Station: Asahikawa. Walk 3 mins. to Malsa Department Store. Turn left to bus stop in front of Central Bus Terminal. Take bus no. 550 for Shi Yakusho (市役所) via Inosawa (伊の沢) to Yuriana Yochien (ユリアナ幼稚園), 15 mins. Hostel is next to Ski Ground.

**¥3,200.** Dinner ¥1,000. Breakfast ¥600.

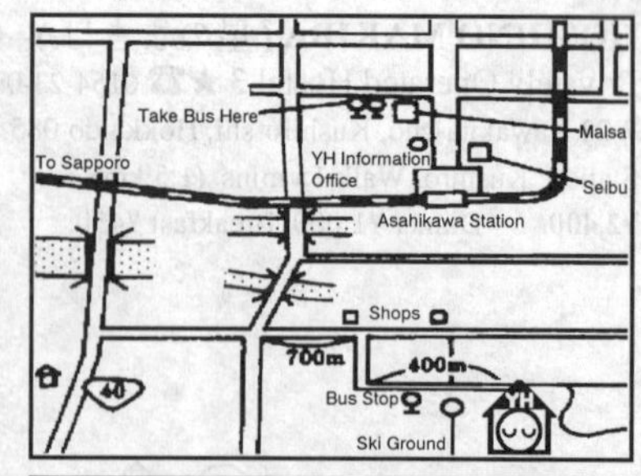


## SHIOKARI ONSEN (塩狩温泉)

Privately Operated Hostel 2★ ☎ 016532-2168. Fax: 2512

3 Shiokari, Wassamu-cho, Hokkaido 098-01. 84 beds

Station: Shiokari (Soya Main Line). Walk 2 mins. (130 m).

**Winter ¥2,670. Summer ¥2,470, both plus Spa Fee ¥30.**

Dinner ¥1,000. Breakfast ¥600. Local Delicacies ¥1,500.

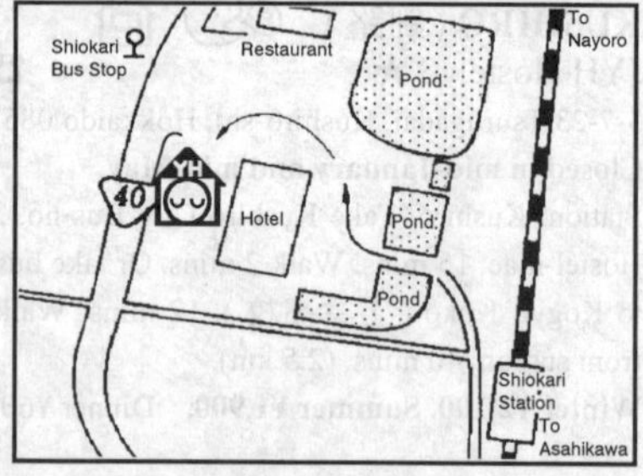


## DAISETSU-ZAN SHIRAKABA-SO (大雪山白樺荘)

Hotel 2★ ☎ 0166-97-2246

Asahi-dake Onsen, 1418 Higashi Kawa-machi, Kamikawa-gun, Hokkaido 071-03. 46 beds

Station: Asahikawa. From main road in front of station, take bus for Asahi-dake Onsen (旭岳温泉) to Camp-jo (キャンプ場), 1 hr. 40 mins. Walk 1 min.

**Caution**: Last bus 15:00. The outward journey is free. For free return, obtain voucher from hostel.

**¥2,700, plus Spa Fee ¥150.** Dinner ¥1,000. Breakfast ¥600.

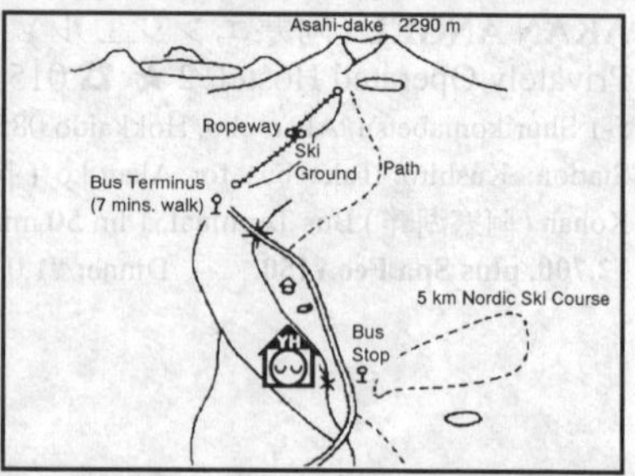


## BIEI POTATO-NO OKA (美瑛ポテトの丘)

Privately Operated Hostel ☎ 0166-92-3255

1087-309 Genya Kukakugai, Biei, Kamikawa-gun, Hokkaido 071-02. 32 beds

Station: Biei (Furano Line). Walk 4 km or request collection.

**¥3,200.** Dinner ¥1,000. Breakfast ¥600.

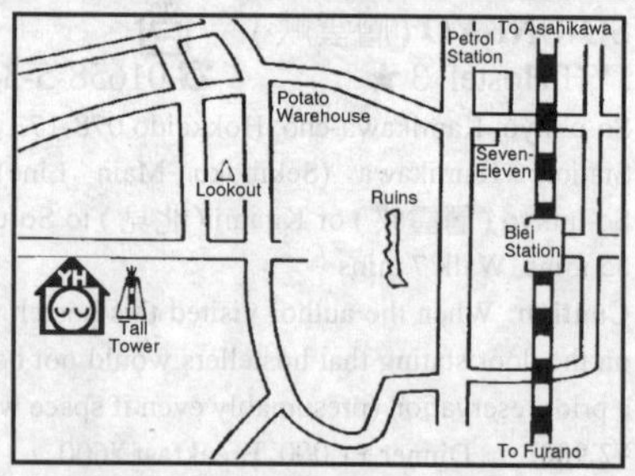


## BIBAUSHI LIBERTY (美馬牛リバティ)

Privately Operated Hostel 4★ ☎ 0166-95-2141

Shigai-chi, Bibaushi, Biei-cho, Hokkaido 071-04. 20 beds

**Closed in March, December and late January.**

Station: Bibaushi (Furano Line). Walk 1 min. Hostel can be seen from station.

**¥3,200.** Dinner ¥1,000. Breakfast ¥600.

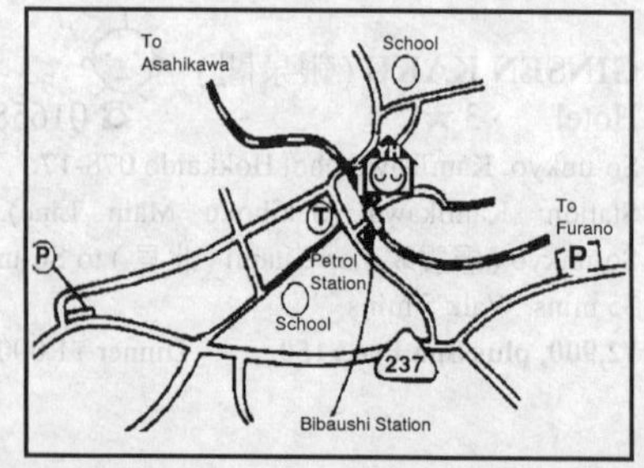

## FURANO WHITE (富良野ホワイト)

Privately Operated Hostel 4★ ☎ 0167-23-4807

14-6 Kitanomine-machi, Furano-shi, Hokkaido 076.

**Closed in April and November.** 40 beds

Station: Furano (Nemuro Main Line). In winter, take bus for Ski-jo (スキー場) to terminus, 10 mins. Walk back 5 mins. In summer, take bus for Goryo (御料) to Kisen (基線), 8 mins. Walk 6 mins.

**¥3,100.** Dinner ¥1,000. Breakfast ¥600.

## SAHORO (サホロ)

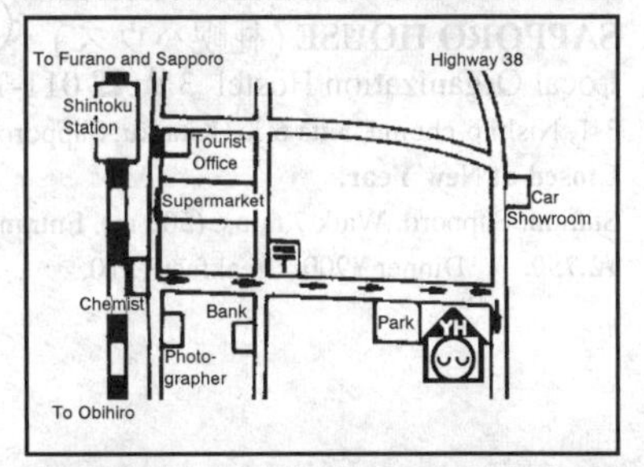


Privately Operated Hostel 4★ ☎ 01566-4-6550

2-26, 4-jo Minami, Shintoku-cho, Hokkaido 081.

**Closed in April and November.** 22 beds

Station: Shintoku (Nemuro Main Line). Walk 7 mins.

**¥3,200.** Dinner ¥1,000. Breakfast ¥600.

## IKEDA KITA-NO-KOTAN (池田北のコタン)

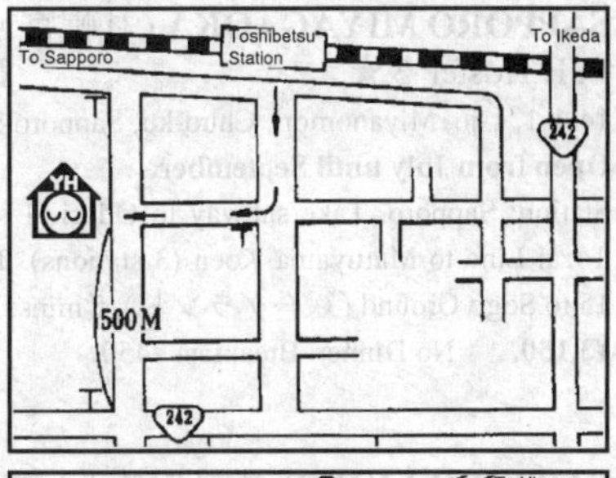


Privately Operated Hostel 3★ ☎ 01557-2-3666

99-4 Toshibetsu Nishi-machi, Ikeda, Hokkaido 083. 14 beds

**Closed in November, December, late January and mid-April.**

Station: Toshibetsu (Nemuro Main Line). Walk 5 mins. (400 m).

**¥2,900.** Dinner ¥1,000. Breakfast ¥500.

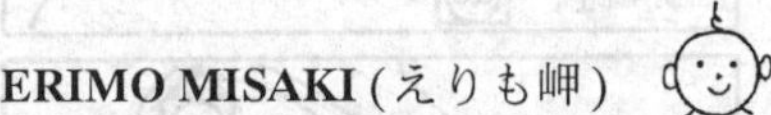

## ERIMO MISAKI (えりも岬)

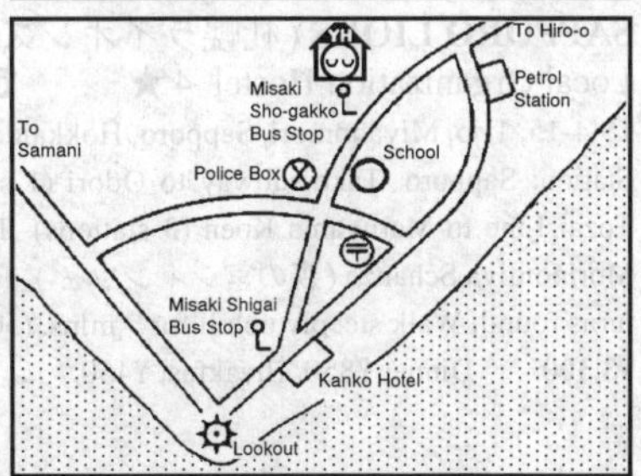


Privately Operated Hostel 2★ ☎ 01466-3-1144. Fax: 1074

236-6 Erimo Misaki, Erimo-machi, Hokkaido 058-03. 100 beds

**Closed in December, January and mid-April.**

Station: Samani (Hidaka Line). Take JR bus for Hiro-o (広尾) to Misaki Sho-gakko (岬小学校), 1 hr. 10 mins. Walk 1 min. Some buses terminate at Misaki Shigai (岬市街), from where 10 mins. walk.

**¥2,700 (Discount ¥500).** Dinner ¥1,000. Breakfast ¥600. Local Delicacies ¥1,500.

## FUNHORSE INN NIIKAPPU

(ファンホース・イン新冠)

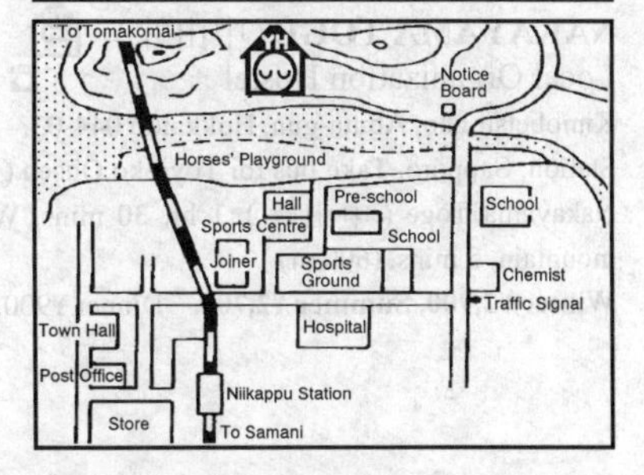


Privately Operated Hostel 3★ ☎ 01464-7-2317

489 Takae, Niikappu-cho, Hokkaido 059-24. 56 beds

**Closed from November until February.**

Station: Niikappu (Hidaka Line). Walk 25 mins. (2 km). On rainy days or at night telephone for collection.

**¥2,700.** Dinner ¥1,000. Breakfast ¥600.

**TOYOSATO MUMIN-MURA** (豊郷夢民村)
Privately Operated Hostel ☎ 01456-2-6388
115 Toyosato, Monbetsu-cho, Hokkaido 059-21. 22 beds
Station: Toyosato (Hidaka Line). Walk 45 mins. (3.6 km) or telephone for collection.
**¥3,200.** Dinner ¥1,000. Breakfast ¥600.

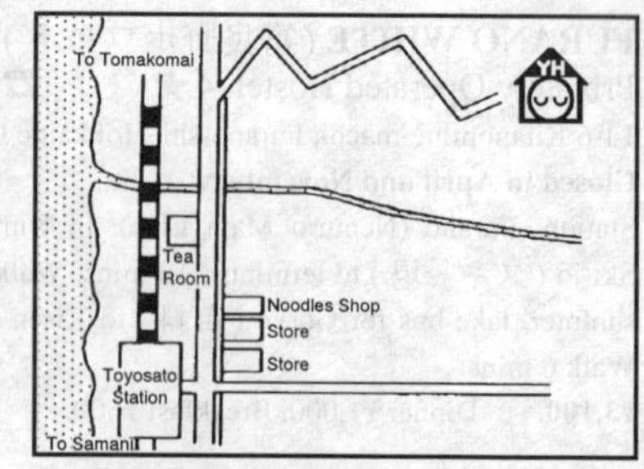


**SAPPORO HOUSE** (札幌ハウス)
Local Organization Hostel 3★ ☎ 011-726-4235, 4236
3-1, Nishi 6-chome, Kita 6-jo, Kita-ku, Sapporo, Hokkaido 060.
**Closed at New Year.** 124 beds
Station: Sapporo. Walk 7 mins. (500 m). Entrance on west side.
**¥2,750.** Dinner ¥900. Breakfast ¥510.

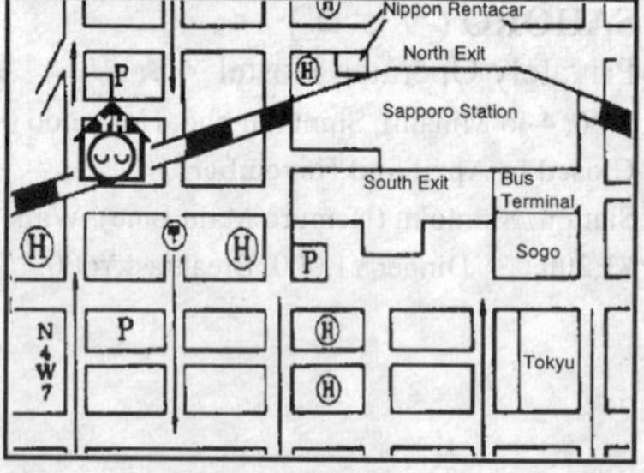


**SAPPORO MIYAGAOKA** (札幌宮ヶ丘)
JYH Hostel 3★ ☎ 011-611-9016
14-1-1, 1-jo, Miyanomori, Chuo-ku, Sapporo-shi, Hokkaido 064.
**Open from July until September.** 52 beds
Station: Sapporo. Take subway to Odori (1 station). Change to Tozai Line to Maruyama Koen (3 stations). Take bus no. 14 or 15 to Sogo Ground (総合グランド), 5 mins. Walk 2 mins.
**¥3,150.** No Dinner. Breakfast ¥450.

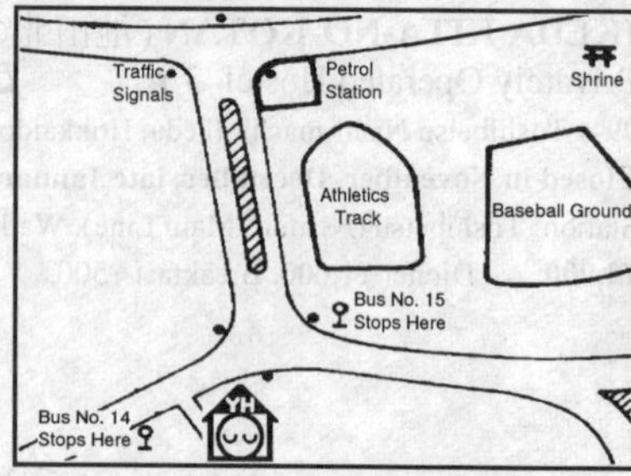


**SAPPORO LIONS** (札幌ライオンズ)
Local Organization Hostel 4★ ☎ 011-611-4709
18-4-15, 1-jo, Miyanomori, Sapporo, Hokkaido 064. 100 beds
Station: Sapporo. Take subway to Odori (1 station). Change to Tozai Line to Maruyama Koen (3 stations). Take bus no. 14 to Morinomiya Schanze (森の宮シャンツェ), 15 mins., where bus turns round. Walk steeply uphill for 7 mins. (500 m).
**¥3,300.** Dinner ¥850. Breakfast ¥450.

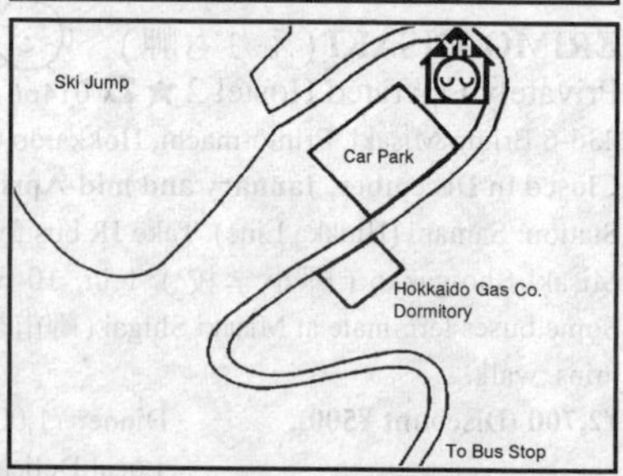


**NAKAYAMA TOGE** (中山峠)
Local Organization Hostel ☎ 0136-33-2668
Kimobetsu-cho, Abuta-gun, Hokkaido 044-03. 58 beds
Station: Sapporo. Take bus for Toya-ko Onsen (洞爺湖温泉) to Nakayama Toge (中山峠), 1 hr. 30 mins. Walk towards the mountain, 5 mins. (600 m).
**Winter ¥2,900. Summer ¥2,700.** Dinner ¥900. Breakfast ¥500.

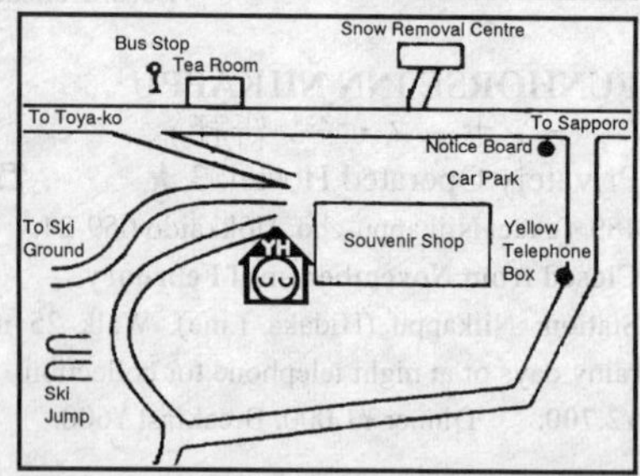

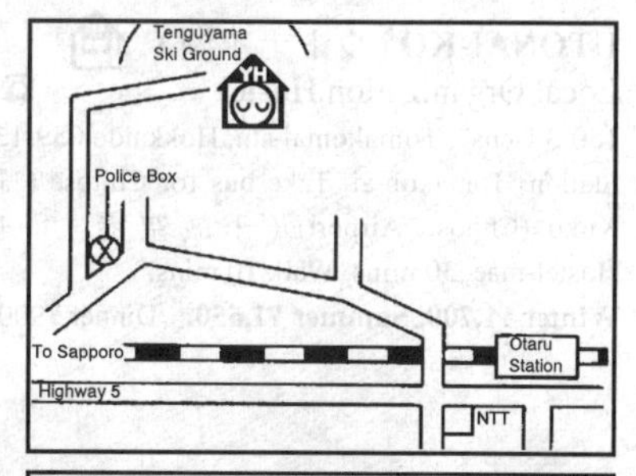


**OTARU TENGUYAMA (小樽天狗山)**
Hotel 2★ ☎ 0134-34-1474. Fax: 24-0422
2-16-22 Mogami, Otaru-shi, Hokkaido 047. 59 beds
Station: Otaru. From bus stop no. 3, take bus no. 9 for Tenguyama (天狗山) to terminus, 20 mins. Walk 1 min.
**¥2,700.** Dinner ¥1,000. Breakfast ¥600. Local Delicacies ¥1,500.

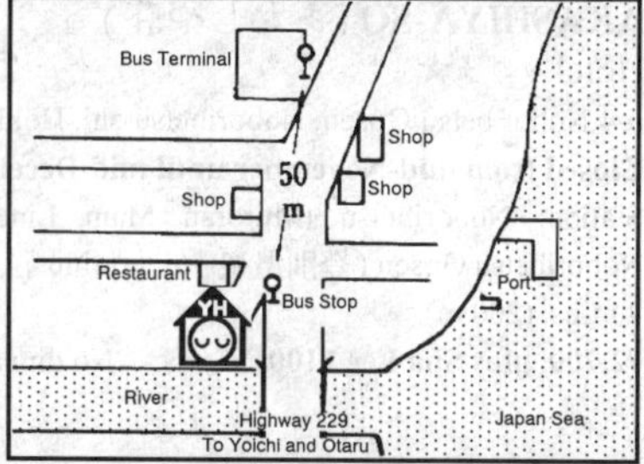


**SHAKOTAN (積丹)**
Privately Operated Hostel 2★ ☎ 0135-46-5051
297 Yobetsu-cho, Shakotan-machi, Hokkaido 046-04. 117 beds
Station: Otaru or Yoichi (Hakodate Main Line). Take bus no. 21 (from bus stop no. 5 at Otaru) for Yobetsu (余別) to Shakotan Youth Hostel-mae, one stop before terminus, 2 hrs. 15 mins. from Otaru or 1 hr. 40 mins. from Yoichi. Hostel is adjacent to bus stop.
**Caution:** Last bus leaves Otaru at 16:35, Yoichi at 17:07.
**¥2,700.** Dinner ¥1,000. Breakfast ¥600. Local Delicacies ¥1,500.

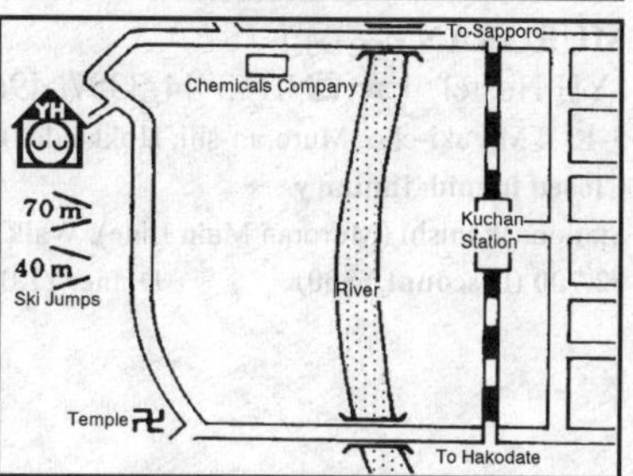


**NISEKO (ニセコ)**
Local Organization Hostel ☎ 0136-22-0553
110 Asahi, Kuchan-cho, Abuta-gun, Hokkaido 044.
**Closed in November and December.** 58 beds
Station: Kuchan (Hakodate Main Line). Cross the river and walk towards the ski jump, 15 mins. (1 km).
**Winter ¥2,300. Summer ¥1,900.** No meals.

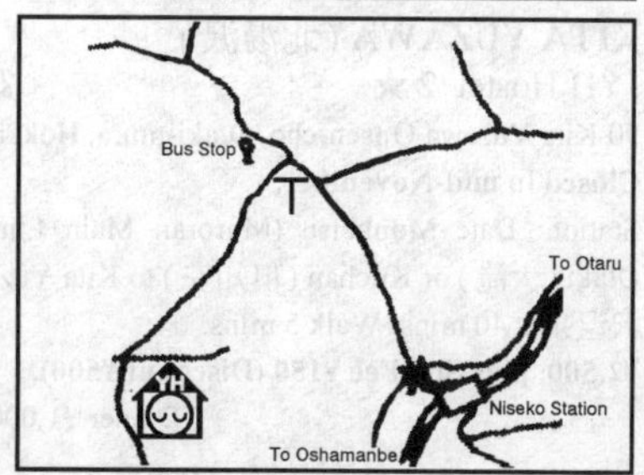


**NISEKO KOGEN (ニセコ高原)**
Privately Operated Hostel 3★ ☎ 0136-44-1171
336 Niseko, Abuta-gun, Hokkaido 048-15. 31 beds
Station: Niseko (Hakodate Main Line). Take bus for Konbu Onsen (昆布温泉) or Yumoto Onsen (湯元温泉) to Fujiyama (藤山), 6 mins. Walk back 20 m and turn right. Walk 15 mins. (1 km).
**Winter ¥2,900. Summer ¥2,700.** Dinner ¥1,000. Breakfast ¥600.

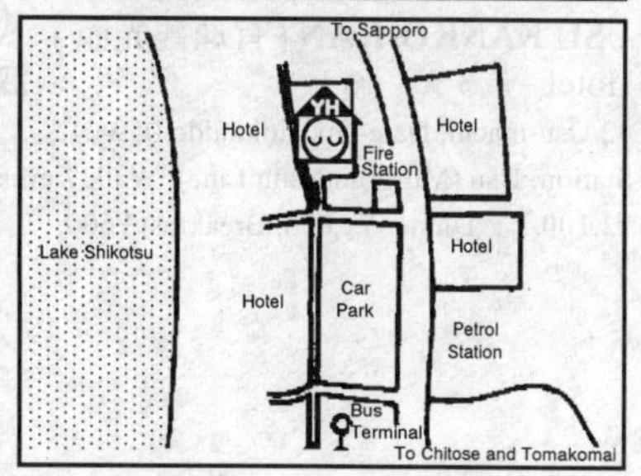


**SHIKOTSU-KO (支笏湖)** IBN
JYH Hostel 4★ ☎ 0123-25-2311. Fax: 2312
Shikotsu Kohan, Chitose-shi, Hokkaido 066-02.
**Closed in early December.** 160 beds
Station: Tomakomai or Shin Chitose Kuko (Chitose Airport). Take bus from either station for Shikotsu-ko (支笏湖) to Shikotsu Kohan (支笏湖畔) Bus Terminal, 40 to 50 mins. Walk 3 mins. (300 m). On request, hostel will collect hostellers from Chitose station at 19:00.
**Summer ¥2,880. Winter ¥2,680, both plus Spa Fee ¥150 (Discount ¥500).** Dinner ¥1,000. Breakfast ¥600.

## UTONAI-KO (ウトナイ湖)

Local Organization Hostel ☎ 0144-58-2153

150-3 Uenae, Tomakomai-shi, Hokkaido 059-13. 68 beds

Station: Tomakomai. Take bus for Chitose (千歳) or Chitose Kuko (Chitose Airport) (千歳空港) to Utonai-ko Youth Hostel-mae, 30 mins. Walk 10 mins.

**Winter ¥1,700. Summer ¥1,550.** Dinner ¥900. Breakfast ¥600.

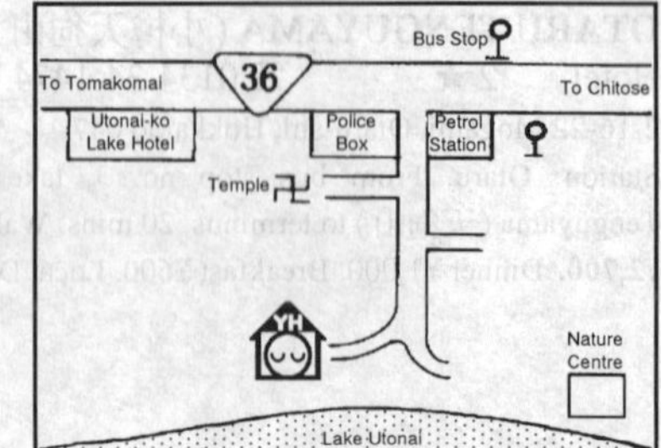


## AKASHIYA-SO (あかしや荘)

Hotel 3★ ☎ 0143-84-2616

6-4 Noboribetsu Onsen, Noboribetsu-shi, Hokkaido 059-05.

**Closed from mid-November until mid-December.** 55 beds

Station: Noboribetsu (Muroran Main Line). Take bus for Noboribetsu Onsen (登別温泉) to terminus, 13 mins. Walk back 2 mins. (200 m).

**¥2,700, plus Spa Fee ¥100.** No dinner. Breakfast ¥600.

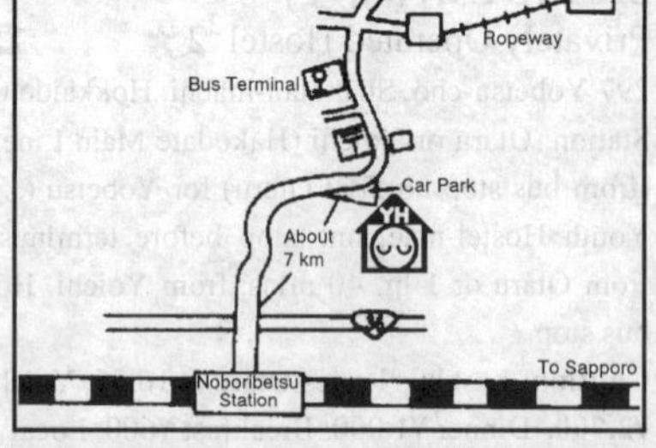


## MURORAN (室蘭)

JYH Hostel 4★ ☎ 0143-44-3357, 4963. Fax: 45-5953

3-12-2 Miyuki-cho, Muroran-shi, Hokkaido 050.

**Closed in mid-January.** 74 beds

Station: Wanishi (Muroran Main Line). Walk 15 mins.

**¥2,700 (Discount ¥500).** Dinner ¥1,000. Breakfast ¥600.

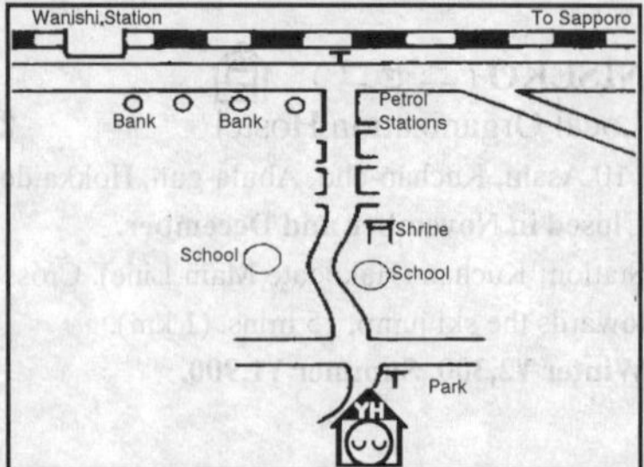


## KITA YUZAWA (北湯沢)

JYH Hostel 2★ ☎ 014268-6552

50 Kita Yuzawa Onsen-cho, Otaki-mura, Hokkaido 052-03.

**Closed in mid-November.** 50 beds

Station: Date Monbetsu (Muroran Main Line). Take bus for Otaki (大滝) or Kuchan (倶知安) to Kita Yuzawa Onsen (北湯沢温泉), 40 mins. Walk 5 mins.

**¥2,500, plus Spa Fee ¥150 (Discount ¥500).**
Dinner ¥1,000. Breakfast ¥600.

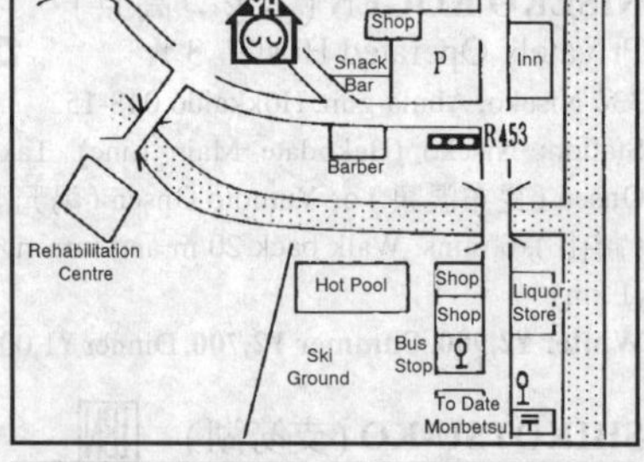


## USU KANKO-KAN (有珠観光館)

Hotel 3★ ☎ 0142-38-2411

32 Usu-machi, Date-shi, Hokkaido 059-01. 80 beds

Station: Usu (Muroran Main Line). Walk 7 mins.

**¥2,100.** Dinner ¥1,000. Breakfast ¥600.

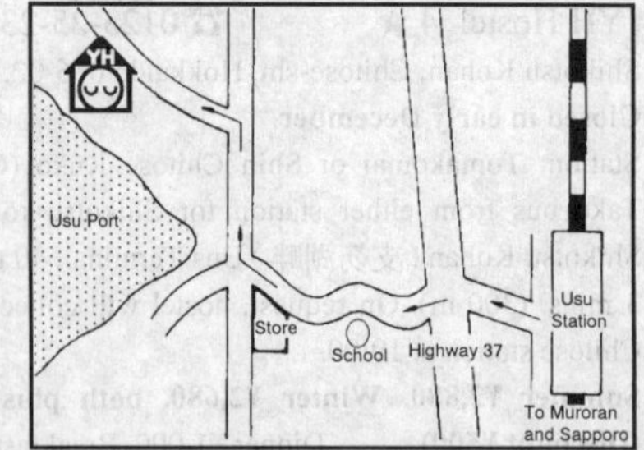

## SHOWA SHINZAN (昭和新山)

Privately Operated Hostel 4 ★ ☎ 0142-75-2283. Fax: 2872
103 Sobetsu Onsen, Usu-gun, Hokkaido 052-01. 67 beds
Station: Toya (Muroran Main Line). Take bus for Toya-ko Onsen (洞爺湖温泉) to terminus, 15 mins. Change to bus for Showa Shinzan (昭和新山) or for Muroran (室蘭) via Sobetsu (壮瞥) to Tozan Guchi (登山口), 8 mins. Walk 1 min.
**¥3,100, plus Spa Fee ¥150.** Dinner ¥1,000. Breakfast ¥600.

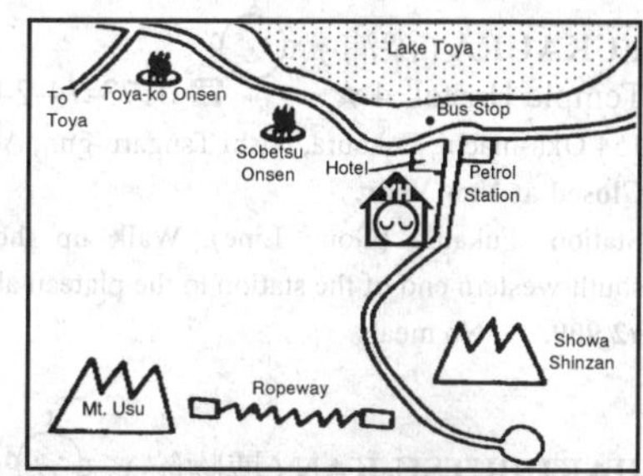


## EXANDER ONUMA (イクサンダー大沼)

Privately Operated Hostel 4 ★ ☎ 0138-67-3419. Fax: 2655
498-7 Onuma-cho, Nanae-machi, Hokkaido 041-13.
**Closed from mid-November until mid-December.** 100 beds
Station: Onuma or Onuma Koen (Hakodate Main Line). Walk 10 mins.
**¥2,900.** Dinner ¥1,000. Breakfast ¥500.

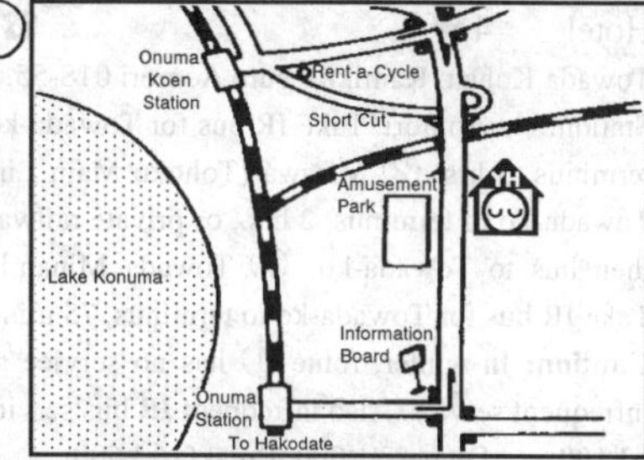


## WAKINOSAWA (脇野沢)

Privately Operated Hostel 3 ★ ☎ 0175-44-2341
41 Senokawame, Wakinosawa-mura, Aomori 039-53.
**Closed at New Year.** 30 beds
Station: Ominato (Ominato Line). Take JR bus to Wakinosawa (脇野沢), 1 hr. 25 mins. Walk 10 mins. (400 m). Also infrequent ferries from Aomori and Kanita.
**¥2,900.** Dinner ¥750. Breakfast ¥450.

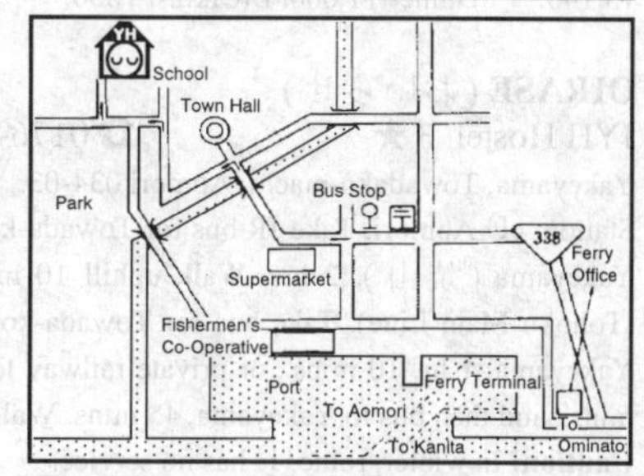


## KAWAYO GREEN (カワヨグリーン)

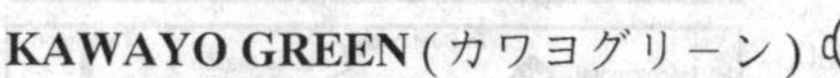

Privately Operated Hostel 4 ★ ☎ 0178-56-2756
3331 Mukaiyama, Shimoda-machi, Aomori 039-21.
**Closed from mid-January until mid-February.** 30 beds
Station: Mukaiyama (Tohoku Main Line). Walk 10 mins. (700 m).
**¥3,100.** Dinner ¥1,000. Breakfast ¥600. Special Barbecue ¥1,500.

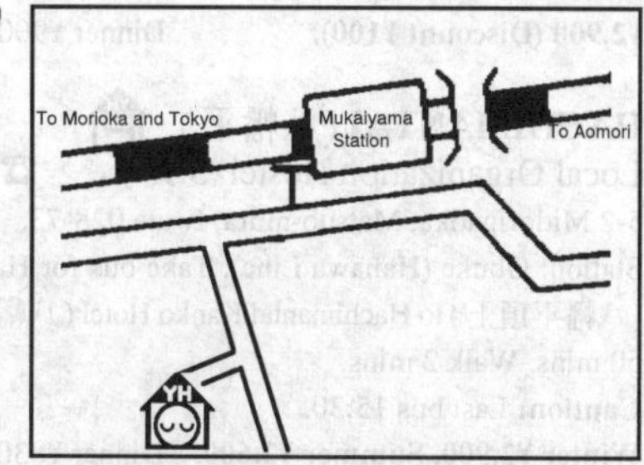


## HIROSAKI (ひろさき)

Privately Operated Hostel 3 ★ ☎ 0172-33-7066
11 Mori-machi, Hirosaki, Aomori 036. 24 beds
Station: Hirosaki (Ou Main Line). From bus stop no. 3, take bus for Shigemori Shin-machi (茂森新町) or Komagoshi (駒越) to Daigaku Byoin (大学病院) or Shi Yaku-sho (市役所), 20 mins. Walk 5 mins.
**¥2,900.** Dinner ¥900. Breakfast ¥500.

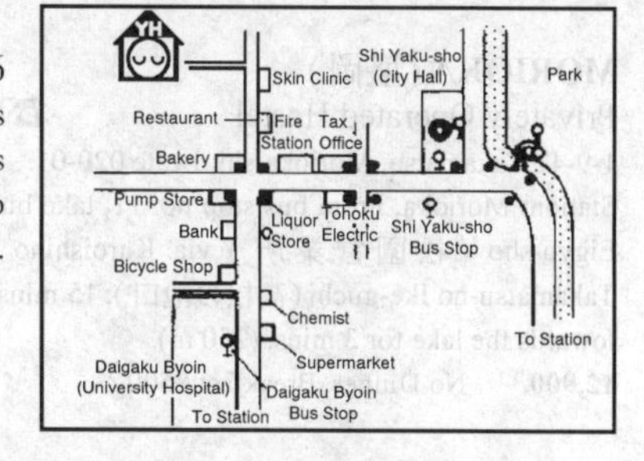

**FUKAURA** (深浦)
Temple Hostel 4★ ☎ 0173-74-2459. Fax: 3785
154 Oka-machi, Fukaura, Nishi Tsugaru-gun, Aomori 038-23.
**Closed at New Year.** 30 beds
Station: Fukaura (Gono Line). Walk up the steps near the south-western end of the station to the plateau above, 7 mins.
**¥2,900.** No meals.

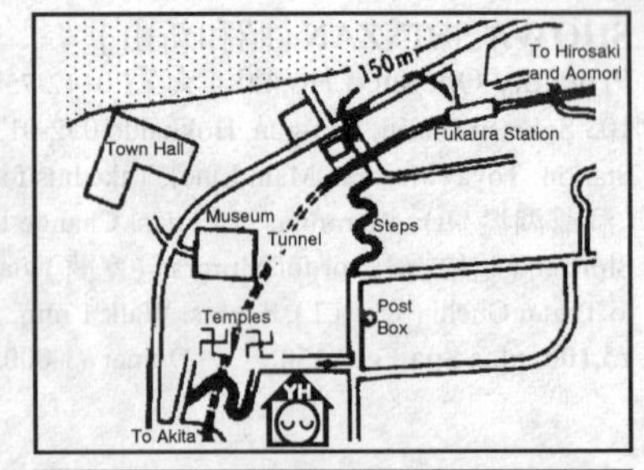


**HAKUBUTSU-KAN** (博物館)
Hotel 4★ ☎ 0176-75-2002
Towada Kohan, Kamikita-gun, Aomori 018-55. 30 beds
Station: ① Aomori. Take JR bus for Towada-ko (十和田湖) to terminus, 3 hrs. ② Misawa (Tohoku Main Line). Take bus for Towada-ko to terminus, 2 hrs., or private railway to Towada-shi, then bus to Towada-ko. ③ Towada Minami (Hanawa Line). Take JR bus for Towada-ko to terminus, 75 mins. Walk 2 mins.
**Caution:** In winter, route ① has no service and route ② has infrequent service. Also infrequent JR bus service from Morioka.
**¥3,100.** Dinner ¥1,000. Breakfast ¥600.

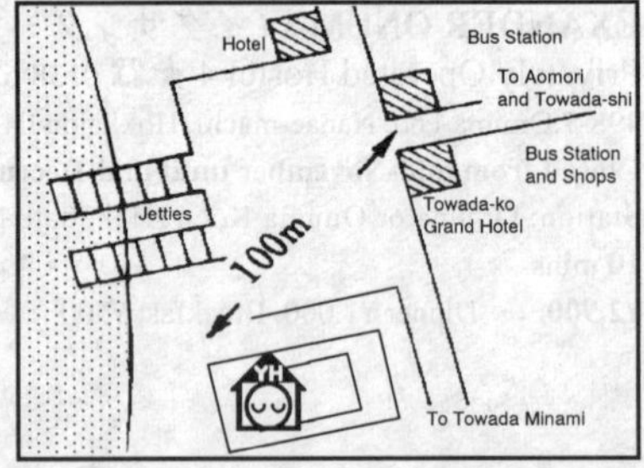


**OIRASE** (おいらせ)
JYH Hostel 3★ ☎ 0176-74-2031, 2032
Yakeyama, Towadako-machi, Aomori 034-03. 60 beds
Station: ① Aomori. Take JR bus for Towada-ko (十和田湖) to Yakeyama (焼山), 2 hrs. Walk uphill 10 mins. ② Misawa (Tohoku Main Line). Take bus for Towada-ko or Yakeyama to Yakeyama, 1 hr. 10 mins., or private railway to Towada-shi, 30 mins., and then bus to Yakeyama, 45 mins. Walk uphill 10 mins.
**Caution:** In winter, route ① has no service.
**¥2,900 (Discount ¥100).** Dinner ¥900. Breakfast ¥500.

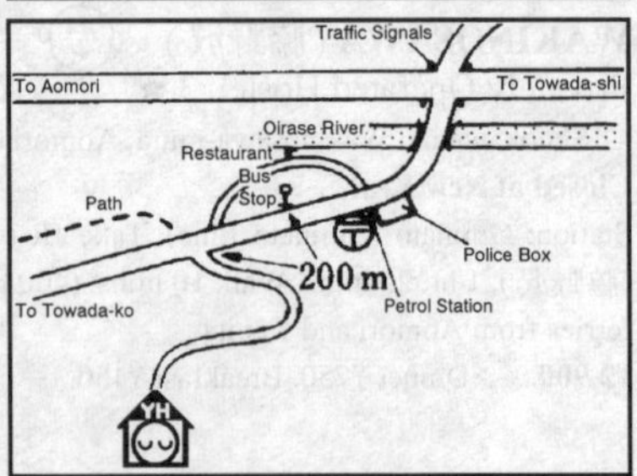


**HACHIMANTAI** (八幡平)
Local Organization Hostel 3★ ☎ 0195-78-2031
5-2 Midorigaoka, Matsuo-mura, Iwate 028-73. 75 beds
Station: Obuke (Hanawa Line). Take bus for Hachimantai Chojo (八幡平頂上) to Hachimantai Kanko Hotel (八幡平観光ホテル), 50 mins. Walk 2 mins.
**Caution:** Last bus 15:30.
**Winter ¥2,900. Summer ¥2,600.** Dinner ¥830. Breakfast ¥520.

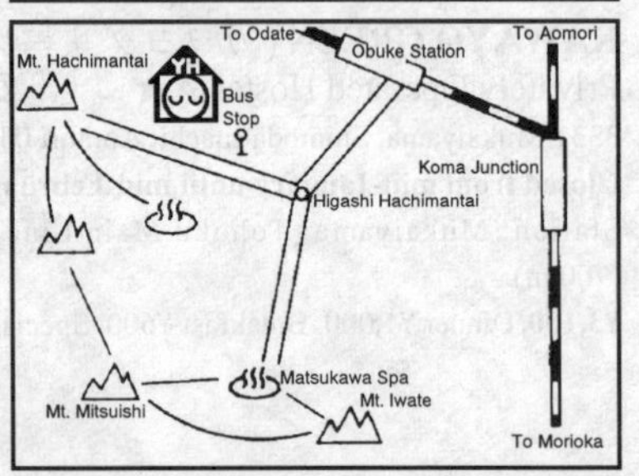


**MORIOKA** (盛岡)
Privately Operated Hostel ☎ 0196-62-2220
1-9-41 Takamatsu, Morioka-shi, Iwate 020-01. 72 beds
Station: Morioka. From bus stop no. 11, take bus for Matsuzono Eigyo-sho (松園営業所) via Kuroishino (黒石野) to Takamatsu-no Ike-guchi (高松の池口), 15 mins. Walk back and towards the lake for 3 mins. (250 m).
**¥2,900.** No Dinner. Breakfast ¥600.

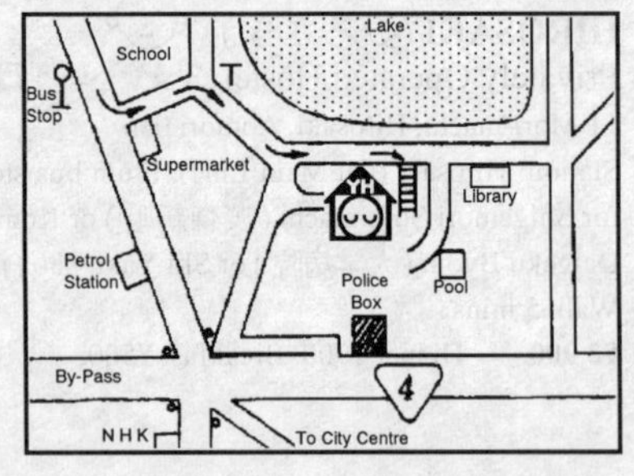

## HANAMAKI NARANOSATO (花巻ならの里)

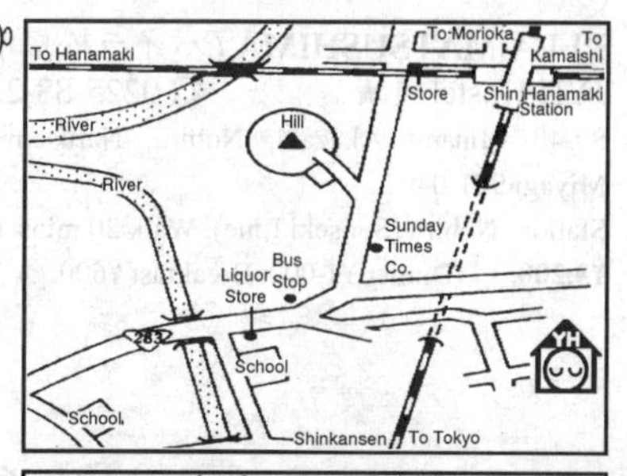


Private Home 4★ ☎ 0198-31-2341

10-16-1 Takamatsu, Hanamaki-shi, Iwate 025.

**Closed on Wednesdays.** 17 beds

Station: ① Shin Hanamaki (Shinkansen or Kamaishi Line). Walk 50 mins.

② Hanamaki (Tohoku Main Line). Take bus for Haruyama (晴山) to Fudanagane (札長根), 15 mins. Walk 20 mins.

**¥2,900.** Dinner ¥1,000. Breakfast ¥600.

## TONO (遠野)

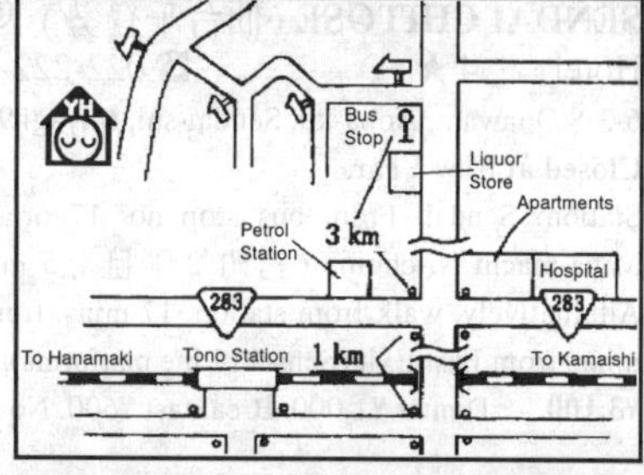


Privately Operated Hostel 4★ ☎ 0198-62-8736

13-39-5 Tsuchibuchi, Tono-shi, Iwate 028-05. 28 beds

Station: Tono (Kamaishi Line). Take bus for Sakanoshita (坂の下) or Oide (大出) to Nitagai (似田貝), 15 mins. Walk 10 mins.

**¥3,100.** Dinner ¥1,000. Breakfast ¥600.

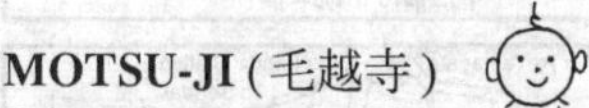

## MOTSU-JI (毛越寺)

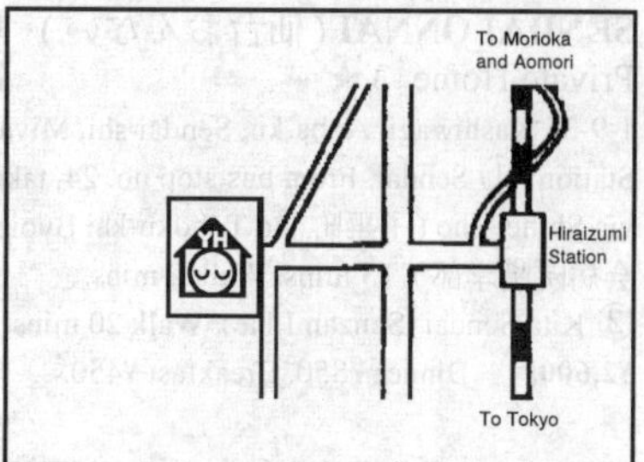


Privately Operated Hostel 3★ ☎ 0191-46-2331. Fax: 4184

58 Osawa, Hiraizumi-machi, Nishi Iwai-gun, Iwate 029-41.

**Closed at New Year.** 66 beds

Station: Hiraizumi (Tohoku Main Line). Walk straight ahead from station exit for 8 mins. Hostel is inside temple complex.

**¥2,800.** Dinner ¥800. Breakfast ¥500.

## RIKUZEN TAKATA (陸前高田)

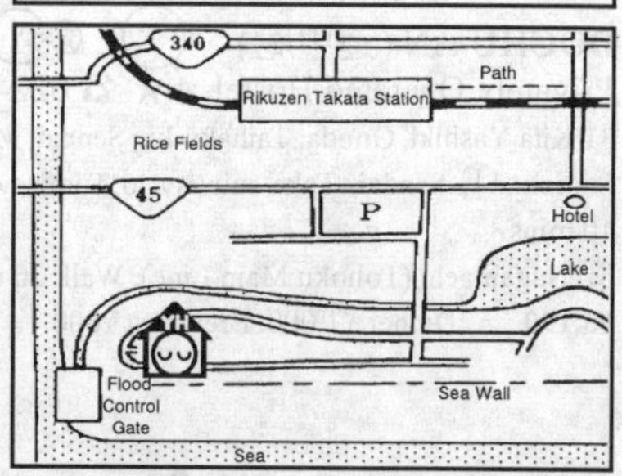


JYH Hostel 3★ ☎ 0192-55-4246

1000 Takata Matsubara, Rikuzen Takata, Iwate 029-22.

**Closed in mid-June.** 84 beds

Station: Rikuzen Takata (Ofunato Line). Walk 20 mins. After dark, hostel is difficult to locate. Hostellers may telephone from station and ask to be collected.

**¥2,600 (Discount ¥100).** Dinner ¥1,000. Breakfast ¥600.

## KARAKUWA (唐桑)

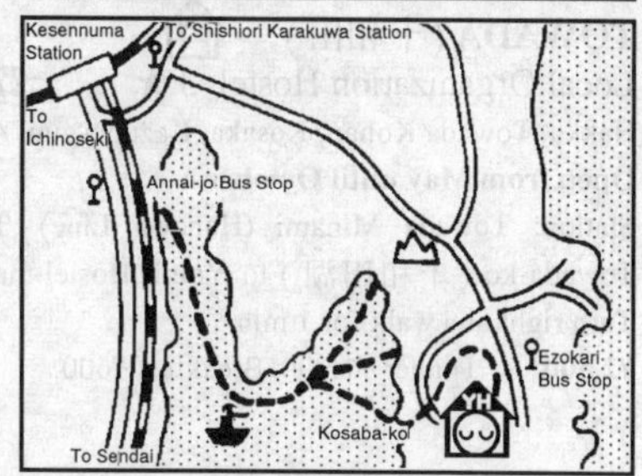


Privately Operated Hostel 4★ ☎ 02263-2-2490

2-8 Nakai, Karakuwa, Motoyoshi-gun, Miyagi 988-05. 33 beds

Station: ① Kesennuma. Take city circular bus (市内回りー 'shi-nai mawari') to Annai-jo (案内所), 10 mins. (or 15 mins. walk). Change to bus for Osaki (御崎) to Ezokari (えぞかり), 40 mins. Walk 1 min. Alternatively, take bus to Annai-jo, then ferry to Kosaba-ko, 40 mins. Walk 15 mins.

② Shishiori Karakuwa (Ofunato Line). Take bus for Osaki to Ezokari, 35 mins. Walk 1 min.

**¥2,900.** Dinner ¥1,000. Breakfast ¥600. Local Delicacies ¥1,500.

## PI LA MATSUSHIMA (パイラ松島)

JYH Hostel 4★ ☎ 0225-88-2220. Fax: 3797

89-48 Minami Akazaki, Nobiru, Naruse-machi, Mono-gun, Miyagi 981-04. 100 beds

Station: Nobiru (Senseki Line). Walk 20 mins. (1.4 km).

**¥3,200.** Dinner ¥1,000. Breakfast ¥600.

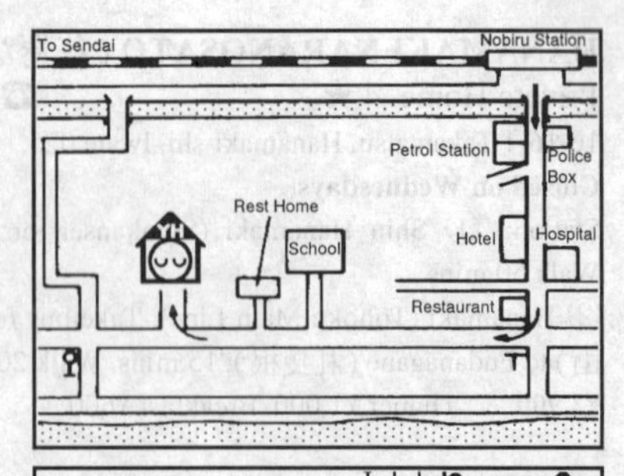


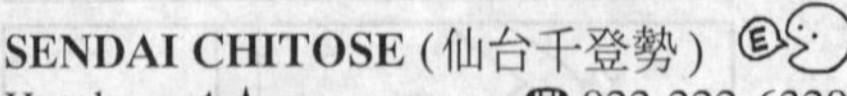

## SENDAI CHITOSE (仙台千登勢)

Hotel 4★ ☎ 022-222-6329, 265-7551

6-3-8 Odawara, Aoba-ku, Sendai-shi, Miyagi 983.

**Closed at New Year.** 50 beds

Station: Sendai. From bus stop no. 17 or 19, take a bus to Miya-machi Ni-chome (宮町２丁目), 5 mins. Walk 3 mins. Alternatively, walk from station, 17 mins. from West Exit or 13 mins. from East Exit (Senseki Line platforms).

**¥3,100.** Dinner ¥1,000. Breakfast ¥600. No meals on holidays.

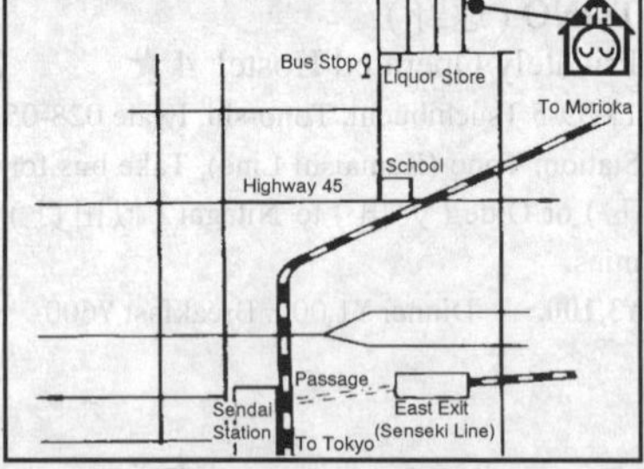


## SENDAI ONNAI (仙台おんない)

Private Home 3★ ☎ 022-234-3922

1-9-35 Kashiwagi, Aoba-ku, Sendai-shi, Miyagi 981. 21 beds

Station: ① Sendai. From bus stop no. 24, take any bus travelling via Shihei-cho (子平町) to Tohoku-kai Byoin Shigaku-bu (東北会病院歯学部), 15 mins. Walk 2 mins.

② Kita Sendai (Senzan Line). Walk 20 mins.

**¥2,600.** Dinner ¥850. Breakfast ¥450.

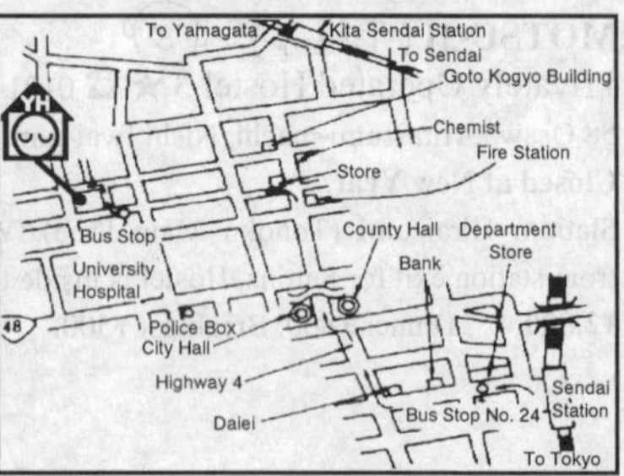


## DOCHU-AN (道中庵)

Privately Operated Hostel 4★ ☎ 022-247-0511, 0759

31 Kita Yashiki, Onoda, Taihaku-ku, Sendai, Miyagi 982. 40 beds

Station: ① Sendai. Take subway to Tomisawa, 12 mins. Walk 10 mins.

② Nagamachi (Tohoku Main Line). Walk 20 mins.

**¥3,190.** Dinner ¥1,000. Breakfast ¥600.

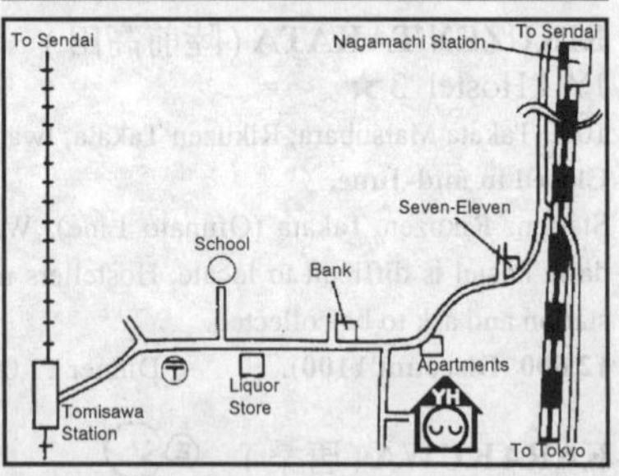


## TOWADA (十和田)

Local Organization Hostel 3★ ☎ 0176-75-2603

Hakka, Towada Kohan, Kosaka, Kazuno-gun, Akita 018-55.

**Open from May until October.** 40 beds

Station: Towada Minami (Hanawa Line). Take JR bus for Towada-ko (十和田湖) to Youth Hostel-mae, 1 hr. 10 mins. Turn right and walk for 1 min.

**¥2,300.** Dinner ¥1,000. Breakfast ¥600.

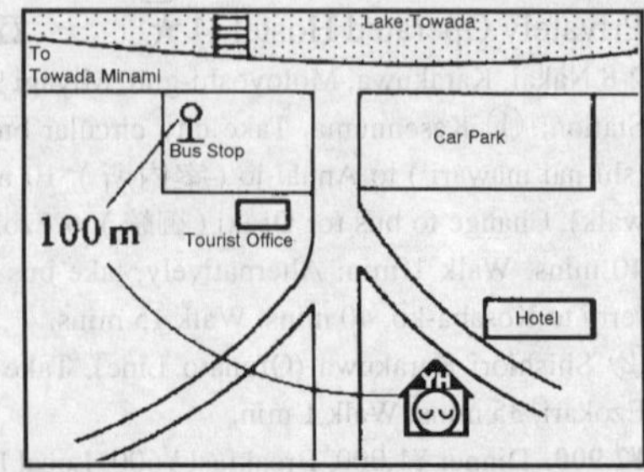

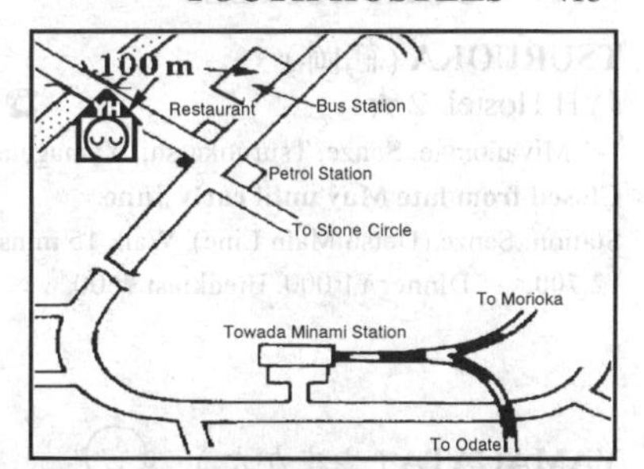


**KUROMORI-SO (黒森荘)**

Local Organization Hostel 4★ ☎ 0186-37-2144

63 Kaminoyu, Towada Oyu, Kazuno-shi, Akita 018-54. 30 beds

Station: Towada Minami (Hanawa Line). Take JR bus for Oyu Onsen (大湯温泉) or Towada-ko (十和田湖) to Oyu Onsen, 17 mins. Walk 2 mins. Also JR bus service from Rikuzen Hanawa (Hanawa Line) and infrequent JR bus service from Morioka.

**Winter ¥2,800. Summer ¥2,700, both plus Spa Fee ¥100.**

Dinner ¥1,000. Breakfast ¥500.

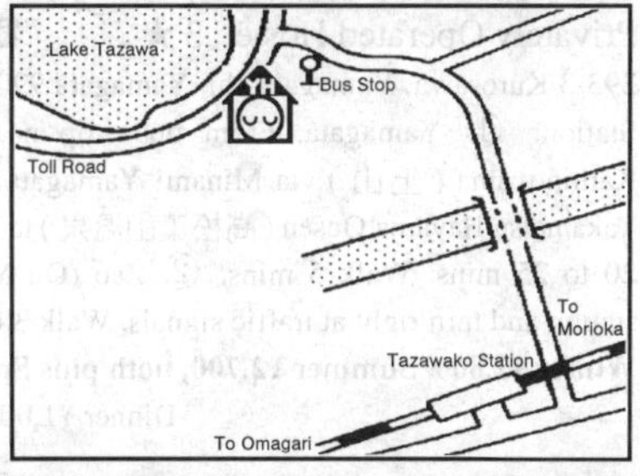


**TAZAWA-KO (田沢湖)**

Privately Operated Hostel 3★ ☎ 0187-43-1281, 0842

33-8 Kami Ishikami, Obonai, Tazawako-machi, Senboku-gun, Akita 014-12. 37 beds

Station: Tazawako (Tazawako Line). Take bus for Tazawa-ko (田沢湖) to Tazawa-ko Koen Iriguchi (田沢湖公園入口), 15 mins. Walk forward a few metres to hostel.

**¥2,400.** Dinner ¥1,000. Breakfast ¥600.

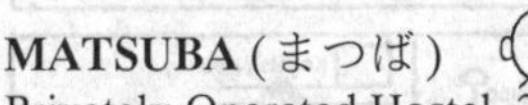

**MATSUBA (まつば)**

Privately Operated Hostel 3★ ☎ 0187-48-2201

58 Matsuba, Shimo Hinokinai, Nishiki-mura, Akita 014-06.

**Closed from November until mid-March.** 25 beds

Station: Matsuba (Akita Nairiku Jiyukan Private Railway), accessible from JR Takanosu (Tazawako Line) or Kakunodate (Ou Line). Walk 7 mins.

**¥2,800.** Dinner ¥900. Breakfast ¥500.

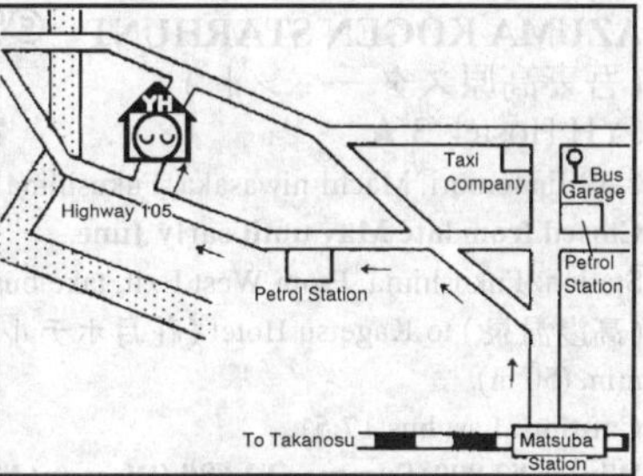


**OGA SEASIDE (男鹿シーサイド)**

JYH Hostel 3★ ☎ 0185-33-3125

Oga Onsen, Kitaura Yumoto, Oga-shi, Akita 010-06.

**Closed in late February.** 96 beds

Station: Hadachi (Oga Line). Take bus for Oga Onsen (男鹿温泉), or a variety of destinations beyond, to Oga Grand Hotel (男鹿グランドホテル), 50 mins., where most buses turn round. Walk towards the sea for 3 mins. (200 m).

**¥2,900 (Discount ¥100).** Dinner ¥1,000. Breakfast ¥600.

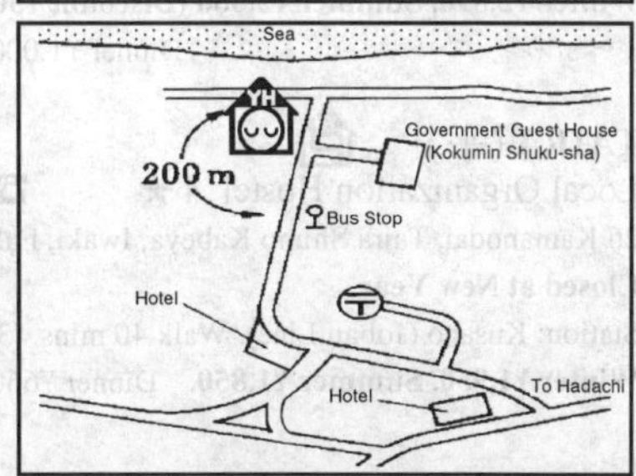


**KISAKATA SEINEN-NO-IE (象潟青年の家)**

Local Organization Hostel 3★ ☎ 0184-43-3154

19-2 Irikonoma, Kisakata-machi, Yuri-gun, Akita 018-01.

**Closed at New Year.** 52 beds

Station: Kisakata (Uetsu Main Line). Walk 10 mins. (1 km).

**¥1,950.** Dinner ¥720. Breakfast ¥460.

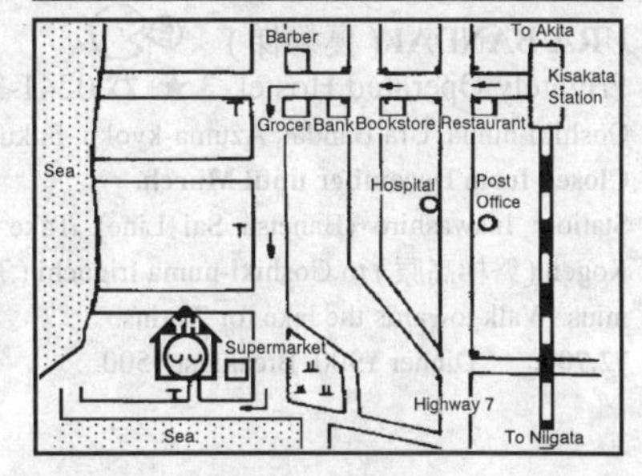

## TSURUOKA (鶴岡)

JYH Hostel 2★ ☎ 0235-73-3205

1-1 Miyanomae, Sanze, Tsuruoka-shi, Yamagata 999-74.

**Closed from late May until early June.** 60 beds

Station: Sanze (Uetsu Main Line). Walk 15 mins. (1 km).

**¥2,700.** Dinner ¥1,000. Breakfast ¥600.

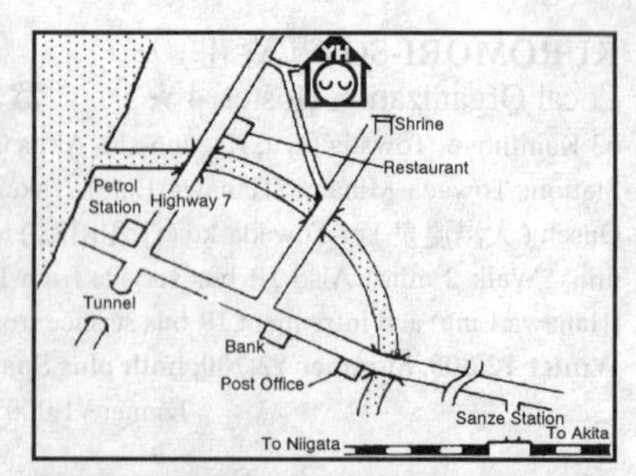


## YAMAGATA (やまがた)

Privately Operated Hostel 3★ ☎ 0236-88-3201

293-3 Kurosawa, Yamagata-shi, Yamagata 990-23. 20 beds

Station: ① Yamagata. From bus stop no. 2, take bus for Kaminoyama (上山) via Minami Yamagata (南山形) or for Takamatsu Hayama Onsen (高松葉山温泉) to Kurosawa (黒沢), 20 to 25 mins. Walk 5 mins. ② Zao (Ou Main Line). Leave station and turn right at traffic signals. Walk 30 mins. (2.2 km).

**Winter ¥2,800. Summer ¥2,700, both plus Spa Fee ¥150.**

Dinner ¥1,000. Breakfast ¥550.

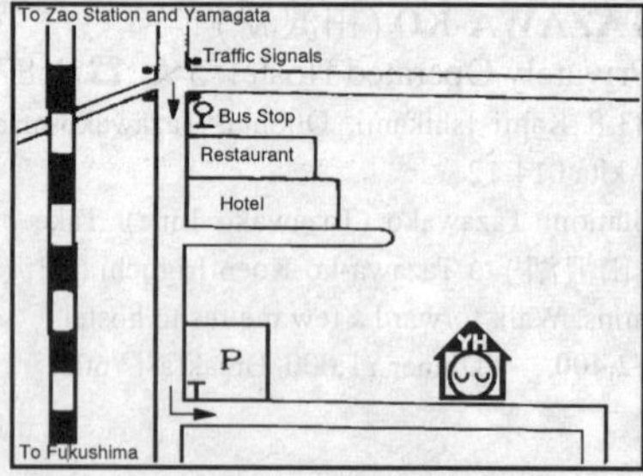


## AZUMA KOGEN STARHUNT (吾妻高原スターハント)

JYH Hostel 3★ ☎ 0245-91-1412

1-49 Jinnomori, Machi-niwasaka, Fukushima 960-22.

**Closed from late May until early June.** 96 beds

Station: Fukushima. From West Exit, take bus for Takayu Onsen (高湯温泉) to Kagetsu Hotel (花月ホテル), 40 mins. Walk 1 min. (50 m).

**Caution:** Last bus 17:51.

**Winter ¥2,890. Summer ¥2,680 (Discount ¥300).**

Dinner ¥1,000. Breakfast ¥600.

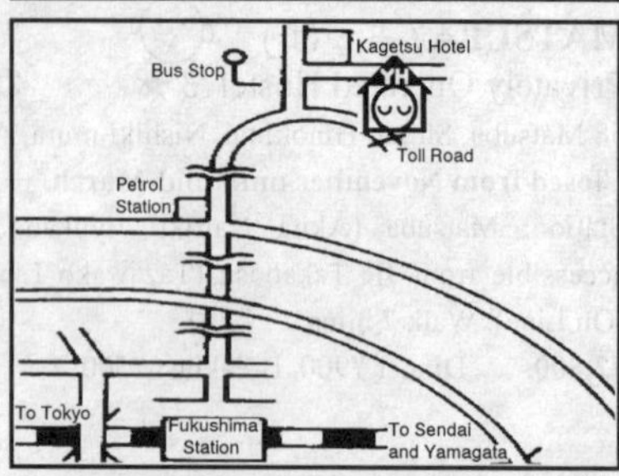


## TAIRA (平)

Local Organization Hostel 4★ ☎ 0246-34-7581

26 Kamanodai, Taira Shimo Kabeya, Iwaki, Fukushima 970-01.

**Closed at New Year.** 60 beds

Station: Kusano (Joban Line). Walk 40 mins. (3 km).

**Winter ¥1,950. Summer ¥1,850.** Dinner ¥660. Breakfast ¥460.

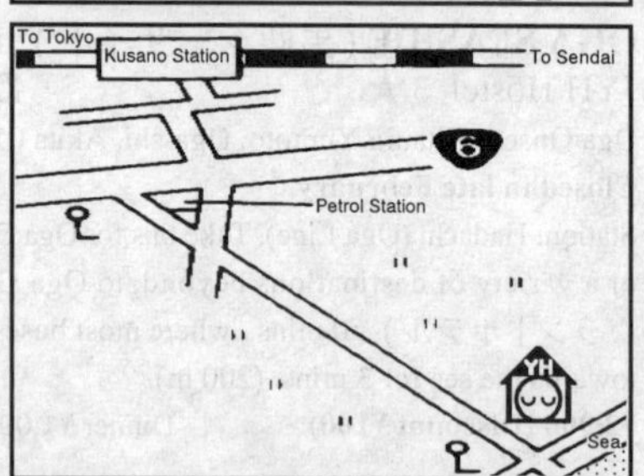


## URA BANDAI (裏磐梯)

Privately Operated Hostel 3★ ☎ 0241-32-2811, 2813

Goshiki-numa, Ura Bandai, Azuma-kyoku, Fukushima 969-27.

**Closed from December until March.** 100 beds

Station: Inawashiro (Banetsu Sai Line). Take bus for Bandai Kogen (磐梯高原) to Goshiki-numa Iriguchi (五色沼入口), 30 mins. Walk towards the lake for 7 mins.

**¥2,700.** Dinner ¥900. Breakfast ¥500.

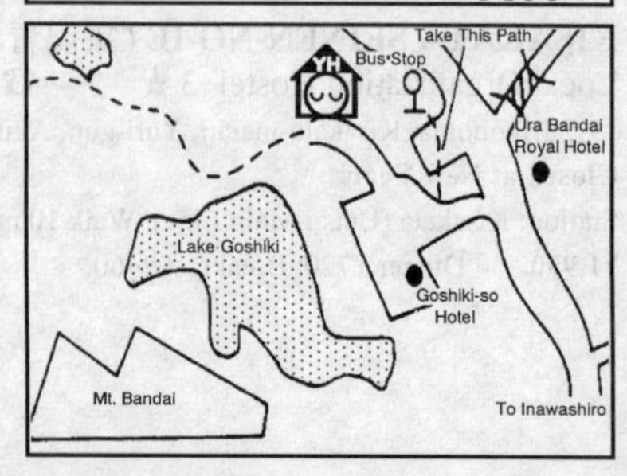

## AIZU-NO-SATO (会津の里)

Private Home 3★ ☎ 0241-27-2054

36 Hatakeda, Kofune, Aizu Shiokawa-cho, Fukushima 969-35.

**Closed at New Year.** 14 beds

Station: Shiokawa (Banetsu Sai Line). Walk 10 mins. (800 m).

**Winter ¥2,300. Summer ¥2,100 (Discount ¥300).** No meals.

## TSUKUBA-SAN (筑波山)

Local Organization Hostel ☎ 0296-54-1200. Fax: 2315

1557 Hatori, Makabe-machi, Makabe-gun, Ibaragi 300-44.

**Closed at New Year. Also second and fourth Tuesday each month.** 56 beds

Station: Tsuchiura (Joban Line). Take bus for Tsukuba Eki (筑波駅) to terminus, 50 mins. Change to bus for Tsukuba Jinja (筑波神社), 15 mins. Alight at terminus and walk ahead for 5 mins. Take funicular railway to mountain top, 8 mins. Turn left before Miyuki Tea House (みゆき茶屋) and walk 20 mins.

**Winter ¥2,150. Summer ¥2,000.** Dinner ¥820. Breakfast ¥600.

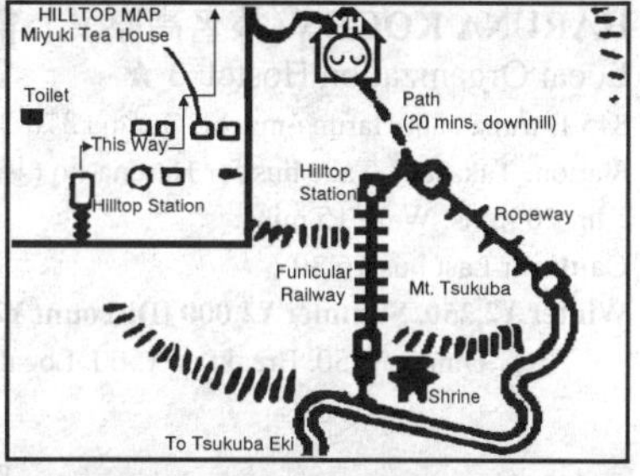


## TSUCHIURA MASUO (土浦増尾)

Private Home 3★ ☎ 0298-21-4430

1-7-14 Komatsu, Tsuchiura-shi, Ibaragi 300.

**Closed on Tuesdays and at New Year.** 10 beds

Station: Tsuchiura (Joban Line). Take bus for Ami (阿見) to Komatsu Sakashita (小松坂下), 5 mins. Walk 1 min. Alternatively, walk from station, 20 mins.

**¥2,600.** Dinner ¥750. Breakfast ¥400.

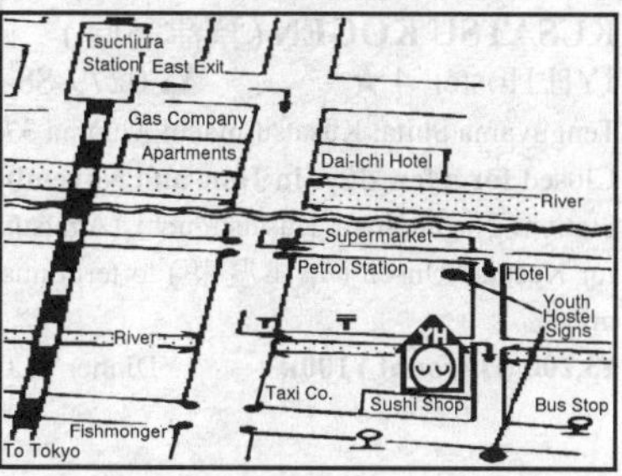


## NIKKO (日光)

Local Organization Hostel ☎ 0288-54-1013

2854 Tokorono, Nikko-shi, Tochigi 321-14.

**Closed at New Year.** 48 beds

Station: JR Nikko or Tobu Nikko. Walk 25 mins. (2 km).

**Winter ¥2,750. Summer ¥2,550.** Dinner ¥720. Breakfast ¥460.

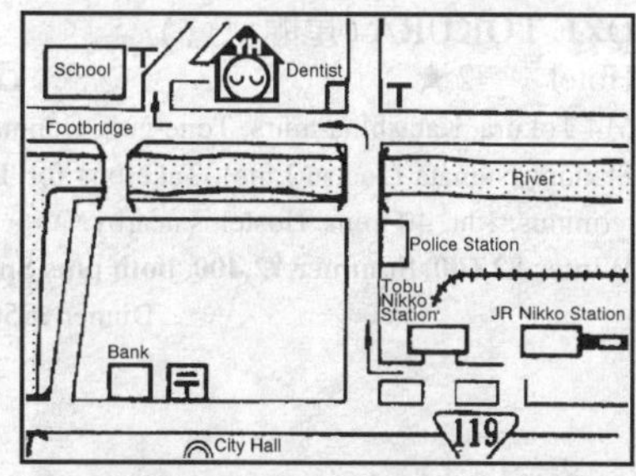


## NIKKO DAIYAGAWA (日光大谷川) 

Privately Operated Hostel 3★ ☎ 0288-54-1974

1075 Naka Hatsuishi-machi, Nikko-shi, Tochigi 321-14.

**Closed in late January.** 26 beds

Station: JR Nikko or Tobu Nikko. Walk 20 mins. (1.5 km).

**¥2,700.** Dinner ¥800. Breakfast ¥400.

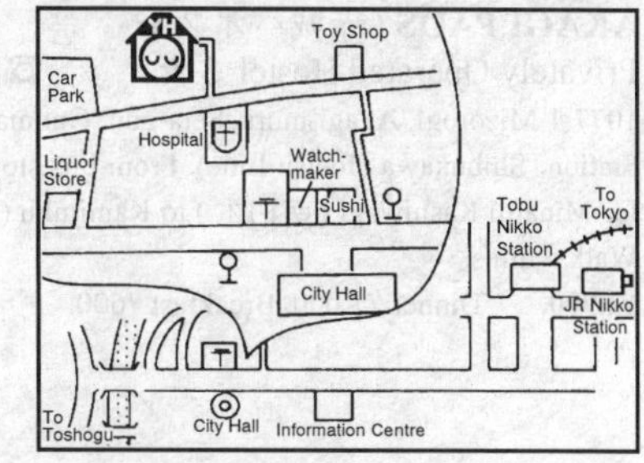

## NIKKO SUGINAMIKI (日光杉並木)

Privately Operated Hostel 3★ ☎ 0288-26-0951, 0817

2112-7 Kiwadajima, Imaichi-shi, Tochigi 321-23. 50 beds

Station: Shimotsuke Osawa (Nikko Line). Walk 20 mins. (2 km).

**¥2,900.** Dinner ¥1,000. Breakfast ¥600.
Local Delicacies ¥1,500 (minimum 2 people).

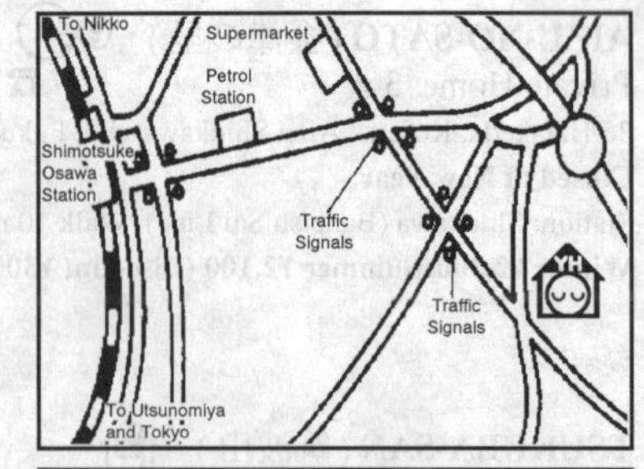


## HARUNA KOGEN (榛名高原)

Local Organization Hostel 3★ ☎ 0273-74-9300

845 Haruna-san, Haruna-machi, Gunma 370-33. 58 beds

Station: Takasaki. Take bus for Haruna-ko (榛名湖) to terminus, 1 hr. 20 mins. Walk 15 mins.

**Caution:** Last bus 16:30.

**Winter ¥2,250. Summer ¥2,000 (Discount ¥200).**
Dinner ¥850. Breakfast ¥500. Local Delicacies ¥1,500.

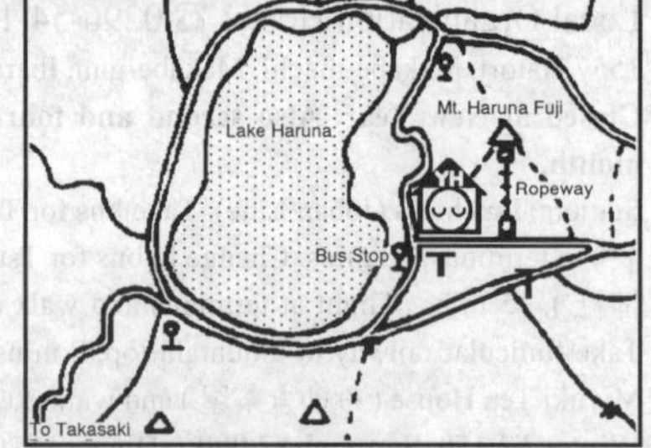


## KUSATSU KOGEN (草津高原)

JYH Hostel 4★ ☎ 0279-88-3895. Fax: 6880

Tenguyama Shita, Kusatsu-machi, Gunma 377-17.

**Closed for a few days in June and November.** 100 beds

Station: Naganohara Kusatsuguchi (Agatsuma Line). Take bus for Kusatsu Onsen (草津温泉) to terminus, 25 mins. Walk 25 mins.

**¥3,200 (Discount ¥100).** Dinner ¥1,000. Breakfast ¥600.

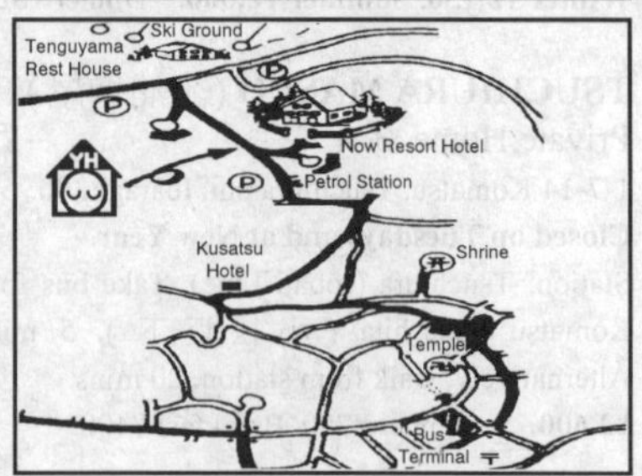


## OZE TOKURA (尾瀬戸倉)

Hotel 2★ ☎ 0278-58-7421

614 Tokura, Katashina-mura, Tone-gun, Gunma 378-04. 45 beds

Station: Numata (Joetsu Line). Take bus for Tokura (戸倉) to terminus, 1 hr. 40 mins. Hostel is nearby.

**Winter ¥2,600. Summer ¥2,400, both plus Spa Fee ¥150.**
Dinner ¥850. Breakfast ¥450.

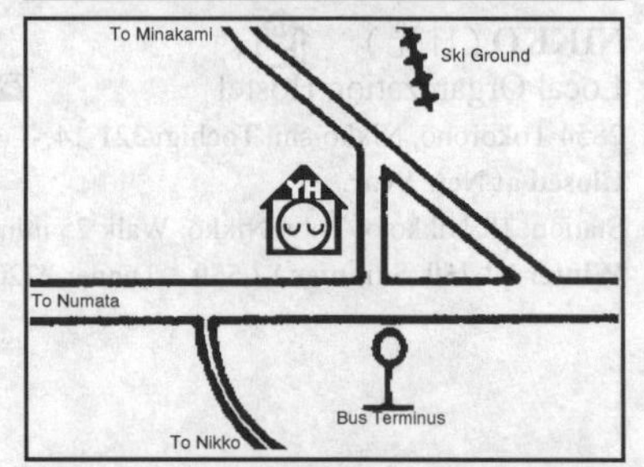


## AKAGI PAOS (赤城パオス)

Privately Operated Hostel 3★ ☎ 0279-56-5731

1077-1 Mizorogi, Akagi-mura, Seta-gun, Gunma 379-11. 15 beds

Station: Shibukawa (Joetsu Line). From bus stop no. 1, take bus for Minami Kashiwagi (南柏木) to Kamijuku (上宿), 20 mins. Walk 5 mins.

**¥2,900.** Dinner ¥1,000. Breakfast ¥600.

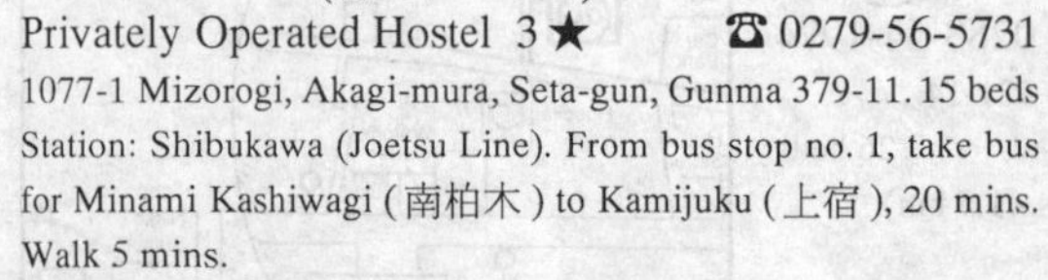

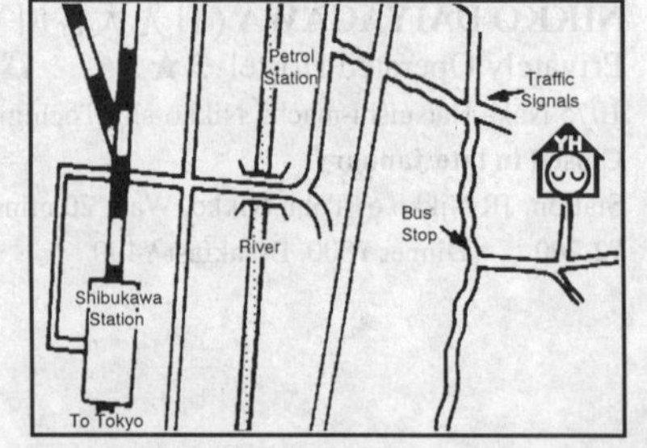

## KAMAKITA LAKE (鎌北レイク)

JYH Hostel ☎ 0492-94-0219

86-1 Gongen-do, Moroyama-machi, Saitama 350-04. 60 beds

Station: ① Moro (JR Hachiko Line). Walk 50 mins.
② Bushu Nagase (Tobu Ogose Line). Walk 60 mins.
③ Higashi Moro (Tobu Ogose Line). Walk 90 mins.
④ Musashi Yokote (Seibu Ikebukuro Line). Walk 90 mins.

Hostellers may telephone and request collection from Moro or Higashi Moro station. In summer, occasional buses run from Higashi Moro and Moro to Kamakita-ko.

**¥2,450.** Dinner ¥880. Breakfast ¥610.

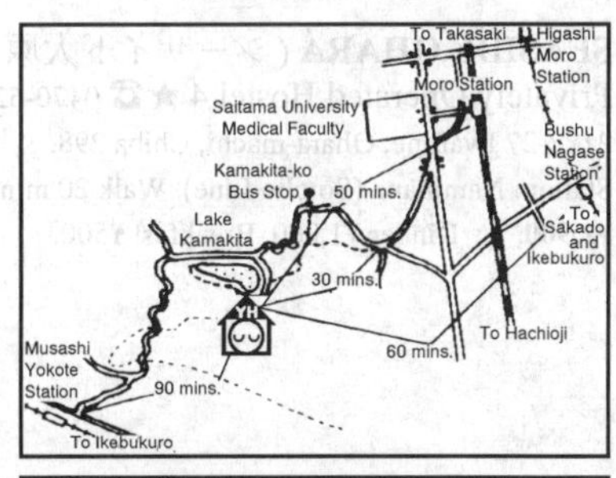


## OKU CHICHIBU LAKE (奥秩父レイク)

JYH Hostel ☎ 0494-55-0056

3755 Otaki, Otaki-mura, Chichibu-gun, Saitama 369-19. 50 beds

Station: Mitsumine-guchi (Chichibu Private Railway). Take bus for Chichibu-ko (秩父湖) to terminus, 35 mins. Walk 15 mins. Direct trains operate from Seibu Ikebukuro to Mitsumine-guchi at 8:36 on weekdays and at 7:16 and 7:56 on holidays. Steam-hauled service operates from Kumagaya (JR Takasaki Line) to Mitsumine-guchi on certain days.

**¥2,450.** Dinner ¥880. Breakfast ¥610.

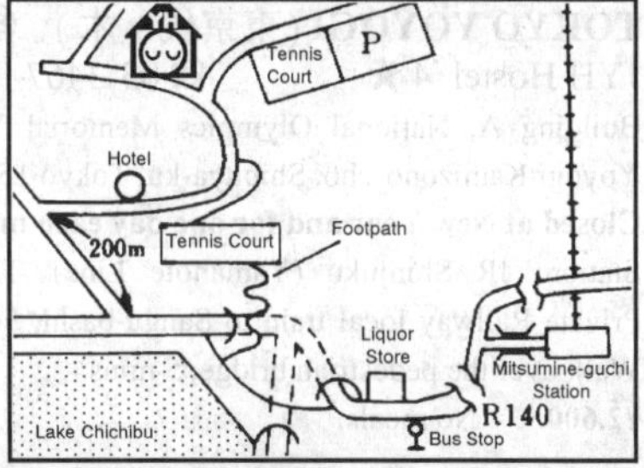


## CHIBA-SHI (千葉市)

Local Organization Hostel 4★ ☎ 043-294-1850

955 Yasashido-cho, Midori-ku, Chiba-shi, Chiba 267.

**Closed at New Year.** 60 beds

Station: Toke (Sotobo Line). Walk 20 mins.

**¥2,200.** Dinner ¥900. Breakfast ¥600.

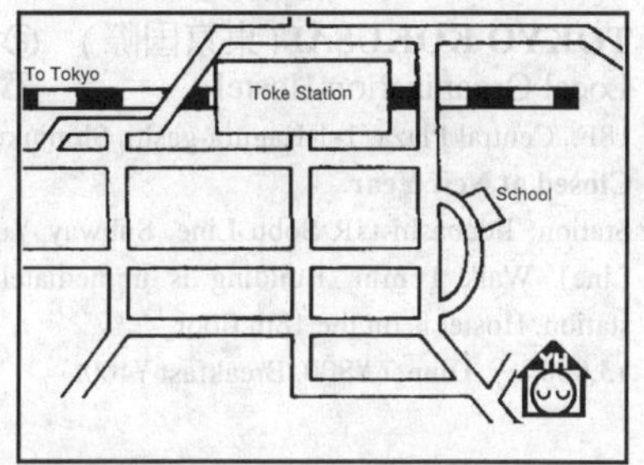


## KUJUKURI-HAMA SHIRAKO (九十九里浜白子)

Private Home 3★ ☎ 0475-33-2254

2722 Sorigane, Shirako-machi, Chiba 299-42. 20 beds

Station: Oami (Sotobo Line). Take bus for Shirako Shako (白子車庫) to Asahi-bashi (旭橋), 40 mins. Walk 3 mins. (300 m). Also buses from Mobara or Honno (both Sotobo Line) to Shirako Shako. Walk 10 mins.

**¥2,900.** Dinner ¥850. Breakfast ¥450.

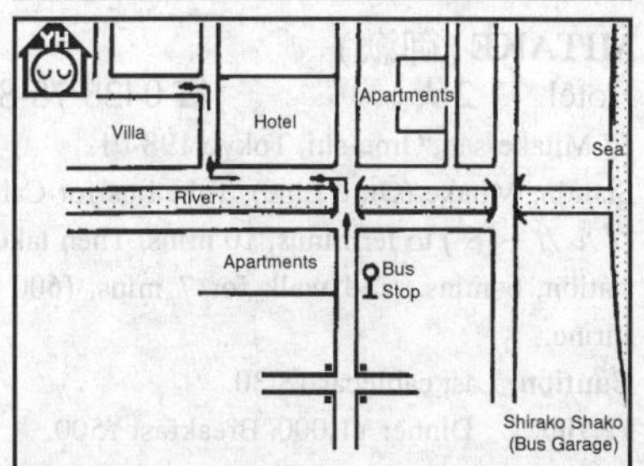


## TATEYAMA (館山)

Local Organization Hostel 3★☎ 0470-28-0073. Fax:0494

1132 Mera, Tateyama-shi, Chiba 294-02.

**Closed in early January.** 52 beds

Station: Tateyama (Uchibo Line). From bus stop no. 3, take bus for Shirahama (白浜) via Shizen-mura (自然村) to Shizen-mura (自然村), 30 mins. Walk 3 mins. (200 m).

**Caution:** The name of this bus stop is expected to change shortly.

**¥1,770.** Dinner ¥870. Breakfast ¥610.

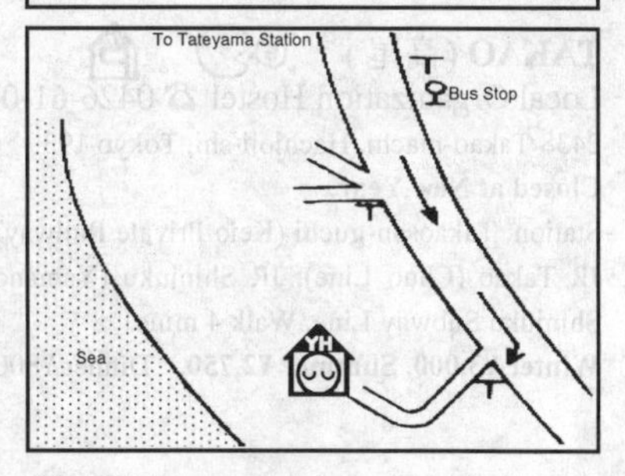

## SEASIDE OHARA (シーサイド大原)

Privately Operated Hostel 4★ ☎ 0470-62-8735. Fax: 8910

2122-27 Iwafune, Ohara-machi, Chiba 298. 16 beds

Station: Namihana (Sotobo Line). Walk 20 mins.

**¥2,900.** Dinner ¥1,000. Breakfast ¥500.

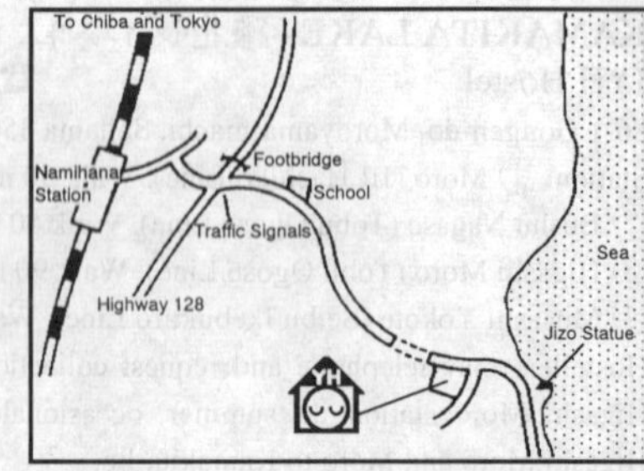


## TOKYO YOYOGI (東京代々木)

JYH Hostel 4★ ☎ 03-3467-9163. Fax: 9417

Building A, National Olympics Memorial Youth Centre, 3-1 Yoyogi Kamizono-cho, Shibuya-ku, Tokyo 151.

**Closed at New Year and for one day each month.** 60 beds

Station: JR Shinjuku (Yamanote Line). Then take Odakyu Private Railway local train to Sangu-bashi, 5 mins. (2 stations). Walk over the pedestrian bridge, 5 mins.

**¥2,600.** No meals.

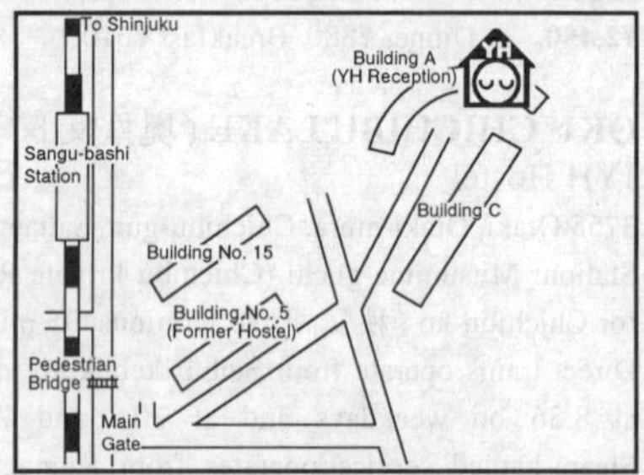

## TOKYO KOKUSAI (東京国際)

Local Organization Hostel ☎ 03-3235-1107.

18F., Central Plaza, 1-1 Kagura-gashi, Shinjuku-ku, Tokyo 162.

**Closed at New Year.** 138 beds

Station: Iidabashi (JR Sobu Line, Subway Yurakucho or Tozai Line). Walk 1 min. Building is immediately in front of JR station. Hostel is on the 18th floor.

**¥3,000.** Dinner ¥800. Breakfast ¥400.

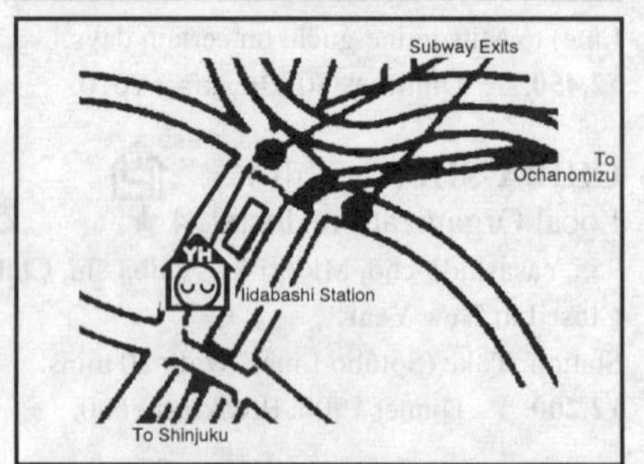


## MITAKE (御嶽)

Hotel 2★ ☎ 0428-78-8501. Fax: 8774

57 Mitake-san, Ome-shi, Tokyo 198-01. 60 beds

Station: Mitake (Ome Line). Take bus for Cablecar Shita (ケーブルカー下) to terminus, 10 mins. Then take cablecar to upper station, 6 mins., and walk for 7 mins. (600 m), towards main shrine.

**Caution:** Last cablecar 18:30.

**¥2,700.** Dinner ¥1,000. Breakfast ¥500.

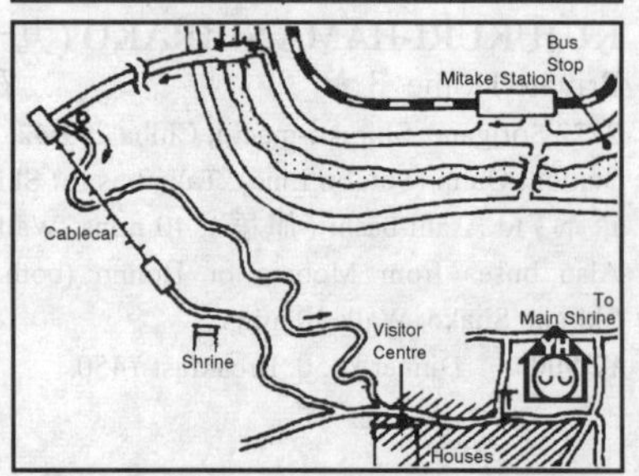


## TAKAO (高尾)

Local Organization Hostel ☎ 0426-61-0437. Fax: 4000

2438 Takao-machi, Hachioji-shi, Tokyo 193.

**Closed at New Year.** 132 beds

Station: Takaosan-guchi (Keio Private Railway), accessible from JR Takao (Chuo Line), JR Shinjuku (Yamanote Line) or Toei Shinjuku Subway Line. Walk 4 mins.

**Winter ¥3,000. Summer ¥2,750.** Dinner ¥800. Breakfast ¥400.

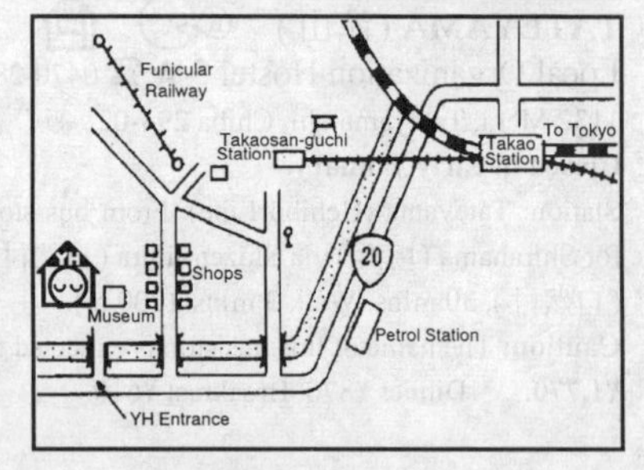

## HINOHARA (ひのはら)

Privately Operated Hostel ☎ 0425-98-1131

7779-10 Hinohara, Nishi Tama-gun, Tokyo 190-02. 15 beds

**Closed from December until March and 2nd Saturday each month.**

Station: Itsukaichi (Itsukaichi Line). Take bus for Fujikura (藤倉) or Koiwa (小岩) to Hinohara-mura Kyodo Shiryo-kan (桧原村郷土資料館). Walk 2 mins.

**¥2,600.** Dinner ¥850. Breakfast ¥400.

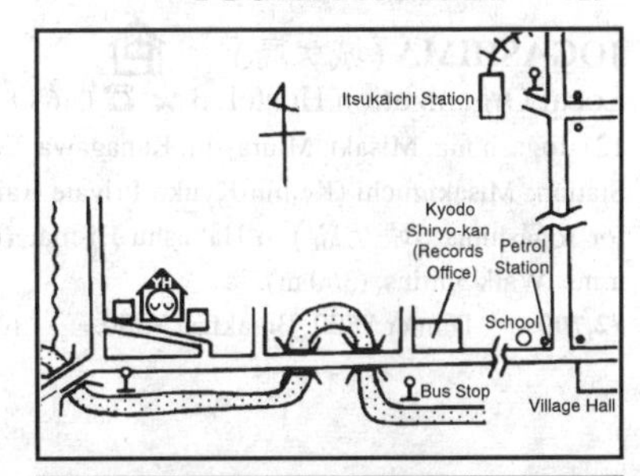


## MIHARA SANSO (三原山荘)

Hotel 4★ ☎ 04992-2-2735

Kandachi, Moto-machi, Oshima-cho, Tokyo 100-01. 65 beds

Station: Hamamatsucho (Yamanote Line). Walk 7 mins. to Takeshiba Sanbashi. Take ferry to Oshima Motomachi, 8 hrs. Walk 15 mins. (1.4 km). Alternatively, take ferry from Atami (Tokaido Line), Ito (Ito Line) or Inatori (Izu Kyuko Private Railway), accessible from JR Ito. However, some ferries go to Okada, from where it is 10 mins. by bus to Motomachi (元町).

**¥3,200.** Dinner ¥1,000. Breakfast ¥600. Local Delicacies ¥1,500.

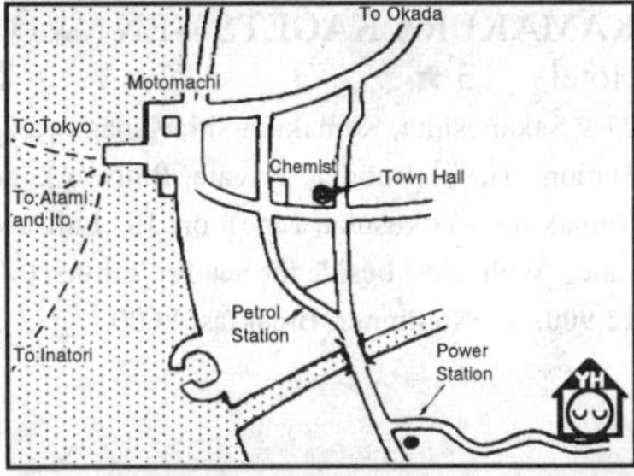


## MIYAKEJIMA AKO (三宅島阿古)

Privately Operated Hostel 2★ ☎ 04994-5-0100

688 Ako, Miyake-mura, Miyakejima, Tokyo 100-12. 38 beds

Station: Hamamatsucho (Yamanote Line). Walk 7 mins. to Takeshiba Sanbashi. Take ferry to Miyakejima Ako Sabigahama, 6 to 8 hrs. Walk 3 mins. Some ferries arrive at Mi-ike, in which case take a bus via Tsubota (坪田) to Sabigahama-ko Iriguchi (錆ヶ浜港入口), 20 mins. Walk 1 min.

**¥2,700.** Dinner ¥900. Breakfast ¥600.

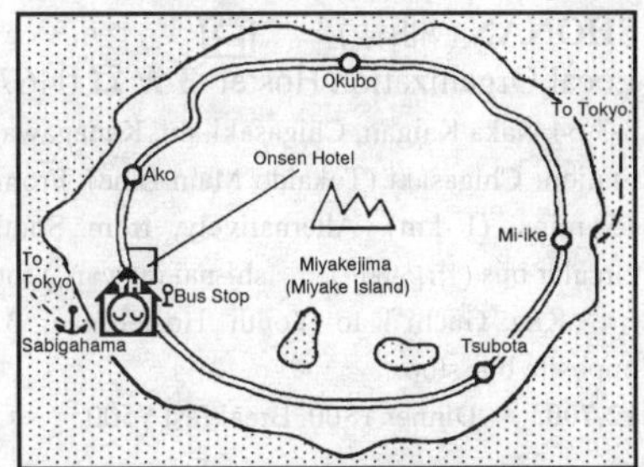


## OGASAWARA (小笠原)

Privately Operated Hostel 3★ ☎ 04998-2-2692

46-12 Nishi-machi, Chichijima, Ogasawara-mura, Tokyo 100-21. 33 beds

Station: Hamamatsucho (Yamanote Line). Walk 7 mins. to Takeshiba Sanbashi. Take ferry to Chichijima Futami, 29 hrs! Walk 10 mins. (600 m).

**Caution:** Ferry operates only once per week. No regular day.

**¥2,800.** Dinner ¥900. Breakfast ¥500.

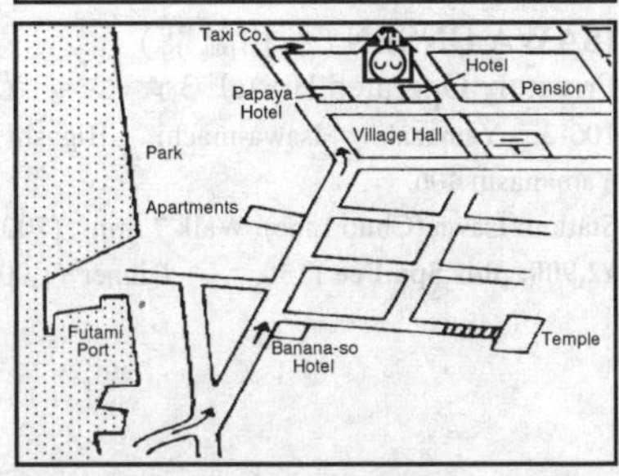


## KANAGAWA (神奈川) IBN

Privately Operated Hostel 3★ ☎ 045-241-6503

1 Momijigaoka, Nishi-ku, Yokohama, Kanagawa 220. 50 beds

Station: Sakuragicho (JR Keihin Tohoku Line, Tokyu Private Railway Toyoko Line or Yokohama subway). Walk 7 mins. (450 m) to Momijizaka (紅葉坂) bus stop. Turn left and walk another 2 mins. (200 m).

**Summer ¥2,900. Winter ¥2,700.** No dinner. Breakfast ¥400.

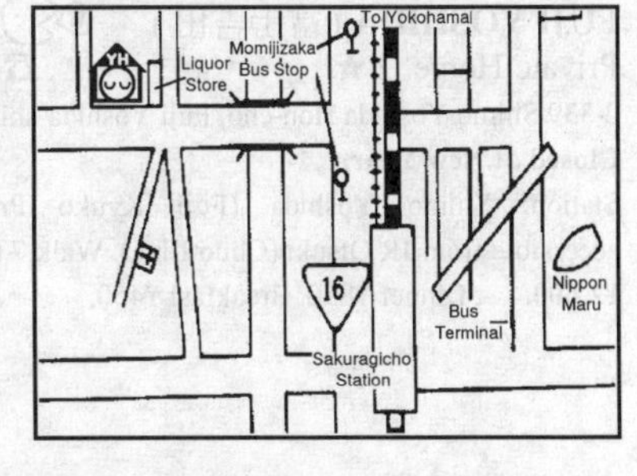

## JOGASHIMA (城ケ島)

Local Organization Hostel 3★ ☎ 0468-81-3893, 82-6103

121 Jogashima, Misaki, Miura-shi, Kanagawa 238-02. 104 beds

Station: Misakiguchi (Keihin Kyuko Private Railway). Take bus for Jogashima (城ケ島) to Hakushu Hi-mae (白秋碑前), 27 mins. Walk 5 mins. (360 m).

**¥2,700.** Dinner ¥800. Breakfast ¥500.

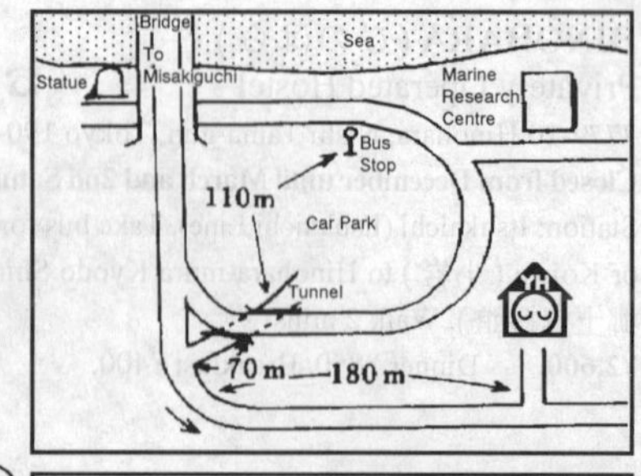


## KAMAKURA KAGETSU-EN (鎌倉花月園)

Hotel 3★ ☎ 0467-25-1238

27-9 Sakanoshita, Kamakura-shi, Kanagawa 248. 48 beds

Station: Hase (Enoden Private Railway), accessible from JR Kamakura (Yokosuka Line) or JR Fujisawa (Tokaido Main Line). Walk west beside the sea for 7 mins. (500 m).

**¥2,900.** No dinner. Breakfast ¥600.

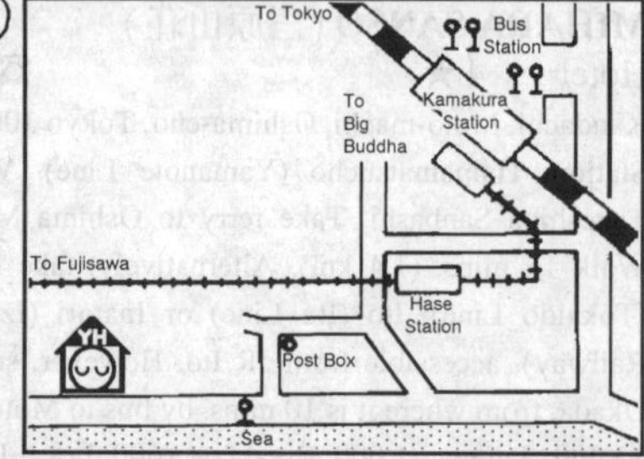


## SHONAN (湘南)

Local Organization Hostel 3★ ☎ 0467-82-2401, 9790

3-3-54 Naka Kaigan, Chigasaki-shi, Kanagawa 253. 132 beds

Station: Chigasaki (Tokaido Main Line). From South Exit, walk 15 mins. (1 km). Alternatively, from South Exit, take city circular bus (市内廻りー 'shi-nai mawari') for North Exit (北口ー 'Kita Guchi') to Youth Hostel-mae, 3 mins. Hostel is opposite bus stop.

**¥2,700.** Dinner ¥800. Breakfast ¥500.

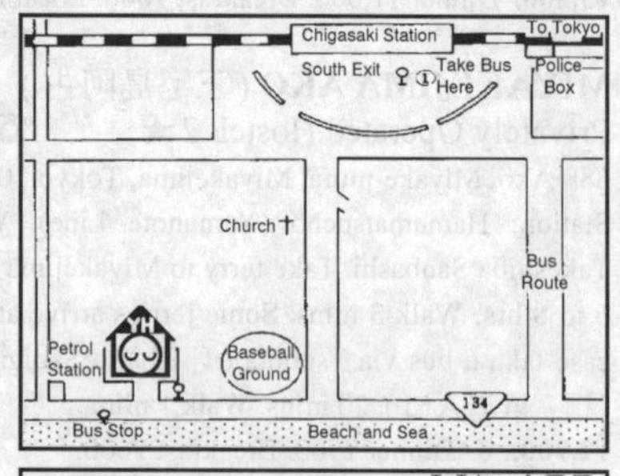


## ISAWA ONSEN (石和温泉)

Privately Operated Hostel 3★ ☎ 0552-62-2110

106-2 Yamazaki, Isawa-machi, Higashi Yatsushiro-gun, Yamanashi 406. 72 beds

Station: Isawa (Chuo Line). Walk 7 mins. (700 m).

**¥2,900, plus Spa Fee ¥150.** Dinner ¥1,000. Breakfast ¥600.

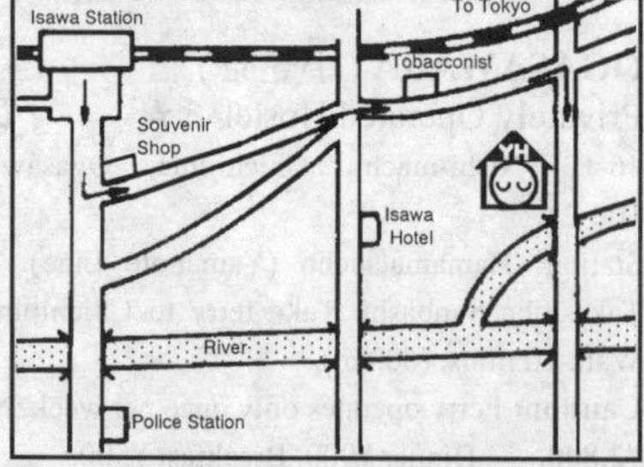


## FUJI YOSHIDA (富士吉田)

Private Home 2★ ☎ 0555-22-0533

2-339 Shimo Yoshida Hon-cho, Fuji Yoshida-shi, Yamanashi 403.

**Closed at New Year.** 30 beds

Station: Shimo Yoshida (Fuji Kyuko Private Railway), accessible from JR Otsuki (Chuo Line). Walk 7 mins.

**¥2,600.** Dinner ¥850. Breakfast ¥450.

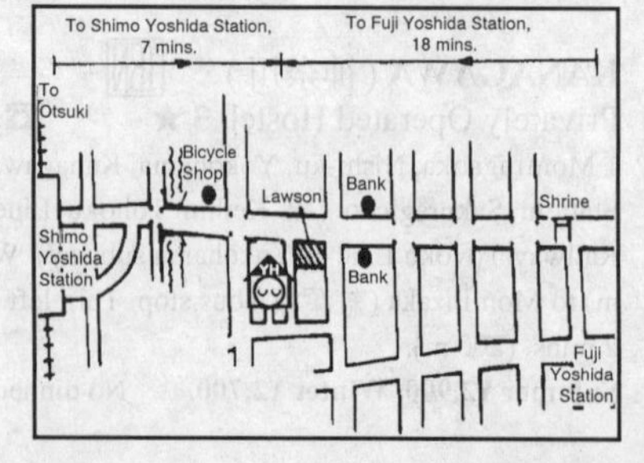

## KAWAGUCHI-KO (河口湖)

Privately Operated Hostel 3★ ☎ 0555-72-1431, 0630

2128 Funazu, Kawaguchiko-machi, Yamanashi 401-30.

**Closed from November until mid-March.** 70 beds

Station: Kawaguchi-ko (Fuji Kyuko Private Railway), accessible from JR Otsuki (Chuo Line). Walk 5 mins. (450 m). Alternatively, take express bus from Shinjuku (Yamanote Line) to Kawaguchi-ko (河口湖), 1 hr. 45 mins. Walk 5 mins.

**¥2,900.** Dinner ¥1,000. Breakfast ¥600.

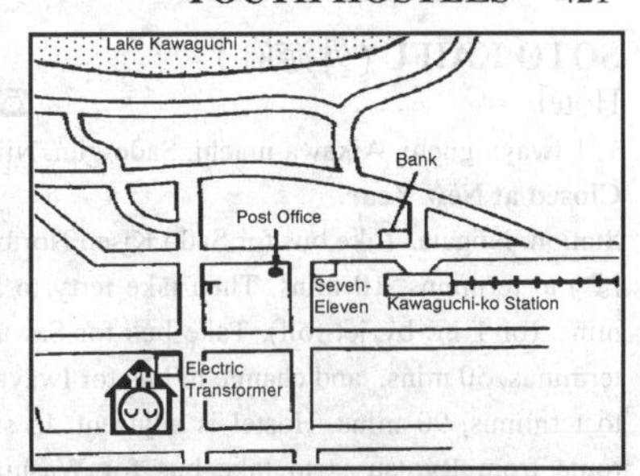


## FUJI SAI-KO (富士西湖) 

Local Organization Hostel ☎ 0555-82-2616

3-1 Saiko Nishi, Ashiwada-mura, Yamanashi 401-04.

**Closed from mid-November until mid-March.** 48 beds

Station: Kawaguchi-ko (Fuji Kyuko Private Railway), accessible from JR Otsuki (Chuo Line). Take bus for Sai-ko Minshuku (西湖民宿) to Youth Hostel-mae, 35 mins. Hostel is adjacent to bus stop. Alternatively, take express bus from Shinjuku (Yamanote Line) to Kawaguchi-ko (河口湖), 1 hr. 45 mins. Then as above.

**Winter ¥2,550. Summer ¥2,400 (Discount ¥500).**

Dinner ¥830. Breakfast ¥520.

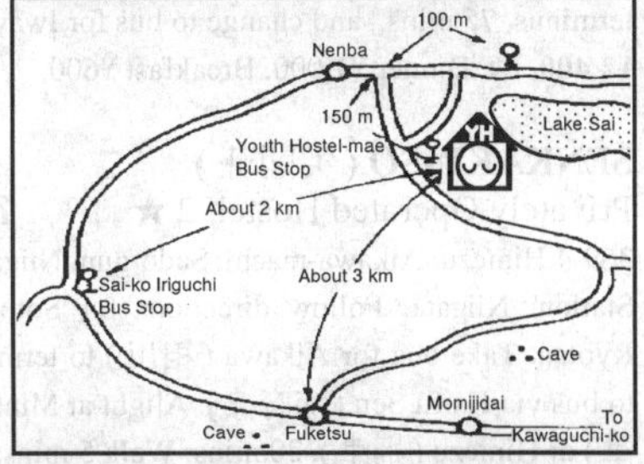


## KOFU HIGHLANDS (甲府ハイランド)

JYH Hostel 3★ ☎ 0552-51-8020

1355 Kami Obina-machi, Kofu-shi, Yamanashi 400-11.

**Closed from December until February.** 50 beds

Station: Kofu (Chuo Line). From North Exit, take bus for Chiyoda-ko (千代田湖) or Kami Obina (上帯那) to Kami Obina, 25 mins. Walk 3 mins. (300 m).

**Caution:** Last bus 17:52.

**¥2,600 (Discount ¥200).** Dinner ¥900. Breakfast ¥500.

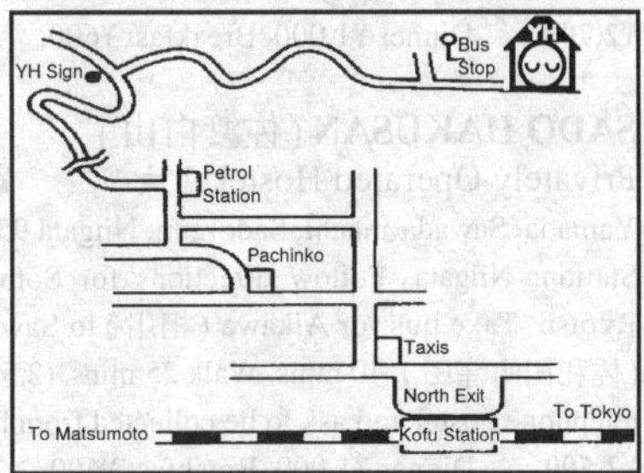


## MINOBU SANSO (身延山荘)

Temple Hostel 3★ ☎ 05566-2-0213

2780 Umedaira, Minobu-machi, Yamanashi 409-25. 50 beds

Station: Minobu (Minobu Line). Take bus for Minobu-san (身延山) to Kyo-enbo (鏡円坊), 7 mins. Walk 3 mins. uphill.

**¥2,900.** Dinner ¥1,000. Breakfast ¥600. Local Delicacies ¥1,250.

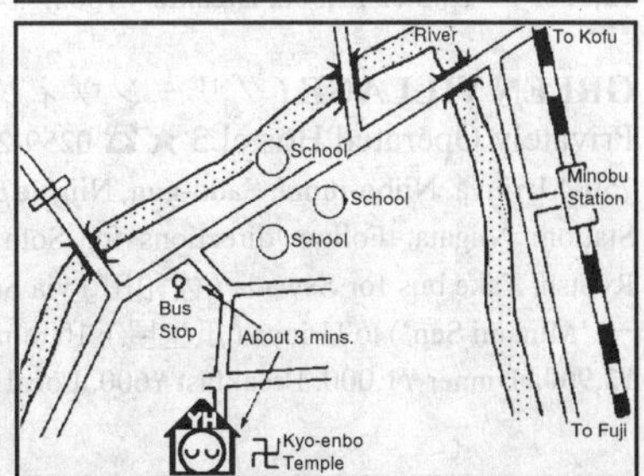


## KIYOSATO (清里)

Privately Operated Hostel 4★ ☎ 0551-48-2125

3545 Kiyosato, Takane-cho, Kita Koma-gun, Yamanashi 407-03. 50 beds

Station: Kiyosato (Koumi Line). Walk 5 mins. (300 m).

**¥3,200.** Dinner ¥900. Breakfast ¥600.

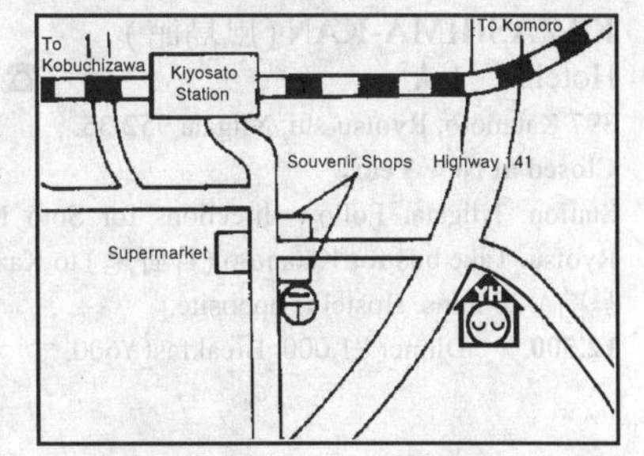

## SOTO KAIFU (外海府)

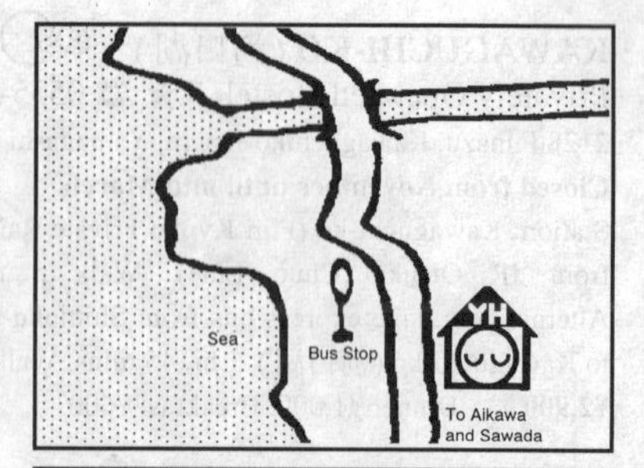


Hotel ☎ 0259-78-2911

131 Iwaya-guchi, Aikawa-machi, Sado-gun, Niigata 952-22.

**Closed at New Year.** 20 beds

Station: Niigata. Take bus for Sado Kisen Noriba (佐渡汽船のりば) to terminus, 10 mins. Then take ferry to Ryotsu, 2 hrs. 20 mins. (or 1 hr. by jet-foil). Take bus for Sawada (佐和田) to terminus, 50 mins., and change to bus for Iwaya-guchi (岩谷口) to terminus, 90 mins. Hostel is adjacent. In summer, a shorter route from Ryotsu is to take bus for Washizaki (鷲崎) to terminus, 75 mins., and change to bus for Iwaya-guchi, 40 mins.

**¥2,400.** Dinner ¥1,000. Breakfast ¥600.

## SENKAKU-SO (尖閣荘)

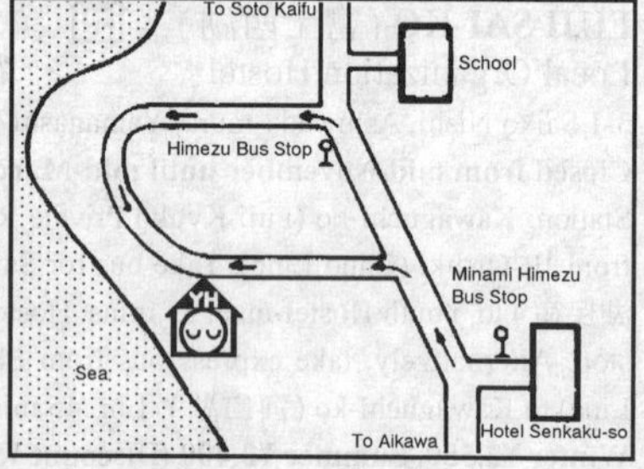


Privately Operated Hostel 2★ ☎ 0259-75-2011

369-4 Himezu, Aikawa-machi, Sado-gun, Niigata 952-21. 19 beds

Station: Niigata. Follow directions for Soto Kaifu (above) to Ryotsu. Take bus for Aikawa (相川) to terminus, 1 hr. Change to bus via Kaifu Sen (海府線). Alight at Minami Himezu (南姫津) or Himezu (姫津), 20 mins. Walk 5 mins.

**¥2,700.** Dinner ¥1,000. Breakfast ¥600.

## SADO HAKUSAN (佐渡白山)

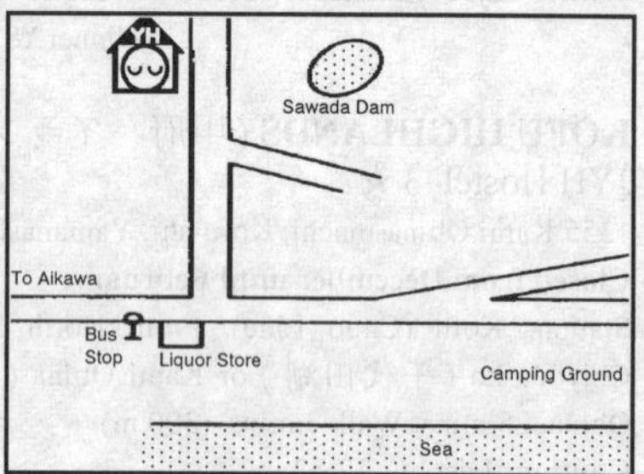


Privately Operated Hostel 1★ ☎ 0259-52-4422

Yamada, Sawada-machi, Sado-gun, Niigata 952-13. 14 beds

Station: Niigata. Follow directions for Soto Kaifu (above) to Ryotsu. Take bus for Aikawa (相川) to Sawada-machi Kubota (佐和田町窪田), 40 mins. Walk 25 mins. (2.5 km). Alternatively, telephone hostel and ask to be collected from bus stop.

**¥2,500.** Dinner ¥1,000. Breakfast ¥600.

## GREEN VILLAGE (グリーンヴィレッヂ)

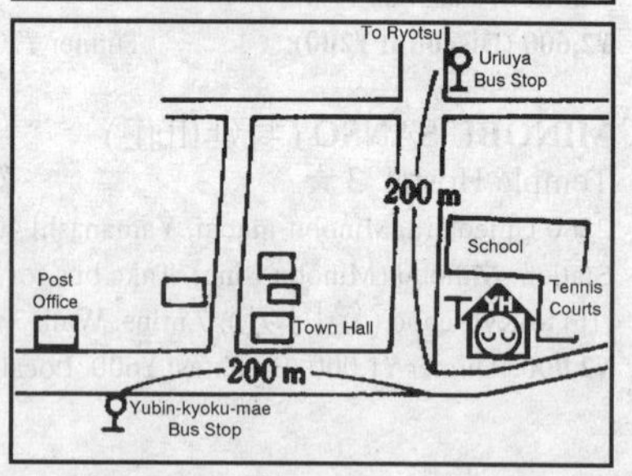


Privately Operated Hostel 3★ ☎ 0259-22-2719. Fax: 3302

750-4 Uriuya, Niibo-mura, Sado-gun, Niigata 952-01. 20 beds

Station: Niigata. Follow directions for Soto Kaifu (above) to Ryotsu. Take bus for Sawada (佐和田) via South Route (南線 – 'Minami Sen') to Uriuya (瓜生屋), 10 mins. Walk 2 mins.

**¥2,900.** Dinner ¥1,000. Breakfast ¥600. Local Delicacies ¥1,500.

## KAZASHIMA-KAN (風島館)

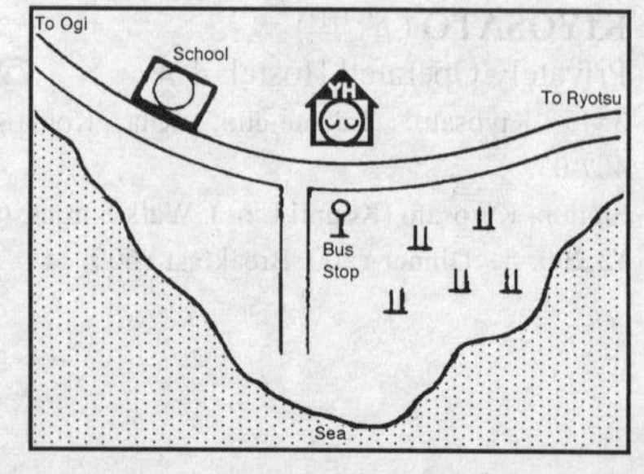


Hotel 1★ ☎ 0259-29-2003

397 Katano-o, Ryotsu-shi, Niigata 952-35.

**Closed at New Year.** 24 beds

Station: Niigata. Follow directions for Soto Kaifu (above) to Ryotsu. Take bus for Katano-o (片野尾) to Kazashima-mae (風島前), 20 mins. Hostel is opposite.

**¥2,500.** Dinner ¥1,000. Breakfast ¥600.

## OGI SAKUMA-SO (小木佐久間荘)

Private Home ☎ 0259-86-2565

1562 Ogi-machi, Sado-gun, Niigata 952-06.

**Closed from December until February.** 19 beds

Station: ① Niigata. Follow directions for Soto Kaifu (previous page) to Ryotsu. Take bus for Sawada (佐和田) via South Route (南線ー 'Minami Sen') to Shin-machi (新町), 40 mins. Change to bus for Ogi (小木) to terminus, 1 hr. 30 mins. Walk 20 mins. ② Naoetsu (Shinetsu Main Line). Take ferry to Ogi, 2 hrs. 30 mins. (or 1 hr. by jet-foil, summer only). Walk 20 mins.

**¥2,500.** Dinner ¥1,000. Breakfast ¥600.

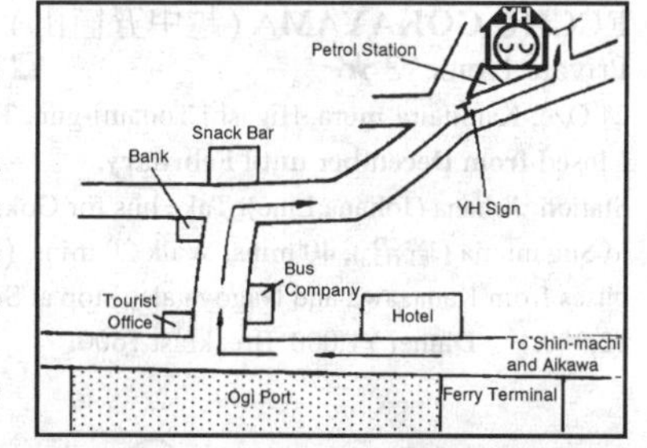


## MUIKA-MACHI ONSEN KOKUSAI (六日町温泉国際)

JYH Hostel 3★ ☎ 0257-72-2842, 73-2069

1920-1 Oguriyama, Muika-machi, Niigata 949-66.

**Closed in late June and late October.** 180 beds

Station: Muikamachi (Joetsu Line). Take bus for Toka-machi (十日町) to Ski-jo (スキー場), 10 mins. Walk 15 mins.

**¥2,700, plus Spa Fee ¥120 (Discount ¥300).**

Dinner ¥1,000. Breakfast ¥600. Local Delicacies ¥1,500.

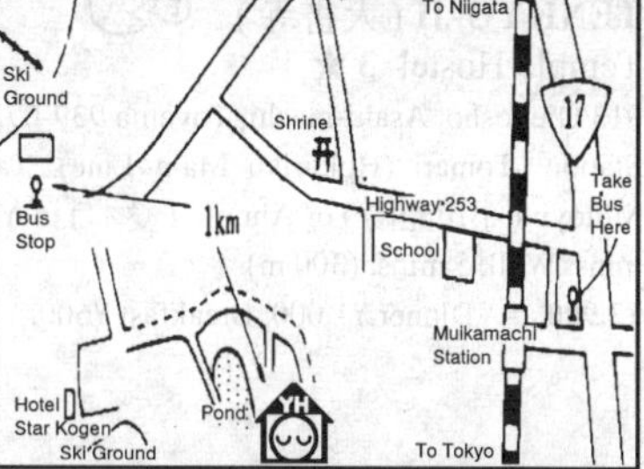


## KIYOTSU-KYO ONSEN (清津峡温泉)

Hotel 2★ ☎ 0257-63-2431

168 Kuramata, Nakazato-mura, Niigata 949-84. 49 beds

Station: ① Echigo Tazawa (Iiyama Line). Walk 5 mins. to Yamazaki Jinja (山崎神社) bus stop. Take bus for Kiyotsu-kyo (清津峡) to Seto-guchi (瀬戸口), 30 mins. Walk 3 mins.

② Echigo Yuzawa (Shinkansen and Joetsu Lines). Take express bus for Morimiya-no-hara (森宮の原) via Kiyotsu-kyo (清津峡) to Seto-guchi (瀬戸口), 30 mins. Walk 3 mins.

**Caution:** Last bus, route ① 17:10, route ② 18:20.

**¥2,700, plus Spa Fee ¥100 (Discount ¥500).**

Dinner ¥1,000. Breakfast ¥600. Local Delicacies ¥1,500.

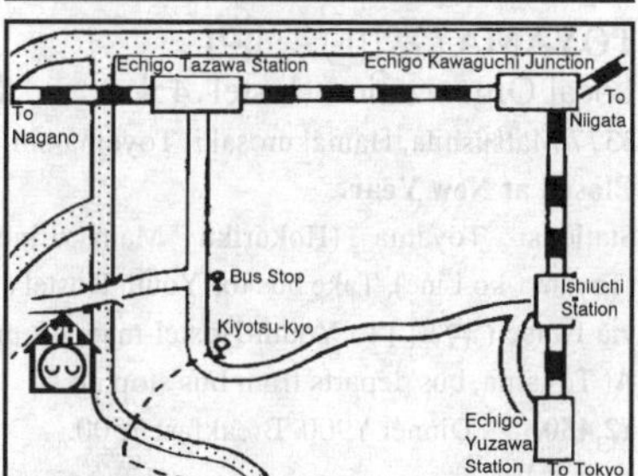


## KASHIWAZAKI (柏崎)

JYH Hostel 2★ ☎ 0257-22-5740. Fax: 5969

7-6 Higashi Minato-machi, Kashiwazaki-shi, Niigata 945.

**Closed at New Year and in late June.** 60 beds

Station: Kashiwazaki (Shinetsu Main Line). Walk towards the sea for 20 mins. (1.8 km).

**Winter ¥2,200. Summer ¥2,100.** Dinner ¥700. Breakfast ¥500.

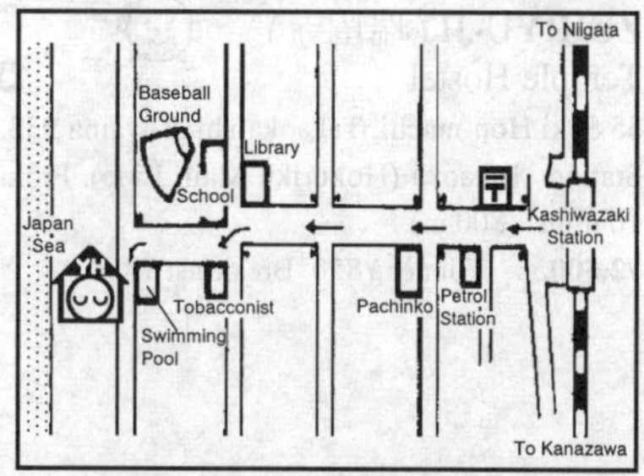


## MYOCHI-JI (妙智寺)

Temple Hostel 2★ ☎ 0257-23-6484

3-7-33 Kujira-nami, Kashiwazaki-shi, Niigata 945.

**Closed at New Year.** 50 beds

Station: Kujiranami (Shinetsu Main Line). Walk 8 mins.

**¥2,700.** Dinner ¥800. Breakfast ¥500.

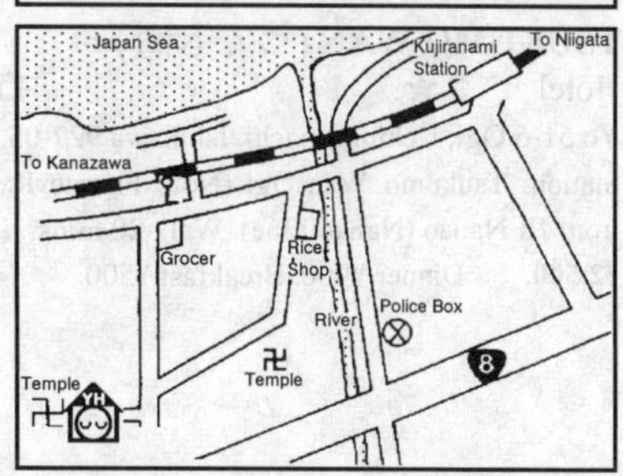

## ECCHU GOKAYAMA (越中五箇山)

Private Home 3★ ☎ 0763-67-3331

24 Oze, Kamitaira-mura, Higashi Tonami-gun, Toyama 939-19.

**Closed from December until February.** 41 beds

Station: Johana (Johana Line). Take bus for Gokayama (五箇山) to Suganuma (菅沼), 40 mins. Walk 20 mins. (1.5 km). Express buses from Kanazawa and Nagoya also stop at Suganuma.

**¥2,900.** Dinner ¥1,000. Breakfast ¥600.

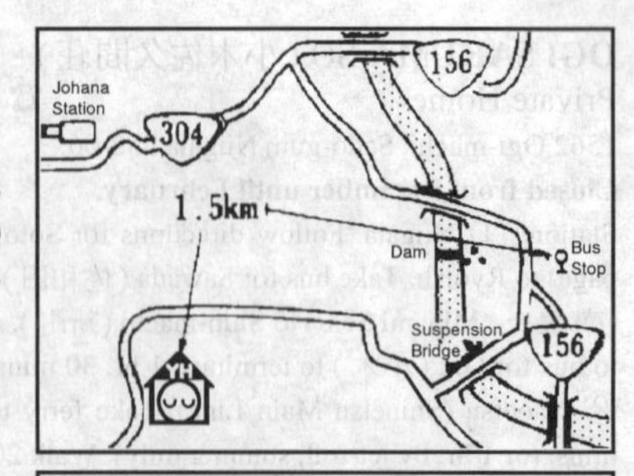


## TENKYO-JI (天香寺)

Temple Hostel 3★ ☎ 0765-82-0580

913 Oienosho, Asahi-machi, Toyama 939-07. 50 beds

Station: Tomari (Hokuriku Main Line). Take bus for Ogawa Motoyu (小川元湯) or Aimoto (愛本) to Yanagida (柳田), 15 mins. Walk 5 mins. (300 m).

**¥2,900.** Dinner ¥1,000. Breakfast ¥600.

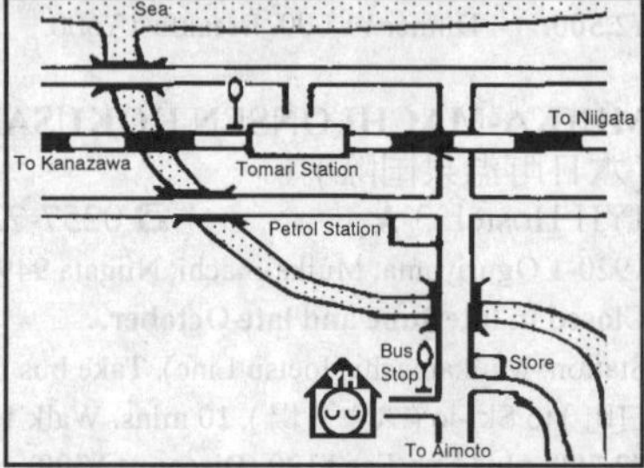


## TOYAMA (富山)

Local Organization Hostel 4★ ☎ 0764-37-9010

3377 Matsushita, Hamakurosaki, Toyama-shi, Toyama 931.

**Closed at New Year.** 41 beds

Stations: Toyama (Hokuriku Main Line) or Iwasehama (Toyama-ko Line). Take bus for Youth Hostel (ユースホステル) via Iwase (岩瀬) to Youth Hostel-mae, 45 mins. from Toyama. At Toyama, bus departs from bus stop no. 7.

**¥2,450.** Dinner ¥900. Breakfast ¥500.

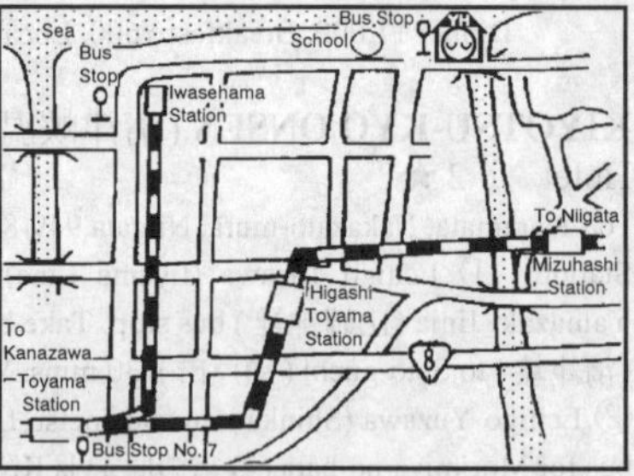


## ZUIRYU-JI (瑞竜寺)

Temple Hostel ☎ 0766-22-0179

35 Seki Hon-machi, Takaoka-shi, Toyama 933. 30 beds

Station: Takaoka (Hokuriku Main Line). From South Exit, walk 10 mins. (800 m).

**¥2,500.** Dinner ¥850. Breakfast ¥450.

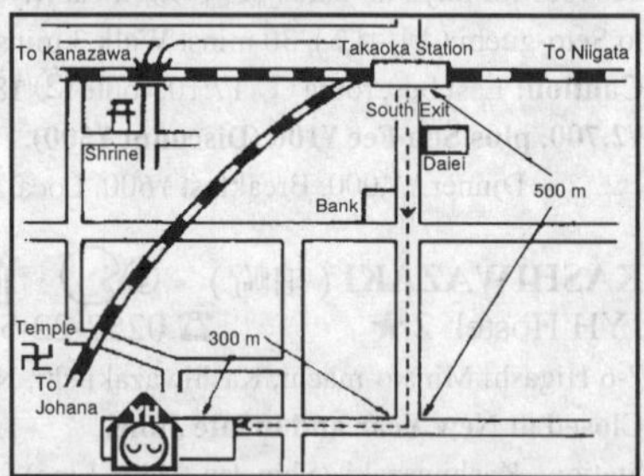


## TSUKUMO WAN (つくも湾)

Hotel 2★ ☎ 0768-74-0150

Yo 51-6 Ogi, Uchiura-machi, Ishikawa 927-05. 50 beds

Station: Tsukumo Wan Ogi (Noto Private Railway), accessible from JR Nanao (Nanao Line). Walk 20 mins.

**¥2,500.** Dinner ¥900. Breakfast ¥500.

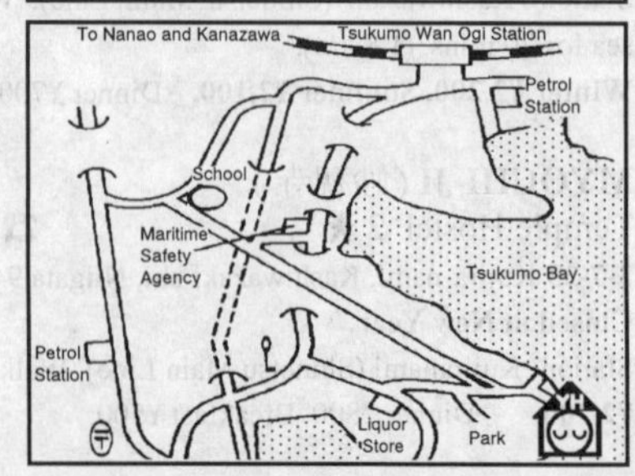

## SOSOGI KAJIYAMA (曽々木梶山)

Hotel 3★ ☎ 0768-32-1145

4-1 Sosogi Kibe, Machino, Wajima, Ishikawa 928-02. 40 beds

Station: Wajima (Noto Private Railway), accessible from JR Nanao (Nanao Line). Take bus for Ushitsu (宇出津) to Sosogi-guchi (曽々木口), 43 mins. Walk 7 mins. Sosogi (曽々木) bus stop is opposite hostel, but is served by few buses from Wajima. Infrequent express sightseeing buses run direct from Kanazawa.

**¥2,900.** Dinner ¥1,000. Breakfast ¥600.

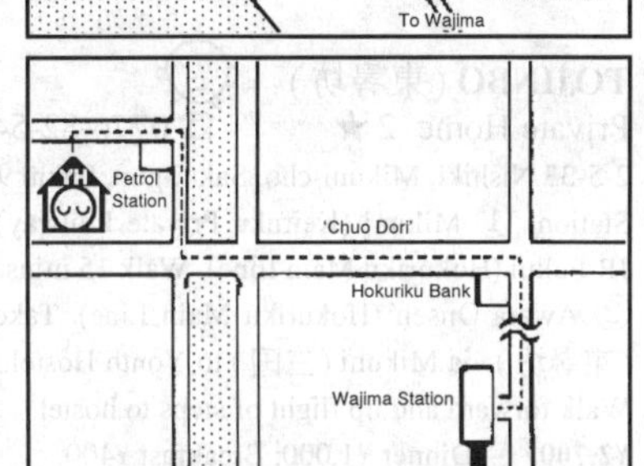


## WAJIMA CHORAKU-JI (輪島長楽寺)

Temple Hostel 2★ ☎ 0768-22-0663

7-104 Shinbashi-dori, Wajima-shi, Ishikawa 928.

**Closed at New Year and in early April.** 52 beds

Station: Wajima (Noto Private Railway), accessible from JR Nanao (Nanao Line). Walk 15 mins. (1.3 km).

**¥2,600.** Dinner ¥900. Breakfast ¥500.

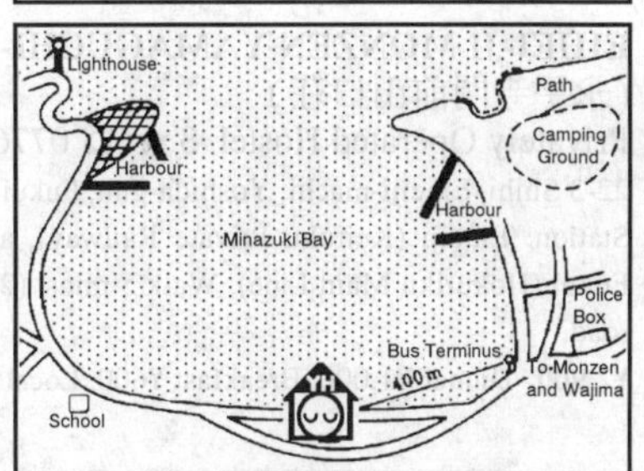


## NOTO MINAZUKI (能登皆月)

Privately Operated Hostel 2★ ☎ 0768-46-2022

Minazuki, Monzen-machi, Fugeshi-gun, Ishikawa 927-22.

**Closed at New Year.** 15 beds

Station: Anamizu (Noto Private Railway), accessible from JR Nanao (Nanao Line). Take bus for Monzen (門前) to terminus, 35 mins. Change to bus for Minazuki (皆月) to terminus, 30 mins. Walk 5 mins. Infrequent express buses run direct from Kanazawa to Monzen and also from Hakui (Nanao Line) to Monzen.

**¥2,700.** Dinner ¥1,000. Breakfast ¥600.

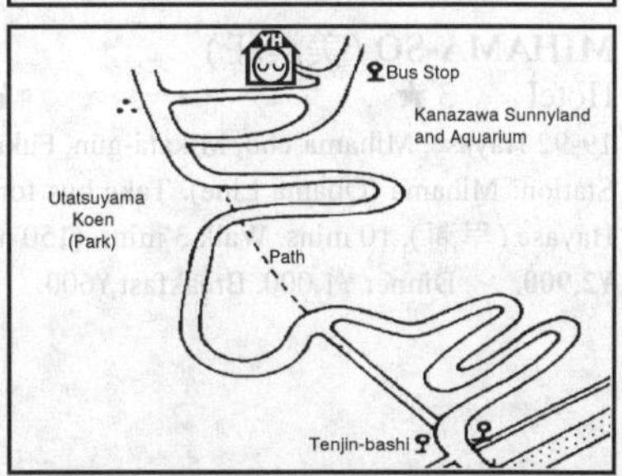


## KANAZAWA (金沢)

JYH Hostel 3★ ☎ 0762-52-3414, 8590

37 Suehiro-machi, Kanazawa-shi, Ishikawa 920.

**Closed in mid-January.** 80 beds

Station: Kanazawa. Take bus for Utatsuyama Koen (卯辰山公園) to Kanazawa Suizoku-kan (金沢水族館), 25 mins. Walk 1 min.

**¥2,900 (Discount ¥200).** Dinner ¥1,000. Breakfast ¥600.

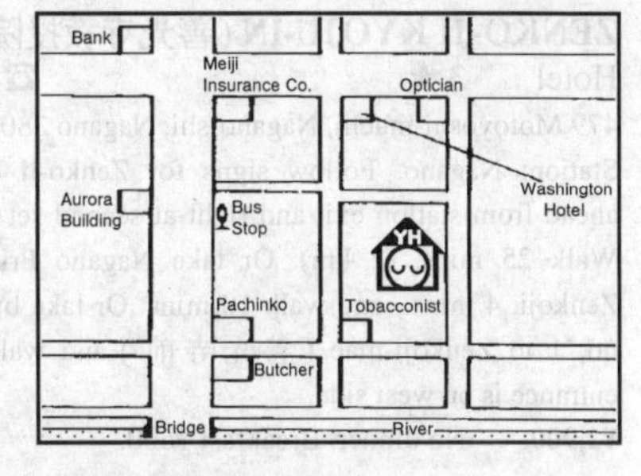


## MATSUI (松井)

Privately Operated Hostel 4★ ☎ 0762-21-0275

1-9-3 Kata-machi, Kanazawa-shi, Ishikawa 920.

**Closed at New Year.** 15 beds

Station: Kanazawa. Take a bus from bus stop no. 7, 8 or 9 to Kata-machi (片町), 14 mins. Walk 4 mins. (310 m).

**¥3,100.** Dinner ¥1,000. Breakfast ¥600.

## FUKUI-KEN FUJIN SEINEN KAIKAN

(福井県婦人青年会館)

Local Organization Hostel 3★ ☎ 0776-22-5625, 5920

3-11-17 Ote, Fukui-shi, Fukui 910. 43 beds

Station: Fukui (Hokuriku Main Line). Walk 7 mins. (700 m). Entrance to hostel is on west side.

**¥2,900.** No dinner. Breakfast ¥600.

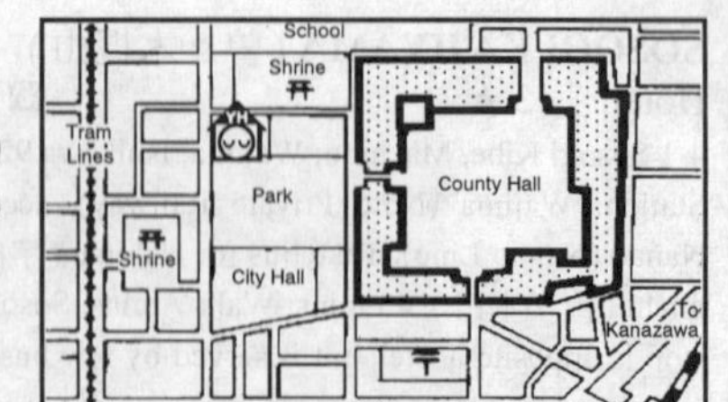


## TOJINBO (東尋坊)

Private Home 2★ ☎ 0776-82-5400. Fax: 5429

2-5-33 Nishiki, Mikuni-cho, Sakai-gun, Fukui 913. 60 beds

Station: ① Mikuni (Keifuku Private Railway), accessible from JR Fukui (Hokuriku Main Line). Walk 15 mins. (700 m).
② Awara Onsen (Hokuriku Main Line). Take bus for Tojinbo (東尋坊) via Mikuni (三国) to Youth Hostel Iriguchi, 30 mins. Walk forward and up flight of steps to hostel.

**¥2,700.** Dinner ¥1,000. Breakfast ¥400.

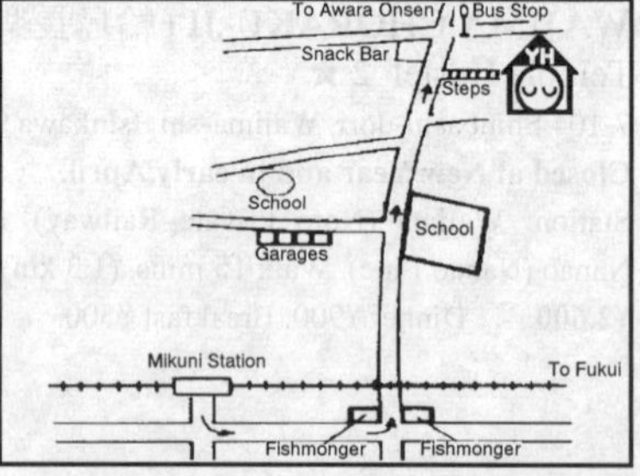


## EIHEI-JI MONZEN YAMAGUCHI-SO

(永平寺門前山口荘)

Privately Operated Hostel 3★ ☎ 0776-63-3123, 3122

22-3 Shihi, Eiheiji-machi, Yoshida-gun, Fukui 910-12. 46 beds

Station: Eiheiji (Keifuku Private Railway), accessible from JR Fukui (Hokuriku Main Line). Walk 5 mins. (250 m) towards toll road.

**¥2,900.** Dinner ¥1,000. Breakfast ¥600. Local Delicacies ¥1,500.

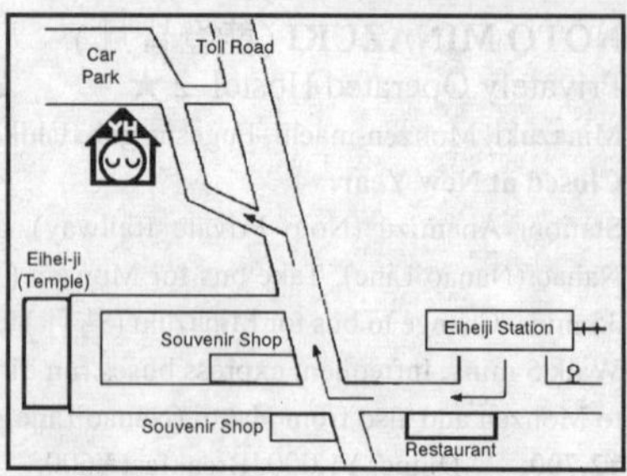


## MIHAMA-SO (美浜荘)

Hotel 3★ ☎ 0770-32-0301

19-92 Hayase, Mihama-cho, Mikata-gun, Fukui 919-11. 27 beds

Station: Mihama (Obama Line). Take bus for Hyuga (日向) to Hayase (早瀬), 10 mins. Walk 3 mins. (150 m).

**¥2,900.** Dinner ¥1,000. Breakfast ¥600.

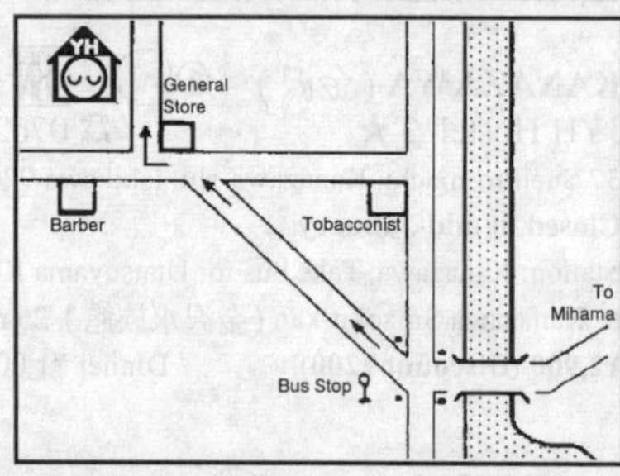


## ZENKO-JI KYOJU-IN (善光寺教授院)

Hotel 3★ ☎ 0262-32-2768

479 Motoyoshi-machi, Nagano-shi, Nagano 380. 30 beds

Station: Nagano. Follow signs for Zenko-ji Temple (straight ahead from station exit and right at second set of traffic lights). Walk 25 mins. (2 km). Or take Nagano Private Railway to Zenkoji, 4 mins., and walk 10 mins. Or take bus from bus stop no. 1 to Zenkoji-mae (善光寺前) and walk 1 min. Hostel entrance is on west side.

**¥2,900.** No dinner. Breakfast ¥600.

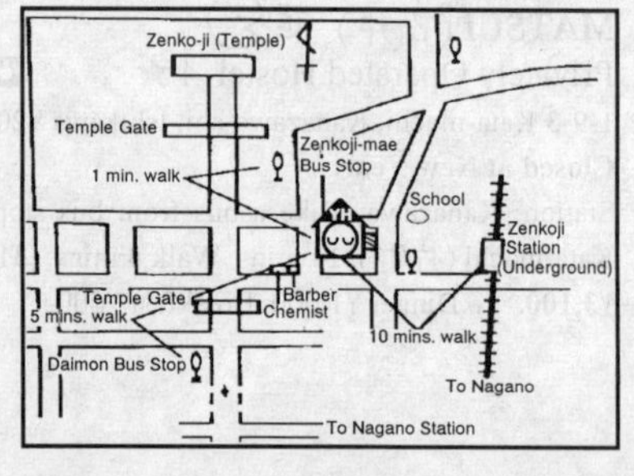

## TOGAKUSHI KOGEN YOKOKURA (戸隠高原横倉)

Hotel 3★ ☎ 0262-54-2030, 2540
3347 Chusha, Togakushi-mura, Nagano 381-41. 100 beds
Station: Nagano. Take bus for Togakushi (戸隠) to Togakushi Chusha Miya-mae (戸隠中社宮前), 1 hr. Walk 2 mins. Some buses terminate at Togakushi Chusha Daimon (戸隠中社大門), from where walk 7 mins.
**Caution:** Last bus 18:48.
**¥2,900.** Dinner ¥1,000. Breakfast ¥600. Local Delicacies ¥1,500.

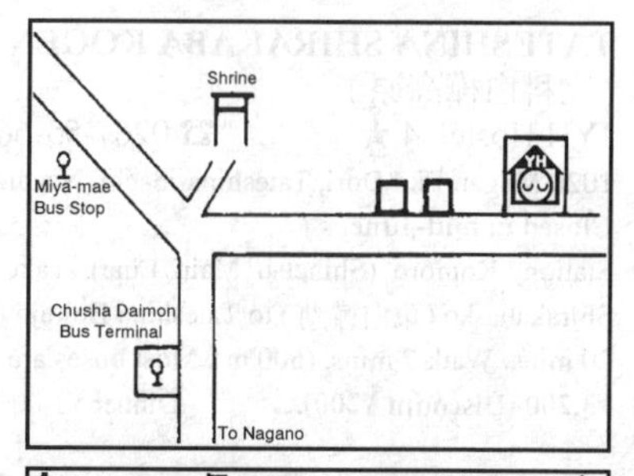


## KOMORO (小諸)

Privately Operated Hostel 4★ ☎ 0267-23-5732
3876-4 Minamigahara, Komoro-shi, Nagano 384. 40 beds
Station: Komoro (Shinetsu Main Line). Take bus for Seinen-no-ie (青年の家) to terminus, 23 mins. Walk 25 mins. (1.8 km) or telephone hostel from telephone by bus stop and ask to be collected.
**Caution:** Last bus 17:35 on weekdays, 16:45 on holidays.
**¥2,900.** Dinner ¥1,000. Breakfast ¥600.

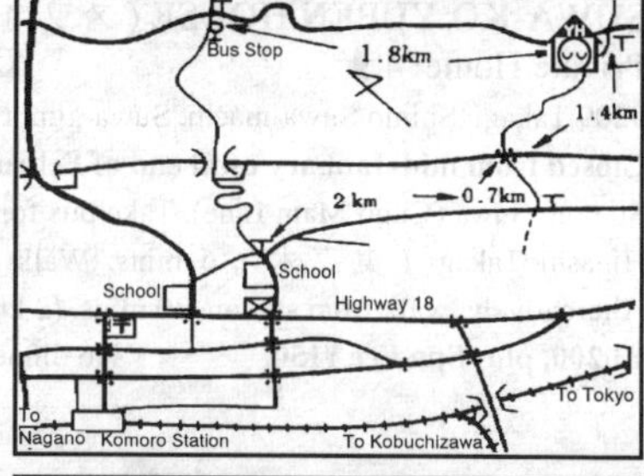


## UEDA MAHOROBA (上田まほろば)

Privately Operated Hostel 3★ ☎ 0268-38-5229
40-1 Bessho Onsen, Ueda-shi, Nagano 386-14. 20 beds
Station: Bessho Onsen (Ueda Private Railway), accessible from JR Ueda (Shinetsu Main Line). Walk 8 mins.
**¥2,900 (Discount ¥500).** Dinner ¥1,000. Breakfast ¥600.

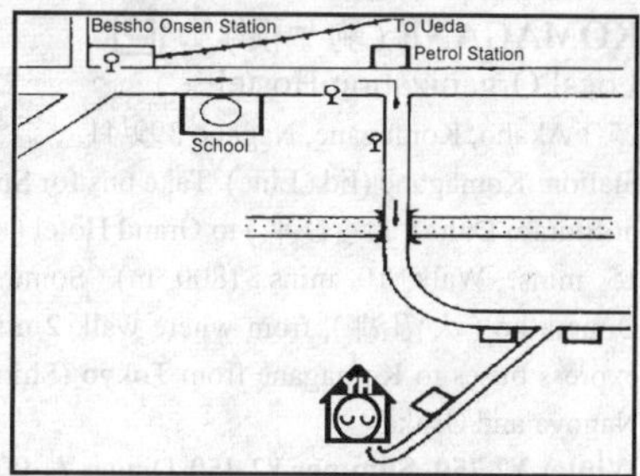


## SHIRAKABA-KO (白樺湖)

JYH Hostel 3★ ☎ 0266-68-2031. Fax: 3378
3418 Kitayama, Chino-shi, Nagano 391-03.
**Closed in early April and late November.** 70 beds
Station: Chino (Chuo Main Line). Take bus for Shirakaba-ko (白樺湖) to Nishi Shirakaba-ko (西白樺湖), 50 mins. Walk 3 mins. JR buses run to Higashi Shirakaba-ko (東白樺湖) from Komoro (Shinetsu Main Line), 1 hr. 30 mins. Walk 10 mins.
**¥2,900.** Dinner ¥1,000. Breakfast ¥450.

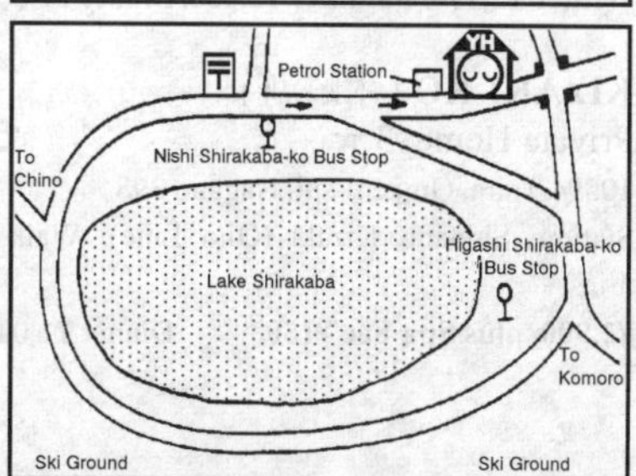


## TATESHINA KLIENE (蓼科クライネ)

Privately Operated Hostel ☎ 0266-77-2077
5890 Kitayama, Chino-shi, Nagano 391-03. 14 beds
Station: Chino (Chuo Main Line). Take bus for Midoriyama (緑山) to Tetsuyama Iriguchi (鉄山入口), 24 mins. Walk 3 mins.
**¥2,700.** Dinner ¥1,000. Breakfast ¥600.

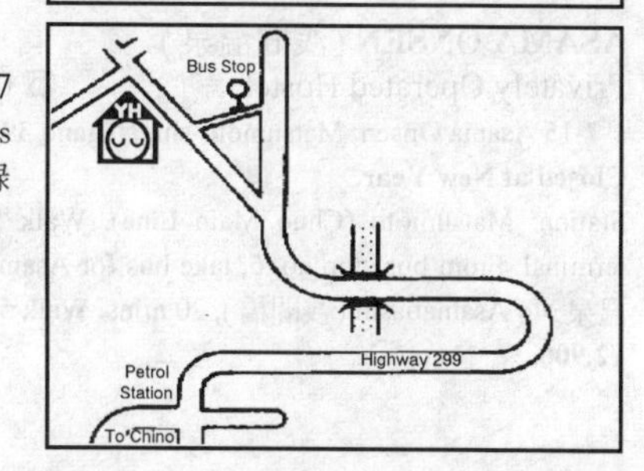

## TATESHINA SHIRAKABA KOGEN (立科白樺高原)

JYH Hostel 4★ ☎ 0267-55-6601. Fax: 7394

1020 Megami-ko Dori, Tateshina-machi, Nagano 384-23.

**Closed in mid-June.** 48 beds

Station: Komoro (Shinetsu Main Line). Take bus for Higashi Shirakaba-ko (東白樺湖) to Tateshina Bokujo (蓼科牧場), 1 hr. 20 mins. Walk 7 mins. (600 m). Most buses are JR buses.

**¥3,200 (Discount ¥200).** Dinner ¥1,000. Breakfast ¥600.

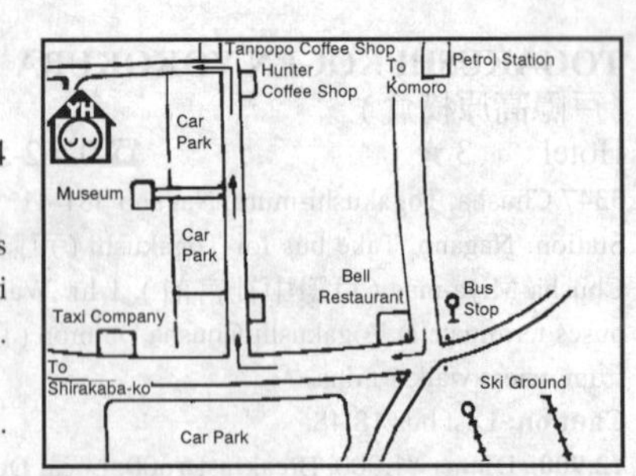


## SUWA-KO YUPEN HOUSE (スワコ遊遍館)

Private Home 4★ ☎ 0266-27-7075

9209 Takagi, Shimo Suwa-machi, Suwa-gun, Nagano 393.

**Closed from mid-January until end of February.** 58 beds

Station: Suwa (Chuo Main Line). Take bus for Okaya (岡谷) to Higashi Takagi (東高木), 6 mins. Walk 4 mins. (200 m). Alternatively, walk from station, 30 mins. (2 km).

**¥3,200, plus Spa Fee ¥150.** No dinner. Breakfast ¥600.

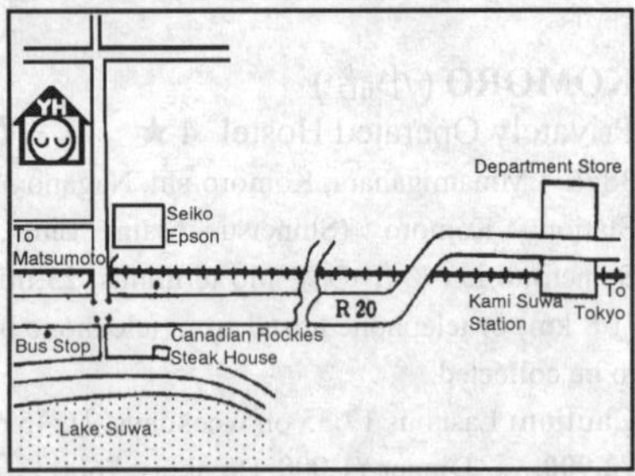


## KOMAGANE (駒ケ根)

Local Organization Hostel ☎ 0265-83-3856

25-1 Akaho, Komagane, Nagano 399-41. 60 beds

Station: Komagane (Iida Line). Take bus for Suganodai (菅の台) or Shirabi Daira (しらび平) to Grand Hotel (グランドホテル), 15 mins. Walk 10 mins. (800 m). Some buses travel via Onuma-ko (大沼湖), from where walk 2 mins. There are also express buses to Komagane from Tokyo (Shinjuku), Yokohama, Nagoya and Osaka.

**Winter ¥2,750. Summer ¥2,450.** Dinner ¥1,000. Breakfast ¥600.

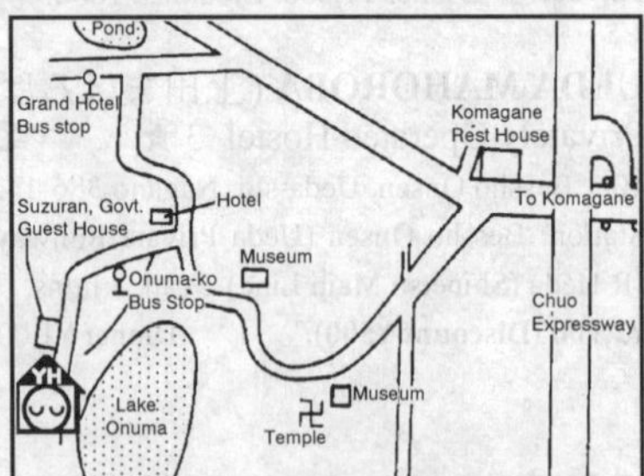


## KIZAKI-KO (木崎湖)

Private Home 3★ ☎ 0261-22-1820

10594 Taira, Omachi-shi, Nagano 398. 48 beds

Station: Shinano Kizaki (Oito Line). Walk towards lake, 15 mins.

**¥2,900, plus Spa Fee ¥150.** Dinner ¥1,000. Breakfast ¥600.

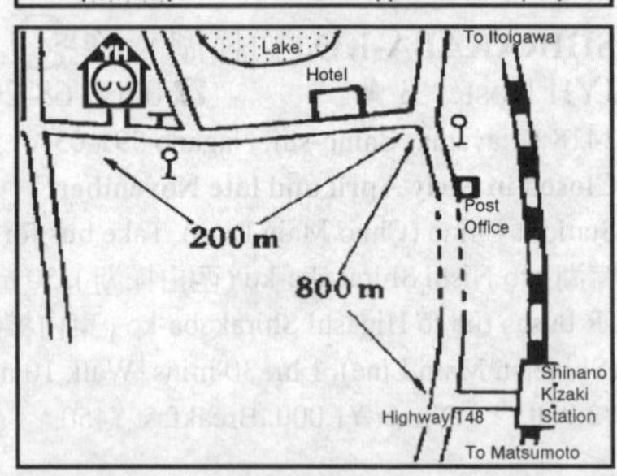


## ASAMA ONSEN (浅間温泉)

Privately Operated Hostel ☎ 0263-46-1335

1-7-15 Asama Onsen, Matsumoto-shi, Nagano 390-03.

**Closed at New Year.** 110 beds

Station: Matsumoto (Chuo Main Line). Walk 5 mins. to bus terminal. From bus stop no. 6, take bus for Asama Onsen (浅間温泉) to Asamabashi (浅間橋), 20 mins. Walk 5 mins. (400 m).

**¥2,900.** No meals.

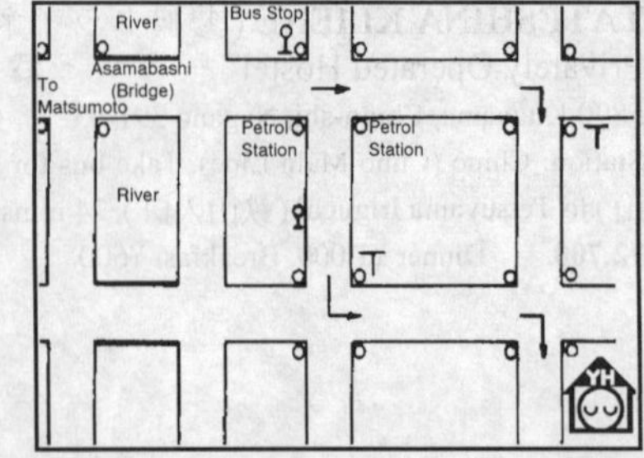

## KISO RYOJO-AN (木曽旅情庵)

Private Home 3★ ☎ 0264-23-7716

634 Shinkai, Kiso Fukushima, Kiso-gun, Nagano 397. 42 beds

Station: Kiso Fukushima (Chuo Main Line). Take bus for Ohara (大原) to terminus at Ohara Ue (大原上), 25 mins. Walk 3 mins.

**¥2,900.** Dinner ¥1,000. Breakfast ¥600.

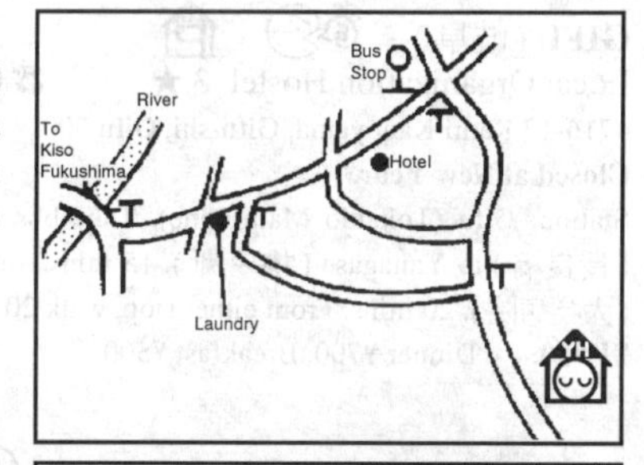


## NORIKURA KOGEN (のりくら高原) 

Privately Operated Hostel 4★ ☎ 0263-93-2748. Fax: 2162

Azumi-mura, Minami Azumi-gun, Nagano 390-15. 51 beds

Station: Shin Shimashima (Matsumoto Private Railway), accessible from JR Matsumoto. Take bus for Norikura Kogen (乗鞍高原) to Suzuran Ski-jo (鈴蘭スキー場), 1 hr. 10 mins. Walk 10 mins. (600 m).

**¥3,200, plus Spa Fee ¥150.** Dinner ¥1,000. Breakfast ¥600.

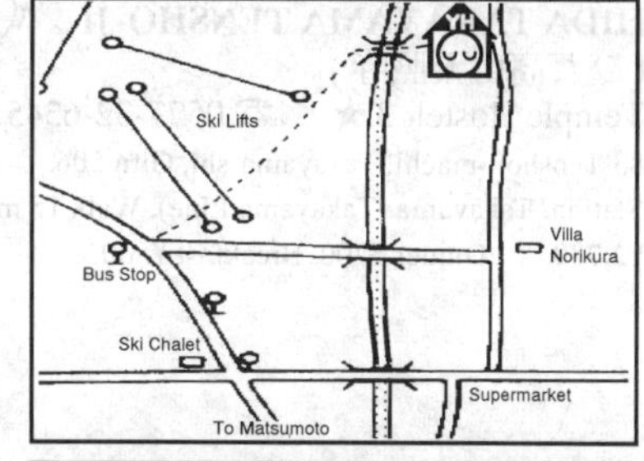


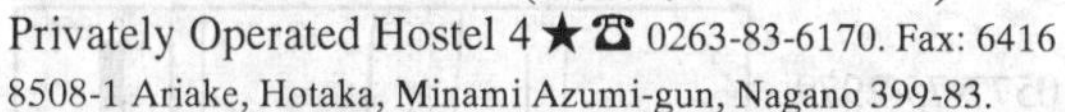

## AZUMINO PASTORAL (安曇野パストラル)

Privately Operated Hostel 4★ ☎ 0263-83-6170. Fax: 6416

8508-1 Ariake, Hotaka, Minami Azumi-gun, Nagano 399-83.

**Closed from mid-January until mid-February.** 32 beds

Station: Hotaka (Oito Line). Walk 1 hr. (4 km). Cross railway and proceed until second set of traffic signals (3.5 km). Then turn left and walk another 700 m. Hostel is a short way along a road on the left. Alternatively, hire a bicycle from the store in front of the station (one-way hire permissible).

**¥3,200.** Dinner ¥1,000. Breakfast ¥600. Local Delicacies ¥1,500.

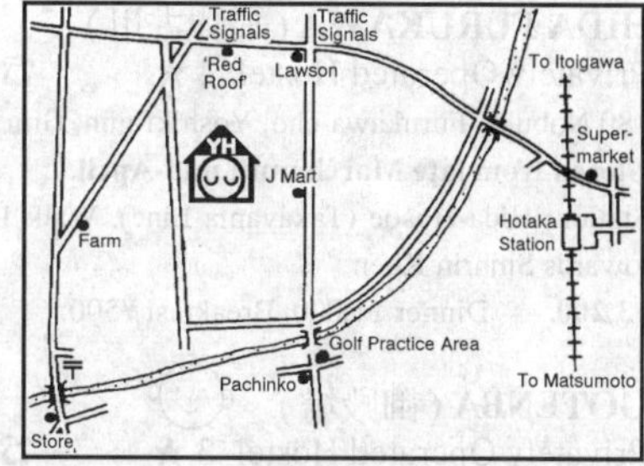


## HOKO-NO-KO (保古の湖)  

Local Organization Hostel 3★ ☎ 0573-65-3534

2390-1 Higashino, Ena-shi, Gifu 509-72. 70 beds

Station: Ena (Chuo Main Line). Take bus for Nenoue Kogen (根ノ上高原) to Hoko-no-ko (保古の湖), 30 mins. Walk 2 mins. See also map for Nenoue Kogen Kohan-no-yado (below).

**Caution:** Bus runs only in mid-summer. At other times ask advice from hostel regarding transport.

**Winter ¥2,110. Summer ¥1,853.** Dinner ¥824. Breakfast ¥515.

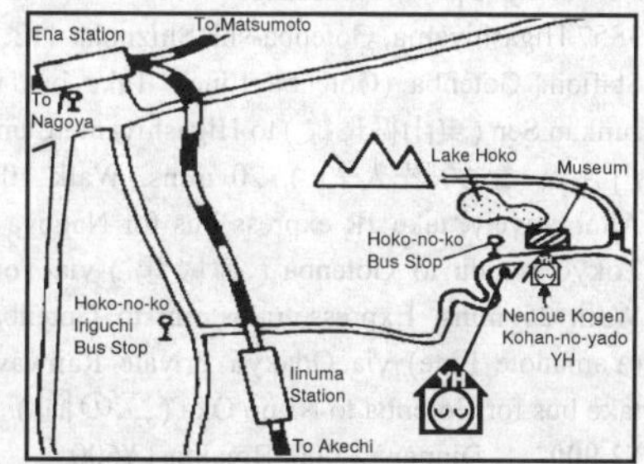


## NENOUE KOGEN KOHAN-NO-YADO (根の上高原湖畔の宿)

Hotel 2★ ☎ 0573-65-4643

Hokono Kohan, Nenoue Kogen, Nakatsugawa-shi, Gifu 508.

**Closed from mid-December until mid-January.** 54 beds

Station: Ena (Chuo Main Line). Take bus for Nenoue Kogen (根ノ上高原) to Hoko-no-ko (保古の湖), 30 mins. Walk 1 min. See also map for Hoko-no-ko (above).

**Caution:** Bus runs only in mid-summer.

**¥2,700.** Dinner ¥850. Breakfast ¥500.

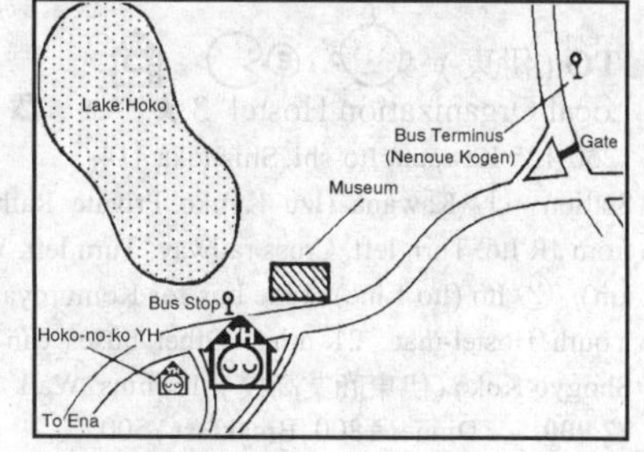

## GIFU (岐阜)

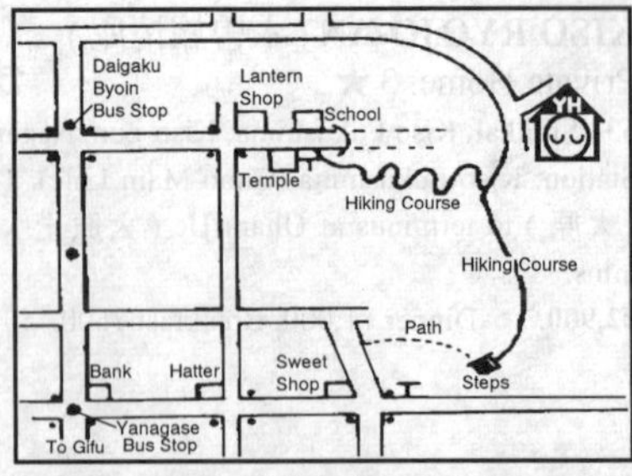


Local Organization Hostel 3★ ☎ 0582-63-6631
4716-17 Kami Kanoyama, Gifu-shi, Gifu 500.
**Closed at New Year.** 60 beds
Station: Gifu (Tokaido Main Line). Take bus for Nagarabashi (長良橋) to Yanagase (柳ヶ瀬), 15 mins., or Daigaku Byoin (大学病院), 20 mins. From either stop, walk 20 mins. (2 km).
**¥1,950.** Dinner ¥700. Breakfast ¥500.

## HIDA TAKAYAMA TENSHO-JI (ひだ高山天照寺)

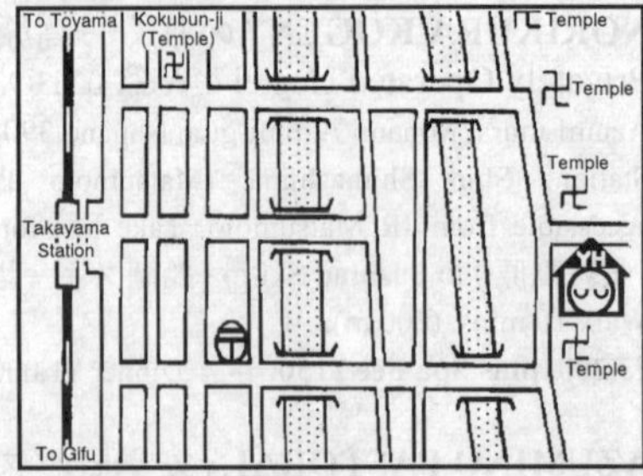


Temple Hostel 3★ ☎ 0577-32-6345. Fax: 35-2986
83 Tenshoji-machi, Takayama-shi, Gifu 506. 114 beds
Station: Takayama (Takayama Line). Walk 15 mins. (1.2 km).
**¥2,700.** Dinner ¥700. Breakfast ¥500.

## HIDA FURUKAWA (飛騨古川)

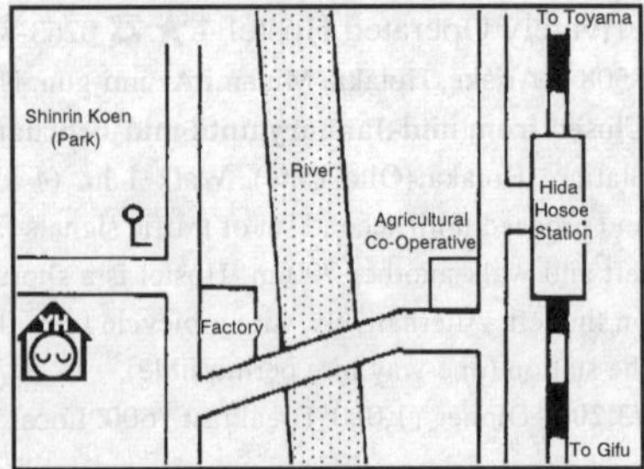


Privately Operated Hostel 4★ ☎ 0577-75-2979
180 Nobuka, Furukawa-cho, Yoshiki-gun, Gifu 509-42.
**Closed from late March until mid-April.** 22 beds
Station: Hida Hosoe (Takayama Line). Walk 15 mins. (1.2 km) towards Shinrin Koen.
**¥3,200.** Dinner ¥1,000. Breakfast ¥500.

## GOTENBA (御殿場)

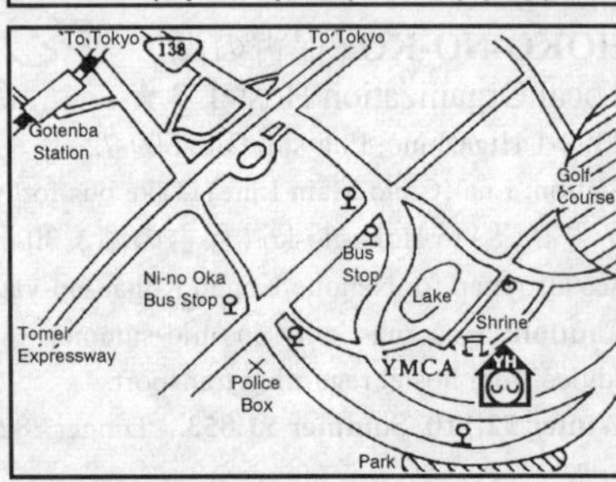


Privately Operated Hostel 3★ ☎ 0550-82-3045
3857 Higashiyama, Gotenba-shi, Shizuoka 412. 52 beds
Station: Gotenba (Gotenba Line). Take bus via Higashiyama Junkan Sen (東山循環線) to Higashiyama Camp-jo Iriguchi (東山キャンプ場入口), 20 mins. Walk 10 mins. (800 m). Alternatively, take JR express bus for Nagoya (名古屋) from Tokyo station to Gotenba (御殿場) via Tomei Expressway. Walk 25 mins. Express trains run to Gotenba from Shinjuku (Yamanote Line) via Odakyu Private Railway. From Hakone, take bus for Gotenba to Ni-no Oka (二の岡). Walk 20 mins.
**¥2,900.** Dinner ¥1,000. Breakfast ¥600.

## ITO (伊東)

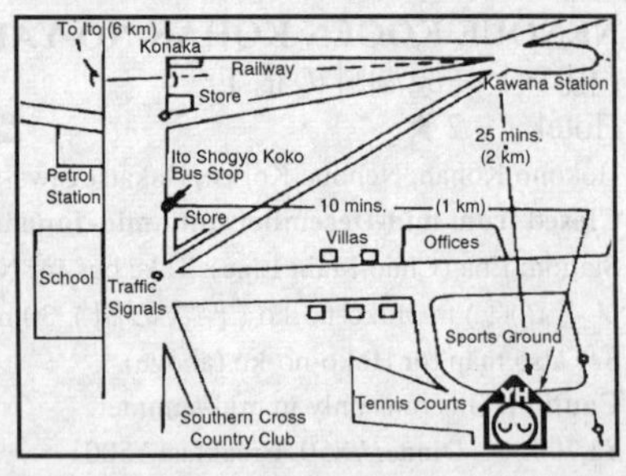


Local Organization Hostel 3★ ☎ 0557-45-0224
1260-125 Kawana, Ito-shi, Shizuoka 414. 100 beds
Station: ① Kawana (Izu Kyuko Private Railway), accessible from JR Ito. Turn left. Cross railway. Turn left. Walk 25 mins. (2 km). ② Ito (Ito Line). Take bus for Komuroyama (小室山) to Youth Hostel-mae, 21 mins. Other buses can be taken to Ito Shogyo Koko (伊東商業高校), 15 mins. Walk 10 mins. (1 km).
**¥2,900.** Dinner ¥800. Breakfast ¥500.

## SHUZENJI (修善寺)

JYH Hostel 3 ★ ☎ 0558-72-1222. Fax: 1771
4279-152 Shuzenji, Tagata-gun, Shizuoka 410-24. 120 beds
**Closed in mid-January and from late May until early June.**
Station: Shuzenji (Izu Hakone Private Railway), accessible from JR Mishima (Shinkansen or Tokaido Main Line). From the bus terminal, bus stop no. 6, take bus for New Town Toda Nijinosato (ニュータウン戸田虹の郷) to New Town Guchi (ニュータウン口), 15 mins. Walk 5 mins. (300 m).
**¥2,900 (Discount ¥200).** Dinner ¥1,000. Breakfast ¥600.

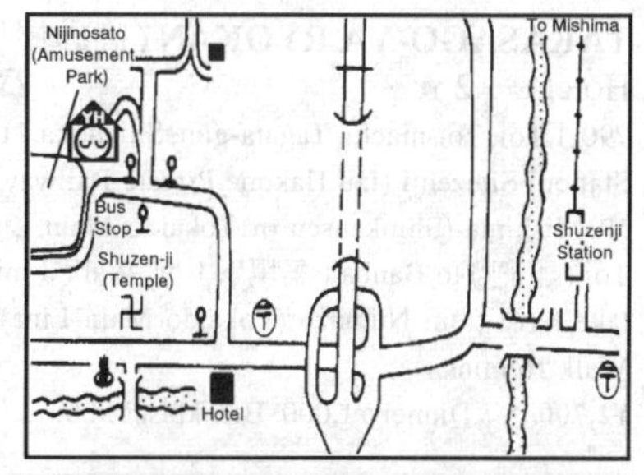


## KIYA RYOKAN (木屋旅館)

Hotel 3 ★ ☎ 0558-83-0146
388 Warabo, Naka Izu, Tagata-gun, Shizuoka 410-25. 20 beds
Station: Shuzenji (Izu Hakone Private Railway), accessible from JR Mishima (Shinkansen or Tokaido Main Line). Take bus for Ikada-ba (筏場) or Jizodo (地蔵堂) to Warabo (原保), 30 mins. Hostel is adjacent to bus stop.
**¥2,900.** Dinner ¥1,000. Breakfast ¥600.

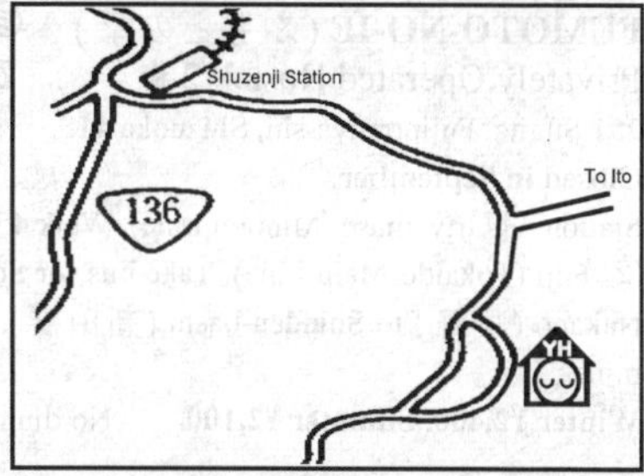


## AMAGI HARRIS COURT (天城ハリスコート)

Privately Operated Hostel 3 ★ ☎ 0558-35-7253
28-1 Nashimoto, Kawazu, Kamo-gun, Shizuoka 413-06. 42 beds
Station: Kawazu (Izu Kyuko Private Railway), accessible from JR Ito (Ito Line). Take bus for Shuzenji (修善寺) to Jigen-in (慈眼院), 20 mins. Walk 1 min.
**¥2,900.** Dinner ¥1,000. Breakfast ¥600. Local Delicacies ¥1,500.

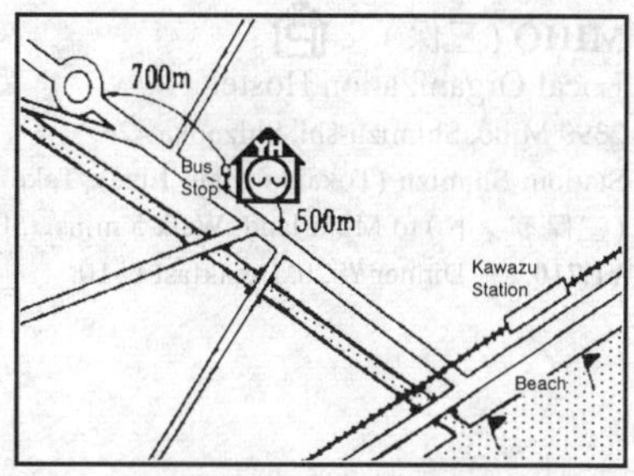


## GENSU (げんす)

Hotel 3 ★ ☎ 0558-62-0035
289 Shimo Kamo, Minami Izu-machi, Shizuoka 415-03. 32 beds
Station: Shimoda (Izu Kyuko Private Railway), accessible from JR Ito (Ito Line). From bus stop no. 2, take bus for Shimo Kamo (下賀茂) to Minami Izu-machi Yaku-ba (南伊豆町役場), 25 mins. Walk 1 min.
**¥2,900, plus Spa Fee ¥130.** Dinner ¥1,000. Breakfast ¥600.

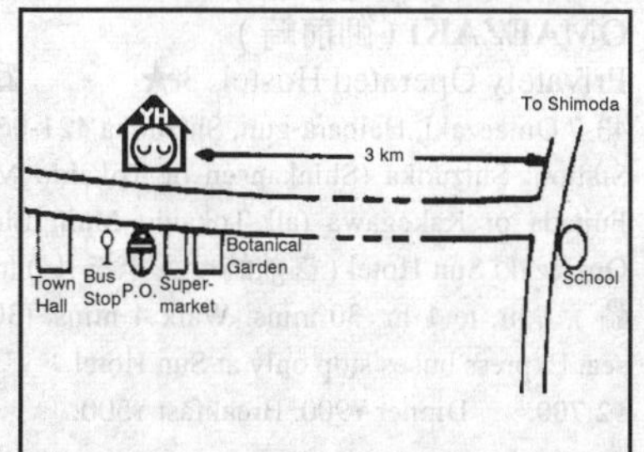


## SANYO-SO (三余荘)

Private Home 3 ★ ☎ 0558-42-0408
73-1 Naka, Matsuzaki, Kamo-gun, Shizuoka 410-36. 77 beds
Station: Shimoda (Izu Kyuko Private Railway), accessible from JR Ito (Ito Line). Take bus for Dogashima (堂ヶ島) to Youth Hostel-mae, 50 mins. Hostel is opposite bus stop.
**¥2,900.** Dinner ¥1,000. Breakfast ¥600.

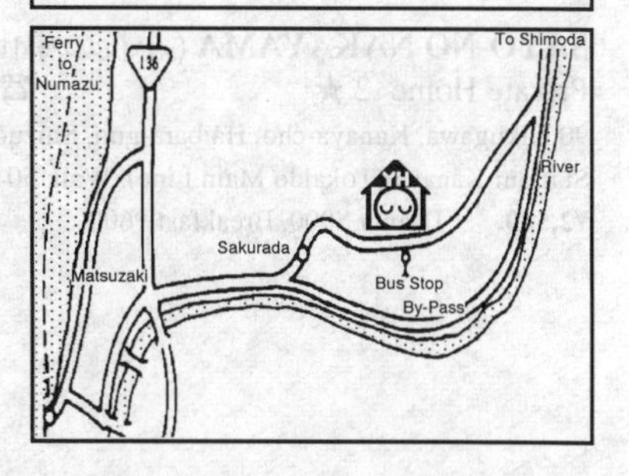

## TAKASAGO-YA RYOKAN (高砂屋旅館)

Hotel 2★ ☎ 0558-98-0200

790-1 Toi, Toi-machi, Tagata-gun, Shizuoka 410-33. 37 beds

Station: Shuzenji (Izu Hakone Private Railway), accessible from JR Mishima (Shinkansen or Tokaido Main Line). Take bus for Toi (土肥) to Banba (馬場), 1 hr. Walk 3 mins. Alternatively, take ferry from Numazu (Tokaido Main Line) to Toi, 40 mins. Walk 15 mins.

**¥2,700.** Dinner ¥1,000. Breakfast ¥500.

## FUMOTO-NO-IE (ふもとの家)

Privately Operated Hostel 2★ ☎ 0544-27-4314

251 Sugita, Fujinomiya-shi, Shizuoka 418.

**Closed in September.** 8 beds

Station: ① Iriyamase (Minobu Line). Walk 45 mins. (3 km). ② Fuji (Tokaido Main Line). Take bus for Sobina (曽比奈) or Nakano (中野) to Shinden-bashi (新田橋), 25 mins. Walk 10 mins.

**Winter ¥2,400. Summer ¥2,100.** No dinner. Breakfast ¥500.

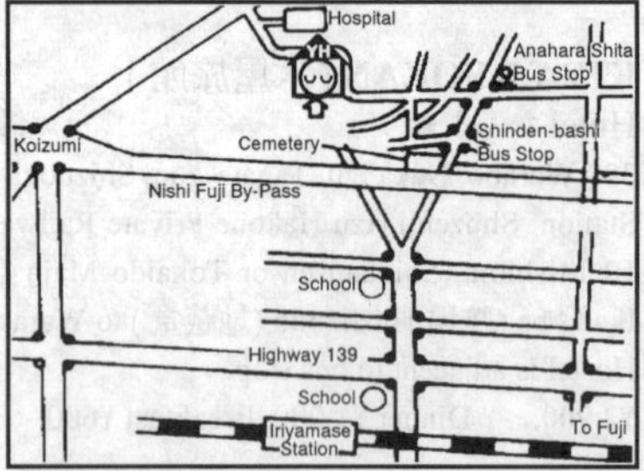


## MIHO (三保)

Local Organization Hostel ☎ 0543-34-0826

2399 Miho, Shimizu-shi, Shizuoka 424. 100 beds

Station: Shimizu (Tokaido Main Line). Take bus for Miho-land (三保ランド) to Miho-land. Walk 5 mins. (500 m).

**¥1,710.** Dinner ¥820. Breakfast ¥510.

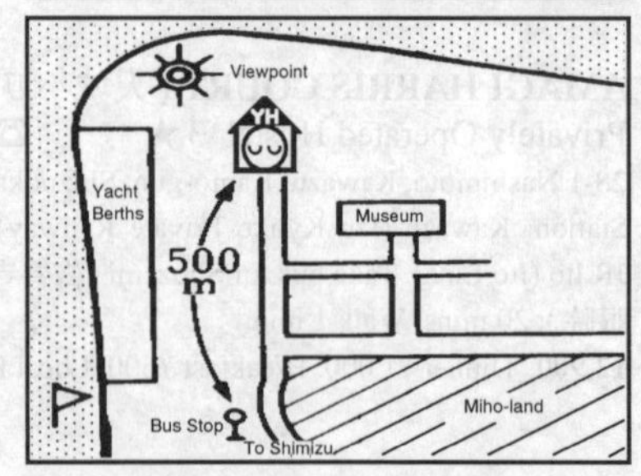


## OMAEZAKI (御前崎)

Privately Operated Hostel 3★ ☎ 0548-63-4518

43-7 Omaezaki, Haibara-gun, Shizuoka 421-06. 38 beds

Station: Shizuoka (Shinkansen or Tokaido Main Line), Yaizu, Fujieda or Kakegawa (all Tokaido Main Line). Take bus for Omaezaki Sun Hotel (御前崎サンホテル) to Omaezaki (御前崎), 1 hr. to 1 hr. 30 mins. Walk 4 mins. (300 m) towards the sea. Express buses stop only at Sun Hotel.

**¥2,700.** Dinner ¥900. Breakfast ¥500.

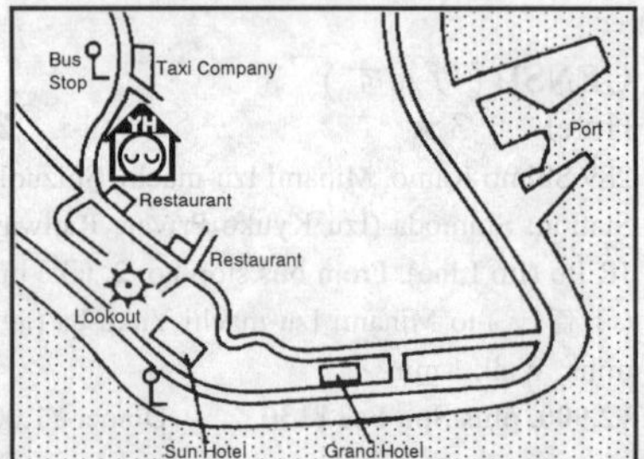


## SAYO-NO NAKAYAMA (小夜の中山)

Private Home 2★ ☎ 0547-46-3284

90 Kikugawa, Kanaya-cho, Haibara-gun, Shizuoka 428. 14 beds

Station: Kanaya (Tokaido Main Line). Walk 50 mins.

**¥2,500.** Dinner ¥900. Breakfast ¥600.

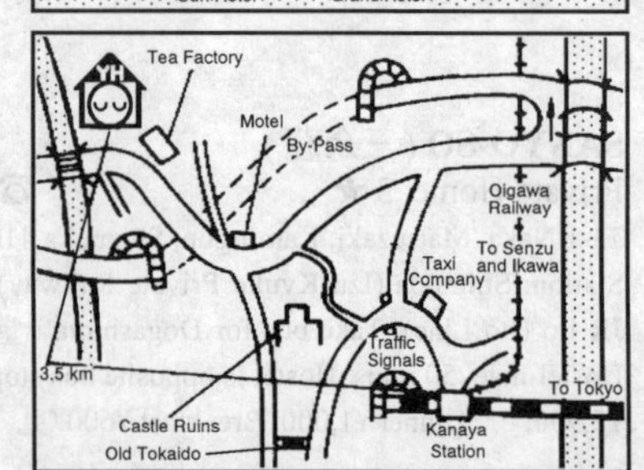

## HAMANA-KO (浜名湖)

Privately Operated Hostel 3★ ☎ 053-594-0670. Fax: 4077

223-2 Uchiyama, Arai-machi, Shizuoka 431-03. 179 beds

Station: Araimachi (Tokaido Main Line). Walk 25 mins. Follow old Tokaido road, at first running parallel with the railway. Turn left and proceed until reaching tobacconist. Then turn right and follow signposted path to hostel.

**¥2,900.** Dinner ¥1,000. Breakfast ¥600.

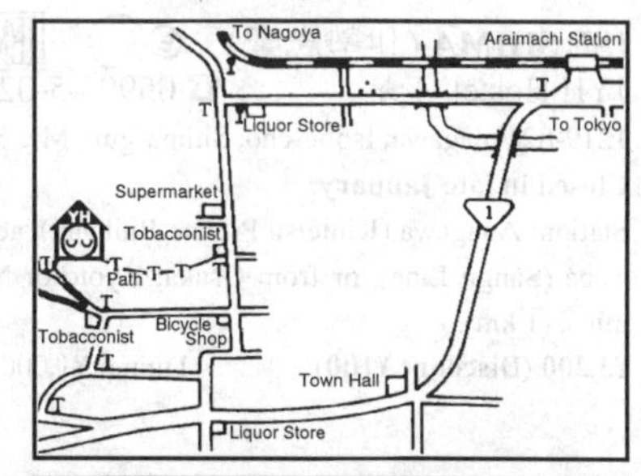


## NAGOYA (名古屋)

Local Organization Hostel 4★ ☎ 052-781-9845. Fax:7023

1-50 Kameiri, Tashiro-cho, Chikusa-ku, Nagoya-shi, Aichi 464.

**Closed at New Year.** 93 beds

Station: Nagoya. Take Higashiyama Subway Line to Higashiyama Koen, 16 mins. Use exit no. 3 and walk uphill 8 mins., following steps to left of zoo entrance.

**¥2,300.** Dinner ¥800. Breakfast ¥600.

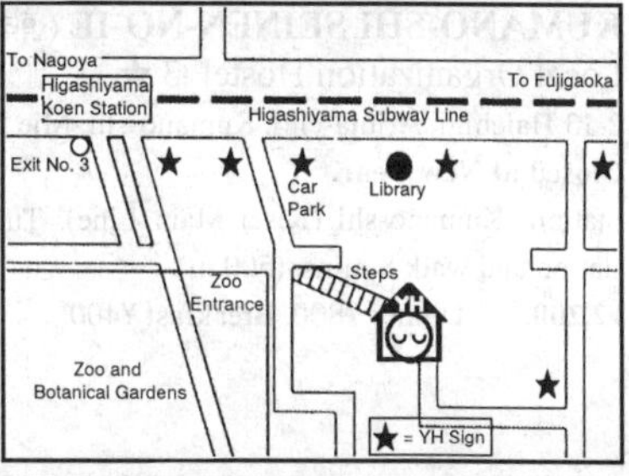


## AICHI-KEN SEINEN KAIKAN (愛知県青年会館)

Local Organization Hostel 4★ ☎ 052-221-6001. Fax:204-3508

1-18-8 Sakae, Naka-ku, Nagoya-shi, Aichi 460.

**Closed at New Year.** 50 beds

Station: Nagoya. From outside Toyota Building, take bus no. 20 or 50 to Nayabashi (納谷橋), 5 mins (1 km). Walk down road next to Asahi Newspaper office to hostel, 3 mins. (300 m). Alternatively, walk from station, 20 mins.

**¥2,900.** Dinner ¥900. Breakfast ¥500.

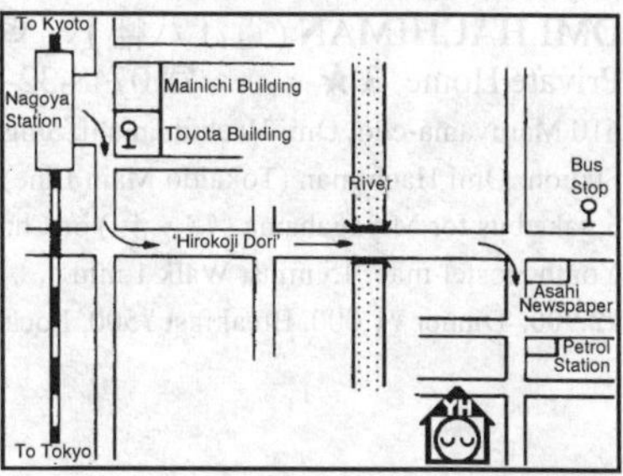


## ATAGO-SAN (愛宕山)

Temple Hostel 2★ ☎ 0598-21-2931

1-4 Atago-machi, Matsusaka-shi, Mie 515. 28 beds

Station: JR Matsusaka (Kisei Main Line) or Kintetsu Matsusaka. Walk south for 10 mins. along Highway 42.

**¥1,800.** No meals.

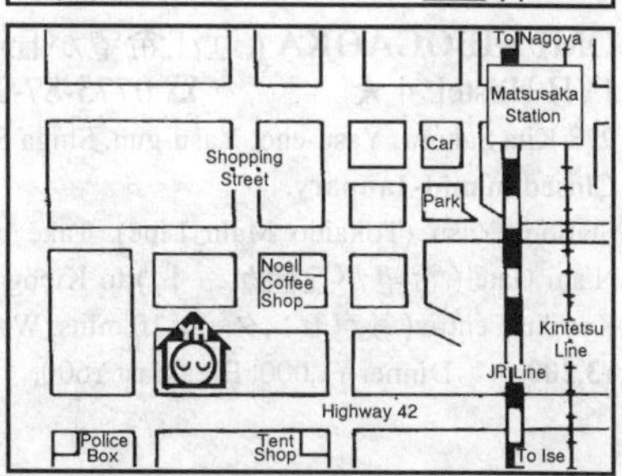


## TAIKO-JI (太江寺)

Temple Hostel 2★ ☎ 05964-3-2283, 2-1952

1659 Ei, Futami-cho, Watarai-gun, Mie 519-06. 28 beds

Station: Futami-no-ura (Sangu Line). Take bus for Toba (鳥羽) or Meoto Iwa (夫婦岩) to Meoto Iwa Higashi Guchi (夫婦岩東口), 3 mins. Walk 10 mins. (1 km). Alternatively, walk from station, 30 mins.

**¥1,800.** Dinner ¥800. Breakfast ¥500.

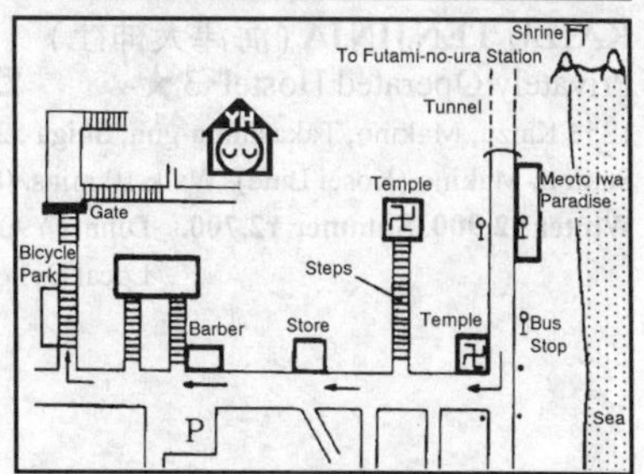

## ISE SHIMA (伊勢志摩)

JYH Hostel 4★ ☎ 05995-5-0226. Fax: 3319

1219-82 Anagawa, Isobe-cho, Shima-gun, Mie 517-02.

**Closed in late January.** 92 beds

Station: Anagawa (Kintetsu Private Railway), accessible from JR Toba (Sangu Line), or from Osaka, Kyoto or Nagoya. Walk 15 mins. (1 km).

**¥3,200 (Discount ¥100).** Dinner ¥1,000. Breakfast ¥600.

## KUMANO-SHI SEINEN-NO-IE (熊野市青年の家)

Local Organization Hostel 3★ ☎ 05978-9-0800

2-13 Haichigi, Arima-cho, Kumano-shi, Mie 519-43.

**Closed at New Year.** 54 beds

Station: Kumano-shi (Kisei Main Line). Turn right on leaving station and walk 8 mins. (500 m).

**¥2,200.** Dinner ¥800. Breakfast ¥400.

## OMI HACHIMAN (近江八幡)

Private Home 3★ ☎ 0748-32-2938. Fax: 7593

610 Maruyama-cho, Omi Hachiman-shi, Shiga 523. 36 beds

Station: Omi Hachiman (Tokaido Main Line). From bus stop no. 6, take bus for Miyagahama (宮ヶ浜) or Chomei-ji (長命寺) to Youth Hostel-mae, 15 mins. Walk 1 min.

**¥2,900.** Dinner ¥1,000. Breakfast ¥500. Local Delicacies ¥1,500.

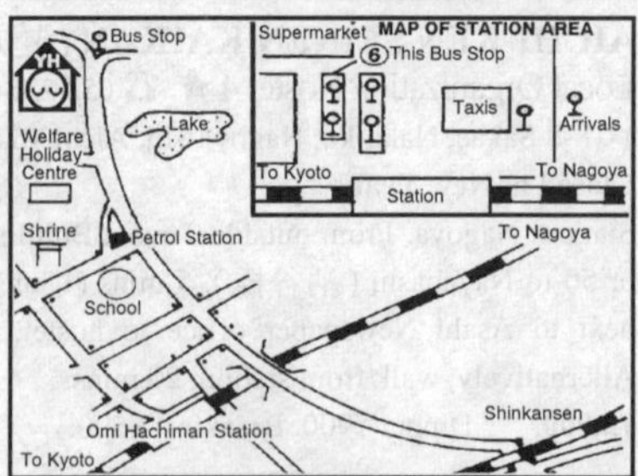


## OMI KIBOGAOKA (近江希望が丘)

JYH Hostel 4★ ☎ 0775-87-2201. Fax: 2008

978 Kita Sakura, Yasu-cho, Yasu-gun, Shiga 520-23.

**Closed in mid-January.** 122 beds

Station: Yasu (Tokaido Main Line). Take bus for Kibogaoka Nishi Gate (希望が丘西ゲート) to Kibogaoka Nishi Gate or Kyoiku Centre (教育センター), 10 mins. Walk 3 mins.

**¥3,200.** Dinner ¥1,000. Breakfast ¥600.

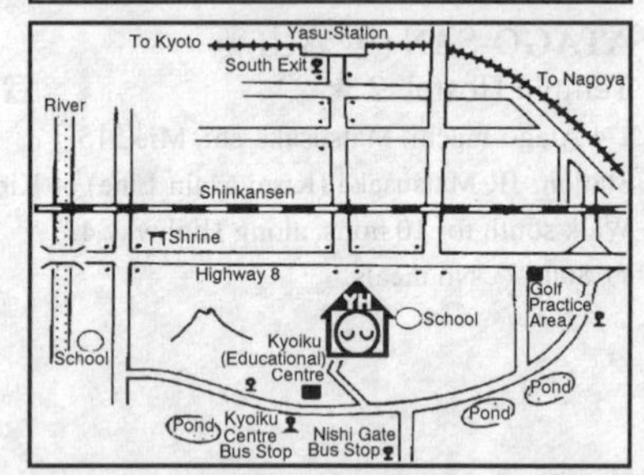


## KAIZU TENJINJA (海津天神社)

Privately Operated Hostel 3★ ☎ 0740-28-0051

1253 Kaizu, Makino, Takashima-gun, Shiga 520-18. 200 beds

Station: Makino (Kosei Line). Walk 10 mins. (800 m).

**Winter ¥2,900. Summer ¥2,700.** Dinner ¥900. Breakfast ¥450. Local Delicacies ¥1,400.

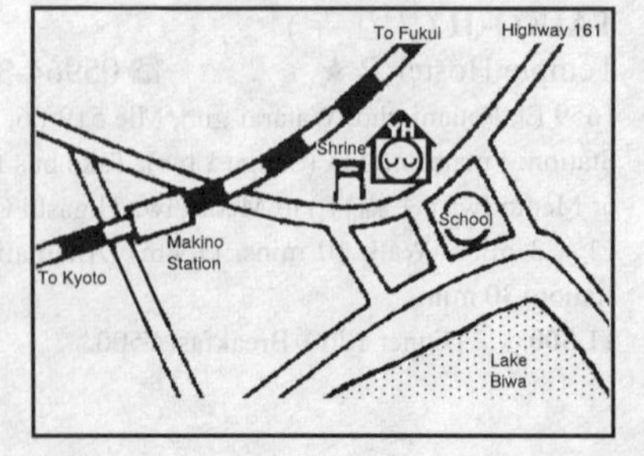

**WANIHAMA SEINEN KAIKAN** (和邇浜青年会館)
Hotel 2★ ☎ 0775-94-4203
403 Minami Hama, Shiga-cho, Shiga 520-05. 160 beds
Station: Wani (Kosei Line). Walk 20 mins. (1.5 km) towards Lake Biwa.
**¥2,600.** Dinner ¥800. Breakfast ¥400.

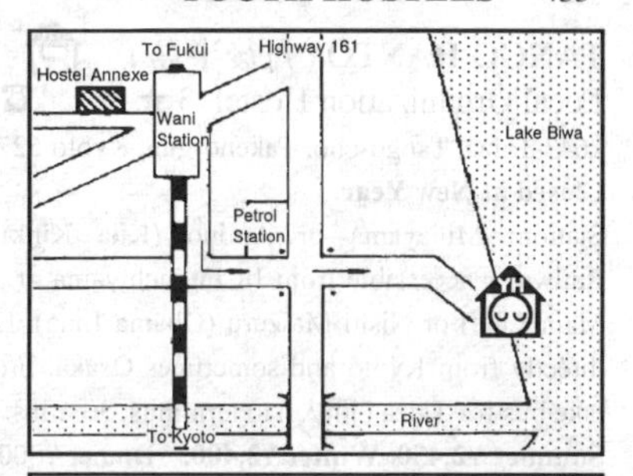


**OTSU YH CENTRE** (大津 YHセンター)
Local Organization Hostel ☎ 0775-22-8009. Fax: 21-0724
18-1 Yamagami-cho, Otsu-shi, Shiga 520. 308 beds
Station: ① Nishi Otsu (Kosei Line). Walk 13 mins. (600 m).
② Ojiyama (Keihan Private Railway). Walk 8 mins.
**¥2,150.** Dinner ¥900. Breakfast ¥570.

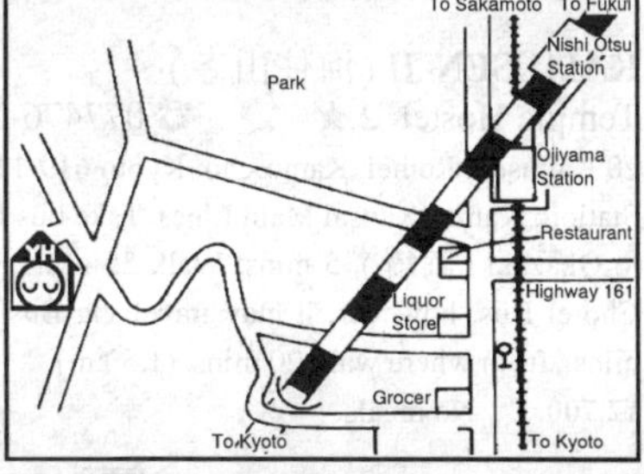


**SAIKYO-JI** (西教寺)
Temple Hostel 3★ ☎ 0775-78-0013
5-13-1 Sakamoto, Otsu-shi, Shiga 520-01. 200 beds
**Closed at New Year and for parts of April, August, November.**
Stations: ① Eizan (Kosei Line). Walk 30 mins.
② Sakamoto (Keihan Private Railway). Walk 25 mins.
**Winter ¥2,200. Summer ¥2,000.** Dinner ¥750. Breakfast ¥450.

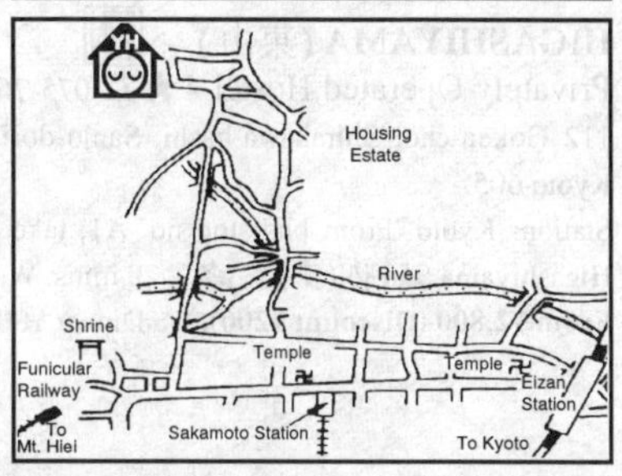


**AMANO HASHIDATE KANKO KAIKAN**
(天橋立観光会館)
Local Organization Hostel 2★ ☎ 0772-27-0046
22 Ogaki, Miyazu-shi, Kyoto 629-22.
**Closed at New Year.** 70 beds
Station: Amano Hashidate (Kita Kinki Tango Private Railway), accessible from JR Fukuchiyama or Toyo-oka (San-in Main Line) or Nishi Maizuru (Obama Line). Express trains run directly from Kyoto and sometimes Osaka. Take ferry to Ichinomiya, 12 mins., and walk 2 mins. Or take bus for Ine (伊根) to Cable Shita (ケーブル下), 20 mins., and walk 2 mins. Or walk from station, 40 mins.
**¥2,450.** Dinner ¥800. Breakfast ¥500.

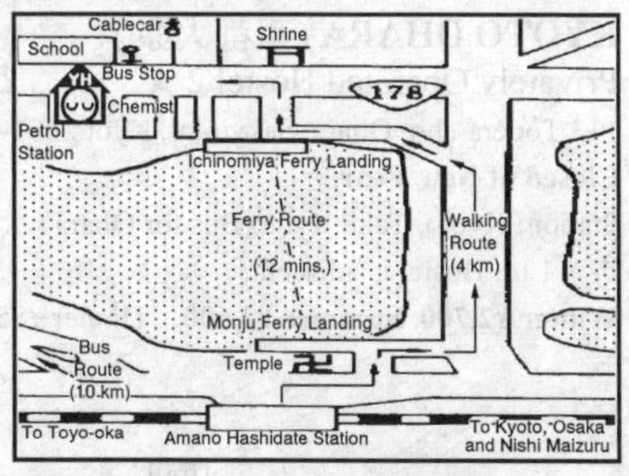


**AMANO HASHIDATE** (天橋立)
JYH Hostel 3★ ☎ 0772-27-0121. Fax: 0939
905 Nakano, Miyazu-shi, Kyoto 629-22.
**Closed third Wednesday and Thursday each month.** 60 beds
Station: Amano Hashidate (see entry above). Take ferry to Ichinomiya, 12 mins., and walk 12 mins. Or take bus for Ine (伊根) to Jinja-mae (神社前), 20 mins., and walk 10 mins. Or walk from station, 45 mins.
**¥2,750.** Dinner ¥800. Breakfast ¥500.

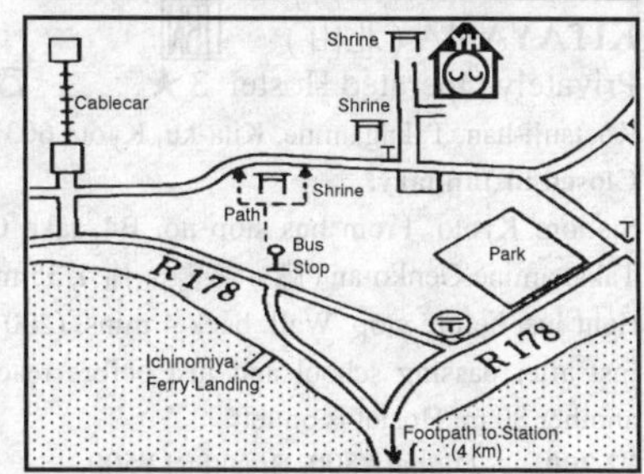

## TANGO HANTO (丹後半島)

Local Organization Hostel 3★ ☎ 0772-75-1529

2643 Taiza, Tango-cho, Takeno-gun, Kyoto 627-02.

**Closed at New Year.** 80 beds

Station: Mineyama or Amino (Kita Kinki Tango Private Railway), accessible from JR Fukuchiyama or Toyo-oka (San-in Main Line) or Nishi Maizuru (Obama Line). Express trains run directly from Kyoto and sometimes Osaka. From either station, take bus for Taiza (間人) to terminus, 30 mins. Walk 5 mins.

**Summer ¥2,450. Winter ¥2,400.** Dinner ¥800. Breakfast ¥500.

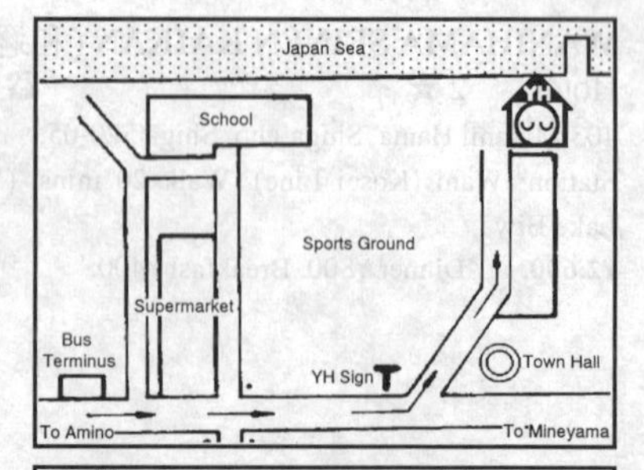


## KAIJUSEN-JI (海住山寺)

Temple Hostel 2★ ☎ 077476-2256. Fax: 7356

20 Kaijusen, Reihei, Kamo-cho, Kyoto 619-11. 17 beds

Station: Kamo (Kansai Main Line). Take bus for Wazuka (和束) to Okazaki (岡崎), 5 mins. Walk 35 mins. If bus is a Wazuka Cho-ei Bus, however, it may travel via Busho-ji (仏生寺), 7 mins., from where walk 20 mins. (1.5 km).

**¥2,700.** No meals.

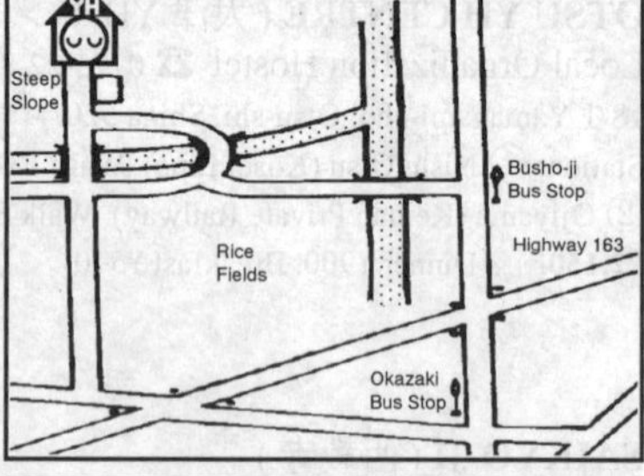


## HIGASHIYAMA (東山)

Privately Operated Hostel 4★ ☎ 075-761-8135. Fax: 8138

112 Goken-cho, Shirakawa-bashi, Sanjo-dori, Higashiyama-ku, Kyoto 605. 150 beds

Station: Kyoto. From bus stop no. A1, take City Bus no. 5 to Higashiyama San-jo (東山三条), 20 mins. Walk 3 mins.

**From ¥2,800 (Discount ¥200).** Dinner ¥800. Breakfast ¥500.

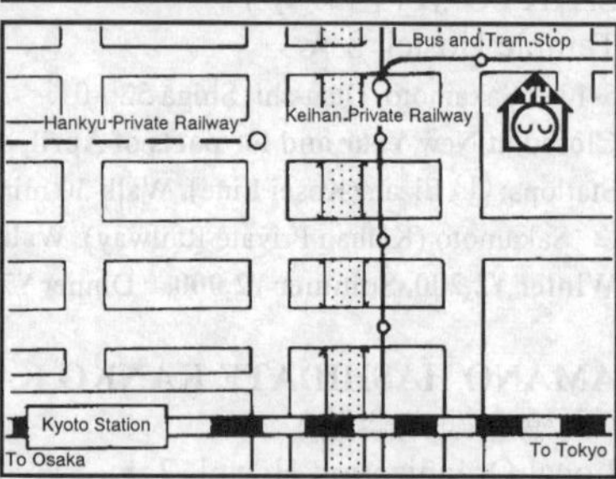


## KYOTO OHARA (京都大原)

Privately Operated Hostel 2★ ☎ 075-744-2528

113 Todera-cho, Ohara, Sakyo-ku, Kyoto 601-12.

**Closed at New Year.** 23 beds

Station: Kyoto. Take Kyoto Bus for Ohara (大原) to Todera (戸寺), 1 hr. Hostel is adjacent.

**Winter ¥2,700. Summer ¥2,600.** Dinner ¥850. Breakfast ¥550.

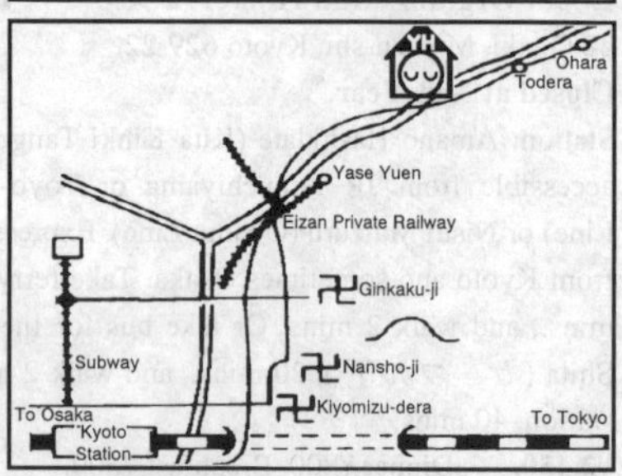


## KITAYAMA (北山)

Privately Operated Hostel 3★ ☎ 075-492-5345

Koetsuji-han, Takagamine, Kita-ku, Kyoto 603.

**Closed in January.** 43 beds

Station: Kyoto. From bus stop no. B4, take City Bus no. 6 to Takagamine Genko-an (鷹ヶ峯源光庵), 35 mins. Bus will turn right just before stop. Walk back 4 mins. (200 m) and turn right just after passing school and just before reaching hotel. Walk another 80 m. Hostel is on left.

**¥2,700.** Dinner ¥800. Breakfast ¥500.

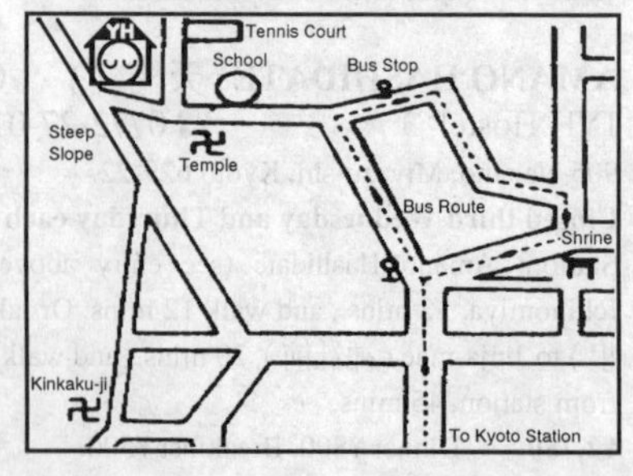

## UTANO (宇多野)

JYH Hostel 4★ ☎ 075-462-2288. Fax: 2289

29 Uzumasa Nakayama-cho, Ukyo-ku, Kyoto 616. 168 beds

Station: Kyoto. From bus stop no. C1, take bus no. 26 to Youth Hostel-mae, 50 mins. Walk 1 min.

**¥2,900.** Dinner ¥750. Breakfast ¥450. Local Delicacies ¥1,000.

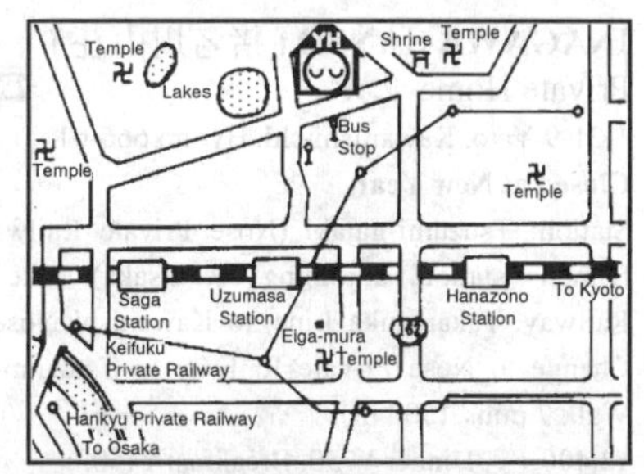


## OSAKA-FU HATTORI RYOKUCHI (大阪府服部緑地)

Local Organization Hostel 3★ ☎ 06-862-0600

1-3 Hattori Ryokuchi, Toyonaka-shi, Osaka 560.

**Closed at New Year.** 108 beds

Station: Osaka or Shin Osaka. Take Midosuji Subway Line northbound (train marked Senri Chuo). Subway trains continue onto Kita Osaka Kyuko Line, the first stop on which is Ryokuchi Koen, where alight. Walk 15 mins. (800 m).

**¥1,800.** Dinner ¥850. Breakfast ¥480.

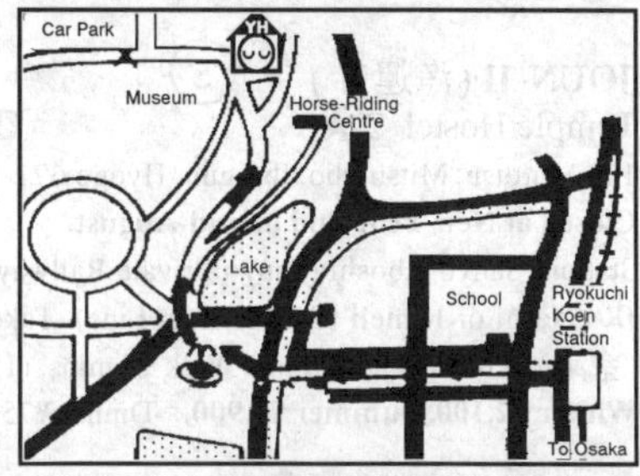


## KAWACHI NAGANO (河内長野)

JYH Hostel 4★ ☎ 0721-53-1010

1305-2 Amano-cho, Kawachi Nagano-shi, Osaka 586.

**Closed in early February and early June.** 80 beds

Station: Kawachi Nagano (Nankai Private Railway or Kintetsu Private Railway). From Osaka or Shin Osaka, take Midosuji Subway Line to Nanba (8 mins. from Osaka). Change to Nankai Private Railway, Takano Line, to Kawachi Nagano, 30 mins. Take bus for Cycle Sports Centre (サイクルスポーツセンター) to Oku Amano-san (奥天野山), 16 mins. Walk 1 min. From New Kansai Airport, take bus to Komyo Ike (光明池), 40 mins. Change to bus for Kawachi Nagano (河内長野) to Amano-san (天野山), 30 mins. Walk 15 mins. or telephone to be collected.

**¥3,200 (Discount ¥500).** Dinner ¥1,000. Breakfast ¥600.

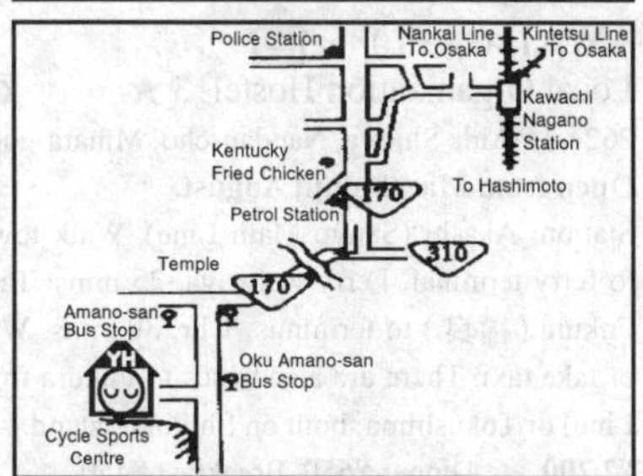


## KOBE TARUMI (神戸垂水)

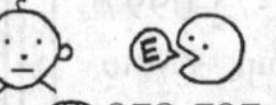

Privately Operated Hostel 3★ ☎ 078-707-2133

5-58 Kaigan-dori, Tarumi-ku, Kobe-shi, Hyogo 655. 28 beds

Station: Tarumi (JR Sanyo Main Line or Sanyo Private Railway). From West Exit, walk 10 mins. (800 m) west along Highway 2.

**¥2,600.** No dinner. Breakfast ¥500.

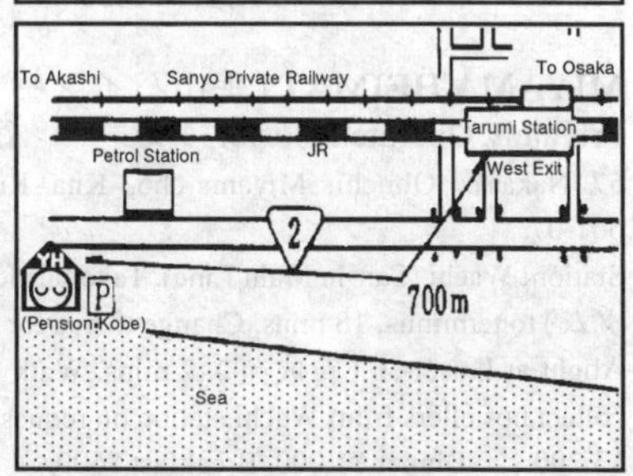


## ROKKO ASHIYA (ろっこう芦屋)

JYH Hostel 3★ ☎ 0797-38-0109

40-30 Okuike Minami-cho, Ashiya-shi, Hyogo 659.

**Closed at New Year.** 92 beds

Station: Ashiya (JR Sanyo Main Line or Hanshin Private Railway) or Ashiyagawa (Hankyu Private Railway). Take bus for Arima (有馬) or Ashiya Highlands (芦屋ハイランド) to Okuike (奥池), 20 mins. Walk 10 mins. (800 m) towards the reservoir.

**Winter ¥2,400. Summer ¥2,200.** Dinner ¥650. Breakfast ¥450.

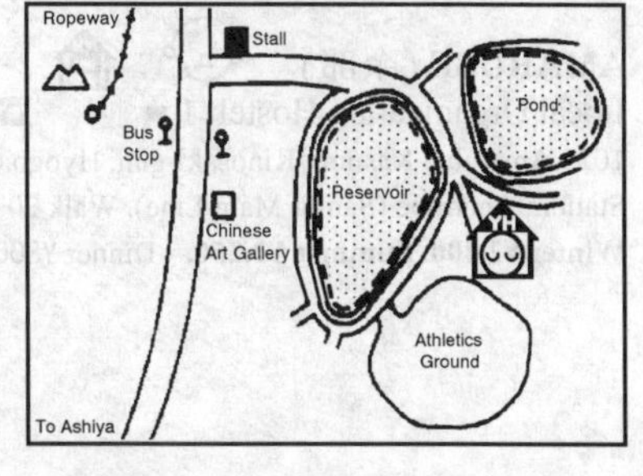

## INAGAWA SANSO (猪名川山荘)

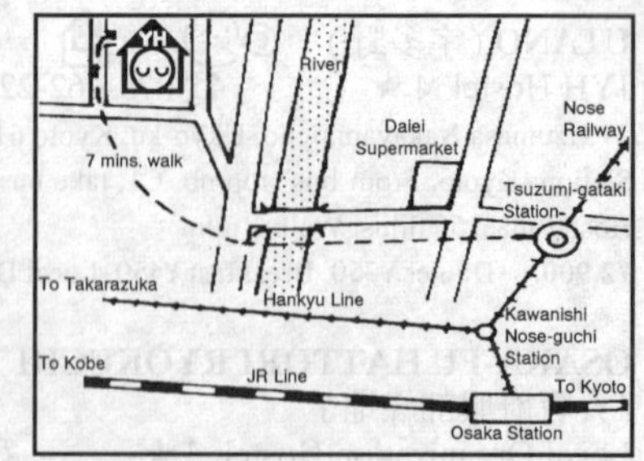


Private Home 2★ ☎ 0727-51-3565
1-21-9 Yato, Kawanishi-shi, Hyogo 666-01.
**Closed at New Year.** 40 beds
Station: Tsuzumi-gataki (Nose Private Railway). From Osaka (Umeda station, adjoining JR Osaka), take Hankyu Private Railway, Takarazuka Line, to Kawanishi Nose-guchi, 23 mins. Change to Nose Private Railway to Tsuzumi-gataki, 10 mins. Walk 7 mins. (500 m).
**¥2,400.** Dinner ¥750. Breakfast ¥450.

## JOUN-JI (浄運寺) 

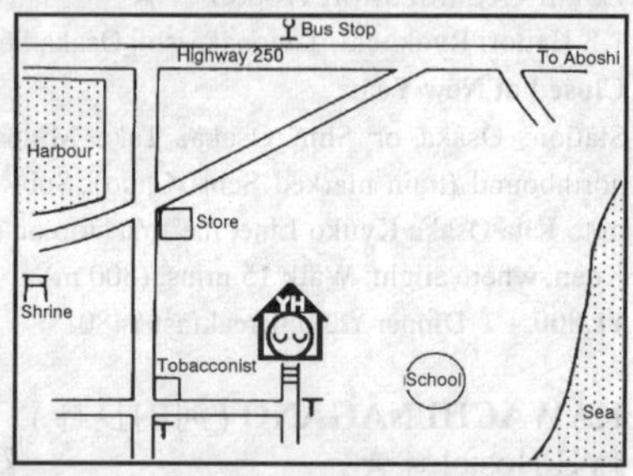


Temple Hostel 2★ ☎ 07932-4-0030
168 Murotsu, Mitsu-cho, Ibo-gun, Hyogo 671-13.
**Closed at New Year and in mid-August.** 50 beds
Station: Sanyo Aboshi (Sanyo Private Railway), accessible from JR Akashi or Himeji (Sanyo Main Line). Take bus for Murotsu (室津) to Murotsu, 25 mins. Walk 15 mins. (1 km).
**Winter ¥2,100. Summer ¥1,900.** Dinner ¥750. Breakfast ¥450.

## AWAJI (淡路) 

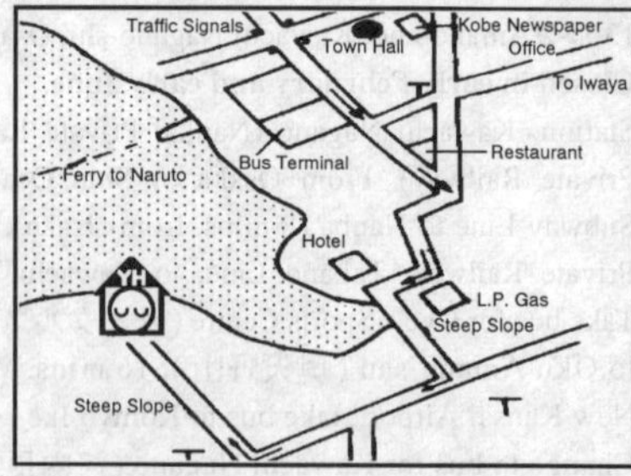


Local Organization Hostel 3★ ☎ 0799-52-0460
2624-16 Ama Shioya, Nandan-cho, Mihara-gun, Hyogo 656-07.
**Open from March until August.** 90 beds
Station: Akashi (Sanyo Main Line). Walk towards sea 10 mins. to ferry terminal. Ferry to Iwaya, 25 mins. Take express bus for Fukura (福良) to terminus, 1 hr. 30 mins. Walk 1 hr. (4.5 km), or take taxi. There are also buses to Fukura from Naruto (Naruto Line) or Tokushima, both on Shikoku Island.
**¥2,200.** Dinner ¥650. Breakfast ¥450.

## MIYAMA HEIMAT (美山ハイマート)

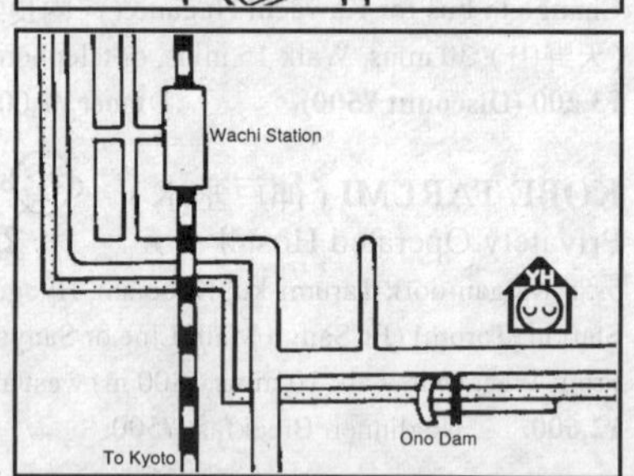


Privately Operated Hostel 4★ ☎ 0771-75-0997
57 Nakasai, Obuchi, Miyama-cho, Kita Kuwata-gun, Kyoto 601-07. 13 beds
Station: Wachi (San-in Main Line). Take bus for Ono Dam (大野ダム) to terminus, 18 mins. Change to bus for Shizuhara (静原). Alight at Ikusei-en (育成苑), 7 mins. Walk 1 min. Hostel will collect hostellers from Wachi station on request.
**¥3,200.** Dinner ¥1,000. Breakfast ¥600.

## AMARUBE (余部) 

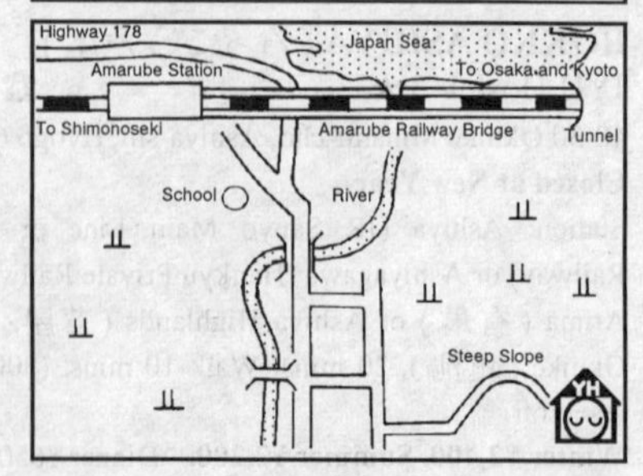


Local Organization Hostel 1★ ☎ 0796-34-0031
1023 Amarube, Kasumi, Kinosaki-gun, Hyogo 669-66. 54 beds
Station: Amarube (San-in Main Line). Walk 20 mins. (2 km).
**Winter ¥2,400. Summer ¥2,250.** Dinner ¥800. Breakfast ¥500.

## HAMASAKA (浜坂) IBN

JYH Hostel 3★ ☎ 0796-82-1282

Shiroyama-enchi, Hamasaka-cho, Mikata-gun, Hyogo 669-67.

**Closed in late January and 2~3 days each month.** 80 beds

Station: ① Moroyose (San-in Main Line). Walk 15 mins.

② Hamasaka (San-in Main Line). Turn left and walk 20 mins. (1.4 km).

**¥2,900 (Discount ¥200).** Dinner ¥1,000. Breakfast ¥600. Local Delicacies ¥1,500 (winter only).

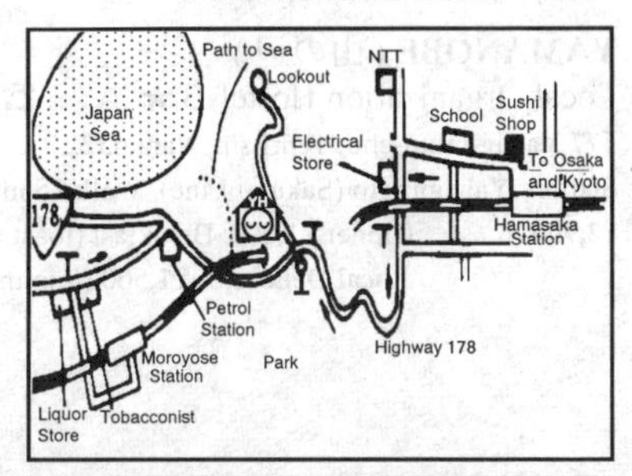


## MOROYOSE-SO (諸寄荘)

Hotel 3★ ☎ 0796-82-1279. Fax: 3614

461 Moroyose, Hamasaka-cho, Mikata-gun, Hyogo 669-67.

**Closed at New Year.** 40 beds

Station: Moroyose (San-in Main Line). Walk 3 mins. (200 m) towards the sea.

**Winter ¥2,500. Summer ¥2,300.** Dinner ¥800. Breakfast ¥500.

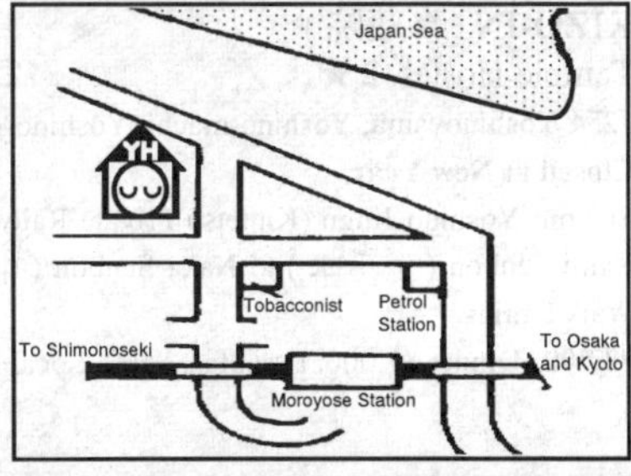


## SENKO-JI (千光寺)

Temple Hostel 3★ ☎ 07454-5-0652

188 Narukawa, Heguri-cho, Ikoma-gun, Nara 636. 35 beds

Station: Moto Sanjo-guchi (Kintetsu Private Railway), accessible from JR Oji (Kansai Main Line) or from Kyoto, Nara or Osaka. Walk 25 mins.

**¥2,900.** Dinner ¥1,000. Breakfast ¥600.

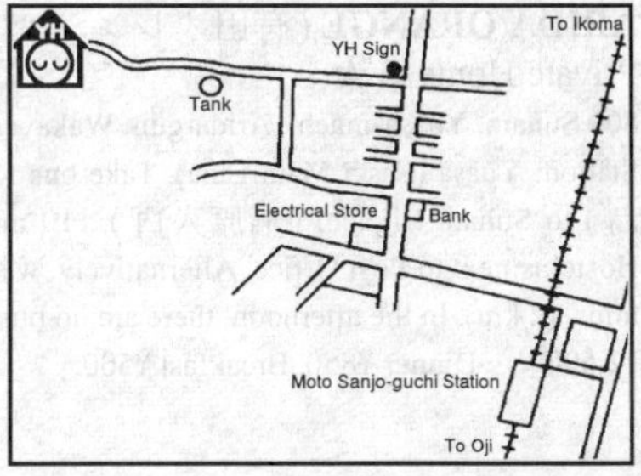


## NARA (奈良)  IBN

JYH Hostel 4★ ☎ 0742-22-1334. Fax: 1335

1716 Horen-cho, Nara-shi, Nara 630.

**Closed in late January and 2~3 days each month.** 200 beds

Station: JR Nara or Kintetsu Nara. Take bus for Kamo (加茂), Takanohara (高の原) or Dreamland (ドリームランド) to Shi-ei Kyu-jo (市営球場), 5 mins. Hostel is adjacent.

**¥2,900 (Discount ¥500).** Dinner ¥1,000. Breakfast ¥600.

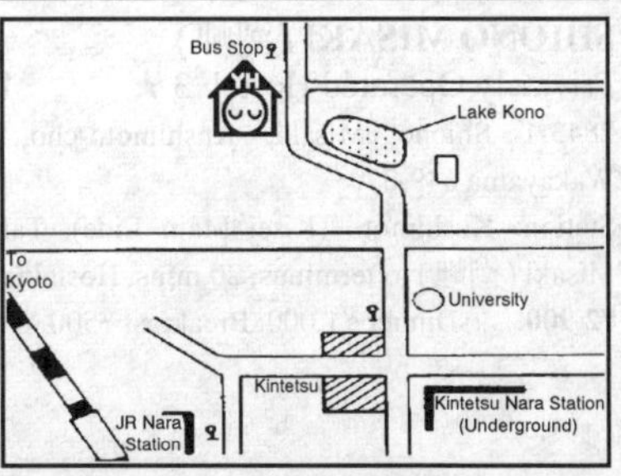


## NARA-KEN SEISHO-NEN KAIKAN (奈良県青少年会館)

Local Organization Hostel 3★ ☎ 0742-22-5540

72-7 Ike-no-ue, Handa Hiraki-cho, Nara-shi, Nara 630.

**Closed at New Year.** 58 beds

Station: JR Nara or Kintetsu Nara. Take bus for Kamo (加茂), Takanohara (高の原) or Dreamland (ドリームランド) to Kono-ike (鴻池), 6 mins. Walk 3 mins. (200 m). After 17:00, bus no. 21 via Dreamland Minami Guchi (ドリームランド南口) stops at Sahoyama (左保山), from where walk 1 min.

**¥2,360.** Dinner ¥800. Breakfast ¥320 (excluding drinks).

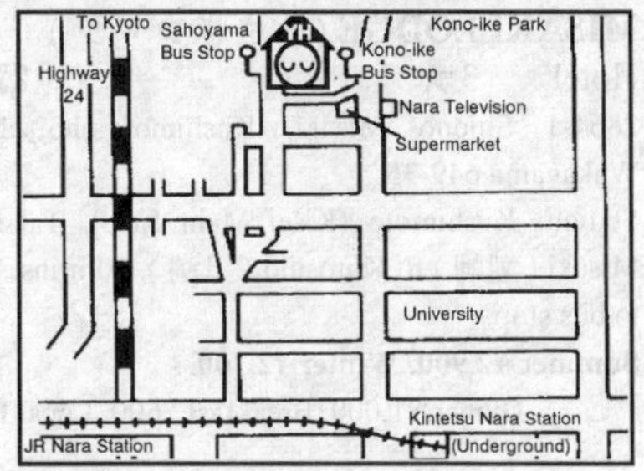

## YAMANOBE ( 山の辺 )

Local Organization Hostel 3★ ☎ 07436-6-2770

577 Yanagimoto-cho, Tenri-shi, Nara 632. 35 beds

Station: Yanagimoto (Sakurai Line). Walk 15 mins. (1.2 km).

**¥2,900.** Dinner ¥1,000. Breakfast (toast and coffee) ¥200. Local Delicacies ¥1,500 (minimum 3 people).

## KIZO-IN ( 喜蔵院 )

Temple Hostel 2★ ☎ 07463-2-3014

1254 Yoshinoyama, Yoshino-machi, Yoshino-gun, Nara 639-31.

**Closed at New Year.** 120 beds

Station: Yoshino Jingu (Kintetsu Private Railway). Take bus for Kami Senbon ( 上千本 ) to Naka Senbon ( 中千本 ), 20 mins. Walk 5 mins.

**¥2,700.** Dinner ¥1,000. Breakfast ¥600. Local Delicacies ¥1,500.

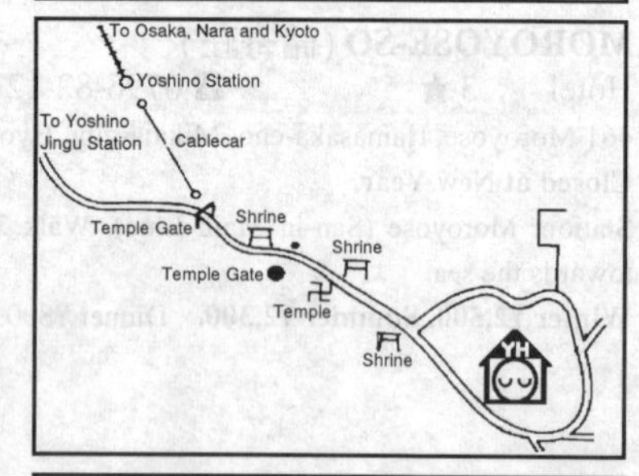


## ARIDA ORANGE ( 有田オレンジ )

Private Home 3★ ☎ 0737-62-4536

809 Suhara, Yuasa-machi, Arida-gun, Wakayama 643. 35 beds

Station: Yuasa (Kisei Main Line). Take bus for Minoshima ( 箕島 ) to Suhara Iriguchi ( 栖原入口 ), 10 mins. Walk 3 mins. Hostel is next to Post Office. Alternatively, walk from station, 30 mins. (2 km). In the afternoon, there are no buses.

**¥2,600.** Dinner ¥850. Breakfast ¥500.

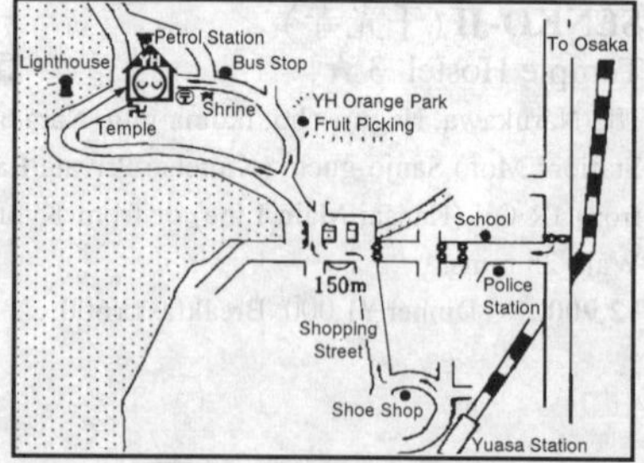


## SHIONO MISAKI ( 潮岬 )

Privately Operated Hostel 3★ ☎ 07356-2-0570

2843-1 Shiono Misaki, Kushimoto-cho, Nishi Muro-gun, Wakayama 649-37. 56 beds

Station: Kushimoto (Kisei Main Line). Take bus for Shiono Misaki ( 潮岬 ) to terminus, 20 mins. Hostel is adjacent.

**¥2,900.** Dinner ¥1,000. Breakfast ¥500.

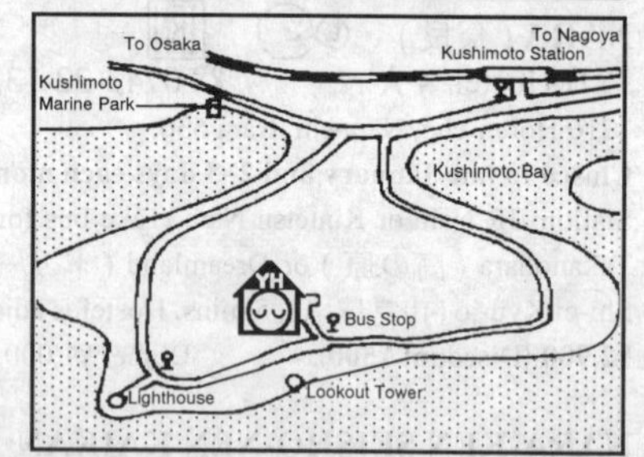


## MISAKI LODGE ( みさきロッジ )

Hotel 3★ ☎ 07356-2-1474

2864-1 Shiono Misaki, Kushimoto-cho, Nishi Muro-gun, Wakayama 649-35. 39 beds

Station: Kushimoto (Kisei Main Line). Take bus for Shiono Misaki ( 潮岬 ) to Kuroshio ( 黒潮 ), 20 mins. Hostel is adjacent to bus stop.

**Summer ¥2,900. Winter ¥2,700.**

Dinner ¥1,000. Breakfast ¥600. Local Delicacies ¥1,500.

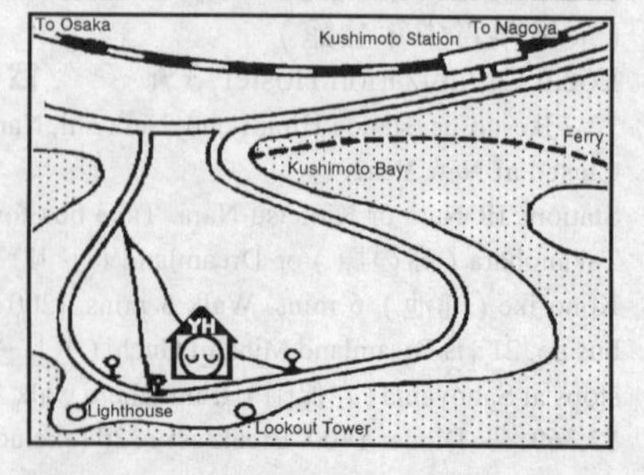

## SHINGU HAYATAMA (新宮早玉)

Hotel 3★ ☎ 0735-22-2309

1-1-9 Kami Hon-machi, Shingu-shi, Wakayama 647.

**Closed at New Year.** 20 beds

Station: Shingu (Kisei Main Line). Walk 15 mins. (1 km) towards Hayatama Jinja (shrine).

**¥2,400.** Dinner ¥850. Breakfast ¥450.

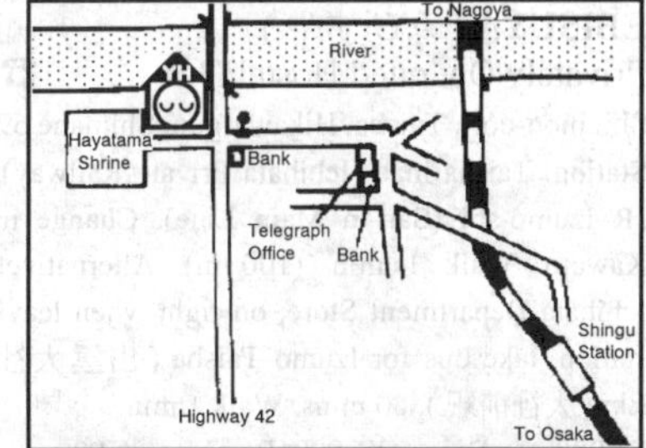


## KAJIKA-SO (河鹿荘)

Hotel 3★ ☎ 07354-2-0518

1408 Kawayu, Hongu-machi, Higashi Muro-gun, Wakayama 647-16. 40 beds

Station: Shingu (Kisei Main Line). Take JR bus for Kawayu Onsen (川湯温泉) via Ukegawa (請川) to Kawayu Onsen, 65 mins. Hostel is near bus stop.

**¥2,900, plus Spa Fee ¥100.** Dinner ¥900. Breakfast ¥600.

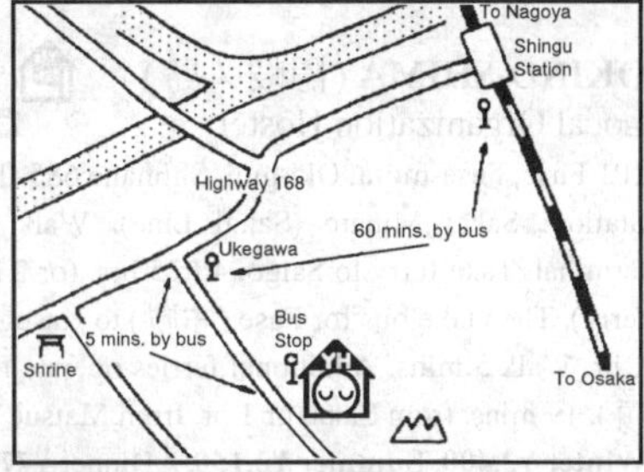


## WAKASA HYO-NO-SEN (若桜氷の山)

JYH Hostel 3★ ☎ 0858-82-1700, 0980. Fax: 1710

631-10 Tsukuyone, Wakasa-machi, Tottori 680-07.

**Closed in mid-June.** 96 beds

Station: Wakasa (Wakasa Private Railway), accessible from JR Koge (Inbi Line). Most trains run directly from Tottori. Take bus for Tsukuyone (舂米) to terminus, 25 mins. Walk 20 mins. towards Ski Ground.

Caution: Last bus 18:54 on weekdays, 17:45 on holidays.

**¥2,900 (Discount ¥100).** Dinner ¥1,000. Breakfast ¥600.

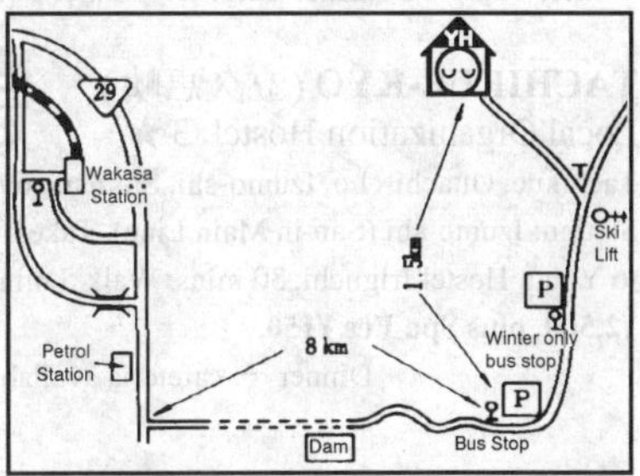


## KOHO-JI (香宝寺)

Temple Hostel 3★ ☎ 0858-35-2054

195 Shimo Asozu, Hawai, Tohaku-gun, Tottori 682-07. 35 beds

Station: Kurayoshi (San-in Main Line). Take bus for Hawai Onsen (羽合温泉) to Kami Asozu (上浅津), 10 mins. Walk 10 mins. (800 m). Ferries run to Hawai from Matsuzaki, 10 mins. Walk 20 mins.

**¥2,900, plus Spa Fee ¥100.** Dinner ¥900. Breakfast ¥500.

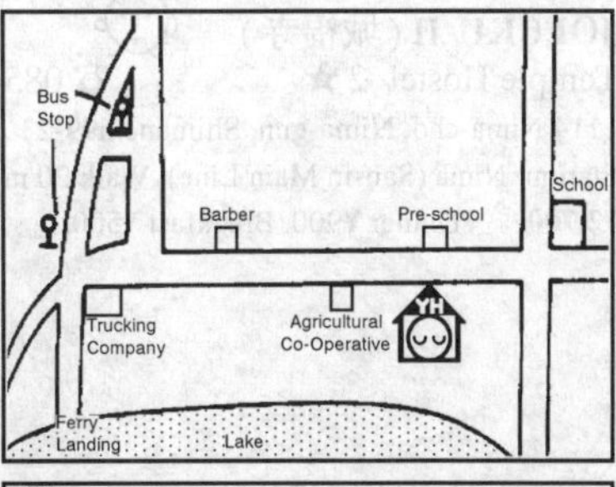


## MATSUE LAKESIDE (松江レークサイド) IBN

JYH Hostel 3★ ☎ 0852-36-8620

1546 Kososhi-cho, Matsue-shi, Shimane 690-01.

**Closed in mid-January.** 50 beds

Station: Furue (Ichibata Private Railway). From JR Matsue (San-in Main Line), bus stop no. 1, take bus to Ichibata Railway Matsue Onsen station, 5 mins., or walk across the river, 15 mins. Take train one station to Furue. Walk 11 mins. (900 m). Alternatively, from bus stop no. 2 at JR Matsue, take bus for Furue (古江) to terminus, 30 mins. Walk 7 mins. (600 m).

**¥2,900 (Discount ¥500).** Dinner ¥1,000. Breakfast ¥600.

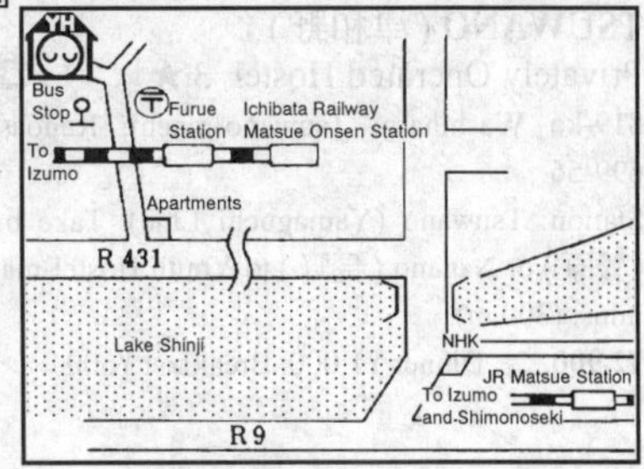

## EBISUYA (ゑびすや)

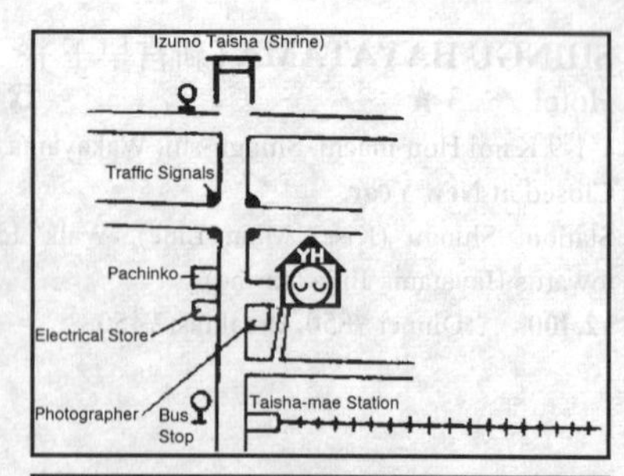


Privately Operated Hostel 3★ ☎ 0853-53-2157

Shinmon-dori, Taisha, Hikawa-gun, Shimane 699-07. 42 beds

Station: Taisha-mae (Ichibata Private Railway), accessible from JR Izumo-shi (San-in Main Line). Change trains en route at Kawato. Walk 1 min. (100 m). Alternatively, from outside Ichibata Department Store, on right when leaving JR Izumo-shi station, take bus for Izumo Taisha (出雲大社) to Taisha-mae Eki (大社前駅), 20 mins. Walk 1 min.

**¥2,900.** Dinner ¥1,000. Breakfast ¥500.

## OKINO-SHIMA (隠岐ノ島)

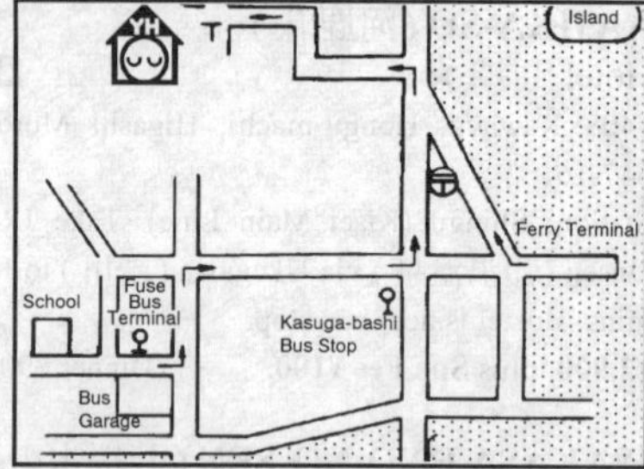


Local Organization Hostel ☎ 08512-7-4321

101 Fuse, Fuse-mura, Oki-gun, Shimane 685-04. 60 beds

Station: Sakai Minato (Sakai Line). Walk 5 mins. to ferry terminal. Take ferry to Saigo, 4 to 5 hrs. (or 2 hrs. by high-speed ferry). Then take bus for Fuse (布施) to Kasuga-bashi (春日橋), 1 hr. Walk 5 mins. Additional ferries operate from Shichirui (七類), 19 mins. from Sakai or 1 hr. from Matsue by bus.

**Winter ¥2,400. Summer ¥2,150.** Dinner ¥770. Breakfast ¥460.

## TACHIKUE-KYO (立久恵峡)

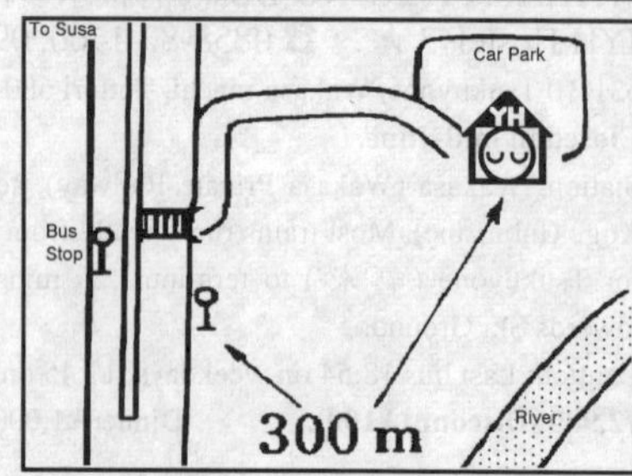


Local Organization Hostel 3★ ☎ 0853-45-0102

Tachikue, Ottachi-cho, Izumo-shi, Shimane 693-03. 30 beds

Station: Izumo-shi (San-in Main Line). Take bus for Susa (須佐) to Youth Hostel Iriguchi, 30 mins. Walk 5 mins.

**¥2,500, plus Spa Fee ¥150.**

Dinner — cafeteria available. Breakfast ¥500.

## JOFUKU-JI (城福寺)

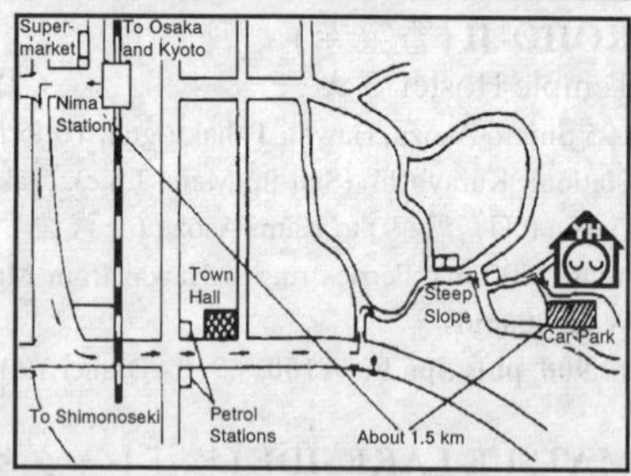


Temple Hostel 2★ ☎ 08548-8-3019, 2233

1114 Nima-cho, Nima-gun, Shimane 699-23. 15 beds

Station: Nima (San-in Main Line). Walk 20 mins. (1.5 km).

**¥2,700.** Dinner ¥900. Breakfast ¥500.

## TSUWANO (津和野)

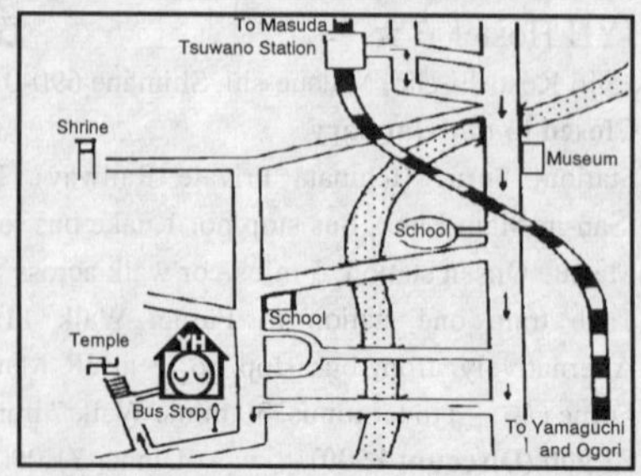


Privately Operated Hostel 3★ ☎ 08567-2-0373

819-ko Washihara, Tsuwano-machi, Kanoashi-gun, Shimane 699-56. 28 beds

Station: Tsuwano (Yamaguchi Line). Take bus for Washihara (鷲原) or Nagano (長野) to Youth Hostel-mae, 8 mins. Walk 3 mins. (300 m).

**¥2,900.** Dinner ¥1,000. Breakfast ¥600.

## OKAYAMA-KEN SEINEN KAIKAN
(岡山県青年会館)
Local Organization Hostel 3★ ☎ 086-252-0651, 7950
1-7-6 Tsukura-cho, Okayama-shi, Okayama 700.
**Closed in late January.** 65 beds
Station: Okayama. Walk 20 mins. (1 km).
**¥2,900.** Dinner ¥850. Breakfast ¥450.

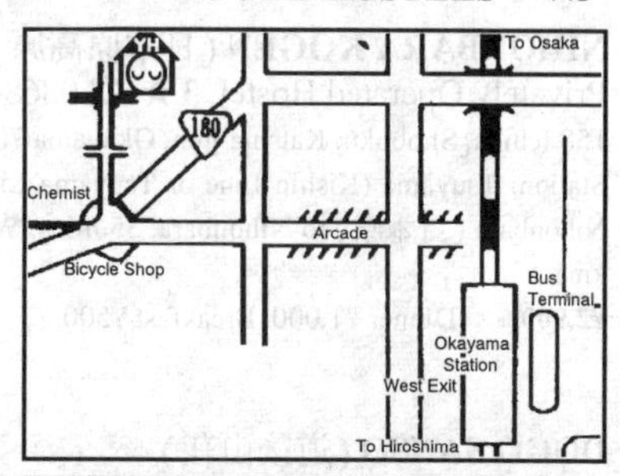


## WASHU-ZAN (鷲羽山)
Local Organization Hostel 3★ ☎ 086-479-9280
1666-1 Obatake, Kurashiki-shi, Okayama 711.
**Closed at New Year.** 60 beds
Station: ① Kojima (Seto Ohashi Line). Take bus for Washu-zan (鷲羽山) to Youth Hostel-mae, 20 mins. Walk 3 mins.
② Kurashiki (Sanyo Main Line). Take bus for Washu-zan to Youth Hostel-mae, 70 mins. Walk 3 mins.
**¥2,060.** Dinner ¥824. Breakfast ¥463.

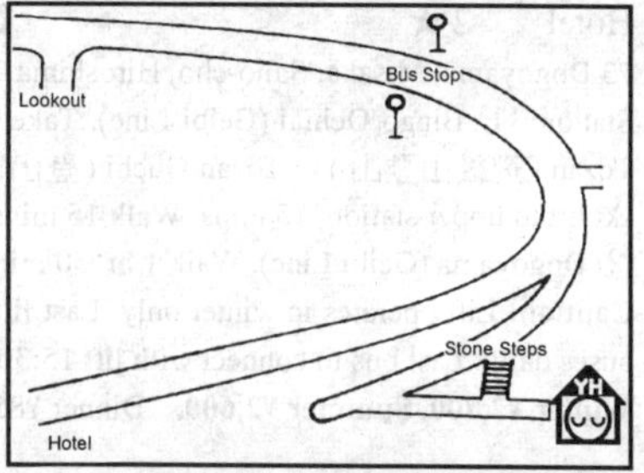


## KASAOKA-YA (笠岡屋)
Hotel 3★ ☎ 0865-63-4188. Fax: 62-4839
5658 Nishi Hon-machi, Kasaoka-shi, Okayama 714.
**Closed at New Year.** 21 beds
Station: Kasaoka (Sanyo Main Line). Walk 8 mins. (500 m).
**¥2,900.** Dinner ¥1,000. Breakfast ¥600.

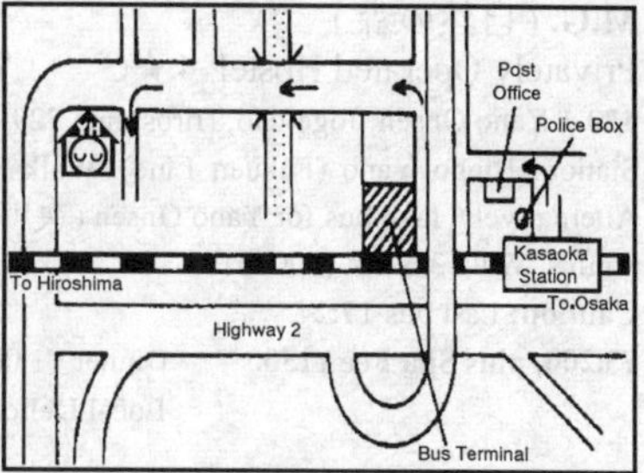


## MANABE SANTORA (まなべ三虎)
Hotel 2★ ☎ 08656-8-3515. Fax: 3516
2224 Manabe-shima, Kasaoka-shi, Okayama 714. 60 beds
Station: Kasaoka (Sanyo Main Line). Walk 7 mins. to ferry terminal. Take ferry for Manabe-shima (Manabe Island), 1 hr. 30 mins. (or 45 mins. by high-speed ferry). Ferry arrives at Motomura, from where walk 9 mins. (500 m).
**¥2,700.** Dinner ¥1,000. Breakfast ¥500.

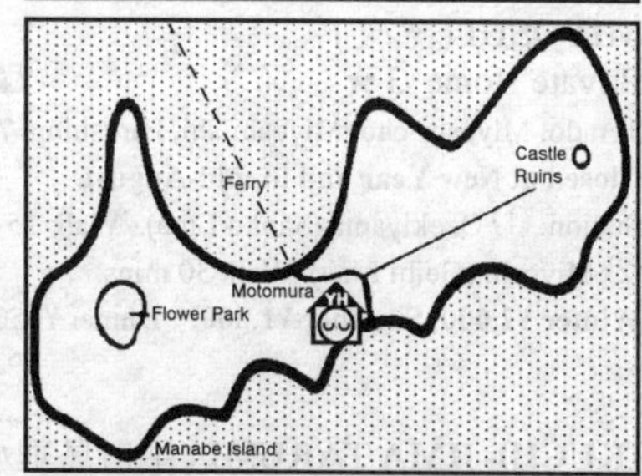


## KURASHIKI (倉敷) 
JYH Hostel 3★ ☎ 086-422-7355. Fax: 7364
1537-1 Mukaiyama, Kurashiki-shi, Okayama 710.
**Closed in mid-June.** 60 beds
Station: Kurashiki (Sanyo Main Line). Walk 30 mins. (1.5 km).
**¥2,900 (Discount ¥100).** Dinner ¥1,000. Breakfast ¥600.

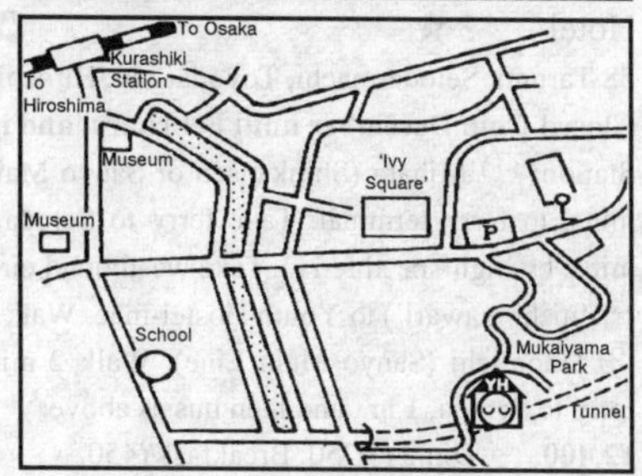

## NIHONBARA KOGEN (日本原高原)

Privately Operated Hostel 3★ ☎ 0868-36-2165, 2940

158 Ichiba, Shoboku, Katsuta-gun, Okayama 708-12. 30 beds

Station: Tsuyama (Kishin Line or Tsuyama Line). Take bus for Nihonbara (日本原) to Nihonbara, 35 mins. Walk 18 mins. (1.5 km).

**¥2,900.** Dinner ¥1,000. Breakfast ¥500.

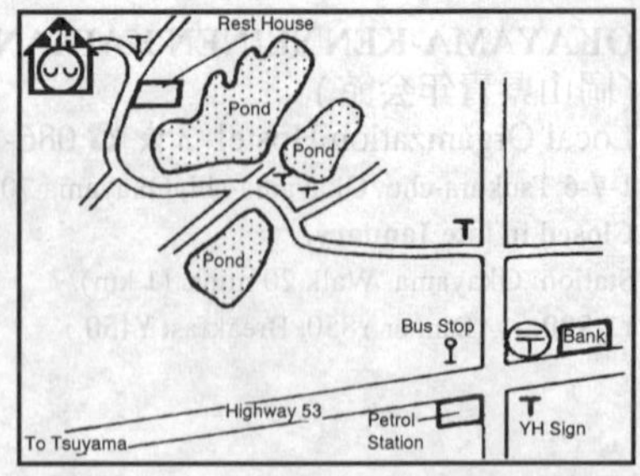


## DOGO SANSO (道後山荘)

Hotel 2★ ☎ 08248-4-2132

73 Dogoyama, Misaka, Saijo-cho, Hiroshima 729-56. 50 beds

Station: ① Bingo Ochiai (Geibi Line). Take bus for Dogoyama Tozan (道後山登山) to Tozan Guchi (登山口), 20 mins. Take ski lift to upper station, 15 mins. Walk 15 mins. (1 km).

② Dogoyama (Geibi Line). Walk 1 hr. 30 mins. (8 km).

**Caution:** Lift operates in winter only. Last lift 17:00. Only three buses daily. Last bus to connect with lift 15:30. Last bus 17:35.

**Winter ¥2,700. Summer ¥2,600.** Dinner ¥850. Breakfast ¥500.

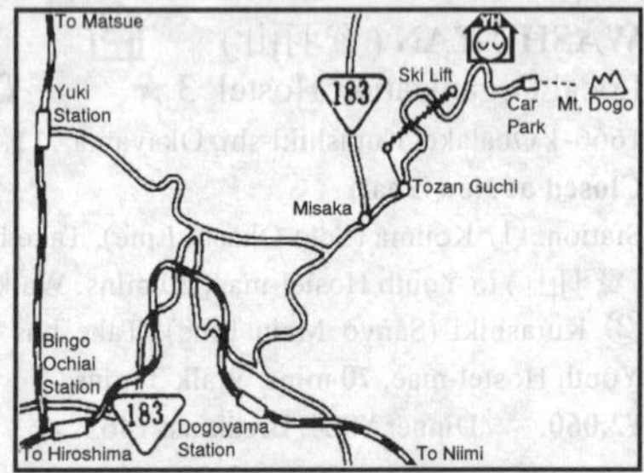


## M.G. (自然の森)

Privately Operated Hostel 4★ ☎ 0847-62-3244

470-1 Yano Onsen, Joge-cho, Hiroshima 729-34. 32 beds

Station: Bingo Yano (Fukuen Line). Walk 30 mins. (1.5 km). Alternatively, take bus for Yano Onsen (矢野温泉) to terminus, 5 mins. Walk 3 mins. (300 m).

**Caution:** Last bus 17:24.

**¥3,200, plus Spa Fee ¥150.** Dinner ¥1,000. Breakfast ¥600. Local Delicacies ¥1,500.

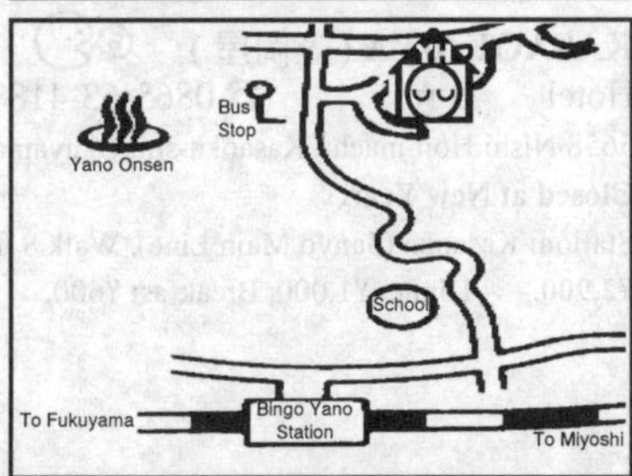


## MIYOSHI (三次)

Private Home 3★ ☎ 08246-3-1759

Terado, Miyoshi-cho, Miyoshi-shi, Hiroshima 728.

**Closed at New Year and in mid-August.** 20 beds

Station: ① Ozekiyama (Sanko Line). Walk 15 mins.

② Miyoshi (Geibi Line). Walk 30 mins.

**Winter ¥2,000. Summer ¥1,800.** Dinner ¥650. Breakfast ¥400.

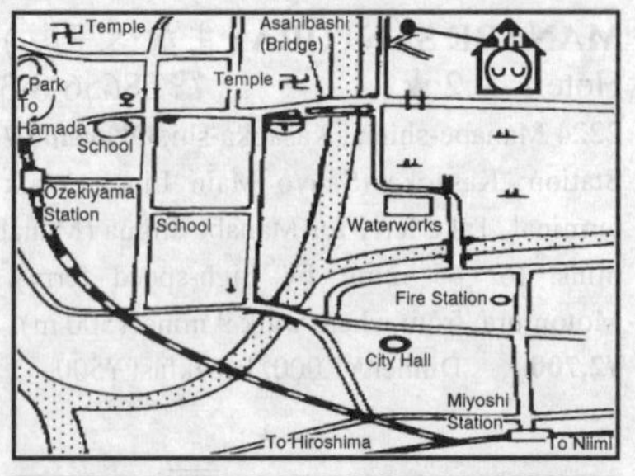


## IKUCHI-JIMA TARUMI (生口島垂水)

Hotel 3★ ☎ 08452-7-3137

58 Tarumi, Setoda-machi, Toyoda-gun, Hiroshima 722-24.

**Closed from December until February, and in June.** 14 beds

Station: ① Mihara (Shinkansen or Sanyo Main Line). Walk 10 mins. to ferry terminal. Take ferry to Setoda, 50 mins. (or 25 mins. by high-speed ferry). Take westbound circular bus (西回り—'nishi mawari') to Youth Hostel-mae. Walk 1 min.

② Onomichi (Sanyo Main Line). Walk 2 mins. to ferry. Take ferry to Setoda, 1 hr., and then bus as above.

**¥2,400.** Dinner ¥750. Breakfast ¥450.

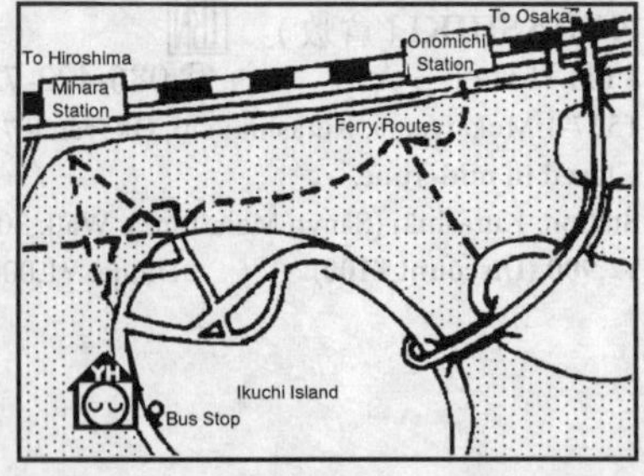

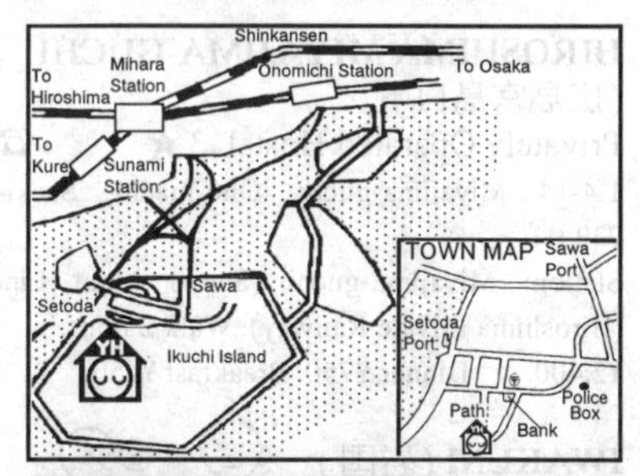


## SETODA (瀬戸田)

Privately Operated Hostel 3★ ☎ 08452-7-0224

668-1 Setoda-machi, Toyoda-gun, Hiroshima 722-24. 48 beds

Station: ① Mihara (Shinkansen or Sanyo Main Line). Walk 10 mins. to ferry terminal. Take ferry to Setoda, 50 mins. (or 25 mins. by high-speed ferry). Walk 6 mins. ② Onomichi (Sanyo Main Line). Walk 2 mins. to ferry. Take ferry to Setoda, 1 hr. Walk 6 mins. ③ Sunami (Kure Line). Take ferry to Sawa, 20 mins. Walk 20 mins.

**¥2,600.** Dinner ¥800. Breakfast ¥400.

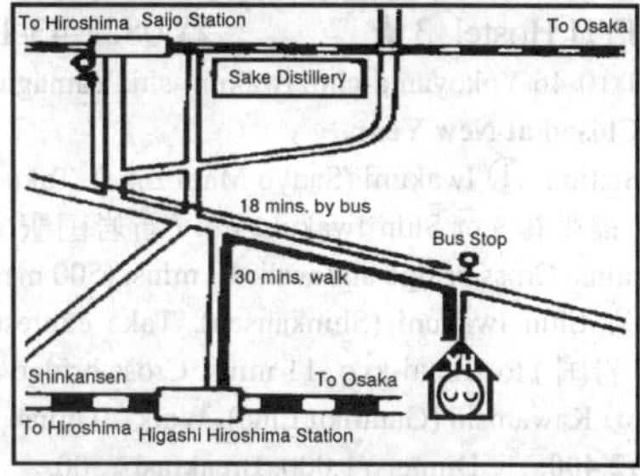


## HIROSHIMA SAIJO (広島西条)

Privately Operated Hostel 3★ ☎ 0824-26-0848

1417-8 Hirata, Kami Minaga, Saijo-cho, Higashi Hiroshima 739.

**Closed at New Year.** 20 beds

Station: ① Saijo (Sanyo Main Line). Take bus for Takehara (竹原) to Kami Minaga (上三永), 18 mins. Walk 4 mins.
② Higashi Hiroshima (Shinkansen). Walk 30 mins.

**¥2,700.** Dinner ¥750. Breakfast ¥400.

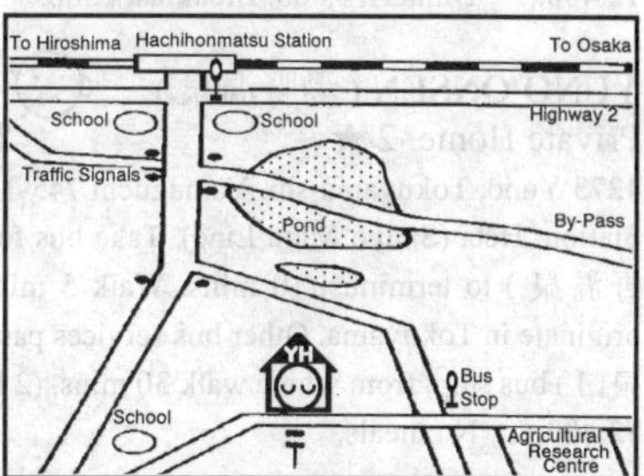


## HIGASHI HIROSHIMA (東広島)

Privately Operated Hostel 3★ ☎ 0824-29-0305

3148 Hara, Hachihonmatsu-machi, Higashi Hiroshima 739-01.

**Closed at New Year.** 27 beds

Station: Hachihonmatsu (Sanyo Main Line). Take bus for Hiroshima Dai-gaku (広島大学) to Nogyo Gijutsu Centre (農業技術センター), 10 mins. Walk 3 mins.

**¥2,800.** Dinner ¥750. Breakfast ¥450.

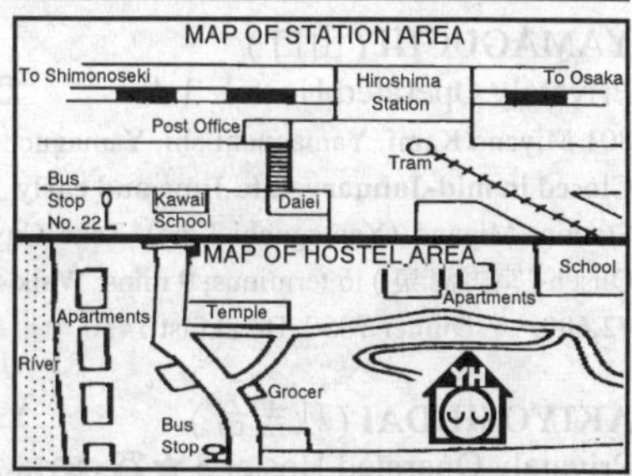


## HIROSHIMA (広島) 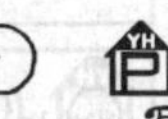

JYH Hostel 3★ ☎ 082-221-5343

1-13-6 Ushita Shin-machi, Higashi-ku, Hiroshima 732. 104 beds

Station: Hiroshima. Take any bus, except a green bus, from bus stop no. 22 to Ushita Shin-machi I-chome (牛田新町一丁目), 10 mins. Walk 8 mins. (600 m) following YH signs. Any bus from bus stop no. 4 in Bus Centre (some are JR buses) will also go to this stop.

**¥2,350 (Discount ¥400).** Dinner ¥750. Breakfast ¥450.

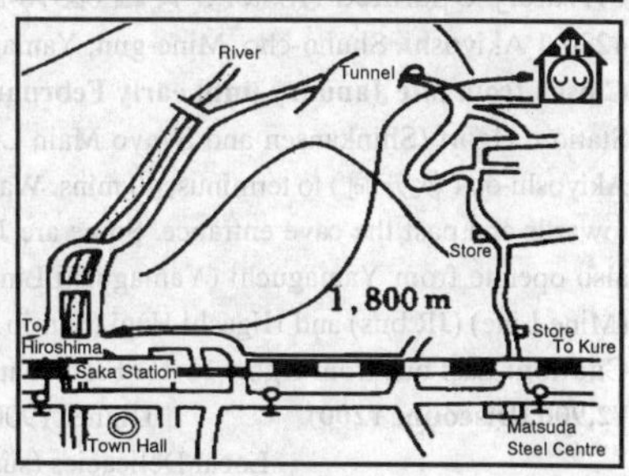


## SAKAMACHI (坂町)

Privately Operated Hostel ☎ 082-885-0700

Ueda, Kogai Sakamachi, Hiroshima 731-43. 12 beds

Station: Saka (Kure Line). Walk 25 mins. (1.8 km). Between 18:00 and 20:00, hostel will collect hostellers from station. Telephone on arrival.

**¥2,600.** Dinner ¥800. Breakfast ¥450.

## HIROSHIMA MIYAJIMA-GUCHI (広島宮島口)

Privately Operated Hostel 3★ ☎ 0829-56-1444

1-4-14 Miyajima-guchi, Ono-machi, Saeki-gun, Hiroshima 739-04. 30 beds

Station: Miyajima-guchi (Sanyo Main Line) or Miyajima (Hiroshima Private Railway). Walk 2 mins.

**¥2,400.** Dinner ¥750. Breakfast ¥450.

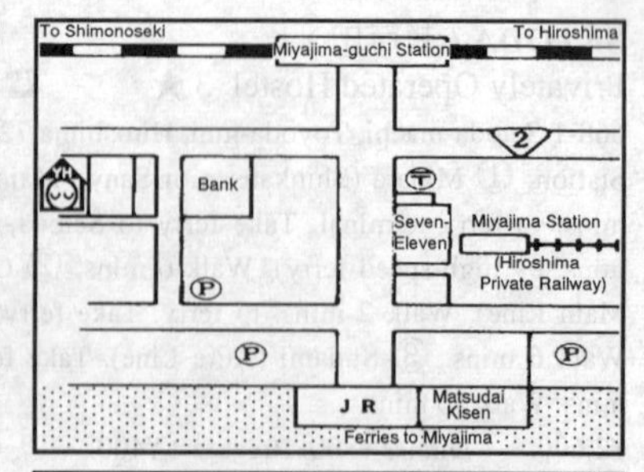


## IWAKUNI (岩国)

JYH Hostel 3★ ☎ 0827-43-1092. Fax: 0123

1-10-46 Yokoyama-cho, Iwakuni-shi, Yamaguchi 741.

**Closed at New Year.** 106 beds

Station: ① Iwakuni (Sanyo Main Line). Take bus for Kintai-kyo (錦帯橋) or Shin Iwakuni Eki (新岩国駅) to Kintai-kyo, 20 mins. Cross bridge and walk 10 mins. (500 m).
② Shin Iwakuni (Shinkansen). Take express bus for Iwakuni (岩国) to Kintai-kyo, 11 mins. Cross bridge and walk 10 mins.
③ Kawanishi (Gantoku Line). Walk 20 mins.

**¥2,400.** Dinner ¥1,000. Breakfast ¥500.

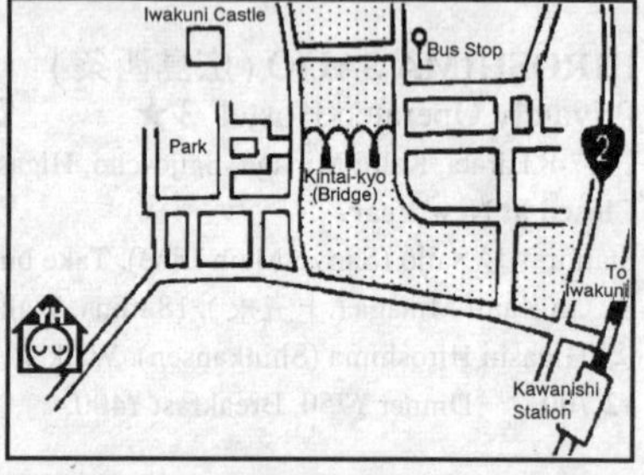


## YUNO ONSEN (湯野温泉)

Private Home 2★ ☎ 0834-83-2104

4273 Yuno, Tokuyama-shi, Yamaguchi 745-11. 15 beds

Station: Heta (Sanyo Main Line). Take bus for Yuno Onsen (湯野温泉) to terminus, 10 mins. Walk 5 mins. (300 m). Buses originate in Tokuyama. Other bus services pass Onsen Guchi (温泉口) bus stop, from where walk 30 mins. (2 km) steadily uphill.

**¥2,400.** No meals.

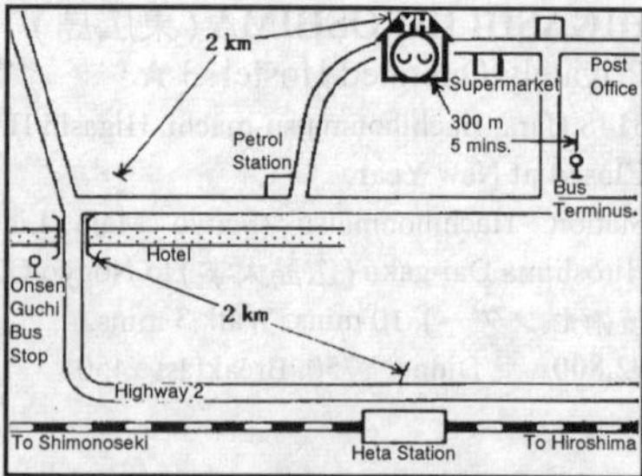


## YAMAGUCHI (山口)

Privately Operated Hostel 3★ ☎ 0839-28-0057

801 Miyano Kami, Yamaguchi-shi, Yamaguchi 753.

**Closed in mid-January, late June and early July.** 30 beds

Station: Miyano (Yamaguchi Line). Take City Bus for Miyano Onsen (宮野温泉) to terminus, 9 mins. Walk 4 mins.

**¥2,600.** Dinner ¥850. Breakfast ¥450.

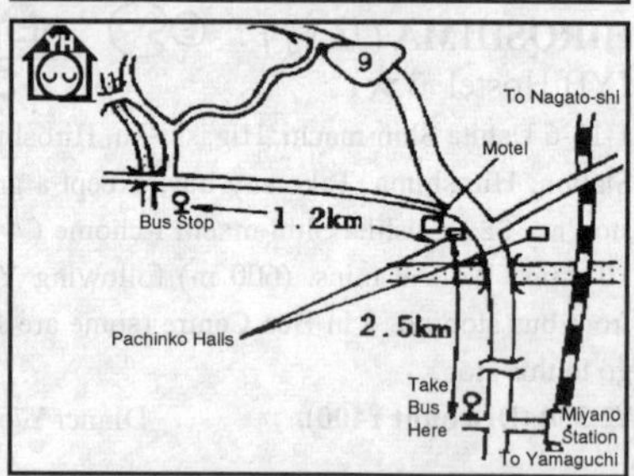


## AKIYOSHIDAI (秋吉台)

Privately Operated Hostel 3★☎ 08376-2-0341. Fax: 1546

4236-1 Akiyoshi, Shuho-cho, Mine-gun, Yamaguchi 754-05.

**Closed from late January until early February.** 76 beds

Station: Ogori (Shinkansen and Sanyo Main Line). Take bus for Akiyoshi-do (秋芳洞) to terminus, 40 mins. Walk 20 mins. (1 km) towards and past the cave entrance. Some are JR buses. Services also operate from Yamaguchi (Yamaguchi Line) (JR bus), Mine (Mine Line) (JR bus) and Higashi Hagi (San-in Main Line).

**Caution:** Last bus from Ogori 16:15. From Yamaguchi 18:20.

**¥2,900 (Discount ¥200).** Dinner ¥900. Breakfast ¥500.
Local Delicacies (sushi menu) ¥1,400.

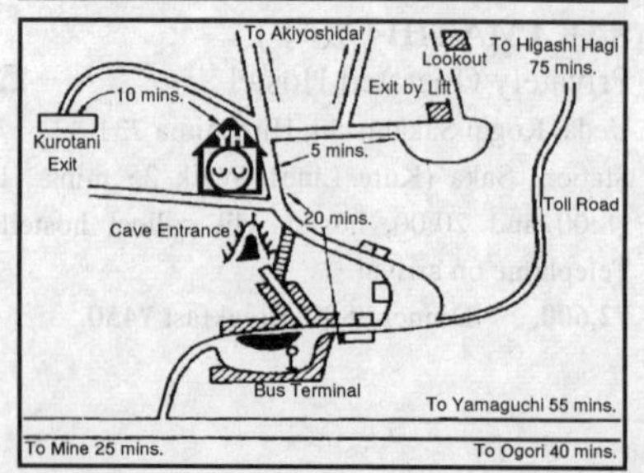

**HAGI** (萩)
Privately Operated Hostel 3★ ☎ 0838-22-0733
109-22 Horinouchi, Hagi-shi, Yamaguchi 758.
**Closed from mid-January until mid-February.** 100 beds
Station: Tamae (San-in Main Line). Walk 15 mins. (1.2 km). It is also possible to walk from Higashi Hagi station (San-in Main Line), 35 mins., or from Hagi Bus Centre, 25 mins.
**¥2,700.** Dinner ¥850. Breakfast ¥500.

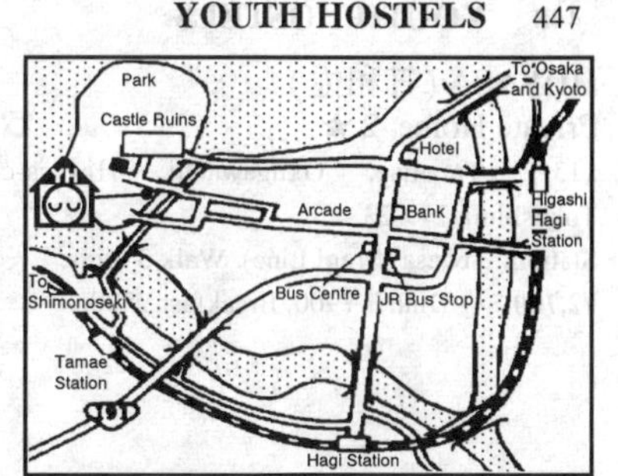


**JINJO-JI** (神上寺)
Temple Hostel 3★ ☎ 08376-6-0286
624 Era, Toyota-cho, Yamaguchi 750-04. 30 beds
Station: ① Ozuki (Sanyo Main Line). Take bus for Omi-jima (青海島) to Ishi-machi (石町), 30 mins. Walk 30 mins. (2 km). Bus originates in Shimonoseki.
② Nagato-shi (San-in Main Line). Take bus for Shimonoseki (下関) to Ishi-machi, 80 mins. Walk 30 mins.
**¥2,700.** Dinner ¥1,000. Breakfast ¥600. Local Delicacies ¥1,200.

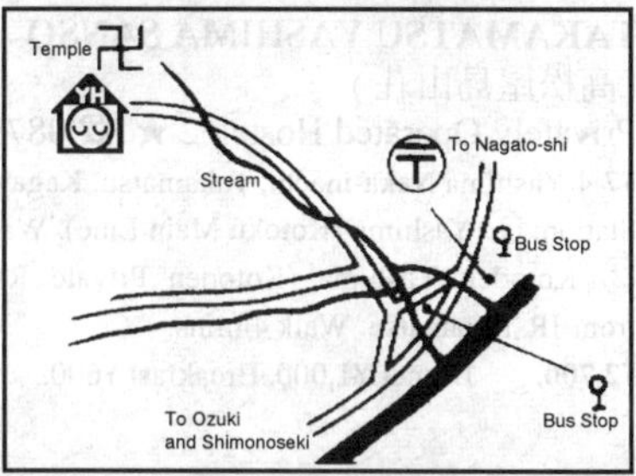


**UBE TOKIWA KOHAN** (宇部ときわ湖畔)
JYH Hostel 2★ ☎ 0836-21-3613
Hiraki, 654 Takahata, Kami Ube, Yamaguchi 755.
**Closed in late January and early June.** 60 beds
Station: Ube Shinkawa (Ube Line). Take bus for Furogasako (風呂ヶ迫) to Hiraki (開), 25 mins. Walk 10 mins. (900 m), or telephone for collection.
**¥2,700.** Dinner ¥900. Breakfast ¥500.

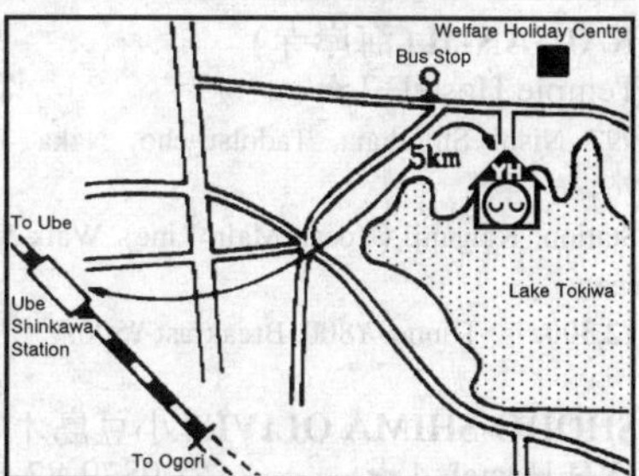


**SHIMONOSEKI HINOYAMA** 
(下関火の山)
JYH Hostel 2★ ☎ 0832-22-3753
3-47 Mimosusogawa, Shimonoseki, Yamaguchi 751.
**Closed in mid-June and early November.** 52 beds
Station: Shimonoseki. From bus stop no. 1, take bus for Hinoyama (火の山) to Ropeway, 15 mins. Walk 2 mins. (80 m).
**Caution:** Last bus 18:00. Other buses from bus stop no. 1 can be taken to Mimosuso-gawa (みもすそ川). Walk 8 mins. Or walk from station along Highway 9, 40 mins.
**¥2,400.** Dinner ¥800. Breakfast ¥600.

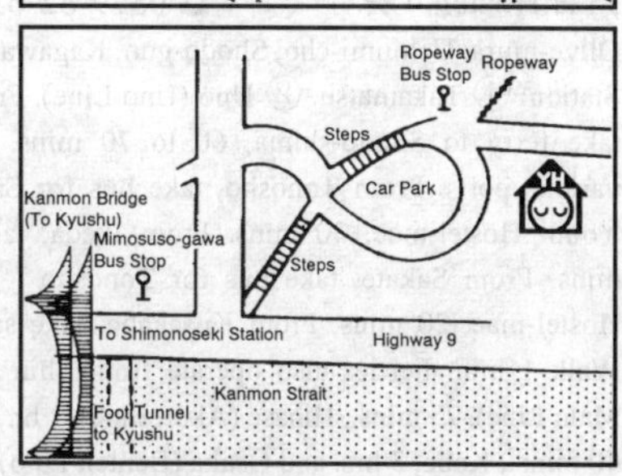


**TOKUSHIMA** (徳島) IBN
JYH Hostel 3★ ☎ 0886-63-1505
7-1 Hama, Ohara-machi, Tokushima-shi, Tokushima 770.
**Closed in late January.** 80 beds
Station: Tokushima. Take bus for Omiko (大神子) to terminus, 30 mins. Walk 2 mins.
**Caution:** Last bus 18:05. After that time, buses operate to Omiko-guchi (大神子口), from where walk 40 mins. (3 km).
**¥2,900 (Discount ¥200).** Dinner ¥900. Breakfast ¥600.

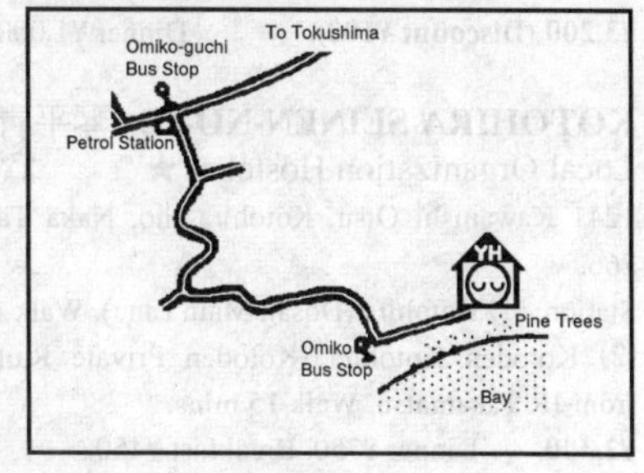

**HIWASA** (日和佐)
Private Home 2★ ☎ 08847-7-0755
113-1 Teramae, Okugawachi, Hiwasa-cho, Kaifu-gun, Tokushima 779-23. 38 beds
Station: Hiwasa (Mugi Line). Walk 3 mins.
**¥2,700.** Dinner ¥900. Breakfast ¥500.

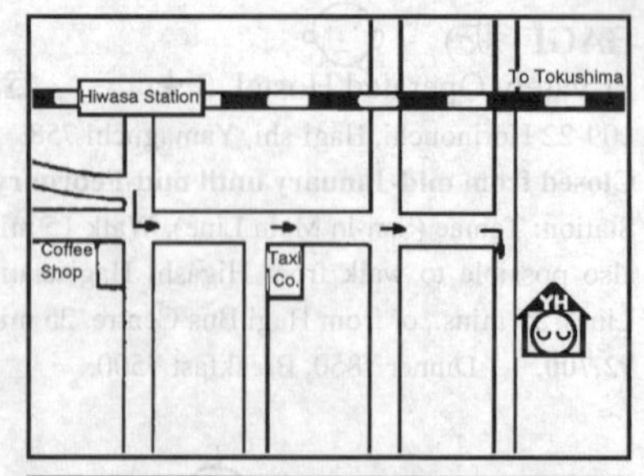


**TAKAMATSU YASHIMA SANSO** 
(高松屋島山荘)
Privately Operated Hostel 2★ ☎ 0878-41-2318, 6010
77-4 Yashima Naka-machi, Takamatsu, Kagawa 761-01. 50 beds
Station: ① Yashima (Kotoku Main Line). Walk 8 mins.
② Kotoden Yashima (Kotoden Private Railway), accessible from JR Takamatsu. Walk 4 mins.
**¥2,700.** Dinner ¥1,000. Breakfast ¥600.

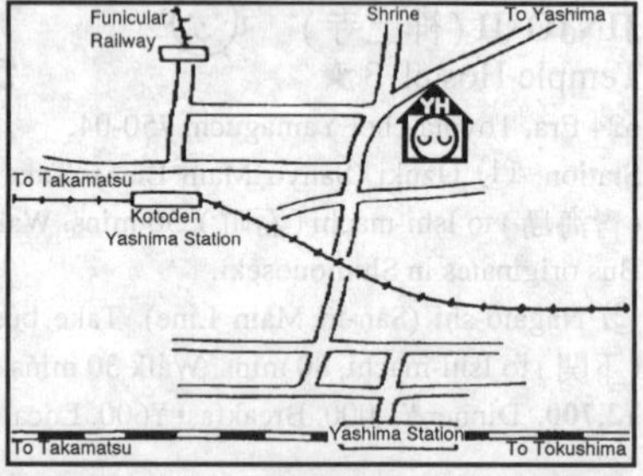


**KAIGAN-JI** (海岸寺)
Temple Hostel 2★ ☎ 0877-33-3333
997 Nishi Shirakata, Tadotsu-cho, Naka Tado-gun, Kagawa 764. 150 beds
Station: Kaiganji (Yosan Main Line). Walk 5 mins. towards the sea.
**¥2,300.** Dinner ¥800. Breakfast ¥500.

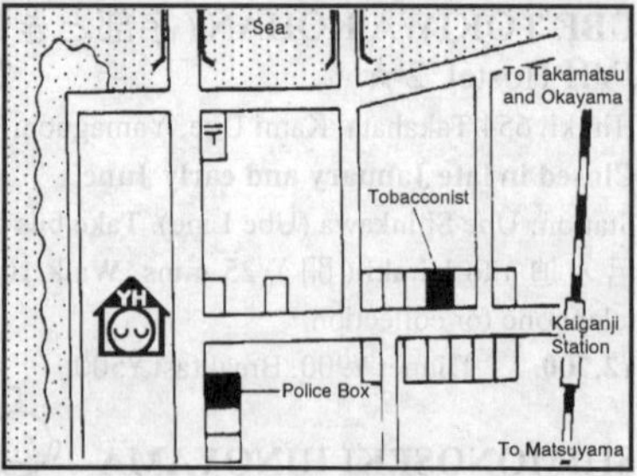


**SHODO-SHIMA OLIVE** (小豆島オリーブ) IBN
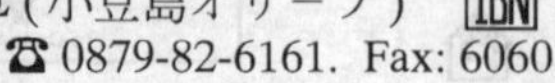
JYH Hostel 4★ ☎ 0879-82-6161. Fax: 6060
Olive-mura, Uchiumi-cho, Shodo-gun, Kagawa 761-44. 123 beds
Station: ① Takamatsu. ② Uno (Uno Line). From either station, take ferry to Shodo-shima, 60 to 70 mins. Ferries arrive at various ports. From Tonosho, take bus for Sakate (坂手) to Youth Hostel-mae, 30 mins. From Ikeda, take same bus, 10 mins. From Sakate, take bus for Tonosho (土庄) to Youth Hostel-mae, 20 mins. From Kusakabe, take same bus, 5 mins. Walk 1 min. Ferries also operate from Shin Okayama (Sanyo Main Line), 75 mins., Hinase (Akou Line), 1 hr., Himeji Port, 1 hr. 40 mins., Kobe, 3 hrs. and Osaka (Benten Futo), 4 hrs. 30 mins.
**¥3,200 (Discount ¥100).** Dinner ¥1,000. Breakfast ¥600.

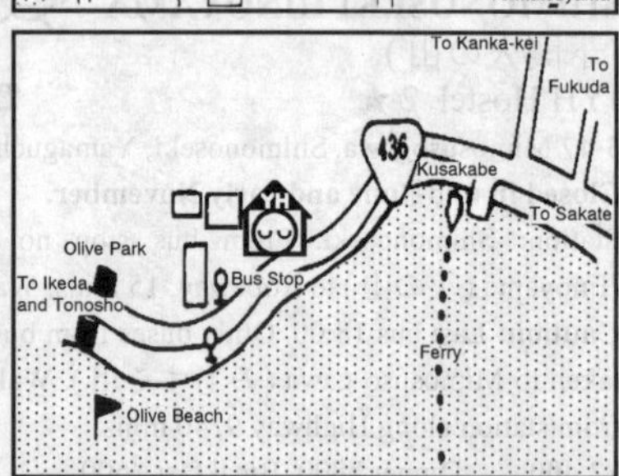


**KOTOHIRA SEINEN-NO-IE** (琴平青年の家)
Local Organization Hostel 1★ ☎ 0877-73-3836
1241 Kawanishi Otsu, Kotohira-cho, Naka Tado-gun, Kagawa 766. 68 beds
Station: ① Kotohira (Dosan Main Line). Walk 18 mins.
② Kotoden Kotohira (Kotoden Private Railway), accessible from JR Takamatsu. Walk 15 mins.
**¥2,300.** Dinner ¥750. Breakfast ¥450.

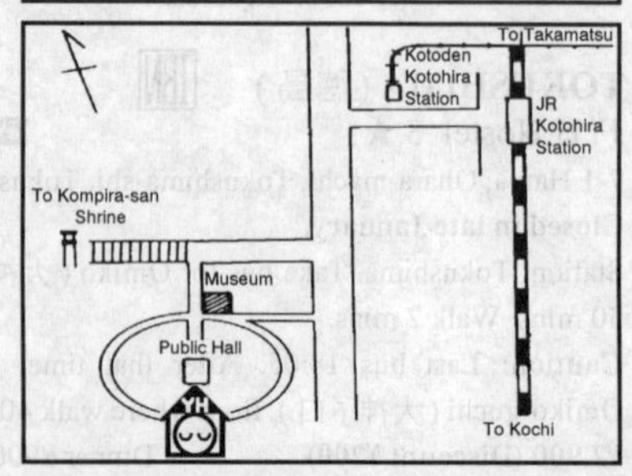

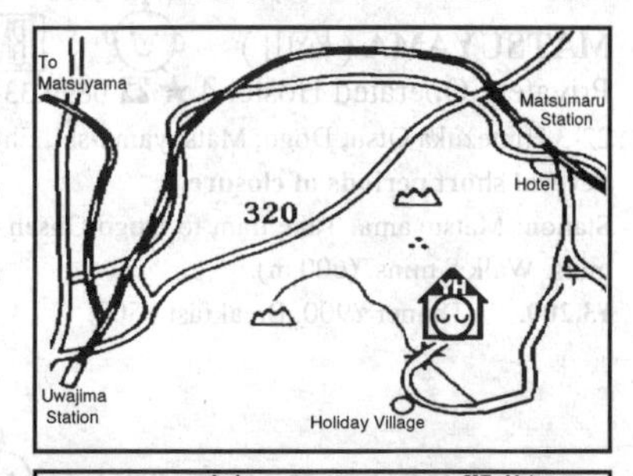


**MANNEN-SO** (万年荘)
Hotel 2★ ☎ 0895-43-0205
Nametoko, Meguro, Matsuno-cho, Ehime 798-21. 35 beds
Station: ① Matsumaru (Yodo Line). Take bus for Nametoko (滑床) to Nametoko, 40 mins. Walk 1 min.
② Uwajima (Yosan Main Line). Take bus for Nametoko to Nametoko, 1 hr. 30 mins. Walk 1 min.
**Caution**: Very few or no buses in winter.
**¥2,400.** Dinner ¥1,000. Breakfast ¥500.

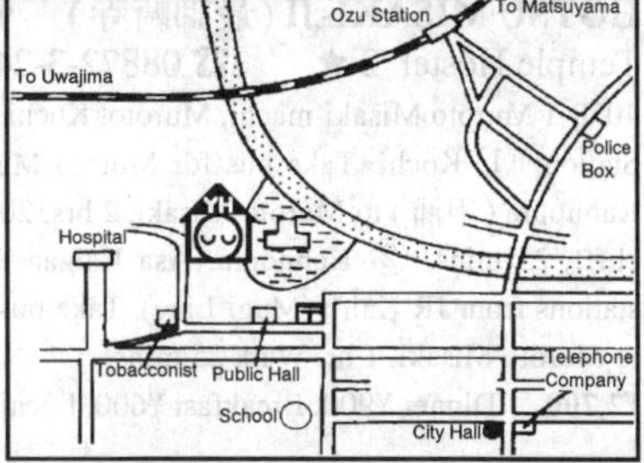


**OZU KYODOKAN** (大洲郷土館)
Private Home 2★ ☎ 0893-24-2258
San-no-maru, Ozu-shi, Ehime 795. 24 beds
Station: Ozu (Yosan Main Line). Walk 20 mins. (2 km).
**¥3,100.** Dinner ¥1,000. Breakfast ¥500.

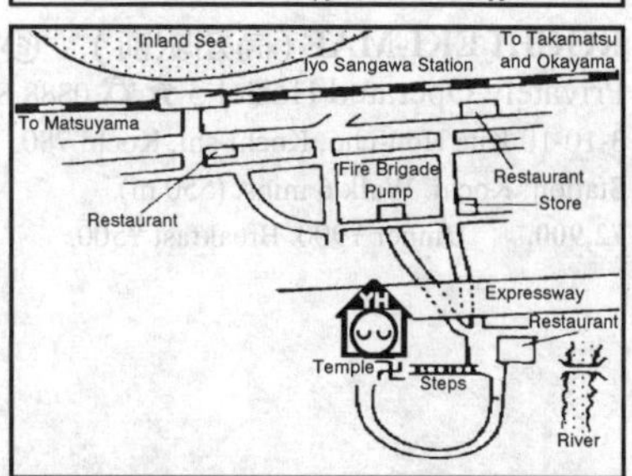


**SHIN HASE-DERA** (新長谷寺)
Temple Hostel 4★ ☎ 0896-25-0202
3214 Sangawa-cho, Iyo Mishima-shi, Ehime 799-04.
**Closed in June and mid-August and at New Year.** 69 beds
Station: Iyo Sangawa (Yosan Main Line). Walk 20 mins. (1 km).
**¥3,200.** Dinner ¥850. Breakfast ¥500.

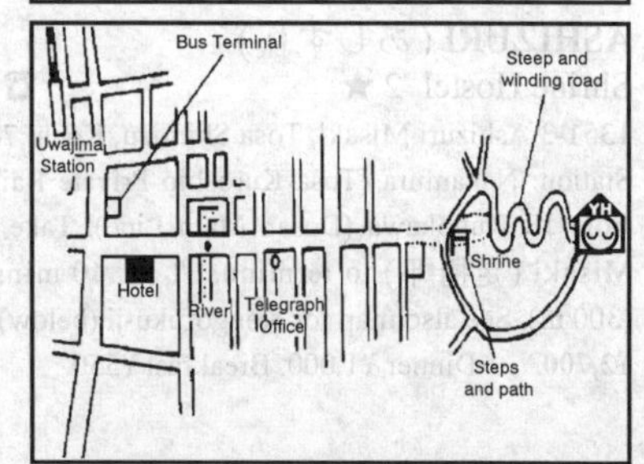


**UWAJIMA** (宇和島)
JYH Hostel 4★ ☎ 0895-22-7177
Atago Koen, Uwajima-shi, Ehime 798.
**Closed in mid-June.** 62 beds
Station: Uwajima (Yosan Main Line). Walk 30 mins. (2 km).
**¥3,200.** Dinner ¥1,000. Breakfast ¥600.

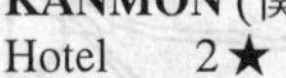

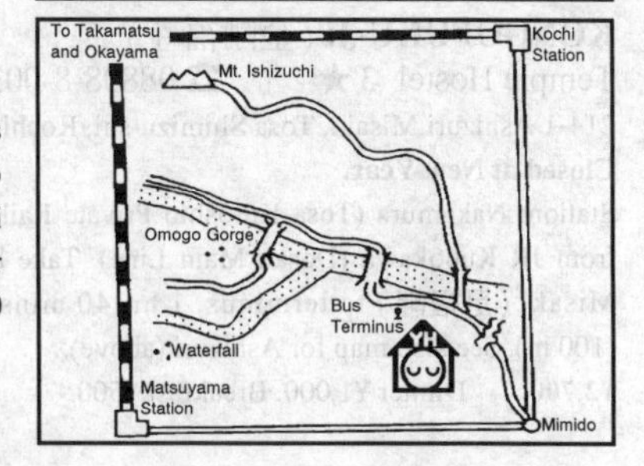


**KANMON** (関門)
Hotel 2★ ☎ 0892-58-2311
620 Wakayama, Omogo-mura, Ehime 791-17. 70 beds
Station: ① Matsuyama. Take bus for Omogo (面河) to terminus, 3 hrs. Walk back a short distance to hostel. ② Kochi or ③ Sakawa (Dosan Main Line). Take JR express bus for Matsuyama (松山) to Mimido (御三戸), 2 hrs. from Kochi, 70 mins. from Sakawa. Change to bus for Omogo, 50 mins.
**Caution:** Last bus from Matsuyama 15:35. From Mimido 17:17.
**¥2,100.** Dinner ¥900. Breakfast ¥500.

## MATSUYAMA (松山)

Privately Operated Hostel 4 ★ ☎ 0899-33-6366. Fax: 6378
22-3 Himezuka Otsu, Dogo, Matsuyama-shi, Ehime 790.
**Several short periods of closure.** 70 beds
Station: Matsuyama. Take tram to Dogo Onsen (道後温泉), 20 mins. Walk 8 mins. (600 m).
**¥3,200.** Dinner ¥900. Breakfast ¥500.

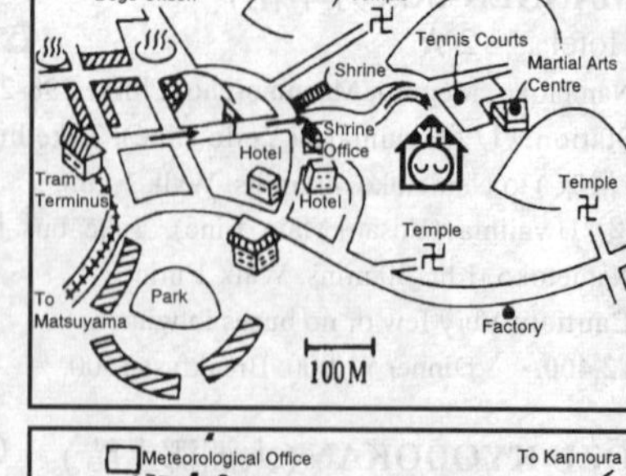


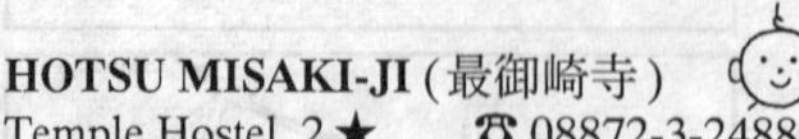

## HOTSU MISAKI-JI (最御崎寺)

Temple Hostel 2 ★ ☎ 08872-3-2488. Fax: 2-0055
4058-1 Muroto Misaki-machi, Muroto, Kochi 781-71. 100 beds
Station: ① Kochi. Take bus for Muroto Misaki (室戸岬) or Kannoura (甲浦) to Muroto Misaki, 2 hrs. 20 mins. Walk up the cliff!, 25 mins. ② Kannoura (Asa Kaigan Private Railway), 2 stations from JR Kaifu (Mugi Line). Take bus for Kochi (高知) to Muroto Misaki, 1 hr. Walk 25 mins.
**¥2,700.** Dinner ¥900. Breakfast ¥600. Local Delicacies ¥1,300.

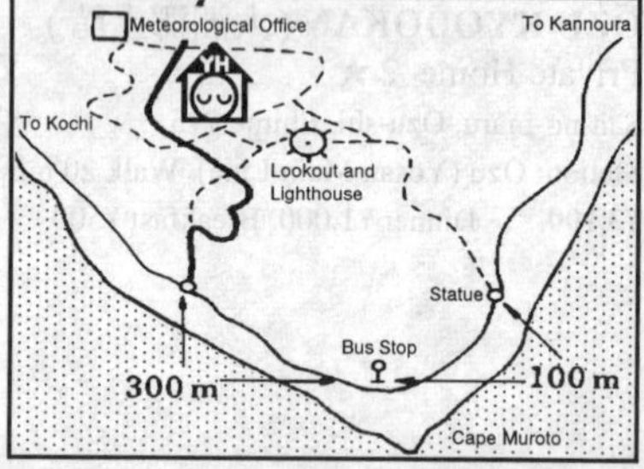


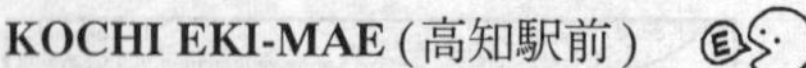

## KOCHI EKI-MAE (高知駅前)

Privately Operated Hostel 3 ★ ☎ 0888-83-5086. Fax: 0925
3-10-10 Kita Hon-cho, Kochi-shi, Kochi 780. 67 beds
Station: Kochi. Walk 6 mins. (550 m).
**¥2,900.** Dinner ¥900. Breakfast ¥500.

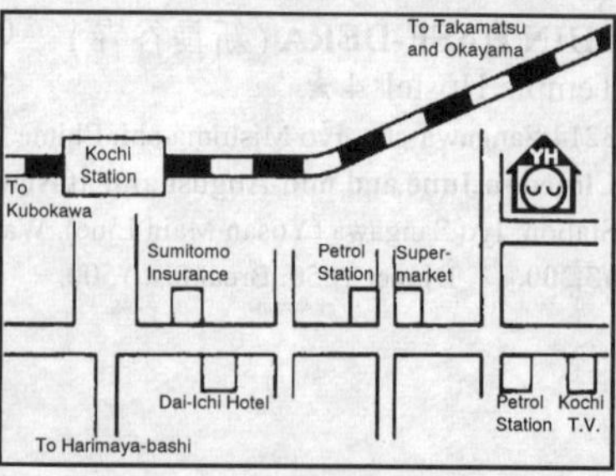


## ASHIZURI (あしずり)

Shrine Hostel 2 ★ ☎ 08808-8-0324
1351-3 Ashizuri Misaki, Tosa Shimizu, Kochi 787-03. 20 beds
Station: Nakamura (Tosa Kuroshio Private Railway), accessible from JR Kubokawa (Dosan Main Line). Take bus for Ashizuri Misaki (足摺岬) to terminus, 1 hr. 40 mins. Walk 3 mins. (300 m). See also map for Kongofuku-ji (below).
**¥2,700.** Dinner ¥1,000. Breakfast ¥550.

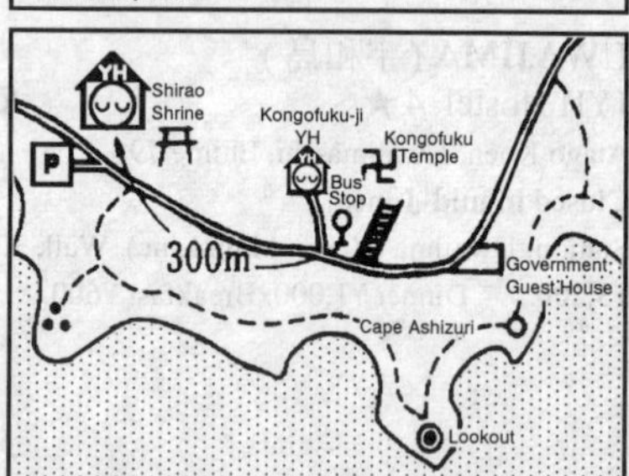


## KONGOFUKU-JI (金剛福寺)

Temple Hostel 3 ★ ☎ 08808-8-0038. Fax: 0688
214-1 Ashizuri Misaki, Tosa Shimizu-shi, Kochi 787-03.
**Closed at New Year.** 100 beds
Station: Nakamura (Tosa Kuroshio Private Railway), accessible from JR Kubokawa (Dosan Main Line). Take bus for Ashizuri Misaki (足摺岬) to terminus, 1 hr. 40 mins. Walk 2 mins. (100 m). See also map for Ashizuri (above).
**¥2,700.** Dinner ¥1,000. Breakfast ¥500.

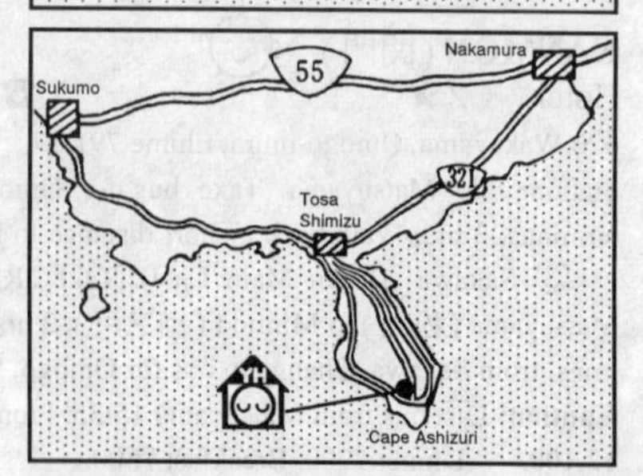

## JOFUKU-JI (定福寺)

Privately Operated Hostel 4★ ☎ 0887-74-0301, 0302
158 Ao, Otoyo-machi, Nagaoka-gun, Kochi 789-01.
**Closed on Mondays, Tuesdays and Wednesdays, except in summer.** 50 beds
Station: Toyonaga (Dosan Main Line). Take bus to Ao (粟生), 7 mins. Walk 2 mins. up the stone steps. Alternatively, walk from station, 25 mins. (1.7 km).
**¥3,200.** Dinner ¥950. Breakfast ¥550. Local Delicacies ¥1,500.

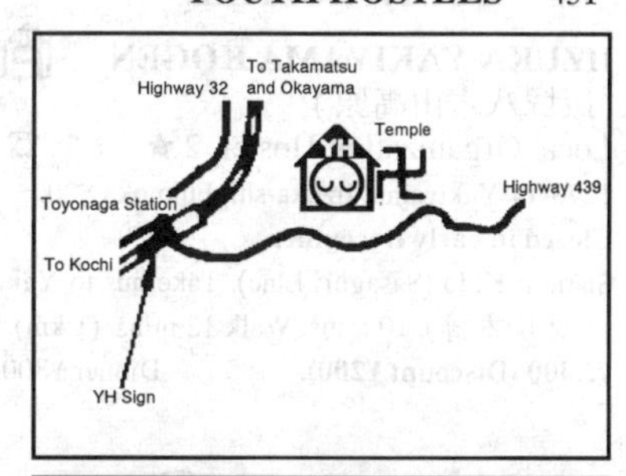


## IWAMOTO-JI (岩本寺)

Temple Hostel 3★ ☎ 08802-2-0376. Fax: 4166
3-13 Shigekushi, Kubokawa-cho, Kochi 786. 20 beds
Station: Kubokawa (Dosan Main Line). Walk 15 mins.
**¥2,900.** Dinner ¥1,000. Breakfast ¥600.

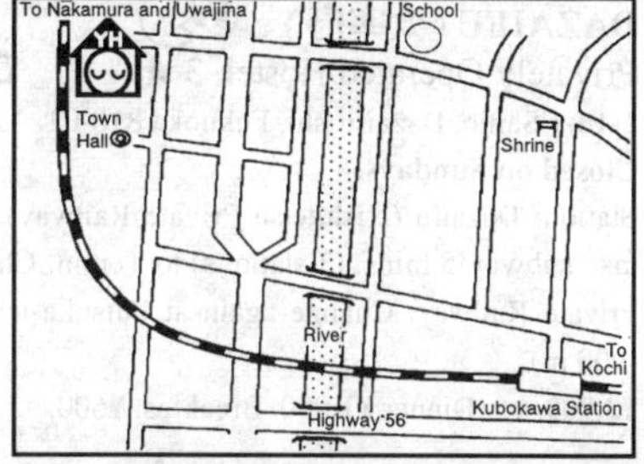


## ODO SUNSET (大堂サンセット)

Hotel 2★ ☎ 0880-76-0222
Kashiwajima, Otsuki-cho, Hata-gun, Kochi 788-04. 20 beds
Station: Nakamura (Tosa Kuroshio Private Railway), accessible from JR Kubokawa (Dosan Main Line). Take bus for Sukumo (宿毛) to terminus, 45 mins. Change to bus for Kashiwa-jima (柏島) to Watashiba (渡場), 90 mins. Hostel is adjacent.
**¥2,700.** Dinner ¥1,000. Breakfast ¥550.

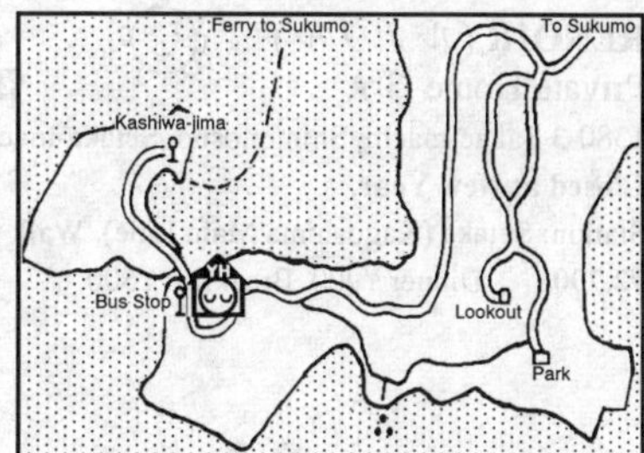


## SUKUMO (宿毛)

Privately Operated Hostel 3★ ☎ 0880-64-0233
196 Kamiari, Hashikami-cho, Sukumo-shi, Kochi 788. 30 beds
**Closed in mid-May and from late September until early October.**
Station: ① Nakamura (Tosa Kuroshio Private Railway), accessible from JR Kubokawa (Dosan Main Line). Take bus for Sukumo (宿毛) to terminus, 45 mins. Change to bus for Kamiari (上有) to Kamiari Yanase (上有柳瀬), 20 mins. Walk 6 mins.
② Uwajima (Yosan Main Line). Take bus to Kamiari, 2 hrs.
**¥2,900.** Dinner ¥1,000. Breakfast ¥500.

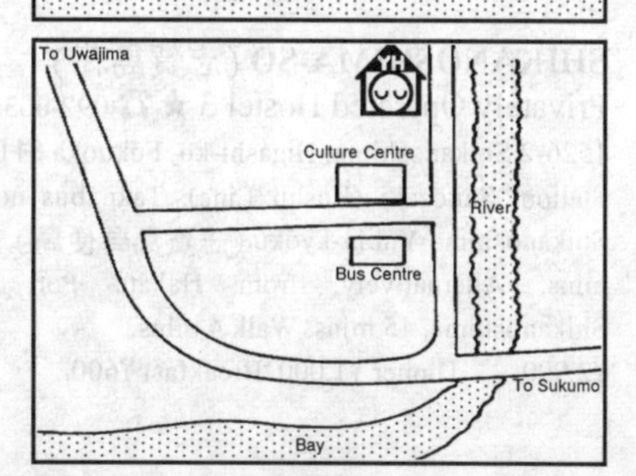


## KITA KYUSHU (北九州)

JYH Hostel 3★ ☎ 093-681-8142
7 Hobashira, Yahata Higashi-ku, Kita Kyushu-shi, Fukuoka 805.
**Closed in mid-June.** 56 beds
Station: Yahata (Kagoshima Main Line). Walk 25 mins. (1.7 km) uphill.
**¥2,700 (Discount ¥300).** Dinner ¥900. Breakfast ¥600.

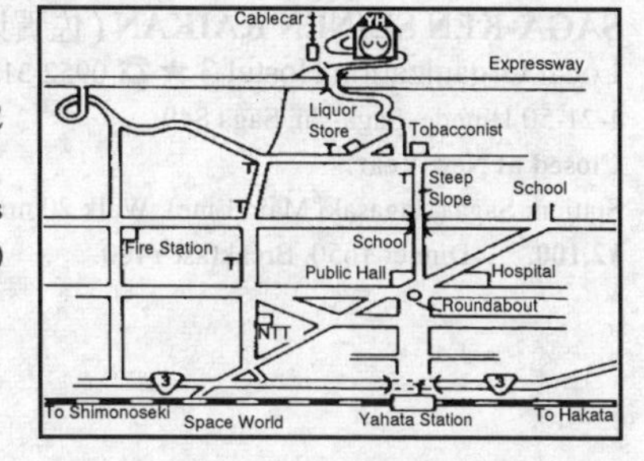

**IIZUKA YAKIYAMA KOGEN**
(飯塚八木山高原)
Local Organization Hostel 2★ ☎ 0948-22-6385
1270-14 Yakiyama, Iizuka-shi, Fukuoka 820.
**Closed in early December.** 90 beds
Station: Kido (Sasaguri Line). Take bus to Yakiyama Motomura (八木山本村), 10 mins. Walk 12 mins. (1 km).
**¥2,400 (Discount ¥200).** Dinner ¥800. Breakfast ¥500.

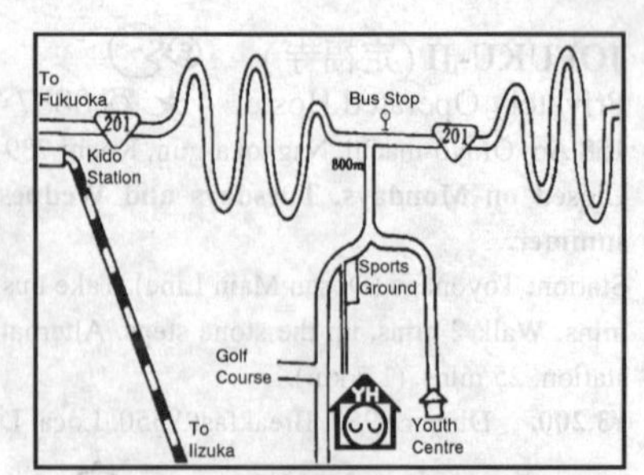


**DAZAIFU** (太宰府)
Privately Operated Hostel 3★ ☎ 092-922-8740
1-18-1 Sanjo, Dazaifu-shi, Fukuoka 818-01.
**Closed on Sundays.** 24 beds
Station: Dazaifu (Nishitetsu Private Railway). From JR Hakata, take subway 5 mins. (3 stations) to Tenjin. Change to Nishitetsu Private Railway. Change again at Futsuka-ichi. Walk 12 mins. (900 m).
**¥2,900.** Dinner ¥1,000. Breakfast ¥600.

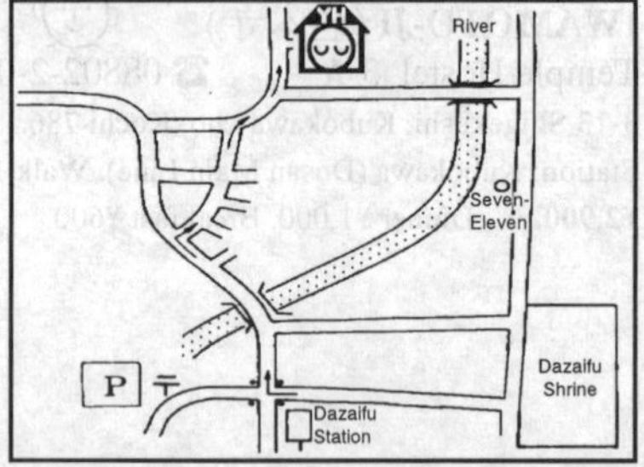


**RENOIR** (ルノワル)
Private Home 3★ ☎ 0944-62-2423
1380-3 Sakae-machi, Shimonosho, Setaka-machi, Fukuoka 835.
**Closed at New Year.** 24 beds
Station: Setaka (Kagoshima Main Line). Walk 13 mins. (800 m).
**¥2,700.** Dinner ¥900. Breakfast ¥500.

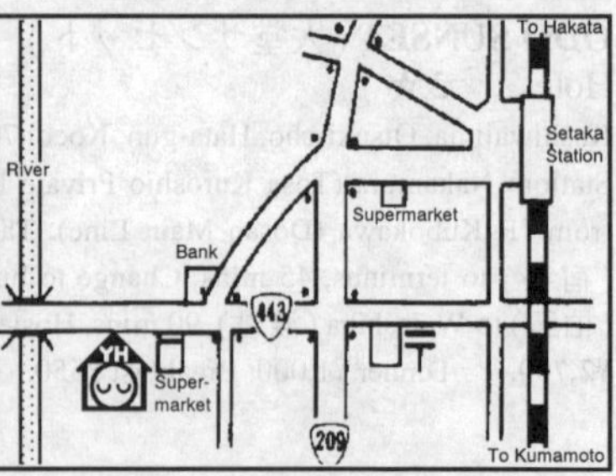


**SHIKANOSHIMA-SO** (志賀島荘)
Privately Operated Hostel 3★ ☎ 092-603-6557. Fax: 0862
1526-2 Shikanoshima, Higashi-ku, Fukuoka 811-03. 50 beds
Station: Saitozaki (Kashii Line). Take bus no. 21 or 21A to Shikanoshima Yubin-kyoku (志賀島郵便局), 13 mins. Walk 2 mins. Alternatively, from Hakata Port take ferry to Shikanoshima, 45 mins. Walk 4 mins.
¥2,900. Dinner ¥1,000. Breakfast ¥600.

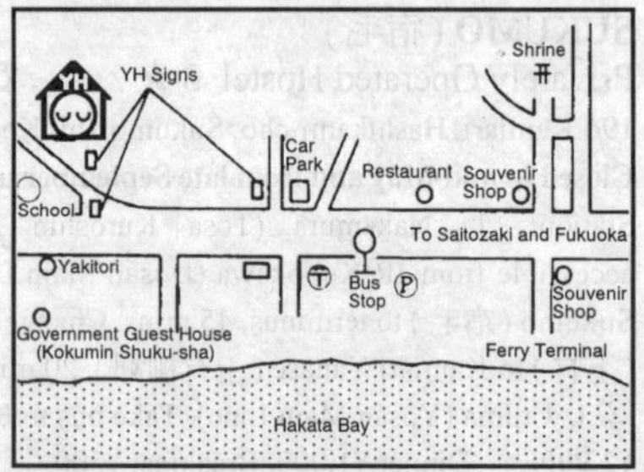


**SAGA-KEN SEINEN KAIKAN** (佐賀県青年会館)
Local Organization Hostel 3★ ☎ 0952-31-2328. Fax:0608
1-21-50 Hinode, Saga-shi, Saga 849.
**Closed at New Year.** 56 beds
Station: Saga (Nagasaki Main Line). Walk 20 mins.
**¥2,100.** Dinner ¥650. Breakfast ¥400.

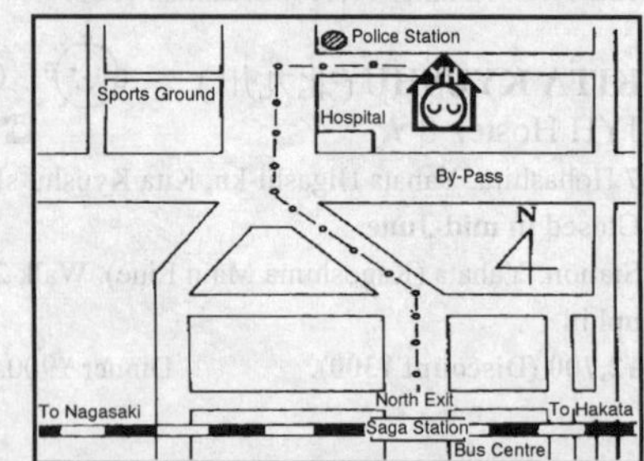

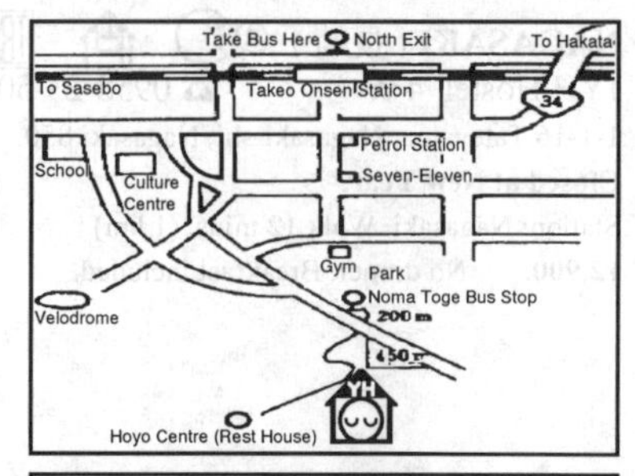


## TAKEO ONSEN (武雄温泉)

IBN

JYH Hostel 3★ ☎ 0954-22-2490

Nagashima, Takeo-machi, Takeo-shi, Saga 843.

**Closed from late May until early June.** 80 beds

Station: Takeo Onsen (Sasebo Line). Take bus for Hoyo Centre (保養センター) to Youth Hostel-mae, 7 mins. Walk 1 min.

**Caution:** Only two buses — at 15:19 and 16:19. At other times, hostellers may telephone hostel if they wish to be collected.

**¥2,500 (Discount ¥100).** Dinner ¥900. Breakfast ¥600.

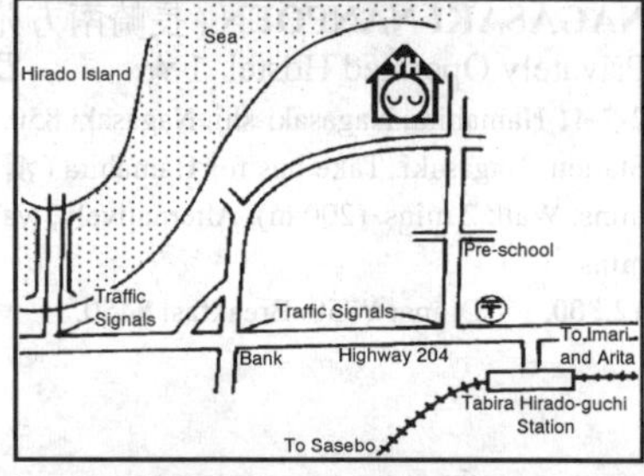


## HIRADO-GUCHI RAINBOW (平戸口レインボー)

JYH Hostel 2★ ☎ 0950-57-1443

1111-3 Nakase, Okubomen, Tabira-cho, Nagasaki 859-48.

**Closed in mid-June.** 100 beds

Station: Tabira Hirado Guchi (Matsuura Private Railway), accessible from JR Sasebo or Arita (Sasebo Line) or Imari (Chikuhi Line). Walk 25 mins. (1.7 km). After leaving station, turn left onto main highway, then right at traffic signals.

**¥2,500 (Discount ¥400).** Dinner ¥900. Breakfast ¥500.

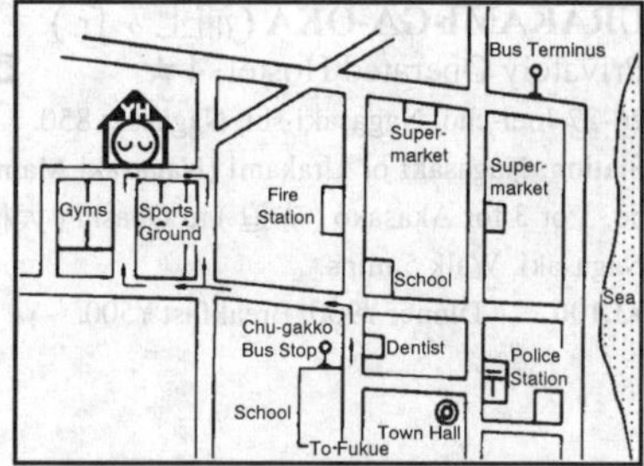


## GOTO MI-IRAKU SUNSET (五島三井楽サンセット)

JYH Hostel 3★ ☎ 0959-84-3151

493 Hamanohango, Miiraku-cho, Nagasaki 853-06.

**Closed in mid-June.** 100 beds

Station: Nagasaki. Walk 15 mins. to port. Take ferry to Fukue, 4 hrs. (or 2 hrs. by jet-foil). Walk 5 mins. to bus terminal. Take bus for Mi-iraku (三井楽) to Mi-iraku Chu-gakko (三井楽中学校), 1 hr. Walk 20 mins. Ferries also operate from Hakata Port (Fukuoka) to Fukue, 9 hrs.

**¥2,500 (Discount ¥500).** Dinner ¥900. Breakfast ¥500.

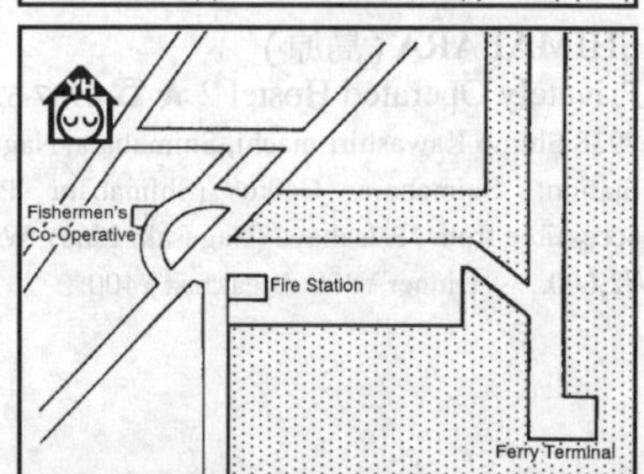


## TSUSHIMA SEIZAN-JI (対馬西山寺)

Temple Hostel 3★ ☎ 09205-2-0444

1453 Kokubu, Izuhara-machi, Nagasaki 817. 16 beds

Station: Hakata. Take bus to port (Hakata-ko — 博多港), 20 mins. Then take ferry for Tsushima to Izuhara, 5 hrs. (or 2 hrs. 10 mins. by jet-foil). Walk 10 mins. (600 m).

**¥2,100.** Dinner ¥800. Breakfast ¥500.

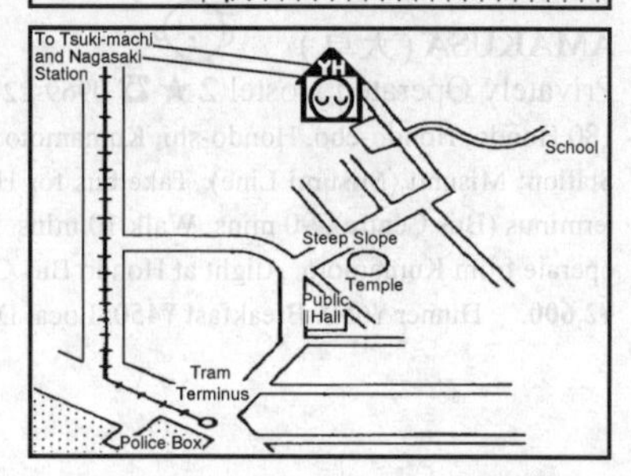


## OLANDA-ZAKA (オランダ坂)

Privately Operated Hostel 2★ ☎ 0958-22-2730

6-14 Higashi Yamate-machi, Nagasaki-shi, Nagasaki 850. 55 beds

Station: Nagasaki. Take tram no. 1 to Tsuki-machi (築町). Obtain transfer ticket and change to tram no. 5 to Ishibashi (石橋), total 20 mins. Walk 5 mins. Alternatively, walk from station, 40 mins. Turn right at main exit and follow tram tracks to Olanda-zaka.

**¥2,500.** No meals.

**NAGASAKI** (長崎)

JYH Hostel 4★ ☎ 0958-23-5032. Fax: 4321

1-1-16 Tateyama, Nagasaki-shi, Nagasaki 850.

**Closed at New Year.** 122 beds

Station: Nagasaki. Walk 12 mins. (1 km).

**¥2,900.** No dinner. Breakfast included.

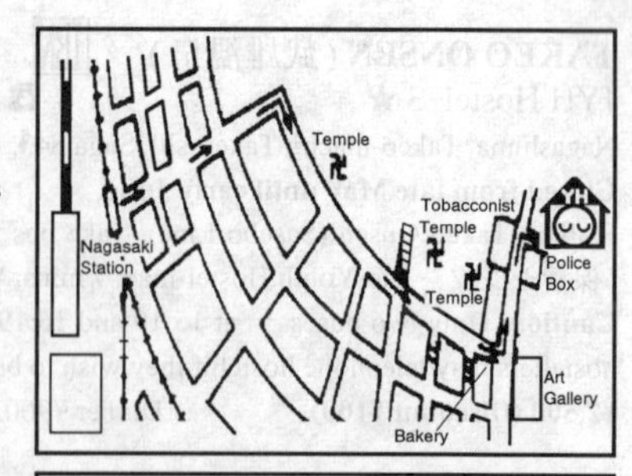


**NAGASAKI NANPOEN** (長崎南方苑)

Privately Operated Hostel 1★ ☎ 0958-23-5526

2-7-41 Hamahira, Nagasaki-shi, Nagasaki 850. 28 beds

Station: Nagasaki. Take bus for Hamahira (浜平) to terminus, 7 mins. Walk 2 mins. (200 m). Alternatively, walk from station, 30 mins.

**¥2,500.** Dinner ¥750. Breakfast ¥450.

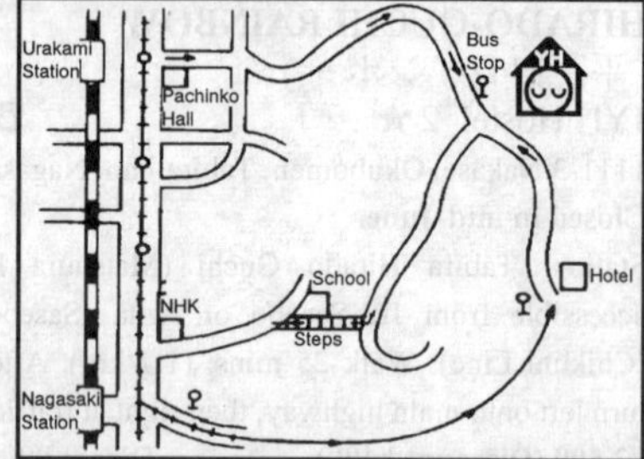


**URAKAMI-GA-OKA** (浦上ヶ丘)

Privately Operated Hostel 4★ ☎ 0958-47-8473

26-27 Joei-cho, Nagasaki-shi, Nagasaki 850. 56 beds

Station: Nagasaki or Urakami (Nagasaki Main Line). Take tram no. 1 or 3 for Akasako (赤迫) to Ohashi (大橋), 10 mins. from Nagasaki. Walk 5 mins.

**¥3,100.** Dinner ¥900. Breakfast ¥500.

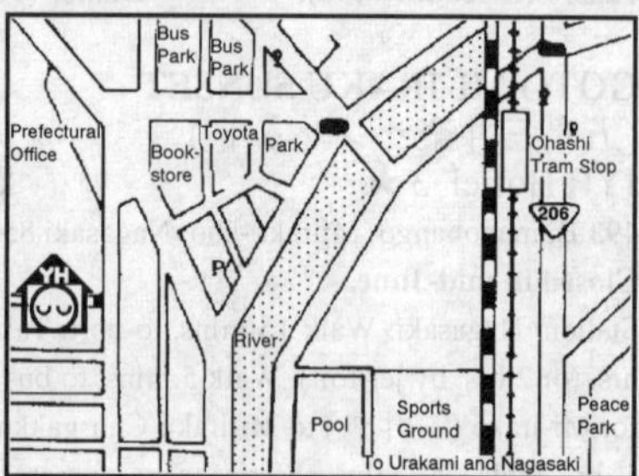


**SHIMABARA** (島原)

Privately Operated Hostel 2★ ☎ 0957-62-4451. Fax: 6107

7938 Shimo Kawashiri-machi, Shimabara, Nagasaki 855. 58 beds

Station: Shimabara Gaiko (Shimabara Private Railway), accessible from JR Isahaya (Nagasaki Line). Walk 1 min.

**¥2,600.** Dinner ¥800. Breakfast ¥400.

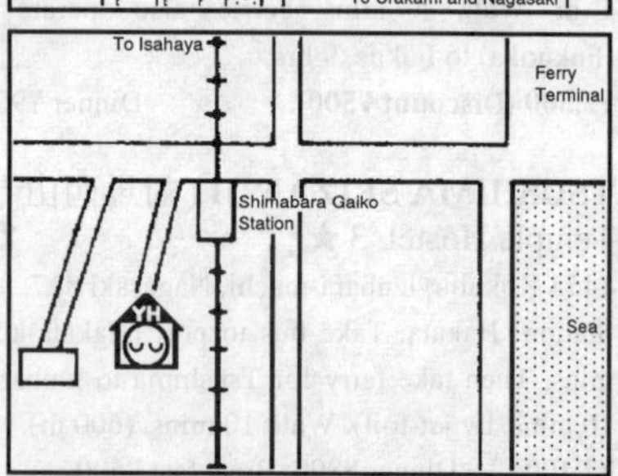


**AMAKUSA** (天草)

Privately Operated Hostel 2★ ☎ 0969-22-3085. Fax: 2257

180 Hondo, Hondo-cho, Hondo-shi, Kumamoto 863. 60 beds

Station: Misumi (Misumi Line). Take bus for Hondo (本渡) to terminus (Bus Centre), 90 mins. Walk 10 mins. Direct buses also operate from Kumamoto. Alight at Hondo Bus Centre.

**¥2,600.** Dinner ¥650. Breakfast ¥450. Local Delicacies ¥1,000.

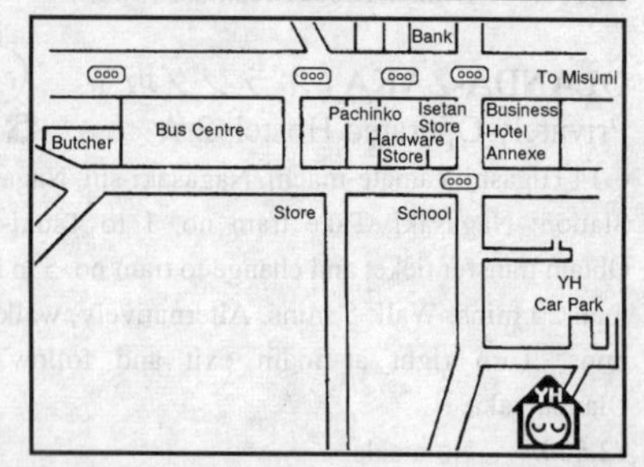

## KUMAMOTO SHI-RITSU (熊本市立)

Local Organization Hostel ☎ 096-352-2441

5-15-55 Shimazaki, Kumamoto-shi, Kumamoto 860.

**Closed at New Year.** 64 beds

Station: Kumamoto. Take tram for Suizenji (水前寺) or Kotsu-kyoku (交通局) to Karashima-cho (辛島町), 10 mins. Walk 2 mins. to Kumamoto Kotsu Centre. From bus stop no. 24, take bus no. 6 for Arao-bashi (荒尾橋) to Kuriyama Youth Hostel-mae, 20 mins. Hostel is opposite. Alternatively, walk to hostel from Kami Kumamoto station. Follow tram lines to bridge shown on map (about 1 km). Turn right shortly afterwards.

**¥1,900.** Dinner ¥600. Breakfast ¥400.

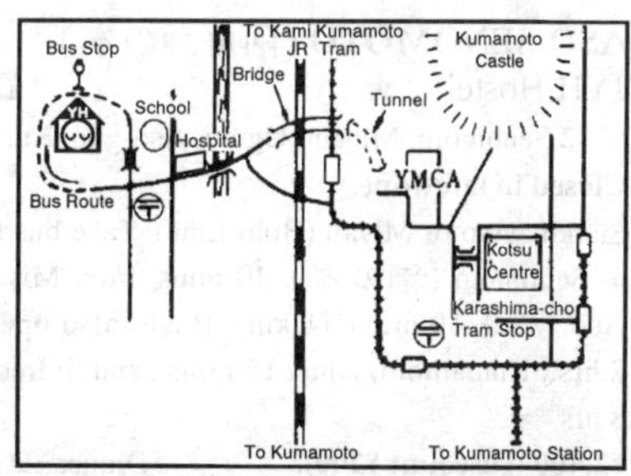


## SUIZENJI (水前寺)

Private Home 3★ ☎ 096-371-9193

1-2-20 Hakusan, Kumamoto-shi, Kumamoto 860.

**Closed at New Year.** 20 beds

Station: ① Shin Suizenji (Hohi Line). Walk 3 mins. Express trains run directly from Hakata.

② Kumamoto. Take tram for Suizenji (水前寺) to Misotenjin (味曽天神), 25 mins. Walk 2 mins.

**¥2,600.** No dinner. Breakfast ¥500.

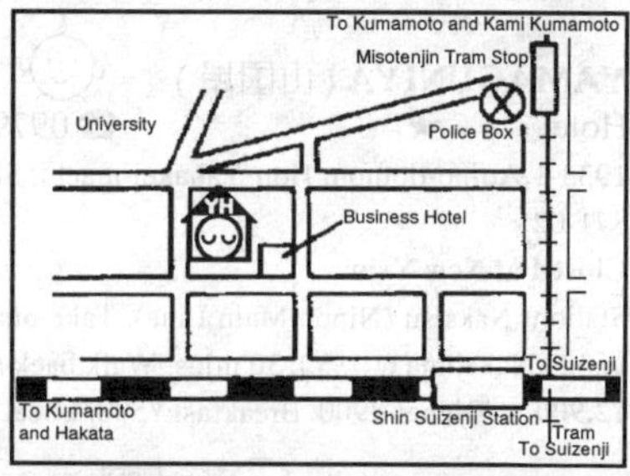


## ASO (阿蘇)

Local Organization Hostel 3★ ☎ 0967-34-0804

922-2 Bochu, Aso-machi, Aso-gun, Kumamoto 869-22.

**Closed at New Year.** 60 beds

Station: Aso (Hohi Line). Walk 16 mins. (1.3 km).

**¥2,100.** Dinner ¥700. Breakfast ¥400.

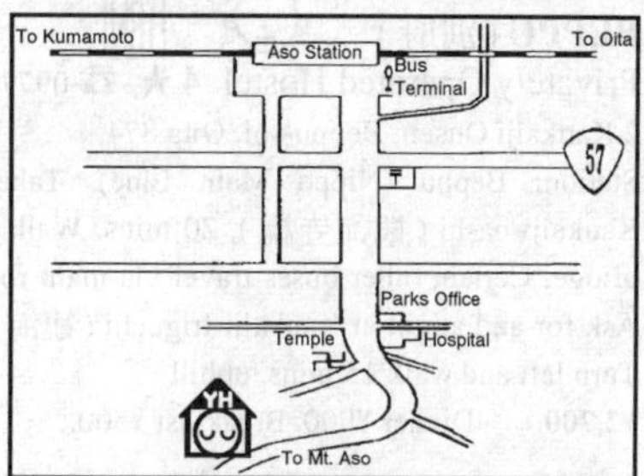


## KUMAMOTO Y.M.C.A. ASO CAMP

(熊本YMCA阿蘇キャンプ)

Local Organization Hostel 3★☎ 0967-35-0124. Fax:1642

Kurumagaeri, Aso-machi, Aso-gun, Kumamoto 869-22. 35 beds

Station: Akamizu (Hohi Line). Walk 30 mins. (2 km).

**¥2,100.** Dinner ¥850. Breakfast ¥450.

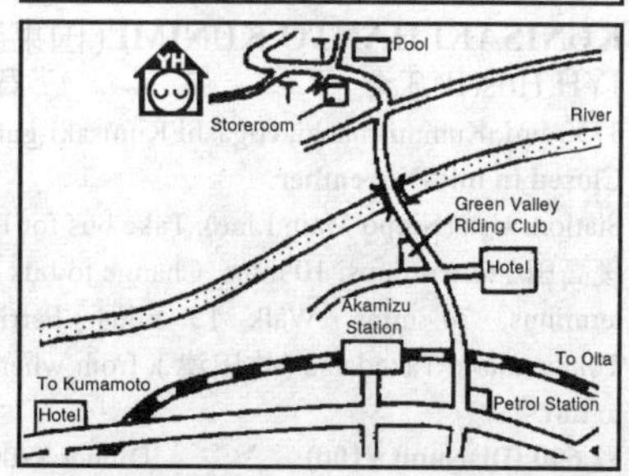


## MURATAYA RYOKAN (村田家旅館)

Hotel 3★ ☎ 09676-2-0066

1672 Takamori, Aso-gun, Kumamoto 869-16. 30 beds

Station: Takamori (Minami Aso Private Railway), accessible from JR Tateno (Hohi Line). Walk 8 mins. (550 m).

**New Year ¥2,900. Otherwise ¥2,700.**

Dinner ¥800. Breakfast ¥500.

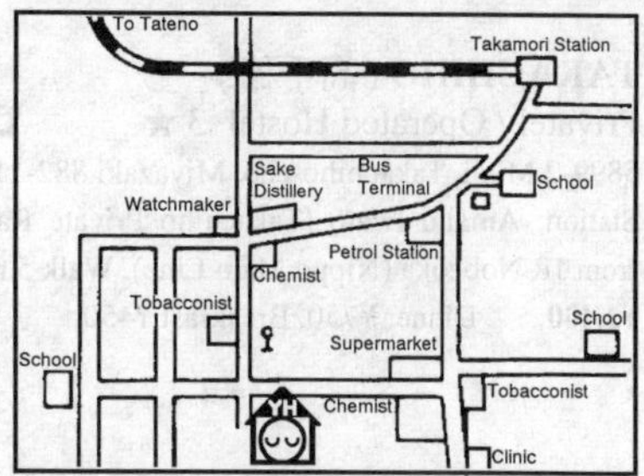

## ASO SENOMOTO (阿蘇瀬の本)

JYH Hostel 2★ ☎ 0967-44-0157

6332 Senomoto, Minami Oguni, Aso-gun, Kumamoto 869-24.

**Closed in late June.** 56 beds

Station: Aso or Miyaji (Hohi Line). Take bus for Beppu (別府) to Senomoto (瀬の本), 40 mins. from Miyaji, 50 mins. from Aso. Walk 10 mins. (1 km). Buses also operate from Beppu, 2 hrs., Kumamoto, 2 hrs. 15 mins., and, infrequently, Nagasaki, 8 hrs.

**¥2,400 (Discount ¥200).** Dinner ¥900. Breakfast ¥500.

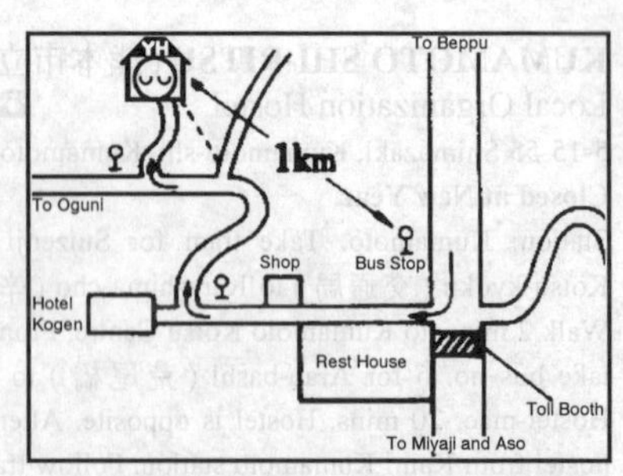


## YAMAGUNIYA (山国屋)

Hotel 3★ ☎ 0979-52-2008, 2711

1933-1 Ao-no-domon, Hon Yabakei-machi, Shimo Ke-gun, Oita 871-02.

**Closed at New Year.** 50 beds

Station: Nakatsu (Nippo Main Line). Take bus for Kakisaka (柿坂) to Nakajima (中島), 30 mins. Walk back across river, 1 min.

**¥2,900.** Dinner ¥900. Breakfast ¥500. Local Delicacies ¥1,500.

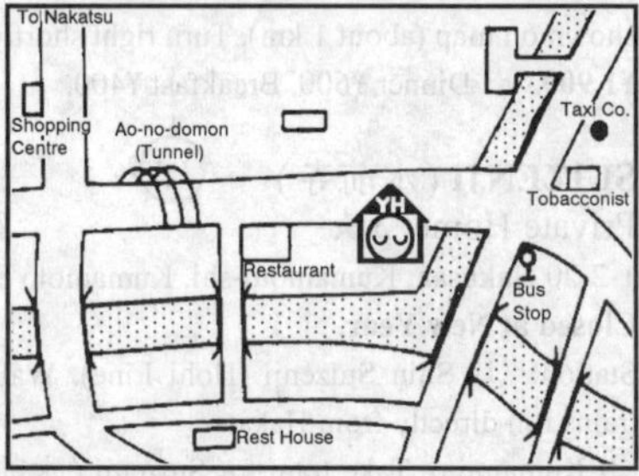


## BEPPU (別府)

Privately Operated Hostel 4★ ☎ 0977-23-4116, 22-0086

2 Kankaiji Onsen, Beppu-shi, Oita 874. 95 beds

Station: Beppu (Nippo Main Line). Take bus no. 10 to Kankaiji-bashi (観海寺橋), 20 mins. Walk 4 mins. across the bridge. Certain other buses travel via main road shown on map. Ask for and alight at Kankaiji Iriguchi (観海寺入口), 15 mins. Turn left and walk 15 mins. uphill.

**¥2,700.** Dinner ¥900. Breakfast ¥500.

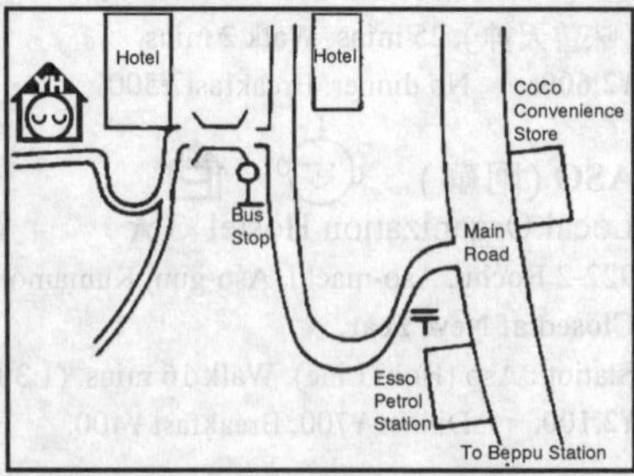


## KUNISAKI HANTO KUNIMI (国東半島国見)

JYH Hostel 3★ ☎ 0978-82-0104

3750 Imi, Kunimi-machi, Higashi Kunisaki-gun, Oita 872-14.

**Closed in mid-November.** 60 beds

Station: Usa (Nippo Main Line). Take bus for Bungo Takada (豊後高田) to terminus, 10 mins. Change to bus for Imi (伊美) to terminus, 70 mins. Walk 15 mins. Ferries operate from Tokuyama to Takedatsu (竹田津), from where 10 mins. by bus to Imi.

**¥2,600 (Discount ¥100).** Dinner ¥900. Breakfast ¥500.

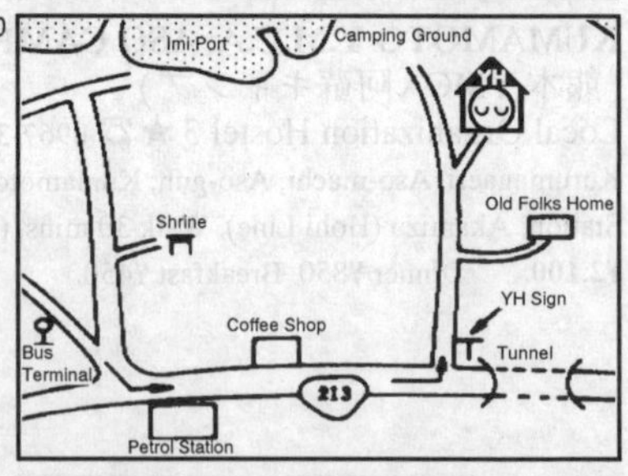


## TAKACHIHO (高千穂)

Privately Operated Hostel 3★ ☎ 0982-72-3021

5899-2 Mitai, Takachiho-cho, Miyazaki 882-11. 50 beds

Station: Amano Iwato (Takachiho Private Railway), accessible from JR Nobeoka (Nippo Main Line). Walk 5 mins. (150 m).

**¥2,400.** Dinner ¥750. Breakfast ¥450.

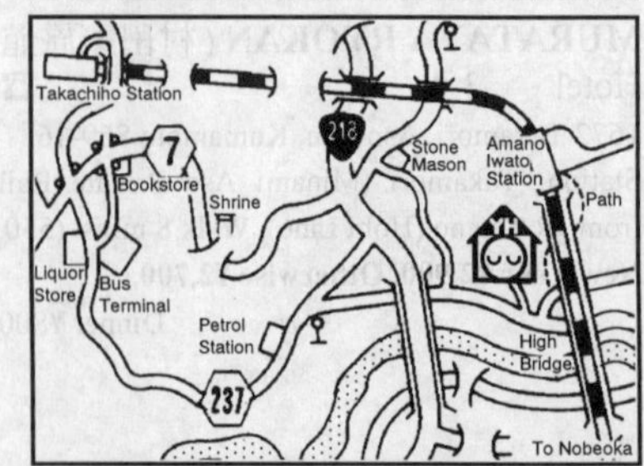

## YAMATOYA (大和屋)

Hotel 3★ ☎ 0982-72-2243, 3808

1148 Mitai, Takachiho-cho, Miyazaki 882-11. 100 beds

Station: Takachiho (Takachiho Private Railway), accessible from JR Nobeoka (Nippo Main Line). Walk 12 mins. (700 m).

**¥2,600.** Dinner ¥900. Breakfast ¥600.

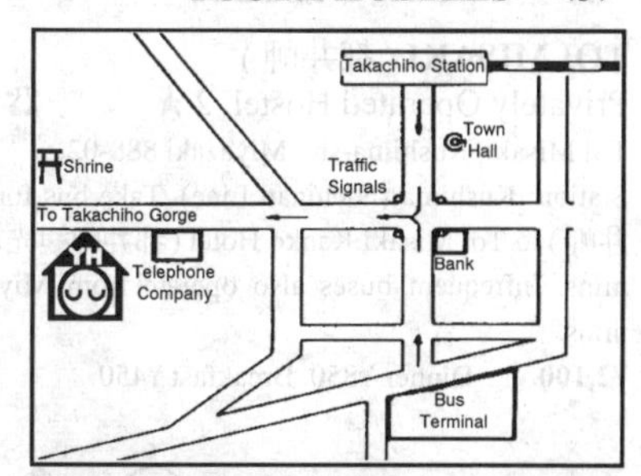


## MIYAKONOJO (都城)

Hotel 3★ ☎ 0986-38-0022

6361-1 Tohoku-cho, Miyakonojo-shi, Miyazaki 885. 17 beds

Station: Miyakonojo (Nippo Main Line). Take bus for Miyazaki (宮崎) via Expressway (高速一 'kosoku'), or for Suzumegano (雀ヶ野), or for Arimizu Drive-in (有水ドライブイン) to Matsunomoto (松の元). Walk 1 min. Alternatively, walk from station, 35 mins. (2.4 km).

**Caution:** Last bus 18:59.

**¥2,400.** Dinner ¥1,000. Breakfast ¥500.

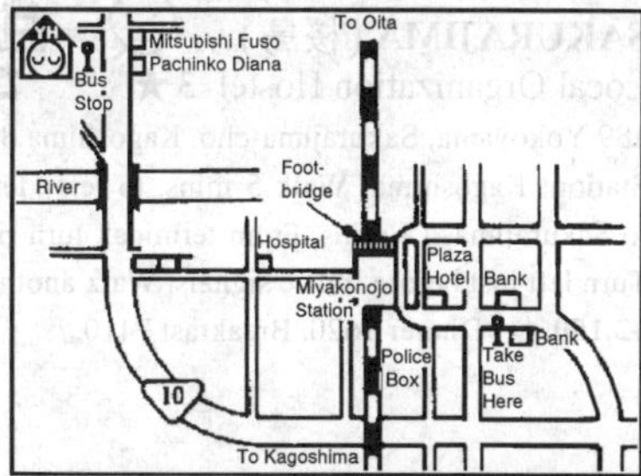


## MIYAZAKI-KEN FUJIN KAIKAN (宮崎県婦人会館)

Local Organization Hostel 3★ ☎ 0985-24-5785.

1-3-10 Asahi, Miyazaki-shi, Miyazaki 880.

**Closed at New Year.** 26 beds

Station: Miyazaki (Nippo Main Line). Walk 15 mins. (1.1 km).

**¥2,400.** No meals.

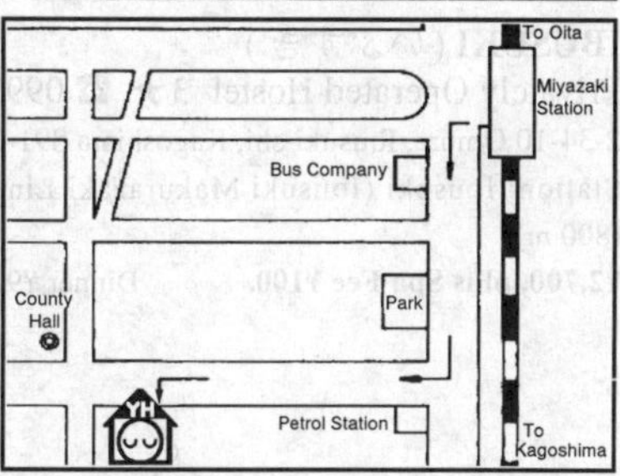


## AOSHIMA (青島)

Local Organization Hostel 3★ ☎ 0985-65-1657

130 Umizoi, Oryuzako, Miyazaki-shi, Miyazaki 889-21.100 beds

Station: Kodomo-no-kuni (Nichinan Line). Walk 8 mins.

**Summer ¥2,300. Winter ¥2,000.** Dinner ¥650. Breakfast ¥400.

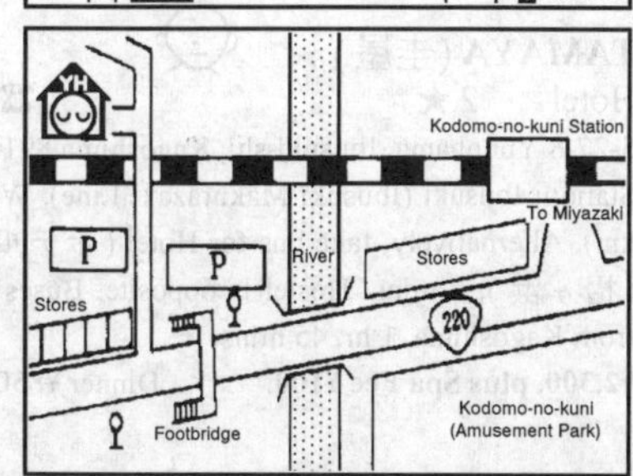


## NICHINAN KAIGAN (日南海岸)

Local Organization Hostel 3★ ☎ 0987-27-0113

Ko 2348 Kumaya, Nichinan-shi, Miyazaki 889-31. 58 beds

Station: Odotsu (Nichinan Line). Walk 20 mins. (1.6 km).

**¥2,400.** Dinner ¥900. Breakfast ¥500.

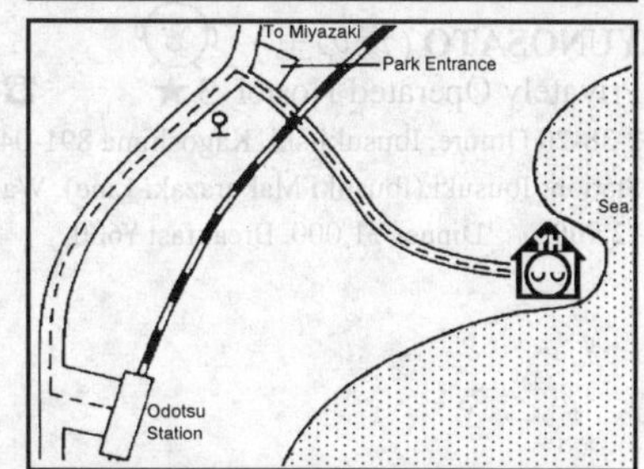

## TOI MISAKI (都井岬)

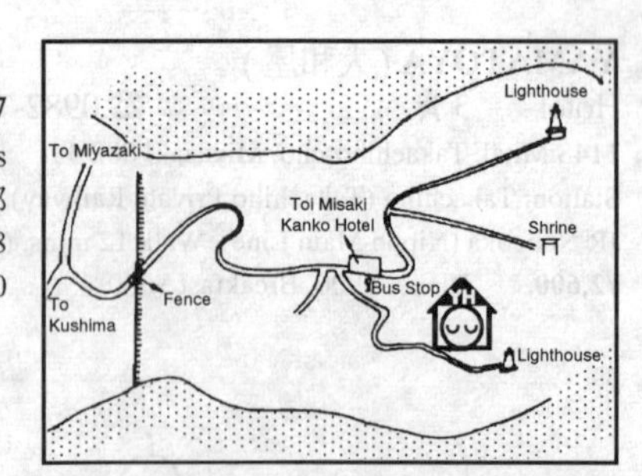


Privately Operated Hostel 2★ ☎ 0987-76-1397

Toi Misaki, Kushima-shi, Miyazaki 888-02. 30 beds

Station: Kushima (Nichinan Line). Take bus for Toi Misaki (都井岬) to Toi Misaki Kanko Hotel (都井岬観光ホテル). Walk 8 mins. Infrequent buses also operate from Miyazaki, 2 hrs. 50 mins.

**¥2,100.** Dinner ¥850. Breakfast ¥450.

## SAKURAJIMA (桜島)

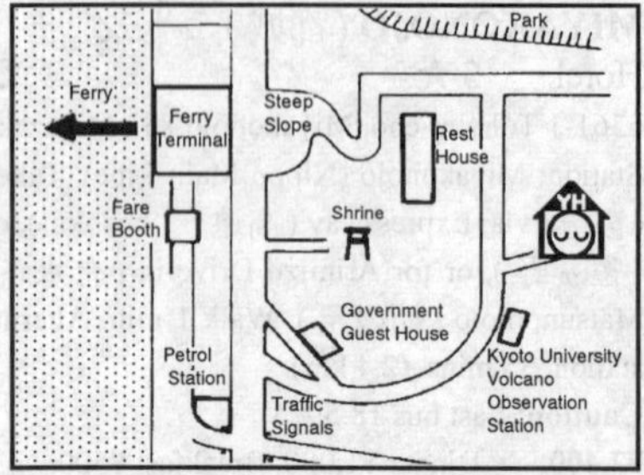


Local Organization Hostel 3★ ☎ 0992-93-2150

189 Yokoyama, Sakurajima-cho, Kagoshima 891-14. 100 beds

Station: Kagoshima. Walk 5 mins. to ferry terminal. Take ferry to Sakurajima, 15 mins. From terminal, turn right. Walk 2 mins. Turn left just before traffic signals. Walk another 5 mins.

**¥2,150.** Dinner ¥620. Breakfast ¥410.

## IBUSUKI (いぶすき)

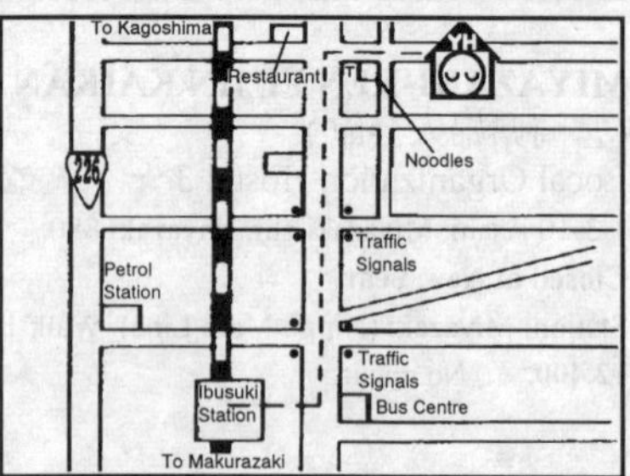


Privately Operated Hostel 3★ ☎ 0993-22-2758, 2271

2-34-10 Omure, Ibusuki-shi, Kagoshima 891-04. 21 beds

Station: Ibusuki (Ibusuki Makurazaki Line). Walk 10 mins. (800 m).

**¥2,700, plus Spa Fee ¥100.** Dinner ¥900. Breakfast ¥500.

## TAMAYA (圭屋)

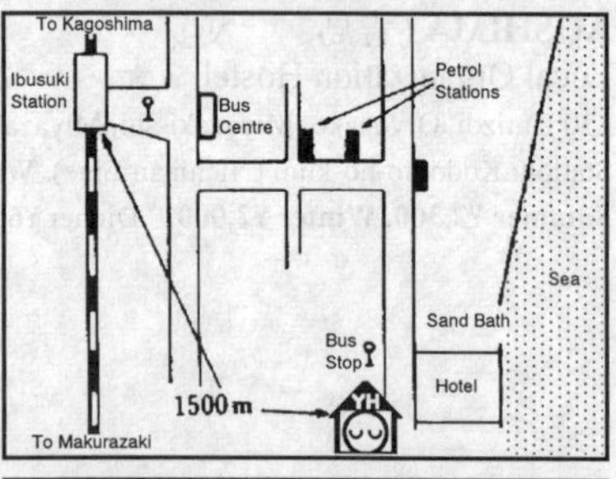


Hotel 2★ ☎ 0993-22-3553

5-27-8 Yunohama, Ibusuki-shi, Kagoshima 891-04. 35 beds

Station: Ibusuki (Ibusuki Makurazaki Line). Walk 20 mins. (1.5 km). Alternatively, take bus for Hotel (ホテル) to Surigahama (摺ヶ浜), 5 mins. Hostel is opposite. Buses also run directly from Kagoshima, 1 hr. 45 mins.

**¥2,300, plus Spa Fee ¥100.** Dinner ¥850. Breakfast ¥450.

## YUNOSATO (湯の里)

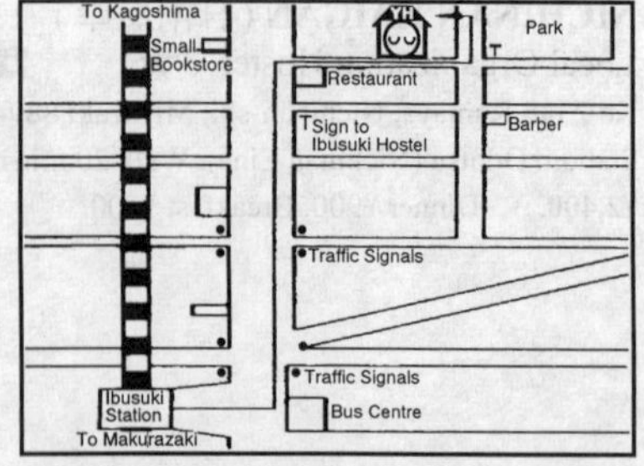


Privately Operated Hostel 3★ ☎ 0993-22-5680

2-38-20 Omure, Ibusuki-shi, Kagoshima 891-04. 20 beds

Station: Ibusuki (Ibusuki Makurazaki Line). Walk 12 mins.

**¥2,900.** Dinner ¥1,000. Breakfast ¥600.

## KIRISHIMA JINGU-MAE (霧島神宮前)

Hotel 2★ ☎ 0995-57-1188

2459 Taguchi, Kirishima-cho, Aira-gun, Kagoshima 899-42.

**Closed at New Year.** 30 beds

Station: Kirishima Jingu (Nippo Main Line). Take bus for Hayashi-da Onsen (林田温泉) to Kirishima Jingu-mae (霧島神宮前), 12 mins. Walk 1 min. (100 m).

**¥2,600, plus Spa Fee ¥150.** Dinner ¥1,000. Breakfast ¥500.

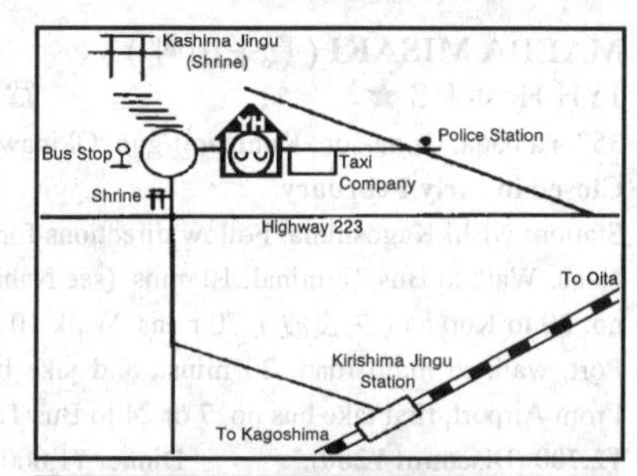


## OKINOERABU (沖永良部)

Privately Operated Hostel ☎ 09979-2-2024

450 Akubo, Furusato, Wadomari-cho, Oshima-gun, Kagoshima 891-91. 20 beds

Station: Nishi Kagoshima. Take bus for Kagoshima Shin-ko (鹿児島新港) to terminus, 20 mins. Then take ferry to Okinoerabu, 18 hrs. From Wadomari Port, take bus for Cheena (知名) to Furusato (古里), 15 mins. Walk 1 min.

**¥2,000.** Dinner ¥1,000. Breakfast available in café.

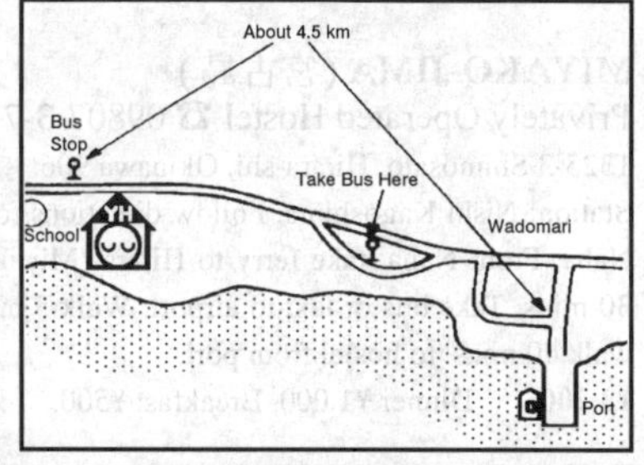


## YORON-TO TAKAKURA-SO (与論島高倉荘)

Privately Operated Hostel ☎ 0997-97-2273

1025 Chabana, Yoron-machi, Oshima-gun, Kagoshima 891-93. 60 beds

Station: Nishi Kagoshima. Take bus for Kagoshima Shin-ko (鹿児島新港) to terminus, 20 mins. Then take ferry to Yoron-to, 20 to 21 hrs. Walk 30 mins. (2.5 km) or look for hostel mini-bus at port.

**¥2,200.** Dinner ¥750. Breakfast ¥450.

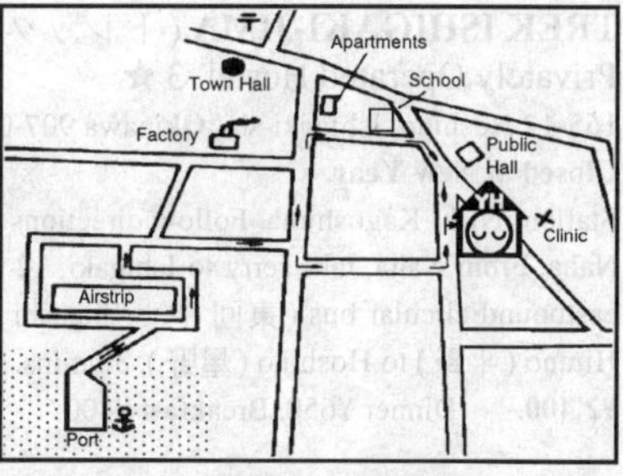


## OKINAWA KOKUSAI (沖縄国際) 

JYH Hostel ☎ 098-857-0073

51 Onoyama-cho, Naha-shi, Okinawa 900. 200 beds

Station: Nishi Kagoshima. Take bus for Kagoshima Shin-ko (鹿児島新港) to terminus, 20 mins. Then take ferry to Naha, 19 to 28 hrs. Walk 15 mins. Ferries also operate from Tokyo, Osaka, Kobe, Fukuoka and Taiwan. Some ferries arrive at New Port, from where take bus no. 101 to Asahi-machi (旭町), 40 mins. From Airport, take bus no. 24 or 102 to Koen-mae (公園前), 5 mins.

**¥3,200 (Discount ¥200).** Dinner ¥1,000. Breakfast ¥600.

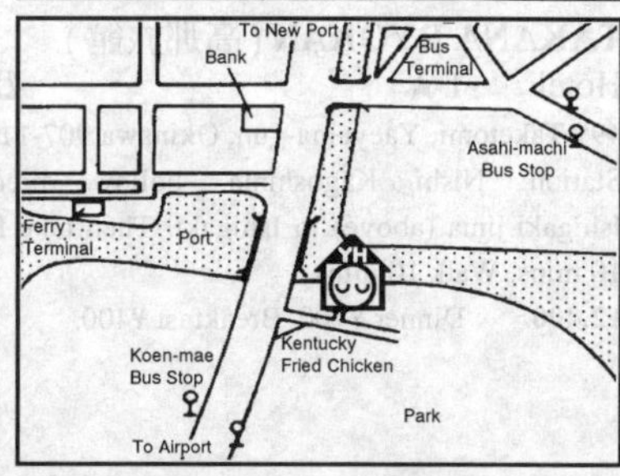


## CITY FRONT HARUMI (シティーフロント春海) IBN

Privately Operated Hostel 4★ ☎ 098-867-3218, 4422

2-22-10 Tomari, Naha-shi, Okinawa 900. 38 beds

Station: Nishi Kagoshima. Follow directions for Naha (above) to Naha. Take bus no. 3 to Tomari Takahashi (泊高橋), 15 mins. Walk 3 mins. From New Port take bus no. 101 to Tomari Takahashi, 15 mins. From Airport, take bus no. 24 to Tomari Takahashi, 25 mins.

**¥3,000 (Discount ¥200).** Dinner ¥1,000. Breakfast ¥600.

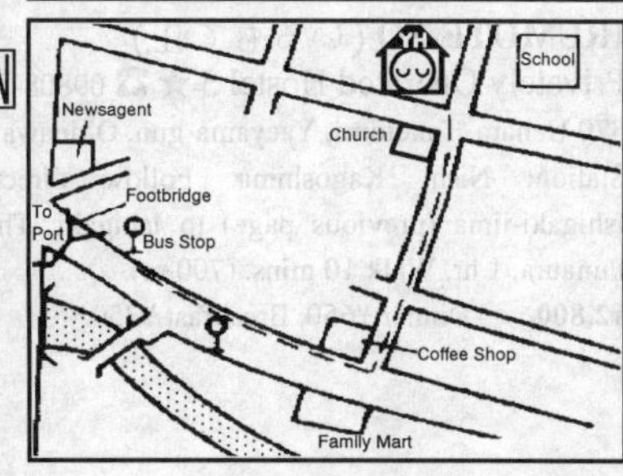

**MAEDA MISAKI** (真栄田岬)

JYH Hostel 3★ ☎ 098-964-2497

357 Yamada, Onna-son, Kunigami-gun, Okinawa 904-04.

**Closed in early February.** 50 beds

Station: Nishi Kagoshima. Follow directions for Naha (above) to Naha. Walk to Bus Terminal, 10 mins. (see Naha map). Take bus no. 20 to Kuraha (久良波), 70 mins. Walk 10 mins. From New Port, walk to main road, 20 mins., and take bus no. 20, 1 hr. From Airport, first take bus no. 7 or 24 to Bus Terminal, 10 mins.

**¥2,700 (Discount ¥200).** Dinner ¥1,000. Breakfast ¥600.

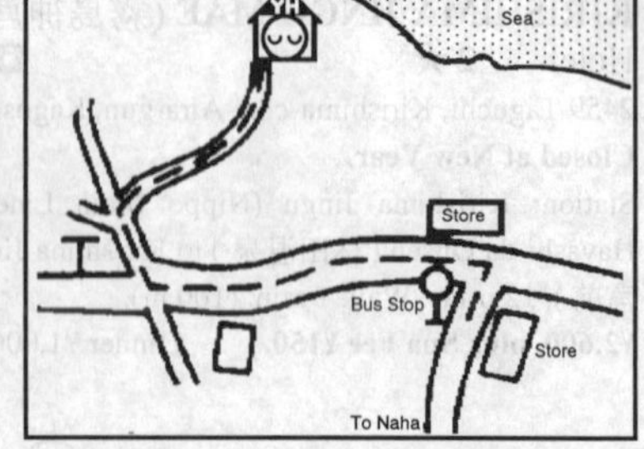


**MIYAKO-JIMA** (宮古島)

Privately Operated Hostel ☎ 09807-3-7700. Fax: 7890

1325-3 Shimosato, Hirara-shi, Okinawa 906. 40 beds

Station: Nishi Kagoshima. Follow directions for Naha (above) to Naha. From Naha, take ferry to Hirara (Miyako Island), 10 hrs. 30 mins. Take bus or taxi to airport. Walk 5 mins. Alternatively, walk 40 mins. to hostel from port.

**¥3,200.** Dinner ¥1,000. Breakfast ¥500.

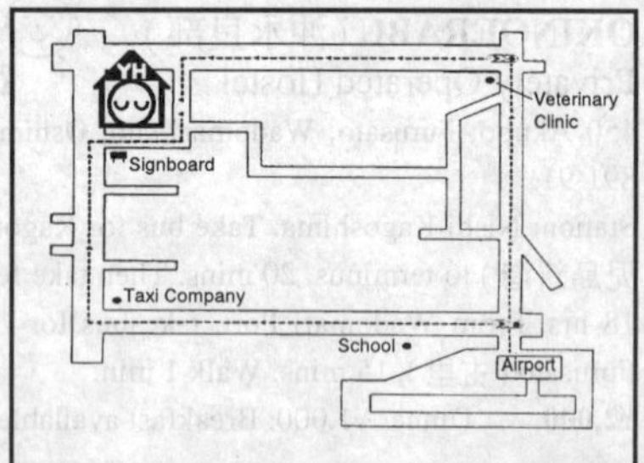


**TREK ISHIGAKI-JIMA** (トレック石垣島)

Privately Operated Hostel 3★ ☎ 09808-6-8257

165-12 Hoshino, Ishigaki-shi, Okinawa 907-02.

**Closed at New Year.** 12 beds

Station: Nishi Kagoshima. Follow directions for Naha (above) to Naha. From Naha, take ferry to Ishigaki, 12 to 19 hrs. Now take eastbound circular bus (東回り一 'higashi mawari') or bus for Hirano (平野) to Hoshino (星野), 30 mins. Walk 1 min.

**¥2,400.** Dinner ¥650. Breakfast ¥400.

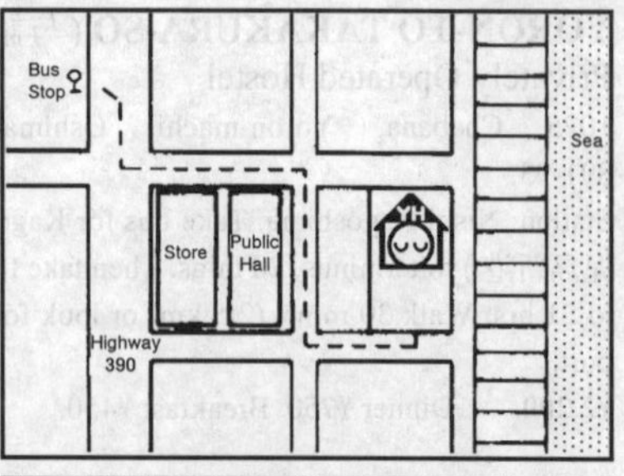


**TAKANA RYOKAN** (高那旅館)

Hotel 1★ ☎ 09808-5-2151

499 Taketomi, Yaeyama-gun, Okinawa 907-11. 35 beds

Station: Nishi Kagoshima. Follow directions for Trek Ishigaki-jima (above) to Ishigaki. Then take ferry to Taketomi, 10 mins. Walk 10 mins.

**¥2,400.** Dinner ¥700. Breakfast ¥400.

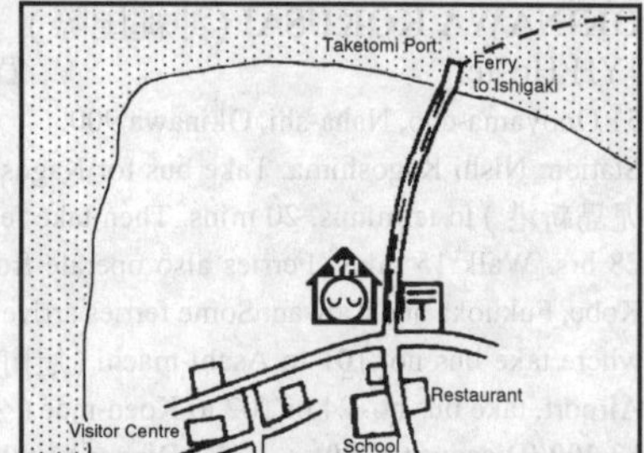


**IRUMOTE-SO** (いるもて荘)

Privately Operated Hostel 3★☎ 09808-5-6255. Fax: 6076

870 Uehara, Taketomi, Yaeyama-gun, Okinawa 907-15. 45 beds

Station: Nishi Kagoshima. Follow directions for Trek Ishigaki-jima (previous page) to Ishigaki. Then take ferry to Funaura, 1 hr. Walk 10 mins. (700 m).

**¥2,800.** Dinner ¥650. Breakfast ¥350.

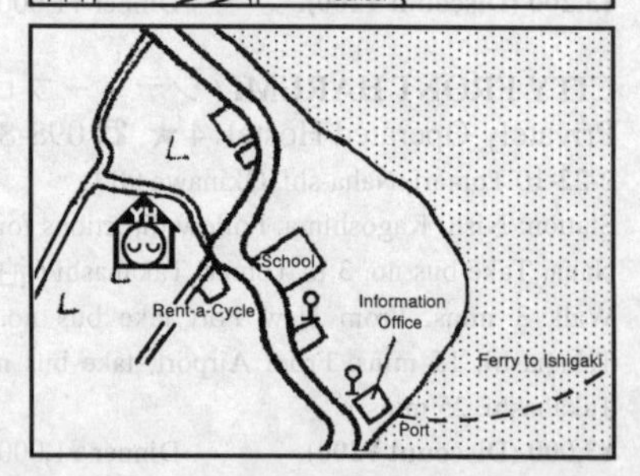

**IRIOMOTE-JIMA MIDORI-SO** (西表島みどり荘)
Hotel 2★ ☎ 09808-5-6526, 6253
572-5 Uehara, Taketomi, Yaeyama-gun, Okinawa 907-11. 32 beds
Station: Nishi Kagoshima. Follow directions for Trek Ishigaki-jima (previous page) to Ishigaki. Then take ferry to Funaura, 1 hr. Take bus for Shirahama (白浜) to Uehara (上原), 5 mins. Walk 1 min. Alternatively, walk from port, 30 mins.
**¥2,400.** Dinner ¥650. Breakfast ¥400.

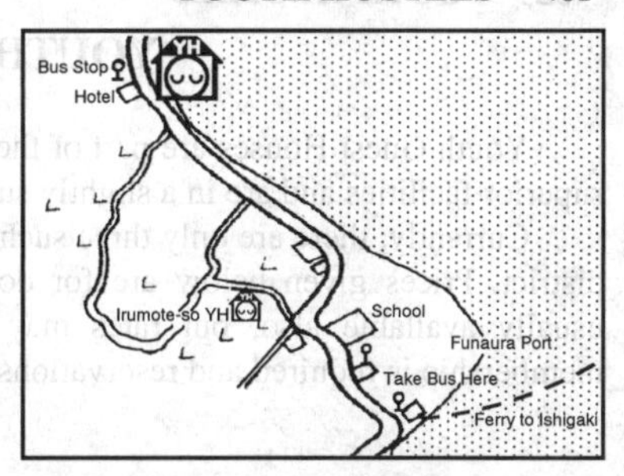


## LATE ADDITIONS

**NASU YUKARA-SO** (那須ゆうから荘)
Privately Operated Hostel ☎ 0287-68-1172
1677-29 Takabayashi, Kuroiso-shi, Tochigi 325-01. 12 beds
Station: Kuroiso (Tohoku Main Line). Take bus for Itamuro Onsen (板室温泉) to Kaitaku Jimsho-mae (開拓事務所前), 15 mins. Walk 20 mins. (1.8 km).
**¥3,200, plus Spa Fee ¥130.** Dinner ¥1,000. Breakfast ¥600.

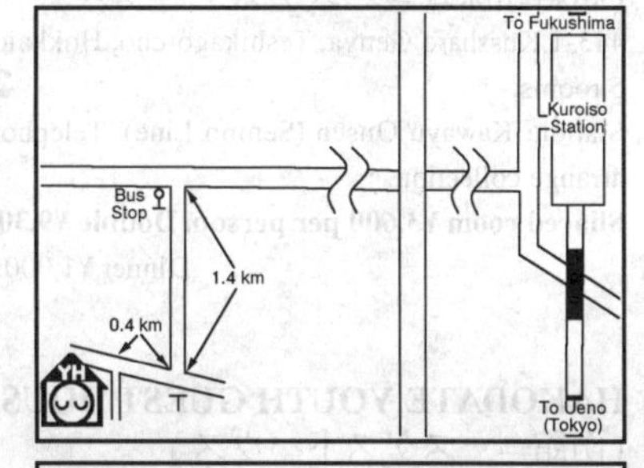


**RIVERSIDE INUYAMA KOKUSAI**
(リバーサイド犬山国際)
Local Organization Hostel ☎ 0568-61-1111
162-1 Himuro, Tsugao, Inuyama, Aichi 484. 80 beds
Station: ① Inuyama Yuen (Meitetsu Private Railway), accessible from JR Nagoya and several other stations. Walk 25 mins.
② Unuma (Takayama Line). Walk 35 mins.
**¥2,900.** Dinner from ¥1,000. Breakfast from ¥600.

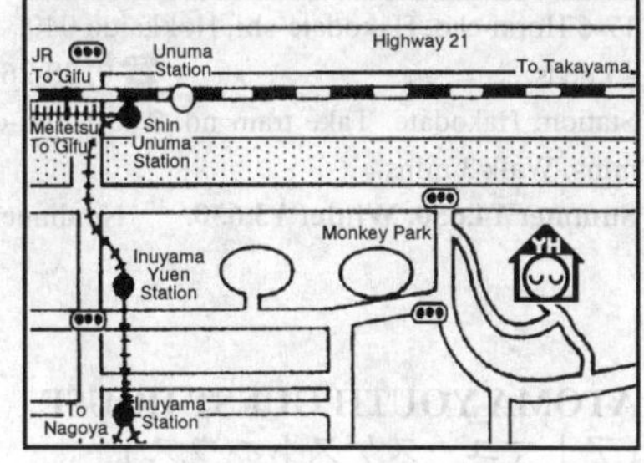

# YOUTH GUEST HOUSES

Youth Guest Houses are part of the Youth Hostels organization, but they offer somewhat superior facilities and are in a slightly superior price range.

Currently, there are only three such guest houses, two in Hokkaido and one in the Tohoku district. Prices given below are for dormitory or shared rooms. Twin or group rooms are usually available also, but rates may be somewhat higher. As with the Youth Hostels, membership is required and reservations should always be made in advance.

## KUSSHARO GENYA YOUTH GUEST HOUSE
(屈斜路原野ユースゲストハウス)

443-1 Kussharo Genya, Teshikago-cho, Hokkaido 088-33.

5 rooms. ☎ 01548-4-2609

Station: Kawayu Onsen (Senmo Line). Telephone in advance to arrange collection.

**Shared room ¥3,600 per person. Double ¥9,300.**

Dinner ¥1,000. Breakfast ¥600.

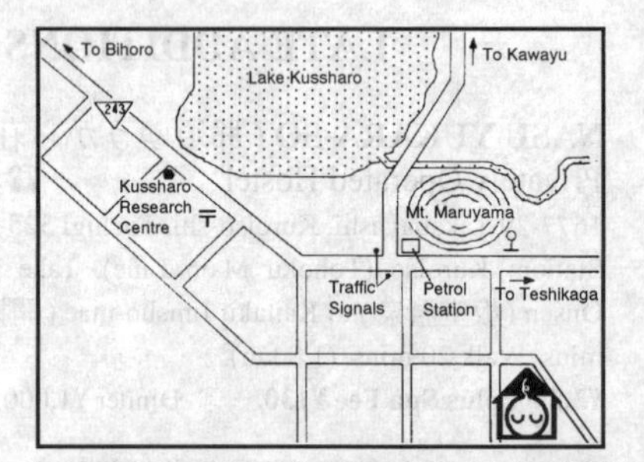


## HAKODATE YOUTH GUEST HOUSE
(函館ユースゲストハウス)

17-6 Horai-cho, Hakodate-shi, Hokkaido 040.

45 beds. ☎ 0138-26-7892. Fax: 0989

Station: Hakodate. Take tram no. 2 to Horai-cho (宝来町), 7 mins. Walk 3 mins.

**Summer ¥4,650. Winter ¥3,650.** No dinner. Breakfast ¥700.

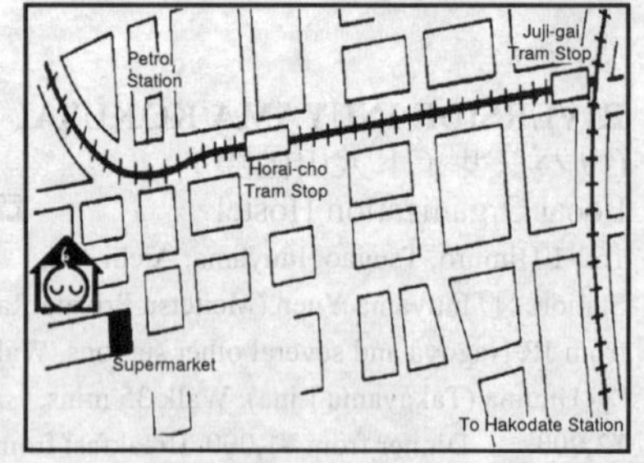


## ATOMA YOUTH GUEST HOUSE
(アトマユースゲストハウス)

15-2 Funaishi, Sakuramoto, Fukushima 960-21.

30 beds. ☎ 0245-91-2523

Station: Fukushima. From West Exit, take bus from bus stop no. 3 for Takayu Onsen (高湯温泉) or Kami Ubado (上姥堂) to Kami Ubado (上姥堂), 20 mins. Walk 5 mins.

**From ¥3,650.** Dinner ¥1,000. Breakfast ¥600.

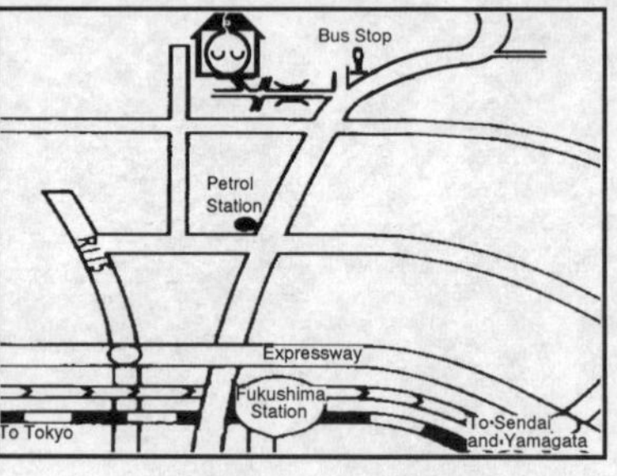

# PRIVATE HOSTELS AND INNS

Private hostels represent both the good and the bad sides of Japanese accommodation. The good side is that they have few restrictions and are cheap. The bad side is that, in Tokyo in particular, demand exceeds supply, so that they often appear to have little interest in attracting new guests. As mentioned earlier in this book, quite often there is nobody to answer the telephone, or the person who does answer knows nothing about the accommodation available, nor when the manager will be back, nor, indeed, whether he will be coming back today, or tomorrow, or this week.

What has happened is that there are many people working in Tokyo and the hostels have turned their attentions gradually to the semi-permanent market, to the disadvantage of the short-term visitor. Many private hostels are no longer interested in those who want to stay only a day or two.

Other books list many such hostels and we tried to contact all we could. About half appeared to have gone out of business. Of the remainder, only a few seemed to have any interest in short-term guests and in some cases that interest was not strong. We have listed only hostels which appeared to be potentially useful to the traveller. Even so, you may encounter some of the difficulties mentioned above. Good advice might be to reserve a place in a youth hostel for the first night or two and have some feeling of security and then look for a private hostel once here.

Kyoto, however, is a different story. Supply and demand are well balanced there, although in mid-summer all accommodation becomes crowded. The hostels there, though, are usually catering for the steady passage of short-term visitors. The private hostels in Kyoto are considerably cheaper than the youth hostels there and tend to have character. They are interesting, although frequently crowded, places to stay. Average price is around ¥2,000 per person per night. In many cases these hostels can also offer private rooms at reasonable rates.

Included in this section are some *ryokan* (Japanese-style hotels) which do not belong to the Japanese Inn Group, but are similar to those which do. Please refer to the introduction to the Japanese Inns (following) for further information regarding such establishments. Rates per person are about ¥4,000 in Kyoto and ¥4,500 in Tokyo. At these types of hotel, it is not appreciably cheaper per person for a couple to stay rather than an individual.

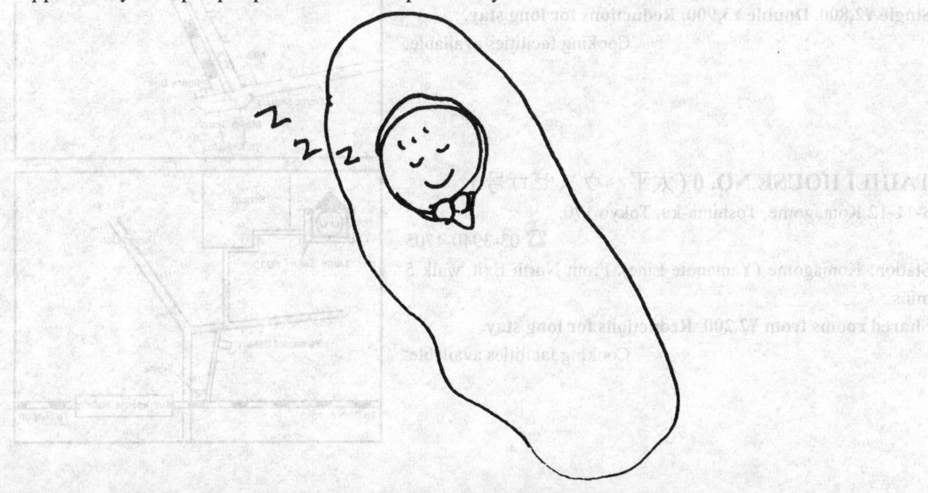

**TOKYO**

## SUZUKI RYOKAN (寿々木旅館)

7-15-23 Yanaka, Taito-ku, Tokyo 110.

15 rooms. ☎ 03-3821-4944

Station: Nippori (Yamanote Line or Keisei Private Railway). Walk 1 min.

**Single ¥3,650. Double ¥7,300.** No meals.

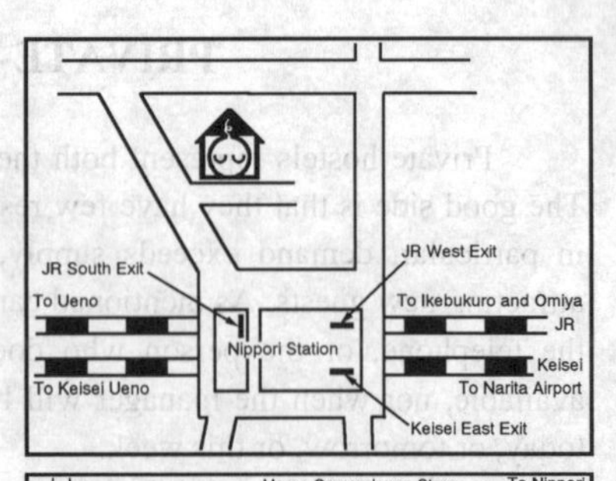


## MARUI HOUSE (丸井ハウス)

3-14-26 Ikebukuro, Toshima-ku, Tokyo 171. ☎ 03-3962-4979

Station: Ikebukuro (Yamanote Line, Marunouchi and Yurakucho Subway Lines). Walk 8 mins.

**Single from ¥2,300. Double from ¥3,600. Reductions for long stay.** Cooking facilities available.

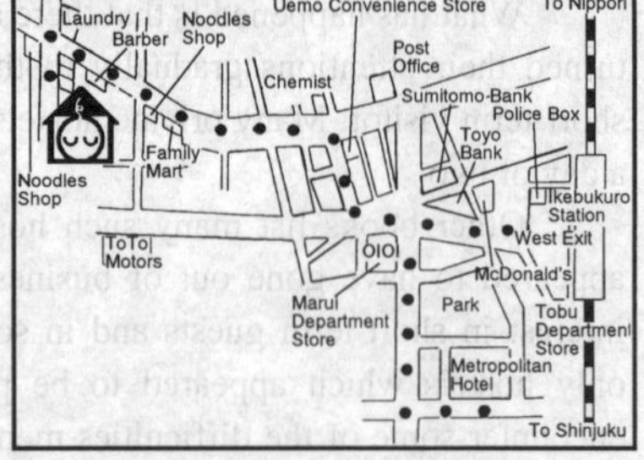


## VILLA YAMANOTE (ヴィラ山手)

3-17-4 Hyakunin-cho, Shinjuku-ku, Tokyo 169.

Annexe of Marui House (above). ☎ 03-3962-4979

Station: Shin Okubo (Yamanote Line). Walk 5 mins.

**Single from ¥2,300. Double from ¥3,600. Reductions for long stay.** Cooking facilities available.

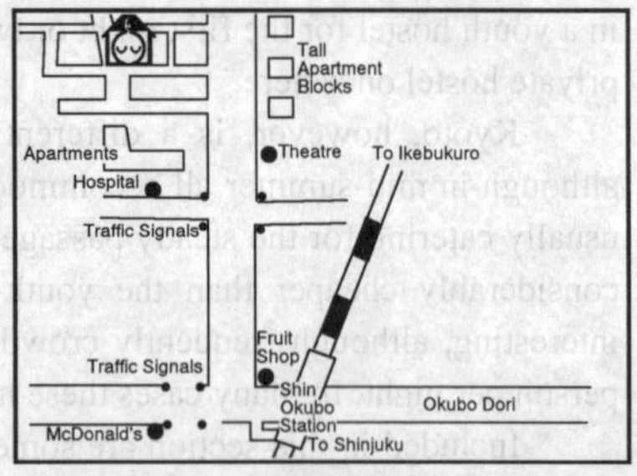


## ENGLISH HOUSE (イングリッシュハウス)

2-23-8 Nishi Ikebukuro, Toshima-ku, Tokyo 171.

☎ 03-3988-1743

Station: Mejiro (Yamanote Line). Walk 6 mins.

**Single ¥2,800. Double ¥3,900. Reductions for long stay.**

Cooking facilities available.

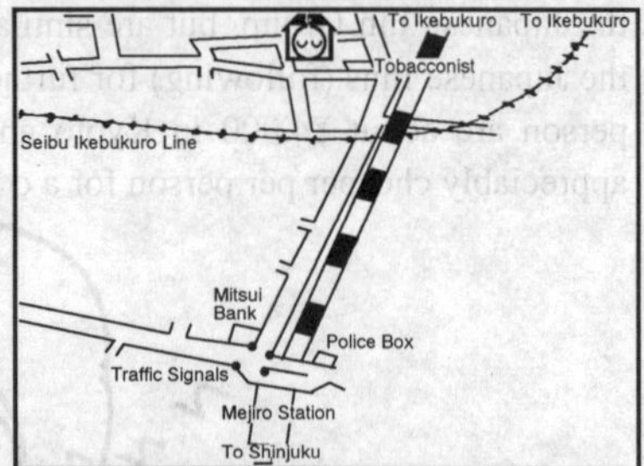


## TAIHEI HOUSE NO. 0 (太平ハウスゼロ号)

3-11-12 Komagome, Toshima-ku, Tokyo 170.

☎ 03-3940-4705

Station: Komagome (Yamanote Line). From North Exit, walk 5 mins.

**Shared rooms from ¥2,200. Reductions for long stay.**

Cooking facilities available.

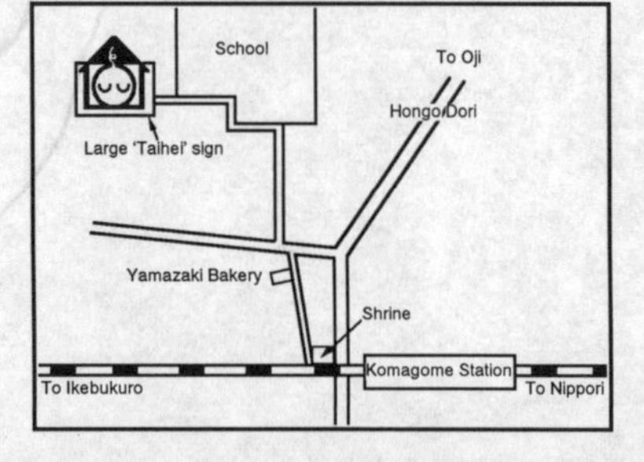

## TAIHEI HOUSE NO. 1 (太平ハウス一号)

23-2 Yamato-cho, Itabashi-ku, Tokyo 173. ☎ 03-3940-4705

Station: Itabashi Hon-cho (Toei Mita Subway Line). Walk 2 mins.

**Shared rooms from ¥1,900. Reductions for long stay.**

Cooking facilities available.

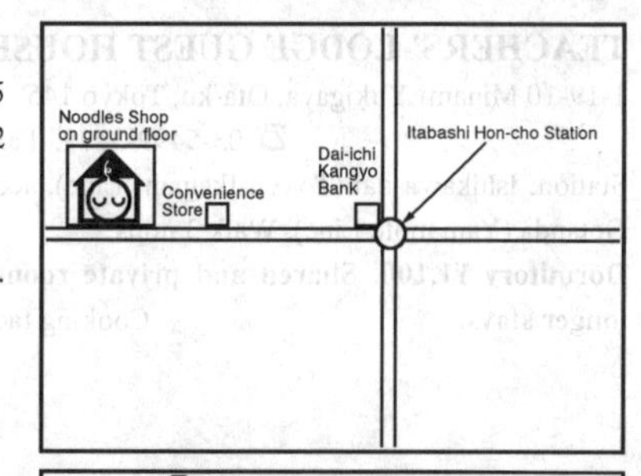


## TAIHEI HOUSE NO. 2 (太平ハウス二号)

3-12-14 Maeno-cho, Itabashi-ku, Tokyo 174. ☎ 03-3940-4705

Station: Tokiwa-dai (Tobu Tojo Line), accessible from JR Ikebukuro (Yamanote Line). From North Exit, walk 10 mins.

**Shared rooms from ¥2,000. Reductions for long stay.**

Cooking facilities available.

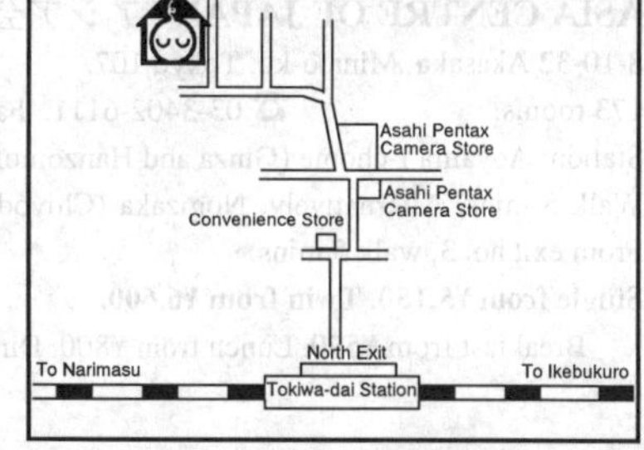


## TAIHEI HOUSE NO. 3 (太平ハウス三号)

3-39-5 Takinogawa, Kita-ku, Tokyo 114. ☎ 03-3940-4705

Station: Nishi Sugamo (Toei Mita Subway Line). Walk 7 mins.

**Note:** Owner says that this hostel is not so clean, but is awfully cheap!

**Dormitory ¥1,500. Reductions for long stay.**

Cooking facilities available.

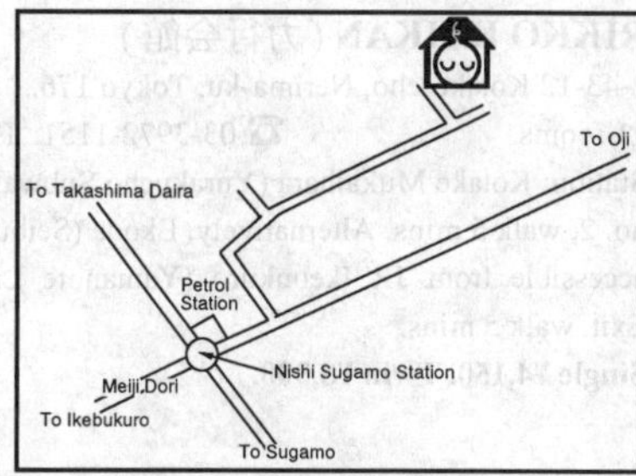


## GREEN PEACE HOUSE
## (グリーンピース留学生宿舎)

3-20-8 Nishigahara, Kita-ku, Tokyo 114.

☎ 03-3915-2572. Fax: 03-3915-5374

Station: Nishigahara (Nanboku Subway Line). Walk 1 min.

**Note:** Accommodation is primarily for those studying in Japan.

**Shared rooms from ¥1,800. Single from ¥2,500. Reductions for long stay.** Cooking facilities available.

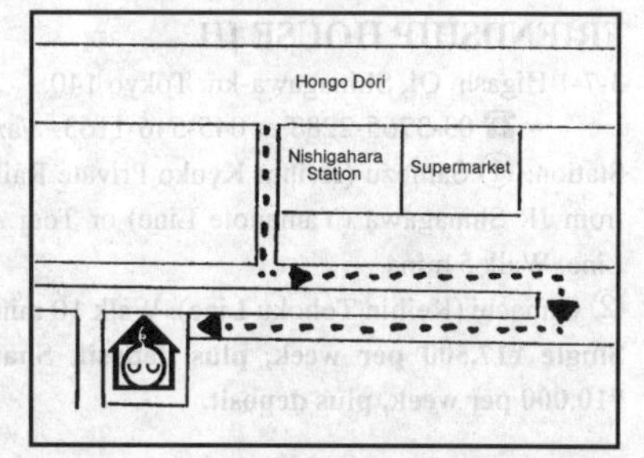


## MAHARAJAH MANSION
## (マハラジャマンション)

3-2-5 Kawagishi, Toda-shi, Saitama 335.

☎ 03-5499-3779. Fax: 03-5499-0977

Station: Toda Koen (Saikyo Line). Walk 5 mins.

**One room apartment from ¥2,700. Reductions for long stay.**

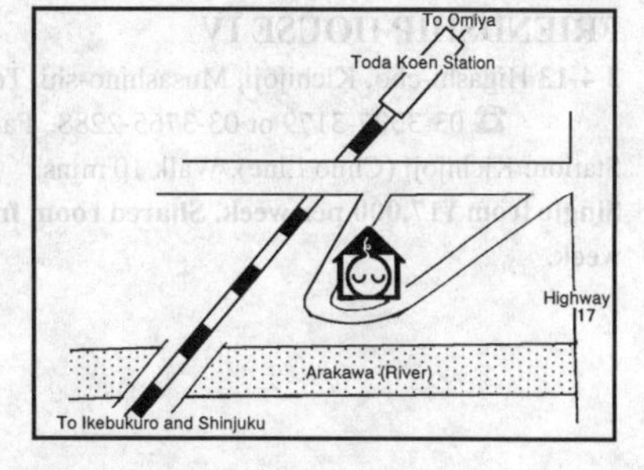

## TEACHERS' LODGE GUEST HOUSE

1-19-10 Minami Yukigaya, Ota-ku, Tokyo 145.

☎ 03-5499-3779. Fax: 03-5499-0977

Station: Ishikawa-dai (Tokyu Ikegami Line), accessible from JR Gotanda (Yamanote Line). Walk 3 mins.

**Dormitory ¥1,100. Shared and private rooms available for longer stays.** Cooking facilities available.

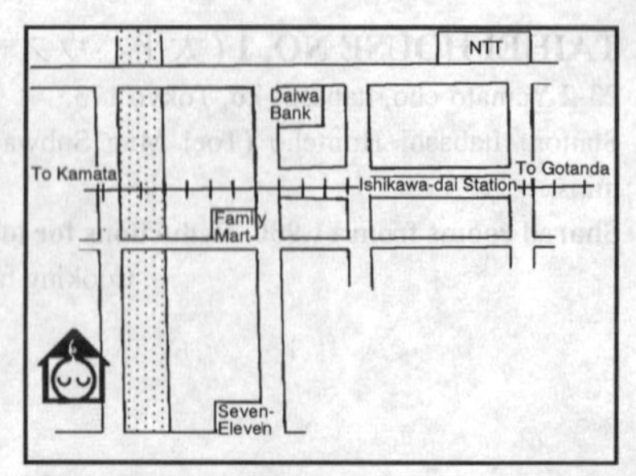


## ASIA CENTRE OF JAPAN (アジア会館)

8-10-32 Akasaka, Minato-ku, Tokyo 107.

173 rooms. ☎ 03-3402-6111. Fax: 03-3402-0738

Station: Aoyama I-chome (Ginza and Hanzomon Subway Lines). Walk 5 mins. Alternatively, Nogizaka (Chiyoda Subway Line). From exit no. 3, walk 5 mins.

**Single from ¥5,150. Twin from ¥6,600.**

Breakfast from ¥570. Lunch from ¥800. Dinner from ¥1,500.

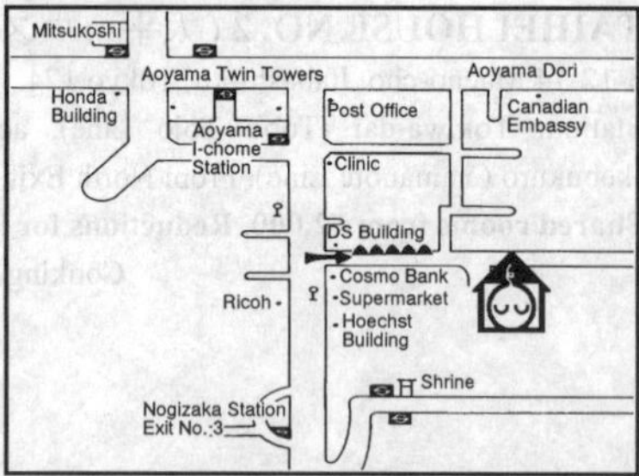


## RIKKO KAIKAN (力行会館)

2-43-12 Kotake-cho, Nerima-ku, Tokyo 176.

11 rooms. ☎ 03-3972-1151. Fax: 03-3972-1264

Station: Kotake Mukaihara (Yurakucho Subway Line). From exit no. 2, walk 5 mins. Alternatively, Ekoda (Seibu Ikebukuro Line), accessible from JR Ikebukuro (Yamanote Line). From North Exit, walk 5 mins.

**Single ¥4,150. Twin ¥8,300.**

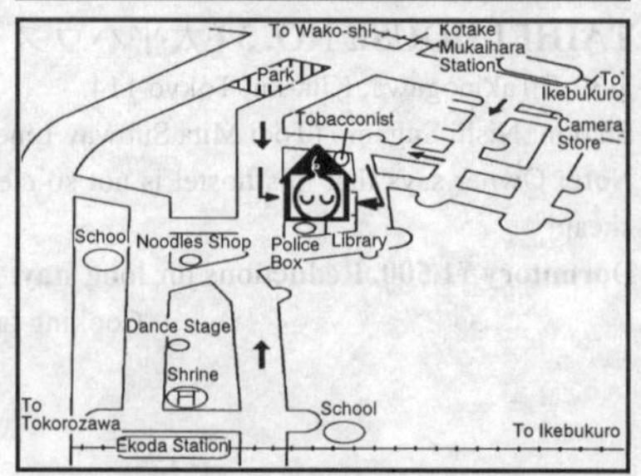


## FRIENDSHIP HOUSE III

3-7-1 Higashi Oi, Shinagawa-ku, Tokyo 140.

☎ 03-3765-2288 or 045-546-1163. Fax: 045-542-9165

Station: ① Samezu (Keihin Kyuko Private Railway), accessible from JR Shinagawa (Yamanote Line) or Toei Asakusa Subway Line. Walk 5 mins.

② Oimachi (Keihin Tohoku Line). Walk 10 mins.

**Single ¥17,500 per week, plus deposit. Shared room from ¥10,000 per week, plus deposit.** No meals.

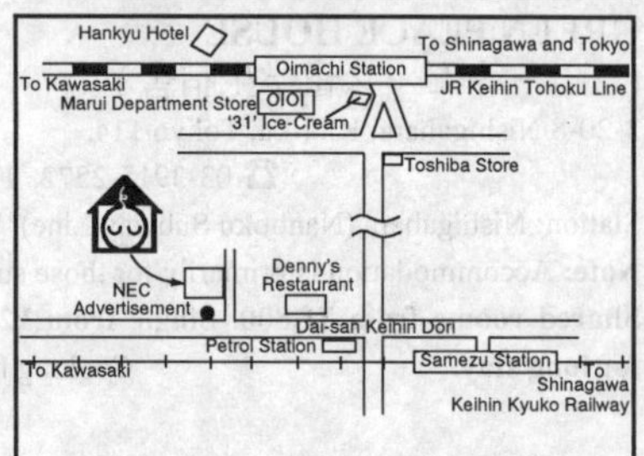


## FRIENDSHIP HOUSE IV

3-4-13 Higashi-cho, Kichijoji, Musashino-shi, Tokyo 180.

☎ 03-3327-3179 or 03-3765-2288. Fax: 045-542-9165

Station: Kichijoji (Chuo Line). Walk 10 mins.

**Single from ¥17,000 per week. Shared room from ¥10,300 per week.** No meals.

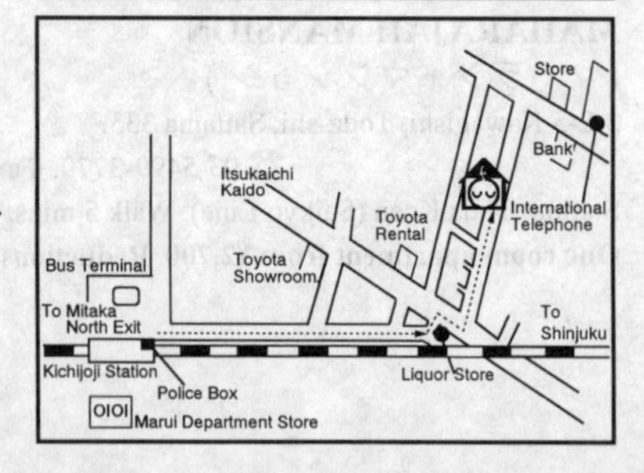

## KYOTO

### TAKAYA (鷹屋)

538 Koji-machi, Muro-machi Ichi-jo Agaru, Kamikyo-ku, Kyoto. ☎ 075-431-5213, 8427

Station: Imadegawa (Kyoto subway). From exit no. 6, walk 5 mins.

**Single ¥3,100. Double ¥6,200. Reductions for long stay.**

Cooking facilities available.

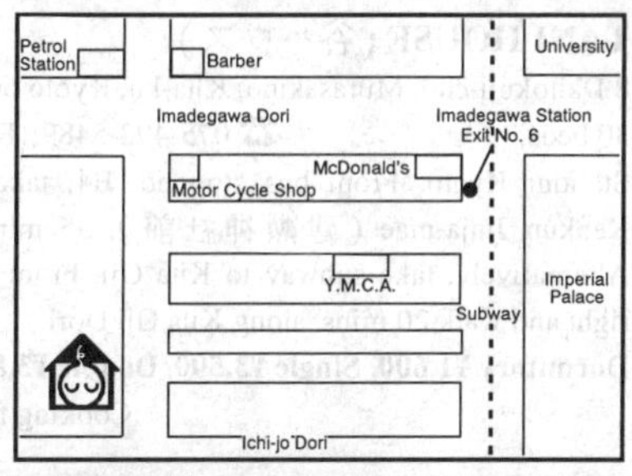


### GREEN PEACE IN KYOTO (グリーン・ピース・イン・京都)

14-1 Shibamoto-cho, Matsugasaki, Sakyo-ku, Kyoto 606. ☎ 075-791-9890

Station: Kitayama (Kyoto subway). From exit no. 1, walk 10 mins.

**Single ¥2,500. Double ¥2,800. Dormitory ¥1,600. Minimum stay 3 days. Reductions for longer stay.**

Cooking facilities available.

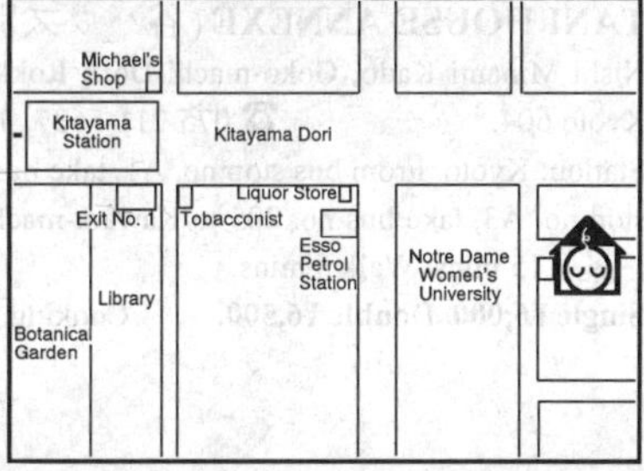


### UNO HOUSE (宇野ハウス)

108 Shin Karasuma Dori, Maruta-machi Sagaru, Nakagyo-ku, Kyoto 604. ☎ 075-231-7763. Fax: 256-0140

Station: Kyoto. From bus stop no. A3, take bus no. 205 or 特 17 to Kawara-machi Maruta-machi (河原町丸太町), 20 mins. Walk 2 mins.

**Dormitory ¥1,750. Private room from ¥2,350 per person.**

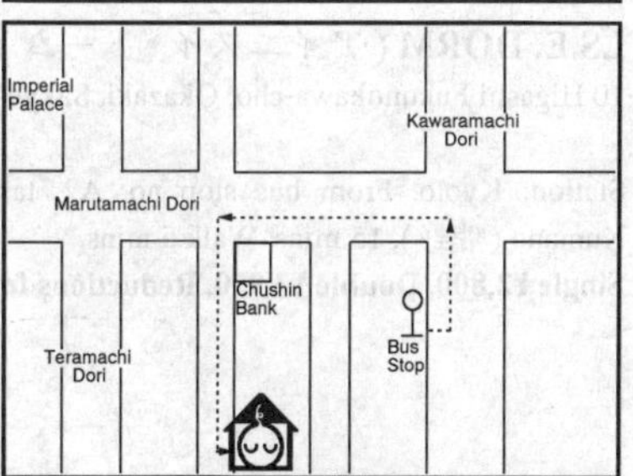


### RYOKAN YUHARA (旅館ゆはら)

Kiya-machi Dori, Shomen Agaru, Shimogyo-ku, Kyoto 600. ☎ 075-371-9583

Station: Kyoto. From bus stop no. A3, take bus no. 205 or 特 17 to Kawara-machi Shomen (河原町正面), 3 stops, 5 mins. Walk 3 mins. Alternatively, walk from Kyoto station, 10 mins.

**Single ¥4,000. Double ¥8,000.**

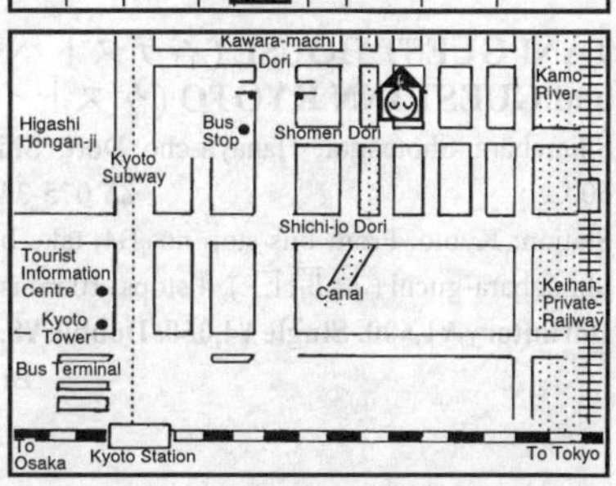


### YOUNG INN KYOTO (ヤングイン京都)

430-1 Kami Benten-cho, Yasaka-no Torii-mae Sagaru, Shimogawara, Higashiyama-ku, Kyoto 605. ☎ 075-541-0349

Station: Kyoto. From bus stop no. A2, take bus no. 206 to Higashiyama Yasui (東山安井), 9 stops, 15 mins. Walk 3 mins.

**Single ¥4,750. Double ¥9,500.** Meals available.

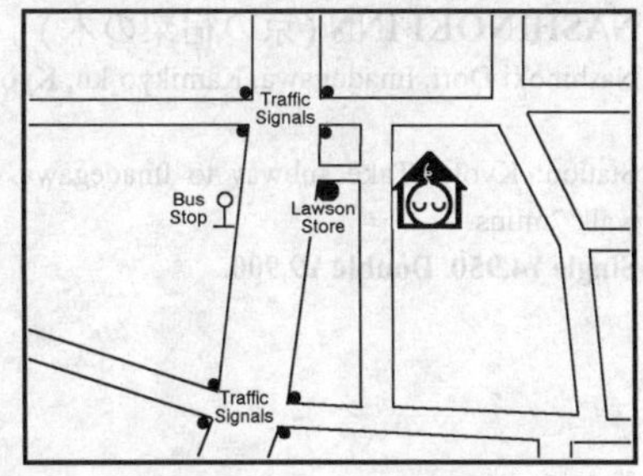

## TANI HOUSE (谷ハウス)

8 Daitokuji-cho, Murasakino, Kita-ku, Kyoto 603.
30 beds. ☎ 075-492-5489. Fax: 075-493-6419
Station: Kyoto. From bus stop no. B4, take bus no. 206 to Kenkun Jinja-mae (建勲神社前), 35 mins. Walk 3 mins. Alternatively, take subway to Kita Oji. From bus terminal turn right and walk 20 mins. along Kita Oji Dori.
**Dormitory ¥1,600. Single ¥3,500. Double ¥3,800.**
Cooking facilities available.

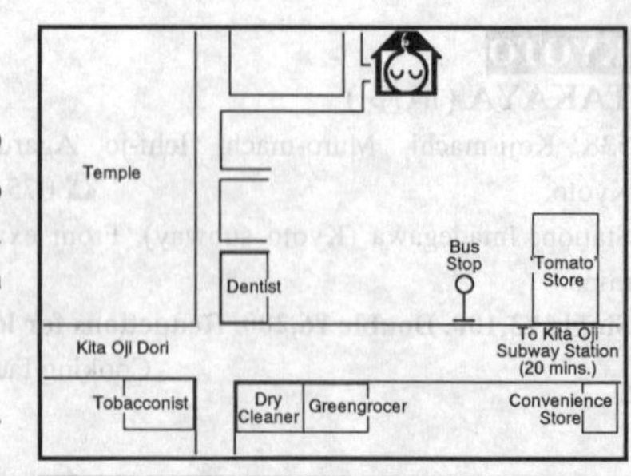


## TANI HOUSE ANNEXE (谷ハウス別館)

Nishi Minami Kado, Goko-machi Dori, Rokkaku, Nakagyo-ku, Kyoto 604. ☎ 075-211-5637. Fax: 075-252-3277
Station: Kyoto. From bus stop no. A1, take bus no. 5 or from bus stop no. A3, take bus no. 205 to Kawara-machi San-jo (河原町三条), 15 mins. Walk 5 mins.
**Single ¥6,000. Double ¥6,500.** Cooking facilities available.

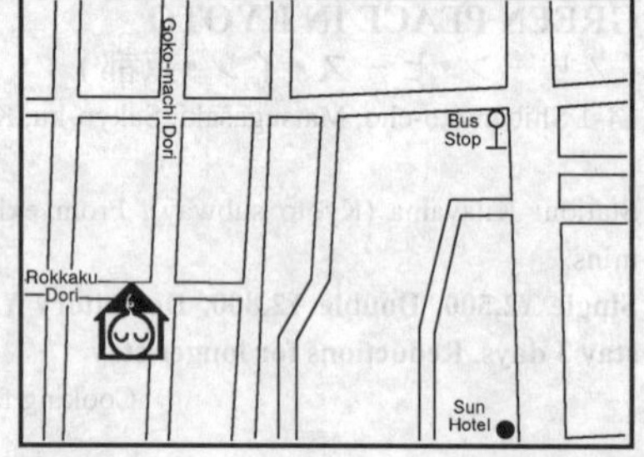


## I.S.E. DORM (アイエスイ・ドーム)

10 Higashi Fukunokawa-cho, Okazaki, Sakyo-ku, Kyoto 606.
☎ 075-771-0566
Station: Kyoto. From bus stop no. A2, take bus no. 206 to Kumano (熊野), 15 mins. Walk 5 mins.
**Single ¥2,800. Double ¥3,950. Reductions for long stay.**

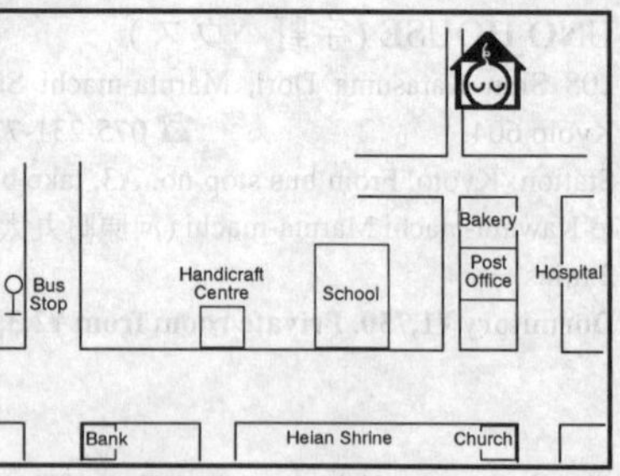


## TANI GUEST HOUSE (谷ゲストハウス) and GUEST INN KYOTO (ゲストイン京都)

Shimabara Shotengai, Hanaya-cho Dori, Shimogyo-ku, Kyoto 600. ☎ 075-341-1344 Fax: same
Station: Kyoto. From bus stop no. B4, take bus no. 6 or 206 to Shimabara-guchi (島原口), 4 stops, 10 mins. Walk 2 mins.
**Dormitory ¥1,600. Single ¥4,050. Double ¥8,100.**
Breakfast from ¥500.

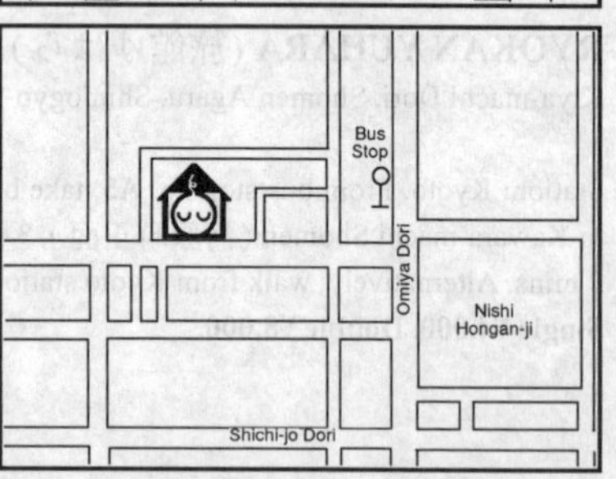


## NASHINOKI INN (京の宿梨の木)

Nashinoki Dori, Imadegawa, Kamikyo-ku, Kyoto 602.
☎ 075-241-1543
Station: Kyoto. Take subway to Imadegawa. From exit no. 3, walk 7 mins.
**Single ¥4,950. Double ¥9,900.**

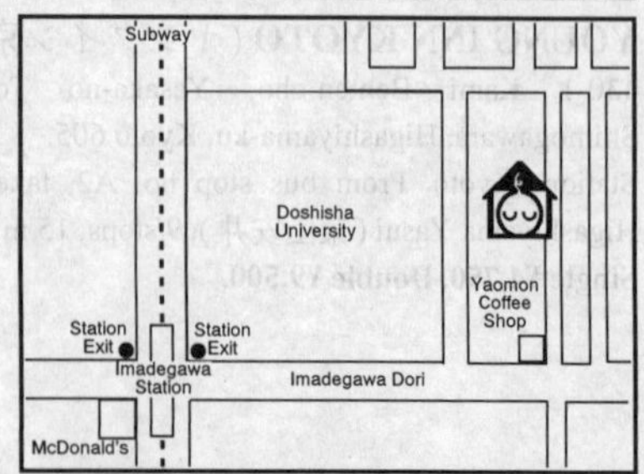

## RYOKAN DAI ICHI INN (旅館大一イン)

1 Otake-cho, Mibu Kami, Nakagyo-ku, Kyoto 604.

☎ 075-882-0546

Station: Kyoto. From bus stop no. B3, take bus no. 75 or 205 to Nishi Oji San-jo (西大路三条), 20 mins. Walk 3 mins.

**Single ¥4,600. Double 8,200**

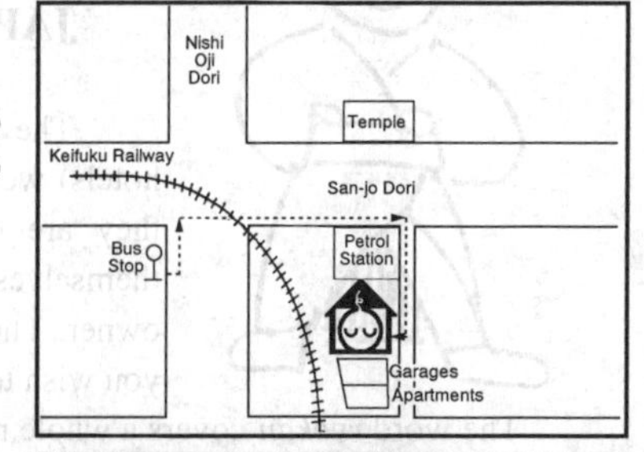


## KUWACHO RYOKAN (桑長旅館)

231 Shichi-jo Agaru, Akezu Dori, Shimogyo-ku, Kyoto 600.

7 rooms. ☎ 075-371-3191

Station: Kyoto. Walk 5 mins.

**Single ¥5,800. Double ¥9,500.**

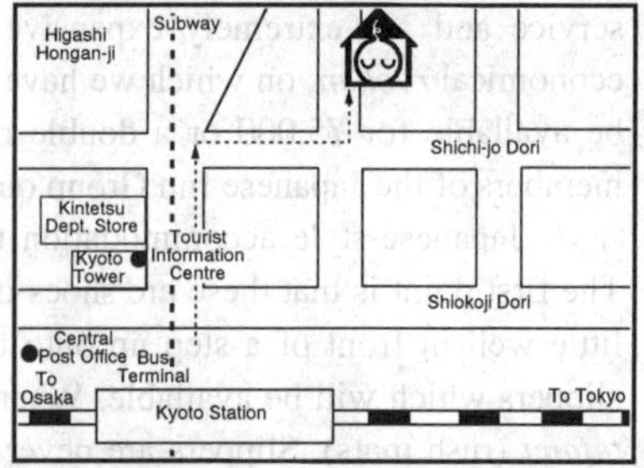


## RYOKAN SANKI (旅館さんき)

Shimono-cho, Nishi Shin Yashiki, Shimabara, Shimogyo-ku, Kyoto 600. ☎ 075-351-6339

Station: Kyoto. From bus stop no. B3, take bus no. 205 to Shichi-jo Mibu (七条壬生), 4 stops, 10 mins. Walk 5 mins.

**Single ¥4,150. Double ¥8,300.**

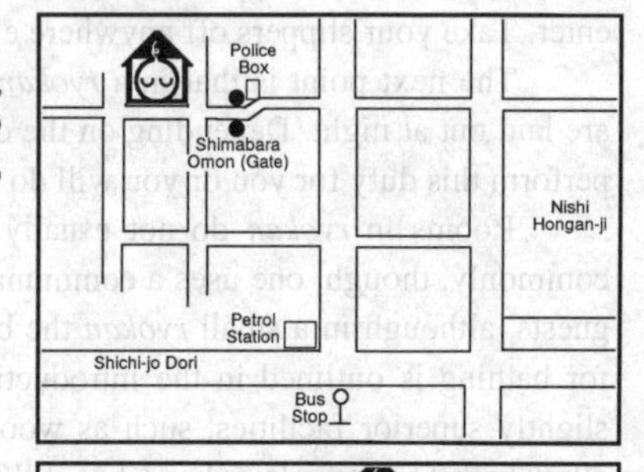


## RYOKAN WAJIMAYA (旅館 わじまや)

Higashi Iru, Karasuma, Kami Juzuya-machi, Shimogyo-ku, Kyoto 600.

9 rooms. ☎ 075-351-7873, 361-5741. Fax: 343-6137

Station: Kyoto. Walk 10 mins.

**Single ¥4,450. Double ¥8,900.**

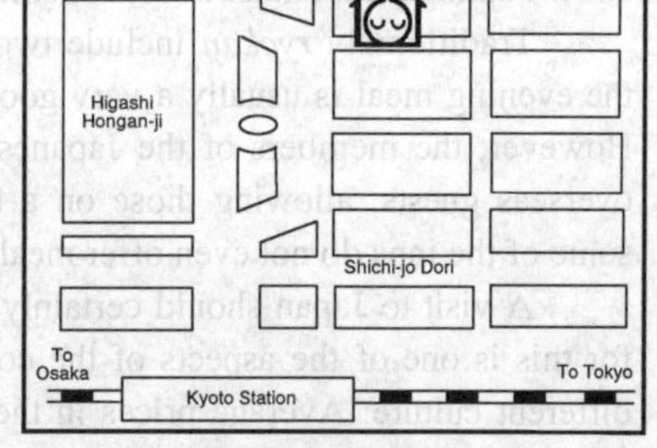


## RYOKAN KITANOYA (旅館北野家)

Higashiyama San-jo Agaru Higashi Iru, Sakyo-ku, Kyoto 606.

10 rooms ☎ 075-771-1488, 751-9926. Fax: 075-761-3386

Station: Kyoto. From bus stop no. A2, take bus no. 206 to Higashiyama San-jo (東山三条), 20 mins. Walk 2 mins.

**Single ¥4,150. Double ¥8,300.** Dinner ¥4,000. Breakfast ¥1,000.

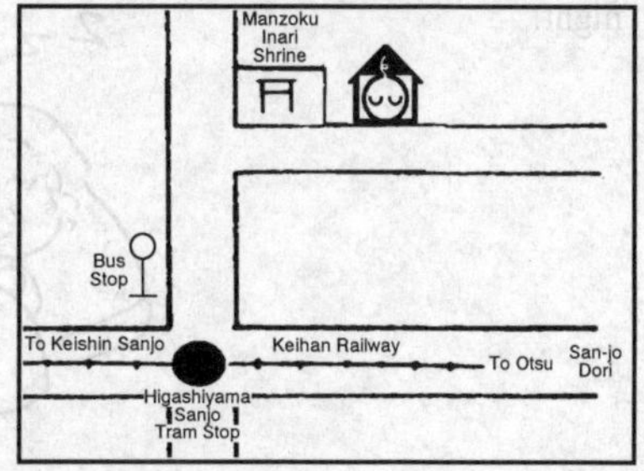

# JAPANESE INNS

The Japanese Inns are a group of *ryokan* (Japanese-style hotels) welcoming guests from overseas. As mentioned earlier, they are only a loose association co-operating to publicize themselves. They are not in any sense a chain with a common owner. Therefore, it is necessary to contact each individually if you wish to stay at such establishments.

The word *ryokan* covers a whole range of hotels. Those of the highest class specialize in service and are extremely expensive. However, those listed in the next dozen pages are economical *ryokan*, on which we have imposed the restriction that either a single room should be available for ¥5,000 or a double room should be available for ¥10,000. There are other members of the Japanese Inn Group outside this price range, not included in this book.

Japanese-style accommodation has some special features which should be mentioned. The first point is that these are shoes-off establishments. As soon as you enter, you will find a little well in front of a step up onto the main floor. Leave your shoes there and put on the slippers which will be available. When you go to your room, you will find that the floor is of *tatami* (rush mats). Slippers are never worn on *tatami*, so remember to take yours off as you enter. Take your slippers off anywhere else in the *ryokan* where there is *tatami* too.

The next point is that in a *ryokan* one sleeps on the floor, on *futon* (mattresses) which are laid out at night. Depending on the class of establishment, either somebody will come and perform this duty for you or you will do it for yourself when ready, but more likely the former.

Rooms in *ryokan* do not usually have attached bathrooms, although a few do. More commonly, though, one uses a communal bathroom. This is a big room with space for several guests, although in a small *ryokan* the bathroom will be of proportionate size. The procedure for bathing is outlined in the introduction to youth hostels on page 386. *Ryokan* may have slightly superior facilities, such as wooden bowls instead of plastic ones, and will probably allow bathing until a later hour, but still the bath will usually be available only in the evening.

Traditionally *ryokan* include two meals, dinner and breakfast, in their rates and, since the evening meal is usually a very good one, this contributes substantially to the high prices. However, the members of the Japanese Inn Group have agreed to make meals optional for overseas guests, allowing those on a budget still to consider such accommodation. Indeed, some of the inns do not even offer meals. Where they do so, prices are indicated.

A visit to Japan should certainly include a sampling of Japanese-style accommodation, for this is one of the aspects of the country which make one feel that one is experiencing a different culture. Average prices in the Japanese Inn Group are about ¥4,500 per person per night.

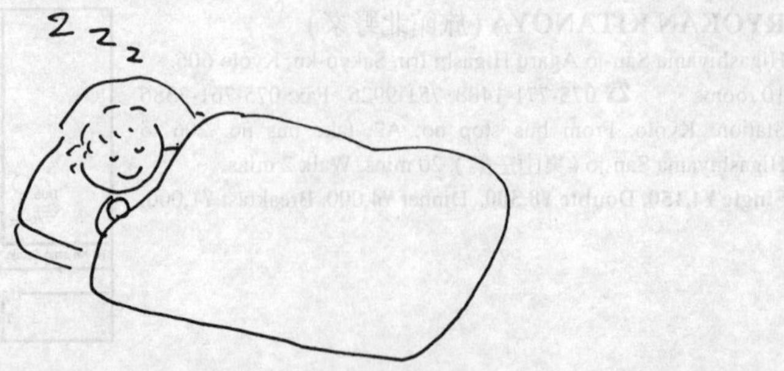

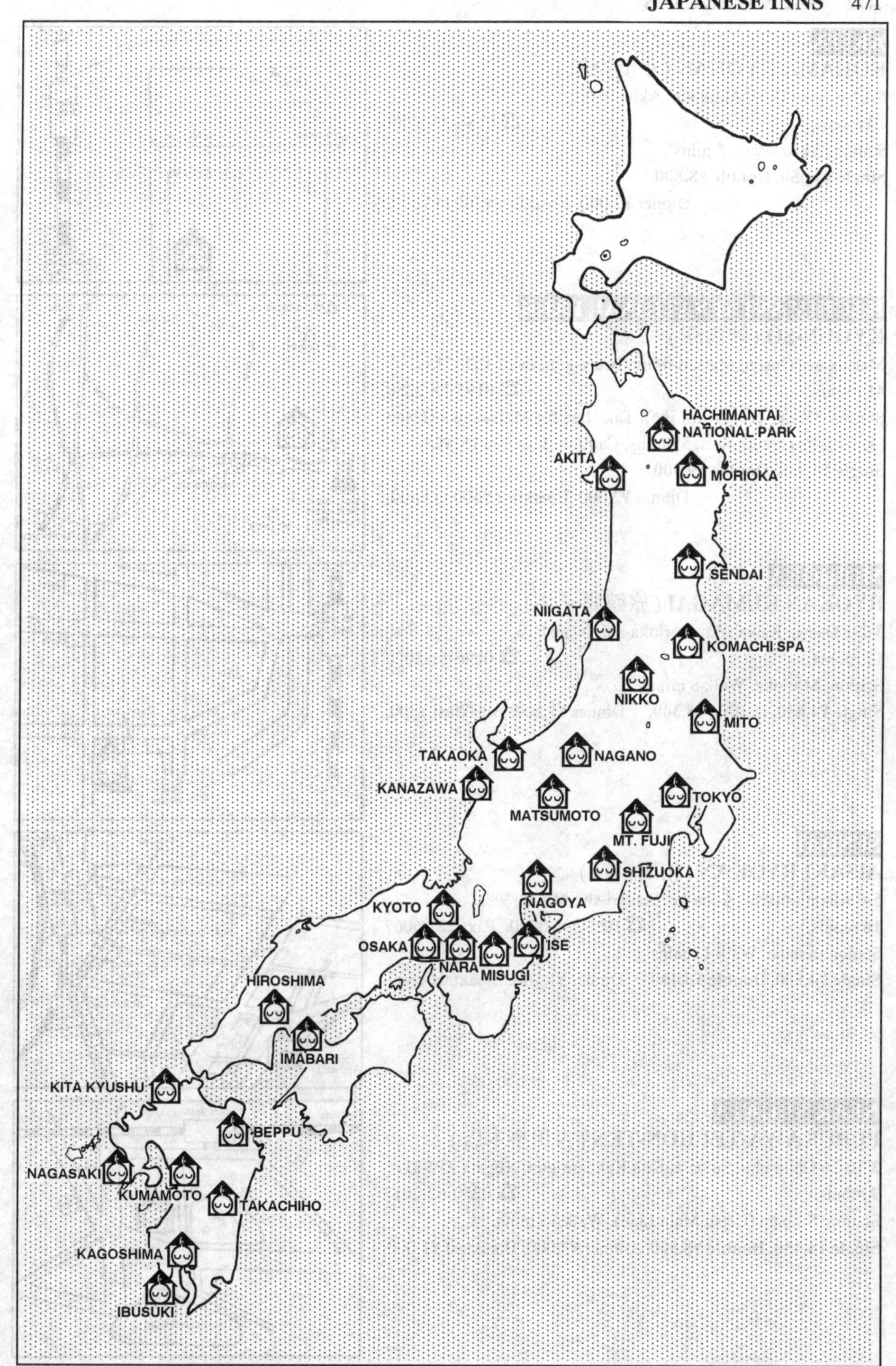
HACHIMANTAI NATIONAL PARK
AKITA
MORIOKA
SENDAI
NIIGATA
KOMACHI SPA
NIKKO
MITO
TAKAOKA
NAGANO
KANAZAWA
MATSUMOTO
TOKYO
MT. FUJI
SHIZUOKA
KYOTO
NAGOYA
OSAKA
NARA
MISUGI
ISE
HIROSHIMA
IMABARI
KITA KYUSHU
BEPPU
NAGASAKI
KUMAMOTO
TAKACHIHO
KAGOSHIMA
IBUSUKI

## AKITA

### KOHAMA RYOKAN (小浜旅館)

6-19-6 Naka Dori, Akita-shi, Akita 010.

10 rooms. ☎ 0188-32-5739

Station: Akita. Walk 5 mins.

**Single ¥4,650. Double ¥8,800.**

Dinner ¥2,000. Breakfast ¥700 to ¥800.

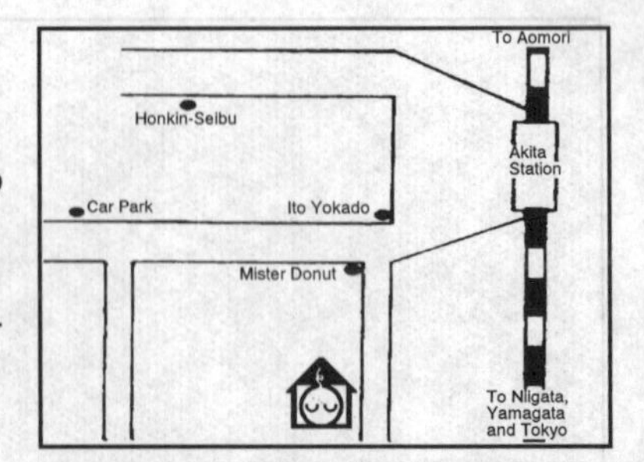


## HACHIMANTAI NATIONAL PARK

### KYOUN-SO (峡雲荘)

Matsukawa Onsen, Matsuo-mura, Iwate-gun, Iwate 028-73.

41 rooms. ☎ 0195-78-2256

Station: Obuke (Hanawa Line). Take bus for Matsukawa Onsen (松川温泉) to terminus, 55 mins. Caution: Last bus 15:31.

**Single ¥4,950. Double ¥9,500.**

Dinner ¥2,000. Breakfast ¥600 to ¥800.

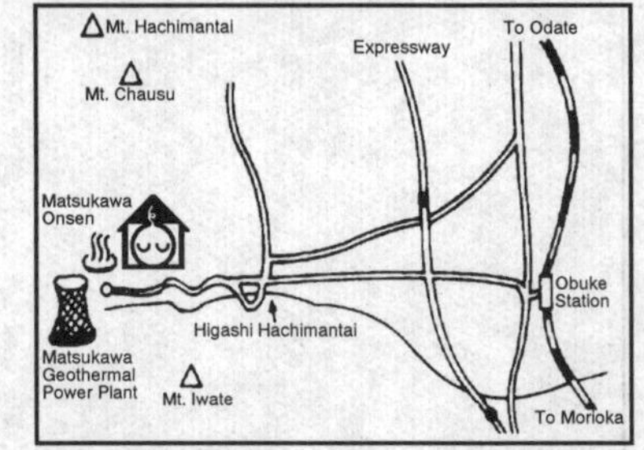


## MORIOKA

### RYOKAN KUMAGAI (旅館熊ヶ井)

3-2-5 Osawa Kawahara, Morioka-shi, Iwate 020.

11 rooms. ☎ 0196-51-3020

Station: Morioka. Walk 8 mins.

**Single ¥4,650. Double ¥8,300.** Dinner ¥1,500. Breakfast ¥800.

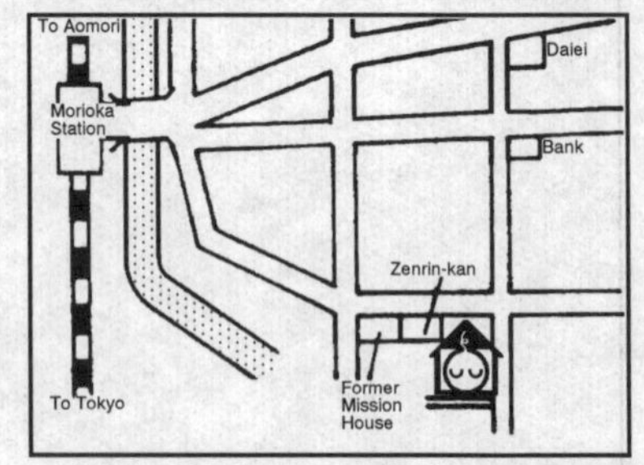


## SENDAI

### AISAKI RYOKAN (相崎旅館)

5-6 Kitame-machi, Aoba-ku, Sendai-shi, Miyagi 980.

16 rooms. ☎ 022-264-0700. Fax: 227-6067

Station: Sendai. Walk 12 mins.

**Single ¥4,500. Double ¥8,400.** Dinner ¥1,700. Breakfast ¥800.

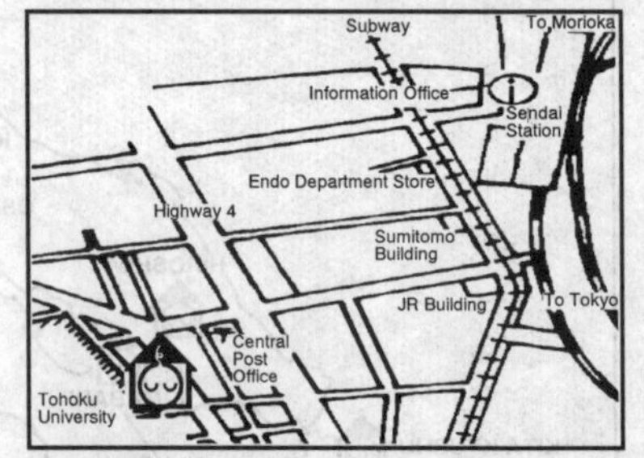


## NEAR NIIGATA

### FURUKAWA-TEI HON-TEN (古川亭本店)

2-10-26 Chuo-cho, Suibara, Kita Kanbara-gun, Niigata 959-21.

7 rooms. ☎ 0250-62-2013

Station: Suibara (Uetsu Main Line). Walk 15 mins.

**Single ¥4,450. Double ¥8,900.** Dinner ¥3,000. Breakfast ¥1,000.

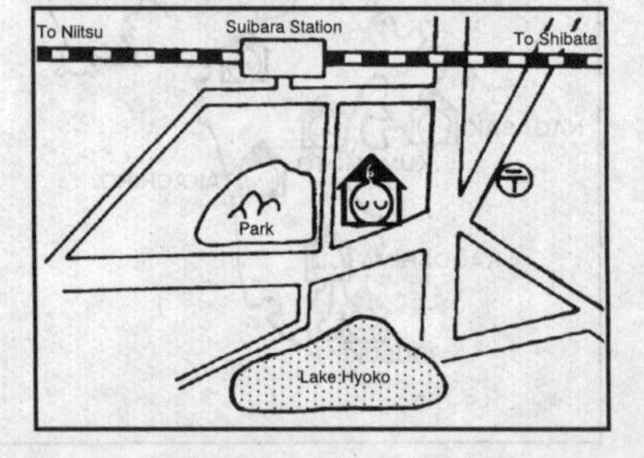

**KOMACHI SPA**

## HIROTAYA (廣太屋)

82 Kojiro, Yatsuzaku, Ono, Tamura-gun, Fukushima 979-34.
9 rooms. ☎ 0247-72-2819. Fax: 2820
Station: Ono Nii-machi (Banetsu To Line). Walk 4 mins.
**Single ¥4,800. Double ¥8,600. (Increased rates in holiday season.)** Dinner ¥3,500. Breakfast ¥800 to ¥1,000.

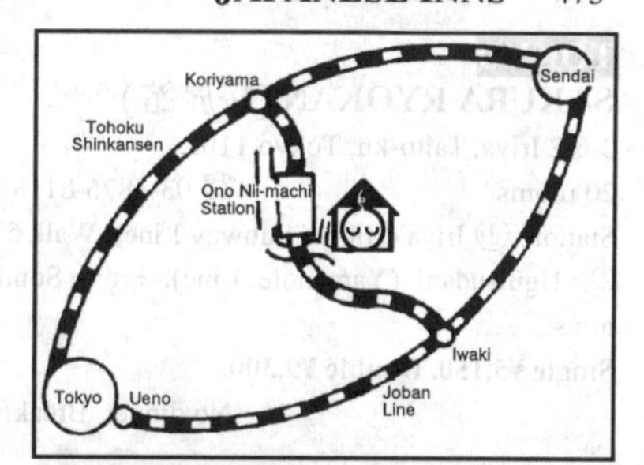


**NIKKO**

## TURTLE INN NIKKO (タートル・イン・日光)

2-16 Takumi-cho, Nikko-shi, Tochigi 321-14.
12 rooms. ☎ 0288-53-3168. Fax: 3883
Station: JR Nikko or Tobu Nikko. Take bus for Nishi Sando (西参道), Chuzenji Onsen (中禅寺温泉) or Yumoto Onsen (湯本温泉) to Sogo Kaikan (総合会館), 10 mins. Walk 5 mins. Alternatively, walk from station, 40 mins.
**Single ¥4,150. Double ¥8,700.**
Dinner ¥2,000. Breakfast ¥800 to ¥1,000.

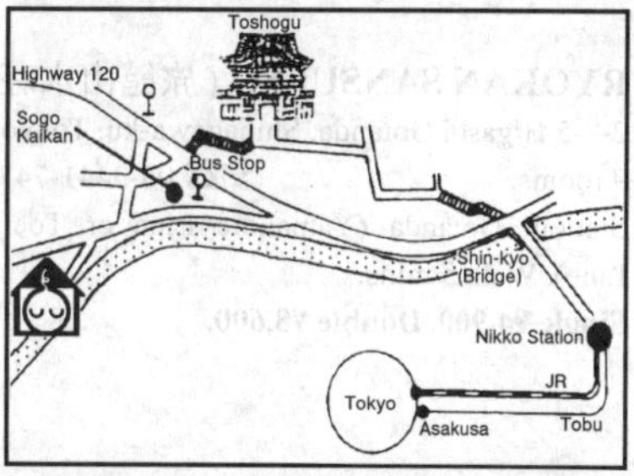

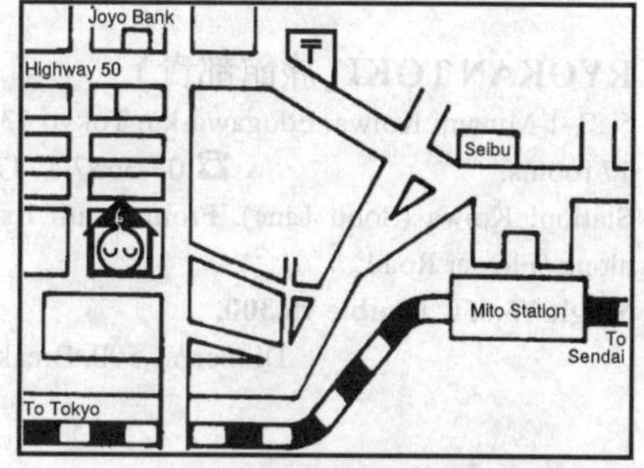


**MITO**

## RYOKAN IZUMI-SO (旅館いずみ荘)

1-3-30 Baiko, Mito-shi, Ibaragi 310.
15 rooms. ☎ 0292-21-3504. Fax: 3505
**Closed at New Year.**
Station: Mito (Joban Line). Walk 15 mins.
**Single ¥4,950. Double ¥9,900.** Dinner ¥2,000. Breakfast ¥700.

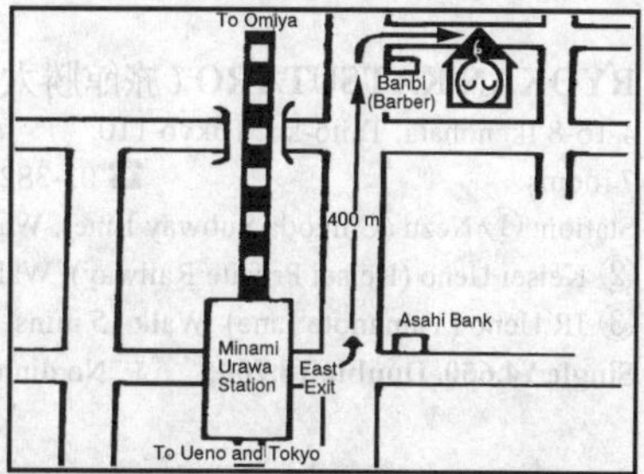


**TOKYO AREA**

## RYOKAN FUKUICHI (旅館福一)

1-33-5 Minami Urawa, Urawa-shi, Saitama 336.
14 rooms. ☎ 048-881-0214. Fax: 887-2557
Station: Minami Urawa (Keihin Tohoku Line). Walk 5 mins.
**Single: ¥4,550. Double ¥8,500.**
Dinner ¥1,500. Breakfast ¥500 to ¥900.



**TOKYO**

## KIKUYA RYOKAN (喜久屋旅館)

2-18-9 Nishi Asakusa, Taito-ku, Tokyo 111.
10 rooms. ☎ 03-3841-6404, 4051. Fax: 6404
Station: Tawaramachi (Ginza Subway Line). Walk 8 mins.
**Single ¥4,950. Double ¥8,500.** No dinner. Breakfast ¥800.

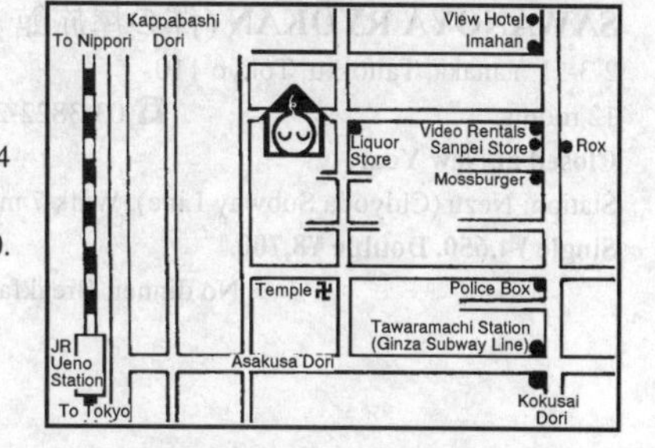

**TOKYO**

## SAKURA RYOKAN (桜旅館)

2-6-2 Iriya, Taito-ku, Tokyo 110.

20 rooms. ☎ 03-3876-8118. Fax: 3873-9456

Station: ① Iriya (Hibiya Subway Line). Walk 5 mins.

② Uguisudani (Yamanote Line). From South Exit, walk 15 mins.

**Single ¥5,150. Double ¥9,300.**

No dinner. Breakfast ¥600 to ¥700.

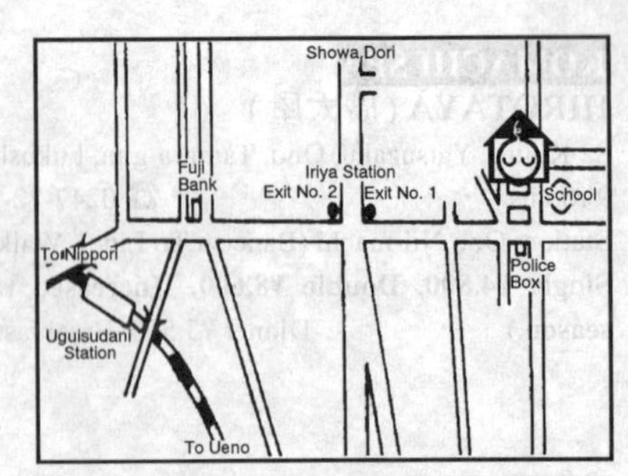


## RYOKAN SANSUI-SO (旅館山水荘)

2-9-5 Higashi Gotanda, Shinagawa-ku, Tokyo 141.

9 rooms. ☎ 03-3441-7475. Fax: 3449-1944

Station: Gotanda (Yamanote Line or Toei Asakusa Subway Line). Walk 5 mins.

**Single ¥4,900. Double ¥8,600.** No meals.

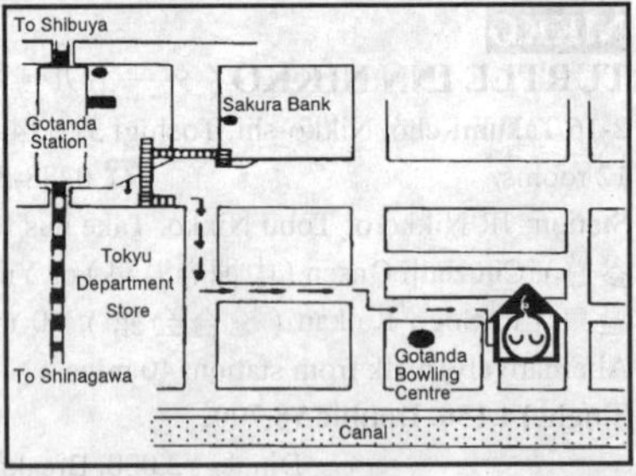


## RYOKAN TOKI (旅館都貴)

5-21-1 Minami Koiwa, Edogawa-ku, Tokyo 133.

17 rooms. ☎ 03-3657-1747. Fax: 3671-0655

Station: Koiwa (Sobu Line). From South Exit, walk 10 mins. along 'Flower Road'.

**Single ¥5,650. Double ¥8,300.**

Dinner ¥1,500. Breakfast ¥700 to ¥800.

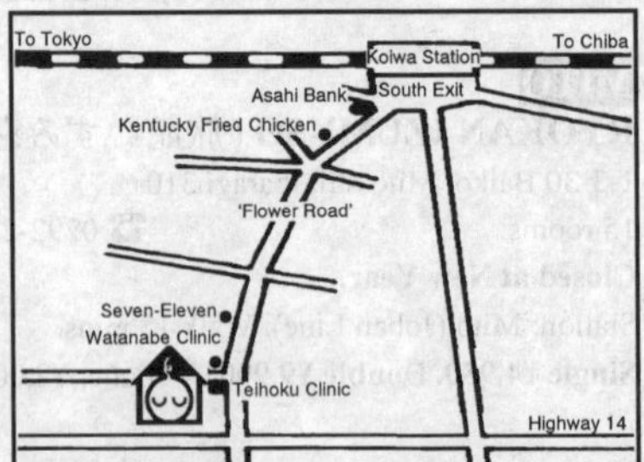


## RYOKAN KATSUTARO (旅館勝太郎)

4-16-8 Ikenohata, Taito-ku, Tokyo 110.

7 rooms. ☎ 03-3821-9808. Fax: 4789

Station: ① Nezu (Chiyoda Subway Line). Walk 7 mins.

② Keisei Ueno (Keisei Private Railway). Walk 10 mins.

③ JR Ueno (Yamanote Line). Walk 15 mins.

**Single ¥4,650. Double ¥8,700.** No dinner. Breakfast ¥500.

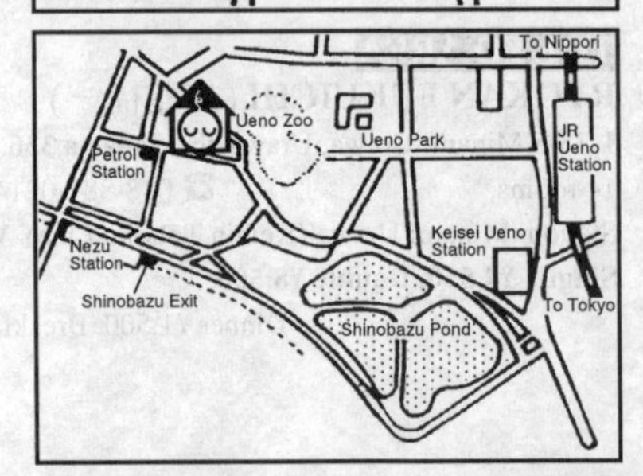


## SAWANOYA RYOKAN (澤の屋旅館)

2-3-11 Yanaka, Taito-ku, Tokyo 110.

12 rooms. ☎ 03-3822-2251. Fax: 2252

**Closed at New Year.**

Station: Nezu (Chiyoda Subway Line). Walk 7 mins.

**Single ¥4,650. Double ¥8,700.**

No dinner. Breakfast ¥300 to ¥900.

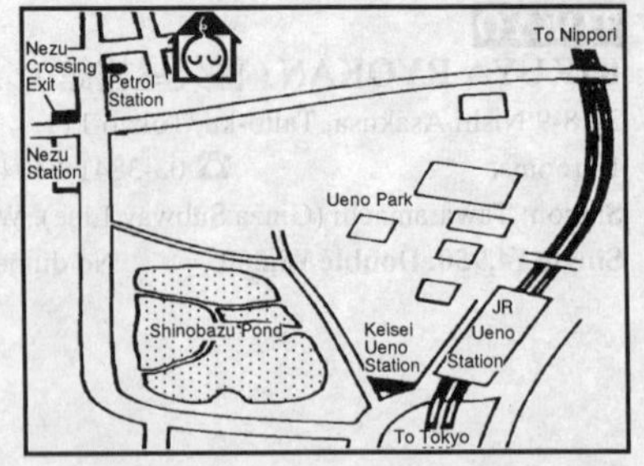

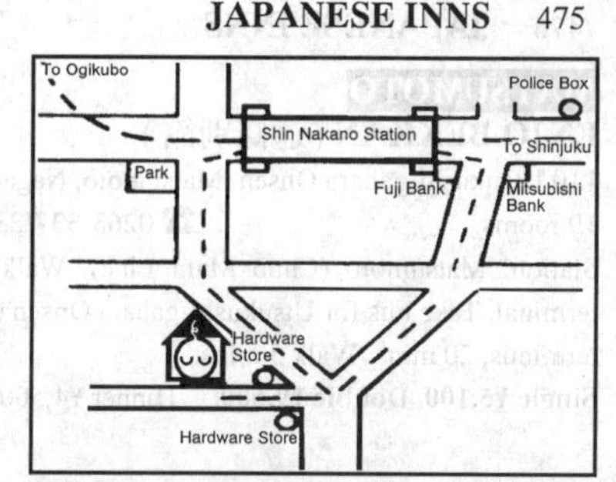


**TOKYO**

## SHIN NAKANO LODGE (新中野ロッヂ)

6-1-1 Hon-cho, Nakano-ku, Tokyo 164.
9 rooms. ☎ 03-3381-4886. Fax: 4219
Station: Shin Nakano (Marunouchi Subway Line). From exit no. 1, walk 5 mins.
**Single ¥4,450. Double ¥9,300.** No meals.

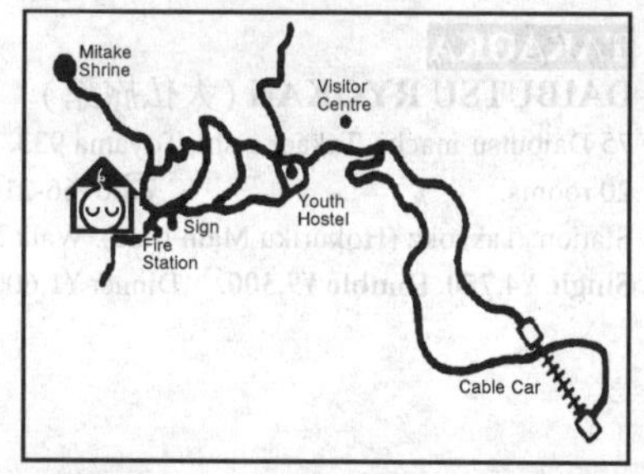


**TOKYO OUTSKIRTS**

## KOMADORI SANSO (駒鳥山荘)

155 Mitake-san, Ome-shi, Tokyo 198-01.
10 rooms. ☎ 0428-78-8472. Fax: same
Station: Mitake (Ome Line). Take bus for Cablecar Shita (ケーブルカー下) to terminus, 10 mins. Then take cablecar to upper station, 6 mins. Walk 15 mins.
**Caution:** Last cablecar 18:30.
**Single ¥4,650. Double ¥8,300. (Increased rates in holiday season.)** Dinner ¥2,000. Breakfast ¥800 to ¥1,000.

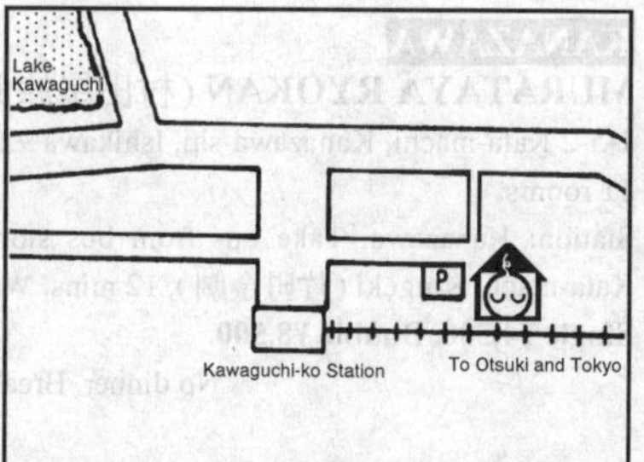


**NEAR MT. FUJI**

## PETIT HOTEL EBISUYA (プチホテルエビスヤ)

3647 Funatsu, Kawaguchiko-machi, Yamanashi 401-03.
9 rooms. ☎ 0555-72-0165
Station: Kawaguchi-ko (Fuji Kyuko Private Railway), accessible from JR Otsuki (Chuo Line). Walk 1 min. Alternatively, take express bus from Shinjuku (Yamanote Line) to Kawaguchi-ko (河口湖), 1 hr. 45 mins. Walk 1 min.
**Single ¥5,000. Double ¥10,000.**
Dinner from ¥2,000. Breakfast from ¥1,000.

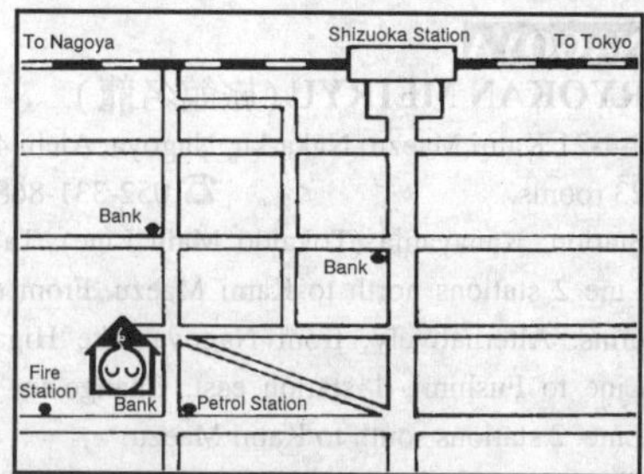


**SHIZUOKA**

## KAGETSU RYOKAN (花月旅館)

1-5-2 Inagawa, Shizuoka-shi, Shizuoka 422.
13 rooms. ☎ 054-281-0034. Fax: 0759
Station: Shizuoka (Shinkansen or Tokaido Main Line). Walk 6 mins.
**Single ¥5,300. Double ¥7,600.**
Dinner ¥1,500 to ¥3,000. Breakfast ¥600 to ¥800.

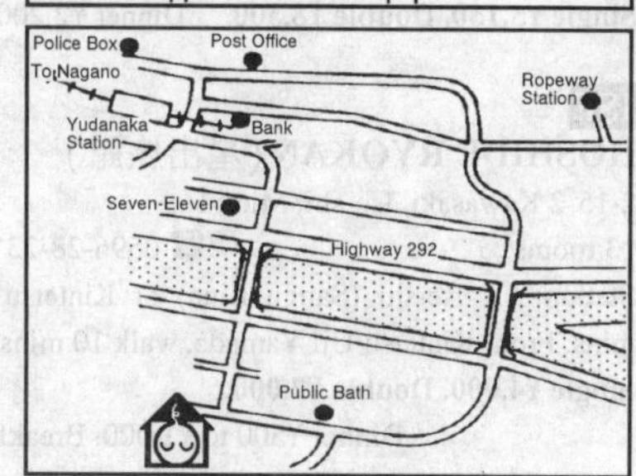


**NEAR NAGANO**

## UOTOSHI RYOKAN (魚敏旅館)

2563 Sano, Yamanouchi, Shimo Takai-gun, Nagano 381-04.
8 rooms. ☎ 0269-33-1215. Fax: 0074
Station: Yudanaka (Nagano Private Railway), accessible from JR Nagano. Walk 7 mins. or telephone to be collected from station.
**Single ¥4,050. Double ¥7,500.**
Dinner ¥2,300 to ¥3,300. Breakfast ¥900.

## MATSUMOTO

### ENJO BEKKAN (遠條別館)

110 Utsukushi-gahara Onsen, Matsumoto, Nagano 390-02.

19 rooms. ☎ 0263-33-7233. Fax: 36-2084

Station: Matsumoto (Chuo Main Line). Walk 5 mins. to bus terminal. Take bus for Utsukushi-gahara Onsen (美ヶ原温泉) to terminus, 20 mins. Walk 5 mins.

**Single ¥5,100. Double ¥9,600.** Dinner ¥4,500. Breakfast ¥800.

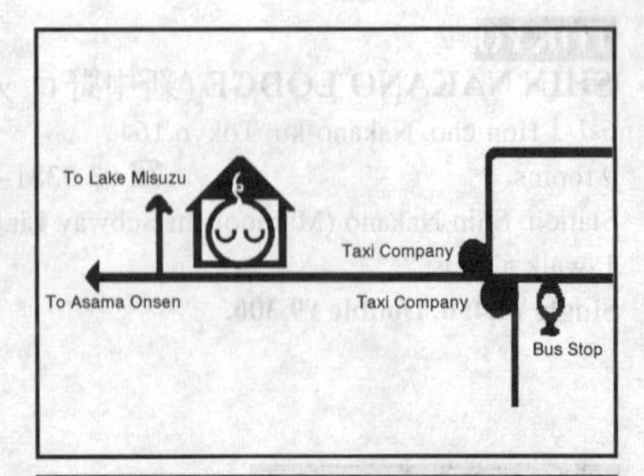


## TAKAOKA

### DAIBUTSU RYOKAN (大仏旅館)

75 Daibutsu-machi, Takaoka-shi, Toyama 933.

20 rooms. ☎ 0766-21-0075. Fax: same

Station: Takaoka (Hokuriku Main Line). Walk 5 mins.

**Single ¥4,750. Double ¥9,300.** Dinner ¥1,600. Breakfast ¥800.

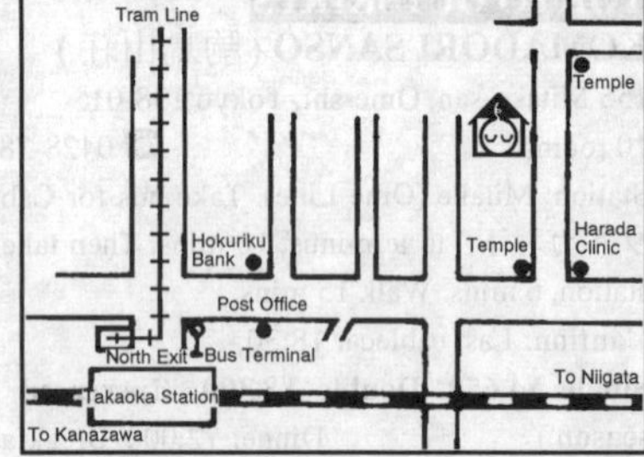


## KANAZAWA

### MURATAYA RYOKAN (村田屋旅館)

1-5-2 Kata-machi, Kanazawa-shi, Ishikawa 920.

11 rooms. ☎ 0762-63-0455

Station: Kanazawa. Take bus from bus stop no. 7, 8 or 9 to Kata-machi Kingeki (片町金劇), 12 mins. Walk 3 mins.

**Single ¥4,500. Double ¥8,500.**

No dinner. Breakfast ¥450 to ¥800.

## NAGOYA

### RYOKAN MEIRYU (旅館名龍)

2-4-21 Kami Maezu, Naka-ku, Nagoya, Aichi 460.

23 rooms. ☎ 052-331-8686. Fax: 321-6119

Station: Kanayama (Tokaido Main Line). Take Meijo Subway Line 2 stations north to Kami Maezu. From exit no. 3, walk 3 mins. Alternatively, from Nagoya take Higashiyama Subway Line to Fushimi, 1 station east. Change to Tsurumai Subway Line. 2 stations south to Kami Maezu.

**Single ¥5,150. Double ¥8,300.** Dinner ¥2,200. Breakfast ¥600.

## ISE

### HOSHIDE RYOKAN (星出旅館)

2-15-2 Kawasaki, Ise-shi, Mie 516.

13 rooms. ☎ 0596-28-2377. Fax: 27-2830

Station: JR Ise-shi (Sangu Line) or Kintetsu Ise-shi. Walk 7 mins. From Kintetsu Uji Yamada, walk 10 mins.

**Single ¥4,000. Double ¥7,000.**

Dinner ¥500 to ¥1,000. Breakfast ¥500 to ¥700.

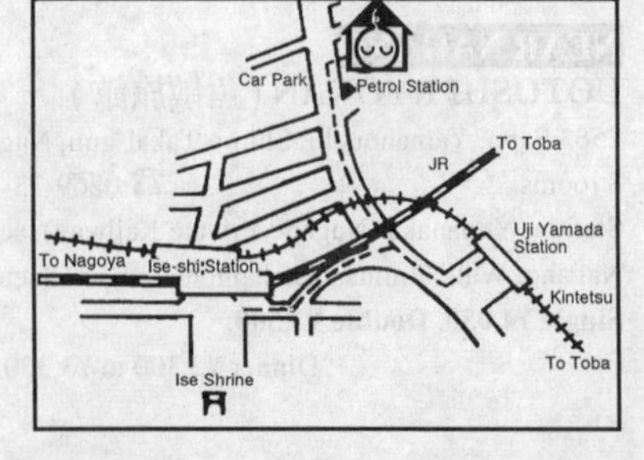

**NEAR ISE**

## RYOKAN ISHIYAMA-SO (旅館石山荘)

Yokoyama-jima, Kashiko-jima, Ago, Shima-gun, Mie 517-05.

12 rooms. ☎ 05995-2-1527. Fax: 1240

Station: Kashikojima (Kintetsu Private Railway), accessible from JR Toba (Sangu Line). Walk to quay and telephone inn for collection by boat (2 mins. ride).

**Single ¥4,800. Double ¥9,600.**

Dinner ¥1,500. Breakfast included.

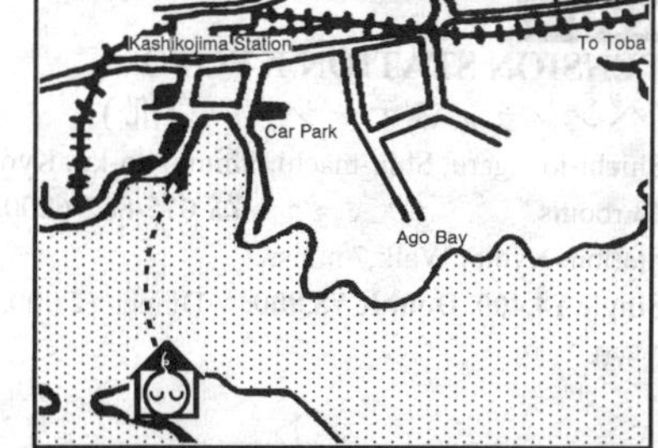


**MISUGI**

## MISUGI KANKO HOTEL UOKU (美杉観光ホテル魚九)

Misugi-mura Yachi, Ichishi-gun, Mie 515-34.

65 rooms. ☎ 05927-2-1155. Fax: 1160

Station: Ise Yachi (Meisho Line). Walk 4 mins.

**Single ¥4,450. Double ¥7,900.** Dinner ¥7,000. Breakfast ¥1,000.

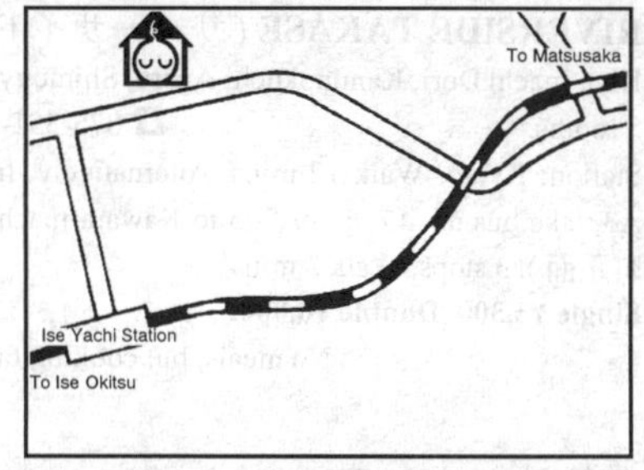


**NARA**

## RYOKAN MATSUMAE (旅館松前)

28-1 Higashi Terabayashi-cho, Nara 630.

20 rooms. ☎ 0742-22-3686. Fax: 26-3927

Station: JR Nara or Kintetsu Nara. From Kintetsu Nara, walk 7 mins. From JR Nara, walk 25 mins.

**Single ¥5,300. Double ¥8,600.**

No dinner. Breakfast ¥1,200 to ¥1,500.

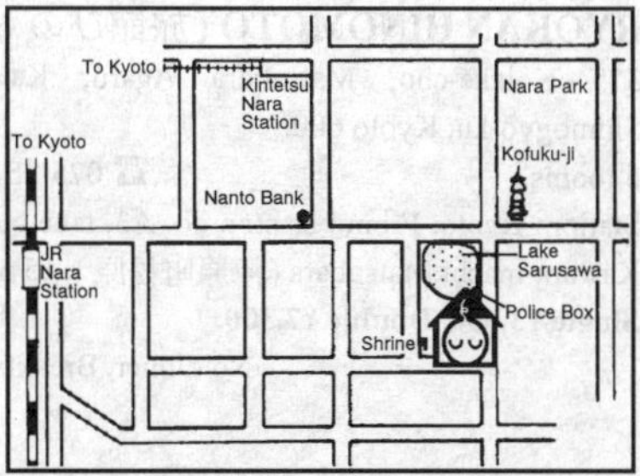


## RYOKAN SEIKAN-SO (旅館静観荘)

29 Higashi Kitsuji-cho, Nara 630.

13 rooms. ☎ 0742-22-2670. Fax: same

Station: JR Nara or Kintetsu Nara. From Kintetsu Nara, walk 12 mins. From JR Nara, walk 25 mins. or take bus no. 1 (circular) to Kita Kyobate, 10 mins.

**Single ¥3,950. Double ¥7,900.**

No dinner. Breakfast ¥450 to ¥700.

**KYOTO**

## MATSUBAYA RYOKAN (松葉家旅館)

Nishi Iru, Higashi-no To-in, Kami Juzuya-machi Dori, Shimogyo-ku, Kyoto 600.

11 rooms. ☎ 075-351-4268, 3727. Fax: 3505

Station: Kyoto. Walk 8 mins.

**Single ¥4,650. Double ¥9,300.** Dinner ¥3,500. Breakfast ¥1,000.

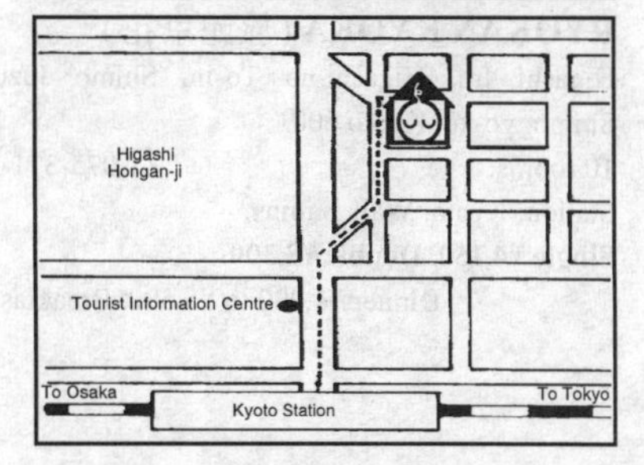

**KYOTO**

## PENSION STATION KYOTO (ペンションステーション京都)

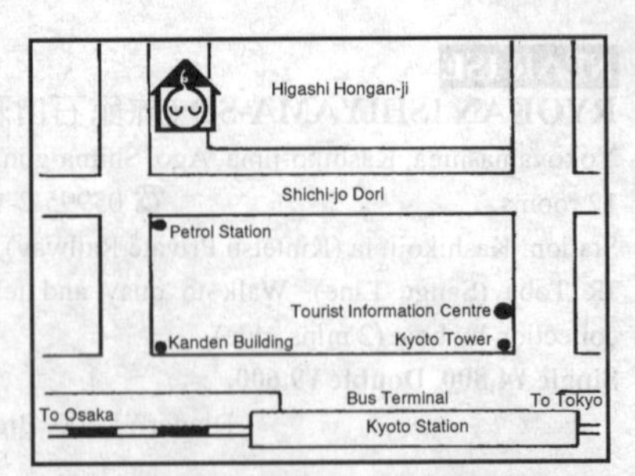


Shichi-jo Agaru, Shin-machi, Shimogyo-ku, Kyoto 600.
13 rooms. ☎ 075-882-6200. Fax: 862-0820
Station: Kyoto. Walk 7 mins.
**Single ¥4,400. Double ¥8,800.** Dinner ¥2,000. Breakfast ¥800.

## RIVERSIDE TAKASE (リバーサイド高瀬)

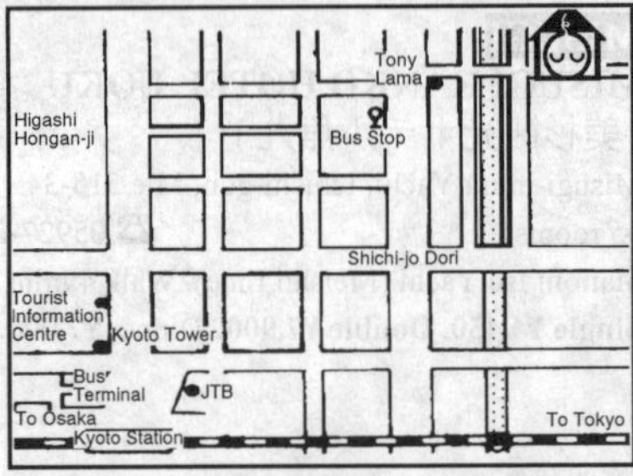


Kiya-machi Dori, Kaminokuchi Agaru, Shimogyo-ku, Kyoto 600.
5 rooms. ☎ 075-351-7920. Fax: same
Station: Kyoto. Walk 12 mins. Alternatively, from bus stop no. A3, take bus no. 17, 42 or 205 to Kawara-machi Shomen (河原町正面), 3 stops. Walk 3 mins.
**Single ¥3,300. Double ¥6,000.**
No meals, but cooking facilities available.

## RYOKAN HINOMOTO (旅館ひのもと)

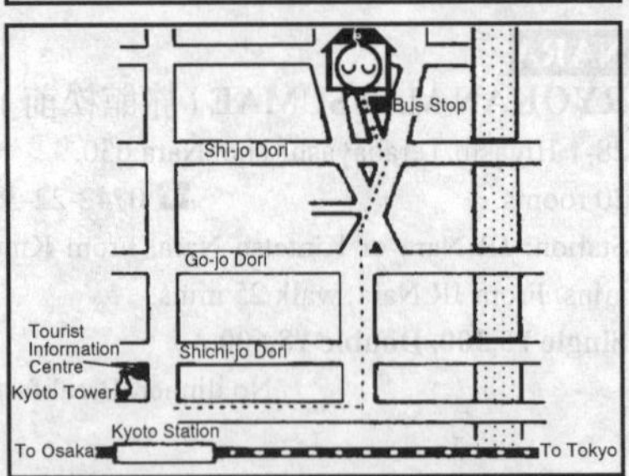


375 Kotake-cho, Matsubara Agaru, Kawara-machi Dori, Shimogyo-ku, Kyoto 600.
6 rooms. ☎ 075-351-4563. Fax: 3932
Station: Kyoto. From bus stop no. A3, take bus no. 17 or 205 to Kawara-machi Matsubara (河原町松原), 15 mins. Walk 3 mins.
**Single ¥3,650. Double ¥7,300.**
No dinner. Breakfast ¥300 to ¥1,000.

## RYOKAN HIRAIWA (旅館平岩)

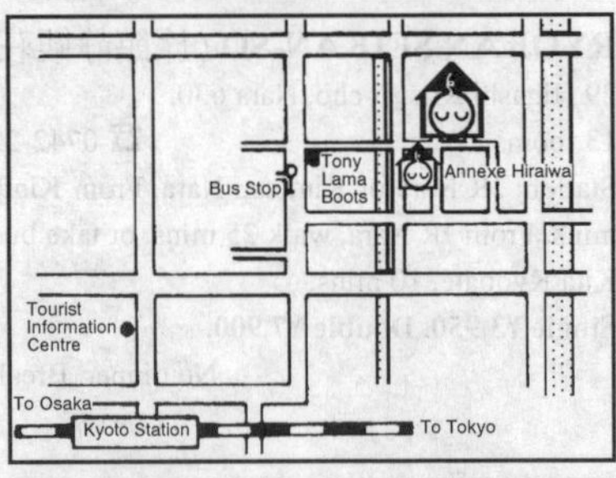


314 Hiyao-cho, Kaminokuchi Agaru, Ninomiya-cho Dori, Shimogyo-ku, Kyoto 600.
21 rooms. ☎ 075-351-6748. Fax: 6969
Station: Kyoto. Walk 12 mins. Alternatively, from bus stop no. A3, take bus no. 17, 42 or 205 to Kawara-machi Shomen (河原町正面), 3 stops. Walk 4 mins.
**Single ¥4,650. Double ¥8,300.**
No dinner. Breakfast ¥300 to ¥1,000.

## RYOKAN KYOKA (旅館京花)

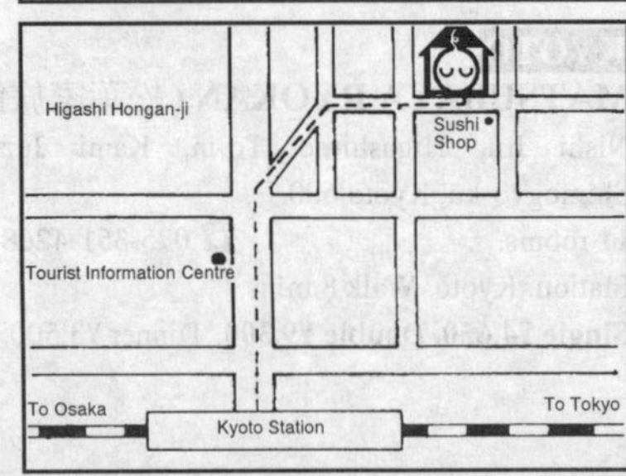


Higashi Iru, Higashi-no To-in, Shimo Juzuya-machi Dori, Shimogyo-ku, Kyoto 600.
10 rooms. ☎ 075-371-2709. Fax: same
Station: Kyoto. Walk 8 mins.
**Single ¥4,150. Double ¥8,300.**
Dinner ¥4,000 to ¥5,500. Breakfast ¥350 to ¥1,500.

**KYOTO**

## RYOKAN MURAKAMIYA (旅館村上家)

270 Sasaya-cho, Shichi-jo Agaru, Higashi-no To-in Dori, Shimogyo-ku, Kyoto 600.

8 rooms. ☎ 075-371-1260. Fax: 7161

Station: Kyoto. Walk 7 mins.

**Single ¥4,150. Double ¥8,300.** No dinner. Breakfast ¥1,000.

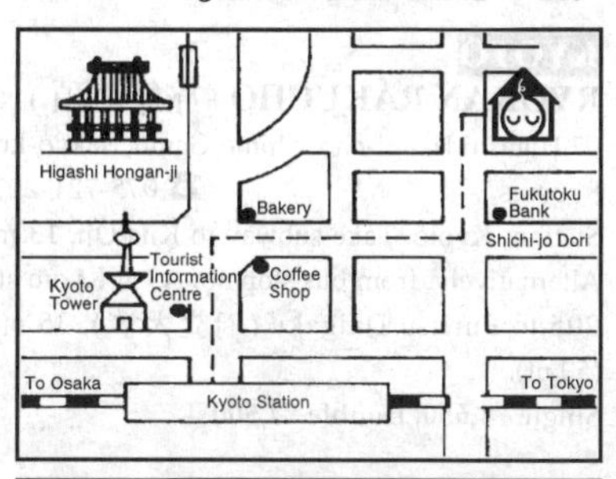


## PENSION HIGASHIYAMA (ペンション東山)

San-jo Sagaru, Shirakawa Suji, Higashiyama-ku, Kyoto 605.

13 rooms. ☎ 075-882-1181. Fax: 862-0820

Station: Kyoto. From bus stop no. A2, take bus no. 206 to Chion-in-mae (知恩院前), 20 mins. Walk 2 mins.

**Single ¥4,400. Double ¥8,800.** Dinner ¥2,000. Breakfast ¥800.

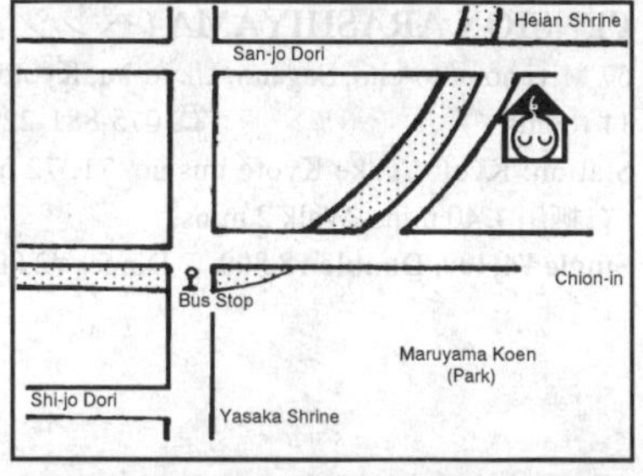


## RYOKAN MISHIMA (旅館みしま)

Uma-machi Dori, Higashi Oji Higashi Iru, Higashiyama-ku, Kyoto 605.

7 rooms. ☎ 075-551-0033. Fax: 531-9768

Station: Kyoto. From bus stop no. A2, take bus no. 206 to Higashiyama Uma-machi (東山馬町), 10 mins. Walk 3 mins.

**Single ¥4,500. Double ¥8,000.** No meals.

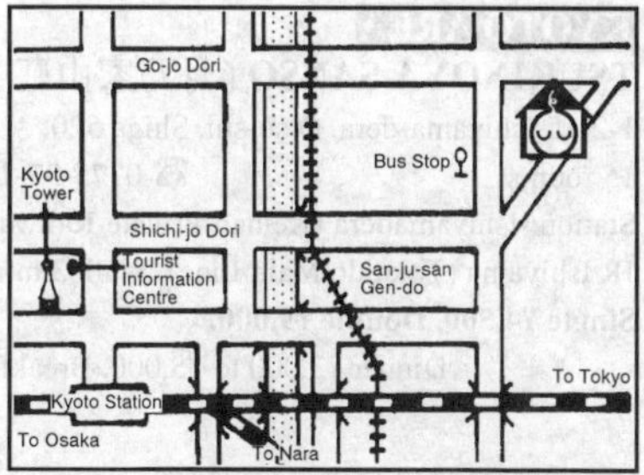


## KYO-NO YADO OHTO (京の宿鴨東)

Hitotsujime Minami Sagaru, Shichi-jo Kamogawa Higashi, Higashiyama-ku, Kyoto 605.

12 rooms. ☎ 075-541-7803. Fax: 561-9751

Station: Kyoto. Walk 20 mins. Alternatively, from bus stop no. A2, take bus no. 206 or 208 to Shichi-jo Ohashi (七条大橋), 7 mins. Walk 2 mins.

**Single ¥3,700. Double ¥7,400.**

Dinner ¥1,500. Breakfast ¥300 to ¥1,000.

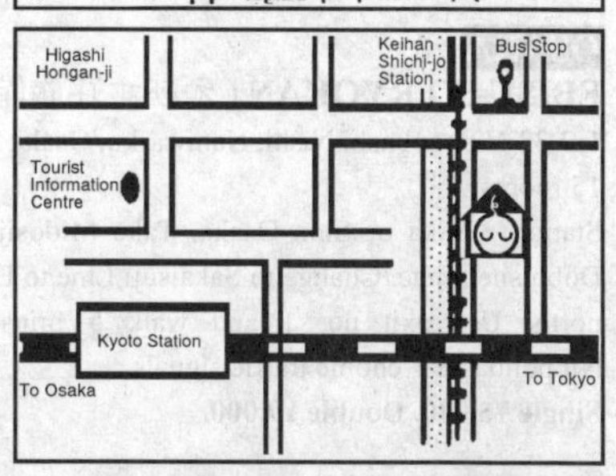


## RYOKAN SEIKI (旅館晴輝)

188-1 Kadowaki-cho, Yamato Oji, Go-jo Agaru Higashi Iru, Higashiyama-ku, Kyoto 605.

9 rooms. ☎ 075-682-0311. Fax: 551-9251

Station: Kyoto. From bus stop no. A2, take bus no. 206 to Go-jo Zaka (五条坂), 15 mins. Walk 2 mins.

**Single ¥3,750. Double ¥7,800.**

Dinner ¥1,000 to ¥2,000. Breakfast ¥300 to ¥1,000.

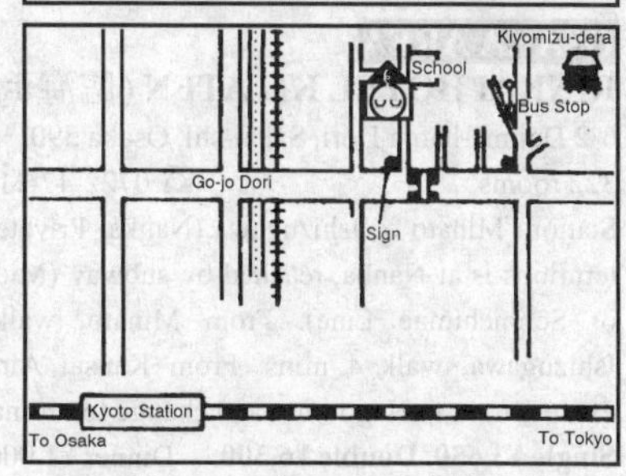

## KYOTO

### RYOKAN RAKUCHO (旅館洛頂)

67 Higashi Hangi-cho, Shimo Gamo, Sakyo-ku, Kyoto 606.
8 rooms. ☎ 075-721-2174. Fax: 791-7202
Station: Kyoto. Take subway to Kita Oji, 13 mins. Walk 8 mins. Alternatively, from bus stop no. A3 at Kyoto station, take bus no. 205 to Furitsu Daigaku (府立大学), 35 mins. Walk 1 min. (50 m).
**Single ¥4,650. Double ¥7,500.** No meals.

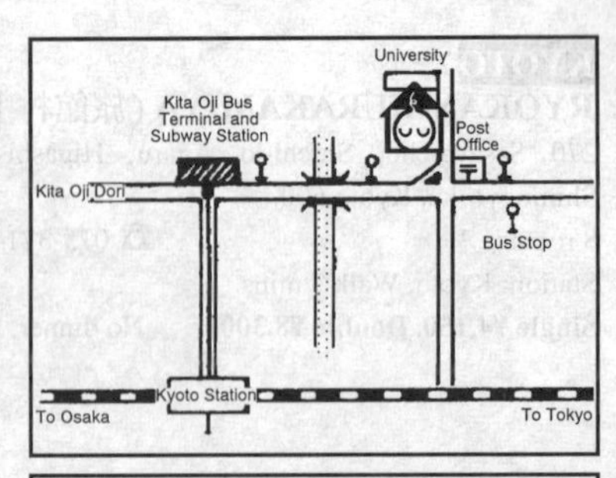


### PENSION ARASHIYAMA (ペンション嵐山)

67 Miyanomoto-cho, Sagano, Ukyo-ku, Kyoto 616.
11 rooms. ☎ 075-881-2294. Fax: 862-0820
Station: Kyoto. Take Kyoto bus no. 71, 72 or 73 to Arisugawa (有栖川), 40 mins. Walk 2 mins.
**Single ¥4,400. Double ¥8,800.** Dinner ¥2,000. Breakfast ¥800.

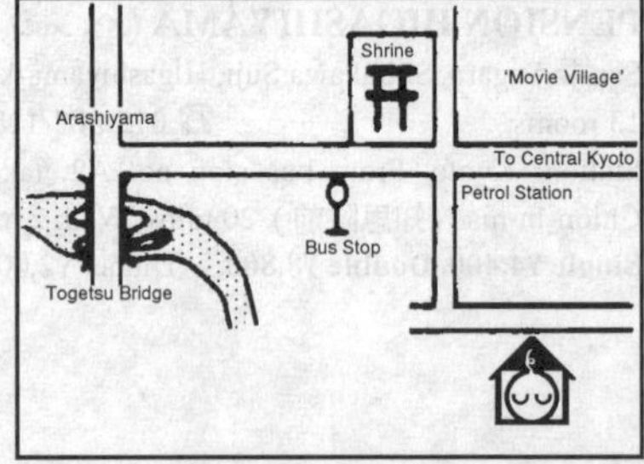


## KYOTO AREA

### TSUKINOYA SANSO (月乃家山荘)

1-2-15 Ishiyama-dera, Otsu-shi, Shiga 520.
15 rooms. ☎ 0775-37-1058. Fax: 33-3551
Station: Ishiyamadera (Keihan Private Railway), accessible from JR Ishiyama (Tokaido Main Line). Walk 3 mins.
**Single ¥4,500. Double ¥9,000.**
Dinner ¥3,000 to ¥5,000. Breakfast ¥500 to ¥1,500.

## OSAKA

### EBISU-SO RYOKAN (えびす荘旅館)

1-7-33 Nipponbashi Nishi, Naniwa-ku, Osaka 556.
15 rooms. ☎ 06-643-4861
Station: Osaka or Shin Osaka. Take Midosiji Subway Line to Dobutsuen-mae. Change to Sakaisuji Line to Ebisu-cho, 1 station north. Use exit no. 1 and walk 5 mins., turning left at Nipponbashi 4-chome traffic signals.
**Single ¥5,000. Double ¥9,000.** No meals.

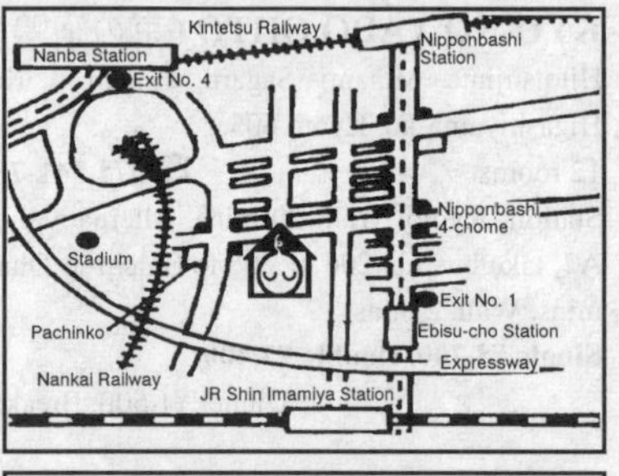

## OSAKA AREA

### RINKAI HOTEL KITATEN (臨海ホテル北店)

6-2 Dejima-hama Dori, Sakai-shi, Osaka 590.
322 rooms. ☎ 0722-47-1111. Fax: 45-8206
Station: Minato or Ishizugawa (Nankai Private Railway). Osaka terminus is at Nanba, reached by subway (Midosuji, Yotsubashi or Sennichimae Line). From Minato, walk 5 mins. From Ishizugawa, walk 4 mins. From Kansai Airport take Nankai express train to Hagoromo and change to ordinary train.
**Single ¥3,650. Double ¥6,300.** Dinner ¥1,000. Breakfast ¥350.

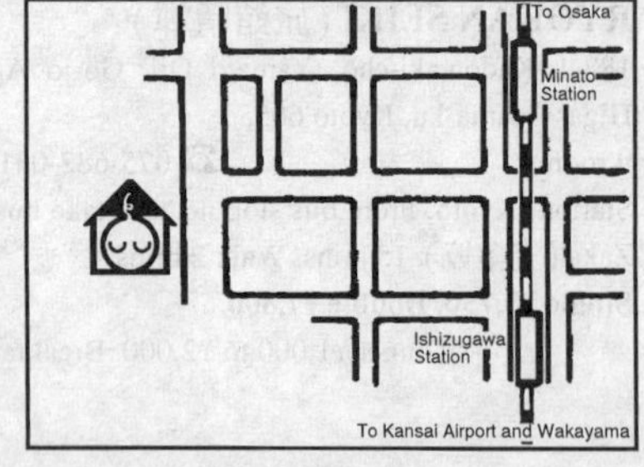

**HIROSHIMA**

## MIKAWA RYOKAN (三河旅館)

9-6 Kyobashi-cho, Minami-ku, Hiroshima 732.

13 rooms. ☎ 082-261-2719

Station: Hiroshima. Walk 7 mins.

**Single ¥3,650. Double ¥6,300.** No dinner. Breakfast ¥700.

## MINSHUKU IKEDAYA (民宿池田屋)

6-36 Dobashi-cho, Naka-ku, Hiroshima 730.

15 rooms. ☎ 082-231-3329. Fax: 7875

Station: Hiroshima. Take tram to Dobashi (土橋), 15 mins. Walk 2 mins.

**Single ¥4,150. Double ¥7,300.** No dinner. Breakfast ¥1,000.

**IMABARI**

## KOMECHO RYOKAN (米長旅館)

1-1-4 Tokiwa-cho, Imabari-shi, Ehime 794.

10 rooms. ☎ 0898-32-0554. Fax: 33-0843

Station: Imabari (Yosan Line). Walk 15 mins. From Imabari Port, walk 1 min.

**Single ¥4,550. Double ¥8,650.**

Dinner ¥2,000 to ¥3,500. Breakfast ¥500 to ¥1,000.

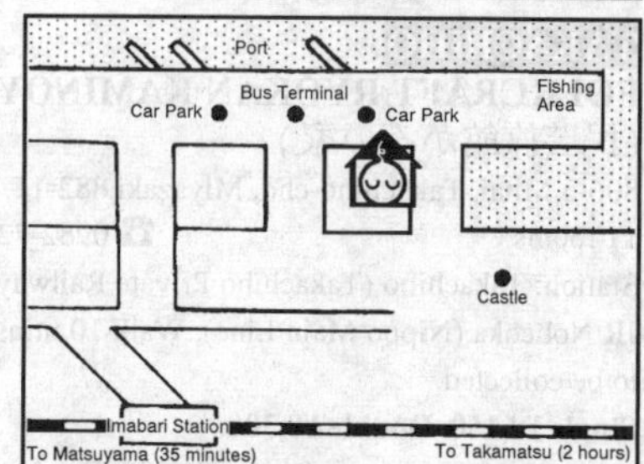


**KITA KYUSHU**

## HOTEL TOWNHOUSE MATSUYA (ホテルタウンハウスまつや)

2-8-3 Nishi Hon-machi, Yahata Higashi-ku, Kita Kyushu, Fukuoka 805.

60 rooms. ☎ 093-661-7890

Station: Yahata (Kagoshima Main Line). Walk 1 min.

**Single ¥5,300. Double ¥9,400.**

Dinner — restaurant available. Breakfast ¥650 to ¥700.

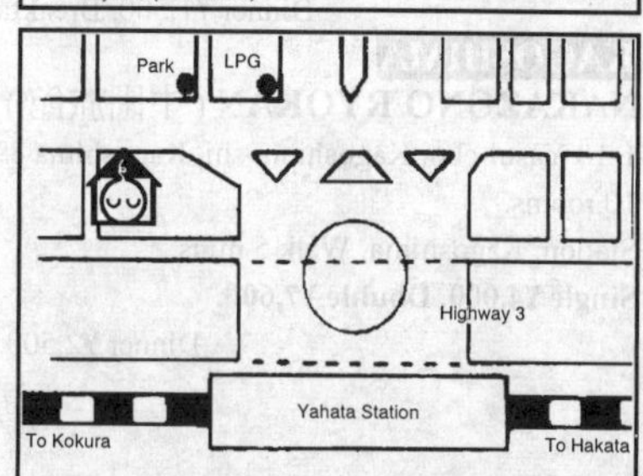


**NAGASAKI**

## MINSHUKU TANPOPO (民宿たんぽぽ)

21-7 Hoei-cho, Nagasaki-shi, Nagasaki 852.

13 rooms. ☎ 0958-61-6230. Fax: 64-0032

Station: Urakami (Nagasaki Main Line). Walk 15 mins.

**Single ¥4,150. Double ¥7,300.** Dinner ¥1,500. Breakfast ¥500.

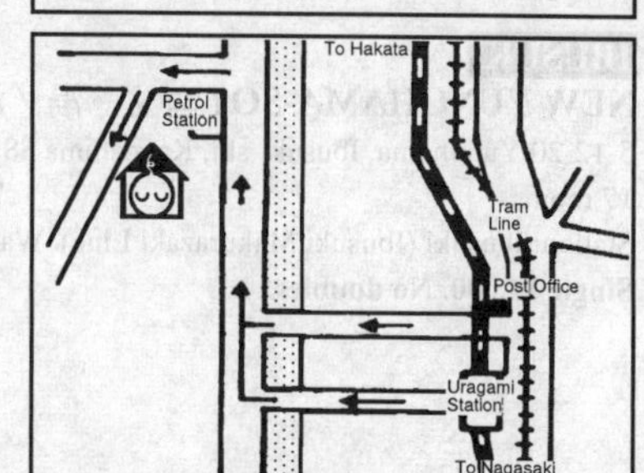

## KUMAMOTO

### MINSHUKU RYOKAN KAJITA (民宿旅館梶田)

1-2-7 Shin-machi, Kumamoto-shi, Kumamoto 860.

10 rooms. ☎ 096-353-1546

Station: Kami Kumamoto (Kagoshima Main Line). Take tram to Shin-machi (新町), 10 mins. Walk 2 mins.

**Single ¥4,150. Double ¥7,900.** Dinner ¥1,500. Breakfast ¥700.

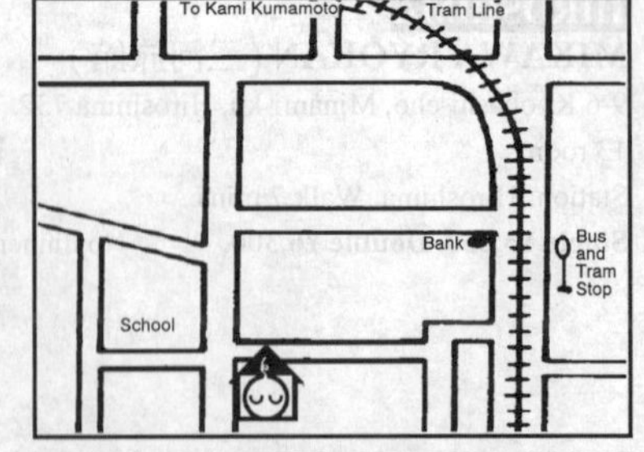


## BEPPU

### MINSHUKU KOKAGE (民宿こかげ)

8-9 Ekimae-cho, Beppu-shi, Oita 874.

16 rooms. ☎ 0977-23-1753. Fax: 3895

Station: Beppu (Nippo Line). Walk 2 mins.

**Single ¥4,300. Double ¥6,600. (Increased rates in holiday season.)** Dinner ¥1,860. Breakfast ¥825.

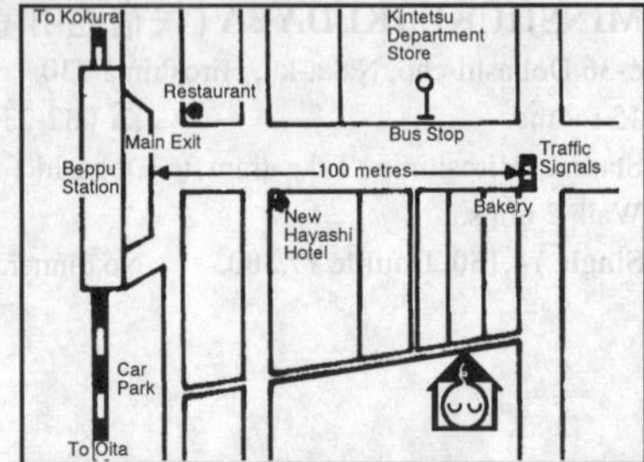


## TAKACHIHO

### FOLKCRAFT RYOKAN KAMINOYA (民芸旅館かみの家)

806-5 Mitai, Takachiho-cho, Miyazaki 882-11.

11 rooms. ☎ 0982-72-2111. Fax: 5040

Station: Takachiho (Takachiho Private Railway), accessible from JR Nobeoka (Nippo Main Line). Walk 10 mins. or telephone inn to be collected.

**Single ¥4,150. Double ¥8,300.**

Dinner ¥1,500. Breakfast ¥500 to ¥1,000.

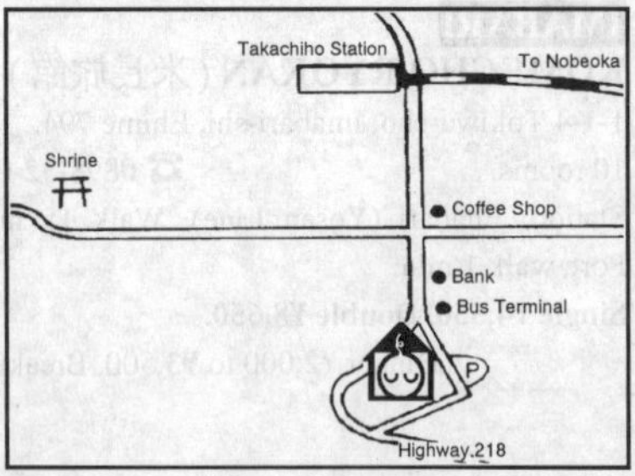

## KAGOSHIMA

### NAKAZONO RYOKAN (中園旅館)

1-18 Yasui-cho, Kagoshima-shi, Kagoshima 892.

10 rooms. ☎ 0992-26-5125

Station: Kagoshima. Walk 5 mins.

**Single ¥4,000. Double ¥7,600.**

Dinner ¥2,500. Breakfast ¥1,500.

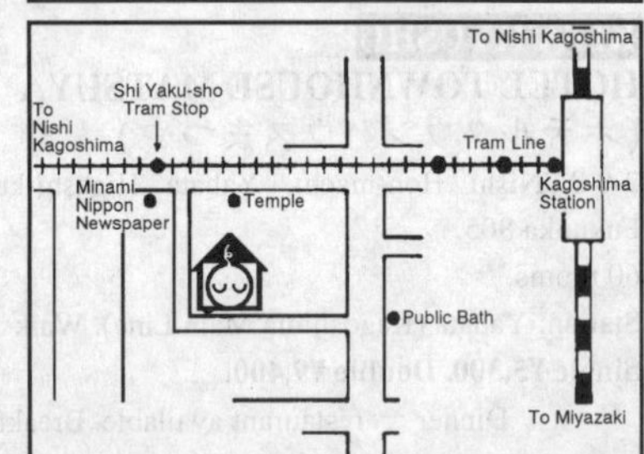


## IBUSUKI

### NEW YUNOHAMA-SO (ニュー湯ノ浜荘)

5-12-20 Yunohama, Ibusuki-shi, Kagoshima 881-04.

17 rooms. ☎ 0993-23-3088

Station: Ibusuki (Ibusuki Makurazaki Line). Walk 10 mins.

**Single ¥3,000. No doubles.** No meals.



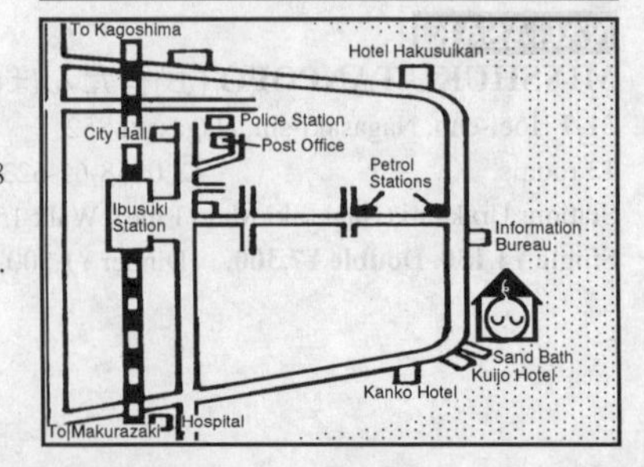

# BUSINESS HOTELS

Business hotels are to be found throughout Japan, not only in the large towns and cities listed here. The reason for our choice of these places is that they are locations likely to be visited by those from overseas and that they are large enough for the location of economical but acceptable accommodation to pose some difficulties.

Business hotels are designed for the travelling businessman, so they tend to have a large proportion of single rooms with some twins and few doubles. Facilities offered are adequate without being glamorous. In smaller places, such hotels tend to congregate around the railway station and are easy to locate, with rates often, but not always, displayed outside or in the entrance lobby. There is sometimes an hotel reservation service in larger stations, although it is unlikely that English will be spoken, while smaller places may have advertisements for accommodation in the station entrance hall. Failing that, station staff may be able to recommend somewhere cheap ('*yasui*'). Usually, however, in places not listed in this book, it is necessary only to have a look round outside.

Business hotels are for those at the most affluent end of our range of readers, the only marginally impoverished, those who want a reasonably comfortable holiday in Japan, but do not want to waste money. What you can expect from business hotels is acceptable levels of accommodation without any frills. In smaller places, most rooms will have attached bathrooms, but in larger towns and cities, such as those listed in this book, the cheaper rooms will be without bath. A communal Japanese-style bathroom will, of course, be available. Instructions for its use are in the introduction to the Youth Hostels section. Most rooms will have facilities for making tea, while other drinks will usually be available from a machine, sometimes at inflated prices.

Again we have imposed a limitation of ¥5,000 for a single room or ¥10,000 for a double or twin. Hotels listed satisfy at least one of these two criteria at the time of writing. However, prices have been increasing rapidly recently in this area, so please be sure to allow 5% per annum (base 1995) when budgeting. Also tax will usually be added to your bill at these hotels. Currently the rate is 3%, but the threat is that it will soon be raised to 7%. Business hotels do not usually impose 'service charges', but there may be just a few which do so, in which case the rate will be 10%. Prices quoted in this book are for the cheapest rooms, which may not always be available, of course. 'Double' means double or twin, whichever is cheaper. You should not expect that any English will be spoken at business hotels, but the words 'single', 'double' and 'twin' are all used in Japanese, as is 'bath' (not 'bathroom'). Average prices for business hotels are approximately ¥5,000 single or ¥8,000 for two. Rates in this book are slightly higher, because listings are given only for major locations. You will generally get better value – a more pleasant hotel with lower prices and superior facilities – by staying in rather smaller towns, rather than those listed here, where possible.

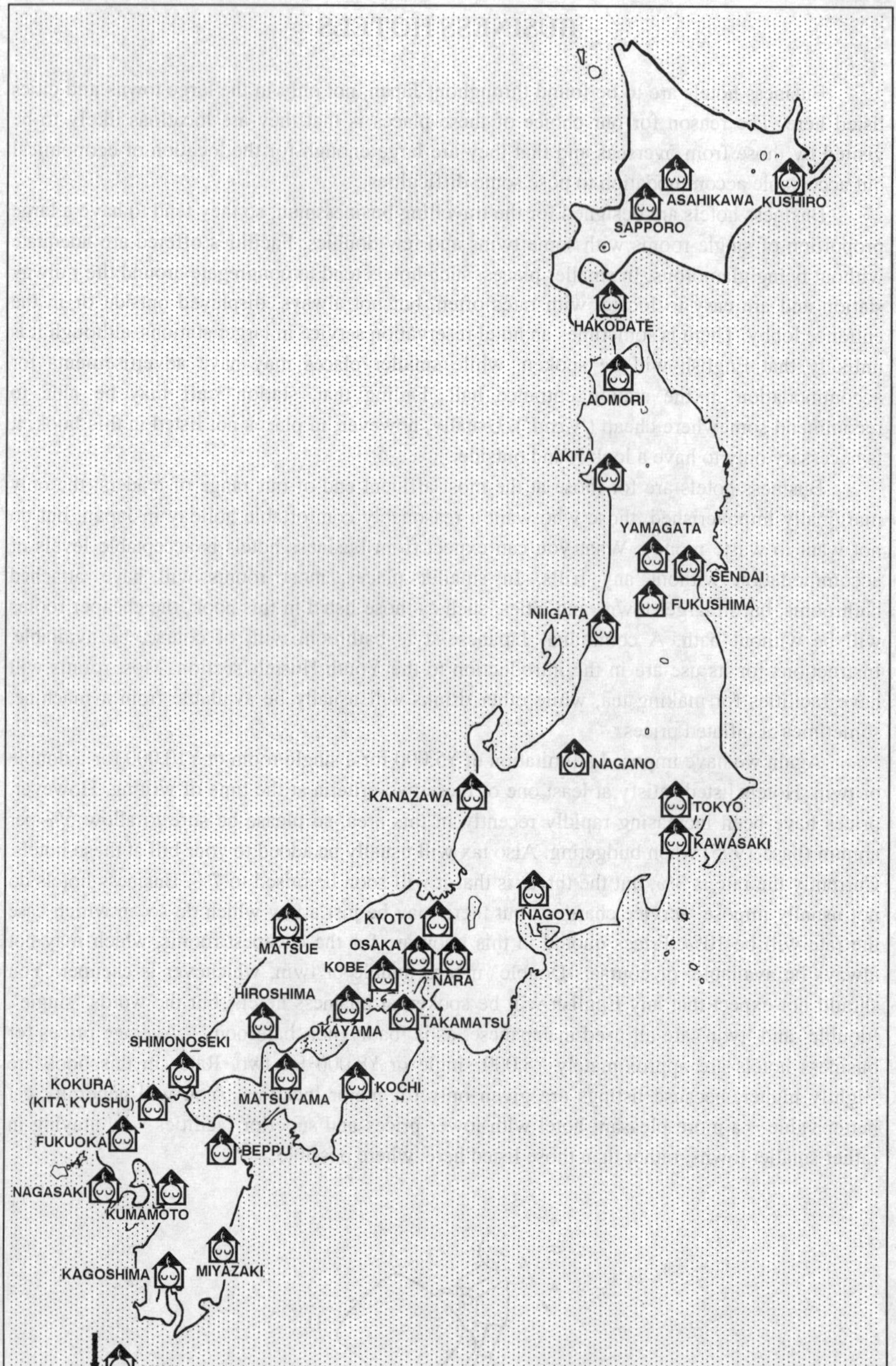

ASAHIKAWA
KUSHIRO
SAPPORO
HAKODATE
AOMORI
AKITA
YAMAGATA
SENDAI
FUKUSHIMA
NIIGATA
NAGANO
KANAZAWA
TOKYO
KAWASAKI
NAGOYA
KYOTO
MATSUE
OSAKA
KOBE
NARA
HIROSHIMA
OKAYAMA
TAKAMATSU
SHIMONOSEKI
KOKURA (KITA KYUSHU)
MATSUYAMA
KOCHI
FUKUOKA
BEPPU
NAGASAKI
KUMAMOTO
KAGOSHIMA
MIYAZAKI
NAHA

## SAPPORO

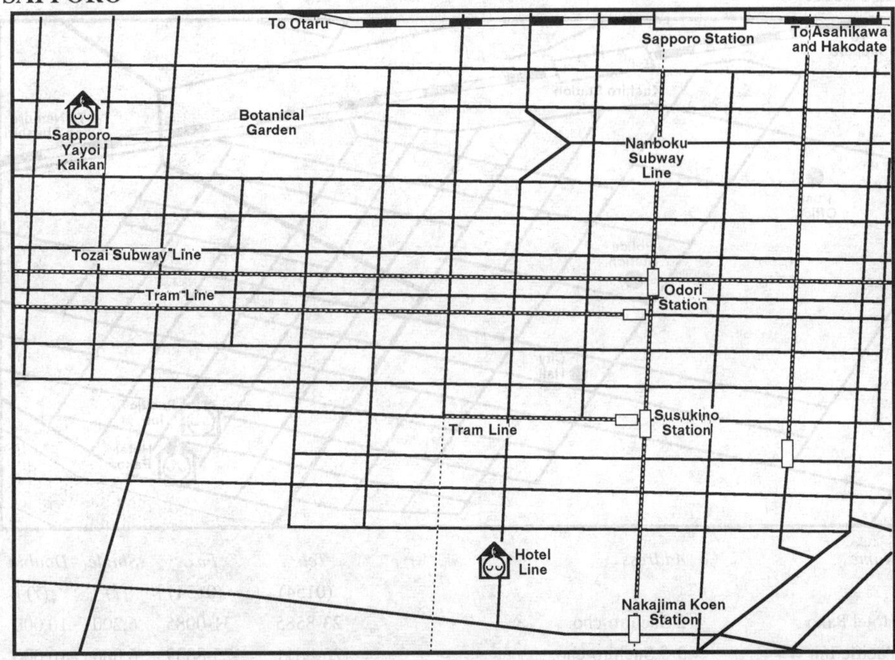


| *Name* | *Address* | *Tel.* (011) | *Fax.* (011) | *Single* (¥) | *Double* (¥) |
|---|---|---|---|---|---|
| Sapporo Yayoi Kaikan | Kita 3-jo Nishi 12-1, Chuo-ku. | 271-2511 | 271-2511 | 5,000 | 8,800 |
| Hotel Line | Minami 8-jo Nishi 6, Chuo-ku. | 521-3371 | 521-3292 | 4,900 | 6,900 |

## ASAHIKAWA

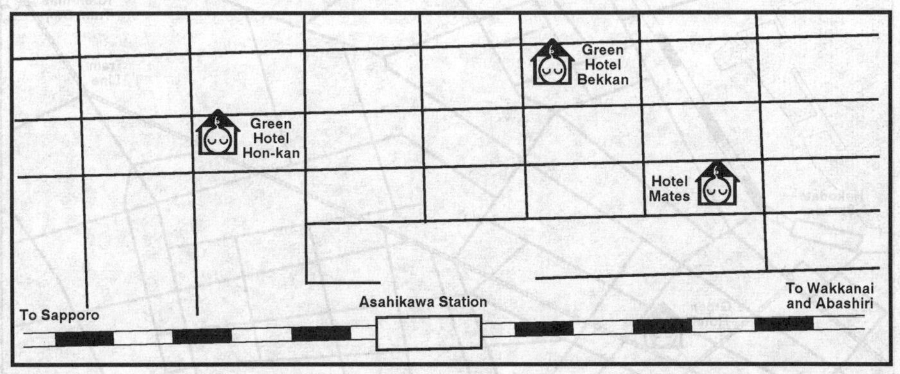


| *Name* | *Address* | *Tel.* (0166) | *Fax.* (0166) | *Single* (¥) | *Double* (¥) |
|---|---|---|---|---|---|
| Green Hotel Hon-kan | 1-jo Dori, 6-chome Migi 1. | 23-2281 | 22-1182 | 5,250 | 9,000 |
| Green Hotel Bekkan | 1-jo Dori, 9-chome Hidari 1. | 26-1414 | 26-1414 | 5,150 | 9,750 |
| Hotel Mates | Miyashita Dori, 10-chome Hidari 5. | 22-0011 | 22-0050 | 5,000 | 9,400 |

## KUSHIRO

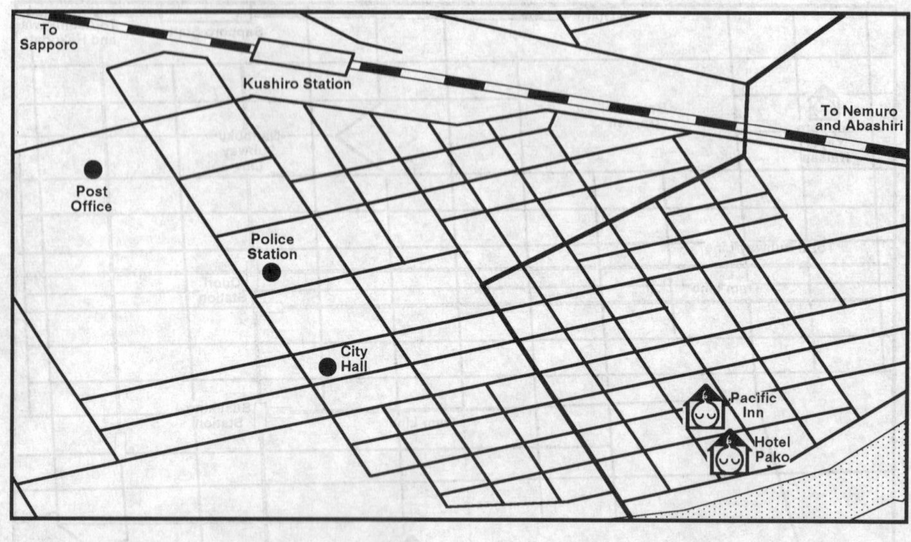


| *Name* | *Address* | *Tel.* (0154) | *Fax.* (0154) | *Single* (¥) | *Double* (¥) |
|---|---|---|---|---|---|
| Hotel Pako | 2 Suehiro-cho. | 23-8585 | 31-0085 | 6,200 | 10,000 |
| Pacific Inn | 3-5 Suehiro-cho. | 25-8811 | 25-8839 | 6,000 | 10,000 |

## HAKODATE

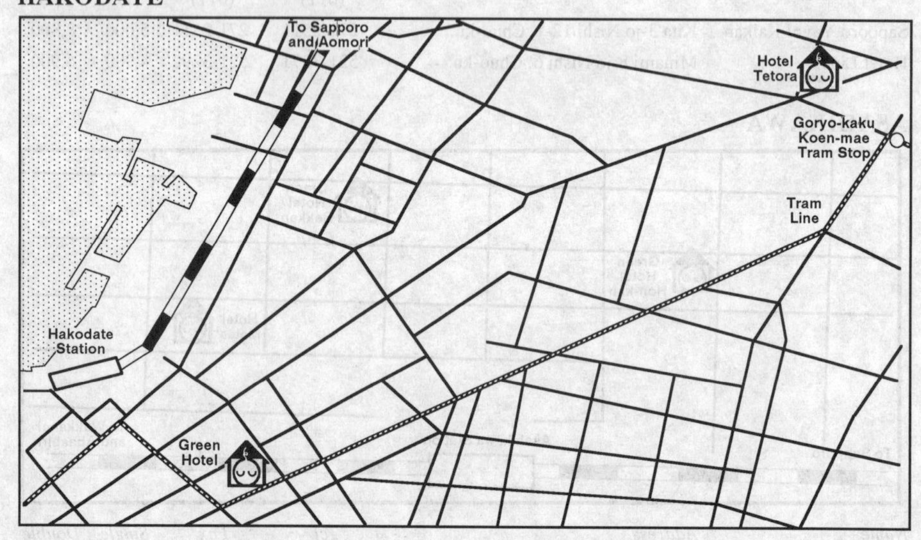


| *Name* | *Address* | *Tel.* (0138) | *Fax.* (0138) | *Single* (¥) | *Double* (¥) |
|---|---|---|---|---|---|
| Green Hotel | 19-19 Matsukaze-cho. | 26-8874 | 26-8876 | 5,300 | 9,100 |
| Hotel Tetora | 17-16 Yanagawa-cho. | 55-1818 | 56-0295 | 5,000 | 10,000 |

## AOMORI

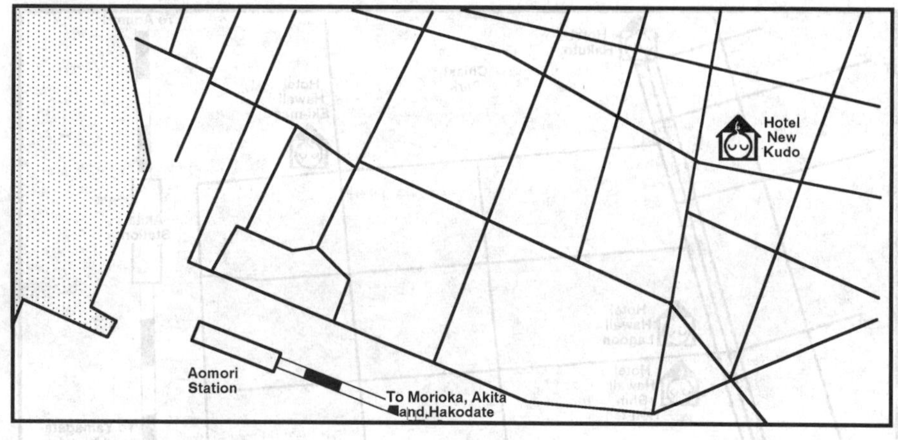


| *Name* | *Address* | *Tel.* | *Fax.* | *Single* | *Double* |
|---|---|---|---|---|---|
| | | (0177) | (0177) | (¥) | (¥) |
| Hotel New Kudo | 2-9-1 Furukawa. | 77-8181 | 77-8190 | 5,500 | 10,000 |

## SENDAI

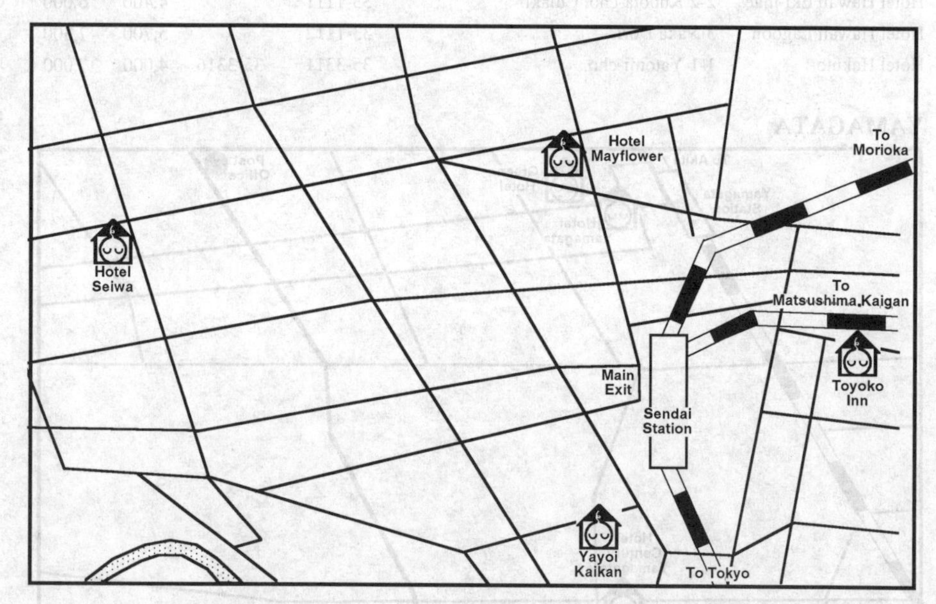


| *Name* | *Address* | *Tel.* | *Fax.* | *Single* | *Double* |
|---|---|---|---|---|---|
| | | (022) | (022) | (¥) | (¥) |
| Yayoi Kaikan | 1-1-1 Itsutsu-bashi, Aoba-ku. | 227-9515 | 227-9519 | 5,900 | 10,000 |
| Hotel Seiwa | 27-32 Tachi-machi, Aoba-ku. | 265-6171 | 265-6149 | 6,200 | 10,000 |
| Hotel Mayflower | 1-13-28 Hon-cho, Aoba-ku. | 262-5411 | 262-5415 | 5,200 | 8,800 |
| Toyoko Inn | 3-4-31 Tsutsuji-ga-oka, Miyagino-ku. | 256-1045 | 293-2045 | 5,800 | 9,000 |

## AKITA

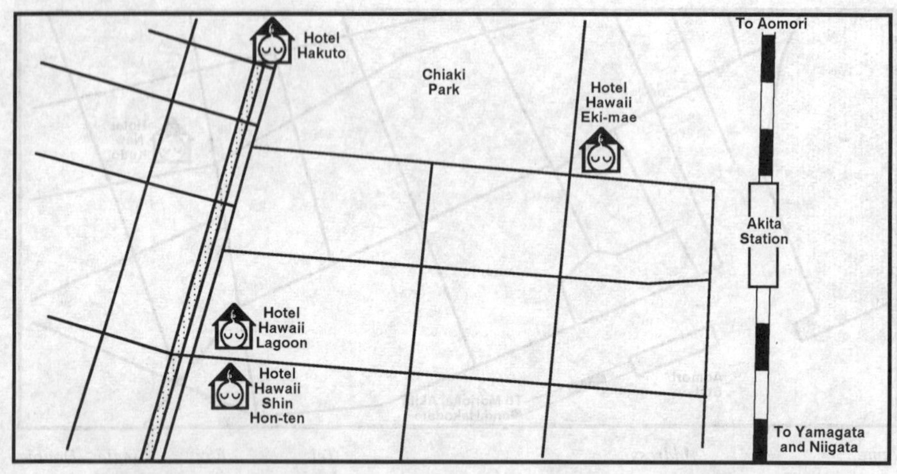


| *Name* | *Address* | *Tel.* (0188) | *Fax.* (0188) | *Single* (¥) | *Double* (¥) |
|---|---|---|---|---|---|
| Hotel Hawaii Shin Hon-ten | 5-1-7 Naka Dori. | 33-1110 | | 5,500 | 7,300 |
| Hotel Hawaii Eki-mae | 2-2 Kubota-cho, Chiaki. | 33-1111 | | 4,400 | 6,000 |
| Hotel Hawaii Lagoon | 3 Naka Dori. | 33-1112 | | 5,700 | 7,300 |
| Hotel Hakuto | 1-1 Yatomi-cho. | 35-3311 | 35-3316 | 4,000 | 7,000 |

## YAMAGATA

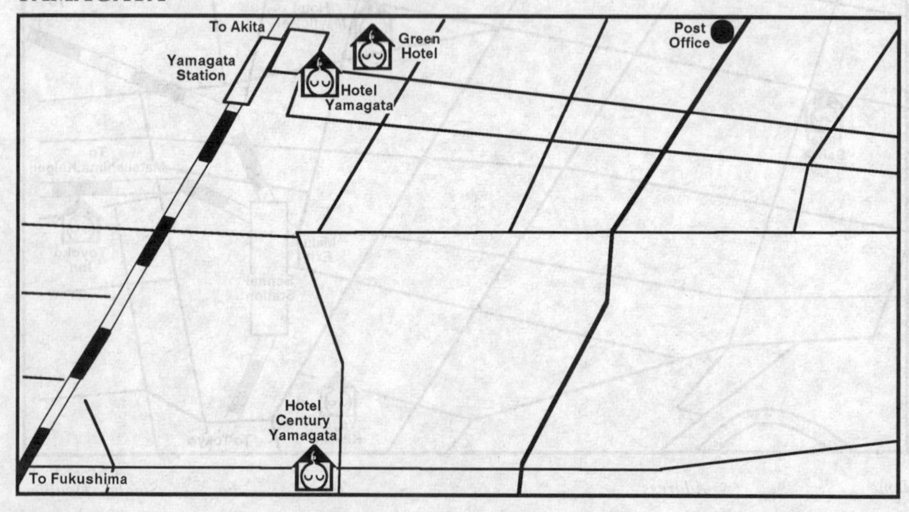


| *Name* | *Address* | *Tel.* (0236) | *Fax.* (0236) | *Single* (¥) | *Double* (¥) |
|---|---|---|---|---|---|
| Green Hotel | 1-3-12 Kasumi-cho. | 22-2636 | 42-8005 | 5,800 | 6,000 |
| Hotel Century Yamagata | 2-13 Minami Yonban-cho. | 31-1766 | 31-1946 | 5,000 | 9,800 |
| Hotel Yamagata | 1-1 Saiwai-cho. | 42-2111 | 42-2119 | 5,500 | 10,000 |

## FUKUSHIMA

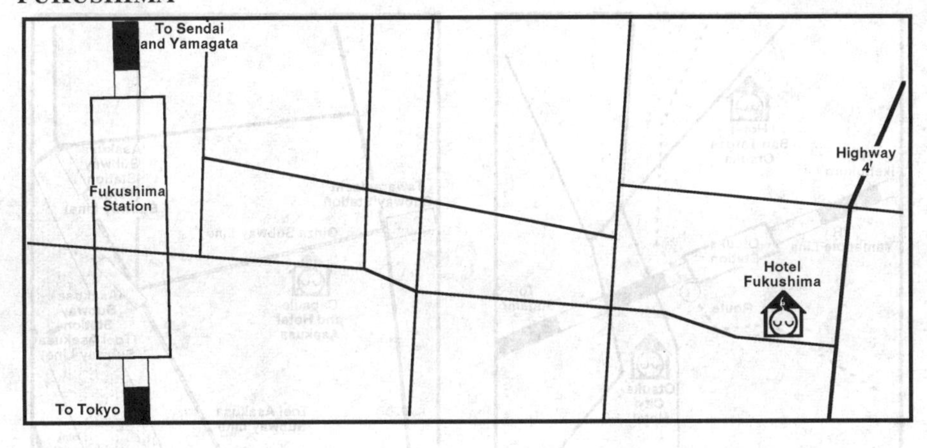


| *Name* | *Address* | *Tel.* (0245) | *Fax.* (0245) | *Single* (¥) | *Double* (¥) |
|---|---|---|---|---|---|
| Hotel Fukushima | 1-24 Funaba-cho. | 21-3211 | 23-5016 | 6,500 | 10,000 |

## TOKYO

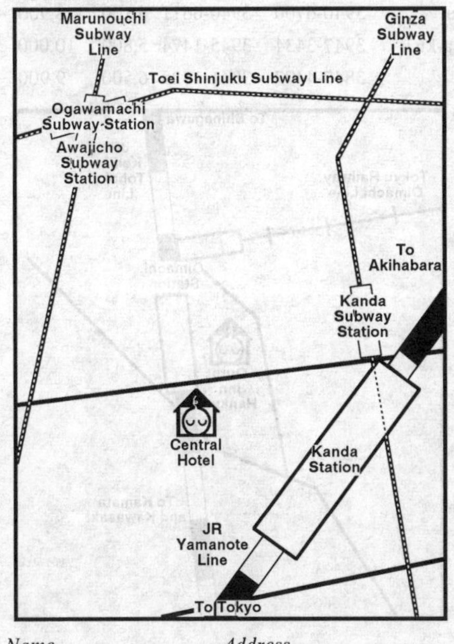


Toei Asakusa
Subway Line
Hotel
Mates
Takanawadai
Subway Station
To
Tamachi
Shinagawa
Station
JR
Yamanote
Line
Keihin
Kyuko
Railway
To Oimachi
and Osaki

| *Name* | *Address* | *Tel.* (03) | *Fax.* (03) | *Single* (¥) | *Double* (¥) |
|---|---|---|---|---|---|
| Central Hotel | 3-17-9 Uchi Kanda, Chiyoda-ku. | 3256-6251 | 3256-6250 | 6,600 | 10,000 |
| Hotel Mates | 2-9-5 Shirogane-dai, Minato-ku. | 3443-4161 | | 6,500 | 8,300 |

## TOKYO

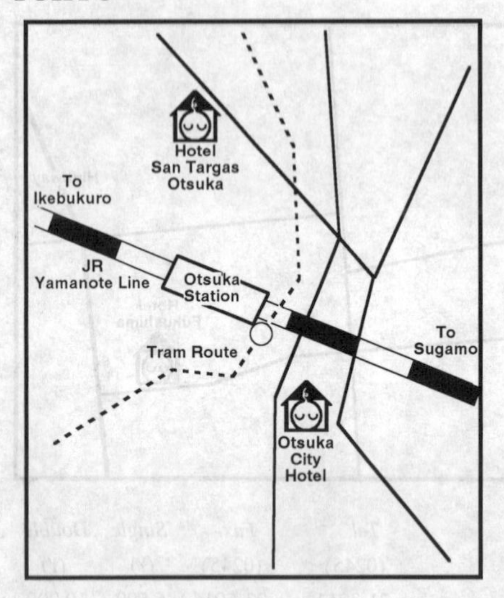


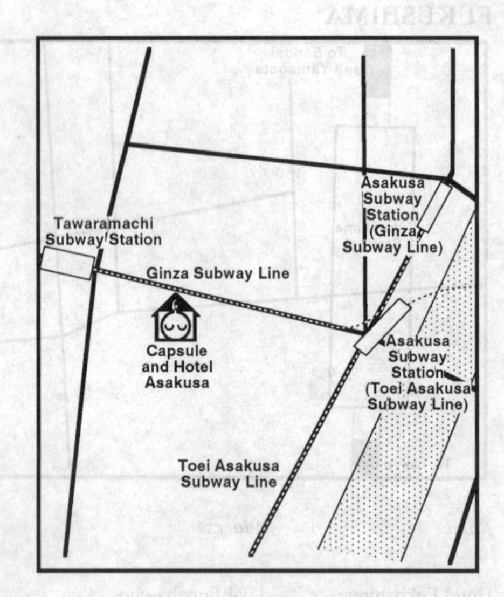


| *Name* | *Address* | *Tel.* | *Fax.* | *Single* | *Double* |
|---|---|---|---|---|---|
| | | (03) | (03) | (¥) | (¥) |
| Hotel San Targas Otsuka | 2-17-5 Kita Otsuka, Toshima-ku. | 3940-6700 | 3940-6611 | 6,100 | 8,900 |
| Otsuka City Hotel | 2-44-5 Minami Otsuka, Toshima-ku. | 3947-3434 | 3945-1474 | 5,800 | 10,000 |
| Capsule and Hotel Asakusa | 4-14-9 Kotobuki, Taito-ku. | 3847-4477 | 3841-1525 | 6,500 | 9,900 |

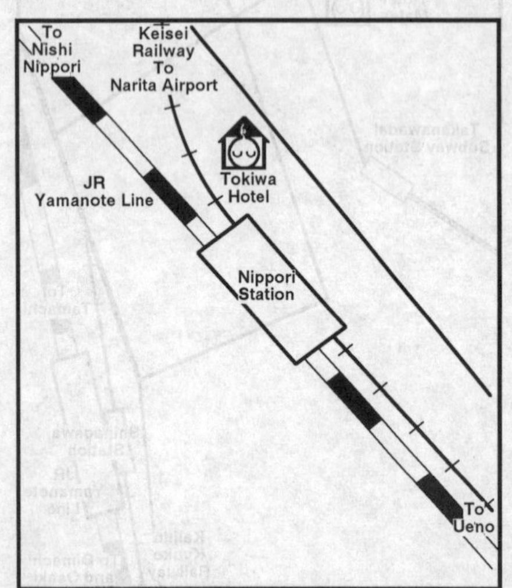


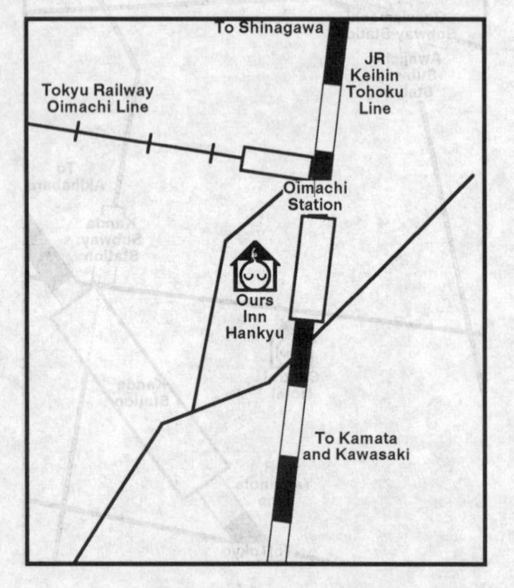


| *Name* | *Address* | *Tel.* | *Fax.* | *Single* | *Double* |
|---|---|---|---|---|---|
| | | (03) | (03) | (¥) | (¥) |
| Tokiwa Hotel | 2-21-11 Nishi Nippori, Arakawa-ku. | 3891-7111 | 3891-7188 | 6,000 | 10,000 |
| Ours Inn Hankyu | 1-50-5 Oi, Shinagawa-ku. | 3775-6121 | 3778-3861 | 5,000 | None |

## KAWASAKI

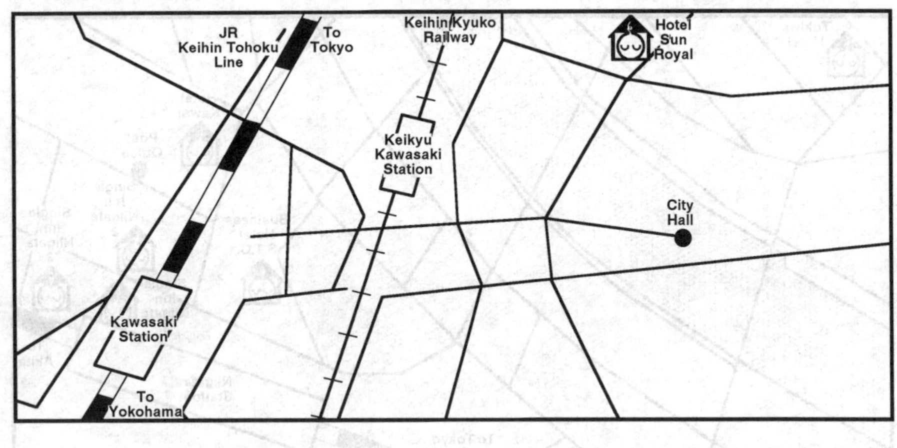


| *Name* | *Address* | *Tel.* | *Fax.* | *Single* | *Double* |
|---|---|---|---|---|---|
| | | (044) | (044) | (¥) | (¥) |
| Hotel Sun Royal | 1-5-11 Hon-cho, Kawasaki-ku. | 244-3711 | 245-0631 | 7,100 | 8,300 |

## NAGANO

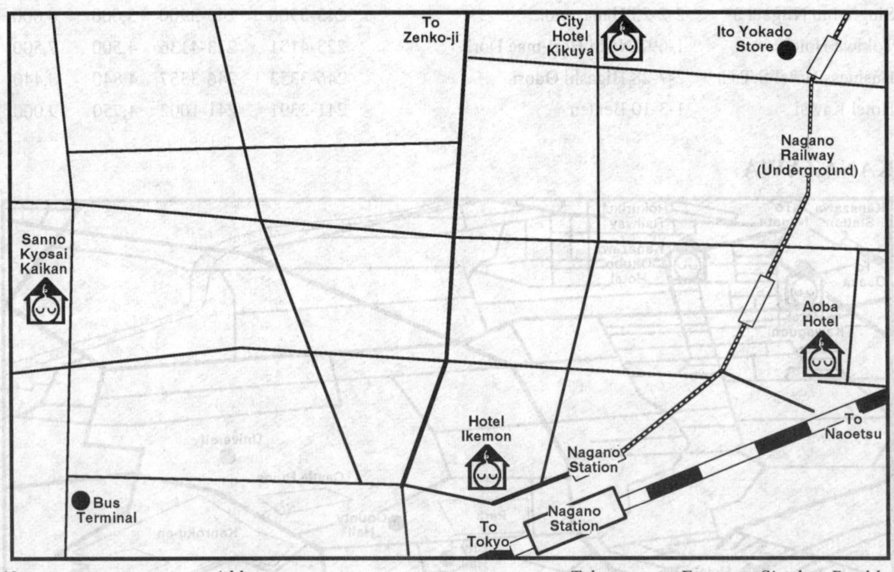


| *Name* | *Address* | *Tel.* | *Fax.* | *Single* | *Double* |
|---|---|---|---|---|---|
| | | (0262) | (0262) | (¥) | (¥) |
| Sanno Kyosai Kaikan | 30-20 Okada-cho. | 28-3011 | 28-8388 | 5,000 | 10,000 |
| City Hotel Kikuya | 2377 Kondo-cho. | 32-4166 | 34-0830 | 5,000 | 8,600 |
| Hotel Ikemon | 1362 Suehiro-cho. | 27-2122 | 27-6600 | 6,000 | 8,800 |
| Aoba Hotel | 2-21-4 Minami Chitose. | 26-3923 | 26-3959 | 5,459 | 9,650 |

## NIIGATA

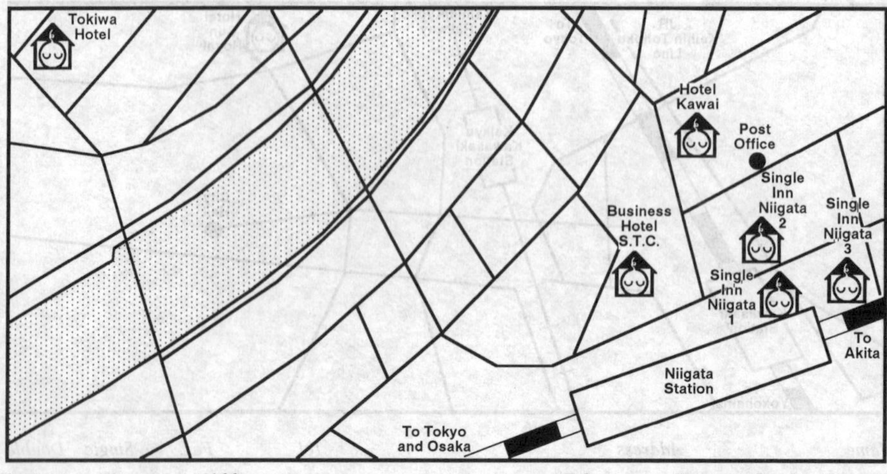


| Name | Address | Tel. (025) | Fax. (025) | Single (¥) | Double (¥) |
|---|---|---|---|---|---|
| Single Inn Niigata 1 | 1-6-1 Hanazono. | 241-3003 | 241-3003 | 5,000 | 8,000 |
| Single Inn Niigata 2 | 1-11-3 Higashi Odori. | 243-3980 | 243-3965 | 5,000 | 8,000 |
| Single Inn Niigata 3 | 2-2-23 Hanazono. | 243-3900 | 243-3900 | 5,000 | 8,000 |
| Tokiwa Hotel | 1-697 Nishi Hori-mae Dori. | 223-4131 | 223-4136 | 4,500 | 7,500 |
| Business Hotel S.T.C. | 2-7-28 Higashi Odori. | 246-3353 | 246-3357 | 4,840 | 8,440 |
| Hotel Kawai | 1-3-10 Benten. | 241-3391 | 241-1002 | 4,750 | 9,000 |

## KANAZAWA

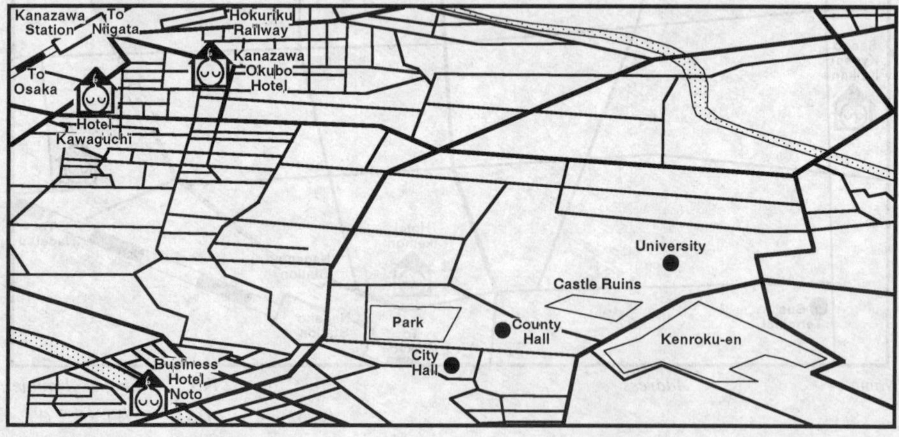


| Name | Address | Tel. (0762) | Fax. (0762) | Single (¥) | Double (¥) |
|---|---|---|---|---|---|
| Business Hotel Noto | 2-1-11 No-machi. | 42-2010 | 42-2071 | 5,000 | 9,200 |
| Hotel Kawaguchi | 2-6-23 Hon-machi. | 23-3155 | 23-2632 | 5,300 | 9,500 |
| Kanazawa Okubo Hotel | 2-20-3 Hon-machi. | 33-3000 | | 5,000 | 9,200 |

## NAGOYA

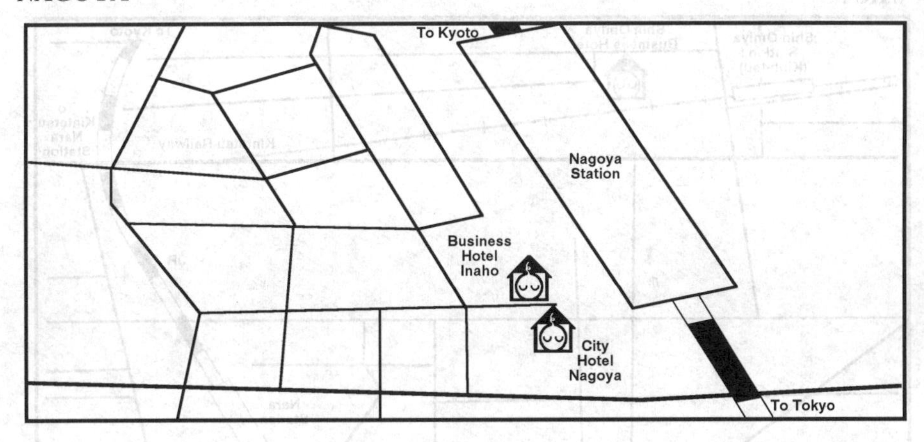


| Name | Address | Tel. (052) | Fax. (052) | Single (¥) | Double (¥) |
|---|---|---|---|---|---|
| Business Hotel Inaho | 15-13 Tsubaki-cho, Nakamura-ku. | 451-1281 | 451-1285 | 6,500 | 10,000 |
| City Hotel Nagoya | 16-21 Tsubaki-cho, Nakamura-ku. | 452-6223 | 451-8792 | 6,000 | 9,900 |

## KYOTO

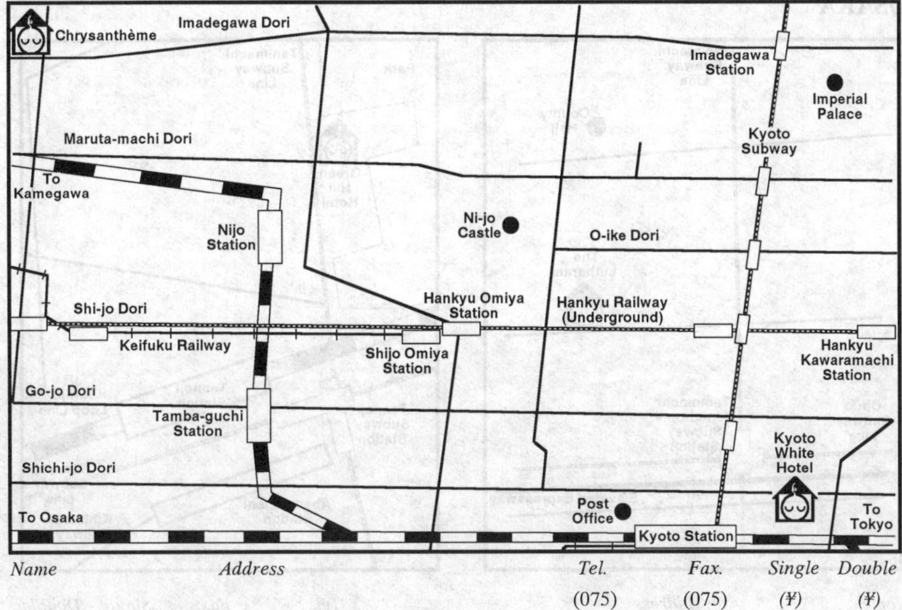


| Name | Address | Tel. (075) | Fax. (075) | Single (¥) | Double (¥) |
|---|---|---|---|---|---|
| Chrysanthème | 51 Yanagi-machi, Hirano Kami Hacho, Kita-ku. | 462-1540 | 462-5489 | 4,650 | None |
| Kyoto White Hotel | Ageru Higashi, Higashi To-in, Shimogyo-ku. | 351-5511 | 351-1226 | 4,600 | 9,200 |

## NARA

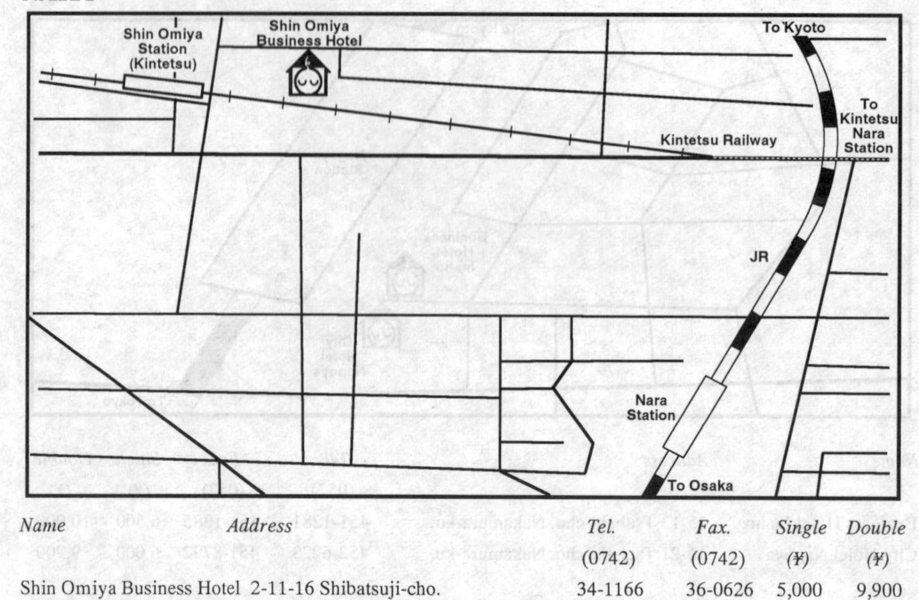


| *Name* | *Address* | *Tel.* | *Fax.* | *Single* | *Double* |
|---|---|---|---|---|---|
| | | (0742) | (0742) | (¥) | (¥) |
| Shin Omiya Business Hotel | 2-11-16 Shibatsuji-cho. | 34-1166 | 36-0626 | 5,000 | 9,900 |

## OSAKA

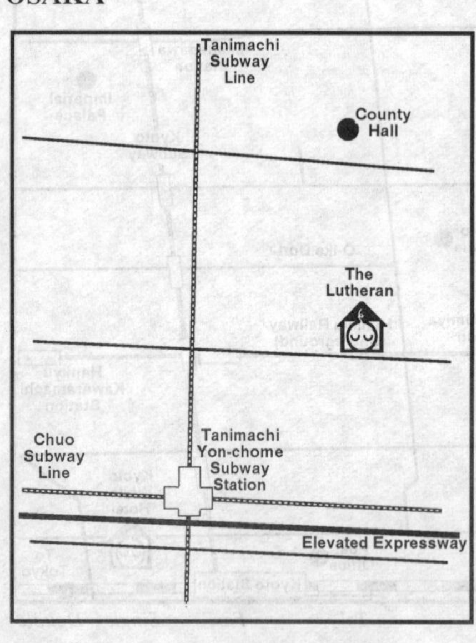


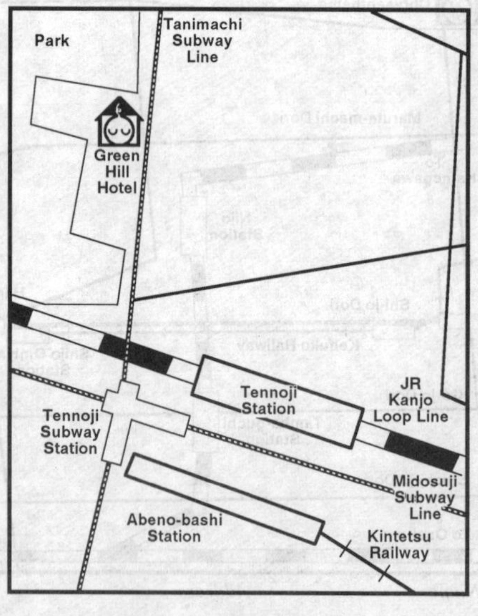


| *Name* | *Address* | *Tel.* | *Fax.* | *Single* | *Double* |
|---|---|---|---|---|---|
| | | (06) | (06) | (¥) | (¥) |
| The Lutheran | 3-1-6 Tani-machi, Chuo-ku. | 942-2281 | 942-0839 | 6,500 | 9,700 |
| Green Hill Hotel | 1-21 Chausu Yama-cho, Tennoji-ku. | 773-0077 | 773-0133 | 6,000 | 10,000 |

## KOBE

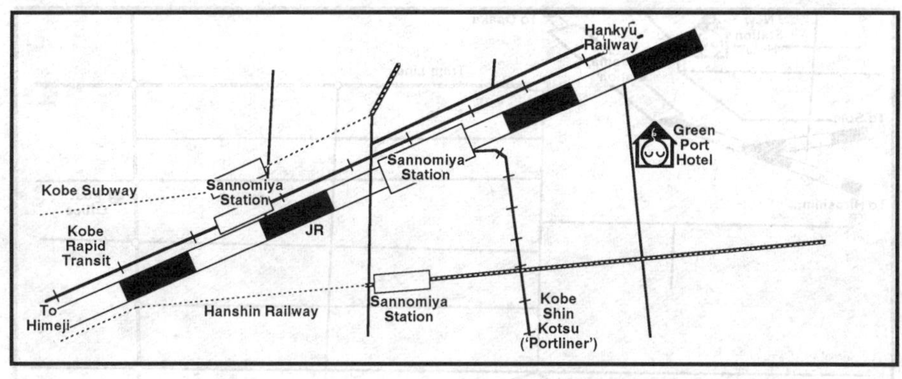


| *Name* | *Address* | *Tel.* | *Fax.* | *Single* | *Double* |
|---|---|---|---|---|---|
| | | (078) | (078) | (¥) | (¥) |
| Green Port Hotel | 4-12-13 Kumoi Dori, Chuo-ku. | 231-6361 | 231-6365 | 5,770 | 7,950 |

## MATSUE

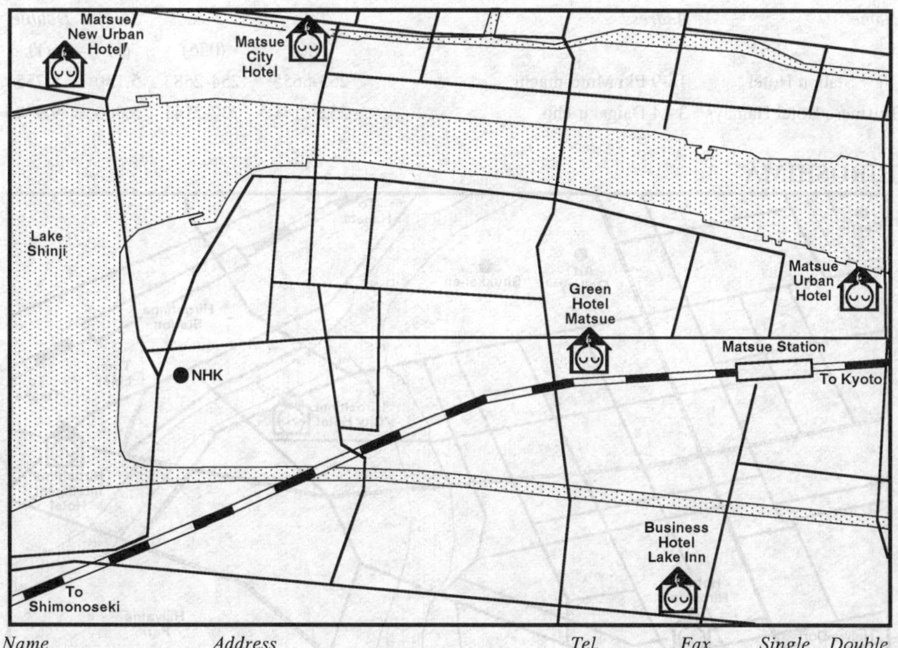


| *Name* | *Address* | *Tel.* | *Fax.* | *Single* | *Double* |
|---|---|---|---|---|---|
| | | (0852) | (0852) | (¥) | (¥) |
| Matsue Urban Hotel | 590-3 Asahi-machi. | 22-0002 | 21-6363 | 5,000 | 8,600 |
| Green Hotel Matsue | 493-1 Asahi-machi. | 27-3000 | 27-3211 | 5,450 | 10,000 |
| Matsue City Hotel | 31 Suetsugu Hon-machi. | 25-4100 | 25-4101 | 5,000 | 7,500 |
| Business Hotel Lake Inn | 153 Saika-machi. | 21-2424 | 24-5594 | 4,500 | 7,800 |
| Matsue New Urban Hotel | 40-1 Nishi Cha-machi. | 23-0002 | 23-0018 | 6,000 | 8,800 |

## OKAYAMA

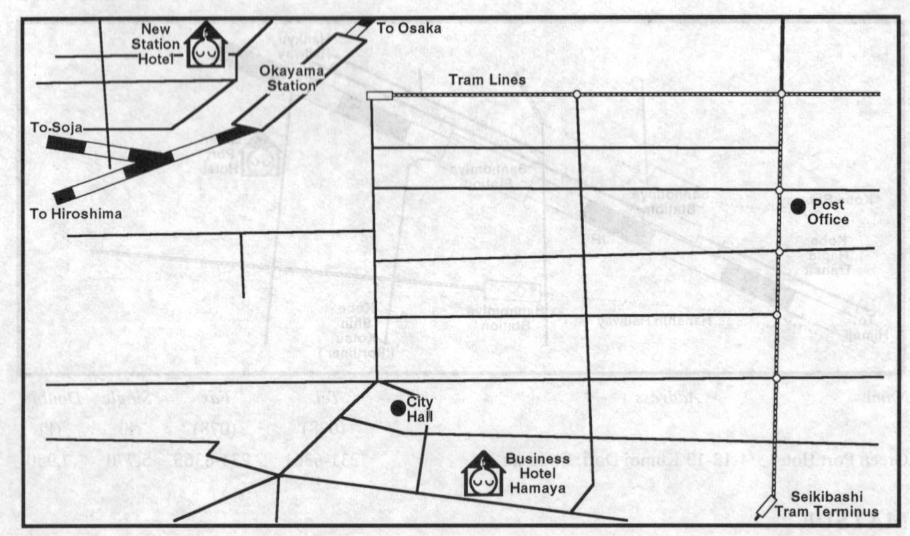


| *Name* | *Address* | *Tel.* (086) | *Fax.* (086) | *Single* (¥) | *Double* (¥) |
|---|---|---|---|---|---|
| New Station Hotel | 18-9 Eki Moto-machi. | 253-6655 | 254-2583 | 5,150 | 8,755 |
| Business Hotel Hamaya | 3-14 Daigaku-cho. | 232-2141 | 232-2141 | 5,000 | 9,900 |

## HIROSHIMA

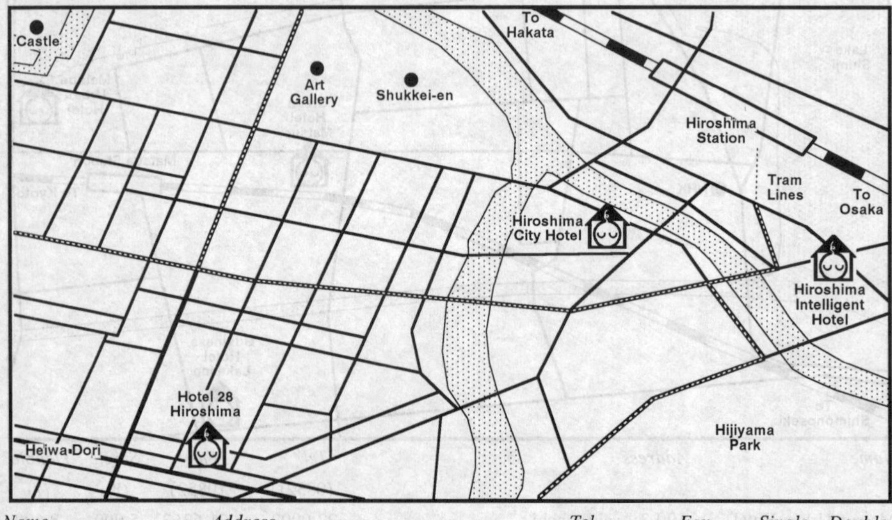


| *Name* | *Address* | *Tel.* (082) | *Fax.* (082) | *Single* (¥) | *Double* (¥) |
|---|---|---|---|---|---|
| Hotel 28 Hiroshima | 6-24 Tanaka-cho, Naka-ku. | 247-2811 | 247-2822 | 4,000 | 6,600 |
| Hiroshima City Hotel | 1-4 Kyobashi-cho, Minami-ku. | 263-5111 | 262-2403 | 7,591 | 9,950 |
| Hiroshima Intelligent Hotel | 3-36 Higashi Kojin-machi, Minami-ku. | 263-7000 | 263-7000 | 5,700 | 9,000 |

## SHIMONOSEKI

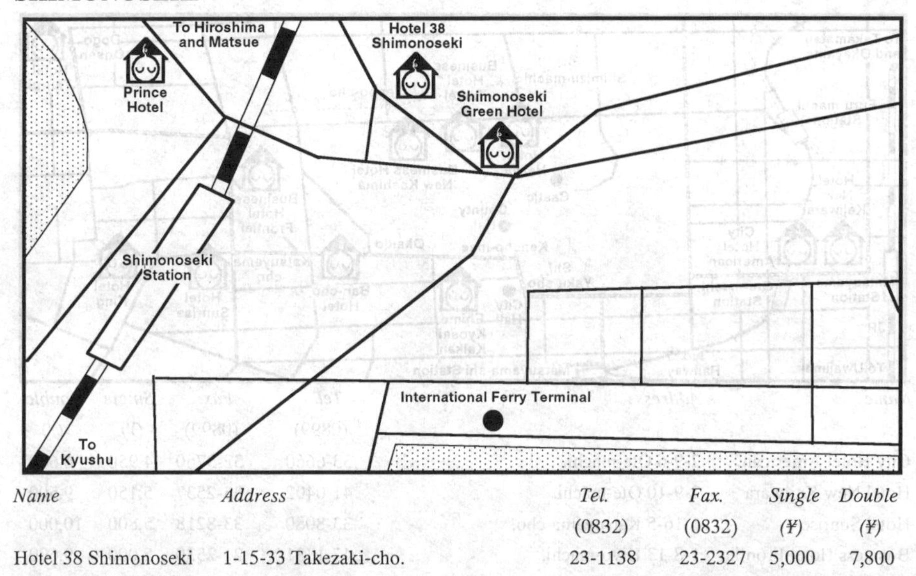


| *Name* | *Address* | *Tel.* | *Fax.* | *Single* | *Double* |
|---|---|---|---|---|---|
| | | (0832) | (0832) | (¥) | (¥) |
| Hotel 38 Shimonoseki | 1-15-33 Takezaki-cho. | 23-1138 | 23-2327 | 5,000 | 7,800 |
| Shimonoseki Green Hotel | 1-16-13 Takezaki-cho. | 31-1007 | 31-3603 | 5,400 | 8,000 |
| Prince Hotel | 3-10-7 Takezaki-cho. | 32-2301 | 34-0459 | 5,500 | 9,400 |

## TAKAMATSU

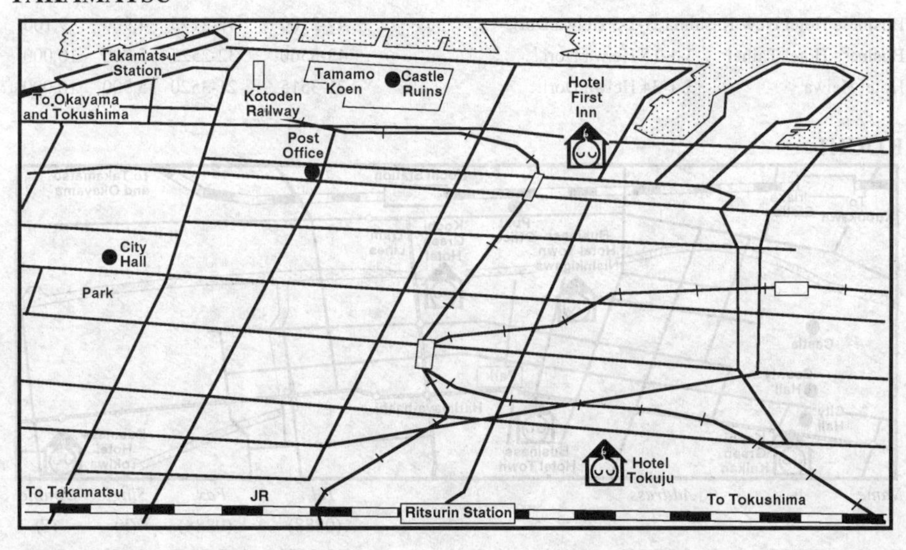


| *Name* | *Address* | *Tel.* | *Fax.* | *Single* | *Double* |
|---|---|---|---|---|---|
| | | (0878) | (0878) | (¥) | (¥) |
| Hotel First Inn | 2-3 Tsuruya-machi. | 22-1919 | 23-2639 | 3,850 | 8,500 |
| Hotel Tokuju | 3-5-5 Hanazono-cho. | 31-0201 | 33-9125 | 5,000 | 10,200 |

## MATSUYAMA

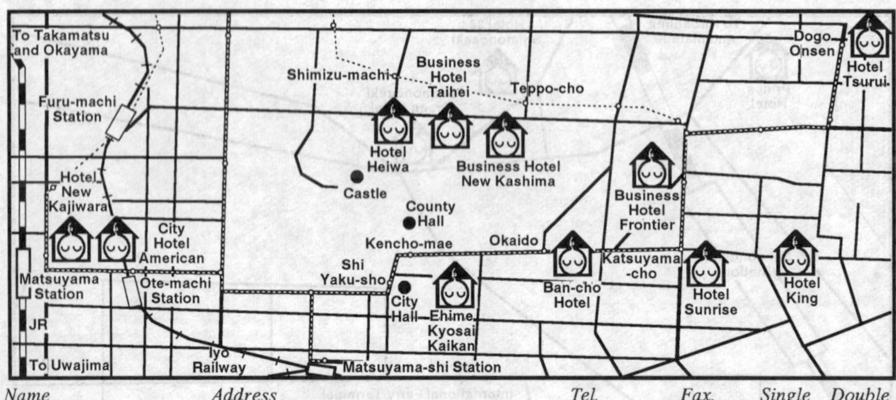


| Name | Address | Tel. (0899) | Fax. (0899) | Single (¥) | Double (¥) |
|---|---|---|---|---|---|
| City Hotel American | 2-9-6 Ote-machi. | 33-6660 | 32-3760 | 4,950 | 6,600 |
| Hotel New Kajiwara | 2-9-10 Ote-machi. | 41-0402 | 33-2537 | 5,150 | 9,500 |
| Hotel Sunrise | 1-16-5 Katsuyama-cho. | 33-8080 | 33-8218 | 5,800 | 10,000 |
| Business Hotel Frontier | 1-8-13 Kiyo-machi. | 47-1331 | 21-2530 | 5,000 | 9,600 |
| Hotel King | 7-14 Konohana-machi. | 46-2511 | 46-2511 | 5,150 | 9,300 |
| Ehime Kyosai Kaikan | 5-13-1 Sanban-cho. | 45-6311 | 45-6311 | 5,000 | 10,640 |
| Hotel Tsurui | 8-22 Kita-machi, Dogo. | 22-2233 | 24-0986 | 4,700 | 8,400 |
| Ban-cho Hotel | 4-3-3 Niban-cho. | 41-4351 | 41-4381 | 5,000 | 9,100 |
| Business Hotel New Kashima | 3-1-3 Heiwa Dori. | 47-2100 | 47-2175 | 4,900 | 9,100 |
| Business Hotel Taihei | 3-1-15 Heiwa Dori. | 43-3560 | 32-2525 | 5,700 | 10,000 |
| Hotel Heiwa | 3-1-34 Heiwa Dori. | 21-3515 | 21-3520 | 5,900 | 10,000 |

## KOCHI

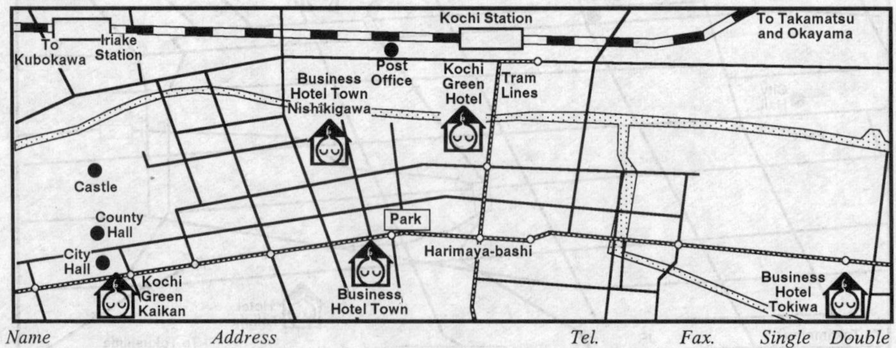


| Name | Address | Tel. (0888) | Fax. (0888) | Single (¥) | Double (¥) |
|---|---|---|---|---|---|
| Business Hotel Town | 1-5-26 Hon-machi. | 25-0055 | 25-0048 | 5,500 | 7,600 |
| Business Hotel Town Nishikigawa | 15-24 Nijudai-cho. | 25-1811 | 25-1814 | 5,500 | 8,000 |
| Kochi Green Hotel | 3-1-11 Harimaya-cho. | 22-1800 | 75-2359 | 6,100 | 10,000 |
| Kochi Green Kaikan | 5-6-11 Hon-machi. | 25-2701 | 25-2703 | 5,100 | 10,000 |
| Business Hotel Tokiwa | 16-12 Minami Hoei-cho. | 84-0111 | 84-0115 | 5,300 | 9,000 |

## FUKUOKA

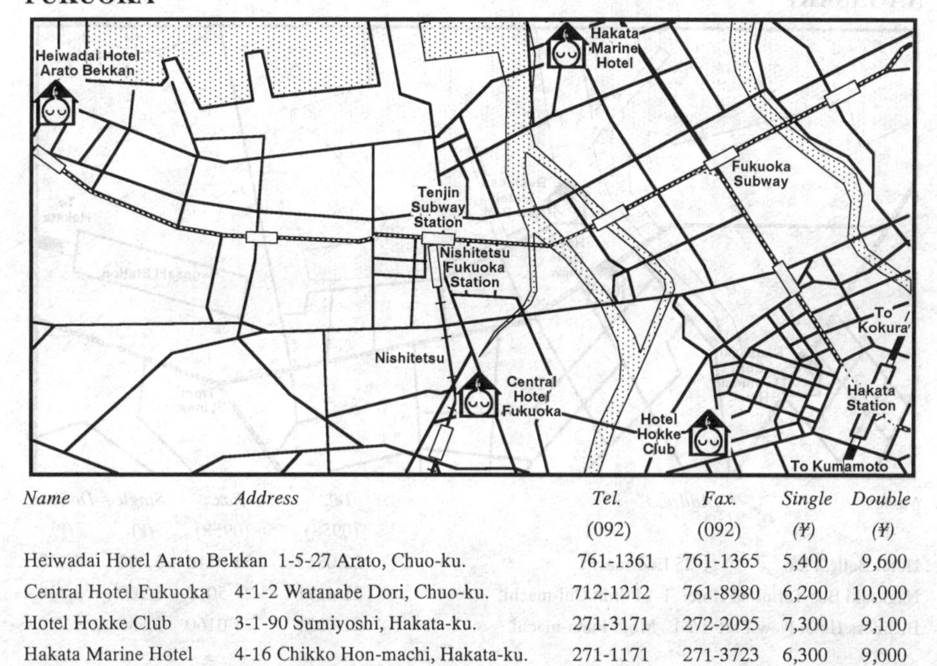


| *Name* | *Address* | *Tel.* | *Fax.* | *Single* | *Double* |
|---|---|---|---|---|---|
| | | (092) | (092) | (¥) | (¥) |
| Heiwadai Hotel Arato Bekkan | 1-5-27 Arato, Chuo-ku. | 761-1361 | 761-1365 | 5,400 | 9,600 |
| Central Hotel Fukuoka | 4-1-2 Watanabe Dori, Chuo-ku. | 712-1212 | 761-8980 | 6,200 | 10,000 |
| Hotel Hokke Club | 3-1-90 Sumiyoshi, Hakata-ku. | 271-3171 | 272-2095 | 7,300 | 9,100 |
| Hakata Marine Hotel | 4-16 Chikko Hon-machi, Hakata-ku. | 271-1171 | 271-3723 | 6,300 | 9,000 |

## KOKURA (KITA KYUSHU)

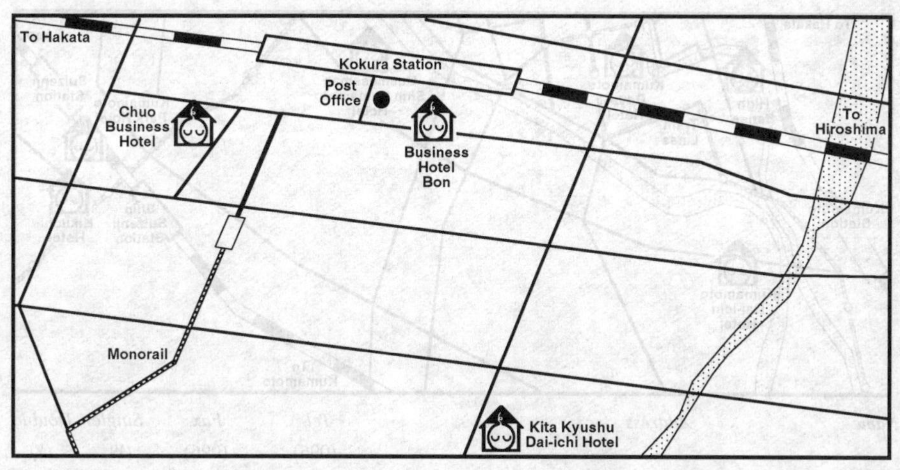


| *Name* | *Address* | *Tel.* | *Fax.* | *Single* | *Double* |
|---|---|---|---|---|---|
| | | (093) | (093) | (¥) | (¥) |
| Chuo Business Hotel | 1-3-21 Uo-machi, Kita-ku, Kokura. | 531-1584 | 551-2296 | 4,500 | 7,400 |
| Business Hotel Bon | 3-10-27 Kyo-machi, Kita-ku, Kokura. | 551-6431 | 551-6434 | 5,974 | 9,270 |
| Kita Kyushu Dai-ichi Hotel | 11-20 Konya-machi, Kita-ku, Kokura. | 551-7331 | 551-7333 | 6,000 | 8,000 |

## NAGASAKI

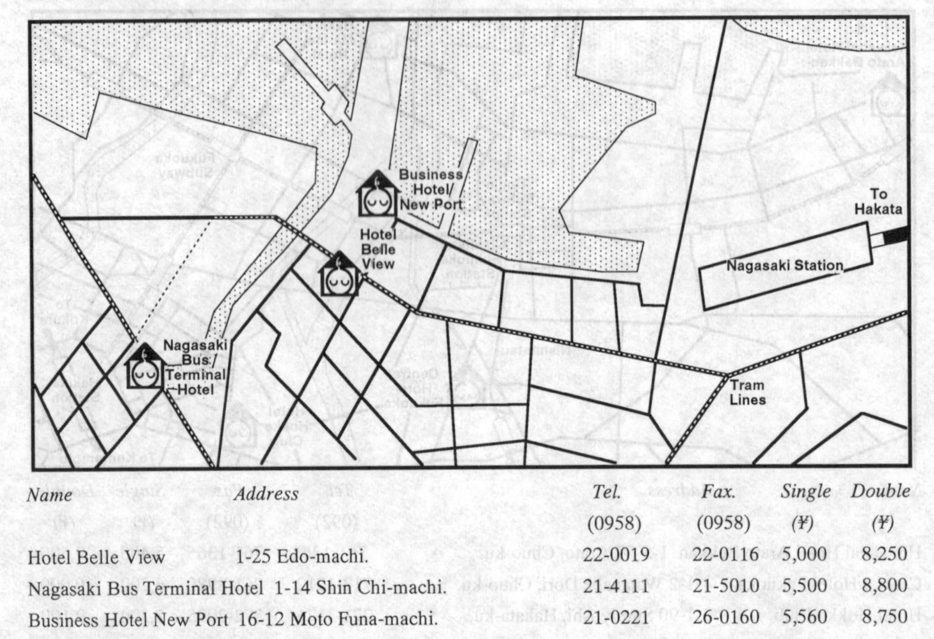


| Name | Address | Tel. (0958) | Fax. (0958) | Single (¥) | Double (¥) |
|---|---|---|---|---|---|
| Hotel Belle View | 1-25 Edo-machi. | 22-0019 | 22-0116 | 5,000 | 8,250 |
| Nagasaki Bus Terminal Hotel | 1-14 Shin Chi-machi. | 21-4111 | 21-5010 | 5,500 | 8,800 |
| Business Hotel New Port | 16-12 Moto Funa-machi. | 21-0221 | 26-0160 | 5,560 | 8,750 |

## KUMAMOTO

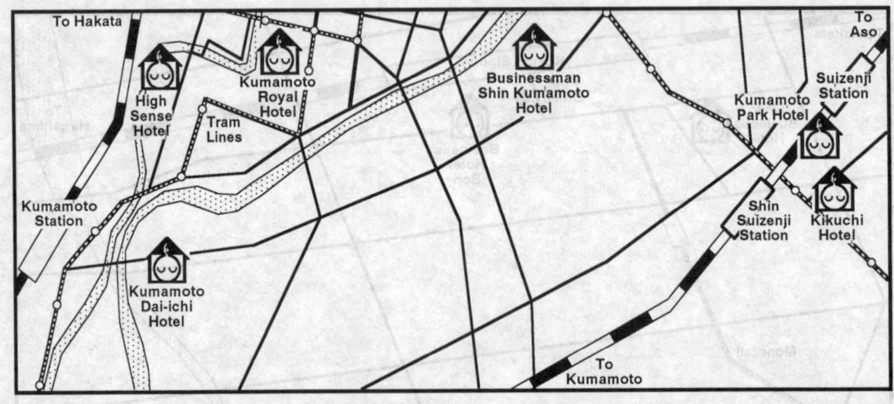


| Name | Address | Tel. (096) | Fax. (096) | Single (¥) | Double (¥) |
|---|---|---|---|---|---|
| High Sense Hotel | 38 Ozawa-cho. | 325-7600 | 325-7607 | 5,000 | 8,800 |
| Kumamoto Royal Hotel | 67-1 Karashima-cho. | 325-0111 | 325-0294 | 6,000 | 10,000 |
| Businessman Shin Kumamoto Hotel | 1-11-17 Kuhonji. | 364-6151 | 364-6151 | 4,800 | 8,400 |
| Kumamoto Park Hotel | 1-2-20 Suizenji. | 382-5454 | 382-7367 | 5,500 | 9,700 |
| Kikuchi Hotel | 1-18-13 Suizenji. | 385-0011 | 384-8315 | 4,750 | 8,000 |
| Kumamoto Dai-ichi Hotel | 3-3-85 Motoyama. | 325-5151 | 354-3337 | 5,800 | 9,900 |

## MIYAZAKI

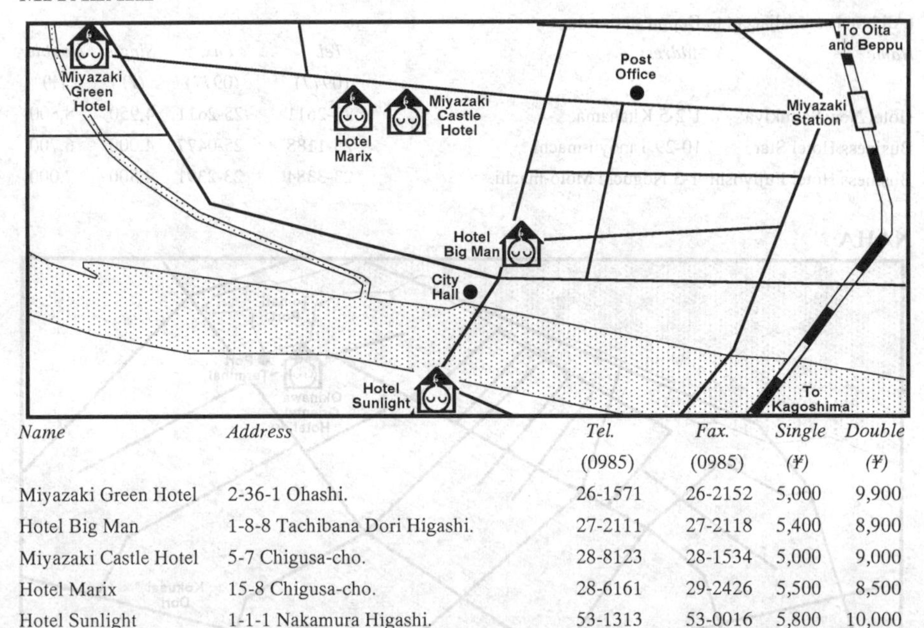


| *Name* | *Address* | *Tel.* (0985) | *Fax.* (0985) | *Single* (¥) | *Double* (¥) |
|---|---|---|---|---|---|
| Miyazaki Green Hotel | 2-36-1 Ohashi. | 26-1571 | 26-2152 | 5,000 | 9,900 |
| Hotel Big Man | 1-8-8 Tachibana Dori Higashi. | 27-2111 | 27-2118 | 5,400 | 8,900 |
| Miyazaki Castle Hotel | 5-7 Chigusa-cho. | 28-8123 | 28-1534 | 5,000 | 9,000 |
| Hotel Marix | 15-8 Chigusa-cho. | 28-6161 | 29-2426 | 5,500 | 8,500 |
| Hotel Sunlight | 1-1-1 Nakamura Higashi. | 53-1313 | 53-0016 | 5,800 | 10,000 |

## KAGOSHIMA

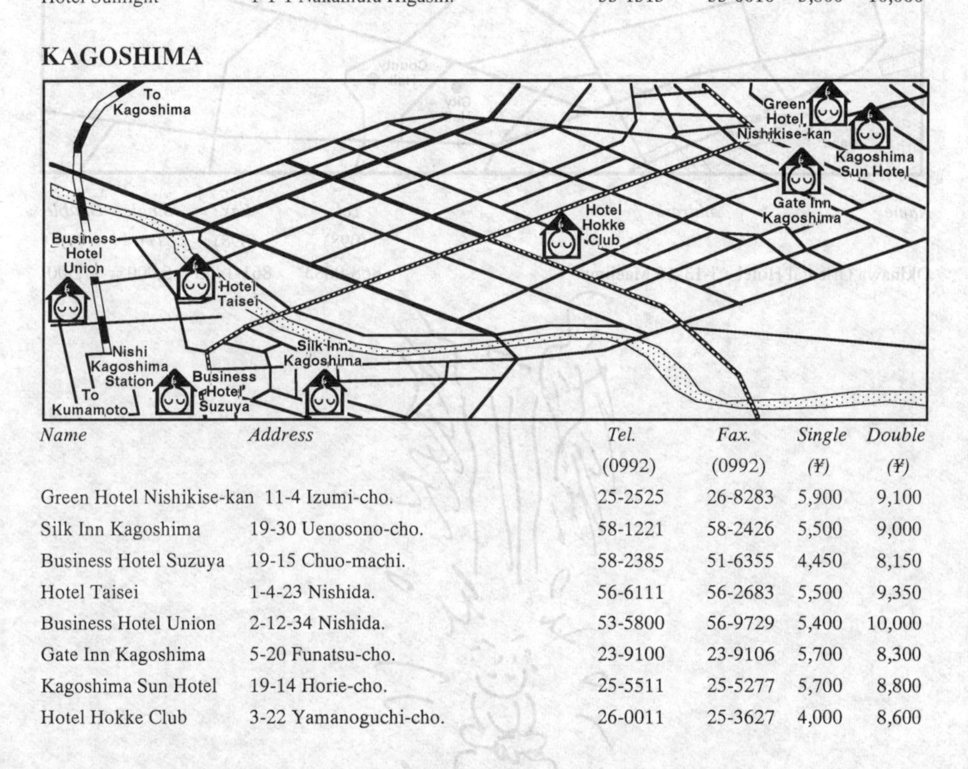


| *Name* | *Address* | *Tel.* (0992) | *Fax.* (0992) | *Single* (¥) | *Double* (¥) |
|---|---|---|---|---|---|
| Green Hotel Nishikise-kan | 11-4 Izumi-cho. | 25-2525 | 26-8283 | 5,900 | 9,100 |
| Silk Inn Kagoshima | 19-30 Uenosono-cho. | 58-1221 | 58-2426 | 5,500 | 9,000 |
| Business Hotel Suzuya | 19-15 Chuo-machi. | 58-2385 | 51-6355 | 4,450 | 8,150 |
| Hotel Taisei | 1-4-23 Nishida. | 56-6111 | 56-2683 | 5,500 | 9,350 |
| Business Hotel Union | 2-12-34 Nishida. | 53-5800 | 56-9729 | 5,400 | 10,000 |
| Gate Inn Kagoshima | 5-20 Funatsu-cho. | 23-9100 | 23-9106 | 5,700 | 8,300 |
| Kagoshima Sun Hotel | 19-14 Horie-cho. | 25-5511 | 25-5277 | 5,700 | 8,800 |
| Hotel Hokke Club | 3-22 Yamanoguchi-cho. | 26-0011 | 25-3627 | 4,000 | 8,600 |

## BEPPU

(All hotels are adjacent to Beppu station.)

| *Name* | *Address* | *Tel.* | *Fax.* | *Single* | *Double* |
|---|---|---|---|---|---|
| | | (0977) | (0977) | (¥) | (¥) |
| Hotel New Sanukiya | 1-2-5 Kitahama. | 25-2611 | 25-2611 | 4,950 | 8,800 |
| Business Hotel Star | 10-29 Tanoyu-machi. | 25-1188 | 25-0477 | 4,000 | 6,700 |
| Business Hotel Fujiyoshi | 1-3 Noguchi Moto-machi. | 23-3384 | 23-2391 | 4,500 | 7,000 |

## NAHA

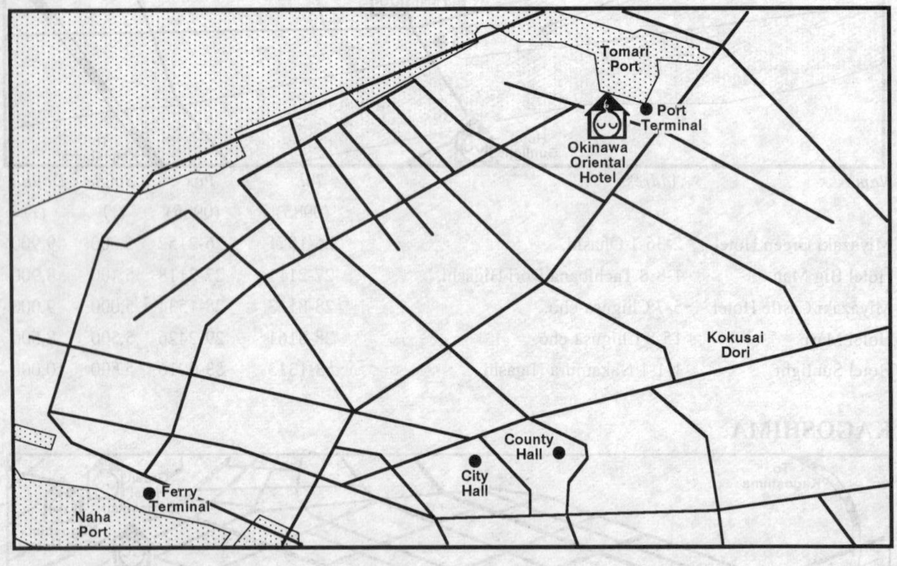


| *Name* | *Address* | *Tel.* | *Fax.* | *Single* | *Double* |
|---|---|---|---|---|---|
| | | (098) | (098) | (¥) | (¥) |
| Okinawa Oriental Hotel | 3-13-16 Maejima. | 868-0883 | 861-1433 | 5,000 | 7,500 |

# PART 4 ITINERARIES

The following suggestions are just a few itineraries which might suit visitors to Japan using various types of tickets and having varying periods of time at their disposal. Of course, the reader is free to add his own modifications or to say, "Oh, I don't want to get up as early as that" and adjust accordingly, but many of the trains have been selected with care and alternatives may not make such good connexions. The tighter the schedule, of course, the harder it was to plan and the fewer the alternatives available, so caution should be exercised in making modifications, particularly where the pace of the tour is brisk.

## TOUR 1 ONE MONTH IN JAPAN USING 21-DAY JAPAN RAIL PASS

This tour allows you to visit the whole of the four main islands. Almost all travelling expenses are covered by the Japan Rail Pass and where they are not, an annotation is made. Visits in the Tokyo area are made using other tickets. The pace of this tour is not too breathless, although it keeps one on the move. Three nights are spent on trains, to economize on time and accommodation expenses. Two of these three trains are quite comfortable.

| Day | Journey | Train | Notes |
|---|---|---|---|
| 1. | Tour of Tokyo. | | Use Eidan Subway One-Day Ticket, ¥650 |
| 2. | Day Trip to Nikko and Lake Chuzenji. | | Tobu Private Railway, ¥1,270 x 2 plus Tobu bus, ¥1,100 x 2 |
| 3. | Visit to Yokohama. | | Use JR *Yokohama Free Kippu*, ¥880 from Tokyo |
| 4. | Day Trip to Kamakura. | | Use JR *Kamakura Enoshima Free Kippu*, ¥1,900 (available for two days, if preferred) |
| 5. | Free Day in Tokyo. | | |
| 6. | Tokyo 7:28. Yamagata 9:55. | Shinkansen | Rail Pass Day 1 |
| | Yamagata 10:13. Yamadera 10:33. | Kaisoku | Sightseeing in Yamadera |
| | Yamadera 13:49. Sendai 14:35. | Kaisoku | |
| 7. | Sendai 9:03. Hon Shiogama 9:19. | Kaisoku | Rail Pass Day 2 |
| | Hon Shiogama 10:00. Matsushima Kaigan 11:00. | | By ferry, ¥1,400. Sightseeing in Matsushima |
| | Matsushima 13:20. Ichinoseki 14:39. | Ordinary | |
| | Ichinoseki 15:00. Hiraizumi 15:08. | Ordinary | Sightseeing in Hiraizumi. Motsuji Y.H. |
| 8. | Hiraizumi 9:27. Ichinoseki 9:37. | Ordinary | Rail Pass Day 3 |
| | Ichinoseki 9:45. Morioka 10:27. | Shinkansen | |
| | Morioka 11:01. Towada Minami 12:51. | Kaisoku | |
| | Towada Minami 13:00. Towada-ko 14:02. | | JR Bus. Summer only. In winter departure from Towada Minami at 16:20 |
| 9. | Towada-ko 7:35. Aomori 10:35. | | JR Bus. Summer only. Rail Pass Day 4 |
| | Aomori 10:49. Hakodate 12:46. | Tokkyu | Through Seikan Tunnel. Sightseeing in Hakodate |
| | Hakodate 23:30. | | |
| 10. | Sapporo 6:30. | Kaisoku | Request 'carpet car'. Rail Pass Day 5 |
| | Sapporo 7:05. Asahikawa 8:39. | Tokkyu | |
| | Asahikawa 8:49. Wakkanai 12:45. | Kyuko | |
| | Wakkanai 13:00. Soya Misaki 13:52. | | Bus, ¥1,230 |

| Day | Journey | Train | Notes |
|---|---|---|---|
| 10. | Soya Misaki 14:20. Wakkanai 15:15. | | Bus ¥1,230. Sightseeing in Wakkanai |
| 11. | Wakkanai 7:52. Asahikawa 11:52. | Kyuko | Rail Pass Day 6 |
| | Asahikawa 15:00. Asahi-dake 16:35. | | Free bus. In summer, additional service available at 13:00 |
| 12. | Walk to So-unkyo. | | Rail Pass Day 7 |
| | So-unkyo 14:15. Kamikawa 14:45. | | Bus, ¥750 |
| | Kamikawa 15:51. Kitami 18:07. | Kaisoku | |
| | Kitami 18:10. Abashiri 19:12. Kitahama 19:36. | Ordinary | |
| 13. | Abashiri 10:00. Kitahama 10:13. Mashu 11:45. | Ordinary | Sightseeing around Mashu-ko. Rail Pass Day 8 |
| 14. | Mashu 8:44. Kushiro 10:00. | Ordinary | Rail Pass Day 9 |
| | Kushiro 11:04. Sapporo 15:56. | Tokkyu | Sightseeing in Sapporo |
| | Sapporo 22:00. | | |
| 15. | Aomori 5:18. | Kyuko | Through Seikan Tunnel. Rail Pass Day 10 |
| | Aomori 6:11. Kanazawa 15:46. | Tokkyu | Sightseeing in Kanazawa |
| 16. | Kanazawa 11:58. Toyama 12:35. | Tokkyu | Rail Pass Day 11 |
| | Toyama 12:43. Takayama 14:13. | Tokkyu | Sightseeing in Takayama |
| 17. | Takayama 7:18. Nagoya 9:35. | Tokkyu | Rail Pass Day 12 |
| | Nagoya 9:50. Himeji 11:28. | Shinkansen | Sightseeing in Himeji |
| | Himeji 13:28. Okayama 13:53. | Shinkansen | |
| | Okayama 13:58. Kurashiki 14:12. | Ordinary | Sightseeing in Kurashiki |
| 18. | Kurashiki 7:26. Okayama 7:40. | Ordinary | Rail Pass Day 13 |
| | Okayama 7:49. Takamatsu 8:51. | Kaisoku | Crossing Seto Ohashi (Bridge) |
| | Takamatsu 8:53. Ritsurin Koen Kita Guchi 8:59. | Ordinary | Sightseeing in Ritsurin Koen |
| | Ritsurin Koen Kita Guchi 10:18. Takamatsu 10:24. | Ordinary | |
| | Takamatsu 11:57. Kotohira 12:34. | Tokkyu | Sightseeing at Kompira-san |
| | Kotohira 15:33. Kochi 16:58. | Tokkyu | |
| 19. | Kochi 9:00. Matsuyama 12:04. | | JR Tokkyu Bus. Sightseeing in Matsuyama. Rail Pass Day 14 |
| 20. | Matsuyama. 7:16. Okayama 10:01. | Tokkyu | Crossing Seto Ohashi again. Rail Pass Day 15 |
| | Okayama 10:15. Hiroshima 11:01. | Shinkansen | Sightseeing in Hiroshima |
| 21. | Hiroshima 7:43. Hakata 9:03. | Shinkansen | Rail Pass Day 16 |
| | Hakata 9:21. Nagasaki 11:26. | Tokkyu | Sightseeing in Nagasaki |
| | Nagasaki 16:01. Tosu 17:37. | Tokkyu | |
| | Tosu 17:41. Kumamoto 18:35. | Tokkyu | |
| 22. | Kumamoto 10:30. Miyaji 12:59. | Steam | Seasonal train. Sightseeing in Kumamoto. Rail Pass Day 17 |
| | Miyaji 13:10. Aso-san Higashi 13:24. | | Bus, ¥300 |
| | Walk to Aso-san Nishi. | | |
| | Aso-san Nishi Eki 17:00. Aso 17:33. | | Bus, ¥610 (via Youth Hostel). Caution: this is the last bus |
| 23. | Aso 9:28. Beppu 11:18. | Tokkyu | Sightseeing in Beppu. Rail Pass Day 18 |
| 24. | Beppu 8:09. Nishi Kagoshima 13:45. | Tokkyu | Sightseeing in Kagoshima. Rail Pass Day 19 |
| | Nishi Kagoshima 19:05. | | |
| 25. | Shin Osaka 9:26. | Tokkyu | Rail Pass Day 20 |
| | Shin Osaka 9:36. Kyoto 9:54. | Shinkansen | Sightseeing in Kyoto |
| 26. | Kyoto 9:45. Nara 10:29. | Kaisoku | Sightseeing in Nara. Rail Pass Day 21 |
| | Nara 16:34. Nagoya 18:48. | Kyuko | |
| | Nagoya 18:55. Tokyo 20:49. | Shinkansen | |
| 27-29. | Visit to Hakone. | | Use 'Hakone Free Pass', ¥5,400 from Shinjuku |

## TOUR 2 MINIMUM 23 DAYS IN JAPAN USING 7-DAY JAPAN RAIL PASS

This tour is something of a mad dash in the middle, with comparative relaxation at each end. However, it is cheaper than the tour above and misses only Shikoku, in exchange for which plenty of time is allowed for Kyoto, and extra days can be added there too if so desired. It makes good use of the rail pass time and includes three nights spent on trains, to economize on accommodation expenses whilst moving from one area to another.

| Day | Journey | Train | Notes |
|---|---|---|---|
| 1. | Tour of Tokyo. | | Use Eidan Subway One-Day Ticket, ¥650 |
| 2. | Day Trip to Nikko and Lake Chuzenji. | | Tobu Private Railway, ¥1,270 x 2 plus Tobu bus, ¥1,100 x 2 |
| 3. | Visit to Yokohama. | | Use JR *Yokohama Free Kippu*, ¥880 from Tokyo |
| 4. | Day Trip to Kamakura. | | Use JR *Kamakura Enoshima Free Kippu*, ¥1,900 (available for two days, if preferred) |
| 5. | Free Day in Tokyo. | | |
| 6. | Tokyo 7:28. Yamagata 9:55. | Shinkansen | Rail Pass Day 1 |
| | Yamagata 10:01. Akita 12:59. | Tokkyu | |
| | Akita 13:03. Aomori 15:38. | Tokkyu | |
| | Aomori 16:08. Hakodate 18:49. | Tokkyu | Through Seikan Tunnel. Sightseeing in Hakodate, especially night view from Mt. Hakodate |
| | Hakodate 23:30. | | |
| 7. | Sapporo 6:30. | Kaisoku | Request 'carpet car'. Rail Pass Day 2 |
| | Sapporo 7:05. Asahikawa 8:39. | Tokkyu | |
| | Asahikawa 8:49. Wakkanai 12:45. | Kyuko | |
| | Wakkanai 13:00. Soya Misaki 13:52. | | Bus, ¥1,230 |
| | Soya Misaki 14:20. Wakkanai 15:15. | | Bus, ¥1,230 |
| | Wakkanai 16:06. Asahikawa 19:57. | Kyuko | |
| | Asahikawa 20:00. Sapporo 21:20. | Tokkyu | |
| | Sapporo 22:00. | | |
| 8. | Aomori 5:18. | Kyuko | Through Seikan Tunnel. Rail Pass Day 3 |
| | Aomori 5:27. Morioka 7:42. | Tokkyu | |
| | Morioka 7:55. Sendai 8:50. | Shinkansen | |
| | Sendai 9:03. Hon Shiogama 9:19. | Kaisoku | |
| | Shiogama 10:00. Matsushima Kaigan 11:00. | | Ferry, ¥1,400. Sightseeing in Matsushima |
| | Matsushima 13:10. Sendai 13:35. | Ordinary | |
| | Sendai 13:39. Yamadera 14:33. | Kaisoku | Sightseeing in Yamadera |
| | Yamadera 16:53. Sendai 17:56. | Kaisoku | |
| | Sendai 18:00. Tokyo 20:12. | Shinkansen | |
| 9. | Tokyo 7:07. Hiroshima 11:47. | Shinkansen | Sightseeing in Hiroshima. Rail Pass Day 4 |
| 10. | Hiroshima 7:43. Hakata 9:03 . | Shinkansen | Rail Pass Day 5 |
| | Hakata 9:21. Nagasaki 11:26. | Tokkyu | Sightseeing in Nagasaki |
| | Nagasaki 16:01. Tosu 17:37. | Tokkyu | |
| | Tosu 17:41. Kumamoto 18:35. | Tokkyu | |
| 11. | Kumamoto 8:31. Aso 9:28. | Tokkyu | Rail Pass Day 6 |
| | Aso 9:51. Aso-san Nishi Eki 10:32. | | Bus, ¥610. Sightseeing at Mt. Aso |

| Day | Journey | Train | Notes |
|---|---|---|---|
| 11. | Aso-san Nishi Eki 13:20. Aso 13:50. | | Bus, ¥610 |
| | Aso 13:58. Beppu 15:51. | Tokkyu | |
| 12. | Beppu 11:33. Nishi Kagoshima 17:14. | Tokkyu | Sightseeing in Beppu. Rail Pass Day 7 |
| | Nishi Kagoshima 19:05. | | |
| 13. | Himeji 8:03. | Tokkyu | Sightseeing in Himeji |
| | Himeji to Kobe, Osaka and Kyoto by JR or private railways. | | Approx. ¥1,500 |
| 14-15. | Sightseeing in Kyoto. | | |
| 16. | Kyoto to Nara by JR or Kintetsu. | | ¥540 by Kintetsu. Sightseeing in Nara |
| 17. | Nara to Ise by Kintetsu. | | Frequent service. ¥1,550. Sightseeing in Ise |
| 18. | Ise to Nagoya by Kintetsu. | | Frequent service. ¥1,260. Sightseeing in Nagoya |
| 19. | Nagoya 9:12. Toyohashi 10:00. | Shin Kaisoku | |
| | Toyohashi 10:04. Hamamatsu 10:38. | Ordinary | |
| | Hamamatsu 10:40. Kanaya 11:19. | Ordinary | Nagoya to Kanaya, ¥2,470 |
| | Kanaya 11:45. Senzu 13:03. | Steam | Oigawa Railway, ¥2,120 |
| | Senzu 13:15. Ikawa 14:59. | Ordinary | Oigawa Railway, ¥1,150 |
| | Ikawa 15:18. Shizuoka 17:39. | | Bus, ¥1,600. Youth hostels available at Miho or Omaezaki |
| 20. | Shizuoka to Numazu by JR. | Ordinary | Frequent service. ¥930 |
| 20-22. | Sightseeing in Hakone. | | Use 'Hakone Free Pass', ¥4,050. Travel area starts in Numazu |
| 22. | Odawara to Shinjuku by Odakyu Railway. | Kyuko | Frequent service. ¥750 |
| 23. | Free day in Tokyo. | | |

## TOUR 3 NORTH OF JAPAN USING *HOKKAIDO WIDE SHU-YU-KEN*

This tour covers the northern half of Japan only and is designed for those who choose to use a *shu-yu-ken* (excursion ticket) rather than a rail pass. It incorporates a visit to Towada-ko (Lake Towada) en route, which is permissible on payment of a small supplement, currently ¥2,880, as explained in the text at the beginning of the Hokkaido section. The requirement for this diversion must be specified when purchasing the ticket, however. It cannot be added later.

The tour is also suitable for those with a Japan Rail Pass, who would be able to save some time by using the *shinkansen* and *tokkyu* trains within the Tohoku region, which is not permitted with the *Hokkaido Wide Shu-yu-ken*, unless very substantial supplements are paid. If a rail pass is used, a suggestion is that, on the last day, an express train could be taken to Kyoto instead of the overnight return to Tokyo and a few days spent exploring that city, which merits having time devoted to it.

| Day | Journey | Train | Notes |
|---|---|---|---|
| 1. | Ueno 7:36. Utsunomiya 9:21 . | Ordinary | |
| | Utsunomiya 9:22. Kuroiso 10:12. | Ordinary | |
| | Kuroiso 10:27. Fukushima 12:20. | Ordinary | |
| | Fukushima 12:32. Sendai 13:53. | Ordinary | |
| | Sendai 13:58. Matsushima 14:22. | Ordinary | Sightseeing in Matsushima |
| | Matsushima 17:20. Ichinoseki 18:39. | Ordinary | |
| | Ichinoseki 19:00. Hiraizumi 19:08. | Ordinary | For Motsuji Youth Hostel |
| 2. | Hiraizumi 9:08. Morioka 10:27. | Ordinary | |
| | Morioka 11:01. Towada Minami 12:51. | Kaisoku | |

| Day | Journey | Train | Notes |
|---|---|---|---|
| 2. | Towada Minami 13:00. Towada-ko 14:02. | | JR Bus. Summer only. Winter departure at 16:20. |
| 3. | Towada-ko 7:35. Aomori 10:35. | | JR Bus. Summer only. |
| | Aomori 10:56. Hakodate 13:34. | Kaisoku | Through Seikan Tunnel. Sightseeing in Hakodate |
| | Hakodate 17:24. Onuma Koen 17:44. | Tokkyu | For Exander Onuma Youth Hostel |
| 4. | Onuma Koen 9:35. Oshamanbe 10:32. | Tokkyu | Seasonal stop at Onuma Koen |
| | Oshamanbe 10:35. Otaru 14:34. | Ordinary | Sightseeing in Otaru |
| | Otaru 17:01. Sapporo 17:30. | Kaisoku | Frequent service. Sightseeing in Sapporo |
| | Sapporo 22:00. | | |
| 5. | Wakkanai 6:00. | Kyuko | |
| | Wakkanai 8:10. Soya Misaki 9:02. | | Bus, ¥1,230 |
| | Soya Misaki 9:35. Wakkanai 10:30. | | Bus, ¥1,230. Sightseeing in Wakkanai |
| | Wakkanai 12:56. Nayoro 15:42. | Kyuko | |
| | Nayoro 16:00. Fukagawa 18:58. | Ordinary | |
| | Fukagawa 19:02. Asahikawa 19:20. | Tokkyu | |
| 6. | Asahikawa 9:00. Asahi-dake 10:35. | | Free bus |
| | Walk to So-unkyo. | | |
| | So-unkyo 16:40. Kamikawa 17:10. | | Bus, ¥750 |
| | Kamikawa 17:47. Rubeshibe 19:36. | Tokkyu | |
| 7. | Rubeshibe 7:30. Abashiri 9:11. | Ordinary | |
| | Abashiri 10:00. Mashu 11:45. | Ordinary | Sightseeing at Mashu-ko |
| 8. | Mashu 8:44. Kushiro 10:00. | Ordinary | |
| | Kushiro 11:44. Obihiro 13:02. | Tokkyu | |
| | Obihiro 13:30. Hiro-o 15:29. | | Bus, ¥1,700 |
| | Hiro-o 16:25. Erimo Misaki 17:25. | | JR Bus |
| 9. | Erimo Misaki Shigai 13:01. Samani 13:56. | | JR Bus. Not Saturdays |
| | Samani 14:22. Tomakomai 17:50. | Ordinary | |
| | Tomakomai 17:55. Minami Chitose 18:11. | Tokkyu | |
| | Minami Chitose 18:16. Chitose 18:21. | Ordinary | |
| | Youth Hostel minibus to Shikotsu-ko. | | |
| 10. | Youth Hostel minibus to Tomakomai. | | |
| | Tomakomai 9:41. Noboribetsu 10:07. | Tokkyu | |
| | Noboribetsu 10:14. Noboribetsu Onsen 10:27. | | Bus, ¥300. Sightseeing in Noboribetsu |
| 11. | Noboribetsu Onsen 13:00. Tozan Guchi 14:35. | | Bus, ¥1,400. Sightseeing around Showa Shin-zan |
| 12. | Tozan Guchi 9:20. Toya-ko Onsen 9:29. | | Bus, ¥200 |
| | Toya-ko Onsen 9:45. Toya 10:00. | | Bus, ¥290 |
| | Toya 10:06. Hakodate 11:36. | Tokkyu | |
| | Hakodate 11:50. Tappi Kaitei 13:20. | Kaisoku | Tour of Seikan Tunnel, ¥820 |
| | Tappi Kaitei 14:10. Aomori 15:15. | Kaisoku | |
| | Aomori 15:56. Hirosaki 16:46. | Ordinary | |
| 13. | Hirosaki 7:08. Odate 7:57. | Ordinary | |
| | Odate 8:19. Akita 9:50. | Kyuko | Time available in Akita |
| | Akita 12:28. Fukura 14:14. | Ordinary | |
| | Fukura 15:12. Tsuruoka 16:14. Sanze 16:39. | Ordinary | Youth Hostel available in Sanze |
| 14. | By bus from Tsuruoka to Haguro-san (all year). | | |
| | Then by bus to Gassan (summer only). | | |
| | Walk to Yudono-san (summer only). | | |
| | Bus back to Tsuruoka. | | |
| | Tsuruoka 20:41. Murakami 22:17. | Ordinary | |
| | Murakami 22:20. | | |
| 15. | Shinjuku 5:10. | Kaisoku | Reserved seats only. ¥500 |

## TOUR 4 CENTRE OF JAPAN USING *SHIKOKU WIDE SHU-YU-KEN*

Here is another tour using a *shu-yu-ken* (excursion ticket). This one is for ten days and covers most of the places which are commonly visited in the Kansai area of central Japan, in addition to which you will get a chance to look at some very pretty but less touristed rural areas of the island of Shikoku. Return is by ferry to Osaka via the island of Shodo-shima, at no extra cost if you use the services of Kansai Kisen, or at a very small extra cost by taking another operator's ferry from Shikoku to Shodo-shima only, because the timing of the Kansai Kisen service is inconvenient. A variation to this plan would be to add a visit to Hiroshima, by ferry from Matsuyama. Details are given under the Matsuyama heading in the Shikoku section of this book. However, this would entail cutting some other part of the plan to make time for such a visit. If necessary, the stop in Nagoya on the first day could be omitted.

| Day | Journey | Train | Notes |
|---|---|---|---|
| 1. | Tokyo 7:15. Shimizu 9:44. | Kyuko | Train destination is Shizuoka, but by changing at Shimizu, you will get a seat from Shizuoka on the next train. |
| | Shimizu 9:47. Hamamatsu 11:15. | Ordinary | Note that only the front three carriages of this train go on to Hamamatsu. The rear three carriages are detached at Shizuoka, so be sure to board at the front. |
| | Hamamatsu 11:18. Nagoya 12:49. | Kaisoku | Sightseeing in Nagoya |
| 2. | Nagoya 8:50. Nara 11:02. | Kyuko | Sightseeing in Nara |
| 3. | Nara 9:00. Osaka 9:46. | Kaisoku | Frequent service. Many other trains available. Sightseeing in Osaka |
| | Osaka 12:00. Sannomiya 12:21. | Shin Kaisoku | Frequent service. Sightseeing in Kobe |
| | Sannomiya 14:21. Himeji 15:01. | Shin Kaisoku | Frequent service. Sightseeing in Himeji |
| | Himeji 17:04. Okayama 18:26. | Ordinary | Hourly service |
| | Okayama 18:28. Kurashiki 18:43. | Ordinary | Frequent service, but outside limits of ticket. Excess fare ¥310 |
| 4. | Kurashiki 11:08. Okayama 11:20. | Kaisoku | Frequent service, ¥310. Sightseeing in Kurashiki and Okayama |
| | Okayama 14:32. Takamatsu 15:27. | Kaisoku | Crossing Seto Ohashi (bridge). Half-hourly service. |
| | Takamatsu 15:37. Ritsurin Koen Kita Guchi 15:43. | Ordinary | Sightseeing in Ritsurin Koen |
| | Ritsurin Koen Kita Guchi 17:17. Yashima 17:27. | Ordinary | Youth Hostel available in Yashima |
| 5. | Yashima 10:21. Ikenotani 11:15. | Tokkyu | Sightseeing in Yashima |
| | Ikenotani 11:37. Naruto 11:54. | Ordinary | Sightseeing in Naruto |
| | Naruto 14:23. Ikenotani 14:41. | Ordinary | |
| | Ikenotani 15:05. Hiwasa 16:11. | Tokkyu | Youth hostel available in Hiwasa |
| 6. | Hiwasa 8:17. Tokushima 9:12. | Tokkyu | |
| | Tokushima 9:18. Awa Ikeda 10:36. | Kyuko | |
| | Awa Ikeda 10:38. Kotohira 11:03. | Tokkyu | Sightseeing at Kompira-san |
| | Kotohira 13:14. Kochi 14:40. | Tokkyu | Sightseeing in Kochi |
| 7. | Kochi 8:38. Kubokawa 9:42. | Tokkyu | |
| | Kubokawa 10:01. Uwajima 11:58. | Ordinary | Sightseeing in Uwajima |
| | Uwajima 15:56. Matsuyama 17:19. | Tokkyu | |
| 8. | Matsuyama 12:18. Takamatsu 14:38. | Tokkyu | |
| | Ferry to Shodo-shima. | | ¥430 |
| 8-9. | Tour of Shodo-shima by bus. | | One-day ticket ¥1,700. Two-day ticket ¥2,200 |

| Day | Journey | Train | Notes |
|---|---|---|---|
| 9. | Sakate (Shodo-shima) 14:40. Osaka 19:10. | | Ferry. Included in *Shikoku Wide Shu-yu-ken* |
| | Osaka to Kyoto by JR. | Shin Kaisoku | Frequent service |
| 10. | Kyoto 21:00. Maibara 21:54. | Shin Kaisoku | Sightseeing in Kyoto |
| | Maibara 22:05. Ogaki 22:37. | Ordinary | |
| | Ogaki 22:40. | | |
| 11. | Tokyo 4:42. | Ordinary | |

## TOUR 5 SOUTH-WEST OF JAPAN USING *KYUSHU WIDE SHU-YU-KEN*

This is another *shu-yu-ken* (excursion ticket) expedition, this time to the south-west of Japan, as far as the tip of Kyushu, but allowing visits to places of interest in the Kansai area on the way there and back. If combined with Tour 3, the Hokkaido expedition, it would allow one to see almost all of the main tourist places in Japan. On the other hand, most visitors could do the same more cheaply, effectively and comfortably with a 21-day Japan Rail Pass. The only obvious advantages to using two *shu-yu-ken* are that one could take a break between the two fortnightly periods and could spend four weeks over the sightseeing, instead of three. Most of the extra week would be spent travelling, however, rather than sightseeing, because of the restrictions of the *shu-yu-ken*. On the whole, the Japan Rail Pass seems better value.

| Day | Journey | Train | Notes |
|---|---|---|---|
| 1. | Tokyo 7:15. Shimizu 9:44. | Kyuko | Train destination is Shizuoka, but by changing at Shimizu, you will get a seat from Shizuoka on the next train. |
| | Shimizu 9:47. Hamamatsu 11:15. | Ordinary | Note that only the front three carriages of this train go on to Hamamatsu. The rear three carriages are detached at Shizuoka, so be sure to board at the front. |
| | Hamamatsu 11:18. Nagoya 12:49. | Kaisoku | Sightseeing in Nagoya |
| 2. | Nagoya 8:50. Nara 11:02. | Kyuko | Sightseeing in Nara |
| 3. | Nara 9:00. Osaka 9:46. | Kaisoku | Frequent service. Many other trains available. Sightseeing in Osaka |
| | Osaka 12:00. Sannomiya 12:21. | Shin Kaisoku | Frequent service. Sightseeing in Kobe |
| | Sannomiya 14:21. Himeji 15:01. | Shin Kaisoku | Frequent service. Sightseeing in Himeji |
| | Himeji 17:04. Okayama 18:26. | Ordinary | Hourly service |
| | Okayama 18:28. Kurashiki 18:43. | Ordinary | Frequent service |
| 4. | Kurashiki 9:58. Hiroshima 12:18. | Kaisoku | Sightseeing in Hiroshima |
| 5. | Hiroshima 7:45. Iwakuni 8:35. | Ordinary | Sightseeing in Iwakuni |
| | Iwakuni 11:17. Shimonoseki 14:31. | Ordinary | Sightseeing in Shimonoseki (or overnight stay, if preferred) |
| | Shimonoseki 17:38. Yahata 18:15. | Ordinary | Youth hostel available in Yahata |
| 6. | Yahata 8:13. Kurosaki 8:16. | Ordinary | |
| | Kurosaki 8:22. Hakata 9:05. | Tokkyu | |
| | Hakata 9:21. Nagasaki 11:26. | Tokkyu | Sightseeing in Nagasaki |
| 7. | Nagasaki 7:57. Isahaya 8:20. | Tokkyu | |
| | Isahaya 8:34. Kuchinotsu 11:02. | Ordinary | Shimobara Railway, ¥1,610. Times subject to variation, since, at time of writing, services are still being slowed due to damage caused by eruption of Mt. Unzen. |

| Day | Journey | Train | Notes |
|---|---|---|---|
| 7. | Kuchinotsu 11:45. Oni-ike 12:15. | | Ferry, ¥320 |
| | Oni-ike to Hondo. | | By bus. Approximately half-hourly service, ¥470. Sightseeing in Hondo. Youth hostel available. |
| 8. | Hondo 7:35. Misumi 8:59. | | Bus, ¥1,350 |
| | Misumi 9:04. Kumamoto 9:55. | Ordinary | |
| | Kumamoto 10:30. Miyaji 12:59. | Steam | Seasonal train. Reserved seats only. ¥800 |
| | Miyaji 13:10. Aso-san Higashi 13:24. | | Bus, ¥300 |
| | Walk to Aso-san Nishi. | | |
| | Aso-san Nishi Eki 17:00. Aso 17:33. | | Bus (via Youth Hostel), ¥610. Caution: this is the last bus. |
| 9. | Aso 9:28. Mie-machi 10:31. | Tokkyu | |
| | Mie-machi 11:02. Usuki Seki-butsu 12:01. | | JR Bus. Look at stone Buddha images |
| | Usuki Seki-butsu 13:39. Usuki 13:57. | | JR Bus |
| | Usuki 13:59. Beppu 14:44. | Tokkyu | Sightseeing in Beppu |
| 10. | Beppu 8:44. Usa 9:21. | Tokkyu | |
| | Usa 9:50 Usa Hachimangu 9:59. | | Bus, ¥230. Sightseeing at Usa Hachiman-gu |
| | Usa Hachimangu 10:42. Usa 10:52. | | Bus, ¥230 |
| | Usa 11:21. Nakatsu 11:38. | Tokkyu | |
| | Nakatsu 11:40. Ao-no-domon 12:09. | | Bus, ¥580. Sightseeing at Ao-no-domon |
| | Ao-no-domon 12:59. Hon Yaba-kei 13:02. | | Bus, ¥140 |
| | Hon Yaba-kei 13:07. Rakan-ji 13:11. | | Bus, ¥140. Sightseeing at Rakan-ji |
| | Walk back to Hon Yaba-kei | | |
| | Hon Yaba-kei 15:02. Bungo Mori 16:03. | | Bus, ¥1,150 |
| | Bungo Mori 16:41. Hita 17:19. | Ordinary | |
| | Hita 17:32. Kurume 18:59. | Ordinary | |
| | Kurume 19:10. Setaka 19:23. | Kaisoku | Youth hostel available at Setaka |
| 11. | Setaka to Yanagawa by youth hostel minibus | | Sightseeing in Yanagawa |
| | Yanagawa to Omuta | | Nishitetsu Railway, ¥310. Frequent service |
| | Omuta 13:06. Kumamoto 13:35. | Tokkyu | Sightseeing in Kumamoto |
| 12. | Kumamoto 8:26. Kobayashi 11:22. | Kyuko | |
| | Kobayashi 12:55. Ebino Kogen 13:45. | | Bus, ¥950. Sightseeing in Ebino Kogen |
| | Ebino Kogen 15:05. Nishi Kagoshima 16:40. | | Bus, ¥1,500. |
| | Nishi Kagoshima 17:09. Ibusuki 18:24. | Ordinary | Sand-bathing in Ibusuki |
| 13. | Ibusuki 7:49. Nishi Kagoshima 9:07. | Ordinary | |
| | Nishi Kagoshima 9:15. Kokura 16:16. | Tokkyu | |
| | Kokura 16:30. Shimonoseki 16:47. | Ordinary | |
| | Shimonoseki 16:54. Miyajima-guchi 20:05. | Ordinary | Youth Hostel available in Miyajima-guchi |
| 14. | Miyajima-guchi 6:32. Okayama 9:50. | Ordinary | |
| | Okayama 10:21. Himeji 11:45. | Ordinary | |
| | Himeji 11:57. Kyoto 13:29. | Shin Kaisoku | Sightseeing in Kyoto |
| | Kyoto 21:00. Maibara 21:54. | Shin Kaisoku | |
| | Maibara 22:05. Ogaki 22:37. | Ordinary | |
| | Ogaki 22:40. | | |
| 15. | Tokyo 4:42. | Ordinary | |

## TOUR 6 FOR THE TRULY IMPOVERISHED. MISERLY 7-DAY RAIL PASS TOUR

This tour is for those who really cannot afford to be here! See Japan in seven days with every night spent on a train, so that accommodation costs are completely eliminated. Public baths (ask for '*sento*') can be found throughout Japan, but are generally easier to locate in smaller towns. Look for a tall chimney. In addition, the trains on nights 1 to 2 and 3 to 4 should have coin-operated showers in some of the sleeper carriages, but you do not get long for your money. Local sightseeing around Tokyo may be added to this tour as in those above.

| Day | Journey | Train | Notes |
|---|---|---|---|
| 1. | Akabane 0:11. Toyama 6:03. | Kyuko | Train starts from Ueno at 23:58. Akabane, on edge of Tokyo, is first stop. Train may be boarded here since it is after midnight. |
| | Toyama 6:06. Takayama 8:13. | Ordinary | Sightseeing in Takayama |
| | Takayama 11:20. Nagoya 13:37. | Tokkyu | |
| | Nagoya 13:50. Kyoto 14:34. | Shinkansen | |
| | Kyoto 14:45. Nara 15:29. | Kaisoku | Sightseeing in Nara |
| | Nara 18:20. Osaka 19:11. | Kaisoku | Frequent service. Many trains available |
| | Shin Osaka 20:26 or Osaka 20:33. | | |
| 2. | Kumamoto 7:09. | Tokkyu | |
| | Kumamoto 7:26. Miyaji 9:10. | Ordinary | |
| | Miyaji 9:25. Aso-san Higashi 9:39. | | Bus, ¥300 |
| | Walk to Aso-san Nishi. | | |
| | Aso-san Nishi Eki 14:18. Aso 14:48. | | Bus, ¥610 |
| | Aso 14:53. Kumamoto 15:48. | Tokkyu | |
| | Kumamoto 16:40. Miyazaki 21:01. | Kyuko | |
| | Miyazaki 23:30. | | |
| 3. | Hakata 6:57. | Tokkyu | |
| | Hakata 7:02. Nagasaki 9:04. | Tokkyu | Sightseeing in Nagasaki |
| | Nagasaki 19:50. | | |
| 4. | Kyoto 7:59. | Tokkyu | Sightseeing in Kyoto |
| | Kyoto 21:37 | | |
| 5. | Nagano 5:24. | Kyuko | Sightseeing at Zenko-ji (temple) |
| | Nagano 7:19. Omiya 9:53. | Tokkyu | |
| | Omiya 9:58. Sendai 11:40. | Shinkansen | |
| | Sendai 12:00. Matsushima Kaigan 12:26. | Kaisoku | Sightseeing in Matsushima |
| | Matsushima Kaigan 14:00. Shiogama 15:00. | | Ferry, ¥1,400 |
| | Hon Shiogama 15:13. Sendai 15:39. | Ordinary | Time for a look around Sendai |
| | Sendai 17:10. Morioka 18:29. | Shinkansen | |
| | Morioka 18:40. Hakodate 22:59. | Tokkyu | Through Seikan Tunnel |
| | Hakodate 23:30. | | |
| 6. | Sapporo 6:30. | Kaisoku | Request 'carpet car'. |
| | Sapporo 7:05. Asahikawa 8:39. | Tokkyu | |
| | Asahikawa 8:49. Wakkanai 12:45. | Kyuko | |
| | Wakkanai 12:56. Nayoro 15:42. | Kyuko | |
| | Nayoro 16:00. Fukagawa 18:58. | Ordinary | Scenic route |
| | Fukagawa 19:19. Sapporo 20:20. | Tokkyu | |
| | Sapporo 22:00. | | |
| 7. | Aomori 5:18. | Kyuko | Through Seikan Tunnel again |
| | Aomori 6:11. Kanazawa 15:46. | Tokkyu | Sightseeing in Kanazawa |
| | Kanazawa 22:32. | | |
| 8. | Ueno 6:05. | Kyuko | |

# INDEX

# LAST MINUTE AMENDMENTS

## SHINMEI LINE (p. 181)

As this book goes to the printer, news has been received that the Shinmei Line in Hokkaido, one of the prettiest routes in Japan, is to be closed before the end of 1995. Therefore, the diversion via Shumarinai mentioned on page 181 and in various other places in this book will no longer be possible.

## PRIVATE RAILWAY FARES

The private railways have just announced that most of their number are to increase their fares from 1st September 1995. JR, however, has decided not to make any increase before 1996, so JR fares stated in this book will remain current for a while at least. For private railways, expect to add about 10% to the fares given. These private railways include the Eidan subway lines in Tokyo, on which the minimum fare will increase to ¥160.

## OFF-PEAK AND HOLIDAY SUBWAY TICKETS

From 1st September 1995, the Eidan subway company in Tokyo will introduce a system of discounted *kai-su-ken* (multiple ride tickets; see pages 70 to 71) for travelling at less congested times. For travelling at off-peak hours (entering the system between 10:00 and 16:00) during the week, you can purchase twelve tickets for the price of ten. Such tickets are distinguished by being blue in colour and are valid for use for three months from the date of purchase. For travelling on Saturdays, Sundays, national holidays, 31st December and 2nd and 3rd January, you can purchase fourteen tickets for the price of ten. These tickets are pink and are also valid for three months. Note that you cannot use the off-peak tickets on holidays, even though you would actually be paying a higher fare by doing so.

## TRIPS TO RYUSEN-DO (pp. 144-145)

JR appears to have ceased operation of the bus from Kuji to Fudai included in the itinerary at the top of page 145. However, this expedition is still possible if one takes the Sanriku Private Railway from Kuji to Fudai (¥660). The train leaves Kuji at 12:23 and reaches Fudai at 12:56. This particular journey is operated by one of the 'retro' rail cars. The time available at Kita Yamazaki Tenbodai has also been reduced to 8 minutes, unfortunately (bus arrives 13:28). The bus listed as leaving Ryusen-do at 16:35 is no longer operating, but the 17:03 journey runs and will allow sufficient time for changing at Iwaizumi station.